i

Wallace Surname Origins

The history of the name Wallace begins in the Scottish/English Borderlands with a family of Strathclyde-Briton ancestry. It is a name for a person who was understood to be foreign. The name is actually an abbreviation of Wallensis, which meant Welsh is derived from the Anglo-Norman French word waleis, meaning foreign. It is sometimes difficult for the layman to understand how such a renowned Scottish Clan could be called, literally, Welsh. Yet from the 3rd to the 8th century the Kingdom of Strathclyde stretched from the northern tip of France to the southern shores of the Clyde in Scotland.

This kingdom was composed of solely coastal territories, of regions including Wales, Lancashire, Westmorland and that part of southwest Scotland known as Galloway. Ironically, the first Scottish poem, dated about 1000 AD, was written in Welsh.

Hence, Richard Wallensis was a vassal in 1174 of Walter FitzAlan, the Norman/ Breton who had settled in Salop in England and then moved north to Scotland. He would later found the great line of Scottish Stewart Kings. The Wallensis were undoubtedly the original natives of the area rather than travelers who moved north from the Welsh border in the train of the Stewarts.

Early Origins of the Wallace family

The surname Wallace was first found in Ayrshire (Gaelic: Siorrachd Inbhir Àir), formerly a county in the southwestern Strathclyde region of Scotland, that today makes up the Council Areas of South, East, and North Ayrshire where in 1173 AD Richard Wallensis obtained the lands that belonged to the former kingdom of Strathclyde called Richardstoun (now Riccarton) by a grant from the King. His son, Richard Walency (or Waleis) witnessed several charters between 1190 and 1220, showing his approval of transfers of land in Molle, Kelso, Cupa and Paisley. The Chiefship passed to his grandson, Sir Malcolm Wallace of Elderslie in Renfrewshire, who had acquired those lands, the ancient Clan territories and other lands in Ayrshire. It was the younger son of Malcolm Wallace, William Wallace, born in 1275, who was Scotland's folklore hero. A knight of no small qualification and skill, throughout his life he had maintained a friendship with the House of Stewart. His many exploits started in 1297 when he killed the Sheriff of Lanark.

Wallace continued to harass the English occupying army with such skill and bewildering speed that the English were demoralized. Wallace unified the Clans of Scotland against a common invader. One of the English captains reported that Wallace was lying in Selkirk forest with his army of Clansmen.

An English force moved northwards to destroy him but found itself under siege in Stirling Castle. The Battle of Stirling Bridge was a decisive victory for Wallace, and he was awarded the guardianship of Scotland. He was probably the greatest unifying factor that Scotland ever had. But the English King once more invaded Scotland, set up his own government and Wallace became an outlaw. Betrayed by Sir John de Menteith near Glasgow, he was tried for treason in London and executed on August 23rd, 1305.

But the Clan Wallace lived on with some forty or fifty branches, most of them having their own lands and territories.

Medieval Scottish names are rife with spelling variations. This is due to the fact that scribes in that era spelled according to the sound of words, rather than any set of rules. Wallace has been spelled Wallace, Wallis, Wallys, Walace, Uallas (Gaelic) and others.

Courtesy of https://www.houseofnames.com/wallace-family-crest

PRO LIBERTATE

THE WALLACES OF MOORE COUNTY, NC

Wallace

MORGAN JACKSON & MALLIE WALLACE

www.MooreCountyWallaces.com

Inside Front & Back Covers:
Wallace Surname Origins
Courtesy of https://www.houseofnames.com/wallace-family-crest

ISBN 978-0-578-79753-3

Published by Morgan Jackson
Raleigh, North Carolina
www.MooreCountyWallaces.com
morganjackson_1997@yahoo.com
919-624-7281

Printed by IngramSpark
www.IngramSpark.com

As always...

For my grandfather Mallie Wallace. You sparked a lifelong love of family and a burning desire to find out more about who we are and where we came from. You are missed every single day. I've finally finished the book!

To my mother, Pat Wallace Jackson. Thank you for the many years of unconditional support, advice and love. And for supporting and nourishing the spark that Pop created. And for being my lifelong Editor!

And to my family...Shawn, thank you for everything, for it all. Nothing in our life happens without you. Emsley and Colt, I hope that my lifelong study of where we came from will help you keep your feet firmly on the ground and your eyes aimed at the sky.

Finally this book is dedicated to the Everet, Nicholas, Joseph, John, Nathan, Josiah, Enoch, Isham, Emsley, Wes, Byrd, Sam, Lane, Quim, Lock, John and all of the old Wallaces who came before us and made it possible for us all to be on this earth. I hope you are proud of the legacy you've left. I certainly am.

Mallie Wallace 1910-2002
The Last of the "Old Wallaces"

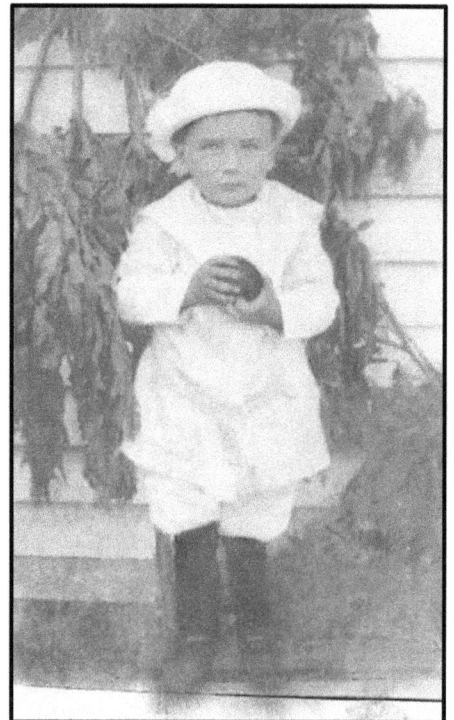

Biography written by granddaughter Jenny Chriscoe Purvis

Mallie L. Wallace was born May 31, 1910 to Lucian and Nancy Jane Williams Wallace. He grew up a farmer's son and was at heart a farmer himself. He married Clara Cockman and was the father to four girls: Jacqueline, Chloe, Doris and Patricia.

A textile mill worker who raised hogs and grew crops as well, he knew how to enjoy life. He delighted in the simple things. Rabbit hunting, auction houses, pumpkins in the fall, and flowers in the spring were among his favorite things. He enjoyed "riding around" and sharing details of old home places and names of creeks while looking at how the crops were doing. He always went home a different way than he came even if it meant taking the long way around. We never, ever saw him rush around or get in a hurry. He savored his time with each of us.

Above all he enjoyed his grandchildren. He taught us about life, how to be positive, laugh, and have a good time. He always kept a "quarter jar" and would take it with us to the beach each year. We'd dump all those quarters in a big pile and divide them out among us. Those were ours to spend however we wanted, and boy did we feel rich. He gave freely of his time and love, showed us what things were most important, and taught us to keep a penny in our pocket so we'd never be broke. In his presence, you always had the feeling that you were his favorite. We never doubted Papa's love.

His house was the Sunday meeting place. Roasted peanuts, Cracker Jacks, and little Cokes in glass bottles were always enjoyed by a big fire in the fireplace or out in the yard in his "tree-house." It was there we listened to him sing songs like "The Man That Rode the Mule around the World" and heard wonderful stories from his life. One of our favorites was when he and his daddy traveled by wagon to Sanford and he got to see electric lights for the first time as they topped the hill that night. It was also there that we learned about our family heritage. Papa was proud of being a Wallace and wanted the younger generations to know their roots and heritage as well. He was the one to ask if you needed to know who was related and how.

Our Papa died in July of 2002, but his life lessons and love live on with us daily. We were so blessed to have such wonderful, unconditional love and support and will forever miss his knowledge and wisdom of life.

Eulogy given by grandson Morgan Jackson

We gather today to celebrate the life of Mallie Lester Wallace. I truly believe that celebrate is the most appropriate word to use for the man that some of you knew as Mr. Wallace, some as Mallie, but to us - he was "Pop." Papa was a man who lived life to the fullest, a day at the time.

Like most in his day, he grew up on the family farm, and later went to work in the textile mills. But unlike most, he was one of those lucky men who got to marry the prettiest girl he ever met. He and Granny were married for more than 54 years when she passed away. Pop spent most of his working life teaching weavers in mills all over North Carolina.

But this does not tell Papa's real story - His real story has a lot more to it. Pop was a man who welcomed each day with a smile and a little song. He was a man who loved his family and who taught us all how to enjoy life. Pop had that special ability to make each of us truly believe that we were his favorite and we all still do. He was a grandfather who always had a dollar for the candy store.

He had such a great way of looking at things. He was a man who believed that the good ol' days were today and tomorrow. He was a man who knew everyone and everything - and most importantly he knew everything about everyone. But he never judged anyone; he believed that every person should live their life as they wanted - as he did.

He loved to talk about those "old" people who just happened to be younger than him. When you asked Papa about his own age, he would tell you that he was signed up for Social Security and he would get his check the first of next month. What he wouldn't tell you was that he had signed up 25 or 30 years ago. He was not old, he would say, just been here a long time.

Over the years, he worked in so many places; from Swepsonsville to Red Springs, from Graham to Rockingham, from Cheraw, SC to Galax, VA - Papa loved to talk about the places he had been and the people he had seen.

He also loved to sit on the porch and enjoy the coolness of the morning and the calmness of the night. He loved to talk of the dances and corn shuckings that he and Hurley used to go to. He loved to eat at those little cafes, but his favorite place was Hardees - where you could find him everyday at two o'clock.

He loved to tell stories about the old Wallaces and prided himself on being the oldest Wallace living. Papa loved to ride around; Lord, did he love to ride - he was so proud - he had just gotten his driver's license renewed for five more years. And he had just returned from the beach. He loved going to the beach and loved the ocean -- or maybe, it was just all the pretty girls. More than anything he was a man who always had a good time.

I hope you will take notice of how many things that I have mentioned that Papa loved to do. We could all learn a lesson from Pop about the preciousness of life and how we need to embrace each morning and live each day to its fullest. So today - we should not mourn for Papa - we should celebrate his life, because that is exactly what he would do.

To end his story - he was a man who married the love of his life, was a wonderful father to four beautiful daughters, grandfather to eleven, great-grandfather to thirteen and great-great grandfather to two - but most importantly he was a friend to us all.

And we will miss him.

Table of Contents

Introduction

My grandfather, Mallie Wallace, loved his family and loved to tell tales of the "old Wallaces". Many of these stories had been passed down to him from his grandfather, Emsley Wallace. Over thirty years ago, my grandfather said, "it's about time somebody started writing this down." As the youngest of his eleven grandchildren, that fortunately became my task. My love of genealogy, history and stories of long ago began with him and we spent the better part of his last twenty years writing it all down. He passed away in 2002 at 92 years old but continues to live on in our hearts and minds. We always planned to write a book on the Wallaces, but I suffered from that familiar foil of most genealogists in that I could never reach a point where I felt it was truly finished. While this research will never be finished, I believe that it was finally time to publish the book he and I started so long ago.

In 2009, I launched *www.MooreCountyWallaces.com* to achieve the goal of publishing the work that he and I started and be able to keep it continually updated with new information. The website, while dedicated and named for our Wallace family, explores and attempts to document all of the families of northern Moore County, NC. As it turns out, the saying, "if you are related to one family, you're related to them all", couldn't be more true. If you descend from the families who resided in or near the towns of Robbins [formerly Hemp and Mechanic's Hill], High Falls or Eagle Springs or current/former communities of Westmoore, Spies, Needham's Grove, Parkwood, Hallison, Putnam, Carter's Mills, Gold Region, Big Oak, Caledonia, Prosperity, Noise, Quiet, Rise, Horners or for that matter anywhere in Bensalem, Ritters, Sheffields, Deep River or Carthage townships or communities in neighboring counties like Candor, Biscoe, Star, Seagrove, Whynot, Bennett or Carbonton, your ancestors can likely be found at *www.MooreCountyWallaces.com*.

Moore County, NC has long been a challenging place to do genealogical research, even more so if your family lived in Northern Moore County. Due to the immense loss of records in the 1889 Moore County courthouse fire combined with Northern Moore's large mix of Scotch-Irish, German, Swiss, English and other settlers who often kept to themselves and left very little evidence behind – genealogical and historical research on these families generally leaves researchers with no shortage of dead ends, brick walls and ancestors who disappear into genealogical black holes.

Utilizing over thirty years of personal research and a multitude of information from numerous sources, the following pages are a collection oral history, land grants, deeds, church records, obituaries, school records, wills, estates, tax lists, military service and pension records, family bibles, newspaper accounts, marriage, death, court records and DNA research.

I am forever indebted to *Ancestry.com* and *Familysearch.org* as well as the NC Archives in Raleigh for making these records available and accessible to research and to the hundreds of Wallace descendants for providing information and photographs. A special thanks to the archivists at the NC Archives for their dedication to preservation and their courteous assistance. And to the staff and volunteers of the Moore County Historical Association in Southern Pines and the Moore County Library in Carthage for all they do to preserve our local history. I have strived to be as accurate as possible, but readily admit that there are likely errors and omissions. Please contact me at *morganjackson_1997@yahoo.com* and I will gladly make any corrections to future editions, print and online.

Along with the *Families of Northern Moore County: Abstracts of Miscellaneous and Rare Records Volumes I 1746-1830, Volume II 1831-1929* and *Families of Moore County, NC: 1790-1850 Census and 1777-1823 Tax Records* this book was inspired by and I hope continues to add to the volumes of genealogical research that came before. *The Williams Family* by Maxine McNeill; *Cockman Family History* by Margaret Cockman Kitchel; *John Phillips Family: Eleven Generations Originating in Moore County* by Emma Phillips Paschal; *The Brady Family of Moore and Chatham Counties* by Lois Smith Phillips and Carol Smith Purvis; *The Stutts Family and their descent from Jacob Stutts of Moore County, NC* by Katherine Shields Melvin; *Brewer families of Moore and southwest Chatham* by David Brewer; *Tales from the Upper End of County* by Lacy Garner, Jr.; *The History of the House in the Horseshoe: her people and her Deep River neighbors* by George W. Willcox; *The Cagle Family in the South to 1850: North Carolina* by John G. Cagle and the *Kennedy and Williamson Families of Upper Moore County* by James Vann Comer are among the incredible resources available on the families of Northern Moore County.

No discussion of Moore County, NC history and genealogy can be complete without paying tribute to *Miscellaneous Ancient Records of Moore County, NC* by Rassie E. Wicker; *A Guide to Moore County Cemeteries* by Anthony E. "Tony" Parker; *Moore County 1747-1847* by Blackwell Robinson, *Moore County 1847-1947* by Manly Wade Wellman and James Vann Comer's *Moore County Bible Projects Vol. I-III, Old Moore County Vital Statistics, Central North Carolina Vital Statistics* and his *Central North Carolina Collection Volume I and II.*

Morgan Jackson
7241 Manor Oaks Drive
Raleigh, NC 27615
Morganjackson_1997@yahoo.com
www.MooreCountyWallaces.com

December 15, 2020

EVERET WALLACE (C1770-C1845)

Everet Wallace is the progenitor of the Moore County Wallaces and any study or analysis of the Wallace family begins and ends with Everet. Every Wallace descendant with roots in northern Moore County descends from him. Everet Wallace appeared for the very first time in the 1790 Census in Moore County, NC. Everet, appearing with his wife, Caty/Catherine and their infant daughter, Celia, were the only Wallaces recorded in the Moore County, NC Census that year. From his first appearance in the 1790 Census to his last in a tax record in 1844/1845, there are over 35 known references to Everet in Moore County, NC records. Among these records, Everet can be found entering land, paying taxes, serving on juries, testifying at trials, and purchasing goods at estate sales.

We are not certain if Everet Wallace was born in Moore County or moved there later but we are confident that he was born in North Carolina. In the 1880 Census, Everet's four living children (Isham, Enoch, Nathan and Franey) all identified their mother and father as being born in North Carolina. Based on DNA research later in this volume, it is also possible that Everet was born or resided in the Yadkin River area in Montgomery and Davidson counties prior to coming to Moore County.

To understand Everet Wallace it is helpful to understand what life was like in northern Moore County in the late 1700's. While it is likely that hunters, trappers and frontiersmen had been visiting the area that would later become Moore County for several years, the first known settlers arrived in the mid-1740's on Deep River near the House in the Horseshoe. In the mid to late 1700's, immigration into the area continued from individuals of English, Scotch, Swiss and German descent. They came many routes to central North Carolina from Pennsylvania and Virginia via the Great Wagon Road, from the ports of Charleston, Wilmington and New Bern and from settlements in eastern North Carolina as the western frontier expanded. A map created in 1959 by D.J. Whitener details the early migration routes into North Carolina.[1]

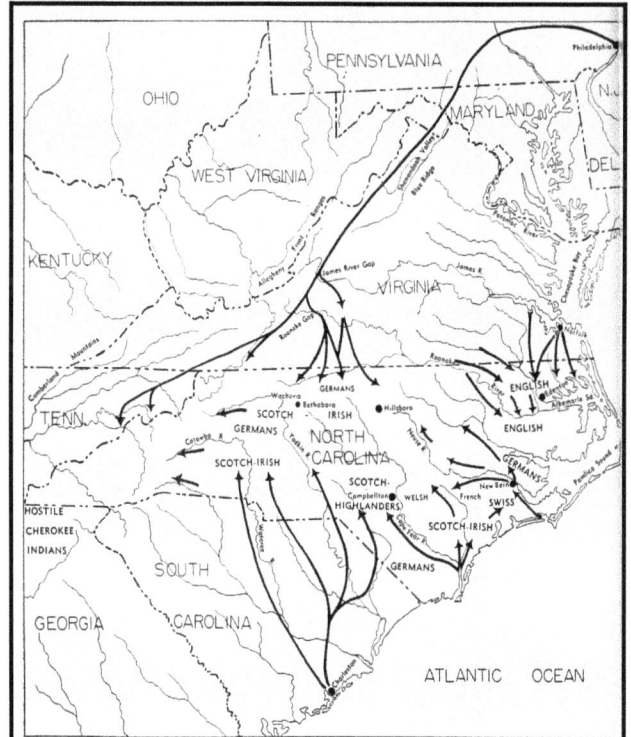

HOW NORTH CAROLINA WAS SETTLED

From *North Carolina History* by D. J. Whitener, 1959

(Courtesy of Harlow Publishing Company, Norman, Oklahoma

Settlers utilized two major throughfares in the mid 1700's that are believed to have originally been Native American trading routes from the Yadkin River Valley to the Cape Fear River Valley. The oldest was the Yadkin Road that was frequently travelled by settlers in the 1750's and by 1770, the Salem-Cross Creek Road was completed providing easier access for traders and merchants from the Moravian settlements around Salem to the markets at Cross Creek.[2] [3] These roads ran directly through northern Moore County and helped connect local settlers with traders and markets to sell their goods. A 1770 map of North Carolina by *John Collet, J. Bayly and Samuel Hooper* provides incredible detail of the roads and waterways at that time.[4] For the purposes of highlighting the area I have selected the portion of the map relating to the Moore County region and annotated the Yadkin and Salem Roads and the approximate locations of the present-day towns of Carthage and Robbins. Moore County was created from Cumberland County in 1784.

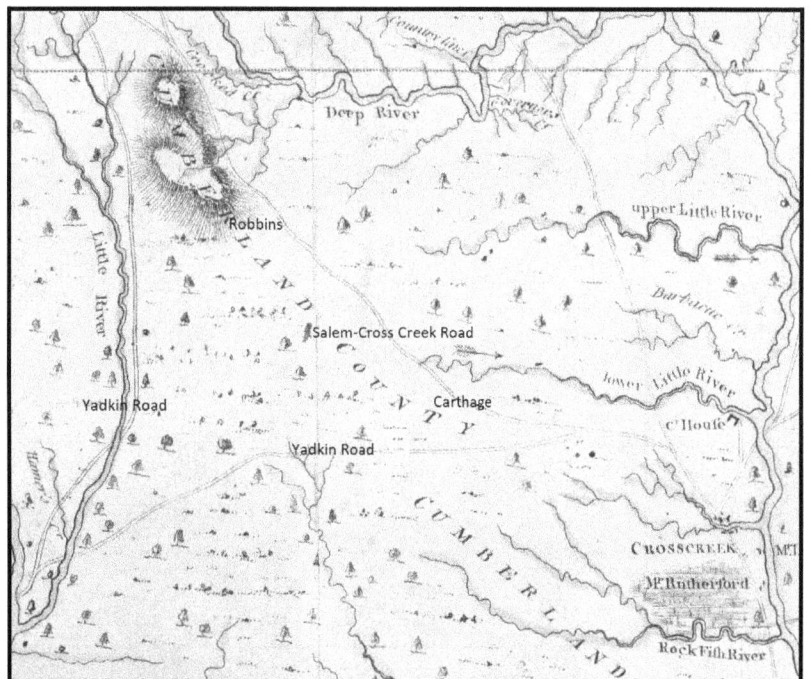

These early settlers claimed the land around rivers and creeks to take advantage of fertile soil and to provide water for their livestock. They lived an agrarian lifestyle and subsisted on crops grown by hand, livestock they kept and the game they hunted or trapped. As more settlers arrived, they spread out laying claim to land further down streams and tributaries. The following maps provide valuable insight into the growth of the region through the early years. The maps were created utilizing original land grants records and *DeedMapper*™ plotting software (http://www.directlinesoftware.com).

Original land grants in northern Moore County by 1750

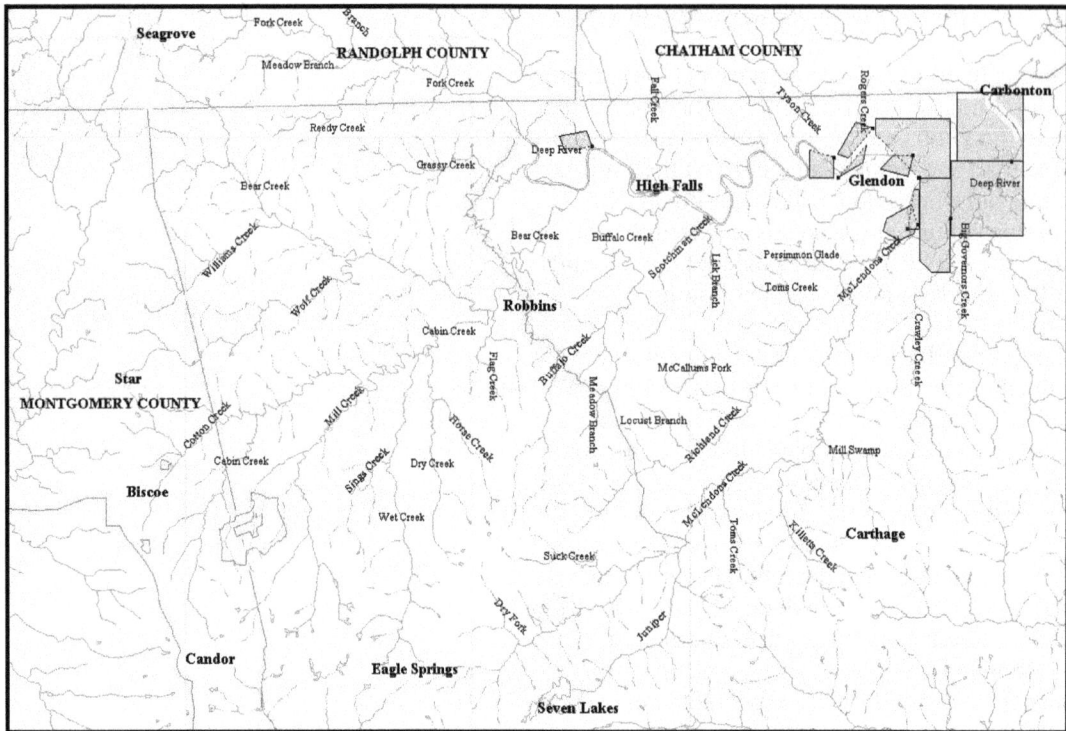

Original land grants in northern Moore County by 1760

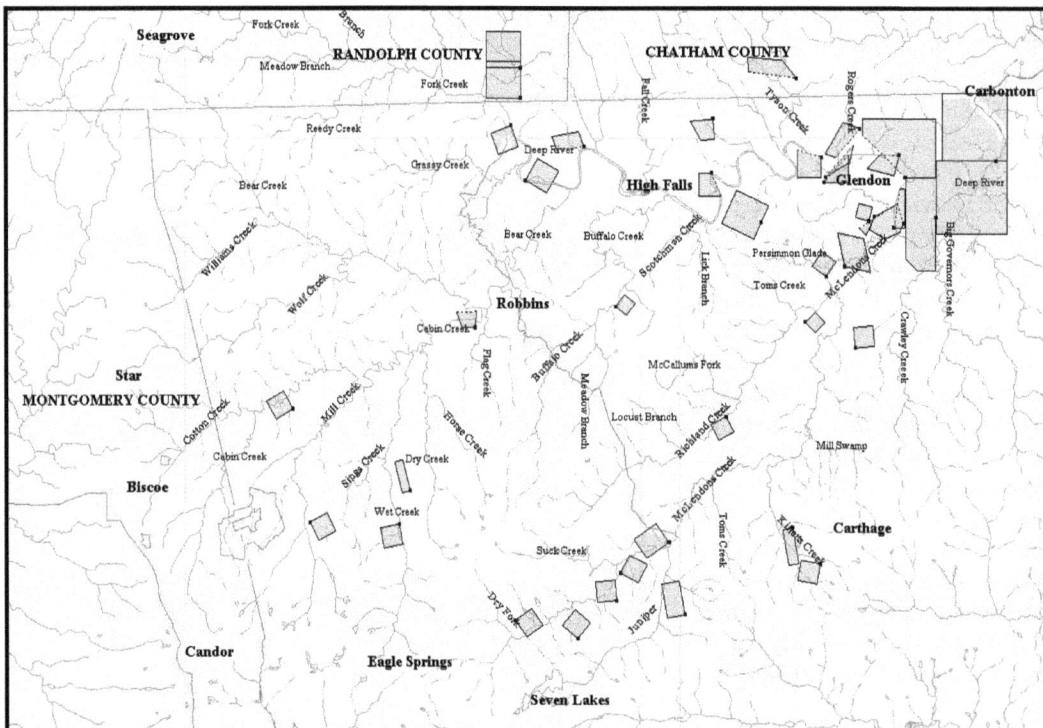

Original land grants in northern Moore County by 1780

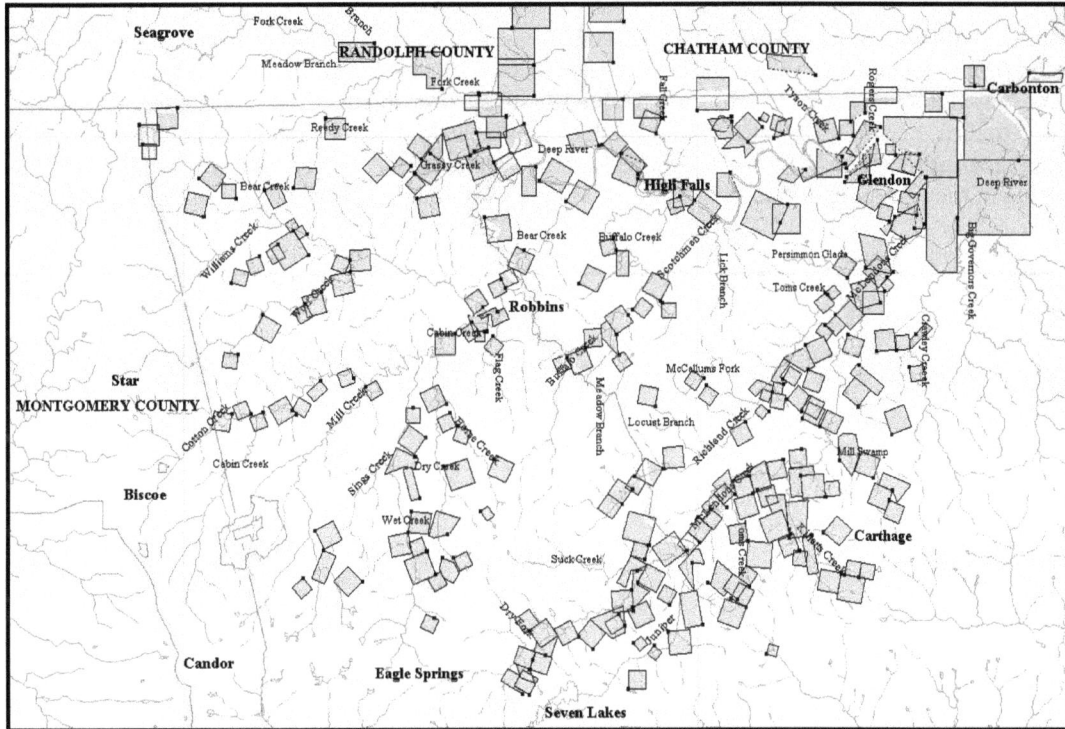

In the first U.S. Census of 1790, Moore County recorded 639 heads of household. It is estimated that 90 percent of the nation's population were farmers and lived in the countryside or in small towns and villages.[5] Like many in his day, Everet Wallace was likely a farmer by trade. Throughout his adult life, Everet and his family resided in upper Moore County, NC south of the present-day town of Robbins. Everet Wallace owned 100 acres of land on Cimlin Branch of Flag Creek, a tributary of Bear Creek in Moore County, NC. He received a land grant from the State of North Carolina for 50 acres in 1794 *(see inset above)* and must have purchased an additional 50 acres as he was listed in Tax Listed in 1815 and 1818-1823 as owning 100 acres. This land is located literally just west of intersection (known as the Robbins Crossroads) of NC Hwy 705 and NC Hwy 24/27 *(see map of original land grants below)*. The original 50-acre tract stayed in the family for over 100 years until it was deeded by his grandson, John Mack Wallace, to William Wesley Brown in 1898.

CATY/CATHERINE, WIFE OF EVERET WALLACE

It is my belief that his wife was named Caty/Catherine. This is based primarily on tax records that list Everet Wallace on an 1844/1845 tax list *(upper image)* and a Caty Wallace in 1846 as owing taxes for 1845 *(lower image)*. In those days, while women were generally not assessed taxes - they are frequently listed after the death of their husbands. In my research, I have not been able to locate another Caty/Catherine Wallace who would have been of age or could have been widowed in order to be paying taxes at this time. Additional circumstantial evidence that Everet's wife was named Caty/Catherine exists in the naming of their grandchildren. Celia Wallace Maness' 1st daughter was named Catherine and her 1st son was named Everet.

Caty/Catherine's maiden name is listed numerous times in online family trees as Horner. There is not one single piece of conclusive evidence to confirm that. Frankly, I believe that it is inaccurate. The Horner family resided in Orange County, NC until the early 1820's when George R. Horner is first recorded Moore County, NC. Everet would have married Catherine prior to 1788 – 30+ years before the George R. Horner arrived in Moore County, NC. There is no evidence that links the Wallace family of Moore County, NC to Orange County, NC.

CHILDREN OF EVERET WALLACE AND CATY/CATHERINE

Everet and Caty/Catherine were known to have raised at least twelve children during their lifetime. Among their known children were Celia, Nicholas, Mary, Joseph, John, Nathan C., Isham, Josiah, Elizabeth, Enoch, Franey, Manda and Susannah.

Other male Wallaces born during the 1810's/1820's include William Lane and Aaron. These individuals are clearly related to Everet but conclusive proof has not been found to establish them as definite children or grandchildren. Both left Moore County, NC with their families and headed south. **William Lane Wallace (1814-1886)** moved to Dillon County, SC where many of his descendants still live. **Aaron Wallace (1818/26-aft 1880)** moved to Richmond and Scotland County, NC and his descendants can still be found in and around the Laurel Hill area.

Celia Wallace (1788-1862) married Shadrach Maness (1770-1858), one of the triplet sons of Revolutionary War soldier William Maness. Celia and Shadrach were the parents of Catherine, Everett, Asa, Lucretia, Alsey, and Ira Lane. Several of their children married into the following families and many of their descendants still reside in upper Moore County, NC: Stutts, Ritter, Shields, and Cagle. Everett Maness and his family moved to Forsyth County, GA

Joseph Wallace (bet 1792/8-bef 1870) married Chaney (1800-bef 1870) and produced the following sons: Ruffin, Seaborne and Alexander. Ruffin and Alexander both left widows with small children when they were killed in the Civil War and Seaborne moved briefly to eastern Tennessee before returning to the Seagrove area of Randolph County, NC where his descendants are located.

Isham Wallace (1801-1882) and Nancy Furr (1806-1881) raised a very large family that for the most part remained in upper Moore County, NC, specifically the area around Buffalo Creek and Meadow Branch near Flint Hill Baptist Church. Isham and Nancy had the following children: Clarkey Ann m. George Cockman; Elizabeth m. J. Sampson Cockman; Mary Ann m. Noah Emsley Cockman; William Wesley m1. Elizabeth Melton, m2. Margaret Louise Seawell; Sarah Ann m. John Garner; Quimby m. Arabella Stewart; Dempsey died young; Lockey m. Susan Muse; Emsley Thomas m. Priscilla Melton; Samuel Bascom m1. Temperance Melton, m2. Nancy Smith; Loveday Jane m. James Washington Horner; Sampson Delaney m. Missouri Hunsucker; Virgil Spinks "Byrd" m1. Regina Hunsucker, m2. Flora Ann Garner; and John M. m1. Candace Melton, later moved to Perry County, AR and married 4 more times.

Josiah Wallace (1807-bef 1880) married Catherine (1808- aft 1880) and was frequently mentioned in Moore County, NC records but to my knowledge yielded no offspring.

Enoch Wallace (1808/15-aft 1880) and Malvina Furr (1810/22- bef 1880) had several children: Hiram W., Hamilton, Isham "Ike", John Spinks and Christian. Hiram died in the Civil War and left a small family that moved to Richmond County, NC. Hamilton died young, while Ike and his family lived in the Calvary Baptist Church area located between Carthage, NC and Robbins, NC. Spinks moved to Lauderdale County, AL and Christian married George Graham.

Franey Wallace (1814-aft 1880) raised four children whose father was Abram Hunsucker. Franey's children were Martha J., Mary Ann, Rebecca Jane, John Mack "Mack" and Julia Frances. Mary Ann died leaving a small family, Mack served in the Civil War and later moved his family to Cumberland County, NC, while Rebecca Jane and Julia Frances all raised families in upper Moore County, NC where their descendants still remain. Martha and her family later migrated to Georgia.

Not much is known about the families of **Manda Wallace (b. 1810)** and **Susannah Wallace (b. 1815)**. Both were listed with small children in the 1850 Census in Moore County, NC and are believed to be daughters of Everet and Caty/Catherine. Manda had the following children: Sarah, Cornelius, Anderson and Isaac Spinks. Isaac Spinks was a very active member of the Beulah Hill Church community (located between Pinehurst, NC and West End, NC) and his family is buried there. Susannah was listed as having two children that little else is known about: Eli and Calvin.

While most of Everet and Catherine's family remained in and around upper Moore County, NC for generations, a few took advantage of the availability of inexpensive land and joined countless others in the westward migration to Tennessee, Alabama, Mississippi and Texas.

Nicholas Wallace (1790/4-aft 1830) was listed with a family in the 1810 and 1820 Moore County, NC Census before moving to Henderson County, TN by 1830. No further record has been found.

Mary Wallace (b. 1790-1794) married Martin Rouse (b. 1792) and migrated to Hall County, GA during the late 1820's. In Martin Rouse's War of 1812 Pension application, he states that he married Mary Wallace in Moore County, NC. Two dates were provided on different versions of the application [20 Oct 1812 and 15 Nov 1821]. It is unclear as to the reason for the different dates, but it could indicate that he was married twice, or the preparer of the application recorded the wrong date.

John Wallace (1798-c1866) married Elizabeth (1800-aft 1866) and raised a large family in Moore County, NC before migrating to Bibb County, AL prior to 1850. John and Elizabeth's children were Nathan, Eli, Isham, Thomas, Raleigh, John Wesley, Josiah/Cyrus, Sarah, Catherine and Franny. While the majority of John and Elizabeth's family remained in the Bibb and Perry County areas of Alabama, a few of their children and descendants continued on to Mississippi, Louisiana, and Texas.

Nathan C. Wallace (1800-aft 1881) was married to Finity Britt (1800-bet 1850/7) and later to Sarah (1829-bef 1870). Nathan and Finity had the following children in North Carolina: Nancy, Deborah, Franey, Mary, Everett and Benjamin. Between 1850-1857, Finity died and Nathan moved his family to Henderson County, TN. Several children were born to Nathan and his second wife Sarah in Tennessee: Sarah Frances, Elizabeth M, William Samuel, Mary A. and Susan Sufronie. Many of Nathan's children intermarried with other Moore County, NC families also migrating to Tennessee. Among those were the Williams, Britt, and Brewer families. Many of their descendants can still be found in the Henderson, McNairy, and Madison County areas of Tennessee.

Elizabeth "Betsy" Wallace (1808-aft 1860) was the second wife of Jeremiah Williams (b. 1775) and according to Williams Family researchers they had a very large family consisting of the following children: Raleigh, Jeremiah D., Mary, Enoch Spinks, Lorenzo D., Amanda Jane, Franey, David Anderson, Caty, Ann, James Wesley, Joseph and Bryant. Jeremiah and Betsy left Moore County, NC and traveled to western TN where most of their family was raised. Their children and descendants can be found in Census data from Madison, McNairy and Henderson County, TN. Several of them moved on further to Texas and Oklahoma.

MIGRATION ROUTES OF EVERET WALLACE'S CHILDREN

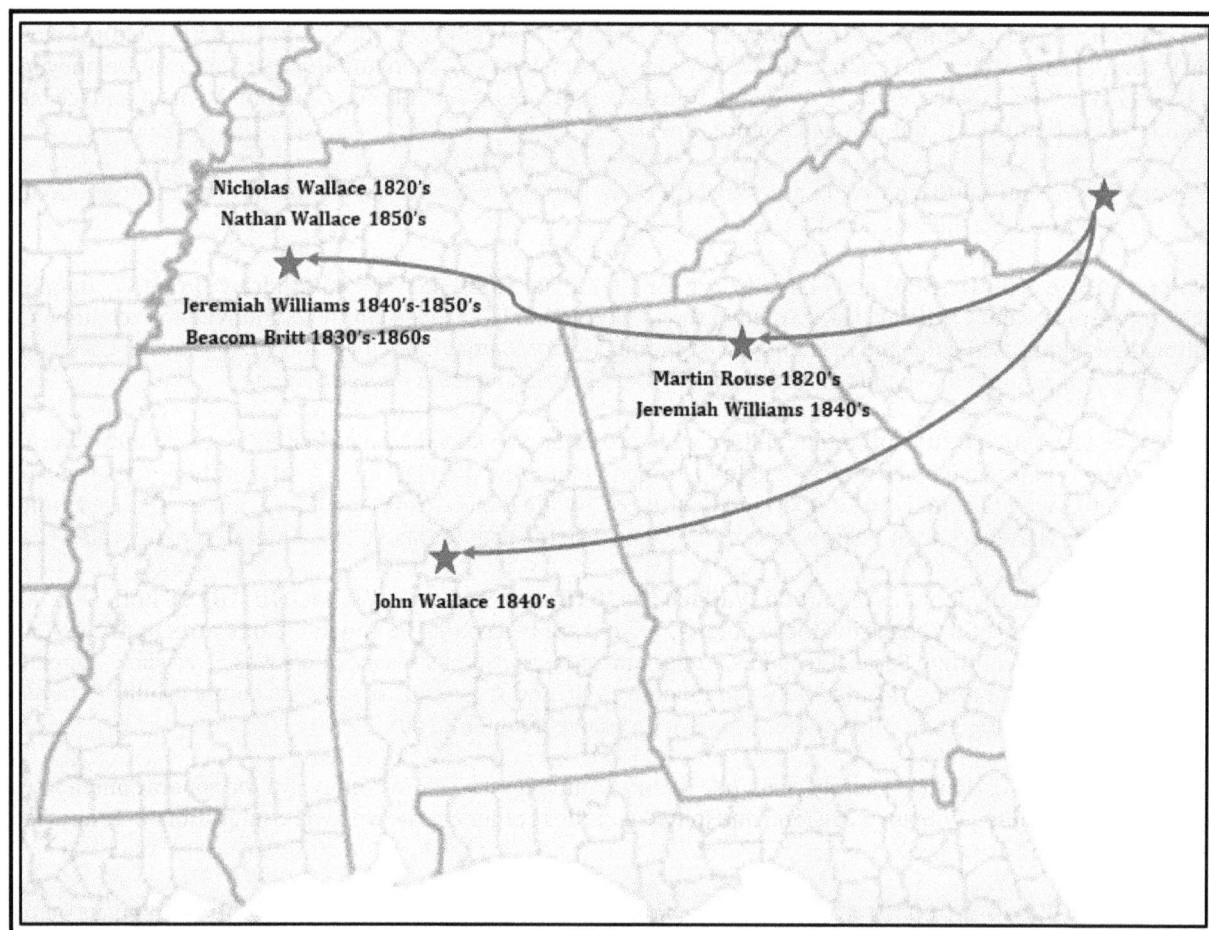

RECORDS OF EVERET WALLACE

1790 -- Census, Moore County, NC Page 154
Everet Wallace
(16+) 1M
(all ages) 2F

1792, May 22 -- Land Entry #451,
Moore County, NC
Everet Wallis entered 50 acres
located on Little Creek

1793, Nov 25 -- Dec 1793-Jan 1794 General Assembly Session Records, Box 3
Moore County residents petitioned the
General Assembly to establish
"Alfordstown" and move the courthouse
there. Petition ultimately failed. Averit
Wallis was listed as a signer.

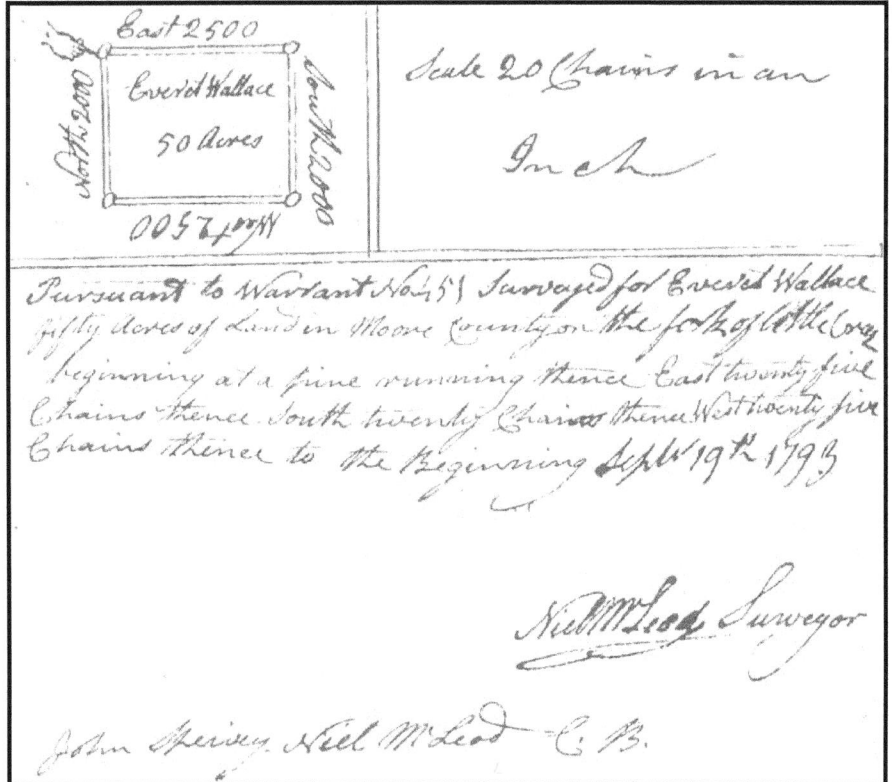

1794, Dec 6 -- Land Grant #508, Moore
County, NC
Everet Wallace received 50 acres located
on Little Creek. John Spivey and Neil
McLeod were chain carriers.

1794, Dec 22 -- Land Grant #1308,
Moore County, NC
Thomas Ritter received 50 acres located
on Richland Creek adjoining Robert
Roan, Rasberry, McSween and McNeill.
Everet Wallace and Jesse Bean were
chain carriers.

1795, Jan -- Petition, Nov 1794-Feb 1795
General Assembly Session Records, Box 3
Folder 15
Citizens of Moore County petitioned the
General Assembly to move the
courthouse to a more suitable location.
Everit Wallis was listed as a signer.

1795, Aug 18 -- 1784-1795 Court of Pleas and Quarter Sessions, Moore County, NC Page 530
Everet Wallace listed as serving Jury Duty

1797, May 10 -- Will Book A, Page 192-193, Moore County, NC
Will of George Williams, Dec'd. Heirs: wife Ann Williams, son James Williams, daughter Nelly Williams, son Jeremiah Williams,
son Thomas Williams, son William Williams, daughter Mary Williams and daughter Sally Williams. Executors: Ann Williams
and Leonard Furr. Witnesses:
Everet Wallis and William
Dunn. Proven Aug 1797.

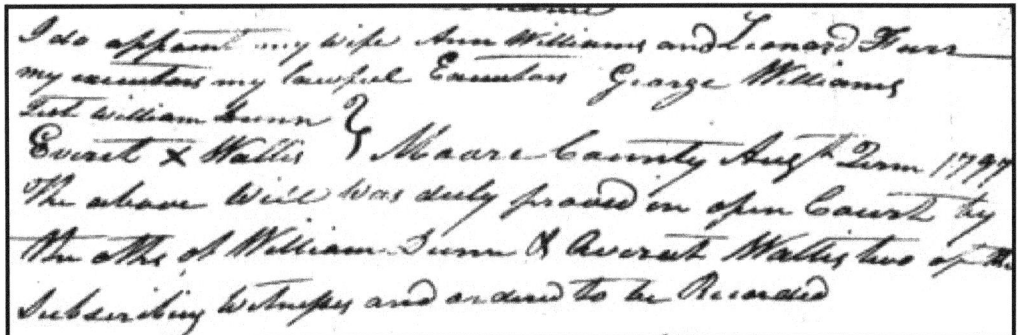

1797, Aug 10 -- Land Grant
#0127, Moore County, NC
Everet Wallis entered 50
acres located on drains of
Flag Creek adjoining his
own line. [*Editor's Note:
never granted*]

1800 -- Census, Moore County, NC Page 57
Evert Wallis
(26-45) 1M 1F
(10-16) 1F
(0-10) 4M 1F

1802, Oct 7 -- Land Grant #0144, Moore County, NC
James Melton entered 300 acres located on Long Meadow Branch adjoining Neil McLeod, Joseph McGee, Robert Wilkins and his own line. Jos. Cockman and Everet Wallis were chain carriers. [*Editor's note: never granted*]

1808, May 7/1811, May 7 -- Land Grant #2209/2136, Moore County, NC
John Cagle received 100 acres located on Flag Creek adjoining Charles Sowell, Jacob Furr, Everet Wallace and William Jones. Everet Wallace and Jacob Furr/Wm. Jones were chain carriers.

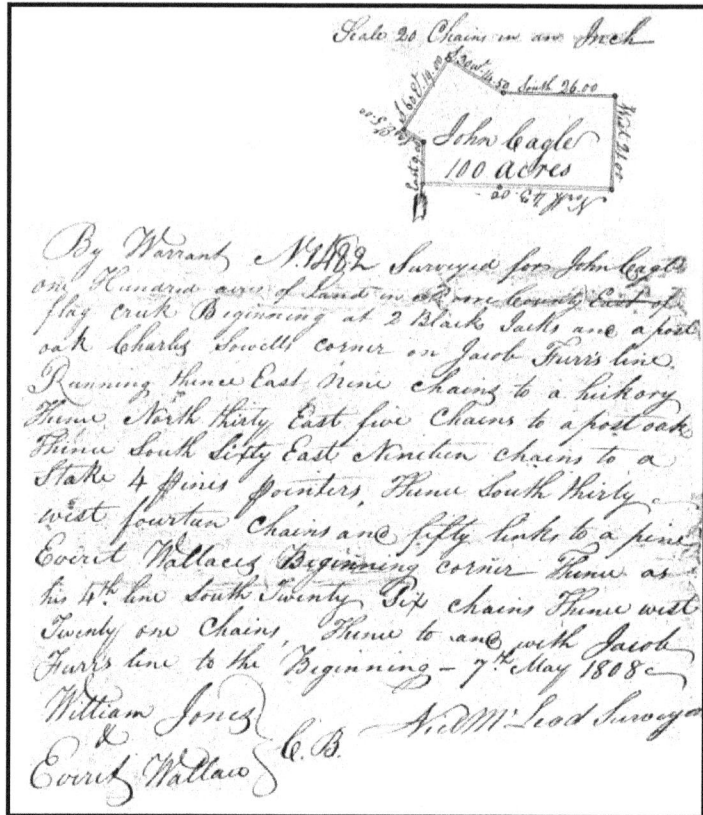

1809, Mar 20 -- Land Grant #2041, Moore County, NC
David Kennedy received 100 acres located on Persimmon Branch. Everet Wallace and Christopher Stutts were chain carriers.

1810 -- Census, Moore County, NC Page 604
Everet Wallace
(26-45) 1M 1F
(16-26) 1M 1F
(10-16) 1M 1F
(0-10) 4M 3F

1811, Feb-Dec [undated estimate] -- Will Book A Page 327, Moore County, NC
Estate of Neill Mathewson, Dec'd.
I account on Everit Wallis for 0"4"6

1811, May 13 -- Deed, Moore County, NC Book 95, Page 25
William Williams deeded Leonard Furr 50 acres located on Flag Creek adjoining Charles Sowell, George Cagle, Graham and Leonard Furr. James Dunlap and Evrett Wallace were witnesses.

1815 -- Tax List, Moore County, NC
Everet Wallis listed 100 acres valued at $100

1816-1827 -- Records of Estates Book B Page 116, Moore County, NC
Estate of Neil McLeod, Dec'd.
1 account on Averet Wallis for 10"27"12
1818-1823 -- Tax List, Moore County, NC
Everet Wallis listed 100 acres valued at $100

1818-1823 -- Tax List, Moore County, NC
Everet Wallis listed 100 acres valued at $100

1820 -- Census, Moore County, NC Page 312
Everet Wallace
(45+) 1M 1F
(16-26) 1M 1F
(10-16) 1M 2F
(0-10) 3F

1825, Apr 12 -- Land Grant #2731, Moore County, NC
William Stutts received 10 acres located on Persimmon Branch adjoining McAulay, Christopher Stutts, William Jones and Neil McLeod. Everet Wallace and William Jones were chain carriers.

1825, May 5 -- Land Grant #2667, Moore County, NC
William Lakey received 14 acres located on Flag Creek adjoining Everet Wallace, Neil McLeod, William Jones and Furr. John Williams and Jacob Stutts were chain carriers.

1825, May 5 -- Land Grant #2668, Moore County, NC
William Lakey received 7 acres located on Flag Creek adjoining Everet Wallace, Jones and McLeod. Henry Stutts and Jacob Stutts were chain carriers.

1825, May 15 -- 1823-1831 Court of Pleas and Quarter Sessions, Moore County, NC Page 80
Everet Wallis listed as serving Jury Duty

1825, Aug 15 -- 1823-1831 Court of Pleas and Quarter Sessions, Moore County, NC Page 81
Everet Wallis listed as serving Jury Duty

1825, Sep 24 -- Land Grant #2687, Moore County, NC
James H. Muse received 150 acres located on Locust Branch adjoining Abraham Stutts, Griffith and William Caddell. Martin Rouse and Everet Wallace were chain carriers.

1828, Nov 9-1831, Aug 16 -- Records of Estates Book B Page 154, 250, Moore County, NC
Estate of George Moore Sr., Dec'd.
1 account on Everet Wallis for $0.50

1829, May 18 -- 1823-1831 Court of Pleas and Quarter Sessions, Moore County, NC Page 263
Everet Wallis listed as serving Jury Duty

1829, Aug 17 -- 1823-1831 Court of Pleas and Quarter Sessions, Moore County, NC Page 272
Everet Wallis listed as serving Jury Duty

1829, Aug 19 -- 1823-1831 Court of Pleas and Quarter Sessions, Moore County, NC Page 277
Everet Wallis listed as serving Jury Duty

1830 -- Census, Moore County, NC Page 447
Everat Wallace
(50-60) 1M 1F
(15-20) 2F
(10-15) 2F
(0-5) 1M

1831 -- Records of Estates Book B Page 246, Moore County, NC
Estate of Jason Sowell, Dec'd.
Everet Wallis purchased 2 barrels of corn for $9.35

1835, Feb -- 1785-1846 Index to Trial Docket, Moore County, NC Page 46
Everet Wallas v. Neil McLeod

1835, May-Feb 1836 -- 1833-1841 County Court Execution Docket, Moore County, NC Pages 28, 32, 39
Everet Wallace [various spellings] v. Neil McLeod

1835, Fall-Spring 1836 -- 1796-1841 County Accounts, Moore County, NC Page 130
State v. Norman Gillis
Everitt Wallace listed as a witness

1840 -- Census, Moore County, NC Page 173 (See image on next page)
Everett Wallace

(70-80) 1M 1F
(20-30) 3F
(10-15) 1M
(5-10) 1F
(0-5) 2F

1844/1845 -- Tax List,
Moore County, NC
Everet Wallis [no land given]

1846 -- Tax List, Moore County, NC
Caty Wallace listed as owing $0.20 for 1845

ADDITIONAL EARLY WALLACES OF MOORE COUNTY, NC

NICHOLAS WALLACE

First and foremost, there are a few mentions of a Nicholas Wallace in between 1784 and 1791 in northern Moore County. He signed a petition in 1784 to divide Cumberland County and create the current county of Moore and in 1785 he signed a petition to establish a courthouse at the center of Randolph County along with other northern Moore County residents and the most informative reference was a 1791 Moore County, NC Land Entry (granted 1793) of 50 acres to Mary Hines. This land was listed as including Nicolas Wallis' improvement. This could have been referencing an actual structure such as a house, barn or fence, etc. or it could have possibly been that Nicolas Wallis simply cleared a portion of the land. This tract of land was located roughly ½ mile north of the Robbins crossroads just west of Hwy 705 and Everet's 50-acre Land Grant. The proximity of these tracts combined with the fact that Everet named his first son Nicholas seem to point to Nicholas potentially being Everet's father. It is my belief that they are closely related but at this point I cannot say with any certainty that Nicholas was Everet's father, brother, cousin or uncle.

The map on the right is of land granted near Everet Wallace by 1800. The highlighted tracks show Everet's 50-acre land grant along with the Mary Hines/Hynes land grant that included Nicholas Wallace's improvement. Finally, the highlighted track of David Cagle was granted in 1769 and sold to William Smith that same year. In the Court of Pleas and Quarter Sessions in 1787, a deed was recorded from William Smith to Mary Hines and proven by Jesse Ritter. While no additional details of the deed remain, I believe that this transaction included all of part of the

land originally granted to David Cagle. Females were rarely deeded land in the late 1700s. It seems likely that Mary was a daughter of William Smith or at the very least a close relative. An additional important part of this deed is that Jesse Ritter was the witness. As you will later see under the DNA analysis, his connection to Everet Wallace is extremely important. William Smith and Nicholas Wallace also happened to sign the 1784 petition (*see image on next page*) in succession. I believe that Mary Hines is a key part of the Wallace puzzle as she appears in records with both Nicholas Wallace and Jesse

Ritter. James Hines can also be found in a few records during this period and appears to be a son or a close relative. Jesse Ritter is also closely connected to the Smith family and sold his initial 1773 land grant to Nathan Smith.

RECORDS OF NICHOLAS WALLACE

1784, May 3 -- Petition, Apr 1784-Jun 1784 General Assembly Session Records, Box 3 Folder 41
Petition of inhabitants of the upper end of Cumberland County to divide the county beginning on the south side of the Cape Fear River at Chatham County line where it crosses the river and runs a direct course to Cole's Bridge on Drowning Creek and so to be bounded by the line of the adjacent counties to make a distinct county. Signers include Nichlos Wallas.

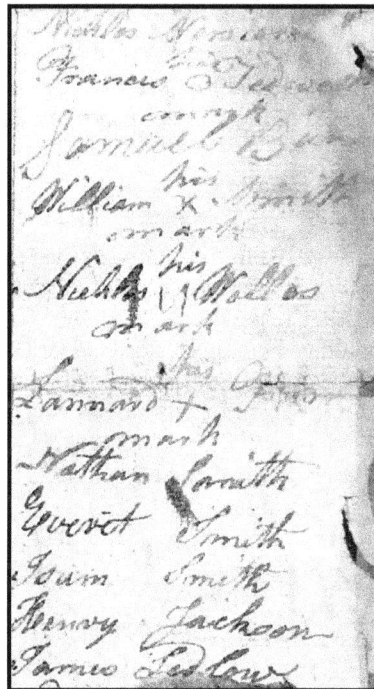

1785, Dec 6 -- Petition, Nov 1785-Dec 1785 General Assembly Session Records, Box 1 Folder 7
Only the petition was included. No details but speculation is that it was a petition to erect a courthouse in the center of Randolph County, NC. There are both Randolph County and Moore County signers including Nicolas Wallis.

1791, Jan 22 -- 1784-1795 Land Entries, Moore County, NC
#317 Mary Hines entered 50 acres located on Persimmon Branch of Flag Creek including Nicholas Wallace's improvement.

1792, May 23 -- Land Grant #432, Moore County, NC
Mary Hines received 50 acres located on Persimmon Branch of Flag Creek including Nicholas Wallace's improvement. Michael Bryant and James Hines were chain carriers.

ADDITIONAL RECORDS OF MARY HINES AND JAMES HINES

1787, Feb 21 -- 1784-1795 Court of Pleas and Quarter Sessions, Moore County, NC Page 140
A deed from William Smith to Mary Hines is proven by Jesse Ritter

1791, Jan 22 -- Land Grant #0190, Moore County, NC
Edward Smith entered 50 acres located on Buffalo Creek adjoining Bean, his own land that he purchased from William Smith and including Hynes' improvement. Warrant sold to James Hynes Nov 24, 1793. Surveyed for James Hines Nov 15, 1794 and Donld. McLeod and James Campbell were chain carriers. [*Editor's Note: grant was never issued*]

1793, Jan 3 -- 1784-1797 Land Entries, Moore County, NC
#532 Christopher Stutts entered 150 acres on Club Branch of Flag Creek adjoining Bartholomew Dunn Sr. and Mary Hynes.

1794, Jun 30 -- Land Grant #402, Moore County, NC
Bartholomew Dunn, Sr. received 50 acres located on Flag Creek adjoining Smith. Henry Cagle and James Hynes were chain carriers.

1800 -- Census, Moore County, NC Page 71
James Hines

(26-45) 1M
(16-26) 1F
(0-10) 2M 1F

1805, Oct 31 -- Land Grant #1904, Moore County, NC
Charles Sowell received 100 acres located on Flag Creek adjoining Mary Hines and his own line. Thomas Williams and Leonard Furr Jr. were chain carriers.

MARY WALLACE

A Mary Wallis was listed in the Moore Court of Pleas and Quarter Sessions in 1788 as being wrongly assessed for a poll tax in 1787. The range of possibilities for who Mary may have been are quite many: [1] She could have been Everet's widowed mother who was assessed for taxes in place of her deceased husband [2] She could've been a widowed sister-in-law [3] She could've been his sister [4] Mary could've have been completely unrelated or she may have even lived in another county and was wrongly assessed. Unfortunately, this record gives no indication as to her location (creek, river, etc.) or any other identifying information. She was not listed in the 1790 Census and no further record of her exists. It is also possible that this Mary Wallis and Mary Hines above are the same person. But again, without any additional information, these possibilities are all just speculation.

1788, Aug 20 -- 1784-1795 Court of Pleas and Quarter Sessions, Moore County, NC Page 203
Ordered that Mary Wallis be exempted from paying poll tax for 1787.

WALLACE DNA ANALYSIS

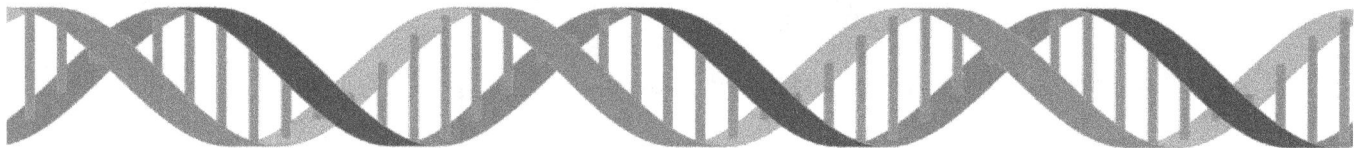

The advance of DNA testing has provided genealogists with an extremely valuable tool in their toolbox. Y-DNA is passed from father to son relatively unchanged for hundreds of years. This is tremendously helpful for surname research where matches between two samples indicate a common male ancestor within a certain period of time based on the number of markers tested and the number of markers that match.

The matches to our results have been interesting and challenging at the same time. To date we have 25 different males that have been tested that share the similar Y-DNA. Due to the advanced testing ability of *FamilyTreeDNA* we know that these men all descend from Haplogroup **R-BY20619**. While a few other DNA testing companies would offer Y-DNA testing in the past, *FamilyTreeDNA* is the only company to offer it currently. The results below and those of other Moore County families can be found at https://www.familytreedna.com/groups/moore-county-nc/about/background

DESCENDANTS OF EVERET WALLACE

• Hurley Wallace Jr. [700 Y-DNA markers analyzed] descends from Everet Wallace 1770-1845 via son Isham Wallace and grandson Emsley Wallace > Lucian Wallace > Hurley Wallace, Sr.

• Ronnie Mitchell "Ron" Wallace [700 markers]. Ron also descends from Isham Wallace via son Virgil Spinks "Byrd" Wallace > Isham Wallace > Claude Cleveland Wallace > William Lewis Wallace.

• Rodney Wallace [700 markers] descends from Everet Wallace through his son John Wallace and grandson Nathan Wallace > Daniel Houston Wallace > David Overton Wallace > Phillip Downy Wallace > Phillip David Wallace. John migrated from Moore County, NC to Bibb County, AL in the 1840's and Nathan and his descendants continued on to Cherokee County, TX during the 1860's.

• David Wallace [700 markers] also descends from John Wallace via son Josiah/Cyrus Wallace > John Wesley Wallace > Noah Columbus Wallace > James Edward Wallace. Josiah/Cyrus Wallace was born in Moore County, NC and migrated with his parents to AL in the 1840's. Many of his descendants can still be found in Bibb County, AL.

• Michael Howard "Mike" Wallace [43 markers] descends from Everet Wallace through his son Joseph Wallace. Joseph's son Ruffin Wallace fought and died in the Civil War. Ruffin was the father of Jerome A. Wallace and grandfather of Audrey Howard Wallace.

ADDITIONAL WALLACE MATCHES

• Neal Wallace [700 markers] descends from Isham Wallace [1778-1853]. Isham was born in North Carolina and resided near the Montgomery and Davidson County line near the Yadkin River. Isham was listed in the 1800 Montgomery County Census, in Tax Lists in Davidson County 1810-1815 and the 1820 Davidson County Census prior to migrating to Calloway and Graves County, KY by 1833. Isham Wallace is believed to have been closely related and possibly a brother to Nathan Wallace [1785-1852] and (see more below) Eli Wallace [1790-1855]. Like Isham, Nathan and Eli migrated with their families to western KY during the late 1820's and early 1830's along with many other neighboring families. Given the prominence of the given names of Isham, Everet, Nathan, Eli in these families it has always been my belief they were connected the to the Wallaces of Moore County, NC. This Y-DNA match is one of the most important discoveries in decades as it confirms that Everet Wallace [b. 1770] and Isham Wallace [b. 1778] share a common male ancestor.

• Edwin E. Wallis II [700 markers] descends from Nathan Wallis [1806-1859] > C.J. Wallis > Joseph J. Wallis > William Cirby Wallis > Edwin E. Wallis Sr. Nathan was born in North Carolina [likely Davidson County, NC], migrated to western Kentucky, died in Obion County, TN and is believed to have been closely related to the families of western Kentucky and may have been a son or nephew of Isham Wallace.

• Jimmy Wallace [700 markers] descends from John Wallace [1809-1893]. John was born in Union County, SC and moved to DeKalb County, AL by 1835. We have not been able to verify John Wallace's father and grandfather yet but there seems to be a connection here. One interesting thing to note is that a Robert Wallace lived in Chatham County, NC during the 1780's-1790's before migrating to Union County, SC where he died in 1800. This Robert owned a tract of land in Moore County, NC [now Lee County]. Jimmy has been trying to confirm a relationship from his John to this Robert but has not been able to verify anything to date. This deed reference is the only mention of Robert Wallace in Moore County and we have never been able to establish a connection with him.

• Terry Smith [700 markers] descends from William Conner Smith [1847-1920] > John Arch Smith > John C. Smith > J.C. Smith. William Conner Smith was the son of Fannie Smith and is listed in the 1850 Census in Moore County, NC next door to Aaron Wallace [1818/1826-aft 1880]. Aaron Wallace and his family moved to the Laurel Hill area of Scotland County, NC by 1870 and William and his mother Fannie did the same. Based on the Y-DNA match, I believe that Aaron was the father of William Conner Smith. Aaron Wallace was likely a child or grandchild of Everet Wallace.

RITTER CONNECTION AND RESULTS

• One of the more monumental findings of our DNA results is the connection to the Ritter family of Moore County, NC. Several male Ritters are very close matches to descendants of Everet Wallace. While we are unsure of the relationship between the Wallace and Ritter families, the Y-DNA matches clearly demonstrate they share a common male ancestor. Many of these men descend from Jesse Ritter [c1735-c1810]. Given these results it is very likely that either Everet Wallace's father or grandfather was a Ritter or that Jesse Ritter, Sr.'s father or grandfather was a Wallace. Recent discoveries suggest that Jesse Ritter's wife Susannah may have been a Wallace adding another complex piece to the puzzle. Ritter Y-DNA matches include:

DESCENDANTS OF JESSE RITTER

• John Ransom Ritter [37 markers] descends from Jesse Sr. > Everett Ritter > Benjamin Franklin Ritter > John Robert Ritter > Elmer Milton Ritter.

• Andy Franklin Ritter [12 markers] descends from Jesse Sr. > Everett Ritter > Everett Ritter Jr. > Isaac A. Ritter > Everett Jackson Ritter > Andrew Jackson Ritter > Alvie Dewitt Ritter.

• Joseph W. Ritter [27 markers] was a descendant of Jesse Sr. > Everett Ritter > James Ritter > John Newton Ritter > William Edwin Ritter > James Benjamin Ritter.

• Eugene L. Ritter [12 markers] was a descendant of Jesse Sr. > Everett Ritter > James Ritter > Benjamin Franklin Ritter > David Martin Ritter > Cecil Franklin Ritter.

• James R. Ritter, [700 markers] descends from Jesse Sr. > John Ritter > Thomas Wesley Ritter > Captain John Ritter > Francis Marion Ritter > Ulysses Grant Ritter > Colon Causey Ritter.

• Eli Ritter, [111 markers] was a descendant of Jesse Sr. > John Ritter > Thomas Wesley Ritter > Captain John Ritter > John Spinks Ritter > Eli Junior Ritter > Gilmer Allison Ritter.

• Morgan Ritter, [37 markers] was a descendant of Jesse Sr. > John Ritter > William D. Ritter > John Henry Ritter > William Thomas Ritter > Charles Edward Ritter > Thomas Alexander Ritter > Charles Edward Ritter

• Darrell Jackson Ritter [37 markers] and his father Nolen Ritter [12 markers] descend from Jesse Sr. > Thomas Ritter [1768-1848 Moore County, NC] > John Thomas Ritter > George D. Ritter > Aaron Ashley Flowers Ritter > Thomas Franklin Ritter.

• James Everett Ritter [111 markers] descends from Jesse Ritter, Sr. > Jesse Ritter, Jr. > Everett Solomon Ritter > James Henry Ritter > James E. Ritter > James Everett Ritter Sr.

• Arbuary Gene Ritter [37 markers] was a descendent of Jesse Sr. > Jesse Ritter Jr. > Everett Solomon Ritter > James Henry Ritter > John Sampson Ritter > Rufus Randolph Ritter

• A Ritter male [37 markers] descends from Jesse Sr. > Jesse Ritter Jr. > Mark Ritter > Wiley Lively Ritter > William Riley Ritter > Aubrey "Blackie" Ritter.

• Timothy Ritter [12 markers] was a descendant of Jesse Sr. > Jesse Ritter Jr. > Mark Ritter > Richardson Ritter > Simon Ritter > Orville Nelson Ritter.

ADDITIONAL RITTER MATCHES

• Bruce Ritter [111 markers], was a descendent of Moses Ritter [1730-1819 New Hanover County, NC] > James Bradbury Ritter [1757-1816 Surry County, NC] > Lazarus Ritter > Joseph Ritter > John Franklin Ritter > Hugh A. Ritter. Moses Ritter was believed to be closely related to Jesse Ritter Sr. of Moore County, NC and may have even been his brother. He lived in Wayne County, NC prior to migrating to New Hanover County, NC [present day Pender County] where he lived near Moore's Creek.

• John Floyd Ritter [700 markers], descends from William Ritter [1789 NC-aft 1870 Claiborne County, TN] > Nathan Silas Ritter > John Franklin Ritter Sr. > Donald Eugene Ritter. William is believed to have been the son of Aaron Ritter [1763-bef 1840] and grandson of Moses Ritter 1730-1819.

• David Thomas Ritter Sr. [700 markers] descends from James Ritter through son William H. Ritter > Thomas Jackson Ritter > Thomas Scofield Ritter. James married Melinda Ballentine in 1841 in Clarksville, Montgomery County, TN. Given the DNA connection, it is very likely that James was a descendant of either Jesse Sr. or Moses Ritter. More research will need to be done to narrow down the connection.

• Gurney Smith Cornwell III [67 markers] can trace his lineage back to Jason Ritter Cornwell [1817-1862 of Southampton County, VA], son of Margaret Cornwell and unknown Ritter.

ADDITIONAL WALLACE RESULTS (DO NOT SHARE SAME Y-DNA AS THE ABOVE MEN)

• John Mack Wallace III and Christopher "Chris" Wallace, descend from John Mack Wallace [1845-1927] and have also been tested. Mack's mother was Franey Wallace, daughter of Everet Wallace and we have been trying to confirm the oral history that had been handed down through generations that Mack's father was a Hunsucker. Both of these samples closely match the Y-DNA of several Hunsucker male descendants likely confirming the oral history. The most likely candidate for John Mack's father was Abraham/Abram C. Hunsucker [1806-1869], son of George Hunsucker [1775-aft 1860] and Sarah Spinks.

• Tom Wallace and Donald Lee Wallace both descend from William Lane Wallace [1814-1886]. William Lane Wallace was born in Moore County, NC and was closely related to Everet and his descendants. We have been unable to identify William Lane's parents but given his date of birth and proximity to Everet it has been believed that he was likely a son or grandson of Everet. Tom and Donald both descend from William Lane > Everett W. Wallace > Charles Chalmers Wallace. Because their Y-DNA does not match any of the tested Wallaces, the results likely indicate that William Lane was the offspring of a Wallace female and unknown male. The most likely scenario would make him Everet's grandson through a daughter.

• Chris Wallace descends from George M. Wallace [1857-1932]. George was born in Moore County, NC, lived near the Moore County Wallaces and even married into a closely related family (Horner), but I am not certain as to the connection. My grandfather told a story of one of Everet's daughters moving to Randolph County and having children by a man named Whistlehunt. Unfortunately, I have not been able to locate any record of a father yet. Chris' Y-DNA does not match any Wallace men but does match the Y-DNA of male Deaton descendants possibly indicating that George's father or grandfather may have been a Deaton.

• Additionally, we have tested three descendants of Eli Wallace [1790-1855]. Eli was born in Montgomery County, NC and migrated to Graves County, KY during the 1830's and is believed to have had brothers Isham and Nathan Wallace [see above]. Clifton Wallace, Chuck Wallace and Charles T. Wallace descend from Eli through his son Kendrick Wallace and three separate sons [Thomas A. Wallace, Ambrose Wallace and Joel Kendrick Wallace]. Their Y-DNA results match each other confirming their ancestral lines back to Kendrick but they do not match any other Wallace men tested above. More research and more samples will need to be tested to gain a better understanding.

• Four descendants of William Wallace [1791/1800-1843] of Montgomery County, NC have also been tested. William resided in the same general vicinity as the Eli, Nathan and Isham Wallace [mentioned above] families of Montgomery/Davidson County, NC and several of William' children migrated to western Kentucky and intermarried with these families. Larry Wallace and his nephew Benjamin G. Wallace descend from William > James Alvis Wallace > Chisholm Clark Wallace > Claude Clark Wallace [Larry's grandfather]. Kurt Wallace also descends from William Wallace via son Alexander Clark Wallace [migrated from Montgomery County, NC to Graves County, KY] > E. Milton Wallace > Herman S. Wallace [Kurt's grandfather] and Ed Wallace who descends from William's son Erasmus Stimpson Wallace > June Harrison Wallace > Verle Lee Wallace [Ed's grandfather]. The results were pretty fascinating as they match a number of Wallaces throughout the country who either trace their ancestry back to Scotch-Irishmen James Wallace [1690-1748] and wife Elizabeth Campbell or Peter Wallace, Sr. [1680-1723] and wife Elizabeth Woods. The connection between James and Peter Sr. has not been established but a number of their descendants share similar Y-DNA. Many of their children immigrated to America and based on the timeframe it is likely that William Wallace was a great-grandson of one of these men. More research is needed to determine the connection, but it is possible that William's father lived in Rowan County, NC and his father came from MD/VA to NC. This likely means that while William Wallace was closely connected to the other Wallace families in the area, he may not have been closely related.

Another nearby Wallace family is that of Thomas Wallis [d. 1800 Randolph County, NC]. There has always been a question as to whether Thomas Wallis was related to the Wallaces of Moore County, NC or the Wallaces of Davidson/Montgomery County, NC. Thomas be found in Randolph County on Brush Creek near the Chatham County line beginning in 1795. Most of his children migrate west in Tennessee and Mississippi. Maxie Wallace and his son Steven Wallis descend from Thomas' son Josiah Wallis [1775 NC -aft 1850 Prentiss County, MS] and match two other Wallace men, Frank Wallace and Julius Wallace. Frank Wallace traces his line back to Henry Wallace [b. 1803] who may be the grandson of Thomas Wallis through his son Timothy Wallis. Julius Wallace seems to descend from Jacob Wallis [b. 1788] who was born in South Carolina and resided in Randolph County, AR. More research and additional samples will be needed to understand these connections.

ANCESTRY OF EVERET WALLACE

Despite over thirty years of research and close examination, Everet Wallace (1770-1845) remains our genealogical roadblock. There have been many theories, close calls, and pure guesses as to who Everet's father was and where the family originated prior to Everet living in Moore County, NC. My belief is that Everet was either born in Moore County, NC or moved there at a young age, possibly from the Yadkin River area of Montgomery and Davidson counties. My grandfather, Mallie Wallace, said his grandfather, Emsley Wallace, told him that Everet was the first Wallace *"in the country."* Now while we know he was nowhere near the first Wallace in the United States, *"in the country"* likely meant *"around here/upper Moore County."*

The following is a list of possible scenarios surrounding the identity of the father of Everet Wallace. In each scenario, the case will be made using records, oral history and lingering questions will be identified.

NICHOLAS WALLACE

Facts. As established earlier, Nicholas Wallace appeared in land records ½ half mile from Everet Wallace. In fact, he is the only Wallace male appearing in records in Moore County, NC during the 1780's. He was likely older than Everet based on the two petitions he signed in 1784 and 1785. Generally, most petition signers were over twenty-one years of age which would place his date of birth before 1763. Everet also named his oldest son Nicholas. A popular English and Scottish cultural naming tradition at the time may hold a clue.[6] If we apply the following to Everet's known children, the results are very interesting.

*The first son was named after the father's father – **Nicholas Wallace***
The second son was named after the mother's father – Joseph Wallace
The third son was named after the father – John Wallace
The fourth son was named after the father's eldest brother – Nathan Wallace
The first daughter after the mother's mother – Celia Wallace
*The second daughter after the father's mother – **Mary Wallace***
The third daughter after the mother – Unknown daughter (1800-1804)
The fourth daughter after the mother's eldest sister – Unknown daughter (1804-1810)

Remember, there was a Mary Wallace listed in 1788 in Moore County as being exempted from poll tax for the prior year of 1787. Poll taxes were due only on free men over the age of twenty-one. A plausible scenario could be that Nicholas died in 1787/1788 and the poll tax was mistakenly applied to his widow Mary.

Questions. If Nicholas was the father of Everet, it would place his birth in the range of 1730-1750. Where was Nicholas prior to 1784? No conclusive records have been located. Another interesting question is what happened to the given name Nicholas in the Wallace line? The given names of Everet, Isham, Nathan, Enoch as well as the more common given names of John and Josiah are prevalent through multiple generations of Everet's descendants, but Nicholas appears to die out with Everet's son. If Nicholas was the father of Everet, it is surprising that Everet did not have one grandchild named Nicholas or any generation thereafter. Numerous online family trees list Nicholas and Mary as the parents of Everet and state Nicholas was from Craven County, NC. Zero proof is offered for this conclusion.

Conclusion. I feel very confident that Nicholas Wallace was a close relative of Everet Wallace. But it is just as possible that he was Everet's brother, cousin or uncle as it was that he was his father. Unless additional records are located, we may never know for certain.

DAVIDSON/ROWAN/MONTGOMERY COUNTY WALLACES

Facts. Isham Wallace (1778-1853), Nathan Wallace (1785-1852) and Eli Wallace (1790-1855) lived in the area in southern Davidson County near the Montgomery County line and all migrated with their young families to western Kentucky during the late 1820's/early 1830's. While I do not have concrete proof that these three men were brothers, and that Mary was their mother – several records point in that direction. Mary Wallace (45+) and Isham Wallace (16-26) are living next door to each other in the 1800 Montgomery County, NC Census. Mary has two sons listed in her household (10-16) & (16-26) that match the ages of Nathan and Eli. Eli Wallace (1790-1855) listed his birthplace as Montgomery County, NC and parents as E. Wallace and M. Wallace on his death certificate in Graves County, KY. Eli Wallace was granted 30 acres in Montgomery County in 1826 adjoining his own tract of 200 acres that was originally purchased by Mary Wallace from John Morris in 1794. Nathan Wallace (1785-1852) was also listed as having been born in North Carolina and in 1850 was living next door to Isham's son Isham (b. 1804) in Graves County, KY. *More information on these Wallace and their descendants can be found starting on Page 534.*

A male descendant of Isham Wallace (1778-1853) shares the same Y-DNA as male descendants of Everet Wallace, Moses Ritter and Jesse Ritter. Nathan Wallis (1806-1859) seems to be clearly connected and likely related to these Wallace families above as he was born in Davidson County and migrated to Kentucky living very near the other Wallaces. A male descendant of Nathan Wallis also shares this same Y-DNA meaning that Isham Wallace and Nathan Wallis share a common male ancestor with Everet Wallace, Moses Ritter and Jesse Ritter.

Jesse Wallace (b. bef 1748) and his wife Susanna also lived in the northwest section of Montgomery County on Mountain Creek in the same vicinity as Mary Wallace and her children and is likely closely connected. Jesse Wallace also owned 200 acres in Montgomery County in 1782.

Questions. Isham Wallace and Everet Wallace sharing a common male ancestor adds another layer to the mystery of the Wallace/Ritter connection. First of all, could Isham have been a brother to Everet Wallace? Comparing Everet's birth date of 1770 along with the birthdates of Isham 1778, Nathan 1785 and Eli 1790, it is possible that Everet could have been an older brother, cousin or even uncle of one or more of these men.

Jesse Wallace was married to Susanna during the 1770's but it is unclear if she was his only wife or first wife. Could Jesse Wallace be the father of Isham, Nathan, and Eli? Could Mary have been his widow? Jesse Wallace listed 200 acres of land on the 1782 Montgomery County tax list. Mary sold 200 acres to John Morris in 1794.

We know that Jesse was at least 21 years of age in 1769 when he signed the Regulators petition, but we do not know old how he actually was. He could have been anywhere from his 20's to 60's. Could Jesse have been Mary's father in law and the grandfather of Isham, Nathan and Eli Wallace?

Jesse Wallace (b. bef 1748) was married to Susannah and during the same period of time that Jesse Ritter (b. 1735) was married to Susannah/Hannah/Anna Wallace. Could it be possible that Jesse Wallace and Jesse Ritter were closely related or potentially even the same person? They appear in enough records consistently in neighboring counties that it seems unlikely they are the same person, but the coincidence is fascinating, nonetheless.

Conclusion. The DNA match between the descendants of Isham Wallace (1778-1853) and Everet is one of the most important discoveries in decades. If we can continue to locate and test additional Wallace men who descend from these western Kentucky Wallaces the results will get us closer and closer to the truth. I believe Jesse Wallace plays an important connection in this puzzle.

JOHN WALLACE [OF CALHOUN COUNTY, AL]

Facts. Male descendants of John Wallace (1809-1839) share the same Y-DNA as male descendants of Everet Wallace (1770-1845). John Wallace was born in Union County, SC and migrated to Benton [later renamed Calhoun] County, AL during the 1830's and resided most of his adult life in DeKalb County, AL. *More information on John and his descendants can be found on Page 559.*

Questions. How does John fit into the picture? Could he be a descendant of the Davidson/Montgomery County Wallaces? An interesting possible connection could possibly be with Robert Wallace who can be found in Chatham County records during the 1780's but it is unclear is there is any connection between John and Robert or Robert and the Moore County Wallaces. Robert died in 1800 owning several tracts of land in Granvillle, Chatham and Moore counties as well as Union County, SC and a large number of slaves.[7] Neither the Moore County Wallaces or John Wallace of SC/AL owned slaves or large tracts of land, so it is possible Robert belonged to an entirely different set of Wallaces.

Conclusion. John was born in 1809 suggesting that he is of the same generation as Everet's children. It is possible that he was as closely related to Everet and could be a nephew, great nephew or cousin of Everet. While the DNA connection is clear, the given names of Everet, Isham, Nathan and Eli are not found among John's descendants as they are in both the Moore County Wallaces and the Montgomery/Davidson County Wallaces which could also point to a connection further back in time.

JESSE RITTER

Facts. Male descendants of Jesse Ritter (1735-1810) share the same Y-DNA as male descendants of Everet Wallace (1770-1845). It is an absolute fact that Jesse Ritter and Everet Wallace share a common male ancestor. *More information on Jesse and his descendants can be found on Page 561.*

Questions. Could Everet be the son of Jesse Ritter? There are several possibilities to consider (1) Everet was the out of wedlock son of Jesse Ritter and a Wallace female (2) Everet's father was a brother or close relative of Jesse Ritter (3) Everet Wallace's grandfather and Jesse Ritter's father were brothers or the common male ancestor could be a generation further removed.

According to the Ritter family oral history, Jesse Ritter was the son of John Henry Ritter Jr. and grandson of German immigrant John Heinrich Ritter. Jesse and his half-brother John left the Salisbury, NC area and settled in Moore County, NC near their uncle Moses Ritter. Was Everet born in the Davidson/Rowan County area and migrated to Moore County with the Ritters? Jesse reportedly married Susannah/Hanna/Anna Wallace and had eleven children. Jesse's wife Susannah apparently left him, and he married Charlotte and had two more children. Susannah returned and "ran off" Charlotte and the kids and they left for South Carolina.

This is the specific account of William Young Ritter, grandson of Everet Ritter: *"Pap [Everet Ritter] said his family came there in the late 1600's when his grandfather was just a boy. His name was John Henry Ritter and when he was grown, him and some of his brothers left Pennsylvania and went further south. John Henry himself settled into Virginia where he married a girl that died giving birth to Pap's father, Jesse Ritter. Later on, he moved to North Carolina and married again to a widow lady named Gussie. They had several children together, I'm not sure of all their names but I know Jesse and his half-brother, John left there and settled in Moore County, North Carolina. There may have been more of them moved there but John was the only one Pap ever talked on about. Another one of their brothers moved to Indiana and there are still people living there who we are related to as well as all over Tennessee. I'm reasonably certain we're related to all the Ritter's in Mississippi and Alabama too. Jesse and John Ritter had an uncle living in Moore County and the story goes that he talked Jesse and John into moving there with the promise of rich farmland to be had for the taking. Pap said Uncle Moses was a mean old bastard and he near worked those boys to death clearing his own land. Once John and Jesse got enough ahead to get their own land, Jesse married a wild woman named either Susannah, Hanna or Anna according to who was telling the story. And there were a lot of stories about her to be sure. Everybody said Jesse was an easygoing, Christian man but his wife made his life miserable and she had been known to take after him with an iron skillet on more than one occasion. She was supposed to be a Wallace, but no one was sure. Lots of Pap's family claimed that woman came straight from the loins of old Scratch. They had eleven younguns together, Everett who was my grandfather, John, Hannah, August who died as a child. Thomas, Cloey, Elizabeth, James (he didn't never marry), Jesse, Nancy, and Susan. It seems like they was all good names cause our family kept on using them through the years. Pap would often tell different ones they had been named after Uncle this or Auntie that. Anyways, Jesse's wife run off and left him after all the younguns were borned. He told everyone it was because his aunt was a bad influence on her but like I said, he was supposedly a sweet natured person who would forgive anything. After some time, he married another woman named Charlotte and they had two more children, Hannah and Daniel. We never knew them and Pap thinks they moved to South Carolina cause Susannah came back one day and chased Charlotte out of the house, telling her she would have her arrested for fornication as she and Grandpa Jesse had never got no divorce. I guess that means we got relations in South Carolina too."* [8]

Everet Ritter (1759-aft 1850) was Jesse and Susanna Ritter's oldest son. The name Everet was not a common name during that period of time and can only be found in the Smith and Sheffield families of northern Moore County. Everet Smith (1751-1822) was the earliest known individual with the given name Everet in northern Moore County. Jesse Ritter was closely connected to the Smith family and sold his original land grant on Wet Creek to Everet Smith's father, Nathan Smith, in 1774. To add to the questions and intrigue – Nathan Smith (1731-1811) not only had a son named Everet, but he also had sons Nicholas and Isham! Nathan and his family migrated to Banks County, GA by 1798 and his children continued west to Lawrence County, MS during the 1810s. These given names continue on through multiple generations of Smith descendants. To add more fuel to the fire, remember Mary Hines? She was granted the land that Nicholas Wallace had improved. In 1787, she was deeded nearby land from William Smith and the witness to the deed was Jesse Ritter. Additionally, Jesse Ritter was a chain carrier on two additional land grants for this same William Smith in 1774. Jesse was granted land on Wet Creek in 1773 and in 1774 he sold it to none other than Nathan Smith. Prior to learning of the oral history suggesting Jesse Ritter's wife was a Wallace, it had long been my belief that he most likely married into the Smith family given the close connection in records. It is certainly possible that he was married twice and that the mother of his Ritter children was a Smith female. It is also just as possible that Susannah was not a Wallace and that the Wallace connection comes through a child out of wedlock. Speaking of given names being passed down through different generations, the given name of Jesse is very rarely found among Everet's descendants.

Conclusion. The DNA match combined with the proximity of Everet Wallace and Jesse Ritter in Moore County paint a fairly strong picture that these two men were very close relatives. The DNA match with Isham Wallace of Davidson County makes it unlikely that Jesse was Everet's father as he would have had to have been Isham's as well. I believe their common male ancestor is likely a generation or two removed from Jesse and Everet such as Jesse's father/grandfather and Everet Wallace's grandfather/great-grandfather were brothers.

MOSES RITTER

Facts. Male descendants of Moses Ritter (1730-1819) share the same Y-DNA as male descendants of Everet Wallace (1770-1845). Similar to Jesse Ritter, it is an absolute fact that Moses Ritter and Everet Wallace share a common male ancestor.

Moses Ritter was believed to be closely related to Jesse Ritter Sr. of Moore County, NC and may have even been his brother. He lived in Wayne County, NC prior to migrating to New Hanover County, NC [present day Pender County] where he lived near Moore's Creek. Moses first appears in Johnston County, NC [the portion that later became Wayne County] in 1753 and can consistently be found in eastern North Carolina until his death in 1819. Moses Ritter's wife was Hannah Bradbury, daughter of James Bradbury (d. 1786). *More information on Moses and his descendants can be found on Page 576.*

Questions. Could this Moses be the uncle that the Ritter oral history stated lived in Moore County? Could he be a brother or cousin of Jesse Ritter? Knowing the DNA connection, we know that Jesse and Moses were closely related. The oral history draws a direct migration path from Pennsylvania to Virginia to Rowan County, NC to Moore County for the Ritter clan. How did Moses end up in eastern North Carolina? When and where did he branch off? Moses can be found consistently in eastern North Carolina from 1753-1819 but no records exist for him in Moore County.

In 1809, Moses Ritter published a notice in a Wilmington, NC newspaper stating that his wife "*Hannah has deserted my bed and board, without any provocation. I do hereby forewarn all persons whatever, from dealing with her, as I am determined not to pay, or answer any of her contracts, to which I requeit all persons to take due notice. Nevertheless, if my said wife Hannah will return to me, I will support her as usual, or procure a good house for her reception.*" The oral history (of Jesse and Susannah Wallace) and the newspaper notice are eerily similar. Maybe it is a coincidence or maybe there are errors in the oral history as it was passed from generation to generation?

Conclusion. The DNA match combined with the oral history of the Ritter family likely point to Moses being a brother or close relative of Jesse Ritter. Similar to his connection to Jesse Ritter, I believe the common male ancestor between Moses Ritter and Everet Wallace is likely a generation or two removed from Moses and Everet and it is possible that that Moses's father/grandfather and Everet Wallace's grandfather/great-grandfather were brothers.

To conclude this section on the possible ancestry of Everet Wallace, it is important to review all the isolated facts, records and oral history and construct a larger narrative. By combining the oral history of the Ritters migrating to a settlement near Salisbury, NC with the Wallace family of Davidson and Montgomery counties sharing the same DNA and the common given names of Everet, Isham, Nathan and Eli it paints a potential picture of the Wallace and Ritter lines crossing in that area and a child or children born out of wedlock being the reason for all of these DNA matches. I have edited an 1808 map of North Carolina by *Jonathan Price* and *John Strother* to illustrate the approximate location of each of these families.[9]

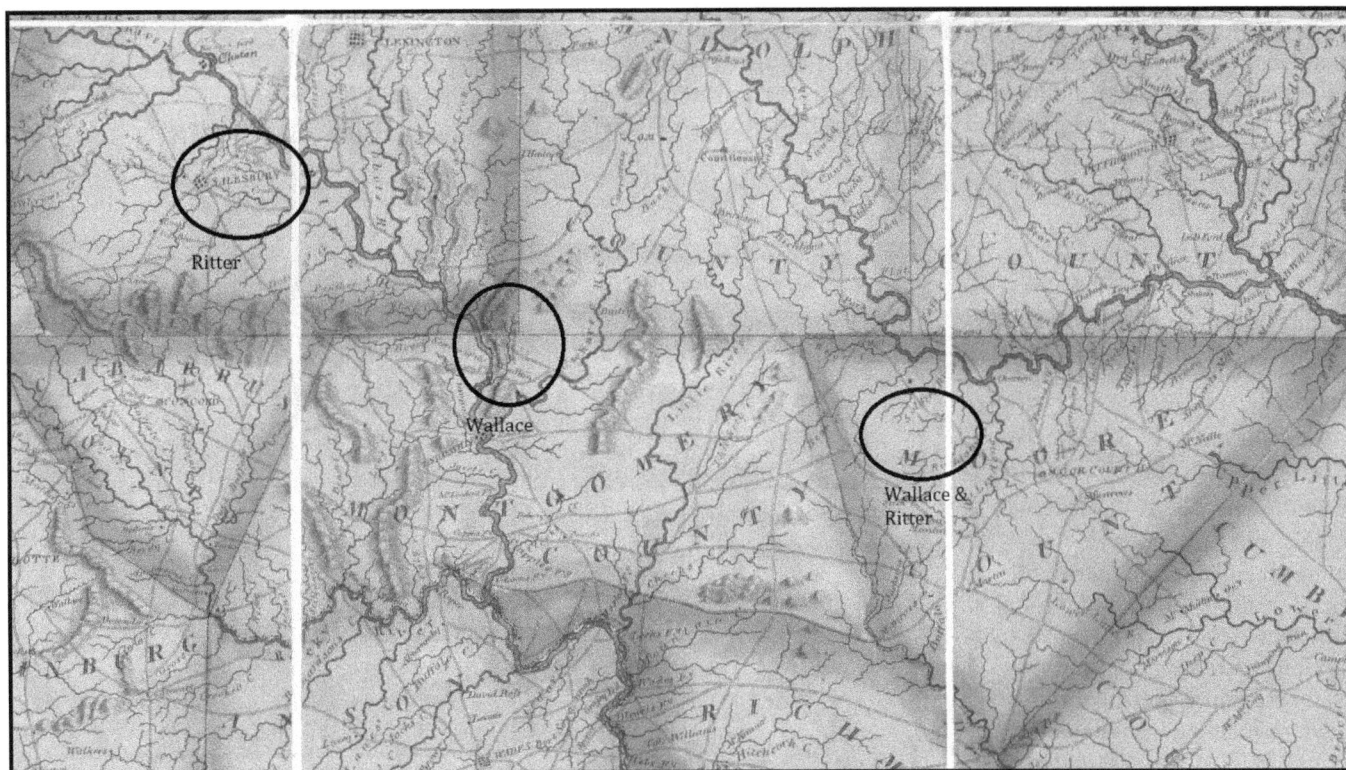

Descendants of Everet Wallace through Five Generations

1. **Everet Wallace** was born circa 1770. He died circa 1845.

> **Caty\Catherine** was born circa 1770. She died between 1845 and 1850. She and Everet Wallace had the following children:

+2	Celia Wallace (1788-1862)
+3	Nicholas Wallace (aft 1790-)
+4	Mary Wallace (aft 1790-)
+5	Joseph Wallace (aft 1792-bef 1870)
+6	John Wallace (1798-c. 1866)
+7	Nathan C. Wallace (1800-1884)
+8	Female2 Wallace (aft 1800-)
+9	Isham Wallace (1801-1882)
+10	Female3 Wallace (aft 1804-)
+11	Josiah Wallace (1807-bef 1880)
+12	Enoch Wallace (c. 1808-aft 1880)
+13	Elizabeth Wallace (1808-)
+14	Manda Wallace (1810-)
+15	Franey Wallace (1814-aft 1880)
+16	Susannah Wallace (1815-)

Second Generation

2. **Celia Wallace**, daughter of Everet Wallace and Caty\Catherine, was born circa 1788 and died 1862. Celia married **Shadrach Maness** (1770-1858), one of the triplet sons of Revolutionary War soldier William Maness Jr. (1738-1832). Shadrach and Celia are believed to have lived near Bear Creek just north of the town of Robbins and were buried near their homeplace (Maness Cemetery #266) at the corner of North Moore Road and Frye Drive at what used to be a planer mill site.[10] Tombstones were erected later for them at the Maness Cemetery (#225) located off North Moore Road near Bear Creek. The map shows the approximate locations of Shadrach and Celia's homeplace and the Maness Cemetery (#225).

Celia and Shadrach were the parents of at least six children: Catherine "Katie", Everett, Asa, Lucretia "Little Cressy", Alsey and Ira Lane "Irely". Mariah Maness (1800-1881), wife of Jacob C. Stutts is also believed to be Shadrach's daughter. It is my belief that Ann Mariah was the child of Shadrach Maness and a previous marriage. I believe the distance between the Ann Mariah (b. 1800) and next child, Catherine (b. 1814) points to a previous marriage. Additional circumstantial evidence of the previous marriage would be the naming of Celia Wallace Maness' oldest daughter and oldest son after her parents Catherine and Everet.

SHADRACH MANESS 1770 1858

(both photographed Jun 13, 2009)

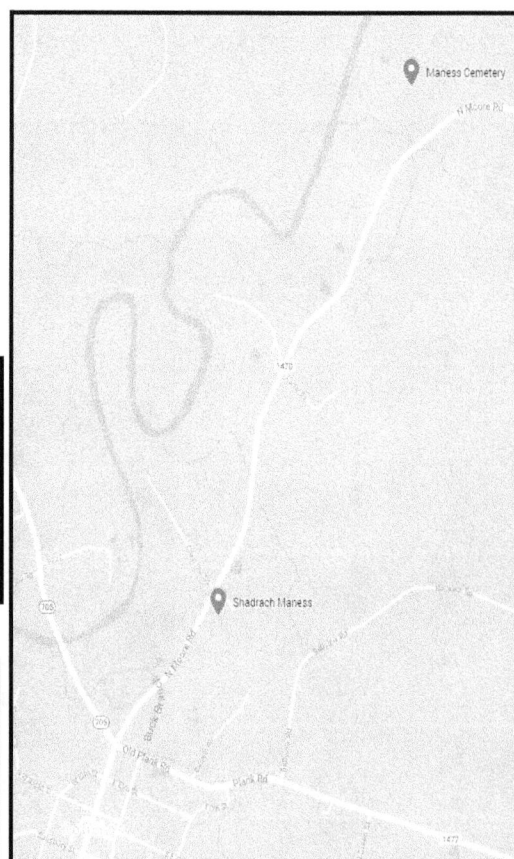

CELIA W. MANESS 1780 — 1862

Shadrach Maness appears in a couple of early petitions during the 1790's but then largely disappears from Records of over a decade. It raises the question did he leave Moore County for a period? It is certainly possible that given the loss of records due to the Moore County courthouse fire in 1889 that he was present, but the records were destroyed. He was granted land in 1810, is listed on the 1815 tax list but is not recorded in the census until 1830. Celia Wallace Maness' age also fluctuates during the census listings from 1830-1850 raising additional questions.

RECORDS OF SHADRACH MANESS AND CELIA WALLACE

1785, Dec 6 -- Petition, Nov 1785-Dec 1785 General Assembly Session Records, Box 1 Folder 7
Only the petition was included. No details but speculation is that it was a petition to erect a courthouse in the center of Randolph County, NC. There are both Randolph County and Moore County signers including Shadrack Maness.

1793, Nov 25 -- Dec 1793-Jan 1794 General Assembly Session Records, Box 3
Moore County residents petitioned the General Assembly to establish "Alfordstown" and move the courthouse there. Petition failed. Shadrach Maness was listed as a signer.

1810, Mar 29 -- Land Grant #2063, Moore County, NC
Shadrach Manes received 50 acres located southeast of Bear Creek adjoining Neil McLeod. Abednego Manes and Howel Brewer were chain carriers.

1810, Apr 12 -- Deed, Moore County, NC
Jesse Ritter Senr. deeded 100 acres to his grandchildren [children of daughter Susanna and husband Daniel Muse] located between Richland and McLendons Creek being part of 200 acres adjoining Jesse Sowell, Everiter Ritter, Donald McQueen, Wm. Barret, Farquard Campbell and McIver (formerly McLeod). Jesse Muse and Shadrach Manes were witnesses. [*Editor's Note: Private deed in possession of Frank Muse, Carthage, NC*]

1815 -- Tax List, Moore County, NC
Shadrick Maness listed 50 acres valued at $70

1826, Nov 8 -- Land Grant #2734, Moore County, NC
Shadrach Manes received 16 acres located south of Bear Creek adjoining Neil McLeod and heirs of John McAulay. Everit Manes and James Manes were chain carriers.

1830 -- Census, Moore County, NC Page 447
Shadrach Manus
(50-60) 1M
(30-40) 1F
(20-30) 1F
(15-20) 1M 1F
(10-15) 1M 1F
(5-10) 1M
(0-5) 1M

1830, May 19 -- 1823-1831 Court of Pleas and Quarter Sessions, Moore County, NC Page 311
A deed from John Sowell to Samuel Jackson was proven by Shadrack Maness

1836, Sep 1 -- Superior Court Minute Docket, Moore County, NC
State v. Celia Mainer

1837, Feb -- County Accounts, Moore County, NC
State v. Sealy Manor

1840 -- Census, Moore County, NC Page 180
Shadrack Maner
(70-80) 1M
(40-50) 1F
(15-20) 1F
(10-15) 2M 1F
(5-10) 1 M

(0-5) 1M

1841, Fall -- 1836-1844 Recognizance Docket
#36 State v. Polly Campbell, Celia Mainer, Delphy Lakey, Betsy Smith, George Hunsucker merchant and William L. Wallace

1842, Spring -- Recognizance Docket & State Docket County Court, Moore County, NC
State v. Polly Campbell, Celia Mainer, Delphy Lakey, Betsy Smith

1842, Spring -- 1836-1844 Recognizance Docket, Moore County, NC
#23 State v. Polly Campbell, Celia Mainer and Betsy Smith (A and B). William L. Wallace and Shadrack Mainer were securities.

1842, Spring -- 1834-1851 State Docket County Court, Moore County, NC Page 165
#23 State v. Polly Campbell, Celia Mainer, Delphy Lakey and Betsy Smith. William L. Wallace was security.

1843, Fall -- 1836-1844 Recognizance Docket, Moore County, NC
#5 State v. Celia Mainer and Polly Campbell. William L. Wallace was a security.

1844, Spring -- 1843-1847 Superior Court Execution Docket, Moore County, NC
#147 State v. Polly Campbell and Celia Mainer. Delphy Wallace and Evirit Mainess were witnesses. Continued Fall 1844
#117 -- Spring 1845 #107 -- Fall 1845 #108 -- Spring 1846 #121 -- Fall 1846 #120 -- Spring 1847 #114 -- Fall 1847 #108

1846 -- Tax List, Moore County, NC
Shadrick Maness listed 84 acres valued at $60 located on Bear Creek in District 9

1847 -- Tax List, Moore County, NC
Shadrick Maness listed 84 acres valued at $84 located on Bear Creek in District 9

1849 -- Tax List, Moore County, NC
Shadrick Maness listed 84 acres valued at $84 located on Bear Creek in District 9

1850 -- Census, Moore County, NC Page 236-B
Shadrack Manus 80 M, Farmer, $62 Real Estate, born in North Carolina
Celia Manus 70 F, born in North Carolina
Lucretia Manus 25 F, born in North Carolina
Irely Manus 16 M, Farmer, born in North Carolina

1852 -- Tax List, Moore County, NC
Shadrac Maness listed 84 acres valued at $84 located on Bear Creek in District 9

1852, Oct 27 -- 1851-1853 Court of Pleas and Quarter Sessions, Moore County, NC Page 347-349
The following lands will be sold at the courthouse in Carthage at the 4th Monday in 1852 to satisfy taxes for 1850 and 1851:
Shadrick Mainess 84 acres

Shadrach Maness and Celia Wallace had the following children:

+17 Catherine "Katie" Maness (1814-1890) married her first cousin Garner Maness (1806-1863), son of Abednego Maness and Susannah "Sukie" Garner and their union produced ten children. Garner owned 278 acres on Bear Creek, and they are both buried at the Maness Cemetery located off North Moore Road near Bear Creek.

+18 Everett Maness (1818-1876) married Lucinda Shields (1818-1884), migrated to Hall County, GA during the 1840's and their union produced eleven children.

+19 Asa Maness (1820-1894) married Mary Ann Ritter (1825-1894), lived south of Deep River on Scotchman's Creek near Buffalo Creek and raised ten children. They are buried in a Maness

Additional Information can be found at www.MooreCountyWallaces.com   22

family cemetery located off NC Highway 22 between Parkwood and McConnell near their homeplace. Asa also fathered a child out of wedlock, Addison Worth Ritter, with his sister-in-law Eliza Ritter.

+20 Lucretia"Little Cressy" Maness (1825-aft 1880) never married nor produced any children and is buried at the Maness Cemetery on North Moore Road.

+21 Alsey Maness (1825-1909) was first married to Catherine Cagle (1833-c1854) and they had two children. After Catherine died, Alsey married Nancy Melton (1833-1899) and they produced ten children.

+22 Ira Lane "Irely" Maness (1832-1912) married Catherine Ritter (1835-bef 1870) and they produced six children. After Catherine's death, Ira married the widow of Bradley "Red Brad" Brady, Nancy A. Hancock (1830-1928) and raised two more children. Ira and Nancy are both buried at Pleasant Hill United Methodist Church.

3. **Nicholas Wallace**, son of Everet Wallace and Caty\Catherine, was born between 1790 and 1794 and died after 1830. Nicholas is believed to have been the oldest son of Everet and Caty/Catherine Wallace. After marriage, Nicholas and his wife lived on Wet Creek near the intersection of NC Highway 705 and Oak Ridge Road between Eagle Springs and Zion Grove. During the 1820's, Nicholas and his family joined other families from northern Moore County and migrated to the western Tennessee counties of Henderson, McNairy and Madison. During the 1830s-1850s, numerous families made this migration including neighboring Britt, Williams, Cagle, Melton, Smith, Spivey, Dunn and Brewer families. Nicholas Wallace can be found on the 1830 Census for Henderson County, TN and is later referenced as owning adjacent property in an 1847 land grant to David O.N. Wadley. Rev. Wadley was a Presbyterian Minister who was active in the founding of the Palestine Church in Henderson County, TN. This is the same church that Nicholas' brother Nathan and nephew Samuel were charter members of in 1881. These are the only two references of Nicholas Wallace in Henderson County, TN and unfortunately, most local records during the period were destroyed in a courthouse fire. It is unclear if Nicholas died in Henderson County or continued migrating further west. Nicholas and his wife appear to have had at least six children but to date the names have not been identified.

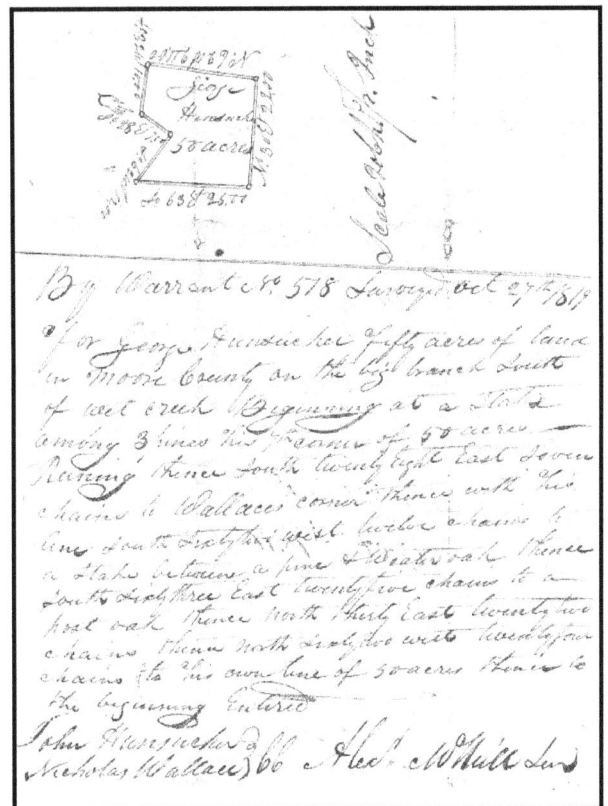

RECORDS OF NICHOLAS WALLACE

1810 -- Census, Moore County, NC Page 599
Nicolas Wallace
(16-26) 1M 1F

1818, Feb 10 -- Land Grant #2490, Moore County, NC
George Hunsucker received 10 acres located East of Wet Creek adjoining his own line, John Gibson, John McKinnon, George Cox, Alexander McKinnon and Donald McKinnon. John Hunsucker and Nicholas Wallace were chain carriers.

1819, Oct 27 -- Land Grant #2508, Moore County, NC
George Hunsucker received 50 acres located South of Wet Creek adjoining Wallace, Neil McLeod, Dunn, John Gibson, his own line, and John McKinnon. John Hunsucker and Nicholas Wallace were chain carriers.

1820 -- Census, Moore County, NC Page 311
Nicholas Wallace
(26-45) 1M 1F
(16-26) 1F
(10-16) 1M 1F
(0-10) 3M 1F

1823, Oct 18 -- Record of Estates Book B Page 76
Estate of Meloney Newton, Dec'd by Administrator Jesse Brown. Notes due on the following: William Dunn, Christopher Stuts, Nicholas Wallis and Malcolm Mathewson.

1830 -- Census, Henderson County, TN Page 98
Nicholas Wallace
(40-50) 1M
(30-40) 1F
(15-20) 1M
(10-15) 1M 1F
(5-10) 1M 1F
(0-5) 1F

1847, Mar 23 -- Land Grant #5345, Book 7 Page 90, Henderson County, TN David O.N. Wadley received 153 acres located in Range 4, Section 8 adjoining Nicholas Wallace, William Wadley and J.R. Mullins.

Nicholas's wife was born between 1790 and 1794. She and Nicholas Wallace had the following children:
+23 Male Wallace (aft 1810-)
+24 Female Wallace (aft 1815-)
+25 Male Wallace (aft 1815-)
+26 Male Wallace (c. 1820-)
+27 Female Wallace (aft 1820-)
+28 Female Wallace (aft 1825-)

4. **Mary Wallace**, daughter of Everet Wallace and Caty\Catherine, was born between 1790 and 1794 and married **Martin Rouse** (b. 1792). Martin served in the War of 1812 under Captain William Dowd and can be found in several records around Locust Branch and Richland Creek. Very little is known about Mary Wallace and her name was only discovered in Martin Rouse's War of 1812 pension application. Everet Wallace had a previously unidentified daughter during this time and Martin Rouse routinely appeared in records with Everet Wallace as well as Mary's brothers Isham Wallace and Enoch Wallace. In this 1871 application, Rouse states that he married Mary Wallace in Moore County, NC although two dates were provided on different versions of the application [20 Oct 1812 and 15 Nov 1821].[11] It is unclear as to the reason for the different dates. Martin (and presumably Mary) migrated to Hall County, GA during the late 1820's and can be found there in the 1830 Census. Martin appears to have been married to Elizabeth by the 1850 Census. Martin listed several children on census records beginning in 1820 but to date, the names of the children or their relationship to Mary cannot be determined. Martin Rouse was likely the son of Joseph Rouse (B. 1760-1770) and brother to Miles and John. Joseph Rouse and his sons all migrated to Georgia during the late 1820's. Many North Carolina families migrated to the state as the frontier moved further westward after multiple treaties forcibly took land from the Creek and Cherokee Indians. An 1830 map of the Cherokee Nation in Georgia depicts Hall County, GA in relation to the lands of the Cherokee Nation.[12]

1820 -- Census, Moore County, NC Page 307
Martin Rouse
(26-45) 1M 1F
(0-10) 2M

1824, Aug 19 -- 1823-1831 Court of Pleas and
Quarter Sessions, Moore County, NC Page 52
Ordered that Daniel Caddell be appointed
overseer of the road from Bean's Bridge to
Flowers Road and have the following hands to work: Leonard Lawhon, John McIntosh, John Murchison, Enoch Wallis, Isham
Wallis, John Rouse, Miles Rouse, Martin Rouse, John McDonald, Hugh Kelly, James Hill, Martin Hill, Dickson Ritter, James Ritter,
Samuel Barrett, Wm. Barrett Esq.'s boy, Simon Murchison and Daniel Murchison.

1825, Aug 15 -- 1823-1831 Court of Pleas and Quarter Sessions, Moore County, NC Page 82
Ordered that Jesse Muse be appointed overseer of the road from Beans Bridge to the hill at the Widow Bethune's and have
the following hands to work: Leonard Lawhon, John Muse, Miles Rouse, John McIntosh, John Rouse, James Hill, Martin Hill, Walter Barrett, Dickson Ritter, Martin Rouse, Daniel Caddell and Enoch Wallis.

1825, Sep 24 -- Land Grant #2687, Moore County, NC
James H. Muse received 150 acres located on both sides of
Locust Branch of Richland Creek adjoining Abraham
Stutts, Griffith and William Caddell. Martin Rouse and
Everit Wallace were chain carriers.

1826, Aug 21 -- 1823-1831 Court of Pleas and Quarter
Sessions, Moore County, NC Page 129
Ordered that John J. McIntosh be appointed overseer of
the road from Bean's Bridge to the hill at the Widow
Bethune's in place of Jesse Muse and have the following
hands to work: Leonard Lawhon, John Muse, Miles
Rouse, John McIntosh, John Rouse, James Hill, Martin Hill,
Walter Barrett, Dickson Ritter, Martin Rouse, Donald
Caddell and Enoch Wallis.

1827, Aug 20 -- 1823-1831 Court of Pleas and Quarter
Sessions, Moore County, NC Page 177
Ordered that James Hill be appointed overseer of the
road from Bean's Bridge to the hill at the Widow
Bethune's in place of John McIntosh and have the
following hands to work: John J. McIntosh, Leonard
Lawhon, John Muse, Miles Rouse, John McIntosh, John
Rouse, Martin Hill, Walter Barrett, Dickson Ritter, Martin Rouse, Daniel Caddell and Enoch Wallis.

1830 -- Census, Hall County, GA Page 74
Martin Rouse
(30-40) 1M 1F
(10-15) 1M
(5-10) 1M 2F
(0-5) 2M 1F

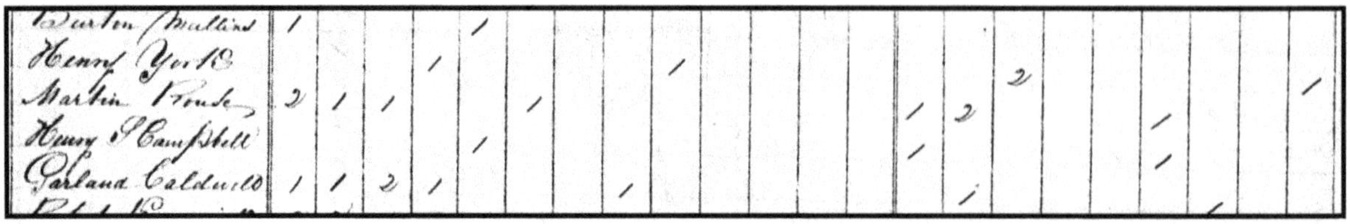
Burton / Mullins
Henry York
Martin Rouse
Henry S Campbell
Garland Caldwell

1840 -- Census,
Cherokee County, GA Page 189-B
Martin Rouce
(40-50) 1M 1F
(20-30) 1M 2F
(15-20) 1M
(10-15) 3M 2F
(0-5) 3M

1850 -- Census, Cass County, GA Page 164
Martin Rouse 48 M, Farmer, born in North Carolina
Elizabeth Rouse 44 F, born in Georgia
Jane Rouse 20 F, born in Georgia
Owen C. Rouse 14 M, born in Georgia
Jacob Rouse 12 M, born in Georgia
William Rouse 10 M, born in Georgia
James Rouse 8 M, born in Georgia
Marion Rouse 4 M, born in Georgia

1860 -- Census, Cass County, GA Page 761
M. Rouse 61 M, Farmer, born in North Carolina

1870 -- Census, Cherokee County, AL Page 307
Geo. W. Redding 48 M, Works for Iron Works, born in Georgia
Elizabeth Redding 25 F, Keeping House, born in Georgia
Sarah Redding 6 F, born in Georgia
Martin Rouse 78 M, Works for Iron Works, born in North Carolina

1871, Oct 13 -- War of 1812 Pension, File 24992, Martin Rouse
Martin Rouse (age 79), resident of Bartow County, GA, applied for a pension. Rouse stated that he served under Captain William Dowd and was drafted in Moore County, NC. Martin Rouse married Mary Wallace in Moore County, NC on 15 Nov 1821. Col. Jurden Leachman and Thomas Leachman attested to his service. He reapplied on 9 Aug 1875 at age 83 with George J. Briant and A.L. Barrow of Cartersville, GA as witnesses. In this application he stated he married Mary Wallace 20 Oct 1812 in Moore County, NC. On 28 Aug 1875 and 2 Sep 1875, John Hancock, of Moore County, NC, and Bartholomew Dunn, of Moore County, submitted affidavits attesting to his service. Rouse reapplied on 12 Aug 1879 at age 88.

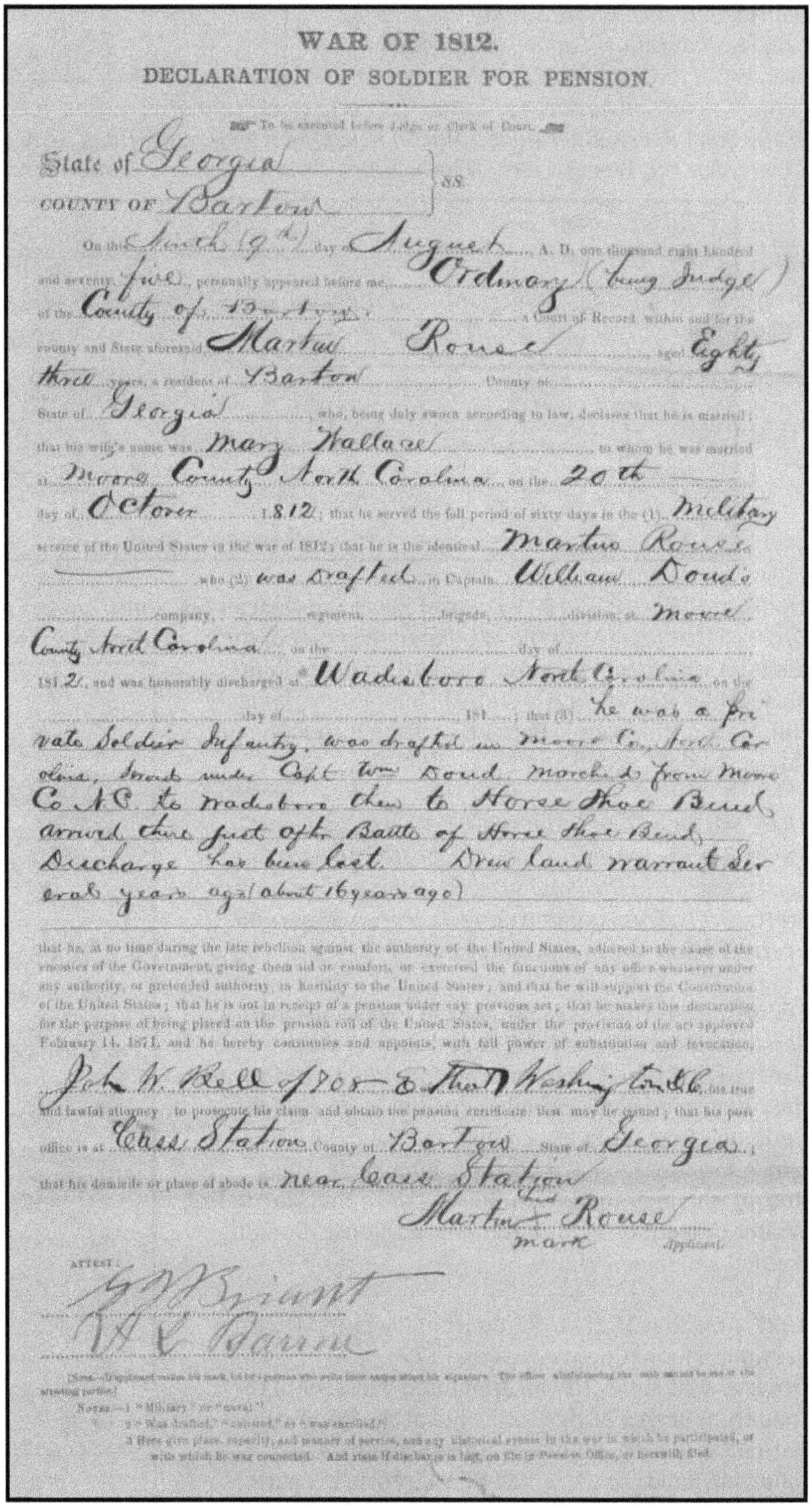
WAR OF 1812.
DECLARATION OF SOLDIER FOR PENSION.

To be executed before Judge or Clerk of Court.

State of Georgia
COUNTY OF Bartow } ss.

On this Ninth (9th) day of August, A. D. one thousand eight hundred and seventy five, personally appeared before me, Ordinary (being Judge) of the County of Bartow, a Court of Record within and for the county and State aforesaid, Martin Rouse, aged Eighty three years, a resident of Barton County of State of Georgia, who, being duly sworn according to law, declares that he is married; that his wife's name was Mary Wallace to whom he was married at Moore County North Carolina on the 20th day of October 1812; that he served the full period of sixty days in the (1) Military service of the United States in the war of 1812; that he is the identical Martin Rouse who (2) was drafted in Captain William Doud's company, regiment, brigade, division, at Moore County North Carolina on the day of 1812, and was honorably discharged at Wadesboro North Carolina on the day of 181 ; that (3) he was a private Soldier Infantry, was drafted in Moore Co. North Carolina, served under Capt Wm Doud marched from Moore Co N C to Wadesboro then to Horse Shoe Bend arrived there just after Battle of Horse Shoe Bend, Discharge has been lost. Drew land warrant several years ago (about 16 years ago)

that he, at no time during the late rebellion against the authority of the United States, adhered to the cause of the enemies of the Government, giving them aid or comfort, or exercised the functions of any office whatever under any authority, or pretended authority, in hostility to the United States; and that he will support the Constitution of the United States; that he is not in receipt of a pension under any previous act; that he makes this declaration for the purpose of being placed on the pension roll of the United States, under the provision of the act approved February 14, 1871, and he hereby constitutes and appoints, with full power of substitution and revocation, John W. Bell of Box 8 Theat Washington D.C. his true and lawful attorney to prosecute his claim and obtain the pension certificate that may be issued; that his post office is at Cass Station County of Bartow State of Georgia; that his domicile or place of abode is near Cass Station

Martin Rouse
mark
Applicant.

ATTEST:
G J Briant
A L Barrow

5. **Joseph Wallace**, was the second son of Everet Wallace and married **Chaney** (1800-bef 1870). Joseph served in the militia during the War of 1812 and later in life can be found owning 100 acres on Jacksons Creek. He and Chaney were parents of at least six children but only the names of three sons are known: Ruffin, Seaborn and Alexander.

RECORDS OF JOSEPH WALLACE

1812/1815 -- North Carolina Militia Muster Roll
Joseph Wallis listed on Muster Roll for Moore County 2nd Regiment

1823, Aug 18 -- 1823-1831 Court of Pleas and Quarter Sessions, Moore County, NC Page 3
Ordered that William Jones be appointed overseer of the road from Kennedy's Mill to the old road at Solomon Brewers and have the following hands to work: Wm. Williams, Joseph Williams, Wm. Dunn, George Williams, John Wallis, John Stuts, Jacob Stuts, George Kenedy, Jacob Stuts (son of Henry), Isham Richardson, William Milton, John Williams, Thomas Williams, Jesse Melton, Henry Melton, Robert Milton and Joseph Wallis.

1827, Aug 22 -- 1823-1831 Court of Pleas and Quarter Sessions, Moore County, NC Page 181
Ordered that Robert Milton be appointed overseer in place of John Cagle of the road from Kennedy's Mill to the old road at Solomon Brewers and have the following hands to work: John Cagle, Wm. Dunn, John Stuts, John Stuts (son of H), Robert Milton, James Milton, Ansel Milton, Nathan Wallis, Matthew Williams, Henry Williams, David Lankford, George Davis, Jethrew Denson, Wm. Wood, John Williams, Daniel McNeill, Wm. Williams, Thomas Williams, Joseph Williams, Josiah Williams, Upshur Furr, Jason Sowell, Hiram Melton, Joseph Wallis and Aaron Kennedy.

1828, Aug 19 -- 1823-1831 Court of Pleas and Quarter Sessions, Moore County, NC Page 226
Ordered that Anderson B. Smith be appointed overseer in place of Robert Milton of the road from Kennedy's Mill to the old road at Solomon Brewers and have the following hands to work: John Cagle, Wm. Dunn, John Stuts, John Stuts (son of H), Robert Milton, James Milton, Ansel Milton, Nathan Wallis, Matthew Williams, Henry Williams, David Lankford, George Davis, Jethrew Denson, Wm. Wood, John Williams, Daniel McNeill, Wm. Williams, Thomas Williams, Joseph Williams, Josiah Williams, Upshur Furr, Isom Sowell, Hiram Melton, Joseph Wallis, Aaron Kennedy, Lewis Garner and Stephen Maness.

1831, May 17 -- 1823-1831 Court of Pleas and Quarter Sessions, Moore County, NC Page 355
Ordered that Simon McNeill be appointed overseer of the road from Flowers' old road to where George Hunsucker formerly lived and have the following hands to work: John Wallis, Nathan Wallis, Thomas Collaer, Joshua Collier, Alexr. Autray, Isiah Smith, Joseph Wallis, Charles Coal and Elisha Cole.

1831, May 19 -- 1823-1831 Court of Pleas and Quarter Sessions, Moore County, NC Page 361
Ordered that James Bryant be appointed overseer of the road from McLendons Creek to Dry Creek and have the following hands to work: Daniel McLean, Murdock McLeod, John Mathewson, Martin Kennedy, Neill Mathewson, Benj. Dunlap, Abil Keys, Joseph Wallis, Alex Kennedy and David Lankford.

1836, Mar 2 -- Land Grant #3044, Moore County, NC
John McNeill received 40 acres located between Cabin Creek and Wet Creek adjoining John Morgan (formerly William Smith), Thomas Harvel, Nathan Smith and his own line. Hardy Sanders and Joseph Wallace were chain carriers.

1840 -- Census, Moore County, NC Page 187
Joseph Wallace
(40-50) 1M
(30-40) 1F
(20-30) 1M 1F

(10-15) 1M 1F
(5-10) 2M

1850, Aug 30 -- Census, Moore County, NC Page 182
Joseph Wallis 52 M, Farmer, born in North Carolina
Chaney Wallis 50 F, born in North Carolina
Ruffin Wallis 18 M, born in North Carolina
Seaborn Wallis 17 M, born in North Carolina
Alexander Wallis 15 M, born in North Carolina

1857 -- Tax List, Moore County, NC
District 6

Wallis	Joseph	Jacksons Creek	100	100

Joseph Wallis listed with 100 acres valued at $100 located on Jackson Creek in District 6

1860, Sep 14 -- Census, Moore County, NC Page 232
Jasiff Wallace 68 M, Farmer, $100 Real Estate, $40 Personal Property, born in North Carolina
Jennet Wallace 60 F, born in North Carolina
Ceaborn Wallace 23 M, Farmer, $200 Real Estate, $50 Personal Property, born in North Carolina

Joseph Wallace and Chaney had the following children:

+29 Ruffin Wallace (1832-1864) married Salina Fry (1840-bef 1885) and they were the parents of three children. Ruffin lived on Jacksons Creek near his father prior to the Civil War. Ruffin served in Company C, 35th Regiment, was captured near Petersburg, VA and later died of pneumonia in the Union prison in Elmira, NY.

+30 Seaborn Wallace (1833-bef 1900) married Tabitha Boone (1842-1914) and their union produced four daughters. Seaborn and family briefly moved to eastern TN before returning to settle down near Tabitha's family in the Seagrove community of Randolph County. Tabitha is buried at Maple Springs Baptist Church in Seagrove.

+31 Alexander Wallace (1835-bef 1870) married Elizabeth Ann Fry (1831-1881), a sister of Salina Fry Wallace. Alexander owned 100 acres on Little River. During the Civil War, Alexander served in Company H, 26th Regiment also known as the "Moore County Independents." Alexander survived the Civil War but died prior to 1870 leaving his widow with three small children to raise.

6. **John Wallace** was the third son of Everet Wallace, married Elizabeth (1800-aft 1866) and they were the parents of ten children: Nathan, Eli, Isham, Thomas, Raleigh, John Wesley, Josiah/Cyrus, Sarah, Catherine and Franny. John can be found in land records in the Bensalem Presbyterian Church community around Cabin, Wet and Dry Creeks during the 1830's and early 1840's. John and Elizabeth's children were Nathan, Eli, Isham, Thomas, Raleigh W., John Wesley, Josiah/Cyrus, Sarah, Catherine and Franny. During the 1840's, John and his family migrated to Bibb County, AL and many of their descendants still live in the area today. They joined a large number of families from Moore and Randolph counties migrating to central Alabama during the period from 1830-1860 including the Barrett, Caddell, Comer, Davis, Deaton, Garner, Glascock, Hunsucker, Kennedy, Latham, Lawrence, McCrimmon, Smitherman, Spinks and Spivey families.

RECORDS OF JOHN WALLACE

1823, Aug 18 -- 1823-1831 Court of Pleas and Quarter Sessions, Moore County, NC Page 3
Ordered that William Jones be appointed overseer of the road from Kennedy's Mill to the old road at Solomon Brewers and have the following hands to work: Wm. Williams, Joseph Williams, Wm. Dunn, George Williams, John Wallis, John Stuts, Jacob Stuts, George Kenedy, Jacob Stuts (son of Henry), Isham Richardson, William Milton, John Williams, Thomas Williams, Jesse Melton, Henry Melton, Robert Milton and Joseph Wallis.

1825, Nov 22 -- 1823-1831 Court of Pleas and Quarter Sessions, Moore County, NC Page 99
Ordered that Matthew Deaton be appointed overseer of the road called the Joel Road from the fork below McIver's to Dry Creek and have the following hands to work: James Kechey, John Wallace, Charles McArthur, Hector McCaskill, Angus McCaskill, Malcolm McCaskill, Mathew Deaton, Donald McDonald one hand, Roderick McAulay one hand, Mary McLeod one hand, John Deaton, Wm. Deaton, Kenneth Morrison, Archibald Munroe, Roderick McLeod and John McLeod.

1830 --
Census, Moore
County, NC
Page 446
John Wallace
(30-40) 1M 1F
(5-10) 3M
(0-5) 3M

Everett Whiffield				2			1						1	2		1
Mathew Whiffield	1			1	1								1		
John Wallace	3	3				1								1		1
Jacob Eagle			2		1						1	1		1		
John Cochman	2	2	3		1						1		1		1

1831, May 17 -- 1823-1831 Court of Pleas and Quarter Sessions, Moore County, NC Page 355
Ordered that Neill Morison be appointed overseer of the road from Cabbin Creek to Hunsuckers old place and have the following hands to work: John Morgan, Avington Britt, Joshua Keys, James Keys, Kenneth Morison, John Wallis, Arch. Munroe hands, John Munroe, Levy Deaton hands, Martin Kennedy, Simon McNeill, Isaac Melton, Daniel Murchison, Joseph Cole, Charles Coal and Thomas Colyer.

1831, May 17 -- 1823-1831 Court of Pleas and Quarter Sessions, Moore County, NC Page 355
Ordered that Simon McNeill be appointed overseer of the road from Flowers' old road to where George Hunsucker formerly lived and have the following hands to work: John Wallis, Nathan Wallis, Thomas Collaer, Joshua Collier, Alexr. Autray, Isiah Smith, Joseph Wallis, Charles Coal and Elisha Cole.

1839, Jun 16 -- Chronicles and Records of Bensalem Presbyterian Church Page 40-41, Moore County, NC
Allan McCaskill was charged with "dancing with negroes and boys" in Mar 1839 at the home of Jesse Sanders. John Wallace and James Hunsucker were witnesses.

1840 -- Census, Moore County, NC Page 171
John Wallace
(40-50) 1M 1F
(30-40) 1F
(15-20) 2M
(10-15) 2M
(5-10) 2M 2F
(0-5) 1F

738	738	John Wallis	51	m	Farmer	150	nc
		Elizabeth "	50	f			nc
		Isom "	25	m	Farmer		nc
		John W "	22	m	none		nc
		Josiah "	21	m	Farmer		nc
		Sarah "	18	f			nc
		Catharine "	16	f			nc
		Franny "	14	f			nc

1850, Nov 20 -- Census, Bibb County, AL
Page 55-B, EC River Township
John Wallis 51 M, Farmer, $150 in Real Estate, born in North Carolina
Elizabeth Wallis 50 F, born in North Carolina
Isom Wallis 25 M, Farmer, born in North Carolina
John W. Wallis 22 M, born in North Carolina
Josiah Wallis 21 M, Farmer, born in North Carolina
Sarah Wallis 18 F, born in North Carolina
Catherine Wallis 16 F, born in North Carolina
Franny Wallis 14 F, born in North Carolina

1850, Aug 10 -- BLM General Land Office Document #38315, Bibb County, AL

John Wallace (of Bibb County) received 39.96 acres from Cahaba Land Office located in southwest Quarter of Section 19, Township 22, Range 12.

1860, Jul 19 -- Census, Perry County, AL Page 685, Plantersville Post Office
John Wallace 63 M, Farmer, $100 Real Estate, $832 Personal Property, born in North Carolina
Elizabeth Wallace 56 F, born in North Carolina
Josiah Wallace 22 M, Laborer, born in Alabama
Frances Wallace 21 F, Domestic, born in Alabama
Martha E. Wallace 1, F, born in Alabama
Thomas Wallace 13 M, born in Alabama
Louis Wallace 7 M, born in Alabama

1866 -- Alabama State Census Schedule 1, Perry County, AL, Page 39, Township 21 Range 11 E
John Wallace
(60-70) 1F
(30-40) 1M
(20-30) 1F
(10-20) 1M
1 Soldier killed and 1 soldier died of sickness

John Wallace and Elizabeth had the following children:

+32   Nathan Wallace (1818-1876) married Mary McCrimmon (1817-1900) and had a total of six children. They were married in Moore County prior to migrating to Bibb County, AL and later continued further west to the state of Texas. Nathan and Mary are buried at Myrtle Springs Cemetery in Cherokee County, TX.

+33   Eli Wallace (1822-1864) married Sina Davis (b. 1821) and they produced five children. Eli served in Company G, 44th Regiment AL Infantry and was killed in action during the Civil War.

+34   Isham Wallace (1825-bef 1864) married Gracy A. Goodwin (b. 1837) and were the parents of one daughter. Isham received land grants on the east side of the Cahaba River in Bibb County, AL.

+35   Thomas Wallace (1826-bef 1864) married Frances "Fanny" Hill (1829-1909) and they produced eight children. Thomas served in the Civil War with Company H, 29th Regiment AL Infantry and was also killed in action.

+36   Raleigh W. Wallace (1827-1898) married Elizabeth Spinks (1831-1902) and they had seven children. Raleigh was born in Moore County, migrated to Bibb County, AL with his family by 1850 and on to Lauderdale County, MS by 1860. He served in Company A, 37th Regiment MS Infantry during the Civil War. Raleigh later died in New Orleans, LA.

+37   John Wesley Wallace (1829-1895) married Frances J. Bearden (1847-1937), they had a large family of eleven children. Wesley was a shoemaker, grocer and farmer at different times in his life. He is buried the Harris Family Cemetery in Bibb County, AL and Frances is buried at Shady Grove Church in Bibb County, AL.

+38   Josiah\Cyrus Wallace (1830-1910) married Frances Jane "Fanny" Bearden (1833-bef 1874) and later after her death married Virginia "Jennie". Josiah and Fanny were the parents of six children. Josiah served in the Civil War with Company F, 4th Regiment AL Infantry

+39   Sarah Wallace (1832-bef 1880) married Isaac Rolley (b. 1829) and they produced three children.

+40   Catherine Wallace (1834-) was listed in the 1850 Census but no further records of her have been located.

+41   Franny Wallace (1836-) was listed in the 1850 Census but no further records of her have been located.

7. **Nathan C. Wallace**, son of Everet Wallace and Caty\Catherine, was born in 1800 in North Carolina and died on February 2, 1884 in Henderson County, TN. Nathan was first married to Finity Britt (1800-bef 1857) and later to Sarah (1829 - bef 1870). Like his brother John, Nathan lived in the Bensalem Presbyterian Church community around Cabin, Wet and Dry Creeks. Finity Britt was the daughter of Benjamin Britt (bef 1774-1810) and Nancy (-). She and Nathan had the following children: Nancy, Deborah, Franey, Mary, Everett and Benjamin. Between 1850-1857, Finity died and Nathan moved his family to Henderson County, TN like his brother Nicholas did two decades prior. Several children were born to Nathan and his second wife Sarah in Tennessee including Sarah Frances, Elizabeth M, William Samuel, Mary A. and Susan Sufronie. Several of Nathan's children intermarried with other Moore County, NC families also migrating to western Tennessee. Among those were the Williams, Britt, and Brewer families. Many of their descendants can still be found in Henderson, McNairy, and Madison counties. Nathan was a founding member of Palestine Church and may be buried in an unmarked grave in the cemetery located south of Lexington, TN.

RECORDS OF NATHAN C. WALLACE

1825, Aug 16 -- 1823-1831 Court of Pleas and Quarter Sessions, Moore County, NC Page 87
Ordered that William Dunn be appointed overseer of the road from Kennedy's Mill to the old road at Solomon Brewers and have the following hands to work: Wm. Jones, John Cagle, John Stuts, John Stuts (son of H), Robert Milton, James Milton, Ansel Milton, Isah Milton, Nathan Wallis, Thomas Williams, Matthew Williams, Henry Williams, David Lankford, Jesse Collar, George Kennedy and George Davis.

1826, Aug 22 -- 1823-1831 Court of Pleas and Quarter Sessions, Moore County, NC Page 133
Ordered that John Cagle be appointed overseer in place of Wm. Dunn of the road from Kennedy's Mill to the old road at Solomon Brewers and have the following hands to work: Wm. Dunn, John Stuts, John Stuts (son of H), Robert Milton, James Milton, Ansel Milton, Nathan Wallis, Matthew Williams, Henry Williams, David Lankford, Jesse Collar, George Davis, Jethrew Denson, Wm. Wood, Jno. Williams and Danl. McNeill.

1827, Aug 22 -- 1823-1831 Court of Pleas and Quarter Sessions, Moore County, NC Page 181
Ordered that Robert Milton be appointed overseer in place of John Cagle of the road from Kennedy's Mill to the old road at Solomon Brewers and have the following hands to work: John Cagle, Wm. Dunn, John Stuts, John Stuts (son of H), Robert Milton, James Milton, Ansel Milton, Nathan Wallis, Matthew Williams, Henry Williams, David Lankford, George Davis, Jethrew Denson, Wm. Wood, John Williams, Daniel McNeill, Wm. Williams, Thomas Williams, Joseph Williams, Josiah Williams, Upshur Furr, Jason Sowell, Hiram Melton, Joseph Wallis and Aaron Kennedy.

1828, Aug 19 -- 1823-1831 Court of Pleas and Quarter Sessions, Moore County, NC Page 226
Ordered that Anderson B. Smith be appointed overseer in place of Robert Milton of the road from Kennedy's Mill to the old road at Solomon Brewers and have the following hands to work: John Cagle, Wm. Dunn, John Stuts, John Stuts (son of H), Robert Milton, James Milton, Ansel Milton, Nathan Wallis, Matthew Williams, Henry Williams, David Lankford, George

Davis, Jethrew Denson, Wm. Wood, John Williams, Daniel McNeill, Wm. Williams, Thomas Williams, Joseph Williams, Josiah Williams, Upshur Furr, Isom Sowell, Hiram Melton, Joseph Wallis, Aaron Kennedy, Lewis Garner and Stephen Maness.

1830 -- Census, Moore County, NC Page 448
Nathan Wallace
(30-40) 1M
(15-20) 1F
(5-10) 1M 1F
(0-5) 2F

1831, May 17 -- 1823-1831 Court of Pleas and Quarter Sessions, Moore County, NC Page 355
Ordered that Simon McNeill be appointed overseer of the road from Flowers' old road to where George Hunsucker formerly lived and have the following hands to work: John Wallis, Nathan Wallis, Thomas Collaer, Joshua Collier, Alexr. Autray, Isiah Smith, Joseph Wallis, Charles Coal and Elisha Cole.

1840 -- Census, Moore County, NC Page 177
Nathan Wallace Jr.
(40-50) 1M 1F
(15-20) 1F
(10-15) 1M 1F
(5-10) 2M 2F
(0-5) 1M

1850, Nov 5 --
Census, Moore County, NC Page 234
Nathan Wallis 50 M, Farmer, born in North Carolina
Finity Wallis 50 F, born in North Carolina
Nancy Wallis 27 F, born in North Carolina
Franey Wallis 21 F, born in North Carolina
Mary Wallis 19 F, born in North Carolina
Everett Wallis 13 M, born in North Carolina
Benjamin Wallis 10 M, born in North
Carolina

1860, Jul 10 -- Census, Henderson County,
TN Page 225, Civil District #6, Middle Fork Post Office
Natha Wallace 57 M, Farm Tenant, $450 Personal Property, born in North Carolina
Sarah Wallace 31 F, born in Virginia
Nancy Wallace 32 F, born in North
Carolina
Mary Seymore 15 F, born in Tennessee
W.H. Pomeroy 5 M, born in Tennessee
H. Davidson 6 M, born in Tennessee
Sarah F. Wallace 3 F, born in Tennessee
M.E.A. Wallace 9/12 F, born in Tennessee
W. Davidson 28 M, born in Virginia

1870, Jun 1 -- Census, McNairy County,
TN Page 348, 14th Civil District, Bethel Springs Post Office
Nathan Wallis 70 M, Farmer, $300 Personal Property, born in North Carolina
Sarah F. Wallis 15 F, Keeping House, born in Tennessee
Elizabeth M. Wallis 10 F, born in Tennessee
Samuel Wallis 8 M, born in Tennessee
Mary A. Wallis 7 F, born in Tennessee
Sefrona Wallis 6 F, born in Tennessee
Bary Rah 15 M, Field Laborer, born in Tennessee

1875 -- Tax List, McNairy County, TN
N. Wallace listed in District 14 (no land given)

1880 -- Census, Henderson County, TN Page 348, Civil District #6
Nathan Wallace 80 M, Head, Widowed, Laborer on Farm, born in North Carolina, father & mother born in North Carolina
William S. Wallace 19 M, Son, Single, Laborer on Farm, born in Tennessee, father & mother born in North Carolina
Susan S. Wallace 16 F, Dau, Single, Laborer on Farm, born in Tennessee, father & mother born in North Carolina

1881, Oct 9 -- Palestine Cumberland Presbyterian Church Minutes, Henderson County, TN
Nathan Wallace/N. C. Wallace listed as a Charter Member

1884, Feb 2 -- Palestine Cumberland Presbyterian Church Register of Deaths, Henderson County, TN
Nathan Wallace – "He died in faith"

Nathan C. Wallace and Finity Britt had the following children:

+42   Nancy Wallace (aft 1823-) married widower Ambrose R. Hart (1816-1886) and had one son.

+43   Deborah Wallace (1828-1897) married her widowed cousin Beacom C. Britt (1804-1876) and had one son. Beacom's first wife was Dallie Wallace (1810/1815-1845/1849) who was likely a close relative of Deborah's. Beacom and Deborah had at least ten children. *(See Page 468 for additional information on Beacom Britt and Dallie Wallace)*

+44   Franey Wallace (1828-) also married a Britt cousin, Benjamin Britt (1835-bef 1880). Benjamin was the son of Beacom Britt and Dallie Wallace. Franey and Benjamin produced seven children.

+45   Mary Wallace (1832-bef 1880) married Harmon Brewer (1832-aft 1800) and they were the parents of ten children. Harmon and Mary migrated from Moore County to Henderson County, TN and later lived in Marshall County, MS and Shelby County, TN.

+46   Everett Wallace (1837-) married Mary Jane Williams (b. 1837) and their union produced two children. Everett served in Company B, 31st Tennessee Infantry during the Civil War.

+47   Benjamin Wallace (1840-1900) married three times (Caty Williams, Holly J. Kizer and Eliza Elizabeth Rivers) and was the father of seven children in total. He migrated from Moore County to McNairy County, TN to St. Francis County, AR and finally to Parker County, TX. Ben is buried at the Jaybird Cemetery in Reno, Parker County, TX. Several Moore County families migrated from western Tennessee to Parker County, TX between 1870-1900.

Sarah was born in 1829 in Virginia. She died between 1863 and 1870 in Tennessee. She and Nathan C. Wallace had the following children:

+48   Sarah Frances Wallace (1857-1941) was the first child of Nathan C. Wallace and Sarah. Sarah Frances married James Columbus Hart (1852-1929) and they are buried in Farmersville, Collin County, TX at the Farmersville IOOF Cemetery.

+49   Elizabeth M. Wallace (1859-) was listed in the 1860 and 1870 censuses but no further records of her have been located.

+50   William Samuel Wallace (1862-1925) married Nancy C. Williams (1865-1945) and they produced seven children. Along with his father, Sam was a founding member of Palestine Church in Henderson County, TN and he and Nancy are both buried there along with a number of family members.

+51   Mary A. Wallace (1863-) was listed in the 1870 Census but no further records of her have been located.

+52   Susan Sufronie Wallace (1864-1926) married Joseph Arch Cox (b. 1848) and they had one child. Frona is buried in Farmersville, Collin County, TX at the Farmersville IOOF Cemetery near his sister Sarah Frances Hart.

9. **Isham Wallace**, son of Everet Wallace and Caty\Catherine, was born on March 6, 1801 and died on January 13, 1882. Isham married Nancy Furr (1806-1884) and is considered one of the mostly widely held common ancestors in northern Moore County. Nancy was the daughter of Charles Furr and Nancy Sowell. Isham, a lifelong farmer, lived on over 1100 acres of land in the Buffalo Creek/Meadow Branch area southeast of Robbins (just east of the intersection of Hwy 24/27 and the Mt. Carmel Road). Isham and Nancy as well as many of their descendants are buried, not far from their home, at Flint Hill Baptist Church.

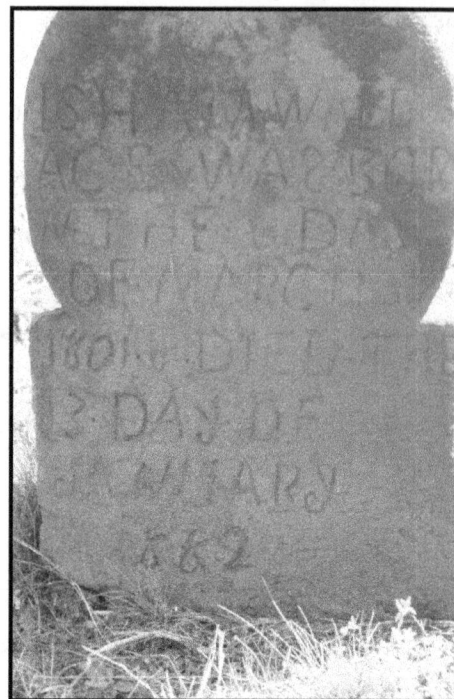

Throughout the years, I was fascinated and amazed by the stories that my grandfather, Mallie Wallace, told about his ancestors. The Wallaces were known to be a rough and tumble crew, spending more time at the County Courthouse for drinking, fighting and so on as they did in church. Isham was always one of his favorite subjects. My grandfather was the grandson of Emsley Wallace and great grandson of Isham. An 1880 article in the *Chatham Record* depicted Isham and his family, much as my grandfather remembered: "*in upper Moore County...an old man named Wallace is over eighty years old, straight as an Indian, six feet high, is capable of doing a good deal of work, has fifteen children living almost in sight of his house, and all of his descendants together amount to about 215 persons. Of the children, six are daughters and nine are sons, and their average height is six feet and their weight two hundred pounds and not one male among the entire family belong to any church.*"[13]

Another story detailed the challenges that many families felt during the Civil War. Many families across central North Carolina did not feel it was their fight and hid their sons from the conscription officers. Isham's family was no different. Only one of Isham's sons fought for the confederacy while his other sons took to the bushes. My grandfather always wondered if Sampson Delaney Wallace volunteered or was conscripted after officers caught up with him. The

(both photographed April 2, 2010)

following narrative shows Isham's desire to keep his sons safe. "*In one instance, a determined father stood down a squad of mounted militia officers sent to arrest him, because two of his sons were [hiding out] in the bushes. In a story related by Bryan Tyson [Object of the Administration, Page 7], the officers informed Isham Wallace, a resident of Moore County, that he must accompany them to their militia camp. Isham refused. When an officer started to dismount to arrest him, Isham warned him that he would shoot him dead before he touched the ground if that was the last thing he ever did. Rather than risk one of them being killed, the militia officers rode off, abandoning their effort to arrest Isham.*"[14]

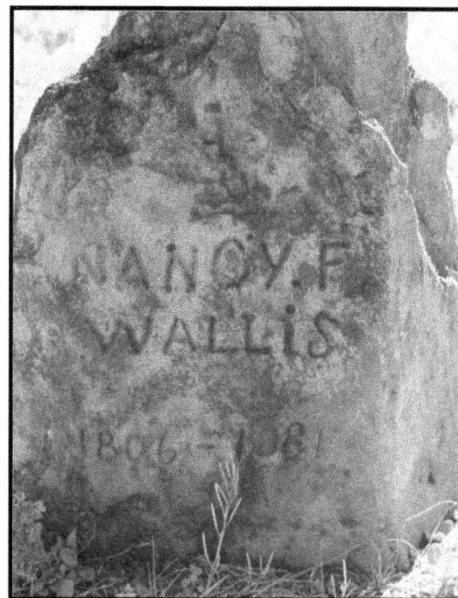

The *Carthage Gazette* eulogized Isham in 1882 saying "*The venerable Isham Wallace leaves behind him a remarkable record which is worthy of mention. He had attained the age of ninety years; and Mr. H. McNeill, Probate Judge-who is closely identified with county history, and knows the people as thoroughly, as any man in Moore-informs us that Mr. Wallace left four generations, of 275 direct descendants. This is certainly an extraordinary page of family history.*"[15] My grandfather would agree Isham was quite the venerable and remarkable man.

Isham and Nancy had the following children: Clarkey Ann, Elizabeth Mary Ann, William Wesley Sarah Ann, Quimby, Dempsey, Lockey, Emsley Thomas, Samuel Bascom, Loveday Jane, Sampson Delaney, Virgil Spinks "Byrd" and John M. Among these children, most resided in close proximately of their parents and raised large families that are still located in northern Moore County. Their children intermarried with the neighboring Cockman, Melton, Hunsucker, Horner and Garner families. The map on the following page shows the approximate location of the homeplaces of Everet Wallace, Isham Wallace and each of his children according to my grandfather Mallie Wallace.

Location of Everet Wallace, Isham Wallace and each of Isham's children

NATIVE AMERICAN HERITAGE?

In most southern families there are stories of Native American ancestry but few if any pan out to be true. One of the more fascinating stories that my grandfather, Mallie Wallace, was told by his grandfather, Emsley Wallace, related to our possible Native American heritage. According to the story, Isham Wallace was married to a full-blooded Cherokee Indian named Nancy Chiffon. One year when her family was traveling on the Salem-Cross Creek road from Salem, NC to Fayetteville, NC to sell furs at the marketplace in Fayetteville, Isham saw her briefly when they camped near his house. The next year when they traveled to Fayetteville again-he married her. According to my grandfather, many of the "older" Wallaces had "jet black hair and darker complexions." He believed that this was a result of the Indian heritage.

While historical research debunks part of this story, I believe the story is too elaborate for some part of it not to be true. From census research and numerous other records, we know that Isham Wallace married Nancy Furr, a daughter of Charles Furr and Nancy Sowell and sister to Malvina Furr, wife of Enoch Wallace. I do not believe that the Furrs were Indians as they are a well-documented family going back to Switzerland. It is very possible that Native Americans were traveling along a trade route to Fayetteville, much earlier than Isham's generation (born 1801) as the Cross Creek-Salem route was established in the mid-1700's and was well traveled by 1770. Whatever the true story was regarding the Native American connection, chances are that it was further back than Isham's generation. It is interesting that one of Everet's children, Susannah, was listed in the census as mulatto (an offspring of a black and a white parent). The children of Everet's daughter Manda were also listed as mulatto while they were younger. It may have been possible that they were listed as mulatto because census takers observed their darker skins and concluded they were of mixed race rather than Native American.

1824, Aug 19 -- 1823-1831 Court of Pleas and Quarter Sessions, Moore County, NC Page 52
Ordered that Daniel Caddell be appointed overseer of the road from Bean's Bridge to Flowers Road and have the following hands to work: Leonard Lawhon, John McIntosh, John Murchison, Enoch Wallis, Isham Wallis, John Rouse, Miles Rouse, Martin Rouse, John McDonald, Hugh Kelly, James Hill, Martin Hill, Dickson Ritter, James Ritter, Samuel Barrett, Wm. Barrett Esq.'s boy, Simon Murchison and Daniel Murchison.

1825, Aug 15 -- 1823-1831 Court of Pleas and Quarter Sessions, Moore County, NC Page 82
Ordered that Danl. Murchison be appointed overseer of the road from the hill at the Widow Bethune's to Flowers Road and have the following hands to work: John Murchison, Alexander Smith, Richmond Smith, John McDonald, Isham Wallis, Samuel Barret, Wm. Barret Esq. Sr. and Hugh Kelly.

1826, Aug 21 -- 1823-1831 Court of Pleas and Quarter Sessions, Moore County, NC Page 129
Ordered that Samuel Barringtine be appointed overseer of the road from the hill at the Widow Bethune's to Flowers Road and have the following hands to work: Alexander Smith, Isham Wallis, Samuel Barret, Wm. Barret Esq. Sr., Angus Kelly, Thomas Dowdy, Wm. McIntosh, John A. McIntosh, Alexander W. McIntosh's boy Tim, James Haines and Jacob Cagle.

1827, Nov 20 -- Petition, Dec 1827-Jan 1828 General Assembly Session Records
Residents of Moore County petitioned to establish a fare [fair] at the Grove in April and October. Isam Wallis signed the petition.

1828, Nov 18 -- 1823-1831 Court of Pleas and Quarter Sessions, Moore County, NC Page 242
Ordered that James Hill be appointed overseer of the road from Kenneth McCaskill's to George Hunsucker's and have the following hands to work: William McIntosh, John McIntosh, Isham Wallis, Martin Hill, Samuel Barrett, John Lawhon, Daniel Caddell, Wm. Ritter, James Ritter, John Ritter, Wm. Barrett Esq. one hand and Hugh Kelly.

1829, Nov 16 -- 1823-1831 Court of Pleas and Quarter Sessions, Moore County, NC Page 283
Ordered that James Hill be appointed the overseer of the road from Bean's Bridge to Flowers Road and work the following hands: Wm. McIntosh, John McIntosh, Alex. McIntosh, Alex. McIntosh Sr.'s hand, Wm. J. McIntosh, Samuel McIntosh, Isham Wallis, Wm. Barrett Esq.'s hand, Samuel Barrett, Willabe Ritter, Henry Ritter, Isaac Lawhon, Daniel Caddell, Jesse Muse, Daniel Muse, Angus Kelly and Alex. McCaskill.

1830, May 18 -- 1823-1831 Court of Pleas and Quarter Sessions, Moore County, NC Page 309
Ordered that Isham Wallis be appointed the overseer of the road from the large sassafras at Alex. McCaskill's to Flowers Road and have the following hands to work: Wm. Barrett Esq. hands, Hiram Melton, Angus Kelly, Alex. McIntosh hands, William McIntosh, John McIntosh and Alex McIntosh Jr.

1839, Feb 20 -- Land Grant #3107, Moore County, NC

Miles Muse received 100 acres located west of Richland Creek on Rutherford Road adjoining Daniel Muse, Thomas Muse, Wallace, McNeill and William Barrett Senr. Daniel Muse and David Jones were chain carriers.

1840 -- Census, Moore County, NC Page 180
Isham Wallace
(40-50) 1M
(30-40) 1F
(15-20) 1M 1F
(10-15) 2M 2F
(5-10) 1M
(0-5) 1M

1840, Jun 24 -- Marriages, Fayetteville Observer [Fayetteville, NC] Newspaper
"In Moore County, on the 18th inst. [Jun 1840], Mr. George Cockman, son of John Cockman to Miss Clarky Wallis, daughter of Isham Wallis-all of Moore County"

1846/1847 -- Tax List, Moore County, NC District 9
Isham Wallace listed 250 acres valued at $300 located on Meadow Branch and 150 acres valued at $450 located on Buffalo Creek

1846, Oct -- 1841-1854 Appearance Docket, Moore County, NC
#20 Amelia Jones v. Henry Yow. William Johnston, Esq., Georg Davis, James Melton and Isham Walase were ordered to lay off years' maintenance for Widow Jones.

1848 -- Tax List, Moore County, NC District 9
Isham Wallace listed 250 acres valued at $300 located on Meadow Branch, 150 acres valued at $450 located on Buffalow Creek and 579 acres valued at $900 located on Buffalow Creek

1849, Jan 23 -- Court of Pleas and Quarter Sessions, Moore County, NC Page 324
A deed from Isaac Jones to Isham Wallace proven by George Cockman

1850, Nov 9 -- Agricultural Census, Moore County, NC Page 989
Isham Wallis listed 200 acres improved, 975 unimproved valued at $800

1850, Nov 12 -- Census, Moore County, NC Page 238
Isham Wallis 49 M, Farmer, $1600 Real Estate, born in North Carolina
Nancy Wallis 44 F, born in North Carolina
Westley Wallis 21 M, Farmer, born in North Carolina
Quimby Wallis 18 M, Farmer, born in North Carolina
Lockey Wallis 14 M, born in North Carolina
Emsley Wallis 12 M, born in North Carolina
Samuel Wallis 9 M, born in North Carolina
Jane Wallis 6 F, born in North Carolina
Sampson Wallis 5 M, born in North Carolina
Virgil Wallis 4 M, born in North Carolina
John Wallis 2/12 M, born in North Carolina

1852 -- Tax List, Moore County, NC District 9
Isham Wallace listed 250 acres valued at $300 located on Meadow Branch, 150 acres valued at $450 located on Meadow Branch and 579 acres valued at $900 located on Meadow Branch

1853 -- Tax List, Moore County, NC District 9
Isham Wallace listed 250 acres valued at $300 located on Meadow Branch, 150 acres valued at $450 located on Meadow Branch and 579 acres valued at $900 located on Meadow Branch

1854 -- Tax List, Moore County, NC District 9
Isham Wallace listed 979 acres valued at $1650

1855 -- Tax List, Moore County, NC District 9
Isham Wallace listed 1142 acres valued at $1650 located on Buffalo Creek

1856 -- Tax List, Moore County, NC District 9
Isaam Wallace listed 1142 acres valued at $1650 located on Buffalo Creek

1857 -- Tax List, Moore County, NC District 9
Isham Wallace listed 1142 acres valued at $1650 located on Buffalo Creek

1857, Oct 31 -- 1856-1858 Court of Pleas and Quarter Sessions, Moore County, NC Page 304
Henry Stutts, Sr., by his guardian Robert W. Goldston, sold 150 acres located on Buffalow Creek adjoining Alexander McNeill, Matthew Yow and Isham Wallace. Stutts had been found to be a lunatic or idiot and the real estate needed to be sold for his support and maintenance.

1858, Oct 18 -- Land Grant #4371, Moore County, NC
Cornelius Stutts received 75 acres located on the waters of Buffalo Creek adjoining Wesly Williams, Isham Wallace and James Stutts. Leonard Stutts and Lindsey Williams were chain carriers.

1858, Oct 18 -- Land Grant #4388, Moore County, NC
James Stutts received 75 acres located on the waters of Buffalo Creek adjoining Wesly Williams, Isham Wallace, Cornelius Stutts, Jones, Ann Tolman and John H. Stutts. Leonard Stutts and Lindsey Williams were chain carriers.

1860, Jul 9 -- Census, Moore County, NC Page 180, Caledonia Post Office
Isam Wallace 56 M, Farmer, $5000 Real Estate, $1000 Personal Property, born in North Carolina
Nancy Wallace 50 F, born in North Carolina
Samuel B. Wallace 17 M, born in North Carolina
Lovedy J. Wallace 15 F, born in North Carolina
Sampson D. Wallace 14 M, born in North Carolina
Virgil A. S. Wallace 12 M, born in North Carolina
John M. Wallace 10 M, born in North Carolina

Dwelling-houses numbered in the order of visitation.	Families numbered in the order of visitation.	The name of every person whose usual place of abode on the first day of June, 1860, was in this family.	Description.			Profession, Occupation, or Trade of each person, male and female, over 15 years of age	Value of Estate Owned.		Place of Birth, Naming the State, Territory, or Country.	Married within the year.	Attended School within the year.	Persons over 20 yrs of age who cannot read & write
			Age.	Sex.	White, black, or mulatto.		Value of Real Estate.	Value of Personal Estate.				
1	2	3	4	5	6	7	8	9	10	11	12	13
626	609	Isam Wallace	56	m		Farmer ✓	5000	1000	NC			1
		Nancy	50	f					NC			
		Samuel B	17	m					NC		1	
		Lovedy J	15	f					NC		1	
		Sampson D	14	m					NC		1	
		Virgil A S	12	m					NC		1	
		John M "	10	m					NC		1	

1860, Jul 16 -- Agricultural Census, Moore County, NC Page 21, Gold Region Post Office
Isham Wallace listed 150 acres improved, 1000 acres unimproved valued at $500

1860, Dec 8 -- Land Grant #4410, Moore County, NC
James Deaton received 26 acres located on the waters of Richland Creek and Meadow Branch adjoining Samuel Barrett, Riley Muse, Isham Wallace and Tolman. George Williams and Samuel Barrett were chain carriers.

1861-1865 [circa] -- Undated Account, *Civil War in the North Carolina Quaker Belt: The Confederate Campaign Against Peace Agitators, Deserters and Draft Dodgers* by William T. Auman, Page 168
"In one instance, a determined father stood down a squad of mounted militia officers sent to arrest him, because two of his sons were [hiding out] in the bushes. In a story related by Bryan Tyson [*Object of the Administration*, Page 7], the officers informed Isham Wallace, a resident of Moore County, that he must accompany them to their militia camp. Isham refused. When an officer started to dismount to arrest him, Isham warned him that he would shoot him dead before he touched the ground if that was the last thing he ever did. Rather than risk one of them being killed, the militia officers rode off, abandoning their effort to arrest Isham."

1861, Feb 14 -- Deed Book 32 Page 194-195, Moore County, NC
James Deaton deeded Samuel Barrett 26 acres located on Richland Creek adjoining Riley Muse, Samuel Barrett, Isham Wallace and Tolman. Neill A. Fry and Alex Barrett were witnesses.

1865, Nov 26 -- Deed Book 127 Page 545, Moore County, NC
Isam Wallis deeded Emsley Wallis 100 acres located on Buffalo Creek adjoining Wesley Wallis. Danl. McIntosh was a witness.

1866, Aug 20 -- Superior Court Minute Docket Book K, Moore County, NC Page 440
Emeline Davis v. Isham Wallace. Ordered that John Davis and Alexander Davis be remanded to Isham Wallace's custody.

1869, Oct 2 -- Deed Book 125 Page 478, Moore County, NC
Isham and Nancy Wallace deeded Virgil Wallace 105 acres located on Buffalo Creek adjoining Emsley Wallace, William Stutts, L.T. Seawell, Stewart and their own line. S.D. Wallace was a witness.

1870, Jul 11 -- Agricultural Census, Moore County, NC Page 3, Bensalem Township, Carters Mill Post Office
Isham Wallis listed 50 acres improved, 50 acres unimproved valued at $150

1870, Jul 14 -- Census, Moore County, NC Page 482, Bensalem Township, Carters Mill Post Office
Isham Wallis 70 M, Farmer, $200 Real Estate, $200 Personal Property, born in North Carolina
Nancy Wallis 65 F, born in North Carolina
John Davis 12 M, born in North Carolina
Alexander Davis 8 M, born in North Carolina
S.D. Wallis 24 M, born in North Carolina
Mosuria Wallis 23 F, born in North Carolina
Charles Wallis 2 M, born in North Carolina

1872, Nov 4 -- Deed Book 127 Page 546, Moore County, NC
Isham and Nancy Wallace deeded Emsley Wallace 2.5 acres located on Buffalo Creek adjoining Bird Wallace.

118	130	Wallace Isham	W M 80				1	Farmer Planter					1	"	"	"	"	"	40
		Nancy	W F 67	wife	1			Keeping House						1	"	"	"	"	"	
		Candis	W F 23	Daughter	1			at home						1	"	"	"	"	"	
		Henry	W M 5	Son grand				at home							"	"	"	"	"	
119	131	Davis John	W M 22	servant				Labor							"	"	"	"	"	

1880, Jun 28 -- Census, Moore County, NC Page 211, Bensalem Township
Isham Wallace 80 M, Head, Married, Farmer/Planter, born in North Carolina, father & mother born in North Carolina
Nancy Wallace 67 F, Wife, Married, Keeping House, born in North Carolina, father & mother born in North Carolina
Candis Wallace 23 F, Dau, Married, At Home, born in North Carolina, father & mother born in North Carolina
Henry Wallace 5 M, GrSon, Single, At Home, born in North Carolina, father & mother born in North Carolina
John Davis 22 M, Servant, Single, Laborer, born in North Carolina, father & mother born in North Carolina

1880, Jun 28 -- Agricultural Census, Moore County, NC Page 20, Bensalem Township
Isam Wallace listed 40 acres improved fields, 225 acres unimproved wooded valued at $325

1880, Oct 9 -- Article, News and Observer [Raleigh, NC] Newspaper
"Pittsboro Record: Rev. J.L. Smith, a zealous Baptist missionary in the upper end of Moore County, gave us at the (Sandy Creek Baptist) Association last week, the following interesting points about a most remarkable family living in that section: an old man named Wallace is over eighty years old, straight as an Indian, six feet high, is capable of doing a good deal of work, has fifteen children living almost in sight of his house and all of his descendants together amount to about 215 persons. Of the children, six are daughters and nine are sons and their average height is six feet and their weight two hundred pounds and not one male among the entire family belong to any church!"

1882, Jan 20 -- Article, The Daily Review [Wilmington, NC] Newspaper
"Carthage Gazette: The venerable Isham Wallace leaves behind him a remarkable record which is worthy of mention. He had attained the age of ninety years; and Mr. H. McNeill, Probate Judge-who is closely identified with county history, and knows the people as thoroughly, as any man in Moore-informs us that Mr. Wallace left four generations, of 275 direct descendants. This is certainly an extraordinary page of family history."

1884, Mar 27-Jun 4, 1906 – Loose Estates, Moore County, NC
Estate of Isham Wallace, Dec'd. by Administrator George Cockman.
Isham Wallace's date of death listed as 12 Jan 1882. On 11 Dec 1889, the estate listed the following heirs: Lovedy Jane Horner, wife of James Horner, Heirs of Elizabeth Cockman, wife of Sampson Cockman (Wesly Cockman, James Cockman, Alice Cockman, Clarky Ann Horner, wife of W.T. Horner, Eliza Horner, wife of Thomas R. Horner), Heirs of Locky Wallace (Mary Maness, wife of Blake Maness, Martha Maness, wife of Lewis Maness, Ruth Ritter, wife of Joseph Ritter, Vandie Maness, wife of McLellan Maness, Ella Blake Wallace), Sarah Garner, wife of John Garner, Samuel B. Wallace, Mary Cockman, wife of Noah Cockman, W.W. Wallace, Clarky Cockman, Quimby Wallace, Emsley Wallace, Virgil Wallace, S.D. Wallace and John Wallace (of Arkansas).

1884, Oct 16 -- 1880-1885 Administrator's Bonds, Moore County, NC Page 68
Wesley W. Wallace appointed Administrator of the Estate of Nancy Wallace, Dec'd. with Lewis Grimm and J.A. Worthy as securities.

A Remarkable Family.

Rev. J. L. Smith, a zealous Baptist missionary in the upper end of Moore county, gave us, at the Association last week, the following interesting points about a most remarkable family living in that section. An old man named Wallace is over eighty years old, straight as an indian, six feet high, is capable of doing a good deal of work, has fifteen children living almost in sight of his house, and all his descendants together amount to about 215 persons. Of the children, six are daughters, and nine are sons, and their average height is six feet and their weight two hundred pounds. And not one male among the entire family belongs to any church !

Carthage *Gazette:* The venerable Isham Wallace leaves behind him a remarkable record which is worthy of mention. He had attained the age of ninety years; and Mr. H. McNeill, Probate Judge—who is as closely identified with county history, and knows the people as thoroughly, as any man in Moore—informs us that Mr. Wallace left four generations, of 275 direct descendants. This is certainly an extraordinary page of family history.

1884, Oct 16-Feb 23, 1886 -- Loose Estates and 1876-1885 Record of Accounts Page 542-544, Moore County, NC
Estate of Nancy Wallace Dec'd.by Administrator W.W. Wallace. *Items were purchased by the following*: Mac. Wallace, Josiah Person, Archd. Seawell, Saml. B. Wallace, John Garner, James Cockman, S.D. Wallace, Quimby Wallace, Sandy Black, Josiah Person, J.W. Horner, George Williams, Sampson Cockman, Charles Cockman, Mrs. Sarah Garner, Frank Wallace, Thomas Horner, Spinks Wallace, Archd. Seawell, J.T. Seawell, Charlie Wallace, Thomas Fry, Parker Stafford and J.M. Davis.

Isham Wallace and Nancy Furr had the following children:

+53   Clarkey Ann Wallace (1820-1891) married George Cockman (1818-1905) and their union produced ten children. George and Clarkey lived on Buffalo Creek and are buried nearby at Flint Hill. Clarkey and her sisters, Elizabeth and Mary Ann, each married sons of John Cockman and Mary Richardson.

+54   Elizabeth Wallace (1825-1871) married J. Sampson Cockman (1819-1905) and they were parents of ten children as well. Sampson and Elizabeth lived on Buffalo Creek and Glade Branch and are also buried at Flint Hill.

+55   Mary Ann Wallace (1826-1892) married Noah Emsley Cockman (1824-aft 1893) and they also had ten children. Noah and Mary lived on Buffalo Creek near the Robbins Crossroads. They are likely buried in unmarked graves at Flint Hill.

+56   William Wesley Wallace (1828-1906) married twice and produced at least fourteen children. He first married Elizabeth Melton (1830-1875) and later in life married Margaret Louise Seawell (1857-1932). Wes lived on the Plank Road east of Robbins and he and Elizabeth are buried at Tabernacle United Methodist Church. After Wes' death, Lou moved the family to Greensboro, and she is buried at Green Hill Cemetery there.

+57   Sarah Ann Wallace (1830-1899) married John Garner (1825-1905) and raised a family of eleven. Sarah and John lived on Buffalo Creek and are buried nearby at Flint Hill.

+58   Quimby Wallace (1832-1895) married Arabella Stewart (1836-1928) and produced nine children. They lived on Ernie Frye Road off Mt. Carmel Road near his parents.

+59   Dempsey Wallace (1833-1839) died at the young age of six and is buried at Flint Hill.

+60   Lochart "Lockey" Wallace (1836-1884) married Susan Muse and raised a family of seven. Lockey and Susan lived on Buffalo Creek in between NC Highway 705 and Mt. Carmel Road and are buried at Flint Hill.

+61   Emsley Thomas Wallace (1837-1918) married Priscilla Melton, daughter of James Melton and Temperance Horner and sister to Elizabeth, Temperance, and Candace who married Emsley's brothers. Emsley and Priscilla went on to raise eight children. Emsley and Priscilla lived on Buffalo Creek near the end of present day Rushwood Road and are buried at a small family cemetery there.

+62   Samuel Bascom Wallace (1841-1913) married Temperance Melton (1839-1906) and produced ten children. Sam also married Nancy Smith (1866-1941) later in life after Tempy died. Sam and Tempy lived near Meadow Branch and are buried at Union Presbyterian Church.

+63   Lovedy Jane Wallace (1844-1916) married James Washington Horner (1842-1921), son of George W. Horner and Mary Ann Ritter and raised a family of six. The Horners lived on Buffalo Creek near Lockey Wallace and are also buried at Flint Hill.

+64   Sampson Delaney "Lane" Wallace (1845-c.1893) married Missouri Hunsucker (1846-1920) and produced eight children. Lane was the only son of Isham to actively fight in the Civil War and served in Company K, 19th Regiment (2nd Regiment Calvary). He became a local deputy sheriff after the war and was a member of the Carthage Masonic Lodge. Lane is buried near the old homeplace on Ernie Frye Road. Upon Lane's death, Missouri moved their family to Rockingham,

NC where several of their descendants still reside. Missouri is buried at East Side Cemetery in Rockingham.

+65   Virgil Spinks "Byrd" Wallace (1846-1917) was married twice and produced a total of eighteen children. Byrd's first marriage was to Regina Hunsucker (1850-bef 1898), daughter of George Hunsucker and Elizabeth Williams and sister to Missouri. Byrd's second marriage was to Flora Ann Garner (1877-1963), daughter of Stedman Garner and Ann Elizabeth Davis. Byrd lived on NC Highway 24/27 on Buffalo Creek and is buried in a large family cemetery directly across the highway.

+66   John M. Wallace (1850-1923) married Candace Melton (1855-1911) and had one son in North Carolina. John later moved to Perry County, AR where he was elected as a Judge and a member of the Arkansas State House of Representatives. John was married four more times, produced at least 13 more children, and is buried at the Perryville Cemetery there.

11. **Josiah Wallace**, son of Everet Wallace and Caty\Catherine, was born in 1807 in North Carolina. He died before 1880 and married Catherine "Katie" (1808-aft 1880). Josiah owned several tracts of land on Scotchmans Creek, Bear Creek and Richland Creek during his life and is believed to have lived between Bear Creek and Buffalo Creek. My grandfather recalled his grandfather Emsley Wallace saying that Josiah was at one time a rock mason at the "Lost City" of Parkwood.[16]

RECORDS OF JOSIAH WALLACE

1830, Nov 16 -- 1823-1831 Court of Pleas and Quarter Sessions, Moore County, NC Page 327
Ordered that Henry Manas be appointed overseer of the road from Bear Creek to Buffalo Creek in place of James Garner and have the following hands to work: James Garner, James Manes, Isaac Maness, Elijah Maness, Hiram Davidson, George Stutts, Wm. Moore, John Hunsucker, John McLeod's hands, Abraham Stutts, David Brewer and Josiah Wallis.

1840 -- Census, Moore County, NC Page 176
Josiah Wallace
(30-40) 1M
(20-30) 1F
(10-15) 1M

1841, Nov 16 -- Land Grant #3204, Moore County, NC
Josiah Wallace received 98 acres located on the waters of Scotchman Creek adjoining John R. Ritter, Matthew Davis and Noah Richardson. William Ritter and Wesly Ritter were chain carriers.

1841, Nov 16 -- Land Grant #3205, Moore County, NC
John R. Ritter received 100 acres located on both sides of Scotchman Creek adjoining Noah Richardson and Josiah Wallas. William Ritter and Wesly Ritter were chain carriers.

1848, May 10 -- Land Grant #3607, Moore County, NC
Josiah Wallace received 28 acres located east of Bear Creek on Lick Branch adjoining Garner Maness, Nall, Henry Stutts, Abel Maness and Jonah B. Maness. John Riddle and William B. Wallace were chain carriers.

1848, Jul 24 -- 1847-1849 Court of Pleas and Quarter Sessions, Moore County, NC Page 227

Ordered that Apr 1848 road order issued to Henry Brown be amended striking out the following names: Stutts hands, Hiram Kelly, Wm. Stewart hands, Edward Stewart, John Denson, Leonard Stutts and Wm. Stutts and inserting the names of: Mark Russel hands, George Cagle, Josiah Wallace, Branson Wallace, Asa Maness and George Hunsucker merchant's hands

1849, Apr 23 -- 1847-1849 Court of Pleas and Quarter Sessions, Moore County, NC Page 399
Ordered that George Cagle be appointed overseer of the road from Bear Creek to William Stewarts' and work the following

hands: Henry Brewer, John McLeod's hands, Mark Russel's hands, George Cagle's hands, Josiah Wallace, Branson Wallace, Ashley Maness, George Hunsucker (merchant)'s hands, John Riddle and Lewis Maness.

1850, Nov 15 -- Census, Moore County, NC Page 242
Josiah Wallis 43 M, Farmer, born in North Carolina
Catherine Wallis 42 F, born in North Carolina

1851, Oct 27 -- 1851-1853 Court of Pleas and Quarter Sessions, Moore County, NC Page 85
A free boy of color Harrison age about 11 and Mary and her sister age about 10 bound to John McLeod with Henry Stutts as a security. Ann, a free girl of color be bound to Josiah Wallace with Henry Stutts as security.

1852 -- Tax List, Moore County, NC District 9
Josiah Wallace listed 28 acres valued at $28

1852, Jan 26 -- 1851-1853 Court of Pleas and Quarter Sessions, Moore County, NC Page 141
Ordered that Josiah Wallace be released from indenture binding him to Ann Caveness, child of Wincy Caveness

1857 -- Tax List, Moore County, NC District 9
Josiah Wallis listed 50 acres valued at $125 located on Richland Creek

1858, Jul 31 -- 1856-1858 Court of Pleas and Quarter Sessions, Moore County, NC Page 491
Persons Involved in Liquor Traffic: Josiah Wallace listed with $100 Capital liquor Traffic and Tax $5

1859, Jan 29 -- Deed Book 32, Page 197-199, Moore County, NC
James Deaton deeded Josiah Wallace 50 acres on Richland Creek adjoining the Grove tract. Danl. McIntosh was a witness.

1859, Sep 1 -- Deed Book 32, Page 199, Moore County, NC
Josiah Wallace deeded Samuel Barrett 50 acres on Richland Creek adjoining the Grove tract. A.M. Branson was a witness.

1860, Aug 6 -- Agricultural Census, Moore County, NC Page 33, Gold Region Post Office
Si Wallace listed 21 acres improved, 50 acres unimproved valued at $160

1860, Aug 9 -- Census, Moore County, NC Page 204, Gold Region Post Office
Si Wallace 52 M, Farmer, $160 Real Estate, $300 Personal Property, born in North Carolina
Catherine Wallace 50 F, born in North Carolina

577	563	Si Wallace	52	m	Farmer		160	300		NC
		Catharine	50	f						NC

1861, Jul 24 -- Deed Book 10, Page 496-498, Moore County, NC

John R. Ritter deeded Wm. L. Ritter three tracts. [1] 45 acres located on Buffalo Creek adjoining Matthew Davis (formerly Wm. Stewart), Noah Richardson and John R. Ritter (formerly Robert Wilson) excluding 0.5 acres for a graveyard and 2 acres for a school house [2] 82 acres on Buffalo Creek [3] 100 acres on Buffalo Creek adjoining Noah Richardson and Josiah Wallace [4] 93 acres on Buffalo Creek adjoining Matthew Davis, Richardson and Ritter excluding 5 acres for Asa Maness' house and land. S.C. Bruce and W.J. King were witnesses.

1867, Mar 7 -- Deed Book 7 Page 438-443, Moore County, NC
Noah Richardson deeded J.B. Richardson several tracts: [1] 10 acres located on Lick Creek deeded by Josiah Wallis [2] 48 acres located on Alder Springs patented by Joshua L. Seawell adjoining Sulivan, Eli Sowell, Brown, Isaac M. Sowell and McLeod [3] 47 acres deeded by Josiah Wallis and I.M. Sowell adjoining McLeod [4] 65 acres located on Weir Branch deeded by Gabriel W. Freeman adjoining Dannelly and John H. Freeman [5] 65 acres located south of Boroughs Road deeded by Joseph Upton adjoining Wm. Reives [6] 95 acres located on McCallums Fork deeded by Joseph Upton adjoining D. Davis [7] 63 acres located east of Buffalo Creek and both sides of Boroughs Road adjoining Wm. Richardson [8] 67 acres located on Kings Street and the Boroughs Road adjoining Wm. Richardson and Upton [9] 150 acres located on Buffalo Creek and Morter Glade deeded by Wm. Dannelly and Michael Cockman adjoining George Cagle, E. Cagle(formerly John Stutts), McLeod, Drury Richardson and Upton [10] 8 acres located on Buffalo Creek patented to Drury Richardson adjoining E. Cagle(formerly John Stutts) [11] 50 acres located on Kings Street west of Boroughs Road patented to William Richardson adjoining John Upton [12] 17.5 acres located on Buffalo Creek [13] a tract purchased from John Stutts located on Buffalo Creek adjoining Drury Richardson [14] 100 acres located on the head of McCallums Fork deeded to Noah Richardson by Wm. Reives and Wm. Reives by Joseph Upton adjoining Polly Upton and her mother. Joseph Upton and W.B. Richardson were witnesses.

1870, Jul 4 -- Agricultural Census, Moore County, NC Page 9, Carthage Township, Carthage Post Office
Josiah Wallis listed 10 acres improved, 100 acres wooded, 90 acres unimproved valued at $75

1870, Jul 8 -- Census, Moore County, NC Page 512, Carthage Township, Carthage Post Office
Josiah Wallis 63 M, Farmer, $200 Real Estate, $75 Personal Property, born in North Carolina
Catherine Wallis 63 F, born in North Carolina

1880, Jun 24 -- Census, Moore County, NC Page 228, Carthage Township
Katie Wallace 70 F, Head, Keeping House, born in North Carolina, father & mother born in North Carolina

1893, Mar 6 -- Deed Book 10, Page 338-340, Moore County, NC
George Cockman, administrator of Isham Wallace, Dec'd. deeded I.W.H. Cockman two tracts. [1] 142 acres located on Meadow Branch adjoining Quimby Wallace, Samuel Wallace and L. Wallace. [2] 10 acres located on Meadow Branch and the Rutherford Road adjoining Armstrong Maness and deeded to Isham Wallace by Josiah Wallace. A.H. McNeill was a witness.

12. **Enoch Wallace**, son of Everet Wallace and Caty\Catherine, was born circa 1808 in North Carolina. He died after 1880 and married Malvina Furr (bet. 1810/1820-aft 1870), sister of Nancy Furr Wallace. Enoch and Malvina were the parents of at least five children: Hiram W., Hamilton, Isham "Ike", John Spinks and Christian. Enoch is listed in records near the McLendons Creek and Juniper Creek area and is believed to have lived nearby.

RECORDS OF ENOCH WALLACE

1823, Nov 17 -- 1823-1831 Court of Pleas and Quarter Sessions, Moore County, NC Page 14

Ordered that William Jones overseer of the road from David Kennedy's bridge to the old road have the following additional hands to work: David Lanckford, Enoch Wallis, Robert Melton Jr., James Milton, William Wood and Matthew Williams.

1824, Aug 19 -- 1823-1831 Court of Pleas and Quarter Sessions, Moore County, NC Page 52
Ordered that Daniel Caddell be appointed overseer of the road from Bean's Bridge to Flowers Road and have the following hands to work: Leonard Lawhon, John McIntosh, John Murchison, Enoch Wallis, Isham Wallis, John Rouse, Miles Rouse, Martin Rouse, John McDonald, Hugh Kelly, James Hill, Martin Hill, Dickson Ritter, James Ritter, Samuel Barrett, Wm. Barrett Esq.'s boy, Simon Murchison and Daniel Murchison.

1825, Aug 15 -- 1823-1831 Court of Pleas and Quarter Sessions, Moore County, NC Page 82
Ordered that Jesse Muse be appointed overseer of the road from Beans Bridge to the hill at the Widow Bethune's and have the following hands to work: Leonard Lawhon, John Muse, Miles Rouse, John McIntosh, John Rouse, James Hill, Martin Hill, Walter Barrett, Dickson Ritter, Martin Rouse, Daniel Caddell and Enoch Wallis.

1826, Aug 21 -- 1823-1831 Court of Pleas and Quarter Sessions, Moore County, NC Page 129
Ordered that John J. McIntosh be appointed overseer of the road from Bean's Bridge to the hill at the Widow Bethune's in place of Jesse Muse and have the following hands to work: Leonard Lawhon, John Muse, Miles Rouse, John McIntosh, John Rouse, James Hill, Martin Hill, Walter Barrett, Dickson Ritter, Martin Rouse, Donald Caddell and Enoch Wallis.

1826, Nov 21 -- 1823-1831 Court of Pleas and Quarter Sessions, Moore County, NC Page 149
Ordered that Daniel McRimson [McCrimmon] be appointed overseer of the road from the Randolph County Line to John
Spivay's and have the following hands to work: Wm. Sheffield, E. Wallis, Jasen Muse, J. Collier, John McDonald, Thomas Williams and Auburn Jones.

1827, Aug 20 -- 1823-1831 Court of Pleas and Quarter Sessions, Moore County, NC Page 177
Ordered that James Hill be appointed overseer of the road from Bean's Bridge to the hill at the Widow Bethune's in place of John McIntosh and have the following hands to work: John J. McIntosh, Leonard Lawhon, John Muse, Miles Rouse, John McIntosh, John Rouse, Martin Hill, Walter Barrett, Dickson Ritter, Martin Rouse, Daniel Caddell and Enoch Wallis.

1827, Nov 20 -- 1823-1831 Court of Pleas and Quarter Sessions, Moore County, NC Page 192
Ordered that Isaac Spivey be appointed overseer of the road in place of Wm. Brewer from Spivey to McNeill's store and have the following hands in addition: Matthew Shuffield, Enoch Wallis and Shadrach Davis.

1835, Fall -- 1834-1851 State Docket County Court. Moore County, NC Page 19
#16 State v. Franklin Muse. Enich Wallis and Joseph Cockman were witnesses.

1835, Fall-Spring 1836 -- 1796-1841 County Accounts, Moore County, NC Page 130
State v. Norman Gillis. Everitt Wallace and Enoch Wallace were witnesses

1837, Spring -- 1834-1851 State Docket County Court, Moore County, NC Page 34
#16 State v. Enich Wallace and Nancy Furr (trespass). Nancy Richison and Ginny Richison were witnesses.

1837, Aug -- 1796-1841 County Accounts, Moore County, NC Page 131-132
#13 State v. Enoch Wallis and William Caldwell
#41 State v. E. Wallis, N. Furr, D. Mews
#42 State v. E. Wallis, N. Furr, J. Melton
#43 State v. E. Wallis, N. Furr, Miles Mews

1840 -- Census, Moore County, NC Page 182
Enoch Wallace
(40-50) 1M
(20-30) 1F
(15-20) 1M
(10-15) 2M 2F
(5-10) 1M
(0-5) 1M

1848 -- Tax List, Moore County, NC
Enoch Wallace listed 1 white poll located on Juniper in District 3

1849 -- Tax List, Moore County, NC
Enoch Wallace listed 1 white poll in District 3

1850, Aug 5 -- Census, Moore County, NC Page 165
Enoch Wallis 36 M, Farmer, born in North Carolina
Malvina Wallis 28 F, born in North Carolina
Hiram Wallis 15 M, born in North Carolina
Hamilton Wallis 12 M, born in North Carolina
Isham Wallis 10 M, born in North Carolina
Spinks Wallis 6 M, born in North Carolina
Christian Wallis 2 F, born in North Carolina

1850, Nov 15 -- Agricultural Census, Moore County, NC Page 993
Enoch Wallis listed 20 acres improved, 230 acres unimproved valued at $300

1860, Sep 13 -- Census, Moore County, NC Page 229-230, Carthage Post Office
Enoch Wallace 45 M, Farmer, $60 Personal Property, born in North Carolina
Malvina Wallace 37 F, born in
Spinks Wallace 12 M, born in North Carolina
Christine Wallace 9 F, born in North Carolina
Isham Wallace 18 M, born in North Carolina

1860, Sep 18 -- Agricultural Census, Moore County, NC Page 49, Lawhons Hill Post Office
Enoch Wallace listed 35 acres improved valued at $10

1870, Jul 4 -- Agricultural Census, Moore County, NC Page 9, Carthage Township, Carthage Post Office
Enoch Wallis listed 10 acres improved valued at $100

1870, Jul 8 -- Census, Moore County, NC Page 513, Carthage Township, Carthage Post Office
Enoch Wallis 62 M, Farmer, $50 Personal Property, born in North Carolina
Molly V. Wallis 60 F, born in North Carolina
George Graham 30 M, born in North Carolina
Christian Graham 17 F, born in North Carolina
Vincy Graham 1 F, born in North Carolina

1880, Jun 15 -- Census, Moore County, NC Page 297, McNeills Township
N.A. Ray 50 M, Head, Married, Farming, born in North Carolina, father & mother born in North Carolina
M.F. Ray 35 F, Wife, Married, Keeping House, born in North Carolina, father & mother born in North Carolina
A.M. Ray 3 M, Son, Single, born in North Carolina, father & mother born in North Carolina
Enouch Wallace 58 M, Servant, Married, Works on Farm, born in North Carolina, father & mother born in North Carolina

Enoch Wallace and Malvina Furr had the following children:

+67 Hiram W. Wallace (1835-1862) married Julia Ann Williams (1838-1921) and their union produced four children. During the Civil War, Hiram served in Company D, 49th Regiment and was killed in action at Sharpsburg, MD.

+68 Hamilton Wallace (1838-bef 1860) appears in the 1850 Census but no further records of him have been located.

+69 Isham "Ike" Wallace (1840-1905) married Matilda Cockman (1845-bef 1924) and they produced four children. He served in the Civil War with his brother Hiram in Company D, 49th Regiment. Isham lived on Meadow Branch and is buried at a small family cemetery near his homeplace on the Plank Road.

+70 John Spinks Wallace (1844-1887) migrated to Lauderdale County, AL and married Nancy Olive "Ollie" Cannerday. Spinks and Ollie were the parents of five children, and they are buried at the Cannerday family cemetery in Lauderdale County, AL.

+71 Christian Wallace (1849-) married George Graham and their union produced at least five children.

13. **Elizabeth "Lizzie" Wallace**, daughter of Everet Wallace and Caty\Catherine, was born in 1808 in North Carolina and died after 1870 in western Tennessee. Elizabeth was the second wife of Jeremiah Williams (b. 1775) and according to Williams Family researchers they had a very large family consisting of the following children: Raleigh, Jeremiah D., Mary, Enoch Spinks, Lorenzo D., Amanda Jane, Franey, David Anderson, Caty, Ann, James Wesley, Joseph and Bryant. Jeremiah Williams' 1st wife is reported to be Florence DeLaney (1774/1780 - c1827). Jeremiah and Florence had the following children: Jeremiah Jr., Elizabeth, John, Matthew, Henry, George and Isaac. The photo on the right is rumored to be of Elizabeth Wallace Williams, "*Mrs. Lizzie Williams*" is handwritten on photo by an individual who the family identifies as having died in 1862.[17]

Jeremiah Williams was the son of George Williams (bef 1750-bef 1797) and Ann (-). He can be consistently found in records on Buffalo Creek in Moore County until he and his family migrated west in the 1840's. During the period from 1820s-1850s a large amount of Moore County families migrated to the western Tennessee counties of Henderson, McNairy and Madison including Elizabeth Wallace's brothers Nicholas and Nathan. Many of these families traveled the southern route through Hall County, GA to avoid the Great Smoky Mountains. Census records show that Jeremiah and Elizabeth's children Ann and James Wesley were born in Georgia en route to Tennessee during the mid-1840's.

According to *The Williams Family* by Maxine Williams McNeill, Jeremiah, Lizzie and "*their children made many trips back and forth from Moore County, NC to Madison County, TN. They made these trips on foot, as there were no roads to support a wagon. He put the smaller children on an old horse called, "a Rat Tail Horse". Jeremiah and Lizzie, along with the older children walked. They were only able to take a few supplies with them, "salt, coffee, flour, beans, and dried beef jerky", in the way of food. They took with them a cook pot, fry pan, coffee pot, bedrolls, and a waterproof tarp for shelter. He carried a musket, a knife, and a hand ax. It has been told by descendants, that Jeremiah was killed by the Indians, but no one knows just when or where. The old homeplace in Tennessee is south of Henderson (Chester County, TN) on Highway 45 across from the Estes Cemetery.*"[18] Their children and descendants can be found in Census data from Madison, McNairy and Henderson County, TN. Several of them later moved on further to Texas and Oklahoma.

"Mrs. Lizzie Williams"
(Courtesy of Judy Little, Lexington, TN)

1797, May 10 -- Will Book A, Page 192-193, Moore County, NC
Will of George Williams, Dec'd. Heirs: wife Ann Williams [*all land*], son James Williams, daughter Nelly Williams, son Jeremiah Williams, son Thomas Williams, son William Williams, daughter Mary Williams and daughter Sally Williams. Executors: Ann Williams and Leonard Furr. Witnesses: Everet Wallis and William Dunn. Proven Aug 1797.

1800 -- Census, Moore County, NC Page 70
Jeremiah Williams
(16-26) 1M 1F
(0-10) 1M

1804, Aug 6 -- Deed Book 127 Page 255, Moore County, NC
Jeremiah Williams deeded John Needham, Sr. 3 tracts (50, 50, 50 acres) located on Cabbin Creek and Dry Creek adjoining Levi Deaton. W. N. Needham and Mathew Deton were witnesses.

1810 -- Census, Moore County, NC Page 611
Jerry Williams
(26-45) 1M 1F
(0-10) 6M

1810, Aug 23 -- Land Grant #2034, Moore County, NC
Charles Sowell received 50 acres located on Flag Creek adjoining his own line, George Cagle, Graham, Leonard Furr, Jacob Furr and Williams. George Cagle and Jeremiah Williams were chain carriers. [*Editor's Note: William Williams deeded to Leonard Furr 1811 --> George Davis 1838*]

1815-Tax List, Moore County, NC
Jeremiah Williams listed with 110 acres valued at $150

1815, Oct 25 -- Land Grant #2255, Moore County, NC
James Hains received 50 acres located east of Buffalo Creek adjoining his own line, James Dunlap and Leonard Furr Senr. (now known as the Moore Place). Normand Matheson and Jeremiah Williams were chain carriers.

1815, Oct 25 -- Land Grant #2257, Moore County, NC
Normand Matheson received 100 acres located on Willow and Long Meadow adjoining his own line (formerly John Carrel). James Hains and Jeremiah Williams were chain carriers.

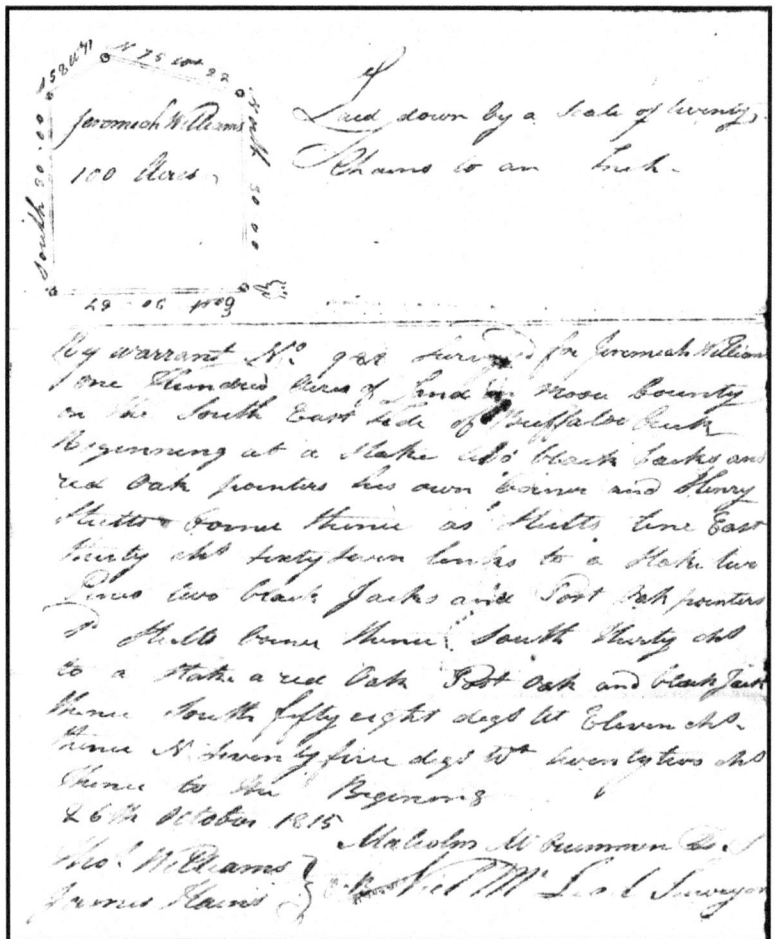

1815, Oct 26 -- Land Grant #2339, Moore County, NC
Jeremiah Williams received 100 acres located southeast of Buffalo Creek adjoining Henry Stutts and own line. Thos. Williams and James Hains were chain carriers.

1818-1823 Tax List, Moore County, NC
Jeremiah Williams listed with 110 acres valued at $140

1823, Dec 31 --- Deed Book 95 Page 22, Moore County, NC
Jeremiah Williams, Thomas Williams, James Williams, Bartholomew Dunn deeded William Williams 2 tracts of land (100 acres and 50 acres) located on Flag Creek. Jesse Brown Junr. and William Dunn were witnesses.

1824, Aug 19 -- 1823-1831 Court of Pleas and Quarter Sessions, Moore County, NC Page 52-53
A deed from Jeremeah Williams, Thomas Williams, James Williams and Bartholomew Dunn to William Williams was proven by Jesse Brown

1825, Feb 24 -- 1823-1831 Court of Pleas and Quarter Sessions, Moore County, NC Page 70
John Richardson to Jeremiah Williams proven by Jesse Brown

1825, May 6 -- Land Grant #2689, Moore County, NC
Jacob Stutts received 41 acres located south of Buffalo Creek adjoining Jeremiah Williams, James Dunlap, Haines and Milton. Henry Stutts and Wm. Lakey were chain carriers.

1830 -- Census, Moore County, NC Page 477
Jeremh. Williams
(50-60) 1M
(20-30) 2M 1F
(15-20) 1M 1F
(10-15) 2M 1F
(5-10) 1M 1F
(0-5) 2M

1835, Nov 21 -- Land Grant #2948, Moore County, NC
Hyram Melton received 25 acres located on the head of Sassafras Branch adjoining Jeremiah Williams and Robert Melton. James Melton and Ansel Melton were chain carriers.

1844 -- Tax List, Moore County, NC
Jeremiah Williams listed 210 acres valued at $210 located on Buffalow Creek in District 6

1844, Apr 23 -- 1844-1847 Court of Pleas and Quarter Sessions, Moore County, NC Page 7
Ordered that Joseph Upton be appointed overseer of the road from George Moores to the branch near McQueens and have the following hands to work: Elisha Cagle, James Melton, Cornl. Mathews, George Williams, David Cockman, Joseph Cockman, Sampson Cockman, Isaac Williams, George Cockman, George W. Horner, Noah Richardson hands, Seburn Jones, John Cockman, Abram Hunsucker, William Williams, James Deaton, Quimby Sowell, William Richardson, John Jones, Allen Jones and Jeremiah Williams.

1860, Jun 15 -- Census, Madison County, TN Page 87, District #1, Mt. Pinson Post Office
Lizzie Williams 51 F, born in North Carolina
L.D. Williams 30 M, Farmer, born in North Carolina
Phrany Williams 23 F, born in North Carolina
Katy Williams 20 F, born in North Carolina
Ann Williams 16 F, born in Georgia
James Williams 15 M, born in North Carolina
Joseph Williams 13 M, born in North Carolina
Bryant Williams 12 M, born in North Carolina

1870, Jun 1 -- Census, McNairy County, TN Page 347-B, 14th Civil District, Bethel Springs Post Office

Enoch Williams 42 M, Farmer, $1500 Real Estate, $1000 Personal Property, born in North Carolina

Rody J. Williams 37 F, Keeping House, born in North Carolina

Jeremiah D. Williams 19 M, born in North Carolina

William B. Williams 17 M, born in North Carolina

Liney E. Williams 14 F, born in Tennessee

Lorenzo D. Williams 6 M, born in Tennessee

Mary A. Williams 3 F, born in Tennessee

John L. Williams 1 M, born in Tennessee

Elizabeth Williams 62 F, born in North Carolina

66	66	Williams Enoch	42	M	W	Farmer	1500	1000	North Carolina
		— Rody J	37	F	W	Keeping house			North Carolina
		— Jeremiah	19	M	W				North Carolina
		— William B	17	M	W				North Carolina
		— Liney E	14	F	W				Tennessee
		— Lorenzo D	6	M	W				Tennessee
		— Mary A	3	F	W				Tennessee
		— John L	1	M	W				Tennessee
		Williams Elizabeth	62	F	W				North Carolina

Jeremiah Williams and Elizabeth Wallace had the following children:

+72   Raleigh Williams (-) is listed as a child of Jeremiah and Elizabeth by Williams family researchers but no further information has been located.

+73   Jeremiah D. Williams (1825-1906) married Rebecca Kizer (1827-1908) and they were the parents of ten children. It is my belief that Jeremiah D. Williams is the son of Jeremiah Williams. This is based on several circumstantial pieces of evidence and backed up by DNA research. (1) Jeremiah D. Williams' migration patterns tracts that of Jeremiah Williams and his children from Moore County to Hall County, GA to McNairy County, TN and then Parker County, TX; (2) Jeremiah D. Williams married Rebecca Kizer in Hall County, GA in 1845. Jeremiah Williams and Elizabeth Wallace had two children who were born in Georgia in 1844 and 1845 (3) Jeremiah D. Williams was listed in the 1870 Census in McNairy County, TN a few houses over from Elizabeth Wallace Williams and son Enoch Spinks Williams. (4) Enoch Spinks Williams, likely brother to Jeremiah D. Williams named his oldest son Jeremiah David Williams.

+74   Mary Williams (1825-1905) was married and outlived three different husbands: Bryant Stafford (1824-1868), Charles G. Clayton (1830-1875) and Aaron W. Williams (1830-1895). There was a close connection between Mary and Elizabeth Susan Williams (1815-1898) and they are both buried at Estes Cemetery in Chester County, TN. Elizabeth Susan married Daniel J. Muse (1808-1878) and it is possible that she was another daughter of Jeremiah.

+75   Enoch Spinks Williams (1827-1894) married Rhoda Jane Morgan (1831-1898) and they migrated from Moore County to McNairy County, TN and finally to Parker County, TX where they are buried at Jaybird Cemetery. They were the parents of ten children.

+76   Lorenzo D. "Low" Williams (1829-1890) married Sarah Elizabeth Hart and their union produced twelve children. Low and Sarah are buried at Palestine Church in Henderson County, TN.

+77   Amanda Jane "Mandy" Williams (1836-1907) married Nathaniel "Nat" Britt (1836-1871), they had six children and Mandy is buried at Palestine Church also.

+78   Franey Williams (1837-) was listed in the 1860 Census but no further record of her has been located.

+79   David Anderson Williams (1838-1900) married Elizabeth Ann Mosier (1845-1876) and had six children. He married Mary J. (b. 1853) after Elizabeth died.

+80   Caty Williams (1840-bef 1870) married her cousin Benjamin Wallace (1840-1900), son of Nathan C. Wallace and their union produced two daughters.

+81   Ann Williams (1844-) was listed in the 1860 Census but no further record of her has been located.

+82   James Wesley Williams (1845-) married Margaret M. Hart (b. 1846) and they produced eight children. James and Margaret are buried at Palestine Church.

+83   Joseph Williams (1847-) was listed in the 1860 Census but no further record of him has been located.

+84   Bryant Williams (1848-) married Mary Latham (b. 1856) and they had four children.

14. **Manda Wallace**, daughter of Everet Wallace and Caty\Catherine, was born in 1810 in North Carolina and very little is known about Manda. She was listed in the 1850 Census with children Sarah, Cornelius, Anderson and Isaac Spinks. In 1900, the North Carolina General Assembly passed a law restricting the rights of North Carolinians to vote. Largely aimed at denying the right of African-Americans to vote, the law said only voters who owned land or had an ancestor who was registered to vote prior to Reconstruction in 1867 (known as the "Grandfather Clause") were eligible to cast a ballot.[19] Isaac Spinks Wallace registered to vote under this law and listed Everet Wallace as his closest male ancestor confirming the relationship between Manda and Everet. Several of her children were listed in the 1850 census as being mulatto (mixed race) likely due to a darker complexion. Their father may have been African American or Native American if the census was correct although Isaac Spinks Wallace was listed as white in every census after 1850.

RECORDS OF MANDA WALLACE

1850, Nov 9 -- Census, Moore County, NC Page 238
Manda Wallis 40 F, born in North Carolina
Sarah Wallis 10 F, born in North Carolina
Corneilus Wallis 5 M (mulatto), born in North Carolina
Anderson Wallis 3 M (mulatto), born in North Carolina
Spinks Wallis 3/12 M (mulatto), born in North Carolina

1870, Jun 24 -- Census, Moore County, NC Page 496, Carthage Township, Carthage Post Office
John W. Warner 48 M, Farmer, $1500 Real Estate, $500 Personal Property, born in North Carolina
Deborah Warner 24 F, born in North Carolina
William T. Warner 5 M, At Home, born in North Carolina
Mary C. Warner 3 F, At Home, born in North Carolina
John A. Warner 1 M, At Home, born in North Carolina
Manda Wallis 50 F, Laborer, born in North Carolina

Manda Wallace had the following children:

+85   Sarah Wallace (1840-) was listed in the 1850 Census and no further record of her has been located.

+86   Cornelius Wallace (1845-) was listed in the 1850 Census and no further record of him has been located.

+87   Anderson Wallace (1847-) was listed in the 1850 Census and no further record of him has been located.

+88   Isaac Spinks Wallace (1849-1912) married Anna Jane McDonald (1852-1928). They lived near
        Pinehurst and were founding members of Beulah Hill Baptist Church in 1897. They are both
        buried at the old Beulah Hill cemetery along with most of their children.

15. **Franey Wallace**, daughter of Everet Wallace and Caty\Catherine, was born in 1814 in North Carolina and she died after 1880. Franey raised five out of wedlock children whose father was believed to be Abram Hunsucker (1806-1869) - (see DNA analysis page 14). Abram was married to Elizabeth Horner during the time that he is believed to have fathered Franey's children Martha J., Mary Ann, Rebecca Jane, John Mack "Mack" and Julia Frances. Franey resided with her parents and her son, John Mack Wallace, inherited the old Everet Wallace home place (located just west of the Robbins crossroads) and was the last Wallace in possession of it. My Grandfather said the spring across from the old home place was known as the "Franey Spring."

RECORDS OF FRANEY WALLACE

1850, Nov 8 -- Census, Moore County, NC Page 236
Franey Wallis 32 F, born in North Carolina
Mary Ann Wallis 14 F, born in North Carolina
Rebecca Wallis 8 F, born in North Carolina
John Wallis 4 M, born in North Carolina
Julia Wallis 4/12 F, born in North Carolina

1860, Aug 31 -- Census, Moore County, NC Page 220, Gold Region Post Office
Franey Wallace 46 F, Farmer, $50 Real Estate, $100 Personal Property, born in North Carolina

1870, Jul 14 -- Census, Moore County, NC Page 481, Bensalem Township, Curriesville Post Office
John M. Wallis 23 M, Farmer, $100 Real Estate, $75 Personal Property, born in North Carolina
Martha A. Wallis 20 M, born in North Carolina
William W. Wallis 9/12 M, born in North Carolina
Franey Wallis 56 F, born in North Carolina

1880, Jun 27 -- Census, Moore County, NC Page 210, Bensalem Township
John M. Wallace 34 M, Head, Married, Farmer/Planter, born in North Carolina, father & mother born in North Carolina
Martha Wallace 30 F, Wife, Married, Keeping House, born in North Carolina, father & mother born in North Carolina
William Wallace 10 M Son, Single, At Home, born in North Carolina, father & mother born in North Carolina
Mary B. Wallace 8 F, Dau, Single, At Home, born in North Carolina, father & mother born in North Carolina
John R. Wallace 6 M, Son, Single, born in North Carolina, father & mother born in North Carolina
Henry Wallace 6 M, Son, Single, born in North Carolina, father & mother born in North Carolina
Margaret Wallace 4 F, Dau, Single, born in North Carolina, father & mother born in North Carolina
Franey Wallace 66 F, Mother, born in North Carolina, father & mother born in North Carolina

Abraham C. Hunsucker, son of George Hunsucker (1775-) and Sarah Spinks (-), was born in 1806. He died in August 1869 in Montgomery County, NC and he was buried in Wadeville, Montgomery County, NC at Liberty Hill Baptist Church. He and Franey Wallace are believed to have had the following children:

+89 Martha J. Wallace (1833-1922) married William Zeno Richardson (1832-1905), had eleven children and later in life moved to Liberty County, GA. They are buried at Deen Cemetery in Appling County, GA.

+90 Mary Ann Wallace (1838-1865) married Anderson Lindo Seawell (1834-1888) and died young leaving four small children. She is buried at Bethlehem Baptist Church near Carthage.

+91 Rebecca Jane Wallace (1842-1875) married Henry Maness (1839-1897) and they produced five children.

+92 John Mack Wallace (1845-1927) served in Company D, 48th Regiment during the Civil War, was married twice and later moved his family to Hope Mills in Cumberland County, NC. Mack married Martha Ann Brown (1849-1902) and they had ten children. After Martha's death Mack married Parthenia Gibsie Bass and their union produced six more children. Mack and both wives are buried at Big Rockfish Presbyterian Church in Hope Mills.

+93 Julia Frances Wallace (1850-1919) married Marshal G. Maness (1844-1907) and they were the parents of two daughters. Frances and Marshal are buried at Tabernacle United Methodist Church in Robbins.

16. **Susannah Wallace**, daughter of Everet Wallace and Caty\Catherine, was born in 1815 in North Carolina. I am less certain that Susannah Wallace (b. 1815) was a daughter of Everet Wallace than any of his other children. The only references found for her are the 1850 and 1860 census where Susannah was listed as having two children: Eli (b. 1838) and Calvin (b. 1841). She was listed as a mulatto (mixed race) in both census records and no further record of her or her descendants has been located.

RECORDS OF SUSANNAH WALLACE

1850, Nov 8 -- Census, Moore County, NC Page 237
Susannah Wallis 35 F (mulatto), born in North Carolina

1850, Nov 8 -- Census, Moore County, NC Page 237
George M. Hunsucker 48 M, Farmer, $800 Real Estate, born in North Carolina
Elizabeth Hunsucker 38 F, born in North Carolina
Loretta Hunsucker 7 F, born in North Carolina
Clarkston Hunsucker 4 M, born in North Carolina
Missouri Hunsucker 2 F, born in North Carolina
Regina Hunsucker 5/12 F, born in North Carolina
Eli Wallis 12 M (mulatto), born in North Carolina
Calvin Wallis 9 M (mulatto), born in North Carolina

1860, Jul 13 -- Census, Moore County, NC Page 204, Gold Region Post Office
George Hunsucker 56 M, Farmer, $500 Real Estate, $500 Personal Property, born in North Carolina
Elizabeth Hunsucker 49 F, born in North Carolina
Clarkson Hunsucker 14 M, born in North Carolina
Missourie Hunsucker 12 F, born in North Carolina
Regina Hunsucker 10 F, born in North Carolina
Loanna M. Hunsucker 6 F, born in North Carolina

Elizabeth Hunsucker 5 F, born in North Carolina
Wesley Brown 23 M, Stage Driver, born in North Carolina
Loretta Brown 17 F, born in North Carolina
Calvin Spiner 19 M (mulatto), born in North Carolina
Susan Wallace 30 F (mulatto), born in North Carolina

Susannah Wallace had the following children:

+94   Eli Wallace (1838-)
+95   Calvin Wallace (1841-)

UNKNOWN DAUGHTERS OF EVERET WALLACE

According to census records, Everet and Caty Wallace had two additional daughters, but their names are unknown at this time. One daughter was born between 1800-1804 and the other was born between 1804-1810. They are believed to have married and left the household by 1830.

Third Generation

17. **Catherine "Katie" Maness**, daughter of Shadrach Maness and Celia Wallace, was born in 1814 and died in 1890. She married **Garner Maness**, son of Abednego Maness (1770-) and Susannah "Sukie" Garner (c. 1780-). Garner was born in 1806 and died in 1863. They were buried in Moore County, NC at Maness Cemetery #225.[20] Garner and Katie owned 278 acres on Bear Creek during their lifetime including the original 200 acre land grant previously owned by his father, Abednego Maness.

RECORDS OF GARNER AND KATIE MANESS

1812, Dec 11 -- Land Grant #2664, Moore County, NC
Abednego Maness received 200 acres located east of Bear Creek adjoining Neil McLeod, John McAulay and Brewer. Gardner Maness and Nathan Maness were chain carriers.

1824, Aug 16 -- 1823-1831 Court of Pleas and Quarter Sessions, Moore County, NC Page 40
Ordered that John Ritter Jr. be appointed overseer in place of Elijah Brewer of the road from Bear Creek to George Moore's and have the following hands to work: Elijah Brewer, Abraham Stuts, Danl. Williams, George Stuts, Jacob Stuts, George Moore Jr., John Hunsucker, Jethrew Denson, Edward Moore, Garner Maness and Bradley Brady.

1825, Aug 15 -- 1823-1831 Court of Pleas and Quarter Sessions, Moore County, NC Page 82
Ordered that George Stuts be appointed overseer in place of John Ritter of the road from Bear Creek to George Moore's and have the following hands to work: John Ritter Jr., Elijah Brewer, Abraham Stuts, Danl. Williams, Jacob Stuts, George

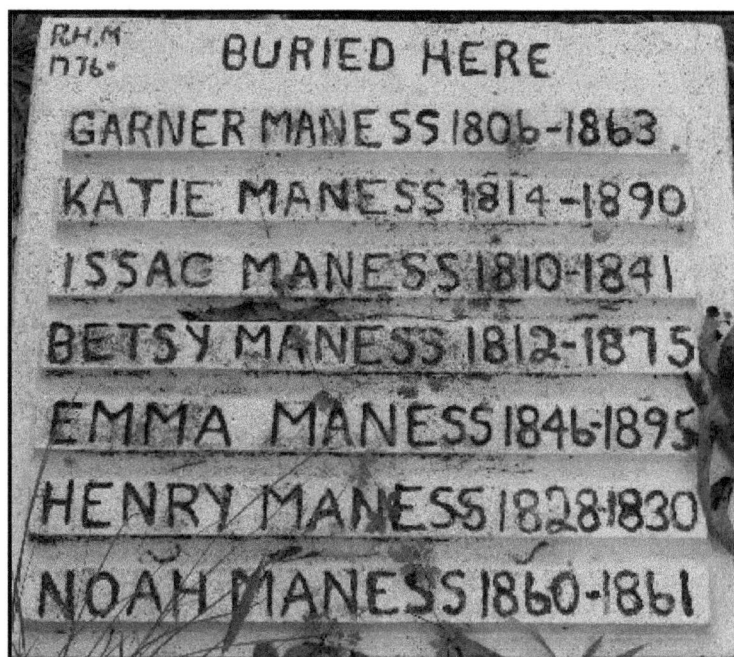

Moore Jr., John Hunsucker, Jethrew Denson, Edward Moore, Garner Maness, Bradley Brady, Willis Brewer, Edmond Boroughs and Robert Hollomon.

(photographed June 13, 2009)

1826, Aug 21 -- 1823-1831 Court of Pleas and Quarter Sessions, Moore County, NC Page 130
Ordered that David Brewer be appointed overseer in place of George Stuts of the road from Bear Creek to George Moore's and have the following hands to work: George Stuts, John Ritter Jr., Elijah Brewer, Abraham Stuts, Daniel Williams, Jacob Stuts, George Moore Jr., John Hunsucker, Jethroe Denson, Edward Moore, Garner Maness, Bradley Brady, Willis Brewer, Edmond Boroughs, Robert Hardin and Stephen Maness.

1836, Mar 12 -- Land Grant #2991, Moore County, NC
Isaac Maness received 100 acres located south of Bear Creek adjoining McAulay, John Maness and Henry Stutts. Garner Maness and Henry Maness were chain carriers.

1836, Sep 21 -- Land Grant #3043, Moore County, NC

Bradley Brady received 100 acres located south of Bear Creek adjoining Isaac Manes and Henry Manes. Henry Manes and Garner Manes were chain carriers.

1840 -- Census, Moore County, NC Page 182
Garner Maner
(30-40) 1M
(20-30) 1F
(5-10) 1M
(0-5) 2F

1841, Dec 29 -- Land Grant #3166, Moore County, NC
Matthew Williams received 100 acres located between Bear Creek and Buffalo Creek adjoining Henry Stutts, Bryant Boroughs and Lamb. Garner Maness and M. Williams were chain carriers.

1844, Apr 24 -- 1844-1847 Court of Pleas and Quarter Sessions, Moore County, NC Page 10
Ordered that Everet Maines be appointed overseer of the road from Bear Creek to Buffalo Creek and work the following hands: John McLeod, George Cagle, Garner Maines, William Stewart, Henry Maines, Matthew Williams, Jethro Denson, Amos Bridges, William L. Wallace, Lauchlin B. Currie and Hiram Kelly.

1845, Jan 30 -- 1844-1847 Court of Pleas and Quarter Sessions, Moore County, NC Page 125
Ordered that Asa Mainess be appointed overseer of the road from Bear Creek to William Stewarts and have the following hands to work: Garner Mainess, John McLeod 1 hand, Henry Mainess, Matthew Williams Senr., Matthew Williams Junr., George Cagle, William Stewart, Henry Stutts (of Jacob) 1 hand and Leonard Stutts (of Jacob).

1846, Apr 28 -- 1844-1847 Court of Pleas and Quarter Sessions, Moore County, NC Page 318
Ordered that William Stewart be appointed overseer of the road from Bear Creek to William Stewart's and have the following hands to work: John McLeod's hands, Henry Stutts' hands, Garner Mainess, Mathew Williams Junr., John Riddle, Hiram Kelly, Edward Stewart, John Denson, George Cagle, Lewis Mainess, William Stutts, Leonard Stutts and Henry Brown.

1846, May 2 -- 1844-1847 Court of Pleas and Quarter Sessions, Moore County, NC Page 333
Ordered that William M. Johnson be appointed the overseer in place of Garner Mainess of the new road from William Ritter's by way of William M. Johnson's mill to the [Chatham] County Line and have the following hands to work: William M. Johnson's hand, James Cavness' hands, Benjamin P. Person's two hands, James Moore, Westley Shields, Hiram Johnson, Jonathan Martindale, Alston Brewer, Henry Brown, Willis Phillips, Jery Phillips, Henry C. Hardin, Calvin C. Myrick, Enoch Powers, Robert L. Purvis, Bailey Brown, Mathew Williams, Henry Stutts, Leonard Stutts, Abram Stutts' one hand, Hiram Kelly, Garner Mainess, James Brady, Bryant Boroughs' hands, Mathew Boroughs' hands and William Hunsucker.

1847 -- Tax List, Moore County, NC District 9
Garner Maness 250 acres valued at $300 1 white poll on Bear Creek

1847, Apr 27 -- 1847-1849 Court of Pleas and Quarter Sessions, Moore County, NC Page 14
Ordered that George Cagle be appointed overseer of the road from Bear Creek to William Stewart's and work the following hands: William Stewart, John McLeod's hands, Henry Stutts' hands, Garner Mainess, Mathew Williams Junr., John Riddle, Hiram Kelly, William Stewart's hands, Edward Stewart's hands, John Denson, George Cagle, Lewis Mainess, Leonard Stutts and Henry Brown.

1848, Apr 24 -- 1847-1849 Court of Pleas and Quarter Sessions, Moore County, NC Page 182
Ordered that Henry Brown be appointed overseer of the road from Bear Creek to William Stuart's and work the following hands: George Cagle, John McLeod's hands, Henry Stutts' hands, Garner Mainess, Matthew Williamson Jr. [error-should be Williams], John Riddle, Hiram Kelly, William Stuart's hands, Edward Stuart's hands, John Denson, Lewis Mainess, Leonard Stutts and William Stutts.

1848, May 10 -- Land Grant #3607, Moore County, NC
Josiah Wallace received 28 acres located east of Bear Creek on Lick Branch adjoining Garner Maness, Nall, Henry Stutts, Abel Maness and Jonah B. Maness. John Riddle and William B. Wallace were chain carriers.

1849 -- Tax List, Moore County, NC District 9
Garner Maness 250 acres valued at $300 1 white poll on Bear Creek

1849, Apr 24 -- 1847-1849 Court of Pleas and Quarter Sessions, Moore County, NC Page 410
Ordered that Enoch Powers be appointed overseer of the new road from near William Ritters to the [Chatham] County line and work the following hands: William M. Johnson's hands, James Caviness' hands, Benjamin P. Person's hands, James Moore, Wesley Shields, Hiram Johnson, Jonathan Martindale, Alston Brown, Henry Brown, Willis Phillips, Henry C. Hardin, Calvin C. Mirick, Enoch Powers, Robert Powers, Bailey Brown, Mathew Williams, Henry Stutts, Hiram Kelly, Garner Maness, James Brady, Bryant Boroughs hands, Mathews Boroughs hands, William Hunsucker, Leonard Stutts and Abram Stutts hands.

1850 -- Census, Moore County, NC Page 241
Garner Manis 44 M, Farmer, $300 Real Estate, born in North Carolina

Additional Information can be found at www.MooreCountyWallaces.com

Catherine Manis 36 F, born in North Carolina
James A. Manis 15 M, born in North Carolina
Mary Manis 14 F, born in North Carolina
Sadberry Manis 6 M, born in North Carolina
A. Spinks Manis 4 M, born in North Carolina
Josiah Manis 2 M, born in North Carolina

1850, Nov 28 -- Deed Book 35 Page 428-430, Moore County, NC
Henry Stutts deeded Duncan McIntosh 28 acres (of 166 acre tract) located south of Bear Creek adjoining Gardner Maness. Murdo Street and A. McKinnon were witnesses.

1851, Apr 28 -- 1851-1853 Court of Pleas and Quarter Sessions, Moore County, NC Page 3
Ordered that Henry Stutts be appointed overseer of the new road from near William Ritters to the [Chatham] county line and have the following hands to work: Enoch Powers, William M. Johnson's hands, James Caveness hands, Benjamin P. Person & hands, James Moore, Westley Shields, Hiram Johnson, Jonathan Martindale, Alston Brewer, Henry Brown, Willis Phillips, Jerry Phillips, Hugh C. Hardin, Calvin C. Myrick, Robert Powers, Bailey Brown, Mathew Williams, Hiram Kelly, Garner Maness, James Brady, Bryan Boroughs hands, Mathew Boroughs & hands, William Hunsucker, Leonard Stutts, Abram Stutts hands, Adam Keeling and Isaiah Caveness.

1852 -- -- Tax List, Moore County, NC District 9
Garner Maness 278 acres valued at $328 on Bear Creek

1853 -- -- Tax List, Moore County, NC District 9
Garner Maness 278 acres valued at $328 on Bear Creek

1854 -- -- Tax List, Moore County, NC District 9
Garner Maness 278 acres valued at $300 on Bear Creek

1854 -- -- Tax List, Moore County, NC District 9
Garner Maness 278 acres valued at $417 on Bear Creek

1855, Nov 12 -- Land Grant #4108, Moore County, NC
John Riddle received 33 acres located between Bear Creek and Buffalo Creek adjoining Garner Maness, Bradley Brady and his own line. Spencer Brown and John Moore were chain carriers.

1854 -- -- Tax List, Moore County, NC District 9
Garner Maness 278 acres valued at $417 on Bear Creek

1860 -- Census, Moore County, NC Page 202-B, Gold Region Post Office
Garner Maner 54 M, Farmer, $600 Real Estate, $400 Personal Property, born in North Carolina
Catharine Maner 45 F, born in North Carolina
Lydia M. Maner 18 F, born in North Carolina
James J. Maner 15 M, born in North Carolina
Alex S. Maner 13 M, born in North Carolina
Sia A. Maner 11 M, born in North Carolina
Mily J. Maner 10 F, born in North Carolina
Presly W. Maner 7 M, born in North Carolina
Emma C. Maner 5 F, born in North Carolina
Noah W. Maner 1 M, born in North Carolina

1860, Mar 15 -- Land Grant #4420, Moore County, NC
P. K. Myrick received 9.5 acres located on both sides of Bear Creek adjoining Jeremiah Williams, Duncan McIntosh, Garner Maness and Alfred Brower. E.T. Williams and Elias Ritter were chain carriers.

1865, Nov 22-Jan 1, 1871 -- 1868-1876 Record of Accounts Page 44,140-141,277, Moore County, NC
Estate of Garner Mainess, Dec'd. by Administrator Jonathan J. Martindale. Noted held on/by the following: H. Brown, Josiah Wallace, John Dixon, Robert Dixon, J.S. Mainess, Catherine Mainess, A.S. Mainess, Lydia Mainess, Elias Mainess, Andrew Mainess and E.T. Williams (Administrator of Jerry Williams Dec'd.).
1870 -- Census, Moore County, NC Page 579-B, Ritters Township, Carter Mill Post Office
Catherine Mainess 55 F, Farmer, $200 Real Estate, $250 Personal Property, born in North Carolina
Jones S. Mainess 25 M, Laborer, born in North Carolina
Miley J. Mainess 18 F, born in North Carolina
Sirah A. Mainess 21 M, born in North Carolina
Presley R. Mainess 16 M, born in North Carolina
Lydia Mainess 27 F, born in North Carolina
Quincy A. Mainess 5 M (Mulatto), born in North Carolina

1880 -- Census, Moore County, NC Page 339-B, Ritters Township
Katie Maness 65 F, Head, Widowed, Farmer, born in North Carolina, father & mother born in North Carolina
Lydia M. Maness 37 F, Dau, Single, Keeps House, born in North Carolina, father & mother born in North Carolina
Sirandra Maness 30 M, Son, Single, Works on Farm, born in North Carolina, father & mother born in North Carolina
Mila Jane Maness 27 F, Dau, Single, born in North Carolina, father & mother born in North Carolina

Garner Maness and Catherine "Katie" Maness had the following children:

+96	James Abel Maness (1835-1907)
+97	Martha "Polly" Maness (1836-bef 1880)
+98	Lydia M. Maness (1842-)
+99	Jonas Sedberry Maness (1844-1898)
+100	Alexander Spinks Maness (1846-1924)
+101	Josiah A. Maness (1848-)
+102	Miley Jane Maness (1851-)
+103	Presley Wright Maness (1854-1935)
+104	Emma C. Maness (1855-)
+105	Noah W. Maness (1860-1861)

18. **Everett Maness**, son of Shadrach Maness and Celia Wallace, was born in 1818 in Moore County, NC. He died on August 15, 1876 in Forsyth County, GA. He married **Lucinda Shields**, daughter of Cornelius Shields (1779-1857) and Mary "Molly" Davis (1776-1832). Lucinda was born in 1818 in Moore County, NC and died on August 22, 1884 in Forsyth County, GA. Everett and Lucinda migrated to Hall County, GA during the mid-1840's. Several Moore County families migrated to Hall County, GA during this period including the Cagle, Hare, Sheffield, Furr families with Everett Maness' Uncle and Aunt Martin Rouse and Mary Wallace among them. Hall County, GA was also along the southern migration route from central North Carolina to western Tennessee.

RECORDS OF EVERETT MANESS

1826, Nov 8 -- Land Grant #2734, Moore County, NC
Shadrach Manes received 16 acres located south of Bear Creek adjoining Neil McLeod and heirs of John McAulay. Everit Manes and James Manes were chain carriers.

1840 -- Census, Moore County, NC Page 169
Everett Maner
(20-30) 1M 1F
(0-5) 1M

1844, Apr 24 -- 1844-1847 Court of Pleas and Quarter Sessions, Moore County, NC Page 10
Ordered that Everet Maines be appointed overseer of the road from Bear Creek to Buffalo Creek and work the following hands: John McLeod, George Cagle, Garner Maines, William Stewart, Henry Maines, Matthew Williams, Jethro Denson, Amos Bridges, William L. Wallace, Lauchlin B. Currie and Hiram Kelly.

1844, Spring -- 1843-1847 Superior Court Execution Docket, Moore County, NC
#147 State v. Polly Campbell and Celia Mainer. Delphy Wallace and Evirit Mainess were witnesses. Continued through Fall 1847 #108

1857, Jul 25 -- Notice, North Carolina Argus [Wadesboro, NC]
Jane Shields v. Archibald Shields. Petition for dower. Appearing that Everet Maness and wife Lucinda are non-residents of the state. They are summoned to appear at the courthouse in Carthage at the fourth Monday in Jul.

1859, Jul 26 -- Orders and Decrees Book 3 Page 147-158, Moore County, NC
K. Matheson, E.N. Moffitt, John Williams, William Jourdan and John Howard appointed to partition the land of Cornelius Shields, Dec'd. as follows: [Lot 1] Children of John W. Shields Dec'd.: Louisa Jane Shields, Henry B. Shields and Mary E. Shields; [Lot 2] Heirs of Henry Brown and wife Catherine: Henry Yow and wife Malsey, Jesse B. Bowden and wife Catherine, Marshal Brown, Henry Brown, Ann Brown, John Brown and Cornelius Brown; [Lot 3] Alex Brewer and wife Mary, daughter of Emily Stutts Dec'd.; [Lot 4] James Stutts and wife Ann R.; [Lot 5] Martin Shields; [Lot 6] Horace Bridges, Mary Bridges in severalty, children of Amos Bridges and wife Sara Dec'd.; [Lot 7] Hector McNeill and wife Elizabeth [Lot 8] Heirs of Wm. Shields: Hiram Johnson and wife Lydia, Wesley Shields, Amos Bridges and wife Sarah and Emily Shields; [Lot 9] Linsey Stutts and wife Isabella; [Lot 10] Robert Shields; [Lot 11] Cornelius Shields; [Lot 12] Heirs of Benjamin Shields Dec'd.: Robert D. Shields, Martha J. Shields, Catherine A. Shields, John W. Shields, Malcolm D. Shields, Mary E. Shields and Daniel Fry and wife Lydia; [Lot 13] Heirs of Robert L. Purvis and wife Polly: Andy J. Purvis, Cornelius Purvis, Montgomery Myrick and wife Missouriann, Haywood Purvis, Joseph Purvis and George Purvis; [Lot 14] Archibald Shields; [Lot 15] Everett Maness and wife Lucinda; [Lot 16] Cassander Shields.

1860 -- Census, Hall County, GA Page 159, 385th District, Gainesville Post Office
E. Maness 41 M, Farmer, $2000 Real Estate, $2000 Personal Property, born in North Carolina
Lucinda Maness 41 F, born in North Carolina
M.A. Maness 20 M, $100 Personal Property, born in North Carolina
Louisa Maness 17 F, born in North Carolina
Lydia Maness 14 F, born in Georgia
Wincy Maness 12 F, born in Georgia
Cornelius Maness 10 M, born in Georgia
Lucinda Maness 8 F, born in Georgia
David Maness 6 M, born in Georgia
Richard Maness 5 M, born in Georgia
John Maness 2 M, born in Georgia

1870 -- Census, Forsyth County, GA Page 424-B, Chattehootche District, Cumming Post Office
Everett Maness 51 M, Farmer, $2000 Real Estate, $500 Personal Property, born in North Carolina
Lucinda Maness 51 F, Keeping House, born in North Carolina
Milton Maness 29 M, Teaching School, born in Georgia
Martha L. Maness 26 F, Teaching School, born in North Carolina
Wincy J. Maness 21 F, Teaching School, born in Georgia
David C, Maness 16 M, Farm Hand, born in Georgia
Lizzie Thompson 17 F, At Home, born in Georgia
John J. Maness 12 M, At Home, born in Georgia
Burrel E. Maness 7 M, At Home, born in Georgia
Walter Thompson 2 M, At Home, born in Georgia

Everett Maness and Lucinda Shields had the following children:

+106	Milton A. Maness (1840-1877)
+107	Martha Louisa Maness (1842-1902)
+108	Lydia Clementine Maness (1847-1901)
+109	Wincy Isabella Maness (1848-1932)
+110	Everett Maness Jr. (1849-1850)
+111	Cornelius E. Maness (1850-bef 1870)
+112	Lucinda E. Maness (1852-bef 1884)
+113	David Cincinnati Maness (1854-1930)
+114	Richard Maness (1855-bef 1870)
+115	John J. Maness (1858-1900)
+116	Burrel E. Maness (1862-1910)

19. **Asa Maness**, son of Shadrach Maness and Celia Wallace, was born on February 7, 1820 and died on April 5, 1894 in Moore County, NC. He married **Mary Ann Ritter**, daughter of Dolly Garner (c. 1790-bef 1848), who was born on February 9, 1825 and died on May 12, 1884. They were buried in Moore County, NC at Maness Cemetery #248.[21] Asa also fathered a child out of wedlock with his sister-in-law, **Eliza Ritter.** Eliza was born in 1834 and died in 1849 and was buried in Moore County, NC at Ritter Cemetery #250.[22] Asa lived on Scotchmans Creek and owned over 400 acres of land between Putnam and High Falls. The *Carthage Blade* eulogized Asa Maness in 1894 saying "*He was 74 years old and was an old-school farmer. We mean one of those good old-fashioned farmers, who made everything he ate and wore at home, except coffee and sugar. Hence, he had accumulated very considerable wealth, and he never made much complaint about hard times. It was said that Mr. Maness had a great deal of money (gold) buried, but we hear that he told his son where it could be found before his death.*"[23]

RECORDS OF ASA MANESS

1845, Jan 30 -- 1844-1847 Court of Pleas and Quarter Sessions, Moore County, NC Page 125
Ordered that Asa Mainess be appointed overseer of the road from Bear Creek to William Stewarts and have the following hands to work: Garner Mainess, John McLeod 1 hand, Henry Mainess, Matthew Williams Senr., Matthew Williams Junr., George Cagle, William Stewart, Henry Stutts (of Jacob) 1 hand and Leonard Stutts (of Jacob).

1847 -- Tax List, Moore County, NC District 9
Asa Maness listed 100 acres valued at $150 and 1 white poll on Scotchmans Creek

1848, May 31 -- Deed Book 10 Page 539-541, Moore County, NC

John Garner and wife Judith, Elias Maness and wife Elizabeth, Asa Maness and wife Ann, Eliza Ritter and John Ritter deeded Lewis Garner 134 acres located on Deep River adjoining Lewis Garner and John Ritter. Jas. L. Garner was a witness. [Editor's Note: heirs of Dolly Garner Ritter Dec'd.]

1848, Jul 24 -- 1847-1849 Court of Pleas and Quarter Sessions, Moore County, NC Page 227
Ordered that Apr 1848 road order issued to Henry Brown be amended striking out the following names: Stutts hands, Hiram Kelly, Wm. Stewart hands, Edward Stewart, John Denson, Leonard Stutts and Wm. Stutts and inserting the names of: Mark Russel hands, George Cagle, Josiah Wallace, Branson Wallace, Asa Maness and George Hunsucker merchant's hands

1849 -- Tax List, Moore County, NC District 9
Asa Maness listed on Cockmans [Scotchmans] Creek

1851, Mar 15 -- Land Grant #3624, Moore County, NC
William Ritter received 25 acres located east of Buffalo Creek adjoining John Ritter Dec'd. and Noah Dannelly. Asa Maness and William D. Ritter were chain carriers.

1851, Oct 28 -- 1851-1853 Court of Pleas and Quarter Sessions, Moore County, NC Page 96
Ordered that Asa Mainess be appointed overseer of the Anson Road from the fork of Boroughs Road near Wm. Ritters to Angus McCaskills and work all the hands liable to duty.

1852 -- Tax List, Moore County, NC District 9
Asha Maness listed 135 acres valued at $175 and 1 white poll on Scotsman Creek

1852, Apr 26 -- 1851-1853 Court of Pleas and Quarter Sessions, Moore County, NC Page 259
Ordered that Asa Mainess be appointed overseer of the Boroughs Road from the fork of near William Ritters to Angus McCaskills and work all the hands liable to duty.

1853 -- Tax List, Moore County, NC District 9
Asha Maness listed 135 acres valued at $175 and 1 white poll on Cockmans [Scotchmans] Creek

1853, Dec 1 -- Land Grant #3941, Moore County, NC
Joseph Beal received 9.5 acres located north of Scotchman Creek adjoining Asa Maness and William Ritter. William Ritter and James Deal were chain carriers.

1854 -- Tax List, Moore County, NC District 9
Asa Maner listed 330 acres valued at $175 and 1 white poll and 200 acres valued at $200

1854, Oct 27 -- 1853-1856 Court of Pleas and Quarter Sessions, Moore County, NC Page 212
Ordered that Asa Maness be appointed overseer of the road from the Island Ford to Phillips Gate and work the following hands: Luther Paschal, Jesse G. Sowell, Joseph Beal, Eli Davis, William King, Riley Oldham, Henry Moore, John Brewer, Elias Brewer, James Davis' hands, Wright Cotton's hands, Robt. W. Goldston hands, Wesley Wood and Stephen Davis

1854 -- Tax List, Moore County, NC District 9
Asa Maness listed 300 acres valued at $600 and 1 white poll on Scotchman Creek

1855, Jan 28 -- Deed Book 86, Page 102, Moore County, NC
John McLeod (of Montgomery County) deeded Asa Maness 200 acres located on Scotchman Creek adjoining Neill McLeod and Beal. Thos. W. Ritter and Joseph Beal were witnesses.

1855, Jul 26 -- 1853-1856 Court of Pleas and Quarter Sessions, Moore County, NC Page 350
Ordered that John R. Ritter be appointed overseer of a new road commencing at the Island Ford on Deep River passing near John R. Ritter's to the point where it intersects with the Fayetteville and Western Plank Road at or near where the Grove Road crosses Plank Road and work the following hands: Luke Brady, James Brady, Bruce Stout, Parham Y. Oats, William Perry, Benjamin Perry, Joseph Beal, Robt. W. Goldston's hands, Noah Richardson hands, George Cockman, James Powers, Newton Woody, Henry Mainess, John S. Ritter, Asa Mainess, Noah Brewer, Spencer Brown, Sampson Cockman, Nelson Hunsucker, John R. Ritter's hands, Armst Stutts and Houston Hunsucker.

1855, Oct 27 -- 1853-1856 Court of Pleas and Quarter Sessions, Moore County, NC Page 404
Ordered that Eli Davis be appointed overseer of the road from the Island Ford to Phillips' Gate and work the following hands: Asa Mainess, Luther Paschal, Jesse G. Sowell, Joseph Beal, William King, Riley Oldham, Henry Moore, John Brewer, Elias Brewer, James Davis' hands, Wright Cotton's hands, Robt. W. Goldston hands, Wesley Wood and Stephen Davis.

1856, Jan 24 -- Deed Book 86, Page 100, Moore County, NC
Joseph Beal deeded Asa Maness 90 acres located on Scotchman Creek adjoining Goldston, Maness and Beal. Danl. McIntosh and H.B. Maness were witnesses.

1856, Oct 28 -- 1856-1858 Court of Pleas and Quarter Sessions, Moore County, NC Page 84
Asa Mainess records his mark to be a half crop off the right ear and a smooth crop of the left ear.

1857 -- Tax List, Moore County, NC District 9
Asa Mainis listed 390 acres valued at $780 and 1 white poll on Scotchmans Creek

1858, May 1 -- 1856-1858 Court of Pleas and Quarter Sessions, Moore County, NC Page 422
Ordered that Asa Maness be appointed overseer of the Boroughs Road near Wm. Ritters to T.N. Vans and work the following hands:
William Ritter, James Brady, Lucas Brady, Alfred Moore, Emsley Moore, Joseph Beal, Noah Richardson's hands, J.J. Richardson and J.J.
Upton.

1858, Jul 31 -- 1856-1858 Court of Pleas and Quarter Sessions, Moore County, NC Page 476
Ordered that William Durham be appointed overseer of the road from Island Ford to Phillips' Gate and work the following hands: Asa
Manes, Eli Davis, Luther Paschal, Jesse G. Sowell, Joseph Beal, William King, Riley Oldham, Henry Moore, John Brewer, Elias Brewer,
James Davis' hands, R.W. Goldston's hands, Wesly Wood, Stephen Davis, P. Robinson, H. Robinson, Malphus Mathis, Wesley Johnson, Wm.
Denson, J. Sullivan, Bryant Caddell, John Cole, Pac Mathis, Elias Moore and Abb. Moor.

1860 -- Census, Moore County, NC Page 201, Carthage Post Office
Asa Maner 40 M, Farmer, $1000 Real Estate, $800 Personal Property, born in North Carolina
Mary A. Maner 32 F, born in North Carolina
Mary C. Maner 13 F, born in North Carolina
Sarah F. Maner 12 F, born in North Carolina
Sinda A. J. Maner 10 F, born in North Carolina
Thos. W. Maner 9 M, born in North Carolina
Ira B. Maner 5 M, born in North Carolina
Joh A. Maner 3 M, born in North Carolina
Martha L. Maner 9/12 F, born in North Carolina

1860, Nov 17 -- Deed Book 86, Page 96, Moore County, NC
Robert W. Goldston deeded Asa Maness 87.5 acres located on both sides of Scotchman Creek. John Allen was a witness.

1861, Jul 24 -- Deed Book 10, Page 496-498, Moore County, NC
John R. Ritter deeded Wm. L. Ritter three tracts. [1] 45 acres located on Buffalo Creek adjoining Matthew Davis (formerly Wm. Stewart),
Noah Richardson and John R. Ritter (formerly Robert Wilson) excluding 0.5 acres for a graveyard and 2 acres for a school house [2] 82
acres on Buffalo Creek [3] 100 acres on Buffalo Creek adjoining Noah Richardson and Josiah Wallace [4] 93 acres on Buffalo Creek
adjoining Matthew Davis, Richardson and Ritter excluding 5 acres for Asa Maness' house and land. S.C. Bruce and W.J. King were
witnesses.

1865, Jan 16 -- Deed Book 86, Page 98, Moore County, NC
Asa Maness deeded John R. Ritter 100 acres located north of Scotchman Creek adjoining J.R. Ritter. Jesse F. Muse and Hugh Leach were
witnesses.

1870 -- Census, Moore County, NC Page 574, Ritters Township, Prosperity Post Office
Asa Mainess 50 M, Farmer, $600 Real Estate, $600 Personal Property, born in North Carolina
Mary A. T. Mainess 49 F, born in North Carolina
Sarah F. Mainess 21 F, born in North Carolina
Sinda A. S. Mainess 20 F, born in North Carolina
Thomas W. Mainess 17 M, born in North Carolina
Ira Blake Mainess 15 M, born in North Carolina
John A. Mainess 13 M, born in North Carolina
Martha L. Mainess 11 F, born in North Carolina
Asa Mc. Mainess 8 M, born in North Carolina
Bid Mainess 5 M, born in North Carolina
Catharine A. Mainess 2 F, born in North Carolina

1875, Jun 9 -- Orders and Decrees Book 1 Page 285-289, Moore County, NC
Green Bailey, Asa Maness and Elisha Cagle appointed to divide the land of William Ritter Dec'd. among the following heirs: [Lot 1] Ira L.
Maness and wife Catherine 36 acres adjoining James Brady and Asa Maness; [Lot 2] T.B. Cagle and wife Nancy 35 acres adjoining James
Brady and Asa Maness; [Lot 3] Elizabeth Ritter 35.5 acres adjoining John R. Ritter and James Brady; [Lot 4] William Ritter 34.5 acres
adjoining James Brady and John R. Ritter; [Lot 5] Asa J. Seawell 33 acres adjoining James Brady [Lot 6] John Ritter adjoining James Brady,
Cotton and William D. Ritter (heirs of Thomas Ritter); [Lot 7] R.L. Purvis and wife Sarah adjoining William D. Ritter (heirs of Thomas
Ritter); [Lot 8] Lydia L. Cheek 36 acres adjoining John Ritter and road from Abram Stutts to William D. Ritter; [Lot 9] N.R. Brady and wife
Martha J. 35 acres adjoining road from Abram Stutts to William D. Ritter; [Lot 10] G.W. Horner and wife Mary Ann 32.5 acres adjoining
John Ritter and William Ritter.

1880 -- Census, Moore County, NC Page 342, Ritters Township

Asa Maness 57 M, Head, Married, Farmer, born in North Carolina, father & mother born in North Carolina
Annie Maness 56 F, Wife, Married, Keeps House, born in North Carolina, father & mother born in North Carolina
Sinda A. Maness 28 F, Single, At Home, born in North Carolina, father & mother born in North Carolina
J. Alston Maness 24 M, Single, Works on Farm, born in North Carolina, father & mother born in North Carolina
Louisa Maness 21 F, Single, born in North Carolina, father & mother born in North Carolina
George McLellan Maness 18 M, Single, Work on Farm, born in North Carolina, father & mother born in North Carolina
Biddie Maness 15 M, Single, born in North Carolina, father & mother born in North Carolina
Alice Maness 12 F, Dau, Single, born in North Carolina, father & mother born in North Carolina

1888, Nov 27 -- Deed Book 3 Page 281-298, Moore County, NC
Wm. Black, Sheriff deeded A.H. McNeill and Lewis Grimm numerous tracts pursuant to judgements against Wm. B. Richardson including 100 acres located on Lick Branch known as the J. Beal place adjoining W.R. Muse previously deeded from Asa Maness to Riley Riddle.

1894, Apr 17 -- Obituary, Carthage Blade [Newspaper], Moore County, NC
"We omitted to mention in last issue the death of Mr. Asa Maness, which occurred at his home on the 5th inst. [Apr], after a short attack of pneumonia. He was 74 years old and was an old-school farmer. We mean one of those good old fashioned farmers, who made everything he ate and wore at home, except coffee and sugar. Hence he had accumulated very considerable wealth, and he never made much complaint about hard times. It was said that Mr. Maness had a great deal of money (gold) buried, but we hear that he told his son where it could be found before his death."

1894, Apr 27 -- 1889-1897 Administrator's Bonds, Moore County, NC Page 52
Thomas W. Maness and Asa McClellan Maness appointed Administrator of the Estate of Asa Maness, Dec'd. with W.L. Ritter, R.R. Riddle and A.H. McNeill as securities.

Asa Maness and Mary Ann Ritter had the following children:

+117	Mary Clementine Maness (1847-1920)
+118	Sarah Frances Maness (1848-1913)
+119	Lucinda Ann Maness (1850-1893)
+120	Thomas Wesley Maness (1851-1905)
+121	Ira Blake Maness (1852-1931)
+122	John Alsey Maness (1856-1885)
+123	Martha Louisa Maness (1858-1885)
+124	Asa McClellan Maness Sr. (1861-1955)
+125	Biddie Maness (1863-1884)
+126	Catherine Alice Maness (1867-1936)

Asa Maness and Eliza Ritter had the following child:

+127	Addison Worth Ritter (1849-1938)

20. **Lucretia"Little Cressy" Maness**, daughter of Shadrach Maness and Celia Wallace, was born in 1825 and died after 1880 and was buried in Moore County, NC at Maness Cemetery #266.[24]

RECORDS OF LUCRETIA MANESS

1850 -- Census, Moore County, NC Page 236-B
Shadrack Manus 80 M, Farmer, $62 Real Estate, born in North Carolina
Celia Manus 70 F, born in North Carolina
Lucretia Manus 25 F, born in North Carolina
Irely Manus 16 M, Farmer, born in North Carolina

1870 -- Census, Moore County, NC Page 576, Ritters Township, Carters Mill Post Office
Crecy Mainess 46 F, House Keeper, $10 Personal Property, born in North Carolina

(photographed June 13, 2009)

1880 -- Census, Moore County, NC Page 340-B, Ritters Township
Lucretia Maness 45 F, Head, Single, Keeps House, born in North Carolina, father & mother born in North Carolina

21. **Alsey Maness**, son of Shadrach Maness and Celia Wallace, was born on March 6, 1825 and died on October 27, 1909. Alsey first married Catherine Cagle who was born in 1833 and died between 1853 and 1854. After her death, Alsey married Nancy Melton, daughter of Robert Melton (1803-bef 1866) and Christian McIntosh (1805-1852). Nancy was born on

November 20, 1833 and died on January 29, 1899. Alsey and Nancy were buried in Biscoe, Montgomery County, NC at Maness Family Cemetery.[25] Alsey and his family moved to Biscoe by 1870 and many of the current Maness families in Montgomery County descend from Alsey Maness.

RECORDS OF ALSEY MANESS

1840, Sep 23 -- Deed Book 63 Page 237-238, Moore County, NC
Nicholas Nall deeded Alsey Maness 133 acres located on Little Creek adjoining Henry Cagle. Wm. Brewer and John McLeod were witnesses. [*Editor's Note: This deed was re-recorded in in 1916 after the original was lost in the courthouse fire of 1889. I believe the original date of the deed was recorded incorrectly as Alsey would only have been 14 at the time.*]

1850 -- Census, Moore County, NC Page 231
Alsey Manis 24 M, Farmer, $150 Real Estate, born in North Carolina
Catharine Manis 17 F, born in North Carolina
Bethuel Manis 1 M, born in North Carolina

1852 -- Tax List, Moore County, NC District 8
Alsey Maness listed 133 acres valued at $150 and 1 white poll on Little Creek

1853 -- Tax List, Moore County, NC District 8
Alsey Maness listed 133 acres valued at $150 and 1 white poll on Little Creek

1854 -- Tax List, Moore County, NC District 8
Alsey Maness listed 133 acres valued at $150 and 1 white poll

1855 -- Tax List, Moore County, NC District 8
Alsey Maness listed 133 acres valued at $25 and 1 white poll on Little Creek

1857 -- Tax List, Moore County, NC District 8
Alsey Maness listed 133 acres valued at $250 and 1 white poll on Little Creek

1857, Nov 30 -- Deed Book 62 Page 583, Moore County, NC
Right W. Williamson deeded Alsey Maness 29 acres located west of Little Creek adjoining Hiram Sheffield. Hector McKenzie and W.M. Brewer, Esq. were witnesses.

1858, Mar 25 -- Deed Book 12 Page 554, Moore County, NC
Robert Melton deeded Henry Brewer, William Hare, Alsey Maness, trustees for the Methodist Episcopal Church at Chapple 2 acres located on Wolf Creek. Neill Melton and William M. Craven was a witness.

1860 -- Census, Moore County, NC Page 249, Calidonia Post Office
Ase Manes 34 M, Farmer, $400 Real Estate, $300 Personal Property, born in North Carolina
Nancy Manes 25 F, born in North Carolina
Bethania Manes 11 F, born in North Carolina
Spinks Manes 5 M, born in North Carolina
Sarah A. Manes 7 F, born in North Carolina
James A. Manes 2 M, born in North Carolina

(Courtesy of Find A Grave)

1866, Dec 20-Apr 2, 1869 -- 1868-1876 Record of Accounts Page 45, Moore County, NC
Estate of Robert Melton Dec'd. by Administrator Neill Melton. Notes held on the following: W.M. Craven, Polly Melton, Alsey Mainess and wife, Malcolm Cole and wife, A.M.D. Williamson, C.D. Williamson, W.J. Williamson, Neill Melton, Sampson Brewer, Martin Sheffield, Aaron Davis, James Melton and John Dunlap.

1870 -- Census, Montgomery County, NC Page 409, Hill Township, Auman's Mill Post Office
Alsa Manis 45 M, Farming, $300 Real Estate, $350 Personal Property, born in North Carolina
Nancy Manis 34 F, Keeping House, born in North Carolina
Spinks Manis 14 M, At Home, born in North Carolina
Sarah Manis 16 F, At Home, born in North Carolina
James Manis 11 M, born in North Carolina
Neill Manis 7 M, born in North Carolina
Mary Manis 5 F, born in North Carolina
Martha Manis 4 F, born in North Carolina
Lucinda Manis 2 F, born in North Carolina

1871, Apr 15 -- Deed Book 11 Page 540-543, Moore County, NC
William M. Craven and wife Eliza, Alsey Maness and wife Nancy, Raleigh Williams and wife Mary, Malcolm Cole and wife Ruth Ann, James Melton and wife Mary and Neill Melton and wife Eliza deeded Polly Melton and Henry Thomas Melton 133 acres located on Wolf Creek adjoining James Melton, Isaac E. Sheffield and Isham Hare. [Editor's Note: heirs of Robert Melton Dec'd.]

1878, Apr 17 -- War of 1812 Pension, File 16714, Martin Cagle
Dicey Cagle (age 92), Troy Post Office, Montgomery County, NC resident and widow of Martin Cagle, applied for a widow's pension in Montgomery County, NC. Cagle stated that her deceased husband served under Captain William Dowd and was drafted in Moore County, NC on Aug 14, 1814 and discharged Mar 15, 1815. At the time of enlistment, he was described as 26 years old, 6' tall, dark complexion, hazel eyes and black hair. Martin Cagle and Dicy Bolin were married Sep 15, 1810 by Michael Haney, JP in Randolph County, NC. Martin Cagle died Mar 20, 1857 in Montgomery County, NC. He obtained a land warrant for his service in 1857. Malcolm M. Leach age 60, of Montgomery County, NC and David Allen age 50, of Montgomery County, NC, testified to having known Dicey Cagle as the wife of Martin Cagle. Wm. Britt and Gardner Boiling declared that Martin Cagle served with them. Bartholomew Dunn age 86, Leachs Store Post Office and Alsey Maness age 53, Leachs Store Post Office, testified to having known Cagle for 56 years and 45 years respectively.

1878, Apr 17 -- War of 1812 Pension, File 32094, Bartholomew Dunn
Bartholomew Dunn (age 86), Moore County, NC resident, applied for a pension in Montgomery County, NC. Dunn stated that he served under Captain William Dowd and was drafted at Shuffields, NC on Aug 14, 1814 and was discharged on Mar 15, 1815. At the time of enlistment, he was described as 22 years old, 5'6" tall, blue eyes, light hair and fair complexion. Alsey Maness age 53, Leachs Store Post Office and Martin Cagle age 53, Leachs Store Post Office, testified to having known Dunn for 45 years each and believed that he served in the War of 1812.

1880 -- Census, Montgomery County, NC Page 126, Hill Township
Alsey Maness 55 M, Head, Married, Farming, born in North Carolina, father & mother born in North Carolina
Nancy Maness 46 F, Wife, Married, Keeping House, born in North Carolina, father & mother born in North Carolina
Sarah Ann Maness 27 F, Dau, Single, born in North Carolina, father & mother born in North Carolina
James A. Maness 22 M, Son, Single, Works on Farm, born in North Carolina, father & mother born in North Carolina
Neill T. Maness 18 M, Son, Single, Work on Farm, born in North Carolina, father & mother born in North Carolina
Mary J. Maness 15 F, Dau, Single, born in North Carolina, father & mother born in North Carolina
Martha C. Maness 14 F, Dau, Single, born in North Carolina, father & mother born in North Carolina
Lucinda Maness 11 F, Dau, Single, born in North Carolina, father & mother born in North Carolina
Francena Maness 9 F, Dau, Single, born in North Carolina, father & mother born in North Carolina
William R. Maness 6 M, Son, Single, born in North Carolina, father & mother born in North Carolina
Tally Maness 4 M, Son, Single, born in North Carolina, father & mother born in North Carolina
Angus C. Maness 1 M, Son, Single, born in North Carolina, father & mother born in North Carolina

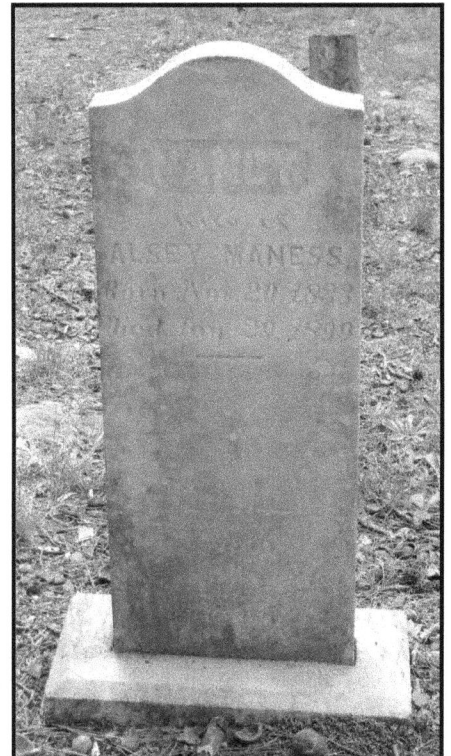

(Courtesy of Find A Grave)

1880, Jan 26 -- Deed Book 63, Page 239, Moore County, NC
Alsey Maness (of Montgomery County) deeded Eli Brown 133 acres located on Little Creek adjoining C.L. Allred, Sampson Brewer and Henry Cagle. Joseph Craven and Hiram Williamson were witnesses.

1900 -- Census, Montgomery County, NC Page 203-B
Alsey Maness 75 M, (Mar 1825) Father, Widowed, Farm Laborer, born in North Carolina, father & mother born in North Carolina listed in the house of his son Spinks Maness.

Alsey Maness and Catherine Cagle had the following children:

+128   Bethuel C. Maness (1849-1924)
+129   Sara Ann Maness (1853-)

Alsey Maness and Nancy Melton had the following children:

+130	Spinks P. Maness (1855-1908)
+131	James Asa Maness (1858-1929)
+132	Neill Tyson Maness (1861-1911)
+133	Mary Jane Maness (1864-1894)
+134	Martha Clementine Maness (1866-1930)
+135	Lucinda Maness (1868-1936)
+136	Francina Maness (1870-1940)
+137	William Robert Maness (1873-1951)
+138	Tally Maness (1875-1892)
+139	Angus Clegg Maness (1878-1956)

22. **Ira Lane "Irely" Maness**, son of Shadrach Maness and Celia Wallace, was born on January 5, 1832 and died on September 17, 1912. He married **Catherine Ritter** on December 13, 1855 in Moore County, NC[26]. Catherine was the daughter of William D. Ritter (1796-1860) and Catherine Melton (1800-1879). She was born in 1835 and died between 1860 and 1870. After her death married **Nancy A. Hancock** circa 1870. daughter of John Hancock (1792-1875) and Clarkie Davis (1795-1873) and the widow of Bradley C. "Red Brad" Brady. Nancy was born on April 22, 1830 and died on June 2, 1928 in Fayetteville, Cumberland County, NC. Irely and Nancy were buried in Moore County, NC at Pleasant Hill United Methodist Church. During the Civil War, Irely served in Company H, 26th Regiment also known as the "Moore County Independents."[27] [28] [29]

RECORDS OF IRA LANE MANESS

1850 -- Census, Moore County, NC Page 236-B
Shadrack Manus 80 M, Farmer, $62 Real Estate, born in North Carolina
Celia Manus 70 F, born in North Carolina
Lucretia Manus 25 F, born in North Carolina
Irely Manus 16 M, Farmer, born in North Carolina

1855 -- Tax List, Moore County, NC District 9
Ira Maness listed 1 white poll on Bear Creek

1855, Dec 13 -- Record of Marriages, Moore County, NC Page 31
Ira Mainess and Catharine Ritter were married by William J. Williamson, JP.

1857 -- Tax List, Moore County, NC District 9
Ira L. Mainis listed 1 white poll on Bear Creek

1858, May 1 -- 1856-1858 Court of Pleas and Quarter Sessions, Moore County, NC Page 422
Ordered that Enoch S. Powers be appointed overseer of the Johnson Road from the Randolph County line to the Boroughs Road near Wm. Ritters and work the following hands: Wm. Caveness, Isaiah Caveness, John Myricks hand, Mac Myrick, Adam Kealin, William Kidd, Tarril Kidd, Cornelius Purvis, Haywood Purvis, Jonathan Martindale, Thomas Maness, Ira Maness, Wm. Perry, Bryan Tyson and hand, Alfred Shields, Wm. Williams, P.Y Oats, Wiley Reynolds and Matthew Williams.

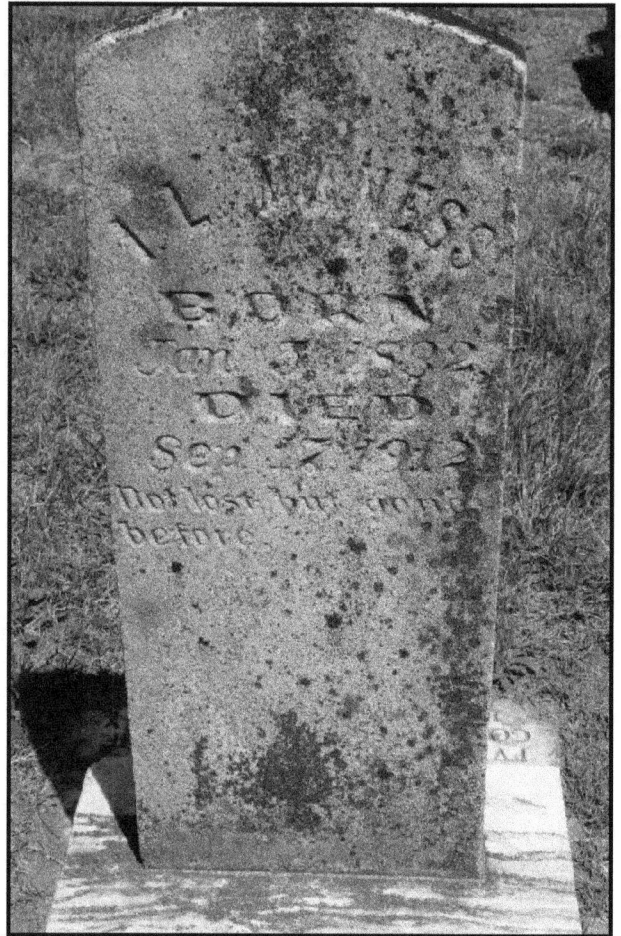

(photographed July 5, 2014)

1858, Jul 31 -- 1856-1858 Court of Pleas and Quarter Sessions, Moore County, NC Page 479
Ordered that Enoch S. Powers be appointed overseer of the Johnson Road from the Randolph County line to the ford on Deep River at Johnson Mills and work the following hands: Ira Maness, Adam Keelin, Matthew Myrick, James Caveness' hands, Edward Kidd and Wiley Reynolds.

1858, Jul 31 -- 1856-1858 Court of Pleas and Quarter Sessions, Moore County, NC Page 479
Ordered that Matthew Williams be appointed overseer of the Johnson Road from the ford on Deep River at Johnson Mills to Boroughs Road near Wm. Ritters and work the following hands: William Ritter, John Riddle, Thomas Maness, Ira Maness, William Perry, Benjamin Perry and William Williams.

1860 -- Census, Moore County, NC Page 201-B, Prosperity Post Office
Ira L. Maness 26 M, Farmer, $300 Real Estate, $500 Personal Property, born in North Carolina

Catharine Maness 25 F, born in North Carolina
Eliza J. Maness 3 F, born in North Carolina
Sarah C. Maness 2 F, born in North Carolina
Nancy E. Maness 1/12 F, born in North Carolina
Wm. R. Maness 1/12 M, born in North Carolina
Alex L. Maness 14 M, born in North Carolina
Mary C. Maness 11 F, born in North Carolina

1860, Oct -- Petition for Dower, Moore County, NC
Catharine Ritter, widow of William Ritter petitioned for dower. William Ritter died with 400 acres located on Buffalo Creek adjoining
John Ritter and leaving the following children: Geo. W. Horner and wife Mary Ann, Elizabeth Ritter, N.R. Brady and wife Martha, R.L.
Purvis and wife Sarah, W.D. Ritter, Ira Maness and wife Catherine, Asa Seawell and wife Emily Francis, Nancy Ritter, John Ritter (minor)
and William Dorras Cheek, son of Lydia Margaret (dead) and Lewis Cheek.[30]

1860, Nov 19-Apr 30, 1861 -- Record of Estates Book H Page 398-400, Moore County, NC
Estate of William Ritter, Dec'd. by Administrators Catherine Ritter and Noah Richardson. *Items were purchased by the following*: William
Ritter, John Morison, A. Williams, James Horner, N.R. Brady, William Williams, Ira Maness, T.W. Ritter, Thomas Horner, Wesly Wallace,
J.A. Stutts, N.E. Ritter, J.H. Ritter, Lauchlin Kelly and C. Purvis. Notes held on the following: John Cole, Bailey Brown, Wiley R. Reynolds and
Henry Brown.

1870 -- Census, Moore County, NC Page 576, Ritters Township, Carters Mill
Post Office
Ira L. Mainess 36 M, Farmer, $300 Real Estate, $200 Real Estate, born in
North Carolina
Nancy A. Mainess 35 F, born in North Carolina
Nancy E. Mainess 10 F, born in North Carolina
William R. Mainess 10 M, born in North Carolina
Emsley R. Mainess 7 F, born in North Carolina
Lavina E. Mainess 3 F, born in North Carolina
Ida F. Brady 9 F, born in North Carolina
John H. Brady 7 M, born in North Carolina
Bradley O. Brady 5 F, born in North Carolina

1871, Feb 20 -- 1869-1873 Superior Court Minute Docket Book N Page 187,
Moore County, NC
State v. Ira L. Mainess [bastardy]. Green Bailey and E.S. Cagle were bondsmen.

1875, Jun 9 -- Orders and Decrees Book 1 Page 285-289, Moore County, NC
Green Bailey, Asa Maness and Elisha Cagle appointed to divide the land of
William Ritter Dec'd. among the following heirs: [Lot 1] Ira L. Maness and
wife Catherine 36 acres adjoining James Brady and Asa Maness; [Lot 2] T.B.
Cagle and wife Nancy 35 acres adjoining James Brady and Asa Maness; [Lot 3]
Elizabeth Ritter 35.5 acres adjoining John R. Ritter and James Brady; [Lot 4]
William Ritter 34.5 acres adjoining James Brady and John R. Ritter; [Lot 5] Asa

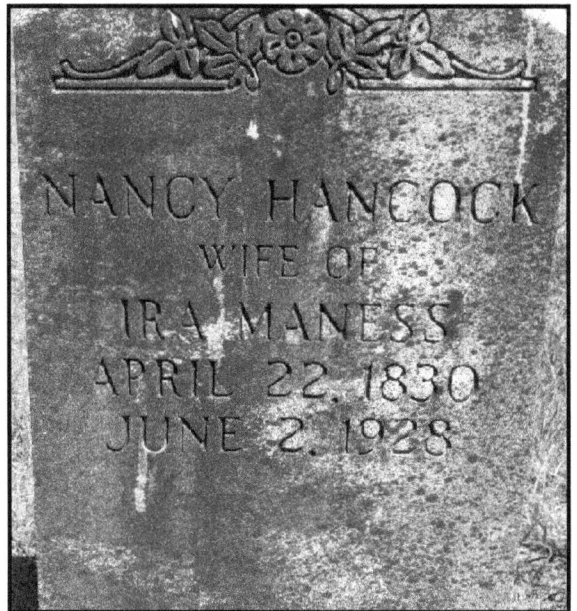

(photographed July 5, 2014)

J. Seawell 33 acres adjoining James Brady [Lot 6] John Ritter adjoining James Brady, Cotton and William D. Ritter (heirs of Thomas
Ritter); [Lot 7] R.L. Purvis and wife Sarah adjoining William D. Ritter (heirs of Thomas Ritter); [Lot 8] Lydia L. Cheek 36 acres adjoining
John Ritter and road from Abram Stutts to William D. Ritter; [Lot 9] N.R. Brady and wife Martha J. 35 acres adjoining road from Abram
Stutts to William D. Ritter; [Lot 10] G.W. Horner and wife Mary Ann 32.5 acres adjoining John Ritter and William Ritter.

1880 -- Census, Moore County, NC Page 341, Ritters Township
Ira L. Maness 46 M, Head, Married, Farmer, born in North Carolina, father & mother born in North Carolina
Nancy A. Maness 44 F, Wife, Married, Keeps House, born in North Carolina, father & mother born in North Carolina
Nancy E. Maness 18 F, Dau, Single, born in North Carolina, father & mother born in North Carolina
William R. Maness 18 M, Son, Single, Works on Farm, born in North Carolina, father & mother born in North Carolina
Emily R. Maness 15 F, Dau, Single, born in North Carolina, father & mother born in North Carolina
Lavina Maness 13 F, Dau, Single, born in North Carolina, father & mother born in North Carolina
Julia M. Maness 8 F, Dau, Single, born in North Carolina, father & mother born in North Carolina
Josaphan Maness 6 F, Dau, Single, born in North Carolina, father & mother born in North Carolina
John Brady 16 M, StepS, Single, Works on Farm, born in North Carolina, father & mother born in North Carolina
Bradly O. Brady 15 M, StepD, Single, born in North Carolina, father & mother born in North Carolina

1900 -- Census, Moore County, NC Page 84, Ritters Township
Ira L. Maness 64 M, Dec 1835, Head, Married-30yrs, Farmer, born in North Carolina, father & mother born in North Carolina
Nancy A. Maness 65 F, Apr 1834, Wife, Married-30yrs, 5 Children (5 Living), born in North Carolina, father & mother born in North
Carolina

1906, Jun 12 -- Confederate Pension Application, Moore County, NC
Ira L. Maness, age 73 of High Falls Post Office, applied for a pension. He served in Company H 26th Regiment.

1910 -- Census, Moore County, NC Page 232, Ritters Township
Ira L. Maness 76 M, Head, Married-2nd-40yrs, born in North Carolina, father & mother born in North Carolina
Nancy Maness 75 F, Wife, Married-2nd-40yrs, 5 Children (3 Living), born in North Carolina, father & mother born in North Carolina

Ira Lane "Irely" Maness and Catherine Ritter had the following children:

+140	Eliza J. Maness (1857-)
+141	Sarah C. Maness (1858-)
+142	William Robert Maness (1859-1920)
+143	Nancy E. Maness (1860-1943)
+144	Emily Rebecca Maness (1866-1944)
+145	Lavina E. Maness (1867-)

Ira Lane "Irely" Maness and Nancy A. Hancock had the following children:

+146	Julia McIntyre Maness (1872-1927)
+147	Josephine A. Maness (1873-1903)

29. Ruffin Wallace, son of Joseph Wallace and Chaney, was born in 1832. He married **Salina Fry** on November 19, 1857 in Moore County, NC.[31] He served in Company C, 35th Regiment in the Civil War and died on September 30, 1864 in Union Prison, Elmira, NY.[32] Salina Fry was the daughter of Thomas B. "Black Tom" Fry (1802-1885) and Philadelphia/Rhodelphia Cox (1803-1884). She was born in 1840 and died before August 5, 1885. Ruffin and family lived on Jacksons Creek.

RECORDS OF RUFFIN WALLACE

1850, Aug 30 -- Census, Moore County, NC Page 182
Joseph Wallis 52 M, Farmer, born in North Carolina
Chaney Wallis 50 F, born in North Carolina
Ruffin Wallis 18 M, born in North Carolina
Seaborn Wallis 17 M, born in North Carolina
Alexander Wallis 15 M, born in North Carolina

1852 -- Tax List, Moore County, NC
Ruffin Wallace listed 1 white poll in District 6

1852, Feb 28 -- Land Grant #3825, Moore County, NC
Ruffin Wallis received 100 acres located on Pineley Branch of Jackson Creek on both sides of the Flowers Road. John McInnis and Alexander Wallis were chain carriers.

1853, Apr 9 -- Land Grant #3810, Moore County, NC
Maurice Q. Waddell received 640 acres located on both sides of Flowers Road on Jacksons Creek east of Drowning Creek adjoining Daniel McKenzie, Alexander Martin, Ruffin Wallis and Aldred. John R. Currie and Daniel McInnis were chain carriers.

1853, Nov 11 -- Land Grant #7063, Montgomery County, NC
Calvin H. Rush received 100 acres located on waters of Mountain Creek and the Fayetteville Road adjoining his own line, John M.N. Clark and Alex. McLeod. William Malloch and Ruffin Wallace were chain carriers.

1854 -- Tax List, Moore County, NC
Ruffin Wallace listed 1 white poll in District 6

1855 -- Tax List, Moore County, NC
Ruffin Wallace listed 1 white poll in District 6

1855, Dec 19 -- Land Grant #4229, Moore County, NC
W. B. Richardson and A. R. McDonald received 640 acres on Suck Branch of Jackson Creek and Flowers Road and path from Asa Smith to Benjamin Bailey adjoining Maurice Q. Waddill, Benjamin Bailey, Daniel McKenzie, Ruffin Wallace, R.A. Stewart and John Jones. R.J. McDonald and Archd. C. Caddell were chain carriers.

1856, Jan 31 -- 1853-1856 Court of Pleas and Quarter Sessions, Moore County, NC Page 450

Richard Street, Ruffin Wallace, James Fields, W.H. Tyson and N.S. Brown appointed patrol in District #2 for one year.

1857, Nov 19 -- Record of Marriages, Moore County, NC Page 48
Ruffin Wallace and Salina Fry were married by William Barrett, JP.

1860, Sep 17 -- Census, Moore County, NC Page 235, Carthage Post Office
Ruffin Wallace 31 M, Farmer, $150 Real Estate, $150 Personal Property, born in North Carolina
Salina Wallace 20 F, born in North Carolina
Elizabeth Wallace 2 F, born in North Carolina

1861, Sept 12 -- Civil War Service Records
Rufus Wallace enlisted in Company C, 35th Regiment in Moore County, NC at age 27. On Jun 17, 1864, Ruffin Wallace was captured near Petersburg, VA at confined at Point Lookout, MD. On Jul 27, 1864, he was transferred to Union Prison in Elmira, NY where he died of pneumonia on Sep 30, 1864.

1870, Sep 27 -- Census, Moore County, NC Page 537, Jackson Springs Township, Jackson Springs PO
Salina Wallace 30 F, Farmer, $70 Real Estate, $13 Personal Property, born in North Carolina
Elizabeth Wallace 11 F, born in North Carolina
Jerome Wallace 9 M, born in North Carolina
Charles Wallace 6 M, born in North Carolina

1870, Sep 27 -- Agricultural Census, Moore County, NC Page 1, Jackson Springs Township, Jackson Springs Post Office
Selena Wallis listed 8 acres of improved land valued at $38

1885, Aug 5 -- 1880-1885 Administrator's Bonds, Moore County, NC Page 78
Richard A. Cole appointed Administrator of the Estate of Salena Wallace, Dec'd. with G.F. Cole and Robt. Cole as securities.

1886, May 29 -- Deed Book 2, Page 302, Moore County, NC
Estate of Salina Wallace (Admst. R.A. Cole) deeded W.W. Cole 66 2/3 acres adjoining Joseph V. Fry. J.C. Black was a witness.

Ruffin Wallace and Salina Fry had the following children:

+148   Elizabeth Wallace (1859-)
+149   Jerome A. Wallace (1861-1923)
+150   Charles Wallace (1864-)

30. **Seaborn Wallace**, son of Joseph Wallace and Chaney, was born in 1833 and died before 1900. Seaborn married Tabitha Boone, daughter of Bird Boone (1790-) and Hannah Costins (1805-). Seaborn and family briefly moved to eastern Tennessee before returning to settle down near Tabitha's family in the Seagrove community of Randolph County. Tabitha was born in May 1842 and died on November 8, 1914 in Seagrove, Randolph County, NC and was buried on November 9, 1914 in Seagrove, Randolph County, NC at Maple Springs Baptist Church.[33]

RECORDS OF SEABORN WALLACE

1850, Aug 30 -- Census, Moore County, NC Page 182
Joseph Wallis 52 M, Farmer, born in North Carolina
Chaney Wallis 50 F, born in North Carolina
Ruffin Wallis 18 M, born in North Carolina
Seaborn Wallis 17 M, born in North Carolina
Alexander Wallis 15 M, born in North Carolina

1853, Apr 26 -- 1851-1853 Court of Pleas and Quarter Sessions, Moore County, NC Page 442-443
Ordered that William Gatlin be appointed overseer of the road leading from Montgomery County line to the fork of the Huary [Uwharrie] Road commencing at the race on the east side of Mill Creek and ending at the fork of the Huary Road and have the following hands to work: Joseph Britt, Westley F. Sowell, Norman McDuffie, Kenneth McCaskill Senr., Kenneth McCaskill Junr., Duncan McInnis, Jesse Thomas, Sebern Wallace, John A. McKinnon & hand, Daniel Chisholm hands, William Williams and Lawrence Williams.

1857, May 2 -- 1856-1858 Court of Pleas and Quarter Sessions, Moore County, NC Page 212
Ordered that Malcolm McCrummin be appointed overseer of the Raleigh Road from the Woolf Pit to Martin's old store and work the following hands: Allen McDonald, John McInnis, John Graham, Sebern Wallace, Green B. Fields, Walter A. Fry, Allen Jones and D.B. Currie.

1857, May 2 -- 1856-1858 Court of Pleas and Quarter Sessions, Moore County, NC Page 213

Ordered that Asa Smith be appointed overseer of a new road from Wm. Gatlin's to Jesse Thomas' Mill and work the following hands: William Gatlin, Sebern Wallace, Benj. Bailey, William Copeland Jr., Daniel Bailey, John Bailey, Burrel Bailey, Danl. B. Campbell and Isabella Morrison two boys [Sandy & Archibald].

1860, Sep 14 -- Census, Moore County, NC Page 232
Jasiff Wallace 68 M, Farmer, $100 Real Estate, $40 Personal Property, born in North Carolina
Jennet Wallace 60 F, born in North Carolina
Ceaborn Wallace 23 M, Farmer, $200 Real Estate, $50 Personal Property, born in North Carolina

1870, Jul 29 -- Census, Jefferson County, TN Page 16, Civil District #9, Mossy Creek Post Office
Seaborn Wallis 30 M, Farm Laborer, born in North Carolina
Tabatha Wallis 28 F, Keeps House, born in North Carolina
Caroline T. Wallis 5 F, born in North Carolina
Annie L. Wallis 1 F, born in North Carolina

1880, Jun 25 -- Census, Randolph County, NC Page 211, Richland Township
Cephas Wallace 49 M, Head, Married, Farm Laborer, born in North Carolina, father & mother born in North Carolina
Tabitha Wallace 35 F, Wife, Married, Keeping House, born in North Carolina, father & mother born in North Carolina
Caroline Wallace 15 F, Dau, Single, Keeping House, born in North Carolina, father & mother born in North Carolina
Annie L. Wallace 11 F, Dau, Single, At Home, born in North Carolina, father & mother born in North Carolina
Jane Wallace 7 F, Dau, Single, At Home, born in North Carolina, father & mother born in North Carolina
Melissa Wallace 1 F, Dau, Single, At Home, born in North Carolina, father & mother born in North Carolina

1900 -- Census, Randolph County, NC Page 242, Richland Township
Bertha Wallas 60 F, May 1840, Head, Widowed, 3 Children(3 Living), Farmer, born in North Carolina, father & mother born in North Carolina
Mauda Wallas 23 F, Apr 1877, Dau, Single, born in North Carolina, father & mother born in North Carolina
Malissie C. Wallas 20 F, Feb 1880, Dau, Single, born in North Carolina, father & mother born in North Carolina
Lula Farlow 25 F, Mar 1875, Dau, Married-2yrs, 5 Children(5 Living), born in North Carolina, father & mother born in North Carolina
Mary E. Farlow 10 F, May 1890, GrDau, Single, born in North Carolina, father & mother born in North Carolina
Maggie V. Farlow 7 F, Nov 1892, GrDau, Single, born in North Carolina, father & mother born in North Carolina
John B. Farlow 5 M, Sep 1894, GrSon, Single, born in North Carolina, father & mother born in North Carolina
William W. Farlow 3 M, Mar 1897, GrSon, Single, born in North Carolina, father & mother born in North Carolina
Colvin Mc. Farlow 3/12 M, Oct 1899, GrSon, Single, born in North Carolina, father & mother born in North Carolina

1910 -- Census, Randolph County, NC Page 261-B, Richland Township, River Road
Lou Wallace 42 F, Head, Single, 7 Children(7 Living), Laborer(Odd Jobs), born in North Carolina, father & mother born in North Carolina
Benjamin Wallace 17 M, Son, Single, Laborer(Odd Jobs), born in North Carolina, father & mother born in North Carolina
Wade Wallace 14 M, Son, Single, born in North Carolina, father & mother born in North Carolina
Wm. Penn Wallace 10 M, Son, Single, born in North Carolina, father & mother born in North Carolina
Thomas Wallace 6 M, Son, Single, born in North Carolina, father & mother born in North Carolina
Raleigh Wallace 2 M, Son, Single, born in North Carolina, father & mother born in North Carolina
Tabitha Wallace 70 F, Mother, Widowed, 4 Children(3 Living), Pauper, born in North Carolina, father & mother born in North Carolina
Elizabeth Boone 75 F, Aunt, Widowed, 1 Child (1 Living), Pauper, born in North Carolina, father & mother born in North Carolina

Seaborn Wallace and Tabitha Boone had the following children:

+151   Caroline Wallace (1864-1909)
+152   Annie Louella Wallace (1868-1948)
+153   Maude Jane Wallace (1870-1956)
+154   Melissa Catherine Wallace (1872-1953)

31. **Alexander Wallace**, son of Joseph Wallace and Chaney, was born in 1835 and died before 1870. He married **Elizabeth "Eliza" Ann Fry** on February 26, 1857 in Moore County, NC.[34] Eliza was the daughter of Thomas B. "Black Tom" Fry (1802-1885) and Philadelphia/Rhodelphia Cox (1803-1884). She was born on January 11, 1831, died on November 10, 1881 and was buried in Moore County, NC at Frye Cemetery #204.[35] Alexander served in Company H, 26th Regiment in the Civil War.[36] [37] Alexander survived the Civil War but died prior to 1870 leaving his widow with three small children to raise.

RECORDS OF ALEXANDER WALLACE

1850, Aug 30 -- Census, Moore County, NC Page 182
Joseph Wallis 52 M, Farmer, born in North Carolina
Chaney Wallis 50 F, born in North Carolina
Ruffin Wallis 18 M, born in North Carolina

Seaborn Wallis 17 M, born in North Carolina
Alexander Wallis 15 M, born in North Carolina

1852, Feb 28 -- Land Grant #3825, Moore County, NC
Ruffin Wallis received 100 acres located on Pineley Branch of Jackson Creek on both sides of the Flowers Road. John McInnis and Alexander Wallis were chain carriers.

1853, Sep 19 -- Chronicles and Records of Bensalem Presbyterian Church, Moore County, NC
Alexander Wallace was baptized

1857, Feb 26 -- Record of Marriages, Moore County, NC Page 45
Alex Wallace and Eliza A. Fry were married by J. Bean, JP.

1858 -- Tax List, Moore County, NC District 3
Alex Wallace listed 100 acres valued at $50 located on Little River

1860, Sep 14 -- Census, Moore County, NC Page 233, Carthage Post Office
Alex Wallace 24 M, Farmer, $100 Real Estate, $100 Personal Property, born in North Carolina
Eliza A. Wallace 29 F, born in North Carolina
Salina Wallace 2 F, born in North Carolina
Flora M. Wallace 2/12 F, born in North Carolina

1862, Jun 16 -- Papers of North Carolina Governor Henry Clark
Alexander Walis and Isam Walis are reported being seen at Lawhon's Hill and refusing to return to duty by L. W. Lawhon, Postmaster at Lawhon's Hill Post Office

1870, Sep 27 -- Census, Moore County, NC Page 537, Jackson Springs Township, Jackson Springs PO
Eula A. Wallace 40 F, born in North Carolina
Salina Wallace 12 F, born in North Carolina
Hanah Wallace 9 F, born in North Carolina
Alexander Wallace 7 M, born in North Carolina

1880, Jun 8 -- Census, Moore County, NC Page 368 B, Mineral Springs Township
Thomas Fry 77 M, Head, Married, Farmer, born in North Carolina, father & mother born in North Carolina
Rodelphia Fry 77 F, Wife, Married, Keeping House, born in North Carolina, father & mother born in North Carolina
Eliza Wallace 48 F, Head, Widowed, Labor, born in North Carolina, father & mother born in North Carolina
Florah Wallace 18 F, Dau, Single, At Home, born in North Carolina, father & mother born in North Carolina
Alex V. Wallace 17 M, Son, Single, Laborer, born in North Carolina, father & mother born in North Carolina

Alexander Wallace and Elizabeth Ann Fry had the following children:

+155	Salina Wallace (1858-)	
+156	Flora M. Wallace (1860-)	
+157	Alexander Vance Wallace (1863-1928)	

32. **Nathan Wallace**, son of John Wallace and Elizabeth, was born on May 4, 1818 in Moore County, NC and he died on June 4, 1876 in Cherokee County, TX and was buried in Cherokee County, TX at Myrtle Springs Cemetery.[38] Nathan married Mary McCrimmon, daughter of Daniel McCrimmon (1784-1873) and Hannah Jane Dunlap (-1822) in Moore County prior to migrating to Bibb County, AL and later they continued further west to the state of Texas during the 1860's. Mary was born on June 22, 1817 in Moore County, NC, died on May 9, 1900 in Smith County, TX and was buried in Troup, Smith County, TX at Troup City Cemetery.[39]

RECORDS OF NATHAN WALLACE

1841, May-Apr 1843 -- County Court Execution Docket, Moore County, NC
Mary McRimmon alias Mary Wallas v. John J. McIntosn, Admst.

1841, Oct 2-Nov 20 -- Notice, The North-Carolinian [Fayetteville, NC] Newspaper
Moore County, NC -- Cornelius Dunlap v. James Dunlap and Others. Appearing that John McCrimmon and wife Sarah, Jacob Cagle and wife Margaret, William Lewis and wife Ann, John Phillips, Mary Phillips, Matthew Deaton and wife Sarah, Nathan Wallas and wife Mary, Martha McCrimmon and John McCrimmon, defendants, are not residents of the state. They are summoned to appear at the courthouse in Carthage on the third Monday in November.

1850 -- Census, Bibb County, AL Page 55, EC River Township

Nathan Wallis 31 M, Farmer, $275 Real Estate, born in North Carolina
Mary Wallis 32 F, born in North Carolina
Sarah Wallis 12 F, born in Alabama
Lucinda Wallis 9 F, born in Alabama
Mary E. Wallis 6 F, born in Alabama
David H. Wallis 3 M, born in Alabama

1860 -- Census, Bibb County, AL Page 751-B, Cahaba River (East side), Randolph Post Office
Nathan Wallace 40 M, Farmer, $800 Real Estate, $1000 Personal Property, born in North Carolina
Mary Wallace 42 F, Domestic, born in North Carolina
Sarah Wallace 21 F, Domestic, born in Alabama
Lucinda Wallace 19 F, Domestic, born in Alabama
Daniel Wallace 13 M, born in Alabama
Clementine Wallace 11 F, born in Alabama
James Wallace 3 M, born in Alabama

(Courtesy of Find A Grave)

Mary McCrimmon Wallace
Courtesy of Ancestry.com [larrylinder38]

1864, Feb 20-Jul 5 1865 -- Probate Records, Bibb County, AL
Estate of Isham/Isam Wallace Dec'd. by Administrator John W. Wallace. Nathan Wallace and Jesse Smitherman were securities to John W. Wallace. The estate references widow Gracy Wallace and minor heir Elizabeth Wallace. *Accounts were held on the following*: Jesse Tucker, John Smitherman, Nathan Horn, D.D. Watson, William Tucker, Mary Smith, John Spinks, Mary Campbell, Marion Griffin, Mariah Dean, Eli Wallis and Michael Pigot. *Notes were held on the following*: L.P.C. Horn, Eli Wallis, G. Smitherman, S. Smitherman, Joseph Lawley, H. McBride, Wm. Tucker, C. Komanger, G. Bowlin and D. Culwell.

1870 -- Census, Cherokee County, TX Page 283, Beat #5
Nathan Wallace 50 M, Farmer, $1500 Real Estate, $400 Personal Property, born in North Carolina
Mary Wallace 50 F, Keeps House, born in North Carolina
Lucinda Wallace 25 F, Works in House, born in Alabama
James M. Wallace 13 M, Works on Farm, born in Alabama
Jane Wallace 30 F (black), Works on Farm, born in North Carolina
David McCrimmon 86 M, Old Gentleman, born in North Carolina\

1880 -- Census, Cherokee County, TX Page 432-D, ED #17

Mary Wallace 63 F, Head, Widow, Housekeeping, born in North Carolina, father & mother born in North Carolina
Maggie Wallace 11 F, Dau, Single, born in Texas, father & mother born in Alabama
Lou Sessions 38 F, Dau, Single, born in Alabama, father & mother born in North Carolina
Nathan Sessions 6 M, GrSon, Single, born in Texas, father born in Georgia, Mother in Alabama
Daniel Sessions 5 M, GrSon, Single, born in Texas, father born in Georgia, Mother in Alabama
Mecky Sessions 18 F, StepDau, Single, born in Alabama, father born in Georgia, Mother in Alabama
Frenchy Sessions 21 F, StepSon, Single, At Home Farming, born in Alabama, father born in Georgia, Mother in Alabama

Nathan Wallace and Mary McCrimmon had the following children:

+158	Sarah Wallace (1839-1913)
+159	Lucinda Wallace (1842-1918)
+160	Mary E. Wallace (1844-)
+161	Daniel Houston Wallace (1848-1927)
+162	Martha Clementine Wallace (1852-1866)
+163	James Monk Wallace (1858-1933)

33. **Eli Wallace**, son of John Wallace and Elizabeth, was born in 1822 in North Carolina. He married **Sina Davis** on April 25, 1846 in Bibb County, AL.[40] Eli served in Company G, 44th Regiment Alabama Infantry and was killed in action during the Civil War in 1864.[41] Eli married Sina Davis, daughter of Hardy Davis (aft 1790-bef 1842) and Rebecca Osborne (-) and was born in 1821 in Alabama. Hardy Davis was the son of Hardy Davis (bef 1755-) of Moore County, NC.

RECORDS OF ELI WALLACE

1844 -- Tax List, Moore County, NC
Eli Wallis listed 1 white poll in District 6

1844, Jul 22 -- 1844-1847 Court of Pleas and Quarter Sessions, Moore County, NC Page 38
State v. John Cole and Eli Wallace (trespass)

1844, Oct -- 1844-1849 County Court Execution Docket, Moore County, NC
#1 State v. Eli Wallace. Alexander Kennedy, Nancy Cox and Angus Morison were witnesses.

1846, Apr 25 -- Marriage Register, Bibb County, AL
Eli Wallis to Sina Davis by John R. Fulghum, JP

1848 -- Tax List, Bibb County, AL
Eli Wallace listed in District 2 with 1 poll, 1 clock and 2 Lots in Section 16 T. 22 R. 11 E. valued at $200

1850, Nov 12 -- Census, Bibb County, AL Page 44, EC River Township
Eli Wallis 28 M, Farmer, $250 Real Estate, born in North Carolina
Sina Wallis 28 F, born in Alabama
Rolly S. Wallis 2 M, born in Alabama
Frances J. Wallis 1 F, born in Alabama
Ann Fittz 11 F, born in Alabama

1860, Jul 27 -- Census, Bibb County, AL Page 751, Cahaba River (East side), Randolph Post Office
Eli Wallace 39 M, Farmer, $250 Real Estate, $250 Personal Property, born in North Carolina
Sinca Wallace 41 F, Domestic, born in Alabama
Rolly Wallace 13 M, born in Alabama
Francis Wallace 11 F, born in Alabama
Joseph M. Wallace 9 M, born in Alabama
Martha Wallace 7 F, born in Alabama
William C. Wallace 4 M, born in Alabama

1864, Feb 20-Jul 5 1865 -- Probate Records, Bibb County, AL
Estate of Isham/Isam Wallace Dec'd. by Administrator John W. Wallace. Nathan Wallace and Jesse Smitherman were securities to John W. Wallace. The estate references widow Gracy Wallace and minor heir Elizabeth Wallace. *Accounts were held on the following*: Jesse Tucker, John Smitherman, Nathan Horn, D.D. Watson, William Tucker, Mary Smith, John Spinks, Mary Campbell, Marion Griffin, Mariah Dean, Eli Wallis and Michael Pigot. *Notes were held on the following*: L.P.C. Horn, Eli Wallis, G. Smitherman, S. Smitherman, Joseph Lawley, H. McBride, Wm. Tucker, C. Komanger, G. Bowlin and D. Culwell.

1866 -- Alabama State Census, Schedule 1, Bibb County, AL, Page 11
Sinah Wallace

(40-50) 1F
(10-20) 2M 2F
(0-10) 1M
1 Soldier was killed in Civil War

1866 -- Alabama State Census, Schedule 3, Bibb County, AL, Page 29/30, Township 22 Range 11
Sina Wallace
(40-50) 1F
(10-20) 2M 2F
(0-10) 1M
1 Soldier was killed in Civil War

1866 -- Alabama State Census, Schedule 3, Bibb County, AL Page 18, Township 22, Range 11 East
Sina Wallace
(20+) 1F
(10-20) 2M 2F
(0-10) 1M

Eli Wallace and Sina Davis had the following children:

+164	Raleigh S. Wallace (1847-1886)
+165	Frances J. Wallace (1849-1891)
+166	Joseph Davis Wallace (1851-1916)
+167	Martha "Patsy" Wallace (1855-1885)
+168	William "Dock" Wallace (1858-1928)

34. **Isham Wallace**, son of John Wallace and Elizabeth, was born in 1825 in North Carolina and died before Feb 20, 1864 in Bibb County, AL. Isham married **Gracy A. Goodwin** on May 14, 1860 in Bibb County, AL.[42] Gracy A. Goodwin was born in 1837 and was the daughter of Lewis H. Goodwin (1810-) and Elizabeth "Betsy" Smitherman (1815-).

RECORDS OF ISHAM WALLACE

1850, Nov 20 -- Census, Bibb County, AL Page 55-B, EC River Township
John Wallis 51 M, Farmer, $150 in Real Estate, born in North Carolina
Elizabeth Wallis 50 F, born in North Carolina
Isom Wallis 25 M, Farmer, born in North Carolina
John W. Wallis 22 M, born in North Carolina
Josiah Wallis 21 M, Farmer, born in North Carolina
Sarah Wallis 18 F, born in North Carolina
Catherine Wallis 16 F, born in North Carolina
Franny Wallis 14 F, born in North Carolina

1852, Feb 2 -- BLM General Land Office Document #40235, Bibb County, AL
Isham Wallace (of Bibb County) received 39.96 acres from Cahaba Land Office located in southwest Quarter of Section 19, Township 22, Range 12.

1854, Apr 1 -- BLM General Land Office Document #73939, Bibb County, AL
Isom Wallace (of Bibb County) received 40.14 acres from Cahaba Land Office located in northeast Quarter of Section 30, Township 22, Range 12.

1860, May 14 -- Marriage Register, Bibb County, AL
Isam Wallace and Gracy A. Goodwin were married by Josiah McGee, JP

1860, Aug 3 -- Census, Bibb County, AL Page 803, Cahaba River (East side), Randolph Post Office
Isham Wallace 35 M, Farmer, $900 Real Estate, $800 Personal Property, born in North Carolina
Lucy Wallace 23 F, Domestic, born in Alabama
J.W. Wallace 29 M, Shoe Maker, born in North Carolina

1864, Feb 20-Jul 5, 1865 -- Probate Records, Bibb County, AL
Estate of Isham/Isam Wallace Dec'd. by Administrator John W. Wallace. Nathan Wallace and Jesse Smitherman were securities to John W. Wallace. The estate references widow Gracy Wallace and minor heir Elizabeth Wallace. Accounts were held on the following: Jesse Tucker, John Smitherman, Nathan Horn, D.D. Watson, William Tucker, Mary Smith, John Spinks, Mary Campbell, Marion Griffin, Mariah Dean, Eli Wallis and Michael Pigot. Notes were held on the following: L.P.C. Horn, Eli Wallis, G. Smitherman, S. Smitherman, Joseph Lawley, H. McBride, Wm. Tucker, C. Komanger, G. Bowlin and D. Culwell.

Isham Wallace and Gracy A. Goodwin had the following child:

+169   Elizabeth Wallace (aft 1860-)

35. Thomas Wallace, son of John Wallace and Elizabeth, was born in 1826 in North Carolina. Thomas served in the Civil War with Company H, 29th Regiment Alabama Infantry and was killed in action prior to November 15, 1864. [43] He married **Frances "Fanny" Hill** on January 9, 1848 in Bibb County, AL. Fanny was the daughter of William Hill (-) and Mary (-), was born in 1829 in Alabama and died on February 27, 1909 in Bibb County, AL. [44]

RECORDS OF THOMAS WALLACE

1848, Jan 9 -- Marriage Register, Bibb County, AL
Thomas Wallace and Fany Hill were married by Jackson Gardner, JP

1850, Nov 12 -- Census, Bibb County, AL Page 44, EC River
Thomas Wallis 24 M, Farmer, born in North Carolina
Fanny Wallis 19 F, born in Alabama
John Wallis 8/12 M, born in Alabama

1860, Jul 27 -- Census, Bibb County, AL Page 751, Cahaba River (East side), Randolph Post Office
Thomas Wallace 36 M, Farmer, $150 Real Estate, $200 Personal Property, born in Alabama
Fannie Wallace 35 F, Domestic, born in Alabama
John Wallace 10 M, born in Alabama
Harrison Wallace 8 M, born in Alabama
Eli Wallace 7 M, born in Alabama
Elizabeth Wallace 4 F, born in Alabama
Charles Wallace 3 M, born in Alabama
Thomas Wallace 3/12 M, born in Alabama

1862, Feb 8 -- Civil War Service Records
Thomas Wallis enlisted at age 33 in 4 Battalion AL Volunteers (Assigned to Company H, 29th Regiment AL Infantry) in Randolph, Bibb County, AL. He was assigned as a Nurse in the Greenville, AL Hospital for part of this time On Nov 15, 1864, Fanny Wallace (widow), filed a claim for Private Thomas Wallace of the Company H, 29th Regiment AL Infantry

1866 -- Alabama State Census Schedule 1, Bibb County, AL, Page 11
Frances Wallace
(30-40) 1F
(10-20) 2M
(0-10) 2M 2F
1 Soldier was killed in Civil War

1866 -- Alabama State Census, Schedule 3, Bibb County, AL, Page 25/26, Township 22 Range 11
Frances Wallace
(30-40) 1F
(10-20) 2M
(0-10) 2M 2F
1 Soldier was killed in Civil War

1866 -- Alabama State Census, Schedule 3, Bibb County, AL Page 18, Township 22, Range 11 East
Francis Wallace
(20+) 1F
(10-20) 2M
(0-10) 2M 2F

1870 -- Census, Bibb County, AL Page 255, Randolph Township, Randolph Post Office
Fanny Wallace 37 F, Farmer, $500 Real Estate, $200 Personal Property, born in Alabama
John Wallace 20 M, Farm Hand, born in Alabama
William Wallace 18 M, Farm Hand, born in Alabama
Mary Wallace 14 F, born in Alabama
Charles Wallace 11 M, born in Alabama
Calhoun Wallace 9 M, born in Alabama
Sarah Wallace 8 F, born in Alabama

1880 -- Census, Bibb County, AL Page 337-D, Randolph Township
Fanny Wallace 50 F, Head, Widow, Farmer, born in Alabama, father & mother born in Alabama
John Wallace 30 M, Son, Single, Works in Farm, born in Alabama, father born in North Carolina, mother born in Alabama
Harrison Wallace 28 M, Son, Married, Works in Farm, born in Alabama, father born in North Carolina, mother born in Alabama
Emily Wallace 30 F, DauLaw, Married, Keeps House, born in Alabama, father & mother born in Alabama
Ann Wallace 4 F, GrDau, Single, At Home, born in Alabama, father & mother born in Alabama
James Wallace 2 M, GrSon, Single, born in Alabama, father & mother born in Alabama

She and Thomas Wallace and Fanny Hill had the following children:

+170	John C. Wallace (1849-1925)
+171	William Harrison Wallace (1852-1926)
+172	Eli Wallace (1853-)
+173	Mary Elizabeth Wallace (1856-)
+174	Charles F. Wallace (1858-1927)
+175	Thomas Wallace (1860-)
+176	J. Henry Calhoun Wallace (1860-1902)
+177	Sarah Wallace (1862-)

36. **Raleigh W. Wallace**, son of John Wallace and Elizabeth, was born on June 17, 1827 in Moore County, NC, migrated to Bibb County, AL with his family by 1850 and on to Lauderdale County, MS by 1860. He served in Company A, 37th Regiment Mississippi Infantry during the Civil War. [45] Raleigh died on December 5, 1898 in New Orleans, Orleans Parish, LA.[46] He married **Elizabeth Spinks** on December 7, 1848 in Bibb County, AL.[47] She was the daughter of Raleigh Spinks (1802-1884) and Elizabeth Cassady (1805-1846) and was born on August 18, 1831. Elizabeth died in 1902 and was buried in Lauderdale County, MS at Coker Chapel Cemetery.[48]

RECORDS OF RALEIGH W. WALLACE

1848 -- Tax List, Bibb County, AL
Raleigh Wallace listed 1 white poll in District 2

1848, Jan 9 -- Marriage Register, Bibb County, AL
Rally Wallace and Elizabeth Spinks were married by B.L. Depreise, JP

1850, Nov 12 -- Census, Bibb County, AL Page 44, EC River Township
Rolley Wallis 24 M, Farmer, $200 Real Estate, born in North Carolina
Elizabeth Wallis 18 F, born in Georgia

1852, Feb 2 -- BLM General Land Office Document #40070, Bibb County, AL
Rolly Wallace (of Bibb County) received 40.02 acres from Cahaba Land Office located in southeast Quarter of Section 17, Township 22, Range 11.

1853, Aug 1 -- BLM General Land Office Document #41911, Bibb County, AL
Rolly Wallace (of Bibb County) received 40.02 acres from Cahaba Land Office located in northeast Quarter of Section 17, Township 22, Range 11.

1860, Aug 20 -- Census, Lauderdale County, MS Page 202, Beat #5, Whynot Post Office
Raleigh Wallace 30 M, Farmer, $1400 Personal Property, born in North Carolina
Elizabeth Wallace 29 F, Domestic Business, born in Georgia
Lawson Wallace 8 M, born in Alabama
Jasper Wallace 1 M, born in Mississippi

Raleigh W. Wallace
(Courtesy of Kelley Cowan-Butler)

1862, Feb 28 -- Civil War Service Records
Raleigh W. Wallis enlisted in Company A, 37th Mississippi Infantry in Marion, MS

1863, Jul 5 -- Civil War Service Records
Rolly W. Wallis, a prisoner of war from Company A, 37th Mississippi Infantry signs letter granting his parole in Vicksburg, MS and pledges not to take up arms against the United States Army after the fall of Vicksburg.

1870, Jun 23 -- Census, Lauderdale County, MS Page 51, Township #1, Meridian Post Office

Raleigh Wallace 41 M, Farmer, $500 Real Estate, $1000 Personal Property, born in North Carolina
Elizabeth Wallace 38 F, Keeping House, born in Georgia
Lawson Wallace 18 M, Farm Laborer, born in Alabama
Jasper Wallace 11 M, Farm Laborer, born in Mississippi
Martha Wallace 5 F, born in Mississippi
Eudora Wallace 3 F, born in Mississippi
Jennie Wallace 2 F, born in Mississippi

1880 -- Census, Winn Parish, LA Page 565-D, 8th Ward
Rolly Wallis 52 M, Head, Married, Farmer, born in North Carolina, father & mother born in North Carolina

(Courtesy of Find a Grave)

Elizabeth Wallis 46 F, Wife, Married, Keeping House, born in Georgia, father & mother born in North Carolina
Jasper Wallis 20 M, Son, Single, Works in Farm, born in Mississippi, father born in North Carolina, mother born in Georgia
Sarah W. Wallis 16 F, Dau, Single, born in Mississippi, father born in North Carolina, mother born in Georgia
Eudora Wallis 14 F, Dau, Single, born in Mississippi, father born in North Carolina, mother born in Georgia
Virginia Wallis 12 F, Dau, Single, born in Mississippi, father born in North Carolina, mother born in Georgia
John Brock 18 M, Other, Single, born in LA, father & mother born in Alabama

Raleigh W. Wallace and Elizabeth Spinks had the following children:

+178	Lawson Wallace (1852-1924)	
+179	Ada Ann Wallace (1857-1860)	
+180	Jasper Wallace (1859-1881)	
+181	Mary Jane Wallace (1861-1863)	
+182	Sarah Martha "Mattie" Wallace (1864-)	
+183	Eudora Ann Wallace (1867-)	
+184	Virginia Wallace (1868-1958)	

37. John Wesley Wallace, son of John Wallace and Elizabeth, was born on February 20, 1829 in Moore County, NC and married **Frances J. Bearden** circa 1863. John Wesley Wallace was a shoemaker, grocer and farmer at different times in his life, died on December 3, 1895 and was buried in Bibb County, AL at Harris Family Cemetery.[49] Frances J. Bearden was born on January 2, 1847 in Chilton County, AL, died on May 20, 1937 in Ashby, Bibb County, AL and was buried on May 20, 1937 in Bibb County, AL at Shady Grove Church Cemetery.[50]

RECORDS OF JOHN WESLEY WALLACE

1850, Nov 20 -- Census, Bibb County, AL Page 55-B, EC River Township
John Wallis 51 M, Farmer, $150 in Real Estate, born in North Carolina
Elizabeth Wallis 50 F, born in North Carolina
Isom Wallis 25 M, Farmer, born in North Carolina
John W. Wallis 22 M, born in North Carolina
Josiah Wallis 21 M, Farmer, born in North Carolina
Sarah Wallis 18 F, born in North Carolina
Catherine Wallis 16 F, born in North Carolina
Franny Wallis 14 F, born in North Carolina

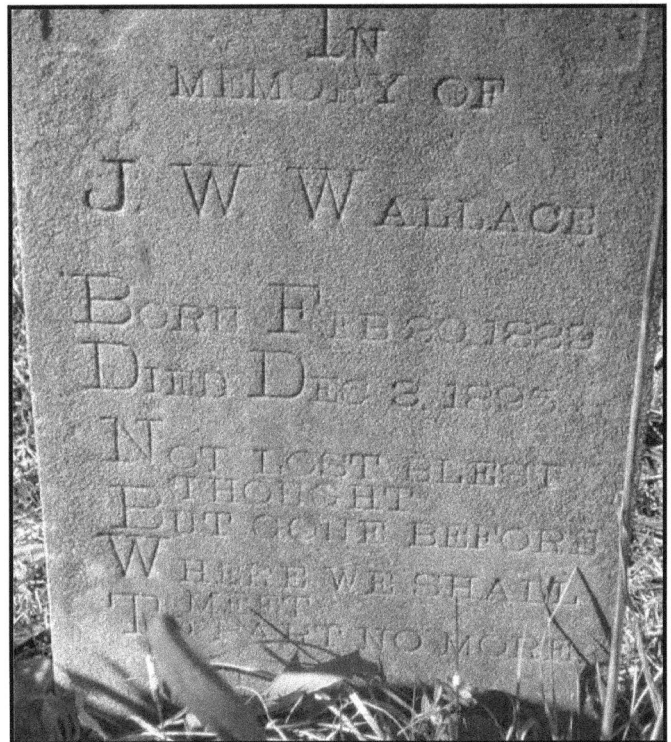

(Courtesy of Find a Grave)

1860, Aug 3 -- Census, Bibb County, AL Page 803, Cahaba River (East side), Randolph Post Office
Isham Wallace 35 M, Farmer, $900 Real Estate, $800 Personal Property, born in North Carolina
Lucy Wallace 23 F, Domestic, born in Alabama
J.W. Wallace 29 M, Shoe Maker, born in North Carolina

1864, Feb 20-Jul 5, 1865 -- Probate Records, Bibb County, AL

Estate of Isham/Isam Wallace Dec'd. by Administrator John W. Wallace. Nathan Wallace and Jesse Smitherman were securities to John W. Wallace. The estate references widow Gracy Wallace and minor heir Elizabeth Wallace. Accounts were held on the following: Jesse Tucker, John Smitherman, Nathan Horn, D.D. Watson, William Tucker, Mary Smith, John Spinks, Mary Campbell, Marion Griffin, Mariah Dean, Eli Wallis and Michael Pigot. Notes were held on the following: L.P.C. Horn, Eli Wallis, G. Smitherman, S. Smitherman, Joseph Lawley, H. McBride, Wm. Tucker, C. Komanger, G. Bowlin and D. Culwell.

1866 -- Alabama State Census Schedule 1, Perry County, AL, Page 39, Township 21 Range 11 E
Wesley Wallace
(30-40) 1M
(20-30) 1F
(0-10) 1M

1866 -- Alabama State Census Schedule 3, Perry County, AL, Page
108, Township 21 Range 11 E
Wes Wallace
(20+) 1M 1F
(0-10) 1M

1870, Jun 6 -- Census, Bibb County, AL Page 250, Randolph
Township, Randolph Post Office
John Wallace 40 M, Grocer, $150 Personal Property, born in North
Carolina
Francis Wallace 23 F, born in Alabama
John Wallace 5 M, born in Alabama
Martha Wallace 2 F, born in Alabama
William Wallace 1 M, born in Alabama

1880 -- Census, Perry County, AL Page 396-C, Perryville Township
John W. Wallace 52 M, Head, Married, Farming, born in North
Carolina, father & mother born in North Carolina
Francis J. Wallace 32 F, Wife, Married, Keeping House, born in
Alabama, father & mother born in Alabama

(Courtesy of Find a Grave)

John M. Wallace 15 M, Son, Single, Farming, born in Alabama, father & mother born in Alabama
Martha F. Wallace 13 F, Dau, Single, Farming, born in Alabama, father & mother born in Alabama
William J. Wallace 11 M, Son, Single, Farming, born in Alabama, father & mother born in Alabama
Andrew J. Wallace 10 M, Son, Single, Farming, born in Alabama, father & mother born in Alabama
Jasper N. Wallace 7 M, Son, , born in Alabama, father & mother born in Alabama
Mary E. Wallace 4 F, Dau, Single, born in Alabama, father & mother born in Alabama
Nancy P. Wallace 8/12 F, Dau, born in Alabama, father & mother born in Alabama

1900 -- Census, Perry County, AL Page 222, Precinct #9 Pinetucky
Fannie Wallace 58 F, May 1841, Head, Widow, 10 Children(10 Living), Farmer, born in Alabama, father & mother born in Alabama
Dovie Wallace 16 F, Apr 1884, Dau, Single, born in Alabama, father & mother born in Alabama
Malvin R. Wallace 13 M, Jan 1887, Son, Single, Farm Laborer, born in Alabama, father & mother born in Alabama
Thomas Wallace 11 M, Mar 1889, Son, Single, Farm Laborer, born in Alabama, father & mother born in Alabama
Mary E. Moton 23 F, Dec 1876, Dau, Widow, 4 Children(2 Living), born in Alabama, father & mother born in Alabama
Samuel Moton 4 M, Mar 1896, GrSon, Single, born in Alabama, father & mother born in Alabama
Ruby Moton, 3/12 F, Nov 1899, GrDau, Single, born in Alabama, father & mother born in Alabama

John Wesley Wallace and Frances J. Bearden had the following children:

+185	John M. Wallace (1864-1928)
+186	William J. Wallace (1866-1940)
+187	Martha F. Wallace (1866-1933)
+188	Andrew Jackson Wallace (1871-1943)
+189	Jasper Newton Wallace Sr (1874-1949)
+190	Mary E. Wallace (1875-1927)
+191	Nancy Paralee Wallace (1879-1966)
+192	Dovie Wallace (c. 1883-1940)
+193	M. G. Wallace (1885-1963)
+194	Melvin Augusta Wallace (1885-1963)
+195	Thomas W. Wallace (1889-1958)

38. Josiah\Cyrus Wallace, son of John Wallace and Elizabeth, was born on February 14, 1830 in Moore County, NC. He married Frances Janes Bearden prior to 1859 and served in the Civil War with Company F, 4th Regiment Alabama Infantry. [51] Frances was born circa 1833 in Jefferson County, AL and died before 1874. Around 1899, Josiah married **Virginia "Jennie"** who was born in October 1865. He died on December 31, 1910 in Lawley, Bibb County, AL and was buried in Bibb County, AL at Rehobeth Church Cemetery. [52]

RECORDS OF JOSIAH WALLACE

1850, Nov 20 -- Census, Bibb County, AL Page 55-B, EC River Township
John Wallis 51 M, Farmer, $150 in Real Estate, born in North Carolina
Elizabeth Wallis 50 F, born in North Carolina
Isom Wallis 25 M, Farmer, born in North Carolina
John W. Wallis 22 M, born in North Carolina
Josiah Wallis 21 M, Farmer, born in North Carolina
Sarah Wallis 18 F, born in North Carolina
Catherine Wallis 16 F, born in North Carolina
Franny Wallis 14 F, born in North Carolina

1860, Jul 19 -- Census, Perry County, AL Page 685, Plantersville Post Office
John Wallace 63 M, Farmer, $100 Real Estate, $832 Personal Property, born in North Carolina
Elizabeth Wallace 56 F, born in North Carolina
Josiah Wallace 22 M, Laborer, born in Alabama
Frances Wallace 21 F, Domestic, born in Alabama
Martha E. Wallace 1, F, born in Alabama
Thomas Wallace 13 M, born in Alabama
Louis Wallace 7 M, born in Alabama

1864, May 31 -- Civil War Service Records
Josiah Wallace enlisted at age 34 in Company F, 4th Regiment AL Infantry in Marion, AL

1865, Feb -- Civil War Service Records
Josiah Wallace listed as AWOL in Company F, 4th Regiment Alabama Infantry. He received a sick furlough in Aug 1864 and never returned to unit. Listed as being age 34 at enlistment, being born in South Carolina, resident of Dixie, AL, married, farmer.

(Courtesy of Find a Grave)

1866 -- Alabama State Census Schedule 1, Perry County, AL, Page 39, Township 21 Range 11 E
Josiah Wallace
(20-30) 1M 1F
(0-10) 2F

1866 -- Alabama State Census Schedule 3, Perry County, AL, Page 108, Township 21 Range 11 E
Josiah Wallace
(20+) 1M 1F
(0-10) 2F

1880 -- Census, Chilton County, AL Page 88-B, Maplesville Township
Josiah Wallis 50 M, Head, Married, Farmer, born in North Carolina, father & mother born in North Carolina
Fanny Wallis 43 F, Wife, Married, Keeping House, born in Alabama, father & mother born in Alabama
Parlee Wallis 17 F, Dau, Single, Works on Farm, born in Alabama, father born in North Carolina, mother born in Alabama
Angeline Wallis 15 F, Dau, Single, Works on Farm, born in Alabama, father born in North Carolina, mother born in Alabama
Sally Wallis 13 F, Dau, Single, Works on Farm, born in Alabama, father born in North Carolina, mother born in Alabama
John Wallis 12 M, Son, Single, Works on Farm, born in Alabama, father born in North Carolina, mother born in Alabama
Thomas Wallis 9 M, Son, Single, born in Alabama, father born in North Carolina, mother born in Alabama

1900, Jun 12 -- Census, Bibb County, AL Page 129, Beat #7, Town of Randolph
Josiah Wallace 68 M, Jun 1832, Head, Married-0yrs, Farmer, born in Alabama, father & mother born in Alabama
Virginia Wallace 35 F, Oct 1865, Wife, Married-0yrs, 0 Children, born in Alabama, father & mother born in Alabama

1910, May 3 -- Census, Bibb County, AL Page 159-B, Precinct #7 Randolph

James S. Wallace 80 M, Head, Married-2nd-10yrs, born in North Carolina, father & mother born in North Carolina
Virginia Wallace 44 F, Wife, Married-2nd-10yrs, 1 Child(1 Living), Home Farm, born in Alabama, father & mother born in Alabama

Josiah\Cyrus Wallace and Frances Jane Bearden had the following children:

+196	Martha E. Wallace (1859-)
+197	Paralee Wallace (1861-1928)
+198	Angeline Wallace (c. 1865-)
+199	Sally Wallace (1866-)
+200	John Wesley Wallace (1868-1947)
+201	Thomas Wesley Wallace (1871-1932)

39. **Sarah Wallace**, daughter of John Wallace and Elizabeth, was born in 1832 in North Carolina and died before 1880. She married **Isaac Rolley** on June 22, 1854 in Bibb County, AL.[53] Isaac Rolley was born in 1829 and was the son of Allen Rolley (1810-) and Sally Latham (1800-).

RECORDS OF ISAAC ROLLEY AND SARAH WALLACE

1854, Jun 22 -- Marriage Register, Bibb County, AL
Isaac Rolly and Sarah Wallace were married by J. Hunt, JP

1860 -- Census, Perry County, AL Page 685, Plantersville Post Office
Isaac Rolla 31 M, Farmer, $321 Personal Property, born in Alabama
Sarah Rolla 22 F, wife, born in North Carolina
Jasper W. Rolla 6 M, born in Alabama
Bray A. E. Rolla 3 F, born in Alabama
Keziah F. Rolla 1 F, born in Alabama

1866 -- Alabama State Census Schedule 1, Perry County, AL, Page 39, Township 21 Range 11 E
Isaac Rowley
(30-40) 1M 1F
(10-20) 1M
(0-10) 2F

1866 -- Alabama State Census Schedule 3, Perry County, AL, Page 108, Township 21 Range 11 E
Isaac Rowley
(20+) 1M 1F
(10-20) 1M
(0-10) 2F

1870 Census Dallas County, AL Page 551, Plantersville Township, Hardy Post Office
Isaac Rolley 45 M, Farmer, $200 Real Estate, $150 Personal Property, born in Alabama
Sarah Rolley 40 F, Keeping House, born in Alabama
Jasper Rolley 15 M, Farm Laborer, born in Alabama
Sallie Rolley 13 F, Farm Laborer, born in Alabama
Francis Rolley 11 F, At Home, born in Alabama

1880 -- Census, Chilton County, AL Page 89-C, Maplesville Township
Isaac Rolley 54 M, Head, Married, Farmer, born in Alabama, father born in South Carolina, mother born in North Carolina
Matilda Rolley 48 F, Wife, Married, Keeping House, born in Georgia, father & mother born in Georgia
Elisabeth Rolley 24 F, Dau, Married, Keeping House, born in Alabama, father & mother born in Alabama

Isaac Rolley and Sarah Wallace had the following children:

+202	Jasper W. Rolley (1854-)
+203	Sarah Elizabeth Rolley (1856-1936)
+204	Keziah Francis Rolley (1859-)

42. **Nancy Wallace**, daughter of Nathan C. Wallace and Finity Britt, was born between 1823 and 1828 in North Carolina and died after 1880. She married widower **Ambrose R. Hart**, son of William D. Hart (-) and Sarah Fort (-), who was born on November 28, 1816 in North Carolina. He died on July 7, 1886 in Henderson County, TN and was buried in Henderson County, TN at Palestine Cemetery.

1850, Nov 5 -- Census, Moore County, NC Page 234
Nathan Wallis 50 M, Farmer, born in North Carolina
Finity Wallis 50 F, born in North Carolina
Nancy Wallis 27 F, born in North Carolina
Franey Wallis 21 F, born in North Carolina
Mary Wallis 19 F, born in North Carolina
Everett Wallis 13 M, born in North Carolina
Benjamin Wallis 10 M, born in North Carolina

1850 -- Census, Henderson County, TN Page 188-B, District 10
Ambrose Hart 34 M, Farmer, $250 Real Estate, born in North Carolina
Nancy Hart 31 F, born in North Carolina
Minerva C. Hart 12 F, born in Tennessee
Mary J. Hart 10 F, born in Tennessee
William T. Hart 8 M, born in Tennessee
Sarah E. Hart 6 F, born in Tennessee
Margaret Hart 4 F, born in Tennessee
Norris H. Hart 4 M, born in Tennessee

1860, Jul 10 -- Census, Henderson County, TN Page 225, Civil District #6, Middle Fork Post Office
Natha Wallace 57 M, Farm Tenant, $450 Personal Property, born in North Carolina
Sarah Wallace 31 F, born in Virginia
Nancy Wallace 32 F, born in North Carolina
Mary Seymore 15 F, born in Tennessee
W.H. Pomeroy 5 M, born in Tennessee
H. Davidson 6 M, born in Tennessee
Sarah F. Wallace 3 F, born in Tennessee
M.E.A. Wallace 9/12 F, born in Tennessee
W. Davidson 28 M, born in Virginia

1860 -- Census, Henderson County, TN Page 244, District 8, Oak Forest Post Office
Ambrose Hart 44 M, Owner of Poor House, $1500 Real Estate, $750 Personal Property, born in North Carolina
M. E. Hart 30 F, born in Tennessee
M. C. Hart 21 F, born in Tennessee
W. T. Hart 18 M, born in Tennessee
S. E. Hart 16 F, born in Tennessee
N. H. Hart 13 M, born in Tennessee
M. H. Hart 13 F, born in Tennessee
J. M. Hart 10 M, born in Tennessee
S. R. Hart 7 M, born in Tennessee
T. S. Hart 6 M, born in Tennessee

1880 -- Census, Henderson County, TN Page 348, District 6
A. R. Hart 64 M, Head, Married, Farmer, born in North Carolina, father & mother born in North Carolina
Nancy Hart 55 F, Wife, Married, Keeping House, born in North Carolina, father & mother born in North Carolina
Minerva Hart 42 F, Dau, Single, Laborer on Farm, born in Tennessee, father & mother born in North Carolina
John L. Hart 16 M, Son, Single, Laborer on Farm, born in Tennessee, father & mother born in North Carolina

Ambrose Hart and Nancy Wallace had the following child:

+205   John Leonard Hart (1863-1930)

43. **Deborah Wallace**, daughter of Nathan C. Wallace and Finity Britt, was born in 1828 in North Carolina and died in 1897. She married a widowed cousin **Beacom C. Britt** between 1845 and 1849. Beacom's first wife was Dallie Wallace (1810/1815-1845/1849) who was likely a close relative of Deborah. Beacom was the son of Ryals Britt (bef 1774-bef 1809) and Rhoda Parrish (1778-aft 1850), was born in 1804 in North Carolina and died in 1876 in western Tennessee.

Britt family history tells of Beacom Britt traveling back and forth several times between Moore County, NC and TN. Records confirm that he resided in Moore County, NC from 1828-1831, 1850-1853 and resided in Tennessee from 1836-1840 and after 1860. One story also said that Beacom was in western Tennessee in 1833 during the Leonid meteor shower "the night the stars fell" and his mother was so frightened that she returned to North Carolina and vowed never to return.[54]

Britt family sources also state that Beacom Britt married Wallace sisters (who were his 1st cousins) and that these sisters had a brother named Sam. I feel strongly that Nathan Wallace and Finity Britt (1st cousin to Beacom) are the most likely candidates to be Deborah's parents. Nathan Wallace lived near Beacom in both Moore County, NC and Henderson County, TN and had a son named William Samuel "Sam" Wallace. While the information passed down through the Britt family state that Dallie and Deborah were sisters, it is my opinion that they were close relatives (such as an aunt/niece or 1st cousins) but probably not sisters. Census records show that Beacom's first wife was born between 1810-1815, which would most likely rule out Nathan Wallace (Born c1800) as the father due to his age. It is much more likely that Dallie was a daughter to Everet Wallace or Nicholas Wallace. Each have an unidentified female child being born in and around 1810-1815. Everet's daughter born between 1810-1815 is listed in his household in the 1820 Census but had moved out by 1830. Beacom and his 1st wife appear together in the 1830 Census in Moore County, NC. Seemingly more likely but maybe less possible is that Nicholas Wallace was her father. Nicholas moved to Henderson County, TN prior to 1830. Beacom and his 1st wife moved west between shortly thereafter. It is quite possible Beacom was following his father-in-law and family. The only snag is that the unidentified daughter that is listed in the 1820 Census with Nicholas in Moore County, NC is also listed with her father in the 1830 Census in Henderson County, TN.

RECORDS OF BEACOM BRITT AND DEBORAH WALLACE

1810, Jul 26 -- Moore County, NC Will Book A, Page 269
Will of Benjamin Britt, Dec'd. Heirs: wife Nancy (plantation where I now live and the profits from the sale of the Harvil place), children Behuver [Belaver], Ispthu [Jeptha], Buldu, Edwin, Tinatee [Finity] and Handay; Rodah, Widow of brother Rial Britt (land containing Bent field); Avington, Prulellah, Billasant [Bellison], Claramon [Cleryman], Becum and Tinsay, orphan children of brother Rial Britt (land north and west of Mill Creek that belonged to Rial). Executor: Joseph Allin. Witnesses: F. Bullock, Alexr. Morrison and Britin Britt. Proven Aug 1810.

1825, Nov 15 -- Land Grant #2742, Moore County, NC
James Key received 50 acres located on Reedy Branch of Mill Creek adjoining the heirs of Ryal Britt. Merryman Britt and Angus McKinnon were chain carriers.

1828, Aug 19 -- 1823-1831 County Court Minutes, Moore County, NC Page 227
Ordered that Mark Allen be appointed overseer in place of Britton Britt for the road from Mill Creek to the fork East of Archd. McNeills and work the following hands: Britton Britt, Alfred Britt, Avington Britt, Daniel Munroe, Jeremiah Renolds, Joseph Allen, John Morgan, Becom Britt, Wm. Morgan, N. Lewis, John Smith, and Hiram Deaton.

1829, May 18 -- 1823-1831 County Court Minutes, Moore County, NC Page 263
Ordered that Jeremiah Renalds be appointed overseer in place of Mark Allen for the road from Mill Creek to the fork East of Archd. McNeills and work the following hands: Mark Allen, Briton Britt, Alfred Britt, Avington Britt, Daniel Munroe, Joseph Allen, John Morgan, Becom Britt, Wm. Morgan, N. Lewis, John Smith, and Hiram Deaton.

1830 -- Census, Moore County, NC Page 449
Becum Britt
(20-30) 1M
(15-20) 1F
(0-5) 1 F

1836 -- Tax List, Henderson County, TN
Beacon Britt listed 1 white poll in Distict 11

1836, Sep 1 -- Land Grant #3027, Moore County, NC
James Key received 68 acres located North of Mill Creek adjoining his own line, Burrell Deaton, Levi Deaton, the heirs of Merryman Britt, Avington Britt, and the heirs of Ryal Britt. Levi Deaton and Ryal Key were chain carriers.

1837 -- Tax List, Henderson County, TN
Beacon Britt listed 1 white poll in District 11

1840 -- Census, Henderson County, TN Page 341
Beacon Britt
(30-40) 1M
(20-30) 1F
(10-15) 1F
(5-10) 1M 1F
(0-5) 2M 1F

1850, Nov 22 -- Census, Moore County, NC Page 250

Beacom Britt 45 M, Farmer, $250 Real Estate, born in North Carolina
Deborah Britt 22 F, born in North Carolina
Benjamin Britt 15 M, born in North Carolina
Nathaniel 12 M, born in North Carolina
Mary A. Britt 10 F, born in North Carolina
Temperance Britt 8 F, born in North Carolina
Sallie Britt 6 F, born in North Carolina
Pattie Britt 1 F, born in North Carolina
Rhody Britt 72 F, born in North Carolina

1850 -- Agricultural Census, Moore County, NC Page 991
Beacom Britt listed 40 acres improved, 160 acres unimproved valued at $250

1852 -- Tax List, Moore County, NC
Becom Britt listed 200 acres valued at $250 located in District 6 on Mill Creek

1853, Apr 2 -- Deed Book 26 Page 457, Moore County, NC
Beacom Brtt deeded Lauchlin B. Monroe 400 acres located on Mill Creek. J.A. McKinnon and Eli Smith were witnesses.

1860, Aug 23 -- Census, McNairy County, NC Page 450, District #8, Anderson Store Post Office
Becom Britt 56 M, Farmer, $430 Real Estate, $280 Personal Property, born in North Carolina
Debby Britt 29 F, born in North Carolina
Mary Britt 20 F, born in Tennessee
Sarah Britt 15 F, born in Tennessee
Martha Britt 10 F, born in North Carolina
Nathan Britt 8 M, born in North Carolina
Andy Britt 7 M, born in North Carolina
Avington Britt 5 M, born in Tennessee
William Britt 2 M, born in Tennessee

1862 -- Federal Tax List, McNairy County, TN
Beacom Britt listed 200 acres valued at $400

1870, Jun 18 -- Census, Henderson County, TN Page 90, District #10, Lexington Post Office
Beacom Britt 56 M, Farmer, $800 Real Estate, $500 Personal Property, born in North Carolina
Debby Britt 40 F, Keeping House, born in North Carolina
Handy Britt 16 M, Works on Farm, born in North Carolina
Nathan Britt 18 M, Works on Farm, born in North Carolina
Avington Britt 14 M, Works on Farm, born in Tennessee
William Britt 12 M, born in Tennessee
John Britt 9 M, born in Tennessee
Nelson Britt 7 M, born in Tennessee
Abe Lincoln Britt 4 M, born in Tennessee
James D. Britt 3 M, born in Tennessee

1880 -- Census, Henderson County, TN Page 386-B, District #10
Debbie Britt 45 F, Head, Widowed, born in North Carolina, father & mother born in North Carolina
Bacom N. Britt 16 M, Son, Single, Laborer, born in Tennessee, father & mother born in North Carolina
Abraham Britt 14 M, Son, Single, born in Tennessee, father & mother born in North Carolina
James A. Britt 12 M, Son, Single, born in Tennessee, father & mother born in North Carolina
Isac Britt 9 M, Son, Single, born in Tennessee, father & mother born in North Carolina

Beacom C. Britt and Deborah Wallace had the following children:

+206	Martha J. Britt (1849-)	
+207	Nathan Britt (1852-)	
+208	Hans Britt (1853-1941)	
+209	William T. Britt (1855-)	
+210	Avington Britt (1856-1928)	
+211	John Britt (1861-)	
+212	Beacom Nelson "Ned" Britt (1862-1909)	
+213	James A. Britt (1865-1937)	
+214	Abraham Lincoln Britt (1865-1916)	

44. Franey Wallace, daughter of Nathan C. Wallace and Finity Britt, was born in May 1828 in North Carolina. She married **Benjamin Britt**, son of Beacom C. Britt (1804-1876) and Dallie Wallace (aft 1810-bef 1849), on October 23, 1853 in Moore County, NC.[55] Benjamin was born in 1835 and died between 1870-1880.

RECORDS OF BENJAMIN BRITT AND FRANEY WALLACE

1850, Nov 22 -- Census, Moore County, NC Page 250
Beacom Britt 45 M, Farmer, $250 Real Estate, born in North Carolina
Deborah Britt 22 F, born in North Carolina
Benjamin Britt 15 M, born in North Carolina
Nathaniel 12 M, born in North Carolina
Mary A. Britt 10 F, born in North Carolina
Temperance Britt 8 F, born in North Carolina
Sallie Britt 6 F, born in North Carolina
Pattie Britt 1 F, born in North Carolina
Rhody Britt 72 F, born in North Carolina

1850, Nov 5 -- Census, Moore County, NC Page 234
Nathan Wallis 50 M, Farmer, born in North Carolina
Finity Wallis 50 F, born in North Carolina
Nancy Wallis 27 F, born in North Carolina
Franey Wallis 21 F, born in North Carolina
Mary Wallis 19 F, born in North Carolina
Everett Wallis 13 M, born in North Carolina
Benjamin Wallis 10 M, born in North Carolina

1853, Oct 23 -- Record of Marriages, Moore County, NC Page 21
Benjamin Britt and Frany Wallace by Eli Smith, JP

1860, Aug 23 -- Census, McNairy County, TN Page 450, District #8, Anderson Store Post Office
Benjamin Brett 23 M, Tenant Farmer, $325 Personal Property, born in Tennessee
Frainey Brett 25 F, born in North Carolina
Evret Brett 5 M, born in Tennessee
Nancy J. Brett 2 F, born in Tennessee
Benjamin Brett 1/12 M, born in Tennessee

1870, Jun 20 -- Census, Henderson County, TN Page 91, 10th Civil District, Lexington Post Office
Benjamin Britt 35 M, Farmer, $500 Personal Property, born in Tennessee
Suffrona Britt 36 F, Keeping House, born in North Carolina
Everitt Britt 15 M, Farmer, born in Tennessee
Nancy J. Britt 12 M, born in Tennessee
Benjamin Britt 8 M, born in Tennessee
George Britt 6 M, born in Tennessee
Mary Britt 5 F, born in Tennessee
Rolley Britt 3 M, born in Tennessee

1880 -- Census, Henderson County, TN Page 348-B, District #6
Phreny Britt 50 M, Head, Widowed, Keeping House, born in North Carolina, father & mother born in North Carolina
George Britt 17 M, Son, Single, Laborer on Farm, born in Tennessee, father born in Tennessee, mother born in North Carolina
Mary A. Britt 15 F, Dau, Single, Laborer on Farm, born in Tennessee, father born in Tennessee, mother born in North Carolina
Rolly Britt 12 M, Son, Single, Laborer on Farm, born in Tennessee, father born in Tennessee, mother born in North Carolina
Debby E. Britt 9 F, Dau, Single, born in Tennessee, father born in Tennessee, mother born in North Carolina

1900, Jun 4 -- Census, Henderson County, TN Page 63-B
Louis Singleton 38 M, Apr 1862, Head, Married-13yrs, Farmer, born in Tennessee, father born in Tennessee, mother born in North Carolina
Debby Singleton 29 F, Jan 1871, Wife, Married-13yrs, 5 Children(4 Living), born in Tennessee, father born in Tennessee, mother born in North Carolina
William Allen Singleton 11 M, Jun 1888, Son, Single, At School, born in Tennessee, father & mother born in Tennessee
Suzanne Singelton 6 F, Jun 1894, Dau, Single, born in Tennessee, father & mother born in Tennessee
Lanbury Singelton 4 M, Mar 1896, Son, Single, born in Tennessee, father & mother born in Tennessee
Alice Singelton 9/12 F, Sep 1899, Dau, Single, born in Tennessee, father & mother born in Tennessee
Franey Britt 72 F, May 1828, MotherL, Widowed, born in North Carolina, father & mother born in North Carolina

Additional Information can be found at www.MooreCountyWallaces.com

Mollie Britt 36 F, Feb 1864, SisterL, Single, Farm Laborer, born in Tennessee, father born in Tennessee, mother born in North Carolina

Benjamin Britt and Franey Wallace had the following children:

+216	Everet Britt (1855-)
+217	Nancy J. Britt (1858-)
+218	Benjamin Britt (1860-)
+219	George Britt (1863-bef 1900)
+220	Mary A. "Mollie" Britt (1864-)
+221	Rolle Allen "Rawl" Britt (1867-1950)
+222	Deborah E. Britt (1871-1908)

45. **Mary Wallace**, daughter of Nathan C. Wallace and Finity Britt, was born in 1832 in North Carolina and died before 1880. She married **Harmon Brewer** before September 10, 1850 in Moore County, NC.[56] Harmon was born on January 9, 1832 and was the son of William M. Brewer (1793-1881) and Elizabeth Jennet Stutts (1793-1876). Harmon and Mary migrated from Moore County to Henderson County, TN and later lived in Marshall County, MS and Shelby County, TN. Harmon served in Company C, 21st Tennessee Calvary.[57]

RECORDS OF HARMON BREWER AND MARY WALLACE

1850 -- Census, Moore County, NC Page 232-B
John Williams 50 M, Farmer, $320 Real Estate, born in North Carolina
Lydia Williams 50 F, born in North Carolina
Milly Williams 21 F, born in North Carolina
Mary Williams 18 F, born in North Carolina
Jerry Williams 16 M, Farmer, born in North Carolina
Rebecca Williams 15 F, born in North Carolina
Edward Williams 11 M, born in North Carolina
Elias Williams 9 M, born in North Carolina
Franey Williams 14 F, born in North Carolina
Harmon Brewer 19 M, born in North Carolina

1850, Nov 5 -- Census, Moore County, NC Page 234
Nathan Wallis 50 M, Farmer, born in North Carolina
Finity Wallis 50 F, born in North Carolina
Nancy Wallis 27 F, born in North Carolina
Franey Wallis 21 F, born in North Carolina
Mary Wallis 19 F, born in North Carolina
Everett Wallis 13 M, born in North Carolina
Benjamin Wallis 10 M, born in North Carolina

1850, Sep 10 -- Marriages, Fayetteville Observer, Fayetteville, NC
In Moore County, by B. Williamson, Esq., Mr. Harmon Brewer to Miss Mary Wallas [*Actual date of marriage not given*]

1860 -- Census, Henderson County, TN Page 222, Civil District #6
Harman Brewer 28 M, Farm Servant, $200 Personal Property, born in Tennessee
Mary Brewer 27 F, born in Tennessee
John Brewer 10 M, born in North Carolina
William Brewer 7 M, born in North Carolina
F.A. Brewer 5 F, born in Tennessee
M.E. Brewer 3 F, born in Tennessee
N.J. Brewer 3/12 F, born in Tennessee

1870, Aug 20 -- Census, Marshall County, MS Page 654, Range #4, Red Banks Post Office
Harmon Brewer 39 M, Farming, $2560 Real Estate, $650 Personal Property, born in North Carolina
Mary Brewer 38 F, Keeping House, born in North Carolina
John W. Brewer 19 M, born in North Carolina
William T. Brewer 18 M, born in North Carolina
Finity A. Brewer 16 F, born in Tennessee
Mary E. Brewer 14 F, born in Tennessee
Nancy J. Brewer 11 F, born in Tennessee
Amanda D. Brewer 9 F, born in Tennessee
Sarah C. Brewer 6 F, born in Mississippi

Jennie F. Brewer 4 M, born in Mississippi
Henry M. Brewer 8/12 M, born in Mississippi

1880 -- Census, Shelby County, TN Page 334, 6th Ward, City of Memphis
H. Brewer 48 M, Head, Married, Street Car Driver, born in North Carolina, father & mother born in North Carolina
Bessie Brewer 24 F, Wife, Keeping House, born in Mississippi, father & mother born in South Carolina
Sallie Brewer 15 F, Dau, Single, born in Mississippi, father born in North Carolina, mother born in NS
Walter Bergin 8 M, Son, Single, born in Mississippi, father & mother born in North Carolina
Jennie B. Bergin 13 F, Dau, Single, born in Mississippi, father & mother born in North Carolina
Henry Bergin 11 M, Son, Single, born in Mississippi, father & mother born in North Carolina

Harmon Brewer and Mary Wallace had the following children:

+223	William Brewer (1852-)
+224	John W. Brewer (1852-)
+225	Finity A. Brewer (1854-)
+226	Mary E. Brewer (1856-)
+227	Nancy J. Brewer (1859-)
+228	Amanda D. Brewer (1862-)
+229	Sarah C. Brewer (1864-)
+230	Geneva F. "Jennie" Brewer (1866-)
+231	Henry Martin Brewer (1869-)
+232	Walter Brewer (1872-)

46. **Everett Wallace**, son of Nathan C. Wallace and Finity Britt, was born in 1837 in North Carolina. He married **Mary Jane Williams** on July 28, 1857 in Madison County, TN. Mary Jane was the daughter of Henry Williams (1805-bef 1878) and Hannah (1810-bef 1860) and was born in 1837 in Tennessee. Everett served in Company B, 31st Tennessee Infantry during the Civil War. [58]

RECORDS OF EVERETT WALLACE AND MARY JANE WILLIAMS

1850, Nov 5 -- Census, Moore County, NC Page 234
Nathan Wallis 50 M, Farmer, born in North Carolina
Finity Wallis 50 F, born in North Carolina
Nancy Wallis 27 F, born in North Carolina
Franey Wallis 21 F, born in North Carolina
Mary Wallis 19 F, born in North Carolina
Everett Wallis 13 M, born in North Carolina
Benjamin Wallis 10 M, born in North Carolina

1857, Aug 26 – Marriage Certificate, Madison County, TN
Nathaniel Britt and Amanda J. Williams were married by P.C. Cowad. Everett Wallace was a witness.

1860, Jun 15 -- Census, Madison County, TN Page 88, District 1, Mt. Pinson Post Office
Everett Wallice 28 M, Farmer, $400 Real Estate, born in North Carolina
Jane Wallice 21 F, born in Tennessee
Jane Wallice, Jr. 1 F, born in Tennessee

1860 -- Agricultural Census, Madison County, TN
Everet Wallice listed 20 acres of improved, 30 acres of unimproved valued at $400

1861, Nov 25 -- Civil War Service Records
Everett Wallace enlisted in Company B, 31st Tennessee Infantry at Trenton, TN.

1878, Feb 4 -- Will Book A, Page 258, Madison County, TN
Will of Henry Williams Dec'd. Heirs: Daughters Mary Jane Wallace, Margaret Williams, son Thomas J. Williams, grandson Hugh A. (son of Elijah Williams), grandson W. Benjamin Wallace. Executor: Pascal Holloway. Witnesses: Hiram Johnson, T. H. Bagwell. Proven Apr 1878.

1879, Aug 27 -- Will Book A, Page 290, Madison County, TN
Will of Margaret Emily Williams Dec'd. Heirs: sister Mary Jane Wallace and mentions her father Henry Williams. Witnesses: Hiram Johnson, Paschal Holloway. Proven Dec 1880.

Everett Wallace and Mary Jane Williams had the following children:

Benjamin Wallace and Eliza Elizabeth Rivers
(Courtesy of Kaye Vernon, Weatherford, TX)

| +233 | W. Benjamin Wallace (-) |
| +234 | Jane Wallace (1859-) |

47. **Benjamin Wallace**, son of Nathan C. Wallace and Finity Britt, was born in April 1840 in North Carolina and died on July 17, 1900 in Reno, Parker County, TX and was buried in Parker County, TX at Jaybird Cemetery.[59] He married **Caty Williams** on January 2, 1862 in McNairy County, TN.[60] Caty was the daughter of Jeremiah Williams (c. 1775-) and Elizabeth Wallace (1808-) and was born in 1840 in North Carolina. She died before 1870.

After Caty's death, Ben married **Holly J. Kizer** on January 23, 1870 in McNairy County, TN.[61] Holly was born in 1842 in Georgia and died between 1872-1880. After her death, he married **Eliza Elizabeth Rivers** on January 9, 1880 in St. Francis County, AR.[62] Eliza Elizabeth Rivers, daughter of W.A. Rivers (1825-), was born on September 29, 1854 in Georgia and died on January 24, 1933 in Brock, Parker County, TX and was buried on January 25, 1933 in Parker County, TX at Brock Cemetery.[63]

During his life, Ben Wallace migrated from Moore County to McNairy County, TN then to St. Francis County, AR and finally to Parker County, TX joining several Moore County families migrating from western Tennessee to Parker County, TX between 1870-1900.

RECORDS OF BENJAMIN WALLACE

1850, Nov 5 -- Census, Moore County, NC Page 234
Nathan Wallis 50 M, Farmer, born in North Carolina
Finity Wallis 50 F, born in North Carolina
Nancy Wallis 27 F, born in North Carolina
Franey Wallis 21 F, born in North Carolina
Mary Wallis 19 F, born in North Carolina
Everett Wallis 13 M, born in North Carolina
Benjamin Wallis 10 M, born in North Carolina

1862, Jan 2 -- Marriage Certificate, McNairy County, TN
Benjamin Wallace and Miss Caty Williams were married by W.L. Gattis, MG. E.S. Williams was a witness.

1870, Jan 23 -- Marriage License, McNairy County, TN
Benjamin Wallace and Holly J. Kizer were married by W.L. Gattis, LC. D.C. Lee was a witness.

1870, Jun 1 -- Census, McNairy County, TN Page 348, 14th Civil District, Bethel Springs Post Office
Benjiman Wallis 31 M, Farmer, $800 Real Estate, $500 Personal Property, born in North Carolina
Holly J. Wallis 28 F, Keeping House, born in Georgia
Sarah E. Wallis 7 F, born in Tennessee
Clark A. Wallis 8 M, born in Tennessee

1871 -- Tax List, McNairy County, TN District 14
Ben Wallace 120 acres valued at $500 and 1 white poll

1872 -- Tax List, McNairy County, TN District 14
B. Wallis 120 acres valued at $500 and 1 white poll

1873 -- Tax List, McNairy County, TN District 14
B. Wallace listed 1 white poll

1880, Jan 9 -- Marriage License, St. Francis County, AR
B. Wallace and E.E. Knight were married by Frank Ritter, MECS

1880 -- Census, St. Francis County, AR Page 148, Town of Madison
B. Wallace 35 M, Head, Married, Farm Laborer, born in NC, father & mother born in North Carolina
E. E. Wallace 28 F, Wife, Married, House Keeper, born in Georgia, father & mother born in South Carolina
C. A. Wallace 14 F, Dau, Single, Farm Laborer, born in Tennessee, father born in North Carolina, mother born in Georgia
M. E. Wallace 8 F, Dau, Single, born in Tennessee, father born in North Carolina, mother born in Tennessee

1900 -- Census, Parker County, TX Page 129-B, Voting Precinct #5, Justice Precinct #2
Benjaman Wallace 60 M, Apr 1840, Head, Married-20yrs, Farmer, born in North Carolina, father & mother born in North Carolina
Elizabeth Wallace 47 F, Sep 1842, Wife, Married-20yrs, 4 Children(4 Living), born in Georgia, father & mother born in South Carolina
Jane Wallace 18 F, July 1881, Dau, Single, born in Texas, father born in North Carolina, mother born in Georgia
Cora Wallace 16 F, Jun 1883, Dau, Single, born in Texas, father born in North Carolina, mother born in Georgia
Benjaman Wallace 14 M, Sep 1885, Son, Single, born in Texas, father born in North Carolina, mother born in Georgia
Dora Wallace 13 F, May 1887, Dau, Single, born in Texas, father born in North Carolina, mother born in Georgia

Benjamin Wallace and Caty Williams had the following children:

+235   Sarah Elizabeth Wallace (1862-1900)
+236   Clarkie Ann Wallace (1866-1889)

Benjamin Wallace and Holly J. Kizer had the following child:

+237   Margaret Emma Wallace (1872-1900)

Benjamin Wallace and Eliza Elizabeth Rivers had the following children:

+238   Josephine Wallace (1881-1970)
+239   Cora Wallace (1883-1948)
+240   Ben Wallace (1885-1929)
+241   Dora Wallace (1887-1969)

48. Sarah Frances Wallace, daughter of Nathan C. Wallace and Sarah, was born on May 17, 1857 in Henderson County, TN and died on May 14, 1941 in Johnson County, TX.[64] She married **James Columbus Hart** on January 7, 1877 in Henderson County, TN. James was the son of Balaam S. Hart (1832-1863) and Louisa Caroline Ramsey (1830-1863). He was born on November 21, 1852 in Henderson County, TN and died on May 5, 1929 in Collin County, TX. Sarah and James were buried in Farmersville, Collin County, TX at Farmersville IOOF Cemetery.[65]

RECORDS OF JAMES COLUMBUS HART AND SARAH FRANCES WALLACE

1880 -- Census, Navarro County, TX Page 290
Columbus Hart 27 M, Head, Married, Farmer, born in Tennessee, father born in Tennessee, mother born in Georgia
Sarah Hart 23 F, Wife, Married, Keeping House, born in Tennessee, father born in ENGLAND, mother born in Tennessee
Moses Hart 4 M, Son, Single, At Home, born in Tennessee, father & mother born in North Carolina
William Hart 7/12 M, Son, Single, born in Texas, father & mother born in Tennessee

James Columbus Hart and Sarah Frances Wallace
(Courtesy of Kaye Vernon, Weatherford, TX)

Family photo c1892-1893. L to R: Luther C. Hart, Sarah Francis Wallace, Hattie Hart(seated), Balaam Moses Hart(standing), James Columbus Hart, Acie Linn Hart(seated), Willie T. Hart(standing), Annie May Hart(standing), Novel Hart(seated)
(Courtesy of Kaye Vernon, Weatherford, TX)

Family photo c1910. Back row L to R: J. Herman Craighead, Luther C. Hart, Balem Mose Hart, Arie Hart, Charles Thomas Wright. Middle row L to R: Eugenia Novel Hart (holding Hershal Craighead), Ella P. Wright (holding Ernest Hart), Rosa Lee Davis (holding Gladys Lucille Hart), Ethel Sophronia Hart. Front row L to R: Sarah Frances Wallace, Luther Columbus Hart, Jr, Grady Hart, James Cecil Hart, Leslie Cardwell, Edna Hart, Bertie May Hart, Willie Craighead, James Columbus Hart
(Courtesy of Kaye Vernon, Weatherford, TX)

1900 -- Census, Ellis County, TX Page 45-B, Precinct #3
James C. Hart 47 M, Nov 1852, Head, Married-22yrs, Farmer, born in Tennessee, father born in Tennessee, mother born in Georgia
Sarah F. Hart 42 F, May 1858, Wife-Married-22yrs, 10 Children(6 Living), born in Tennessee, father born in North Carolina, mother born in Virginia
William T. Hart 20 M, Nov 1879, Son, Widowed, Farm Laborer, born in Texas, father & mother born in Tennessee
Luther C. Hart 16 M, Mar 1884, Son, Single, At School, born in Texas, father & mother born in Tennessee
Eugenie N. Hart 14 F, Apr 1886, Dau, Single, At School, born in Texas, father & mother born in Tennessee
Hattie L. Hart 10 F, Dec 1889, Dau, Single, At School, born in Texas, father & mother born in Tennessee
Acy L. Hart 8 M, Sep 1891, Son, Single, born in Texas, father & mother born in Tennessee
Ethel S. Hart 5 F, Oct 1894, Dau, Single, born in Texas, father & mother born in Tennessee
Ira Hart 1 M, Aug 1898, Son, Single, born in Texas, father & mother born in Tennessee

(Courtesy of Find A Grave)

1920 Census Collin County, TX Page 123, Justice Precinct #2
James H. Hart 67 M, Head, Married, Farmer, born in Tennessee, father born in North Carolina, mother born in Tennessee
Sarah F. Hart 62 F, Wife, Married, born in Tennessee, father born in North Carolina, mother born in Virginia
Edna Hart 17 F, Dau, Single, Attending School, born in Tennessee, father & mother born in Tennessee

James Columbus Hart and Sarah Frances Wallace had the following children:

+242	Mary Hart (1877-1878)	
+243	William T. Hart (1879-1903)	
+244	Annie May Hart (1882-1899)	
+245	Luther Columbus Hart (1884-1950)	
+246	Eugenia Novel Hart (1886-1967)	
+247	Bennie F. Hart (1888-1888)	
+248	Hattie Lee Hart (1889-1923)	
+249	Acie Linn Hart (1891-1962)	
+250	Ethel Sophronia Hart (1894-1961)	
+251	Arie L. Hart (1898-1970)	
+252	Edna Hart (1902-1944)	

50. **William Samuel Wallace**, son of Nathan C. Wallace and Sarah, was born on January 15, 1862 in Tennessee and died on October 14, 1925 in Jackson, Madison County, TN[66]. He married **Nancy C. Williams** circa 1881. Nancy was the daughter of Lorenzo D. "Low" Williams (1829-1890) and Sarah Elizabeth Hart (1844-1885). She was born on July 15, 1865 in Tennessee and died on September 7, 1945 in Henderson County, TN.[67] Along with his father, Sam was a founding member of Palestine Church in Henderson County, TN. He and Nancy are both buried in the cemetery there along with several family members.[68]

RECORDS OF WILLIAM SAMUEL WALLACE

1880 -- Census, Henderson County, TN Page 348, Civil District #6
Nathan Wallace 80 M, Laborer on Farm, born in North Carolina, father & mother born in North Carolina

William S. Wallace 19 M, Laborer on Farm, born in Tennessee, father & mother born in North Carolina
Susan S. Wallace 16 F, Laborer on Farm, born in Tennessee, father & mother born in North Carolina

(Courtesy of Find A Grave)

1881, Oct 9 -- Palestine Cumberland Presbyterian Church, Henderson County, TN
Nathan C. Wallace and W. Saml. Wallace were listed among the founding members.

1900 -- Census, Henderson County, TN Page 65-B
Samuel W. Wallace 37 M, Aug 1862, Head, Married-19yrs, Farmer, born in Tennessee, father born in North Carolina, mother born in Tennessee

Nancy A. Wallace 34 F, 1866, Wife, Married-19yrs, 7 Children(6 Living), born in Tennessee, father born in North Carolina, mother born in Tennessee
Mary Ann Wallace 15 F, Jul 1884, Dau, Single, born in Tennessee, father & mother born in Tennessee
James O. Wallace 13 M, Aug 1886, Son, Single, born in Tennessee, father & mother born in Tennessee
Birdie L. Wallace 10 M, Aug 1889, Son, Single, born in Tennessee, father & mother born in Tennessee
Lummy T. Wallace 8 M, Sep 1891, Son, Single, born in Tennessee, father & mother born in Tennessee
Ida J. Wallace 4 F, Oct 1895, Dau, Single, born in Tennessee, father & mother born in Tennessee
Harvey E. Wallace 1 M, May 1899, Son, Single, born in Tennessee, father & mother born in Tennessee

1910 -- Census, Henderson County, TN Page 101, Civil District #5
William S. Wallace 50 M, Head, Married-28yrs, Farmer(General Farm), born in Tennessee, father & mother born in Tennessee
Nan Wallace 45 F, Wife, Married-28yrs, 10 Children(9 Living), born in Tennessee, father & mother born in Tennessee
Ollie Wallace 21 M, Son, Single, Farm Laborer, born in Tennessee, father & mother born in Tennessee
Burt Wallace 19 M, Son, Single, Farm Laborer, born in Tennessee, father & mother born in Tennessee
Tanie Wallace 15 M, Son, Single, Farm Laborer, born in Tennessee, father & mother born in Tennessee
Ida Wallace 13 F, Dau, Single, born in Tennessee, father & mother born in Tennessee
Harvey Wallace 11 M, Son, Single, born in Tennessee, father & mother born in Tennessee
Hermin Wallace 8 M, Son, Single, born in Tennessee, father & mother born in Tennessee
Ella Wallace 5 F, Dau, Single, born in Tennessee, father & mother born in Tennessee
Ethirge Wallace 3 M, Son, Single, born in Tennessee, father & mother born in Tennessee

1920 -- Census, Henderson County, TN Page 107, District #5
Sam Wallace 59 M, Head, Married, Farmer-General Farm, born in Tennessee, father born in North Carolina, mother born in Tennessee
Nan Wallace 45 F, Wife, Married, born in Tennessee, father born in North Carolina, mother born in Tennessee
Olie Wallace 30 M, Son, Single, Farm Laborer, born in Tennessee, father & mother born in Tennessee
Harvey Wallace 20 M, Son, Single, Farm Laborer, born in Tennessee, father & mother born in Tennessee
Eller Wallace 15 F, Dau, Single, born in Tennessee, father & mother born in Tennessee
Ethridge Wallace 12 M, Son, Single, born in Tennessee, father & mother born in Tennessee

William Samuel Wallace and Nancy C. Williams had the following children:

+253	Mary Ann "Molly" Wallace (1884-1967)
+254	James Oliver "Ollie" Wallace (1888-1950)
+255	Bert Lee Wallace (1890-1982)
+256	Lummie Tanie Wallace (1891-)
+257	Ida Victoria Wallace (1895-1975)
+258	Harve D. Wallace (1900-1941)
+259	Hermin Wallace (1902-)
+260	L. Ella Wallace (1905-1932)
+261	Emerson Ethridge Wallace (1908-1936)

52. **Susan Sufronie Wallace**, daughter of Nathan C. Wallace and Sarah, was born in 1864 in Tennessee. She died on January 3, 1926 in Collin County, TX and was buried on January 4, 1926 in Farmersville, Collin County, TX at Farmersville IOOF Cemetery.[6970] She married **Joseph Arch Cox** in 1892. He was born in 1848 in Tennessee.

RECORDS OF JOSEPH ARCH COX AND SUSAN SUFRONIE WALLACE

1880 -- Census, Henderson County, TN Page 348, Civil District #6
Nathan Wallace 80 M, Laborer on Farm, born in North Carolina, father & mother born in North Carolina
William S. Wallace 19 M, Laborer on Farm, born in Tennessee, father & mother born in North Carolina
Susan S. Wallace 16 F, Laborer on Farm, born in Tennessee, father & mother born in North Carolina

1900 -- Census, Henderson County, TN Page 65
Arch J. Cox 53 M, Jun 1846, Head, Married-7yrs, Farmer, born in Virginia, father & mother born in Virginia
Susan F. Cox 34 F, Oct 1865, Wife, Married-7yrs, 1 Child(1 Living), born in Tennessee, father born in North Carolina, mother born in Virginia
Mary A. Cox 6 F, Dec 1893, Dau, Single, born in Tennessee, father born in Virginia, mother born in Tennessee
Rebecca Cox 56 F, Mar 1844, Sister, Single, born in Virginia, father & mother born in Virginia

1910 -- Census, Henderson County, TN Page 46, 2nd Civil District
Joseph A. Cox 62 M, Head, Married-1st-18yrs, Laborer(Farm Laborer), born in Tennessee, father & mother born in Virginia
Susin S. Cox 44 F, Wife, Married-1st-18yrs, 1 Child(1 Living), born in Tennessee, father born in North Carolina
Mary A. Cox 16 F, Dau, Single, born in Tennessee, father & mother born in Tennessee

Joseph Arch Cox and Susan Sufronie Wallace had the following child:

+262   Mary Ann Cox (1893-1915)

53. Clarkey Ann Wallace, daughter of Isham Wallace and Nancy Furr, was born on March 2, 1820 and died August 24m 1891. She married **George Cockman** on June 18, 1840 in Moore County, NC.[71] George was the son of John Cockman (1785-bef 1861) and Mary Richardson (1783-1868), was born in 1818 and died on August 13, 1905. George and Clarkey were buried in Moore County, NC at Flint Hill Baptist Church.

RECORDS OF GEORGE COCKMAN AND CLARKEY WALLACE

1836, Nov 4 -- Land Grant #2957, Moore County, NC
David Cockman received 100 acres located on Locust Branch of Richland Creek adjoining McKay, Griffith and James H. Muse. John Cockman and George Cockman were chain carriers.

1840, Jun 24 -- Marriages, Fayetteville Observer [Fayetteville, NC] Newspaper
"In Moore County, on the 18th inst. [Jun 1840], Mr. George Cockman, son of John Cockman to Miss Clarky Wallis, daughter of Isham Wallis - all of Moore County"

1844, Apr 23 -- 1844-1847 Court of Pleas and Quarter Sessions, Moore County, NC Page 7
Ordered that Joseph Upton be appointed overseer of the road from George Moores to the branch near McQueens and have the following hands to work: Elisha Cagle, James Melton, Cornl. Mathews, George Williams, David Cockman, Joseph Cockman, Sampson Cockman, Isaac Williams, George Cockman, George W. Horner, Noah Richardson hands, Seburn Jones, John Cockman, Abram Hunsucker, William Williams, James Deaton, Quimby Sowell, William Richardson, John Jones, Allen Jones and Jeremiah Williams.

1846, Apr 28 -- 1844-1847 Court of Pleas and Quarter Sessions, Moore County, NC Page 319
Ordered that George W. Horner be appointed overseer of the road from George Moore's to the branch near McQueen's and work the following hands: Elisha Cagle, James Melton, Cornelius Mathews, George Williams, David Cockman, Joseph Cockman, Sampson Cockman, Isaac Williams, George Cockman, Noah Richardson and hands, Seburn Jones, Abram Hunsucker, James Deaton, Quimby Sowell, William Richardson, John Jones, Allan Jones, John W. Jackson, Westly Wallace, Chesly Horner, Enoch Williams, William Reaves and Richard Phillips.

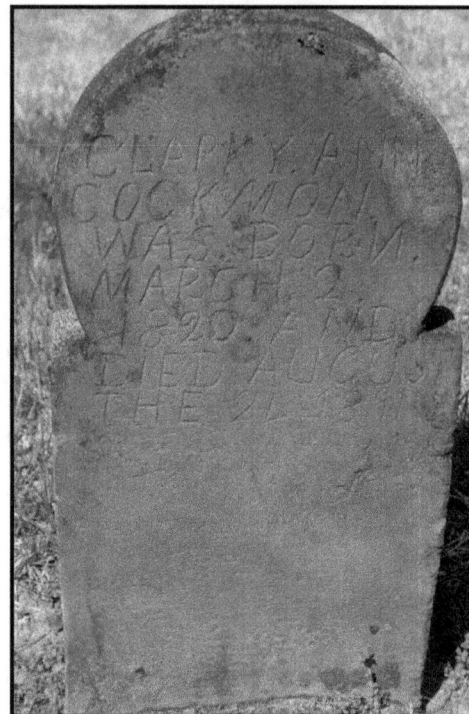

(photographed April 2, 2010)

1847 -- Tax List, Moore County, NC
George Cockman listed 200 acres valued at $200 and 1 white poll on Glades Branch in District 9

1848, Apr 27 -- 1847-1849 Court of Pleas and Quarter Sessions, Moore County, NC Page 198
George Hunsucker, overseer of the road from the fork at George Cockmans to Mechanics Hill resigned. The court divided the road and ordered the appointment of two overseers.

1848, Apr 27 -- 1847-1849 Court of Pleas and Quarter Sessions, Moore County, NC Page 199
Ordered that William H. Stutts be appointed overseer of the road from the fork of the Fayetteville Road at George Cockmans to the Bars at Thomas Williams' south of his house and work the following hands: James Stutts, Lindsay Stutts, George Stutts, George Williams, William Williams, Westley Williams, John H. Stutts and John Garner.

1848, Oct 24 -- 1847-1849 Court of Pleas and Quarter Sessions, Moore County, NC Page 274
Ordered that John Jones be appointed overseer of the road from George Moore's to the branch near McQueen's and work the following hands: Josiah Cockman, George

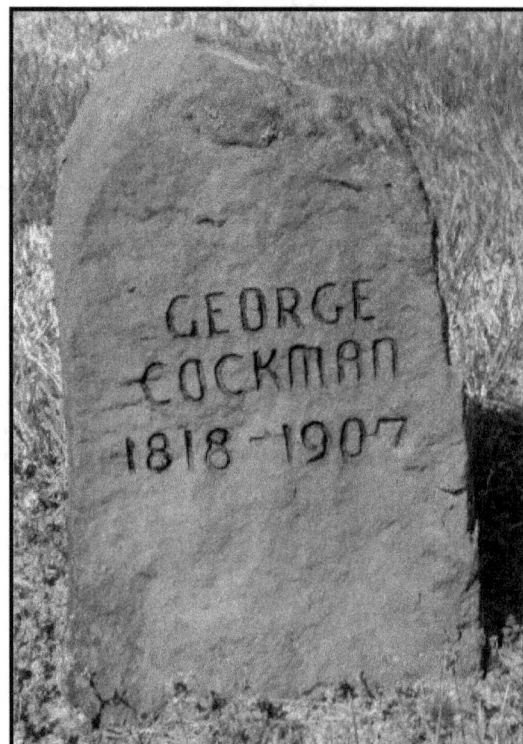

W. Horner, Elisha Cagle, James Melton, Cornelius Mathews, George Williams, David Cockman, Joseph Cockman, Sampson Cockman, Isaac Williams, George Cockman, Noah Richardson and hands, Seburn Jones, Abram Hunsucker, James Deaton, Quimby Sowell, William Richardson, Allen Jones, Westley Wallace, Chesley Horner, Enoch Williams, William Reaves, Richard Phillips and James Jones.

1849 -- Tax List, Moore County, NC
George Cockman listed 200 acres valued at $200 and 1 white poll on Glades Branch in District 9

1849, Jan 23 -- Court of Pleas and Quarter Sessions, Moore County, NC Page 324
A deed from Isaac Jones to Isham Wallace proven by George Cockman

1849, Apr 23 -- 1847-1849 Court of Pleas and Quarter Sessions, Moore County, NC Page 399
Ordered that Upshur Furr be appointed overseer of the road from the fork of the Fayetteville Road at George Cockman to the Bars at Thomas Williams south of his house and work the following hands: James Stutts, Lindsey Stutts, George Stutts, George Williams, William Williams, Wesley Williams, John H. Stutts and John Garner.

1850 -- Census, Moore County, NC Page 238
George Cockman 32 M, Farmer, $200 Real Estate, born in North Carolina
Clarkey Cockman 26 F, born in North Carolina
William M. Cockman 8 M, born in North Carolina
Mary E. Cockman 6 F, born in North Carolina
Sarah L. Cockman 4 F, born in North Carolina
Isham W. Cockman 2 M, born in North Carolina
Nancy J. Cockman 3/12 F, born in North Carolina

1851, Oct 28 -- 1851-1853 Court of Pleas and Quarter Sessions, Moore County, NC Page 97
Ordered that James Stutts be appointed overseer of the road from the fork at the Fayetteville Road at Geo. Cockmans to the Bars of Thomas Williams and work the following hands: James Stutts, Lindsey Stutts, George Williams, William Williams, Westley Williams, Alstin Williams, John Garner, Edmond Garner, Leonard Stutts and Lindsey Williams.

1852 -- Tax List, Moore County, NC
George Cockman listed 200 acres valued at $200 and 1 white poll on Glades Branch in District 9

1853 -- Tax List, Moore County, NC
George Cockman listed 200 acres valued at $200 and 1 white poll on Meadow Branch in District 9

1853, Jul 26 -- 1853-1856 Court of Pleas and Quarter Sessions, Moore County, NC Page 13
Ordered that Westley Wallace be appointed overseer of the road from George Moore's to the branch near McQueen's and work the following hands: Joseph Upton, Cornelius Dowdy, Zeno Cockman, Henry Melton, George Cockman, Noah Richardson & hands, Noah Cockman, David Cockman, Armstead Stutts, Isaac Williams, George W. Horner, John Jones and Quimby Wallace.

1853, Jul 26 -- 1853-1856 Court of Pleas and Quarter Sessions, Moore County, NC Page 18-19
The following appointed to superintend elections in 1853: [District 9] Robert W. Goldston Esq. and E.Q. Sowell for Congress; Henry B. Maness and Presly Caddell for for Superior Court Clerk; Abram Stutts Esq. and George Cockman for County Court Clerk.

1854 -- Tax List, Moore County, NC
George Cockman listed 200 acres valued at $200 and 1 white poll in District 9

1854, Oct 24 -- 1853-1856 Court of Pleas and Quarter Sessions, Moore County, NC Page 205
Ordered that Leonard Stutts be appointed overseer of the road from the ford at George Cockmans to the Bars of Thomas Williams and work the following hands: James Stutts, Lindsey Stutts, George Williams, John Garner, Edmond Garner, Lindsey Williams, Henry Yow, William Garner, Henry Williams, Branson Williams and Derick Yow.

1855 -- Tax List, Moore County, NC
George Cockman listed 200 acres valued at $200 and 1 white poll on Buffalo Creek in District 9

1855, Jul 26 -- 1853-1856 Court of Pleas and Quarter Sessions, Moore County, NC Page 350
Ordered that John R. Ritter be appointed overseer of a new road commencing at the Island Ford on Deep River passing near John R. Ritter's to the point where it intersects with the Fayetteville and Western Plank Road at or near where the Grove Road crosses Plank Road and work the following hands: Luke Brady, James Brady, Bruce Stout, Parham Y. Oats, William Perry, Benjamin Perry, Joseph Beal, Robt. W. Goldston's hands, Noah Richardson hands, George Cockman, James Powers, Newton Woody, Henry Mainess, John S. Ritter, Asa Mainess, Noah Brewer, Spencer Brown, Sampson Cockman, Nelson Hunsucker, John R. Ritter's hands, Armst Stutts and Houston Hunsucker.

1856, Feb 2 -- 1853-1856 Court of Pleas and Quarter Sessions, Moore County, NC Page 466
Ordered that William Stutts be appointed overseer of the road from George Moore's to the branch near McQueen's and work the following hands: Westley Wallace, Cornelius Dowdy, Zeno Cockman, Henry Melton, George Cockman, Sampson Cockman, Noah Cockman,

David Cockman, Noah Richardson & hands, Armstead Stutts, Isaac Williams, G.W. Horner, John Jones, Quimby Wallace, Joseph Upton, Lochart Wallace, Geo. Williams and Jefferson Williams.

1857 -- Tax List, Moore County, NC
George Cockman listed 200 acres valued at $300 and 1 white poll on Buffalo Creek in District 9

1858, May 1 -- 1856-1858 Court of Pleas and Quarter Sessions, Moore County, NC Page 422
Ordered that George Cockman be appointed overseer of the road from George Moore's to the branch near McQueen's and work the following hands: William Stutts, Wesley Wallace, Cornelius Dowdy, Zeno Cockman, Henry Melton, Sampson Cockman, Noah Cockman, David Cockman, Noah Richardson hands, Armsted Stutts, Isaac Williams, G.W. Horner, John Jones, Quimby Wallace, Joseph Upton, Lochart Wallace, George Williams and Jefferey Williams.

1858, Jul 31 -- 1856-1858 Court of Pleas and Quarter Sessions, Moore County, NC Page 475
Ordered that John Gardner be appointed overseer of the road from the fork at George Cockman to the Bar at Thomas Williams and work the following hands: James Stutts, Lindsy Stutts, John Garner, Edmond Garner, Lindsey Williams, Henry Yow, Henry Williams, Branson Williams, Derick Yow, Alex. Williams, Harbert Williams, Andrew Yow and Wm. Yow.

1860 -- Census, Moore County, NC Page 204, Gold Region Post Office
George Cockman 44 M, Farmer, $800 Real Estate, $100 Personal Property, born in North Carolina
Clarkey Cockman 40 F, born in North Carolina
William Mc. Cockman 18 M, born in North Carolina
Ellen E. Cockman 16 F, born in North Carolina
Sarah L. Cockman 15 F, born in North Carolina
Isham W. Cockman 11 M, born in North Carolina
Nancy J. Cockman 9 F, born in North Carolina
Rebecca F. Cockman 6 F, born in North Carolina
Eli E. Cockman 3 M, born in North Carolina
Delphina Cockman 1 F, born in North Carolina

1861, May 21-Apr 1862 -- Record of Estates Book H Page 406-409, Moore County, NC
Estate of John Cockman, Dec'd. by Administrator George Cockman. *Items were purchased by the following*: Noah Richardson, Noah Cockman, D. Davis, Bryant Tyson, D.F. Muse, J.A. Stutts, Enoch Stewart, J.J. Richardson, Saml. Wallace, C.T. Horner, Mary Cockman, J.S. Ritter, L.M. Seawell, Emsley Wallace, Miles Muse, Thomas Horner, Sampson Cockman, S.W. Seawell, James Horner, M.A. Cockman, B.C. Brady, Z.B. Moore, D. Stutts, W. Wallace, J.H. Williams, Isham Wallace, Zeno Richardson, Armstrong Maness, N.R. Currie, John Muse, Henry Brown, George Horner, A. Brown, W. Williams and Wm. King.

1861, Jun 2-Jul 8 -- Notice, Fayetteville Weekly Observer [Fayetteville, NC] Newspaper
Moore County, NC -- Mary Cockman v. George Cockman et al. Petition for Dower. Appearing that Michael Cockman and David Cockman, defendants, are not inhabitants of this State. They are summoned to appear at the courthouse in Carthage on the fourth Monday in Jul.

1870 -- Census, Moore County, NC Page 578, Ritters Township, Carters Mill Post Office
George Cockman 53 M, Farmer, $600 Real Estate, $500 Personal Property, born in North Carolina
Clarkey Cockman 47 F, born in North Carolina
Rebecca Cockman 16 F, born in North Carolina
Eli E. T. Cockman 13 M, born in North Carolina
Belfina Cockman 11 F, born in North Carolina
Charles E. Cockman 9 M, born in North Carolina

1871, Mar 11-Apr 3 -- Orders and Decrees Book 1 Page 66, Moore County, NC
George Cockman, Administrator of John Cockman Dec'd. ExParte. Ordered that administrator have leave to sell evidence of debt.

1871, Oct 9 -- Deed Book 82 Page 6, Moore County, NC
Levi Sheffield and wife Jane/Jenny deeded W.T. Horner two tracts located on the Plank Road [1] 50 acres adjoining George Cockman, Sampson Cockman and his own line [2] 40 acres adjoining Rachel Dowdy and Noah Cockman. Danl. McIntosh was a witness.

1873, Jan 21 -- Land Grant #4487, Moore County, NC
Sampson Cockman received 42 acres located on the waters of Glade Branch adjoining Presley Caddell, George Cockman and Joseph Caddell. A.W. Cagle and Elisha Cagle were chain carriers.

1874, Oct 2 -- Orders and Decrees Book 1 Page 355, Moore County, NC
Sampson Cockman and George Cockman appointed to review the stock and crops of A.H. Williams Dec'd.to determine the amount available for a year's maintenance for widow Nannie Williams and their two children under ten.

1880 -- Census, Moore County, NC Page 337, Ritters Township
George Cockman 66 M, Head, Married, Farmer, born in North Carolina, father & mother born in North Carolina
Clarkey Cockman 59 F, Wife, Married, Keeps House, born in North Carolina, father & mother born in North Carolina

Charley Cockman 19 M, Son, Single, Works on Farm, born in North Carolina, father & mother born in North Carolina

1884 -- Branson's NC Business Directory Page 468-474, Moore County, NC
Geo. Knockman [Cockman] listed as a farmer at Carters Mill Post Office

1884, Mar 27 -- 1880-1885 Administrator's Bonds, Moore County, NC Page 58
George Cockman appointed Administrator of the Estate of Isham Wallace, Dec'd. with David S. Barrett and M. McL. Kelly as securities.

1884, Apr 4 -- Deed Book 12 Page 533, Moore County, NC
J.S. Cockman deeded W.J. Cockman, Jas. A. Cockman and W.L. Cockman 190 acres located on Meadow Branch adjoining Samuel B. Wallace. Comprised of the following tracts deeded to J.S. Cockman: 47 acres from Wm. Stutts and L. Grimm, 50 acres from Mary Cockman, 24 acres from George Melton, 24 acres from Candy Melton, 8 acres from George Cockman, 36 acres of Melton land. R.L. McNeill was a witness.

1886, Jan 5 -- Deed Book 49 Page 444, Moore County, NC
James H. Shields and wife Nannie M. Shields deeded Lewis S. Maness 32 acres adjoining Lewis S. Maness, William Stutts, George Cockman and lot #5 assigned to Nannie M. Wallace. E.T. Williams was a witness.

1889, Dec 11 -- Orders and Decrees Book 3 Page 80-82, Moore County, NC
George Cockman, Admst. of Isham Wallace Dec'd. v. Samuel B. Wallace, W.W. Wallace, Quimby Wallace. John Wallace, Virgil Wallace and other heirs. Division of Land mentions neighbors Quimby Wallace, Samuel Wallace; 10a tract deeded from Joseph Wallace to Isham Wallace. Heirs: Lovedy Jane Horner, wife of James Horner, Heirs of Elizabeth Cockman, wife of Sampson Cockman (Wesly Cockman, James Cockman, Alice Cockman, Clarky Ann Horner, wife of W.T. Horner, Eliza Horner, wife of Thomas R. Horner), Heirs of Locky Wallace (Mary Maness, wife of Blake Maness, Martha Maness, wife of Lewis Maness, Ruth Ritter, wife of Joseph Ritter, Vandie Maness, wife of McLellan Maness, Ella Blake Wallace), Sarah Garner, wife of John Garner, Samuel B. Wallace, Mary Cockman, wife of Noah Cockman, W.W. Wallace, Clarky Cockman, Quimby Wallace, Emsley Wallace, Virgil Wallace, S.D. Wallace and John Wallace (of Arkansas).

1890 -- Branson's NC Business Directory Page 457-466, Moore County, NC
Geo. Knockman [Cockman] listed as a farmer at Carters Mill Post Office

1891, Sep 15 -- Deed Book 126 Page 378, Moore County, NC
S.D. Garner and wife Lillie Ellen deeded W.T. Garner and wife Martha 40 acres adjoining Alexander Williams and George Cockman. M.McL. Kelly was a witness.

1893, Mar 6 -- Deed Book 10, Page 338-340, Moore County, NC
George Cockman, administrator of Isham Wallace, Dec'd. deeded I.W.H. Cockman two tracts. [1] 142 acres located on Meadow Branch adjoining Quimby Wallace, Samuel Wallace and L. Wallace. [2] 10 acres located on Meadow Branch and the Rutherford Road adjoining Armstrong Maness and deeded to Isham Wallace by Josiah Wallace. A.H. McNeill was a witness.

1893, Dec 23 -- Deed Book 22 Page 400, Moore County, NC
Sampson Cockman deeded S. Alice Cockman 40 acres adjoining George Cockman and N. Cockman. Jos. T. Seawell was a witness.

1894, Jul 30 -- Will Book E Page 528-531, Moore County, NC
Will of George Cockman Dec'd. Heirs: son W. McSwain Cockman; daughter Elizabeth Caddell, wife of Bias Caddell; son-law Leander Hare; daughter Nancy Jane Stafford; Becky Williams, wife of Richard Williams; Delphiny Williams, wife of Murdock Williams; son Eli Cockman; son Charles Edward Cockman; son I.W.H. Cockman. Executor: W. McSwain Cockman. Witnesses: John J. Shaw, A.F. Seawell and S.M. Jones. Proven Aug 13, 1907.

1895, Mar 12 -- 1889-1897 Administrator's Bonds, Moore County, NC Page 68
George Cockman appointed Administrator of the Estate of Isham Wallace, Dec'd. with W. McS. Cockman and Robert W. Barrett as securities.

1898 -- Branson's Business Directory, Moore County, NC
Geo. Cockman listed 152 acres valued at $200 located at Horners Post Office in Bensalem Township / George Cockman listed 200 acres valued at $275 located at Horners Post Office in Ritters Township

1905, Aug 16 -- Local News, Carthage Blade [Carthage, NC] Newspaper
"Death of Mr. Geo. Cockman. Mr. Geo. Cockman, age about 93 years, died at Mr. Eli Cockman's in Ritter's township Sunday and was buried at Flint Hill Baptist church, of which he was a member, Monday afternoon. Another ancient landmark, another victim of old age has been removed."

1906, Jan 30 -- 1896-1908 Administrator's Bonds, Moore County, NC Page 448-449
C.E. Cockman appointed Administrator of the Estate of Geo. Cockman, Dec'd. with John L. Currie and Gilbert McLeod as securities. Heirs: W. McS. Cockman, Elizabeth Caddell, Sarah Hair, Jane Stafford and husband Parker Stafford, I.W.H. Cockman, Rebecca Williams and husband R.M. Williams, Eli T. Cockman, Della Williams and husband Murd. Williams and C.E. Cockman.

1906, Mar 13 -- Deed Book 33 Page 512, Moore County, NC

John M. Wallace [Perry County, AR] deeded Geo. W Horner his 1/3 interest and 52 2/3 of 158 acre tract known as the Isham Wallace homestead adjoining the heirs of Lockey Wallace, Isham Cockman and Quimby Wallace. Land includes the 21 acres deeded to Elizabeth Cockman prior to Isham Wallace's death and the 21 acres provided to John M. Wallace and Clarkie Cockman of the remaining 137 acres.

George Cockman and Clarkey Ann Wallace had the following children:

+263	William McSwain Cockman (1842-1906)
+264	Mary Elizabeth Cockman (1844-)
+265	Sarah Lee Cockman (1845-1887)
+266	Isham Wallace Haig Cockman (1848-1909)
+267	Nancy Jane Cockman (1850-1921)
+268	Sindi Ann Cockman (1852-1856)
+269	Rebecca Francis Cockman (1854-1928)
+270	Eli Terry Cockman (1857-1946)
+271	Delphina Cockman (1859-1910)
+272	Charles Edward Cockman (1860-1938)

54. Elizabeth Wallace, daughter of Isham Wallace and Nancy Furr, was born on April 24, 1825 and died August 28, 1871. She married **J. Sampson Cockman** circa 1841. Sampson was a brother to George Cockman and son of John Cockman and Mary Richardson. Sampson was born on November 7, 1819 and died on January 28, 1909. They are buried in Moore County, NC at Flint Hill Baptist Church.

RECORDS OF SAMPSON COCKMAN AND ELIZABETH WALLACE

1843, Mar 1 -- Deed Book 61 Page 26, Moore County, NC
John Cockman deeded 2 tracts (100a and 9a) to Sampson Cockman on Buffalo Creek. A. McKinnon was a witness.

1844, Apr 23 -- 1844-1847 Court of Pleas and Quarter Sessions, Moore County, NC Page 7
Ordered that Joseph Upton be appointed overseer of the road from George Moores to the branch near McQueens and have the following hands to work: Elisha Cagle, James Melton, Cornl. Mathews, George Williams, David Cockman, Joseph Cockman, Sampson Cockman, Isaac Williams, George Cockman, George W. Horner, Noah Richardson hands, Seburn Jones, John Cockman, Abram Hunsucker, William Williams, James Deaton, Quimby Sowell, William Richardson, John Jones, Allen Jones and Jeremiah Williams.

1846, Apr 28 -- 1844-1847 Court of Pleas and Quarter Sessions, Moore County, NC Page 319
Ordered that George W. Horner be appointed overseer of the road from George Moore's to the branch near McQueen's and work the following hands: Elisha Cagle, James Melton, Cornelius Mathews, George Williams, David Cockman, Joseph Cockman, Sampson Cockman, Isaac Williams, George Cockman, Noah Richardson and hands, Seburn Jones, Abram Hunsucker, James Deaton, Quimby Sowell, William Richardson, John Jones, Allan Jones, John W. Jackson, Westly Wallace, Chesly Horner, Enoch Williams, William Reaves and Richard Phillips.

Elizabeth Wallace Cockman
(photographed April 2, 2010)

1847 -- Tax List, Moore County, NC
Sampson Cockman listed 100 acres valued at $100 and 1 white poll on Glades Branch in District 9

1847, Oct 25 -- 1847-1849 Court of Pleas and Quarter Sessions, Moore County, NC Page 81
Ordered that Josiah Cockman be appointed overseer of the road from George Moore's to the branch near McQueen's and work the following hands: George W. Horner, Elisha Cagle, James Melton, Cornelius Mathews, George Williams, David Cockman, Joseph Cockman, Sampson Cockman, Isaac Williams, George C. Cockman, Noah Richardson & hands, Seburn Jones, Abram Hunsucker, James Deaton, Quimby Sowell, Wm. Richardson, John Jones, Allan Jones, John W. Jackson, Westley Wallace, Chesley Horner, Enoch Williams, William Reaves, Richard Phillips and James Jones.

1848, Oct 24 -- 1847-1849 Court of Pleas and Quarter Sessions, Moore County, NC Page 274
Ordered that John Jones be appointed overseer of the road from George Moore's to the branch near McQueen's and work the following hands: Josiah Cockman, George W. Horner, Elisha Cagle, James Melton, Cornelius Mathews, George Williams, David Cockman, Joseph Cockman, Sampson Cockman, Isaac Williams, George Cockman, Noah Richardson and hands, Seburn Jones, Abram Hunsucker, James Deaton, Quimby Sowell, William Richardson, Allen Jones, Westley Wallace, Chesley Horner, Enoch Williams, William Reaves, Richard Phillips and James Jones.

1849 -- Tax List, Moore County, NC
Sampson Cockman listed 100 acres valued at $100 and 1 white poll on Glades Branch in District 9

1850 -- Census, Moore County, NC Page 239
Sampson Cockman 31 M, Farmer, born in North Carolina
Elizabeth Cockman 26 F, born in North Carolina
Clarkey Cockman 8 F, born in North Carolina
Noah Cockman 6 M, born in North Carolina
Sarah Cockman 4 F, born in North Carolina
Isham Cockman 4/12 M, born in North Carolina

1851, Apr 29 -- 1851-1853 Court of Pleas and Quarter Sessions, Moore County, NC Page 14
Saml. Barrett, Jno. Stutts, John Stuart, W.M. Person, William Cole, Neill Caddell, J. Bean. Alexr. W. Campbell, Lauchlin Kelly, Henry Stutts, Jacob Stutts and Garner Maines reviewed the premises of Sampson Cockman and found the Fayetteville and Western Plank Road to have taken up 1.7 acres owned by Cockman and assessed the damage at $8.

1852 -- Tax List, Moore County, NC
Sampson Cockman listed 100 acres valued at $100 and 1 white poll on Buffalo Creek in District 9

1853 -- Tax List, Moore County, NC
Sampson Cockman listed 100 acres valued at $100 and 1 white poll on Buffalo Creek in District 9

1855 -- Tax List, Moore County, NC
Sampson Cockman listed 109 acres valued at $250 and 1 white poll on Buffalo Creek in District 9

1855, Jul 26 -- 1853-1856 Court of Pleas and Quarter Sessions, Moore County, NC Page 350
Ordered that John R. Ritter be appointed overseer of a new road commencing at the Island Ford on Deep River passing near John R. Ritter's to the point where it intersects with the Fayetteville and Western Plank Road at or near where the Grove Road crosses Plank Road and work the following hands: Luke Brady, James Brady, Bruce Stout, Parham Y. Oats,

Sampson Cockman *(photographed April 2, 2010)*

William Perry, Benjamin Perry, Joseph Beal, Robt. W. Goldston's hands, Noah Richardson hands, George Cockman, James Powers, Newton Woody, Henry Mainess, John S. Ritter, Asa Mainess, Noah Brewer, Spencer Brown, Sampson Cockman, Nelson Hunsucker, John R. Ritter's hands, Armst Stutts and Houston Hunsucker.

1856, Feb 2 -- 1853-1856 Court of Pleas and Quarter Sessions, Moore County, NC Page 466
Ordered that William Stutts be appointed overseer of the road from George Moore's to the branch near McQueen's and work the following hands: Westley Wallace, Cornelius Dowdy, Zeno Cockman, Henry Melton, George Cockman, Sampson Cockman, Noah Cockman, David Cockman, Noah Richardson & hands, Armstead Stutts, Isaac Williams, G.W. Horner, John Jones, Quimby Wallace, Joseph Upton, Lochart Wallace, Geo. Williams and Jefferson Williams.

1857 -- Tax List, Moore County, NC
Samson Cockman listed 109 acres valued at $250 and 1 white poll on Buffalo Creek in District 9

1857, Oct 29 -- 1856-1858 Court of Pleas and Quarter Sessions, Moore County, NC Page 288
Deed from John Cockman to Sampson Cockman acknowledged

1858, May 1 -- 1856-1858 Court of Pleas and Quarter Sessions, Moore County, NC Page 422
Ordered that George Cockman be appointed overseer of the road from George Moore's to the branch near McQueen's and work the following hands: William Stutts, Wesley Wallace, Cornelius Dowdy, Zeno Cockman, Henry Melton, Sampson Cockman, Noah Cockman,

David Cockman, Noah Richardson hands, Armsted Stutts, Isaac Williams, G.W. Horner, John Jones, Quimby Wallace, Joseph Upton, Lochart Wallace, George Williams and Jefferey Williams.

1860 -- Census, Moore County, NC Page 214, Gold Region Post Office
Sampson Cockman 41 M, Farmer, $500 Real Estate, $700 Personal Property, born in North Carolina
Elizabeth Cockman 35 F, born in North Carolina
Clarkey Cockman 18 F, born in North Carolina
Noah W. Cockman 15 M, born in North Carolina
John Mc. Cockman 5 M, born in North Carolina
Louisa Cockman 2 F, born in North Carolina

1861, May 21-Apr 1862 -- Record of Estates Book H Page 406-409, Moore County, NC
Estate of John Cockman, Dec'd. by Administrator George Cockman. *Items were purchased by the following*: Noah Richardson, Noah Cockman, D. Davis, Bryant Tyson, D.F. Muse, J.A. Stutts, Enoch Stewart, J.J. Richardson, Saml. Wallace, C.T. Horner, Mary Cockman, J.S. Ritter, L.M. Seawell, Emsley Wallace, Miles Muse, Thomas Horner, Sampson Cockman, S.W. Seawell, James Horner, M.A. Cockman, B.C. Brady, Z.B. Moore, D. Stutts, W. Wallace, J.H. Williams, Isham Wallace, Zeno Richardson, Armstrong Maness, N.R. Currie, John Muse, Henry Brown, George Horner, A. Brown, W. Williams and Wm. King.

1870 -- Census, Moore County, NC Page 577, Ritters Township, Carters Mill Post Office
Sampson Cockman 51 M, Farmer, $250 Real Estate, $250 Personal Property, born in North Carolina
Elizabeth Cockman 45 F, Housekeeper, born in North Carolina
Louiza Cockman 11 F, born in North Carolina
James A. Cockman 8 M, born in North Carolina
Susannah A. Cockman 6 F, born in North Carolina
William T. S. Cockman 4 M, born in North Carolina
Nancy Furr 79 F, born in North Carolina

1871, Oct 9 -- Deed Book 82 Page 6, Moore County, NC
Levi Sheffield and wife Jane/Jenny deeded W.T. Horner two tracts located on the Plank Road [1] 50 acres adjoining George Cockman, Sampson Cockman and his own line [2] 40 acres adjoining Rachel Dowdy and Noah Cockman. Danl. McIntosh was a witness.

1873, Jan 21 -- Land Grant #4487, Moore County, NC
Sampson Cockman received 42 acres located on the waters of Glade Branch adjoining Presley Caddell, George Cockman and Joseph Caddell. A.W. Cagle and Elisha Cagle were chain carriers.

1874, Oct 2 -- Orders and Decrees Book 1 Page 355, Moore County, NC
Sampson Cockman and George Cockman appointed to review the stock and crops of A.H. Williams Dec'd.to determine the amount available for a year's maintenance for widow Nannie Williams and their two children under ten.

1880 -- Census, Moore County, NC Page 337-B, Ritters Township
Sampson Cockman 60 M, Head, Widowed, Farmer, born in North Carolina, father & mother born in North Carolina
James Cockman 19 M, Son, Single, Works on Farm, born in North Carolina, father & mother born in North Carolina
Alice Cockman 17 F, Dau, Single, born in North Carolina, father & mother born in North Carolina

1884, Sep 9 -- Orders and Decrees Book 2 Page 251-254, Moore County, NC
Green Baily, John Jones and E.T. Williams appointed to partition the land of Lockey Wallace, Dec'd. located on Buffalo Creek and Meadow Branch adjoining Jas. Melton, Mrs. Jones, Horner, Stutts, Sampson Cockman and L.T. Seawell. Heirs: I.B. Maness and wife Mary E., Joseph Ritter and wife Ruth J., Lewis S. Maness and wife Martha A., Nannie M. Wallace, Vandie L. Wallace and Ella B. Wallace.

1884, Oct 16-Feb 23, 1886 -- Loose Estates and 1876-1885 Record of Accounts Page 542-544, Moore County, NC
Estate of Nancy Wallace Dec'd.by Administrator W.W. Wallace. *Items were purchased by the following*: Mac. Wallace, Josiah Person, Archd. Seawell, Saml. B. Wallace, John Garner, James Cockman, S.D. Wallace, Quimby Wallace, Sandy Black, Josiah Person, J.W. Horner, George Williams, Sampson Cockman, Charles Cockman, Mrs. Sarah Garner, Frank Wallace, Thomas Horner, Spinks Wallace, Archd. Seawell, J.T. Seawell, Charlie Wallace, Thomas Fry, Parker Stafford and J.M. Davis.

1887, Sep 12 -- Deed Book 5 Page 541, Moore County, NC
J.S. Cockman and wife L.A deeded Samp. Cockman, D.C. Barrett, Mary Cockman and W.C. Wallace, trustees for Flint Hill Missionary Baptist Church 3 acres [including graveyard] located on Meadow Branch adjoining Emsley Wallace. J.S. Barrett was a witness.

1887, Nov 11 -- Deed Book 59 Page 555, Moore County, NC
Polly Ann Lockwood and Jane Jackson (of Saline County, AR) appoint Sampson Cockman their power of attorney in the sale of the 40 acres that they received as an heir to their grandfather, John Cockman, Dec'd. Jno. L. Parham was a witness.

1888, Oct 28 -- Flint Hill Baptist Church Minutes, Moore County, NC
Sampson Cockman, K.C. Horner, Susan Wallace, Martha Maness and Sarah A. Wallace were admitted by experience.

1889, Dec 11 -- Orders and Decrees Book 3 Page 80-82, Moore County, NC
George Cockman, Admst. of Isham Wallace Dec'd. v. Samuel B. Wallace, W.W. Wallace, Quimby Wallace. John Wallace, Virgil Wallace and other heirs. Division of Land mentions neighbors Quimby Wallace, Samuel Wallace; 10a tract deeded from Joseph Wallace to Isham Wallace. Heirs: Lovedy Jane Horner, wife of James Horner, Heirs of Elizabeth Cockman, wife of Sampson Cockman (Wesly Cockman, James Cockman, Alice Cockman, Clarky Ann Horner, wife of W.T. Horner, Eliza Horner, wife of Thomas R. Horner), Heirs of Locky Wallace (Mary Maness, wife of Blake Maness, Martha Maness, wife of Lewis Maness, Ruth Ritter, wife of Joseph Ritter, Vandie Maness, wife of McLellan Maness, Ella Blake Wallace), Sarah Garner, wife of John Garner, Samuel B. Wallace, Mary Cockman, wife of Noah Cockman, W.W. Wallace, Clarky Cockman, Quimby Wallace, Emsley Wallace, Virgil Wallace, S.D. Wallace and John Wallace (of Arkansas)

1890 -- Branson's NC Business Directory Page 457-466, Moore County, NC
Smason Knockman [Cockman] listed as a farmer at Carters Mill Post Office

1893, Dec 23 -- Deed Book 22 Page 400, Moore County, NC
Sampson Cockman deeded S. Alice Cockman 40 acres adjoining George Cockman and N. Cockman. Jos. T. Seawell was a witness.

1900 -- Census, Moore County, NC Page 85, Ritters Township
Sampson Cockman 80 M, Nov 1819, Head, Widow, Farmer, born in North Carolina, father & mother born in North Carolina
Jonah Maness 25 M, 1875, SonL, Married-1yr, Farmer, born in North Carolina, father & mother born in North Carolina
Alice Maness 36 F, Sep 1863, Wife, Married-1yr, 1 Child(1 Living), born in North Carolina, father & mother born in North Carolina
Sherman L. Maness 9 M, Jul 1890, Son, Single, born in North Carolina, father & mother born in North Carolina

Sampson Cockman and Elizabeth Wallace had the following children:

+273	Clarkey Ann Cockman (1842-1919)
+274	Noah Wesley Cockman (1845-1929)
+275	Mary Sarah Cockman (1845-)
+276	Isham Pilgram Cockman (1851-)
+277	Adeline Haseltine Cockman (1852-1856)
+278	John Gillery Cockman (1855-1864)
+279	Lena Louisa Cockman (1859-1920)
+280	James Alexander Cockman (1861-1933)
+281	Alice Susannah Cockman (1863-1949)
+282	William E. Sherman Cockman (1865-1878)

55. **Mary Ann Wallace**, daughter of Isham Wallace and Nancy Furr, was born in 1826 and died on July 1, 1892 in Moore County, NC.[72] She married Noah Emsley Cockman, a brother to George and Sampson. Noah was born in 1824 and died after November 7, 1893. Noah and Mary lived on Buffalo Creek near the Robbins Crossroads and are likely buried in unmarked graves at Flint Hill.

Noah Cockman was known throughout the county for the elaborate names he gave to their children. Dr. H.B. Shields recounted, "Noah Cockman who lived on Buffalo Creek certainly had a fertile imagination, as regards names. He gave each of his children a generous supply and then probably some left over. In this family, I am sure nicknames would have been a blessing. Here follows the names of his children: The oldest boy was George Mendenhall Dempsy O'Laurence Henry Durant Isham Chambers; the second son, John Shuford Sampson Gadlock Wesley Swain Quimby Addison; the third son, Charles Riley O'Leonard Emmsley Rufus; the fourth son, Thomas Bias Noah Louweed; his daughters were Marthy Anne Alonzo; Maggie Delaney Deleeny Priscilla Alice; and Mary Jane Sarah Emmoline Camilla Hazeltine."[73] Another account from the *Chatham Record* detailed even more names, "Peculiar Names - A citizen of Moore county informs us that there is a family in that county, consisting of four brother and four sister, who together have 49 Christian names as follows: George Mendenhall Dempsey Laurance Henry Durant Isham Chalmers, Johnny Shuford Sampson Goudlock Wesley Swain Quimby Addison, James Lockey Silvanus Thomas Byas Noah Lewede, Charles Riley Arlewood Emsley Ruford, William Burton Ceclage, Martha Ann Alonzo, Loveday Arabella Alamina Eliza, Mary Jane Sarah Emeline Camilla Haseltine, and Maggie Delaney Delena Priscilla Alice. The same family owns a cat named Sib Sally Jane Jiglena Jerome Bruce Gus Sanders Silvanus Stutts. Now, if anybody can beat these names let us hear from him!"[74]

RECORDS OF NOAH COCKMAN AND MARY ANN WALLACE

1843, Apr 25 -- Land Grant #3324, Moore County, NC
David Cockman received 40 acres located on both sides of Locust Branch adjoining McKay, John Cockman, Griffith and James H. Muse. John Cockman and Noah Cockman were chain carriers.

1847 -- Tax List, Moore County, NC
Noah Cockman listed 1 white poll in District 9

1849 -- Tax List, District 9, Moore County, NC
Noah Cockman listed 1 white poll in District 9

1849, Nov-Jan 31, 1850 -- Record of Estates Book F Page 179-183
Estate of Joseph Cockman, Dec'd. by Noah Richardson, Administrator. *Items were purchased by the following*: Lydia Cockman, Geo. Williams, P. Morgan, Josiah Wallace, S. Cockman, A. Kelly, L.H. Ritter, M. Taylor, C. Horner, H.C. Harden, Jno. J. McIntosh, Geo. McIntosh, A. Fry, James Stutts, James Dowdy, Lindsay Stutts and N. Cockman.

1850 -- Census, Moore County, NC Page 239
Noah Cockman 24 M, Farmer, born in North Carolina
Mary Cockman 22 F, born in North Carolina
George Cockman 3 M, born in North Carolina
John Cockman 2 M, born in North Carolina

1852 -- Tax List, Moore County, NC
Noah Cockman listed 100 acres valued at $100 and 1 white poll on Buffalo Creek in District 9

1853 -- Tax List, District 9, Moore County, NC
Noah Cockman listed 100 acres valued at $100 and 1 white poll on Meadow Branch in District 9

1853, Jul 26 -- 1853-1856 Court of Pleas and Quarter Sessions, Moore County, NC Page 13
Ordered that Westley Wallace be appointed overseer of the road from George Moore's to the branch near McQueen's and work the following hands: Joseph Upton, Cornelius Dowdy, Zeno Cockman, Henry Melton, George Cockman, Noah Richardson & hands, Noah Cockman, David Cockman, Armstead Stutts, Isaac Williams, George W. Horner, John Jones and Quimby Wallace.

1854 -- Tax List, Moore County, NC
Noah Cockman listed 100 acres valued at $100 and 1 white poll in District 9

1855 -- Tax List, District 9, Moore County, NC
Noah Cockman listed 100 acres valued at $200 and 1 white poll located on Buffalo Creek in District 9

1855, Jul 27 -- 1853-1856 Court of Pleas and Quarter Sessions, Moore County, NC Page 370-372
Ordered that the following lands be sold at the courthouse on 4th Monday in September to pay back taxes: Noah Cockman 100 acres on Meadow Branch for 1853

1856, Feb 2 -- 1853-1856 Court of Pleas and Quarter Sessions, Moore County, NC Page 466
Ordered that William Stutts be appointed overseer of the road from George Moore's to the branch near McQueen's and work the following hands: Westley Wallace, Cornelius Dowdy, Zeno Cockman, Henry Melton, George Cockman, Sampson Cockman, Noah Cockman, David Cockman, Noah Richardson & hands, Armstead Stutts, Isaac Williams, G.W. Horner, John Jones, Quimby Wallace, Joseph Upton, Lochart Wallace, Geo. Williams and Jefferson Williams.

1857 -- Tax List, District 9, Moore County, NC
Noah Cockman listed 100 acres valued at $200 and 1 white poll located on Meadow Branch in District 9

1858, May 1 -- 1856-1858 Court of Pleas and Quarter Sessions, Moore County, NC Page 422
Ordered that George Cockman be appointed overseer of the road from George Moore's to the branch near McQueen's and work the following hands: William Stutts, Wesley Wallace, Cornelius Dowdy, Zeno Cockman, Henry Melton, Sampson Cockman, Noah Cockman, David Cockman, Noah Richardson hands, Armsted Stutts, Isaac Williams, G.W. Horner, John Jones, Quimby Wallace, Joseph Upton, Lochart Wallace, George Williams and Jefferey Williams.

1860 -- Census, Moore County, NC Page 214, Gold Region Post Office
Noah Cockman 37 M, Farmer, $300 Real Estate, $450 Personal Property, born in North Carolina
Mary Cockman 34 F, born in North Carolina
George Cockman 13 M, born in North Carolina
John S. Cockman 11 M, born in North Carolina
Martha A. Cockman 9 F, born in North Carolina
I. L. S. Cockman 7 F, born in North Carolina
William B. Cockman 5 M, born in North Carolina
L. A. B. Cockman 2 F, born in North Carolina

1861, May 21-Apr 1862 -- Record of Estates Book H Page 406-409, Moore County, NC
Estate of John Cockman, Dec'd. by Administrator George Cockman. *Items were purchased by the following*: Noah Richardson, Noah Cockman, D. Davis, Bryant Tyson, D.F. Muse, J.A. Stutts, Enoch Stewart, J.J. Richardson, Saml. Wallace, C.T. Horner, Mary Cockman, J.S. Ritter, L.M. Seawell, Emsley Wallace, Miles Muse, Thomas Horner, Sampson Cockman, S.W. Seawell, James Horner, M.A. Cockman, B.C.

Brady, Z.B. Moore, D. Stutts, W. Wallace, J.H. Williams, Isham Wallace, Zeno Richardson, Armstrong Maness, N.R. Currie, John Muse, Henry Brown, George Horner, A. Brown, W. Williams and Wm. King.

1870 -- Census, Moore County, NC Page 481, Bensalem Township, Curriesville Post Office
Noah Cockman 45 M, Farmer, $750 Real Estate, $250 Personal Property, born in North Carolina
Mary Cockman 42 F, born in North Carolina
Martha A. Cockman 19 F, born in North Carolina
Lovedy A. B. Cockman 12 F, born in North Carolina
Charles R. Cockman 9 M, born in North Carolina
Thomas B. N. L. Cockman 7 M, born in North Carolina
Mary J. S. E. C. H. Cockman 3 F, born in North Carolina

1871, Oct 9 -- Deed Book 82 Page 6, Moore County, NC
Levi Sheffield and wife Jane/Jenny deeded W.T. Horner two tracts located on the Plank Road [1] 50 acres adjoining George Cockman, Sampson Cockman and his own line [2] 40 acres adjoining Rachel Dowdy and Noah Cockman. Danl. McIntosh was a witness.

1876, Dec 22 -- Deed Book 82 Page 4, Moore County, NC
Adam Tyson and wife Ann deeded W.T. Horner two tracts [1] 50 acres adjoining John Jones, G.W. Horner and Williams [2] 40 acres adjoining Noah Cockman, Jones, Williams and Dowdy. A.H. McNeill was a witness.

1880 -- Census, Moore County, NC Page 212, Bensalem Township
Noah Cockman 56 M, Head, Married, Farmer, born in North Carolina, father & mother born in North Carolina
Marria Cockman 54 F, Wife, Married, Keeping House, born in North Carolina, father & mother born in North Carolina
Martha Cockman 29 F, Dau, Single, At Home, born in North Carolina, father & mother born in North Carolina
Wrily Cockman 19 M, Son, Single, At Home, born in North Carolina, father & mother born in North Carolina
Thomas L. Cockman 17 M, Son, Single, At Home, born in North Carolina, father & mother born in North Carolina
Sarrah Cockman 12 F, Dau, Single, At Home, born in North Carolina, father & mother born in North Carolina
Maggie Cockman 9 F, Dau, Single, At Home, born in North Carolina, father & mother born in North Carolina

1881, Mar 30 -- Deed Book 42 Page 430, Moore County, NC
Matthew and Lydia Williams deeded Henry Williams 125 acres adjoining their own line and Noah Cockman. H.B. Shields and J.M. Hunsucker were witnesses.

1881, Mar 30 -- Deed Book 49 Page 262, Moore County, NC
Matthew and Lydia Williams deeded John Williams 30 acres adjoining E. Wallace, Mary A. Carroll, Noah Cockman, L. Stutts, Wm. Jones and John Williams. J.M. Hunsucker was a witness.

1884 -- Branson's NC Business Directory Page 468-474, Moore County, NC
Noah Knockman [Cockman] listed as a farmer at Carters Mill Post Office

1887, Oct 27 -- Article, Chatham Record [Pittsboro, NC] Newspaper
"Peculiar Names - A citizen of Moore county informs us that there is a family in that county, consisting of four brother and four sister, who together have 49 Christian names as follows: George Mendenhall Dempsey Laurance Henry Durant Isham Chalmers, Johnny Shuford Sampson Goudlock Wesley Swain Quimby Addison, James Lockey Silvanus Thomas Byas Noah Lewede, Charles Riley Arlewood Emsley Ruford William Burton Ceclage, Martha Ann Alonzo, Loveday Arabella Alamina Eliza, Mary Jane Sarah Emeline Camilla Haseltine, and Maggie Delaney Delena Priscilla Alice. The same family owns a cat named Sib Sally Jane Jiglena Jerome Bruce Gus Sanders Silvanus Stutts. Now, if anybody can beat these names let us hear from him!"

1889, Dec 11 -- Orders and Decrees Book 3 Page 80-82, Moore County, NC
George Cockman, Admst. of Isham Wallace Dec'd. v. Samuel B. Wallace, W.W. Wallace, Quimby Wallace. John Wallace, Virgil Wallace and other heirs. Division of Land mentions neighbors Quimby Wallace, Samuel Wallace; 10a tract deeded from Joseph Wallace to Isham Wallace. Heirs: Lovedy Jane Horner, wife of James Horner, Heirs of Elizabeth Cockman, wife of Sampson Cockman (Wesly Cockman, James Cockman, Alice Cockman, Clarky Ann Horner, wife of W.T. Horner, Eliza Horner, wife of Thomas R. Horner), Heirs of Locky Wallace (Mary Maness, wife of Blake Maness, Martha Maness, wife of Lewis Maness, Ruth Ritter, wife of Joseph Ritter, Vandie Maness, wife of McLellan Maness, Ella Blake Wallace), Sarah Garner, wife of John Garner, Samuel B. Wallace, Mary Cockman, wife of Noah Cockman, W.W. Wallace, Clarky Cockman, Quimby Wallace, Emsley Wallace, Virgil Wallace, S.D. Wallace and John Wallace (of Arkansas)

PECULIAR NAMES.—A citizen of Moore county informs us that there is a family in that county, consisting of four brothers and four sisters, who together have 49 Christian names, as follows: George Mendenhall Demsey Laurance Henry Durant Isham Chalmers, Johnny Shuford Sampson Goudlock Wesley Swaim Quimby Addison, James Lockey Silvanus Thomas Byas Noah Lewede, Charles Riley Arleword Emsley Ruford William Burton Ceclage. Martha Ann Alonzo, Loveday Arabella Alamina Eliza, Mary Jane Sarah Emeline Camilla Haseltine; and Maggie Delaney Delena Priscilla Alice. The same family owns a cat named Sib Sally Jane Jiglena Jerome Bruce Gus Sanders Silvanus Stutts. Now, if anybody can beat these names let us hear from him!

1890 -- Branson's NC Business Directory Page 457-466, Moore County, NC
Additional Information can be found at www.MooreCountyWallaces.com

Noah Knockman [Cockman] listed as a farmer at Carters Mill Post Office

1892, July 13 -- Obituary, Biblical Recorder, Raleigh, NC
Died - Cockmon: Fell asleep in Jesus, near Flint Hill Baptist Church, Moore County, NC., July 1, 1892, our kind and beloved sister, Mary Cockmon, aged 67 years. Sister Cockmon joined the church at the age of 12 years...She will be greatly missed by her husband and children. Her funeral was conducted by the writer, KCH. [Editor's Note: KCH referred to her nephew, Rev. Kenneth Cassidy Horner.]

1893, Jan 27 -- Deed Book 80 Page 476, Moore County, NC
Noah Cockman deeded M.J. Brown 15 acres adjoining John Garner. C.R. Cockman and M.D. Cockman were witnesses.

1893, Dec 23 -- Deed Book 22 Page 400, Moore County, NC
Sampson Cockman deeded S. Alice Cockman 40 acres adjoining George Cockman and N. Cockman. Jos. T. Seawell was a witness.

1893, Nov 7 -- Mortgage Book 5 Page 22, Moore County, NC
Noah Cockman mortgaged Ann R. Burns 150 acres located on Buffalo Creek adjoining Isham Wallace, J. Stutts, James Garner, Mrs. Jones and William Stutts. J.R. Marley was a witness.

1898 -- Branson's Business Directory, Moore County, NC
Noah Cockman listed 105 acres valued at $200 located at Horners Post Office in Bensalem Township

COCKMON—Fell asleep in Jesus, near Flint Hill Baptist church, Moore county, N. C., July 1st, 1892, our kind and beloved sister, Mary Cockmon, aged sixty-seven years. Sister Cockmon joined the church at the age of twelve years. She lived a consistent christian life. All the time she strove and fought against the great adversary of souls. As a wife and mother she was kind, affectionate, and devoted. As a christian she was a model. Always ready to help build up the kingdom of Christ in the earth.. She never seemed to grow weary in well doing. As a neighbor she was ever ready and willing to do what she could to relieve those who were in trouble and distress. We are ready to exclaim as did Solomon in his proverb, " Who can find a virtuous woman? for her price is far above rubies. She stretcheth out her hand to the poor; yea, she reacheth forth her hands to the needy. She openeth her mouth with wisdom; and in her tongue is the law of kindness. Her children arise up and call her blessed; her husband also, and he praiseth her." She will be greatly missed by her husband, children, and many friends who knew her. As her christian character was without spot or blemish, we believe that we can safely say, therefore, that she is in the land of bliss, where there is no more sorrow, pain or death, and where parting is unknown. Her funeral was conducted by the writer.
K. C. H.

Noah Cockman and Mary Ann Wallace had the following children:

+283	George MDOHDIC Cockman (1847-1907)
+284	John SSGWSQA "Jack" Cockman (1848-1912)
+285	Martha Anna Alonzo Cockman (1851-)
+286	I. Louise S. Cockman (1853-)
+287	William Burton Ceclage Cockman (1855-)
+288	Lovedy Arabella Alamina Eliza Cockman (1857-)
+289	Charles Riley O'Leonard Emsley Rufus Cockman (1860-1922)
+290	Thomas Bias Noah Louweed Cockman (1862-1942)
+291	Mary Jane "Sarah" Emmoline Camilla Hazeltine Cockman (1867-1944)
+292	Maggie Delaney Deleeny Cockman (1877-1957)

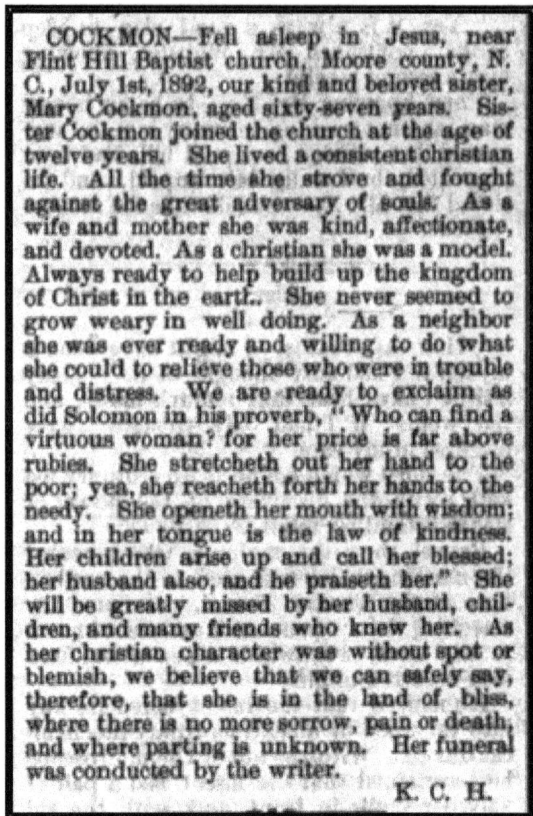

56. **William Wesley Wallace**, son of Isham Wallace and Nancy Furr, was born on June 1, 1828 and died on October 4, 1906 in Greensboro, Guilford County, NC and was buried in Robbins, Moore County, NC at Tabernacle United Methodist Church.[75] Wes first married **Elizabeth Melton**, daughter of James Melton (1805-1857) and Temperance Horner (1814-aft 1880). Elizabeth was born on March 1, 1830, died on October 15, 1875, and was also buried in Robbins, Moore County, NC at Tabernacle United Methodist Church. After Elizabeth died, Wes married **Margaret Louise "Lou" Seawell** on February 22, 1880 in Moore County, NC. Lou was the daughter of Isaac McLendon Seawell (1810-bef 1870) and Catherine Patterson (1815-c. 1875). She was born in 1857 in Moore County, NC, died on October 18, 1932 in Greensboro, Guilford County, NC and buried in Greensboro, Guilford County, NC at Green Hill Cemetery.[76] [77]

RECORDS OF WILLIAM WESLEY WALLACE

1846, Apr 28 -- 1844-1847 Court of Pleas and Quarter Sessions, Moore County, NC Page 319
Ordered that George W. Horner be appointed overseer of the road from George Moore's to the branch near McQueen's and work the following hands: Elisha Cagle, James Melton, Cornelius Mathews, George Williams, David Cockman, Joseph Cockman, Sampson Cockman, Isaac Williams, George Cockman, Noah Richardson and hands, Seburn Jones, Abram Hunsucker, James Deaton, Quimby Sowell, William Richardson, John Jones, Allan Jones, John W. Jackson, Westly Wallace, Chesly Horner, Enoch Williams, William Reaves and Richard Phillips.

1847, Oct 25 -- 1847-1849 Court of Pleas and Quarter Sessions, Moore County, NC Page 81

Ordered that Josiah Cockman be appointed overseer of the road from George Moore's to the branch near McQueen's and work the following hands: George W. Horner, Elisha Cagle, James Melton, Cornelius Mathews, George Williams, David Cockman, Joseph Cockman, Sampson Cockman, Isaac Williams, George C. Cockman, Noah Richardson & hands, Seburn Jones, Abram Hunsucker, James Deaton, Quimby Sowell, Wm. Richardson, John Jones, Allan Jones, John W. Jackson, Westley Wallace, Chesley Horner, Enoch Williams, William Reaves, Richard Phillips and James Jones.

1848, Oct 24 -- 1847-1849 Court of Pleas and Quarter Sessions, Moore County, NC Page 274
Ordered that John Jones be appointed overseer of the road from George Moore's to the branch near McQueen's and work the following hands: Josiah Cockman, George W. Horner, Elisha Cagle, James Melton, Cornelius Mathews, George Williams, David Cockman, Joseph Cockman, Sampson Cockman, Isaac Williams, George Cockman, Noah Richardson and hands, Seburn Jones, Abram Hunsucker, James Deaton, Quimby Sowell, William Richardson, Allen Jones, Westley Wallace, Chesley Horner, Enoch Williams, William Reaves, Richard Phillips and James Jones.

1850, Nov 12 -- Census, Moore County, NC Page 238
Isham Wallis 49 M, Farmer, $1600 Real Estate, born in North Carolina
Nancy Wallis 44 F, born in North Carolina
Westley Wallis 21 M, Farmer, born in North Carolina
Quimby Wallis 18 M, Farmer, born in North Carolina
Lockey Wallis 14 M, born in North Carolina
Emsley Wallis 12 M, born in North Carolina
Samuel Wallis 9 M, born in North Carolina
Jane Wallis 6 F, born in North Carolina
Sampson Wallis 5 M, born in North Carolina
Virgil Wallis 4 M, born in North Carolina
John Wallis 2/12 M, born in North Carolina

1853, Jul 26 -- 1853-1856 Court of Pleas and Quarter Sessions, Moore County, NC Page 13
Ordered that Westley Wallace be appointed overseer of the road from George Moore's to the branch near McQueen's and work the following hands: Joseph Upton, Cornelius Dowdy, Zeno Cockman, Henry Melton, George Cockman, Noah Richardson & hands, Noah Cockman, David Cockman, Armstead Stutts, Isaac Williams, George W. Horner, John Jones and Quimby Wallace.

1854 -- Tax List, Moore County, NC
Wesley Wallace listed 1 white poll in District 9

1855 -- Tax List, Moore County, NC
Wesly Wallace listed 1 white poll in District 9 on Buffalo Cree

William Wesley Wallace
(Courtesy of Hazel Kennedy Hamilton, Robbins, NC)

1856, Feb 2 -- 1853-1856 Court of Pleas and Quarter Sessions, Moore County, NC Page 466
Ordered that William Stutts be appointed overseer of the road from George Moore's to the branch near McQueen's and work the following hands: Westley Wallace, Cornelius Dowdy, Zeno Cockman, Henry Melton, George Cockman, Sampson Cockman, Noah Cockman, David Cockman, Noah Richardson & hands, Armstead Stutts, Isaac Williams, G.W. Horner, John Jones, Quimby Wallace, Joseph Upton, Lochart Wallace, Geo. Williams and Jefferson Williams.

1857 -- Tax List, Moore County, NC
Westly Wallas listed 1 white poll in District 9 on Buffalo Creek

1858, May 1 -- 1856-1858 Court of Pleas and Quarter Sessions, Moore County, NC Page 422
Ordered that George Cockman be appointed overseer of the road from George Moore's to the branch near McQueen's and work the following hands: William Stutts, Wesley Wallace, Cornelius Dowdy, Zeno Cockman, Henry Melton, Sampson Cockman, Noah Cockman, David Cockman, Noah Richardson hands, Armsted Stutts, Isaac Williams, G.W. Horner, John Jones, Quimby Wallace, Joseph Upton, Lochart Wallace, George Williams and Jefferey Williams.

1860, Aug 31 -- Census, Moore County, NC Page 220, Gold Region Post Office
Wesly Wallace 29 M, Farmer, $500 Personal Property, born in North Carolina
Elizabeth Wallace 29 F, born in North Carolina
Margaret Wallace 7 F, born in North Carolina
Martha J. Wallace 5 F, born in North Carolina

1860, Sep 1 -- Agricultural Census, Moore County, NC Page 43, Gold Region Post Office
Wesly Wallace listed 35 acres improved, 0 acres unimproved valued at $50

1865, Nov 26 -- Deed Book 127 Page 545, Moore County, NC
Isam Wallis deeded Emsley Wallis 100 acres located on Buffalo Creek adjoining Wesley Wallis.
Danl. McIntosh was a witness.

1870, Aug 6 -- Agricultural Census, Moore County, NC Page 5, Ritters Township, Carters Mills
Post Office
W. W. Wallis listed 75 acres improved valued at $300
1870, Aug 10 -- Census, Moore County, NC Page 578, Ritters Township, Carters Mill Post Office
W.W. Wallis 41 M, Farmer, $700 Real Estate, $500 Personal Property, born in North Carolina
Elizabeth Wallis 39 F, born in North Carolina
Margaret L. Wallis 16 F, born in North Carolina
James C. Wallis 7 M, born in North Carolina
William C. Wallis 3 M, born in North Carolina
Lydia Melton 32 F, born in North Carolina

(photographed April 7, 2010)

1872, Dec 12 -- Orders and Decrees Book 1 Page 159-165, Moore County, NC
K. Matheson, J.J. Richardson and Samuel McIntosh appointed to partition the land of James
Melton, Dec'd. as follows: [Lot 1] W.W. Wallace assignee of James Melton 15 acres on home
tract adjoining Matheson and 8 acres on chalk level tract; [Lot 2] Lovedy A. Melton 15 acres on
home tract and 8 acres on chalk level tract; [Lot 3] W.W. Wallace and wife Elizabeth 15 acres
on home tract and 9 acres on chalk level tract; [Lot 4] Candis E. Melton 15 acres on home tract
and 8 acres on chalk level tract; [Lot 5] Lydia Melton 15 acres on home tract and 9 acres on chalk
level tract; [Lot 6] George W. Melton 15 acres on home tract and 8 acres on chalk
level tract; [Lot 7] Emsley Wallace and wife Priscilla 16 acres on home tract and
9 acres on chalk level tract; [Lot 8] George M. Cockman and wife Lucinda 16
acres on home tract and 8 acres on chalk level tract; [Lot 9] John Cockman and
wife Nancy Jane 16 acres on home tract and 15 acres on chalk level tract; [Lot
10] Margaret E. Melton 16 acres on home tract and 9 acres on chalk level tract;
[Lot 11] Daniel McNeill and wife Amanda 16 acres on home tract and 8 acres on
chalk level tract; [Lot 12] Samuel B. Wallace and wife Tempy 160 acres on home
tract adjoining S.B. Wallace and James Melton and 8 acres on the chalk level tract
and Tempy Wallace. The more valuable dividends are charged to pay the others
to ensure an equitable division.

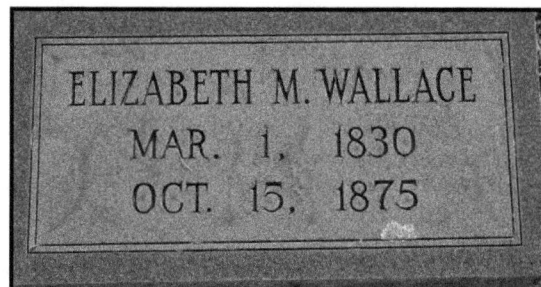

1874, Nov 28 -- 1875-1878 Judgment Docket #2, Moore County, NC Page 91-93
#2049 George Melton and Others Ex Parte. Judgments: W.W. Wallace and wife,
Daniel McNeill and wife, Emsly Wallace and wife, Lydia Melton, Saml. Wallace
and wife, John Cockman and wife, George Melton, Geo. M. Cockman and wife,
James Melton, Margaret E. Melton, Lovedy Adline Melton, Candis Ellen Melton.
Division of Land occurred on Dec 12, 1872.

1875, Feb -- Superior Court Minute Docket Book M, Moore County, NC Page
380
Tempy Melton v. W.W. Wallace et ux -- Petition for Dower

1880, Mar 11 -- Marriages, The Farmer and Mechanic, Raleigh, NC
On Sunday, Feb 22, Mr. W. W. Wallace, of Moore County, and Miss M. L. Seawell

1880, Jun 14 -- Census, Moore County, NC Page 337-B, Ritters Township
W.W. Wallace 52 M, Head, Married, Farmer, born in North Carolina, father &
mother born in North Carolina
Lou Wallace 23 F, Wife, Married, Keeping House, born in North Carolina, father

(Courtesy of Find A Grave)

& mother born in North Carolina
Charlie Wallace 18 M, Son, Single, Works on Farm, born in North Carolina, father &
mother born in North Carolina
Clark Wallace 12 M, Son, Single, Works on Farm, born in North Carolina, father & mother born in North Carolina

Laura Wallace 6 F, Dau, Single, born in North Carolina, father &
mother born in North Carolina
Nash Jordan 17 M, (black), Servant, Single, born in North Carolina,
father & mother born in North Carolina

1880, Jun 14 -- Agricultural Census, Moore County, NC Page 11,
Ritters Township
W. W. Wallace listed 75 acres improved fields; 200 acres
unimproved wooded valued at $1000

1884 -- Branson Business Directory, Moore County, NC
W. W. Wallace listed as a farmer at Carters Mills Post Office

1884, Oct 16 -- 1880-1885 Administrator's Bonds, Moore County,
NC Page 68
Wesley W. Wallace appointed Administrator of the Estate of Nancy
Wallace, Dec'd. with Lewis Grimm and J.A. Worthy as securities.

1884, Oct 16-Feb 23, 1886 -- Loose Estates and 1876-1885 Record
of Accounts Page 542-544, Moore County, NC
Estate of Nancy Wallace Dec'd. by Administrator W.W. Wallace.
Items were purchased by the following: Mac. Wallace, Josiah Person,
Archd. Seawell, Saml. B. Wallace, John Garner, James Cockman, S.D.
Wallace, Quimby Wallace, Sandy Black, Josiah Person, J.W. Horner,
George Williams, Sampson Cockman, Charles Cockman, Mrs. Sarah
Garner, Frank Wallace, Thomas Horner, Spinks Wallace, Archd.
Seawell, J.T. Seawell, Charlie Wallace, Thomas Fry, Parker Stafford
and J.M. Davis.

1889, Dec 11 -- Orders and Decrees Book 3 Page 80-82, Moore
County, NC
George Cockman, Admst. of Isham Wallace Dec'd. v. Samuel B.
Wallace, W.W. Wallace, Quimby Wallace. John Wallace, Virgil
Wallace and other heirs. Division of Land mentions neighbors
Quimby Wallace, Samuel Wallace; 10a tract deeded from Joseph
Wallace to Isham Wallace. Heirs: Lovedy Jane Horner, wife of James
Horner, Heirs of Elizabeth Cockman, wife of Sampson Cockman
(Wesly Cockman, James Cockman, Alice Cockman, Clarky Ann
Horner, wife of W.T. Horner, Eliza Horner, wife of Thomas R. Horner),
Heirs of Locky Wallace (Mary Maness, wife of Blake Maness, Martha
Maness, wife of Lewis Maness, Ruth Ritter, wife of Joseph Ritter, Vandie
Maness, wife of McLellan Maness, Ella Blake Wallace), Sarah Garner, wife
of John Garner, Samuel B. Wallace, Mary Cockman, wife of Noah
Cockman, W.W. Wallace, Clarky Cockman, Quimby Wallace, Emsley
Wallace, Virgil Wallace, S.D. Wallace and John Wallace (of Arkansas)
1890 -- Branson Business Directory, Moore County, NC
W. W. Wallace listed as a farmer at Carters Mills Post Office

**Margaret Louise Seawell Wallace and
daughters. [L-R] Hattie Wallace, Martha
Wallace, Lou Wallace, Belle Wallace and Nannie
Wallace**
(Courtesy of Mike Cross, Panama City, FL)

1892, Dec 6 -- Deed Book 24 Page 8, Moore County, NC
W. W. & Louisa M. Wallace, J. C. Wallace, Laura L. Wallace deeded L. B. Maness 75 acres located in Ritters township adjoining Jack
Cockman, S.D. Wallace and Isham Wallace. E.T. Williams was a witness.

1898 – Branson's Business Directory. Moore County, NC
W.W. Wallace listed 266 acres valued at $350 located at Horners Post Office in Ritters Township

1900, Jun 13 -- Census, Moore County, NC Page 86, Ritters Township
Wesley W. Wallace 71 M, Jun 1828, Head, Married-20yrs, Farmer, born in North Carolina, father & mother born in North Carolina
Lou Wallace 46 F, Jul 1853, Wife, Married-20yrs, 9 Children(9 Living), born in North Carolina, father & mother born in North Carolina
Maggie E. Wallace 18 F, Aug 1881, Dau, Single, born in North Carolina, father & mother born in North Carolina
Jessie T. Wallace 17 M, Apr 1883, Son, Single, At School, born in North Carolina, father & mother born in North Carolina
John Wallace 14 M, Apr 1886, Son, Single, born in North Carolina, father & mother born in North Carolina
Martha J. Wallace 11 F, Aug 1888, Dau, Single, born in North Carolina, father & mother born in North Carolina
Kinnie C. Wallace 10 M, Dec 1889, Son, Single, born in North Carolina, father & mother born in North Carolina
Annie B. Wallace 7 F, Nov 1892, Dau, Single, born in North Carolina, father & mother born in North Carolina
Eddie L. Wallace 5 M, Jan 1895, Son, Single, born in North Carolina, father & mother born in North Carolina
Nannie Wallace 3 F, Jan 1897, Dau, Single, born in North Carolina, father & mother born in North Carolina

Hattie Wallace 3 F, Jan 1897, Dau, Single, born in North Carolina, father & mother born in North Carolina

1906, Oct 11 -- Obituary, Carthage Blade [Carthage, NC] Newspaper
"Mr. Wesley W. Wallace died at his home in Greensboro Friday Oct 5th and his body brought to this county and the burial took place in the cemetery of Tabernacle church at Elise Saturday. Mr. Wallace had lived the larger part of his life in this, his native county. A few years ago he moved his family to Greensboro where he lived until his death at the age of 79. Mr. Wallace was a respected citizen and reared a useful family of children among whom are Rev. W.C. Wallace of Hamer, SC and Mr. J.C. Wallace of Carthage."

William Wesley Wallace and Elizabeth Melton had the following children:

+293	Margaret L. Wallace (1854-1876)
+294	Martha Wallace (1855-)
+295	James Charles Wallace (1863-1930)
+296	William Clark Wallace (1867-1937)
+297	Laura Louise Wallace (1873-1931)

William Wesley Wallace and Margaret Louise "Lou" Seawell had the following children:

+298	Maggie Elizabeth Wallace (1881-1969)
+299	Jesse Lee Wallace (1883-1946)
+300	John Stellings Wallace (1886-1939)
+301	Martha Jane Wallace (1888-1956)
+302	Kenneth Carson "Kennie" Wallace (1889-1972)
+303	Anne Belle Wallace (1892-1963)
+304	Edward Lee Wallace (1895-1966)
+305	Mary Hattie Wallace (1896-1967)
+306	Nannie Florence Wallace (1896-1978)

Death of Mr. W. W. Wallace.

Mr. Wesley W. Wallace died at his home in Greensboro, Friday, Oct. 5th and his body brought to this county and the burial took place in the cemetery of Tabernacle church at Elise Saturday.

Mr. Wallace had lived the larger part of his life in this, his native county. A few years ago he moved with his family to Greensboro where he lived until his death at the age of 79.

Mr. Wallace was a respected citizen and reared a useful family of children among whom are Rev. W. C. Wallace of Hamer, S. C., and Mr. J. C. Wallace of Carthage.

57. **Sarah Ann Wallace**, daughter of Isham Wallace and Nancy Furr, was born on January 20, 1830 and died on June 25, 1899 in Moore County, NC. Sarah married **John Garner**, son of James Garner (1792-1882) and Margaret "Peggy" Davis (1797-1867), who was born on May 24, 1825 and died on February 2, 1905 in Moore County, NC. John and Sarah were buried in Moore County, NC at Flint Hill Baptist Church.

RECORDS OF JOHN GARNER AND SARAH WALLACE

1847 -- Tax List, Moore County, NC
John Garner listed 155 acres valued at $250 and 1 white poll on Buffalo Creek in District 9

1847, Oct 25 -- 1847-1849 Court of Pleas and Quarter Sessions, Moore County, NC Page 82
Ordered that George Hunsucker be appointed overseer of the road from the [Bear] creek at Kennedy's Bridge to the fork of the Salem Road and work the following hands: Milly Jones' hands, Nancy Furr's hands, John Cagle's hands, Noah Brewer, John H. Stutts, Stephen Davis, James Davis, Wm. C. Stutts, Wm. H. Stutts, James Stutts, George Stutts, Leonard C. Stutts, George Williams, Linzey Stutts, Wm. Williams, Upshur [Furr], R.K. Smith's hands, Stephen Williams, Wesley Williams, Thomas Morris, Robert W. Goldston, James Gordon, E. Bryant's hands, H. Kelly, John Garner and Lorenzo Williams.

1848, Apr 27 -- 1847-1849 Court of Pleas and Quarter Sessions, Moore County, NC Page 199
Ordered that William H. Stutts be appointed overseer of the road from the fork of the Fayetteville Road at George Cockmans to the Bars at Thomas Williams' south of his house and work the following hands: James Stutts, Lindsay Stutts, George Stutts, George Williams, William Williams, Westley Williams, John H. Stutts and John Garner.

1849 -- Tax List, Moore County, NC
John Garner listed 155 acres valued at $250 and 1 white poll on Buffalo Creek in District 9

1850, Nov 12 -- Census, Moore County, NC Page 238
John Gardiner 24 M, Farmer, $140 Real Estate, born in North Carolina
Sarah Gardiner 20 F, born in North Carolina
Stephen Gardiner 3/12 M, born in North Carolina

1851, Oct 28 -- 1851-1853 Court of Pleas and Quarter Sessions, Moore County, NC
Page 97
Ordered that James Stutts be appointed overseer of the road from the fork at the
Fayetteville Road at Geo. Cockmans to the Bars of Thomas Williams and work the
following hands: James Stutts, Lindsey Stutts, George Williams, William Williams,
Westley Williams, Alstin Williams, John Garner, Edmond Garner, Leonard Stutts and
Lindsey Williams.

1852 -- Tax List, Moore County, NC
John Garner listed 80.33 acres valued at $240 and 1 white poll on Meadow Branch
on District 9

1854 -- Tax List, Moore County, NC
John Garner listed 155 acres valued at $250 and 1 white poll in District 9

1854, Oct 24 -- 1853-1856 Court of Pleas and Quarter Sessions, Moore County, NC
Page 205
Ordered that Leonard Stutts be appointed overseer of the road from the ford at
George Cockmans to the Bars of Thomas Williams and work the following hands:
James Stutts, Lindsey Stutts, George Williams, John Garner, Edmond Garner, Lindsey
Williams, Henry Yow, William Garner, Henry Williams, Branson Williams and Derick
Yow.

1855 -- Tax List, Moore County, NC
John Garner listed 1 white poll on Buffalo Creek in District 9

(photographed Jul 16, 2014)

1857 -- Tax List, Moore County, NC
John Garner listed 155 acres valued at $250 and 1 white poll on Buffalo Creek in
District 9

1858, Jul 31 -- 1856-1858 Court of Pleas and Quarter Sessions, Moore County, NC
Page 475
Ordered that John Gardner be appointed overseer of the road from the fork at
George Cockman to the Bar at Thomas Williams and work the following hands:
James Stutts, Lindsy Stutts, John Garner, Edmond Garner, Lindsey Williams, Henry
Yow, Henry Williams, Branson Williams, Derick Yow, Alex. Williams, Harbert
Williams, Andrew Yow and Wm. Yow.

1859, Sep 23 -- Deed Book 11, Page 429, Moore County, NC
Wm. A. Brown deeded Abner Brown 105 acres located on Buffalo Creek adjoining
Richardson. Elisha Cagle and John Garner were witnesses.

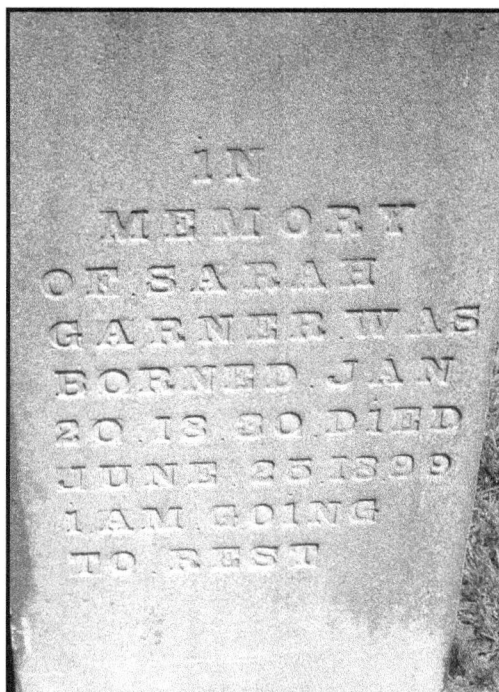

1860, Aug 31 -- Census, Moore County, NC Page 220, Gold Region Post Office
John Garner 30 M, Farmer, $500 Real Estate, born in North Carolina
Sarah Garner 29 F, born in North Carolina
Stephen Garner 11 M, born in North Carolina
Leonard Garner 9 M, born in North Carolina
James Garner 5 M, born in North Carolina
Martha J. Garner 4 F, born in North Carolina
Peter Garner 2 M, born in North Carolina
Mary A. Garner 1/12 F, born in North Carolina

1870, Aug 4 -- Census, Moore County, NC Page 575, Bensalem Township, Carters Mill Post Office
John Garner 45 M, Farmer, $700 Real Estate, $500 Personal Property, born in North Carolina
Sarah Garner 40 F, born in North Carolina
Stephen Garner 21 M, born in North Carolina
Leonard Garner 19 M, born in North Carolina
James D. Garner 15 M, born in North Carolina
Martha Garner 13 F, born in North Carolina

Laney Garner 5 M, born in North Carolina
Elias Garner 4 M, born in North Carolina
Anna Garner 2 F, born in North Carolina

1880, Jun 14 -- Census, Moore County, NC Page 337-B, Ritters Township
John Gardner 52 M, Head, Married, Farmer, born in North Carolina, father & mother born in North Carolina
Sarah Garner 48 F, Wife, Married, Keeping House, born in North Carolina, father & mother born in North Carolina
Lane Garner 17 M, Son, Single, Works on Farm, born in North Carolina, father & mother born in North Carolina
Elias Garner 15 M, Son, Single, Works on Farm, born in North Carolina, father & mother born in North Carolina
Annie Garner 12 F, Dau, Single, born in North Carolina, father & mother born in North Carolina
Duncan Garner 9 M, Son, Single, born in North Carolina, father & mother born in North Carolina
Fannie Garner 7 F, Dau, Single, born in North Carolina, father & mother born in North Carolina

1882, Mar 4 -- Deed Book 85 Page 226, Moore County, NC
L.T. Seawell and wife Catherine and Albert Seawell and wife Mary A. deeded James W. Horner four tracts [1] 120 acres adjoining William Jones, Danl. McNeill and John Garner [2] 39.50 acres known as lot #1 in William Jones division [3] 39.50 acres known as lot #2 in William Jones division [4] 39.50 acres known as lot #13 in William Jones division. A.H. McNeill was a witness.

1884, Oct 16-Feb 23, 1886 -- Loose Estates and 1876-1885 Record of Accounts Page 542-544, Moore County, NC
Estate of Nancy Wallace Dec'd. by Administrator W.W. Wallace. *Items were purchased by the following*: Mac. Wallace, Josiah Person, Archd. Seawell, Saml. B. Wallace, John Garner, James Cockman, S.D. Wallace, Quimby Wallace, Sandy Black, Josiah Person, J.W. Horner, George Williams, Sampson Cockman, Charles Cockman, Mrs. Sarah Garner, Frank Wallace, Thomas Horner, Spinks Wallace, Archd. Seawell, J.T. Seawell, Charlie Wallace, Thomas Fry, Parker Stafford and J.M. Davis.

1885, Nov 5 -- Deed Book 39 Page 38-41, Moore County, NC
J.J. Wicker, Sheriff deeded John Garner 121.5 acres located on Buffalo Creek adjoining Isham Wallace.

1889, Dec 11 -- Orders and Decrees Book 3 Page 80-82, Moore County, NC
George Cockman, Admst. of Isham Wallace Dec'd. v. Samuel B. Wallace, W.W. Wallace, Quimby Wallace. John Wallace, Virgil Wallace and other heirs. Division of Land mentions neighbors Quimby Wallace, Samuel Wallace; 10a tract deeded from Joseph Wallace to Isham Wallace. Heirs: Lovedy Jane Horner, wife of James Horner, Heirs of Elizabeth Cockman, wife of Sampson Cockman (Wesly Cockman, James Cockman, Alice Cockman, Clarky Ann Horner, wife of W.T. Horner, Eliza Horner, wife of Thomas R. Horner), Heirs of Locky Wallace (Mary Maness, wife of Blake Maness, Martha Maness, wife of Lewis Maness, Ruth Ritter, wife of Joseph Ritter, Vandie Maness, wife of McLellan Maness, Ella Blake Wallace), Sarah Garner, wife of John Garner, Samuel B. Wallace, Mary Cockman, wife of Noah Cockman, W.W. Wallace, Clarky Cockman, Quimby Wallace, Emsley Wallace, Virgil Wallace, S.D. Wallace and John Wallace (of Arkansas)

1893, Jan 27 -- Deed Book 80 Page 476, Moore County, NC
Noah Cockman deeded M.J. Brown 15 acres adjoining John Garner. C.R. Cockman and M.D. Cockman were witnesses.

1898 – Branson's Business Directory. Moore County, NC
John Garner listed 377 acres valued at $825 located at Horners Post Office in Ritters Township

1900 -- Census, Moore County, NC Page 85-B, Ritters Township
John Garner 72 M, May 1828, Widowed, born in North Carolina, father & mother born in North Carolina

1905, Feb 7 -- 1896-1908 Administrator's Bonds, Moore County, NC Page 394-395
Stephen Garner appointed Administrator of the Estate of John Garner, Dec'd. with C.F. Garner and A.H. McNeill as securities. Heirs: Steven Garner, Lenard Garner, J.D. Garner, Lindsy Burns and wife Martha Burns, Laney Garner, Frany Yow and wife Annie Yow, Fanny Williams and husband Offie Williams, Duncan Garner and the heirs of Elias Garner.

1905, Oct 10 -- Deed Book 35 Page 592-595, Moore County, NC
Samuel B. Wallace and wife T.L. deeded J.D. Cockman 266 acres located on both sides of the Long Meadow Branch adjoining Jack Cockman, John Jones, Blake Maness and Jno. Garner. Harry S. Jones was a witness.

1906, Mar 21 -- Deed Book 33 Page 515, Moore County, NC
Leonard Garner and wife Ella deeded Geo. W Horner their interest in 100 acres of the estate of John Garner adjoining Leonard Garner and Emsley Wallace.

1906, Jun 4 -- 1896-1908 Administrator's Bonds, Moore County, NC Page 476-477
C.E. Cockman appointed Administrator of the Estate of Isham Wallace, Dec'd. with A.J. Lawhon and W.L. Ritter as securities. Heirs: Wes Wallace, Clarky Ann Cockman, Quimby Wallace, Lock Wallace, Sam Wallace, Bird Wallace, Emsly Wallace, Lane Wallace, John Wallace, Sarah Garner, Jane Horner, Elizabeth Cockman and Mary A. Cockman.

John Garner and Sarah Ann Wallace had the following children:

+307	Stephen Garner (1850-1928)	
+308	Leonard Garner (1851-1922)	
+309	James Douglas Garner (1855-1935)	
+310	Martha Jane Garner (1856-1933)	
+311	Peter Garner (1858-)	
+312	Mary Ann Garner (1860-)	
+313	Sampson Delaney Garner (1863-1937)	
+314	Elias "Lizard" Garner (1865-1898)	
+315	Anna Margaret Garner (1867-1917)	
+316	Duncan G. Garner (1871-1945)	
+317	Fannie Garner (1873-1938)	

58. **Quimby Wallace**, son of Isham Wallace and Nancy Furr, was born in 1832 in Moore County, NC and died on October 15, 1895 in Moore County, NC. He married **Arabella Stewart** on December 30, 1855 in Moore County, NC.[78] Arabella Stewart, daughter of William Stewart (1803-aft 1880) and Annie Shields (1813-), was born on April 24, 1836 in Moore County, NC, died on July 17, 1928 in Moore County, NC and was buried at Flint Hill Baptist Church.[79] Quimby was conscripted into Company D, 49th Regiment during the Civil War but Shadrach Maness (1848-1864) served as his substitute.[80] Quimby is rumored to have been buried in a shared family cemetery off Old Carthage Road near the entrance to Camp Reeves Boy Scout Camp.[81]

RECORDS OF QUIMBY WALLACE

1850, Nov 12 -- Census, Moore County, NC Page 238
Isham Wallis 49 M, Farmer, $1600 Real Estate, born in North Carolina
Nancy Wallis 44 F, born in North Carolina
Westley Wallis 21 M, Farmer, born in North Carolina
Quimby Wallis 18 M, Farmer, born in North Carolina
Lockey Wallis 14 M, born in North Carolina
Emsley Wallis 12 M, born in North Carolina
Samuel Wallis 9 M, born in North Carolina
Jane Wallis 6 F, born in North Carolina
Sampson Wallis 5 M, born in North Carolina
Virgil Wallis 4 M, born in North Carolina
John Wallis 2/12 M, born in North Carolina

1853, Jul 26 -- 1853-1856 Court of Pleas and Quarter Sessions, Moore County, NC Page 13
Ordered that Westley Wallace be appointed overseer of the road from George Moore's to the branch near McQueen's and work the following hands: Joseph Upton, Cornelius Dowdy, Zeno Cockman, Henry Melton, George Cockman, Noah Richardson & hands, Noah Cockman, David Cockman, Armstead Stutts, Isaac Williams, George W. Horner, John Jones and Quimby Wallace.

1855 -- Tax List, Moore County, NC
Quimby Wallace listed 1 white poll on Buffalo Creek in District 9

1855, Dec 30 -- Record of Marriages, Moore County, NC Page 31
Quimby Wallace and Arabella Stewart were married by K. Matheson, JP.

1856, Feb 2 -- 1853-1856 Court of Pleas and Quarter Sessions, Moore County, NC Page 466

Ordered that William Stutts be appointed overseer of the road from George Moore's to the branch near McQueen's and work the following hands: Westley Wallace, Cornelius Dowdy, Zeno Cockman, Henry Melton, George Cockman, Sampson Cockman, Noah Cockman, David Cockman, Noah Richardson & hands, Armstead Stutts, Isaac Williams, G.W. Horner, John Jones, Quimby Wallace, Joseph Upton, Lochart Wallace, Geo. Williams and Jefferson Williams.

1857 -- Tax List, Moore County, NC
Quimby Wallas listed 1 white poll on Buffalo Creek in District 9

1858, May 1 -- 1856-1858 Court of Pleas and Quarter Sessions, Moore County, NC Page 422
Ordered that George Cockman be appointed overseer of the road from George Moore's to the branch near McQueen's and work the following hands: William Stutts, Wesley Wallace, Cornelius Dowdy, Zeno Cockman, Henry Melton, Sampson Cockman, Noah Cockman, David Cockman, Noah Richardson hands, Armsted Stutts, Isaac Williams, G.W. Horner, John Jones, Quimby Wallace, Joseph Upton, Lochart Wallace, George Williams and Jefferey Williams.

1860, Aug 31 -- Census, Moore County, NC Page 220, Gold Region Post Office
Quimby Wallace 28 M, Farmer, born in North Carolina
Arabella Wallace 26 F, born in North Carolina
William W. Wallace 3 M, born in North Carolina
Martha A. Wallace 2 F, born in North Carolina
Sharruck Maner 12 M, born in North Carolina

1860, Sep 1 -- Agricultural Census, Moore County, NC Page 43, Gold Region Post Office
Quimby Wallace listed 45 acres improved, 0 acres unimproved valued at $

1863, Jan 27 -- Civil War Service Records
Shadrack Maness enlisted in Company D, 49th Regiment as a substitute for Quimby Wallace

1870, Jul 11 -- Agricultural Census, Moore County, NC Page 3, Bensalem Township, Carters Mill Post Office
Quimby Wallis listed 40 acres improved, 70 acres wooded valued at $150

1870, Jul 15 -- Census, Moore County, NC Page 482, Bensalem Township, Carters Mill Post Office
Quimby Wallis 38 M, Farmer, $200 Real Estate, $1000 Personal Property, born in North Carolina
Arabella Wallis 33 F, born in North Carolina
William W. Wallis 13 M, born in North Carolina
Martha A. Wallis 11 F, born in North Carolina
Nancy Wallis 7 F, born in North Carolina
Rufus Wallis 5 M, born in North Carolina
Charlotte Wallis 3 F, born in North Carolina
Eli Wallis 8/12 M, born in North Carolina

1880, Jun 28 -- Census, Moore County, NC Page 211, Bensalem Township
Quimby Wallace 50 M, Head, Married, Farmer/Planter, born in North Carolina, father & mother born in North Carolina
Arabella Wallace 44 F, Wife, Married, Keeping House, born in North Carolina, father & mother born in North Carolina
William Wallace 22 M, Son, Single, At Home, born in North Carolina, father & mother born in North Carolina
Martha Wallace 21 F, Dau, Single, At Home, born in North Carolina, father & mother born in North Carolina
Nancy Wallace 18 F, Dau, Single, At Home, born in North Carolina, father & mother born in North Carolina
Rufus Wallace 15 M, Son, Single, At Home, born in North Carolina, father & mother born in North Carolina
Charlott Wallace 12 F, Dau, Single, At Home, born in North Carolina, father & mother born in North Carolina
Eli Wallace 10 M, Son, Single, At Home, born in North Carolina, father & mother born in North Carolina
Eliza A. Wallace 8 F, Dau, Single, At Home, born in North Carolina, father & mother born in North Carolina
James Y. Wallace 4 M, Son, Single, born in North Carolina, father & mother born in North Carolina
Bettie Wallace 1 F, Dau, Single, born in North Carolina, father & mother born in North Carolina

1880, Jun 28 -- Agricultural Census, Moore County, NC Page 20, Bensalem Township
Quimby Wallace listed 50 acres improved fields, 2 acres improved meadows, 90 acres unimproved wooded valued at $140

1884, Oct 16-Feb 23, 1886 -- Loose Estates and 1876-1885 Record of Accounts Page 542-544, Moore County, NC
Estate of Nancy Wallace Dec'd.by Administrator W.W. Wallace. *Items were purchased by the following*: Mac. Wallace, Josiah Person, Archd. Seawell, Saml. B. Wallace, John Garner, James Cockman, S.D. Wallace, Quimby Wallace, Sandy Black, Josiah Person, J.W. Horner, George Williams, Sampson Cockman, Charles Cockman, Mrs. Sarah Garner, Frank Wallace, Thomas Horner, Spinks Wallace, Archd. Seawell, J.T. Seawell, Charlie Wallace, Thomas Fry, Parker Stafford and J.M. Davis.

1886, Jan 6 -- Deed Book 85 Page 350, Moore County, NC
W.B. Furr deeded L.S. Furr 120 acres located on both sides of Flag Creek adjoining Quimby Wallace. J.F. Cole was a witness.

1886, Jan 6 -- Deed Book 112 Page 512, Moore County, NC

L.S. Furr and wife C.J deeded J.B. Davis 80 acres located west of Flag Creek adjoining Quimby Wallace and former Upshur Furr land. J.F. Cole was a witness.

1888, Nov 27 -- Deed Book 3 Page 281-298, Moore County, NC
Wm. Black, Sheriff deeded A.H. McNeill and Lewis Grimm numerous tracts pursuant to judgements against Wm. B. Richardson including 550 acres located on Richland Creek and Buffalo Creek known as the Grove place whereon Samuel Barrett now lives adjoining Wesley Williams, David Jones, James Deaton and Quimby Wallace.

1889, Dec 11 -- Orders and Decrees Book 3 Page 80-82, Moore County, NC
George Cockman, Admst. of Isham Wallace Dec'd. v. Samuel B. Wallace, W.W. Wallace, Quimby Wallace. John Wallace, Virgil Wallace and other heirs. Division of Land mentions neighbors Quimby Wallace, Samuel Wallace; 10a tract deeded from Joseph Wallace to Isham Wallace. Heirs: Lovedy Jane Horner, wife of James Horner, Heirs of Elizabeth Cockman, wife of Sampson Cockman (Wesly Cockman, James Cockman, Alice Cockman, Clarky Ann Horner, wife of W.T. Horner, Eliza Horner, wife of Thomas R. Horner), Heirs of Locky Wallace (Mary Maness, wife of Blake Maness, Martha Maness, wife of Lewis Maness, Ruth Ritter, wife of Joseph Ritter, Vandie Maness, wife of McLellan Maness, Ella Blake Wallace), Sarah Garner, wife of John Garner, Samuel B. Wallace, Mary Cockman, wife of Noah Cockman, W.W. Wallace, Clarky Cockman, Quimby Wallace, Emsley Wallace, Virgil Wallace, S.D. Wallace and John Wallace (of Arkansas)

1893, Mar 6 -- Deed Book 10, Page 338-340, Moore County, NC
George Cockman, administrator of Isham Wallace, Dec'd. deeded I.W.H. Cockman two tracts. [1] 142 acres located on Meadow Branch adjoining Quimby Wallace, Samuel Wallace and L. Wallace. [2] 10 acres located on Meadow Branch and the Rutherford Road adjoining Armstrong Maness and deeded to Isham Wallace by Josiah Wallace. A.H. McNeill was a witness.

1895, Nov 27 -- Record of Widows' Year's Support, Moore County, NC
Arabella Wallace, widow of Quimby Wallace allowed $52.35 year's support

1896, Apr 6 -- 1889-1897 Administrator's Bonds, Moore County, NC Page 82
R.J. Morgan appointed Administrator of the Estate of Quimby Wallace, Dec'd. with K.M. McDonald and B. Deaton as securities.

1896, Apr 6 -- Probate Docket, Moore County, NC
R.J. Morgan, Admst. of Quimby Wallace v. W.W. Wallace, Martha Wallace, Eli Wallace heirs, Elias & Charlotte Williams, John & Alice Hooker, James Wallace

1898 -- Branson's Business Directory, Moore County, NC
J.L. Wallace (agent for Q. Wallace heirs) listed 277 acres valued at $340 at Mt. Carmel Post Office in Bensalem Township

1899, Nov 15 -- Deed Book 21, Page 358-360, Moore County, NC
Mausia C. Wallace, Charlie A. Wallace, Effie Wallace, A.B. Wallace, F.A. Wallace, B.H. Wallace, C.E. Wallace, R.F. Wallace and W.H. Wallace deeded J.M. Worth 100 acres (Timber Deed) known as the home tract adjoining Jas. W. Horner, Lewis Maness and the heirs of Quimby Wallace. Charlie and Wade Wallace now live on this tract and it is the undivided tract of S.D. Wallace.

1903, Feb 17 -- 1896-1908 Administrator's Bonds, Moore County, NC Page 282-283
J.F. Cole appointed Administrator of the Estate of Quimby Wallace, Dec'd. with Gilbert McLeod and S.M. Jones as securities after death of former Administrator R.J. Morgan. Heirs: W.W. Wallace, Nancy Morgan, Charlotte Williams, wife of Elias Williams, Bertha Wallace, James Quimby Wallace, Eli Wallace, Alice Hooker, wife of John Hooker and James Lewis Wallace.

1903, Mar 9-Jun 12 -- Record of Dowers Book A Page 78-85, Moore County, NC
Arabella Wallace, widow of Quimby Wallace Dec'd. v. W.W. Wallace, Nancy Morgan, Elias Williams and wife Charlotte, heirs of Eli Wallace Dec'd. of Montgomery County, NC (Bertha Wallace, James Quimby Wallace, Eli Wallace), John Hooker and wife Alice and James Wallace, heirs at law. Quimby Wallace died Oct 15, 1895 possessing the following land: [1] 110 acres located on the head of Meadow Branch known as the home place [2] 117 acres Quimby Wallace purchased from Margaret Kennedy 1882 adjoining Noah Williams, Alexander Williams, Martin Morgan and John Williams [3] 29.5 acres located on both sides of the Horsepen Branch of Richland Creek purchased from Margaret J. Williams 1880 [4] tract located on both sides of Horsepen Branch of Richland Creek purchased from Martha F. Fry 1880 and adjoining tract #3 above. C.C. Hunsucker, J.D. Henson and M. McL. Kelly allotted Arabella Wallace the 110 acre home tract as her dower.

1906, Mar 13 -- Deed Book 33 Page 512, Moore County, NC
John M. Wallace [Perry County, AR] deeded Geo. W Horner his 1/3 interest and 52 2/3 of 158 acre tract known as the Isham Wallace homestead adjoining the heirs of Lockey Wallace, Isham Cockman and Quimby Wallace. Land includes the 21 acres deeded to Elizabeth Cockman prior to Isham Wallace's death and the 21 acres provided to John M. Wallace and Clarkie Cockman of the remaining 137 acres.

1906, Jun 4 -- 1896-1908 Administrator's Bonds, Moore County, NC Page 476-477
C.E. Cockman appointed Administrator of the Estate of Isham Wallace, Dec'd. with A.J. Lawhon and W.L. Ritter as securities. Heirs: Wes Wallace, Clarky Ann Cockman, Quimby Wallace, Lock Wallace, Sam Wallace, Bird Wallace, Emsly Wallace, Lane Wallace, John Wallace, Sarah Garner, Jane Horner, Elizabeth Cockman and Mary A. Cockman.

Quimby Wallace and Arabella Stewart had the following children:

+318	William Wesley Wallace (1857-1944)	
+319	Martha A. Wallace (1859-bef 1900)	
+320	Nancy Wallace (1862-1928)	
+321	Rufus Wallace (1865-1892)	
+322	Charlotte Wallace (1867-1938)	
+323	Eli Wallace (1869-bef 1903)	
+324	Eliza Alice Wallace (1871-1940)	
+325	James Lewis Wallace (1875-1950)	
+326	Betty Wallace (1879-)	

59. **Dempsey Wallace**, son of Isham Wallace and Nancy Furr, was born on February 21, 1833. He died on October 12, 1839 in Moore County, NC and was buried in Moore County, NC at Flint Hill Baptist Church.

60. **Lochart "Lockey" Wallace**, son of Isham Wallace and Nancy Furr, was born on February 6, 1836 and died on June 11, 1884 in Moore County, NC. He married **Susan Muse** on December 27, 1855 in Moore County, NC.[82] Susan was the daughter of Jesse Muse (1804-1878) and Nancy J. (1810-1880). She was born on February 23, 1836 and died on February 18, 1911 in Moore County, NC. They were buried in Moore County, NC at Flint Hill Baptist Church.

RECORDS OF LOCKEY WALLACE

1850, Nov 12 -- Census, Moore County, NC Page 238
Isham Wallis 49 M, Farmer, $1600 Real Estate, born in North Carolina
Nancy Wallis 44 F, born in North Carolina
Westley Wallis 21 M, Farmer, born in North Carolina
Quimby Wallis 18 M, Farmer, born in North Carolina
Lockey Wallis 14 M, born in North Carolina
Emsley Wallis 12 M, born in North Carolina
Samuel Wallis 9 M, born in North Carolina
Jane Wallis 6 F, born in North Carolina
Sampson Wallis 5 M, born in North Carolina
Virgil Wallis 4 M, born in North Carolina
John Wallis 2/12 M, born in North Carolina

1855, Dec 27 -- Record of Marriages, Moore County, NC Page 30
Lochart Wallace and Susan Muse were married by J. Bean, JP

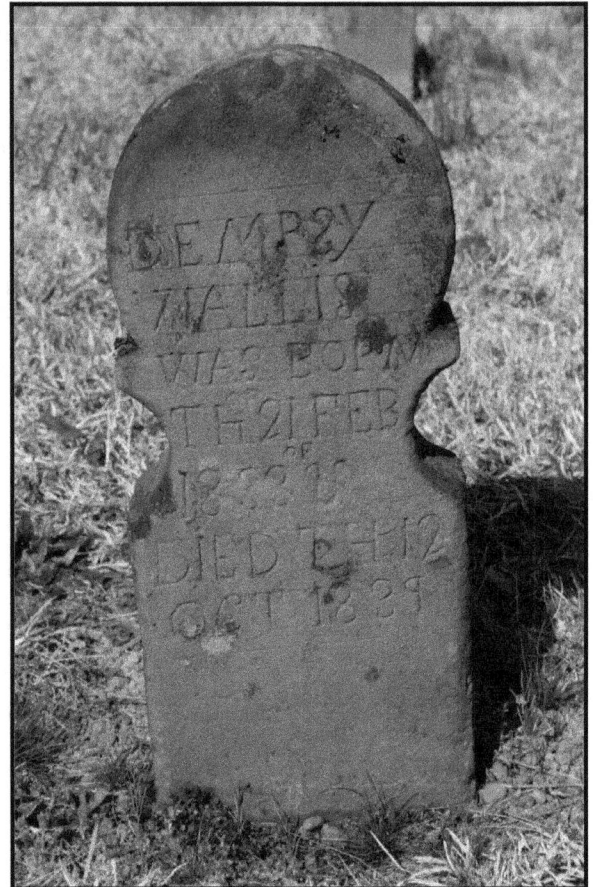

(photographed April 7, 2010)

1856, Feb 2 -- 1853-1856 Court of Pleas and Quarter Sessions, Moore County, NC Page 466
Ordered that William Stutts be appointed overseer of the road from George Moore's to the branch near McQueen's and work the following hands: Westley Wallace, Cornelius Dowdy, Zeno Cockman, Henry Melton, George Cockman, Sampson Cockman, Noah Cockman, David Cockman, Noah Richardson & hands, Armstead Stutts, Isaac Williams, G.W. Horner, John Jones, Quimby Wallace, Joseph Upton, Lochart Wallace, Geo. Williams and Jefferson Williams.

1858, May 1 -- 1856-1858 Court of Pleas and Quarter Sessions, Moore County, NC Page 422
Ordered that George Cockman be appointed overseer of the road from George Moore's to the branch near McQueen's and work the following hands: William Stutts, Wesley Wallace, Cornelius Dowdy, Zeno Cockman, Henry Melton, Sampson Cockman, Noah Cockman, David Cockman, Noah Richardson hands, Armsted Stutts, Isaac Williams, G.W. Horner, John Jones, Quimby Wallace, Joseph Upton, Lochart Wallace, George Williams and Jefferey Williams.

1860, Aug 31 -- Census, Moore County, NC Page 220, Gold Region Post Office
Locky Wallace 25 M, Farmer, $350 Personal Property, born in North Carolina
Susan Wallace 21 F, born in North Carolina
Mary Wallace 2 F, born in North Carolina

1860, Sep 1 -- Agricultural Census, Moore County, NC Page 43, Gold Region Post Office
Locky Wallace listed 20 acres improved, 0 acres unimproved valued at $35

Additional Information can be found at www.MooreCountyWallaces.com

1870, Aug 6 -- Agricultural Census, Moore County, NC Page 5, Ritters Township, Carters Mills Post Office
Lockey Wallis listed 60 acres improved, 130 acres wooded, 10 acres other unimproved valued at $300

1870, Aug 9 -- Census, Moore County, NC Page 578, Ritters Township, Carters Mill Post Office
Lockey Wallis 34 M, Farmer, $400 Real Estate, $1000 Personal Property, born in North Carolina
Susan Wallis 34 F, born in North Carolina
Mary E. Wallis 12 F, born in North Carolina
Martha A. Wallis 7 F, born in North Carolina
Rutha J. Wallis 3 F, born in North Carolina
Nancy M. Wallis 4/12 F, born in North Carolina

1880, Jun 14 -- Agricultural Census, Moore County, NC Page 10, Ritters Township
Lock Wallace listed 100 acres improved Fields, 50 acres unimproved wooded, 30 acres unimproved non-wooded valued at $400

1880, Jun 25 -- Census, Moore County, NC Page 337-B, Ritters Township
Lock Wallace 45 M, Head, Married, Farmer, born in North Carolina, father & mother born in North Carolina
Susan Wallace 45 F, Wife, Married, Keeping House, born in North Carolina, father & mother born in North Carolina
Rutha Wallace 12 F, Dau, Single, born in North Carolina, father & mother born in North Carolina
Nannie Wallace 10 F, Dau, Single, born in North Carolina, father & mother born in North Carolina
Vandie L. Wallace 7 F, Dau, Single, born in North Carolina, father & mother born in North Carolina
Ella B. Wallace 3 F, Dau, Single, born in North Carolina, father & mother born in North Carolina

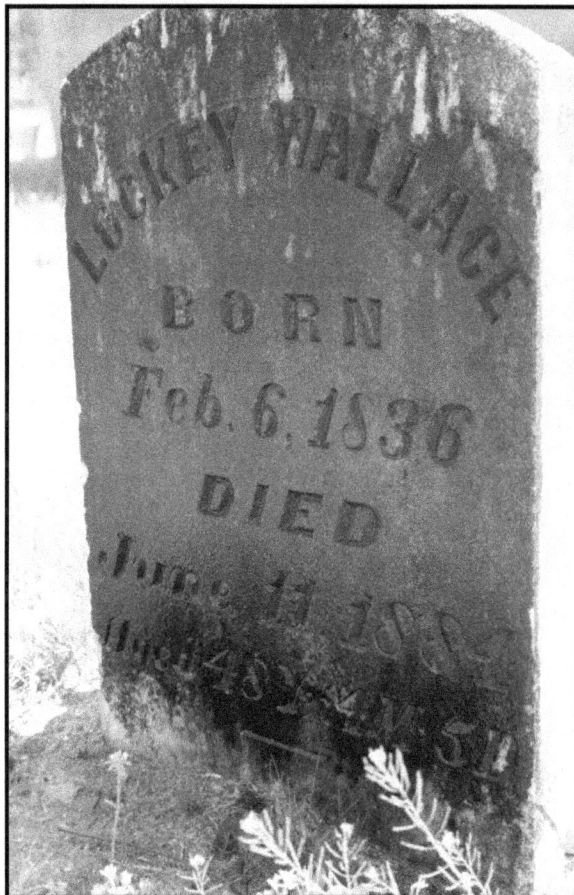

(photographed Jul 16, 2014)

1884 -- Branson Business Directory, Moore County, NC
Lack Wallace listed as a farmer at Carters Mills Post Office

1884, Aug 19 -- 1880-1885 Administrator's Bonds, Moore County, NC Page 66
Susan Wallace appointed Administrator of the Estate of Lockey Wallace, Dec'd. with I.B. Maness, Joseph Ritter and Lewis S. Maness as securities.

1884, Aug 19 -- 1869-1897 Probate Docket #1, Moore County, NC Page 238-239
#470 Susan Wallace, Widow of Locky Wallace v. I.B. Maness and wife Mary Eliza, Joseph Ritter and wife Ruthy Jane Florence, Lewis Maness and wife Martha, Nannie Margaret Wallace, Vandy Lee Wallace, Ella Blake Wallace; Petition for Dower. #471 I.B. Maness and wife Mary Eliza v. Joseph and Rutha Jane Florence Ritter, Lewis and Martha Maness, Nannie Margaret Wallace, Vandy Lee Wallace, Ella Blake Wallace. Petition for Partition. Susan Wallace appointed Guardian ad litem for minor heirs.

1884, Sep 9 -- Orders and Decrees Book 2 Page 251-254, Moore County, NC
Green Baily, John Jones and E.T. Williams appointed to partition the land of Lockey Wallace, Dec'd. located on Buffalo Creek and Meadow Branch adjoining Jas. Melton, Mrs. Jones, Horner, Stutts, Sampson Cockman and L.T. Seawell. Heirs: I.B. Maness and wife Mary E., Joseph Ritter and wife Ruth J., Lewis S. Maness and wife Martha A., Nannie M. Wallace, Vandie L. Wallace and Ella B. Wallace.

1886, Feb 11 -- Deed Book 49 Page 448, Moore County, NC
Joseph Ritter and wife Ruth J. Ritter deeded Lewis S. Maness 31 acres located on Buffalo Creek adjoining Stutts being lot #3 in the division of Lockey Wallace Dec'd. E.T. Williams was a witness.

1889, Dec 11 -- Orders and Decrees Book 3 Page 80-82, Moore County, NC
George Cockman, Admst. of Isham Wallace Dec'd. v. Samuel B. Wallace, W.W. Wallace, Quimby Wallace. John Wallace, Virgil Wallace and other heirs. Division of Land mentions neighbors Quimby Wallace, Samuel Wallace; 10a tract deeded from Joseph Wallace to Isham Wallace. Heirs: Lovedy Jane Horner, wife of James Horner, Heirs of Elizabeth Cockman, wife of Sampson Cockman (Wesly Cockman, James Cockman, Alice Cockman, Clarky Ann Horner, wife of W.T. Horner, Eliza Horner, wife of Thomas R. Horner), Heirs of Locky Wallace (Mary Maness, wife of Blake Maness, Martha Maness, wife of Lewis Maness, Ruth Ritter, wife of Joseph Ritter, Vandie Maness, wife of McLellan Maness, Ella Blake Wallace), Sarah Garner, wife of John Garner, Samuel B. Wallace, Mary Cockman, wife of Noah Cockman, W.W. Wallace, Clarky Cockman, Quimby Wallace, Emsley Wallace, Virgil Wallace, S.D. Wallace and John Wallace (of Arkansas)

1898 -- Branson's Business Directory, Moore County, NC
Susan Wallace listed 194 acres valued at $265 located at Horners Post Office in Bensalem Township

1906, Mar 13 -- Deed Book 33 Page 512, Moore County, NC
John M. Wallace [Perry County, AR] deeded Geo. W Horner his 1/3 interest and 52 2/3 of 158 acre tract known as the Isham Wallace homestead adjoining the heirs of Lockey Wallace, Isham Cockman and Quimby Wallace. Land includes the 21 acres deeded to Elizabeth Cockman prior to Isham Wallace's death and the 21 acres provided to John M. Wallace and Clarkie Cockman of the remaining 137 acres.

1906, Jun 4 -- 1896-1908 Administrator's Bonds, Moore County, NC Page 476-477
C.E. Cockman appointed Administrator of the Estate of Isham Wallace, Dec'd. with A.J. Lawhon and W.L. Ritter as securities. Heirs: Wes Wallace, Clarky Ann Cockman, Quimby Wallace, Lock Wallace, Sam Wallace, Bird Wallace, Emsly Wallace, Lane Wallace, John Wallace, Sarah Garner, Jane Horner, Elizabeth Cockman and Mary A. Cockman.

Lochart "Lockey" Wallace fathered the following child out of wedlock. We are unsure who the mother was:

+327   Isaac Frank Wallace (1856-1925)

Lochart "Lockey" and Susan Muse had the following children:

+328   Mary Ellis Wallace (1857-1920)
+329   Male Wallace (1860-1860)
+330   Martha Ann Wallace (1862-1902)
+331   Rutha Jane Florence Wallace (1867-1936)
+332   Nancy Margaret "Nannie" Wallace (1870-c. 1888)
+333   Vandie Lee Wallace (1874-1929)
+334   Ella Blake Wallace (1877-1950)

61. **Emsley Thomas Wallace**, son of Isham Wallace and Nancy Furr, was born on February 15, 1837 in Moore County, NC and died on July 25, 1918 in Moore County, NC.[83] He married **Priscilla Melton**, daughter of James Melton (1805-1857) and Temperance Horner (1814-aft 1880) on August 25, 1859.[84] Priscilla was born on September 29, 1834 in Moore County, NC and died on August 18, 1909 in Moore County, NC. They were buried in Moore County, NC at Emsley Wallace Cemetery.

The Wallaces and the Meltons were close neighbors and there were four marriages between the families. Emsley and three of his brothers went on to marry four of James Melton's daughters. Emsley and Priscilla lived just southeast of the town of Robbins at the end of the present day Rushwood Road. Like many of his time, Emsley spent much of his life farming the 230 acres of land he owned near Buffalo Creek.

Emsley and Priscilla had seven daughters and one son during their life together: Elizabeth Jane (1861-1934), Sindy Ann (1863-1930), Louisa Elipher (1865-1944), Sarah Catherine (1868-1941), Callie Lee (1870-1916), Addie Florence (1872-1943), Lucian Thomas (1876-1935), and Martha (1878-1955). Most of their children married and raised large families in upper Moore County, NC as well.

Elizabeth Jane married Baxter Williams and produced 9 children. Sindy Ann married Lineberry B. Maness and had 8 children. Louisa married James P. Garner and they had six children and lived in the vicinity of the present-day Yates Thagard Baptist Church near Vass, NC. Sarah Catherine married George Williams (brother to Baxter Williams) and produced a family of eleven children. Callie Lee married James Britt and died at 46 years old without children. Addie Florence lived with Emsley throughout her life and never married. Lucian Thomas was the only son of the union. He married Nancy Jane Williams and they produced seven children including my grandfather Mallie Wallace. Martha was the youngest child of Emsley and Priscilla and she married Daniel Bethune Britt, Jr. (brother to James Britt). They lived on Cedar Lane in Eagle Springs and had two children. Emsley and Priscilla both lived long lives – Emsley dying at 81 and Priscilla at 74.

In addition, and arguably more important than Emsley's biography, he was the inspiration and focus of admiration of a young boy. My grandfather, Mallie Wallace, was enamored with his grandfather from the very beginning. Looking back it is easy to see why; Emsley was colorful character, standing over six feet tall, possessing a long white beard and a deep, booming voice. His wife, Priscilla, had died in 1909 a year before my grandfather was born and from an early age, Mallie would spend as many waking hours and nights with Emsley as his parents would let him. He was his constant companion and side kick. Emsley truly had a soft spot for his young grandson and Mallie worshipped the ground Ems walked on.

Emsley told him the stories of the old Wallaces like Everet, Isham, Enoch, Josiah, Aaron, and so many others who had passed long ago. He lectured as to how the Wallaces were related to every family in upper Moore County except the Morgans and the Moores. Not surprising, it turns out that we are related to both families, but apparently Ems and his brothers had a few run-ins with them and had declared them off-limits. An undated account found among Artemus Caddell's personal papers mention a fight between "the Moores, Wes Wallis, Ems Wallis, Nick Shields and Ike Wallis" saying "you've never seen such a time." [85] This may explain why we aren't "related" to the Moores...

Emsley told of how he and several of his brothers (Wes, Sam, and Lockey) had laid in the creek beds during the Civil War to avoid the conscription officers. Only Emsley's brother Sampson Delaney "Lane" Wallace fought in the War. It was often speculated that he did not volunteer, but just had been "found."

While Emsley Wallace was admired and loved by his grandson Mallie, he was not generally thought of as a kind and loving man and was more often described by

Emsley Wallace and Priscilla Melton

others as ill-tempered and even as "meaner than the Devil." One of the more telling stories of Emsley's character and personal notoriety was the story about the time that he claimed to have met the Devil. One-night walking home late from a gathering, Emsley claimed to have met the Devil on a narrow path. He knew it to be the Devil, because he could see his pitchfork tail, horns and red eyes in the light of the moon. The Devil growled and told Emsley to step aside so he could pass. Emsley proceeded to go "eyeball to eyeball" with him and eventually the Devil stepped aside and let ol' Ems pass to which began the "legend" that he actually was meaner than the Devil.

As such, Emsley and his only son, Lucian, never particularly got along well. As a direct result, Lucian unfortunately did not fare as well in his son Mallie's memory. My grandfather often recalled Lucian as a hard man to get to know and one who spent too much time working and not enough time talking and visiting with people. Mallie's brothers and sisters though remembered their father in a much more favorable light, especially when compared to ol' Ems. Lucian was well loved by his children, a highly regarded member of the community, he took handwriting classes and had wonderful penmanship in a day when few did, and even sang in the choir at Tabernacle Methodist Church. In comparison, Mallie's siblings were leery of Emsley and probably much like the Devil got out of his way and allowed him to pass.

One particular example of Lucian and Emsley's chilly relationship is the location of Emsley's grave. When Emsley's wife, Priscilla, died she was buried at the end of Emsley's field beside a small grove of trees. As time passed, Emsley decided that he wanted to be buried at the new, nicer cemetery at Tabernacle Church when he died. Lucian bid his time and when Emsley died, Lucian declared defiantly, "if the old field was good enough for Mam it is good enough for you" and the old field is where Emsley remains. In the end, my grandfather Mallie always believed that Emsley haunted Lucian for that act.

My grandfather would tell us many stories about Emsley and his rough and tumble brothers. Two of the most memorable involved his younger brothers, Byrd and John. In 1914, Virgil Spinks "Byrd" Wallace's young daughter, Dora Wallace, was killed when she was badly burned in a fire. Byrd moved his family into Emsley's house for a few days after her death. During the next couple of days, Byrd and Emsley got into an argument that became so heated that Byrd packed up the family and left. As they were walking away from Emsley's house, Byrd and Emsley were yelling back and forth at each other. Emsley got so mad that he picked up a rock and threw it at Byrd and his family narrowly missing them. According to my grandfather Mallie, Ems threw the rock so hard that it knocked a plank off a nearby corn crib. All this towards his closest brother who had just lost his daughter. Maybe the Devil was smarter than we thought.

(photographed Jul 23, 2020)

Another was the time Emsley's brother John M. Wallace came in on the train from Arkansas to stay with Emsley for a few weeks. My grandfather and Emsley had waited at the station until midnight for the train to arrive. John was the youngest of Emsley's siblings and had been one of his favorites. John had gotten married to Candace Melton (Priscilla's younger sister) when he was young and she was pregnant. Not long after, John slipped off and headed west. In Arkansas, John got along well, was married a few times and raised a family. He had also recently been elected as a Judge. After his arrival by train, John and Emsley spent the entire day catching up and planning his stay. Then they got the word that John's former family, currently living in Rockingham, had heard about his arrival and were headed their way. John slipped away that night on the midnight train much the same way he had arrived. It is interesting to note that John gave a quite embellished biographical sketch of his family in *Goodspeed's Biographical and Historical Memoirs of Central Arkansas* in which he listed his brother Emsley, a successful member of the state legislature.[86] Maybe my grandfather Mallie wasn't the only one with a high opinion of ol' Ems after all.

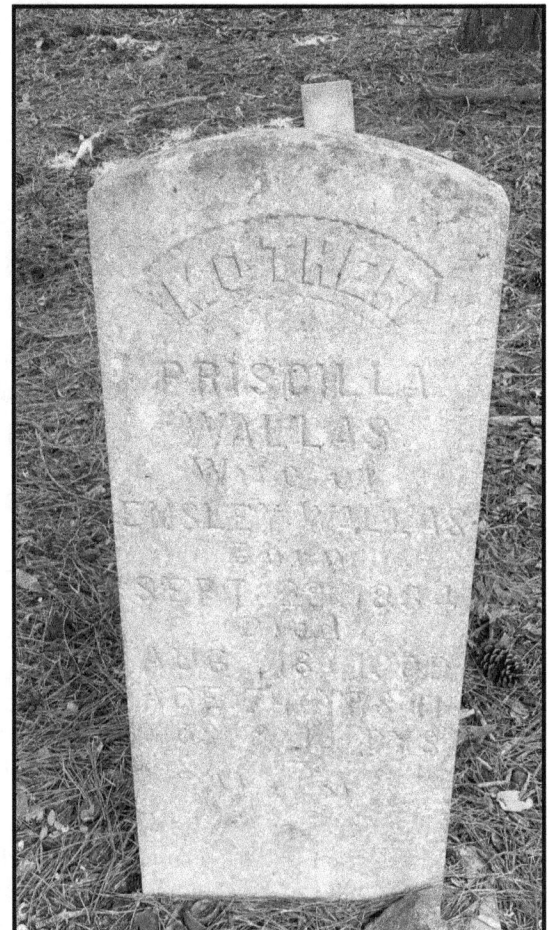

One final story that has always been one of my favorites and helps demonstrate that while Emsley had a soft spot for his young grandson Mallie in his final years – the Devil still would have been wise to step aside and let him pass. Duncan Garner was the son of John Garner and Sarah Ann Wallace and a nephew to Emsley. Duncan owned land that adjoined Emsley's property down by Buffalo Creek. One day Duncan was cutting down a tree and it happened to fall down over on Emsley's property and tear up Emsley's fence. When Duncan came to tell Emsley that it had happened and that he intended to rebuild the fence, Ems flew into a rage right in front of my grandfather. Mallie told of how an eighty year old man picked up his walking cane and went to beating Duncan with it. Duncan, a mere forty-five years old and quite a strapping fellow himself, took off running down the road with Emsley close behind in hot pursuit swinging the walking cane. Mallie said he had never seen anything like it. Duncan went on to press charges but later dropped them due to the embarrassment that he was assaulted by an eighty year old man.

The stories are just a few of many that Emsley told Mallie. One of the most amazing facts was that when Emsley died, Mallie was only eight years old. What an effect Emsley had on his grandson Mallie as over the next eighty four years Mallie himself became a great spinner of yarns and had many, many stories for his children and grandchildren but you could always count on him coming back to his favorite topic, Emsley Wallace.

Just like my grandfather Mallie before me, my love of the Wallaces began with Emsley. I saw him through the same eyes as my grandfather did many, many years before. So much so, that my daughter now bears Emsley's name as a testament to my own grandfather and his love for Emsley Wallace. I have always believed that Emsley's relationship with Mallie was the foundation for my grandfather's relationship with his children and grandchildren. My grandfather was so beloved and so special to all of us that almost twenty years after his death, he is missed as painfully as he was the day he died. And just like my grandfather Mallie did with us, we talk frequently about our grandfather to our children and to others who will always know him in the way that we have.

My grandfather built his house on the very same spot as Emsley's house and proudly kept the large rocks used as foundation for Emsley's house in his yard. It was in that same yard and under those same trees that he passed down the stories of long ago and sparked an interest in several more generations of Wallaces. While we may now all be called by other names like Jackson, Chriscoe, Parker, Moore, Dodson, and Purvis – we will always be Wallaces.

RECORDS OF EMSLEY WALLACE

1850, Nov 12 -- Census, Moore County, NC Page 238
Isham Wallis 49 M, Farmer, $1600 Real Estate, born in North Carolina
Nancy Wallis 44 F, born in North Carolina
Westley Wallis 21 M, Farmer, born in North Carolina
Quimby Wallis 18 M, Farmer, born in North Carolina
Lockey Wallis 14 M, born in North Carolina
Emsley Wallis 12 M, born in North Carolina
Samuel Wallis 9 M, born in North Carolina
Jane Wallis 6 F, born in North Carolina
Sampson Wallis 5 M, born in North Carolina
Virgil Wallis 4 M, born in North Carolina
John Wallis 2/12 M, born in North Carolina

1855, Oct 1 -- School Roster, Moore County, NC
List of school attendees and days attending during session: Artimas S. Caddell [teacher] 60 days, George Melton 49 days, James W. Melton 59 days, Lucinda Melton 59 days, Margret Melton 59 days, Thomas Horner 42 days, James Horner 47 days, Elizabeth Horner 43 days, Katharine Horner 51 days, Tempy Melton 19 days, Misouri Melton 29 days, Susan Williams 51 days, Loveda J. Wallis 51 days, Arren Jones 40 days, Nelson Jones 17 days, Jefferson W. Williams 31 days, Tempy Muse 7 days, Elizabeth Muse 6 days, Margret Dowdy 8 days, Rebecca Dowdy 30 days, James S. Dowdy 7 days, George Williams 14 days, Maryann Williams 10 days, Emerson Jones 36 days, Martha Black 14 days, Ann E. Muse 4 days, George D. Stuts 13 days, Noah B. Stuts 15 days, Samuel Wallis 5 days, Emsly Wallis 3 days and Jane Melton 4 days. [Editor's Note: Papers of Artemus Caddell, Special Collections, David M. Rubenstein Library, Duke University, Durham, NC]

1859, Aug 25 -- Record of Marriages, Moore County, NC Page 67
Emsly Wallace and Priscilla Melton were married by John Shaw, JP.

1859, Sep 19 -- Marriages, Fayetteville Observer [Fayetteville, NC] Newspaper
"In Moore County, at the residence of the bride's mother, on the 25th ult. [Aug], by Dr. John Shaw, Mr. Emsley Wallace and Miss Priscilla Melton, daughter of Robert Melton, Dec'd." [Editor's Note: Priscilla was the daughter of James Melton]

1860, Aug 31 -- Census, Moore County, NC Page 220, Gold Region Post Office
Emsley Wallace 23 M, Farmer, $400 Personal Property, born in North Carolina
Priscilla Wallace 24 F, born in North Carolina

1860, Sep 1 -- Agricultural Census, Moore County, NC Page 43, Gold Region Post Office
Emsly Wallace listed 25 acres improved valued at $40

1865, Nov 26 -- Deed Book 127 Page 545, Moore County, NC
Isam Wallis deeded Emsley Wallis 100 acres located on Buffalo Creek adjoining Wesley Wallis. Danl. McIntosh was a witness.

1869, Oct 2 -- Deed Book 125 Page 478, Moore County, NC
Isham and Nancy Wallace deeded Virgil Wallace 105 acres located on Buffalo Creek adjoining Emsley Wallace, William Stutts, L.T. Seawell, Stewart and their own line. S.D. Wallace was a witness.

1870, Jul 6 -- Agricultural Census, Moore County, NC Page 1, Bensalem Township, Curriesville Post Office
Emsley Wallis listed 40 acres improved, 35 acres wooded, 30 acres other unimproved valued at $150

1870, Jul 14 -- Census, Moore County, NC Page 481, Bensalem Township, Curriesville Post Office
Emsly Wallis 33 M, Farmer, $200 Real Estate, $400 Personal Property, born in North Carolina
Priscilla Wallis 36 F, born in North Carolina
Elizabeth J. Wallis 9 F, born in North Carolina
Cinda A. Wallis 7 F, born in North Carolina
Louiza E. Wallis 5 F, born in North Carolina
Sarah C. Wallis 2 F, born in North Carolina
James Lilly 15 M (mulatto), Laborer, born in North Carolina

1872, Nov 4 -- Deed Book 127 Page 546, Moore County, NC
Isham and Nancy Wallace deeded Emsley Wallace 2.5 acres located on Buffalo Creek adjoining Bird Wallace.

1872, Dec 12 -- Orders and Decrees Book 1 Page 159-165, Moore County, NC
K. Matheson, J.J. Richardson and Samuel McIntosh appointed to partition the land of James Melton, Dec'd. as follows: [Lot 1] W.W. Wallace assignee of James Melton 15 acres on home tract adjoining Matheson and 8 acres on chalk level tract; [Lot 2] Lovedy A. Melton 15 acres on home tract and 8 acres on chalk level tract; [Lot 3] W.W. Wallace and wife Elizabeth 15 acres on home tract and 9 acres on chalk level tract; [Lot 4] Candis E. Melton 15 acres on home tract and 8 acres on chalk level tract; [Lot 5] Lydia Melton 15 acres on home tract and 9 acres on chalk level tract; [Lot 6] George W. Melton 15 acres on home tract and 8 acres on chalk level tract; [Lot 7] Emsley Wallace and wife Priscilla 16 acres on home tract and 9 acres on chalk level tract; [Lot 8] George M. Cockman and wife Lucinda 16 acres on home tract and 8 acres on chalk level tract; [Lot 9] John Cockman and wife Nancy Jane 16 acres on home tract and 15 acres on chalk level tract; [Lot 10] Margaret E. Melton 16 acres on home tract and 9 acres on chalk level tract; [Lot 11] Daniel McNeill and wife Amanda 16 acres on home tract and 8 acres on chalk level tract; [Lot 12] Samuel B. Wallace and wife Tempy 160 acres on home tract adjoining S.B. Wallace and James Melton and 8 acres on the chalk level tract and Tempy Wallace. The more valuable dividends are charged to pay the others to ensure an equitable division.

1874, Nov 28 -- 1875-1878 Judgment Docket #2, Moore County, NC Page 91-93
#2049 George Melton and Others Ex Parte. Judgments: W.W. Wallace and wife, Daniel McNeill and wife, Emsly Wallace and wife, Lydia Melton, Saml. Wallace and wife, John Cockman and wife, George Melton, Geo. M. Cockman and wife, James Melton, Margaret E. Melton, Lovedy Adline Melton, Candis Ellen Melton. Division of Land occurred on Dec 12, 1872.

1880, Jun 28 -- Census, Moore County, NC Page 211-B, Bensalem Township
Emesly Wallace 43 M, Head, Married, Farmer/Planter, born in North Carolina, father & mother born in North Carolina
Priscilla Wallace 45 F, Wife, Married, Keeping House, born in North Carolina, father & mother born in North Carolina
Elizabeth Wallace 18 F, Dau, Single, At Home, born in North Carolina, father & mother born in North Carolina
Cindia A. Wallace 16 F, Dau, Single, At Home, born in North Carolina, father & mother born in North Carolina
Louisa Wallace 14 F, Dau, Single, At Home, born in North Carolina, father & mother born in North Carolina
Sarrah C. Wallace 11 F, Dau, Single, At Home, born in North Carolina, father & mother born in North Carolina
Callie Lee Wallace 10 F, Dau, Single, At Home, born in North Carolina, father & mother born in North Carolina
Adia L. Wallace 8 F, Dau, Single, At Home, born in North Carolina, father & mother born in North Carolina
Lucien Wallace 4 M, Son, Single, born in North Carolina, father & mother born in North Carolina
Mattie Wallace 1 F, Dau, Single, born in North Carolina, father & mother born in North Carolina
Upshur Rouse 25 M, Servant, Single, Laborer, born in North Carolina, father & mother born in North Carolina

1880, Jun 28 -- Agricultural Census, Moore County, NC Page 21, Bensalem Township
Emsley Wallace listed 50 acres improved fields, 150 acres unimproved wooded, 20 acres unimproved non-wooded valued at $150

1882, Dec 30 -- Deed Book 95 Page 529, Moore County, NC
John M. Fry and Lucy A. E. Fry (of Lauderdale County, AL) deeded Emsly Wallace 100 acres on Buffalo Creek. J.C. Parker was a witness.

1884 -- Branson's Business Directory, Moore County, NC
Emsley Wallace listed as a farmer at Carters Mills Post Office

1887, Sep 12 -- Deed Book 5 Page 541, Moore County, NC
J.S. Cockman and wife L.A deeded Samp. Cockman, D.C. Barrett, Mary Cockman and W.C. Wallace, trustees for Flint Hill Missionary Baptist Church 3 acres [including graveyard] located on Meadow Branch adjoining Emsley Wallace. J.S. Barrett was a witness.

1889, Dec 11 -- Orders and Decrees Book 3 Page 80-82, Moore County, NC
George Cockman, Admst. of Isham Wallace Dec'd. v. Samuel B. Wallace, W.W. Wallace, Quimby Wallace. John Wallace, Virgil Wallace and other heirs. Division of Land mentions neighbors Quimby Wallace, Samuel Wallace; 10a tract deeded from Joseph Wallace to Isham

Wallace. Heirs: Lovedy Jane Horner, wife of James Horner, Heirs of Elizabeth Cockman, wife of Sampson Cockman (Wesly Cockman, James Cockman, Alice Cockman, Clarky Ann Horner, wife of W.T. Horner, Eliza Horner, wife of Thomas R. Horner), Heirs of Locky Wallace (Mary Maness, wife of Blake Maness, Martha Maness, wife of Lewis Maness, Ruth Ritter, wife of Joseph Ritter, Vandie Maness, wife of McLellan Maness, Ella Blake Wallace), Sarah Garner, wife of John Garner, Samuel B. Wallace, Mary Cockman, wife of Noah Cockman, W.W. Wallace, Clarky Cockman, Quimby Wallace, Emsley Wallace, Virgil Wallace, S.D. Wallace and John Wallace (of Arkansas)

1890 -- Branson's Business Directory, Moore County, NC
Emsley Wallace listed as a farmer at Carters Mills Post Office

1898 -- Branson's Business Directory, Moore County, NC
Emesley Wallace listed 230 acres valued at $250 at Horners Post Office

1900 -- Tax List, Moore County, NC
Emsley Wallace (age 62) listed 232 acres valued at $250 located in Bensalem Township on Buffalo Creek

1900, Jun 22 -- Census, Moore County, NC Page 49, Bensalem Township
Emsley Wallace 62 M, Feb 1838, Head, Married-41yrs, Farmer, born in North Carolina, father & mother born in North Carolina
Priscilla Wallace 64 F, Jul 1835, Wife, Married-41yrs, 8 Children(8 Living), born in North Carolina, father & mother born in North Carolina
Adda F. Wallace 28 F, Apr 1872, Dau, Single, born in North Carolina, father & mother born in North Carolina

1906, Mar 21 -- Deed Book 33 Page 515, Moore County, NC
Leonard Garner and wife Ella deeded Geo. W Horner their interest in 100 acres of the estate of John Garner adjoining Leonard Garner and Emsley Wallace.

1906, Jun 4 -- 1896-1908 Administrator's Bonds, Moore County, NC Page 476-477
C.E. Cockman appointed Administrator of the Estate of Isham Wallace, Dec'd. with A.J. Lawhon and W.L. Ritter as securities. Heirs: Wes Wallace, Clarky Ann Cockman, Quimby Wallace, Lock Wallace, Sam Wallace, Bird Wallace, Emsly Wallace, Lane Wallace, John Wallace, Sarah Garner, Jane Horner, Elizabeth Cockman and Mary A. Cockman.

1910 -- Census, Moore County, NC Page 96-B, Bensalem Township
Emsley Wallace 74 M, Head, Widowed, Farmer(Home Farm), born in North Carolina, father & mother born in North Carolina
Addie Wallace 37 F, Dau, Single, Farm Laborer(Home Farm), born in North Carolina, father & mother born in North Carolina

1910, Nov 21 -- Deed Book 46 Page 88, Moore County, NC
Emsley Wallace deeded John J. Britt (of Saint Lusy County, FL) two tracts: [1] 100 acres located on Buffalo Creek adjoining Wesley Wallace; [2] 2.5 acres located on Buffalo Creek adjoining Bird Wallace. L.T. Wallace was a witness.

1916, Mar 20 -- Deed Book 64 Page 95, Moore County, NC
Emsley Wallace deeded L.T. Wallace 60 acres located on Buffalo Creek. E.C. Matheson was a witness.

1918, July 24 - Death Certificate, Moore County, NC
Emsley Wallace died in Bensalem Township. Widowed. Age: 81y 5m 9d. Occupation: Farmer. Birthplace: NC
Father: Isham Wallace. Birthplace of Father: NC. Mother: Priscilla Melton. Birthplace of Mother: NC. Cause of Death: Chronic Prostatitis. Place of Burial: Home Cemetery. Date of Burial: July 26, 1918. Undertaker: W.R. Kennedy, Hemp
Informant: Lucian Wallace, Eagle Springs.

Emsley Thomas Wallace and Priscilla Melton had the following children:

+335	Elizabeth Jane Wallace (1861-1934)
+336	Sindy Ann "Annie" Wallace (1863-1930)
+337	Louisa Elafair Wallace (1865-1944)
+338	Sarah Catherine "Kate" Wallace (1868-1941)
+339	Callie Lee Wallace (1870-1916)
+340	Addie Florence Wallace (1872-1943)
+341	Lucian Thomas Wallace (1876-1935)
+342	Martha "Mattie" Wallace (1878-1955)

62. **Samuel Bascom Wallace**, son of Isham Wallace and Nancy Furr, was born on February 10, 1841 in Moore County, NC and died on January 1, 1913 in Moore County, NC. He married **Temperance Levina Melton** on March 21, 1864 in Moore County, NC.[87] Tempy was the daughter of James Melton (1805-1857) and Temperance Horner (1814-aft 1880). She was born in August 1839 in Moore County, NC and died on June 26, 1906 in Moore County, NC. Tempy had previously married William Yow on June 13, 1861 in Moore County, NC.[88] Sam and Tempy were buried in Moore County, NC at Union Presbyterian Church.

After Tempy died, Sam married **Nancy Smith** on May 15, 1908 in Moore County, NC.[89] Nancy Smith, daughter of Hiram Smith (1832-1898) and Mary Ann Freeman (1841-1903), was born on February 6, 1866 in Moore County, NC. She first married R. Matthew Britt circa 1885. After Sam's death, she married Riley M. Britt on March 6, 1918 in Moore County, NC. She died on March 11, 1941 in Moore County, NC and was buried in Moore County, NC at Brown's Chapel Christian Church.

RECORDS OF SAMUEL BASCOM WALLACE

1850, Nov 12 -- Census, Moore County, NC Page 238
Isham Wallis 49 M, Farmer, $1600 Real Estate, born in North Carolina
Nancy Wallis 44 F, born in North Carolina
Westley Wallis 21 M, Farmer, born in North Carolina
Quimby Wallis 18 M, Farmer, born in North Carolina
Lockey Wallis 14 M, born in North Carolina
Emsley Wallis 12 M, born in North Carolina
Samuel Wallis 9 M, born in North Carolina
Jane Wallis 6 F, born in North Carolina
Sampson Wallis 5 M, born in North Carolina
Virgil Wallis 4 M, born in North Carolina
John Wallis 2/12 M, born in North Carolina

1860, Jul 9 -- Census, Moore County, NC Page 180, Caledonia Post Office
Isam Wallace 56 M, Farmer, $5000 Real Estate, $1000 Personal Property, born in North Carolina
Nancy Wallace 50 F, born in North Carolina
Samuel B. Wallace 17 M, born in North Carolina
Lovedy J. Wallace 15 F, born in North Carolina
Sampson D. Wallace 14 M, born in North Carolina
Virgil A. S. Wallace 12 M, born in North Carolina
John M. Wallace 10 M, born in North Carolina

1864, Mar 31 -- Record of Marriages, Moore County, NC Page 97
Samuel Wallace and Tempy Yow were married by Jesse Muse, JP.

1870, Jul 6 -- Agricultural Census, Moore County, NC Page 1, Bensalem Township, Curriesville Post Office
Samuel Wallis listed 35 acres improved, 65 acres wooded valued at $125

Samuel Bascom Wallace
(Courtesy of Maxine Auman, Sanford, NC)

1870, Jul 14 -- Census, Moore County, NC Page 482, Bensalem Township, Carters Mill Post Office
Samuel B. Wallas 27 M, Farmer, $200 Real Estate, $300 Personal Property, born in North Carolina
Tempy L. Wallas 30 F, born in North Carolina
Mary J. Wallas 5 F, born in North Carolina
Isham S.R.R. Wallas 1 M, born in North Carolina
Thomas Yow 9 M, born in North Carolina

1872, Dec 12 -- Orders and Decrees Book 1 Page 159-165, Moore County, NC
K. Matheson, J.J. Richardson and Samuel McIntosh appointed to partition the land of James Melton, Dec'd. as follows: [Lot 1] W.W. Wallace assignee of James Melton 15 acres on home tract adjoining Matheson and 8 acres on chalk level tract; [Lot 2] Lovedy A. Melton 15 acres on home tract and 8 acres on chalk level tract; [Lot 3] W.W. Wallace and wife Elizabeth 15 acres on home tract and 9 acres on chalk level tract; [Lot 4] Candis E. Melton 15 acres on home tract and 8 acres on chalk level tract; [Lot 5] Lydia Melton 15 acres on home tract and 9 acres on chalk level tract; [Lot 6] George W. Melton 15 acres on home tract and 8 acres on chalk level tract; [Lot 7] Emsley Wallace and wife Priscilla 16 acres on home tract and 9 acres on chalk level tract; [Lot 8] George M. Cockman and wife Lucinda 16 acres on home tract and 8 acres on chalk level tract; [Lot 9] John Cockman and wife Nancy Jane 16 acres on home tract and 15 acres on chalk level tract; [Lot 10] Margaret E. Melton 16 acres on home tract and 9 acres on chalk level tract; [Lot 11] Daniel McNeill and wife Amanda 16 acres on home tract and 8 acres on chalk level tract; [Lot 12] Samuel B. Wallace and wife Tempy 160 acres on home tract adjoining S.B. Wallace and James Melton and 8 acres on the chalk level tract and Tempy Wallace. The more valuable dividends are charged to pay the others to ensure an equitable division.

1874, Nov 28 -- 1875-1878 Judgment Docket #2, Moore County, NC Page 91-93
#2049 George Melton and Others Ex Parte. Judgments: W.W. Wallace and wife, Daniel McNeill and wife, Emsly Wallace and wife, Lydia Melton, Saml. Wallace and wife, John Cockman and wife, George Melton, Geo. M. Cockman and wife, James Melton, Margaret E. Melton, Lovedy Adline Melton, Candis Ellen Melton. Division of Land occurred on Dec 12, 1872.

1880, Jun 28 -- Census, Moore County, NC Page 211-B, Bensalem Township
Sam Wallace 40 M, Head, Married, Farmer/Planter, born in North Carolina, father & mother born in North Carolina

Tempy Y. Wallace 41 F, Wife, Married, Keeping House, born in North Carolina, father & mother born in North Carolina
Matthew Wallace 18 M, Son, Single, At Home, born in North Carolina, father & mother born in North Carolina
Mary Jane Wallace 13 F, Dau, Single, At Home, born in North Carolina, father & mother born in North Carolina
Isham S. Wallace 11 M, Son, Single, At Home, born in North Carolina, father & mother born in North Carolina
Daisy Wallace 9 F, Dau, Single, At Home, born in North Carolina, father & mother born in North Carolina
Cinthia Ann Wallace 7 F, Dau, Single, born in North Carolina, father & mother born in North Carolina
Sarrah L. Wallace 5 F, Dau, Single, born in North Carolina, father & mother born in North Carolina
Josiah T. S. Wallace 4 M, Son, Single, born in North Carolina, father & mother born in North Carolina
Jesse L. Wallace 1 M, Son, Single, born in North Carolina, father & mother born in North Carolina

1880, Jun 28 -- Agricultural Census, Moore County, NC Page 20, Bensalem Township
Samuel B. Wallace listed 60 acres improved fields, 50 acres unimproved wooded valued at $300

1884 -- Branson Business Directory, Moore County, NC
Sam Wallace listed as a farmer in Carters Mill Township

1884, Apr 4 -- Deed Book 12 Page 533, Moore County, NC
J.S. Cockman deeded W.J. Cockman, Jas. A. Cockman and W.L. Cockman 190 acres located on Meadow Branch adjoining Samuel B. Wallace. Comprised of the following tracts deeded to J.S. Cockman: 47 acres from Wm. Stutts and L. Grimm, 50 acres from Mary Cockman, 24 acres from George Melton, 24 acres from Candy Melton, 8 acres from George Cockman, 36 acres of Melton land. R.L. McNeill was a witness.

1884, Oct 16-Feb 23, 1886 -- Loose Estates and 1876-1885 Record of Accounts Page 542-544, Moore County, NC
Estate of Nancy Wallace Dec'd.by Administrator W.W. Wallace. *Items were purchased by the following*: Mac. Wallace, Josiah Person, Archd. Seawell, Saml. B. Wallace, John Garner, James Cockman, S.D. Wallace, Quimby Wallace, Sandy Black, Josiah Person, J.W. Horner, George Williams, Sampson Cockman, Charles Cockman, Mrs. Sarah Garner, Frank Wallace, Thomas Horner, Spinks Wallace, Archd. Seawell, J.T. Seawell, Charlie Wallace, Thomas Fry, Parker Stafford and J.M. Davis.

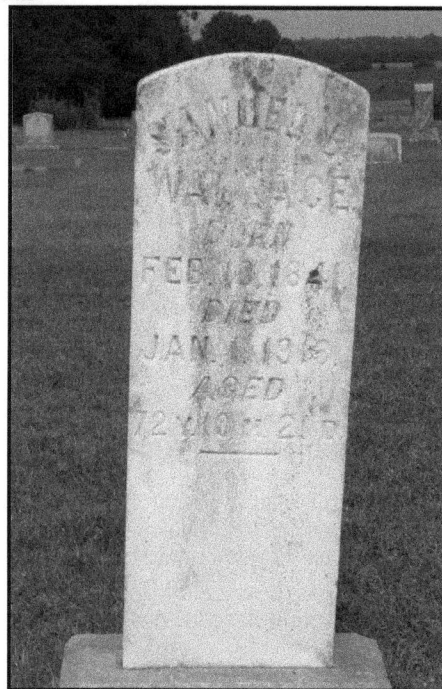

(photographed July 12, 2010)

1889, Dec 11 -- Orders and Decrees Book 3 Page 80-82, Moore County, NC
George Cockman, Admst. of Isham Wallace Dec'd. v. Samuel B. Wallace, W.W. Wallace, Quimby Wallace. John Wallace, Virgil Wallace and other heirs. Division of Land mentions neighbors Quimby Wallace, Samuel Wallace; 10a tract deeded from Joseph Wallace to Isham Wallace. Heirs: Lovedy Jane Horner, wife of James Horner, Heirs of Elizabeth Cockman, wife of Sampson Cockman (Wesly Cockman, James Cockman, Alice Cockman, Clarky Ann Horner, wife of W.T. Horner, Eliza Horner, wife of Thomas R. Horner), Heirs of Locky Wallace (Mary Maness, wife of Blake Maness, Martha Maness, wife of Lewis Maness, Ruth Ritter, wife of Joseph Ritter, Vandie Maness, wife of McLellan Maness, Ella Blake Wallace), Sarah Garner, wife of John Garner, Samuel B. Wallace, Mary Cockman, wife of Noah Cockman, W.W. Wallace, Clarky Cockman, Quimby Wallace, Emsley Wallace, Virgil Wallace, S.D. Wallace and John Wallace (of Arkansas)

1890 -- Branson Business Directory, Moore County, NC
Sam Wallace listed as a farmer at Carters Mill Post Office

1891, Oct 3-4 -- Flint Hill Baptist Church Minutes, Moore County, NC
Willie T. Horner, Duncan Garner, A. Fry, S.B. Wallace, Mary E. Fry, A.C. Maness and Mattie J. Horner were admitted by letter and experience.

1893, Mar 6 -- Deed Book 10, Page 338-340, Moore County, NC
George Cockman, administrator of Isham Wallace, Dec'd. deeded I.W.H. Cockman two tracts. [1] 142 acres located on Meadow Branch adjoining Quimby Wallace, Samuel Wallace and L. Wallace. [2] 10 acres located on Meadow Branch and the Rutherford Road adjoining Armstrong Maness and deeded to Isham Wallace by Josiah Wallace. A.H. McNeill was a witness.

1898 -- Branson Business Directory, Moore County, NC
S.B. Wallace listed 283 acres valued at $350 located at Horners Post Office in Bensalem Township

1899, Oct 18 -- Deed Book 21 Page 323, Moore County, NC
Mary Horner deeded J.M. Worth 54 acres (Timber Deed) adjoining Sam Wallace, V.S. Garner, W.T. Horner and L.B. Maness, known as the old Geo. Horner place. C.C. Hunsucker was a witness.

1900, Jun 22 -- Census, Moore County, NC Page 49, Bensalem Township
Samuel B. Wallace 59 M, Mar 1841, Head, Married-40yrs, Farmer, born in North Carolina, father & mother born in North Carolina
Tempy L. Wallace 60 F, Aug 1839, Wife, Married-40yrs, 12 Children(10 Living), born in North Carolina, father & mother born in North Carolina
Jesse L. Wallace 20 M, Jun 1879, Son, Single, Farm Laborer, born in North Carolina, father & mother born in North Carolina
Mattie E. Wallace 19 F, Feb 1881, Dau, Single, born in North Carolina, father & mother born in North Carolina
Samuel H. Wallace 15 M, Apr 1885, Son, Single, At School, born in North Carolina, father & mother born in North Carolina

1905, Oct 4 -- Local News, Carthage Blade [Carthage, NC] Newspaper
"Mr. and Mrs. Sam Wallace who formerly lived near Elise have sold their farm and will move to Carthage and will live with their son-in-law, Mr. Ever McLeod. Their children are all married and they are not able to work the farm, hence they are making this move."

1905, Oct 10 -- Deed Book 35 Page 592-595, Moore County, NC
Samuel B. Wallace and wife T.L. deeded J.D. Cockman 266 acres located on both sides of the Long Meadow Branch adjoining Jack Cockman, John Jones, Blake Maness and Jno. Garner. Harry S. Jones was a witness.

1906, Jun 4 -- 1896-1908 Administrator's Bonds, Moore County, NC Page 476-477
C.E. Cockman appointed Administrator of the Estate of Isham Wallace, Dec'd. with A.J. Lawhon and W.L. Ritter as securities. Heirs: Wes Wallace, Clarky Ann Cockman, Quimby Wallace, Lock Wallace, Sam Wallace, Bird Wallace, Emsly Wallace, Lane Wallace, John Wallace, Sarah Garner, Jane Horner, Elizabeth Cockman and Mary A. Cockman.

1908, May 17 -- Marriage Certificate, Moore County, NC
S.B. Wallace (age 66) and Nancy Britt (age 41) were married by J.M. Deaton, JP at J. Tay Wallace's in Bensalem Township. John Sanders, D.T. Britt and Annie Sanders were witnesses.

1910 -- Census, Moore County, NC Page 104, Bensalem Township
S. B. Wallace 68 M, Head, Married-2nd-1yr, born in North Carolina, father & mother born in North Carolina
Nancy Wallace 43 F, Wife, Married-2nd-1yr, Farm Laborer(Own Garden), born in North Carolina, father & mother born in North Carolina

Samuel Bascom Wallace and Temperance Levina Melton had the following children:

+343	James Arthur Mason Bethune Wallace (-)
+344	Mary Jane Nancy Regina Ledbetter "Mamie" Wallace (1867-1936)
+345	Isham Sedman Robert Renfro "Bob" Wallace (1870-1933)
+346	Daisy Arnold Irene Wallace (1872-1909)
+347	Cynthia Ann "Annie" Wallace (1873-1906)
+348	Josiah Tay Settle Wallace (1877-1946)
+349	Sarah Lee Nettie Wallace (1878-1941)
+350	Jesse Lewis Smith Wallace (1879-1946)
+351	Eliza Rosetta Mattie Evelyn "Mattie" Wallace (1882-1924)
+352	Samuel Henry Bascom "Bass" Wallace (1885-1949)

63. **Lovedy Jane Wallace**, daughter of Isham Wallace and Nancy Furr, was born on January 12, 1844 in Moore County, NC and died on December 13, 1916 in Moore County, NC.[90] She married **James Washington Horner** on August 25, 1861 in Moore County, NC.[91] James was the son of George Washington Horner (1817-1885) and Mary Ann Ritter (1821-) He was born on August 11, 1842 in Moore County, NC and died on November 9, 1921 in Moore County, NC.[92] They were buried in Moore County, NC at Flint Hill Baptist Church.

RECORDS OF JAMES WASHINGTON HORNER AND LOVEDY JANE WALLACE

1850, Nov 12 -- Census, Moore County, NC Page 238
Isham Wallis 49 M, Farmer, $1600 Real Estate, born in North Carolina
Nancy Wallis 44 F, born in North Carolina
Westley Wallis 21 M, Farmer, born in North Carolina
Quimby Wallis 18 M, Farmer, born in North Carolina
Lockey Wallis 14 M, born in North Carolina
Emsley Wallis 12 M, born in North Carolina
Samuel Wallis 9 M, born in North Carolina
Jane Wallis 6 F, born in North Carolina
Sampson Wallis 5 M, born in North Carolina
Virgil Wallis 4 M, born in North Carolina
John Wallis 2/12 M, born in North Carolina

1860, Jul 9 -- Census, Moore County, NC Page 180, Caledonia Post Office
Isam Wallace 56 M, Farmer, $5000 Real Estate, $1000 Personal Property, born in
North Carolina
Nancy Wallace 50 F, born in North Carolina
Samuel B. Wallace 17 M, born in North Carolina
Lovedy J. Wallace 15 F, born in North Carolina
Sampson D. Wallace 14 M, born in North Carolina
Virgil A. S. Wallace 12 M, born in North Carolina
John M. Wallace 10 M, born in North Carolina

1861, Aug 25 -- Records of Marriages, Moore County, NC Page 81
Jas. W. Horner and Lovedy Wallace by Jesse Muse, JP

1870, Jul 14 -- Census, Moore County, NC Page 482, Bensalem Township, Carters
Mill Post Office
James W. Horner 27 M, Farmer, $200 Real Estate, $300 Personal Property, born
in North Carolina
Lovedy J. Horner 26 F, born in North Carolina
Josiah T. Horner 9/12 (Oct) M, born in North Carolina

1873, Mar 4 -- Land Grant #4492, Moore County, NC
J.R. Cagle received 32.5 acres located on Buffalo Creek adjoining Isham Wallace,
William Stutts, James Horner and George Milton. I.W.H Cockman and A.W. Cagle
were chain carriers.

1880 -- Census, Moore County, NC Page 211-B, Bensalem Township
James Horner 37 M, Head, Married, Farmer/Planter, born in North Carolina,
father & mother born in North Carolina
Lovedy Jane Horner 35 F, Wife, Married, Keeping House, born in North Carolina,
father & mother born in North Carolina
Josiah Horner 10 M, Son, Single, At Home, born in North Carolina, father &
mother born in North Carolina
William Horner 8 M, Son, Single, born in North Carolina, father & mother born in
North Carolina
John W. Horner 5 M, Son, Single, born in North Carolina, father & mother born in
North Carolina
Mary A. Horner 1 F, Dau, Single, born in North Carolina, father & mother born in
North Carolina

1882, Mar 4 -- Deed Book 85 Page 226, Moore County, NC
L.T. Seawell and wife Catherine and Albert Seawell and wife Mary A. deeded
James W. Horner four tracts [1] 120 acres adjoining William Jones, Danl. McNeill
and John Garner [2] 39.50 acres known as lot #1 in William Jones division [3]
39.50 acres known as lot #2 in William Jones division [4] 39.50 acres known as
lot #13 in William Jones division. A.H. McNeill was a witness.

1884 -- Branson's Business Directory, Moore County, NC
J.W. Horner listed as a farmer at Carters Mills Post Office

1884, Sep 9 -- Orders and Decrees Book 2 Page 251-254, Moore County, NC
Green Baily, John Jones and E.T. Williams appointed to partition the land of
Lockey Wallace, Dec'd. located on Buffalo Creek and Meadow Branch adjoining
Jas. Melton, Mrs. Jones, Horner, Stutts, Sampson Cockman and L.T. Seawell.
Heirs: I.B. Maness and wife Mary E., Joseph Ritter and wife Ruth J., Lewis S.
Maness and wife Martha A., Nannie M. Wallace, Vandie L. Wallace and Ella B.
Wallace.

1884, Oct 16-Feb 23, 1886 -- Loose Estates and 1876-1885 Record of Accounts
Page 542-544, Moore County, NC
Estate of Nancy Wallace Dec'd.by Administrator W.W. Wallace. *Items were
purchased by the following*: Mac. Wallace, Josiah Person, Archd. Seawell, Saml. B. Wallace, John Garner, James Cockman, S.D. Wallace,
Quimby Wallace, Sandy Black, Josiah Person, J.W. Horner, George Williams, Sampson Cockman, Charles Cockman, Mrs. Sarah Garner,
Frank Wallace, Thomas Horner, Spinks Wallace, Archd. Seawell, J.T. Seawell, Charlie Wallace, Thomas Fry, Parker Stafford and J.M. Davis.

1885, Nov 20 -- Orders and Decrees Book 2 Page 305,308-310, Moore County, NC

(photographed July 6, 2010)

M.M.L. Kelly, Edmond Waddell and B.P. Phillips commissioner to partition land of George W. Horner, Dec'd. located on Meadow Branch and the Plank Road adjoining S. Cockman. Heirs: Sarah Francis Horner (Widow), G.B. Horner, James W. Horner, John and Nancy Kennedy, Eli and Frances Cockman, W.W. and Jane Wallace, heirs of George Wallace (J.C. Wallace, S.A. Wallace), A.J. and Catherine Williams and T.W. Horner.

1889, Dec 11 -- Orders and Decrees Book 3 Page 80-82, Moore County, NC
George Cockman, Admst. of Isham Wallace Dec'd. v. Samuel B. Wallace, W.W. Wallace, Quimby Wallace. John Wallace, Virgil Wallace and other heirs. Division of Land mentions neighbors Quimby Wallace, Samuel Wallace; 10a tract deeded from Joseph Wallace to Isham Wallace. Heirs: Lovedy Jane Horner, wife of James Horner, Heirs of Elizabeth Cockman, wife of Sampson Cockman (Wesly Cockman, James Cockman, Alice Cockman, Clarky Ann Horner, wife of W.T. Horner, Eliza Horner, wife of Thomas R. Horner), Heirs of Locky Wallace (Mary Maness, wife of Blake Maness, Martha Maness, wife of Lewis Maness, Ruth Ritter, wife of Joseph Ritter, Vandie Maness, wife of McLellan Maness, Ella Blake Wallace), Sarah Garner, wife of John Garner, Samuel B. Wallace, Mary Cockman, wife of Noah Cockman, W.W. Wallace, Clarky Cockman, Quimby Wallace, Emsley Wallace, Virgil Wallace, S.D. Wallace and John Wallace (of Arkansas)

1890 -- Branson's Business Directory, Moore County, NC
J.W. Horner listed as a farmer at Carters Mills Post Office

1891, Jan 6 -- Land Grant #4708, Moore County, NC
A.H. McNeill received 41.39 acres located on the waters of Flag Creek adjoining James Horner, Melton, Garner, A. Williams, M.G. Maness, Parrish. Steadman Garner and A.D. Garner were chain carriers.

1898 -- Branson's Business Directory, Moore County, NC
J.W. Horner listed 350 acres valued at $ located at Horners Post Office in Bensalem Township

1899, Sep 29 -- Deed Book 21 Page 319, Moore County, NC
Steadman Garner and wife Ann Elizabeth deeded J.M. Worth (Timber Deed) [no acreage listed] adjoining J.W. Horner and Causey Cox. W.J. Page was a witness.

1899, Sep 29 -- Deed Book 21 Page 320, Moore County, NC
S.D. Garner and wife Lillie E. deeded J.M. Worth 40 acres (Timber Deed) adjoining J.W. Horner, W.T. Garner and Marshall Maness.

1899, Sep 29 -- Deed Book 21 Page 325, Moore County, NC
J.W. Horner and wife L.J. deeded J.M. Worth 120 acres (Timber Deed) adjoining Steadman Garner, W.W. Williams, Enoch Rouse and Lona Garner, sold by L.T. Seawell and Albert Seawell to J.W. Horner in 1882. W.J. Page was a witness.

1899, Sep 29 -- Deed Book 21 Page 351, Moore County, NC
W.W. Williams and wife Margaret deeded J.M. Worth 37 acres (Timber Deed) adjoining Enoch Rouse, J.W. Horner and K.K. Williams.

1899, Nov 15 -- Deed Book 21, Page 358-360, Moore County, NC
Mausia C. Wallace, Charlie A. Wallace, Effie Wallace, A.B. Wallace, F.A. Wallace, B.H. Wallace, C.E. Wallace, R.F. Wallace and W.H. Wallace deeded J.M. Worth 100 acres (Timber Deed) known as the home tract adjoining Jas. W. Horner, Lewis Maness and the heirs of Quimby Wallace. Charlie and Wade Wallace now live on this tract and it is the undivided tract of S.D. Wallace.

1900 -- Census, Moore County, NC Page 49-B, Bensalem Township
James W. Horner 57 M, Aug 1842, Head, Married-39yrs, Farmer, born in North Carolina, father & mother born in North Carolina
Lovedy J. Horner 57 F, Jan 1843, Wife, Married-39yrs, 6 Children(5 Living), born in North Carolina, father & mother born in North Carolina
William B. Horner 28 M, May 1872, Son, Single, Farm Laborer, born in North Carolina, father & mother born in North Carolina
Louvina Horner 17 F, Oct 1882, Dau, Single, At School, born in North Carolina, father & mother born in North Carolina
Joseph L. Horner 30 M, Oct 1869, Son, Widow, Engineer(Cotton Mill), born in North Carolina, father & mother born in North Carolina
Carson L. Horner 5 M, Aug 1894, GrSon, Single, born in North Carolina, father & mother born in North Carolina
Bulah Horner 4 F, Feb 1896, GrDau, Single, born in North Carolina, father & mother born in North Carolina

1900, Jan 23 -- Deed Book 21 Page 355, Moore County, NC
W.C. Stutts and wife Clarkie deeded J.M. Worth [no acreage listed] (Timber Deed) adjoining J.W. Horner, J.S. Cockman and Lewis Maness, being the home tract which he has owned since 1855. C.A. Wallace and W.J. Page were witnesses.

1906, Jun 4 -- 1896-1908 Administrator's Bonds, Moore County, NC Page 476-477
C.E. Cockman appointed Administrator of the Estate of Isham Wallace, Dec'd. with A.J. Lawhon and W.L. Ritter as securities. Heirs: Wes Wallace, Clarky Ann Cockman, Quimby Wallace, Lock Wallace, Sam Wallace, Bird Wallace, Emsly Wallace, Lane Wallace, John Wallace, Sarah Garner, Jane Horner, Elizabeth Cockman and Mary A. Cockman.

1910 -- Census, Moore County, NC Page 97, Bensalem Township
James W. Horner 67 M, Head, Married-1st--48yrs, Farmer, born in North Carolina, father & mother born in North Carolina
Lovedy J. Horner 66 F, Wife, Married-1st-48yrs, 6 Children(5 Living), Farm Laborer, born in North Carolina, father & mother born in North Carolina

Carson L. Horner 15 M, GrSon, Married-1st, born in North Carolina, father & mother born in North Carolina

1912, May 13 -- Deed Book 53 Page 35-36, Moore County, NC
J.W. Horner and wife Lovedy deeded Lewis S. Maness 88 acres adjoining his own line, Stephen Garner, S.D. Wallace heirs, J.S. Cockman heirs, W.C. Morgan and W.C. Stutts.

1916, Dec 13 --Death Certificate, Moore County, NC
Lovedy Jane Horner died in Bensalem Township. Married. Date of birth: 1844. Age: 72. Birthplace: Moore County, NC. Father: Isham Wallace. Birthplace of Father: NC. Mother: Nancy Furr. Birthplace of Mother: NC. Cause of Death: Endo Carditis and Bright's Disease. Place of Burial: Flint Hill. Date of Burial: Dec 14, 1916. Undertaker: W.R. Kennedy, Hemp. Informant: John M. McMillan, Hemp.

1921, Oct 11 -- Will Book H Page 201-204, Moore County, NC
Will of James W. Horner Dec'd. Heirs: Edna Williams and Luther Williams (of Eagle Springs), children of Mary Ann Williams and Kinneth Williams [39 acres being Lot #1 in the division of Billie Jones], Martha L. Ritter and her children (of Hemp) [78 acres excepting the 2 acres sold to W.B. Horner consisting of Lot #2 and #3 of Billie Jones division including the house tract where James W. Horner now resides], grandson Carson L. Horner (of Fayetteville), son J.T. Horner (of Fayetteville), W.B. Horner (State Hospital, Raleigh) and son John W. Horner (Norfolk, VA). Executor: son J.T. Horner. Witnesses: E.T. Williams and S.H. Garner. Proven May 15, 1922.

James Washington Horner and Lovedy Jane Wallace had the following children:

+353	Josiah Turner Horner (1869-1923)	
+354	William Branson "Bud" Horner (1872-1925)	
+355	John W. Horner (1874-)	
+356	Mary Ann Horner (1878-1914)	
+357	Maggie C. Horner (1880-1880)	
+358	Martha Louvina Horner (1882-1958)	

64. **Sampson Delaney Wallace**, son of Isham Wallace and Nancy Furr, was born in 1845 and died circa 1893 in Moore County, NC and was buried in Moore County, NC at Sampson Delaney Wallace Grave Site near his home.[93] Lane Wallace married **Missouri Coleman Hunsucker**, daughter of George M. Hunsucker (1802-aft 1880) and Elizabeth Williams (1811-1879), was born in November 1846. She died on August 10, 1920 in Rockingham, Richmond County, NC and was buried on August 12, 1920 in Rockingham, Richmond County, NC at East Side Cemetery.[94] Lane served in Company K, 19th Regiment, 2nd Regiment Calvary during the Civil War. [95]

RECORDS OF SAMPSON DELANEY WALLACE

1850, Nov 12 -- Census, Moore County, NC Page 238
Isham Wallis 49 M, Farmer, $1600 Real Estate, born in North Carolina
Nancy Wallis 44 F, born in North Carolina
Westley Wallis 21 M, Farmer, born in North Carolina
Quimby Wallis 18 M, Farmer, born in North Carolina
Lockey Wallis 14 M, born in North Carolina
Emsley Wallis 12 M, born in North Carolina
Samuel Wallis 9 M, born in North Carolina
Jane Wallis 6 F, born in North Carolina
Sampson Wallis 5 M, born in North Carolina
Virgil Wallis 4 M, born in North Carolina
John Wallis 2/12 M, born in North Carolina

1860, Jul 9 -- Census, Moore County, NC Page 180, Caledonia Post Office
Isam Wallace 56 M, Farmer, $5000 Real Estate, $1000 Personal Property, born in North Carolina
Nancy Wallace 50 F, born in North Carolina
Samuel B. Wallace 17 M, born in North Carolina
Lovedy J. Wallace 15 F, born in North Carolina
Sampson D. Wallace 14 M, born in North Carolina
Virgil A. S. Wallace 12 M, born in North Carolina
John M. Wallace 10 M, born in North Carolina

(photographed June 13, 2009)

1861, Sep 10 -- Civil War Service Records
Delany Wallace enlisted in Company K, 19th Regiment (2nd Regiment Calvary) in Moore County, NC at age 17

1861, Sep 12 -- Fayetteville Observer, Fayetteville, NC
Delaney Wallace listed as having joined the 2nd Regiment Calvary

1864, Jul 31 -- Civil War Service Records
Delany Wallace was dropped from Company K, 19th Regiment (2nd Regiment Calvary) for being absent without leave

1867, Nov -- Carthage Masonic Lodge #181 Minutes, Moore County, NC
S. D. Wallace raised for membership

1869, Oct 2 -- Deed Book 125 Page 478, Moore County, NC
Isham and Nancy Wallace deeded Virgil Wallace 105 acres located on Buffalo Creek adjoining Emsley Wallace, William Stutts, L.T. Seawell, Stewart and their own line. S.D. Wallace was a witness.

1870, Jul 15 -- Census, Moore County, NC Page 482, Bensalem Township, Carters Mill Post Office
Isham Wallis 70 M, Farmer, $200 Real Estate, $200 Personal Property, born in North Carolina
Nancy Wallis 65 F, born in North Carolina

John Davis 12 M, born in North Carolina
Alexander Davis 8 M, born in North Carolina
S.D. Wallis 24 M, born in North Carolina
Mosuria Wallis 23 F, born in North Carolina
Charles Wallis 2 M, born in North Carolina

1870, Dec 1 -- Carthage Masonic Lodge #181 Minutes, Moore County, NC
S. D. Wallace listed as present

1872 – Bransons Business Directory, Moore County, NC
S. D. Wallace, Carters Mills listed as the Clerk of Bensalem Township

1872, Nov 27 -- Carthage Masonic Lodge #181 Minutes, Moore County, NC
S. D. Wallace listed as present

1873, Nov 22 -- Carthage Masonic Lodge #181 Minutes, Moore County, NC
S. D. Wallace listed as suspended for present year

1880, Jun 28 -- Census, Moore County, NC Page 211, Bensalem Township
Delaney Wallace 35 M, Head, Married, Farmer/Planter, born in North Carolina, father & mother born in North Carolina
Mousura Wallace 33 F, Wife, Married, Keeping House, born in North Carolina, father & mother born in North Carolina
Charles A. Wallace 12 M, Son, Single, At Home, born in North Carolina, father & mother born in North Carolina
Wade Hampton Wallace 10 M, Single, Son, At Home, born in North Carolina, father & mother born in North Carolina
Euphernia Wallace 7 F, Dau, Single, born in North Carolina, father & mother born in North Carolina
Ashley B. Wallace 5 M, Son, Single, At Home, born in North Carolina, father & mother born in North Carolina
Catherine Wallace 1 F, Dau, Single, born in North Carolina, father & mother born in North Carolina

1880, Jun 28 -- Agricultural Census, Moore County, NC Page 20, Bensalem Township

(photographed May 1, 2010)

Missouri Hunsucker Wallace

Delaney Wallace listed 35 acres improved fields, 35 acres unimproved wooded valued at $75

1884, Oct 16-Feb 23, 1886 -- Loose Estates and 1876-1885 Record of Accounts Page 542-544, Moore County, NC
Estate of Nancy Wallace Dec'd.by Administrator W.W. Wallace. *Items were purchased by the following*: Mac. Wallace, Josiah Person, Archd. Seawell, Saml. B. Wallace, John Garner, James Cockman, S.D. Wallace, Quimby Wallace, Sandy Black, Josiah Person, J.W. Horner, George Williams, Sampson Cockman, Charles Cockman, Mrs. Sarah Garner, Frank Wallace, Thomas Horner, Spinks Wallace, Archd. Seawell, J.T. Seawell, Charlie Wallace, Thomas Fry, Parker Stafford and J.M. Davis.

1889, Dec 11 -- Orders and Decrees Book 3 Page 80-82, Moore County, NC
George Cockman, Admst. of Isham Wallace Dec'd. v. Samuel B. Wallace, W.W. Wallace, Quimby Wallace. John Wallace, Virgil Wallace and other heirs. Division of Land mentions neighbors Quimby Wallace, Samuel Wallace; 10a tract deeded from Joseph Wallace to Isham Wallace. Heirs: Lovedy Jane Horner, wife of James Horner, Heirs of Elizabeth Cockman, wife of Sampson Cockman (Wesly Cockman, James Cockman, Alice Cockman, Clarky Ann Horner, wife of W.T. Horner, Eliza Horner, wife of Thomas R. Horner), Heirs of Locky Wallace (Mary Maness, wife of Blake Maness, Martha Maness, wife of Lewis Maness, Ruth Ritter, wife of Joseph Ritter, Vandie Maness, wife of McLellan Maness, Ella Blake Wallace), Sarah Garner, wife of John Garner, Samuel B. Wallace, Mary Cockman, wife of Noah Cockman, W.W. Wallace, Clarky Cockman, Quimby Wallace, Emsley Wallace, Virgil Wallace, S.D. Wallace and John Wallace (of Arkansas)

1892, Dec 6 -- Deed Book 24 Page 8, Moore County, NC
W. W. & Louisa M. Wallace, J. C. Wallace, Laura L. Wallace deeded L. B. Maness 75 acres located in Ritters Township adjoining Jack Cockman, S.D. Wallace and Isham Wallace. E.T. Williams was a witness.

1898 -- Branson Business Directory, Moore County, NC
C.A. Wallace (agent for S.D. Wallace heirs) listed 100 acres valued at $140 at Horners Post Office in Bensalem Township

1899, Nov 15 -- Deed Book 21, Page 358-360, Moore County, NC
Mausia C. Wallace, Charlie A. Wallace, Effie Wallace, A.B. Wallace, F.A. Wallace, B.H. Wallace, C.E. Wallace, R.F. Wallace and W.H. Wallace deeded J.M. Worth 100 acres (Timber Deed) known as the home tract adjoining Jas. W. Horner, Lewis Maness and the heirs of Quimby Wallace. Charlie and Wade Wallace now live on this tract and it is the undivided tract of S.D. Wallace.

1900, Jun 13 -- Census, Richmond County, NC Page 145-B, Wolf Pit Upper Precinct
Masoria Wallace 52 F, Nov 1847, Head, Widow, 8 Children(8 Living), born in North Carolina, father & mother born in North Carolina
Ashley B. Wallace 23 M, Dec 1876, Son, Single, Cotton Mill Weaver, born in North Carolina, father & mother born in North Carolina
Catherine Wallace 21 F, Apr 1879, Dau, Single, Cotton Mill Spool, born in North Carolina, father & mother born in North Carolina
Flossie Wallace 18 F, Feb 1882, Dau, Single, Cotton Mill Spinner, born in North Carolina, father & mother born in North Carolina
Rushie Wallace 16 F, May 1884, Dau, Single, Cotton Mil Spinner, born in North Carolina, father & mother born in North Carolina
Ben H. Wallace 10 M, July 1889, Son, Single, born in North Carolina, father & mother born in North Carolina
Joseph T. Horner 30 M, Oct 1869, Boarder, Widow, Carpenter, born in North Carolina, father & mother born in North Carolina

1903, Apr 24 -- Confederate Pension Application, Richmond NC
M.C. Wallace, age 56 of Rockingham Post Office applied for Widow's Pension for S.D. Wallace. He served in Company B, 2nd NC Calvary. J.M. Ledbetter was a witness.[96]

1906, Jun 4 -- 1896-1908 Administrator's Bonds, Moore County, NC Page 476-477
C.E. Cockman appointed Administrator of the Estate of Isham Wallace, Decd. with A.J. Lawhon and W.L. Ritter as securities. Heirs: Wes Wallace, Clarky Ann Cockman, Quimby Wallace, Lock Wallace, Sam Wallace, Bird Wallace, Emsly Wallace, Lane Wallace, John Wallace, Sarah Garner, Jane Horner, Elizabeth Cockman and Mary A. Cockman.

1910, May 13 -- Census, Richmond County, NC Page 173, Rockingham Township
Misouria Wallace 64 F, Head, Widow-17yrs(Married), 8 Children(8 Living), born in North Carolina, father & mother born in North Carolina
Ashley B. Wallace 33 M, Son, Single, Salesman-Dry Goods Store, born in North Carolina, father & mother born in North Carolina
Benj. H. Wallace 20 M, Son, Single, Salesman-Grocery Store, born in North Carolina, father & mother born in North Carolina

1912, May 13 -- Deed Book 53 Page 35-36, Moore County, NC
J.W. Horner and wife Lovedy deeded Lewis S. Maness 88 acres adjoining his own line, Stephen Garner, S.D. Wallace heirs, J.S. Cockman heirs, W.C. Morgan and W.C. Stutts.

1920, Jan 17 -- Census, Richmond County, NC Page 181, Rockingham Township, Town of Rockingham
Alfred P. Barrett 42 M, Head, Married, Merchant, born in North Carolina, father & mother born in North Carolina
Ruth Barrett 27 F, Wife, Married, born in North Carolina, father & mother born in North Carolina
Alberta Barrett 12 F, Dau, Single, born in North Carolina, father & mother born in North Carolina
Grace Barrett 10 F, Dau, Single, born in North Carolina, father & mother born in North Carolina
Mary Barrett 4 7/12 F, Dau, Single, born in North Carolina, father & mother born in North Carolina
A. P. Barrett, Jr. 3 1/12, M, Son, Single, born in North Carolina, father & mother born in North Carolina
Robert Barrett 1 11/12 M, Son, Single, born in North Carolina, father & mother born in North Carolina
Missouri Wallace 72 F, MotherL, Widowed, born in North Carolina, father & mother born in North Carolina

Sampson Delaney Wallace and Missouri Coleman Hunsucker had the following children:

+359 Charles A. Wallace (1867-)
+360 Wade Hampton Wallace (1870-1947)
+361 Euphernia S. "Effie" Wallace (1872-1915)
+362 Ashley Braxton Wallace (1876-1925)
+363 Catherine E. Wallace (1881-1910)
+364 Flossie Alma Wallace (1883-1912)
+365 Jerusha Francis "Ruth" Wallace (1887-1982)
+366 Benjamin Harrison Wallace (1891-1956)

65. Virgil Spinks "Byrd" Wallace, son of Isham Wallace and Nancy Furr, was born on August 10, 1846 in Moore County, NC and died on August 1, 1917 in Moore County, NC.[97] Byrd married **Regina Hunsucker**, daughter of George M. Hunsucker (1802-aft 1880) and Elizabeth Williams (1811-1879). Regina was born in 1850 in Moore County, NC and died between 1888 and 1898 in Moore County, NC. After Regina's death, Byrd married **Flora Ann Garner** on September 15, 1898 in Moore County, NC.[98] Flora Ann Garner was the daughter of Steadman Garner (1843-1928) and Ann Elizabeth Davis (1843-1925). She was born on November 8, 1877 in Moore County, NC on November 4, 1963 in Moore County, NC.[99] After Byrd's death she married James Lewis Wallace on August 1, 1921 in Moore County, NC.[100] Byrd, Regina and Flora Ann were buried in Moore County, NC at Virgil (Byrd) Wallace Cemetery.[101]

RECORDS OF VIRGIL SPINKS "BYRD" WALLACE

1850, Nov 12 -- Census, Moore County, NC Page 238
Isham Wallis 49 M, Farmer, $1600 Real Estate, born in North Carolina
Nancy Wallis 44 F, born in North Carolina
Westley Wallis 21 M, Farmer, born in North Carolina
Quimby Wallis 18 M, Farmer, born in North Carolina
Lockey Wallis 14 M, born in North Carolina
Emsley Wallis 12 M, born in North Carolina
Samuel Wallis 9 M, born in North Carolina
Jane Wallis 6 F, born in North Carolina
Sampson Wallis 5 M, born in North Carolina
Virgil Wallis 4 M, born in North Carolina
John Wallis 2/12 M, born in North Carolina

1860, Jul 9 -- Census, Moore County, NC Page 180, Caledonia Post Office
Isam Wallace 56 M, Farmer, $5000 Real Estate, $1000 Personal Property, born in North Carolina
Nancy Wallace 50 F, born in North Carolina
Samuel B. Wallace 17 M, born in North Carolina
Lovedy J. Wallace 15 F, born in North Carolina
Sampson D. Wallace 14 M, born in North Carolina
Virgil A. S. Wallace 12 M, born in North Carolina
John M. Wallace 10 M, born in North Carolina

1869, Oct 2 -- Deed Book 125 Page 478, Moore County, NC
Isham and Nancy Wallace deeded Virgil Wallace 105 acres located on Buffalo Creek adjoining Emsley Wallace, William Stutts, L.T. Seawell, Stewart and their own line. S.D. Wallace was a witness.

1870, Jul 6 -- Agricultural Census, Moore County, NC Page 1, Bensalem Township, Curriesville Post Office
Virgald Wallis listed 15 acres improved, 65 acres wooded, 25 acres other unimproved valued at $100

1870, Jul 14 -- Census, Moore County, NC Page 481, Bensalem Township, Curriesville Post Office
Virgil S. Wallis 22 M, Farmer, $150 Real Estate, $200 Personal Property, born in North Carolina

Virgil Spinks "Byrd" Wallace
(Courtesy of Evelyn Sanders Spivey, Robbins, NC)

Regina Wallis 21 F, born in North Carolina
William B. Wallis 3 M, born in North Carolina
Lovda A. Wallis 1 F, born in North Carolina
John M. Wallis 20 M, Laborer, born in North Carolina

1872, Nov 4 -- Deed Book 127 Page 546, Moore County, NC
Isham and Nancy Wallace deeded Emsley Wallace 2.5 acres located on Buffalo Creek adjoining Bird Wallace.

1880, Jun 28 -- Census, Moore County, NC Page 211-B, Bensalem Township
Virgil Wallace 33 M, Head, Married, Farmer/Planter, born in North Carolina, father & mother born in North Carolina
Regina Wallace 30 F, Wife, Married, Keeping House, born in North Carolina, father & mother born in North Carolina
William B. Wallace 13 M, Son, Single, At Home, born in North Carolina, father & mother born in North Carolina
Lovedy Wallace 11 F, Dau, Single, At Home, born in North Carolina, father & mother born in North Carolina
John Morrison Wallace 9 M, Son, Single, At Home, born in North Carolina, father & mother born in North Carolina
Lovena Wallace 6 F, Dau, Single, At Home, born in North Carolina, father & mother born in North Carolina
Hattie Wallace 4 F, Dau, Single, born in North Carolina, father & mother born in North Carolina
Martha E. Wallace 1 F, Dau, Single, born in North Carolina, father & mother born in North Carolina

1880, Jun 28 -- Agricultural Census, Moore County, NC Page 21, Bensalem Township
Virgill Wallace listed 30 acres improved fields, 75 acres unimproved wooded valued at $100

(photographed April 2, 2010)

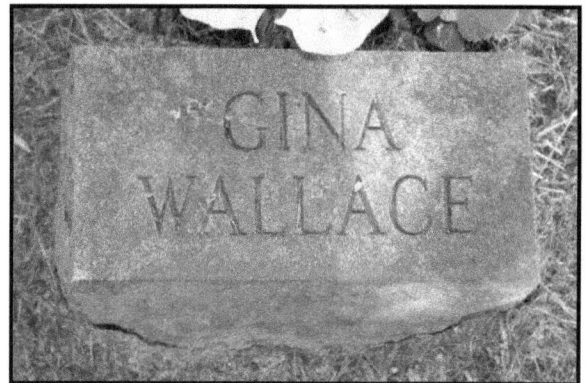

1889, Dec 11 -- Orders and Decrees Book 3 Page 80-82, Moore County, NC
George Cockman, Admst. of Isham Wallace Dec'd. v. Samuel B. Wallace, W.W. Wallace, Quimby Wallace. John Wallace, Virgil Wallace and other heirs. Division of Land mentions neighbors Quimby Wallace, Samuel Wallace; 10a tract deeded from Joseph Wallace to Isham Wallace. Heirs: Lovedy Jane Horner, wife of James Horner, Heirs of Elizabeth Cockman, wife of Sampson Cockman (Wesly Cockman, James Cockman, Alice Cockman, Clarky Ann Horner, wife of W.T. Horner, Eliza Horner, wife of Thomas R. Horner), Heirs of Locky Wallace (Mary Maness, wife of Blake Maness, Martha Maness, wife of Lewis Maness, Ruth Ritter, wife of Joseph Ritter, Vandie Maness, wife of McLellan Maness, Ella Blake Wallace), Sarah Garner, wife of John Garner, Samuel B. Wallace, Mary Cockman, wife of Noah Cockman, W.W. Wallace, Clarky Cockman, Quimby Wallace, Emsley Wallace, Virgil Wallace, S.D. Wallace and John Wallace (of Arkansas)

1898 -- Branson Business Directory, Moore County, NC
V.S. Wallace listed $100 acres valued at $150 located at Mt. Carmel Post Office in Bensalem Township

1898, Sep 15 -- Marriage Certificate, Moore County, NC
Virgily S. Wallace (age 49) and Flora Ann Garner (age 23) were married by J.M Deaton, JP in Bensalem Township. S.G Garner, J.H. Myrick and L.G. Myrick were witnesses. S.B. Wallace applied for the license.

Flora Ann Garner Wallace and son James Andrew "Jim Whit" Wallace *(Courtesy of James R. Ritter, Columbia, SC)*

1900, Jun 22 -- Census, Moore County, NC Page 49, Bensalem Township
Virgil S. Wallace 51 M, Apr 1849, Head, Married-2yrs, Farmer, born in North Carolina, father & mother born in North Carolina
Flora A. Wallace 23 F, Nov 1876, Wife, Married-2yrs, 2 Children(2 Living), born in North Carolina, father & mother born in North Carolina
Hattie L. Wallace 23 F, Oct 1876, Dau, Single, born in North Carolina, father & mother born in North Carolina
Lula F. Wallace 15 F, Dec 1884, Dau, Single, At School, born in North Carolina, father & mother born in North Carolina
Verney L. Wallace 10 M, Sep 1889. Son, Single, At School, born in North Carolina, father & mother born in North Carolina
Bulah F. Wallace 9/12 F, Aug 1899, Dau, Single, born in North Carolina, father & mother born in North Carolina

1906, Jun 4 -- 1896-1908 Administrator's Bonds, Moore County, NC Page 476-477
C.E. Cockman appointed Administrator of the Estate of Isham Wallace, Dec'd. with A.J. Lawhon and W.L. Ritter as securities. Heirs: Wes Wallace, Clarky Ann Cockman, Quimby Wallace, Lock Wallace, Sam Wallace, Bird Wallace, Emsly Wallace, Lane Wallace, John Wallace, Sarah Garner, Jane Horner, Elizabeth Cockman and Mary A. Cockman.

1910 -- Census, Moore County, NC Page 96-B, Bensalem Township
Bird Virgil Wallace 62 M, Head, Married-2nd-11yrs, Farmer, born in North Carolina, father & mother born in North Carolina
Flora A. Wallace 34 F, Wife, Married-1st-11yrs, 5 Children(5 Living), Farm Laborer(Home Farm), born in North Carolina, father & mother born in North Carolina
Bernne L. Wallace 19 M, Son, Single, Farm Laborer(Home Farm), born in North Carolina, father & mother born in North Carolina
Bulah F. Wallace 10 F, Dau, Single, born in North Carolina, father & mother born in North Carolina
Flora B. Wallace 8 F, Dau, Single, born in North Carolina, father & mother born in North Carolina
Steadman T. Wallace 6 M, Son, Single, born in North Carolina, father & mother born in North Carolina
Jeanette Wallace 4 F, Dau, Single, born in North Carolina, father & mother born in North Carolina
Baby Wallace 2 M, Son, Single, born in North Carolina, father & mother born in North Carolina

1917, Aug 1 – Death Certificate, Moore County, NC
V. S. Wallace died in Bensalem Township. Date of birth: Aug 10, 1849. Age: 67y 11m 21d. Occupation: Farmer. Birthplace: Moore County, NC. Father: Isham Wallace. Birthplace of Father: Moore County, NC. Mother: Nancy Furr. Birthplace of Mother: Moore County, NC. Cause of Death: Mitral Insufficiency. Place of Burial: Home Graveyard. Date of Burial: Aug 2, 1917. Undertaker: W.R. Kennedy, Hemp. Informant: Not Listed

1920, May 25 -- Order and Decrees Book 14 Page 224-227, Moore County, NC
Flora A. Wallace, widow of Virgil (Bird) Wallace Dec'd., petitioned the court for dower. As part of the dower petition, the court case listed all living heirs of Byrd Wallace. Heirs listed: Martha Deaton and husband George Deaton, Isham Wallace, Bernie Wallace, (H.T McNeill, Archibald McNeill, Hattie Jane Davis and husband, George Davis) children and heirs at law of Annie Wallace McNeill Dec'd., and her husband Alex McNeill, Dec'd.; Wilbur Brown and Lillian Brown, minor children of Effie McNeill Brown, Dec'd. and her husband, George Brown, Dec'd. and grandchildren of Annie Wallace McNeill, Dec'd.; Dock Williams, husband of Hattie Wallace Williams, Dec'd., and their children, Grady Williams and Bertha Williams, Charles Williams, husband of Lula Williams Dec'd., and their children Dawson Williams, minor, Regina Williams, minor, Virgil Williams, minor, Flossie Williams and James Williams, minors. The above named children and grandchildren being the heirs at law of the said Virgil Wallace by his first wife Regina Wallace. Bulah McNeill and husband Thomas McNeill, Cora Wallace, Steadman Wallace, Jeannette Wallace, James Wallace, Millard Wallace and Swannie Wallace all being the children and heirs at law of the said Virgil Wallace, Dec'd. by his second wife, Flora A. Wallace.

Virgil Spinks "Byrd" Wallace and Regina Hunsucker had the following children:

+367	Vann Wallace (-)	
+368	West Wallace (-)	
+369	William B. Wallace (1867-)	
+370	Lovedy Ann "Annie" Wallace (1868-1896)	
+371	John Morrison Wallace (1871-)	
+372	Lovena Wallace (1874-)	
+373	Hattie Jane Wallace (1875-1905)	
+374	Martha Elizabeth Wallace (1879-1947)	
+375	Isham Wallace (1882-1962)	
+376	Lula Florence Wallace (1886-1915)	
+377	Burney Leason Wallace (1888-1955)	

Virgil Spinks "Byrd" Wallace and Flora Ann Garner had the following children:

+378	Beulah Hazel Wallace (1898-1976)	
+379	Cora Bell Wallace (1901-1988)	
+380	Steadman McLendon Wallace (1903-1973)	
+381	Jeanette "Nettie" Wallace (1906-1985)	
+382	James Andrew "Jim Whit" Wallace (1908-1979)	

66. John M. Wallace, son of Isham Wallace and Nancy Furr, was born on March 4, 1850 in Moore County, NC died on January 3, 1923 in Perryville, Perry County, AR and was buried in Perryville, Perry County, AR at Perryville Cemetery. He married **Candace Ellen Melton** before 1875. Candace was daughter of James Melton (1805-1857) and Temperance Horner (1814-aft 1880). She was born on September 25, 1855 in Moore County, NC, died on July 29, 1911 in Rockingham, Richmond County, NC and was buried in Rockingham, Richmond County, NC at Northam Cemetery. He married **Emma Mitchell** on December 3, 1875 in Perryville, Perry County, AR.[102] He married **Dora Laughlin** on August 3, 1881 in Perryville, Perry County, AR.[103] He married **Tommie Powell** on January 16, 1894 in Perryville, Perry County, AR. He married **Cora Irene Reed** April 4, 1899 in Little Rock, Pulaski County, AR.[104]

RECORDS OF JOHN M. WALLACE

1850, Nov 12 -- Census, Moore County, NC Page 238
Isham Wallis 49 M, Farmer, $1600 Real Estate, born in North Carolina
Nancy Wallis 44 F, born in North Carolina
Westley Wallis 21 M, Farmer, born in North Carolina
Quimby Wallis 18 M, Farmer, born in North Carolina
Lockey Wallis 14 M, born in North Carolina
Emsley Wallis 12 M, born in North Carolina
Samuel Wallis 9 M, born in North Carolina
Jane Wallis 6 F, born in North Carolina
Sampson Wallis 5 M, born in North Carolina
Virgil Wallis 4 M, born in North Carolina
John Wallis 2/12 M, born in North Carolina

1860, Jul 9 -- Census, Moore County, NC Page 180, Caledonia Post Office
Isam Wallace 56 M, Farmer, $5000 Real Estate, $1000 Personal Property, born in North Carolina
Nancy Wallace 50 F, born in North Carolina
Samuel B. Wallace 17 M, born in North Carolina
Lovedy J. Wallace 15 F, born in North Carolina
Sampson D. Wallace 14 M, born in North Carolina
Virgil A. S. Wallace 12 M, born in North Carolina
John M. Wallace 10 M, born in North Carolina

1870, Jul 14 -- Census, Moore County, NC Page 481, Bensalem Township, Curriesville Post Office
Virgil S. Wallis 22 M, Farmer, $150 Real Estate, $200 Personal Property, born in North Carolina
Regina Wallis 21 F, born in North Carolina
William B. Wallis 3 M, born in North Carolina
Lovda A. Wallis 1 F, born in North Carolina
John M. Wallis 20 M, Laborer, born in North Carolina

1880 -- Census, Perry County, AR Page 164, Perryville Township
John H. Wallace 26 M, Farmer, Single, born in North Carolina, father born in North Carolina, mother born in Scotland
Living with family of Jacob & Eliza Smyers (no relation)

1889 -- Goodspeed's Biographical and Historical Memoirs of Central Arkansas Counties: Pulaski, Jefferson, Lonoke, Faulkner, Grant, Saline, Perry, Garland, and Hot Springs, Chapter 22 Perry County -- Page 700-701
"J.M. Wallace has been occupied as a farmer and stock-raiser of Fourche LaFave Township with good results. A native of Carthage, Moore County, N.C., he was born on March 4, 1850 his parents being Isham and Nancy Wallace, both born in the same state who were the parents of fifteen children, eleven of them still living: William W. (residing in North Carolina, where he is a farmer and has been sheriff of Moore County for three terms), Quimby (a farmer and residing in the same county), Emsby (a farmer also of the same county, who represented them in the State Legislature in 1868), S.D. (a farmer and at one time sheriff of the county), V.A and Samuel B. (both farmers of Moore County), Clarkie (wife of George Corkman), Sarah (wife of John Garner), Hettie (wife of James Horner), Marty (also married), and all residing in Moore County. The father of these children died Jun 15, 1885, his wife following him on August 3, 1886. J.M. Wallace remained with his father and attended public schools at Carthage in his youth, and when eighteen years of age went to college at Greensboro, Guilford County, N.C. He afterward taught school for about two years, and then moved to Little Rock, Ark., where he entered into business and from there to Texarkana, where he engaged in the cigar business. He again returned to Little Rock, but not remain long before he moved to Dardanelle, Yell County, and from there to Perry County, where he took charge and conducted a saw-mill. From Aplin he came to Perryville, where he bought a farm of eighty acres, with about fifty-three acres under cultivation, and has resided these since. On December 3, 1875, he was married to Miss Emma Mitchell, a daughter of William Mitchell, by whom he had one child: Byrdee (born Jun 1877, and dying in August if the same year), the mother dying some time afterward in Texarkana. Mr. Wallace was again married, his

second union taking place August 3, 1881, to Miss Dora Laughlin, a daughter of S.H. and I.F. Laughlin of Perryville, by whom he had five children: Ernest I. (born Jun 13, 1882), Myrtle (born December 13, 1883), Jessie (born August 15, 1885), Johnie Ellen (born December 27, 1887). Mr. Wallace became well and favorably known after a short residence in Perry County, and for two years was constable of Fourche LaFave Township, during which period the county was without a sheriff. He and his wife are both members of the Methodist Episcopal Church, and in politics, Mr. Wallace is a strong Democrat and a valuable support to that party." [*Editor's Note: There are several errors in this sketch as well as some embellishments.*]

1889, Dec 11 -- Orders and Decrees Book 3 Page 80-82, Moore County, NC
George Cockman, Admst. of Isham Wallace Dec'd. v. Samuel B. Wallace, W.W. Wallace, Quimby Wallace. John Wallace, Virgil Wallace and other heirs. Division of Land mentions neighbors Quimby Wallace, Samuel Wallace; 10a tract deeded from Joseph Wallace to Isham Wallace. Heirs: Lovedy Jane Horner, wife of James Horner, Heirs of Elizabeth Cockman, wife of Sampson Cockman (Wesly Cockman, James Cockman, Alice Cockman, Clarky Ann Horner, wife of W.T. Horner, Eliza Horner, wife of Thomas R. Horner), Heirs of Locky Wallace (Mary Maness, wife of Blake Maness, Martha Maness, wife of Lewis Maness, Ruth Ritter, wife of Joseph Ritter, Vandie Maness, wife of McLellan Maness, Ella Blake Wallace), Sarah Garner, wife of John Garner, Samuel B. Wallace, Mary Cockman, wife of Noah Cockman, W.W. Wallace, Clarky Cockman, Quimby Wallace, Emsley Wallace, Virgil Wallace, S.D. Wallace and John Wallace (of Arkansas)

1894-1898 -- Perry County, AR
John M. Wallace listed as County Judge

1899, Feb 23 -- Article, Arkansas Democrat [Little Rock, AR] Newspaper
Judge John M. Wallace, representative of Perry County, has returned after attending the funeral of his little daughter.

1899, Mar 14 -- Article, Arkansas Democrat [Little Rock, AR] Newspaper
Judge John M. Wallace, the member from Perry County, returned this morning from his home at Aplin, and is receiving the condolence of his confreres in his sad bereavement in the death of his wife and two daughters within three months.

John M. Wallace *(Courtesy of Mike Cross, Panama City, FL)*

1899, Mar 17 -- Article, The Southern Standard [Arkadelphia, AR] Newspaper
Mrs. John M. Wallace, wife of the member of the lower house of the legislature from Perry county, died the other day. Only a short time ago he was summoned home by the death of his daughter, and just before the convening of the legislature another child died. His confreres in the general assembly sympathize deeply with Judge Wallace in is triple bereavement. He was at his wife's bedside when the end came.

1899, Apr 5 -- Article, Arkansas Democrat [Little Rock, AR] Newspaper
John M. Wallace, representative from Perry County, stole a march on his friends last evening by getting married quietly. None of his friends in the general assembly were aware of his intentions. His bride was Miss Cora McDonald, of this city. It will be remembered that within the last three months Judge Wallace's wife and two daughters have died, his wife having died only three weeks ago at their home at Aplin, Perry County. Judge Wallace was granted leave of absence this morning.

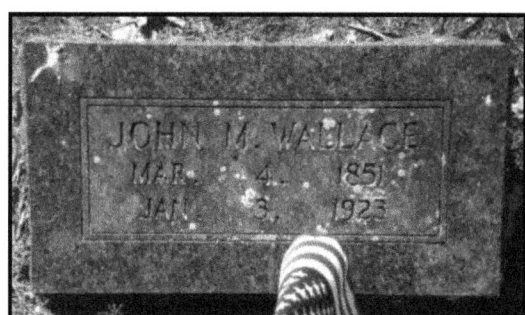

(Courtesy of Cassandra Shrum)

1900, Jun 4 -- Census, Perry County, AR Page 336-B, Aplin Township
John M. Wallace 50 M, Mar 1850, Head, Married-1yr, Farmer, born in North Carolina, father born in North Carolina, mother born in Scotland
Cora I. Wallace 26 F, Sep 1873, Wife, Married-1yr, 1 Child(1 Living), born in AR, father born in IN, mother born in KY
Earnest Wallace 18 M, Jun 1881, Son, Single, Farm Laborer, born in AR, father & mother born in North Carolina
Jessie Wallace 14 F, Sep 1885, Dau, Single, born in AR, father & mother born in North Carolina
Fred Wallace 11 M, Jun 1889, Son, Single, born in AR, father & mother born in North Carolina
Loch Wallace 4 M, Feb 1896, Son, Single, born in AR, father & mother born in North Carolina
Ruth Wallace 2 F, Sep 1897, Dau, Single, born in AR, father born in North Carolina, mother born in AR
Dewie Wallace 1 M, Sep 1898, Son, Single, born in AR, father born in North Carolina, mother born in AR
Eva Wallace 4 F, Oct 1895, S-Dau, Single, born in AR, father & mother born in AR

Additional Information can be found at www.MooreCountyWallaces.com

1906, Apr 5 -- Local News, Carthage Blade [Carthage, NC] Newspaper
"Mr. J.M. Wallace, of Arkansas, visited his relatives and friends in this county for the last three weeks and returned to Arkansas Tuesday. Mr. Wallace left this county when a young man, in 1874, for his adopted state and this was his first visit to his native state since he left. He has been successful and has accumulated considerable property and has been honored several times with office."

1906, Mar 13 -- Deed Book 33 Page 512, Moore County, NC
John M. Wallace [Perry County, AR] deeded Geo. W Horner his 1/3 interest and 52 2/3 of 158 acre tract known as the Isham Wallace homestead adjoining the heirs of Lockey Wallace, Isham Cockman and Quimby Wallace. Land includes the 21 acres deeded to Elizabeth Cockman prior to Isham Wallace's death and the 21 acres provided to John M. Wallace and Clarkie Cockman of the remaining 137 acres.

1906, Jun 4 -- 1896-1908 Administrator's Bonds, Moore County, NC Page 476-477
C.E. Cockman appointed Administrator of the Estate of Isham Wallace, Dec'd. with A.J. Lawhon and W.L. Ritter as securities. Heirs: Wes Wallace, Clarky Ann Cockman, Quimby Wallace, Lock Wallace, Sam Wallace, Bird Wallace, Emsly Wallace, Lane Wallace, John Wallace, Sarah Garner, Jane Horner, Elizabeth Cockman and Mary A. Cockman.

1908-1910 Listed as County Judge for Perry County, AR

1910, Apr 18 -- Census, Perry County, AR Page 43, Fourche-la-Fave Township, Town of Perryville
John M. Wallace 60 M, Head, Married-4th-11yrs, County Judge, born in North Carolina, father & mother born in North Carolina
Cora I. Wallace 36 F, Wife, Married-2nd--11yrs, 5 Children(5 Living), born in AR, father born in IN, mother born in KY
Lock Wallace 16 M, Son, Single, born in AR, father born in North Carolina, mother born in AR
Ruth Wallace 14 F, Dau, Single, born in AR, father born in North Carolina, mother born in AR
Eva Wallace 14 F, Dau, Single, born in AR, father born in North Carolina, mother born in AR
Fleet Wallace 9 M, Son, Single, born in AR, father born in North Carolina, mother born in AR
Reed Wallace 7 M, Son, Single, born in AR, father born in North Carolina, mother born in AR
Olga Wallace 5 M, Son, Single, born in AR, father born in North Carolina, mother born in AR
John Wallace 3 M, Son, Single, born in AR, father born in North Carolina, mother born in AR

1920, Jan 3 -- Census, Perry County, AR Page 28-B, Fourche Lafave Towship, Perryville Town
John M. Wallace 69 M, Head, Married, Operator-Farm, born in North Carolina, father & mother born in North Carolina
Cora I. Wallace 47 F, Wife, Married, Operator-Farm, born in AR, father born in IN, mother born in KY
Olga W. Wallace 14 M, Son, Single, born in AR, father born in North Carolina, mother born in AR
John M. Wallace 13 M, Son, Single, born in AR, father born in North Carolina, mother born in AR

1923, Jan -- Obituary, Daily Arkansas Gazette [Little Rock, AR] Newspaper
Solon from Perry County dies here: Representative J.M Wallace is a victim of Paralysis.
J.M. Wallace, aged 73, representative-elect of Perry County, died at the home of Mason Allen, 309 West Fourteenth Street, at 2:30 o'clock yesterday afternoon following a stroke of paralysis yesterday morning. He arrived here last Sunday to await the convening of the legislature. He Had been ill since last August, when he suffered a stroke of paralysis. Mr. Wallace has served a previous term in the legislature as representative of Perry County, and also was county judge for several terms. He was a well-known planted of Perryville. Mr. Wallace was born in North Carolina, but had been a resident of Perry County for many years. He is survived by his wife, two daughters and seven sons. The body was sent to Perryville early this (Thursday) morning by Healey & Roth

John M. Wallace and Candace Ellen Melton had the following child:

+386   Henry Clay Wallace (1875-1938)

John M. Wallace and Emma Mitchell had the following child:

+387   Byrdee Wallace (1877-1877)

John M. Wallace and Dora Laughlin had the following children:

+388   Phil Earnest I. Wallace (1882-1956)
+389   Myrtle Wallace (1883-)
+390   Jessie Nancy Wallace (1885-)
+391   Johnnie Ellen Wallace (1887-)
+392   Fred I. Wallace (1889-1954)

Tommie Powell was born on August 12, 1876. She died on March 10, 1898. She and John M. Wallace and Tommie Powell had the following children:

+393	Lock T. Wallace (1894-1956)
+394	Ruth Wallace (1897-)
+395	Dewey Wallace (1898-)

Cora Irene Reed was born circa 1873. She and John M. Wallace had the following children:

+396	Bertram Fleet Wallace (1900-1943)
+397	Charles Reed Wallace (c. 1903-)
+398	Olga William Wallace (c. 1905-)
+399	John Murriston Wallace (c. 1907-)

67. Hiram W. Wallace, son of Enoch Wallace and Malvina Furr, was born in 1835. He married **Julia Ann Williams** on August 12, 1855 in Moore County, NC.[105] He died on September 17, 1862 in Sharpsburg, MD in Civil War. [106]

RECORDS OF HIRAM W. WALLACE

1850, Aug 5 -- Census, Moore County, NC Page 165
Enoch Wallis 36 M, Farmer, born in North Carolina
Malvina Wallis 28 F, born in North Carolina
Hiram Wallis 15 M, born in North Carolina
Hamilton Wallis 12 M, born in North Carolina
Isham Wallis 10 M, born in North Carolina
Spinks Wallis 6 M, born in North Carolina
Christian Wallis 2 F, born in North Carolina

1854, Dec 9 -- Land Grant #4010, Moore County, NC
Jesse Thomas received 90 acres located on Big Branch of Drowning Creek adjoining his own line, Norman Morison, John Morison and Alexander McKenzie. James D. Thomas and Hiram Wallace were chain carriers.

1855, Aug 12 -- Record of Marriages, Moore County, NC Page 26
Hiram Wallace and Julia A. Williams were married by A. Stutts, JP.

1856, Jul 31 -- 1856-1858 Court of Pleas and Quarter Sessions, Moore County, NC Page 64
Ordered that Neill McIntosh be appointed overseer of the road from Bean's Bridge to the sassafras at McCaskill's and work the following hands: Wesley B. Muse, Benjamin Medlin, Franklin Muse, William H. Muse, Neill Caddell hands, A.B. Kelly, D.C. Kelly, Alexander Davis, Lochart Davis, William Bryant, Alvin Smith, William Fry, Calvin Crabtree
Jackson Crabtree and Hiram Wallace.

1858, Jan 30 -- 1856-1858 Court of Pleas and Quarter Sessions, Moore County, NC Page 354
Ordered that Wesley B. Muse be appointed overseer of the road from Bean's Bridge to the sassafras at McCaskill's and work the following hands: Neill McIntosh, Benjamin Medlin, Franklin Muse, W.H. Muse , Neill Caddell's hands, A.B. Kelly, D.C. Kelly, Alex Davis, L. Davis, Wm. Bryant, Alvin Smith, William Fry, C. Crabtree, J. Crabtree and H. Wallace.

[L-R] sisters Candis L. Williams and Julia Ann Williams Wallace
(Courtesy of Sarah Lawn, Carthage, NC)

1860, Sep 1 -- Census, Moore County, NC Page 221, Carthage Post Office
Hiram Wallace 25 M, $50 Personal Property, born in North Carolina
Julia A. Wallace 23 F, born in North Carolina
Martha J. Wallace 4 F, born in North Carolina
Louisa Wallace 1 F, born in North Carolina

1862, Mar 13 -- Civil War Service Records
Hiram Wallis enlisted in Company D, 49th Regiment in Moore County, NC at 24. Hiram was killed at Sharpsburg, MD on Sep 17, 1862.

1911, Jul 3 -- Confederate Widow's Pension Application, Moore County, NC
Julia Ann Brown, age 74 of Carthage Post Office, applied for a pension for Hiram Wallace Dec'd. Her husband served in Company D 49th Regiment. W.A. Fry and E.P. Seawell were witnesses. D.S. Barrett submitted an affidavit of support. [107]

Julia Ann Williams, daughter of George Williams (1812-1896) and Doxy Horner (1815-), was born on February 16, 1838 in Moore County, NC. She later married William Wesley Brown circa 1884. She died on June 16, 1921 in Moore County, NC.[108] She and Hiram W. Wallace had the following children:

+400   Martha Jane Wallace (1856-1929)
+401   Louisa Elizabeth Wallace (1859-1936)
+402   Hiram Walker Wallace (1862-1938)

69. Isham "Ike" Wallace, son of Enoch Wallace and Malvina Furr, was born in 1840. He married **Matilda Cockman** on April 18, 1861 in Moore County, NC.[109] He died on March 9, 1905 and was buried in Moore County, NC at Isham (Ike) Wallace Cemetery. Isham served in Company D, 49th Regiment in the Civil War. [110]

RECORDS OF ISHAM "IKE" WALLACE

1850, Aug 5 -- Census, Moore County, NC Page 165
Enoch Wallis 36 M, Farmer, born in North Carolina
Malvina Wallis 28 F, born in North Carolina
Hiram Wallis 15 M, born in North Carolina
Hamilton Wallis 12 M, born in North Carolina
Isham Wallis 10 M, born in North Carolina
Spinks Wallis 6 M, born in North Carolina
Christian Wallis 2 F, born in North Carolina

1860, Sep 13 -- Census, Moore County, NC Page 229-230, Carthage Post Office
Enoch Wallace 45 M, Farmer, $60 Personal Property, born in North Carolina
Malvina Wallace 37 F, born in
Spinks Wallace 12 M, born in North Carolina
Christine Wallace 9 F, born in North Carolina
Isham Wallace 18 M, born in North Carolina

(photographed June 13, 2009)

1861, Apr 18 -- Record of Marriages, Moore County, NC Page 85
Isham Wallace and Malinda Cockman were married by Corn. Dunlap, JP.

1862, Mar 13 -- Civil War Service Records
Isham Wallis enlisted in Company D, 49th Regiment in Moore County, NC at age 21

1862, Jun 16 -- Papers of North Carolina Governor Henry Clark
Alexander Walis and Isam Walis are reported being seen at Lawhon's Hill and refusing to return to duty by L. W. Lawhon, Postmaster at Lawhon's Hill Post Office

1870, Jul 4 -- Agricultural Census, Moore County, NC Page 9, Carthage Township, Carthage Post Office
Isham Wallace listed 10 acres improved, 8 acres wooded valued at $75

1870, Jul 6 -- Census, Moore County, NC Page 510, Carthage Township, Carthage Post Office
Isham Wallace 36 M, Farmer, $100 Real Estate, $150 Personal Property, born in North Carolina
Matilda Wallace 27 F, born in North Carolina
Spinks Wallace 8 M, born in North Carolina
Elias Wallace 5 M, born in North Carolina
Malinda Wallace 5/12 F, born in North Carolina

1877, Feb 25 -- 1875-1895 Appointment of Road Overseers Page 7, Moore County, NC
Ordered that J.J. Phillips be appointed overseer of the Plank Road from Richland Creek to the township line and have the following hands to work: Alex Black, W. Black, G.R. Fry, Pilot Fry, Isham Wallace, Thomas Fry, John Muse, Jerry Phillips, G. Williams and John Crabtree.

1879, Oct 5 -- Deed Book 127 Page 302
Mark Cockman and Alexander Cockman deeded Isham Wallace Jr. 100 acres located on Richland and Buffalo Creeks adjoining John Cockman, Griffith, Donald McQueen and McKay. C.E. Cockman and J.N. Green were witnesses.

1880, Jun 25 -- Census, Moore County, NC Page 228 B, Carthage Township
Isham Wallace Jr. 42 M, Head, Married, Farmer, born in North Carolina, father & mother born in North Carolina
Matilda Wallace 36 F, Wife, Married, Keeping House, born in North Carolina, father & mother born in North Carolina
Spinx Wallace 17 M, Son, Single, Works on Farm, born in North Carolina, father & mother born in North Carolina

Elias Wallace 15 M, Son, Single, Works on Farm, born in North Carolina, father & mother born in North Carolina
Malinda Wallace 12 F, Dau, Single, At Home, born in North Carolina, father & mother born in North Carolina

1880, Jun 25 -- Agricultural Census, Moore County, NC Page 18, Carthage Township
Isham Wallace, Jr. listed 40 acres improved fields, 100 unimproved wooded valued at $3000

1880, May 3 -- 1875-1895 Appointment of Road Overseers Page 21, Moore County, NC
Ordered that Emerson Jones be appointed overseer of the Plank Road from Richland Creek to the township line and have the following hands to work: J.W. Muse, John Crabtree, W.A. Fry, T.M. Fry, A.N. Fry, W.J. Black, A.M. Black and Isham Wallace.

1882, Aug 7 -- 1875-1895 Appointment of Road Overseers, Moore County, NC Page 37
Ordered that John Crabtree be appointed overseer of the Plank Road from Richland Creek to the township line and have the following hands to work: J.W. Muse, W.A. Fry, T.M. Fry, W.J. Black, A.M. Black, Isham Wallis and Ed Jones.

1883, Feb 14 -- 1875-1895 Appointment of Road Overseers, Moore County, NC Page 42
Ordered that Josiah Seawell be appointed overseer of the Plank Road from Richland Creek to the township line and have the following hands to work: J.W. Muse, W.A. Fry, T.M. Fry, W.J. Black, A.M. Black, Isham Wallace and Ed Jones.

1884 -- Branson's Business Directory, Moore County, NC
Ike Wallace listed as a farmer in Carters Mill Township

1886, Sep 18 -- 1875-1895 Appointment of Road Overseers, Moore County, NC Page 68
Ordered that Emerson Jones be appointed overseer of the new road from Plank Road at Isham Wallace's to township line and have the following hands to work: W.J. Black, Lurrence Jones and William Wallace.

1889, Oct 3 -- Article, Carthage Blade, Carthage, NC
"The item going the rounds of the grand jury at Carthage had indicted a father and son for larceny is incorrect. The facts are these. A white man by the name of Isham Wallace was taken before the Justice of the Peace upon the charge of stealing a sheep, his own son being the prosecutor. At the trial Wallace procured a warrant for his son, charging him with stealing (Wallace's) clothes. After hearing the evidence the Justice bound both father and son to the next Term of the Superior Court. The son was jailed not being able to give bond. The father afterwards mortgaged his property and secured bail for his son. The son is trying to get his father in the penitentiary and the father is trying to get his son there. The Justice thought that they both should go. The father is prosecuting the son, and at the same time procured bail for his appearance at court. It is somewhat a family affair."

1889, Nov 7 -- Article, Carthage Blade, Carthage, NC (follow up)
"Perhaps the most amusing cases tried at the late tern of court were the two which Lias Wallace indicted his father, Isham Wallace, for stealing sheep, and the father had a countersuit against the son for stealing a suit of clothes. The old man was called up first to testify against his son. He knew nothing about his son's connection with the theft of his clothes. As the State could make no case, at the suggestion of the Solicitor the prosecutor was taxed with the cost. Lias was next called to testify against the old man. He never owned a sheep, never saw the old man with one, and knew nothing about anybody stealing a sheep. In fact from his appearance, one would suppose that he had never seen a sheep. He was also taxed with the cost. While coming to court Monday morning Lias was met by a gentleman who enquired what was going to be done about the case and replied "The old man is going to do all he can to get me off, and I'm going to do all I can to get him off, but what I said about the old man stealing the sheep is so, I be d--n if he didn't steal him" Book these men are bad characters. The son ran away the day after the trial to avoid arrest for another offence."

1890 -- Branson's Business Directory, Moore County, NC
Ike Wallace listed as a farmer in Carters Mill Township

1898 -- Branson's Business Directory, Moore County, NC
Isham Wallace listed 140 acres valued at $200 located in Carthage Township at Carthage Post Office

1900, Jun 1 -- Census, Moore County, NC Page 19, West Carthage Precinct
Isam Wallace 59 M, 1841, Head, Married-40yrs, Farmer, born in North Carolina, father & mother born in North Carolina
Matilda Wallace 60 F, 1840, Wife, Married-40yrs, 5 Children(3 Living), born in North Carolina, father & mother born in North Carolina
Malinda Wallace 27 F, 1873, Dau, Single, 1 Child(1 Living), born in North Carolina, father & mother born in North Carolina
Torla E. Wallace 11 F, Dec 1888, GrDau, Single, born in North Carolina, father & mother born in North Carolina

1905, Apr 6 -- Record of Widow's Year Support, Moore County, NC
Matilda Wallace, widow of Isham Wallace allowed support

1924, Nov 15 -- 1923-1931 Administrator's Bonds, Moore County, NC Page 118-119
Geo. W. McNeill appointed Administrator of the Estate of Miltilda Wallace, Dec'd. with Spinks Wallace as security. Heirs: Spinks Wallace, Elias Wallace and Toad Wallace.

Matilda Cockman, daughter of Josiah Cockman (1813-1849) and Lydia Morgan (1814-), was born in 1845. She died before November 15, 1924 and was buried in Moore County, NC at Isham (Ike) Wallace Cemetery. She and Isham "Ike" Wallace had the following children:

+403	Sarah Wallace (-)
+404	Spinks Wallace (1862-1930)
+405	Elias W. Wallace (1865-1926)
+406	Malinda "Toad" Wallace (1870-)

70. **John Spinks Wallace**, son of Enoch Wallace and Malvina Furr, was born in 1844 in North Carolina. He married **Nancy Olive "Ollie" Canaday** on December 22, 1875 in Lauderdale County, AL.[111] He died on May 16, 1887 in Lauderdale County, AL and was buried in Lauderdale County, AL at Canerday Cemetery.[112]

RECORDS OF JOHN SPINKS WALLACE

1850, Aug 5 -- Census, Moore County, NC Page 165
Enoch Wallis 36 M, Farmer, born in North Carolina
Malvina Wallis 28 F, born in North Carolina
Hiram Wallis 15 M, born in North Carolina
Hamilton Wallis 12 M, born in North Carolina
Isham Wallis 10 M, born in North Carolina
Spinks Wallis 6 M, born in North Carolina
Christian Wallis 2 F, born in North Carolina

1860, Sep 13 -- Census, Moore County, NC Page 229-230, Carthage Post Office
Enoch Wallace 45 M, Farmer, $60 Personal Property, born in North Carolina
Malvina Wallace 37 F, born in
Spinks Wallace 12 M, born in North Carolina
Christine Wallace 9 F, born in North Carolina
Isham Wallace 18 M, born in North Carolina

1880 -- Census, Lauderdale County, AL Page 104, Township 1, Beat #5
Spinks Wallace 34 M, Head, Married, Farmer, born in North Carolina, Father and mother born in North Carolina
Olivy Wallace 32 F, Wife, Married, Keeping House, born in Alabama, Father and mother born in Alabama
Mary Wallace 4 F, Dau, Single, born in Alabama, father born in North Carolina, mother born in Alabama
Linnie Wallace 1 F, Dau, Single, born in Alabama, father born in North Carolina, mother born in Alabama
John Anderson 25 M(b), Other, Single, Laborer on Farm, born in Alabama, Father and mother born in Tennessee

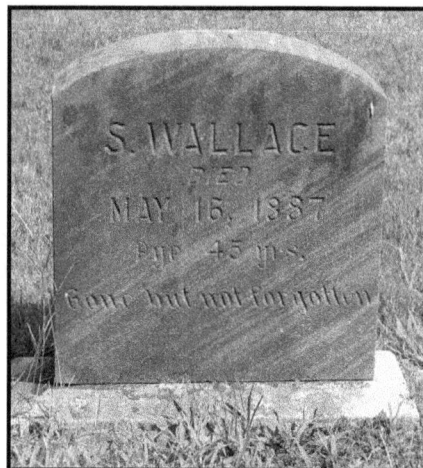

(Courtesy of Find A Grave)

Nancy Olive "Ollie" Canaday, daughter of Curtis Canaday (-) and Mary Robertson (-), was born on May 28, 1848 in Alabama. She died on January 16, 1944 and was buried in Lauderdale County, AL at Canerday Cemetery. She and John Spinks Wallace had the following children:

+407	Mary Wallace (1876-)
+408	Malinda A. Wallace (1879-1962)
+409	George Washington Wallace (1880-1926)
+410	Chappel Elizabeth Wallace (1884-1967)
+411	Thomas Evit Wallace (1887-1968)

71. **Christian Wallace**, daughter of Enoch Wallace and Malvina Furr, was born in 1849. Christian married **George Graham** in the late 1860's. George was born circa 1840.

RECORDS OF GEORGE GRAHAM AND CHRISTIAN WALLACE

1850, Aug 5 -- Census, Moore County, NC Page 165
Enoch Wallis 36 M, Farmer, born in North Carolina
Malvina Wallis 28 F, born in North Carolina
Hiram Wallis 15 M, born in North Carolina

Hamilton Wallis 12 M, born in North Carolina
Isham Wallis 10 M, born in North Carolina
Spinks Wallis 6 M, born in North Carolina
Christian Wallis 2 F, born in North Carolina

1856, Oct 30 -- 1856-1858 Court of Pleas and Quarter Sessions, Moore County, NC Page 102
Ordered that R.A. Cole be appointed overseer of the road from Elkins Branch to Beans Bridge and have the following hands to work: Jesse Bean's hands, John Warner, Burrel Ritter, Benjamin Barber, John Morrison's (Dick and Alston), B. Phillips, S. Phillips, R.A. Cole's hand, Daniel Fry, Noah Smith, Anderson Smith, W.L. Sullivan, A.W. Bean, George Graham and William Fry.

1860, Sep 13 -- Census, Moore County, NC Page 229-230, Carthage Post Office
Enoch Wallace 45 M, Farmer, $60 Personal Property, born in North Carolina
Malvina Wallace 37 F, born in
Spinks Wallace 12 M, born in North Carolina
Christine Wallace 9 F, born in North Carolina
Isham Wallace 18 M, born in North Carolina

1870, Jul 8 -- Census, Moore County, NC Page 513, Carthage Township, Carthage Post Office
Enoch Wallis 62 M, Farmer, $50 Personal Property, born in North Carolina
Molly V. Wallis 60 F, born in North Carolina
George Graham 30 M, born in North Carolina
Christian Graham 17 F, born in North Carolina
Vincy Graham 1 F, born in North Carolina

1880, Jun 28 -- Census, Moore County, NC Page 231-B, Carthage Township
George Graham 40 M, Head, Married, Farm Laborer, born in North Carolina, father & mother born in North Carolina
Christian Graham 30 F, Wife, Married, Keeping House, born in North Carolina, father & mother born in North Carolina
Malvina Graham 8 F, Dau, Single, born in North Carolina, father & mother born in North Carolina
Charlie Graham 6 M, Son, Single, born in North Carolina, father & mother born in North Carolina
Matilda Graham 4 F, Dau, Single, born in North Carolina, father & mother born in North Carolina
Sallie Graham 2 F, Dau, born in North Carolina, father & mother born in North Carolina
Infant Graham 2/12 F, Dau, born in North Carolina, father & mother born in North Carolina

George Graham and Christian Wallace had the following children:

+412	Vincy Graham (1869-)
+413	Malvina Graham (1872-)
+414	Charlie Graham (1874-)
+415	Matilda Graham (1876-)
+416	Sallie Graham (1878-)
+417	Infant Graham (1880-)

73. **Jeremiah D. Williams**, son of Jeremiah Williams and Elizabeth Wallace, was born in October 1825 in North Carolina. He married **Rebecca Kizer** on October 22, 1845 in Hall County, GA.[113] He died on March 1, 1906 in Springtown, Parker County, TX.[114]

RECORDS OF JEREMIAH D. WILLIAMS

1860 -- Census, McNairy County, TN Page 483
Jerry Williams 34 M, Farmer, $400 Real Estate, $400 Personal Property, born in North Carolina
Rebecca Williams 32 F, born in Georgia
William W. Williams 13 M, born in Georgia
Malissy Williams 12 F, born in Georgia
Sarah A. Williams 11 F, born in Georgia
Susanna Williams 7 F, born in Georgia
Mary J. Williams 5 F, born in Tennessee
Joseph B. Williams 3 M, born in Tennessee
John S. Williams 1 M, born in Tennessee

1862 -- Tax List, McNairy County, TN
Jeremiah Williams listed 84 acres valued at $350 and 1 white poll in District 16

1867 -- Tax List, McNairy County, TN
Jraymiah Williams listed 1 white poll in District 14

1868 -- Tax List, McNairy County, TN
Jerry Williams listed 125 acres valued at $300 and 1 white poll in District 14

1869 -- Tax List, McNairy County, TN
Jerrie Williams listed 125 acres valued at $300 and 1 white poll in District 14

1870 -- Tax List, McNairy County, TN
Jerry Williams listed 125 acres valued at $300 and 1 white poll in District 14

1870 -- Census, McNairy County, TN Page 347
Jeremiah Williams 44 M, Farmer, $1000 Real Estate, $1200 Personal Property, born in North Carolina
Rebecca Williams 43 F, Keeping House, born in Georgia
Sarah A. Williams 20 F, born in Georgia
Susanah 17 F, born in Georgia
Joseph B. Williams 13 M, born in Tennessee
John L. Williams 11 M, born in Tennessee
Henry D. Williams 8 M, born in Tennessee
Nancy M. Williams 5 F, born in Tennessee
Jerry L. Williams 2 M, born in Tennessee

1871 -- Tax List, McNairy County, TN
Jerry Williams listed 125 acres valued at $939 and 1 white poll in District 14

1872 -- Tax List, McNairy County, TN
Jerry Williams listed 125 acres valued at $900 and 1 white poll in District 14

1873 -- Tax List, McNairy County, TN
Jeremiah Williams listed 125 acres valued at $1275 and 1 white poll in District 14

1874 -- Tax List, McNairy County, TN
Jeremiah Williams listed 125 acres valued at $1275 and 1 white poll in District 14

1875 -- Tax List, McNairy County, TN
Jeremiah Williams listed 125 acres valued at $1300 and 1 white poll in District 14

1876 -- Tax List, McNairy County, TN
Jeremiah Williams listed 125 acres valued at $1300 and 1 white poll in District 14

1877 -- Tax List, McNairy County, TN
Jeremiah Williams listed 125 acres valued at $800 and 1 white poll in District 14

1880 -- Census, Parker County, TX Page 486
J. Williams 55 M, Head, Married, Farmer, born in North Carolina, father & mother born in North Carolina
R. Williams 53 F, Wife, Married, Keeping House, born in Georgia, father & mother born in South Carolina
H.D. Williams 19 M, Son, Single, Works on Farm, born in Tennessee, father born in North Carolina, mother born in Georgia
N. M. Williams 16 F, Dau, Single, At Home, born in Tennessee, father born in North Carolina, mother born in Georgia
J. T. Williams 13 M, Son, Single, Works on Farm, born in Tennessee, father born in North Carolina, mother born in Georgia
R. L. Kiser 9 M, Nephew, Single, born in Tennessee, father born in Georgia, mother born in ?

1900 -- Census, Parker County, TX Page 134-B
James S. Williams 41 M, Sep 1859, Head, Married-9yrs, Farmer, born in Tennessee, father & mother born in Tennessee
Lilly Williams 26 F, Mar 1874, Wife, Married-9yrs, 5 Children(2 Living), born in Texas, father & mother born in AR
Hassie Williams 2 F, Aug 1897, Dau, Single, born in Texas, father & mother born in AR
May Williams 2/12 F, May 1900, Dau, Single, born in Texas, father & mother born in AR
Jermiah Williams 74 M, Father, Married-52 years, Farm Hand, born in Georgia, father & mother born in Georgia
Rebecka Williams 72 F, Oct 1827, Mother, Married-52 years, 1 Child (1 Living), born in Georgia, father & mother born in Georgia
[Editors's Note: There are clear errors in this census listing]

1906, Mar 1 -- Death Certificate, Parker County, TX
Jeremiah Williams died in Springtown, Parker County, TX. Age: 80 yrs. Residence: Springtown, TX. Native of Tennessee. Cause of Death: Senile decay heart failure.

1906, Mar 16 – Obituary, The Plain Texan and Democrat [Weatherford, TX] Newspaper
"J.D. Williams, familiarly known as "Uncle Jerry" died at the home of his son, John Williams, in Springtown. Mr. Williams was 83 years of age."

Rebecca Kizer was born in October 1827 in Georgia. She died on May 24, 1908 in Wise County, TX. She and Jeremiah D. Williams had the following children:

+418   William W. Williams (1846-1868)
+419   Melissa Williams (1848-)
+420   Sarah Ann Williams (1849-)
+421   Susanna Williams (1852-1935)
+422   Mary J. Williams (1855-)
+423   Joseph Benjamin Williams (1857-)
+424   John S. Williams (1859-)
+425   Henry D. Williams (1862-)
+426   Nancy Margaret Williams (1864-1949)
+427   Jeremiah Thomas Williams (1868-bef 1930)

74. Mary Williams, daughter of Jeremiah Williams and Elizabeth Wallace, was born on December 9, 1825. She died on May 22, 1905 in Chester County, TN and was buried in Chester County, TN at Estes Cemetery.[115]

RECORDS OF MARY WILLIAMS

1850 -- Census, Moore County, NC Page 243-B
Bryant Stafford 24 M, Farmer, $1000 Real Estate, born in North Carolina
Mary Stafford 25 F, born in North Carolina
Henry C. Brewer 12 M, born in North Carolina
Rebecca Cockman 30 F, born in North Carolina

1860 -- Census, McNairy County, TN Page 508-B
Bryant Stafford 38 M, Farmer, $1000 Real Estate, $550 Personal Property, born in North Carolina
Mary Stafford 35 F, born in North Carolina
Losara Stafford 7 F, born in Tennessee
Rebecca Williams 37 F, born in North Carolina

1862 -- Tax List, McNairy County, TN
B. Stafford listed 202 acres valued at $950 and 1 white poll in District 14

1867 -- Tax List, McNairy County, TN
Bryant Stafford listed 286 acres valued at $1500 and 1 white poll in District 14

1868 -- Tax List, McNairy County, TN
Bryant Stafford listed 286 acres valued at $1500 and 1 white poll in District 14

1869 -- Tax List, McNairy County, TN
Mary Stafford listed 286 acres valued at $1200 in District 14

1870 -- Census, McNairy County, TN Page 346
Charly Clayton 40 M, Farmer, $3000 Real Estate, $1000 Personal Property, born in Tennessee
Mary Clayton 45 F, Keeping House, born in North Carolina

1870 -- Tax List, McNairy County, TN
Chas. Clayton listed 286 acres valued at $1200 and 1 white poll in District 14

1871 -- Tax List, McNairy County, TN
C.G. Clayton listed 286 acres valued at $2185 and 1 white poll in District 14

1873 -- Tax List, McNairy County, TN
C.G. Clayton listed 250 acres valued at $1700 and 1 white poll in District 14

1874-- Tax List, McNairy County, TN
C.G. Clayton listed 250 acres valued at $1700 and 1 white poll in District 14

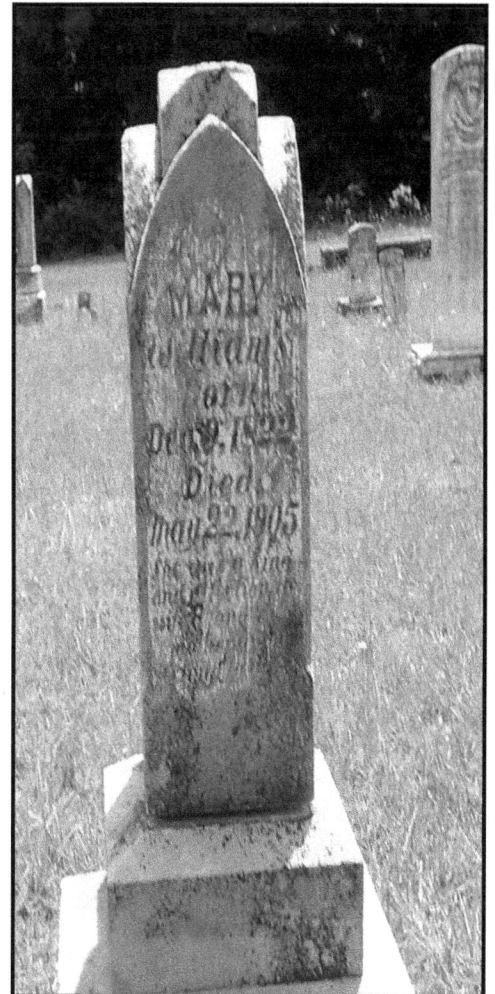

(Courtesy of Find A Grave)

1875 -- Tax List, McNairy County, TN
C.G. Clayton listed 250 acres valued at $1700 and 1 white poll in District 14

1876 -- Tax List, McNairy County, TN
C.G. Clayton listed 250 acres valued at $1700 and 1 white poll in District 14

1877 -- Tax List, McNairy County, TN
A.W. Williams listed 385 acres valued at $1400 and 1 white poll in District 14

1878 -- Tax List, McNairy County, TN
A.W. Williams listed 385 acres valued at $1400 and 1 white poll in District 14

1879 -- Tax List, McNairy County, TN
A.W. Williams listed 385 acres valued at $1200 and 1 white poll in District 14

1880 -- Tax List, McNairy County, TN
A.W. Williams listed 385 acres valued at $1200 and 1 white poll in District 14

1880 -- Census, McNairy County, TN Page 123
A.W. Williams 50 M, Head, Married, born in Tennessee, father born in North Carolina, mother born in Tennessee
Mary Williams 54 F, Wife, Married, Keeping House, born in North Carolina, father & mother born in North Carolina
Jos. F. Williams 23 M, Son, Single, Works on Farm, born in Tennessee, father born in Tennessee, mother born in Virginia

1881 -- Tax List, McNairy County, TN
A.W. Williams listed 385 acres valued at $1200 and 1 white poll in District 14

1882 -- Tax List, McNairy County, TN
A.W. Williams listed 355 acres valued at $1100 and 1 white poll in District 14

1897, Jan 15 -- Will, Chester County, TN
Will of Mary Williams Dec'd. Heirs: T.H. Williams, E.S. Muse and David Williams. Executor: S.J. Patterson. Witnesses: W.A. Scott and A.T. Williams. Codicil directing all land to T.H. Williams was witnessed by A.B. Patterson and D.M. Smith 7 Mar 1898.

1900 -- Census, Chester County, TN Page 194
Thomas H. Williams 36 M, Nov 1863, Head, Married-15yrs, Farmer, born in Tennessee, father born in North Carolina, mother born in MS
Martha A. Williams 42 F, Oct 1857, Wife, Married-15yrs, 9 Children(9 Living), born in Tennessee, father born in North Carolina, mother born in Virginia
Bettie O. Williams 14 F, Jan 1886, Dau, Single, In School, born in Tennessee, father & mother born in Tennessee
Benjamin D. Williams 12 M, Nov 1887, Son, Single, Farm Laborer, born in Tennessee, father & mother born in Tennessee
Thomas J. Williams 10 M, Mar 1890, Son, Single, In School, born in Tennessee, father & mother born in Tennessee
Mary A. Williams 7 F, Jun 1893, Dau, Single, In School, born in Tennessee, father & mother born in Tennessee
Elisus E. Williams 6 M, May 1894, Son, Single, born in Tennessee, father & mother born in Tennessee
Willis L. Williams 3 M, Dec 1896, Son, Single, born in Tennessee, father & mother born in Tennessee
Mona D. Williams 1 F, Dec 1898, Dau, Single, born in Tennessee, father & mother born in Tennessee
Polly Williams 76 F, Nov 1823, Aunt, Widowed, born in North Carolina, father & mother born in North Carolina
Estelle Webster 21 F, Mar 1879, Cook, Single, Cook, born in Tennessee, father & mother born in Tennessee
Frank Webster 1 M, Jan 1899, Servant, Single, born in Tennessee, father & mother born in Tennessee

Bryant Stafford was born on August 20, 1824. He died on April 19, 1868 and was buried in Chester County, TN at Estes Cemetery. He and Mary Williams had the following children:

+428   Losara Stafford (1853-)

Charles G. Clayton was born on February 1, 1830. He died on October 9, 1875 and was buried in Chester County, TN at Estes Cemetery.

Aaron W. Williams was born on January 19, 1830. He died on January 8, 1895 and was buried in Chester County, TN at Estes Cemetery.

75. **Enoch Spinks Williams**, son of Jeremiah Williams and Elizabeth Wallace, was born on July 6, 1827 in Moore County, NC. He died on April 6, 1894 in Parker County, TX and he was buried in Parker County, TX at Jaybird Cemetery.

RECORDS OF ENOCH SPINKS WILLIAMS

1846, Apr 28 -- 1844-1847 Court of Pleas and Quarter Sessions, Moore County, NC Page 319
Ordered that George W. Horner be appointed overseer of the road from George Moore's to the branch near McQueen's and work the following hands: Elisha Cagle, James Melton, Cornelius Mathews, George Williams, David Cockman, Joseph Cockman, Sampson Cockman, Isaac Williams, George Cockman, Noah Richardson and hands, Seburn Jones, Abram Hunsucker, James Deaton, Quimby Sowell, William Richardson, John Jones, Allan Jones, John W. Jackson, Westly Wallace, Chesly Horner, Enoch Williams, William Reaves and Richard Phillips.

1847, Oct 25 -- 1847-1849 Court of Pleas and Quarter Sessions, Moore County, NC Page 81
Ordered that Josiah Cockman be appointed overseer of the road from George Moore's to the branch near McQueen's and work the following hands: George W. Horner, Elisha Cagle, James Melton, Cornelius Mathews, George Williams, David Cockman, Joseph Cockman, Sampson Cockman, Isaac Williams, George C. Cockman, Noah Richardson & hands, Seburn Jones, Abram Hunsucker, James Deaton, Quimby Sowell, Wm. Richardson, John Jones, Allan Jones, John W. Jackson, Westley Wallace, Chesley Horner, Enoch Williams, William Reaves, Richard Phillips and James Jones.

1848, Apr 27 -- 1847-1849 Court of Pleas and Quarter Sessions, Moore County, NC Page 199
Ordered that George Hunsucker be appointed overseer of the road from the Bars at Thomas Williams' south of his house to Bear Creek at Mechanics Hill and work the following hands: James Hunsucker, Asa Hunsucker, H.K. Kelly, Stephen D. Williams, Emsley Jones' hand (Cob), Enoch Williams, Low Williams, Noah Brewer, John Cagle's hands, (Tyce and Jerry), Robert W. Goldston's hand (Wesley), Upshur [Furr]'s hands (Charles, Martin and Wesley), Leonard C. Stutts, Stephen Davis, James Davis, Matthew Williams and Linzy Williams.

1848, Oct 24 -- 1847-1849 Court of Pleas and Quarter Sessions, Moore County, NC Page 274
Ordered that John Jones be appointed overseer of the road from George Moore's to the branch near McQueen's and work the following hands: Josiah Cockman, George W. Horner, Elisha Cagle, James Melton, Cornelius Mathews, George Williams, David Cockman,

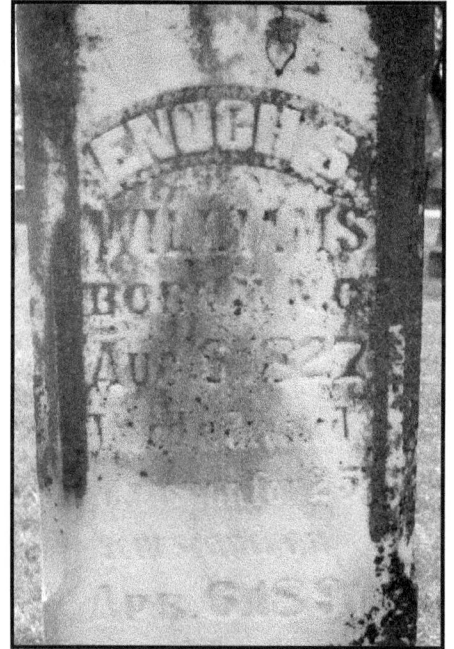
(Courtesy of Find A Grave)

Joseph Cockman, Sampson Cockman, Isaac Williams, George Cockman, Noah Richardson and hands, Seburn Jones, Abram Hunsucker, James Deaton, Quimby Sowell, William Richardson, Allen Jones, Westley Wallace, Chesley Horner, Enoch Williams, William Reaves, Richard Phillips and James Jones.

1849, Apr 23 -- 1847-1849 Court of Pleas and Quarter Sessions, Moore County, NC Page 399
Ordered that Robert W. Goldston be appointed overseer of the road from the Bars at Thomas Williams' to Mechanics Hill and work the following hands: George Hunsucker, James M. Hunsucker, Asa Hunsucker, H.K. Kelly, Stephen D. Williams, Amelia Jones (Bob), Enoch Williams, Low Williams, Noah Brewer, John Cagle (Tice & Jerry), Robert W. Goldston &hand, Upshur Furr & hands (Charles, Martin & Isaac), Stephen Davis, James Davis, Shadrick Williams, George W. Hunsucker, William Henly, William C. Stutts, Elijah Wilson, Upshur Sowell, Kinchen Fields and James H. Gordon.

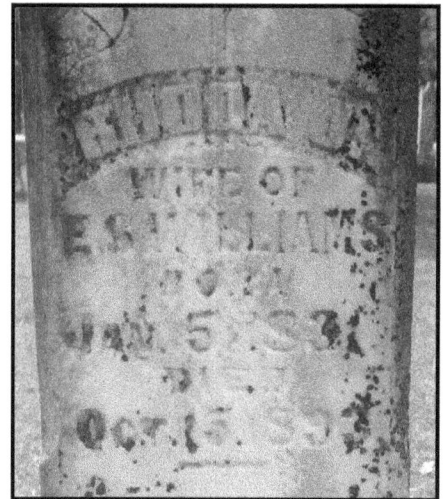

1850 -- Census, Moore County, NC Page 233
Enoch Williams 24 M, Laborer, born in North Carolina
Jane Williams 20 F, born in North Carolina

1852 -- Tax List, Moore County, NC
Enoch S. Williams listed 1 white poll in District 6

1852, Oct 27 -- 1851-1853 Court of Pleas and Quarter Sessions, Moore County, NC Page 340
Ordered that John Rouse be appointed overseer of the road from the fork of Cabbin Creek to the upper end of Alexr. Morison's old field and have the following hands to work: William Deaton, John Freeman, Jesse Sanders, Noah Williams, Enoch Richardson, Wesley Moore, Joseph Morgan, Britton Sanders, Enoch Williams, William Britt, Archd. McNeill, Isham Sanders, Noah Britt, Bazzel Deaton and Thomas Richardson.

1860, Jun 15 -- Census, Madison County, TN Page 87, District #1, Mt. Pinson Post Office
Enoch Williams 32 M, Farmer, born in North Carolina
Rodie Williams 29 F, born in North Carolina
Jerry William 9 M, born in North Carolina
Wm. Williams 7 M, born in North Carolina
Tensy Williams 5 F, born in Tennessee

Enoch Williams Jr. 1/12 M, born in Tennessee

1862, Jan 2 -- Marriage Certificate, McNairy County, TN
Benjamin Wallace and Miss Caty Williams were married by W.L. Gattis, MG. E.S. Williams was a witness.

1867 -- Tax List, McNairy County, TN
Enoch Williams listed 1 white poll in District 14

1868 -- Tax List, McNairy County, TN
Enoch Williams listed 150 acres valued at $750 and 1 white poll in District 14

1869 -- Tax List, McNairy County, TN
Enoch Williams listed 342 acres valued at $800 and 1 white poll in District 14

1870 -- Tax List, McNairy County, TN
Enoch Williams listed 342 acres valued at $800 and 1 white poll in District 14

1870, Jun 1 -- Census, McNairy County, TN Page 347-B, 14th Civil District, Bethel Springs Post Office
Enoch Williams 42 M, Farmer, $1500 Real Estate, $1000 Personal Property, born in North Carolina
Rody J. Williams 37 F, Keeping House, born in North Carolina
Jeremiah D. Williams 19 M, born in North Carolina
William B. Williams 17 M, born in North Carolina
Liney E. Williams 14 F, born in Tennessee
Lorenzo D. Williams 6 M, born in Tennessee
Mary A. Williams 3 F, born in Tennessee
John L. Williams 1 M, born in Tennessee
Elizabeth Williams 62 F, born in North Carolina

1871 -- Tax List, McNairy County, TN
E.S. Williams listed 30 acres valued at $150 and 1 white poll in District 14

1872 -- Tax List, McNairy County, TN
E.S. Williams listed 185 acres valued at $1250 and 1 white poll in District 14

1873 -- Tax List, McNairy County, TN
E.S. Williams listed 185 acres valued at $1600 and 1 white poll in District 14

1874 -- Tax List, McNairy County, TN
E.S. Williams listed 185 acres valued at $1604 and 1 white poll in District 14

**Enoch Spinks Williams Homeplace,
Montezuma, TN**
(Courtesy of Judy Little, Lexington, NC)

1875 -- Tax List, McNairy County, TN
E.S. Williams listed 185 acres valued at $2000 and 1 white poll in District 14

1876 -- Tax List, McNairy County, TN
E.S. Williams listed 185 acres valued at $2000 and 1 white poll in District 14

1877 -- Tax List, McNairy County, TN
E.S. Williams listed 185 acres valued at $1500 and 1 white poll in District 14

1880 -- Census, Parker County, TX Page 396, Precinct #2
E. F. Williams 51 M, Head, Married, Farmer, born in North Carolina, father born in Virginia, mother born in North Carolina
R. J. Williams 48 F, Wife, Married, Keeping House, born in North Carolina, father & mother born in North Carolina
R. D. Williams 16 M, Son, Single, Work on Farm, born in Tennessee, father & mother born in North Carolina
M. A. Williams 14 F, Dau, Single, At Home, born in Tennessee, father & mother born in North Carolina
J. S. Williams 11 M, Son, Single, Work on Farm, born in Tennessee, father & mother born in North Carolina
H. A. Williams 7 M, Son, Single, born in Tennessee, father & mother born in North Carolina
B. J. Williams 4 F, Dau, Single, born in Tennessee, father & mother born in North Carolina

Rhoda Jane Morgan was born on January 5, 1831 in Moore County, NC. She died on October 5, 1898 in Parker County, TX and was buried in Parker County, TX at Jaybird Cemetery. She and Enoch Spinks Williams had the following children:

+429   Jeremiah David Williams (1850-1917)
+430   William Birch Williams (1853-1926)
+431   Lency Elizabeth "Tennsy" Williams (1855-)

+432	Roda Jane Williams (1858-)
+433	Enoch L. Williams (1860-)
+434	Lorenzo Dewel "Lowe" Williams (1863-1942)
+435	Mary Ann "Mollie" Williams (1866-1962)
+436	John L. Williams (1868-)
+437	Hubert Andrew Williams (1873-1959)
+438	Rebecca Jane Williams (1875-1952)

76. Lorenzo D. "Low" Williams, son of Jeremiah Williams and Elizabeth Wallace, was born on December 2, 1829 in Moore County, NC. He died on August 3, 1890 in Henderson County, TN and was buried in Henderson County, TN at Palestine Cemetery.

RECORDS OF LORENZO D. "LOW" WILLIAMS

1850 -- Census, Moore County, NC Page 236-B
Stephen D. Williams 25 M, born in North Carolina
Franey Williams 24 F, born in North Carolina
William T. Williams 2 M, born in North Carolina
Richard M. Williams 1 M, born in North Carolina
Lorenzo Williams 21 M, born in North Carolina

1851, Jul 29 -- 1851-1853 Court of Pleas and Quarter Sessions, Moore County, NC Page 55
Ordered that James Davis be appointed overseer of the road from the Bars at Thomas Williams to Mechanics Hill and work the following hands: Stephen D. Williams, Andrew Hunsucker, James Hunsucker, Asa Hunsucker, Levi Deaton, Low Williams, Upshur Fur's hands, Jno. Cagle's hands, Jacob Stutts, James Davis, Stephen Davis, Robert Davis, Kinchen Fields, Thomas Henby, Noah Brewer, William Stutts, Enoch Rouse, Wesly Hunsucker, James H. Gordon, Hiram Kelly and Nathaniel Marley.

1852, Jul 27 -- 1851-1853 Court of Pleas and Quarter Sessions, Moore County, NC Page 306
Ordered that Lemu Sowell be appointed overseer of the road from the Bars at Thomas Williams to Machancis [Mechanics] Hill and work the following hands: Stephen D. Williams, Andrew Hunsucker, James Hunsucker, Asa Hunsucker, Levi Deaton, Low Williams, Upshur Furr hands, John Cagle hands, Jacob Stutts, James Davis, Stephen Davis, Robert Davis, Kinchin Fields, Thomas Henley, Noah Brewer, William Stutts, Enoch Rouse, Westley Hunsucker, James H. Gordon, Hiram Kelly and Nathaniel Marley.

1860, Jun 15 -- Census, Madison County, TN Page 87, District #1, Mt. Pinson Post Office
Lizzie Williams 51 F, born in North Carolina
L.D. Williams 30 M, Farmer, born in North Carolina
Phrany Williams 23 F, born in North Carolina
Katy Williams 20 F, born in North Carolina
Ann Williams 16 F, born in Georgia
James Williams 15 M, born in North Carolina
Joseph Williams 13 M, born in North Carolina
Bryant Williams 12 M, born in North Carolina

1867 -- Tax List, McNairy County, TN
L.D. Williams listed 1 white poll in District 14

1870 -- Census, Henderson County, TN Page 55, Lexington Post Office
Low D. Williams 40 M, Farmer, born in North Carolina
Sarah E. Williams 26 F, Keeping House, born in Tennessee
John W. Williams 7 M, born in Tennessee
Nancy C. Williams 5 F, born in Tennessee
Ambros A. Williams 3 M, born in Tennessee
Jerry W. Williams 3 M, born in Tennessee
Sarah M. Williams 1 F, born in Tennessee
Louisa M. Williams 1 F, born in Tennessee

Lorenzo D. "Low" Williams
(Courtesy of Judy D. Little, Lexington, TN)

1880 -- Census, Henderson County, TN Page 343, District #6
L.D. Williams 51 M, Head, Married, Farmer, born in North Carolina, father & mother born in North Carolina
Sarah E. Williams 33 F, Wife, Married, Keeping House, born in Tennessee, father & mother born in North Carolina
John W. Williams 17 M, Son, Single, Laborer on Farm, born in Tennessee, father born in North Carolina, mother born in Tennessee
Nancy C. Williams 14 F, Dau, Single, Laborer on Farm, born in Tennessee, father born in North Carolina, mother born in Tennessee

Jerrymiah Williams 13 M, Son, Single, Laborer on Farm, born in Tennessee, father born in North Carolina, mother born in Tennessee
Louisa Williams 11 F, Dau, Single, Laborer on Farm, born in Tennessee, father born in North Carolina, mother born in Tennessee
William T. Williams 8 M, Son, Single, Laborer on Farm, born in Tennessee, father born in North Carolina, mother born in Tennessee
Clarka A. Williams 6 F, Dau, Single, born in Tennessee, father born in North Carolina, mother born in Tennessee
Allice V. Williams 5 F, Dau, Single, born in Tennessee, father born in North Carolina, mother born in Tennessee
George W. Williams 3 M, Son, Single, born in Tennessee, father born in North Carolina, mother born in Tennessee
David L. Williams 11/12 M, Son, Single, born in Tennessee, father born in North Carolina, mother born in Tennessee
Benjaman Britt 20 M, Other, Single, Laborer on Farm, born in Tennessee, father & mother born in North Carolina

Sarah Elizabeth Hart, daughter of Ambrose R. Hart (1816-1886) and Nancy E. Reed (1819-bef 1860), was born on August 14, 1844 in Tennessee. She died on May 14, 1885 in Henderson County, TN and was buried in Henderson County, TN at Palestine Cemetery. She and Lorenzo D. "Low" Williams had the following children:

+439	John W. Williams (1863-1903)
+440	Nancy C. Williams (1865-1945)
+441	Ambrose A. Williams (1867-)
+442	Jeremiah W. Williams (1867-)
+443	Sarah M. Williams (1869-)
+444	Louisa M. Williams (1869-)
+445	William T. Williams (1872-)
+446	Clarkie Ann Williams (1874-1914)
+447	Alice V. Williams (1875-1907)
+448	George W. Williams (1877-1900)
+449	David L. Williams (1879-1924)
+450	Joseph Park Williams (1884-1962)

77. **Amanda Jane "Mandy" Williams**, daughter of Jeremiah Williams and Elizabeth Wallace, was born on July 16, 1836 in North Carolina. She married **Nathaniel "Nat" Britt** on August 26, 1857 in Madison County, TN.[116] She died on July 27, 1907 in Henderson County, TN and was buried in Henderson County, TN at Palestine Cemetery.

RECORDS OF NATHANIEL "NAT" BRITT AND AMANDA JANES "MANDY" WILLIAMS

1857, Aug 26 – Marriage Certificate, Madison County, TN
Nathaniel Britt and Amanda J. Williams were married by P.C. Cowad. Everett Wallace was a witness.

1860 -- Census, Madison County, TN Page 87, District #1, McTinson Post Office
Natt Britt 25 M, Farmer, born in Tennessee
Amanda Britt 22 F, born in Tennessee
David Britt 1 M, born in Tennessee
Jane Britt 6/12 F, born in Tennessee
David Williams 21 M, born in North Carolina

1867 -- Tax List, McNairy County, TN
Natanl. Britt listed 1 white poll in District 14

1868 -- Tax List, McNairy County, TN
Natanel Britt listed 1 white poll in District 14

1869 -- Tax List, McNairy County, TN
Nathaniel Britt listed 1 white poll in District 14

1870 -- Census, Madison County, TN Page 103, Jackson Post Office
N. Britt 30 M, Farmer, $1000 Personal Property, born in Tennessee
M. Britt 26 F, born in Tennessee
D. Britt 12 M, born in Tennessee
B. Britt 10 F, born in Tennessee
H. Britt 8 M, born in Tennessee
T. Britt 6 M, born in Tennessee
S. Britt 3 M, born in Tennessee

1880 -- Census, Henderson County, TN Page 393-B, District #10
Mandy Britt 40 F, Head, Widowed, Laborer, born in North Carolina, father & mother born in North Carolina
Davy J. Britt 21 M, Son, Single, Laborer, born in Tennessee, father & mother born in North Carolina

1880 -- Census, Henderson County, TN Page 393-B, District #10
Bettie Crow 20 F, Head, Married, Keeping House, born in Tennessee, father & mother born in North Carolina
Tom Crow 20 M, Husband, Married, Laborer, born in Tennessee, father & mother LEFT BLANK
Henry Britt 18 M, BroL, Single, Laborer, born in Tennessee, father & mother born in North Carolina
Tommie Britt 15 M, BroL, Single, Laborer, born in Tennessee, father & mother born in North Carolina
Savage Britt 12 M, Brother, Single, Laborer, born in Tennessee, father & mother born in North Carolina
Clarkey Britt 9 F, Sister, Single, born in Tennessee, father & mother born in North Carolina
Florency Britt 5 F, Sister, Single, born in Tennessee, father & mother born in North Carolina

1900, Jun 4 -- Census, Henderson County, TN Page 63-B
Joe C. Hart 28 M, Dec 1871, Head, Married-3yrs, Farmer, born in Tennessee, father & mother born in Tennessee
Florence Hart 25 F, Jun 1875, Wife, Married-3yrs, 3 Children(3 Living), born in Tennessee, father & mother born in Tennessee
Roy E. Hart 6 M, Oct 1893, Son, Single, born in Tennessee, father & mother born in Tennessee
Bettie L. Hart 3 F, Mar 1896, Dau, Single, born in Tennessee, father & mother born in Tennessee
Ernest W. Hart 1 M, Sep 1898, Son, Single, born in Tennessee, father & mother born in Tennessee
Mandy Britt 64 F, Jun 1835, MotherL, Widowed, 7 Children(1 Living), born in North Carolina, father & mother born in North Carolina

Amanda Jane "Mandy" Williams had the following children:

+451   Florence "Retta" Britt (1875-1944)

Nathaniel "Nat" Britt, son of Beacom C. Britt (1804-1876) and Dallie Wallace (aft 1810-bef 1849), was born in June 1836 in Moore County, NC. He died on February 19, 1871 in Henderson County, TN. He and Amanda Jane "Mandy" Williams had the following children:

+452   David James Britt (1857-1953)
+453   Elizabeth Jane Britt (1860-)
+454   Henry Clay Britt (1862-1946)
+455   Thomas Jefferson Britt (1865-1942)
+456   William Salvage Britt (1868-1951)
+457   Clarkie Ann Britt (1872-1906)

79. **David Anderson Williams**, son of Jeremiah Williams and Elizabeth Wallace, was born on December 14, 1838 in Moore County, NC. He died on January 25, 1900 in Tennessee and was buried in Chester County, TN at Estes Cemetery.[117]

RECORDS OF DAVID ANDERSON WILLIAMS

1860 -- Census, Madison County, TN Page 87, District #1, McTinson Post Office
Natt Britt 25 M, Farmer, born in Tennessee
Amanda Britt 22 F, born in Tennessee
David Britt 1 M, born in Tennessee
Jane Britt 6/12 F, born in Tennessee
David Williams 21 M, born in North Carolina

1867 -- Tax List, McNairy County, TN
David Williams listed 1 white poll in District 14

1868 -- Tax List, McNairy County, TN
David Williams listed 1 white poll in District 14

1869 -- Tax List, McNairy County, TN
David Williams listed 1 white poll in District 14

1870 -- Census, Madison County, TN Page 103, Jackson Post Office
D. Williams 27 M, Farmer, $500 Personal Property, born in Tennessee
B. Williams 26 F, born in Tennessee
A. Williams 10 M, born in Tennessee
T. Williams 8 M, born in Tennessee
B. Williams 6 F, born in Tennessee

1880 -- Census, Madison County, TN Page 109, District #1

(Courtesy of Find A Grave)

David A. Williams 42 M, Head, Married, Farmer, born in North Carolina, father born in Virginia, mother born in North Carolina
Mary J. Williams 27 F, Wife, Married, Keeping House, born in North Carolina, father & mother born in North Carolina
Thomas Williams 16 M, Son, Single, Work on Farm, born in Tennessee, father born in North Carolina, mother born in MS
Archy Williams 15 M, Son, Single, Work on Farm, born in Tennessee, father born in North Carolina, mother born in MS
Mary J. Williams 10 F, Dau, Single, born in Tennessee, father born in North Carolina, mother born in MS
Robt. H. Williams 7 M, Son, Single, born in Tennessee, father born in North Carolina, mother born in MS
Henry Collins 21 M, Other, Single, Work on Farm, born in North Carolina, father & mother born in North Carolina
John E. Mosier 72 M, FatherL, Widowed, born in North Carolina, father & mother born in North Carolina

> **Elizabeth Ann Mosier**, daughter of John E. Mosier (1808-), was born on May 11, 1845 in Mississippi. She died on April 12, 1876 in Tennessee. She and David Anderson Williams had the following children:

+458	Thomas Henry Williams (1863-1918)
+459	Archibald Theodore Williams (1865-1899)
+460	Milissey Williams (1868-1870)
+461	Mary Jane Williams (1870-)
+462	Robert H. Williams (1873-)
+463	Susan Williams (1875-1876)

> **Mary J.** was born in 1853.

80. **Caty Williams**, daughter of Jeremiah Williams and Elizabeth Wallace, was born in 1840 in North Carolina. She married **Benjamin Wallace** on January 2, 1862 in McNairy County, TN.[118] She died before 1870.

> Benjamin Wallace, son of Nathan C. Wallace (1800-1884) and Finity Britt (1800-bef 1857), was born in April 1840 in North Carolina. He married Holly J. Kizer on January 23, 1870 in McNairy County, TN.[119] He married Eliza Elizabeth Rivers on January 9, 1880 in St. Francis County, AR.[120] He died on July 17, 1900 in Reno, Parker County, TX and was buried in Parker County, TX at Jaybird Cemetery. He and Caty Williams had the following children:

+235	Sarah Elizabeth Wallace (1862-1900)
+236	Clarkie Ann Wallace (1866-1889)

82. **James Wesley Williams**, son of Jeremiah Williams and Elizabeth Wallace, was born in 1845 in Georgia. He married **Margaret M. Hart** on September 28, 1868 in Madison County, TN and was buried in Henderson County, TN at Palestine Cemetery.[121]

RECORDS OF JAMES WESLEY WILLIAMS

1860, Jun 15 -- Census, Madison County, TN Page 87, District #1, Mt. Pinson Post Office
Lizzie Williams 51 F, born in North Carolina
L.D. Williams 30 M, Farmer, born in North Carolina
Phrany Williams 23 F, born in North Carolina
Katy Williams 20 F, born in North Carolina
Ann Williams 16 F, born in Georgia
James Williams 15 M, born in North Carolina
Joseph Williams 13 M, born in North Carolina
Bryant Williams 12 M, born in North Carolina

1880 -- Census, Henderson County, TN Page 344-B, District #6
James M. Williams 33 M, Head, Married, Farmer, born in Georgia, father & mother born in North Carolina
Margaret M. Williams 29 F, Wife, Married, Keeping House, born in Tennessee, father & mother born in Tennessee
Mollie A. Williams 9 F, Dau, Single, Laborer on Farm, born in Tennessee, father born in Georgia, mother born in Tennessee
Ada F. Williams 7 F, Dau, Single, born in Tennessee, father born in Georgia, mother born in Tennessee
Martha C. Williams 5 F, Dau, Single, born in Tennessee, father born in Georgia, mother born in Tennessee
Lewis C. Williams 2 M, Son, Single, born in Tennessee, father born in Georgia, mother born in Tennessee
Adel Williams 6/12 F, Dau, Single, born in Tennessee, father born in Georgia, mother born in Tennessee

> Margaret M. Hart, daughter of Ambrose R. Hart (1816-1886) and Nancy E. Reed (1819-bef 1860), was born in 1846 in Tennessee and was buried in Henderson County, TN at Palestine Cemetery. She and James Wesley Williams had the following children:

+464	Mollie Ann Williams (1869-1962)

+465	Ada F. Williams (1873-)
+466	Martha Catherine Williams (1874-1918)
+467	Lewis Cager Williams (1876-1909)
+468	Adele Williams (1879-)
+469	Dovie A. Williams (1881-1968)
+470	Daisy E. Williams (1885-)
+471	Westly Tom Williams (1886-)

84. Bryant Williams, son of Jeremiah Williams and Elizabeth Wallace, was born in 1848 in Tennessee. He married **Mary Latham** on January 27, 1874 in McNairy County, TN.[122]

RECORDS OF BRYANT WILLIAMS

1880 -- Census, Henderson County, TN Page 393-B, District #10
Bryant Williams 31 M, Head, Married, Laborer, born in North Carolina, father born in Virginia, mother born in North Carolina
Mary Williams 23 F, Wife, Married, Keeping House, born in Tennessee
Ella Williams 5 F, Dau, Single, born in Tennessee, father born in North Carolina, mother born in Tennessee
Docey Williams 11/12 F, Dau, Single, born in Tennessee, father born in North Carolina, mother born in Tennessee

Mary Latham, daughter of Carter Latham (1830-) and Rhoda Britt (1834-1891), was born on November 25, 1856 in Tennessee. She and Bryant Williams had the following children:

+472	Ella Williams (1875-)
+473	Docey Williams (1879-)
+474	Dave Williams (1883-1909)
+475	Jerry Hubert Williams Sr. (1886-1931)

88. Isaac Spinks Wallace, son of Manda Wallace, was born on October 1, 1849. He died on March 23, 1912 and was buried in Moore County, NC at Old Beulah Hill Cemetery.

RECORDS OF ISAAC SPINKS WALLACE

1850, Nov 9 -- Census, Moore County, NC Page 238
Manda Wallis 40 F, born in North Carolina
Sarah Wallis 10 F, born in North Carolina
Corneilus Wallis 5 M (mulatto), born in North Carolina
Anderson Wallis 3 M (mulatto), born in North Carolina
Spinks Wallis 3/12 M (mulatto), born in North Carolina

1880, Jun 14 -- Agricultural Census, Moore County, NC Page 6, Mineral Spings Township
Spinks Wallace listed 5 acres improved fields, 45 acres unimproved wooded valued at $50

1880, Jun 16 -- Census, Moore County, NC Page 371, Mineral Springs Township
Spinx Wallace 29 M, Head, Married, Farmer, born in North Carolina, father & mother born in North Carolina
Anna Jane Wallace 25 F, Wife, Married, Keeping House, born in North Carolina, father & mother born in North Carolina
Sarah C. Wallace 8 F, Dau, Single, born in North Carolina, father & mother born in North Carolina
Archibald A. Wallace 5 M, Son, Single, born in North Carolina, father & mother born in North Carolina
James M. Wallace 2 M, Son, Single, born in North Carolina, father & mother born in North Carolina

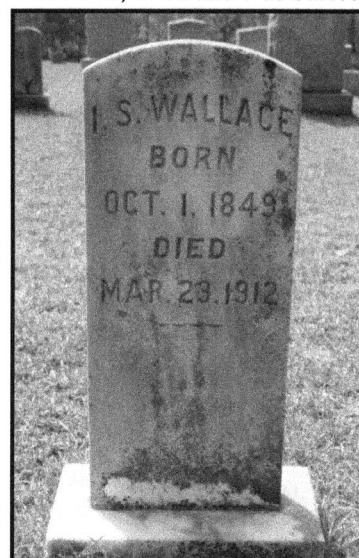

I. S. WALLACE
BORN
OCT. 1. 1849
DIED
MAR. 23. 1912

(photographed April 25, 2010)

1897, Oct 15 -- Article, The Pinehurst Outlook [Newspaper] Pinehurst, NC
I.S. Wallace, Archie Wallace, and Mrs. Ann Wallace listed as founding members of Beulah Hill Baptist Church. The original article can be found in the History of Beulah Hill Baptist Church at http://www.beulahhillbaptistchurch.com/id4.html

1898 -- Branson Business Directory, Moore County, NC
Mrs. Ann J. Wallace listed $50 acres valued at $93 located at Pinehurst Post Office in Mineral Springs Township

1900, Jun 27 -- Census, Moore County, NC Page 207-B, Mineral Springs Township
Ivy S. Wallace 49 M, Oct 1850, Head, Married-27yrs, Gardner, born in North Carolina, father & mother born in North Carolina
Annie J. Wallace 49 F, 1851, Wife, Married-27yrs, 6 Children(5 Living), born in North Carolina, father & mother born in North Carolina
Archie A. Wallace 24 M, Oct 1875, Son, Single, Farmer, born in North Carolina, father & mother born in North Carolina

Additional Information can be found at www.MooreCountyWallaces.com

James M. Wallace 21 M, Sep 1878, Son, Single, Gardner, born in North Carolina, father & mother born in North Carolina
Kinnie M. Wallace 15 M, 1885, Son, Single, Assisting on Farm, born in North Carolina, father & mother born in North Carolina
Florence J. Wallace 11 F, Oct 1888, Dau, Single, At School, born in North Carolina, father & mother born in North Carolina

1902 -- Voter Registration Rolls, Moore County, NC
I.S. Wallace listed as a registered voter and Everet Wallace as a male ancestor who voted prior to 1867.

1910, May 6 -- Census, Moore County, NC Page 216-B, Mineral Springs Township
Spinks Wallice 57 M, Head, Married-1st-39yrs, Farmer, born in North Carolina, father & mother born in North Carolina
Annie Wallice 56 F, Wife, Married-1st-39yrs, born in North Carolina, father & mother born in North Carolina
James M. Wallice 34 M, Son, Single, Farm Laborer, born in North Carolina, father & mother born in North Carolina
Kenneth Wallice 26 M, Son, Single, Laborer-Odd Jobs, born in North Carolina, father & mother born in North Carolina
Florence Wallice 20 F, Dau, Single, Farm Laborer, born in North Carolina, father & mother born in North Carolina
Carson Black 6 M, GrSon, Single, born in North Carolina, father & mother born in North Carolina
Myrtle Black 4 F, GrDau, Single, born in North Carolina, father & mother born in North Carolina
James Q. Wallice 26 M, Head, Married-6mos, Laborer-Jobs, born in North Carolina, father & mother born in North Carolina
Maggie Wallice 17 F, Wife, Married-6mos, born in North Carolina, father & mother born in North Carolina

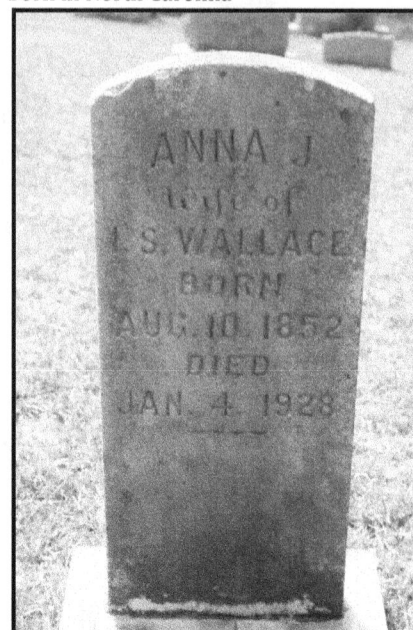

(photographed April 25, 2010)

Anna Jane McDonald, daughter of James William McDonald (1824-1865) and Catherine Ray (1824-1864), was born on August 10, 1852. She died on January 4, 1928 and was buried in Moore County, NC at Old Beulah Hill Cemetery. She and Isaac Spinks Wallace had the following children:

+476	Sarah C. Wallace (1872-)	
+477	Ella Wallace (1873-1936)	
+478	Archibald Alexander "Archie" Wallace (1875-1939)	
+479	James M. "Jim" Wallace (1878-1931)	
+480	Kenneth Martin Wallace (1883-1966)	
+481	Florence Jane Wallace (1888-1973)	
+482	Mary A. E. Wallace (1891-1893)	

89. **Martha J. Wallace**, daughter of Abraham C. Hunsucker and Franey Wallace, was born on March 10, 1833. She died on January 22, 1922 and was buried in Appling County, GA at Deen Cemetery.[123]

RECORDS OF WILLIAM ZENO RICHARDSON AND MARTHA J. WALLACE

1850 -- Census, Moore County, NC Page 239
John Cockman 64 M, Farmer, $350 Real Estate, born in North Carolina
Mary Cockman 66 F, born in North Carolina
Leno Richardson 18 M, born in North Carolina

1853, July 26 -- 1853-1856 County Court Minutes Page 13
Ordered that Westley Wallace be appointed overseer of the road from George Moore's to the branch near McQueen's and work the following hands: Joseph Upton, Cornelius Dowdy, Zeno Cockman, Henry Melton, George Cockman, Noah Richardson and hands, Noah Cockman, David Cockman, Armstead Stutts, Isaac Williams, George W. Horner, John Jones, and Quimby Wallace.

1856, Jan 31 -- 1853-1856 County Court Minutes Page 456
Ordered that William Stutts be appointed overseer of the road from George Moore's to the branch near McQueen's and work the following hands: Westley Wallace, Cornelius Dowdy, Zeno Cockman, Henry Melton, George Cockman, Sampson Cockman, Noah Cockman, David Cockman, Noah Richardson and hands, Armstead Stutts, Isaac Williams, G.W. Horner, John Jones, Quimby Wallace, Joseph Upton, Lochart Wallace, Geo. Williams and Jefferson Williams.

1858, May 1 -- 1856-1858 County Court Minutes Page 422
Ordered that George Cockman be appointed overseer of the road from George Moore's to the branch near McQueen's and work the following hands: William Stutts, Wesley Wallace, Cornelius Dowdy, Zeno Cockman, Henry Melton, Sampson Cockman, Noah Cockman,

David Cockman, Noah Richardson hands, Armsted Stutts, Isaac Williams, G.W. Horner, John Jones, Quimby Wallace, Joseph Upton, Lochart Wallace, George Williams and Jefferey Williams.

1860, Sep 14 -- Census, Moore County, NC Page 232, Carthage Post Office
W. Z. Richardson 28 M, born in North Carolina
Martha Richardson 26 F, born in North Carolina
Alfred Richardson 5 M, born in North Carolina
Margaret R. Richardson 4 F, born in North Carolina
John A. Richardson 2 M, born in North Carolina
William A. Richardson 1/12 M, born in North Carolina
Rebecca Wallace 16 F, born in North Carolina

1870, Jun 29 -- Census, Moore County, NC Page 501, Carthage Township, Carthage Post Office
Wm. Z. Richardson 38 M, Farmer, $500 Personal Property, born in North Carolina
Martha J. Richardson 37 F, born in North Carolina
Alfred D. Richardson 14 M, Laborer, born in North Carolina
Margaret R. Richardson 13 F, At Home, born in North Carolina
John A. Richardson 12 M, At Home, born in North Carolina
William A. Richardson 9 M, At Home, born in North Carolina
Mary Richardson 6 F, At Home, born in North Carolina
Charles R. Richardson 4 M, At Home, born in North Carolina
Noah B. Richardson 1 M, At Home, born in North Carolina

1880 -- Census, Cumberland County, NC Page 521-B, Quewhiffle Township
William Richardson 48 M, Head, Married, Mechanic, born in North Carolina, father & mother born in North Carolina
Salla M. Richardson 46 F, Wife, Married, Keeping House, born in North Carolina, father & mother born in North Carolina
John Richardson 23 M, Son, Single, Farmer, born in North Carolina, father & mother born in North Carolina
Mary Richardson 17 F, Dau, Single, born in North Carolina, father & mother born in North Carolina
Carles R. Richardson 12 M, Son, Single, born in North Carolina, father & mother born in North Carolina
Noah B. Richardson 11 M, Son, Single, born in North Carolina, father & mother born in North Carolina
Zena W. Richardson 9 M, Son, Single, born in North Carolina, father & mother born in North Carolina
Tommy F. Richardson 8 M, Son, Single, born in North Carolina, father & mother born in North Carolina
Matty J. Richardson 5 F, Dau, Single, born in North Carolina, father & mother born in North Carolina
Stevan Richardson 3 M, Son, Single, born in North Carolina, father & mother born in North Carolina
William Newell 19 M, Other, Married, Turpentine Labor, born in North Carolina, father & mother born in North Carolina

1900 -- Census, Liberty County, GA Page
W. Z. Richardson 68 M, 1832, Head, Married, Distiller, born in Georgia, father & mother born in Georgia
Martha J. Richardson 69 F, 1831, Wife, Married, 2 Children(2 Living), born in Georgia, father & mother born in Georgia
Mattie J. Richardson 24 F, 1876, Daughter, Single, born in Georgia, father & mother born in Georgia
Z. C. West 20 M, 1880, Grandson, Single, Cooper, born in Georgia, father & mother born in Georgia

William Zeno Richardson, son of Richardson (-) and Sarah (aft 1800-), was born on January 15, 1832. He died on October 27, 1905 and was buried in Appling County, GA at Deen Cemetery.[124] He and Martha J. Wallace had the following children:

+483	Alfred D. Richardson (1855-)
+484	Margaret R. Richardson (1856-)
+485	John A. Richardson (1858-)
+486	William A. Richardson (1860-)
+487	Mary Richardson (1864-)
+488	Charles R. Richardson (1866-)
+489	Noah Bazzel Richardson (1868-1906)
+490	Zeno Worth Richardson (1871-)
+491	Tommy F. Richardson (1872-)
+492	Matty J. Richardson (1875-)
+493	Stephen O. Richardson (1877-)

90. **Mary Ann Wallace**, daughter of Abraham C. Hunsucker and Franey Wallace, was born on June 16, 1838. She married **Anderson Lindo Seawell** on August 7, 1856 in Moore County, NC.[125] She died on September 6, 1865 and was buried in Moore County, NC at Bethlehem Baptist Church.

RECORDS OF ANDERSON LINDO SEAWELL AND MARY ANN WALLACE

1850, Nov 8 -- Census, Moore County, NC Page 236
Franey Wallis 32 F, born in North Carolina
Mary Ann Wallis 14 F, born in North Carolina
Rebecca Wallis 8 F, born in North Carolina
John Wallis 4 M, born in North Carolina
Julia Wallis 4/12 F, born in North Carolina

1854, Oct 24 -- 1853-1856 Court of Pleas and Quarter Sessions, Moore County, NC
Page 207-208
Ordered that Chesley T. Horner be appointed overseer of the road from the mouth
of Kelly's lane to the McQueen Branch and work the following hands: Daniel
McIntosh, Joseph Caddell, William R. Muse, William R. Sowell, Presley Caddell,
Duncan McIntosh, Neill Black, Noah H. Muse, George Williams, Bryant Caddell,
Devotion Davis, John Davis, Jason Sowell, Lendo Sowell, Absalom Fry, Eli Sowell,
Duncan Black, D.F. Muse, Artimus S. Caddell and Kindred Muse.

1855, Oct 22 -- 1853-1856 Court of Pleas and Quarter Sessions, Moore County, NC
Page 383
Ordered that William R. Sowell be appointed overseer of the road from the mouth
of Kelly's lane to McQueen's Branch and work the following hands: Daniel
McIntosh, W.H. Muse, Neil Black, Noah F. Muse, George Williams, Bryant Caddell,
Devotion Davis, John M. Davis, Jason Sowell, Lendo Sowell, Abraham Fry, Eli Sowell,
D.F. Muse, Artemas S. Caddell, Kindred Muse, Neodom Yarn, James Dowdy hands,
Jefferson Williams, Josiha Wallace and Joseph Fry.

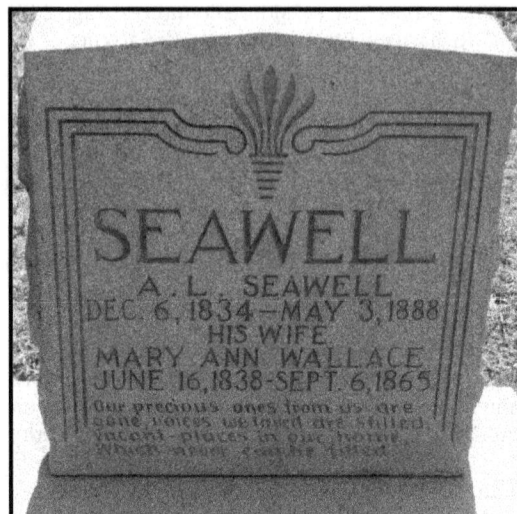

(photographed July 5, 2010)

1856, Aug 7 -- Marriage Register, Moore County, NC Page 38
A. L. Sowell and Mary A. Wallace by Jesse Bean, JP

1857, May 2 -- 1856-1858 Court of Pleas and Quarter Sessions, Moore County, NC Page 214
Ordered that Neill Black be appointed overseer of the road from the mouth of Kelly's lane to McQueen's Branch and work the following
hands: Chestly T. Horner, Daniel McIntosh, Wm. H. Muse, Noah F. Muse, George Williams, Bryant Caddell, Devotion Davis, John Davis,
Jason Sowell, Lendo Sowell, Absalom Fry, Eli Sowell, D.F. Muse, Artemas S. Caddell, Kindred Muse, Nedom Vann, James Dowdy hands,
Wm. Sowell hands, Jefferson Williams, Josiah Wallace and Joseph C. Fry.

1860, Aug 9 -- Census, Moore County, NC Page 204, Gold Region Post Office
Lendo Seawell 25 M, Farmer, $250 Real Estate, $500 Personal Property, born in North Carolina
Mary A. Seawell 21 F, born in North Carolina
Archibald W. Seawell 3 M, born in North Carolina
Martha A. Seawell 1 F, born in North Carolina
Frances Wallace 12 F, born in North Carolina

Anderson Lindo Seawell, son of Quimby Seawell (1809-1859) and Emaline Furr (1814-1892), was born on
December 6, 1834. He married Nancy Jane Cagle on November 7, 1867 in Moore County, NC. He died on May 3,
1888 in Moore County, NC and was buried in Moore County, NC at Bethlehem Baptist Church. He and Mary Ann
Wallace had the following children:

+494	Archibald Winston Seawell (1857-1928)
+495	Martha A. Seawell (1859-1905)
+496	Sara Eliza Seawell (1861-1880)
+497	John Wesley P. Seawell (1862-1936)

91. **Rebecca Jane Wallace**, daughter of Abraham C. Hunsucker and Franey Wallace, was born in 1842. She married **Henry
Maness** on July 30, 1863 in Moore County, NC.[126] She died in 1875.

RECORDS OF HENRY MANESS AND REBECCA JANE WALLACE

1850, Nov 8 -- Census, Moore County, NC Page 236
Franey Wallis 32 F, born in North Carolina
Mary Ann Wallis 14 F, born in North Carolina
Rebecca Wallis 8 F, born in North Carolina
John Wallis 4 M, born in North Carolina
Julia Wallis 4/12 F, born in North Carolina

1860, Sep 14 -- Census, Moore County, NC Page 232, Carthage Post Office
W. L. Richardson 28 M, born in North Carolina
Martha Richardson 26 F, born in North Carolina
Alfred Richardson 5 M, born in North Carolina
Margaret R. Richardson 4 F, born in North Carolina
John A. Richardson 2 M, born in North Carolina
William A. Richardson 1/12 M, born in North Carolina
Rebecca Wallace 16 F, born in North Carolina

1863, Jul 30 -- Marriage Register, Moore County, NC
Henry Maness and Rebecca Jane Wallace by K. Matheson, JP

1870, Aug 30 -- Census, Moore County, NC Page 610, Sheffields Township, Carters Mill Post Office
Henry Mainess 35 M, Farmer, $200 Real Estate, born in North Carolina
Rebecca J. Mainess 24 F, born in North Carolina
Henry A. Mainess 3 M, born in North Carolina
Columbus Mainess 1 M, born in North Carolina
Marshal G. Mainess 22 M, born in North Carolina

Henry Maness, son of Lewis Washington Maness (1813-bef 1880) and Ann Jones (1817-bef 1870), was born in 1839 and died in 1897. He married Nancy S. McQueen on January 14, 1877 in Montgomery County, NC. Henry and Rebecca Jane Wallace had the following children:

+498	Henry Alexander Maness (1865-1949)
+499	Christopher Columbus Maness (1870-1958)
+500	Julia Ann Maness (1871-1946)
+501	Martha L. "Mattie" Maness (1873-1899)
+502	George W. Maness (1874-1948)

92. **John Mack Wallace**, son of Abraham C. Hunsucker and Franey Wallace, was born on August 3, 1845 in Moore County, NC. He married **Martha Ann Brown** on October 15, 1867 in Moore County, NC and later married **Parthenia Gibsie Bass** on July 5, 1903 in Cumberland County, NC. John died on July 20, 1927 in Cumberland County, NC and was buried in Hope Mills, Cumberland County, NC at Big Rockfish Presbyterian Cemetery.[127]

RECORDS OF JOHN MACK WALLACE

1850, Nov 8 -- Census, Moore County, NC Page 236
Franey Wallis 32 F, born in North Carolina
Mary Ann Wallis 14 F, born in North Carolina
Rebecca Wallis 8 F, born in North Carolina
John Wallis 4 M, born in North Carolina
Julia Wallis 4/12 F, born in North Carolina

1860, Sep 14 -- Census, Moore County, NC Page 232-233, Carthage Post Office
Jesse Harmon 50 M, Farmer, $1200 Real Estate, $1000 Personal Property, born in North Carolina
Anna Harmon 50 F, born in North Carolina
John Harmon 25 M, MF Spirits & Turpentine, $150 Real Estate, $1000 Personal Property, born in North Carolina
William Harmon, 24 M, born in North Carolina
Neil Harmon 22 M, born in North Carolina
Malcolm Harmon 19 M, born in North Carolina
Archd. Harmon 17 M, born in North Carolina
Flora Harmon 13 F, born in North Carolina
Daniel Jackson 18 M, Laborer, born in North Carolina
Mack Wallace 16 M, Laborer, born in North Carolina

1862, Feb 28 -- Civil War Service Records
John M. Wallace enlisted in Company D, 48th Regiment in Moore County, NC at age 17. On Dec 13, 1862, he was wounded in the lung at Fredericksburg, VA and was hospitalized at Richmond, VA. On Oct 18, 1863, he hospitalized at Charlottesville, VA with a gunshot wound. On May 12, 1864, he was captured at Spotsylvania

**John Mack Wallace and
Martha Ann Brown**
(Courtesy of Gail S. Dupree)

Courthouse, VA and confined at Point Lookout, MD. On Jun 20, 1864. John M. Wallace was released from Point Lookout, MD after taking Oath of Allegiance. He joined the US Army and assigned Company D, 1st Regiment US Volunteer Infantry.[128]

1870, Jul 6 -- Agricultural Census, Moore County, NC Page 1, Bensalem Township, Curriesville Post Office
John M. Wallis listed 12 acres improved, 38 acres wooded valued at$70

1870, Jul 14 -- Census, Moore County, NC Page 481, Bensalem Township, Curriesville Post Office
John M. Wallis 23 M, Farmer, $100 Real Estate, $75 Personal Property, born in North Carolina
Martha A. Wallis 20 M, born in North Carolina
William W. Wallis 9/12 M, born in North Carolina
Franey Wallis 56 F, born in North Carolina

1875, Oct 5 -- Deed Book 51 Page 431, Moore County, NC
Mary E. Furr deeded John Williams 20 acres located on Flag Creek adjoining Stephen D. Williams. Hector McKenzie and John Mc. Wallace listed as witnesses.

1880, Jun 27 -- Census, Moore County, NC Page 210, Bensalem Township
John M. Wallace 34 M, Head, Farmer/Planter, born in North Carolina, father & mother born in North Carolina
Martha Wallace 30 F, Wife, Keeping House, born in North Carolina, father & mother born in North Carolina
William Wallace 10 M Son, At Home, born in North Carolina, father & mother born in North Carolina
Mary B. Wallace 8 F, Dau, At Home, born in North Carolina, father & mother born in North Carolina
John R. Wallace 6 M, Son, born in North Carolina, father & mother born in North Carolina
Henry Wallace 6 M, Son, born in North Carolina, father & mother born in North Carolina
Margaret Wallace 4 F, Dau, born in North Carolina, father & mother born in North Carolina
Franey Wallace 66 F, Mother, born in North Carolina, father & mother born in North Carolina

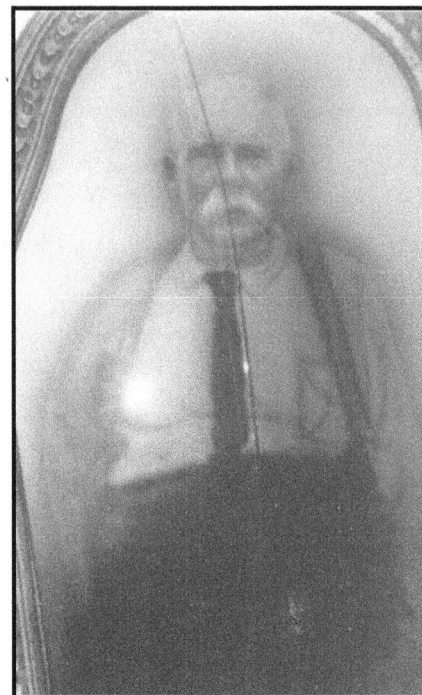

John Mack Wallace
(Courtesy of Gail S. Dupree)

(Courtesy of Find A Grave)

1880 -- Agricultural Census, Moore County, NC Page 19, Bensalem Township
John Mc. Wallace listed 20 acres improved fields, 25 unimproved wooded valued at $150

1884, Oct 16-Feb 23, 1886 -- Loose Estates and 1876-1885 Record of Accounts Page 542-544, Moore County, NC
Estate of Nancy Wallace Dec'd. by Administrator W.W. Wallace. *Items were purchased by the following*: Mac. Wallace, Josiah Person, Archd. Seawell, Saml. B. Wallace, John Garner, James Cockman, S.D. Wallace, Quimby Wallace, Sandy Black, Josiah Person, J.W. Horner,

George Williams, Sampson Cockman, Charles Cockman, Mrs. Sarah Garner, Frank Wallace, Thomas Horner, Spinks Wallace, Archd. Seawell, J.T. Seawell, Charlie Wallace, Thomas Fry, Parker Stafford and J.M. Davis.

1890 -- Veteran's Census, Moore County, NC
John M. Wallace listed as a Private in Company D of the 1st US Volunteers. Enlistment Dates Jan 20, 1864 - Nov 1, 1865. Disability listed as "shot in the right breast"

1898, Oct 23 -- Deed Book 28, Page 349-351, Moore County, NC
J.M. and Martha Wallace (by Mortgagee W.K. Jackson) deeded William W. Brown 50 acres located on Cymbling Creek adjoining Monroe Carroll.

1900, Jun 4 -- Census, Cumberland County, NC Page 249-B, Rockfish Township, Town of Hope Mills
John M. Wallace 54 M, Aug 1845, Head, Married-32yrs, Regulator-Cotton Mill, born in North Carolina, father & mother born in North Carolina
Martha Wallace 50 F, Dec 1849, Wife, Married-32yrs, 11 Children(9 Living), born in North Carolina, father & mother born in North Carolina
John R. Wallace 26 M, Sep 1873, Son, Married-0yr, Weaver-Cotton Mill, born in North Carolina, father & mother born in North Carolina
Nora Wallace 23 F, Oct 1876, DauL, Married-0yr, 0 Children, Weaver-Cotton Mill, born in North Carolina, father & mother born in North Carolina
Charles M. Wallace 15 M, May 1885, Son, Single, Day Laborer, born in North Carolina, father & mother born in North Carolina
Joseph G. Wallace 3 M, Aug 1896, GrSon, Single, born in North Carolina, father & mother born in North Carolina
Sarah E. Wallace 11 F, Aug 1889, Dau, Single, Spinner-Cotton Mill, born in North Carolina, father & mother born in North Carolina
Franklin Warner 19 M, Mar 1881, SonL, Married-0yr, Spinner-Cotton Mill, born in North Carolina, father & mother born in North Carolina
Mianna J. Warner 17 F, May 1883, Dau, Married-0yr, 0 Children, Realer-Cotton Mill, born in North Carolina, father & mother born in North Carolina

(Courtesy of Janice Barefoot Suggs, Fayetteville, NC)

1910, May 21 -- Census, Cumberland County, NC Page 21, Quewhiffle Township
John M. Wallace 64 M, Head, Married-2nd-6yrs, Farmer, born in North Carolina, father & mother born in North Carolina
Parthenia Wallace 34 F, Wife, Married-2nd-6yrs, 6 Children(4 Living), born in North Carolina, father & mother born in North Carolina
Archibald T. Wallace 11 M, Son, Single, Labor, born in North Carolina, father & mother born in North Carolina
Henriettie Wallace 4 F, Dau, Single, born in North Carolina, father & mother born in North Carolina
Tishie E. Wallace 2 F, Dau, Single, born in North Carolina, father & mother born in North Carolina
Walter W. Wallace 4/12 M, Son, Single, born in North Carolina, father & mother born in North Carolina
George Graham 82 M, None, Widow, Farmer, born in North Carolina, father & mother born in North Carolina
Nell Graham 29 F, Dau, Single, Teacher, born in North Carolina, father & mother born in North Carolina

1920, Jan 17 -- Census, Cumberland County, NC Page 43, Pearces Mill Township
John Wallace 74 M, Head, Married, born in North Carolina, father & mother born in North Carolina
Parthenia Wallace 43 F, Wife, Married, Spooler(Cotton Mill), born in North Carolina, father & mother born in North Carolina
Harriett Wallac 14 F, Dau, Single, Spooler(Cotton Mill), born in North Carolina, father & mother born in North Carolina
Tishie Wallace 12 F, Dau, Single, born in North Carolina, father & mother born in North Carolina
Walter W. Wallace 10 M, Son, Single, born in North Carolina, father & mother born in North Carolina
James M. Wallace 8 M, Son, Single, born in North Carolina, father & mother born in North Carolina
Lillie Wallace 5 F, Dau, Single, born in North Carolina, father & mother born in North Carolina
Sallie A. Wallace 3 F, Dau, Single, born in North Carolina, father & mother born in North Carolina
Amy Bass 72 F, MotherL, Widowed, born in North Carolina, father & mother born in North Carolina
Archie Kinsaw 21 M, StepSon, Single, Farmer(Cotton Mill), born in North Carolina, father & mother born in North Carolina

1927, July 20 -- Death Certificate, Cumberland County, NC
James M. Wallace [error - should be John] died in Cross Creek Township. Husband of Parthena Bass. Age: 83y. Occupation: Farmer. Birthplace: NC. Cause of Death: Mitral Heart Disease. Place of Burial: Hope Mills Cemetery. Undertaker: Rogers & Breast, Fayetteville. Informant: Archie Kinsauls, Linden, NC

Martha Ann Brown was born on December 27, 1849 in Moore County, NC. She died on January 15, 1902 in Cumberland County, NC and was buried in Hope Mills, Cumberland County, NC at Big Rockfish Presbyterian Cemetery. She and John Mack Wallace had the following children:

+503	William Wesley Wallace (1869-1929)	
+504	Mary Blake Wallace (1871-1939)	
+505	Henry Lee Wallace (1873-1953)	
+506	John Robert Wallace (1873-1930)	
+507	Margaret Rosetta Wallace (1875-1948)	
+508	Martha Ann Wallace (1880-1924)	
+509	Mianna J. "Annie" Wallace (1883-1960)	
+510	Charles Mack Wallace (1886-1966)	
+511	Sarah Elizabeth Wallace (1888-1992)	
+512	George W. Wallace (1892-1893)	

Parthenia Gibsie Bass, daughter of Melvin Bass (-) and Amy Honeycutt (-), was born on April 1, 1875 in Sampson County, NC. She died on December 9, 1957 in Kenansville, Duplin County, NC and was buried in Hope Mills, Cumberland County, NC at Big Rockfish Presbyterian Cemetery. She and John Mack Wallace had the following children:

+513	Harriet Wallace (1905-1997)	
+514	Tishi Evelyn Wallace (1907-2003)	
+515	Walter Watson Wallace (1909-1995)	
+516	James Madison Wallace (1911-1992)	
+517	Lillie Al Rhoney Wallace (1914-1993)	
+518	Sallie Adelaide Wallace (1917-2003)	

93. **Julia Frances Wallace**, daughter of Abraham C. Hunsucker and Franey Wallace, was born in December 1850 in Moore County, NC. She died on February 6, 1919 in Moore County, NC and was buried on February 8, 1919 in Robbins, Moore County, NC at Tabernacle United Methodist Church.[129]

RECORDS OF JULIA FRANCES WALLACE AND MARSHAL G. MANESS

1850, Nov 8 -- Census, Moore County, NC Page 236
Franey Wallis 32 F, Born in NC

Mary Ann Wallis 14 F, Born in NC
Rebecca Wallis 8 F, Born in NC
John Wallis 4 M, Born in NC
Julia Wallis 4/12 F, Born in NC

1860, Aug 9 -- Census, Moore County, NC Page 204, Gold Region Post Office
Lendo Seawell 25 M, Farmer, $250 Real Estate, $500 Personal Property, Born in NC
Mary A. Seawell 21 F, Born in NC
Archibald W. Seawell 3 M, Born in NC
Martha A. Seawell 1 F, Born in NC
Frances Wallace 12 F, Born in NC

1880, Jun 25 -- Census, Moore County, NC Page 210, Bensalem Township
Marshal Maness 35 M, Head, Married, Laborer, Born in NC, father & Mother Born in NC
Julia F. Maness 29 F, Wife, Married, Keep House, Born in NC, father & Mother Born in NC
Mary Ann Maness 12 F, Dau, Single, At Home, Born in NC, father & Mother Born in NC
Rebecca J. Maness 11 F, Dau, Single, At Home, Born in NC, father & Mother Born in NC

1891, Jan 6 -- Land Grant #4708, Moore County, NC
A.H. McNeill received 41.39 acres located on the waters of Flag Creek adjoining James Horner, Melton, Garner, A. Williams, M.G. Maness, Parrish. Steadman Garner and A.D. Garner were chain carriers.

1899, Sep 29 -- Deed Book 21 Page 320, Moore County, NC
S.D. Garner and wife Lillie E. deeded J.M. Worth 40 acres (Timber Deed) adjoining J.W. Horner, W.T. Garner and Marshall Maness.

1900 -- Census, Moore County, NC Page 50, Bensalem Township
Martial Maness 57 M, May 1843, Head, Married-32yrs, Teamster, Born in NC, father & Mother Born in NC
Francis Maness 49 F, Dec 1850, WIfe, Married-32yrs, 2 Children(2 Living), Born in NC, father & Mother Born in NC

1908, Jul 6 -- Confederate Widow's Pension Application, Moore County, NC
Julia Francis Maness, age 59 of Hemp Post Office, applied for a pension for Marshall G. Maness Dec'd. John Williams and Henry Williams were witnesses. She reapplied at age 68 on 2 Jul 1917.[130]

1910 -- Census, Moore County, NC Page 96, Bensalem Township
Malcolm Rouse 44 M, Head, Married-21yrs, Farmer(Home Farm), Born in NC, father & Mother Born in NC
Becky Jane Rouse 43 F, Wife, Married-21yrs, 9 Children(8 Living), Born in NC, father & Mother Born in NC
Doral Rouse 21 F, Dau, Single, Farm Laborer, Born in NC, father & Mother Born in NC
Effie S. Rouse 17 F, Dau, Single, Farm Laborer, Born in NC, father & Mother Born in NC
Willie Rouse 15 M, Son, Single, Laborer(Saw Mill), Born in NC, father & Mother Born in NC
Harrison Rouse 12 M, Son, Single, Laborer(Saw Mill), Born in NC, father & Mother Born in NC
Dewy Rouse 9 M, Son, Single, Born in NC, father & Mother Born in NC
Hurley Rouse 6 M, Son, Single, Born in NC, father & Mother Born in NC
Grady Rouse 4 M, Son, Single, Born in NC, father & Mother Born in NC
Pearl Rouse 4/12 F, Dau, Single, Born in NC, father & Mother Born in NC
Francis Maness 61 F, MotherL, Widowed, 2 Children(2 Living), Farm Laborer(Working Out), Born in NC, father & Mother Born in NC

Marshal G. Maness, son of Lewis Washington Maness (1813-bef 1880) and Ann Jones (1817-bef 1870), was born on May 8, 1844. He died on July 20, 1907 and was buried in Robbins, Moore County, NC at Tabernacle United Methodist Church. He and Julia Frances Wallace had the following children:

+519   Mary Ann Maness (1867-1942)
+520   Rebecca Jane Maness (1869-1951)

Fourth Generation

96. **James Abel Maness**, son of Garner Maness and Catherine "Katie" Maness, was born in April 1835. He married **Deborah Eliza "Debby" Brown** on August 10, 1854 in Moore County, NC. He died in 1907 and was buried in Moore County, NC at Pleasant Hill United Methodist Church.

Deborah Eliza "Debby" Brown, daughter of William Brown (1793-bef 1851) and Elizabeth (1796-), was born in 1831. She died before 1900 and was buried in Moore County, NC at Maness Cemetery #247. She and James Abel Maness had the following children:

+521   James R. Maness (1856-bef 1900)

+522	Parthenia Maness (1861-)
+523	Jonah Baxter Maness (1870-1961)

97. Martha "Polly" Maness, daughter of Garner Maness and Catherine "Katie" Maness, was born in 1836. She married **Robert Newton Dixon** on February 10, 1859 in Moore County, NC. She died before 1880 and was buried in Moore County, NC at Pleasant Hill United Methodist Church.

Robert Newton Dixon was born on June 15, 1835. He died on July 17, 1896 and was buried in Moore County, NC at Pleasant Hill United Methodist Church. He and Martha "Polly" Maness had the following children:

+524	David Dixon (1859-)
+525	John T. Dixon (1861-)
+526	Joseph Dixon (1862-)
+527	Rosina S. Dixon (1863-1883)
+528	Lucy J. Dixon (1865-)
+529	Robert Newton Dixon Jr. (1868-)
+530	Martha Ann Dixon (1869-1895)
+531	Mary Dixon (1869-1873)
+532	Silas F. Dixon (1875-)
+533	Emma Ellen Dixon (1876-1963)

98. Lydia M. Maness, daughter of Garner Maness and Catherine "Katie" Maness, was born in 1842.

Alex Pleasant "Plez" Williams, son of Matthew Bryant Williams (1818-1885) and Elizabeth C. Stutts (1825-1896), was born on August 1, 1842. He died on April 21, 1918. He and Lydia M. Maness had the following children:

+534	Quincy Addison Maness (1865-1922)

99. Jonas Sedberry Maness, son of Garner Maness and Catherine "Katie" Maness, was born on June 11, 1844. He died on June 11, 1898 and was buried in Eden, Rockingham County, NC at Lawson Cemetery.

Rosanna Pearl Boroughs was born on December 23, 1857. She died on November 25, 1923 and was buried in Eden, Rockingham County, NC at Lawson Cemetery. She and Jonas Sedberry Maness had the following children:

+535	Reuben Luther Maness (-)
+536	Siddie Rosetta Maness (-)
+537	Elvira Allie Maness (-)
+538	Minnie Ola Maness (-)
+539	Bertie Lee Maness (-)
+540	Mary Catherine \"Kate\" Maness (-)
+541	Troy Everett Maness (1881-1967)

100. Alexander Spinks Maness, son of Garner Maness and Catherine "Katie" Maness, was born on October 20, 1846. He married **Mary Elizabeth Riddle** circa 1868. He died on March 27, 1924 in Lee County, NC and was buried in Moore County, NC at Pleasant Hill United Methodist Church.

Mary Elizabeth Riddle, daughter of John W. Riddle (1816-1893) and Lydia Williams (1820-1914), was born on January 16, 1847. She died on February 8, 1939 and was buried in Moore County, NC at Pleasant Hill United Methodist Church. She and Alexander Spinks Maness had the following children:

+542	Sarah Elizabeth Maness (1877-1954)

102. Miley Jane Maness, daughter of Garner Maness and Catherine "Katie" Maness, was born in 1851. She married **Bethuel Coffin Brown** on August 15, 1889 in Moore County, NC.

Bethuel Coffin Brown, son of Henry Brown (1821-bef 1880) and Mary (1825-bef 1860), was born in April 1851. He died on August 21, 1920 in Sampson County, NC.

103. **Presley Wright Maness**, son of Garner Maness and Catherine "Katie" Maness, was born on July 30, 1854. He married **Martha Jane Riddle** circa 1872. He died on July 30, 1935 and was buried in Moore County, NC at Pleasant Hill United Methodist Church.

Martha Jane Riddle, daughter of John W. Riddle (1816-1893) and Lydia Williams (1820-1914), was born on February 5, 1852. She died on September 18, 1940 and was buried in Moore County, NC at Pleasant Hill United Methodist Church. She and Presley Wright Maness had the following children:

+543	Annie Mae Maness (1875-1942)
+544	Mintie G. Maness (1877-1905)
+545	William Right Maness (1879-1964)
+546	John Spinks Maness (1883-1965)
+547	Mary J. Maness (1886-)
+548	Benjamin Harrison Maness (1887-1979)
+549	Henry Clay Maness (1894-1978)

104. **Emma C. Maness**, daughter of Garner Maness and Catherine "Katie" Maness, was born in 1855 and was buried in Moore County, NC at Maness Cemetery #225.

105. **Noah W. Maness**, son of Garner Maness and Catherine "Katie" Maness, was born in 1860. He died in 1861 and was buried in Moore County, NC at Maness Cemetery #225.

106. **Milton A. Maness**, son of Everett Maness and Lucinda Shields, was born in 1840 in Moore County, NC. He married **Emma Harriet Hicks** circa 1873. He died on September 10, 1877 in Bibb County, AL.

Emma Harriet Hicks, daughter of Isaac Madison Hicks (1815-1886) and Mary Ann Smitherman (1826-1897), was born on April 29, 1853 in Bibb County, AL. She and Milton A. Maness had the following children:

+550	Plato Griffin Maness (1874-1944)
+551	Euturphy Maness (1876-1887)
+552	Bonner Purvis Maness (1877-1950)
+553	Floyd W. Maness (1878-1953)

107. **Martha Louisa Maness**, daughter of Everett Maness and Lucinda Shields, was born in September 1842. She died on March 24, 1902.

108. **Lydia Clementine Maness**, daughter of Everett Maness and Lucinda Shields, was born in 1847. She married **Lisbon Fales Gober** on September 19, 1866. She died in 1901.

Lisbon Fales Gober, son of John Wesley Gober (1821-1896) and Temperance B. Chastine (1817-1877), was born in 1845. He married Caroline Elizabeth Rowlen on October 2, 1901. He died on November 28, 1921. He and Lydia Clementine Maness had the following children:

+554	Bartus Lee Gober (1874-1931)
+555	Cally Lucinda Gober (1875-1947)

109. **Wincy Isabella Maness**, daughter of Everett Maness and Lucinda Shields, was born in 1848. She married **Jonathan Roach** on February 22, 1871. She died in 1932.

Jonathan Roach, son of William McDaniel Roach (-) and Nancy Cook (-), was born in 1853 and in 1930. He and Wincy Isabella Maness had the following children:

+556	Lou Ella Roach (1873-1941)
+557	Lula Belle Roach (1873-1945)
+558	Julia Victoria Roach (1876-1962)
+559	Sam B. Roach (1878-1888)
+560	Rosa Loyd Roach (1879-1973)
+561	Mamie Roach (1884-1941)

110. **Everett Maness Jr.**, son of Everett Maness and Lucinda Shields, was born in September 1849. He died in 1850.

111. **Cornelius E. Maness**, son of Everett Maness and Lucinda Shields, was born in 1850. He died between 1860 and 1870.

112. **Lucinda E. Maness**, daughter of Everett Maness and Lucinda Shields, was born in 1852. She died between 1880 and 1884.

    Robert A. Thompson was born in 1849. He and Lucinda E. Maness had the following children:

+562	Walter Thompson (1868-)
+563	Mary L. Thompson (1872-)
+564	Elissna Thompson (1873-)
+565	Wiley L. Thompson (1877-)
+566	John B. Thompson (1879-)

113. **David Cincinnati Maness**, son of Everett Maness and Lucinda Shields, was born in 1854. He married **Nancy Hughes** on August 20, 1871. He died in 1930.

    Nancy Hughes was born in 1854. She died on March 17, 1910. She and David Cincinnati Maness had the following children:

+567	William Mark Maness (1872-1906)
+568	Beulah Maness (1874-)
+569	Hermon Everette Maness (1877-)
+570	Arthur Hughes Maness (1880-1967)
+571	Henry Bascom Maness (1883-1972)
+572	Roy Brewer Maness (1886-1934)
+573	Callie Lee Maness (1889-)
+574	Charlie G. Maness (1895-)
+575	Lula Maness (1902-)

114. **Richard Maness**, son of Everett Maness and Lucinda Shields, was born in 1855. He died between 1860 and 1870.

115. **John J. Maness**, son of Everett Maness and Lucinda Shields, was born in 1858. He married **Mary T. Crow** on December 13, 1874 in Forsyth County, GA. He died on May 9, 1900 and was buried in Forsyth County, GA at Pleasant Grove Baptist Church.

    Mary T. Crow was born on June 28, 1857. She died on October 20, 1922 and was buried in Forsyth County, GA at Pleasant Grove Baptist Church. She and John J. Maness had the following children:

+576	Lilous E. Maness (1876-)
+577	Julius B. Maness (1879-)
+578	Auda Maness (1883-)
+579	Ada Maness (1884-)
+580	Genie Maness (1885-)
+581	James Harris Maness (1887-)
+582	Nannie Maness (1890-)
+583	Velmie Maness (1891-)
+584	Carl Maness (1893-)
+585	Cora Maness (1895-)
+586	Huston W. Maness (1897-)

116. **Burrel E. Maness**, son of Everett Maness and Lucinda Shields, was born in June 1862. He died in 1910.

117. **Mary Clementine Maness**, daughter of Asa Maness and Mary Ann Ritter, was born on November 8, 1847. She married **James Bailey Caddell** on September 27, 1866 in Moore County, NC. She died on January 13, 1920.

    James Bailey Caddell, son of Joseph Hurley Caddell (1811-1896) and Sarah Stafford (1819-1860), was born on March 17, 1847. He died on July 26, 1921. He and Mary Clementine Maness had the following children:

+587	Eddie Caddell (-)
+588	John Spinks Caddell (1867-1937)
+589	Annie Cornelia Florence Caddell (1869-1954)
+590	Infant Caddell (1870-1870)
+591	Mary Emma Caddell (1871-1891)
+592	Sarah Otelia Caddell (1873-1939)
+593	Lily Caddell (1874-1912)
+594	Asa Bascom Caddell (1876-1905)
+595	Margaret Louisa Caddell (1878-1960)
+596	Eva Augusta Caddell (1880-1971)
+597	Artie Peoples "Mishie" Caddell (1881-)
+598	James Clyde Caddell (1883-)
+599	Infant Caddell (1884-1884)
+600	Dora Alice Caddell (1886-1965)
+601	Clement Caddell (1889-)

118. Sarah Frances Maness, daughter of Asa Maness and Mary Ann Ritter, was born on August 31, 1848. She married **Riley Roderick Riddle** on February 22, 1875 in Moore County, NC. She died on May 19, 1913 and was buried in Moore County, NC at High Falls United Methodist Church.

Riley Roderick Riddle, son of John W. Riddle (1816-1893) and Lydia Williams (1820-1914), was born on September 5, 1852. He married Mary Elizabeth "Betty" Phillips on January 17, 1915 in Moore County, NC. He died on September 10, 1936 and was buried in Moore County, NC at High Falls United Methodist Church. He and Sarah Frances Maness had the following children:

+602	Thomas Lee Riddle (1877-1951)
+603	Laura Brantley Riddle (1879-1931)
+604	Addie Camilla Riddle (1880-1961)
+605	Annie Jane Riddle (1882-1956)
+606	Maude Alice Riddle (1884-1962)
+607	Sarah Emma Riddle (1886-1928)
+608	Mary Louise Riddle (1889-)
+609	Margaret Mae Riddle (1891-1929)
+610	Alma Estelle Clementine Riddle (1894-1964)

119. Lucinda Ann Maness, daughter of Asa Maness and Mary Ann Ritter, was born in 1850. She married **Thomas Branson Cagle** circa 1887. She died in 1893.

Thomas Branson Cagle, son of George Cagle (1814-bef 1890) and Elizabeth Williams (1814-bef 1860), was born on March 18, 1836 in Moore County, NC. He married Nancy E. Ritter in September 1861 in Moore County, NC. He married Sallie Brown on April 11, 1895 in Moore County, NC. He died on January 4, 1917 in Greensboro, Guilford County, NC and was buried on January 21, 1917 in Carthage, Moore County, NC at Cross Hill Cemetery. He and Lucinda Ann Maness had the following children:

+611	Blake Cagle (-)
+612	Eli Lee Cagle (1887-)
+613	Annie B. Cagle (1888-)
+614	Edna Alice Cagle (1890-1935)
+615	Bessie Lee Cagle (1892-1918)
+616	Samantha Beulah Cagle (1893-)

120. Thomas Wesley Maness, son of Asa Maness and Mary Ann Ritter, was born in November 1851. He died on February 24, 1905 and was buried in Moore County, NC at Maness Cemetery #248.

Sarah Frances Williams, daughter of Abram M. Williams (1835-bef 1867) and Sarah L. Stutts (1837-1920), was born in 1863. She died in 1895 and was buried in Moore County, NC at Pleasant Hill United Methodist Church. She and Thomas Wesley Maness had the following children:

+617	Sindia Ann Maness (1883-1911)
+618	Lulu Maness (1885-1905)
+619	Rossie Maness (1887-)
+620	Culbertha Maness (1889-1972)
+621	Sallie Louisa Maness (1894-1938)

121. Ira Blake Maness, son of Asa Maness and Mary Ann Ritter, was born on October 24, 1852. He died on January 2, 1931.

Mary Ellis Wallace, daughter of Lochart "Lockey" Wallace (1836-1884) and Susan Muse (1836-1911), was born on March 15, 1857 and died on October 20, 1920. She and Ira Blake Maness had the following children:

+622	Annie Louisa Maness (1875-1957)
+623	Ida C. Maness (1878-)
+624	Neelie Maness (1880-1930)
+625	Mattie Austin Maness (1881-1926)
+626	Mary Blake "Molly" Maness (1882-1944)
+627	W. Walter Maness (1883-1918)
+628	Maggie Mae Maness (1885-1937)
+629	Claude Ellis Maness (1887-1947)

122. John Alsey Maness, son of Asa Maness and Mary Ann Ritter, was born on December 20, 1856. He died on April 4, 1885 and was buried in Moore County, NC at Russell/Maness Cemetery #103.

Frances Eugenia Hughes, daughter of Joseph E. "Joe" Hughes (1829-1872) and Martha "Patsy" Phillips (1831-1876), was born on April 14, 1856. She died on March 21, 1926 and was buried in Moore County, NC at Russell/Maness Cemetery #103. She and John Alsey Maness had the following children:

+630	Callie Maness (1882-1884)
+631	Herbert L. Maness (1884-1967)
+632	John Alsey Maness Jr. (1885-1958)

123. Martha Louisa Maness, daughter of Asa Maness and Mary Ann Ritter, was born in 1858. She died in 1885 and was buried in Moore County, NC at Maness Cemetery #248.

Benjamin M. Howard, son of John Howard (1812-1893) and Julia Ann Moffitt (1824-1889), was born on October 4, 1852. He died on August 12, 1885 and was buried in Moore County, NC at Smyrna Methodist Church. He and Martha Louisa Maness had the following children:

+633	Mattie Ann Howard (1883-1955)
+634	Benjamin Franklin Howard (1884-1973)

124. Asa McClellan Maness Sr., son of Asa Maness and Mary Ann Ritter, was born on December 1, 1861. He married **Vandie Lee Wallace** circa 1889. He died on October 10, 1955 and was buried in Moore County, NC at Pleasant Hill United Methodist Church.

Vandie Lee Wallace, daughter of Lochart "Lockey" Wallace (1836-1884) and Susan Muse (1836-1911), was born on July 15, 1874 and was buried on January 12, 1929 in Moore County, NC at Pleasant Hill United Methodist Church. She died on June 11, 1929 in Moore County, NC. She and Asa McClellan Maness Sr. had the following children:

+635	Duffy Maness (1886-)
+636	Asa McClellan Maness Jr. (1889-1970)
+637	Alexander Lee Maness (1894-1972)
+638	Arthur Maness (1897-1935)
+639	Ralph Maness (1899-1957)
+640	Johnny Carson Maness (1901-1975)
+641	Montie Lee Maness (1902-1975)
+642	Annie Ruth Maness (1908-)

125. **Biddie Maness**, son of Asa Maness and Mary Ann Ritter, was born on June 10, 1863. He died on October 24, 1884 and was buried in Moore County, NC at Maness Cemetery #248.

126. **Catherine Alice Maness**, daughter of Asa Maness and Mary Ann Ritter, was born on November 17, 1867. She married **William Turner Seawell** circa 1890. She died on October 30, 1936 and was buried in Moore County, NC at High Falls United Methodist Church.

> William Turner Seawell, son of Lemuel Turner Seawell (1828-1901) and Catherine McNeill (1828-bef 1891), was born on February 25, 1861. He died on February 11, 1948 and was buried in Moore County, NC at High Falls United Methodist Church. He and Catherine Alice Maness had the following children:

> | +643 | Asa H. Seawell (1890-) |
> | +644 | William Walter Seawell (1893-) |
> | +645 | Edna Alice Seawell (1895-1936) |
> | +646 | Ola Belle Seawell (1898-1942) |
> | +647 | Clem Floyd Seawell (1900-1963) |
> | +648 | Gilmer Flowers Seawell (1902-1976) |
> | +649 | Dewey C. Seawell (1903-1926) |
> | +650 | Ollie Seawell (1907-1964) |
> | +651 | Homer Seawell (1910-1992) |

127. **Addison Worth Ritter**, son of Asa Maness and Eliza Ritter, was born on July 9, 1849. He married **Catherine Maness** circa 1874. He married **Hannah Jane "Janie" Cox** after 1912. He died on August 15, 1938 and was buried in Moore County, NC at Smyrna Methodist Church.

> Catherine Maness, daughter of Lewis Grant Maness (1816-1913) and Rebecca Williams (1818-1894), was born on July 5, 1853. She died on November 27, 1912 and was buried in Moore County, NC at Smyrna Methodist Church. She and Addison Worth Ritter had the following children:

> | +652 | William Lewis Ritter (1873-) |
> | +653 | Mary Elizabeth Ritter (1875-1943) |
> | +654 | Martha Jane Ritter (1878-1964) |
> | +655 | Joseph Thomas Ritter (1880-1923) |
> | +656 | John Addison Ritter (1886-1942) |
> | +657 | Sarah Alice Ritter (1888-1936) |
> | +658 | Julia Ann Ritter (1888-1972) |

128. **Bethuel C. Maness**, son of Alsey Maness and Catherine Cagle, was born in 1849 and died in 1924. He married **Catherine Cole** circa 1870. He married **Sarah Jane Martin** on March 28, 1872 in Montgomery County, NC. He married **Louisa Jane Britt** circa 1886. He married **Lydia Ann Williams** after 1913.

> Catherine Cole was born in 1851. She died before 1872.

> Sarah Jane Martin, daughter of Norman Martin (1805-1879) and Sarah Lewis (1810-1894), was born in 1843 and died before 1886. She and Bethuel C. Maness had the following children:

> | +659 | John Alsey Maness (-) |
> | +660 | Martha L. Maness (1873-) |
> | +661 | Mary Catherine Maness (1874-1948) |
> | +662 | Sarah Elizabeth Maness (1879-1943) |
> | +663 | Norman Martin Maness (1882-1960) |

> Louisa Jane Britt, daughter of Bryant Britt (1820-1903) and Barbara Ann Myrick (1826-1883), was born on May 30, 1847. She died on November 13, 1913 and was buried in Moore County, NC at Bensalem Presbyterian Church.

> Lydia Ann Williams, daughter of Isaac Williams (1825-1871) and Martha Williamson (1825-), was born on August 26, 1860. She married Alexander Teague circa 1884. She died on February 29, 1932 in Moore County, NC.

129. **Sara Ann Maness**, daughter of Alsey Maness and Catherine Cagle, was born in 1853. She married **Wesley Thaddeus Dunn** on March 10, 1887.

Wesley Thaddeus Dunn, son of Wesley Dunn (1827-1873) and Amanda Deaton (1825-1912), was born in January 1865. He and Sara Ann Maness had the following children:

+664	John Lindon Dunn (-)
+665	Daisy E. Dunn (1896-)

130. **Spinks P. Maness**, son of Alsey Maness and Nancy Melton, was born on May 14, 1855 in North Carolina. He married **Rose Anna Leach** on January 30, 1878. He died on March 3, 1908 and was buried in Biscoe, Montgomery County, NC at Maness Family Cemetery.

Rose Anna Leach, daughter of Alexander Patterson Leach (1830-1915) and Mary McLeod (1834-1902), was born on September 27, 1858 in Montgomery County, NC. She died on June 3, 1924 and was buried in Biscoe, Montgomery County, NC at Maness Family Cemetery. She and Spinks P. Maness had the following children:

+666	Paul Maness (-)
+667	David Calvin Maness (1879-)
+668	Alsey Alexander Maness (1880-1953)
+669	Nancy Lou Maness (1881-1976)
+670	Mary Dell Maness (1884-1979)
+671	Martha Ellen Maness (1885-)
+672	Daisy Blanche Maness (1886-1978)
+673	Deborah Ethel Maness (1888-)
+674	Rose Lee Maness (1889-1982)
+675	Lillian Christian Maness (1891-)
+676	Elizabeth Pearl Maness (1892-1985)
+677	Margaret Myrtle Maness (1894-1986)
+678	John Ray Maness (1895-1967)
+679	Frances Esther Maness (1897-1974)
+680	Leslie Gold Maness (1902-1966)

131. **James Asa Maness**, son of Alsey Maness and Nancy Melton, was born on February 5, 1858. He married **Nancy Louise Leach** on January 24, 1883 in Montgomery County, NC. He died on April 14, 1929 and was buried in Biscoe, Montgomery County, NC at Maness Family Cemetery.

Nancy Louise Leach, daughter of Alexander Patterson Leach (1830-1915) and Mary McLeod (1834-1902), was born on March 11, 1863 in Montgomery County, NC. She died on October 13, 1936 and was buried in Biscoe, Montgomery County, NC at Maness Family Cemetery. She and James Asa Maness had the following children:

+681	Neil Wade Maness (1884-1948)
+682	Thomas Lester Maness (1886-1944)
+683	William Spinks Maness (1887-1958)
+684	Charles Alexander Maness (1889-1944)
+685	Mary Lula Maness (1891-1953)
+686	John Calvin Maness (1893-1951)
+687	James Edgar Maness (1896-1963)
+688	Minnie Blanche Maness (1898-1973)
+689	Bertie Jane Maness (1900-1989)
+690	Anne Lee Maness (1902-1992)
+691	Jesse Brown Maness (1902-1986)
+692	Elva Ellen Maness (1905-1984)
+693	Claude Leach Maness (1908-1913)

132. **Neill Tyson Maness**, son of Alsey Maness and Nancy Melton, was born on June 24, 1861. He married **Martha Leutitia Leach** on March 16, 1892. He died on August 17, 1911.

Martha Leutitia Leach, daughter of Alexander Patterson Leach (1830-1915) and Mary McLeod (1834-1902), was born on October 4, 1868 in Montgomery County, NC. She died on January 29, 1941 in North Carolina. She and Neill Tyson Maness had the following children:

+694	Ruth D. Maness (1892-1964)
+695	James Leach Maness (1894-1977)
+696	Archibald Kelly Maness (1895-1974)
+697	Ernest Grady Maness (1898-1950)
+698	Isaac Leland Maness (1900-1981)
+699	Mary Maness (1902-1973)
+700	Maude Maness (1904-1971)
+701	Della Maness (1906-1988)
+702	Jewell Maness (1908-2002)
+703	Maness (1910-1910)

133. **Mary Jane Maness**, daughter of Alsey Maness and Nancy Melton, was born in 1864. She died in 1894.

William Wright Dunn, son of Bartholomew Dunn (1792-1879) and Nancy Williams (aft 1832-), was born in October 1855. He died on May 12, 1930 in State Hospital, Raleigh, Wake County, NC and was buried in Star, Montgomery County, NC. He and Mary Jane Maness had the following children:

+704	Alsey Dunn (-)
+705	Fannie H. Dunn (1884-)
+706	William W. Dunn (1886-)
+707	Ada L. Dunn (1889-1974)
+708	Martha May Dunn (1891-1947)

134. **Martha Clementine Maness**, daughter of Alsey Maness and Nancy Melton, was born on May 28, 1866. She died on August 17, 1930 and was buried in Moore County, NC at Dover Baptist Church.

Lewis Washington Davis, son of Archibald McNeill Davis (1819-1879) and Mary S. Maness (1827-1858), was born on May 15, 1857. He died on December 15, 1928 and was buried in Moore County, NC at Dover Baptist Church. He and Martha Clementine Maness had the following children:

+709	Neil Webster Davis (1884-1952)
+710	Mary M. Davis (1885-1913)
+711	John Archie Davis (1888-1965)
+712	Nancy Francena Davis (1890-1960)
+713	Alsey Cleveland Davis (1892-1958)
+714	Ira Spinks Davis (1893-1950)
+715	Cora Helen Davis (1895-1941)
+716	Snoten M. Davis (1898-1961)
+717	Asa Lewis Davis (1900-1962)
+718	Ruth Bernice Davis (1903-)
+719	Glennie Esther Davis (1904-1979)
+720	Claude Roosevelt Davis (1906-1972)
+721	Frank Taft Davis (1909-1949)

135. **Lucinda Maness**, daughter of Alsey Maness and Nancy Melton, was born in 1868. She died in 1936.

Joseph Franklin Deaton was born in 1866. He died in 1953. He and Lucinda Maness had the following children:

+722	Eleanor Deaton (-)
+723	Wiley Carr Deaton (-)
+724	Tally Deaton (-)
+725	Carson Deaton (-)
+726	Ollie Deaton (-)
+727	Luther Deaton (-)
+728	Willie Deaton (-)

+729	Ira Deaton (-)
+730	Mentie Deaton (-)
+731	Dossie Deaton (-)
+732	Dora Deaton (1902-1983)
+733	Hattie F. Deaton (1904-1994)

136. **Francina Maness**, daughter of Alsey Maness and Nancy Melton, was born on October 18, 1870. She married **William Cornelius Kerns** circa 1890. She died on March 19, 1940 and was buried in Montgomery County, NC at Shady Grove Christian Church Cemetery.

William Cornelius Kerns was born on December 15, 1854. He died on February 8, 1941 and was buried in Montgomery County, NC at Shady Grove Christian Church Cemetery. He and Francina Maness had the following children:

+734	Catherine Kerns (1900-1963)
+735	Richard Kerns (1901-1922)
+736	Ida Kerns (1903-1977)

137. **William Robert Maness**, son of Alsey Maness and Nancy Melton, was born on August 28, 1873. He married **Martha Matilda Wallace** circa 1900. He died on July 1, 1951.

Martha Matilda Wallace, daughter of Chisholm Clark Wallace (1848-1932) and Martha Jane Reynolds (1854-1918), was born on October 23, 1874 in Montgomery County, NC. She died on August 15, 1966 in Montgomery Memorial Hospital, Troy, Montgomery County, NC and was buried in Star, Montgomery County, NC at United Methodist Church. She and William Robert Maness had the following children:

+737	Nora Belle Maness (1900-1979)
+738	Dossie Carl Maness (1902-)
+739	Chisholm M. Maness (1904-)
+740	Robert L. Maness (1906-)
+741	Riley Colon Maness (1908-1963)
+742	Martha Gladys Maness (1909-)
+743	Joseph Peele Maness (1911-1986)
+744	William Wallace Maness (1914-)
+745	Fred H. Maness (1915-)
+746	Nancy Lucille Maness (1919-)

138. **Tally Maness**, daughter of Alsey Maness and Nancy Melton, was born in 1875. She died in 1892 and was buried in Biscoe, Montgomery County, NC at Maness Family Cemetery.

139. **Angus Clegg Maness**, son of Alsey Maness and Nancy Melton, was born on October 21, 1878 in North Carolina. He married **Christian Nall** circa 1903. He died on October 26, 1956 in Amarillo, Potter County, TX.

Christian Nall, daughter of Wright William Nall (1857-1938) and Eliza Jane McLeod (1855-1947), was born in March 1884 in North Carolina. She and Angus Clegg Maness had the following children:

+747	Leo Maness (-)
+748	Nell Maness (-)
+749	Lola Maness (-)
+750	Mable Wright Maness (1915-2009)

142. **William Robert Maness**, son of Ira Lane "Irely" Maness and Catherine Ritter, was born on August 15, 1859. He married **Lucy Ella Davis** on January 17, 1895 in Moore County, NC. He died on March 2, 1920 and was buried in Moore County, NC at Pleasant Hill United Methodist Church.

Lucy Ella Davis, daughter of Martin D. Davis (1846-1922) and Nancy Jane Black (-1880), was born on September 15, 1878. She died on June 5, 1932 and was buried in Moore County, NC at Pleasant Hill United Methodist Church. She and William Robert Maness had the following children:

+751	William Arley Maness (1897-1972)
+752	Annie Jane Maness (1899-1990)
+753	Maggie L. Maness (1900-)
+754	Cary Etta Maness (1903-)
+755	Ada M. Maness (1904-)
+756	Martin J. Maness (1906-)
+757	Edna M. Maness (1909-)
+758	Ida B. Maness (1912-)
+759	Maude L. Maness (1914-)
+760	Racy Hugh Maness (1917-1996)
+761	Beulah Irene Maness (1920-)

143. **Nancy E. Maness**, daughter of Ira Lane "Irely" Maness and Catherine Ritter, was born on August 10, 1860. She died on February 16, 1943 and was buried in Moore County, NC at Pleasant Hill United Methodist Church.

Nancy E. Maness had the following children:

| +762 | Aggie Donner Maness (1894-1972) |

144. **Emily Rebecca Maness**, daughter of Ira Lane "Irely" Maness and Catherine Ritter, was born on January 8, 1866. She died on August 7, 1944 and was buried in Siler City, Chatham County, NC at Edwards Hill Friends Meeting Cemetery.

Charles Wesley Phillips, son of Berry Phillips (1828-1903) and Mary Ann Shields (1826-1876), was born in 1849. He died on May 12, 1921 and was buried in Siler City, Chatham County, NC at Edwards Hill Friends Meeting Cemetery. He and Emily Rebecca Maness had the following children:

| +763 | Ruby Kathleen Phillips (1906-2002) |

146. **Julia McIntyre Maness**, daughter of Ira Lane "Irely" Maness and Nancy A. Hancock, was born on September 11, 1872. She married **George Luther Paschal** circa 1889. She died on October 1, 1927 and was buried in Moore County, NC at Fair Promise Methodist Church.

George Luther Paschal, son of Richard Street (1822-1899) and Esperan Paschal (1832-1857), was born on January 4, 1854. He died on June 19, 1932 in Cameron County, TX and was buried in Moore County, NC at Fair Promise Methodist Church. He and Julia McIntyre Maness had the following children:

+764	Archie Lane Paschal (1889-)
+765	Mollie Cora Paschal (1891-1980)
+766	Nannie Florence Paschal (1892-)
+767	Baxter Worth Paschal (1894-1971)
+768	Josephine Paschal (1896-1963)
+769	Virginia Oppie Paschal (1899-1991)
+770	Julian Carr Paschal (1901-2001)
+771	Ernest Hurley Paschal (1903-)
+772	Luther George Paschal (1906-1982)
+773	Lawrence Hughes Paschal (1908-1999)
+774	Donald Ira Paschal (1910-1976)
+775	Arthur Garner Paschal (1912-)
+776	Henry Phillips Paschal (1913-1914)

147. **Josephine A. Maness**, daughter of Ira Lane "Irely" Maness and Nancy A. Hancock, was born on February 4, 1873. She married **George W. Brady** circa 1897. She died on February 5, 1903 and was buried in Moore County, NC at Pleasant Hill United Methodist Church.

George W. Brady, son of William Brady (1853-1923) and Millie Ann Maness (1861-1895), was born on July 15, 1877. He died on October 28, 1952 and was buried in High Falls, Moore County, NC at Prosperity Friends Meeting Cemetery. He and Josephine A. Maness had the following children:

| +777 | Addie Marie Brady (1899-1999) |

149. **Jerome A. Wallace**, son of Ruffin Wallace and Salina Fry, was born in 1861. He married **Ella Bennett** circa 1897. He died in 1923 and was buried in Echols County, GA at Wayfare Cemetery.

Ella Bennett was born in 1880. She died in 1954 and was buried in Echols County, GA at Wayfare Cemetery. She and Jerome A. Wallace had the following children:

+778	Claude E. Wallace (1898-)
+779	Ollie Mae Wallace (1900-)
+780	Maggie L. Wallace (1904-)
+781	Edna Wallace (1908-)
+782	Jewel Wallace (1909-1987)
+783	Drew Wallace (1912-)
+784	Earl Wallace (1913-)
+785	Mildred Doris Wallace (1915-2005)
+786	Audrey Howard Wallace (1918-1994)

150. **Charles Wallace**, son of Ruffin Wallace and Salina Fry, was born in 1864.

151. **Caroline Wallace**, daughter of Seaborn Wallace and Tabitha Boone, was born on September 5, 1864. She married **James Marion Harper** on January 15, 1885 in Randolph County, NC. She died on November 1, 1909 and was buried in Seagrove, Randolph County, NC at Maple Springs Baptist Church.

James Marion Harper, son of James Edward Harper (1841-1926) and Caroline Dean (1841-1926), was born on November 7, 1862. He married Nettie between 1910 and 1920. He died on February 13, 1928 and was buried in Seagrove, Randolph County, NC at Maple Springs Baptist Church. He and Caroline Wallace had the following children:

+787	Sabina Harper (1886-)
+788	James Oliver Harper (1888-1953)
+789	Mary E. Harper (1891-)
+790	John Thomas Harper (1895-1897)
+791	William Elmer Harper (1898-)
+792	Burnie Alfine Harper (1901-1979)
+793	Ella Harper (1903-)
+794	Esther Harper (1903-)
+795	Della Harper (1906-)
+796	Effie Dosie Harper (1910-)

152. **Annie Louella Wallace**, daughter of Seaborn Wallace and Tabitha Boone, was born on March 10, 1868. She died on October 31, 1948 in Randolph County, NC and was buried on November 1, 1948 in Seagrove, Randolph County, NC at Maple Springs Baptist Church.

Robert Lee Farlow and Annie Louella Wallace had the following children:

+797	Maggie V. Farlow (1892-)
+798	William Penn Farlow (1899-1961)
+799	Colvin Mc. Farlow (1899-)
+800	Thomas Kenyon Farlow (1904-1978)
+801	Raleigh L. Wallace (1907-1926)
+802	Zora Della Wallace (1912-1996)

Willard Webster Boone, son of Daniel Henry Boone (1825-1910) and Amy Lucas (1823-1875), was born on July 26, 1858. He married Mahaley Bean on May 16, 1876 in Randolph County, NC. He married Sara Levicey Jordan between 1881 and 1885. He died on May 13, 1945 and was buried in Seagrove, Randolph County, NC at Boone Family Cemetery. He and Annie Louella Wallace had the following children:

+803	Mary Elizabeth Wallace (1884-1974)

Reece Blair and Annie Louella Wallace had the following children:

> +804   Wade C. Wallace (1893-1970)

153. Maude Jane Wallace, daughter of Seaborn Wallace and Tabitha Boone, was born on January 7, 1870. She married **William M. Kennedy** on March 8, 1903 in Randolph County, NC. She died on January 14, 1956 in Seagrove, Randolph County, NC and was buried on January 16, 1956 in Seagrove, Randolph County, NC at Union Grove Baptist Church.

> William M. Kennedy, son of David R. Kennedy (1825-1894) and Amy Freeman (1823-1878), was born on December 25, 1856. He married Martha Ellen Luck circa 1886. He died on July 2, 1931 and was buried in Seagrove, Randolph County, NC at Union Grove Baptist Church. He and Maude Jane Wallace had the following children:

> > +805   George Washington Kennedy (1903-1967)
> > +806   Lucy Jane Kennedy (1907-1993)
> > +807   Daniel A. Kennedy (1910-)
> > +808   Dewey Ernest Kennedy (1913-1978)
> > +809   May Elizabeth Kennedy (1919-)

154. Melissa Catherine Wallace, daughter of Seaborn Wallace and Tabitha Boone, was born on July 15, 1872. She died on November 5, 1953 in Griffin Clinic, Asheboro, Randolph County, NC and was buried on November 7, 1953 in Seagrove, Randolph County, NC at Union Grove Baptist Church.

157. Alexander Vance Wallace, son of Alexander Wallace and Elizabeth Ann Fry, was born on April 11, 1863 in Moore County, NC. He married **Leander Frances Sheffield** on November 1, 1884 in Richmond County, NC. He died on April 21, 1928 in Scotland County, NC and was buried on April 22, 1928 in Scotland County, NC at Sutherland Cemetery.

> Leander Frances Sheffield was born on October 27, 1864 in Moore County, NC. She died on May 14, 1944 in Charlotte, Mecklenburg County, NC and was buried on May 15, 1944 in Scotland County, NC at Sutherland Cemetery. She and Alexander Vance Wallace had the following children:

> > +810   Octavius Wallace (-)
> > +811   Hattie Wallace (1890-)
> > +812   William Wallace (1894-)
> > +813   John Dixon Wallace (1899-1987)
> > +814   Viola Blanche Wallace (1902-)
> > +815   Ida Lee Wallace (1907-)

158. Sarah Wallace, daughter of Nathan Wallace and Mary McCrimmon, was born on October 15, 1839 in Moore County, NC. She married **Cornelius Hasseltine Jones** on July 20, 1860 in Bibb County, AL. She died on September 2, 1913 and was buried in Jacksonville, Cherokee County, TX at Jacksonville City Cemetery.

> **Jeptha C. Bowden** was born on September 16, 1826 in Putnam County, GA. He died on August 28, 1884 and was buried in Cherokee County, TX at Myrtle Springs Cemetery.

> Cornelius Hasseltine Jones was born on March 27, 1831 in Elbert County, GA. He died on February 1, 1872 and was buried in Cherokee County, TX at Myrtle Springs Cemetery. He and Sarah Wallace had the following children:

> > +816   John Jones (1858-)
> > +817   Mary Alice Jones (1861-1892)
> > +818   Lucy Jones (1864-)
> > +819   Bernice Jones (1868-)
> > +820   Walter Jones (1868-)
> > +821   Margaret Jones (1870-)
> > +822   Laura C. Jones (1870-)

159. Lucinda Wallace, daughter of Nathan Wallace and Mary McCrimmon, was born on July 16, 1842 in Bibb County, AL. She died in 1918 in Mineral Wells, Palo Pinto County, TX.

> **S.R. Sessions** died before 1880. He and Lucinda Wallace had the following children:

+823	Nathan Sessions (1874-)
+824	Winnie E. Sessions (1875-1876)
+825	Daniel M. Sessions (1877-)

160. **Mary E. Wallace**, daughter of Nathan Wallace and Mary McCrimmon, was born in 1844 in Bibb County, AL.

161. **Daniel Houston Wallace**, son of Nathan Wallace and Mary McCrimmon, was born on January 12, 1848 in Bibb County, AL. He married **Laura Ellen Knight** on July 14, 1870 in Cherokee County, TX. He died on September 9, 1927 in Palestine, Anderson County, TX.

Laura Ellen Knight was born on April 5, 1852 in Texas. She died on January 18, 1915. She and Daniel Houston Wallace had the following children:

+826	David Overton Wallace (1872-)
+827	Martha Clementine Wallace (1874-1965)
+828	Lilly Wallace (1876-)
+829	Briston McCrimmon Wallace (1879-1948)
+830	Sarah Wallace (1881-1911)
+831	James Britian Wallace (1885-1937)
+832	Fred F. Wallace (1888-1933)
+833	Mary L. Wallace (1890-1891)

162. **Martha Clementine Wallace**, daughter of Nathan Wallace and Mary McCrimmon, was born on March 14, 1852 in Bibb County, AL. She died on July 26, 1866 in Cherokee County, TX and was buried in Cherokee County, TX at Myrtle Springs Cemetery.

163. **James Monk Wallace**, son of Nathan Wallace and Mary McCrimmon, was born on March 21, 1858 in Selma, Dallas County, AL. He married **Lily Wiggins Knight** circa 1879. He died on February 8, 1933 in Mineral Wells, Palo Pinto County, TX and was buried on February 10, 1933 in Mineral Wells, Palo Pinto County, TX at Elmwood Cemetery.

Lily Wiggins Knight, daughter of John Knight (-) and Sarah Payne (-), was born on March 18, 1862 in Cherokee County, TX. She died on August 11, 1943 in Mineral Wells, Palo Pinto County, TX and was buried in Mineral Wells, Palo Pinto County, TX at Elmwood Cemetery. She and James Monk Wallace had the following children:

+834	Byrd Wallace (1880-1956)
+835	Winnie Elizabeth Wallace (1882-1967)
+836	Verna Wallace (1885-)
+837	Ernest Joe Wallace (1887-1960)
+838	Elsie Bess Wallace (1889-1968)
+839	Laura Wallace (1892-1981)
+840	Allen B. Wallace (1899-1989)

164. **Raleigh S. Wallace**, son of Eli Wallace and Sina Davis, was born on June 25, 1847 in Bibb County, AL. He married **Dolly Smitherman** on July 27, 1868 in Bibb County, AL. He died on July 11, 1886 in Bibb County, AL.

Dolly Smitherman was born in 1852 in Alabama. She and Raleigh S. Wallace had the following children:

+841	Julia Ann Wallace (1870-)
+842	Viola Wallace (1873-1913)
+843	Victoria Wallace (1874-)
+844	Sina Wallace (1877-1963)
+845	Rufus Cobb Wallace (1877-1920)
+846	Sallie Wallace (1880-)
+847	John Hardy Wallace (1883-1959)

165. **Frances J. Wallace**, daughter of Eli Wallace and Sina Davis, was born on June 12, 1849 in Bibb County, AL. She married **Alfred Smitherman** on September 11, 1868 in Bibb County, AL. She died on October 10, 1891 in Bibb County, AL and was buried in Bibb County, AL at Shady Grove Church Cemetery.

Alfred Smitherman, son of John M. Smitherman (1818-1883) and Delilah Lawley (1822-1857), was born in 1847 in Bibb County, AL. He died on June 15, 1907 in Bibb County, AL and was buried in Bibb County, AL at Shady Grove Church Cemetery. He and Frances J. Wallace had the following children:

+848	Martha Isabell Smitherman (1869-1945)
+849	Lila Smitherman (1871-)
+850	Levi Smitherman (1872-1901)
+851	John A. Smitherman (1875-)
+852	Rachel Smitherman (1879-)

166. **Joseph Davis Wallace**, son of Eli Wallace and Sina Davis, was born on June 12, 1851 in Bibb County, AL. He married **Elizabeth Caldwell** on January 2, 1870 in Bibb County, AL. He died on May 16, 1916 in Bibb County, AL and was buried in Bibb County, AL at Shady Grove Church Cemetery.

Elizabeth Caldwell was born on September 15, 1855 in Bibb County, AL. She died on September 17, 1905 in Bibb County, AL and was buried in Bibb County, AL at Shady Grove Church Cemetery. She and Joseph Davis Wallace had the following children:

+853	John W. Wallace (1871-)
+854	Walter Wallace (1873-)
+855	Luther Wallace (1878-)
+856	Rhoday M. "Rocky" Wallace (1882-1942)

167. **Martha "Patsy" Wallace**, daughter of Eli Wallace and Sina Davis, was born on January 22, 1855 in Bibb County, AL. She died on April 21, 1885 in Bibb County, AL and was buried in Bibb County, AL at Shady Grove Church Cemetery.

James Pinkney Smitherman, son of John M. Smitherman (1818-1883) and Delilah Lawley (1822-1857), was born on October 15, 1850 in Bibb County, AL. He died on August 24, 1924 in Bibb County, AL. He and Martha "Patsy" Wallace had the following children:

+857	Laura Smitherman (1875-1945)
+858	Lillian Smitherman (1876-1939)
+859	William James Smitherman (1880-1962)

168. **William "Dock" Wallace**, son of Eli Wallace and Sina Davis, was born on October 20, 1858 in Chilton County, AL. He died on October 17, 1928 in Bessemer, Jefferson County, AL and was buried on October 19, 1928 in Randolph, AL.

169. **Elizabeth Wallace**, daughter of Isham Wallace and Gracy A. Goodwin, was born between 1860 and 1864.

170. **John C. Wallace**, son of Thomas Wallace and Frances "Fanny" Hill, was born in 1849. He married **Mary J. Henderson** on March 3, 1882 in Bibb County, AL. He died on April 10, 1925 in Lawley, Bibb County, AL and was buried on April 11, 1925 in Bibb County, AL at Tabernacle Methodist Church Cemetery.

Mary J. Henderson, daughter of Franklin Henderson (-) and Katie Langford (-), was born in 1856. She died on July 8, 1913 in Bibb County, AL and was buried in Bibb County, AL at Tabernacle Methodist Church Cemetery. She and John C. Wallace had the following children:

+860	Eula Wallace (1886-)
+861	Minerva Mae Wallace (1888-1969)
+862	Melford V. Wallace (1889-)
+863	Sarah M. Wallace (1890-1948)
+864	Reuben Franklin Wallace (1893-1966)
+865	Stella Wallace (1895-)
+866	Luther Wallace (1899-)

171. **William Harrison Wallace**, son of Thomas Wallace and Frances "Fanny" Hill, was born in 1852 in Lawley, Bibb County, AL. He died on August 11, 1926 in Lawley, Bibb County, AL and was buried in Bibb County, AL at Tabernacle Methodist Church Cemetery.

Frances Emily Edwards was born in 1850. She died on November 15, 1924 in Bibb County, AL and was buried in Bibb County, AL at Tabernacle Methodist Church Cemetery. She and William Harrison Wallace had the following children:

+867	Anna Ludelia Wallace (1874-1957)
+868	James Edward Wallace (1878-1945)
+869	Maudie Estelle Wallace (1888-1956)
+870	Louisa Wallace (1890-)

174. **Charles F. Wallace**, son of Thomas Wallace and Frances "Fanny" Hill, was born on August 15, 1858. He married **Jeneria Jane Langford** circa 1890. He died on March 13, 1927 in Tuscaloosa County, AL and was buried on March 14, 1927 in Bucksville, Tuscaloosa County, AL at Bucksville Cemetery.

Jeneria Jane Langford, daughter of David Crockett Langford (1848-1920) and Sarah Elizabeth Gentry (1849-1911), was born on December 20, 1872 in Bibb County, AL. She died on February 2, 1933 in Tuscaloosa County, AL and was buried on February 3, 1933 in Bucksville, Tuscaloosa County, AL at Bucksville Cemetery. She and Charles F. Wallace had the following children:

+871	Lodie Wallace (1896-)
+872	Clarence Wallace (1899-)
+873	Howard Houston Wallace (1901-1962)
+874	Roscoe A. Wallace (1904-1973)
+875	Ella Wallace (1907-)
+876	Josie Wallace (1910-)

176. **J. Henry Calhoun Wallace**, son of Thomas Wallace and Frances "Fanny" Hill, was born on April 13, 1860. He married **Mary Henry "Mollie" Cash** on October 19, 1882 in Bibb County, AL. He died on January 3, 1902 and was buried in Bibb County, AL at Tabernacle Methodist Church Cemetery.

Mary Henry "Mollie" Cash, daughter of Henry Cash (-) and Martha Pounds (-), was born on November 16, 1862. She died on July 23, 1923 and was buried in Bibb County, AL at Tabernacle Methodist Church Cemetery. She and J. Henry Calhoun Wallace had the following children:

+877	Henry Calhoun Wallace (1883-1949)
+878	Charles T. Wallace (1886-1969)
+879	Jasper Decaster Wallace (1887-1960)
+880	William Augusta Wallace (1889-1956)
+881	Rebecca Wallace (1891-1964)
+882	John Columbus Wallace (1894-1973)
+883	Felix E. Wallace (1896-)
+884	Miranda Idell Wallace (1897-1983)
+885	Robert Vandon Wallace (1899-1942)
+886	Ruth M. Wallace (1902-)

178. **Lawson Wallace**, son of Raleigh W. Wallace and Elizabeth Spinks, was born on May 3, 1852 in Alabama. He married **Mary Catherine Pigford** on September 7, 1870. He died in August 1924.

Mary Catherine Pigford, daughter of Wright Pigford (-) and Lucretia Harris Rodgers (-), was born on August 1, 1854 in Mississippi. She and Lawson Wallace had the following children:

+887	Minnie Virginia Wallace (1871-1966)
+888	Cevilla Arrie Wallace (1874-1956)
+889	Lillian Avice Wallace (1876-1877)
+890	Daisy Edna Wallace (1881-1946)

179. **Ada Ann Wallace**, daughter of Raleigh W. Wallace and Elizabeth Spinks, was born on October 1, 1857. She died on January 4, 1860.

180. **Jasper Wallace**, son of Raleigh W. Wallace and Elizabeth Spinks, was born on June 18, 1859. He died on December 30, 1881.

181. **Mary Jane Wallace**, daughter of Raleigh W. Wallace and Elizabeth Spinks, was born on November 25, 1861. She died on June 29, 1863.

182. **Sarah Martha "Mattie" Wallace**, daughter of Raleigh W. Wallace and Elizabeth Spinks, was born on April 12, 1864.

   Robert Lee Deen and Sarah Martha "Mattie" Wallace had the following children:

+891	Jasper Arthur Deen (1884-)
+892	Lessie Deen (1885-)
+893	Lena Deen (1887-)
+894	Marion Deen (1889-1973)
+895	Mollie E. Deen (1890-)
+896	Carrie E. Deen (1891-1998)
+897	Jesse Randall Deen (1895-1971)
+898	Floyd Virgil Deen (1899-)
+899	Ebbin O. Deen (1903-1983)
+900	Harrison Irvin Deen (1905-)

183. **Eudora Ann Wallace**, daughter of Raleigh W. Wallace and Elizabeth Spinks, was born on July 1, 1867.

184. **Virginia Wallace**, daughter of Raleigh W. Wallace and Elizabeth Spinks, was born on October 14, 1868. She married **John Gary Maggard** on December 12, 1888. She died on March 13, 1958 and was buried in Lauderdale County, MS at Coker Chapel Cemetery.

   John Gary Maggard was born on August 16, 1869. He died on February 10, 1943 and was buried in Lauderdale County, MS at Coker Chapel Cemetery. He and Virginia Wallace had the following children:

+901	Jessie Maggard (1889-)
+902	Charles Maggard (1892-)
+903	David Maggard (1894-1967)
+904	Pernita Maggard (1896-)
+905	Wesley Maggard (1898-)
+906	Johnnye Maggard (1902-)
+907	Pauline Maggard (1905-1933)

185. **John M. Wallace**, son of John Wesley Wallace and Frances J. Bearden, was born on October 6, 1864 in Alabama. He married **Emma Parker** on July 13, 1883 in Bibb County, AL. He died on December 23, 1928 and was buried in Bibb County, AL at Tabernacle Methodist Church Cemetery.

   Emma Parker was born on August 7, 1860 in Alabama. She died on March 22, 1945 and was buried in Bibb County, AL at Tabernacle Methodist Church Cemetery. She and John M. Wallace had the following children:

+908	Thomas Jefferson "Jeff" Wallace (1884-1959)
+909	Henry W. Wallace (1886-1967)
+910	Marvin Jackson Wallace (1889-1962)
+911	Oma Wallace (1893-)
+912	Ola Wallace (1897-1924)
+913	Harvey Wallace (1902-1958)

186. **William J. Wallace**, son of John Wesley Wallace and Frances J. Bearden, was born on October 12, 1866 in Perry County, AL. He married **Roxie A. Hollie** circa 1887. He married **Fannie Jackson** after 1910. He died on August 14, 1940 and was buried on August 14, 1940 in Bibb County, AL at Harris Family Cemetery.

   Roxie A. Hollie was born in July 1868 in Alabama. She died circa 1908 and was buried in Bibb County, AL at Harris Family Cemetery. She and William J. Wallace had the following children:

+914	James F. Wallace (1891-)
+915	Robert C. Wallace (1893-1944)
+916	John William Wallace (1896-)
+917	Belle Wallace (1898-)
+918	Dock Wallace (1900-1992)
+919	Rosa Bell Wallace (1900-1981)
+920	Jennie Wallace (c. 1904-)

Fannie Jackson was born in 1880 and was buried in Bibb County, AL at Harris Family Cemetery. She and William J. Wallace had the following children:

+921	Rich Wallace (1914-)
+922	Lottie Wallace (1915-)
+923	Henry Wallace (1918-)

187. **Martha F. Wallace**, daughter of John Wesley Wallace and Frances J. Bearden, was born on October 23, 1866 in Perry County, AL. She married **Marcus D. Cochran** circa 1890. She died on January 30, 1933 in Bibb County, AL and was buried in Bibb County, AL at Shady Grove Church Cemetery.

Marcus D. Cochran was born on January 6, 1850 in Mississippi. He died on August 7, 1927 and was buried in Bibb County, AL at Shady Grove Church Cemetery. He and Martha F. Wallace had the following children:

+924	Charlie Cochran (-1991)
+925	Lizzie Cochran (-)
+926	Julie Cochran (-)
+927	George Cochran (1892-1922)
+928	Dave Cochran (1898-1973)
+929	N. Pete Cochran (1902-1972)
+930	Jessie Cochran (1904-1967)

188. **Andrew Jackson Wallace**, son of John Wesley Wallace and Frances J. Bearden, was born on November 24, 1871 in Alabama. He married **Mary Susan Stewart** on July 8, 1890 in Bibb or Chilton County, AL at home of Richard McKinley. He died on November 12, 1943 in Bibb County, AL and was buried on November 14, 1943 in Bibb County, AL at Shady Grove Church Cemetery.

Mary Susan Stewart was born on April 17, 1871 in Alabama. She died on June 9, 1913 and was buried in Bibb County, AL at Harris Family Cemetery. She and Andrew Jackson Wallace had the following children:

+931	Richard Albert Wallace (1891-1969)
+932	Luther Columbus Wallace (1892-1973)
+933	Lilly Belle Wallace (1894-1922)
+934	James Jackson Wallace (1896-1972)
+935	Houston Shivers Wallace (1898-1973)
+936	Eva Dee Wallace (1900-1988)
+937	Dan Crawford Wallace (1902-1911)
+938	Ollie Mae Wallace (1904-1986)
+939	Odell Wallace (1906-1985)
+940	Maude Lee Wallace (1908-1989)
+941	Lehman Grundy Wallace (1909-1987)
+942	Infant Wallace (1913-1913)

189. **Jasper Newton Wallace Sr.**, son of John Wesley Wallace and Frances J. Bearden, was born on May 19, 1874 in Alabama. He married **Eller Moton** circa 1899. He married **Dolly Mae Solomon** after 1929. He died on June 4, 1949 in Bibb County, AL and was buried on June 5, 1949 in Bibb County, AL at Shady Grove Church Cemetery.

Eller Moton was born circa 1875 in Alabama. She died circa 1929 and was buried in Bibb County, AL at Shady Grove Church Cemetery. She and Jasper Newton Wallace Sr had the following children:

+943	Harmon Wallace (-)

+944	Livie Wallace (-)
+945	King Cornelius Wallace (1900-1981)
+946	Virgil Wallace (1907-1963)

Dolly Mae Solomon was buried in Bibb County, AL at Shady Grove Church Cemetery. She and Jasper Newton Wallace Sr had the following children:

+947	Annie Murrell Wallace (-)
+948	Allen Wallace (-)
+949	Marie Wallace (-)
+950	Ishmeal Wallace (1931-1981)
+951	Mary Ruth Wallace (1932-1933)
+952	Jasper Newton Wallace Jr (1939-1939)

190. **Mary E. Wallace**, daughter of John Wesley Wallace and Frances J. Bearden, was born on April 23, 1875 in Alabama. She died on May 28, 1927 and was buried in Perry County, AL at Mt. Olive Church Cemetery.

Zake Moton died before 1900 and was buried in Perry County, AL at Mt. Olive Church Cemetery. He and Mary E. Wallace had the following children:

+953	Samuel Moton (1896-c. 1948)
+954	Ruby B. Moton (1899-1965)

Jack C. Cochran was buried in Perry County, AL at Mt. Olive Church Cemetery. He and Mary E. Wallace had the following children:

+955	Columbus Cochran (-1957)
+956	Lorena Cochran (-)
+957	William Alfred Cochran (-)
+958	Bela Cochran (1901-1987)
+959	Zula Cochran (1906-1986)
+960	Lena Mae Cochran (1915-1948)

191. **Nancy Paralee Wallace**, daughter of John Wesley Wallace and Frances J. Bearden, was born on September 13, 1879 in Alabama. She married **Joe Cochran** circa 1899. She died on June 4, 1966 and was buried in Bibb County, AL at Shady Grove Church Cemetery.

Joe Cochran was born on July 8, 1879 in Alabama. He died on November 27, 1964 and was buried in Bibb County, AL at Shady Grove Church Cemetery. He and Nancy Paralee Wallace had the following children:

+961	Earnest Cochran (-)
+962	Louvenia Cochran (-)
+963	Grady Cochran (-)
+964	Virginia Cochran (-)
+965	Freeman Cochran (1903-1986)
+966	Lester Cochran (1916-1958)
+967	Vester Cochran (1916-1990)
+968	Lehman Cochran (1919-1997)

192. **Dovie Wallace**, daughter of John Wesley Wallace and Frances J. Bearden, was born circa 1883 in Perry County, AL. She died on December 13, 1940 in Maplesville, Chilton County, AL and was buried on December 14, 1940 in Bibb County, AL at Shady Grove Church Cemetery.

Dovie Wallace had the following children:

+969	Ward Wilson Wallace (-)
+970	Arthur Wallace (1906-1988)

193. **M. G. Wallace**, son of John Wesley Wallace and Frances J. Bearden, was born on January 11, 1885 in Alabama. He married **Myrtle Bearden** circa 1903. He married **Gertrude Bearden** after 1935. He died on June 7, 1963 and was buried in Chilton County, AL at Pleasant Grove Baptist Church Cemetery.

Myrtle Bearden was born on March 24, 1886 in Alabama. She died on March 2, 1935 and was buried in Chilton County, AL at Pleasant Grove Baptist Church Cemetery. She and M. G. Wallace had the following children:

+971	Roy M. Wallace Sr (-)	
+972	Ida Mae Wallace (-)	
+973	Euna Wallace (-)	
+974	Harvey Wallace (-)	

Gertrude Bearden was born on December 25, 1897 in Alabama. She died on November 30, 1953 and was buried in Chilton County, AL at Pleasant Grove Baptist Church Cemetery.

194. **Melvin Augusta Wallace**, son of John Wesley Wallace and Frances J. Bearden, was born on January 11, 1885. He married **Myrtle Bearden** on August 16, 1906 in Bibb County, AL. He died on June 7, 1963 in Clanton, Chilton County, AL and was buried on June 10, 1963 in Maplesville, Chilton County, AL at Pleasant Grove Cemetery #2.

Myrtle Bearden was born on March 24, 1886. She died on March 2, 1935. She and Melvin Augusta Wallace had the following children:

+975	Roy Moody Wallace (1909-1990)	

195. **Thomas W. Wallace**, son of John Wesley Wallace and Frances J. Bearden, was born on May 19, 1889 in Perry County, AL. He married **Vadna Doss** on January 30, 1910. He died on November 11, 1958 in Bibb County, AL and was buried on November 12, 1958 in Bibb County, AL at Shady Grove Church Cemetery.

Vadna Doss was born on February 9, 1892 in Alabama. She died on April 27, 1975 and was buried in Bibb County, AL at Shady Grove Church Cemetery. She and Thomas W. Wallace had the following children:

+976	Lucille Wallace (-)	
+977	Bobby Gene Wallace (-)	
+978	John Wesley Wallace (1910-1964)	
+979	Katie Wallace (1912-1983)	

197. **Paralee Wallace**, daughter of Josiah\Cyrus Wallace and Frances Jane Bearden, was born on October 5, 1861. She married **Emmet Casey Lawrence** on September 28, 1883 in Bibb County, AL. She died on September 19, 1928.

Emmet Casey Lawrence, son of Nancy Lawrence (1835-1904), was born circa 1865 in Alabama. He died on July 27, 1929. He and Paralee Wallace had the following children:

+980	Emmet Joseph Lawrence (1886-1962)	
+981	Lee Edward Lawrence Sr (1887-1912)	
+982	Lola M. Lawrence (1888-1966)	
+983	Zeke Lawrence (1890-1917)	

198. **Angeline Wallace**, daughter of Josiah\Cyrus Wallace and Frances Jane Bearden, was born circa 1865 in Alabama. She married **Robert Harrison** on December 28, 1885 in Chilton County, AL and was buried in Chilton County, AL at Chestnut Hill Cemetery.

Robert Harrison and Angeline Wallace had the following children:

+984	Essie Harrison (-)	
+985	Lillie Harrison (-)	
+986	Cleveland Harrison (-)	
+987	Julia Harrison (-)	
+988	Harrison (-)	

199. **Sally Wallace**, daughter of Josiah\Cyrus Wallace and Frances Jane Bearden, was born in 1866 in Alabama.

    Dave Leach and Sally Wallace had the following children:

        +989   Nora Agnes Leach\Wallace (1893-1971)

200. **John Wesley Wallace**, son of Josiah\Cyrus Wallace and Frances Jane Bearden, was born on April 30, 1868 in Alabama. He died on December 24, 1947.

    Markie Baker and John Wesley Wallace had the following children:

        +990   Tommy Wallace (-)
        +991   Johnny Wallace (-)
        +992   Mary Wallace (-)
        +993   Donald Wallace (-)
        +994   Emmer Charity Wallace (-)

    Susan Latham, daughter of Wesley E. Latham (1841-1864) and Julia Ann Hicks (1843-1914), was born on July 12, 1868 in Alabama. She died on July 14, 1921. She and John Wesley Wallace had the following children:

        +995   Julia Wallace (-)
        +996   Infant Wallace (-)
        +997   Infant Wallace (-)
        +998   Infant Wallace (-)
        +999   Janie Wallace (1891-)
        +1000   Noah Columbus Wallace (1894-1965)
        +1001   Eula Wallace (1899-)
        +1002   Robert Monroe Wallace (1905-1982)

201. **Thomas Wesley Wallace**, son of Josiah\Cyrus Wallace and Frances Jane Bearden, was born on October 13, 1871 in Chilton County, AL. He married **Mary Frances Lawrence** circa 1894. He died on March 21, 1932 in Lawley, Bibb County, AL and was buried in Bibb County, AL at Rehobeth Church Cemetery.

    Mary Frances Lawrence was born on April 7, 1875 in Spraytown, Jackson County, IN. She died on March 30, 1955 and was buried in Bibb County, AL at Rehobeth Church Cemetery.

203. **Sarah Elizabeth Rolley**, daughter of Isaac Rolley and Sarah Wallace, was born on September 11, 1856. She died on January 24, 1936 and was buried in Stanton, Chilton County, AL at Ebenezer Baptist Church.

    Moses Jefferson Mull was born on June 29, 1854. He died on September 16, 1939 and was buried in Stanton, Chilton County, AL at Ebenezer Baptist Church. He and Sarah Elizabeth Rolley had the following children:

        +1003   Bevie Waloner Mull (1882-1964)

205. **John Leonard Hart**, son of Ambrose R. Hart and Nancy Wallace, was born in June 1863 in Tennessee. He married **Mary Jane Stewart** circa 1884. He died on September 4, 1930 in Henderson County, TN and was buried in Henderson County, TN at Palestine Cemetery.

    Mary Jane Stewart, daughter of John Wesley Stewart (1818-1855) and Eliza Jane Watkins (1822-), was born in 1848. She died in 1932 and was buried in Henderson County, TN at Palestine Cemetery. She and John Leonard Hart had the following children:

        +1004   James Marion Hart (1890-1941)

206. **Martha J. Britt**, daughter of Beacom C. Britt and Deborah Wallace, was born in 1849. She married **Alexander Rector** on October 12, 1867 in McNairy County, TN.

207. **Nathan Britt**, son of Beacom C. Britt and Deborah Wallace, was born in 1852. He married **Sarah Ann Williams** on November 25, 1874 in McNairy County, TN.

Sarah Ann Williams, daughter of Jeremiah D. Williams (1825-1906) and Rebecca Kizer (1827-1908), was born in 1849 in Georgia.

208. **Hans Britt**, son of Beacom C. Britt and Deborah Wallace, was born on April 17, 1853 in North Carolina. He married **Martha Elizabeth Powers** circa 1878. He died on January 9, 1941 and was buried in Henderson County, TN at Union Grove Baptist Church.

Martha Elizabeth Powers was born on March 9, 1861 in Tennessee. She died on March 26, 1933 and was buried in Henderson County, TN at Union Grove Baptist Church. She and Hans Britt had the following children:

+1005	Nathan Wesley Britt (1878-1962)
+1006	W.J. Britt (1880-1880)
+1007	Lee A. Britt (1881-1900)
+1008	John Henry Britt (1884-1980)
+1009	James Edward Britt (1887-1918)
+1010	Jennie F. Britt (1891-)
+1011	Robert Britt (1894-1900)

209. **William T. Britt**, son of Beacom C. Britt and Deborah Wallace, was born in 1855. He married **Eliza Ann Kizer** on August 22, 1877 in McNairy County, TN. He married **Eliza Jane Cagle** circa 1888.

Eliza Ann Kizer, daughter of Benjamin W. Kizer (1825-) and Margaret Hanes (1824-), was born in 1856. She and William T. Britt had the following children:

+1012	Hayden W. Britt (1879-)

Eliza Jane Cagle, daughter of Robert Cagle (1826-bef 1880) and Anna (1826-), was born in 1852. She died on May 10, 1916 in Henderson County, TN.

210. **Avington Britt**, son of Beacom C. Britt and Deborah Wallace, was born on January 12, 1856 in Henderson County, TN. He married **Nancy Powers** circa 1877. He died on January 25, 1928 in Henderson County, TN and was buried on January 26, 1928 in Henderson County, TN at Maple Springs Cemetery.

Nancy Powers was born in 1856 in Tennessee. She died before 1900. She and Avington Britt had the following children:

+1013	James Britt (1878-)
+1014	Martha Britt (1879-)
+1015	Charles Garfield Britt (1880-1964)
+1016	Caswell Melton Britt (1884-1974)
+1017	Amanda Elizabeth "Mandy" Britt (1886-1978)

212. **Beacom Nelson "Ned" Britt**, son of Beacom C. Britt and Deborah Wallace, was born in June 1862 in Henderson County, TN. He married **Sarah "Sallie" Cagle** circa 1887. He died on December 2, 1909 in Henderson County, TN.

Sarah "Sallie" Cagle, daughter of Robert Cagle (1826-bef 1880) and Anna (1826-), was born on May 6, 1867 in Tennessee. She died on May 18, 1934 in Dunklin County, MO. She and Beacom Nelson "Ned" Britt had the following children:

+1018	Debby Annie Britt (1888-)
+1019	Mary Lula Britt (1890-)
+1020	Joe T. Britt (1892-)
+1021	Gertrude Britt (1895-)
+1022	William Hobert Britt (1897-)
+1023	Myrtle Britt (1906-)

213. **James A. Britt**, son of Beacom C. Britt and Deborah Wallace, was born in March 1865 in Tennessee. He married **Nancy E. Cagle** circa 1887. He died in 1937 and was buried in Henderson County, TN at Maple Springs Cemetery.

Nancy E. Cagle, daughter of Robert Cagle (1826-bef 1880) and Anna (1826-), was born on April 2, 1854 in Tennessee. She died on February 21, 1916 and was buried in Henderson County, TN at Maple Springs Cemetery. She and James A. Britt had the following children:

+1024   James Henry Britt (1891-1969)

Charity Jane Western was born in 1867. She died on February 20, 1944 in Henderson County, TN and was buried on February 21, 1944 in Henderson County, TN at Maple Springs Cemetery.

214. **Abraham Lincoln Britt**, son of Beacom C. Britt and Deborah Wallace, was born in April 1865 in Tennessee. He married **Martha E. "Patsy" Cagle** circa 1887. He died on September 15, 1916 in Henderson County, TN.

Martha E. "Patsy" Cagle, daughter of Robert Cagle (1826-bef 1880) and Anna (1826-), was born in January 1858 in Tennessee. She died on July 28, 1955. She and Abraham Lincoln Britt had the following children:

+1025   Eliza F. Britt (1889-)
+1026   Sarah Jane "Sallie" Britt (1891-1981)
+1027   George W. Britt (1893-)
+1028   Nancy L. Britt (1896-)
+1029   Bertha M. Britt (1898-)
+1030   Jennie E. Britt (1900-)

215. **Joseph Isaac "Ike" Britt**, son of Beacom C. Britt and Deborah Wallace, was born in June 1871. He married **Ada E. Horton** on October 11, 1902 in Henderson County, TN. He died on October 16, 1948 in Jackson, Madison County, TN and was buried on October 17, 1948 in Cedar Grove, Carroll County, TN at Hickory Flat United Methodist Church.

Ada E. Horton was born on December 25, 1882. She died on October 11, 1966 in Madison County, TN and was buried in Cedar Grove, Carroll County, TN at Hickory Flat United Methodist Church. She and Joseph Isaac "Ike" Britt had the following children:

+1031   Jennie Frances Britt (1907-1999)

216. **Everet Britt**, son of Benjamin Britt and Franey Wallace, was born in October 1855. He married **Frances Josephine McCarrell** circa 1878.

Frances Josephine McCarrell was born in 1858. She and Everet Britt had the following children:

+1032   Eliza A. Britt (1879-)
+1033   Esther Francis Britt (1881-1934)
+1034   Melvina Britt (1885-)
+1035   Robert G. Britt (1886-)
+1036   Minnie T. Britt (1889-)
+1037   John W. Britt (1896-)

219. **George Britt**, son of Benjamin Britt and Franey Wallace, was born in 1863. He died before 1900.

Louisa M. Williams, daughter of Lorenzo D. "Low" Williams (1829-1890) and Sarah Elizabeth Hart (1844-1885), was born in February 1869. She and George Britt had the following children:

+1038   Ella L. "Nettie" Britt (1889-)
+1039   Mary Emma Britt (1892-)
+1040   Sarah Elizabeth "Bessie" Britt (1894-1973)
+1041   James Richard Britt (1896-1946)

**[Above L-R] Charles Wallace
and Jerome Wallace**
*(sons of Ruffin Wallace and Salina Fry - Courtesy
of Pam Sherman, Valdosta, GA)*

[Top Right] Hans Britt
*(son of Beacom Britt and Deborah Wallace -
Courtesy of Ancestry.com user brandywine_97)*

[Above] Daniel Houston Wallace *(son of
Nathan Wallace and Mary McCrimmon)*
and Laura Ellen Knight *(Courtesy of
Ancestry.com user larrylinder38)*
**[Left] Harvey Gassaway and Sarah
Elizabeth Wallace** *(daughter of Benjamin
Wallace and Caty Williams - Courtesy of Kaye
Vernon, Weatherford, TX)*

[Above] John Gary Maggard and Virginia Wallace *(daughter of Raleigh Wallace and Elizabeth Spinks - Courtesy of Robert Miller, Findagrave.com)*
[Below] Back row [L to R] Sidney Horace Hart, Harvey Lafayette Hart, Margaret Emma Wallace *(daughter of Ben Wallace and Holly Kizer).* Front row [L to R] Thomas Benjamin Hart, William Bennett Williams, Jr., Abbie May Hart.
(Courtesy of Kaye Vernon, Weatherford, TX)

[Above L-R] Rolle Allen "Rawl" Britt *(son of Benjamin Britt and Franey Wallace),* Flossie Britt, Dee Elliott, and Gracie Britt. *(Courtesy of Bradley D. Britt).* [Below] Ben Wallace Jr. *(son of Ben Wallace and Eliza Elizabeth Rivers - Courtesy of Kaye Vernon, Weatherford, TX)*

David Cincinnati Maness *(son of Everett Maness and Lucinda Shields)* **and Nancy Hughes**. *(Courtesy of Charlotte Maness)*

[Right] Julia McIntyre Maness *(daughter of Ira Lane Maness and Nancy Hancock)* **and George Luther Paschal** *(Courtesy of Scott Paschal, findagrave.com)*

[Below] L-R Cora Wallace, Dora Wallace and Josephine Wallace *(daughters of Ben Wallace and Eliza Elizabeth Rivers – Courtesy of Kaye Vernon. Weatherford, TX)*

[Above] James Bailey Caddell, Mary Clementine Maness and family. *(daughter of Asa Maness and Mary Ann Ritter – Courtesy of Robert M. Griffith, Ancestry.com)*

[Left] Jonas Sedberry Maness
(son of Garner Maness and Katie Maness – Courtesy of Lacy Garner, Jr., Carthage, NC)

[Top Left] Joseph Park Williams *(son of Low Williams and Sarah Elizabeth Hart)* **and Maggie Horton.**

[Above] John W. Williams *(son of Low Williams and Sarah Elizabeth Hart)* **and Clarkie Ann Britt** *(daughter of Nat Britt and Amanda Jane Williams). Children on left and right are sons David J. and William T. but unsure which is which. Minnie Lillian is in Clarkie Ann's lap and John W. is on right. Unsure as to the older lady standing but believe her to be Amanda Jane Williams Britt (mother of Clarkie Ann).*

[Left] Clarkie Ann Williams *(daughter of Low Williams and Sarah Elizabeth Hart)* **and William Salvage Britt** *(son of Nat Britt and Amanda Jane Williams)*
(all Courtesy of Judy Little, Lexington, TN)

221. **Rolle Allen "Rawl" Britt**, son of Benjamin Britt and Franey Wallace, was born in 1867. He married **Mary A. "Molly" Lee** circa 1887. He married **Azalee Frances "Dee" Elliot** on February 20, 1910 in Henderson County, TN. He died on May 18, 1950 and was buried in Henderson County, TN at Palestine Cemetery.

Mary A. "Molly" Lee was born in December 1869. She died before 1910 and was buried in Henderson County, TN at Palestine Cemetery. She and Rolle Allen "Rawl" Britt had the following children:

+1042	Felix R. Britt (1889-1909)
+1043	Frona Esther Britt (1892-)
+1044	Franey Azilee Britt (1893-1935)
+1045	Hubert Jefferson Britt (1896-1969)
+1046	Gracie Britt (1903-)
+1047	Flossie Britt (1906-1932)

Azalee Frances "Dee" Elliot was born in 1880. She died on February 24, 1922 in Henderson County, TN and was buried in Henderson County, TN at Palestine Cemetery.

222. **Deborah E. Britt**, daughter of Benjamin Britt and Franey Wallace, was born in January 1871 in Tennessee. She married **Louis Singleton** circa 1887. She died in 1908.

Louis Singleton was born in April 1862 in Tennessee. He died on October 21, 1930. He and Deborah E. Britt had the following children:

+1048	William Allen Singleton (1888-)
+1049	Suzanne Singleton (1894-)
+1050	Lanebury Singleton (1896-)
+1051	Alice Singleton (1899-)
+1052	Robert Sherman Singleton (1902-1929)

223. **William Brewer**, son of Harmon Brewer and Mary Wallace, was born in 1852.

Henrietta Clements was born in 1856. She and William Brewer had the following children:

+1053	Mary Brewer (1876-)
+1054	William Morgan Brewer (1886-1949)

230. **Geneva F. "Jennie" Brewer**, daughter of Harmon Brewer and Mary Wallace, was born in 1866. She married **John A. Clements** on March 5, 1884 in Shelby County, TN.

John A. Clements and Geneva F. "Jennie" Brewer had the following children:

+1055	Ina Inez Clements (1886-1950)

231. **Henry Martin Brewer**, son of Harmon Brewer and Mary Wallace, was born on November 29, 1869. He married **Annie Lorene Joyner** on February 24, 1892 in Tipton County, TN.

Annie Lorene Joyner was born on August 8, 1872. She died on August 13, 1914. She and Henry Martin Brewer had the following children:

+1056	Willie H. Brewer (1893-)
+1057	Margie D. Brewer (1896-)
+1058	Martin T. Brewer (1899-)
+1059	Lillie Brewer (1905-1980)

235. **Sarah Elizabeth Wallace**, daughter of Benjamin Wallace and Caty Williams, was born on November 16, 1862. She married **Harvey R. Gassaway** on November 23, 1879. She died on November 16, 1900 in Mankin, Henderson County, TX.

Harvey R. Gassaway was born on November 15, 1854. He died on July 20, 1902 in Antelope, Jack County, TX. He and Sarah Elizabeth Wallace had the following children:

+1060 Farry M. Gassaway (1880-1946)
+1061 Clarkie Lee Gassaway (1882-1946)
+1062 Emma Francis Gassaway (1885-1959)
+1063 Male Gassaway (1889-1889)
+1064 Harvey Gassaway (1890-1956)
+1065 Mary Penina Gassaway (1893-1972)
+1066 Male Gassaway (1897-1897)
+1067 Infant Gassaway (1900-1900)

236. **Clarkie Ann Wallace**, daughter of Benjamin Wallace and Caty Williams, was born on March 24, 1866. She married **Sidney Horace Hart** on October 6, 1886. She died in 1889 in Navarro County, TX.

Sidney Horace Hart was born on July 22, 1865 in Tennessee. He married Margaret Emma Wallace circa 1893. He married Ollie L. McCarley circa 1902. He and Clarkie Ann Wallace had the following children:

+1068 Harvey Lafayette Hart (1887-1974)
+1069 Thomas Benjamin Hart (1888-1928)

237. **Margaret Emma Wallace**, daughter of Benjamin Wallace and Holly J. Kizer, was born in April 1872 in Tennessee. She married **William Bennett Williams** on February 10, 1889 in Parker County, TX. She married **Sidney Horace Hart** circa 1893. She died on September 30, 1900 in Navarro County, TX.

William Bennett Williams, son of Thomas Jefferson Williams (1844-1924) and Bethany J. Naylor (-), was born on March 11, 1868 in Tennessee. He died on February 28, 1891 in Parker County, TX. He and Margaret Emma Wallace had the following children:

+1070 Female Williams (1890-1890)
+1071 William Bennett Williams Jr. (1891-1995)

Sidney Horace Hart was born on July 22, 1865 in Tennessee. He married Clarkie Ann Wallace on October 6, 1886. He married Ollie L. McCarley circa 1902. He and Margaret Emma Wallace had the following children:

+1072 Abbie May Hart (1893-)
+1073 Eunice Hart (1895-)
+1074 Leona B. Hart (1898-)
+1075 Chester Hart (1900-)

238. **Josephine Wallace**, daughter of Benjamin Wallace and Eliza Elizabeth Rivers, was born on July 2, 1881 in Parker County, TX. She married **Henry "Dock" Cross** on June 26, 1898. She died on July 6, 1970 in Parker County, TX.

Henry "Dock" Cross was born on August 24, 1859 in Camden, AR. He died on February 7, 1953 in Parker County, TX.

239. **Cora Wallace**, daughter of Benjamin Wallace and Eliza Elizabeth Rivers, was born on June 20, 1883 in Parker County, TX. She died on November 24, 1948 in Prairie Grove, AR.

William Mattison Henry was born on October 2, 1876. He died on August 26, 1963 in Prairie Grove, AR. He and Cora Wallace had the following children:

+1076 Mamie Jessie Henry (1913-2009)

240. **Ben Wallace**, son of Benjamin Wallace and Eliza Elizabeth Rivers, was born on September 13, 1885 in Parker County, TX. He married **Eula Bantau** on January 23, 1906. He died on June 29, 1929 in Weatherford, Parker County, TX and was buried on July 1, 1929 in Weatherford, Parker County, TX at Greenwood Cemetery.

Eula Bantau was born on May 17, 1882 in Parker County, TX. She died on January 17, 1971 in Parker County, TX.

241. **Dora Wallace**, daughter of Benjamin Wallace and Eliza Elizabeth Rivers, was born on March 18, 1887 in Parker County, TX. She died on December 26, 1969 in Anaheim, Orange County, CA.

242. **Mary Hart**, daughter of James Columbus Hart and Sarah Frances Wallace, was born on December 14, 1877 in Henderson County, TN. She died on August 5, 1878 in Navarro County, TX.

243. **William T. Hart**, son of James Columbus Hart and Sarah Frances Wallace, was born on May 5, 1879 in Navarro County, TX. He married **Clarkie Lee Gassaway** on February 23, 1902. He died on November 19, 1903 in Navarro County, TX.

    Clarkie Lee Gassaway, daughter of Harvey R. Gassaway (1854-1902) and Sarah Elizabeth Wallace (1862-1900), was born on July 24, 1882 in Parker County, TX. She died in May 1946 in Dallas, TX.

244. **Annie May Hart**, daughter of James Columbus Hart and Sarah Frances Wallace, was born on January 25, 1882 in Navarro County, TX. She died on December 22, 1899 in Navarro County, TX.

245. **Luther Columbus Hart**, son of James Columbus Hart and Sarah Frances Wallace, was born on March 16, 1884 in Navarro County, TX. He married **Ella Pearl Wright** on April 28, 1907. He died on May 26, 1950 in Fort Worth, Tarrant County, TX and was buried on June 29, 1950 in Fort Worth, Tarrant County, TX at Rose Hill Cemetery.

    Ella Pearl Wright, daughter of William T. Wright (1864-) and Mary Jane "Mollie" King (1870-), was born on December 6, 1883 in Coweta County, GA. She died on October 17, 1968 in Fort Worth, Tarrant County, TX. She and Luther Columbus Hart had the following children:

    | +1077 | Ernest Hart (-) |
    | +1078 | Luther Columbus Hart Jr. (1908-1970) |

246. **Eugenia Novel Hart**, daughter of James Columbus Hart and Sarah Frances Wallace, was born on April 16, 1886 in Texas. She married **John Herman Craighead** on August 7, 1904 in Johnson County, TX. She died on October 14, 1967 in Collin County, TX.

    John Herman Craighead was born on September 14, 1884 in Nashville, Davidson County, TN. He died on April 16, 1952 in Collin County, TX. He and Eugenia Novel Hart had the following children:

    | +1079 | Willie Craighead (-) |
    | +1080 | Hershal Craighead (-) |

247. **Bennie F. Hart**, son of James Columbus Hart and Sarah Frances Wallace, was born on January 12, 1888. He died on September 25, 1888.

248. **Hattie Lee Hart**, daughter of James Columbus Hart and Sarah Frances Wallace, was born on December 2, 1889 in Texas. She married **Isom Daniel Dansby** on December 24, 1905. She died on December 24, 1923 in Hunt County, TX and was buried in Farmersville, Collin County, TX at Farmersville IOOF Cemetery.

    Isom Daniel Dansby was born on July 22, 1880 in Heard County, GA. He died on December 4, 1953 in Stringtown, OK and was buried in Farmersville, Collin County, TX at Farmersville IOOF Cemetery. He and Hattie Lee Hart had the following children:

    | +1081 | Arthur Dovard Dansby (1913-2007) |
    | +1082 | Ethel Pauline Dansby (1918-2008) |
    | +1083 | Peggy Dansby (1921-2012) |
    | +1084 | Acie Willard \"Bill\" Dansby (1923-1997) |

249. **Acie Linn Hart**, son of James Columbus Hart and Sarah Frances Wallace, was born on September 16, 1891 in Parker County, TX. He married **Linnie May Criswell** on July 10, 1915 in Collin County, TX. He died on December 10, 1962 in Orange County, CA.

Linnie May Criswell was born on May 31, 1894 in Collin County, TX. She died on December 8, 1968 in Orange County, CA.

250. **Ethel Sophronia Hart**, daughter of James Columbus Hart and Sarah Frances Wallace, was born on October 2, 1894 in Henderson County, TX. She married **Charles Thomas Wright** on November 27, 1910. She died on July 22, 1961 in Orange County, CA.

Charles Thomas Wright, son of William T. Wright (1864-) and Mary Jane "Mollie" King (1870-), was born on March 13, 1886 in Newnan, Coweta County, GA. He died on April 5, 1946 in Orange County, CA.

251. **Arie L. Hart**, son of James Columbus Hart and Sarah Frances Wallace, was born on August 21, 1898 in Navarro County, TX. He married **Stella Killian** in July 1917. He died on March 21, 1970 in Jackson County, OK.

Stella Killian was born in 1901 in Grayson County, TX. She died in 1984.

252. **Edna Hart**, daughter of James Columbus Hart and Sarah Frances Wallace, was born on January 7, 1902 in Texas. She married **William Martin** on February 21, 1921. She died on August 31, 1944 in Johnson County, TX.

253. **Mary Ann "Molly" Wallace**, daughter of William Samuel Wallace and Nancy C. Williams, was born in July 1884. She died in 1967 in Henderson County, TN.

Isaac Neal "Ike" Daws was born on October 20, 1881. He died on January 31, 1968. He and Mary Ann "Molly" Wallace had the following children:

+1085	Lessie Daws (1909-1936)
+1086	Charlie Washington Daws (1921-1987)

254. **James Oliver "Ollie" Wallace**, son of William Samuel Wallace and Nancy C. Williams, was born on October 2, 1888. He died on December 16, 1950 in Henderson County, TN and was buried in Henderson County, TN at Palestine Cemetery.

255. **Bert Lee Wallace**, son of William Samuel Wallace and Nancy C. Williams, was born in August 1890 in Tennessee. He married **Sarah Elizabeth "Bessie" Britt** on July 18, 1911 in Henderson County, TN. He died on September 18, 1982 and was buried in Henderson County, TN at Palestine Cemetery.

Sarah Elizabeth "Bessie" Britt, daughter of George Britt (1863-bef 1900) and Louisa M. Williams (1869-), was born in July 1894. She died in 1973 and was buried in Henderson County, TN at Palestine Cemetery. She and Bert Lee Wallace had the following children:

+1087	Billy Joe Wallace (-)
+1088	Melvin L. Wallace (1912-2003)
+1089	Inez Wallace (1915-)
+1090	J. Murray Wallace (1920-)
+1091	D. L. Wallace (1923-)
+1092	E. Louise Wallace (1925-)
+1093	Ruby M. Wallace (1928-)
+1094	Cletus Lee Wallace (1931-1999)
+1095	Ruthie Dean Wallace (1938-1988)

257. **Ida Victoria Wallace**, daughter of William Samuel Wallace and Nancy C. Williams, was born on October 8, 1895. She married **George Washington Pollock** on September 14, 1913. She died on April 20, 1975 in Henderson County, TN.

George Washington Pollock, son of James Pollock (1852-1933) and Tabitha Cagle (1850-1895), was born on February 1, 1891. He died on November 25, 1977. He and Ida Victoria Wallace had the following children:

+1096	Delta Mae Pollock (1925-1970)

258. **Harve D. Wallace**, son of William Samuel Wallace and Nancy C. Williams, was born on June 7, 1900 in Tennessee. He died on August 31, 1941 and was buried in Henderson County, TN at Palestine Cemetery.

Fannie C. Britt, daughter of John Henry Britt (1884-1980) and Tempie Daws (1882-1921), was born in 1910. She and Harve D. Wallace had the following children:

+1097   J. S. Wallace (1926-1926)

260. **L. Ella Wallace**, daughter of William Samuel Wallace and Nancy C. Williams, was born in 1905 in Tennessee. She married **Bob Little** circa 1921. She died in 1932.

Bob Little died before 1930. He and L. Ella Wallace had the following children:

+1098   Clayton Little (1923-)
+1099   C. Thomas Little (1925-)
+1100   W. Edward Little (1927-)
+1101   Robert Little (1928-)

261. **Emerson Ethridge Wallace**, son of William Samuel Wallace and Nancy C. Williams, was born in 1908 in Tennessee. He died in 1936 and was buried in Henderson County, TN at Palestine Cemetery.

Lula Mae Hart was born in 1914. She died in 1993 and was buried in Henderson County, TN at Palestine Cemetery. She and Emerson Ethridge Wallace had the following children:

+1102   Emerson Wallace (1934-1970)

262. **Mary Ann Cox**, daughter of Joseph Arch Cox and Susan Sufronie Wallace, was born on December 8, 1893. She died on September 29, 1915 and was buried in Henderson County, TN at Nebo Methodist Church.

Robert Cagle, son of George Washington Cagle (1868-1953) and Elizabeth "Lizzie" Crittenden (1876-1926), was born on February 17, 1891. He died on August 12, 1981 and was buried in Poplar Springs, Henderson County, TN at Independence Cemetery. He and Mary Ann Cox had the following children:

+1103   Johnnie Adams Cagle (1913-1976)

263. **William McSwain Cockman**, son of George Cockman and Clarkey Ann Wallace, was born in April 1842. He married **Julia Ann Cagle** on December 6, 1864 in Moore County, NC. He died in 1906 and was buried in Moore County, NC at Cockman Cemetery #41.

Julia Ann Cagle, daughter of George Cagle (1814-bef 1890) and Elizabeth Williams (1814-bef 1860), was born on April 4, 1842. She married William Moffitt on January 16, 1862 in Moore County, NC. She died on December 8, 1917 and was buried on December 9, 1917 in Moore County, NC at Cockman Cemetery #41. She and William McSwain Cockman had the following children:

+1104   Louvene Cockman (1865-1943)
+1105   Annette E. Cockman (1868-1921)
+1106   Florence Ruthie Cockman (1870-)
+1107   Ulysses Franklin Cockman (1871-1935)
+1108   Ira Lee "Arlee" Cockman (1873-1960)
+1109   Ida G. Cockman (1876-)
+1110   Jerome Cockman (1878-1883)
+1111   Ernest Cockman (1879-1883)
+1112   Charles Turner Cockman (1884-1949)
+1113   Lewis Graham Cockman (1885-1926)

264. **Mary Elizabeth Cockman**, daughter of George Cockman and Clarkey Ann Wallace, was born in 1844. She married **Tobias B. Caddell** on February 14, 1861 in Moore County, NC.

Tobias B. Caddell, son of Daniel Caddell (1800-1861) and Charity Bean (1801-), was born on April 21, 1826. He died on January 11, 1906 and was buried in Moore County, NC at Bethlehem Baptist Church. He and Mary Elizabeth Cockman had the following children:

+1114	Daniel Turner Caddell (1864-1922)
+1115	George M. Caddell (1870-)

265. **Sarah Lee Cockman**, daughter of George Cockman and Clarkey Ann Wallace, was born in 1845. She married **John Russell Hare** on November 5, 1863 in Moore County, NC. She died in 1887 and was buried in Daingerfield, Morris County, TX at Daingerfield Cemetery.

John Russell Hare, son of Isham Hare (1811-1883) and Mary "Molcy" Hussey (1812-1864), was born on January 24, 1839. He died on September 2, 1881 and was buried in Daingerfield, Morris County, TX at Daingerfield Cemetery. He and Sarah Lee Cockman had the following children:

+1116	Peter Thomas Hare (1864-1933)
+1117	William James Hare (1865-1941)
+1118	Alfred W. Hare (1869-)
+1119	Isom Hegler Hare (1871-1950)
+1120	Sarah Lee "Trannie" Hare (1874-1922)
+1121	Mary M. Hare (1877-)
+1122	John Kendrick "Kinnie" Hare (1880-1960)

266. **Isham Wallace Haig Cockman**, son of George Cockman and Clarkey Ann Wallace, was born on March 27, 1848. He married **Camilla Haseltine Cagle** on January 11, 1872 in Moore County, NC. He died in October 1909.

Camilla Haseltine Cagle, daughter of Elisha Cagle (1816-1895) and Ann Elizabeth Stutts (1816-1902), was born on May 7, 1853. She died on March 4, 1907 in Greensboro, Guilford County, NC and was buried in Moore County, NC at Bethlehem Baptist Church. She and Isham Wallace Haig Cockman had the following children:

+1123	Loretta B. Cockman (1873-1893)
+1124	Henrietta E. Cockman (1875-1917)
+1125	Robert Addison Cockman (1877-1971)
+1126	Madison B. Cockman (1879-1918)
+1127	Dorietta Cockman (1881-1918)
+1128	Ellen Vetta Cockman (1884-1981)
+1129	Beretta Cockman (1886-1974)
+1130	George Elisha Cockman (1888-1976)
+1131	Isham Wallace Haig Cockman Jr. (1889-1938)
+1132	Lottie Haseltine Cockman (1894-1959)

267. **Nancy Jane Cockman**, daughter of George Cockman and Clarkey Ann Wallace, was born on August 27, 1850. She died on January 9, 1921 in Charlotte, Mecklenburg County, NC and was buried in Whitney, Spartanburg County, SC at Liberty United Methodist Church.

Jesse Parker Stafford, son of Isaac Stafford (1823-1898) and Sarah Williams (1820-1881), was born on December 14, 1847. He died on December 8, 1910 and was buried in Whitney, Spartanburg County, SC at Liberty United Methodist Church. He and Nancy Jane Cockman had the following children:

+1133	Cinda A. Stafford (1869-)
+1134	Eli W. Stafford (1871-)
+1135	George A. Stafford (1875-)
+1136	James Charles "Jein" Stafford (1876-1951)
+1137	Barbara E. Stafford (1879-)
+1138	Walter Branson Stafford (1884-1965)

268. **Sindi Ann Cockman**, daughter of George Cockman and Clarkey Ann Wallace, was born on October 21, 1852. She died on January 1, 1856 and was buried in Moore County, NC at Flint Hill Baptist Church.

269. **Rebecca Francis Cockman**, daughter of George Cockman and Clarkey Ann Wallace, was born on August 30, 1854. She died on July 11, 1928 and was buried in Moore County, NC at Bethlehem Baptist Church.

Richard McCoy Williams, son of Stephen D. Williams (1823-1894) and Franey Jones (1826-bef 1860), was born on April 8, 1848. He died on January 24, 1936 and was buried in Moore County, NC at Bethlehem Baptist Church. He and Rebecca Francis Cockman had the following children:

+1139	Mary Lee Williams (1875-1945)	
+1140	Charles L. "Charlie" Williams (1876-1937)	
+1141	Nannie Clark Williams (1879-1950)	
+1142	Jesse Bice Williams (1881-1965)	
+1143	Mattie Jane Williams (1883-1935)	
+1144	George Archie Williams (1883-1891)	
+1145	Lillian Florence Williams (1891-1984)	
+1146	Myrtle Ruth Williams (1894-1960)	
+1147	Eugene Stephen Williams (1898-1958)	

270. **Eli Terry Cockman**, son of George Cockman and Clarkey Ann Wallace, was born on February 7, 1857. He died on September 2, 1946 and was buried in Moore County, NC at Pleasant Hill United Methodist Church.

Silla Frances Horner, daughter of George Washington Horner (1817-1885) and Mary Ann Ritter (1821-), was born on March 25, 1854. She died on May 24, 1903 and was buried in Moore County, NC at Pleasant Hill United Methodist Church. She and Eli Terry Cockman had the following children:

+1148	John Huey Cockman (1880-1957)	
+1149	Mary Clark Cockman (1881-1957)	
+1150	Sarah Emma Cockman (1883-1976)	
+1151	Martha A. Cockman (1885-1974)	
+1152	Purcilla Florence Cockman (1888-1943)	
+1153	George Thomas Cockman (1889-1971)	
+1154	Kenny Harrison Cockman (1891-1980)	
+1155	Betty Jane "Janie" Cockman (1892-1965)	
+1156	Lizzie C. Cockman (1895-1975)	
+1157	Lula L. Cockman (1897-1923)	
+1158	Ruth Adlaide Cockman (1899-1970)	

271. **Delphina Cockman**, daughter of George Cockman and Clarkey Ann Wallace, was born in April 1859. She died on January 2, 1910 and was buried in Greensboro, Guilford County, NC at Green Hill Cemetery.

Murdock M. Williams, son of Stephen D. Williams (1823-1894) and Franey Jones (1826-bef 1860), was born on March 4, 1847 in Moore County, NC. He died on April 17, 1916 in Greensboro, Guilford County, NC and was buried in Greensboro, Guilford County, NC at Green Hill Cemetery. He and Delphina Cockman had the following children:

+1159	Callie J. Williams (1874-1957)	
+1160	William M. Williams (1878-1954)	
+1161	Daniel W. Williams (1880-1965)	
+1162	Martha Williams (1885-1965)	
+1163	Iola Williams (1888-1964)	
+1164	Lillie May Williams (1892-1965)	

272. **Charles Edward Cockman**, son of George Cockman and Clarkey Ann Wallace, was born on February 21, 1860 in Moore County, NC. He died on December 15, 1938 in Randolph County, NC and was buried on December 16, 1938 in Moore County, NC at Flint Hill Baptist Church.

Myca Jane "Millie" Cagle, daughter of Abraham W. Cagle (1841-1876) and Sara Welch (1847-1918), was born on July 6, 1869. She died on March 5, 1899 and was buried in Moore County, NC at Flint Hill Baptist Church. She and Charles Edward Cockman had the following children:

+1165	Walston Leonidas Cockman (1886-1971)
+1166	Barbara Anna Cockman (1888-1974)
+1167	Lucy Jane Cockman (1892-1972)
+1168	Peter Wesley Cockman (1896-1973)
+1169	Sarah C. Cockman (1899-)

273. **Clarkey Ann Cockman**, daughter of J. Sampson Cockman and Elizabeth Wallace, was born on August 13, 1842 in Moore County, NC. She married **William Thomas Horner** on November 9, 1860 in Moore County, NC. She died on October 8, 1919 in Ramseur, Randolph County, NC and was buried in Robbins, Moore County, NC at Tabernacle United Methodist Church.

William Thomas Horner, son of George Washington Horner (1817-1885) and Mary Ann Ritter (1821-), was born on August 29, 1840. He died on April 1, 1919 and was buried in Robbins, Moore County, NC at Tabernacle United Methodist Church. He and Clarkey Ann Cockman had the following children:

+1170	Sarah Annette Horner (1862-1913)
+1171	Kenneth Cassidy Horner (1864-1931)
+1172	John A. Horner (1865-1882)
+1173	George Washington Horner (1867-1937)
+1174	Daniel Hopkins Horner (1869-1919)
+1175	William Thomas "Will" Horner Jr. (1872-1936)
+1176	Mary Elizabeth Horner (1874-1933)
+1177	Jennie P. Horner (1875-1927)
+1178	Martha L. "Mattie" Horner (1878-1934)
+1179	James Robert Horner (1880-1958)

Children of George Cockman and Clarkey Ann Cockman

[Left] **Murdock Williams and Delphina Cockman** *(Courtesy of Lee Williams)*
[Right] **Isham Wallace Haig Cockman and Carmilla Cagle**

Eli Terry Cockman and his children (1940's): Front row, [L-R] Harrison, Adelaid and Eli. Back row [L-R] Lizzie, George, Florence, Emma, Mary and John. *(Courtesy of Stacey Hugo Mansfield)*

Children of Sampson Cockman and Elizabeth Wallace

William Thomas Horner and Clarkey Ann Cockman with sons [L-R] John A. Horner and Kenneth Cassiday Horner *(Courtesy of Cockman Family History by Margaret Cockman Kitchel)*

Noah Wesley Cockman and Sarah Ann Cagle *(Courtesy of Cockman Family History by Margaret Cockman Kitchel)*

Lena Louisa Cockman Horner and family
(Courtesy of Janice Hullender)

274. **Noah Wesley Cockman**, son of J. Sampson Cockman and Elizabeth Wallace, was born on March 16, 1845 in Moore County, NC. He married **Sarah Ann Cagle** on January 25, 1865 in Moore County, NC. He died on January 6, 1929 in Randolph County, NC and was buried on January 7, 1929 in Randolph County, NC at Beulah Baptist Church.

Sarah Ann Cagle, daughter of Elisha Cagle (1816-1895) and Ann Elizabeth Stutts (1816-1902), was born on June 25, 1848 in Moore County, NC. She died on November 20, 1938 in Randolph County, NC and was buried on November 22, 1938 in Randolph County, NC at Beulah Baptist Church. She and Noah Wesley Cockman had the following children:

+1180	John Ransom D. Cockman (1866-1948)
+1181	Joseph Islem Haglem Cockman (1869-1953)
+1182	Exer Ann Elizabeth Cockman (1870-1929)
+1183	Lucretia Morndia Cockman (1872-1958)
+1184	Globina Hill Cockman (1874-1962)
+1185	Abraham Rommie Cockman (1876-1949)
+1186	Noah Wesley Cockman Jr. (1878-1943)
+1187	Magaline D. "Maggie" Cockman (1879-1960)
+1188	Ashley Carson Cockman (1881-1963)
+1189	Mittie Mammie Cockman (1883-1902)
+1190	Jerome Cassidy Cockman (1885-1952)
+1191	Arlen Well Cockman (1887-1962)
+1192	Ommie Cornelia Cockman (1889-1966)

Children of Noah Cockman and Mary Ann Wallace

Clockwise from top left:

John S. "Jack" Cockman
(Courtesy of Lacy Garner, Jr., Carthage, NC)

Sarah Cockman Brown
(Courtesy of Margaret Brown Shepherd)

Charles Riley Cockman
(Courtesy of Lacy Garner, Jr., Carthage, NC)

275. **Mary Sarah Cockman**, daughter of J. Sampson Cockman and Elizabeth Wallace, was born on July 30, 1845.

276. **Isham Pilgram Cockman**, son of J. Sampson Cockman and Elizabeth Wallace, was born on March 10, 1851 and was buried in Moore County, NC at Flint Hill Baptist Church.

277. **Adeline Haseltine Cockman**, daughter of J. Sampson Cockman and Elizabeth Wallace, was born on November 12, 1852. She died on April 23, 1856 and was buried in Moore County, NC at Flint Hill Baptist Church.

278. **John Gillery Cockman**, son of J. Sampson Cockman and Elizabeth Wallace, was born on May 5, 1855. He died on July 15, 1864 and was buried in Moore County, NC at Flint Hill Baptist Church.

279. **Lena Louisa Cockman**, daughter of J. Sampson Cockman and Elizabeth Wallace, was born on July 26, 1859 in Moore County, NC. She died on February 19, 1920 in Guilford County, NC and was buried on February 21, 1920 in Moore County, NC at Bethlehem Baptist Church.

Thomas R. Horner, son of Chestley Thomas Horner (1827-1900) and Candace Muse (1829-1893), was born on December 31, 1859. He died on May 17, 1900 and was buried in Moore County, NC at Bethlehem Baptist Church. He and Lena Louisa Cockman had the following children:

+1193	Mary Camilla Horner (1880-1936)
+1194	Norris Fulton Horner (1881-1952)
+1195	Fairly Arthur Horner (1883-1951)
+1196	William Sampson "Bill" Horner (1884-1952)
+1197	Chestley Paisley Horner (1886-1927)
+1198	Hurley Harrison Horner (1889-1959)
+1199	John Lawrence Horner (1889-1963)
+1200	Mittie Tom Horner (1893-1923)
+1201	Monica Horner (1895-1895)
+1202	Martha Jane Horner (1896-1896)
+1203	Walter Wesley Horner (1898-1898)
+1204	Jesse Horner (1900-1900)

280. **James Alexander Cockman**, son of J. Sampson Cockman and Elizabeth Wallace, was born on May 20, 1861 in Moore County, NC. He died on September 13, 1933 in Moore County, NC and was buried on September 14, 1933 in Moore County, NC at Flint Hill Baptist Church.

Mary Alice Horner, daughter of Chestley Thomas Horner (1827-1900) and Candace Muse (1829-1893), was born on August 23, 1865. She died on February 6, 1948. She and James Alexander Cockman had the following children:

+1205	Marchia Alberta Lee Cockman (1881-1966)
+1206	John William Cockman (1883-1916)
+1207	George Charles Cockman (1886-1959)
+1208	Etta Mae Cockman (1904-1933)

281. **Alice Susannah Cockman**, daughter of J. Sampson Cockman and Elizabeth Wallace, was born on September 11, 1863. She married **Jonah Baxter Maness** on February 10, 1899. She died on December 20, 1949 and was buried in Moore County, NC at Flint Hill Baptist Church.

Alice Susannah Cockman had the following children:

+1209	Sherman L. Maness (1890-)

Jonah Baxter Maness, son of James Abel Maness (1835-1907) and Deborah Eliza "Debby" Brown (1831-bef 1900), was born on February 15, 1870. He died on August 21, 1961 and was buried in Moore County, NC at Flint Hill Baptist Church. He and Alice Susannah Cockman had the following children:

+1210	William Maness (1901-)

+1211	James Laborn Maness (1902-1982)
+1212	Arthur Edmund Maness (1903-1989)
+1213	Kenny Cassidy Maness (1905-1981)
+1214	Rosa Maggie Maness (1907-1962)

282. **William E. Sherman Cockman**, son of J. Sampson Cockman and Elizabeth Wallace, was born on September 19, 1865. He died on October 29, 1878 and was buried in Moore County, NC at Flint Hill Baptist Church.

283. **George MDOHDIC Cockman**, son of Noah Emsley Cockman and Mary Ann Wallace, was born on March 24, 1847 in Moore County, NC. He died on November 6, 1907 in Rockingham, Richmond County, NC and was buried in Rockingham, Richmond County, NC at Northam Cemetery.

Lucinda Melton, daughter of James Melton (1805-1857) and Temperance Horner (1814-aft 1880), was born on November 12, 1845. She died on August 3, 1908 in Rockingham, Richmond County, NC and was buried in Rockingham, Richmond County, NC at Northam Cemetery. She and George MDOHDIC Cockman had the following children:

+1215	Fonnie F. Cockman (1867-1915)
+1216	Anna Jane "Janie" Cockman (1869-1913)
+1217	Laura Luvenia Cockman (1870-1954)
+1218	Isham Delaney Cockman (1874-1938)
+1219	Ida Delaney Priscilla Alice Cockman (1877-1968)
+1220	Delilah Cockman (1881-1961)
+1221	Dora Cockman (1883-1906)
+1222	Lexie Green Cockman (1885-1915)
+1223	George Hurley Cockman Sr. (1886-1955)

284. **John SSGWSQA "Jack" Cockman**, son of Noah Emsley Cockman and Mary Ann Wallace, was born on June 7, 1848 in Moore County, NC. He married **Nancy Jane Riddle** on April 15, 1900. He died on April 7, 1912 in Moore County, NC and was buried in Robbins, Moore County, NC at Tabernacle United Methodist Church.

Nancy Jane Melton, daughter of James Melton (1805-1857) and Temperance Horner (1814-aft 1880), was born on July 21, 1841. She died on June 15, 1886 and was buried in Robbins, Moore County, NC at Tabernacle United Methodist Church. She and John SSGWSQA "Jack" Cockman had the following children:

+1224	James Atlas Cockman (1868-1937)
+1225	William Lockie Cockman (1871-1919)
+1226	Temperance Levina "Erie" Cockman (1875-1940)
+1227	Mary Ann "Tanie" Cockman (1876-1958)
+1228	Armittie Evelyn Cockman (1879-1954)
+1229	John Wesley Cockman (1881-1920)
+1230	Noah Bethune Cockman (1882-1966)

Lovedy Adaline Melton, daughter of James Melton (1805-1857) and Temperance Horner (1814-aft 1880), was born in 1852. She died in 1891 and was buried in Moore County, NC at Flint Hill Baptist Church. She and John SSGWSQA "Jack" Cockman had the following children:

| +1231 | Nancy Jane "Florence" Cockman (1887-1927) |
| +1232 | Jennette B. "Nettie" Cockman (1891-1955) |

Nancy Jane Riddle, daughter of Wiley Riddle (1825-1897) and Elizabeth Ann Gore (1828-1900), was born in March 1869. She died on June 16, 1920 and was buried in Rockingham, Richmond County, NC at Zion Methodist Church. She and John SSGWSQA "Jack" Cockman had the following children:

| +1233 | Londia Ann "Lovedy" Cockman (1903-) |

+1234   Lottie M. Cockman (1905-bef 1910)
+1235   Gonzalee Cockman (1909-1956)

289. **Charles Riley O'Leonard Emsley Rufus Cockman**, son of Noah Emsley Cockman and Mary Ann Wallace, was born on November 8, 1860 in Moore County, NC. He married **Lou Vicie Brown** circa 1881. He died on June 8, 1922 in Moore County, NC and was buried in Moore County, NC at Flint Hill Baptist Church.

Lou Vicie Brown, daughter of William Wesley Brown (1837-1906) and Loretta T. Hunsucker (1842-1916), was born on April 27, 1863 in Moore County, NC. She died on April 4, 1942 in Moore Regional Hospital, Pinehurst, Moore County, NC and was buried in Moore County, NC at Flint Hill Baptist Church. She and Charles Riley O'Leonard Emsley Rufus Cockman had the following children:

+1236   Monnie Cockman (1881-1881)
+1237   William Jerome Cockman (1883-1947)
+1238   Noah Wesley Cockman (1884-1971)
+1239   Louis Delaney Cockman (1887-1973)
+1240   Atlas Franklin Cockman (1889-1970)
+1241   Branson Cockman (1891-1891)
+1242   Maggie Cockman (1893-1893)
+1243   Martha Alice Cockman (1896-1972)
+1244   Henry Harrison "Bud" Cockman (1898-1969)
+1245   Burley Leaton Cockman (1901-1968)
+1246   Nepsie Mae Cockman (1904-1964)
+1247   Gurney Raeford Cockman (1906-1966)

290. **Thomas Bias Noah Louweed Cockman**, son of Noah Emsley Cockman and Mary Ann Wallace, was born on August 20, 1862 in Moore County, NC. He married **Indiana Brown** circa 1885. He died on August 8, 1942 in Greensboro, Guilford County, NC and was buried on August 9, 1942 in Moore County, NC at Brown's Chapel Christian Church.

Indiana Brown, daughter of Eli Brown (1840-) and Martha Sheffield (1848-), was born on September 4, 1864. She died on June 24, 1938 in Guilford County, NC and was buried on June 26, 1938 in Moore County, NC at Brown's Chapel Christian Church. She and Thomas Bias Noah Louweed Cockman had the following children:

+1248   Eli Cockman (1887-)
+1249   Mattie Elizabeth Cockman (1889-)
+1250   Causey Belton Cockman (1892-)
+1251   Burton Cockman (1895-1976)
+1252   Altie Cockman (1897-1975)
+1253   Hardin Cockman (1901-1962)
+1254   Mary Delila Cockman (1904-1978)
+1255   Joe Branson Cockman (1907-1975)

291. **Mary Jane "Sarah" Emmoline Camilla Hazeltine Cockman**, daughter of Noah Emsley Cockman and Mary Ann Wallace, was born on August 15, 1867. She married **William Wesley Brown** circa 1884. She died on July 26, 1944 and was buried in Moore County, NC at Flint Hill Baptist Church.

William Wesley Brown was born on April 20, 1863. He died on May 22, 1925 and was buried in Moore County, NC at Flint Hill Baptist Church. He and Mary Jane "Sarah" Emmoline Camilla Hazeltine Cockman had the following children:

+1256   Duke Brown (-)
+1257   Maggie Brown (-)
+1258   Nettie Louise Brown (1886-1968)
+1259   Benjamin Harrison Brown (1888-1964)
+1260   James Arnold Brown (1890-1952)
+1261   Neil Lee Brown (1895-1923)
+1262   Jennie Brown (1895-)

+1263	Walter Branson Brown (1897-1975)
+1264	Mittie M. Brown (1899-1981)
+1265	Bertha Ethel Brown (1902-1950)
+1266	Arthur Edd Brown (1903-1983)
+1267	Lena Brown (1905-1985)
+1268	John Wesley Brown (1907-1985)

292. **Maggie Delaney Deleeny Cockman**, daughter of Noah Emsley Cockman and Mary Ann Wallace, was born on November 12, 1877. She married **Dock F. Maness** on September 14, 1893 in Moore County, NC. She died on July 4, 1957 and was buried in Moore County, NC at Flint Hill Baptist Church.

Dock F. Maness, son of George H. Maness (1844-1918) and Sarah Elizabeth Brown (1844-bef 1885), was born in 1871. He died on March 22, 1934 in Richmond County, NC and was buried on March 23, 1934 in Rockingham, Richmond County, NC at Mizpah Church Cemetery.

Wade Hampton Wallace, son of Sampson Delaney Wallace (1845-c. 1893) and Missouri Coleman Hunsucker (1846-1920), was born on July 21, 1870. He died on March 15, 1947 and was buried in Moore County, NC at Flint Hill Baptist Church. He and Maggie Delaney Deleeny Cockman had the following child out of wedlock:

      +1269   Gurtie Cockman (1909-1962)

293. **Margaret L. Wallace**, daughter of William Wesley Wallace and Elizabeth Melton, was born on February 2, 1854. She married **Josiah Tay Seawell** on December 24, 1875 in Moore County, NC. She died on October 28, 1876 and was buried in Moore County, NC at Friendship Baptist Church.

Josiah Tay Seawell, son of Eleazer Quimby Seawell (1808-1893) and Mary Dickerson Phillips (1808-1899), was born on January 23, 1849. He married Mattie E. Johnson on February 23, 1879 in Moore County, NC. He died on June 18, 1934 and was buried in Moore County, NC at Friendship Baptist Church.

295. **James Charles Wallace**, son of William Wesley Wallace and Elizabeth Melton, was born on September 17, 1863 in Moore County, NC. He married **Arnettie Maness** on March 6, 1881 in Moore County, NC. He died on September 1, 1930 in Carthage, Moore County, NC and was buried on September 2, 1930 in Carthage, Moore County, NC at Cross Hill Cemetery.

Arnettie Maness, daughter of William Armstrong Maness (1833-1895) and Rebecca E. Seawell (1833-1920), was born on April 6, 1864 in Moore County, NC. She died on July 15, 1948 in Moore County, NC and was buried on July 17, 1948 in Carthage, Moore County, NC at Cross Hill Cemetery. She and James Charles Wallace had the following children:

+1270	Coy Carlton Wallace (1882-1966)
+1271	Offie Doyle Wallace (1883-1945)
+1272	Walter Lee Wallace (1885-1956)
+1273	Luther Class Wallace (1886-1968)
+1274	Burnie Clyde Wallace (1888-1976)
+1275	Loula Maude Wallace (1890-1943)
+1276	Lora Almar Wallace (1892-1894)
+1277	Molly Viola Wallace (1894-1951)
+1278	Ruley Gart Wallace (1895-1967)
+1279	Lizzie F. Wallace (1899-1978)
+1280	Bonnie J. Wallace (1904-1972)

Children of William Wesley Wallace and Elizabeth Melton

Margaret L. Wallace Seawell
(Courtesy of Hazel Kennedy Hamilton, Robbins, NC)

[Above Left] Laura Louise Wallace McNeill
[Left] Sandy McNeill and Laura Louise Wallace
McNeill *(Courtesy of Donald Wallace, Robbins, NC)*

William Clark Wallace (left), his first
wife Mollie Lee Gaitley is below him
holding Edna Wallace. The couple on
the right are unknown.
(Courtesy of Tim Anderson, LeRoy, NY)

Rev. William Clark Wallace (center
with hand raised) baptizing members
of Lexington Baptist Church in
Lexington, SC during the 1920's.
(Courtesy of Tim Anderson, LeRoy, NY)

Children of William Wesley Wallace and Margaret Louise Seawell

E. Richard Kennedy and Maggie Wallace
(Courtesy of Cindi Rigsbee, Durham, NC)

[Below] John Stellings Wallace and Pearl Phillips *(Courtesy of Donald Wallace, Robbins, NC)*
Martha Jane Wallace Broadstreet *(Courtesy of Martha Jane Broadstreet Edwards Asheboro, NC)*

Daughters of W.W. and Lou Wallace: [Top Left L-R] Nannie Wallace, Laura Hinshaw, unknown male (Kenneth C. Wallace???), Hattie Wallace & Belle Wallace **[Top Right L-R]** unknown & Mary Hattie Wallace **[Bottom Right L-R]** Unidentified daughter, Hattie Wallace & Nannie Wallace **[Bottom Left L-R]** Hattie Wallace, Laura Hinshaw and Nannie Wallace *(Courtesy of Mike Cross, Panama City, FL)*

296. **William Clark Wallace**, son of William Wesley Wallace and Elizabeth Melton, was born on February 13, 1867. He married **Mollie Lee Gaitley** on February 14, 1895. He married **Gabriella "Ella" Ford** on November 17, 1915 in Rennert, Robeson County, NC. He died on March 5, 1937 and was buried in Lakeview, Dillon County, SC at Lakeview Cemetery.

Mollie Lee Gaitley, daughter of Isaac Gaitley (-) and Catherine (-), was born on August 20, 1867. She died on July 31, 1914 and was buried in Lakeview, Dillon County, SC at Lakeview Cemetery. She and William Clark Wallace had the following children:

+1281	Edna Elizabeth Wallace (1899-1977)
+1282	Mary L. "Molly" Wallace (1903-1981)
+1283	William Gaitley Wallace (1907-1971)

Gabriella "Ella" Ford, daughter of Luther Thomas Ford (-) and Margaret Victoria Revell (1860-1933), was born on June 25, 1884. She died on October 29, 1932 in Dillon County, SC and was buried in Lakeview, Dillon County, SC at Lakeview Cemetery. She and William Clark Wallace had the following children:

+1284	Robert Dall Wallace (1917-1977)
+1285	William Manning Wallace (1919-1986)
+1286	Joseph Thomas Wallace (1921-2004)
+1287	Margaret Victoria "Peggy" Wallace (1924-2017)
+1288	Celeste Annette Wallace (1926-2013)

297. **Laura Louise Wallace**, daughter of William Wesley Wallace and Elizabeth Melton, was born on August 1, 1873 in Moore County, NC. She married **Lemeul Alexander McNeill** on December 29, 1892 in Moore County, NC. She died on October 8, 1931 in Moore County, NC and was buried on October 10, 1931 in Robbins, Moore County, NC at Tabernacle United Methodist Church.

Lemeul Alexander McNeill, son of Alexander McNeill (1822-1886) and Celia Elizabeth Yow (1838-1923), was born on December 4, 1868. He died on December 4, 1939 and was buried in Robbins, Moore County, NC at Tabernacle United Methodist Church. He and Laura Louise Wallace had the following children:

+1289	Infant McNeill (1901-1901)
+1290	Ethel McNeill (1908-1995)
+1291	Charlie C. McNeill (1911-1911)

298. **Maggie Elizabeth Wallace**, daughter of William Wesley Wallace and Margaret Louise "Lou" Seawell, was born on August 29, 1881 in Moore County, NC. She married **Elias Richard Kennedy** on April 15, 1903 in Moore County, NC. She died on January 1, 1969 in Moore County, NC and was buried on January 3, 1969 in Moore County, NC at Pleasant Hill United Methodist Church.

Elias Richard Kennedy, son of Elias Kennedy (1845-1924) and Lydia M. Hare (1843-1911), was born on August 22, 1876. He died on June 1, 1962 and was buried in Moore County, NC at Pleasant Hill United Methodist Church. He and Maggie Elizabeth Wallace had the following children:

+1292	Lydia Rossie Kennedy (1903-1995)
+1293	John Wesley Raymond Kennedy (1916-1978)
+1294	Hazel Ailene Kennedy (1922-)

299. **Jesse Lee Wallace**, son of William Wesley Wallace and Margaret Louise "Lou" Seawell, was born on April 13, 1883 in Moore County, NC. He died on April 21, 1946 in Greensboro, Guilford County, NC and was buried on April 23, 1946 in Greensboro, Guilford County, NC at Green Hill Cemetery.

Mary Caroline Hilliard was born in 1891 in Georgia. She and Jesse Lee Wallace had the following children:

+1295	Donna Inez Wallace (1915-2006)
+1296	William Emerson Wallace (1917-1991)

300. **John Stellings Wallace**, son of William Wesley Wallace and Margaret Louise "Lou" Seawell, was born on April 14, 1886 in Moore County, NC. He married **Pearl Phillips** on February 28, 1909 in Guilford County, NC. He died on February 6, 1939 in Greensboro, Guilford County, NC and was buried on February 7, 1939 in Greensboro, Guilford County, NC at Green Hill Cemetery.

Pearl Phillips, daughter of Thomas Phillips (-) and Margaret Hughes (-), was born on August 15, 1887 in North Carolina. She died on August 31, 1941 in Guilford County, NC and was buried on September 1, 1941 in Greensboro, Guilford County, NC at Green Hill Cemetery. She and John Stellings Wallace had the following children:

+1298	Louise Wallace (1914-)
+1299	Elva Wallace (1918-)
+1300	Fred Thomas Wallace (1920-1965)
+1301	Lois Wallace (1922-)

301. **Martha Jane Wallace**, daughter of William Wesley Wallace and Margaret Louise "Lou" Seawell, was born on August 6, 1888 in Moore County, NC. She married **Oscar Azle Broadstreet** on April 28, 1910 in Guilford County, NC. She died on August 24, 1956 in Mt. Gilead, Montgomery County, NC and was buried on August 26, 1956 in Troy, Montgomery County, NC at Southside Cemetery.

Oscar Azle Broadstreet was born on March 13, 1886. He died on January 25, 1950 and was buried in Troy, Montgomery County, NC at Southside Cemetery. He and Martha Jane Wallace had the following children:

+1302	Jesse Edward Broadstreet (1912-1989)
+1303	Merrill Rex Broadstreet (1916-2008)
+1304	Margaret Broadstreet (1921-1998)
+1305	Catherine Broadstreet (1927-)

302. **Kenneth Carson "Kennie" Wallace**, son of William Wesley Wallace and Margaret Louise "Lou" Seawell, was born on December 6, 1889 in Moore County, NC. He married **Laura A. Hinshaw** on June 14, 1914 in Guilford County, NC. He married **Bessie Andrews** after 1931. He died on December 27, 1972 in Gibsonville, Guilford County, NC and was buried on December 30, 1972 in Graham, Alamance County, NC at Providence Memorial Church.

Laura A. Hinshaw, daughter of J. T Hinshaw (-) and Etta Mulligan (-), was born on January 8, 1895 in Randolph County, NC. She died on November 15, 1931 in Greensboro, Guilford County, NC and was buried on November 17, 1931 in Greensboro, Guilford County, NC at Green Hill Cemetery. She and Kenneth Carson "Kennie" Wallace had the following children:

+1306	Ruby Mae Wallace (1915-)
+1307	Lindsay Lee Wallace (1917-1919)
+1308	Carl Edison Wallace (1919-1989)
+1309	Mary Frances Wallace (1922-1974)
+1310	Norman Hinshaw "Stick" Wallace (1924-2007)
+1311	Bettie Marie Wallace (1929-)
+1312	Dallas Lane Wallace (1931-)

Bessie Andrews was born on December 12, 1906. She died on September 6, 1985 and was buried in Graham, Alamance County, NC at Providence Memorial Church.

303. **Anne Belle Wallace**, daughter of William Wesley Wallace and Margaret Louise "Lou" Seawell, was born on November 27, 1892 in Moore County, NC. She married **Raymond Taylor Ferree** on December 24, 1913 in Guilford County, NC. She died on March 9, 1963 in Butner Hospital, Granville County, NC and was buried on March 10, 1963 in Guilford County, NC at Forest Lawn Cemetery.

Raymond Taylor Ferree, son of David Ferree (-), was born on August 12, 1892. He married Marie Floyd after 1963. He died on May 4, 1973. He and Anne Belle Wallace had the following children:

+1313	Ruth Ferree (1915-)

304. Edward Lee Wallace, son of William Wesley Wallace and Margaret Louise "Lou" Seawell, was born on January 5, 1895 in Moore County, NC. He married **Paley Ellice** on December 26, 1917 in Guilford County, NC. He married **Allie Gibson** on December 26, 1924 in Guilford County, NC. He died on May 21, 1966 in Greensboro, Guilford County, NC and was buried on May 23, 1966 in Greensboro, Guilford County, NC at Guilford Memorial Park.

Paley Ellice and Edward Lee Wallace had the following children:

+1314   Gladys Lee Wallace (1918-)

Allie Gibson was born on July 28, 1905. She died on March 20, 1993 and was buried in Greensboro, Guilford County, NC at Guilford Memorial Park. She and Edward Lee Wallace had the following children:

+1315   Helen Wallace (-)
+1316   Margaret Wallace (-)
+1317   Edward Lee Wallace Jr. (-)
+1318   Hildred Pauline Wallace (1925-2006)
+1319   Mildred Louvene Wallace (1925-2008)
+1320   Doris K. Wallace (1926-)
+1321   Billie M. Wallace (1929-)
+1322   William Wesley Wallace (1942-1999)

305. Mary Hattie Wallace, daughter of William Wesley Wallace and Margaret Louise "Lou" Seawell, was born on January 5, 1896 in Moore County, NC. She married **Fred Walker Martin** on October 2, 1919 in Moore County, NC. She died on December 1, 1967 in Greensboro, Guilford County, NC and was buried on December 3, 1967 in Burlington, Alamance County, NC at Alamance Memorial Park.

Fred Walker Martin, son of Luther Wesley Martin (-) and Emma Petty (-), was born on September 14, 1891 in Orange County, NC. He died on February 2, 1964 in Virginia Hospital, Durham, Durham County, NC and was buried in Burlington, Alamance County, NC at Alamance Memorial Park. He and Mary Hattie Wallace had the following children:

+1323   Carl Martin (-)
+1324   Wallace Martin (-)
+1325   Tom Martin (-)
+1326   Mary Lou Martin (-)
+1327   Wesley Martin (-)
+1328   Fred Martin Jr. (-)

306. Nannie Florence Wallace, daughter of William Wesley Wallace and Margaret Louise "Lou" Seawell, was born on January 5, 1896 in Moore County, NC. She married **Robert Cummings Morphis** on June 15, 1914 in Guilford County, NC. She died on November 11, 1978 and was buried in Robbins, Moore County, NC at Pine Rest Cemetery.

Robert Cummings Morphis was born on September 27, 1892. He died on January 29, 1982 and was buried in Robbins, Moore County, NC at Pine Rest Cemetery. He and Nannie Florence Wallace had the following children:

+1329   Rebecca Morphis (1915-1991)
+1330   Charles Wallace Morphis (1917-1917)
+1331   Beatrice Morphis (1918-2003)
+1332   Donald Barrymore Morphis (1923-1997)

307. Stephen Garner, son of John Garner and Sarah Ann Wallace, was born on March 17, 1850. He died on December 29, 1928 and was buried in Moore County, NC at Flint Hill Baptist Church.

Catherine Elizabeth Yow, daughter of Henry Clay Yow (1830-1905) and Mary Molsey Brown (1834-1900), was born in 1854. She died in 1929. She and Stephen Garner had the following children:

+1333   William Hampton "Bud" Garner (1873-1925)
+1334   John Marshall Garner (1873-1942)
+1335   Charles Frank Garner (1879-1956)

+1336	Claudia J. Garner (1881-)
+1337	Henry B. Garner (1884-)
+1338	Myrtle E. Garner (1884-1971)
+1339	Nettie J. Garner (1887-1922)
+1340	Tessa Ada Garner (1887-1965)
+1341	Clem Cassidy "Cass" Garner (1890-1963)
+1342	James Hampton B. Garner (1892-1939)

308. **Leonard Garner**, son of John Garner and Sarah Ann Wallace, was born on August 22, 1851 in Moore County, NC. He married **Mary Ella Maness** on September 15, 1890 in Moore County, NC. He died on November 16, 1922 in Moore County, NC and was buried on November 17, 1922 in Moore County, NC at Flint Hill Baptist Church.

Ann Williams and Leonard Garner had the following children:

| +1343 | John Fuller Williams (1867-1945) |

Sarah Emmaline Stutts, daughter of Leonard C. Stutts (1815-1897) and Margaret Patterson Leach (1828-1852), was born on July 8, 1850. She died on September 19, 1888 and was buried in Moore County, NC at Stutts Cemetery #147. She and Leonard Garner had the following children:

| +1344 | James Frank Garner (1878-1953) |
| +1345 | William G. Garner (1882-1945) |

Mary Ella Maness, daughter of Thomas P. Maness (1834-1900) and Mary Eliza Stewart (1845-1897), was born on August 29, 1862. She died on January 25, 1942 and was buried in Moore County, NC at Flint Hill Baptist Church. She and Leonard Garner had the following children:

+1346	Sarah Eliza Garner (1891-1974)
+1347	John Thomas Garner (1893-1974)
+1348	Edgar Addison Garner (1896-1932)
+1349	Delaney Harrison Garner (1899-1990)
+1350	Maggie Mae Garner (1902-)
+1351	Mary Alice Rebecca "Mamie" Garner (1905-1969)

309. **James Douglas Garner**, son of John Garner and Sarah Ann Wallace, was born on February 15, 1855 in Moore County, NC. He married **Lillie Alma Maness** on July 21, 1895 in Moore County, NC. He died on November 3, 1935 in Moore County, NC and was buried on November 5, 1935 in Moore County, NC at Flint Hill Baptist Church.

Lydia Ann Riddle, daughter of John W. Riddle (1816-1893) and Lydia Williams (1820-1914), was born on September 5, 1858. She died on September 1, 1895 and was buried in Moore County, NC at Flint Hill Baptist Church. She and James Douglas Garner had the following children:

+1352	John Peter Garner (1881-)
+1353	Lucy Jane Garner (1883-1966)
+1354	Infant Garner (1884-1884)
+1355	Riley Blake Garner (1886-1972)
+1356	James Alfred Garner (1888-1956)
+1357	William Lewis Garner (1893-1969)

Lillie Alma Maness, daughter of Mary Ella Maness (1862-1942), was born on October 7, 1880. She died on June 14, 1972 and was buried in Moore County, NC at Flint Hill Baptist Church. She and James Douglas Garner had the following children:

+1358	John Earlie Garner (1896-1987)
+1359	William Addison Garner (1898-1965)
+1360	Elias Garner (1901-1972)
+1361	Mary Eliza Garner (1904-)
+1362	Lockey Merriott Garner (1905-1992)
+1363	James Douglas Garner Jr. (1908-1928)

+1364	Sarah Ella Garner (1910-2005)
+1365	Pressley Robert Garner (1912-1994)
+1366	Stephen Harrison Garner Sr. (1915-1999)
+1367	Laura Alma Garner (1917-1997)
+1368	Ruby Helen Garner (1920-1939)

310. **Martha Jane Garner**, daughter of John Garner and Sarah Ann Wallace, was born on January 18, 1856. She married **Henry Lindsey Burns** circa 1872. She died on November 14, 1933 and was buried in Robbins, Moore County, NC at Tabernacle United Methodist Church.

Henry Lindsey Burns, son of Enoch Burns (1801-1878) and Catherine Beckerdite (1805-1880), was born on February 19, 1844. He died on October 30, 1906 and was buried in Robbins, Moore County, NC at Tabernacle United Methodist Church. He and Martha Jane Garner had the following children:

+1369	Sarah Catherine Elizabeth Burns (1876-1927)
+1370	Zemery Mitchell Burns (1876-1945)
+1371	Barney Leason Burns (1878-1904)
+1372	John Elsevand Burns (1880-)
+1373	Annie Jane Burns (1883-1932)
+1374	Enoch Harrison "Buddy" Burns (1885-1949)
+1375	Hattie Bell Burns (1887-1963)
+1376	Ira Nelson Burns (1889-1889)
+1377	George Ariah Burns (1890-1918)
+1378	Mary Ellen "Minerva" Burns (1893-1893)

312. **Mary Ann Garner**, daughter of John Garner and Sarah Ann Wallace, was born on June 24, 1860. She died Sep 1830 (no year) and was buried in Moore County, NC at Flint Hill Baptist Church.

313. **Sampson Delaney Garner**, son of John Garner and Sarah Ann Wallace, was born on March 10, 1863 in Moore County, NC. He married **Lillie E. Stutts** circa 1885. He died on April 3, 1937 in Moore Regional Hospital, Pinehurst, Moore County, NC and was buried on April 5, 1937 in Robbins, Moore County, NC at Tabernacle United Methodist Church.

Lillie E. Stutts, daughter of Cornelius Alexander Stutts (1840-1869) and Lydia Jane Yow (1843-1920), was born on June 17, 1866. She died on May 12, 1958 and was buried in Robbins, Moore County, NC at Tabernacle United Methodist Church. She and Sampson Delaney Garner had the following children:

+1379	Sarah Jane Garner (1886-1967)
+1380	Connie B. Garner (1888-1979)
+1381	Nancy L. Garner (1890-1972)
+1382	Cornelius Robert Garner (1893-1917)
+1383	Katie L. Garner (1895-1988)

314. **Elias "Lizard" Garner**, son of John Garner and Sarah Ann Wallace, was born in 1865. He married **Anna Jane "Janie" Cockman** circa 1887. He died in 1898 and was buried in Moore County, NC at Flint Hill Baptist Church.

Anna Jane "Janie" Cockman, daughter of George MDOHDIC Cockman (1847-1907) and Lucinda Melton (1845-1908), was born on June 18, 1869. She married Josiah Turner Horner circa 1901. She died on April 26, 1913. She and Elias "Lizard" Garner had the following children:

+1384	Kinnie Carson Garner (1888-1955)
+1385	Margaret B. Garner (1890-)
+1386	Josephine Garner (1893-1948)
+1387	Sara Lucinda Garner (1895-1935)

Children of John Garner and Sarah Ann Wallace

James Douglas Garner and Lillie Alma Maness
(Courtesy of Billy Garner)

Stephen Garner [Below] and
Martha Jane Garner Burns [Below Right]
(Courtesy of Anthony Garner)

315. **Anna Margaret Garner**, daughter of John Garner and Sarah Ann Wallace, was born on October 15, 1867. She married **Charles Frank Yow** circa 1889. She died on December 30, 1917 in Lee County, NC and was buried in Sanford, Lee County, NC at Euphronia Presbyterian Church.

Charles Frank Yow, son of David Darrow Yow (1837-1896) and Malinda Seawell (1838-1884), was born on August 4, 1867. He died on October 2, 1938 and was buried in Sanford, Lee County, NC at Euphronia Presbyterian Church. He and Anna Margaret Garner had the following children:

+1388	Nannie Yow (-)
+1389	Offie Yow (-)
+1390	Mittie Jane Yow (1890-1969)
+1391	Archie L. Yow (1893-)
+1392	John Franklin Yow (1897-1975)
+1393	Charles Scott Yow (1898-1971)
+1394	Arlie Dewey Yow (1908-2001)

316. **Duncan G. Garner**, son of John Garner and Sarah Ann Wallace, was born on January 22, 1871. He died on June 26, 1945 in Moore County, NC and was buried in Moore County, NC at Flint Hill Baptist Church.

Laura Luvenia Cockman, daughter of George MDOHDIC Cockman (1847-1907) and Lucinda Melton (1845-1908), was born on February 23, 1870 in Moore County, NC. She died on September 9, 1954 in Moore County, NC and was buried in Moore County, NC at Flint Hill Baptist Church. She and Duncan G. Garner had the following children:

+1395	Mollie Green Garner (1897-1928)
+1396	Alexander Garner (1903-1967)
+1397	Katie Jane Garner (1905-1952)
+1398	Ashley Lee Garner (1907-1924)
+1399	Ethel Marie Garner (1913-)

317. **Fannie Garner**, daughter of John Garner and Sarah Ann Wallace, was born on January 15, 1873 in Moore County, NC. She married **Offie Alson Williams** on October 28, 1894 in Moore County, NC. She died on March 14, 1938 in Moore County, NC and was buried on March 15, 1938 in Moore County, NC at Flint Hill Baptist Church.

Offie Alson Williams, son of Doctor Murdock Williams (1848-1922) and Sarah L. Stutts (1837-1920), was born on February 21, 1875. He died on April 7, 1950 in Moore County, NC and was buried on April 9, 1950 in Moore County, NC at Flint Hill Baptist Church. He and Fannie Garner had the following children:

+1400	Hampton Williams (-)
+1401	Elizabeth Williams (-)
+1402	John Williams (-)
+1403	Kenny C. Williams (1896-)
+1404	Sarah Sadie Williams (1904-1967)
+1405	George P. Williams (1906-)
+1406	Clarence Williams (1910-1997)
+1407	Fletcher Williams (1912-)
+1408	Mary H. Williams (1915-)

318. **William Wesley Wallace**, son of Quimby Wallace and Arabella Stewart, was born on April 1, 1857 in Moore County, NC. He married **Elizabeth Jane McIntosh** circa 1886. He died on January 11, 1944 in Moore County, NC and was buried in Carthage, Moore County, NC at Cross Hill Cemetery.

Elizabeth Jane McIntosh, daughter of Samuel J. McIntosh (1809-bef 1880) and Nancy Jackson (1809-1890), was born on October 1, 1850. She died on December 7, 1909 and was buried in Carthage, Moore County, NC at Cross Hill Cemetery. She and William Wesley Wallace had the following children:

+1409	Stephen C. Wallace (1888-1923)
+1410	Hattie Mae Wallace (1890-1944)

319. **Martha A. Wallace**, daughter of Quimby Wallace and Arabella Stewart, was born in 1859. She died before 1900.

320. **Nancy Wallace**, daughter of Quimby Wallace and Arabella Stewart, was born on September 28, 1862 in Moore County, NC. She married **Reuben Jackson Morgan** circa 1886. She died on January 17, 1928 in Moore County, NC and was buried on January 18, 1928 in Moore County, NC at Morgan Cemetery #418.

Reuben Jackson Morgan, son of George Troy Morgan (1822-1897) and Elizabeth Margaret Ann Allen (1830-1909), was born on January 31, 1850. He died on January 7, 1902 and was buried in Moore County, NC at Morgan Cemetery #418. He and Nancy Wallace had the following children:

+1411	George Quimby Morgan (1886-1966)
+1412	James Martin Morgan (1889-1945)
+1413	Daniel J. Morgan (1891-)
+1414	Charlotte Ann Morgan (1893-)
+1415	Etta Ada Morgan (1896-1913)
+1416	Reuben Rufus Morgan (1902-)

321. **Rufus Wallace**, son of Quimby Wallace and Arabella Stewart, was born in 1865. He died on July 1, 1892 in Moore County, NC.

322. **Charlotte Wallace**, daughter of Quimby Wallace and Arabella Stewart, was born on May 10, 1867 in Moore County, NC. She married **Elias Spinks Williams** circa 1885. She died on September 17, 1938 in Moore County, NC and was buried on September 18, 1938 in Moore County, NC at Pleasant View Evangelical Church.

Elias Spinks Williams, son of Noah Williams (1826-1904) and Mary Ann Davis (1833-1896), was born on June 11, 1862. He died on April 26, 1952 and was buried in Moore County, NC at Pleasant View Evangelical Church. He and Charlotte Wallace had the following children:

+1417	Eli Williams (1885-1960)
+1418	James Rufus "Duck" Williams (1888-1965)
+1419	Robert Lewis Williams (1892-1925)
+1420	Mary Alice Williams (1893-1971)
+1421	Eddie Carson Williams (1897-1954)
+1422	George Branson Williams (1899-1975)
+1423	Ocia Ometa Williams (1904-1991)
+1424	Dossie Ethel Williams (1910-1942)

323. **Eli Wallace**, son of Quimby Wallace and Arabella Stewart, was born in 1869. He married **Mary Mourning Allen** on July 3, 1892 in Moore County, NC. He died before March 9, 1903 in Montgomery County, NC.

Mary Mourning Allen, daughter of James Allen (1855-1930) and Annie T. Capel (1862-1942), was born on February 10, 1879. She married Beauregard J. Arendell circa 1903. She died on October 22, 1919 in Wilson, Wilson County, NC and was buried in Wendell, Wake County, NC at Greenmount Cemetery. She and Eli Wallace had the following children:

+1425	Eli Wallace (-)
+1426	Bertha Elizabeth Wallace (1894-)
+1427	James Quimby Wallace (1895-1956)
+1428	Carl Wallace (1897-)

Children of Quimby Wallace and Arabella Stewart

Charlotte Wallace and Elias Spinks Williams
(Courtesy of The Williams Family by Maxine W. McNeill)

James Lewis Wallace [Right]
(Courtesy of Becky Wallace Gilmore, West End, NC)

324. **Eliza Alice Wallace**, daughter of Quimby Wallace and Arabella Stewart, was born on December 24, 1871 in Moore County, NC. She married **John M. Hooker** circa 1897. She died on September 8, 1940 in Moore County, NC and was buried on September 10, 1940 in Moore County, NC at Flint Hill Baptist Church.

John M. Hooker, son of John Marshall Cox (1847-) and Sarah Hooker (1844-), was born on December 24, 1866. He died on November 18, 1948 and was buried in Moore County, NC at Flint Hill Baptist Church. He and Eliza Alice Wallace had the following children:

+1429	Oscar Lee Hooker (1898-1957)	
+1430	Elias Spinks Hooker (1899-1975)	
+1431	Benjamin F. Hooker (1902-1973)	
+1432	Rosanna M. Hooker (1905-1992)	
+1433	Alfred N. Hooker (1913-1986)	

325. **James Lewis Wallace**, son of Quimby Wallace and Arabella Stewart, was born on February 9, 1875. He married **Lillie Jane Maness** on July 7, 1900 in Moore County, NC.[131] He married **Flora Ann Garner** on August 1, 1921 in Moore County, NC.[132] He died on February 27, 1950 in Moore County, NC and was buried on March 1, 1950 in Robbins, Moore County, NC at Tabernacle United Methodist Church.

Lillie Jane Maness, daughter of Lewis Scott Maness (1855-1943) and Martha Ann Wallace (1862-1902), was born on September 22, 1884 in Moore County, NC. She died on October 6, 1919 in Moore County, NC and was buried on October 7, 1919 in Robbins, Moore County, NC at Tabernacle United Methodist Church. She and James Lewis Wallace had the following children:

+1434	Etta Jennette Wallace (1903-1984)	
+1435	Quimby Lewis Wallace (1906-1977)	
+1436	William Howard Taft Wallace (1908-1987)	
+1437	Lizar Myrtle Wallace (1911-1988)	
+1438	Montie Bertha Wallace (1914-1977)	
+1439	Maggie Wallace (1916-)	
+1440	Infant Wallace (1919-1919)	

Flora Ann Garner, daughter of Steadman Garner (1843-1928) and Ann Elizabeth Davis (1843-1925), was born on November 8, 1877 in Moore County, NC. She married Virgil Spinks "Byrd" Wallace on September 15, 1898 in Moore County, NC. She died on November 4, 1963 in Moore County, NC and was buried on November 6, 1963 in Moore County, NC at Virgil (Byrd) Wallace Cemetery.

327. **Isaac Frank Wallace**, son of Lochart "Lockey" Wallace, was born on March 15, 1856 in Moore County, NC. He married **Sarah Annette Horner** circa 1879. He died on September 5, 1925 in Danville, VA.

Sarah Annette Horner, daughter of William Thomas Horner (1840-1919) and Clarkey Ann Cockman (1842-1919), was born on March 15, 1862 in Moore County, NC. She died on November 20, 1913 in Randolph County, NC and was buried on November 21, 1913 in Ramseur, Randolph County, NC at First Christian Church AKA Sunset Knoll Cemetery. She and Isaac Frank Wallace had the following children:

+1441	Ella Wallace (1886-1923)
+1442	Sarah A. Wallace (1889-1910)
+1443	Aggie E. Wallace (1892-1906)
+1444	Leora Wallace (1900-)

328. **Mary Ellis Wallace**, daughter of Lochart "Lockey" Wallace and Susan Muse, was born on March 15, 1857. She died on October 20, 1920.

Ira Blake Maness, son of Asa Maness (1820-1894) and Mary Ann Ritter (1825-1884), was born on October 24, 1852. He died on January 2, 1931. He and Mary Ellis Wallace had the following children:

+622	Annie Louisa Maness (1875-1957)
+623	Ida C. Maness (1878-)
+624	Neelie Maness (1880-1930)
+625	Mattie Austin Maness (1881-1926)
+626	Mary Blake "Molly" Maness (1882-1944)
+627	W. Walter Maness (1883-1918)
+628	Maggie Mae Maness (1885-1937)
+629	Claude Ellis Maness (1887-1947)

329. **Male Wallace**, son of Lochart "Lockey" Wallace and Susan Muse, was born on September 15, 1860. He died on September 21, 1860 and was buried in Moore County, NC at Flint Hill Baptist Church.

330. **Martha Ann Wallace**, daughter of Lochart "Lockey" Wallace and Susan Muse, was born on December 10, 1862. She married **Lewis Scott Maness** circa 1879. She died on February 27, 1902 and was buried in Robbins, Moore County, NC at Tabernacle United Methodist Church.

Lewis Scott Maness, son of Lewis Grant Maness (1816-1913) and Rebecca Williams (1818-1894), was born on April 12, 1855. He married Mary L. Brown circa 1905. He died on August 14, 1943 and was buried in Robbins, Moore County, NC at Tabernacle United Methodist Church. He and Martha Ann Wallace had the following children:

+1445	Offie Thomas Maness (1879-1951)
+1446	Mary Alice Maness (1881-1912)

+1447	James Charles "Charlie" Maness (1882-1959)
+1448	Lillie Jane Maness (1884-1919)
+1449	Nettie F. Maness (1886-1964)
+1450	John Lockey Maness (1887-1973)
+1451	William Lewis "Willie" Maness (1890-1985)
+1452	Eli Carson Maness (1891-1968)
+1453	Lewis Rufus Maness (1893-1974)
+1454	Dora Lee Maness (1895-1966)
+1455	Garrett Hobert Maness (1896-1981)
+1456	Jerusha Annie Maness (1898-1987)
+1457	Rosa Pearl Maness (1901-1901)

Children of Lockey Wallace and Susan Muse

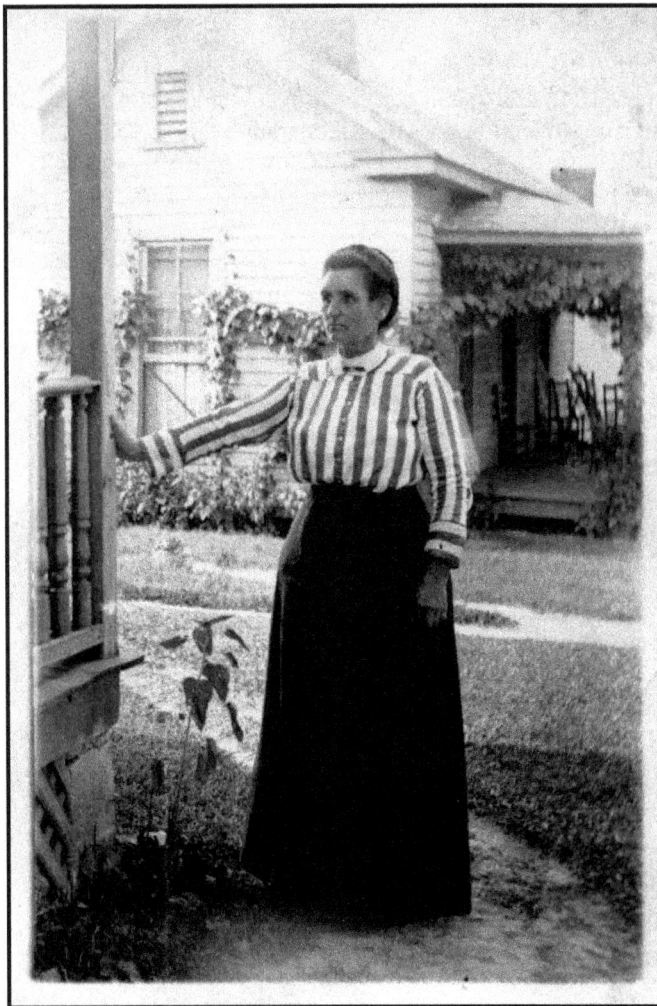

Rutha Jane Wallace Ritter
(Courtesy of Susan Peurifoy)

Martha Ann Wallace Maness
(Courtesy of Ancestry.com user leannb21)

Lewis Scott Maness and family circa 1915

[Front Row L-R] Charlie Williams, ?, Dewey Maness, ?, Vandie Williams Chisholm, Etta Wallace, Mamie Williams, H. Taft Williams, Mazie Maness Wallace, child of Offie Maness, child of Offie Maness, ?, ?, Taft Wallace, ?, ?, ? [Second Row L-R seated] Dora Lee Maness, Annie Covington Maness, Beulah McNeill Maness, Lewis Scott Maness, Mary Brown Maness, Nettie Maness Marley, Dora Hayes Maness, Lillie Jane Maness Wallace, Mattie Howard Maness [Third Row L-R standing] Jerusha Maness Kennedy, Willie Lloyd Maness, Eli Maness, child of Eli Maness, Willie Maness, child of Willie Maness, Ira Williams, Lee Williams Maness, Ben Marley, child of Charlie Maness, Charlie Maness, Montie Wallace, James Lewis Wallace, child of Offie Maness, Offie Maness, Madia Williams Garner [Fourth Row L-R standing] ?, Hobert Maness, John Maness, child of John Maness, Rufus Williams, Laney Williams *(Courtesy of Becky Wallace Gilmore, West End, NC)*

Lewis Scott Maness and sons circa 1915
[Front L-R] Lewis Scott Maness, Offie Maness, Charlie Maness, John Maness
[Back L-R] Willie Maness, Eli Maness, Rufus Maness, Hobert Maness
(Courtesy of Ancestry.com user leannb21)

331. **Rutha Jane Florence Wallace**, daughter of Lochart "Lockey" Wallace and Susan Muse, was born on April 22, 1867 in Moore County, NC. She married **Joseph Ritter** circa 1883. She died on July 7, 1936 in Greensboro, Guilford County, NC and was buried on July 9, 1936 in Greensboro, Guilford County, NC at Green Hill Cemetery.

Joseph Ritter, son of John Ritter (1816-1902) and Sara Ann Myrick (1818-1905), was born on December 2, 1857 in Moore County, NC. He died on February 19, 1936 in Greensboro, Guilford County, NC. He and Rutha Jane Florence Wallace had the following children:

+1458	William Walter Ritter (1883-1959)
+1459	John A. Ritter (1884-)
+1460	Maggie L. Ritter (1887-)
+1461	Flossie F. Ritter (1892-1955)
+1462	Herbert B. Ritter (1895-)
+1463	Annie Aggie Ritter (1898-)
+1464	Maudie Ritter (1900-1900)
+1465	Mattie Ritter (1902-1902)
+1466	Lennie Ritter (1904-)
+1467	Fannie Ritter (1906-)

332. **Nancy Margaret "Nannie" Wallace**, daughter of Lochart "Lockey" Wallace and Susan Muse, was born in January 1870. She died circa 1888.

James Hector Shields, son of James Martin Shields (1836-1912) and Amanda J. Burns (1836-1932), was born on December 11, 1861. He married Annie Casina Burns circa 1888. He died on December 4, 1941 and was buried in Robbins, Moore County, NC at Tabernacle United Methodist Church.

333. **Vandie Lee Wallace**, daughter of Lochart "Lockey" Wallace and Susan Muse, was born on July 15, 1874. She married **Asa McClellan Maness Sr.** circa 1889 and was buried on January 12, 1929 in Moore County, NC at Pleasant Hill United Methodist Church. She died on June 11, 1929 in Moore County, NC.

Asa McClellan Maness Sr., son of Asa Maness (1820-1894) and Mary Ann Ritter (1825-1884), was born on December 1, 1861. He died on October 10, 1955 and was buried in Moore County, NC at Pleasant Hill United Methodist Church. He and Vandie Lee Wallace had the following children:

+635	Duffy Maness (1886-)
+636	Asa McClellan Maness Jr. (1889-1970)
+637	Alexander Lee Maness (1894-1972)
+638	Arthur Maness (1897-1935)
+639	Ralph Maness (1899-1957)
+640	Johnny Carson Maness (1901-1975)
+641	Montie Lee Maness (1902-1975)
+642	Annie Ruth Maness (1908-)

334. **Ella Blake Wallace**, daughter of Lochart "Lockey" Wallace and Susan Muse, was born on May 21, 1877. She married **Stephen Harrison "Frog" Garner** on May 20, 1895 in Moore County, NC. She died on November 12, 1950 and was buried in Robbins, Moore County, NC at Tabernacle United Methodist Church.

Stephen Harrison "Frog" Garner, son of Steadman Garner (1843-1928) and Ann Elizabeth Davis (1843-1925), was born on February 22, 1874. He died on January 31, 1954 and was buried in Robbins, Moore County, NC at Tabernacle United Methodist Church. He and Ella Blake Wallace had the following children:

+1468	Maggie S. Garner (1896-1922)
+1469	William McLenon Garner (1897-1979)
+1470	Annie May Garner (1900-1920)
+1471	John Spinx Garner (1905-1969)
+1472	Mandie Alma Garner (1910-1974)
+1473	Myrtle Lee Garner (1914-1995)
+1474	Cornelius Blanche Garner (1918-1968)

335. **Elizabeth Jane Wallace**, daughter of Emsley Thomas Wallace and Priscilla Melton, was born on April 28, 1861 in Moore County, NC. She married **Baxter Williams** circa 1883. She died on August 25, 1934 in Moore County, NC and was buried on August 27, 1934 in Robbins, Moore County, NC at Tabernacle United Methodist Church.

Baxter Williams, son of Noah Williams (1826-1904) and Mary Ann Davis (1833-1896), was born on May 4, 1859 in Moore County, NC. He died on March 15, 1938 in Moore County, NC and was buried on March 17, 1938 in Robbins, Moore County, NC at Tabernacle United Methodist Church. He and Elizabeth Jane Wallace had the following children:

+1475	Katherine Marticia "Katie" Williams (1884-1968)
+1476	Walter W. Williams (1885-1951)
+1477	Emsley Thomas Williams (1888-1963)
+1478	Stephen Devotion Williams (1890-1972)
+1479	Noah Raleigh Williams (1892-1974)
+1480	Robert Henry Williams (1894-1918)
+1481	Annie Cindie Williams (1898-1994)
+1482	Cora Ida Williams (1900-1957)
+1483	Newton James Williams (1904-)

Stephen Harrison "Frog" Garner and grandson Tracy Garner *(Courtesy of Lacy Garner Jr., Carthage, NC)*

Bottom row (L-R) Lacy Garner, Sr., Stephen Harrison (Frog) Garner, Myrlean Garner Welch, Ella May Garner Watson. Top row (L-R) William McLenon Garner, Cecil Ruth Garner Sanders, Martha Alice Cockman Garner
(Courtesy of Lacy Garner, Jr., Carthage, NC)

Children of Emsley Wallace and Priscilla Melton

Front Row [L-R] **Baxter Williams, Elizabeth Wallace Williams, Katie Williams, Walter Williams, Emsley Williams. Back Row [L-R] Newton Williams, Cora Williams, Robert Williams, Raleigh Williams, Annie Williams, Stephen Williams**

Circa 1923 [Seated] **George Williams and Kate Wallace Williams** [Standing L-R] **Mollie Williams Lewis, Nannie Williams Morrison, Minnie Williams McNeill, Ellie Williams, Ruth Williams Brewer, Jim Williams, Dora Williams Henson, Norman Williams, Curtis Williams, Josie Williams Thomas.** *(Courtesy of The Williams Family by Maxine W. McNeill)*

Clockwise from above:

[L-R] Nancy Jane Williams Wallace
and Addie Florence Wallace.

Louisa Wallace Garner
(Courtesy of Kay Daunheimer)

George Williams and Kate Wallace
*(Courtesy of The Williams Family
by Maxine Williams McNeill)*

Lucian Wallace, Nancy Jane Williams Wallace and
sons Roscoe, Hurley and Alton (*oldest to youngest*)

Lucian Wallace and Nancy Jane Williams Wallace

336. **Sindy Ann "Annie" Wallace**, daughter of Emsley Thomas Wallace and Priscilla Melton, was born on March 10, 1863 in Moore County, NC. She married **Lineberry B. Maness** circa 1882. She died on December 13, 1930 in Rockingham, Richmond County, NC and was buried on December 14, 1930 in Rockingham, Richmond County, NC at Northam Cemetery.

Lineberry B. Maness, son of William Armstrong Maness (1833-1895) and Rebecca E. Seawell (1833-1920), was born on March 27, 1862. He died on April 25, 1903 and was buried in Rockingham, Richmond County, NC at Northam Cemetery. He and Sindy Ann "Annie" Wallace had the following children:

+1484	Cora Isabelle Maness (1883-1951)
+1485	Lewis A. Maness (1885-1932)
+1486	William C. Maness (1887-)
+1487	Dossie L. Maness (1889-)
+1488	Josie M. Maness (1892-1953)
+1489	Barney Armstrong Maness (1896-)
+1490	Dewey Rosco Maness (1899-)
+1491	Charlie T. Maness (1903-)

337. **Louisa Elafair Wallace**, daughter of Emsley Thomas Wallace and Priscilla Melton, was born on April 13, 1865 in Moore County, NC. She married **James Poling Garner** on March 17, 1892 in Moore County, NC. She died on March 9, 1944 in Moore County, NC and was buried on March 11, 1944 in Vass, Moore County, NC at Johnson Grove Cemetery.

James Poling Garner, son of Edmund Garner (1833-1905) and R. Margaret McNeill (1836-), was born on July 13, 1864. He died on July 9, 1921 and was buried in Vass, Moore County, NC at Johnson Grove Cemetery. He and Louisa Elafair Wallace had the following children:

+1492	Claude Lee Garner (1893-1967)
+1493	Ira Jason Garner (1895-1972)
+1494	Radie Florence Garner (1897-1983)
+1495	Arthur Garner (1900-1992)
+1496	Magaret "Maggie" Garner (1901-1985)
+1497	Hugh Lineberry Garner (1906-1987)

338. **Sarah Catherine "Kate" Wallace**, daughter of Emsley Thomas Wallace and Priscilla Melton, was born on October 13, 1868. She married **George W. Williams** circa 1885. She died on August 29, 1941 and was buried in Robbins, Moore County, NC at Tabernacle United Methodist Church.

George W. Williams, son of Noah Williams (1826-1904) and Mary Ann Davis (1833-1896), was born on August 26, 1865 in Moore County, NC. He died on March 25, 1942 in Moore County, NC and was buried on March 27, 1942 in Robbins, Moore County, NC at Tabernacle United Methodist Church. He and Sarah Catherine "Kate" Wallace had the following children:

+1498	Lou Minnie Williams (1885-1936)
+1499	Infant Williams (1887-1887)
+1500	Ruth Elizabeth Williams (1888-1966)
+1501	Ellis Lewis Williams (1891-1973)
+1502	James Lucian Williams (1893-1970)
+1503	Curtis Daniel Williams (1896-1933)
+1504	Dora Lee Williams (1898-1982)
+1505	Callie Florence Williams (1900-1982)
+1506	Josie Ella Williams (1903-1924)
+1507	Mollie Priscilla Williams (1905-2001)
+1508	Nannie Verona Williams (1909-2004)
+1509	William Norman Williams (1911-2007)

339. **Callie Lee Wallace**, daughter of Emsley Thomas Wallace and Priscilla Melton, was born on June 30, 1870. She married **James Britt** on October 26, 1899 in Moore County, NC. She died on November 23, 1916 in Presbyterian Hospital,

Charlotte, Mecklenburg County, NC and was buried on November 24, 1916 in Moore County, NC at Bensalem Presbyterian Church.

James Britt, son of Daniel Bethune Britt (1845-1927) and Lydia Freeman (1848-1918), was born on September 16, 1870. He died on September 22, 1917.

340. **Addie Florence Wallace**, daughter of Emsley Thomas Wallace and Priscilla Melton, was born on March 7, 1872. She died on August 18, 1943 in Moore County, NC and was buried in Robbins, Moore County, NC at Tabernacle United Methodist Church.

341. **Lucian Thomas Wallace**, son of Emsley Thomas Wallace and Priscilla Melton, was born on January 15, 1876 in Moore County, NC. He married **Nancy Jane "Nan" Williams** on December 24, 1896 in John Spanker Williams/Mary Catherine Williams Homeplace, Moore County, NC. He died on July 1, 1935 in Moore Regional Hospital, Pinehurst, Moore County, NC and was buried in Robbins, Moore County, NC at Tabernacle United Methodist Church.

Nancy Jane "Nan" Williams, daughter of John Spanker Williams (1842-1924) and Mary Catherine Williams (1848-1935), was born on December 21, 1875 in Moore County, NC. She died on August 15, 1967 in Moore Regional Hospital, Pinehurst, Moore County, NC and was buried on August 17, 1967 in Robbins, Moore County, NC at Tabernacle United Methodist Church. She and Lucian Thomas Wallace had the following children:

+1510	Infant Wallace (-)
+1511	Roscoe Greene Wallace (1900-1960)
+1512	Hurley Carlton Wallace (1905-1994)
+1513	Chester Alton Wallace (1907-1982)
+1514	Mallie Lester Wallace (1910-2002)
+1515	Sadie Lou Wallace (1912-1992)
+1516	Verdia Lee Wallace (1914-1998)
+1517	Connie Thomas Wallace (1916-1972)

342. **Martha "Mattie" Wallace**, daughter of Emsley Thomas Wallace and Priscilla Melton, was born on October 28, 1878 in Moore County, NC. She married **Daniel Bethune Britt Jr.** on February 15, 1900 in Moore County, NC. She died on October 9, 1955 in St. Joseph of Pines Hospital, Pinehurst, Moore County, NC and was buried on October 10, 1955 in Moore County, NC at Bensalem Presbyterian Church.

Daniel Bethune Britt Jr., son of Daniel Bethune Britt (1845-1927) and Lydia Freeman (1848-1918), was born on September 16, 1875 in Moore County, NC. He died on August 18, 1933 in Moore Regional Hospital, Pinehurst, Moore County, NC and was buried on August 19, 1933 in Moore County, NC at Bensalem Presbyterian Church. He and Martha "Mattie" Wallace had the following children:

+1518	Isham Thomas Britt (1900-1980)
+1519	Gertie Lee Britt (1906-1980)

344. **Mary Jane Nancy Regina Ledbetter "Mamie" Wallace**, daughter of Samuel Bascom Wallace and Temperance Levina Melton, was born on February 16, 1867 in Moore County, NC. She died on June 5, 1936 in Moore County, NC and was buried on June 6, 1936 in Carthage, Moore County, NC at Cross Hill Cemetery.

Jesse Samuel Barrett, son of John Andrew Barrett (1837-1912) and Mary Elizabeth Bean (1838-1898), was born on March 7, 1862. He died on July 29, 1933 and was buried in Carthage, Moore County, NC at Cross Hill Cemetery. He and Mary Jane Nancy Regina Ledbetter "Mamie" Wallace had the following children:

+1520	Annette Barrett (1884-1956)

345. **Isham Sedman Robert Renfro "Bob" Wallace**, son of Samuel Bascom Wallace and Temperance Levina Melton, was born on March 2, 1870 in Moore County, NC. He married **Bura S. Stutts** on September 24, 1893 in Richmond County, NC. He died on December 4, 1933 in Newton, Catawba County, NC and was buried on December 6, 1933 in Marion, McDowell County, NC at Oak Grove Cemetery.

Bura S. Stutts, daughter of John Armstead Stutts (1830-) and Mary J. Seawell (1836-1889), was born on April 2, 1872. She died on April 2, 1938 and was buried in Marion, McDowell County, NC at Oak Grove Cemetery. She and Isham Sedman Robert Renfro "Bob" Wallace had the following children:

+1521   Mary Pauline Wallace (1895-1958)

346. **Daisy Arnold Irene Wallace**, daughter of Samuel Bascom Wallace and Temperance Levina Melton, was born in 1872. She married **Evander Kelly McLeod** on June 17, 1894 in Moore County, NC. She died on October 4, 1909 in Moore County, NC and was buried in Moore County, NC at Union Presbyterian Church.

Evander Kelly McLeod, son of James Wesley McLeod (1830-1885) and Jeanette "Jane" McCaskill (1835-aft 1910), was born on February 17, 1872. He died on February 11, 1960 and was buried in Asheboro, Randolph County, NC at Neighbors Grove Wesleyan Church. He and Daisy Arnold Irene Wallace had the following children:

+1522   Maggie Lee McLeod (1895-1975)
+1523   William C. McLeod (1898-)
+1524   James Samuel McLeod (1900-1918)
+1525   Mamie McLeod (1901-1904)
+1526   Jesse Lewis McLeod (1906-1949)
+1527   Claude McLeod (1909-)
+1528   Maude Daisy McLeod (1909-)

347. **Cynthia Ann "Annie" Wallace**, daughter of Samuel Bascom Wallace and Temperance Levina Melton, was born on April 9, 1873. She married **David Newton Morgan** on November 7, 1895 in Moore County, NC. She died on April 28, 1906 and was buried in Moore County, NC at Brown Cemetery #280.

David Newton Morgan, son of John Martin Morgan (1837-1913) and Maloney Richardson (1836-bef 1900), was born on January 29, 1873. He married Alberta Alma "Bertie" Sanders circa 1918. He died on January 19, 1943 and was buried in Moore County, NC at Brown Cemetery #280. He and Cynthia Ann "Annie" Wallace had the following children:

+1529   Daisy Morgan (-)
+1530   William Morgan (-)
+1531   Etta Bell Morgan (1896-1920)
+1532   Eli Samuel Morgan (1897-1919)
+1533   Arthur Clemons "Offie" Morgan (1899-1957)
+1534   Charles M. Morgan (1901-)
+1535   Daniel E. Morgan (1905-)

348. **Josiah Tay Settle Wallace**, son of Samuel Bascom Wallace and Temperance Levina Melton, was born on October 9, 1877 in Moore County, NC. He married **Annie Jane Sanders** on December 6, 1898 in Moore County, NC. He died on October 15, 1946 in Stanly County, NC and was buried on October 17, 1946 in Albemarle, Stanly County, NC at Fairview Cemetery.

Annie Jane Sanders, daughter of John Sanders (1859-1933) and Delitha Smith (1863-1894), was born on July 5, 1881 in Moore County, NC. She died on March 28, 1943 in Albemarle, Stanly County, NC and was buried on March 30, 1943 in Albemarle, Stanly County, NC at Fairview Cemetery. She and Josiah Tay Settle Wallace had the following children:

+1536   Ursula M. "Shulie" Wallace (1899-1901)
+1537   Shelly R. Wallace (1902-)
+1538   Maggie Pearl Wallace (1906-1973)
+1539   Thelma Devina Wallace (1910-)
+1540   Charles Evans Wallace (1916-1981)
+1541   James Wallace (1922-)

Children of Samuel B. Wallace and Tempy Melton

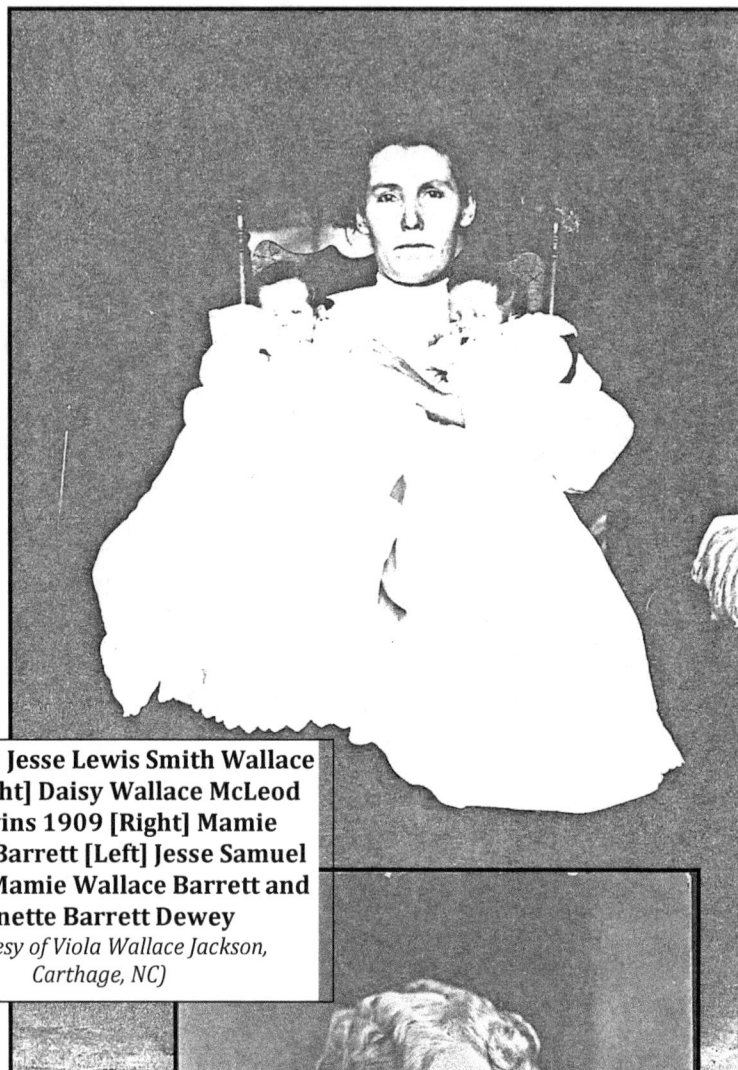

[Top Left] Jesse Lewis Smith Wallace
[Top Right] Daisy Wallace McLeod
and twins 1909 [Right] Mamie
Wallace Barrett [Left] Jesse Samuel
Barrett, Mamie Wallace Barrett and
Annette Barrett Dewey
*(Courtesy of Viola Wallace Jackson,
Carthage, NC)*

349. Sarah Lee Nettie Wallace, daughter of Samuel Bascom Wallace and Temperance Levina Melton, was born on February 28, 1878. She married **Lonnie Lee Stewart** on June 4, 1899 in Moore County, NC. She died on May 9, 1941 and was buried in Coats, Harnett County, NC at Coats City Cemetery.

Lonnie Lee Stewart, son of Archie Stewart (-) and Betty (-), was born on December 15, 1870. He died on December 30, 1940 and was buried in Coats, Harnett County, NC at Coats City Cemetery. He and Sarah Lee Nettie Wallace had the following children:

| +1542 | Ila Myrtle Stewart (1900-1969) |
| +1543 | Archie Lee Stewart (1902-1950) |

350. Jesse Lewis Smith Wallace, son of Samuel Bascom Wallace and Temperance Levina Melton, was born on June 5, 1879. He died on November 28, 1946 and was buried in Moore County, NC at Union Presbyterian Church.

Sarah Catherine "Cassie" Hunsucker, daughter of William Wesley Hunsucker (1829-1896) and Christian McDonald (1842-1906), was born on August 2, 1887 in Moore County, NC. She died on April 13, 1972 in Moore Regional Hospital, Pinehurst, Moore County, NC and was buried on April 14, 1972 in Moore County, NC at Union Presbyterian Church. She and Jesse Lewis Smith Wallace had the following children:

+1544	Viola Mae Wallace (1907-1994)
+1545	Blanche Gretchen Wallace (1909-1991)
+1546	Roberta Wallace (1915-1915)
+1547	Jessie Lazell Wallace (1922-2002)

351. Eliza Rosetta Mattie Evelyn "Mattie" Wallace, daughter of Samuel Bascom Wallace and Temperance Levina Melton, was born on September 22, 1882 in Moore County, NC. She married **Troy Van Truelove** on September 22, 1900 in Moore County, NC. She married **George W. Fields** on September 7, 1921 in Sanford, Lee County, NC. She died on October 12, 1924 in State Hospital, Raleigh, Wake County, NC and was buried in Sanford, Lee County, NC at Shallow Well Cemetery.

Troy Van Truelove, son of Henry Alfred Truelove (1848-1913) and Mary Elizabeth "Minnie" Spence (1846-1922), was born on December 17, 1871 in Harnett County, NC. He died on April 6, 1915 in Sanford, Lee County, NC and was buried in Sanford, Lee County, NC at Shallow Well Cemetery. He and Eliza Rosetta Mattie Evelyn "Mattie" Wallace had the following children:

+1548	Roland Truelove (1902-)
+1549	Samuel Estis Truelove (1903-1957)
+1550	Pauline Truelove (1905-)
+1551	Alford Raeford Truelove (1909-1978)
+1552	Margie Truelove (1914-)

George W. Fields was born on February 22, 1866. He died on May 29, 1921.

352. Samuel Henry Bascom "Bass" Wallace, son of Samuel Bascom Wallace and Temperance Levina Melton, was born on April 29, 1885 in Moore County, NC. He died on September 26, 1949 in Lexington, Davidson County, NC and was buried on September 28, 1949 in Lexington, Davidson County, NC at Forest Hill Memorial Park.

Nettie J. Britt, daughter of Allen Emmerson Britt (1866-1951) and Lydia M. Morgan (1869-bef 1907), was born on July 7, 1890. She died in February 1984 and was buried in Lexington, Davidson County, NC at Forest Hill Memorial Park. She and Samuel Henry Bascom "Bass" Wallace had the following children:

+1553	Oscar Emerson Wallace (1910-1970)
+1554	Floyd Lee Wallace (1913-1997)
+1555	Beulah M. Wallace (1918-)
+1556	Jesse Wallace (1923-)

353. Josiah Turner Horner, son of James Washington Horner and Lovedy Jane Wallace, was born in October 1869. He married **Agnes Chalmers Barrett** on December 25, 1892 in Moore County, NC. He married **Anna Jane "Janie"**

Cockman circa 1901. He married **Hattie Belle McLean** on May 3, 1914 in Cumberland County, NC. He died on June 24, 1923 in Cumberland County, NC.

Agnes Chalmers Barrett, daughter of Doctor Chalmers Barrett (1846-1891) and Margaret H. Stewart (1854-1918), was born on October 26, 1869. She died in 1899. She and Josiah Turner Horner had the following children:

+1557	Carson Lee Horner (1894-1979)
+1558	Beulah Horner (1896-1979)

Anna Jane "Janie" Cockman, daughter of George MDOHDIC Cockman (1847-1907) and Lucinda Melton (1845-1908), was born on June 18, 1869. She married Elias "Lizard" Garner circa 1887. She died on April 26, 1913.

Hattie Belle McLean was born on May 3, 1883 in Cumberland County, NC. She died on June 19, 1964 in Fayetteville, Cumberland County, NC. She and Josiah Turner Horner had the following children:

+1559	James Thomas "Jack" Horner Sr. (1915-2013)
+1560	Mabel Agnes Horner (1916-1992)
+1561	Joseph Winford Horner (1919-1963)
+1562	Hattie Pauline Horner (1921-2008)

354. **William Branson "Bud" Horner**, son of James Washington Horner and Lovedy Jane Wallace, was born in May 1872. He married **Martha Jane Garner** circa 1900. He died in June 1925 and was buried in Robbins, Moore County, NC at Tabernacle United Methodist Church.

Martha Jane Garner, daughter of Steadman Garner (1843-1928) and Ann Elizabeth Davis (1843-1925), was born on July 15, 1881. She died on December 16, 1920 in Moore County, NC and was buried in Robbins, Moore County, NC at Tabernacle United Methodist Church. She and William Branson "Bud" Horner had the following children:

+1563	Mollie Horner (1902-1921)
+1564	Mamie Horner (1905-1999)
+1565	Archie Daniel Horner (1907-1980)
+1566	Carl Horner (1910-)
+1567	James Washington Horner (1912-1914)
+1568	Bonnie Mae Horner (1915-)
+1569	Dola Fonnie Horner (1918-2002)
+1570	Rady Ora Horner (1920-1921)

355. **John W. Horner**, son of James Washington Horner and Lovedy Jane Wallace, was born in September 1874. He married **Lena Mercer** on February 14, 1898 in Moore County, NC.

Lena Mercer, daughter of George Mercer (-) and Annie Jane (-), was born in October 1880. She and John W. Horner had the following children:

+1571	Thelma Horner (1900-1965)

356. **Mary Ann Horner**, daughter of James Washington Horner and Lovedy Jane Wallace, was born on September 13, 1878 in Moore County, NC. She married **Kenneth K. Williams** on March 16, 1899 in Moore County, NC. She died on February 15, 1914 in Moore County, NC and was buried on February 17, 1914 in Robbins, Moore County, NC at Tabernacle United Methodist Church.

Kenneth K. Williams, son of Wesley William Williams (1823-1911) and Margaret Garner (1822-1906), was born on November 15, 1854. He died on January 7, 1935 and was buried in Robbins, Moore County, NC at Tabernacle United Methodist Church. He and Mary Ann Horner had the following children:

+1572	Edna Williams (1899-1972)
+1573	Luther Clegg Williams (1909-1962)
+1574	Grover Williams (1914-1914)

357. **Maggie C. Horner**, daughter of James Washington Horner and Lovedy Jane Wallace, was born on June 22, 1880. She died on October 14, 1880 and was buried in Moore County, NC at Flint Hill Baptist Church.

358. **Martha Louvina Horner**, daughter of James Washington Horner and Lovedy Jane Wallace, was born on October 30, 1882. She married **Noah R. Ritter** on March 13, 1907 in Moore County, NC. She died on September 19, 1958 and was buried in Moore County, NC at Flint Hill Baptist Church.

Noah R. Ritter, son of John Henry Ritter (1842-1927) and Nancy Jane Cole (1848-1923), was born on March 2, 1880. He died on July 1, 1953 and was buried in Moore County, NC at Flint Hill Baptist Church. He and Martha Louvina Horner had the following children:

+1575	Eli Ritter (1907-1994)
+1576	Eulis Alfred Ritter (1909-1968)
+1577	Flossie Jenettie Ritter (1913-1988)
+1578	Etta Agnes Ritter (1915-)
+1579	Stella Marie Ritter (1918-)
+1580	Charlie Mason Ritter (1921-)
+1581	Jesse Vander Ritter (1925-1994)

360. **Wade Hampton Wallace**, son of Sampson Delaney Wallace and Missouri Coleman Hunsucker, was born on July 21, 1870. He died on March 15, 1947 and was buried in Moore County, NC at Flint Hill Baptist Church.

Rosanna M. Hooker, daughter of John M. Hooker (1866-1948) and Eliza Alice Wallace (1871-1940), was born on November 23, 1905. She died on October 15, 1992 and was buried in Moore County, NC at Flint Hill Baptist Church. She and Wade Hampton Wallace had the following children:

+1582	Amaryllis Jean Wallace (1932-)

Maggie Delaney Deleeny Cockman, daughter of Noah Emsley Cockman (1824-aft 1893) and Mary Ann Wallace (1826-1892), was born on November 12, 1877. She married Dock F. Maness on September 14, 1893 in Moore County, NC. She died on July 4, 1957 and was buried in Moore County, NC at Flint Hill Baptist Church. She and Wade Hampton Wallace had the following children:

+1269	Gurtie Cockman (1909-1962)

Sarah Louisa Williamson, daughter of Mary A. Williamson (1855-), was born in February 1883. She married Daniel H. Moore on April 11, 1903 in Moore County, NC. She died in 1932. She and Wade Hampton Wallace had the following children:

+1583	Josie Ora Moore (1914-1989)

Annie Lakey, daughter of William Lakey (-) and Jane (-), was born in 1872. She married Joseph S. Riddle on November 9, 1897 in Moore County, NC. She and Wade Hampton Wallace had the following children:

+1584	Mamie Riddle (1893-1958)
+1585	Benjamin Harrison Riddle (1895-1949)

361. **Euphernia S. "Effie" Wallace**, daughter of Sampson Delaney Wallace and Missouri Coleman Hunsucker, was born in March 1872 in Moore County, NC. She died on December 7, 1915 in Moore County, NC and was buried on December 9, 1915 in Moore County, NC at Rock Hill Church.

Euphernia S. "Effie" Wallace had the following children:

+1586	Pearl M. Wallace (1898-)

362. **Ashley Braxton Wallace**, son of Sampson Delaney Wallace and Missouri Coleman Hunsucker, was born on December 26, 1876. He died on March 23, 1925 in Rockingham, Richmond County, NC and was buried on March 24, 1925 in Rockingham, Richmond County, NC at East Side Cemetery.

Children of Sampson Delaney Wallace and Missouri Hunsucker

[Right and Below]
Benjamin Harrison Wallace
(Courtesy of Jeri Dearing)

[Below] Carter Family. Ruth Wallace Carter [4th from left], standing next to her 3 daughters and 2 of her 3 sons. Far right is James Ford Carter and wife [holding oldest daughter]. The shorter stout lady in black was "Aunt Georgia" who owned a home at the beach (unclear how she was related) [Bottom] **John Carter and Ruth Wallace** on their wedding day circa 1908. *(Courtesy of Janet Carter)* [Bottom Left] **Wade Hampton Wallace**

363. **Catherine E. Wallace**, daughter of Sampson Delaney Wallace and Missouri Coleman Hunsucker, was born on April 26, 1881. She married **Archibald Asa Muse** on September 28, 1900 in Moore County, NC. She died on June 29, 1910 and was buried in Moore County, NC at Friendship Baptist Church.

Archibald Asa Muse, son of Archibald Buckley Muse (1838-1903) and Martha Jane Johnson (1841-1904), was born on February 10, 1876. He died on April 21, 1961 and was buried in Moore County, NC at Friendship Baptist Church. He and Catherine E. Wallace had the following children:

+1587	Claude Muse (1902-)	
+1588	Archie Braxton Muse (1903-)	
+1589	Josie A. Muse (1906-1976)	
+1590	Johnsie M. Muse (1909-1910)	

364. **Flossie Alma Wallace**, daughter of Sampson Delaney Wallace and Missouri Coleman Hunsucker, was born on February 10, 1883 in Moore County, NC. She married **Alfred Powell Hill Barrett** on June 5, 1905. She died on January 22, 1912 in Rockingham, Richmond County, NC and was buried on January 23, 1912 in Rockingham, Richmond County, NC at East Side Cemetery.

Alfred Powell Hill Barrett, son of Robert Williams Barrett (1829-1897) and Louise Charity Cox (1840-1900), was born on January 16, 1876. He died on December 10, 1933 and was buried in Rockingham, Richmond County, NC at East Side Cemetery. He and Flossie Alma Wallace had the following children:

+1591	Fred Lewis Barrett (1906-1907)	
+1592	Alberta Ulysses Barrett (1907-1924)	
+1593	Minnie Grace Barrett (1909-)	

365. **Jerusha Francis "Ruth" Wallace**, daughter of Sampson Delaney Wallace and Missouri Coleman Hunsucker, was born on May 1, 1887. She died on February 5, 1982 and was buried in Rockingham, Richmond County, NC at East Side Cemetery.

John D. Carter was born on September 19, 1878. He died on September 22, 1930 and was buried in Rockingham, Richmond County, NC at East Side Cemetery. He and Jerusha Francis "Ruth" Wallace had the following children:

+1594	John Ashley Carter (1908-1981)	
+1595	Addie Webb Carter (1912-2008)	
+1596	James Ford Carter (1916-1983)	
+1597	Ruth Coleman "Coley" Carter (1920-1997)	
+1598	Mary Louise Carter (1923-2009)	
+1599	Billy Braxton Carter (1928-2011)	

366. **Benjamin Harrison Wallace**, son of Sampson Delaney Wallace and Missouri Coleman Hunsucker, was born on July 20, 1891 in Moore County, NC. He married **Luna Clementine Coble** circa 1924. He died on November 14, 1956 in Albemarle, Stanly County, NC and was buried on November 15, 1956 in Albemarle, Stanly County, NC at Fairview Cemetery.

Ruth Mable Dawson was born on June 18, 1892. She died on February 19, 1919 and was buried in Rockingham, Richmond County, NC at East Side Cemetery. She and Benjamin Harrison Wallace had the following children:

+1600	Mildred Hamer Wallace (1913-1998)	
+1601	Benjamin Harrison Wallace Jr. (1915-1994)	
+1602	Annie Ruth Wallace (1917-1993)	
+1603	Mary Missouri Wallace (1919-1994)	

Luna Clementine Coble, daughter of Ephriam Coble (-) and Elizabeth Burgess (-), was born on February 7, 1898 in North Carolina. She died on September 24, 1971 in Albemarle, Stanly County, NC and was buried on September 26, 1971 in Albemarle, Stanly County, NC at Fairview Cemetery. She and Benjamin Harrison Wallace had the following children:

+1604	Elizabeth Delaney Wallace (1925-2006)	

+1605   Calvin Coble Wallace (1928-1991)

370. **Lovedy Ann "Annie" Wallace**, daughter of Virgil Spinks "Byrd" Wallace and Regina Hunsucker, was born on September 9, 1868. She died on October 9, 1896 and was buried in Moore County, NC at Brown's Chapel Christian Church.

Alexander McNeill, son of Archibald McNeill (1818-1880) and Jennet "Jane" Brewer (1820-1908), was born on February 11, 1861. He died on September 6, 1899 and was buried in Moore County, NC at Brown's Chapel Christian Church. He and Lovedy Ann "Annie" Wallace had the following children:

+1606   Hattie Jane McNeill (1886-1945)
+1607   Archibald Daniel "Archie" McNeill (1887-1965)
+1608   Effie R. McNeill (1889-1913)
+1609   Virgil L. McNeill (1891-1892)
+1610   Nettie F. McNeill (1892-1893)
+1611   Hugh T. McNeill (1895-)

373. **Hattie Jane Wallace**, daughter of Virgil Spinks "Byrd" Wallace and Regina Hunsucker, was born in October 1875 in Moore County, NC. She married **George Dock Williams** on October 21, 1900 in Moore County, NC. She died in 1905 in Moore County, NC and was buried in Moore County, NC at Virgil (Byrd) Wallace Cemetery.

George Dock Williams, son of Jefferson H. Williams (1836-bef 1910) and Avena Jane Medlin (1842-bef 1888), was born on July 15, 1876. He married Lucinda Florence Morgan circa 1907. He died on May 17, 1940 and was buried in Eagle Springs, Moore County, NC at Eagle Springs Baptist Church. He and Hattie Jane Wallace had the following children:

+1612   Grady Lester Williams (1901-1957)
+1613   Bertha Rodela Williams (1903-1977)

374. **Martha Elizabeth Wallace**, daughter of Virgil Spinks "Byrd" Wallace and Regina Hunsucker, was born on April 30, 1879 in Moore County, NC. She married **George Sanderlin Deaton** on May 17, 1894 in Moore County, NC. She died on March 12, 1947 in Moore County, NC and was buried on March 14, 1947 in Moore County, NC at Pine Grove Baptist Church.

George Sanderlin Deaton, son of John M. Deaton (1838-1919) and Lydia Morgan (1845-1914), was born on January 21, 1871 in Montgomery County, NC. He died on January 26, 1929 in High Point, Guilford County, NC and was buried on January 28, 1929 in Moore County, NC at Pine Grove Baptist Church. He and Martha Elizabeth Wallace had the following children:

+1614   Bertha May Deaton (1895-1895)
+1615   Ida Florence Deaton (1896-1961)
+1616   Maudie Easter Deaton (1899-1951)
+1617   Gurney Carlton Deaton (1902-1967)
+1618   Lillie Jane Deaton (1908-1972)
+1619   John Earl Deaton (1910-1984)
+1620   Virgil Pearl "Bird" Deaton (1910-1968)
+1621   Isham Deaton (1913-1947)
+1622   Lettie Ethel Deaton (1916-)
+1623   Joseph Franklin Deaton (1918-)
+1624   Charles Hoyt Deaton (1921-1926)
+1625   Willie Paul Deaton (1923-)

375. **Isham Wallace**, son of Virgil Spinks "Byrd" Wallace and Regina Hunsucker, was born on May 11, 1882 in Moore County, NC. He married **Bertha Hall** on November 9, 1900 in Moore County, NC. He married **Flora Britt** on January 14, 1907 in Moore County, NC. He died on September 2, 1962 in St. Joseph of Pines Hospital, Pinehurst, Moore County, NC and was buried on September 4, 1962 in Moore County, NC at Virgil (Byrd) Wallace Cemetery.

Bertha Hall, daughter of Elisha Calvin Hall (-) and Nancy Marian Rich (-), was born on July 17, 1884. She died on November 15, 1906 and was buried in Moore County, NC at Virgil (Byrd) Wallace Cemetery. She and Isham Wallace had the following children:

+1626   Minnie Lee Wallace (1902-1972)
+1627   Hattie Jane Wallace (1904-1981)

Flora Britt, daughter of Daniel Bethune Britt (1845-1927) and Lydia Freeman (1848-1918), was born on November 4, 1884 in Moore County, NC. She died on October 23, 1946 in Moore County, NC and was buried on October 25, 1946 in Moore County, NC at Virgil (Byrd) Wallace Cemetery. She and Isham Wallace had the following children:

+1628   Emma Mae Wallace (1908-1995)
+1629   Willis Wallace (1909-1919)
+1630   John Wallace (1911-1913)
+1631   Lydia Annie Wallace (1914-1982)
+1632   Clyde Grover Wallace (1917-1983)
+1633   Claude Cleveland Wallace (1920-1981)
+1634   Beulah Wallace (1923-1923)

376. **Lula Florence Wallace**, daughter of Virgil Spinks "Byrd" Wallace and Regina Hunsucker, was born on November 16, 1886 in Moore County, NC. She married **Charles Benjamin Williams** on April 27, 1902 in Moore County, NC. She died on June 15, 1915 in Moore County, NC and was buried on June 17, 1915 in Moore County, NC at Virgil (Byrd) Wallace Cemetery.

Charles Benjamin Williams, son of Jefferson H. Williams (1836-bef 1910) and Avena Jane Medlin (1842-bef 1888), was born on August 31, 1873 in Moore County, NC. He married Rossie Belle Williams circa 1926. He died on June 3, 1943 in Moore County, NC and was buried on June 5, 1943 in Moore County, NC at Virgil (Byrd) Wallace Cemetery. He and Lula Florence Wallace had the following children:

+1635   Dossie L. Williams (1903-1949)
+1636   Regina Williams (1905-1984)
+1637   Virgil "Bird" Williams (1907-)
+1638   Flossie Williams (1911-)
+1639   Janie Williams (1913-)

377. **Burney Leason Wallace**, son of Virgil Spinks "Byrd" Wallace and Regina Hunsucker, was born on September 30, 1888 in Moore County, NC. He married **Bessie Lee Needham** on April 11, 1912 in Montgomery County, NC. He died on November 29, 1955 in Moore County, NC and was buried on December 1, 1955 in Moore County, NC at Calvary Baptist Church.

Bessie Lee Needham, daughter of Eli Needham (1851-1923) and Susannah Fox (1873-1952), was born on November 17, 1894. She died on March 7, 1971 in St. Joseph of Pines Hospital, Pinehurst, Moore County, NC and was buried on March 10, 1971 in Moore County, NC at Calvary Baptist Church. She and Burney Leason Wallace had the following children:

+1640   Hazel Wallace (1913-1967)
+1641   Dewey Green Wallace (1915-1979)
+1642   Dora Leason Wallace (1918-1985)
+1643   Essie Lee Wallace (1921-1988)
+1644   Annie Ruth Wallace (1924-)
+1645   Johnsie Grier Wallace (1931-)

378. **Beulah Hazel Wallace**, daughter of Virgil Spinks "Byrd" Wallace and Flora Ann Garner, was born on August 31, 1898. She died on August 24, 1976 in Sanford, Lee County, NC and was buried in Seagrove, Randolph County, NC at Union Grove Baptist Church.

William Thomas McNeill, son of William C. McNeill (1845-1931) and Elizabeth Louisa Yow (1856-1920), was born on December 3, 1883 in Randolph County, NC. He died on December 25, 1959 in Moore County, NC and was buried on December 27, 1959 in Seagrove, Randolph County, NC at Union Grove Baptist Church. He and Beulah Hazel Wallace had the following children:

+1646	Garvin McNeill (-)	
+1647	Marjorie McNeill (-)	
+1648	Rellie McNeill (-)	
+1649	Dora E. McNeill (1920-)	
+1650	Richard Thomas McNeill (1926-2017)	
+1651	Clarence McNeill (1928-2000)	
+1652	Dorothy Mae McNeill (1931-2001)	
+1653	Annie Mozelle McNeill (1938-1940)	
+1654	Peter Paul McNeill (1939-2020)	
+1655	Maxine Annie McNeill (1941-)	
+1656	Mazie Lorene McNeill (1941-)	
+1657	Roy Thomas McNeill (1945-)	

379. **Cora Bell Wallace**, daughter of Virgil Spinks "Byrd" Wallace and Flora Ann Garner, was born on May 15, 1901 in Moore County, NC. She died on June 10, 1988 in Moore County, NC and was buried in Moore County, NC at Virgil (Byrd) Wallace Cemetery.

Barney Edward Britt, son of General Street Britt (1874-1965) and Lucinda Frances Bruce (1873-), was born on June 24, 1898. He died on October 9, 1981 and was buried in Moore County, NC at Virgil (Byrd) Wallace Cemetery. He and Cora Bell Wallace had the following children:

+1658	Roy Edward Britt (-)	
+1659	Nora Jane Britt (1928-)	
+1660	James Robert Britt (1931-1998)	
+1661	Esther Lene Britt (1933-)	
+1662	Annie Helen Britt (1938-)	
+1663	Bettie Lou Britt (1944-1944)	

Stephen Devotion Williams, son of Baxter Williams (1859-1938) and Elizabeth Jane Wallace (1861-1934), was born on April 29, 1890. He died on April 8, 1972. He and Cora Bell Wallace had the following children:

+1664	Dora Mae Wallace (1921-)	

380. **Steadman McLendon Wallace**, son of Virgil Spinks "Byrd" Wallace and Flora Ann Garner, was born on October 9, 1903 in Moore County, NC. He married **Annie Boder York** on January 5, 1926 in Moore County, NC. He died on November 15, 1973 in St. Joseph of Pines Hospital, Pinehurst, Moore County, NC and was buried on November 17, 1973 in Biscoe, Montgomery County, NC at Biscoe Cemetery.

Annie Boder York, daughter of John York (-) and Mary (-), was born on August 2, 1906 in Randelman, Randolph County, NC. She died on March 11, 1993 in Montgomery County, NC and was buried in Biscoe, Montgomery County, NC at Biscoe Cemetery. She and Steadman McLendon Wallace had the following children:

+1665	June Wallace (-)	
+1666	Anna Lee Wallace (-)	
+1667	Johnsie Elizabeth Wallace (1928-1996)	
+1668	Irma Jean Wallace (1931-2007)	
+1669	Steadman McLendon Wallace Jr. (1934-1983)	

381. **Jeanette "Nettie" Wallace**, daughter of Virgil Spinks "Byrd" Wallace and Flora Ann Garner, was born on March 30, 1906 in Moore County, NC. She married **Canoy Allen "Ned" Sanders** on February 11, 1921 in Moore County, NC. She died on January 18, 1985 in Moore County, NC and was buried in Moore County, NC at Virgil (Byrd) Wallace Cemetery.

Canoy Allen "Ned" Sanders, son of Malinda Sanders (1866-1905), was born on April 12, 1897. He died on July 17, 1977 and was buried in Moore County, NC at Virgil (Byrd) Wallace Cemetery. He and Jeanette "Nettie" Wallace had the following children:

+1670	Dora Wilma Sanders (1923-1998)
+1671	Swannie Evelyn Sanders (1924-2001)
+1672	Bertha Elizabeth Sanders (1927-1988)
+1673	Ethel Marie Sanders (1929-2002)
+1674	Gyles Lewis "Bud" Saunders (1931-2010)
+1675	Nora Kathleen Sanders (1935-2000)
+1676	James Holt "Gboe" Sanders (1941-1993)

382. **James Andrew "Jim Whit" Wallace**, son of Virgil Spinks "Byrd" Wallace and Flora Ann Garner, was born on March 26, 1908 in Moore County, NC. He died on January 3, 1979 in Moore County, NC and was buried in Moore County, NC at Unity Grove Baptist Church.

Mazie Florence Maness, daughter of John Lockey Maness (1887-1973) and Mary Lee Williams (1891-1978), was born on June 11, 1912. She died on May 21, 2008 and was buried in Moore County, NC at Unity Grove Baptist Church. She and James Andrew "Jim Whit" Wallace had the following children:

+1677	Brenda Kay Wallace (1953-)
+1678	Julia Catherine Wallace (1938-2005)
+1679	Faye Lavone Wallace (1936-)
+1680	Annie Carolyn Wallace (1941-2019)
+1681	Margaret Lee Wallace (1944-)

383. **Dora Wallace**, daughter of Virgil Spinks "Byrd" Wallace and Flora Ann Garner, was born on November 3, 1910 in Moore County, NC. She died on October 18, 1915 in Moore County, NC and was buried in Moore County, NC at Virgil (Byrd) Wallace Cemetery.

384. **Millard Fillmore Wallace**, son of Virgil Spinks "Byrd" Wallace and Flora Ann Garner, was born on September 14, 1913. He married **Eula Mae Garner** on April 26, 1935 in Moore County, NC. He died on February 23, 1974 in Moore Regional Hospital, Pinehurst, Moore County, NC and was buried on February 25, 1974 in Moore County, NC at Virgil (Byrd) Wallace Cemetery.

Eula Mae Garner, daughter of William Curtis Garner (1889-1971) and Mary H. Hussey (1891-1958), was born on March 26, 1917. She died on August 6, 2011 and was buried in Robbins, Moore County, NC at Acorn Ridge Baptist Church. She and Millard Fillmore Wallace had the following children:

+1682	Paul Brackmon Wallace (1936-2009)
+1683	Daisy Lorene Wallace (1939-2018)
+1684	William Russell "Billy" Wallace (1942-2020)
+1685	Thelma Jean Wallace (1948-1948)
+1686	Sandra Mae Wallace (1952-)
+1687	Phyllis Ann Wallace (1956-)

385. **Swannie Esther Wallace**, daughter of Virgil Spinks "Byrd" Wallace and Flora Ann Garner, was born on October 1, 1916 in Moore County, NC. She died on March 20, 2001 and was buried in Siler City, Chatham County, NC at Oakley Baptist Church.

Wiley Russell Maness, son of Samuel Wiley Maness (1889-1963) and Lola Brewer (1892-1976), was born on May 3, 1920. He died on April 15, 1987 and was buried in Siler City, Chatham County, NC at Oakley Baptist Church. He and Swannie Esther Wallace had the following children:

| +1688 | Barbara Jean Maness (1946-2003) |

Grover C. McQuargin and Swannie Esther Wallace had the following children:

| +1689 | David Edward Wallace (1936-) |

Children of Virgil Spinks "Byrd" Wallace and Regina Hunsucker

[L-R] **Minnie Lee Wallace, Isham Wallace, Hattie Jane Wallace** (in lap) [Below] **Isham Wallace** *(Courtesy of Roxanne Johnson)*

[Bottom Left] **George Dock Williams and Hattie Jane Wallace**
(Courtesy of Barbara Harris)

Children of Virgil Spinks "Byrd" Wallace and Flora Ann Garner

[Above L-R] **John Lockey Maness, Cora Bell Wallace Britt, Steadman Wallace and James Andrew Wallace.** [Below Right] **Swannie Wallace Maness and daughter Barbara Jean** [Left] **James Andrew "Jim Whit" Wallace** *(Courtesy of James R. Ritter, Columbia, SC)*

James Andrew "Jim Whit" Wallace and Mazie Maness
(Courtesy of James R. Ritter, Columbia, SC)

386. **Henry Clay Wallace**, son of John M. Wallace and Candace Ellen Melton, was born on June 22, 1875 in Moore County, NC. He married **Camilla Drake Talley** on November 22, 1896 in Richmond County, NC. He died on April 29, 1938 in Sanford, Lee County, NC and was buried on May 1, 1938 in Rockingham, Richmond County, NC at Northam Cemetery.

Camilla Drake Talley was born on December 11, 1871. She died on December 21, 1955 in Richmond County, NC and was buried in Rockingham, Richmond County, NC at Northam Cemetery. She and Henry Clay Wallace had the following children:

+1690	Lonnie Wilson Wallace (1899-1958)
+1691	Henry Rufus Wallace (1905-1978)
+1692	William M. Wallace (1908-1988)
+1693	Emmett Lee Wallace (1909-1971)

387. **Byrdee Wallace**, daughter of John M. Wallace and Emma Mitchell, was born in June 1877. She died in August 1877.

388. **Phil Earnest I. Wallace**, son of John M. Wallace and Dora Laughlin, was born on June 13, 1882. He married **May Thompson** on December 27, 1901 in Conway County, AR. He died on November 1, 1956 in Chickasha, Grady County, OK.

Naomi Ester York was born in Tennessee. She and Phil Earnest I. Wallace had the following children:

+1694	Fay Dora Wallace (1906-1995)
+1695	Raymond Wallace (1916-1975)

May Thompson was born circa 1883 in AR. She and Phil Earnest I. Wallace had the following children:

+1696	Sewell Wallace (c. 1904-1932)

390. **Jessie Nancy Wallace**, daughter of John M. Wallace and Dora Laughlin, was born on August 15, 1885.

Jack McRae Harper was born in 1886. He died in 1941. He and Jessie Nancy Wallace had the following children:

+1697	Martha Jean Harper (1914-1993)

392. **Fred I. Wallace**, son of John M. Wallace and Dora Laughlin, was born on November 27, 1889 in Perryville, Perry County, AR. He married **Emma Rickman** on July 1, 1909 in Perryville, Perry County, AR. He died on June 10, 1954 in Gonzales County, TX and was buried on June 14, 1954 in Hochheim, DeWitt County, TX at Hochheim Cemetery.

Blan Rickman was born on February 11, 1898 in Perryville, Perry County, AR. She died on July 6, 1987 in Sugar Land, Fort Bend County, TX and was buried in Hochheim, DeWitt County, TX at Hochheim Cemetery. She and Fred I. Wallace had the following children:

+1698	Fred Wallace Jr. (1920-1973)

Emma Rickman was born on March 30, 1893 in Perryville, Perry County, AR. She married William Addison Garner on May 7, 1922 in Pottawatomie County, OK. She died on March 18, 1928 in Shawnee, Pottawatomie County, OK and was buried in Shawnee, Pottawatomie County, OK at Fairview Cemetery. She and Fred I. Wallace had the following children:

+1699	Thelma Dora Wallace (1910-2001)
+1700	Jessie Velma Wallace (1914-)
+1701	Georgia Baxter Wallace (1916-)

393. **Lock T. Wallace**, son of John M. Wallace and Tommie Powell, was born on December 27, 1894 in Perryville, Perry County, AR. He married **Effie Beck** on July 3, 1916 in Perry County, AR. He died in 1956 in Perryville, Perry County, AR and was buried in Perryville, Perry County, AR at Perryville Cemetery.

Effie Beck was born in 1892. She died in 1976 in Perryville, Perry County, AR and was buried in Perryville, Perry County, AR at Perryville Cemetery. She and Lock T. Wallace had the following children:

+1702	Lucille E. Wallace (1918-)
+1703	Jessie Mae Wallace (1919-)

396. **Bertram Fleet Wallace**, son of John M. Wallace and Cora Irene Reed, was born on July 16, 1900 in AR. He married **Amanda John Thompson** on December 13, 1922 in Perryville, Perry County, AR. He died on August 17, 1943 and was buried in Perryville, Perry County, AR at Perryville Cemetery.

Amanda John Thompson was born circa 1906 in AR. She and Bertram Fleet Wallace had the following children:

+1704	Johnnie Corinne Wallace (1923-)
+1705	Helen Virginia Wallace (1925-c. 1932)
+1706	Dimple Bernice Wallace (1926-)
+1707	Bertram Fleet Wallace (1929-)
+1708	Stanley Newton Orville Wallace (1933-)
+1709	Betty Maxine Wallace (1935-)
+1710	Charles Wayne Wallace (1937-)

397. **Charles Reed Wallace**, son of John M. Wallace and Cora Irene Reed, was born circa 1903 and was buried in California.

398. **Olga William Wallace**, son of John M. Wallace and Cora Irene Reed, was born circa 1905 and was buried in California.

399. **John Murriston Wallace**, son of John M. Wallace and Cora Irene Reed, was born circa 1907 and was buried in California.

400. **Martha Jane Wallace**, daughter of Hiram W. Wallace and Julia Ann Williams, was born on May 29, 1856 in Moore County, NC. She married **James M. Brown** circa 1877. She died on May 29, 1929 in Moore County, NC and was buried on June 3, 1929 in Moore County, NC at Mt. Carmel United Methodist Church.

James M. Brown, son of William Wesley Brown (1826-bef 1910) and Margaret "Peggy" Williams (1824-bef 1884), was born on April 10, 1856 in Moore County, NC. He died on June 7, 1928 in Moore County, NC and was buried on June 9, 1928 in Moore County, NC at Mt. Carmel United Methodist Church. He and Martha Jane Wallace had the following children:

+1711	Julia Maggie Brown (1878-)
+1712	Margaret Lurinda "Rindy" Brown (1879-1957)
+1713	William Thomas Brown (1885-1977)
+1714	George A. Brown (1887-1914)
+1715	Mary Blake "Molly" Brown (1891-1979)
+1716	Lillie Mae Brown (1895-1980)
+1717	Flossie Elizabeth Brown (1898-1987)

401. **Louisa Elizabeth Wallace**, daughter of Hiram W. Wallace and Julia Ann Williams, was born on April 18, 1859 in Moore County, NC. She died on March 26, 1936 in Guilford County, NC and was buried on March 29, 1936 in Guilford County, NC at Forest Lawn Cemetery.

William Henry Gordon, son of William A. Gordon (1831-) and Martha A. Sheffield (1835-1903), was born on November 29, 1857. He died on March 18, 1943 in Piedmont Hospital, Greensboro, Guilford County, NC and was buried on March 21, 1943 in Guilford County, NC at Forest Lawn Cemetery. He and Louisa Elizabeth Wallace had the following children:

+1718	Fonnie Gordon (-)
+1719	John Gordon (-)
+1720	Luther Gordon (-)
+1721	Virginia Gordon (-)
+1722	Kizzie Flowers Gordon (1879-1952)
+1723	Laura Ann Gordon (1883-1961)

+1724	Sallie Jane Gordon (1887-)
+1725	Addie Florence Gordon (1894-)
+1726	Ebell Gordon (1896-)

402. **Hiram Walker Wallace**, son of Hiram W. Wallace and Julia Ann Williams, was born on October 29, 1862 in Moore County, NC. He married **Jane Sanders** on January 6, 1881 in Moore County, NC. He died on May 29, 1938 in Rockingham, Richmond County, NC and was buried on May 30, 1938 in Rockingham, Richmond County, NC at Mizpah Church Cemetery.

Jane Sanders, daughter of Brittan Sanders (1831-1913) and Ann "Spicy" Morgan (1837-1913), was born on January 6, 1862 in Moore County, NC. She died on November 11, 1937 in Rockingham, Richmond County, NC and was buried on November 12, 1937 in Rockingham, Richmond County, NC at Mizpah Church Cemetery. She and Hiram Walker Wallace had the following children:

+1727	Hugh T. Wallace (1883-1924)
+1728	Julia Florence Wallace (1885-1965)
+1729	John C. Wallace (1887-1959)
+1730	Camilla F. Wallace (1890-)
+1731	Mary Alice Wallace (1891-1965)
+1732	Louella Wallace (1893-1978)
+1733	Ida F. Wallace (1895-1966)
+1734	Maggie Mae Wallace (1898-1966)
+1735	Maude Eva Wallace (1902-1955)
+1736	Fairley Ledbetter Wallace (1904-1915)

403. **Sarah Wallace**, daughter of Isham "Ike" Wallace and Matilda Cockman, was buried in Moore County, NC at Isham (Ike) Wallace Cemetery.

404. **Spinks Wallace**, son of Isham "Ike" Wallace and Matilda Cockman, was born on April 4, 1862. He married **Martha Ann Johnson** circa 1882. He died on August 5, 1930 and was buried in Moore County, NC at Calvary Baptist Church.

Martha Ann Johnson was born on January 17, 1864. She died on February 15, 1935 and was buried in Moore County, NC at Calvary Baptist Church. She and Spinks Wallace had the following children:

+1737	Katherine E. Wallace (1889-1953)
+1738	Ruth Jane Wallace (1889-1944)
+1739	William Lincoln Wallace (1892-1966)
+1740	Daniel Isaac Wallace (1896-1956)
+1741	Ellen Barber Wallace (1903-1975)

405. **Elias W. Wallace**, son of Isham "Ike" Wallace and Matilda Cockman, was born in August 1865 in Moore County, NC. He died on November 26, 1926 in Candor, Montgomery County, NC and was buried on November 27, 1926 in Candor, Montgomery County, NC at Macedonia Presbyterian Church.

Lydia Frances Muse, daughter of Doctor Franklin Muse (1816-1891) and Jennet\Josiah Melton (1816-1868), was born in May 1857 in Moore County, NC. She died on October 12, 1927 in Montgomery County, NC and was buried on October 13, 1927 in Candor, Montgomery County, NC at Macedonia Presbyterian Church. She and Elias W. Wallace had the following children:

+1742	Fannie C. Wallace (1885-1959)
+1743	William Lewis Wallace (1890-1951)
+1744	Laura Lee Wallace (1893-1963)
+1745	Alexander Wallace (1893-1980)
+1746	Loutishie J. Wallace (1899-)

Celie Ann McGee &
George Washington Wallace
abt. 1900

[Top Left] **Fred Wallace Sr., son of John M. Wallace and Dora Laughlin.** *(Courtesy of Cassandra Shrum).* [Top Right] **George Washington Wallace (son of John Spinks Wallace) and Celia Ann McGee** *(Courtesy of Ancestry.com user marilynadams10)* [Bottom Right] **Hiram Walker Wallace (son of Hiram W. Wallace) and Jane Sanders.** *(Courtesy of Lucy Oakes)* [Bottom Left] **Louisa Elizabeth Wallace Gordon, daughter of Hiram W. Wallace.** *(Courtesy of Betty Jo Forrest)*

406. **Malinda "Toad" Wallace**, daughter of Isham "Ike" Wallace and Matilda Cockman, was born in January 1870 and was buried in Moore County, NC at Isham (Ike) Wallace Cemetery.

Malinda "Toad" Wallace had the following children:

+1747   Torla B. "Toadie" Wallace (1888-bef 1909)

407. **Mary Wallace**, daughter of John Spinks Wallace and Nancy Olive "Ollie" Canaday, was born in 1876.

408. **Malinda A. Wallace**, daughter of John Spinks Wallace and Nancy Olive "Ollie" Canaday, was born on January 10, 1879 in Lauderdale County, AL. She married **Isaac D. Richardson** on December 9, 1898 in Lauderdale County, AL. She died on November 27, 1962 in Lauderdale County, AL and was buried in Lauderdale County, AL at Canerday Cemetery.

Isaac D. Richardson was born on January 1, 1879. He died on October 15, 1947 and was buried in Lauderdale County, AL at Canerday Cemetery. He and Malinda A. Wallace had the following children:

+1748   Ollie Leola Richardson (1899-1916)

409. **George Washington Wallace**, son of John Spinks Wallace and Nancy Olive "Ollie" Canaday, was born on November 6, 1880 in Lauderdale County, AL. He married **Celia Ann McGee** on June 2, 1900 in Lauderdale County, AL. He died on January 15, 1926 in Lauderdale County, AL and was buried in Lauderdale County, AL at Canerday Cemetery.

Celia Ann McGee was born on January 23, 1881. She died on October 19, 1965 and was buried in Lauderdale County, AL at Canerday Cemetery. She and George Washington Wallace had the following children:

+1749   Maudie Lee Wallace (1901-1901)
+1750   Ira Leland Wallace (1904-)
+1751   Ollie Irene Wallace (1907-1994)
+1752   Fletcher Alan Wallace (1910-)
+1753   Homer Wallace (1913-)
+1754   Oscar Wallace (1916-2005)
+1755   A.D. Wallace (1919-)
+1756   Ruby Wallace (1922-)
+1757   Reba Wallace (1922-)

410. **Chappel Elizabeth Wallace**, daughter of John Spinks Wallace and Nancy Olive "Ollie" Canaday, was born on November 8, 1884. She died on December 15, 1967 and was buried in Lauderdale County, AL at Canerday Cemetery.

John Wiley Jenkins, son of William B. "Sam" Jenkins (1846-1877) and Dollie Ann McGee (1855-1889), was born on August 30, 1879. He died on October 8, 1949 and was buried in Lauderdale County, AL at Canerday Cemetery. He and Chappel Elizabeth Wallace had the following children:

+1758   Gentry Wiley Jenkins (1922-1993)

411. **Thomas Evit Wallace**, son of John Spinks Wallace and Nancy Olive "Ollie" Canaday, was born on July 5, 1887 in Lauderdale County, AL. He married **Cynthia Virginia McMurtey** on February 3, 1909 in Lauderdale County, AL. He died on January 5, 1968 in Lauderdale County, AL and was buried in Lauderdale County, AL at Canerday Cemetery.

Cynthia Virginia McMurtey was born on February 21, 1884 in Lauderdale County, AL. She died on May 5, 1962 in Lauderdale County, AL. She and Thomas Evit Wallace had the following children:

+1759   John Albert Wallace (1910-)
+1760   Thomas Alvin Wallace (1910-)
+1761   Melvin Eli Wallace (1913-)
+1762   Evelyn Ann Wallace (1918-)
+1763   Mable Eunice Wallace (1921-)

418. **William W. Williams**, son of Jeremiah D. Williams and Rebecca Kizer, was born on November 6, 1846 in Georgia. He died on August 6, 1868 and was buried in Chester County, TN at Estes Cemetery.

419. **Melissa Williams**, daughter of Jeremiah D. Williams and Rebecca Kizer, was born in 1848 in Georgia. She married **Jasper M. Davis** on October 23, 1866 in McNairy County, TN.

Jasper M. Davis was born in 1841. He and Melissa Williams had the following children:

+1764   William Davis (1868-)
+1765   Mary Davis (1869-)

420. **Sarah Ann Williams**, daughter of Jeremiah D. Williams and Rebecca Kizer, was born in 1849 in Georgia. She married **Nathan Britt** on November 25, 1874 in McNairy County, TN.

Nathan Britt, son of Beacom C. Britt (1804-1876) and Deborah Wallace (1828-1897), was born in 1852.

421. **Susanna Williams**, daughter of Jeremiah D. Williams and Rebecca Kizer, was born on September 15, 1852 in Georgia. She married **Joseph Allen Nall** circa 1875. She died on November 2, 1935 in Lockney, Floyd County, TX and was buried on November 3, 1935 in Lockney, Floyd County, TX at Lockney Cemetery.

Joseph Allen Nall, son of Nicholas Nall (1812-1887) and Lydia Williamson (1821-1897), was born on October 22, 1849 in Moore County, NC. He died on July 15, 1935 in Tulia, Swisher County, TX and was buried on July 16, 1935 in Lockney, Floyd County, TX at Lockney Cemetery. He and Susanna Williams had the following children:

+1766   Lydia A. Nall (1878-1912)
+1767   Ira Lawson Nall (1880-1893)
+1768   Sarah Eveline Nall (1883-1959)
+1769   John Harding Nall (1885-1966)
+1770   Jerry Hall Nall (1891-1898)

422. **Mary J. Williams**, daughter of Jeremiah D. Williams and Rebecca Kizer, was born in 1855 in Tennessee. She married **William Birch Williams** on February 7, 1876 in McNairy County, TN.

William Birch Williams, son of Enoch Spinks Williams (1827-1894) and Rhoda Jane Morgan (1831-1898), was born on October 15, 1853 in Moore County, NC. He married Addie Comfort Sewell on August 20, 1893 in Parker County, TX. He died on August 12, 1926 in Boyd, Wise County, TX and was buried in Parker County, TX at Jaybird Cemetery. He and Mary J. Williams had the following children:

+1771   Edna Williams (1877-)

426. **Nancy Margaret Williams**, daughter of Jeremiah D. Williams and Rebecca Kizer, was born on October 3, 1864 in Tennessee. She died on December 31, 1949.

Mackay Morrison was born on June 18, 1850. He died on July 20, 1927. He and Nancy Margaret Williams had the following children:

+1772   Walter Wilson Morrison (1892-1977)

427. **Jeremiah Thomas Williams**, son of Jeremiah D. Williams and Rebecca Kizer, was born in 1868 in Tennessee. He married **Georgia Glover** on September 4, 1890 in Parker County, TX. He died between 1920 and 1930.

Georgia Glover was born in December 1874. She died between 1913 and 1920. She and Jeremiah Thomas Williams had the following children:

+1773   Oscar Williams (1893-)
+1774   Erah L. Williams (1895-)
+1775   Ivie Williams (1901-)
+1776   Pearlie Williams (1905-)

+1777	Irving Williams (1906-)
+1778	Earnest Freeman Williams (1909-)
+1779	Audie Williams (1913-)

429. **Jeremiah David Williams**, son of Enoch Spinks Williams and Rhoda Jane Morgan, was born on September 9, 1850 in Moore County, NC. He married **Samantha J. Gattis** on October 9, 1872 in McNairy County, TN. He died on August 19, 1917 in Wise County, TX and was buried in Parker County, TX at Jaybird Cemetery.

Samantha J. Gattis, daughter of W. L. Gattis (-) and Mary Davis (-), was born on February 18, 1849 in Tennessee. She died on December 7, 1930 in Boyd, Wise County, TX and was buried on December 9, 1930 in Parker County, TX at Jaybird Cemetery. She and Jeremiah David Williams had the following children:

+1780	Female Williams (-)
+1781	Ada Angeline Williams (1873-1951)
+1782	Alice Williams (1876-)
+1783	Cora D. Williams (1881-)

430. **William Birch Williams**, son of Enoch Spinks Williams and Rhoda Jane Morgan, was born on October 15, 1853 in Moore County, NC. He married **Mary J. Williams** on February 7, 1876 in McNairy County, TN. He married **Addie Comfort Sewell** on August 20, 1893 in Parker County, TX. He died on August 12, 1926 in Boyd, Wise County, TX and was buried in Parker County, TX at Jaybird Cemetery.

Mary J. Williams, daughter of Jeremiah D. Williams (1825-1906) and Rebecca Kizer (1827-1908), was born in 1855 in Tennessee. She and William Birch Williams had the following children:

+1771	Edna Williams (1877-)

Addie Comfort Sewell was born on September 3, 1871 in Montague County, TX. She died on March 18, 1954 in Springtown, Parker County, TX and was buried on March 20, 1954 in Parker County, TX at Jaybird Cemetery.

431. **Lency Elizabeth "Tennsy" Williams**, daughter of Enoch Spinks Williams and Rhoda Jane Morgan, was born on October 16, 1855 in Madison County, TN. She married **James Latham** on April 16, 1874 in McNairy County, TN.

James Latham, son of Carter Latham (1830-) and Rhoda Britt (1834-1891), was born on May 15, 1851. He died in Texas.

432. **Roda Jane Williams**, daughter of Enoch Spinks Williams and Rhoda Jane Morgan, was born on September 8, 1858 in Tennessee.

433. **Enoch L. Williams**, son of Enoch Spinks Williams and Rhoda Jane Morgan, was born in 1860 in Madison County, TN.

434. **Lorenzo Dewel "Lowe" Williams**, son of Enoch Spinks Williams and Rhoda Jane Morgan, was born on April 26, 1863 in McNairy County, TN. He died on December 29, 1942 in Springtown, Parker County, TX and was buried on December 30, 1942 in Springtown, Parker County, TX at Springtown Cemetery.

Mary E. "Mollie" Cockburn was born on April 27, 1867 in Parker County, TX. She died on September 1, 1929 in Springtown, Parker County, TX and was buried on September 1, 1929 in Springtown, Parker County, TX at Springtown Cemetery. She and Lorenzo Dewel "Lowe" Williams had the following children:

+1784	Eudora Williams (1885-1966)

435. **Mary Ann "Mollie" Williams**, daughter of Enoch Spinks Williams and Rhoda Jane Morgan, was born on November 6, 1866 in McNairy County, TN. She married **John William Medcalf** on January 5, 1888 in Parker County, TX. She died on January 17, 1962 in Cushing, OK.

John William Medcalf was born on November 23, 1866. He died on February 21, 1958. He and Mary Ann "Mollie" Williams had the following children:

+1785	Viola Marie \"Bygie\" Medcalf (1912-1979)

436. **John L. Williams**, son of Enoch Spinks Williams and Rhoda Jane Morgan, was born on August 23, 1868 in Tennessee. He married **Betty Ann Cherry** circa 1895.

Betty Ann Cherry was born in 1876. She died in 1953. She and John L. Williams had the following children:

+1786	Bula Williams (1895-)
+1787	James R. Williams (1897-)
+1788	Minnie M. Williams (1900-)
+1789	Alma V. Williams (1903-)
+1790	Carrie Williams (1905-)
+1791	Jessie L. Williams (1907-)
+1792	Carl E. Williams (1909-)

437. **Hubert Andrew Williams**, son of Enoch Spinks Williams and Rhoda Jane Morgan, was born on April 30, 1873 in Henderson, Madison County, TN. He married **Henrietta Georgia Parker** on September 8, 1901 in Marietta, Love, OK. He died on June 12, 1959 in Ardmore, Carter County, OK.

Henrietta Georgia Parker was born on November 19, 1884 in Fannin County, TX. She died on June 22, 1981 in Ardmore, Carter County, OK. She and Hubert Andrew Williams had the following children:

+1793	Mollie Williams (1902-1986)
+1794	Archie Lorenzo Williams (1905-1971)
+1795	Hardie Elisha "Boag" Williams (1907-)
+1796	Ernest Lee "Bob" Williams (1910-1981)
+1797	John Sydney Williams (1912-)
+1798	Hubert Cecil Williams (1916-2000)
+1799	Gladys Georgia Williams (1919-)
+1800	Kathryn Marie Williams (1922-)
+1801	Lela Lavella Williams (1924-)

438. **Rebecca Jane Williams**, daughter of Enoch Spinks Williams and Rhoda Jane Morgan, was born on October 4, 1875. She died on December 22, 1952.

439. **John W. Williams**, son of Lorenzo D. "Low" Williams and Sarah Elizabeth Hart, was born in July 1863 in Henderson County, TN. He married **Clarkie Ann Britt** circa 1888. He died in 1903 in Henderson County, TN and was buried in Henderson County, TN at Palestine Cemetery.

Clarkie Ann Britt, daughter of Nathaniel "Nat" Britt (1836-1871) and Amanda Jane "Mandy" Williams (1836-1907), was born in April 1872. She died in 1906 and was buried in Henderson County, TN at Palestine Cemetery. She and John W. Williams had the following children:

+1802	William T. Williams (1889-)
+1803	David J. Williams (1891-1957)
+1804	Minnie Lillian Williams (1894-1935)
+1805	John T. Williams (1897-)
+1806	Luther Anderson Williams (1899-1967)
+1807	Coy Williams (1901-1972)

440. **Nancy C. Williams**, daughter of Lorenzo D. "Low" Williams and Sarah Elizabeth Hart, was born on July 15, 1865 in Tennessee. She married **William Samuel Wallace** circa 1881. She died on September 7, 1945 in Henderson County, TN and was buried in Henderson County, TN at Palestine Cemetery.

William Samuel Wallace, son of Nathan C. Wallace (1800-1884) and Sarah (1829-bef 1870), was born on January 15, 1862 in Tennessee. He died on October 14, 1925 in Jackson, Madison County, TN and was buried on October 15, 1925 in Henderson County, TN at Palestine Cemetery. He and Nancy C. Williams had the following children:

+253	Mary Ann "Molly" Wallace (1884-1967)
+254	James Oliver "Ollie" Wallace (1888-1950)

+255	Bert Lee Wallace (1890-1982)
+256	Lummie Tanie Wallace (1891-)
+257	Ida Victoria Wallace (1895-1975)
+258	Harve D. Wallace (1900-1941)
+259	Hermin Wallace (1902-)
+260	L. Ella Wallace (1905-1932)
+261	Emerson Ethridge Wallace (1908-1936)

444. Louisa M. Williams, daughter of Lorenzo D. "Low" Williams and Sarah Elizabeth Hart, was born in February 1869.

George Britt, son of Benjamin Britt (1835-bef 1880) and Franey Wallace (1828-), was born in 1863. He died before 1900. He and Louisa M. Williams had the following children:

+1038	Ella L. "Nettie" Britt (1889-)
+1039	Mary Emma Britt (1892-)
+1040	Sarah Elizabeth "Bessie" Britt (1894-1973)
+1041	James Richard Britt (1896-1946)

446. Clarkie Ann Williams, daughter of Lorenzo D. "Low" Williams and Sarah Elizabeth Hart, was born on March 15, 1874 in Henderson County, TN. She married **William Salvage Britt** on December 17, 1894 in Henderson County, TN. She died on April 10, 1914 in Henderson County, TN and was buried on April 11, 1914 in Henderson County, TN at Palestine Cemetery.

William Salvage Britt, son of Nathaniel "Nat" Britt (1836-1871) and Amanda Jane "Mandy" Williams (1836-1907), was born on April 8, 1868 in Henderson County, TN. He died on July 6, 1951 in Henderson County, TN and was buried on July 7, 1951 in Henderson County, TN at Palestine Cemetery. He and Clarkie Ann Williams had the following children:

+1808	John Walter Britt (1894-1947)
+1809	Amanda Elvira "Mandy" Britt (1896-1966)
+1810	Luther T. Britt (1898-1917)
+1811	Lonnie Britt (1901-)
+1812	Ethel Britt (1903-)
+1813	Allie Britt (1906-)
+1814	Bertha Britt (1907-)
+1815	Guy Britt (1909-1924)
+1816	Hugh Britt (1912-)
+1817	Noah Britt (1914-)

447. Alice V. Williams, daughter of Lorenzo D. "Low" Williams and Sarah Elizabeth Hart, was born on June 1, 1875 in Henderson County, TN. She died on December 7, 1907 in Henderson County, TN.

Miles L. Wallace was born on August 24, 1874. He died on November 7, 1958 in Henderson County, TN.

448. George W. Williams, son of Lorenzo D. "Low" Williams and Sarah Elizabeth Hart, was born on January 13, 1877 in Henderson County, TN. He married **Tempie Daws** on November 11, 1897 in Henderson County, TN. He died on January 23, 1900 in Henderson County, TN and was buried in Henderson County, TN at Palestine Cemetery.

Tempie Daws was born in September 1882. She died on September 21, 1921 and was buried in Henderson County, TN at Union Grove Baptist Church.

449. David L. Williams, son of Lorenzo D. "Low" Williams and Sarah Elizabeth Hart, was born in June 1879 in Henderson County, TN. He married **Sallie** circa 1900. He died in 1924 in Henderson County, TN.

Sallie was born in 1880. She and David L. Williams had the following children:

+1818	Lula Williams (1901-)
+1819	Warne Williams (1908-)

450. **Joseph Park Williams**, son of Lorenzo D. "Low" Williams and Sarah Elizabeth Hart, was born in March 1884. He married **Maggie Horton** circa 1903. He died in 1962 and was buried in Henderson County, TN at Palestine Cemetery.

Maggie Horton was born in 1884. She died in 1963 and was buried in Henderson County, TN at Palestine Cemetery. She and Joseph Park Williams had the following children:

+1820   Flossie Ann Williams (1905-1953)
+1821   Joseph E. Williams (1907-)

451. **Florence "Retta" Britt**, daughter of Amanda Jane "Mandy" Williams, was born on June 9, 1875. She married **Joseph C. Hart** in 1897. She died on March 27, 1944.

Joseph C. Hart was born on December 27, 1871. He died on October 16, 1920. He and Florence "Retta" Britt had the following children:

+1822   Lala Lucille Hart (1904-1941)

452. **David James Britt**, son of Nathaniel "Nat" Britt and Amanda Jane "Mandy" Williams, was born on August 27, 1857 in Henderson County, TN. He married **Elvira "Kizzie" Daws** circa 1883. He died on January 8, 1953 in Henderson County, TN and was buried on January 9, 1953 in Henderson County, TN at Palestine Cemetery.

Elvira "Kizzie" Daws was born on November 8, 1857 in Tennessee. She died on June 8, 1924 and was buried in Henderson County, TN at Palestine Cemetery.

453. **Elizabeth Jane Britt**, daughter of Nathaniel "Nat" Britt and Amanda Jane "Mandy" Williams, was born in 1860 in Tennessee.

Tom Crow was born in 1860.

454. **Henry Clay Britt**, son of Nathaniel "Nat" Britt and Amanda Jane "Mandy" Williams, was born on September 26, 1862 in Henderson County, TN. He died on April 18, 1946 in Lexington, Henderson County, TN and was buried on April 19, 1946 in Lexington, Henderson County, TN at Lexington Cemetery.

Tenie Adeline Barker was born in 1870. She died in 1922. She and Henry Clay Britt had the following children:

+1823   Liston Britt (1907-1995)

455. **Thomas Jefferson Britt**, son of Nathaniel "Nat" Britt and Amanda Jane "Mandy" Williams, was born on May 3, 1865 in Henderson County, TN. He married **Mollie Ann Williams** circa 1888. He died on January 19, 1942 in Henderson County, TN and was buried in Henderson County, TN at Palestine Cemetery.

Mollie Ann Williams, daughter of James Wesley Williams (1845-) and Margaret M. Hart (1846-), was born in 1869. She died in 1962 in Henderson County, TN and was buried in Henderson County, TN at Palestine Cemetery. She and Thomas Jefferson Britt had the following children:

+1824   Lula Britt (1889-1896)
+1825   Casie Britt (1891-1894)
+1826   Murray L. Britt (1894-1918)
+1827   Margie Britt (1896-)
+1828   Millie Britt (1899-)
+1829   Elbert Anderson Britt (1904-1994)
+1830   Ruby Britt (1907-)
+1831   Wess T. Britt (1909-)

456. **William Salvage Britt**, son of Nathaniel "Nat" Britt and Amanda Jane "Mandy" Williams, was born on April 8, 1868 in Henderson County, TN. He married **Clarkie Ann Williams** on December 17, 1894 in Henderson County, TN. He died on July 6, 1951 in Henderson County, TN and was buried on July 7, 1951 in Henderson County, TN at Palestine Cemetery.

Clarkie Ann Williams, daughter of Lorenzo D. "Low" Williams (1829-1890) and Sarah Elizabeth Hart (1844-1885), was born on March 15, 1874 in Henderson County, TN. She died on April 10, 1914 in Henderson County, TN and was buried on April 11, 1914 in Henderson County, TN at Palestine Cemetery. She and William Salvage Britt had the following children:

+1808	John Walter Britt (1894-1947)	
+1809	Amanda Elvira "Mandy" Britt (1896-1966)	
+1810	Luther T. Britt (1898-1917)	
+1811	Lonnie Britt (1901-)	
+1812	Ethel Britt (1903-)	
+1813	Allie Britt (1906-)	
+1814	Bertha Britt (1907-)	
+1815	Guy Britt (1909-1924)	
+1816	Hugh Britt (1912-)	
+1817	Noah Britt (1914-)	

457. **Clarkie Ann Britt**, daughter of Nathaniel "Nat" Britt and Amanda Jane "Mandy" Williams, was born in April 1872. She married **John W. Williams** circa 1888. She died in 1906 and was buried in Henderson County, TN at Palestine Cemetery.

John W. Williams, son of Lorenzo D. "Low" Williams (1829-1890) and Sarah Elizabeth Hart (1844-1885), was born in July 1863 in Henderson County, TN. He died in 1903 in Henderson County, TN and was buried in Henderson County, TN at Palestine Cemetery. He and Clarkie Ann Britt had the following children:

+1802	William T. Williams (1889-)	
+1803	David J. Williams (1891-1957)	
+1804	Minnie Lillian Williams (1894-1935)	
+1805	John T. Williams (1897-)	
+1806	Luther Anderson Williams (1899-1967)	
+1807	Coy Williams (1901-1972)	

458. **Thomas Henry Williams**, son of David Anderson Williams and Elizabeth Ann Mosier, was born on November 4, 1863 in Madison County, TN. He died on December 18, 1918 in Chester County, TN and was buried in Chester County, TN at Estes Cemetery.

Martha A. was born on October 21, 1857. She died on October 27, 1939 and was buried in Chester County, TN at Estes Cemetery.

459. **Archibald Theodore Williams**, son of David Anderson Williams and Elizabeth Ann Mosier, was born on February 28, 1865 in Madison County, TN. He died on October 12, 1899 in Chester County, TN and was buried in Chester County, TN at Estes Cemetery.

Fronia was born in 1859. She died in 1934 and was buried in Chester County, TN at Estes Cemetery.

460. **Milissey Williams**, daughter of David Anderson Williams and Elizabeth Ann Mosier, was born on July 19, 1868 in Madison County, TN. She died on October 31, 1870 in Madison County, TN.

461. **Mary Jane Williams**, daughter of David Anderson Williams and Elizabeth Ann Mosier, was born on December 12, 1870 in Madison County, TN.

Charles W. Coleman was born in July 1866 in Alabama.

462. **Robert H. Williams**, son of David Anderson Williams and Elizabeth Ann Mosier, was born on January 10, 1873 in Madison County, TN.

463. **Susan Williams**, daughter of David Anderson Williams and Elizabeth Ann Mosier, was born on February 27, 1875 in Madison County, TN. She died on July 31, 1876 in Madison County, TN.

464. **Mollie Ann Williams**, daughter of James Wesley Williams and Margaret M. Hart, was born in 1869. She married **Thomas Jefferson Britt** circa 1888. She died in 1962 in Henderson County, TN and was buried in Henderson County, TN at Palestine Cemetery.

Thomas Jefferson Britt, son of Nathaniel "Nat" Britt (1836-1871) and Amanda Jane "Mandy" Williams (1836-1907), was born on May 3, 1865 in Henderson County, TN. He died on January 19, 1942 in Henderson County, TN and was buried in Henderson County, TN at Palestine Cemetery. He and Mollie Ann Williams had the following children:

+1824	Lula Britt (1889-1896)
+1825	Casie Britt (1891-1894)
+1826	Murray L. Britt (1894-1918)
+1827	Margie Britt (1896-)
+1828	Millie Britt (1899-)
+1829	Elbert Anderson Britt (1904-1994)
+1830	Ruby Britt (1907-)
+1831	Wess T. Britt (1909-)

465. **Ada F. Williams**, daughter of James Wesley Williams and Margaret M. Hart, was born in 1873.

466. **Martha Catherine Williams**, daughter of James Wesley Williams and Margaret M. Hart, was born on October 16, 1874. She married **William Henry Weatherington** circa 1892. She died on April 28, 1918 and was buried in Henderson County, TN at Center Hill Cemetery.

William Henry Weatherington, son of Thomas Benton Weatherington (1843-1911) and Sarah Ann "Sallie" Britt (1843-1891), was born on August 9, 1870. He died on February 11, 1955 and was buried in Henderson County, TN at Center Hill Cemetery. He and Martha Catherine Williams had the following children:

+1832	Hettie V. Weatherington (1893-1925)
+1833	Hautie A. Weatherington (1895-1985)
+1834	Dossie Benton Weatherington (1896-)
+1835	Toker Z. Weatherington (1900-1918)
+1836	Milburn Otral Weatherington (1909-1998)

467. **Lewis Cager Williams**, son of James Wesley Williams and Margaret M. Hart, was born on April 23, 1876 in Henderson County, TN. He married **Margaret Emma Weatherington** on December 26, 1896 in Chester County, TN. He died on August 28, 1909 in AR and was buried in Henderson County, TN at Palestine Cemetery.

Margaret Emma Weatherington, daughter of Thomas Benton Weatherington (1843-1911) and Sarah Ann "Sallie" Britt (1843-1891), was born on February 23, 1880. She died on October 1, 1960 in Chester County, TN and was buried in Henderson County, TN at Palestine Cemetery.

468. **Adele Williams**, daughter of James Wesley Williams and Margaret M. Hart, was born in December 1879.

469. **Dovie A. Williams**, daughter of James Wesley Williams and Margaret M. Hart, was born on October 13, 1881 in Henderson County, TN. She married **Joel B. Maness** on August 31, 1900 in Henderson County, TN. She died on July 29, 1968 and was buried in Henderson County, TN at Palestine Cemetery.

Joel B. Maness was born on August 10, 1881. He died on November 20, 1952 in Henderson County, TN and was buried in Henderson County, TN at Palestine Cemetery.

471. **Westly Tom Williams**, son of James Wesley Williams and Margaret M. Hart, was born in June 1886 in Henderson County, TN. He died in AR.

Ella Williams, daughter of Bryant Williams (1848-) and Mary Latham (1856-), was born in 1875 in Tennessee. She married William Melton on December 21, 1892 in Chester County, TN.

472. **Ella Williams**, daughter of Bryant Williams and Mary Latham, was born in 1875 in Tennessee. She married **William Melton** on December 21, 1892 in Chester County, TN.

Westly Tom Williams, son of James Wesley Williams (1845-) and Margaret M. Hart (1846-), was born in June 1886 in Henderson County, TN. He died in AR.

473. **Docey Williams**, daughter of Bryant Williams and Mary Latham, was born in July 1879 in Henderson County, TN. She married **John S. Byrd** on September 28, 1895 in Chester County, TN.

474. **Dave Williams**, son of Bryant Williams and Mary Latham, was born in 1883 in Chester County, TN. He married **Martha Emmaline Hart** circa 1904 in Henderson County, TN. He died on November 7, 1909 in Henderson County, TN and was buried in Henderson County, TN at Palestine Cemetery.

Martha Emmaline Hart, daughter of James M. Hart (1850-) and Vellera Whitenton (1849-), was born in April 1884 in Henderson County, TN. She died in 1965 in Henderson County, TN and was buried in Henderson County, TN at Palestine Cemetery. She and Dave Williams had the following children:

    +1837   Clyde Williams (1910-1989)

475. **Jerry Hubert Williams Sr.**, son of Bryant Williams and Mary Latham, was born on February 27, 1886. He married **Nona Ann Green** on July 6, 1915 in Crocket County, TN. He died on February 27, 1931 in Madison County, TN.

Nona Ann Green was born on January 10, 1896 in Crocket County, TN. She died on September 9, 1975 in Madison County, TN. She and Jerry Hubert Williams Sr. had the following children:

    +1838   Jerry Hubert Williams Jr. (1921-2001)

476. **Sarah C. Wallace**, daughter of Isaac Spinks Wallace and Anna Jane McDonald, was born in 1872.

Black and Sarah C. Wallace had the following children:

    +1839   Carson Roy Black (1904-1999)
    +1840   Myrtle Black (1906-)

477. **Ella Wallace**, daughter of Isaac Spinks Wallace and Anna Jane McDonald, was born on September 20, 1873. She married **John Angus Deaton Kennedy** on May 9, 1896 in Moore County, NC. She died on November 24, 1936 in Moore County, NC and was buried on November 26, 1936 in Moore County, NC at Old Beulah Hill Cemetery.

John Angus Deaton Kennedy, son of William Martin Kennedy (1841-1913) and Sarah Bethune Deaton (1840-1924), was born on February 9, 1868. He died on March 29, 1938 and was buried in Moore County, NC at Old Beulah Hill Cemetery. He and Ella Wallace had the following children:

    +1841   Elvira Kennedy (1903-1904)
    +1842   Bessie Sarah Kennedy (1905-1989)
    +1843   Alexander Martin Kennedy (1908-2001)
    +1844   John Deaton Kennedy (1910-2001)

478. **Archibald Alexander "Archie" Wallace**, son of Isaac Spinks Wallace and Anna Jane McDonald, was born on October 1, 1875 in Moore County, NC. He married **Mary Jane Shaw** on May 10, 1902 in Moore County, NC. He died on June 19, 1939 in Moore County, NC and was buried on June 21, 1939 in Moore County, NC at Old Beulah Hill Cemetery.

Mary Jane Shaw, daughter of James Allen "Jim" Shaw (1860-1925) and Flora Ellen Spivey (1872-1937), was born on August 14, 1885. She died on January 5, 1965 and was buried in Moore County, NC at Old Beulah Hill Cemetery. She and Archibald Alexander "Archie" Wallace had the following children:

    +1845   Charlie James Wallace (1904-1977)
    +1846   John Daniel Wallace (1906-1981)
    +1847   Lula Florence Wallace (1908-1983)
    +1848   Mary Ann Wallace (1910-1991)
    +1849   Jessie Wallace (1913-1916)
    +1850   Janie Wallace (1915-1982)
    +1851   Mack Wallace (1917-1918)

+1852	Evelyn Wallace (1919-)
+1853	George Wallace (1921-1921)
+1854	Elizabeth Wallace (1924-)
+1855	Edgar Wallace (1927-1930)

479. **James M. "Jim" Wallace**, son of Isaac Spinks Wallace and Anna Jane McDonald, was born on September 20, 1878 in Moore County, NC. He died on June 9, 1931 in Moore Regional Hospital, Pinehurst, Moore County, NC and was buried on June 10, 1931 in Moore County, NC at Culdee Presbyterian Church.

Margaret Leo Oliver and James M. "Jim" Wallace had the following children:

+1856	Beulah May Wallace (1910-1990)
+1857	Margaret Ann Wallace (1915-1931)

480. **Kenneth Martin Wallace**, son of Isaac Spinks Wallace and Anna Jane McDonald, was born on November 30, 1883 in Moore County, NC. He married **Ella May Juline Frye** on June 24, 1917 in Moore County, NC. He died on May 21, 1966 in Moore Regional Hospital, Pinehurst, Moore County, NC and was buried on May 26, 1966 in Moore County, NC at Beulah Hill Baptist Church.

Ella May Juline Frye, daughter of John M. Frye (1871-) and Lydia Ann Caddell (1873-), was born on February 20, 1900. She died on January 24, 1996 and was buried in Moore County, NC at Beulah Hill Baptist Church. She and Kenneth Martin Wallace had the following children:

+1858	Chris Hugh Wallace (1918-1973)
+1859	Aretia Mae "Rita" Wallace (1920-)
+1860	Annie Louise Wallace (1923-1942)
+1861	Mattie Frances Wallace (1925-2010)
+1862	Kenneth Charles Wallace (1927-2001)
+1863	John Edgar Wallace (1930-)
+1864	Betty Ray Wallace (1933-2006)

481. **Florence Jane Wallace**, daughter of Isaac Spinks Wallace and Anna Jane McDonald, was born in October 1888. She married **Christ Anels** on April 30, 1916 in Moore County, NC. She died in 1973.

Christ Anels, son of John Anels (-) and Annie (-), was born in 1893 in Cypress Island, Greece. He died in 1973.

482. **Mary A. E. Wallace**, daughter of Isaac Spinks Wallace and Anna Jane McDonald, was born on October 3, 1891. She died on February 8, 1893 and was buried in Moore County, NC at Old Beulah Hill Cemetery.

486. **William A. Richardson**, son of William Zeno Richardson and Martha J. Wallace, was born in August 1860.

Lila Leila Susannah Jones and William A. Richardson had the following children:

+1865	Olan Curtis Richardson (-)

489. **Noah Bazzel Richardson**, son of William Zeno Richardson and Martha J. Wallace, was born on August 5, 1868. He married **Bessie** circa 1897. He died on March 19, 1906 and was buried in Appling County, GA at Deen Cemetery.

Bessie was born in January 1869. She and Noah Bazzel Richardson had the following children:

+1866	Ethel Richardson (1897-)
+1867	Noah J. Richardson (1902-1989)

493. **Stephen O. Richardson**, son of William Zeno Richardson and Martha J. Wallace, was born in 1877. He married **Fannie E.** in 1899.

Fannie E. was born in 1878. She and Stephen O. Richardson had the following children:

+1868	Oscar A. Richardson (1900-)

+1869	Eva B. Richardson (1903-)
+1870	Zeno Ellis Richardson (1906-)
+1871	Estella Richardson (1908-)
+1872	Odessa C. Richardson (1910-)
+1873	Ernest W. Richardson (1916-)

494. **Archibald Winston Seawell**, son of Anderson Lindo Seawell and Mary Ann Wallace, was born on July 16, 1857. He married **Mary Hadley Williams** circa 1884. He died on October 1, 1928 and was buried in Moore County, NC at Bethlehem Baptist Church.

Mary Hadley Williams, daughter of Abram M. Williams (1835-bef 1867) and Sarah L. Stutts (1837-1920), was born on April 18, 1865 in Moore County, NC. She died on August 30, 1925 in Moore County, NC and was buried on August 31, 1925 in Moore County, NC at Bethlehem Baptist Church. She and Archibald Winston Seawell had the following children:

+1874	Lilly F. Seawell (1885-)
+1875	Arthur L. Seawell (1886-1907)
+1876	Flossie Lee Seawell (1888-1936)
+1877	John Quincy Seawell (1891-)
+1878	Mamie K. Seawell (1893-1945)
+1879	Fodie H. Seawell (1895-1971)
+1880	Wesley Herbert Seawell (1897-)
+1881	Hattie Seawell (1900-)
+1882	Lettie D. Seawell (1900-1910)
+1883	Efland Archie Seawell (1904-1973)

495. **Martha A. Seawell**, daughter of Anderson Lindo Seawell and Mary Ann Wallace, was born on January 15, 1859. She died on February 21, 1905 and was buried in Moore County, NC at Bethlehem Baptist Church.

496. **Sara Eliza Seawell**, daughter of Anderson Lindo Seawell and Mary Ann Wallace, was born on September 8, 1861. She died on March 30, 1880 in Moore County, NC and was buried in Moore County, NC at Bethlehem Baptist Church.

497. **John Wesley P. Seawell**, son of Anderson Lindo Seawell and Mary Ann Wallace, was born on September 22, 1862. He married **Florence Jackson** on January 12, 1888 in Moore County, NC. He married **Fannie Elizabeth Gilliam** on June 4, 1921. He died on January 27, 1936 and was buried in Moore County, NC at Bethlehem Baptist Church.

Florence Jackson, daughter of John A. Jackson (1828-1896) and Sarah Ann Currie (1843-1923), was born on March 20, 1867 in Moore County, NC. She died on July 19, 1919 in Charlotte, Mecklenburg County, NC and was buried on July 20, 1919 in Moore County, NC at Bethlehem Baptist Church. She and John Wesley P. Seawell had the following children:

+1884	J. Clinton Seawell (1889-)
+1885	Gladys Gertrude Seawell (1891-1958)
+1886	Cecil Ann Seawell (1895-)
+1887	Bertie E. Seawell (1897-)
+1888	Geneva Jackson Seawell (1901-)
+1889	Mary Robert Seawell (1905-)
+1890	Hubert Wesley Seawell (1907-)
+1891	Ester Florence Seawell (1911-1959)

Fannie Elizabeth Gilliam was born on November 28, 1875.

498. **Henry Alexander Maness**, son of Henry Maness and Rebecca Jane Wallace, was born on June 10, 1865. He married **Julie Ann Johnson** circa 1888. He died on September 18, 1949 in Biscoe, Montgomery County, NC and was buried in Biscoe, Montgomery County, NC at Biscoe Cemetery.

Julie Ann Johnson was born on June 11, 1873. She died on December 11, 1970 in Biscoe, Montgomery County, NC and was buried in Biscoe, Montgomery County, NC at Biscoe Cemetery. She and Henry Alexander Maness had the following children:

+1892	Lillie D. Maness (1896-1952)
+1893	Dillian Ruffin "Dill" Maness (1898-1974)
+1894	David Willie Maness (1902-1956)
+1895	Henry Harris Maness (1903-1971)
+1896	Mary Ellen Maness (1905-1984)
+1897	Howard Taft Maness (1908-1965)
+1898	Robert Paige Maness (1910-1966)

499. **Christopher Columbus Maness**, son of Henry Maness and Rebecca Jane Wallace, was born on October 4, 1870. He married **Jennie Ervin** on May 5, 1892 in Cabarrus County, NC. He died on November 6, 1958 in Statesville, Iredell County, NC and was buried in Mooresville, Iredell County, NC at Rocky Mount United Methodist Church.

Jennie Ervin and Christopher Columbus Maness had the following children:

+1899	Carl Samuel Maness (1893-1982)
+1900	Cora Lee Maness (1896-1974)
+1901	Marshall M. Maness (1905-1967)

500. **Julia Ann Maness**, daughter of Henry Maness and Rebecca Jane Wallace, was born on July 4, 1871 in Montgomery County, NC. She married **Adam Jackson Pinion** on November 26, 1888 in Troy, Montgomery County, NC. She died on May 4, 1946 in Troy, Montgomery County, NC and was buried in Troy, Montgomery County, NC at Mt. Olivet Methodist Church.

Adam Jackson Pinion and Julia Ann Maness had the following children:

+1902	Maggie J. Pinion (1889-)
+1903	John S. Pinion (1891-bef 1910)
+1904	James C. Pinion (1893-bef 1910)
+1905	Lou Ella Pinion (1894-1971)
+1906	Dorothy Pinion (1898-)
+1907	Dossie Franklin Pinion (1900-)
+1908	Theodore Pinion (c. 1904-)
+1909	Mary Elizabeth Pinion (1906-1992)
+1910	Mittie Beulah Pinion (1908-)

501. **Martha L. "Mattie" Maness**, daughter of Henry Maness and Rebecca Jane Wallace, was born on March 4, 1873. She married **William Henry Kellis** on February 15, 1891 in Troy, Montgomery County, NC. She died on December 3, 1899.

William Henry Kellis was born on December 8, 1870. He died on January 10, 1938. He and Martha L. "Mattie" Maness had the following children:

+1911	Robert Lee Kellis (1898-1977)

502. **George W. Maness**, son of Henry Maness and Rebecca Jane Wallace, was born on January 5, 1874 in Montgomery County, NC. He married **Elizabeth J. Pinion** on December 16, 1894 in Troy, Montgomery County, NC. He married **M. Eliza Hicks** on October 7, 1922. He died on August 6, 1948 in Biscoe, Montgomery County, NC and was buried on August 7, 1948 in Troy, Montgomery County, NC at Mt. Carmel Baptist Church.

Elizabeth J. Pinion and George W. Maness had the following children:

+1912	Ellis Guy Maness Sr. (1894-1963)
+1913	Mary M. Maness (1897-)
+1914	Bertie E. Maness (1899-1902)
+1915	Gladys Ethel Maness (1911-)

503. **William Wesley Wallace**, son of John Mack Wallace and Martha Ann Brown, was born on August 27, 1869 in Moore County, NC. He married **Ira Lee "Arlee" Cockman** on December 20, 1891. He died on September 5, 1929 in

Cumberland County, NC and was buried on September 7, 1929 in Hope Mills, Cumberland County, NC at Big Rockfish Presbyterian Cemetery.

Ira Lee "Arlee" Cockman, daughter of William McSwain Cockman (1842-1906) and Julia Ann Cagle (1842-1917), was born on May 24, 1873. She died on March 8, 1960 in Cumberland County, NC and was buried on March 10, 1960 in Hope Mills, Cumberland County, NC at Big Rockfish Presbyterian Cemetery. She and William Wesley Wallace had the following children:

+1916	William Roscoe Wallace (1894-)
+1917	Rupert Oliver Wallace (1896-1969)
+1918	Robert D. Wallace (1896-1897)
+1919	John Mack Wallace II (1898-1955)
+1920	Dewey Edgar Wallace (1900-1936)
+1921	Bessie Wallace (1904-1904)
+1922	Glenna Velma Wallace (1905-2001)
+1923	Theodore Wesley Wallace (1908-)
+1924	Lillian Gertrude Wallace (1912-)
+1925	Ruby Pearl Wallace (1915-)
+1926	James Franklin Wallace (1918-)

504. **Mary Blake Wallace**, daughter of John Mack Wallace and Martha Ann Brown, was born on October 6, 1871 in Moore County, NC. She married **George Washington Williams** on May 22, 1920 in Durham, Durham County, NC. She died on February 16, 1939 and was buried in Durham, Durham County, NC at Maplewood Cemetery.

William Judson Coleman was born on August 17, 1853 in Sampson County, NC. He died on February 2, 1920 in Durham County, NC. He and Mary Blake Wallace had the following children:

+1927	Lydia Coleman (-)
+1928	Annie Douglas Coleman (1900-)
+1929	Maggie P. Coleman (1903-)
+1930	Benjamin Franklin Coleman (1905-)
+1931	Willie May Coleman (1906-1938)
+1932	Luther Judson Coleman (1908-)
+1933	Ruth F. Coleman (1910-)

Isaac W. Rose, son of Henry Rose (1819-) and Catherine (1825-), was born in 1859. He died on July 6, 1896. He and Mary Blake Wallace had the following children:

+1934	John Wesley Rose (1892-1970)
+1935	Charles Anderson James Fox Rose (1896-1943)

George Washington Williams was born in 1861. He died on March 30, 1952 and was buried in Durham, Durham County, NC at Maplewood Cemetery.

505. **Henry Lee Wallace**, son of John Mack Wallace and Martha Ann Brown, was born on September 7, 1873 in Moore County, NC. He married **Della Adelaide Horne** on June 19, 1895 in Cumberland County, NC. He married **Lula Smith** on October 31, 1950 in Cumberland County, NC. He died on May 24, 1953 in Fayetteville, Cumberland County, NC and was buried on May 26, 1953 in Cumberland County, NC at Judson Baptist Church.

Della Adelaide Horne, daughter of John Horn (-) and Mary McDaniel (-), was born on March 29, 1876 in Cumberland County, NC. She died on June 29, 1949 in Durham, Durham County, NC and was buried on July 1, 1949 in Cumberland County, NC at Judson Baptist Church. She and Henry Lee Wallace had the following children:

+1936	John Lee Wallace (1896-1957)
+1937	Lester Mack Wallace (1898-1970)
+1938	Nellie Maggie Wallace (1900-1959)
+1939	Carl Clevin Wallace (1902-1994)
+1940	Jasper Conley Wallace (1904-1980)
+1941	Flavius A. Wallace (1906-1999)

+1942	Luther Edward Wallace (1909-1962)
+1943	Henry Clayton Wallace (1911-1977)
+1944	Polly Ruth Wallace (1912-1994)
+1945	Etta Mae Wallace (1915-1915)
+1946	Maxine Naomi Wallace (1917-)
+1947	Esther Della Wallace (1920-1986)

506. **John Robert Wallace**, son of John Mack Wallace and Martha Ann Brown, was born on September 7, 1873 in Moore County, NC. He married **Minnie J. Hair** on June 18, 1893 in Cumberland County, NC. He married **Nora Bell Brady** on February 24, 1900 in Cumberland County, NC. He married **Pauline Victoria Tew** on July 4, 1909 in Cumberland County, NC. He died on December 17, 1930 in Durham, Durham County, NC and was buried on December 18, 1930 in Durham, Durham County, NC at Maplewood Cemetery.

Minnie J. Hair was born in 1876 in Bladen County, NC. She and John Robert Wallace had the following children:

| +1948 | Joseph Garland Wallace (1896-) |

Nora Bell Brady, daughter of Charles Underwood Brady (1844-1935) and Elizabeth E. Moore (1854-1906), was born on October 9, 1877. She died on October 16, 1908 and was buried in High Falls, Moore County, NC at Prosperity Friends Meeting Cemetery. She and John Robert Wallace had the following children:

+1949	Nellie Ann Wallace (-)
+1950	Bessie Lee Wallace (-)
+1951	Dewey Winfred (Wallace) Lambert (-)

Pauline Victoria Tew was born on April 20, 1873 in Sampson County, NC. She died on August 24, 1957 in Durham, Durham County, NC. She and John Robert Wallace had the following children:

| +1952 | John Lucian Wallace (1910-1977) |
| +1953 | Cecil Ernest Wallace (1912-1965) |

507. **Margaret Rosetta Wallace**, daughter of John Mack Wallace and Martha Ann Brown, was born in May 1875 in Moore County, NC. She married **Charles Chalmers Wallace** on September 22, 1895 in Cumberland County, NC. She married **Walter Jackson Yates** on October 14, 1933 in Caswell County, NC. She died on July 30, 1948 and was buried in Durham, Durham County, NC at Maplewood Cemetery.

Charles Chalmers Wallace, son of Everett W. Wallace (1837-1916) and Nancy Lett (1843-), was born on September 30, 1869 in Moore County, NC. He died on April 26, 1930 in Durham, Durham County, NC and was buried on April 27, 1930 in Durham, Durham County, NC at Cedar Hill Cemetery. He and Margaret Rosetta Wallace had the following children:

+1954	James Fletcher Wallace (1898-1979)
+1955	Daisy Mae Wallace (1901-1985)
+1956	Lelia Georgia Wallace (1903-1997)
+1957	Lawrence Craven Wallace (1905-1987)
+1958	Alvin Vernon Wallace (1908-1983)
+1959	Forrest Lee Wallace (1912-1982)

Walter Jackson Yates was born on December 25, 1878. He died on December 25, 1955 and was buried in Durham, Durham County, NC at Maplewood Cemetery.

508. **Martha Ann Wallace**, daughter of John Mack Wallace and Martha Ann Brown, was born on October 10, 1880 in Moore County, NC. She married **Charlie Fletcher Wrenn** on April 10, 1898 in Cumberland County, NC. She died on March 10, 1924 in Cumberland County, NC.

Charlie Fletcher Wrenn was born on May 14, 1872 in Liberty, Randolph County, NC. He and Martha Ann Wallace had the following children:

| +1960 | Lula May Wrenn (1899-) |

+1961	Nora B. Wrenn (1900-)
+1962	Bessie L. Wrenn (1903-1979)
+1963	Mamie E. Wrenn (1905-)
+1964	Lillian Bertrude Wrenn (1907-2000)
+1965	Wilma Nevada Wrenn (1910-)
+1966	Ruby Juanita Wrenn (1912-)
+1967	James Fletcher Wrenn (1914-1917)
+1968	Edna Elvira Wrenn (1917-1990)
+1969	Charlie Fletcher Wrenn Jr. (1919-)

509. **Mianna J. "Annie" Wallace**, daughter of John Mack Wallace and Martha Ann Brown, was born on May 15, 1883 in Moore County, NC. She married **Franklin J. Warner** on December 24, 1899 in Cumberland County, NC. She died on June 22, 1960 and was buried in Danville, VA at Mountain View Cemetery.

Franklin J. Warner was born on April 26, 1878. He died on September 16, 1952 and was buried in Danville, VA at Mountain View Cemetery.

510. **Charles Mack Wallace**, son of John Mack Wallace and Martha Ann Brown, was born on May 13, 1886 in Moore County, NC. He married **Lula Ellen McKinney** on April 2, 1905 in Cumberland County, NC. He died on November 6, 1966 in Fayetteville, Cumberland County, NC and was buried on November 8, 1966 in Fayetteville, Cumberland County, NC at Lafayette Memorial Park.

Gertrude Pully was born on September 30, 1912. She died on January 7, 1995 in Rural Retreat, VA. She and Charles Mack Wallace had the following children:

| +1970 | Margaret Maxine Wallace (1929-) |

Lula Ellen McKinney, daughter of John Albert McKinney (1867-1943) and Margaret Jane Biggs (1868-1947), was born on June 30, 1889 in Robeson County, NC. She died on August 12, 1984 in McLean, VA. She and Charles Mack Wallace had the following children:

+1971	Thelma Lorraine Wallace (-)
+1972	Vivian Alma Wallace (1906-1998)
+1973	Oliver Lacy Wallace (1908-1995)
+1974	Albert Mack Wallace (1911-1992)
+1975	Margaret Louise Wallace (1914-1955)
+1976	Clyde Leroy Wallace (1916-1971)
+1977	Doris Ruth Wallace (1919-2011)
+1978	Pauline Wallace (1921-1923)
+1979	Charles Kenneth Wallace (1922-2011)
+1980	Iris Natalie Wallace (1925-2007)
+1981	Infant Wallace (1926-1926)
+1982	Arthur Clifton Wallace (1927-1927)

511. **Sarah Elizabeth Wallace**, daughter of John Mack Wallace and Martha Ann Brown, was born on August 17, 1888 in Moore County, NC. She married **Luther Regan** on November 20, 1904 in Cumberland County, NC. She died on April 6, 1992 in Durham, Durham County, NC and was buried in Durham, Durham County, NC at Maplewood Cemetery.

512. **George W. Wallace**, son of John Mack Wallace and Martha Ann Brown, was born on May 15, 1892. He died on October 22, 1893 and was buried in Hope Mills, Cumberland County, NC at Big Rockfish Presbyterian Cemetery.

513. **Harriet Wallace**, daughter of John Mack Wallace and Parthenia Gibsie Bass, was born on October 12, 1905 in Fayetteville, Cumberland County, NC. She married **William James Grice** on July 8, 1922. She died on February 9, 1997 in Fayetteville, Cumberland County, NC.

William James Grice was born on August 30, 1904. He died on March 13, 1936 in Fayetteville, Cumberland County, NC. He and Harriet Wallace had the following children:

| +1983 | Lela Mae Grice (1923-) |

+1984	Mabel Agnes Grice (1925-)
+1985	Virginia Fay Grice (1926-2000)
+1986	Myrtle Marie Grice (1928-)
+1987	William Lloyd Grice (1929-1930)

Walter C. Whitfield died on July 7, 1985 in Fayetteville, Cumberland County, NC.

514. **Tishi Evelyn Wallace**, daughter of John Mack Wallace and Parthenia Gibsie Bass, was born on June 30, 1907 in Cumberland County, NC. She married **Charles Gentry Dees** on September 2, 1922 in Dillon, Dillon County, SC. She died on December 3, 2003.

Charles Gentry Dees was born on April 18, 1905 in Cumberland County, NC. He died on June 18, 1988 in Fayetteville, Cumberland County, NC. He and Tishi Evelyn Wallace had the following children:

+1988	Charles Gentry Dees Jr. (-)
+1989	Edith Frances Dees (-)
+1990	Edith Frances Dees (1923-)
+1991	Charles Gentry Dees Jr. (1926-)
+1992	Glenn Dees (1927-1929)
+1993	Edna Maxine Dees (1929-)
+1994	Robert Grant Dees (1931-1996)
+1995	Ida Jean Dees (1933-)
+1996	Hilda Gibsie Dees (1934-)
+1997	Martha Carleen Dees (1940-)

515. **Walter Watson Wallace**, son of John Mack Wallace and Parthenia Gibsie Bass, was born on December 28, 1909 in Cumberland County, NC. He married **Lillian Parker** on February 27, 1928 in Cumberland County, NC. He married **Edith Clifton** on August 29, 1936 in Cumberland County, NC. He married **Helen Carter** on February 5, 1939 in Cumberland County, NC. He died on December 4, 1995.

Lillian Parker was born in 1910. She died on March 10, 1935. She and Walter Watson Wallace had the following children:

+1998	Atha Lee Wallace (-)
+1999	Joyce Wallace (-)
+2000	Leigh Wallace (-)
+2001	stillborn (1929-)
+2002	Robert Wallace (1931-1931)
+2003	Evelyn Joyce Wallace (1932-)
+2004	Oscar Lloyd Wallace (1933-)
+2005	Male Wallace (1935-1935)

Edith Clifton and Walter Watson Wallace had the following children:

| +2006 | Alice Roberta Wallace (1936-) |

516. **James Madison Wallace**, son of John Mack Wallace and Parthenia Gibsie Bass, was born on December 21, 1911 in Cumberland County, NC. He married **Donnie Rachel Noble** on March 26, 1932 in Fayetteville, Cumberland County, NC. He died on June 8, 1992.

Donnie Rachel Noble was born on September 10, 1912 in Goldsboro, Wayne County, NC. She died on April 10, 1966. She and James Madison Wallace had the following children:

+2007	Jewell Marie Wallace (1933-2003)
+2008	James Madison "Billy Mack" Wallace Jr. (1934-)
+2009	Dwight Thomas Wallace (1944-)

517. **Lillie Al Rhoney Wallace**, daughter of John Mack Wallace and Parthenia Gibsie Bass, was born on July 13, 1914 in Cumberland County, NC. She married **Ray Thurman Collins** on August 23, 1930 in Dillon, Dillon County, SC. She died on September 21, 1993 in Fayetteville, Cumberland County, NC.

Ray Thurman Collins was born on December 20, 1910 in Verona, Onslow, NC. He died on March 28, 1997 in Fayetteville, Cumberland County, NC. He and Lillie Al Rhoney Wallace had the following children:

+2010	Elsie Vernell Collins (1931-)
+2011	Ray Thurman Collins Jr. (1934-1985)
+2012	George Wayne Collins (1944-1980)
+2013	Linda Sue Collins (1947-)

518. **Sallie Adelaide Wallace**, daughter of John Mack Wallace and Parthenia Gibsie Bass, was born on January 1, 1917 in Linden, Cumberland County, NC. She married **Nathan Joy Cannon** on June 9, 1930 in Dillon, Dillon County, SC. She died on October 9, 2003 in Fayetteville, Cumberland County, NC and was buried in Fayetteville, Cumberland County, NC at Cumberland Memorial Gardens.

Nathan Joy Cannon was born on April 1, 1911 in Lake City, SC. He died on August 23, 1988 in Fayetteville, Cumberland County, NC and was buried in Fayetteville, Cumberland County, NC at Cumberland Memorial Gardens. He and Sallie Adelaide Wallace had the following children:

+2014	Patricia Ann Cannon (1935-)
+2015	Juanita Rhea Cannon (1936-1988)
+2016	Gwendolyn Hope Cannon (1938-1996)
+2017	Nathan Joy Cannon Jr. (1940-2005)
+2018	Brenda Carol Cannon (1941-2015)
+2019	Mary Angela Cannon (1944-)
+2020	Marie Elaina Cannon (1945-2006)
+2021	Timothy Mackins Cannon (1947-)

519. **Mary Ann Maness**, daughter of Marshal G. Maness and Julia Frances Wallace, was born in November 1867. She married **George Rufus Brown** circa 1880. She died on September 16, 1942 and was buried in Linden, Cumberland County, NC at Collier's Chapel Church.

George Rufus Brown, son of William Wesley Brown (1837-1906) and Loretta T. Hunsucker (1842-1916), was born on February 4, 1862 in Moore County, NC. He died on January 3, 1944 in Cumberland County, NC and was buried on January 4, 1944 in Linden, Cumberland County, NC at Collier's Chapel Church. He and Mary Ann Maness had the following children:

+2022	George W. Brown (1886-1947)
+2023	Charles Worthy Brown (1888-1942)
+2024	William Walter Brown (1890-1964)
+2025	Hattie J. Brown (1890-)
+2026	Florence Camellia Brown (1894-1974)
+2027	James Curtis Brown (1895-1972)
+2028	Cindy Brown (1898-)
+2029	Maggie Brown (1900-)
+2030	Donnie Carson Brown (1901-1982)
+2031	Bertha Loretta Brown (1906-1958)
+2032	Swannie Brown (1909-)
+2033	Floyd Rufus Brown (1912-)

520. **Rebecca Jane Maness**, daughter of Marshal G. Maness and Julia Frances Wallace, was born on September 23, 1869. She married **Malcolm Street Rouse** on August 25, 1889 in Moore County, NC. She died on September 30, 1951 in Moore County, NC and was buried on October 2, 1951 in Robbins, Moore County, NC at Tabernacle United Methodist Church.

Malcolm Street Rouse, son of Enoch Rouse (1833-1905) and Deborah Richardson (1840-), was born in August 1871. He died in 1948 and was buried in Robbins, Moore County, NC at Tabernacle United Methodist Church. He and Rebecca Jane Maness had the following children:

+2034   Ida Louise Rouse (1890-1894)
+2035   Dora F. Rouse (1891-1984)
+2036   Effie Jane Rouse (1893-1941)
+2037   Willie Marshall Rouse (1896-1966)
+2038   Harrison G. Rouse (1898-1914)
+2039   Dewey Hobson Rouse (1901-1975)
+2040   Hurley Lee Rouse (1904-1986)
+2041   Grady Worthy Rouse (1907-1982)
+2042   Pearl Lillian Rouse (1909-1970)
+2043   Stella Rouse (1913-)

Fifth Generation

521. **James R. Maness**, son of James Abel Maness and Deborah Eliza "Debby" Brown, was born in 1856. He died before 1900.

Emily B. Lambert, daughter of Daniel Lambert (1821-) and Elizabeth Maness (1819-), was born on February 24, 1860. She died on May 16, 1933 and was buried in Robbins, Moore County, NC at Tabernacle United Methodist Church. She and James R. Maness had the following children:

2044   Eli Bray Maness (1877-1953). *Eli was born on March 30, 1877. He married **Cary Alice Garner** on December 21, 1898 in Moore County, NC. He died on May 30, 1953 and was buried in Randolph County, NC at Beulah Baptist Church.*

2045   William A. Maness (1878-1925). *William was born on December 27, 1878 in Moore County, NC. He died on March 13, 1925 in Greensboro, Guilford County, NC and was buried on March 15, 1925 in Moore County, NC at Flint Hill Baptist Church.*

2046   Jenette Green Maness (1883-1939). *Jenette was born on June 15, 1883. She married **Noah Wesley Cockman** on September 23, 1905 in Moore County, NC. She died on March 10, 1939 and was buried in Robbins, Moore County, NC at Tabernacle United Methodist Church.*

523. **Jonah Baxter Maness**, son of James Abel Maness and Deborah Eliza "Debby" Brown, was born on February 15, 1870. He married **Alice Susannah Cockman** on February 10, 1899. He died on August 21, 1961 and was buried in Moore County, NC at Flint Hill Baptist Church.

Alice Susannah Cockman, daughter of J. Sampson Cockman (1819-1909) and Elizabeth Wallace (1825-1871), was born on September 11, 1863. She died on December 20, 1949 and was buried in Moore County, NC at Flint Hill Baptist Church. She and Jonah Baxter Maness had the following children:

2047   William Maness (1901-). *William was born in 1901.*

2048   James Laborn Maness (1902-1982). *James was born on February 22, 1902. He died on March 31, 1982 and was buried in Moore County, NC at Pleasant Hill United Methodist Church.*

2049   Arthur Edmund Maness (1903-1989). *Arthur was born on April 2, 1903. He died on November 14, 1989 and was buried in Robbins, Moore County, NC at Acorn Ridge Baptist Church.*

2050   Kenny Cassidy Maness (1905-1981). *Kenny was born on April 10, 1905. He married **Lydia Annie Wallace** on October 1, 1932. He died on March 8, 1981 and was buried in Moore County, NC at Virgil (Byrd) Wallace Cemetery.*

2051   Rosa Maggie Maness (1907-1962). *Rosa was born on July 17, 1907 in Moore County, NC. She married **Presley Parker Floyd** on April 16, 1960 in Davidson County, NC. She died on April 4, 1962 in Winston-Salem, Forsyth County, NC and was buried in Asheboro, Randolph County, NC at Pleasant Cross Christian Church.*

529. Robert Newton Dixon Jr., son of Robert Newton Dixon and Martha "Polly" Maness, was born in 1868. He married **Agnes Louisa Davis** on December 24, 1890 in Moore County, NC.

Agnes Louisa Davis, daughter of Archibald McNeill Davis (1819-1879) and Lucinda King (1836-1932), was born in 1871.

533. Emma Ellen Dixon, daughter of Robert Newton Dixon and Martha "Polly" Maness, was born on December 14, 1876. She married **William Garner** on November 19, 1896. She married **John Thomas Chriscoe** on June 3, 1906 in Randolph County, NC. She died on September 27, 1963 and was buried in Seagrove, Randolph County, NC at New Center Christian Church.

William Garner, son of Peter Garner (1783-aft 1860) and Elizabeth "Betsy" Morgan (1790-), was born in September 1829. He married Dolly Ann Williamson on August 7, 1855 in Randolph County, NC. He died in August 1905. He and Emma Ellen Dixon had the following children:

2052	Julian Zebulon Garner (1897-1973). *Julian was born on December 2, 1897. He died on September 2, 1973 and was buried in Seagrove, Randolph County, NC at New Center Christian Church.*
2053	Leonard Garner (1900-). *Leonard was born on May 19, 1900.*

John Thomas Chriscoe was born in 1860. He and Emma Ellen Dixon had the following children:

2054	Marvin Hoyette Chriscoe (1907-). *Marvin was born on February 17, 1907.*
2055	John Lester Chriscoe (1915-). *John was born on June 19, 1915.*

541. Rev. Troy Everett Maness, son of Jonas Sedberry Maness and Rosanna Pearl Boroughs, was born on December 5, 1881. He died on July 19, 1967.

Sarah Jane Gowens was born on May 7, 1883. She died in February 1961. She and Troy Everett Maness had the following children:

2056	Raymond Luther Maness (1917-1973). *Raymond was born on May 29, 1917. He died on January 8, 1973.*

542. Sarah Elizabeth Maness, daughter of Alexander Spinks Maness and Mary Elizabeth Riddle, was born on September 6, 1877. She married **John H. Kennedy** on July 20, 1894 in Moore County, NC. She died on April 23, 1954.

John H. Kennedy, son of Duncan Kennedy (1848-1927) and Elizabeth F. Maness (1853-1930), was born on March 20, 1873. He died on October 14, 1950. He and Sarah Elizabeth Maness had the following children:

2057	Herman Kennedy (-)
2058	Ollie Kennedy (-)
2059	Ralph Kennedy (-)
2060	Ernest Kennedy (-)
2061	John H. Kennedy Jr. (-)
2062	Dorothy Kennedy (-)
2063	Harvey Kennedy (1899-1989). *Harvey was born in 1899. He died in October 1989 in Lee County, NC.*

543. Annie Mae Maness, daughter of Presley Wright Maness and Martha Jane Riddle, was born on January 6, 1875. She married **Reuben Addison Maness** on October 18, 1890 in Moore County, NC. She died on August 8, 1942 and was buried in Moore County, NC at Pleasant Hill United Methodist Church.

Reuben Addison Maness, son of Thomas P. Maness (1834-1900) and Mary Eliza Stewart (1845-1897), was born on August 6, 1865. He married Louella Brown Bullington in 1943. He married Jane Parsons on July 24, 1946 in Moore County, NC. He died on May 1, 1953 and was buried in Moore County, NC at Pleasant Hill United Methodist Church. He and Annie Mae Maness had the following children:

2064	Annie Katie Maness (1891-1932). *Annie was born on September 16, 1891. She died on*

November 13, 1932 and was buried in Moore County, NC at Pleasant Hill United Methodist Church.

2065	Clinton Bevin Maness (1892-1987). *Clinton was born on November 9, 1892. He died on January 12, 1987 and was buried in Moore County, NC at Pleasant Hill United Methodist Church.*
2066	Frank H. Maness (1895-1955). *Frank was born on July 1, 1895. He died on March 9, 1955 and was buried in Troy, Montgomery County, NC at Lovejoy Methodist Church.*
2067	John Hobart Maness (1897-1986). *John was born on March 29, 1897. He died on March 12, 1986 and was buried in Moore County, NC at Pleasant Hill United Methodist Church.*
2068	Quincy Addison Maness (1899-1993). *Quincy was born on September 1, 1899. He died on February 2, 1993 and was buried in Moore County, NC at Pleasant Hill United Methodist Church.*
2069	Mary E. Maness (1901-1919). *Mary was born on August 16, 1901. She died on March 29, 1919 and was buried in Moore County, NC at Pleasant Hill United Methodist Church.*
2070	Martha L. Maness (1903-1975). *Martha was born on August 27, 1903. She died on October 27, 1975 and was buried in Asheboro, Randolph County, NC at Randolph Memorial Park.*
2071	Dewey Wright Maness (1905-1967). *Dewey was born on June 22, 1905. He died on December 26, 1967 and was buried in Moore County, NC at Pleasant Hill United Methodist Church.*
2072	Coble Maie Maness (1907-1969). *Coble was born on May 26, 1907 in Moore County, NC. He married **Lillie Viola Wallace** on January 24, 1925. He died on September 14, 1969 in Asheboro, Randolph County, NC and was buried in Moore County, NC at Pleasant Hill United Methodist Church.*
2073	Thurman Dosson Maness (1909-2010). *Thurman was born on July 27, 1909. He married **Verdia Lee Wallace** on February 26, 1937 in Moore County, NC. He died on August 8, 2010 in St. Joseph of Pines Hospital, Pinehurst, Moore County, NC.*
2074	Annie Tonie Maness (1912-2005). *Annie was born on January 30, 1912. She died on January 17, 2005 and was buried in Robbins, Moore County, NC at Acorn Ridge Baptist Church.*
2075	McClellan "Mack" Maness (1915-1988). *McClellan was born on January 23, 1915. He died on December 10, 1988 and was buried in Bennett, Chatham County, NC at Fall Creek Baptist Church Cemetery.*
2076	Rency Hurdle Maness (1918-1993). *Rency was born on April 3, 1918. He died on October 5, 1993 and was buried in Moore County, NC at Pleasant Hill United Methodist Church.*

544. **Mintie G. Maness**, daughter of Presley Wright Maness and Martha Jane Riddle, was born in 1877. She married **William James "Willie" Williams** on March 18, 1897 in Moore County, NC. She died in 1905 and was buried in Moore County, NC at Pleasant Hill United Methodist Church.

William James "Willie" Williams, son of Matthew Bryant Williams (1818-1885) and Elizabeth C. Stutts (1825-1896), was born in 1858. He died in 1940 and was buried in Moore County, NC at Pleasant Hill United Methodist Church. He and Mintie G. Maness had the following children:

2077	Annie J. Williams (1898-1985). *Annie was born on January 25, 1898. She died on April 16, 1985 and was buried in Robbins, Moore County, NC at Acorn Ridge Baptist Church.*
2078	Mary H. Williams (1899-). *Mary was born in May 1899.*
2079	William Ernest Williams (1902-1996). *William was born on March 6, 1902. He died on May 20, 1996 and was buried in Moore County, NC at Brown's Chapel Christian Church.*
2080	Maggie Lueola Williams (1904-1962). *Maggie was born on April 29, 1904. She married **Lloyd Ritter** on January 9, 1923 in Moore County, NC. She died on May 18, 1962 and was buried in Asheboro, Randolph County, NC at Randolph Memorial Park.*

545. **William Right Maness**, son of Presley Wright Maness and Martha Jane Riddle, was born on September 9, 1879. He died on October 21, 1964 in Randolph County, NC and was buried in Ramseur, Randolph County, NC at First Christian Church AKA Sunset Knoll Cemetery.

Loveday Elizabeth Jordan, daughter of Martha Jane Jordan (1851-), was born on February 22, 1882. She died on November 17, 1966 in Randolph County, NC and was buried in Ramseur, Randolph County, NC at First Christian Church AKA Sunset Knoll Cemetery. She and William Right Maness had the following children:

> 2081   Jesse Walton Maness (-)

546. **John Spinks Maness**, son of Presley Wright Maness and Martha Jane Riddle, was born on February 7, 1883. He died on February 25, 1965 and was buried in Moore County, NC at Pleasant Hill United Methodist Church.

Maggie Loretta Reynolds, daughter of Elijah Reynolds (1835-1914) and Martha Jane Williams (1850-1917), was born on July 22, 1893. She died on December 14, 1983 and was buried in Moore County, NC at Pleasant Hill United Methodist Church. She and John Spinks Maness had the following children:

> 2082   Bessie Maness (1917-1918). *Bessie was born on October 23, 1917. She died on March 14, 1918 and was buried in Moore County, NC at Pleasant Hill United Methodist Church.*
>
> 2083   Thomas Julian Maness (1919-2003). *Thomas was born in 1919. He died on December 19, 2003 in Moore County, NC.*

548. **Benjamin Harrison Maness**, son of Presley Wright Maness and Martha Jane Riddle, was born on January 30, 1887. He died on January 31, 1979 and was buried in Moore County, NC at Pleasant Hill United Methodist Church.

Nancy Beulah Russell, daughter of Leach Russell (-) and Lucinda Reynolds (-), was born on March 9, 1880. She died on May 19, 1963 and was buried in Moore County, NC at Pleasant Hill United Methodist Church. She and Benjamin Harrison Maness had the following children:

> 2084   Bradford Leo Maness (1915-1992). *Bradford was born on February 16, 1915 in Moore County, NC. He died on September 29, 1992 and was buried in Moore County, NC at Pleasant Hill United Methodist Church.*
>
> 2085   Esther Pearl Maness (1917-1991). *Esther was born on May 22, 1917. She died on March 9, 1991.*
>
> 2086   Infant Maness (1920-1920). *Infant was born on April 29, 1920. He died on April 29, 1920 and was buried in Moore County, NC at Pleasant Hill United Methodist Church.*

549. **Henry Clay Maness**, son of Presley Wright Maness and Martha Jane Riddle, was born on August 15, 1894. He died on January 22, 1978 and was buried in Moore County, NC at Smyrna Methodist Church.

Aggie Emma Hussey, daughter of John Madison Hussey (1865-1948) and Lydia Jane Garner (1870-1937), was born on October 14, 1898. She died on June 27, 1980 and was buried in Moore County, NC at Smyrna Methodist Church. She and Henry Clay Maness had the following children:

> 2087   Lillian E. Maness (1918-). *Lillian was born on March 16, 1918 in Moore County, NC.*
>
> 2088   Annie B. Maness (1919-1919). *Annie was born on July 16, 1919. She died on December 20, 1919 and was buried in Moore County, NC at Pleasant Hill United Methodist Church.*
>
> 2089   James Lester Maness (1920-1993). *James was born on September 22, 1920. He died on December 17, 1993 and was buried in Robbins, Moore County, NC at Pine Rest Cemetery.*
>
> 2090   Nellie G. Maness (1923-). *Nellie was born in 1923.*
>
> 2091   Lacy J. Maness (1925-1977). *Lacy was born on January 13, 1925 in Moore County, NC. She died on February 12, 1977 and was buried in Moore County, NC at Smyrna Methodist Church.*
>
> 2092   Jim Newlan Maness (1926-). *Jim was born on October 14, 1926.*
>
> 2093   Henry Clay Maness Jr. (1928-1970). *Henry was born on November 20, 1928. He died on January 23, 1970 and was buried in Moore County, NC at Smyrna Methodist*

2094   Carl Leroy Maness (1931-2003). *Carl was born on January 20, 1931. He died on July 4, 2003.*

558. **Julia Victoria Roach**, daughter of Jonathan Roach and Wincy Isabella Maness, was born on July 27, 1876. She died on May 11, 1962.

     James L. Pendley and Julia Victoria Roach had the following children:

2095   Bertis Belle Pendley (-)

571. **Henry Bascom Maness**, son of David Cincinnati Maness and Nancy Hughes, was born on May 22, 1883. He died on March 9, 1972.

     Carrie Ophelia Bishop was born on July 5, 1888. She died on June 25, 1954. She and Henry Bascom Maness had the following children:

2096   Carolyn Maness (1924-2004). *Carolyn was born on July 18, 1924. She died on March 8, 2004.*

588. **John Spinks Caddell**, son of James Bailey Caddell and Mary Clementine Maness, was born on July 23, 1867. He died on September 20, 1937.

     Minnie Robbins and John Spinks Caddell had the following children:

2097   Eliza Sarah Clementine Caddell (-)
2098   Robert E. Lee Caddell (-)
2099   James Bailey Caddell (-)
2100   Pauline Caddell (-)
2101   George Washington Caddell (-)
2102   David Bivens Caddell (-)
2103   Nona Elizabeth Caddell (-)
2104   Minnie Elsie Caddell (-)

602. **Thomas Lee Riddle**, son of Riley Roderick Riddle and Sarah Frances Maness, was born on February 12, 1877. He married **Mabel Pearl Reid** on June 16, 1908 in Moore County, NC. He died on March 23, 1951 and was buried in Carthage, Moore County, NC at Cross Hill Cemetery.

     Mabel Pearl Reid, daughter of Henry S. Reid (1864-1928) and Annie Jackson (1867-1894), was born in 1889. She died in 1966 and was buried in Carthage, Moore County, NC at Cross Hill Cemetery. She and Thomas Lee Riddle had the following children:

2105   Frances J. Riddle (1909-1971). *Frances was born on April 10, 1909. She died on January 30, 1971 and was buried in Sanford, Lee County, NC at Buffalo Presbyterian Church.*

603. **Laura Brantley Riddle**, daughter of Riley Roderick Riddle and Sarah Frances Maness, was born on March 3, 1879. She married **John Franklin Scott** on March 11, 1906 in Moore County, NC. She died on October 26, 1931 and was buried in Moore County, NC at High Falls United Methodist Church.

     John Franklin Scott, son of Ira Scott (1855-1941) and Rebecca Finnison (1856-1934), was born on April 10, 1882. He died on August 8, 1965 and was buried in Moore County, NC at High Falls United Methodist Church. He and Laura Brantley Riddle had the following children:

2106   Theodore Franklin Scott (-)
2107   Lucille Scott (-)
2108   Kathleen Scott (-)

Children of David Cincinnati Maness and Nancy Hughes

[Clockwise from Top Left] **Roy Brewer Maness; Henry Bascom Maness, Arthur Hughes Maness, Hermon Everette Maness and William "Will" Mark Maness.** [Above] **Callie Lee Maness** [Below] **Roy Brewer Maness** [Left] **Lula Maness** *(All Courtesy of Charlotte Maness)*

[Above] **Reuben Maness, Annie Maness and son John Maness c. 1919** *(Courtesy of Stacey Hugo Mansfield)*

[Right] **Willis Moses Williams and Annie Louisa Maness**

[Below] **Alsey Cleveland Davis and Daphne Lury Sheffield** *(Courtesy of Ruby Jewell Cockman Jones)*

604. **Addie Camilla Riddle**, daughter of Riley Roderick Riddle and Sarah Frances Maness, was born on October 20, 1880. She married **Charlie A. Wilson** on November 11, 1900 in Moore County, NC. She died on October 25, 1961.

Charlie A. Wilson, son of Robert W. Wilson (1841-1895) and Elizabeth A. Dorsett (1845-1923), was born in 1877.

605. **Annie Jane Riddle**, daughter of Riley Roderick Riddle and Sarah Frances Maness, was born on October 4, 1882. She married **Hayes Downing Phillips** on December 26, 1902 in Moore County, NC. She died on April 15, 1956.

Hayes Downing Phillips, son of Ira P. Phillips (1844-1908) and Nancy Jane Bray (1847-1910), was born in 1880. He died on January 16, 1945. He and Annie Jane Riddle had the following children:

2109   Ira Glenn Phillips (1907-1976). *Ira was born on June 2, 1907. He died in September 1976.*

606. **Maude Alice Riddle**, daughter of Riley Roderick Riddle and Sarah Frances Maness, was born on November 13, 1884. She married **D. Houston Parks** on November 25, 1906 in Moore County, NC. She died on April 17, 1962.

D. Houston Parks was born in 1885.

607. **Sarah Emma Riddle**, daughter of Riley Roderick Riddle and Sarah Frances Maness, was born on December 24, 1886. She died on December 31, 1928 and was buried in Moore County, NC at High Falls United Methodist Church.

608. **Mary Louise Riddle**, daughter of Riley Roderick Riddle and Sarah Frances Maness, was born on May 14, 1889. She married **W. Vestra Brewer** on February 22, 1916 in Moore County, NC.

609. **Margaret Mae Riddle**, daughter of Riley Roderick Riddle and Sarah Frances Maness, was born on May 30, 1891. She died on January 1, 1929 and was buried in Moore County, NC at High Falls United Methodist Church.

610. **Alma Estelle Clementine Riddle**, daughter of Riley Roderick Riddle and Sarah Frances Maness, was born on May 5, 1894. She died on October 14, 1964 and was buried in Robbins, Moore County, NC at Pine Rest Cemetery.

Frank Hampton Upchurch, son of William Henry Upchurch (1852-1925) and Emily Bell Carroll (1865-1930), was born in 1892. He died in 1970 and was buried in Robbins, Moore County, NC at Pine Rest Cemetery. He and Alma Estelle Clementine Riddle had the following children:

2110   Sarah Margaret Upchurch (1935-1935). *Sarah was born on November 15, 1935. She died on November 15, 1935 and was buried in Moore County, NC at High Falls United Methodist Church.*

614. **Edna Alice Cagle**, daughter of Thomas Branson Cagle and Lucinda Ann Maness, was born on May 29, 1890. She married **George Frank Pace** on June 28, 1908. She died on December 26, 1935.

George Frank Pace and Edna Alice Cagle had the following children:

2111   Annie Pace (-)
2112   Gertrude Pace (-)
2113   Ruby Pace (-)
2114   Frank Pace Jr. (-)
2115   Catherine Pace (-)

615. **Bessie Lee Cagle**, daughter of Thomas Branson Cagle and Lucinda Ann Maness, was born on May 4, 1892. She married **Fletcher Brooks** on October 9, 1910. She died on October 26, 1918.

Fletcher Brooks and Bessie Lee Cagle had the following children:

2116   Ruth Brooks (-)
2117   Carl Brooks (-)
2118   Tom Brooks (-)

616. **Samantha Beulah Cagle**, daughter of Thomas Branson Cagle and Lucinda Ann Maness, was born on August 22, 1893. She married **Herbert Cox** on June 8, 1913.

Herbert Cox and Samantha Beulah Cagle had the following children:

2119	Thelma Cox (-)
2120	Curtis Cox (-)
2121	Rudolph Cox (-)
2122	Sherman Cox (-)

617. **Sindia Ann Maness**, daughter of Thomas Wesley Maness and Sarah Frances Williams, was born on February 25, 1883. She died on November 3, 1911 and was buried in Moore County, NC at High Falls United Methodist Church.

618. **Lulu Maness**, daughter of Thomas Wesley Maness and Sarah Frances Williams, was born in 1885. She died on May 28, 1905 and was buried in Moore County, NC at Pleasant Hill United Methodist Church.

620. **Culbertha Maness**, daughter of Thomas Wesley Maness and Sarah Frances Williams, was born on August 26, 1889. She married **James Addison Williams** on March 8, 1906 in Moore County, NC. She died on July 26, 1972 and was buried in Robbins, Moore County, NC at Pine Rest Cemetery.

James Addison Williams, son of William James "Willie" Williams (1858-1940) and Sarah Ann Garner (1858-1895), was born on July 14, 1882. He died on July 5, 1962 and was buried in Robbins, Moore County, NC at Pine Rest Cemetery. He and Culbertha Maness had the following children:

2123	Floyd Williams (1908-). *Floyd was born in 1908.*
2124	Glossie Mae Williams (1909-1975). *Glossie was born on January 5, 1909. She died on January 25, 1975 in Moore Regional Hospital, Pinehurst, Moore County, NC and was buried on January 27, 1975 in Moore County, NC at Brown's Chapel Christian Church.*
2125	Beulah Williams (1912-). *Beulah was born in 1912.*
2126	Nina Vaugn Williams (1914-). *Nina was born on December 14, 1914.*
2127	Jay Rusha Williams (1915-). *Jay was born on November 30, 1915.*
2128	James Robert Williams (1918-1989). *James was born on April 25, 1918. He died on April 1, 1989 and was buried in Robbins, Moore County, NC at Pine Rest Cemetery.*
2129	Lenear Roberta Williams (1920-). *Lenear was born on July 13, 1920.*
2130	Paul Edgar Williams (1922-1979). *Paul was born on June 30, 1922. He died on April 23, 1979 and was buried in Robbins, Moore County, NC at Pine Rest Cemetery.*
2131	Leroy Quincy Williams (1926-). *Leroy was born on January 29, 1926.*
2132	Eugene Thomas Williams (1928-). *Eugene was born on September 23, 1928.*
2133	Asa Alexander Williams (1931-). *Asa was born on January 15, 1931.*

621. **Sallie Louisa Maness**, daughter of Thomas Wesley Maness and Sarah Frances Williams, was born on March 12, 1894. She married **Junius Allen** on December 29, 1912. She died on June 24, 1938 and was buried in Moore County, NC at Brown's Chapel Christian Church.

Junius Allen, son of James Terrell Moore (1859-1935) and Margaret Ann Elizabeth Allen (1868-1930), was born in May 1894. He died in 1953 and was buried in Moore County, NC at Brown's Chapel Christian Church. He and Sallie Louisa Maness had the following children:

2134	Malon Gonsbee Allen (1913-1962). *Malon was born on November 14, 1913. He died on August 21, 1962 and was buried in Moore County, NC at Brown's Chapel Christian Church.*
2135	Annie Frances Allen (1919-). *Annie was born on January 29, 1919.*
2136	Irene Allen (1921-1921). *Irene was born on August 27, 1921. She died on August 27, 1921 and was buried in Moore County, NC at Brown's Chapel Christian Church.*
2137	James Harding Allen (1922-). *James was born on September 5, 1922.*

622. **Annie Louisa Maness**, daughter of Ira Blake Maness and Mary Ellis Wallace, was born on June 17, 1875. She died on January 7, 1957 and was buried in Robbins, Moore County, NC at Tabernacle United Methodist Church.

Willis Moses Williams, son of John Spanker Williams (1842-1924) and Mary Catherine Williams (1848-1935), was born on June 12, 1878 in Moore County, NC. He died on September 1, 1957 in Moore Regional Hospital, Pinehurst, Moore County, NC and was buried on September 3, 1957 in Robbins, Moore County, NC at Tabernacle United Methodist Church. He and Annie Louisa Maness had the following children:

2138	Pearlie Williams (1903-). *Pearlie was born on November 18, 1903.*
2139	Asa Doyle Williams (1905-). *Asa was born on March 16, 1905.*
2140	Valley Edna Williams (1907-1909). *Valley was born in February 1907. She died in 1909.*
2141	John Fletcher Williams (1909-1912). *John was born in May 1909. He died in 1912.*
2142	Dossie Williams (1910-). *Dossie was born on December 4, 1910.*
2143	May Myrtle Williams (1913-1977). *May was born on February 10, 1913. She died on December 24, 1977 and was buried in Robbins, Moore County, NC at Tabernacle United Methodist Church.*
2144	Marvin J. Williams (1917-1996). *Marvin was born on April 18, 1917. He died on August 27, 1996.*

625. **Mattie Austin Maness**, daughter of Ira Blake Maness and Mary Ellis Wallace, was born on August 9, 1881. She married **Alonzo Williams** in 1909. She died on November 9, 1926 and was buried in Moore County, NC at Pleasant Hill United Methodist Church.

Alonzo Williams and Mattie Austin Maness had the following children:

2145	Harrison Williams (1910-). *Harrison was born in 1910.*
2146	Jessie Williams (1912-). *Jessie was born in 1912.*
2147	Arnold Williams (1914-). *Arnold was born in 1914.*
2148	Madgie Williams (1916-). *Madgie was born in 1916.*
2149	F.A. Williams (1919-). *F.A. was born on June 14, 1919.*
2150	Ruby Williams (1920-). *Ruby was born in 1920.*

626. **Mary Blake "Molly" Maness**, daughter of Ira Blake Maness and Mary Ellis Wallace, was born on August 5, 1882. She married **Jesse E. Faucette** on May 20, 1900. She died on July 9, 1944.

Jesse E. Faucette and Mary Blake "Molly" Maness had the following children:

2151	Lonza Alexander Faucette (1908-1975). *Lonza was born on July 19, 1908. He died in September 1975.*
2152	Isabell Faucette (1914-1975). *Isabell was born in 1914. She died on May 20, 1975.*
2153	Leon Faucette (1918-1921). *Leon was born on March 23, 1918. He died on May 3, 1921.*

627. **W. Walter Maness**, son of Ira Blake Maness and Mary Ellis Wallace, was born on December 19, 1883. He died on October 13, 1918 and was buried in Fayetteville, Cumberland County, NC at Cross Creek Cemetery #3.

Julia Musselwhite, daughter of Archie Musselwhite (-) and Hattie (-), was born in 1884. She died in 1951. She and W. Walter Maness had the following children:

2154	Ellis Blake Maness (1904-1941). *Ellis was born on August 5, 1904. He died on December 17, 1941 and was buried in Fayetteville, Cumberland County, NC at Cross Creek Cemetery #3.*
2155	Tracy Archie Maness (1906-1973). *Tracy was born on May 11, 1906. He married **Millie Blue Edge** on August 13, 1928. He died on November 20, 1973.*
2156	Dewey Belmont Maness (1908-1968). *Dewey was born on March 28, 1908. He died on October 11, 1968 and was buried in Fayetteville, Cumberland County, NC at Cross Creek Cemetery #3.*
2157	Addie Mabel Maness (1910-). *Addie was born on August 17, 1910. She married **John B. Edge** on September 14, 1929.*
2158	Willie Paul Maness (1913-1968). *Willie was born on March 25, 1913. He died on June 1, 1968 and was buried in Fayetteville, Cumberland County, NC at Cross Creek Cemetery #3.*

2159   Montie Mae Maness (1916-1916). *Montie was born on July 3, 1916. She died on December 15, 1916.*

2160   Walter Winford Maness (1918-1966). *Walter was born on November 29, 1918. He died on July 12, 1966.*

628. Maggie Mae Maness, daughter of Ira Blake Maness and Mary Ellis Wallace, was born on September 26, 1885 in Moore County, NC. She died on January 1, 1937 in Fayetteville, Cumberland County, NC.

629. Claude Ellis Maness, son of Ira Blake Maness and Mary Ellis Wallace, was born on February 10, 1887. He married **Mamie Vick Melvin** on March 19, 1912. He died on April 23, 1947 and was buried in Fayetteville, Cumberland County, NC at Cross Creek Cemetery #3.

Mamie Vick Melvin was born in 1894. She died in 1960. She and Claude Ellis Maness had the following children:

2161   Willie Thelma Maness (1912-). *Willie was born in 1912.*

2162   Ira Belmont Maness (1914-1992). *Ira was born on October 6, 1914. He died on January 5, 1992 and was buried in Fayetteville, Cumberland County, NC at Cross Creek Cemetery #3.*

2163   Mary Dollie Maness (1916-). *Mary was born on December 9, 1916.*

2164   Juanita Maness (1919-). *Juanita was born on February 20, 1919.*

2165   Ruby Maness (1921-). *Ruby was born on August 21, 1921.*

2166   Coolidge Poindexter Maness (1923-). *Coolidge was born on September 25, 1923.*

2167   Danie Kerbel Maness (1925-1995). *Danie was born on October 3, 1925. He died on December 29, 1995 and was buried in Fayetteville, Cumberland County, NC at Cross Creek Cemetery #3.*

2168   Claudia Mae Maness (1927-). *Claudia was born on September 24, 1927.*

2169   Jean Maness (1929-). *Jean was born on December 14, 1929.*

2170   Peggy Victoria Maness (1931-). *Peggy was born on December 17, 1931.*

2171   Bettie Lee Maness (1933-1996). *Bettie was born on June 22, 1933. She died on August 3, 1996.*

630. Callie Maness, daughter of John Alsey Maness and Frances Eugenia Hughes, was born on September 19, 1882. She died on April 12, 1884 and was buried in Moore County, NC at Russell/Maness Cemetery #103.

631. Herbert L. Maness, son of John Alsey Maness and Frances Eugenia Hughes, was born on January 12, 1884. He married **Mary Lulsa Kennedy** on March 7, 1915 in Moore County, NC. He died on May 4, 1967 and was buried in Moore County, NC at Pleasant Hill United Methodist Church.

Mary Lulsa Kennedy, daughter of William Wesley Kennedy (1865-1918) and Etta Jane Brown (1868-1928), was born on June 11, 1894. She died on October 17, 1945 and was buried in Moore County, NC at Pleasant Hill United Methodist Church.

Mary Alma Cagle, daughter of John Ransom Cagle (1839-1922) and Margaret Corinne Ritter (1858-1935), was born on May 23, 1891. She died on August 11, 1960 and was buried in Carthage, Moore County, NC at Cross Hill Cemetery.

632. John Alsey Maness Jr., son of John Alsey Maness and Frances Eugenia Hughes, was born on August 15, 1885. He married **Nancy Jane "Florence" Cockman** on February 10, 1905 in Moore County, NC. He married **Lizzie C. Cockman** on June 30, 1928 in Moore County, NC. He died on December 13, 1958 and was buried in Moore County, NC at Pleasant Hill United Methodist Church.

Nancy Jane "Florence" Cockman, daughter of John SSGWSQA "Jack" Cockman (1848-1912) and Lovedy Adaline Melton (1852-1891), was born on May 9, 1887. She died on August 4, 1927 and was buried in Moore County, NC at Pleasant Hill United Methodist Church. She and John Alsey Maness Jr. had the following children:

2172   Leta F. Maness (1907-1997). *Leta was born on March 20, 1907. She died on November 11, 1997 and was buried in Randolph County, NC at Beulah Baptist Church.*

2173   Claude Herbert Maness (1908-1998). *Claude was born on October 17, 1908. He married Lydia Martha Morgan on October 20, 1938 in Moore County, NC. He died on*

February 9, 1998 and was buried in Moore County, NC at Pleasant Hill United Methodist Church.

2174   Alton Marvin Maness (1910-1970). *Alton was born on May 15, 1910. He married **Eula Bristow** on December 25, 1935 in Moore County, NC. He died on March 23, 1970 and was buried in Moore County, NC at Pleasant Hill United Methodist Church.*

2175   John Edgar Maness (1913-1984). *John was born on January 4, 1913. He died on September 4, 1984.*

2176   Nova Belle Maness (1915-1989). *Nova was born on January 20, 1915. She died on July 17, 1989 and was buried in Moore County, NC at Pleasant Hill United Methodist Church.*

2177   Norman Harrison Maness (1918-1993). *Norman was born on June 14, 1918. He married **Hattie Mae Ross** on December 24, 1942. He died on December 14, 1993 and was buried in Moore County, NC at Pleasant Hill United Methodist Church.*

2178   Theodore Houston Maness (1921-). *Theodore was born on November 8, 1921. He married **Mary Margaret Cameron** on December 23, 1960 in Moore County, NC and was buried in Moore County, NC at Pleasant Hill United Methodist Church.*

2179   Mary Catherine Maness (1924-1931). *Mary was born on August 3, 1924. She died on September 25, 1931 and was buried in Moore County, NC at Pleasant Hill United Methodist Church.*

Lizzie C. Cockman, daughter of Eli Terry Cockman (1857-1946) and Silla Frances Horner (1854-1903), was born on February 23, 1895. She died on December 27, 1975 and was buried in Moore County, NC at Pleasant Hill United Methodist Church. She and John Alsey Maness Jr. had the following children:

2180   Joe Alsey Maness (1934-2000). *Joe was born on October 20, 1934. He died on February 9, 2000 and was buried in Moore County, NC at Pleasant Hill United Methodist Church.*

2181   Lonnie Franklin Maness (1936-). *Lonnie was born on September 3, 1936.*

633. **Mattie Ann Howard**, daughter of Benjamin M. Howard and Martha Louisa Maness, was born on February 1, 1883. She married **Offie Thomas Maness** on December 25, 1904. She died on March 24, 1955 and was buried in Moore County, NC at Smyrna Methodist Church.

Offie Thomas Maness, son of Lewis Scott Maness (1855-1943) and Martha Ann Wallace (1862-1902), was born on November 9, 1879. He died on September 2, 1951 in Moore County, NC and was buried in Moore County, NC at Smyrna Methodist Church. He and Mattie Ann Howard had the following children:

2182   Dewey Franklin Maness (1905-1974). *Dewey was born on November 5, 1905. He died in February 1974 in Guilford County, NC.*

2183   Mamie Flossie Maness (1907-1928). *Mamie was born on January 7, 1907. She died on July 26, 1928 and was buried in Moore County, NC at Smyrna Methodist Church.*

2184   Theodore Thomas Maness (1908-1976). *Theodore was born on February 27, 1908. He died on May 28, 1976 and was buried in Moore County, NC at Smyrna Methodist Church.*

2185   Myrtie Ethel Maness (1909-). *Myrtie was born in 1909.*

2186   Bertha A. Maness (1910-). *Bertha was born on September 3, 1910.*

2187   Essie Luola Maness (1912-1987). *Essie was born on July 5, 1912. She died on September 22, 1987 and was buried in Moore County, NC at Smyrna Methodist Church.*

2188   Lewis Clarence Maness (1914-1983). *Lewis was born on November 4, 1914. He died on May 15, 1983 and was buried in Moore County, NC at Smyrna Methodist Church.*

2189   Beulah Mae Maness (1916-1988). *Beulah was born on May 13, 1916. She died on September 15, 1988 and was buried in Moore County, NC at Smyrna Methodist Church.*

2190   Edith Esther Maness (1918-1979). *Edith was born on July 7, 1918. She died on October 26, 1979 and was buried in Moore County, NC at Smyrna Methodist Church.*

2191   Eli Darlington Maness (1920-2000). *Eli was born on March 11, 1920. He died on December 5, 2000 and was buried in Moore County, NC at Smyrna Methodist Church.*

2192   William Herbert Maness (1922-). *William was born on March 20, 1922.*

2193	Mattie Gertrude Maness (1924-1925). *Mattie was born on December 8, 1924. She died on April 26, 1925 and was buried in Moore County, NC at Smyrna Methodist Church.*
2194	Ruth Helen Maness (1930-1994). *Ruth was born on April 1, 1930. She died on October 11, 1994 in Moore County, NC and was buried in Moore County, NC at Smyrna Methodist Church.*

634. Benjamin Franklin Howard, son of Benjamin M. Howard and Martha Louisa Maness, was born on July 1, 1884. He married **Flossie Adelaide Purvis** on August 5, 1906 in Moore County, NC. He died on October 28, 1973 and was buried in Moore County, NC at Pleasant Hill United Methodist Church.

Flossie Adelaide Purvis, daughter of Nathaniel Green Purvis (1868-1958) and Aggie Norah Reynolds (1871-1919), was born on November 20, 1889. She died on March 22, 1965 and was buried in Moore County, NC at Pleasant Hill United Methodist Church. She and Benjamin Franklin Howard had the following children:

2195	V. A. Howard (1908-). *V. was born in 1908.*
2196	Benjamin Green Howard (1908-1993). *Benjamin was born on October 17, 1908. He died on March 6, 1993 and was buried in Moore County, NC at Pleasant Hill United Methodist Church.*
2197	Maude Louise Howard (1910-1994). *Maude was born on November 22, 1910. She died on June 26, 1994 and was buried in Carthage, Moore County, NC at Cross Hill Cemetery.*
2198	Edith Aggie Howard (1913-). *Edith was born on March 7, 1913.*
2199	Leon Franklin Howard (1915-). *Leon was born on April 27, 1915.*
2200	Mays Howard (1917-). *Mays was born on May 25, 1917.*
2201	Robert Lee Howard (1920-1996). *Robert was born on June 6, 1920. He married **Audrey Mae Booth** on December 1, 1944 in Moore County, NC. He died on April 10, 1996 and was buried in Moore County, NC at Pleasant Hill United Methodist Church.*
2202	Lennings McClennon Howard (1922-). *Lennings was born on August 21, 1922.*
2203	Wendell Reynolds Howard (1926-). *Wendell was born on May 14, 1926.*

635. Duffy Maness, daughter of Asa McClellan Maness Sr. and Vandie Lee Wallace, was born in 1886. She married **Azel Spinks Martindale** on June 6, 1912 in Moore County, NC and was buried in Moore County, NC at High Falls First Wesleyan Church.

Azel Spinks Martindale, son of Samuel Thomas Martindale (1869-1960) and Mary Elizabeth Ellen Kennedy (1875-1941), was born on April 15, 1896. He died on March 22, 1950 and was buried in Moore County, NC at High Falls First Wesleyan Church. He and Duffy Maness had the following children:

2204	Ervin McClendon Martindale (1916-1986). *Ervin was born on July 15, 1916 in Moore County, NC. He died on April 10, 1986 in Moore County, NC.*
2205	Dewey Houston Martindale (1921-2009). *Dewey was born on February 24, 1921 in Moore County, NC. He died on August 4, 2009 in Moore Regional Hospital, Pinehurst, Moore County, NC.*

636. Asa McClellan Maness Jr., son of Asa McClellan Maness Sr. and Vandie Lee Wallace, was born on September 23, 1889. He died on January 24, 1970 and was buried in Moore County, NC at Pleasant Hill United Methodist Church.

Nora Emily Jordan, daughter of James T. Jordan (1850-) and Martha Rosanna Maness (1859-), was born on December 31, 1896. She died on March 27, 1978. She and Asa McClellan Maness Jr. had the following children:

2206	Norman Harrison Maness (-)
2207	Eva Maness (1912-). *Eva was born on December 3, 1912.*
2208	Gladys Maness (1914-1992). *Gladys was born on June 10, 1914. She died on June 18, 1992 in Asheboro, Randolph County, NC.*
2209	Otis McLendon Maness (1916-). *Otis was born on May 22, 1916.*
2210	James Alton Maness (1919-2010). *James was born on December 10, 1919 in Montgomery County, NC. He died on July 24, 2010 in Randolph County Hospital, Asheboro, Randolph County, NC.*

Della Elizabeth Garner, daughter of Charles Oliver Garner (1875-1953) and Margaret Katherine Brown (1877-1951), was born on May 9, 1904. She died on December 27, 1992 in Moore County, NC and was buried in Moore County, NC at Pleasant Hill United Methodist Church. She and Asa McClellan Maness Jr. had the following children:

2211	Cathy Maness (-)
2212	Glenn Edward Maness (1943-2002). *Glenn was born on June 25, 1943. He died on September 22, 2002 and was buried in Robbins, Moore County, NC at Acorn Ridge Baptist Church.*
2213	Betty Jean Maness (1945-). *Betty was born on April 11, 1945.*
2214	Donald Asa Maness (1949-2009). *Donald was born on February 21, 1949 in Moore County, NC. He died on May 2, 2009 in Troy, Montgomery County, NC and was buried in Moore County, NC at Pleasant Hill United Methodist Church.*

637. **Alexander Lee Maness**, son of Asa McClellan Maness Sr. and Vandie Lee Wallace, was born on October 15, 1894. He married **Annie Jane Kennedy** on April 4, 1915 in Moore County, NC. He died on April 30, 1972 and was buried in Moore County, NC at Pleasant Hill United Methodist Church.

Annie Jane Kennedy, daughter of William Wesley Kennedy (1865-1918) and Etta Jane Brown (1868-1928), was born on August 16, 1898. She died on May 17, 1956 and was buried in Moore County, NC at Pleasant Hill United Methodist Church. She and Alexander Lee Maness had the following children:

2215	Etta Grace Maness (1916-1983). *Etta was born on January 16, 1916. She died on February 10, 1983 and was buried in Moore County, NC at Pleasant Hill United Methodist Church.*
2216	Flossie Ruth Maness (1919-). *Flossie was born on January 29, 1919.*
2217	Ann Kennedy Maness (1924-). *Ann was born on December 14, 1924.*

638. **Arthur Maness**, son of Asa McClellan Maness Sr. and Vandie Lee Wallace, was born in April 1897. He died on December 25, 1935.

Glenna Lee Howard, daughter of Solomon M. Howard (1860-1902) and Annie Magdaline "Maggie" Carter (1871-1956), was born in January 1897. She and Arthur Maness had the following children:

2218	Julius Carlton Maness (1921-1999). *Julius was born on May 9, 1921. He died on January 27, 1999 in Moore County, NC and was buried in Moore County, NC at Pleasant Hill United Methodist Church.*

Straudie J. Hussey, daughter of William Thomas Hussey (1870-1949) and Sallie Jane Welch (1873-1957), was born on April 13, 1908. She died on April 27, 1988 and was buried in Moore County, NC at Smyrna Methodist Church. She and Arthur Maness had the following children:

2219	Mack T. Maness (1935-1935). *Mack was born on February 12, 1935. He died on December 25, 1935 and was buried in Moore County, NC at Smyrna Methodist Church.*

639. **Ralph Maness**, son of Asa McClellan Maness Sr. and Vandie Lee Wallace, was born on January 16, 1899. He married **Glenna Caviness** on December 22, 1927 in Moore County, NC. He died on May 28, 1957 and was buried in Moore County, NC at Pleasant Hill United Methodist Church.

Glenna Caviness was born on December 26, 1910 and was buried in Moore County, NC at Pleasant Hill United Methodist Church. She and Ralph Maness had the following children:

2220	Montie Mae Maness (1928-2020). *Montie was born on October 6, 1928. She died on February 2, 2020 and was buried in Moore County, NC at Pleasant Hill United Methodist Church.*
2221	Billy James McLellan Maness (1930-). *Billy was born on July 31, 1930.*
2222	Johnny Ralph Maness (1938-2020). *Johnny was born on May 17, 1938. He died on June 10, 2020 and was buried in Asheboro, Randolph County, NC at Randolph*

640. **Johnny Carson Maness**, son of Asa McClellan Maness Sr. and Vandie Lee Wallace, was born on May 17, 1901. He married **Eva Mae Purvis** on February 15, 1929 in Moore County, NC. He died on December 14, 1975 and was buried in Moore County, NC at Pleasant Hill United Methodist Church.

Eva Mae Purvis, daughter of Nathaniel Green Purvis (1868-1958) and Aggie Norah Reynolds (1871-1919), was born on August 8, 1911. She died on August 31, 1997 and was buried in Moore County, NC at Pleasant Hill United Methodist Church. She and Johnny Carson Maness had the following children:

2223	Hilda Gray Maness (-)

641. **Montie Lee Maness**, daughter of Asa McClellan Maness Sr. and Vandie Lee Wallace, was born on May 15, 1902. She married **Theodore Lennings Howard** on March 27, 1920 in Moore County, NC. She died on December 30, 1975 and was buried in Moore County, NC at Pleasant Hill United Methodist Church.

Theodore Lennings Howard, son of Solomon M. Howard (1860-1902) and Annie Magdaline "Maggie" Carter (1871-1956), was born on December 15, 1900. He died on February 15, 1977 and was buried in Moore County, NC at Pleasant Hill United Methodist Church. He and Montie Lee Maness had the following children:

2224	Lillian Mae Howard (1921-1990). *Lillian was born on March 19, 1921. She died on November 15, 1990 and was buried in Moore County, NC at Pleasant Hill United Methodist Church.*
2225	Winfred Theodore Howard (1922-). *Winfred was born on December 7, 1922. He married **Clara Marguerite Wallace** on October 23, 1947 in Moore County, NC.*
2226	Charles Edward Howard (1924-). *Charles was born on November 25, 1924.*
2227	Jacqueline Mae Howard (1934-). *Jacqueline was born on January 17, 1934.*

645. **Edna Alice Seawell**, daughter of William Turner Seawell and Catherine Alice Maness, was born in October 1895. She died in 1936 and was buried in Carthage, Moore County, NC at Cross Hill Cemetery.

John Wiley Myrick, son of William Robert Myrick (1855-1930) and Lydia Alice Martindale (1869-1897), was born on August 16, 1893. He died on April 16, 1947 and was buried in Carthage, Moore County, NC at Cross Hill Cemetery. He and Edna Alice Seawell had the following children:

2228	William Holt Myrick (1914-1963). *William was born in 1914. He died in 1963 and was buried in Carthage, Moore County, NC at Cross Hill Cemetery.*
2229	Annie Loue Myrick (1917-). *Annie was born in 1917.*
2230	John Howard Myrick (1918-). *John was born in 1918.*
2231	Paul Seawell Myrick (1920-2011). *Paul was born on April 9, 1920. He died on January 5, 2011 and was buried in Asheboro, Randolph County, NC at Randolph Memorial Park.*
2232	May Bell Myrick (1921-). *May was born in 1921.*
2233	Catherine Alice Myrick (1924-). *Catherine was born in 1924.*
2234	Maude Lee Myrick (1926-). *Maude was born in 1926.*
2235	Hurley Ebert Myrick (1928-). *Hurley was born in 1928.*

646. **Ola Belle Seawell**, daughter of William Turner Seawell and Catherine Alice Maness, was born on July 6, 1898. She married **Cornelius Wiley Purvis** on October 7, 1922 in Moore County, NC. She died on May 16, 1942 and was buried in Moore County, NC at Pleasant Hill United Methodist Church.

Cornelius Wiley Purvis, son of Nathaniel Green Purvis (1868-1958) and Aggie Norah Reynolds (1871-1919), was born on July 10, 1894. He married Maggie S. Garner on February 25, 1912 in Moore County, NC. He married Ida Mae Flinchum in December 1942. He died on July 14, 1989 and was buried in Moore County, NC at Pleasant Hill United Methodist Church. He and Ola Belle Seawell had the following children:

2236	Franklin Purvis (-)
2237	Virginia Dare Purvis (-)
2238	Lester Purvis (-)

| 2239 | Arthur Linton Purvis (1927-). *Arthur was born on September 28, 1927.* |

647. Clem Floyd Seawell, son of William Turner Seawell and Catherine Alice Maness, was born on July 23, 1900. He died on August 20, 1963 and was buried in Moore County, NC at Flint Hill Baptist Church.

Bessie Maness was born on January 20, 1907. She died on July 7, 1968 and was buried in Moore County, NC at Flint Hill Baptist Church. She and Clem Floyd Seawell had the following children:

2240	Giles Turner Seawell (1923-1987). *Giles was born on April 14, 1923. He died on March 4, 1987.*
2241	William Arthur Seawell (1925-2004). *William was born on August 24, 1925. He died on April 29, 2004.*
2242	Ester Mae Seawell (1927-1935). *Ester was born on October 26, 1927. She died on April 7, 1935 and was buried in Moore County, NC at Flint Hill Baptist Church.*
2243	James Curtis Seawell (1930-2001). *James was born on January 6, 1930. He died on October 15, 2001 and was buried in Moore County, NC at Flint Hill Baptist Church.*
2244	Clem Floyd Seawell Jr. (1932-1933). *Clem was born on September 17, 1932. He died on June 5, 1933 and was buried in Moore County, NC at Flint Hill Baptist Church.*

648. Gilmer Flowers Seawell, son of William Turner Seawell and Catherine Alice Maness, was born on February 17, 1902. He died on September 20, 1976 and was buried in Moore County, NC at High Falls United Methodist Church.

Mary Elvia Phillips, daughter of John Wesley Phillips (1874-1934) and Nancy Caroline Hill (1875-1954), was born on May 3, 1904. She died on October 18, 1980 and was buried in Moore County, NC at High Falls United Methodist Church. She and Gilmer Flowers Seawell had the following children:

| 2245 | Herman Obert Seawell (1927-). *Herman was born on December 12, 1927.* |

649. Dewey C. Seawell, son of William Turner Seawell and Catherine Alice Maness, was born on December 27, 1903. He died on February 21, 1926 and was buried in Moore County, NC at High Falls United Methodist Church.

650. Ollie Seawell, son of William Turner Seawell and Catherine Alice Maness, was born on January 19, 1907. He died on November 16, 1964 and was buried in Moore County, NC at High Falls United Methodist Church.

Mittie Green was born on April 29, 1914.

651. Homer Seawell, son of William Turner Seawell and Catherine Alice Maness, was born on December 15, 1910. He died on November 10, 1992 and was buried in Moore County, NC at Friendship Baptist Church.

Ethel Pearl Williams, daughter of Sampson Delaney Williams (1875-1939) and Artie Mishie Maness (1887-1956), was born on January 27, 1916. She and Homer Seawell had the following children:

| 2246 | Alvin Linton Seawell (1934-2012). *Alvin was born on September 2, 1934. He died on March 2, 2012 and was buried in Moore County, NC at Friendship Baptist Church.* |
| 2247 | June Seawell (1938-). *June was born on January 8, 1938.* |

652. William Lewis Ritter, son of Addison Worth Ritter and Catherine Maness, was born on October 16, 1873. He married **Martha A. "Doonie" Maness** on August 29, 1895 in Moore County, NC.

Martha A. "Doonie" Maness, daughter of Thomas P. Maness (1834-1900) and Mary Eliza Stewart (1845-1897), was born on April 15, 1880. She and William Lewis Ritter had the following children:

2248	Etta Gertrude Ritter (1896-1961). *Etta was born on August 16, 1896. She died on January 22, 1961.*
2249	Joe E. Ritter (1899-). *Joe was born in 1899.*
2250	Oscar M. Ritter (1902-). *Oscar was born in 1902.*
2251	William Ritter (1903-). *William was born in 1903.*

| 2252 | Leroy Ritter (1906-). *Leroy was born in 1906.* |
| 2253 | Corneila C. Ritter (1908-). *Corneila was born in 1908.* |

653. **Mary Elizabeth Ritter**, daughter of Addison Worth Ritter and Catherine Maness, was born on December 15, 1875. She married **Abijah Herbert Bray** on January 5, 1896 in Moore County, NC. She died on January 16, 1943 and was buried in Moore County, NC at Smyrna Methodist Church.

Abijah Herbert Bray, son of Henry Thomas Bray (1852-) and Artie Mishe Trogdon (1852-), was born on May 16, 1878. He died on June 30, 1944 and was buried in Moore County, NC at Smyrna Methodist Church. He and Mary Elizabeth Ritter had the following children:

2254	Arthur W. Bray (1896-). *Arthur was born in August 1896. He married **Maggie M. Brown** on January 23, 1918 in Moore County, NC.*
2255	Mamie Ethel Bray (1898-1978). *Mamie was born on October 19, 1898. She died on May 4, 1978 and was buried in Robbins, Moore County, NC at Tabernacle United Methodist Church.*
2256	Herbert T. Bray (1900-). *Herbert was born in April 1900.*
2257	Shelly R. Bray (1906-). *Shelly was born in 1906.*
2258	Blanche Bray (1911-2012). *Blanche was born on May 7, 1911. She died on June 13, 2012 in Biscoe, Montgomery County, NC and was buried on June 16, 2012 in Asheboro, Randolph County, NC at Randolph Memorial Park.*
2259	Lewis Ritter Bray (1914-1987). *Lewis was born on June 1, 1914. He died on January 26, 1987 and was buried in Moore County, NC at Pine Grove Baptist Church.*

654. **Martha Jane Ritter**, daughter of Addison Worth Ritter and Catherine Maness, was born on November 29, 1878. She married **Rufus Bryant Reynolds** circa 1901. She died on July 1, 1964 and was buried in Moore County, NC at Pleasant Hill United Methodist Church.

Rufus Bryant Reynolds, son of Wiley Ruben Reynolds (1829-1899) and Mary Elizabeth Williams (1844-1909), was born on October 16, 1875. He died on May 7, 1954 and was buried in Moore County, NC at Pleasant Hill United Methodist Church. He and Martha Jane Ritter had the following children:

2260	James Reynolds (1902-). *James was born in 1902.*
2261	Lacy Catherine Reynolds (1903-1991). *Lacy was born on April 9, 1903. She died on July 26, 1991.*
2262	Savannah A. Reynolds (1906-). *Savannah was born in 1906.*
2263	Rufus W. Reynolds (1908-). *Rufus was born in 1908.*
2264	Lucy Jane Reynolds (1909-1984). *Lucy was born on October 14, 1909. She died on January 17, 1984 and was buried in Moore County, NC at Pleasant Hill United Methodist Church.*
2265	Ervin T. Reynolds (1913-). *Ervin was born in 1913.*
2266	Neulan Bryant Reynolds (1914-1987). *Neulan was born on August 17, 1914 in Moore County, NC. He died on October 15, 1987 and was buried in Moore County, NC at Pleasant Hill United Methodist Church.*
2267	Ethalene Reynolds (1918-). *Ethalene was born in 1918.*
2268	Geneva Reynolds (1920-2007). *Geneva was born in 1920. She died on January 2, 2007 in Seagrove, Randolph County, NC and was buried in Moore County, NC at Pleasant Hill United Methodist Church.*

655. **Joseph Thomas Ritter**, son of Addison Worth Ritter and Catherine Maness, was born on October 22, 1880. He died on October 16, 1923 in Sanford, Lee County, NC and was buried in Carthage, Moore County, NC at Cross Hill Cemetery.

Mamie K. Seawell, daughter of Archibald Winston Seawell (1857-1928) and Mary Hadley Williams (1865-1925), was born on March 23, 1893. She died on May 14, 1945 and was buried in Carthage, Moore County, NC at Cross Hill Cemetery. She and Joseph Thomas Ritter had the following children:

| 2269 | Josie Ritter (-) |
| 2270 | David A. Ritter (1917-1934). *David was born in 1917. He died in 1934 and was buried in Carthage, Moore County, NC at Cross Hill Cemetery.* |

2271   Mary Catherine Ritter (1920-1964). *Mary was born in 1920. She died in 1964 and was buried in Carthage, Moore County, NC at Cross Hill Cemetery.*

Beulah Stout was born on July 31, 1885. She died on June 19, 1907 and was buried in Moore County, NC at Smyrna Methodist Church.

656. **John Addison Ritter**, son of Addison Worth Ritter and Catherine Maness, was born on May 5, 1886. He died on January 11, 1942.

Maude May Roller was born in 1895. She died in 1985. She and John Addison Ritter had the following children:

2272   Norma Jane Ritter (1927-). *Norma was born on September 25, 1927.*

657. **Sarah Alice Ritter**, daughter of Addison Worth Ritter and Catherine Maness, was born on March 5, 1888. She married **Walter R. Kennedy** on January 20, 1914 in Moore County, NC. She died on July 13, 1936 and was buried in Moore County, NC at Pleasant Hill United Methodist Church.

Walter R. Kennedy, son of Elias Kennedy (1845-1924) and Lydia M. Hare (1843-1911), was born on January 15, 1878. He died on November 24, 1964 and was buried in Moore County, NC at Pleasant Hill United Methodist Church. He and Sarah Alice Ritter had the following children:

2273   Wayland Rite Kennedy (1913-1996). *Wayland was born on August 15, 1913. He died on January 2, 1996 and was buried in Robbins, Moore County, NC at Pine Rest Cemetery.*
2274   Walter Royster Kennedy (1914-1915). *Walter was born on September 25, 1914. He died on February 14, 1915 and was buried in Moore County, NC at Pleasant Hill United Methodist Church.*

658. **Julia Ann Ritter**, daughter of Addison Worth Ritter and Catherine Maness, was born on October 30, 1888. She died on October 21, 1972 and was buried in Robbins, Moore County, NC at Pine Rest Cemetery.

William Herbert Kennedy, son of Alexander Spinks Kennedy (1862-1953) and Addie Arisdale Brown (1866-1941), was born on May 9, 1886. He died on February 7, 1975 and was buried in Robbins, Moore County, NC at Pine Rest Cemetery. He and Julia Ann Ritter had the following children:

2275   Irene Kennedy (-)
2276   Norman Lee Kennedy (1911-1997). *Norman was born on September 24, 1911. He died on March 30, 1997 and was buried in Robbins, Moore County, NC at Pine Rest Cemetery.*
2277   Edgar Carlton Kennedy (1915-1999). *Edgar was born on November 27, 1915. He died on August 27, 1999 and was buried in Robbins, Moore County, NC at Pine Rest Cemetery.*
2278   Mable Kennedy (1917-). *Mable was born on August 28, 1917.*

659. **John Alsey Maness** was the son of Bethuel C. Maness and Sarah Jane Martin.

Eliza Ellen McLeod was the daughter of John McLeod (-) and Martha Moore (-). She and John Alsey Maness had the following children:

2279   Ollie Martin Maness (1901-1967). *Ollie was born on May 24, 1901. He died on June 4, 1967 and was buried in Moore County, NC at Brown's Chapel Christian Church.*

660. **Martha L. Maness**, daughter of Bethuel C. Maness and Sarah Jane Martin, was born in 1873. She married **William N. Parrish** on May 21, 1891 in Moore County, NC.

William N. Parrish, son of Ashley Parrish (1802-) and Deborah Dunn (1832-), was born in 1869. He married Laura A. circa 1905. He and Martha L. Maness had the following children:

2280   John F. Parrish (1891-). *John was born in June 1891.*

2281   Maggie E. Parrish (1893-). *Maggie was born in October 1893.*

661. Mary Catherine Maness, daughter of Bethuel C. Maness and Sarah Jane Martin, was born on June 17, 1874. She married **William L. Britt** on August 2, 1891 in Moore County, NC. She died on December 2, 1948 in Asheboro, Randolph County, NC and was buried on December 4, 1948 in Moore County, NC at Bensalem Presbyterian Church.

William L. Britt, son of Bryant Britt (1820-1903) and Barbara Ann Myrick (1826-1883), was born on November 4, 1852. He died on March 29, 1930 and was buried in Moore County, NC at Bensalem Presbyterian Church. He and Mary Catherine Maness had the following children:

2282   Eunice J. Britt (1892-1928). *Eunice was born on February 20, 1892. She died on October 16, 1928 and was buried in Moore County, NC at Bensalem Presbyterian Church.*

2283   Rufus Howell Britt (1894-). *Rufus was born in 1894.*

2284   Minnie A. Britt (1896-1960). *Minnie was born on June 12, 1896. She died on December 12, 1960.*

2285   Curtis Luke Britt (1899-1961). *Curtis was born on May 27, 1899. He died on November 12, 1961 and was buried in Moore County, NC at Bensalem Presbyterian Church.*

2286   Myrtle M. Britt (1901-). *Myrtle was born in 1901.*

2287   Arnold L. Britt (1905-). *Arnold was born in 1905. He married **Annie May Blake** circa 1925.*

2288   Mary D. Britt (1909-). *Mary was born in 1909.*

662. Sarah Elizabeth Maness, daughter of Bethuel C. Maness and Sarah Jane Martin, was born on December 22, 1879. She married **Elias Babe Maness** on October 27, 1898 in Moore County, NC. She married **Joseph C. Garner** circa 1904. She died on June 24, 1943 and was buried in Moore County, NC at Smyrna Methodist Church.

Elias Babe Maness, son of Elias Maness (1819-1890) and Elizabeth Ritter (1822-1880), was born on May 5, 1860. He married Sarah Elizabeth Garner on February 7, 1893 in Moore County, NC. He died on May 23, 1903 and was buried in Robbins, Moore County, NC at Acorn Ridge Baptist Church.

Joseph C. Garner, son of John Harrison Garner (1840-1913) and Julia Ann Maness (1842-1914), was born on May 31, 1872. He died on November 10, 1947 and was buried in Moore County, NC at Smyrna Methodist Church.

663. Norman Martin Maness, son of Bethuel C. Maness and Sarah Jane Martin, was born on April 14, 1882. He married **Martha Emily Garner** on March 22, 1902 in Moore County, NC. He married **Ethel Florence Garner** on June 11, 1932 in Moore County, NC. He died on December 16, 1960 and was buried in Moore County, NC at Smyrna Methodist Church.

Martha Emily Garner, daughter of William Bradley Garner (1846-1899) and Carrie Emily Maness (1845-1926), was born on November 3, 1867. She died on September 10, 1931 and was buried in Moore County, NC at Smyrna Methodist Church. She and Norman Martin Maness had the following children:

2289   Rosa Maness (1906-). *Rosa was born in 1906.*

2290   Theodore Mitchell "Teddy" Maness (1907-1995). *Theodore was born on October 1, 1907. He died on February 26, 1995 and was buried in Moore County, NC at Smyrna Methodist Church.*

Ethel Florence Garner, daughter of Charles Oliver Garner (1875-1953) and Margaret Katherine Brown (1877-1951), was born on November 9, 1898. She died on January 30, 1969 and was buried in Moore County, NC at Smyrna Methodist Church.

664. John Lindon Dunn, son of Wesley Thaddeus Dunn and Sara Ann Maness, married **Deborah Elizabeth Deaton** on November 14, 1909 in Montgomery County, NC.

Deborah Elizabeth Deaton, daughter of Erwin Paschal Deaton (1857-1928) and Emeline Freeman (1858-1943), was born in 1891.

667. David Calvin Maness, son of Spinks P. Maness and Rose Anna Leach, was born in 1879 in North Carolina. He married **Frances White** circa 1902.

Frances White was born in 1884. She and David Calvin Maness had the following children:

    2291   Clara Maness (1904-). *Clara was born in 1904.*
    2292   Harvey Maness (1906-). *Harvey was born in 1906.*

668. **Alsey Alexander Maness**, son of Spinks P. Maness and Rose Anna Leach, was born in May 1880 in North Carolina. He married **Stella Dickens** circa 1904. He died on September 16, 1953.

Stella Dickens was born in 1885. She and Alsey Alexander Maness had the following children:

    2293   Ruth Maness (1907-). *Ruth was born in 1907.*
    2294   Colleen Maness (1909-). *Colleen was born in 1909.*

669. **Nancy Lou Maness**, daughter of Spinks P. Maness and Rose Anna Leach, was born in September 1881 in North Carolina. She died on September 26, 1976 in Montgomery County, NC and was buried in Candor, Montgomery County, NC at Macedonia Presbyterian Church.

Daniel Atlas McLeod was born circa 1880. He and Nancy Lou Maness had the following children:

    2295   Edgar McLeod (-)
    2296   Robert McLeod (-)
    2297   Walter McLeod (-)
    2298   Frank McLeod (-)
    2299   Grace McLeod (-)

670. **Mary Dell Maness**, daughter of Spinks P. Maness and Rose Anna Leach, was born on January 9, 1884 in North Carolina. She married **Manly Luck** on December 19, 1900 in Montgomery County, NC. She died on July 16, 1979.

Manly Luck, son of William Henry Luck (1846-1918) and Caroline Kennedy (1851-1944), was born on February 1, 1875 in Randolph County, NC. He died in 1932.

673. **Deborah Ethel Maness**, daughter of Spinks P. Maness and Rose Anna Leach, was born in May 1888 in North Carolina.

Ernest Cashwell Johnson and Deborah Ethel Maness had the following children:

    2300   Leach Maness Johnson (1912-). *Leach was born in 1912.*

674. **Rose Lee Maness**, daughter of Spinks P. Maness and Rose Anna Leach, was born on September 22, 1889 in North Carolina. She died on December 25, 1982 in Montgomery County, NC and was buried in Asheboro, Randolph County, NC at Pleasant Hill Primitive Baptist Church Cemetery.

676. **Elizabeth Pearl Maness**, daughter of Spinks P. Maness and Rose Anna Leach, was born on August 30, 1892 in North Carolina. She died in April 1985 in Wake County, NC.

Burney A. Britt was born in February 1900. He died in September 1984 in Wake County, NC.

677. **Margaret Myrtle Maness**, daughter of Spinks P. Maness and Rose Anna Leach, was born on February 6, 1894 in North Carolina. She died on February 4, 1986 in Montgomery County, NC and was buried in Maness Family Cemetery.

678. **John Ray Maness**, son of Spinks P. Maness and Rose Anna Leach, was born on September 18, 1895 in North Carolina. He died in October 1967 in Montgomery County, NC.

Christian McLeod was born on November 17, 1896. She died in March 1980 in Montgomery County, NC.

680. **Leslie Gold Maness**, son of Spinks P. Maness and Rose Anna Leach, was born in 1902. He died on March 22, 1966.

Mary Ruth Melton, daughter of John Melton (1881-1945) and Lalon Jenetta Cagle (1886-1924), was born in 1915. She died in 1966.

681. **Neil Wade Maness**, son of James Asa Maness and Nancy Louise Leach, was born in February 1884 in North Carolina. He married **Maggie McMillan** circa 1908. He died in 1948.

Maggie McMillan was born in 1883. She and Neil Wade Maness had the following children:

      2301   Wade Maness (1909-). *Wade was born in 1909.*

683. **William Spinks Maness**, son of James Asa Maness and Nancy Louise Leach, was born in March 1887 in North Carolina. He died in 1958.

Onnie McMillan was born in 1891. She died in 1948. She and William Spinks Maness had the following children:

      2302   Willine Maness (-)
      2303   Max Maness (-)
      2304   John Murrey Maness (-)
      2305   Paul Maness (-)

687. **James Edgar Maness**, son of James Asa Maness and Nancy Louise Leach, was born on March 4, 1896 in North Carolina. He married **Bonnie Martin** in October 1921. He died on June 6, 1963 and was buried in Biscoe, Montgomery County, NC at Biscoe Cemetery.

Bonnie Martin, daughter of Daniel Alexander Martin (1843-1911) and Margaret Ann McKenzie (1851-1926), was born on February 10, 1898. She died on August 11, 1989 in Cary, Wake County, NC and was buried in Biscoe, Montgomery County, NC at Biscoe Cemetery. She and James Edgar Maness had the following children:

      2306   Harold M. Maness (-)
      2307   Myra M. Maness (-)
      2308   Margaret Faye Maness (1925-2012). *Margaret was born on July 2, 1925. She died on November 5, 2012 and was buried in Biscoe, Montgomery County, NC at Biscoe Cemetery.*

688. **Minnie Blanche Maness**, daughter of James Asa Maness and Nancy Louise Leach, was born on January 28, 1898 in North Carolina. She died in September 1973 in Biscoe, Montgomery County, NC.

689. **Bertie Jane Maness**, daughter of James Asa Maness and Nancy Louise Leach, was born on April 7, 1900 in North Carolina. She died on October 19, 1989 in Biscoe, Montgomery County, NC.

690. **Anne Lee Maness**, daughter of James Asa Maness and Nancy Louise Leach, was born on September 25, 1902. She died on April 24, 1992 and was buried in Moore County, NC at Bensalem Presbyterian Church.

John Archie Kelly was born on January 23, 1894. He died on December 1, 1964 and was buried in Moore County, NC at Bensalem Presbyterian Church.

692. **Elva Ellen Maness**, daughter of James Asa Maness and Nancy Louise Leach, was born on December 20, 1905 in North Carolina. She died in August 1984 in Biscoe, Montgomery County, NC.

Thomas Wade Hurley was born in 1908.

694. **Ruth D. Maness**, daughter of Neill Tyson Maness and Martha Leutitia Leach, was born on November 26, 1892. She married **Carl Clarence Stout** on December 25, 1912. She died on August 24, 1964.

Carl Clarence Stout was born on February 25, 1892. He died on November 18, 1963 in North Carolina. He and Ruth D. Maness had the following children:

      2309   Stout (-)
      2310   Stout (-)
      2311   Carl Clarence Stout Jr. (1913-1998). *Carl was born on October 4, 1913. He married Annie Pearl Raines on April 14, 1938. He died on January 28, 1998 in North*

Carolina.

2312	Cecil Maness Stout (1914-2000). *Cecil was born on October 17, 1914. He married **Cleo Garrison** on October 27, 1943. He died on June 13, 2000 in Virginia.*
2313	Mary Kathleen Stout (1916-). *Mary was born on October 28, 1916. She married **Glendil Leon Tucker, Sr.** on April 18, 1945.*
2314	Francis Edward Stout (1918-). *Francis was born on February 13, 1918. He married **Felipa Lerma** in 1944.*
2315	Ralph Leach Stout (1920-). *Ralph was born on June 10, 1920.*
2316	Martha Caroline Stout (1922-1999). *Martha was born on June 2, 1922. She married **Lewellyn MacDonald Alexander** on September 3, 1952. She died on March 12, 1999 in Virginia.*
2317	Frederick Douglas Stout (1923-1993). *Frederick was born on August 18, 1923. He married **Kathryn Ward** on June 9, 1956. He died in October 1993 in Maryland.*
2318	Archie Mangum Stout (1925-). *Archie was born on August 2, 1925.*
2319	Neil Taylor Stout (1927-). *Neil was born on August 6, 1927.*
2320	Ruth Stout (1929-). *Ruth was born on August 21, 1929. She married **Bill Burgess** on February 11, 1951.*

695. **James Leach Maness**, son of Neill Tyson Maness and Martha Leutitia Leach, was born on May 9, 1894. He married **Gaye Smith** on January 31, 1918. He died on June 7, 1977 in Hickory, Catawba County, NC and was buried on June 9, 1977.

Gaye Smith was born on October 9, 1898. She died in March 1974 in Hickory, Catawba County, NC. She and James Leach Maness had the following children:

2321	Rachel Elizabeth Maness (1918-). *Rachel was born on November 29, 1918. She married **Thomas Richard Williams Jr.** on June 28, 1941.*
2322	Morell Elaine Maness (1920-). *Morell was born on August 7, 1920. She married **William Abel Fritz** on November 24, 1938.*
2323	James Leach Maness Jr. (1923-1923). *James was born on January 4, 1923. He died on February 1, 1923 and was buried in Bird City, Cheyenne, Kansas at Bird City Cemetery.*

696. **Archibald Kelly Maness**, son of Neill Tyson Maness and Martha Leutitia Leach, was born on November 14, 1895. He married **Nellie Jewel Almon** on May 30, 1931. He died on December 12, 1974 in Greensboro, Guilford County, NC.

Nellie Jewel Almon was born on October 13, 1906. She died on July 27, 2002 in Greensboro, Guilford County, NC. She and Archibald Kelly Maness had the following children:

2324	Maness (-)
2325	Archibald Kelly Maness Jr. (1936-2001). *Archibald was born on September 1, 1936. He died on October 2, 2001 in Greensboro, Guilford County, NC.*

698. **Isaac Leland Maness**, son of Neill Tyson Maness and Martha Leutitia Leach, was born on February 18, 1900. He died on October 9, 1981 in Biscoe, Montgomery County, NC and was buried on October 11, 1981 in Biscoe, Montgomery County, NC at Maness Family Cemetery.

699. **Mary Maness**, daughter of Neill Tyson Maness and Martha Leutitia Leach, was born on July 24, 1902. She married **John Elsa Allen** on May 31, 1922. She died on July 10, 1973 in Biscoe, Montgomery County, NC.

John Elsa Allen was born on November 21, 1888. He died in December 1968 in North Carolina. He and Mary Maness had the following children:

2326	John O'Henry Allen (1923-). *John was born on September 28, 1923. He married **Sue Barton** on March 17, 1944.*

701. **Della Maness**, daughter of Neill Tyson Maness and Martha Leutitia Leach, was born on January 3, 1906. She died on September 25, 1988 in Charlotte, Mecklenburg County, NC and was buried on September 27, 1988 in Biscoe, Montgomery County, NC at Maness Family Cemetery.

Jack Albert was born on May 2, 1896. He died in May 1973.

702. **Jewell Maness**, daughter of Neill Tyson Maness and Martha Leutitia Leach, was born on March 6, 1908. She married **Richard Turner Elmore** on April 20, 1938. She died on March 26, 2002.

Richard Turner Elmore was born on May 1, 1905. He died on August 9, 1983 in Charlotte, Mecklenburg County, NC and was buried on August 12, 1983 in Biscoe, Montgomery County, NC at Maness Family Cemetery. He and Jewell Maness had the following children:

| 2327 | Elmore (-) |
| 2328 | Elmore (-) |

707. **Ada L. Dunn**, daughter of William Wright Dunn and Mary Jane Maness, was born on February 9, 1889. She died on June 7, 1974 and was buried in Moore County, NC at Dover Baptist Church.

Oscar L. Miller was born on May 19, 1882. He married Mary M. Davis circa 1905. He died on January 10, 1962 and was buried in Moore County, NC at Dover Baptist Church.

708. **Martha May Dunn**, daughter of William Wright Dunn and Mary Jane Maness, was born on July 23, 1891. She died on October 18, 1947 and was buried in Moore County, NC at Dover Baptist Church.

Dossie W. Miller was born on March 24, 1886. He died on July 20, 1970 and was buried in Moore County, NC at Dover Baptist Church. He and Martha May Dunn had the following children:

| 2329 | Mary Lucille Miller (1912-1915). *Mary was born on December 8, 1912. She died on January 10, 1915 and was buried in Moore County, NC at Dover Baptist Church.* |
| 2330 | Nancy Irene Miller (1919-). *Nancy was born on December 9, 1919.* |

709. **Neil Webster Davis**, son of Lewis Washington Davis and Martha Clementine Maness, was born on January 13, 1884. He died on November 24, 1952 and was buried in Moore County, NC at Dover Baptist Church.

Elma Susanna Hancock, daughter of W. Henderson Hancock (1865-1919) and Rena Simmons (1859-1928), was born on October 2, 1887. She died on December 18, 1975 and was buried in Moore County, NC at Dover Baptist Church. She and Neil Webster Davis had the following children:

2331	Clarence Webster Davis (1912-1979). *Clarence was born on December 31, 1912. He died on October 31, 1979 and was buried in Robbins, Moore County, NC at Pine Rest Cemetery.*
2332	Howard F. Davis (1915-). *Howard was born in 1915.*
2333	Tallie Richard Davis (1917-1981). *Tallie was born on July 11, 1917. He died on May 21, 1981 and was buried in Moore County, NC at Dover Baptist Church.*
2334	Thelma A. Davis (1920-). *Thelma was born in 1920.*
2335	Ray Lewis Davis (1922-2010). *Ray was born on June 27, 1922. He died on December 8, 2010.*
2336	Charlie H. Davis (1925-). *Charlie was born in 1925.*
2337	Lelan Dawson Davis (1929-). *Lelan was born in 1929.*

710. **Mary M. Davis**, daughter of Lewis Washington Davis and Martha Clementine Maness, was born on December 31, 1885. She married **Oscar L. Miller** circa 1905. She died on February 9, 1913 and was buried in Moore County, NC at Dover Baptist Church.

Oscar L. Miller was born on May 19, 1882. He died on January 10, 1962 and was buried in Moore County, NC at Dover Baptist Church. He and Mary M. Davis had the following children:

2338	Martha E. Miller (1906-). *Martha was born in 1906.*
2339	Lucy A. Miller (1907-1987). *Lucy was born on June 17, 1907. She died on March 31, 1987 and was buried in Moore County, NC at Dover Baptist Church.*
2340	Nancy E. Miller (1909-). *Nancy was born in 1909.*

711. **John Archie Davis**, son of Lewis Washington Davis and Martha Clementine Maness, was born on February 11, 1888. He died on December 3, 1965 and was buried in Orange County, NC at Mars Hill Baptist Church.

Lillie Smith, daughter of Enoch Turner Smith (1849-1934) and Louisa Jane Deaton (1854-1937), was born on March 21, 1885. She died on May 20, 1971 and was buried in Orange County, NC at Mars Hill Baptist Church. She and John Archie Davis had the following children:

    2341   Davis (-)

712. **Nancy Francena Davis**, daughter of Lewis Washington Davis and Martha Clementine Maness, was born on January 19, 1890. She died on May 18, 1960 and was buried in Moore County, NC at Dover Baptist Church.

Numa C. Hare, son of Isham Zebedee Hare (1863-1951) and Hulda Matilda Jane Trogdon (1865-1958), was born on December 19, 1891. He died on April 18, 1961 and was buried in Moore County, NC at Dover Baptist Church. He and Nancy Francena Davis had the following children:

    2342   Graham Maxton Hare (1915-1980). *Graham was born on October 25, 1915. He died on August 27, 1980 and was buried in Moore County, NC at Dover Baptist Church.*
    2343   James B. Hare (1917-1969). *James was born on September 4, 1917. He died on April 8, 1969 and was buried in Moore County, NC at Dover Baptist Church.*
    2344   Nellie Rue Hare (1919-). *Nellie was born on February 13, 1919.*
    2345   Jesse Harden Hare (1921-1963). *Jesse was born on July 21, 1921. He died on February 15, 1963 and was buried in Moore County, NC at Dover Baptist Church.*

713. **Alsey Cleveland Davis**, son of Lewis Washington Davis and Martha Clementine Maness, was born on January 3, 1892 in Seagrove, Randolph County, NC. He married **Daphne Lury Sheffield** on March 7, 1915 in Montgomery County, NC. He married **Sarah Isabelle Jordan** on October 30, 1936. He died on December 12, 1958 in Moore County, NC and was buried in Candor, Montgomery County, NC at Old Center Baptist Church.

Daphne Lury Sheffield, daughter of Emery Sheffield (1865-1932) and Margaret Frances Williams (1857-1942), was born on June 12, 1896. She died on January 12, 1936 and was buried in Candor, Montgomery County, NC at Old Center Baptist Church. She and Alsey Cleveland Davis had the following children:

    2346   James H. Davis (1919-). *James was born in 1919.*
    2347   Frances Davis (1920-). *Frances was born in 1920.*
    2348   Bernice Jewell Davis (1921-2018). *Bernice was born on September 8, 1921. She married* **William Fletcher Cockman** *on January 2, 1943. She died on January 5, 2018.*
    2349   Miriam B. Davis (1924-). *Miriam was born in 1924.*
    2350   Foster L. Davis (1926-). *Foster was born in 1926.*
    2351   Rachel E. Davis (1927-). *Rachel was born in 1927.*
    2352   Alton A. Davis (1929-). *Alton was born in 1929.*
    2353   Elva C. Davis (1931-). *Elva was born in 1931.*
    2354   Dossie Davis (1933-). *Dossie was born in 1933.*
    2355   Emery Lewis Davis (1935-). *Emery was born in 1935. He married* **Mildred Irene Green** *on September 1, 1956 in Montgomery County, NC.*

Sarah Isabelle Jordan, daughter of William S. Jordan (1863-1943) and Sarah Francena Brown (1861-1919), was born on November 26, 1896. She married John Robert McNeill on February 4, 1916 in Moore County, NC. She died on July 17, 1957 and was buried in Candor, Montgomery County, NC at Old Center Baptist Church. She and Alsey Cleveland Davis had the following children:

    2356   Harold Edward Davis (1937-). *Harold was born on June 8, 1937.*

714. **Ira Spinks Davis**, son of Lewis Washington Davis and Martha Clementine Maness, was born on December 27, 1893. He married **Martha Elizabeth Brewer** on December 7, 1919 in Montgomery County, NC. He died on January 14, 1950 and was buried in Moore County, NC at Dover Baptist Church.

Martha Elizabeth Brewer, daughter of Stephen Brewer (1877-1953) and Caroline Dunn (1873-1951), was born on December 30, 1899. She died on August 1, 1982 and was buried in Moore County, NC at Dover Baptist Church. She and Ira Spinks Davis had the following children:

> 2357   Edith Pearl Davis (1922-1999). *Edith was born on June 18, 1922. She died on January 30, 1999 and was buried in Moore County, NC at Dover Baptist Church.*
>
> 2358   Lena Mae Davis (1930-2015). *Lena was born on November 15, 1930. She died on May 24, 2015.*

Annie Bell Spivey, daughter of James Martin Spivey (1871-1929) and Mary Caroline Sheffield (1870-1921), was born on August 19, 1900 in Moore County, NC. She died on September 3, 1978 in Montgomery County, NC and was buried in Moore County, NC at Dover Baptist Church. She and Ira Spinks Davis had the following children:

> 2359   Myrtle Mae Spivey (1920-1957). *Myrtle was born on June 5, 1920. She died on March 30, 1957 and was buried in Moore County, NC at Dover Baptist Church.*

715. **Cora Helen Davis**, daughter of Lewis Washington Davis and Martha Clementine Maness, was born on December 31, 1895. She died on July 12, 1941 and was buried in Mt. Gilead, Montgomery County, NC at Stoney Fork Baptist Church.

> **William Sydney Harris** was born on March 5, 1888 in Montgomery County, NC. He died on January 8, 1973 in Norfolk, VA and was buried in Mt. Gilead, Montgomery County, NC at Stoney Fork Baptist Church. He and Cora Helen Davis had the following children:
>
> 2360   Harris (-)

716. **Snoten M. Davis**, son of Lewis Washington Davis and Martha Clementine Maness, was born on March 10, 1898. He died on June 8, 1961 and was buried in Moore County, NC at Dover Baptist Church.

> **Emma Williams** was born on March 11, 1902. She died on June 15, 1981 and was buried in Moore County, NC at Dover Baptist Church.

717. **Asa Lewis Davis**, son of Lewis Washington Davis and Martha Clementine Maness, was born on April 14, 1900. He died on October 2, 1962 and was buried in Moore County, NC at Dover Baptist Church.

> **Lona F. Dunn** was born on February 6, 1907. She died on August 2, 1996 and was buried in Moore County, NC at Dover Baptist Church.

718. **Ruth Bernice Davis**, daughter of Lewis Washington Davis and Martha Clementine Maness, was born in 1903.

> **Dossie Orlando Comer**, son of Adam Franklin Comer (1870-1957) and Margaret Dunn (1870-1947), was born in June 1896. He and Ruth Bernice Davis had the following children:
>
> 2361   Mabel Comer (-)
> 2362   Doris Blanche Comer (-)
> 2363   James Everette Comer (1922-1990). *James was born on January 10, 1922. He died on December 26, 1990 and was buried in Eagle Springs, Moore County, NC at Eagle Springs United Methodist Church.*
> 2364   Treva Estelle Comer (1923-). *Treva was born on July 6, 1923.*
> 2365   Roy S. Comer (1925-). *Roy was born in 1925.*
> 2366   Wayne M. Comer (1926-). *Wayne was born in 1926.*
> 2367   D. Reese Comer (1928-1978). *D. was born on August 25, 1928. He died on May 2, 1978 and was buried in Eagle Springs, Moore County, NC at Eagle Springs United Methodist Church.*
> 2368   Melvin Comer (1930-1990). *Melvin was born on June 11, 1930. He died on December 16, 1990 and was buried in Moore County, NC at Bensalem Presbyterian Church.*

719. **Glennie Esther Davis**, daughter of Lewis Washington Davis and Martha Clementine Maness, was born on August 9, 1904. She died on December 14, 1979 and was buried in Moore County, NC at Dover Baptist Church.

Willie James Brewer, son of Stephen Brewer (1877-1953) and Caroline Dunn (1873-1951), was born on April 25, 1898. He died on January 16, 1982 and was buried in Moore County, NC at Dover Baptist Church. He and Glennie Esther Davis had the following children:

2369	Dorothy Brewer (-)
2370	Ruth Brewer (-)
2371	Marie Brewer (-)
2372	Geraldine Brewer (-)
2373	Joe Brewer (-)
2374	Thomas Lewis Brewer (1923-1946). *Thomas was born on November 16, 1923. He died on June 23, 1946 and was buried in Moore County, NC at Dover Baptist Church.*
2375	Vernon Leroy Brewer (1932-2001). *Vernon was born on August 14, 1932. He died on July 26, 2001.*
2376	Female Brewer (1934-1934). *Female was born on July 18, 1934. She died on July 18, 1934 and was buried in Moore County, NC at Dover Baptist Church.*
2377	Betty Sue Brewer (1935-2020). *Betty was born on August 10, 1935. She died on April 28, 2020 and was buried in Moore County, NC at Smyrna Methodist Church.*
2378	Gurney Clinton Brewer (1938-1995). *Gurney was born on January 12, 1938. He married* **Dora Helen Kennedy** *on April 1, 1961. He died on October 14, 1995 and was buried in Moore County, NC at Dover Baptist Church.*
2379	Barbara Ann Brewer (1940-). *Barbara was born on February 14, 1940.*

720. **Claude Roosevelt Davis**, son of Lewis Washington Davis and Martha Clementine Maness, was born on September 24, 1906. He died on August 15, 1972 and was buried in Moore County, NC at Dover Baptist Church.

Nonnie A. Spivey, daughter of Nancy Jane Spivey (1881-1975), was born on August 5, 1917. She died on May 2, 1998 and was buried in Moore County, NC at Dover Baptist Church. She and Claude Roosevelt Davis had the following children:

2380	Annie Mae Davis (-)
2381	Lennie Melvin Davis (1934-1987). *Lennie was born on January 20, 1934. He died on September 25, 1987 and was buried in Robbins, Moore County, NC at Acorn Ridge Baptist Church.*

732. **Dora Deaton**, daughter of Joseph Franklin Deaton and Lucinda Maness, was born in 1902 in Moore County, NC. She died on June 10, 1983 in Pinehurst, Moore County, NC and was buried in Biscoe, Montgomery County, NC at Deaton Family Cemetery.

Charles Leach, son of David Archibald Leach (1861-1921) and Martha Adeline Skeen (1866-1918), was born on June 29, 1897 in Randolph County, NC. He married Bessie Marie Franklin on June 1, 1924 in Kansas City, Wyandotte, Kansas. He died on August 19, 1971 in St. Francis, KS and was buried in Bird City, Cheyenne County, KS.

733. **Hattie F. Deaton**, daughter of Joseph Franklin Deaton and Lucinda Maness, was born on January 11, 1904. She died on June 25, 1994 and was buried in Moore County, NC at Dover Baptist Church.

Willie Kitchen Melton, son of John Melton (1881-1945) and Lalon Jenetta Cagle (1886-1924), was born on October 5, 1908. He died on May 6, 1971 and was buried in Moore County, NC at Dover Baptist Church.

734. **Catherine Kerns**, daughter of William Cornelius Kerns and Francina Maness, was born on July 19, 1900. She died on October 14, 1963 and was buried in Montgomery County, NC at Shady Grove Christian Church Cemetery.

William Thomas Shankle and Catherine Kerns had the following children:

2382	Clem Harry Shankle (1935-2015). *Clem was born in 1935. He died in 2015.*

735. **Richard Kerns**, son of William Cornelius Kerns and Francina Maness, was born on October 24, 1901. He died on December 25, 1922 and was buried in Montgomery County, NC at Shady Grove Christian Church Cemetery.

737. **Nora Belle Maness**, daughter of William Robert Maness and Martha Matilda Wallace, was born on July 26, 1900. She died on July 16, 1979 and was buried in Moore County, NC at Bascom Chapel United Methodist Church.

Daniel A. Dunlap, son of John William Dunlap (1858-1916) and Mary Jane Cole (1857-1920), was born on February 11, 1889. He died on March 23, 1970 and was buried in Moore County, NC at Bascom Chapel United Methodist Church. He and Nora Belle Maness had the following children:

2383	Mary Jane Dunlap (1921-2001). *Mary was born on February 2, 1921. She married **June Atlas Cockman** on September 16, 1939. She died on December 31, 2001 and was buried in Robbins, Moore County, NC at Pine Rest Cemetery.*
2384	Lynnie Kate Dunlap (1923-). *Lynnie was born in 1923.*
2385	Nannie Lou Dunlap (1924-). *Nannie was born on September 17, 1924.*
2386	Daniel C. Dunlap (1926-). *Daniel was born in 1926.*
2387	William Alfred Dunlap (1928-2006). *William was born on October 17, 1928. He married **Lillie Eljean Barber** on December 23, 1953. He died on May 2, 2006 in Moore County, NC.*
2388	Oliver Max Dunlap (1930-). *Oliver was born on August 24, 1930 in Moore County, NC. He married **Annie Ruth Kidd** on January 26, 1954 in Moore County, NC.*

741. **Riley Colon Maness**, son of William Robert Maness and Martha Matilda Wallace, was born in 1908. He died on November 24, 1963 in Guilford County, NC.

Lucille Robbins was born on November 3, 1911. She died on April 12, 1979 in Guilford County, NC. She and Riley Colon Maness had the following children:

2389	Riley Colon Maness Jr. (-)
2390	Rubin Maness (1950-1999). *Rubin was born in 1950. He died in 1999.*

743. **Joseph Peele Maness**, son of William Robert Maness and Martha Matilda Wallace, was born on August 19, 1911 in Montgomery County, NC. He married **Marjorie Morrison** on November 26, 1935 in Randolph County, NC. He died on February 5, 1986 in Thomasville, Davidson County, NC and was buried in Thomasville, Davidson County, NC at Holly Hill Memorial Park.

Marjorie Morrison died in December 2005 and was buried in Thomasville, Davidson County, NC at Holly Hill Memorial Park. She and Joseph Peele Maness had the following children:

2391	Marjorie Gwendolyn Maness (1937-). *Marjorie was born on July 17, 1937.*

750. **Mable Wright Maness**, daughter of Angus Clegg Maness and Christian Nall, was born on May 13, 1915. She died on February 15, 2009.

Vinoka Audrey Holland was born on February 14, 1913. He died on September 11, 2000. He and Mable Wright Maness had the following children:

2392	Janice Holland (-)

751. **William Arley Maness**, son of William Robert Maness and Lucy Ella Davis, was born on March 12, 1897. He died on June 29, 1972 and was buried in Moore County, NC at Pleasant Hill United Methodist Church.

Ida Elizabeth Siler was born on February 6, 1898. She died on May 18, 1968 and was buried in Moore County, NC at Pleasant Hill United Methodist Church. She and William Arley Maness had the following children:

2393	Tillett Leo Maness (1937-1964). *Tillett was born on July 14, 1937. He died on April 27, 1964 and was buried in Moore County, NC at Pleasant Hill United Methodist Church.*

752. Annie Jane Maness, daughter of William Robert Maness and Lucy Ella Davis, was born on February 28, 1899. She married **Lonnie Watson Lambert** on April 6, 1929 in Moore County, NC. She died on October 14, 1990 and was buried in Moore County, NC at Pleasant Hill United Methodist Church.

Lonnie Watson Lambert, son of Robartis Lambert (1854-1929) and Sarah Hadley Maness (1855-1912), was born on October 12, 1899. He died on October 12, 1957 and was buried in Moore County, NC at Pleasant Hill United Methodist Church. He and Annie Jane Maness had the following children:

2394	Lonnie Watson Lambert Jr. (1930-1946). *Lonnie was born on May 20, 1930. He died on January 7, 1946 and was buried in Moore County, NC at Pleasant Hill United Methodist Church.*

760. Racy Hugh Maness, son of William Robert Maness and Lucy Ella Davis, was born on February 15, 1917. He died on February 28, 1996 and was buried in Moore County, NC at High Falls Friends Meeting Cemetery.

Beulah Edith Kennedy, daughter of John Biddle Kennedy (1884-1971) and Mary Katherine Brewer (1888-1963), was born on October 25, 1921. She died on April 21, 2009 in Moore County, NC and was buried in High Falls, Moore County, NC at Prosperity Friends Meeting Cemetery. She and Racy Hugh Maness had the following children:

2395	Lester Gerald Maness (1943-2001). *Lester was born on December 14, 1943. He died on January 22, 2001 and was buried in Moore County, NC at Providence Chapel Church.*

761. Beulah Irene Maness, daughter of William Robert Maness and Lucy Ella Davis, was born in 1920.

Albert Everette Paschal and Beulah Irene Maness had the following children:

2396	Paschal (-)

762. Aggie Donner Maness, daughter of Nancy E. Maness, was born on June 10, 1894. She died on July 19, 1972 and was buried in Moore County, NC at Pleasant Hill United Methodist Church.

Kenny Harrison Cockman, son of Eli Terry Cockman (1857-1946) and Silla Frances Horner (1854-1903), was born on March 21, 1891. He died on June 12, 1980 and was buried in Moore County, NC at Pleasant Hill United Methodist Church. He and Aggie Donner Maness had the following children:

2397	Josie Mae Cockman (1914-1999). *Josie was born on May 23, 1914. She married **Earl Carter Stutts** on June 5, 1937. She died on December 25, 1999 and was buried in Robbins, Moore County, NC at Pine Rest Cemetery.*
2398	Kennie Eli Cockman (1916-1919). *Kennie was born on July 10, 1916. He died on January 17, 1919 and was buried in Moore County, NC at Pleasant Hill United Methodist Church.*
2399	Roland Harrison Cockman (1918-). *Roland was born on April 15, 1918.*
2400	Female Cockman (1919-1919). *Female was born on December 24, 1919. She died on December 24, 1919 and was buried in Moore County, NC at Pleasant Hill United Methodist Church.*
2401	Male Cockman (1919-1919). *Male was born on December 24, 1919. He died on December 24, 1919 and was buried in Moore County, NC at Pleasant Hill United Methodist Church.*
2402	Calvin Harding Cockman (1921-1998). *Calvin was born on March 22, 1921. He died on September 12, 1998 and was buried in Moore County, NC at Calvary Baptist Church.*
2403	Nancy Frances Cockman (1923-1998). *Nancy was born on April 15, 1923 in Moore County, NC. She died on December 4, 1998 and was buried in Robbins, Moore County, NC at Pine Rest Cemetery.*
2404	Lacy J. Cockman (1925-1925). *Lacy was born on May 23, 1925. He died on July 3, 1925 and was buried in Moore County, NC at Pleasant Hill United Methodist Church.*
2405	Donner Lee Cockman (1928-2009). *Donner was born on May 9, 1928. She married **Robert Mack Beck** on September 29, 1946 in Moore County, NC. She died on*

2406   Kerney Elbert Cockman (1930-1994). *Kerney was born on March 24, 1930 in Moore County, NC. He died on October 3, 1994 and was buried in Robbins, Moore County, NC at Pine Rest Cemetery.*

2407   Benjamin Franklin Cockman (1932-2000). *Benjamin was born on July 21, 1932 in Moore County, NC. He died on June 23, 2000 and was buried in Robbins, Moore County, NC at Pine Rest Cemetery.*

763. **Ruby Kathleen Phillips**, daughter of Charles Wesley Phillips and Emily Rebecca Maness, was born on July 12, 1906. She died on March 20, 2002 and was buried in Chatham County, NC at Gaines Grove Cemetery.

Paul Alexander Wilson, son of Daniel Lewis Wilson (1875-1928) and Mary Catherine Groce (1877-1941), was born on March 10, 1908. He died on November 24, 1957 and was buried in Goldston, Chatham County, NC at Antioch Baptist Church. He and Ruby Kathleen Phillips had the following children:

2408   Jerry Wilson (-)

764. **Archie Lane Paschal**, son of George Luther Paschal and Julia McIntyre Maness, was born in December 1889.

765. **Mollie Cora Paschal**, daughter of George Luther Paschal and Julia McIntyre Maness, was born on July 26, 1891. She died on November 29, 1980 and was buried in Moore County, NC at Fair Promise Methodist Church.

Fred Lee Shields, son of Arabelle Shields (1868-), was born on July 10, 1889. He died on December 6, 1959 and was buried in Moore County, NC at Fair Promise Methodist Church. He and Mollie Cora Paschal had the following children:

2409   Julia Belle Shields (-)
2410   Vincent Shields (-)
2411   Fred W. Shields (-)
2412   Norris Shields (-)
2413   Alfred Holten Shields (1914-1975). *Alfred was born on August 29, 1914. He died on February 18, 1975 and was buried in Fayetteville, Cumberland County, NC at Lafayette Memorial Park.*

767. **Baxter Worth Paschal**, son of George Luther Paschal and Julia McIntyre Maness, was born on October 17, 1894. He died on November 29, 1971 and was buried in Moore County, NC at Fair Promise Methodist Church.

768. **Josephine Paschal**, daughter of George Luther Paschal and Julia McIntyre Maness, was born on September 20, 1896. She died on July 15, 1963 and was buried in Fayetteville, Cumberland County, NC at Lafayette Memorial Park.

Leonidas Stacy McDaniel was born on November 27, 1891. He died on September 24, 1970 and was buried in Fayetteville, Cumberland County, NC at Lafayette Memorial Park.

769. **Virginia Oppie Paschal**, daughter of George Luther Paschal and Julia McIntyre Maness, was born on January 18, 1899. She died on January 28, 1991 and was buried in Moore County, NC at Fair Promise Methodist Church.

William Christian Goodall Jr., son of William Christian Goodall Sr. (1869-1943) and Grace Darling Dunn (-), was born on May 4, 1893. He died on December 8, 1972 and was buried in Moore County, NC at Fair Promise Methodist Church.

770. **Julian Carr Paschal**, son of George Luther Paschal and Julia McIntyre Maness, was born on July 29, 1901. He died on January 27, 2001 and was buried in Moore County, NC at Fair Promise Methodist Church.

Carrie "Mackie" Muse, daughter of Murdoch Lee Muse (1889-1928) and Wilbert Dixon "Willie" Phillips (1897-1926), was born on September 17, 1920. She died on September 12, 2013 and was buried in Moore County, NC at Fair Promise Methodist Church. She and Julian Carr Paschal had the following children:

2414   Nancy Paschal (-)
2415   Julian Carr Paschal Jr. (1942-1959). *Julian was born on July 13, 1942. He died on*

February 10, 1959 and was buried in Moore County, NC at Fair Promise Methodist Church.

771. **Ernest Hurley Paschal**, son of George Luther Paschal and Julia McIntyre Maness, was born in 1903.

772. **Luther George Paschal**, son of George Luther Paschal and Julia McIntyre Maness, was born on April 22, 1906. He died on March 25, 1982 and was buried in Moore County, NC at Fair Promise Methodist Church.

773. **Lawrence Hughes Paschal**, son of George Luther Paschal and Julia McIntyre Maness, was born on February 23, 1908. He died on June 25, 1999 and was buried in Moore County, NC at Fair Promise Methodist Church.

774. **Donald Ira Paschal**, son of George Luther Paschal and Julia McIntyre Maness, was born on March 14, 1910. He died on September 18, 1976 and was buried in Moore County, NC at Fair Promise Methodist Church.

775. **Arthur Garner Paschal**, son of George Luther Paschal and Julia McIntyre Maness, was born in 1912.

776. **Henry Phillips Paschal**, son of George Luther Paschal and Julia McIntyre Maness, was born on December 29, 1913. He died on March 25, 1914 and was buried in Moore County, NC at Fair Promise Methodist Church.

777. **Addie Marie Brady**, daughter of George W. Brady and Josephine A. Maness, was born on February 20, 1899. She died on December 26, 1999 and was buried in High Falls, Moore County, NC at Prosperity Friends Meeting Cemetery.

782. **Jewel Wallace**, daughter of Jerome A. Wallace and Ella Bennett, was born on January 19, 1909. She died on October 8, 1987.

>   **John L. Dasher** was born on August 12, 1911. He died on January 31, 1966. He and Jewel Wallace had the following children:
>
> | 2416 | Dasher (-) |
> |---|---|

785. **Mildred Doris Wallace**, daughter of Jerome A. Wallace and Ella Bennett, was born on February 20, 1915. She married **George Ivey** on August 2, 1937 in Lowndes County, GA. She died on February 5, 2005.

>   George Ivey was born on March 12, 1915. He died on November 29, 2004. He and Mildred Doris Wallace had the following children:
>
> | 2417 | Ivey (-) |
> |---|---|

786. **Audrey Howard Wallace**, son of Jerome A. Wallace and Ella Bennett, was born on September 10, 1918. He died on April 29, 1994.

>   **Dorothy E. Crumpton** was born on March 4, 1927. She died on August 1, 2006. She and Audrey Howard Wallace had the following children:
>
> | 2418 | Michael Howard Wallace (-) |
> |---|---|

787. **Sabina Harper**, daughter of James Marion Harper and Caroline Wallace, was born in February 1886.

788. **James Oliver Harper**, son of James Marion Harper and Caroline Wallace, was born on May 8, 1888. He died on December 24, 1953 and was buried in Seagrove, Randolph County, NC at Maple Springs Baptist Church.

>   **Nannie Irene Purvis**, daughter of William Garrett Purvis (1860-1928) and Irene "Rena" Johnson (1865-1909), was born on August 20, 1893. She died on July 15, 1972 and was buried in Seagrove, Randolph County, NC at Maple Springs Baptist Church. She and James Oliver Harper had the following children:
>
> | 2419 | Jessie J. Harper (1912-1912). *Jessie was born on July 3, 1912. He died on December 3, 1912 and was buried in Seagrove, Randolph County, NC at Maple Springs Baptist Church.* |
> |---|---|
> | 2420 | Rena Harper (1915-). *Rena was born in 1915.* |

2421	Rosa Harper (1916-1990). *Rosa was born on August 25, 1916. She died on August 17, 1990 and was buried in Seagrove, Randolph County, NC at Maple Springs Baptist Church.*
2422	Howard Lee Harper (1918-1988). *Howard was born on October 14, 1918. He died on November 20, 1988 and was buried in Seagrove, Randolph County, NC at Maple Springs Baptist Church.*
2423	Helen Pauline Harper (1921-). *Helen was born on June 20, 1921 in Randolph County, NC.*
2424	Canary Belle Harper (1923-). *Canary was born on September 8, 1923 in Randolph County, NC.*
2425	Mary Allene Harper (1926-). *Mary was born on April 10, 1926 in Randolph County, NC.*

789. **Mary E. Harper**, daughter of James Marion Harper and Caroline Wallace, was born in May 1891.

790. **John Thomas Harper**, son of James Marion Harper and Caroline Wallace, was born on June 11, 1895. He died on June 12, 1897 and was buried in Seagrove, Randolph County, NC at Maple Springs Baptist Church.

791. **William Elmer Harper**, son of James Marion Harper and Caroline Wallace, was born in August 1898.

Tishie Eugenia Plummer was born in 1903. She and William Elmer Harper had the following children:

2426	Mary Edith Harper (1920-). *Mary was born in 1920.*
2427	James Robert Harper (1921-). *James was born on September 23, 1921 in Randolph County, NC.*
2428	Minnie Kathalene Harper (1923-). *Minnie was born on December 21, 1923.*
2429	William Ernest Harper (1926-). *William was born on May 12, 1926 in Randolph County, NC.*
2430	Elizabeth Ann Harper (1930-). *Elizabeth was born on October 18, 1930 in Randolph County, NC.*
2431	Martha Harper (1936-). *Martha was born on March 17, 1936 in Randolph County, NC.*

792. **Burnie Alfine Harper**, son of James Marion Harper and Caroline Wallace, was born on May 19, 1901. He died on April 12, 1979 in Randolph County, NC.

798. **William Penn Farlow**, son of Robert Lee Farlow and Annie Louella Wallace, was born on March 1, 1899 in Randolph County, NC. He married **Elizabeth Hogan** circa 1923. He died on December 24, 1961 in Asheboro, Randolph County, NC and was buried on December 26, 1961 in Asheboro, Randolph County, NC at Marlboro Friends Church.

Elizabeth Hogan was born in 1903 in Montgomery County, NC. She and William Penn Farlow had the following children:

2432	John F. Farlow (1924-). *John was born in 1924.*
2433	Blanche Farlow (1926-). *Blanche was born in 1926.*
2434	Pearlie Farlow (1928-). *Pearlie was born in 1928.*
2435	Dee Ette Farlow (1939-). *Dee was born on November 12, 1939 in Randolph County, NC.*
2436	Dee Farlow (1939-). *Dee was born on November 12, 1939 in Randolph County, NC.*
2437	Alberta Farlow (1942-). *Alberta was born on April 1, 1942 in Randolph County, NC.*

800. **Thomas Kenyon Farlow**, son of Robert Lee Farlow and Annie Louella Wallace, was born on June 6, 1904. He died on September 22, 1978 in UNC Hospital, Chapel Hill, Orange County, NC and was buried in Seagrove, Randolph County, NC at Maple Springs Baptist Church.

801. **Raleigh L. Wallace**, son of Robert Lee Farlow and Annie Louella Wallace, was born on December 4, 1907. He died on April 26, 1926 and was buried in Seagrove, Randolph County, NC at Maple Springs Baptist Church.

802. **Zora Della Wallace**, daughter of Robert Lee Farlow and Annie Louella Wallace, was born on December 15, 1912 in Randolph County, NC. She married **James Goodmon Green** circa 1929. She died on June 15, 1996 and was buried in Seagrove, Randolph County, NC at Maple Springs Baptist Church.

James Goodmon Green was born on April 25, 1905 in Montgomery County, NC. He died on February 28, 1992 and was buried in Seagrove, Randolph County, NC at Maple Springs Baptist Church. He and Zora Della Wallace had the following children:

2438   James Ray Green (1928-1977). *James was born on June 30, 1928 in Randolph County, NC. He died on November 24, 1977 and was buried in Seagrove, Randolph County, NC at Maple Springs Baptist Church.*

2439   Janie Elizabeth Green (1931-). *Janie was born on March 5, 1931 in Randolph County, NC.*

2440   Kenneth Lee Green (1933-). *Kenneth was born on June 9, 1933 in Randolph County, NC.*

2441   Colon Wesley Green (1934-). *Colon was born on December 14, 1934 in Randolph County, NC.*

803. **Mary Elizabeth Wallace**, daughter of Willard Webster Boone and Annie Louella Wallace, was born on July 24, 1884 in Randolph County, NC. She married **Artemus Kennedy** on December 20, 1906 in Randolph County, NC. She died on March 24, 1974 in Pine Ridge Nursing Home, Sanford, Lee County, NC and was buried on March 26, 1974 in Seagrove, Randolph County, NC at Maple Springs Baptist Church.

Artemus Kennedy, son of William M. Kennedy (1856-1931) and Martha Ellen Luck (1862-bef 1910), was born on December 25, 1885 in Moore County, NC. He died on January 3, 1962 and was buried in Seagrove, Randolph County, NC at Maple Springs Baptist Church. He and Mary Elizabeth Wallace had the following children:

2442   May Kennedy (1906-). *May was born in 1906. She married **Velty Greene** on November 3, 1923 in Montgomery County, NC.*

2443   Etta Kennedy (1909-). *Etta was born in 1909. She married **Henry H. Singleton** on November 7, 1923 in Montgomery County, NC.*

2444   Walter Carson Kennedy (1911-1994). *Walter was born on April 2, 1911. He died on July 10, 1994.*

2445   Annie Kennedy (1915-1994). *Annie was born in 1915. She died on February 25, 1994 in Montgomery County, NC and was buried in Thomasville, Davidson County, NC at Holly Hill Memorial Park.*

2446   Cora Lee Kennedy (1916-1998). *Cora was born on July 4, 1916. She died on July 21, 1998 and was buried in Seagrove, Randolph County, NC at Maple Springs Baptist Church.*

2447   Carl Chesley Kennedy (1919-1933). *Carl was born on May 20, 1919 in Randolph County, NC. He died on April 17, 1933 in Randolph County, NC and was buried in Seagrove, Randolph County, NC at Maple Springs Baptist Church.*

2448   Colvin Kennedy (1923-2015). *Colvin was born on June 24, 1923 in Randolph County, NC. He married **Connie Ellen Greene** on December 1, 1943. He died on March 31, 2015 and was buried in Seagrove, Randolph County, NC at Maple Springs Baptist Church.*

2449   Lacy Kennedy (1926-). *Lacy was born on January 12, 1926 in Randolph County, NC.*

2450   Mary Magdalene Kennedy (1928-). *Mary was born on June 26, 1928 in Randolph County, NC.*

804. **Wade C. Wallace**, son of Reece Blair and Annie Louella Wallace, was born on December 25, 1893. He married **Dora Christian Hall** circa 1914. He died on July 17, 1970 and was buried in Sanford, Lee County, NC at Buffalo Presbyterian Church.

Dora Christian Hall, daughter of Fern George Hall (1867-1942) and Nancy Lucinda Cole (1871-1956), was born on September 10, 1895. She died on March 4, 1988 and was buried in Sanford, Lee County, NC at Buffalo Presbyterian Church. She and Wade C. Wallace had the following children:

2451   Verona Belle Wallace (1916-1998). *Verona was born on January 7, 1916. She died on July 1, 1998 and was buried in Moore County, NC at Culdee Presbyterian Church.*

2452   George Reece Wallace (1917-1997). *George was born on July 7, 1917. He married **Mamie Lee McNeill** on February 3, 1945 in Bennettsville, Marlboro County, SC. He died on October 5, 1997 and was buried in Sanford, Lee County, NC at Buffalo Presbyterian Church.*

2453   James Dixon Wallace (1919-1920). *James was born on June 16, 1919 in Moore County,*

NC. He died on January 24, 1920 in Moore County, NC and was buried in Eagle Springs, Moore County, NC at Eagle Springs United Methodist Church.

2454   Francis Theodore Wallace (1921-1992). *Francis was born on February 21, 1921 in Moore County, NC. He died on May 5, 1992 in Myrtle Beach, SC and was buried in Sanford, Lee County, NC at Buffalo Presbyterian Church.*

2455   Leanora Helen Wallace (1924-2004). *Leanora was born on April 15, 1924 in Moore County, NC. She died on February 22, 2004 in Moore County, NC and was buried in Sanford, Lee County, NC at Buffalo Presbyterian Church.*

2456   Bertha Inez Wallace (1927-). *Bertha was born on July 23, 1927 in Moore County, NC.*

2457   Hazel Marie Wallace (1930-). *Hazel was born on September 15, 1930 in Moore County, NC.*

2458   Robert Rolland Wallace (1933-2004). *Robert was born on August 28, 1933 in Moore County, NC. He died on June 7, 2004 and was buried in Sanford, Lee County, NC at Buffalo Presbyterian Church.*

2459   Betty Jean Wallace (1936-2005). *Betty was born on January 1, 1936 in Moore County, NC. She died on May 26, 2005 and was buried in Sanford, Lee County, NC at Buffalo Presbyterian Church.*

2460   Harold L. Wallace (1940-1941). *Harold was born on November 25, 1940 in Moore County, NC. He died on March 5, 1941 in Lee County Hospital, Sanford, Lee County, NC and was buried on March 6, 1941 in Eagle Springs, Moore County, NC at Eagle Springs United Methodist Church.*

805. George Washington Kennedy, son of William M. Kennedy and Maude Jane Wallace, was born on April 4, 1903. He died on July 18, 1967 in Randolph County, NC.

Mishie Owens and George Washington Kennedy had the following children:

2461   Dorothy Kennedy (-)

2462   Daughter Kennedy (-)

2463   Daughter Kennedy (-)

2464   George Washington Kennedy Jr. (c. 1942-1986). *George was born circa 1942. He died on August 14, 1986.*

806. Lucy Jane Kennedy, daughter of William M. Kennedy and Maude Jane Wallace, was born on April 2, 1907. She died on September 21, 1993 and was buried in Moore County, NC at Cool Springs United Methodist Church.

Norman Loflin Yow, son of Reuben Spinks Yow (1879-1943) and Elizabeth Hicks (1891-1918), was born on July 15, 1905. He died on August 27, 1970 in Montgomery County, NC and was buried in Moore County, NC at Cool Springs United Methodist Church. He and Lucy Jane Kennedy had the following children:

2465   Jesse J. Yow (1928-). *Jesse was born on November 12, 1928 in Randolph County, NC.*

2466   Cay Lee Yow (1931-). *Cay was born on March 26, 1931 in Randolph County, NC.*

2467   Ernest Eugene Yow (1933-). *Ernest was born on July 30, 1933 in Randolph County, NC.*

2468   Everett William Yow (1941-). *Everett was born on May 1, 1941 in Randolph County, NC.*

813. John Dixon Wallace, son of Alexander Vance Wallace and Leander Frances Sheffield, was born on July 4, 1899 in Scotland County, NC. He died in April 1987.

Eney Wiley and John Dixon Wallace had the following children:

2469   John Dixon Wallace Jr. (1926-1970). *John was born on October 21, 1926. He married **Evelyn Mooring** on September 10, 1950. He died on December 23, 1970.*

814. Viola Blanche Wallace, daughter of Alexander Vance Wallace and Leander Frances Sheffield, was born on March 16, 1902 in Scotland County, NC.

Langford and Viola Blanche Wallace had the following children:

2470   John Langford (-)

2471	Boyce Langford (-)

817. Mary Alice Jones, daughter of Cornelius Hasseltine Jones and Sarah Wallace, was born on July 30, 1861 in Alabama. She died on May 10, 1892 and was buried in Cherokee County, TX at Myrtle Springs Cemetery.

819. Bernice Jones, daughter of Cornelius Hasseltine Jones and Sarah Wallace, was born in 1868 in Texas.

R. H. Hunter and Bernice Jones had the following children:

2472	Bonnie Hunter (-)
2473	Mary Hunter (-)
2474	Lulu Hunter (-)
2475	Rush Hunter (-)
2476	Sarah Hunter (-)
2477	Harold Hunter (-)

822. Laura C. Jones, daughter of Cornelius Hasseltine Jones and Sarah Wallace, was born in January 1870 in Texas.

John N. Chandler was born in May 1868. He and Laura C. Jones had the following children:

2478	Alton B. Chandler (1897-). *Alton was born in October 1897.*

824. Winnie E. Sessions, daughter of S.R. Sessions and Lucinda Wallace, was born on December 13, 1875. She died on November 17, 1876 and was buried in Cherokee County, TX at Myrtle Springs Cemetery.

826. David Overton Wallace, son of Daniel Houston Wallace and Laura Ellen Knight, was born in 1872.

Nita Montgomery and David Overton Wallace had the following children:

2479	Phillip Downy Wallace (-)
2480	Marjorie Wallace (-)

827. Martha Clementine Wallace, daughter of Daniel Houston Wallace and Laura Ellen Knight, was born on February 12, 1874. She died on October 5, 1965.

829. Briston McCrimmon Wallace, son of Daniel Houston Wallace and Laura Ellen Knight, was born on January 3, 1879. He married **Grace Fetters** on October 19, 1902 in Anderson County, TX. He died on November 30, 1948.

Grace Fetters was born on July 5, 1882. She died on October 29, 1977. She and Briston McCrimmon Wallace had the following children:

2481	James Lionell Wallace (-)
2482	Anna Mae Wallace (-)
2483	Weldon Wallace (-)
2484	Eugene Wallace (-)
2485	June Wallace (-)
2486	Elmo LeRoy Wallace (1914-1966). *Elmo was born on April 19, 1914. He died on February 13, 1966.*

831. James Britian Wallace, son of Daniel Houston Wallace and Laura Ellen Knight, was born on April 20, 1885. He died on July 7, 1937.

Flavia Alice Stubbs was born in 1894. She and James Britian Wallace had the following children:

2487	James Britian Wallace Jr. (1918-). *James was born in 1918.*
2488	Gloria Jacquelyn Wallace (1921-). *Gloria was born in 1921.*
2489	William O'Brien Wallace (1925-). *William was born in 1925.*

832. **Fred F. Wallace**, son of Daniel Houston Wallace and Laura Ellen Knight, was born on February 15, 1888. He died on December 27, 1933.

> **Ethel Whidden** and Fred F. Wallace had the following children:
>
> | 2490 | Jack Wallace (-) |
> |------|------------------|
> | 2491 | Morgan Wallace (-) |

833. **Mary L. Wallace**, daughter of Daniel Houston Wallace and Laura Ellen Knight, was born on November 30, 1890. She died on February 7, 1891 and was buried in Cherokee County, TX at Myrtle Springs Cemetery.

834. **Byrd Wallace**, daughter of James Monk Wallace and Lily Wiggins Knight, was born on December 2, 1880 in Cherokee County, TX. She died on March 9, 1956 in Mineral Wells, Palo Pinto County, TX and was buried on March 10, 1956 in Mineral Wells, Palo Pinto County, TX at Elmwood Cemetery.

835. **Winnie Elizabeth Wallace**, daughter of James Monk Wallace and Lily Wiggins Knight, was born on October 3, 1882. She died on May 2, 1967 in Mineral Wells, Palo Pinto County, TX and was buried in Mineral Wells, Palo Pinto County, TX at Elmwood Cemetery.

> **James Henry Hester** was born on October 25, 1878. He died on April 26, 1966 and was buried in Mineral Wells, Palo Pinto County, TX at Elmwood Cemetery. He and Winnie Elizabeth Wallace had the following children:
>
> 2492   Bonnie Lou Hester (1916-2004). *Bonnie was born on November 20, 1916. She died on September 1, 2004 and was buried in Mineral Wells, Palo Pinto County, TX at Elmwood Cemetery.*

837. **Ernest Joe Wallace**, son of James Monk Wallace and Lily Wiggins Knight, was born on April 20, 1887 in Cherokee County, TX. He died on February 13, 1960 in Mineral Wells, Palo Pinto County, TX and was buried in Mineral Wells, Palo Pinto County, TX at Elmwood Cemetery.

838. **Elsie Bess Wallace**, daughter of James Monk Wallace and Lily Wiggins Knight, was born on December 4, 1889. She died on March 21, 1968 in Mineral Wells, Palo Pinto County, TX and was buried in Mineral Wells, Palo Pinto County, TX at Elmwood Cemetery.

839. **Laura Wallace**, daughter of James Monk Wallace and Lily Wiggins Knight, was born on April 16, 1892. She died on October 28, 1981 in Mineral Wells, Palo Pinto County, TX and was buried in Mineral Wells, Palo Pinto County, TX at Elmwood Cemetery.

840. **Allen B. Wallace**, son of James Monk Wallace and Lily Wiggins Knight, was born on February 20, 1899. He died on November 28, 1989 and was buried in Mineral Wells, Palo Pinto County, TX at Elmwood Cemetery.

> **Brownie** was born on December 4, 1902. She died on December 4, 1990 and was buried in Mineral Wells, Palo Pinto County, TX at Elmwood Cemetery.

841. **Julia Ann Wallace**, daughter of Raleigh S. Wallace and Dolly Smitherman, was born in 1870.

842. **Viola Wallace**, daughter of Raleigh S. Wallace and Dolly Smitherman, was born on September 11, 1873. She married **John Frank Scoggins** on November 13, 1898 in Bibb County, AL. She died on November 12, 1913.

> John Frank Scoggins was born in 1874. He died on March 14, 1920. He and Viola Wallace had the following children:
>
> 2493   Marvin Scoggins (1903-1958). *Marvin was born on June 8, 1903. He died on July 21, 1958.*

844. **Sina Wallace**, daughter of Raleigh S. Wallace and Dolly Smitherman, was born in 1877. She died on March 7, 1963 in Bibb County, AL.

James Manley Smith was born in 1874 in Fayette County, AL. He died on December 7, 1939 in Bibb County, AL. He and Sina Wallace had the following children:

> 2494   James Arthur Smith (-)

845. **Rufus Cobb Wallace**, son of Raleigh S. Wallace and Dolly Smitherman, was born in November 1877 in Bibb County, AL. He died on August 31, 1920 in Phoenix, Maricopa County, AZ and was buried in Phoenix, Maricopa County, AZ at Cementario Lindo Cemetery.

> **Mary Elizabeth Scroggins** was born in December 1876 in Alabama. She died in 1913 in Bibb County, AL. She and Rufus Cobb Wallace had the following children:

> > 2495   K. C. Wallace (-)
> > 2496   April Wallace (-)
> > 2497   Charles Wallace (-)
> > 2498   Clyde J. Wallace (1899-). *Clyde was born in October 1899.*
> > 2499   Mamie Alice Wallace (1902-1986). *Mamie was born on December 15, 1902. She married* **Norman Leslie "Pete" Saylor** *on July 3, 1923 in Phoenix, Maricopa County, AZ. She died on July 1, 1986 in Clovis, Curry County, NM.*

847. **John Hardy Wallace**, son of Raleigh S. Wallace and Dolly Smitherman, was born in 1883. He died on January 22, 1959 in Bibb County, AL and was buried on January 23, 1959 in Tuscaloosa, Tuscaloosa County, AL at Tuscaloosa Memorial Park Cemetery.

848. **Martha Isabell Smitherman**, daughter of Alfred Smitherman and Frances J. Wallace, was born on August 3, 1869 in Bibb County, AL. She died on April 11, 1945.

> **John Thomas Anderson** was born in 1850. He died in 1911.

850. **Levi Smitherman**, son of Alfred Smitherman and Frances J. Wallace, was born in May 1872 in Bibb County, AL. He married **Ada Obrantine Smitherman** on December 29, 1892 in Bibb County, AL. He died in December 1901.

> Ada Obrantine Smitherman was born on October 25, 1878 in Bibb County, AL. She died on September 11, 1968.

853. **John W. Wallace**, son of Joseph Davis Wallace and Elizabeth Caldwell, was born in 1871. He married **Pearl G. "Lula" Smitherman** on December 13, 1894 in Bibb County, AL.

> Pearl G. "Lula" Smitherman was born in 1873. She died on April 21, 1921 in Bibb County, AL. She and John W. Wallace had the following children:

> > 2500   Addie Wallace (1896-). *Addie was born in 1896.*
> > 2501   Effie Wallace (1898-). *Effie was born in 1898.*
> > 2502   Clarence Wallace (1902-). *Clarence was born in 1902.*
> > 2503   Gaston Wallace (1904-). *Gaston was born in 1904.*
> > 2504   Fannie Wallace (1907-). *Fannie was born in 1907.*
> > 2505   Eliza B. Wallace (1910-). *Eliza was born in 1910.*

854. **Walter Wallace**, son of Joseph Davis Wallace and Elizabeth Caldwell, was born in 1873. He married **Clemie Smitherman** on December 23, 1894 in Bibb County, AL.

856. **Rhoday M. "Rocky" Wallace**, daughter of Joseph Davis Wallace and Elizabeth Caldwell, was born on November 17, 1882. She died on September 28, 1942 and was buried in Bibb County, AL at Shady Grove Church Cemetery.

> **William Henry "Will" Smitherman** was born on October 6, 1874. He died on December 18, 1950 and was buried in Bibb County, AL at Shady Grove Church Cemetery. He and Rhoday M. "Rocky" Wallace had the following children:

> > 2506   Moody L. Smitherman (1917-1982). *Moody was born on September 27, 1917. He died on July 9, 1982.*

857. **Laura Smitherman**, daughter of James Pinkney Smitherman and Martha "Patsy" Wallace, was born on December 25, 1875 in Bibb County, AL. She married **Robert Brown** on November 20, 1895 in Bibb County, AL. She died on August 17, 1945.

858. **Lillian Smitherman**, daughter of James Pinkney Smitherman and Martha "Patsy" Wallace, was born on May 5, 1876 in Bibb County, AL. She died on July 18, 1939.

   Rome J. Payne was born on January 19, 1881 in Bibb County, AL. He died on December 9, 1941 in Bibb County, AL.

859. **William James Smitherman**, son of James Pinkney Smitherman and Martha "Patsy" Wallace, was born on May 20, 1880 in Bibb County, AL. He married **Myrtle Evelyn Payne** on November 14, 1907 in Bibb County, AL. He died on November 4, 1962 in Bibb County, AL and was buried in Bibb County, AL at Shady Grove Church Cemetery.

   Myrtle Evelyn Payne, daughter of Jonathan Geoffrey Payne (1858-1937) and Manila Alice Lawrence (1859-1929), was born on June 6, 1890 in Bibb County, AL. She died on November 28, 1958 in Bibb County, AL and was buried in Bibb County, AL at Shady Grove Church Cemetery. She and William James Smitherman had the following children:

   2507   Eloise Smitherman (1927-2014). *Eloise was born on August 30, 1927. She died on December 12, 2014 and was buried in Bibb County, AL at Shady Grove Church Cemetery.*

860. **Eula Wallace**, daughter of John C. Wallace and Mary J. Henderson, was born in August 1886.

861. **Minerva Mae Wallace**, daughter of John C. Wallace and Mary J. Henderson, was born on December 7, 1888. She married **Henry W. Wallace** circa 1907. She died on May 26, 1969 in Bibb County, AL and was buried in Bibb County, AL at Tabernacle Methodist Church Cemetery.

   Henry W. Wallace, son of John M. Wallace (1864-1928) and Emma Parker (1860-1945), was born on September 23, 1886. He died on December 6, 1967 and was buried in Bibb County, AL at Tabernacle Methodist Church Cemetery. He and Minerva Mae Wallace had the following children:

   2508   Grady Wallace (1909-). *Grady was born in 1909.*
   2509   Alvis Wallace (1914-). *Alvis was born in 1914.*
   2510   Willard Wallace (1915-). *Willard was born in 1915.*
   2511   Joyce Wallace (1920-). *Joyce was born in 1920.*

862. **Melford V. Wallace**, son of John C. Wallace and Mary J. Henderson, was born in March 1889.

863. **Sarah M. Wallace**, daughter of John C. Wallace and Mary J. Henderson, was born in August 1890. She died on June 29, 1948 in Bessemer, Jefferson County, AL.

   Marvin Jackson Wallace, son of John M. Wallace (1864-1928) and Emma Parker (1860-1945), was born on September 19, 1889. He died on June 1, 1962 in Houston, Harris County, TX and was buried in Vance, Bibb County, AL at Evergreen Baptist Church. He and Sarah M. Wallace had the following children:

   2512   Carl Edison Wallace (1915-). *Carl was born in 1915.*
   2513   Jesse May Wallace (1917-). *Jesse was born in 1917.*
   2514   Mary Wallace (1920-). *Mary was born in 1920.*

864. **Reuben Franklin Wallace**, son of John C. Wallace and Mary J. Henderson, was born on December 20, 1893. He died on October 10, 1966 and was buried in Bibb County, AL at Tabernacle Methodist Church Cemetery.

867. **Anna Ludelia Wallace**, daughter of William Harrison Wallace and Frances Emily Edwards, was born on December 16, 1874. She died on June 3, 1957 and was buried in Bibb County, AL at Tabernacle Methodist Church Cemetery.

   William Henry Thomas Riley was born in July 1874. He died on December 16, 1949 and was buried in Marion, Perry County, AL at Paynes Chapel Cemetery. He and Anna Ludelia Wallace had the following children:

2515	Lula F. Riley (1898-1989). *Lula was born on September 23, 1898. She died on September 2, 1989 and was buried in Jemison, Chilton County, AL at Macedonia Baptist Church Cemetery.*
2516	Ethel M. Riley (1901-). *Ethel was born in 1901.*
2517	Bevie O. Riley (1903-). *Bevie was born in 1903.*

868. **James Edward Wallace**, son of William Harrison Wallace and Frances Emily Edwards, was born on July 19, 1878. He died on December 9, 1945 in Selma, Dallas County, AL and was buried in Bibb County, AL at Tabernacle Methodist Church Cemetery.

Martha Ina Gentry was born on October 28, 1880. She died on June 10, 1970 and was buried in Bibb County, AL at Tabernacle Methodist Church Cemetery. She and James Edward Wallace had the following children:

2518	Iva Wallace (1901-). *Iva was born in 1901.*
2519	Clayton R. Wallace (1906-1974). *Clayton was born on June 19, 1906. He died on March 2, 1974 and was buried in Bibb County, AL at Tabernacle Methodist Church Cemetery.*
2520	Clyde Wallace (1908-). *Clyde was born in 1908.*
2521	Ina Wallace Jr. (1922-1922). *Ina was born on August 26, 1922 in Bibb County, AL. She died on August 29, 1922 in Bibb County, AL and was buried in Bibb County, AL at Tabernacle Methodist Church Cemetery.*

869. **Maudie Estelle Wallace**, daughter of William Harrison Wallace and Frances Emily Edwards, was born on February 22, 1888. She married **George Calhoun Langford** on November 11, 1905 in Bibb County, AL. She died on March 18, 1956 and was buried in Bibb County, AL at Tabernacle Methodist Church Cemetery.

George Calhoun Langford was born on February 4, 1878. He died on October 10, 1939 and was buried in Bibb County, AL at Tabernacle Methodist Church Cemetery. He and Maudie Estelle Wallace had the following children:

2522	Luman Gates Langford Sr. (1907-1967). *Luman was born on October 7, 1907. He died on August 31, 1967.*

874. **Roscoe A. Wallace**, son of Charles F. Wallace and Jeneria Jane Langford, was born in 1904. He died on October 10, 1973 in Birmingham, Jefferson County, AL and was buried in Bucksville, Tuscaloosa County, AL at Bucksville Cemetery.

877. **Henry Calhoun Wallace**, son of J. Henry Calhoun Wallace and Mary Henry "Mollie" Cash, was born in November 1883. He died on May 3, 1949 in Macon County, AL and was buried in Bibb County, AL at Tabernacle Methodist Church Cemetery.

Qunicy was born in 1891. She and Henry Calhoun Wallace had the following children:

2523	Grady Wallace (1910-). *Grady was born in 1910.*
2524	Alina Wallace (1912-). *Alina was born in 1912.*
2525	Nevada Wallace (1916-). *Nevada was born in 1916.*
2526	Male Wallace (1920-). *Male was born in 1920.*

878. **Charles T. Wallace**, son of J. Henry Calhoun Wallace and Mary Henry "Mollie" Cash, was born in March 1886. He died on October 2, 1969 in Birmingham, Jefferson County, AL.

Cora Jane was born in 1894.

879. **Jasper Decaster Wallace**, son of J. Henry Calhoun Wallace and Mary Henry "Mollie" Cash, was born on July 23, 1887. He died on November 16, 1960 in Bibb County, AL and was buried in Bibb County, AL at Tabernacle Methodist Church Cemetery.

880. **William Augusta Wallace**, son of J. Henry Calhoun Wallace and Mary Henry "Mollie" Cash, was born on November 16, 1889. He died on March 27, 1956 in Bibb County, AL and was buried in Bibb County, AL at Tabernacle Methodist Church Cemetery.

Lurania was born on December 29, 1899. She died on June 11, 1987 and was buried in Bibb County, AL at Tabernacle Methodist Church Cemetery.

881. **Rebecca Wallace**, daughter of J. Henry Calhoun Wallace and Mary Henry "Mollie" Cash, was born on October 12, 1891. She died on December 4, 1964 in Tuscaloosa, Tuscaloosa County, AL and was buried in Bibb County, AL at Tabernacle Methodist Church Cemetery.

   J. Frank Wooddell was born on November 10, 1891 and was buried in Bibb County, AL at Tabernacle Methodist Church Cemetery.

882. **John Columbus Wallace**, son of J. Henry Calhoun Wallace and Mary Henry "Mollie" Cash, was born on May 27, 1894. He died on October 25, 1973 in Bibb County, AL and was buried in Bibb County, AL at Tabernacle Methodist Church Cemetery.

884. **Miranda Idell Wallace**, daughter of J. Henry Calhoun Wallace and Mary Henry "Mollie" Cash, was born on December 30, 1897. She died on December 10, 1983 and was buried in Bibb County, AL at Tabernacle Methodist Church Cemetery.

   George Clemon Smith was born on January 13, 1900. He died on April 13, 1964 and was buried in Bibb County, AL at Tabernacle Methodist Church Cemetery.

885. **Robert Vandon Wallace**, son of J. Henry Calhoun Wallace and Mary Henry "Mollie" Cash, was born on October 4, 1899 in Bibb County, AL. He died on November 25, 1942 in Bessemer, Jefferson County, AL and was buried in Bibb County, AL at Tabernacle Methodist Church Cemetery.

887. **Minnie Virginia Wallace**, daughter of Lawson Wallace and Mary Catherine Pigford, was born on August 9, 1871. She married **James Wilson Coker** on October 4, 1892. She married **Charles Desseso Maury** on May 1, 1898. She died on July 3, 1966.

   James Wilson Coker died in 1897. He and Minnie Virginia Wallace had the following children:

2527	Irenne L. Coker (1894-). *Irenne was born in 1894.*
2528	Maggie M. Coker (1895-). *Maggie was born in 1895.*

   Charles Desseso Maury was born in 1871. He died in 1939. He and Minnie Virginia Wallace had the following children:

2529	Lucy G. Maury (1901-). *Lucy was born in 1901. She married **Sam B. Erice** in 1923.*
2530	Wallace Gilbert Maury (1902-1960). *Wallace was born on October 18, 1902. He died in August 1960.*
2531	Julian C. Maury (1907-). *Julian was born in 1907.*

888. **Cevilla Arrie Wallace**, daughter of Lawson Wallace and Mary Catherine Pigford, was born on September 10, 1874. She married **John Wesley Thompson** on November 21, 1895. She died on August 12, 1956.

   John Wesley Thompson was born on August 6, 1873. He died on March 19, 1940. He and Cevilla Arrie Wallace had the following children:

2532	Percy Wallace Thompson (1897-1984). *Percy was born on April 9, 1897. He died in 1984.*
2533	Edison Ray Thompson (1901-). *Edison was born in 1901.*
2534	Starr Kenneth Thompson (1902-1923). *Starr was born on May 20, 1902. He died on December 12, 1923.*
2535	Gladys Thompson (1905-). *Gladys was born in 1905.*
2536	Walton Ernest Thompson (1906-1990). *Walton was born on March 15, 1906. He married **Gerta Farmer Sharp** in 1926. He died on May 30, 1990.*
2537	Fred Leo Thompson (1908-). *Fred was born in 1908.*
2538	Lillian Avice Thompson (1911-). *Lillian was born in 1911.*

2539   Edith Mae Thompson (1914-). *Edith was born in 1914.*

890. **Daisy Edna Wallace**, daughter of Lawson Wallace and Mary Catherine Pigford, was born on September 13, 1881. She married **Marion Clinton Wilson** on December 22, 1900. She died on December 22, 1946.

Marion Clinton Wilson was born on September 18, 1882. He died on April 16, 1945. He and Daisy Edna Wallace had the following children:

2540   Julia Alica Wilson (1909-1986). *Julia was born on July 25, 1909. She married **Jeffery Leroy Lawrence** on October 17, 1925. She died on May 9, 1986.*

891. **Jasper Arthur Deen**, son of Robert Lee Deen and Sarah Martha "Mattie" Wallace, was born in July 1884.

Amelia was born in 1895. She and Jasper Arthur Deen had the following children:

2541   Leroy Deen (1911-). *Leroy was born in 1911.*
2542   Ardette Deen (1913-). *Ardette was born in 1913.*
2543   Maxina Deen (1915-). *Maxina was born in 1915.*
2544   Jasper Arthur Deen Jr. (1919-2006). *Jasper was born on October 25, 1919. He died on October 22, 2006.*
2545   Jewel Deen (1923-). *Jewel was born in 1923.*

894. **Marion Deen**, son of Robert Lee Deen and Sarah Martha "Mattie" Wallace, was born on March 12, 1889. He married **Minnie D. Durham** in 1910. He died in 1973.

Minnie D. Durham was born in 1889. She died in 1973. She and Marion Deen had the following children:

2546   Lucille Deen (-)
2547   Jessie C. Deen (-)
2548   Marion Lee Deen (1912-). *Marion was born in 1912.*
2549   Hazel Deen (1915-2012). *Hazel was born on April 3, 1915. She died on August 4, 2012.*
2550   Otha Deen (1917-). *Otha was born in December 1917.*

896. **Carrie E. Deen**, daughter of Robert Lee Deen and Sarah Martha "Mattie" Wallace, was born on December 22, 1891. She married **Gus Creed** in 1924. She died on June 19, 1998.

Gus Creed and Carrie E. Deen had the following children:

2551   Charles Creed (-)
2552   Clyde Creed (-)

897. **Jesse Randall Deen**, son of Robert Lee Deen and Sarah Martha "Mattie" Wallace, was born on May 29, 1895. He died on December 11, 1971.

Pearl Lanier was born in September 1896. She and Jesse Randall Deen had the following children:

2553   Randall E. Deen (-)
2554   Robert L. Deen (-)

898. **Floyd Virgil Deen**, son of Robert Lee Deen and Sarah Martha "Mattie" Wallace, was born in December 1899. He married **Eva** in 1923.

Eva and Floyd Virgil Deen had the following children:

2555   Audry Deen (-)

899. **Ebbin O. Deen**, son of Robert Lee Deen and Sarah Martha "Mattie" Wallace, was born in 1903. He married in 1924. He died in August 1983.

Ebbin O. Deen had the following children:

>2556   Jessie Lee Deen (1926-). *Jessie was born in 1926.*
>2557   Annie O. Deen (1929-). *Annie was born in 1929.*

901. **Jessie Maggard**, daughter of John Gary Maggard and Virginia Wallace, was born on December 15, 1889.

Monroe Butler was born on May 8, 1880. He and Jessie Maggard had the following children:

>2558   Agnes Thelma Butler (1912-1988). *Agnes was born on April 24, 1912. She died on September 11, 1988.*
>2559   Dave M. Butler (1915-). *Dave was born in 1915.*
>2560   Elton J. Butler (1921-). *Elton was born in 1921.*
>2561   James M. Butler (1928-). *James was born in 1928.*

902. **Charles Maggard**, son of John Gary Maggard and Virginia Wallace, was born in December 1892.

Ora M. Butler was born in 1894. She and Charles Maggard had the following children:

>2562   Weldon C. Maggard (1914-). *Weldon was born in 1914.*

903. **David Maggard**, son of John Gary Maggard and Virginia Wallace, was born on April 24, 1894. He died in January 1967.

Ina Mae Butler was born on December 25, 1896. She died on March 15, 1991. She and David Maggard had the following children:

>2563   Ruby Maggard (1913-). *Ruby was born in 1913.*
>2564   Marie Maggard (1915-). *Marie was born in 1915.*
>2565   Virginia Maggard (1916-). *Virginia was born in 1916.*
>2566   Allen Maggard (1918-). *Allen was born in 1918.*
>2567   Freida Fae Maggard (1922-). *Freida was born in 1922.*
>2568   Dave Gene Maggard (1925-). *Dave was born in 1925.*

904. **Pernita Maggard**, daughter of John Gary Maggard and Virginia Wallace, was born on October 9, 1896. She married **William Ernest Butler** on January 3, 1912.

William Ernest Butler was born on May 1, 1891. He died on June 15, 1972. He and Pernita Maggard had the following children:

>2569   William Clyde Butler (-)
>2570   Eloise Butler (1936-1994). *Eloise was born on March 2, 1936. She married **Willis Frederick Scarborough** on May 16, 1953. She died on April 9, 1994.*

905. **Wesley Maggard**, son of John Gary Maggard and Virginia Wallace, was born on September 4, 1898.

Maggie Corrine Smith was born on April 7, 1900. She died on January 29, 1952. She and Wesley Maggard had the following children:

>2571   Eugene C. Maggard (-)
>2572   Stella Maggard (-)
>2573   Raynell Maggard (-)
>2574   Cecil Maggard (-)
>2575   John Wesley Maggard (1922-1990). *John was born on December 28, 1922. He died on October 16, 1990.*

906. **Johnnye Maggard**, son of John Gary Maggard and Virginia Wallace, was born on May 21, 1902.

Everett Hollis Hughes was born on February 8, 1900. She died on March 14, 1985. She and Johnnye Maggard had the following children:

2576   Virginia Ann Maggard (-)

907. Pauline Maggard, daughter of John Gary Maggard and Virginia Wallace, was born on May 21, 1905. She died on April 10, 1933 and was buried in Lauderdale County, MS at Coker Chapel Cemetery.

> **William Bryan Hughes** was born on January 8, 1903. He died on May 6, 1989 and was buried in Lauderdale County, MS at Coker Chapel Cemetery. He and Pauline Maggard had the following children:

>> 2577   Helen Hughes (1933-). *Helen was born on March 27, 1933.*

908. Thomas Jefferson "Jeff" Wallace, son of John M. Wallace and Emma Parker, was born on August 12, 1884 in Alabama. He married **Ida Lee Smith** in 1907. He died on August 1, 1959 in Selma, Dallas County, AL and was buried in Bibb County, AL at Tabernacle Methodist Church Cemetery.

> Ida Lee Smith was born on August 20, 1885 in Alabama. She died on February 9, 1963 in Bibb County, AL and was buried in Bibb County, AL at Tabernacle Methodist Church Cemetery. She and Thomas Jefferson "Jeff" Wallace had the following children:

>> 2578   Cozy Lee Wallace (1910-2000). *Cozy was born on March 10, 1910. She married **Doris Jackson Cook** in 1930. She married **Teddy James McFarland** on March 8, 1940 in Clanton, Chilton County, AL. She married **John Foshee** in 1960. She died on December 29, 2000 in Tarrant, Jefferson County, AL and was buried in Bibb County, AL at Tabernacle Methodist Church Cemetery.*

>> 2579   Woodford Wallace (1913-1925). *Woodford was born in May 1913 in Bibb County, AL. He died on June 11, 1925 in Maplesville, Chilton County, AL and was buried in Bibb County, AL at Tabernacle Methodist Church Cemetery.*

>> 2580   Fondon Wallace (1916-1992). *Fondon was born on June 29, 1916. He married **Ophelia Hill** on December 10, 1945 in Brent, Bibb County, AL. He died on November 2, 1992 in Selma, Dallas County, AL and was buried in Bibb County, AL at Tabernacle Methodist Church Cemetery.*

>> 2581   Flossie Estelle Wallace (1918-1989). *Flossie was born on October 4, 1918 in Chilton County, AL. She married **O. V. Wright** on November 20, 1937 in Stanton, Chilton County, AL at Ebenezer Baptist Church. She died on November 5, 1989 in Selma, Dallas County, AL and was buried in Stanton, Chilton County, AL at Ebenezer Baptist Church.*

>> 2582   Flessie Bethertina Wallace (1920-1983). *Flessie was born on September 23, 1920. She died on December 26, 1983.*

>> 2583   Cillian Louise Wallace (1922-1971). *Cillian was born on September 8, 1922 in Maplesville, Chilton County, AL. She married **John Thomas Pope Sr** on May 20, 1940. She died on September 9, 1971 in Pell City, St. Clair County, AL and was buried in Bibb County, AL at Tabernacle Methodist Church Cemetery.*

909. Henry W. Wallace, son of John M. Wallace and Emma Parker, was born on September 23, 1886. He married **Minerva Mae Wallace** circa 1907. He died on December 6, 1967 and was buried in Bibb County, AL at Tabernacle Methodist Church Cemetery.

> Minerva Mae Wallace, daughter of John C. Wallace (1849-1925) and Mary J. Henderson (1856-1913), was born on December 7, 1888. She died on May 26, 1969 in Bibb County, AL and was buried in Bibb County, AL at Tabernacle Methodist Church Cemetery. She and Henry W. Wallace had the following children:

>> 2584   Grady Wallace (1909-). *Grady was born in 1909.*
>> 2585   Alvis Wallace (1914-). *Alvis was born in 1914.*
>> 2586   Willard Wallace (1915-). *Willard was born in 1915.*
>> 2587   Joyce Wallace (1920-). *Joyce was born in 1920.*

910. Marvin Jackson Wallace, son of John M. Wallace and Emma Parker, was born on September 19, 1889. He died on June 1, 1962 in Houston, Harris County, TX and was buried in Vance, Bibb County, AL at Evergreen Baptist Church.

Sarah M. Wallace, daughter of John C. Wallace (1849-1925) and Mary J. Henderson (1856-1913), was born in August 1890. She died on June 29, 1948 in Bessemer, Jefferson County, AL. She and Marvin Jackson Wallace had the following children:

2588	Carl Edison Wallace (1915-). *Carl was born in 1915.*
2589	Jesse May Wallace (1917-). *Jesse was born in 1917.*
2590	Mary Wallace (1920-). *Mary was born in 1920.*

911. **Oma Wallace**, daughter of John M. Wallace and Emma Parker, was born in October 1893 and was buried in Bibb County, AL at Tabernacle Methodist Church Cemetery.

    Jasper Smith was born in 1888. He died in 1946 and was buried in Bibb County, AL at Tabernacle Methodist Church Cemetery.

912. **Ola Wallace**, daughter of John M. Wallace and Emma Parker, was born on February 4, 1897. She married **James A. Smith** in 1918. She died on June 20, 1924 and was buried in Bibb County, AL at Tabernacle Methodist Church Cemetery.

    James A. Smith was born on September 18, 1888 in Alabama. He died on January 11, 1962 and was buried in Chilton County, AL at Smith-Campbellite Church Cemetery.

913. **Harvey Wallace**, son of John M. Wallace and Emma Parker, was born on January 13, 1902. He died on October 12, 1958 and was buried in Bibb County, AL at Tabernacle Methodist Church Cemetery.

    Sarah O'Neal was born on January 13, 1900 and was buried in Bibb County, AL at Tabernacle Methodist Church Cemetery.

919. **Rosa Bell Wallace**, daughter of William J. Wallace and Roxie A. Hollie, was born on November 12, 1900. She died on February 28, 1981.

    Jesse B. Smith was born on April 21, 1903. He died on December 13, 1968. He and Rosa Bell Wallace had the following children:

2591	Thomas Allen Smith (1939-2005). *Thomas was born on March 10, 1939. He died on September 24, 2005.*

927. **George Cochran**, son of Marcus D. Cochran and Martha F. Wallace, was born on July 23, 1892. He died on April 27, 1922 and was buried in Bibb County, AL at Shady Grove Church Cemetery.

    Mary Emma Aultman was born on August 16, 1895. She died on April 16, 1976. She and George Cochran had the following children:

2592	Leola Cochran (1918-2005). *Leola was born on February 28, 1918. She died on October 31, 2005.*

930. **Jessie Cochran**, son of Marcus D. Cochran and Martha F. Wallace, was born on September 25, 1904. He died on February 11, 1967 and was buried in Bibb County, AL at Shady Grove Church Cemetery.

931. **Richard Albert Wallace**, son of Andrew Jackson Wallace and Mary Susan Stewart, was born on June 25, 1891. He married **Eliza Agnes Hopper** on January 3, 1909. He died on July 3, 1969 and was buried in Tuscaloosa, Tuscaloosa County, AL at Tuscaloosa Memorial Park Cemetery.

    Eliza Agnes Hopper was born on April 9, 1890. She died on January 30, 1966 and was buried in Tuscaloosa, Tuscaloosa County, AL at Tuscaloosa Memorial Park Cemetery.

932. **Luther Columbus Wallace**, son of Andrew Jackson Wallace and Mary Susan Stewart, was born on September 10, 1892. He married **Mary Mable Rogers** on December 18, 1910 in Bibb County, AL at Bethleham Baptist Church. He died on April 17, 1973 and was buried in Bibb County, AL at Sandy Chapel Methodist Cemetery.

Mary Mable Rogers was born on September 4, 1882. She died on October 1, 1965 and was buried in Bibb County, AL at Sandy Chapel Methodist Cemetery.

933. **Lilly Belle Wallace**, daughter of Andrew Jackson Wallace and Mary Susan Stewart, was born on July 1, 1894. She died on July 14, 1922 and was buried in Moundville Cemetery, Moundville, AL.

Abner Crowe was buried in Moundville Cemetery, Moundville, AL.

934. **James Jackson Wallace**, son of Andrew Jackson Wallace and Mary Susan Stewart, was born on July 2, 1896. He married **Mamie E. Williams** on October 12, 1928. He died on February 18, 1972 and was buried in West Blockton, Bibb County, AL at Hill Crest Cemetery.

Mamie E. Williams was born on July 28, 1906. She died on March 31, 1988 and was buried in West Blockton, Bibb County, AL at Hill Crest Cemetery.

935. **Houston Shivers Wallace**, son of Andrew Jackson Wallace and Mary Susan Stewart, was born on September 10, 1898. He died on March 7, 1973.

936. **Eva Dee Wallace**, daughter of Andrew Jackson Wallace and Mary Susan Stewart, was born on March 1, 1900 in Perry County, AL. She married **Luther Rezzie Robinson** on September 16, 1920. She died on August 10, 1988.

Luther Rezzie Robinson was born on November 26, 1893 in Bibb County, AL. He died on June 3, 1979.

937. **Dan Crawford Wallace**, son of Andrew Jackson Wallace and Mary Susan Stewart, was born on January 8, 1902. He died on February 12, 1911 and was buried in Bibb County, AL at Harris Family Cemetery.

938. **Ollie Mae Wallace**, daughter of Andrew Jackson Wallace and Mary Susan Stewart, was born on March 2, 1904. She died on March 9, 1986 and was buried in Bibb County, AL at Sandy Chapel Methodist Cemetery.

Victor Stacey Robinson was born on November 11, 1890. He died on July 21, 1958 and was buried in Bibb County, AL at Sandy Chapel Methodist Cemetery.

939. **Odell Wallace**, daughter of Andrew Jackson Wallace and Mary Susan Stewart, was born on January 9, 1906. She married **Clyde Lee Smitherman** on June 19, 1927. She died on April 5, 1985 and was buried in Hueytown, Jefferson County, AL at Pleasant Ridge Baptist Church Cemetery.

Clyde Lee Smitherman was born on March 18, 1903. He died on June 3, 1994 and was buried in Hueytown, Jefferson County, AL at Pleasant Ridge Baptist Church Cemetery.

940. **Maude Lee Wallace**, daughter of Andrew Jackson Wallace and Mary Susan Stewart, was born on February 15, 1908. She married **George David Lanston** circa 1927. She died on February 13, 1989 and was buried in Birmingham, Jefferson County, AL at Elmwood Cemetery.

George David Lanston was born on December 13, 1904. He died on September 27, 1969 and was buried in Birmingham, Jefferson County, AL at Elmwood Cemetery.

941. **Lehman Grundy Wallace**, son of Andrew Jackson Wallace and Mary Susan Stewart, was born on August 18, 1909. He married **Esther Owens** on April 7, 1928. He died on July 24, 1987 and was buried in Bibb County, AL at Little Hope Baptist Church Cemetery.

Esther Owens was born on February 12, 1910. She died on December 23, 1985 and was buried in Bibb County, AL at Little Hope Baptist Church Cemetery.

945. **King Cornelius Wallace**, son of Jasper Newton Wallace Sr. and Eller Moton, was born on October 8, 1900. He married **Nellie Dennis** on October 17, 1926. He died on March 4, 1981 and was buried in Bibb County, AL at Shady Grove Church Cemetery.

Nellie Dennis was born on May 5, 1906. She died on February 13, 1990 and was buried in Bibb County, AL at Shady Grove Church Cemetery.

950. **Ishmeal Wallace**, son of Jasper Newton Wallace Sr. and Dolly Mae Solomon, was born on February 6, 1931. He died on November 18, 1981 and was buried in Chilton County, AL at Mineral Springs Cemetery.

953. **Samuel Moton**, son of Zake Moton and Mary E. Wallace, was born in March 1896. He died circa 1948 and was buried in Perry County, AL at Mt. Olive Church Cemetery.

Evie Doss was born circa 1896. She died circa 1955 and was buried in Perry County, AL at Mt. Olive Church Cemetery.

954. **Ruby B. Moton**, daughter of Zake Moton and Mary E. Wallace, was born on October 16, 1899. She died on February 15, 1965 and was buried in Bibb County, AL at Tabernacle Methodist Church Cemetery.

958. **Bela Cochran**, daughter of Jack C. Cochran and Mary E. Wallace, was born on August 16, 1901. She married **William L. Blocker** on May 17, 1919. She died on August 9, 1987.

William L. Blocker was born on April 2, 1896.

959. **Zula Cochran**, daughter of Jack C. Cochran and Mary E. Wallace, was born on February 6, 1906. She died on November 3, 1986.

960. **Lena Mae Cochran**, daughter of Jack C. Cochran and Mary E. Wallace, was born on August 6, 1915. She died on October 7, 1948.

Luman Gates Langford Sr., son of George Calhoun Langford (1878-1939) and Maudie Estelle Wallace (1888-1956), was born on October 7, 1907. He died on August 31, 1967. He and Lena Mae Cochran had the following children:

    2593   Voncile Edith Langford (1935-2010). *Voncile was born on February 18, 1935. She died on November 18, 2010.*

971. **Roy M. Wallace Sr.** was the son of M. G. Wallace and Myrtle Bearden.

Vannie Mae White was born on March 2, 1912. She died on May 21, 2000 and was buried in Maplesville, Chilton County, AL at Pleasant Grove Cemetery #2. She and Roy M. Wallace Sr had the following children:

    2594   Aubry Wallace (-)
    2595   Jesse Wallace (-)
    2596   Roy M. Wallace Jr (-)
    2597   Myrtle Wallace (-)

972. **Ida Mae Wallace** was the daughter of M. G. Wallace and Myrtle Bearden.

Noah Wesley Latham Jr Jr was born on September 18, 1894 in Chilton County, AL. He died on April 11, 1974 and was buried in Chilton County, AL at Pleasant Grove Baptist Church Cemetery. He and Ida Mae Wallace had the following children:

    2598   Henry Latham (-)

975. **Roy Moody Wallace**, son of Melvin Augusta Wallace and Myrtle Bearden, was born on September 4, 1909. He died on September 3, 1990.

Vannie Mae White was born on March 2, 1912. She died on May 21, 2000. She and Roy Moody Wallace had the following children:

    2599   Wallace (-)

978. **John Wesley Wallace**, son of Thomas W. Wallace and Vadna Doss, was born on November 21, 1910 in Perry County, AL. He died on March 16, 1964 and was buried in Bibb County, AL at Shady Grove Church Cemetery.

979. **Katie Wallace**, daughter of Thomas W. Wallace and Vadna Doss, was born on April 27, 1912. She died in October 1983.

980. **Emmet Joseph Lawrence**, son of Emmet Casey Lawrence and Paralee Wallace, was born on January 31, 1886 in Alabama. He married **Junie Pearl Adams** circa 1905. He died on June 22, 1962.

Junie Pearl Adams was born on June 5, 1886 in Alabama. She and Emmet Joseph Lawrence had the following children:

2600	Herman Lawrence (-)	
2601	Hollis Lawrence (-)	
2602	Doris E. Lawrence (1923-2013). *Doris was born on September 29, 1923. She died on March 14, 2013.*	

981. **Lee Edward Lawrence Sr.**, son of Emmet Casey Lawrence and Paralee Wallace, was born on April 6, 1887 in Alabama. He married **Fannie E. Johnson** circa 1907. He died on September 2, 1912.

Fannie E. Johnson was born on January 4, 1886 in Alabama. She died on June 25, 1937 and was buried in Bibb County, AL at Rehobeth Church Cemetery. She and Lee Edward Lawrence Sr had the following children:

2603	Flemon Lawrence (-)	
2604	Judson Lawrence (-)	
2605	Thomas Lee Lawrence (1912-1996). *Thomas was born on November 12, 1912. He died on March 7, 1996 and was buried in Chilton County, AL at Liberty Hill Cemetery.*	

982. **Lola M. Lawrence**, daughter of Emmet Casey Lawrence and Paralee Wallace, was born on October 13, 1888. She married **Luther Alonza Kelley** on December 23, 1903 in Bibb County, AL. She died on April 13, 1966 and was buried in Chilton County, AL at Pleasant Grove Baptist Church Cemetery.

Luther Alonza Kelley was born on September 30, 1880 in Bibb County, AL. He died on July 13, 1965 in Selma, Dallas County, AL and was buried in Chilton County, AL at Pleasant Grove Baptist Church Cemetery. He and Lola M. Lawrence had the following children:

2606	Grady Kelley (-)	
2607	Percy Kelley (1904-1980). *Percy was born on October 7, 1904. He died on May 9, 1980 and was buried in Chilton County, AL at Pleasant Grove Baptist Church Cemetery.*	

983. **Zeke Lawrence**, son of Emmet Casey Lawrence and Paralee Wallace, was born on March 3, 1890 in Alabama. He married **Reba Threadgill** circa 1909. He died on August 3, 1917 and was buried in Bibb County, AL at Lawley Cemetery.

Reba Threadgill was born circa 1890 in Alabama. She and Zeke Lawrence had the following children:

2608	Carrie Lawrence (-)	
2609	Ollie Lawrence (-)	
2610	Maggie Lawrence (-)	
2611	Bertha Lawrence (1916-1919). *Bertha was born on February 7, 1916. She died on September 18, 1919 and was buried in Bibb County, AL at Lawley Cemetery.*	

986. **Cleveland Harrison** was the son of Robert Harrison and Angeline Wallace.

Bessie Fuller and Cleveland Harrison had the following children:

2612	Ruth Harrison (-)	
2613	Annie Mae Harrison (-)	
2614	Harrison (-)	
2615	Harrison (-)	

987. Julia Harrison was the daughter of Robert Harrison and Angeline Wallace.

988. Harrison, daughter of Robert Harrison and Angeline Wallace, was buried in Chilton County, AL at Chestnut Hill Cemetery.

989. Nora Agnes Leach\Wallace, daughter of Dave Leach and Sally Wallace, was born on July 14, 1893. She married **John Franklin Lovelady** on August 30, 1925. She died on December 12, 1971 and was buried in Bibb County, AL at Cox Chapel Cemetery.

John Franklin Lovelady was born on February 13, 1880 in Medline, Perry County, AL. He died on March 15, 1952 in Maplesville, Chilton County, AL and was buried in Bibb County, AL at Cox Chapel Cemetery. He and Nora Agnes Leach\Wallace had the following children:

2616	Thomas Edward Lovelady (-)
2617	Mary Ruth Lovelady (-)

1000. Noah Columbus Wallace, son of John Wesley Wallace and Susan Latham, was born on July 12, 1894 in Alabama. He died in May 1965.

Lula F. Riley, daughter of William Henry Thomas Riley (1874-1949) and Anna Ludelia Wallace (1874-1957), was born on September 23, 1898. She died on September 2, 1989 and was buried in Jemison, Chilton County, AL at Macedonia Baptist Church Cemetery. She and Noah Columbus Wallace had the following children:

2618	Mildred S. Wallace (1915-2010). *Mildred was born on September 26, 1915. She died on February 23, 2010 and was buried in Jemison, Chilton County, AL at Macedonia Baptist Church Cemetery.*
2619	Curdie Pauline Wallace (1921-1987). *Curdie was born on February 15, 1921. She died in January 1987.*
2620	James Edward Wallace (1927-1995). *James was born on August 17, 1927. He died on January 8, 1995.*

1002. Robert Monroe Wallace, son of John Wesley Wallace and Susan Latham, was born on March 21, 1905. He died on August 27, 1982.

Camilla Elizabeth Brownlow was born on August 7, 1904. She died on January 23, 1973. She and Robert Monroe Wallace had the following children:

2621	Wallace (-)

1003. Bevie Waloner Mull, daughter of Moses Jefferson Mull and Sarah Elizabeth Rolley, was born on May 8, 1882. She died on September 18, 1964 and was buried in Chilton County, AL at Alpine Baptist Church Cemetery.

Buckner Houston "Buck" Keener was born on August 11, 1877. He died on March 31, 1947 and was buried in Chilton County, AL at Alpine Baptist Church Cemetery. He and Bevie Waloner Mull had the following children:

2622	Leon Keener (1913-1984). *Leon was born on June 3, 1913. He died on January 30, 1984 and was buried in Cooper, Chilton County, AL at Floyd Cemetery.*

1004. James Marion Hart, son of John Leonard Hart and Mary Jane Stewart, was born on October 3, 1890. He died on September 16, 1941 and was buried in Henderson County, TN at Palestine Cemetery.

Evie Lena Wallace was born on December 24, 1893. She died on October 9, 1976 and was buried in Henderson County, TN at Palestine Cemetery. She and James Marion Hart had the following children:

2623	Ruth Hart (1923-2001). *Ruth was born on May 30, 1923. She died on February 14, 2001 and was buried in Henderson County, TN at Palestine Cemetery.*

1005. **Nathan Wesley Britt**, son of Hans Britt and Martha Elizabeth Powers, was born in July 1878. He married **Dona Cogdell** on January 9, 1897 in Henderson County, TN. He died in 1962.

Dona Cogdell was born in February 1878. She died in 1953. She and Nathan Wesley Britt had the following children:

2624	Pulie Britt (1898-). *Pulie was born in July 1898.*
2625	William Wyley Britt (1899-). *William was born in October 1899.*
2626	John Jessie Britt (1902-1980). *John was born on February 15, 1902. He married **Luziane Annie Bybee** on June 25, 1922 in Henderson County, TN. He died on August 11, 1980.*
2627	Clyde Wesley Britt (1904-1975). *Clyde was born on April 5, 1904. He died on February 11, 1975.*
2628	Beulah Britt (1909-). *Beulah was born in 1909.*
2629	Flossie Britt (1913-1979). *Flossie was born on December 13, 1913. She died on June 19, 1979.*
2630	James A. Britt (1919-1978). *James was born in 1919. He died in 1978.*

1008. **John Henry Britt**, son of Hans Britt and Martha Elizabeth Powers, was born on October 5, 1884. He died on January 8, 1980 and was buried in Henderson County, TN at Union Grove Baptist Church.

Tempie Daws was born in September 1882. She married George W. Williams on November 11, 1897 in Henderson County, TN. She died on September 21, 1921 and was buried in Henderson County, TN at Union Grove Baptist Church. She and John Henry Britt had the following children:

2631	Fannie C. Britt (1910-). *Fannie was born in 1910.*
2632	Floyd D. Britt (1913-1996). *Floyd was born on April 22, 1913. He married **Dorothy Victoria Pollock** on September 21, 1941. He died on April 11, 1996 and was buried in Henderson County, TN at Union Grove Baptist Church.*
2633	Mary E. Britt (1916-). *Mary was born in 1916.*
2634	Fulton Terry Britt (1918-1999). *Fulton was born on September 12, 1918. He married **Ruby** on February 18, 1942. He died on February 18, 1999 and was buried in Henderson County, TN at Union Grove Baptist Church.*

Sarah Frances Hicks was born on June 7, 1888. She died on September 2, 1969 and was buried in Henderson County, TN at Union Grove Baptist Church. She and John Henry Britt had the following children:

2635	Lula M. Britt (1922-). *Lula was born in 1922.*
2636	Opal L. Britt (1923-). *Opal was born in 1923.*
2637	Elmo Euel Britt (1924-1964). *Elmo was born on October 24, 1964 and was buried in Henderson County, TN at Union Grove Baptist Church.*
2638	Elmer D. Britt (1926-1945). *Elmer was born on April 23, 1926. He died on March 27, 1945 and was buried in Henderson County, TN at Union Grove Baptist Church.*
2639	Hattie M. Britt (1929-). *Hattie was born in 1929.*

1009. **James Edward Britt**, son of Hans Britt and Martha Elizabeth Powers, was born in February 1887. He died in 1918.

Emma McDonald was born in 1882. She and James Edward Britt had the following children:

2640	Lessie M. Britt (1909-). *Lessie was born in 1909.*

1015. **Charles Garfield Britt**, son of Avington Britt and Nancy Powers, was born on February 9, 1880. He married **Hariett Mullins** on March 21, 1901. He died on October 22, 1964 in Madison County, TN and was buried in Henderson County, TN at Palestine Cemetery.

Hariett Mullins, daughter of William Wesley Mullins (1844-1918) and Evaline A. Smothers (1838-1911), was born in 1879. She died in 1941 and was buried in Henderson County, TN at Palestine Cemetery. She and Charles Garfield Britt had the following children:

2641	Alice E. Britt (-)
2642	Mildred Britt (-)
2643	Flossie Britt (-)

1016. Caswell Melton Britt, son of Avington Britt and Nancy Powers, was born on April 15, 1884. He died on December 15, 1974 and was buried in Henderson County, TN at Palestine Cemetery.

Josie Feki Mullins, daughter of William Wesley Mullins (1844-1918) and Evaline A. Smothers (1838-1911), was born on April 5, 1874. She died on December 28, 1926 and was buried in Henderson County, TN at Palestine Cemetery. She and Caswell Melton Britt had the following children:

2644	Raymon Melton Britt (1908-1971). *Raymon was born on May 27, 1908. He died on October 3, 1971 and was buried in Henderson County, TN at Nebo Methodist Church.*

1017. Amanda Elizabeth "Mandy" Britt, daughter of Avington Britt and Nancy Powers, was born on May 13, 1886 in Henderson County, TN. She died in January 1978.

1024. James Henry Britt, son of James A. Britt and Nancy E. Cagle, was born on April 22, 1891. He married **Myrtle M. Adcox** on October 1, 1911 in Henderson County, TN. He died on August 8, 1969 and was buried in Henderson County, TN at Nebo Methodist Church.

Myrtle M. Adcox was born on July 11, 1888. She died on November 14, 1967 and was buried in Henderson County, TN at Nebo Methodist Church. She and James Henry Britt had the following children:

2645	Infant Britt (1912-1912). *Infant was born on August 29, 1912. He died on August 29, 1912 and was buried in Henderson County, TN at Nebo Methodist Church.*
2646	Lula O. Britt (1914-). *Lula was born in 1914.*
2647	Noel S. Britt (1917-). *Noel was born in 1917.*
2648	Virginia R. Britt (1918-). *Virginia was born in 1918.*
2649	Jack R. Britt (1920-). *Jack was born in 1920.*

1026. Sarah Jane "Sallie" Britt, daughter of Abraham Lincoln Britt and Martha E. "Patsy" Cagle, was born on May 30, 1891. She died on May 7, 1981 and was buried in Henderson County, TN at Nebo Methodist Church.

John Riley Wynn Hinson was born in 1896. He died on February 24, 1966. He and Sarah Jane "Sallie" Britt had the following children:

2650	Annie Mae Hinson (1912-2009). *Annie was born on July 7, 1912. She died on November 1, 2009 and was buried in Henderson County, TN at Nebo Methodist Church.*

1031. Jennie Frances Britt, daughter of Joseph Isaac "Ike" Britt and Ada E. Horton, was born on March 4, 1907. She died on April 29, 1999.

Clyde Washington Cagle was born on May 27, 1901. He died on October 3, 1983. He and Jennie Frances Britt had the following children:

2651	Clyde Cagle Jr. (1927-1994). *Clyde was born on May 27, 1927. He died on September 25, 1994.*

1033. Esther Francis Britt, daughter of Everet Britt and Frances Josephine McCarrell, was born in 1881. She died in 1934.

Robert Lee "Bud" Ford was born on November 16, 1866. He died on April 13, 1937. He and Esther Francis Britt had the following children:

2652	Jewell William Ford (1911-2000). *Jewell was born on March 13, 1911. He died on January 1, 2000.*

1036. Minnie T. Britt, daughter of Everet Britt and Frances Josephine McCarrell, was born in March 1889.

William E. Johnson was born in 1889. He and Minnie T. Britt had the following children:

2653   Tildon Johnson (1911-). *Tildon was born in 1911.*

1038. Ella L. "Nettie" Britt, daughter of George Britt and Louisa M. Williams, was born in September 1889.

Jim Mullins and Ella L. "Nettie" Britt had the following children:

2654   Lillian Mullins (1912-2001). *Lillian was born in 1912. She died in 2001 and was buried in Henderson County, TN at Palestine Cemetery.*

1040. Sarah Elizabeth "Bessie" Britt, daughter of George Britt and Louisa M. Williams, was born in July 1894. She married **Bert Lee Wallace** on July 18, 1911 in Henderson County, TN. She died in 1973 and was buried in Henderson County, TN at Palestine Cemetery.

Bert Lee Wallace, son of William Samuel Wallace (1862-1925) and Nancy C. Williams (1865-1945), was born in August 1890 in Tennessee. He died on September 18, 1982 and was buried in Henderson County, TN at Palestine Cemetery. He and Sarah Elizabeth "Bessie" Britt had the following children:

2655   Billy Joe Wallace (-)
2656   Melvin L. Wallace (1912-2003). *Melvin was born in 1912. He died in 2003 and was buried in Henderson County, TN at Palestine Cemetery.*
2657   Inez Wallace (1915-). *Inez was born in 1915.*
2658   J. Murray Wallace (1920-). *J. was born in 1920.*
2659   D. L. Wallace (1923-). *D. was born in 1923.*
2660   E. Louise Wallace (1925-). *E. was born in 1925.*
2661   Ruby M. Wallace (1928-). *Ruby was born in 1928.*
2662   Cletus Lee Wallace (1931-1999). *Cletus was born on September 18, 1931 in Henderson County, TN. He died on March 5, 1999 in Henderson County, TN and was buried in Henderson County, TN at Palestine Cemetery.*
2663   Ruthie Dean Wallace (1938-1988). *Ruthie was born in 1938. She died in 1988.*

1041. James Richard Britt, son of George Britt and Louisa M. Williams, was born in July 1896. He died in 1946 and was buried in Henderson County, TN at Palestine Cemetery.

Eva T. was born in 1905. She died in 1987 and was buried in Henderson County, TN at Palestine Cemetery.

1042. Felix R. Britt, son of Rolle Allen "Rawl" Britt and Mary A. "Molly" Lee, was born in October 1889. He died in 1909 and was buried in Henderson County, TN at Palestine Cemetery.

1044. Franey Azilee Britt, daughter of Rolle Allen "Rawl" Britt and Mary A. "Molly" Lee, was born on February 10, 1893. She married **Edmond R. Pollock** on December 9, 1909 in Henderson County, TN. She died on October 5, 1935 and was buried in Lexington, Henderson County, TN at Chapel Hill Cemetery.

Edmond R. Pollock, son of James Pollock (1852-1933) and Tabitha Cagle (1850-1895), was born on June 4, 1893. He died on February 9, 1961 and was buried in Lexington, Henderson County, TN at Chapel Hill Cemetery. He and Franey Azilee Britt had the following children:

2664   Willie Pollock (1913-). *Willie was born in 1913.*
2665   George Pollock (1914-). *George was born in 1914.*
2666   Annie Bill Pollock (1918-). *Annie was born in 1918.*
2667   Ludell Pollock (1919-). *Ludell was born in 1919.*

1045. Hubert Jefferson Britt, son of Rolle Allen "Rawl" Britt and Mary A. "Molly" Lee, was born on April 3, 1896. He died on June 8, 1969 and was buried in Henderson County, TN at Palestine Cemetery.

Edna Daisy Hart was born on July 28, 1908 in Henderson County, TN. She died on December 12, 1988 in Henderson County, TN. She and Hubert Jefferson Britt had the following children:

2668	Callie Marie Britt (1932-). *Callie was born on January 16, 1932 in Henderson County, TN.*
2669	Margie Lee Britt (1933-). *Margie was born on August 25, 1933 in Henderson County, TN.*
2670	Willie Sue Britt (1936-2014). *Willie was born on March 7, 1936 in Henderson County, TN. She died on September 17, 2014 in Jackson, Madison County, TN and was buried in Lexington, Henderson County, TN at Dyers Chapel Church Of Christ.*
2671	Paul Hulon Britt (1939-1995). *Paul was born on January 21, 1939 in Henderson County, TN. He died on December 26, 1995 in Madison County, TN and was buried in Henderson County, TN at Palestine Cemetery.*
2672	Billy Allen Britt (1942-). *Billy was born on May 13, 1942 in Henderson County, TN. He married **Judy Kay Roberts** on May 15, 1975 in Henderson County, TN.*
2673	Robert Felix Britt (1952-1952). *Robert was born on February 4, 1952 in Henderson County, TN. He died on March 3, 1952 in Henderson County, TN and was buried in Henderson County, TN at Palestine Cemetery.*

1052. **Robert Sherman Singleton**, son of Louis Singleton and Deborah E. Britt, was born on September 13, 1902. He died on December 1, 1929.

Mary Magdalene Harrell was born on December 2, 1902. She died on March 30, 1928. She and Robert Sherman Singleton had the following children:

2674	Velma Louise Singleton (1922-2011). *Velma was born on August 23, 1922. She died on November 10, 2011.*

1054. **William Morgan Brewer**, son of William Brewer and Henrietta Clements, was born on November 22, 1886. He died on June 20, 1949.

Mamie Celeste Thompson was born in 1893. She died on February 27, 1971. She and William Morgan Brewer had the following children:

2675	Harry P. Brewer (1919-1993). *Harry was born on September 10, 1919. He died on March 5, 1993.*

1055. **Ina Inez Clements**, daughter of John A. Clements and Geneva F. "Jennie" Brewer, was born on October 6, 1886. She died on August 22, 1950.

John Joseph Looney was born on April 11, 1889. He died on May 4, 1986. He and Ina Inez Clements had the following children:

2676	Irene Geneva Looney (1912-1989). *Irene was born on June 7, 1912. She died on March 26, 1989.*
2677	Mary Katherine Looney (1916-1997). *Mary was born on October 22, 1916. She died on March 17, 1997.*
2678	Margaret Elizabeth Looney (1924-1992). *Margaret was born in 1924. She died in 1992.*

1059. **Lillie Brewer**, daughter of Henry Martin Brewer and Annie Lorene Joyner, was born on April 13, 1905. She died on June 27, 1980.

Frederick Albert Pinner was born on March 2, 1901. He died on November 26, 1977. He and Lillie Brewer had the following children:

2679	Russell James Pinner (1921-1993). *Russell was born in 1921. He died in 1993.*
2680	Albert Buford Pinner (1925-2000). *Albert was born on September 23, 1925. He died on April 24, 2000.*

1060. **Farry M. Gassaway**, daughter of Harvey R. Gassaway and Sarah Elizabeth Wallace, was born on October 30, 1880. She married **E. T. "Tabe" Stone** on March 5, 1899. She died on February 4, 1946 in Mankin, Henderson County, TX.

1061. **Clarkie Lee Gassaway**, daughter of Harvey R. Gassaway and Sarah Elizabeth Wallace, was born on July 24, 1882 in Parker County, TX. She married **William T. Hart** on February 23, 1902. She died in May 1946 in Dallas, TX.

William T. Hart, son of James Columbus Hart (1852-1929) and Sarah Frances Wallace (1857-1941), was born on May 5, 1879 in Navarro County, TX. He died on November 19, 1903 in Navarro County, TX.

1062. **Emma Francis Gassaway**, daughter of Harvey R. Gassaway and Sarah Elizabeth Wallace, was born on September 23, 1885. She married **W. T. Oaks** on June 21, 1903. She died on June 15, 1959.

1063. **Male Gassaway**, son of Harvey R. Gassaway and Sarah Elizabeth Wallace, was born on September 3, 1889. He died on September 7, 1889.

1064. **Harvey Gassaway**, son of Harvey R. Gassaway and Sarah Elizabeth Wallace, was born on May 8, 1890 in Navarro County, TX. He married **Julia Rogers** on December 1, 1912. He died on February 15, 1956 in Dallas, TX.

Julia Rogers was born on April 20, 1894. She died on August 2, 1982 in Kemp, Kaufman County, TX.

1065. **Mary Penina Gassaway**, daughter of Harvey R. Gassaway and Sarah Elizabeth Wallace, was born on October 8, 1893 in Malakoff, Henderson County, TX. She married **William Alonzo "Lonnie" Reed** in February 1910. She married **Andrew Ray Pool** in April 1957. She died in January 1972 in Portales, Roosevelt County, NM.

William Alonzo "Lonnie" Reed was born in 1888. He died in 1938 and was buried in Wilbarger County, TX at Eastview Memorial Park. He and Mary Penina Gassaway had the following children:

2681	Evelyn Reed (-)
2682	Erwin Winfred Reed (1912-1997). *Erwin was born on November 4, 1912. He died on February 13, 1997.*

1066. **Male Gassaway**, son of Harvey R. Gassaway and Sarah Elizabeth Wallace, was born on September 17, 1897 in Mankin, Henderson County, TX. He died in September 1897 in Mankin, Henderson County, TX.

1067. **Infant Gassaway**, daughter of Harvey R. Gassaway and Sarah Elizabeth Wallace, was born in November 1900 in Mankin, Henderson County, TX. She died in November 1900 in Mankin, Henderson County, TX.

1068. **Harvey Lafayette Hart**, son of Sidney Horace Hart and Clarkie Ann Wallace, was born on July 19, 1887 in Garrett, TX. He married **Myrtle Nancy Davis** on December 18, 1910 in Mitchell County, TX. He died on February 25, 1974.

Myrtle Nancy Davis was born on June 17, 1893. She died on March 31, 1971. She and Harvey Lafayette Hart had the following children:

2683	James Dorwin Hart (-2004). *James died in 2004.*

1069. **Thomas Benjamin Hart**, son of Sidney Horace Hart and Clarkie Ann Wallace, was born in March 1888 in Ellis County, TX. He died in 1928 in Clara, TX.

1070. **Female Williams**, daughter of William Bennett Williams and Margaret Emma Wallace, was born on January 13, 1890 in Parker County, TX. She died on January 13, 1890 in Parker County, TX and was buried in Parker County, TX at Jaybird Cemetery.

1071. **William Bennett Williams Jr.**, son of William Bennett Williams and Margaret Emma Wallace, was born on February 13, 1891 in Parker County, TX. He died on December 13, 1995 in Blanco, TX.

1076. **Mamie Jessie Henry**, daughter of William Mattison Henry and Cora Wallace, was born on December 8, 1913. She died on July 26, 2009.

Glenn Pridemore was born on April 17, 1915. He died in 1986. He and Mamie Jessie Henry had the following children:

2684   Pridemore (-)

1078. **Luther Columbus Hart Jr.**, son of Luther Columbus Hart and Ella Pearl Wright, was born on January 15, 1908. He married **Claudia Greenway** on November 14, 1931 in Bryan County, OK. He died on November 8, 1970.

Claudia Greenway was born on October 14, 1914. She died on August 9, 2008. She and Luther Columbus Hart Jr. had the following children:

2685   Hart (-)

1081. **Arthur Dovard Dansby**, son of Isom Daniel Dansby and Hattie Lee Hart, was born on July 5, 1913. He died on May 19, 2007.

Mary Marie Weddel was born on December 21, 1920. She died "12-9-2011". She and Arthur Dovard Dansby had the following children:

2686   Dansby (-)
2687   Joanna Dansby (1944-2013). *Joanna was born on June 4, 1944. She died on December 14, 2013.*

1082. **Ethel Pauline Dansby**, daughter of Isom Daniel Dansby and Hattie Lee Hart, was born on June 25, 1918. She died on May 5, 2008.

Delmar Franklin Brumley was born on August 14, 1906. He died on July 5, 2005. He and Ethel Pauline Dansby had the following children:

2688   Brumley (-)

1083. **Peggy Dansby**, daughter of Isom Daniel Dansby and Hattie Lee Hart, was born on March 20, 1921. She died on April 2, 2012.

John Roy Toney was born on October 10, 1914. He died on October 4, 2001. He and Peggy Dansby had the following children:

2689   Marcia Toney (-)

1084. **Acie Willard \"Bill\" Dansby**, son of Isom Daniel Dansby and Hattie Lee Hart, was born on October 5, 1923. He died on April 24, 1997.

Glenna Faye Castleberry was born on August 12, 1927. She died on December 29, 2014. She and Acie Willard "Bill" Dansby had the following children:

2690   Melanie Dansby (-)

1085. **Lessie Daws**, daughter of Isaac Neal "Ike" Daws and Mary Ann "Molly" Wallace, was born on March 27, 1909. She died on November 17, 1936.

Earnest Waddle was born on June 9, 1903. He died on March 1, 1945. He and Lessie Daws had the following children:

2691   Waddle (-)

1086. **Charlie Washington Daws**, son of Isaac Neal "Ike" Daws and Mary Ann "Molly" Wallace, was born on November 21, 1921. He died on January 11, 1987.

Velma Mae McCollum was born on May 4, 1921. She died on January 31, 1990. She and Charlie Washington Daws had the following children:

2692   Bonnie Daws (1940-2014). *Bonnie was born on July 31, 1940. She died on August 4,*

1087. Billy Joe Wallace was the son of Bert Lee Wallace and Sarah Elizabeth "Bessie" Britt.

Johnnie Faye and Billy Joe Wallace had the following children:

> 2693   Terry Joe Wallace (1957-2009). *Terry was born on February 15, 1957. He died on June 19, 2009 and was buried in Henderson County, TN at Palestine Cemetery.*

1088. Melvin L. Wallace, son of Bert Lee Wallace and Sarah Elizabeth "Bessie" Britt, was born in 1912. He died in 2003 and was buried in Henderson County, TN at Palestine Cemetery.

Elizabeth S. Hart was born in 1911. She died in 1999 and was buried in Henderson County, TN at Palestine Cemetery. She and Melvin L. Wallace had the following children:

> 2694   Bobby Gene Wallace (1933-2008). *Bobby was born on September 12, 1933 in Henderson County, TN. He died on February 2, 2008 and was buried in Henderson County, TN at Palestine Cemetery.*

1094. Cletus Lee Wallace, son of Bert Lee Wallace and Sarah Elizabeth "Bessie" Britt, was born on September 18, 1931 in Henderson County, TN. He died on March 5, 1999 in Henderson County, TN and was buried in Henderson County, TN at Palestine Cemetery.

Cletus Lee Wallace had the following children:

> 2695   Rocky Leon Wallace (-)

1096. Delta Mae Pollock, daughter of George Washington Pollock and Ida Victoria Wallace, was born on June 6, 1925. She married **Paul Hulon Holmes** on March 30, 1946 in Alcorn County, MS. She died on August 12, 1970.

Paul Hulon Holmes, son of Sidney Thomas Holmes (1902-1987) and Lala Lucille Hart (1904-1941), was born on August 19, 1924. He died on June 15, 2009. He and Delta Mae Pollock had the following children:

> 2696   Holmes (-)

1097. J. S. Wallace, son of Harve D. Wallace and Fannie C. Britt, was born on October 11, 1926. He died on October 13, 1926 and was buried in Henderson County, TN at Palestine Cemetery.

1103. Johnnie Adams Cagle, son of Robert Cagle and Mary Ann Cox, was born on December 30, 1913. He died on January 13, 1976 and was buried in Lexington, Henderson County, TN at Sand Ridge Church.

Elizabeth Rhodes was born on June 10, 1915. She died on November 26, 1998 and was buried in Lexington, Henderson County, TN at Sand Ridge Church.

1104. Louvene Cockman, daughter of William McSwain Cockman and Julia Ann Cagle, was born on October 24, 1865. She married **Elias Hector McNeill** on November 9, 1884. She died on August 19, 1943 and was buried in Moore County, NC at Bensalem Presbyterian Church.

Elias Hector McNeill, son of Hector McNeill (1829-1862) and Elizabeth J. Shields (1837-1910), was born on September 16, 1861. He died on September 14, 1946 and was buried in Moore County, NC at Bensalem Presbyterian Church. He and Louvene Cockman had the following children:

> 2697   Jerome Carson McNeill (1885-1965). *Jerome was born on August 20, 1885. He died on August 20, 1965 and was buried in Moore County, NC at Bensalem Presbyterian Church.*
> 2698   Lillie Isobel McNeill (1888-1969). *Lillie was born on January 23, 1888. She died on March 13, 1969 in Raleigh, Wake County, NC and was buried on March 17, 1969 in Raleigh, Wake County, NC at Oakwood Cemetery.*
> 2699   John Robert McNeill (1889-1970). *John was born on November 3, 1889. He died on*

November 13, 1970.

2700   Mary Elizabeth McNeill (1892-1974). *Mary was born on November 12, 1892. She died on June 20, 1974 and was buried in Moore County, NC at Bensalem Presbyterian Church.*

2701   Julia Ann McNeill (1903-1993). *Julia was born on November 1, 1903. She died on June 2, 1993 and was buried in Moore County, NC at Mt. Carmel United Methodist Church.*

1105. **Annette E. Cockman**, daughter of William McSwain Cockman and Julia Ann Cagle, was born on April 3, 1868 in Moore County, NC. She married **Jason Mc. Seawell** circa 1889. She died on April 22, 1921 in Greensboro, Guilford County, NC and was buried on April 24, 1921 in Greensboro, Guilford County, NC at Green Hill Cemetery.

Jason Mc. Seawell was born on September 8, 1864. He died on July 16, 1937 in Greensboro, Guilford County, NC and was buried on July 17, 1937 in Greensboro, Guilford County, NC at Green Hill Cemetery. He and Annette E. Cockman had the following children:

2702   Catherine Ann "Cattie" Seawell (1891-1972). *Catherine was born on October 9, 1891. She married **John Turner Jordan** on October 12, 1912 in Guilford County, NC. She died on November 11, 1972.*

2703   Offie Seawell (1895-). *Offie was born in 1895.*

2704   Turner Seawell (1897-). *Turner was born in 1897.*

1106. **Florence Ruthie Cockman**, daughter of William McSwain Cockman and Julia Ann Cagle, was born in 1870. She married **John C. Wright** on December 25, 1895 in Moore County, NC.

John C. Wright, son of A. D. Wright (-) and Mary A. (-), was born in 1869. He and Florence Ruthie Cockman had the following children:

2705   Jenettie Wright (1899-). *Jenettie was born in 1899.*

2706   Cora Lee Wright (1901-). *Cora was born in 1901.*

2707   Lacy L. Wright (1905-). *Lacy was born in 1905.*

2708   Willie H. Wright (1908-). *Willie was born in 1908.*

1107. **Ulysses Franklin Cockman**, son of William McSwain Cockman and Julia Ann Cagle, was born on April 16, 1871. He married **Margaret Melissa Myrick** circa 1901. He died on September 15, 1935 and was buried in Carthage, Moore County, NC at Cross Hill Cemetery.

Margaret Melissa Myrick, daughter of William Lewis Myrick (1834-1904) and Millie A. Jones (1840-1883), was born on September 6, 1871. She died on February 13, 1959 and was buried in Carthage, Moore County, NC at Cross Hill Cemetery. She and Ulysses Franklin Cockman had the following children:

2709   Edwin B. Cockman (1903-). *Edwin was born in 1903.*

2710   Dewey Cockman (1904-). *Dewey was born in 1904.*

2711   Annie May Cockman (1906-). *Annie was born in 1906.*

2712   Ulysses Franklin Cockman Jr. (1908-). *Ulysses was born in 1908.*

1108. **Ira Lee "Arlee" Cockman**, daughter of William McSwain Cockman and Julia Ann Cagle, was born on May 24, 1873. She married **William Wesley Wallace** on December 20, 1891. She died on March 8, 1960 in Cumberland County, NC and was buried on March 10, 1960 in Hope Mills, Cumberland County, NC at Big Rockfish Presbyterian Cemetary.

William Wesley Wallace, son of John Mack Wallace (1845-1927) and Martha Ann Brown (1849-1902), was born on August 27, 1869 in Moore County, NC. He died on September 5, 1929 in Cumberland County, NC and was buried on September 7, 1929 in Hope Mills, Cumberland County, NC at Big Rockfish Presbyterian Cemetary. He and Ira Lee "Arlee" Cockman had the following children:

2713   William Roscoe Wallace (1894-). *William was born in May 1894.*

2714   Rupert Oliver Wallace (1896-1969). *Rupert was born on October 2, 1896. He died on August 9, 1969 and was buried in Moore County, NC at Bethlehem Baptist*

Church.

2715	Robert D. Wallace (1896-1897). *Robert was born on October 2, 1896 in Moore County, NC. He died on August 9, 1897 in Moore County, NC.*
2716	John Mack Wallace II (1898-1955). *John was born on September 30, 1898. He died in 1955.*
2717	Dewey Edgar Wallace (1900-1936). *Dewey was born on September 6, 1900. He died on May 15, 1936 in Hope Mills, Cumberland County, NC.*
2718	Bessie Wallace (1904-1904). *Bessie was born on February 23, 1904. She died on February 26, 1904 and was buried in Hope Mills, Cumberland County, NC at Big Rockfish Presbyterian Cemetery.*
2719	Glenna Velma Wallace (1905-2001). *Glenna was born on August 15, 1905. She married* **James H. Davis** *on June 20, 1929 in Cumberland County, NC. She died in 2001.*
2720	Theodore Wesley Wallace (1908-). *Theodore was born on April 26, 1908 in Hope Mills, Cumberland County, NC. He married* **Velma Adelle Moore** *on June 3, 1928 in Kinston, NC.*
2721	Lillian Gertrude Wallace (1912-). *Lillian was born in 1912.*
2722	Ruby Pearl Wallace (1915-). *Ruby was born in 1915.*
2723	James Franklin Wallace (1918-). *James was born in 1918.*

1110. Jerome Cockman, son of William McSwain Cockman and Julia Ann Cagle, was born on March 28, 1878. He died on September 18, 1883 and was buried in Moore County, NC at Cockman Cemetery #41.

1111. Ernest Cockman, son of William McSwain Cockman and Julia Ann Cagle, was born on September 23, 1879. He died on September 16, 1883 and was buried in Moore County, NC at Cockman Cemetery #41.

1112. Charles Turner Cockman, son of William McSwain Cockman and Julia Ann Cagle, was born in December 1884 in Moore County, NC. He married **Sallie Elizabeth Jessup** circa 1905. He died on October 28, 1949 in Wadesboro, Anson County, NC.

Sallie Elizabeth Jessup was born in 1885 in Bladen County, NC. She died on December 26, 1940 in Rockingham, Richmond County, NC. She and Charles Turner Cockman had the following children:

2724	Charles L. Cockman (1907-). *Charles was born in 1907.*
2725	Mary L. Cockman (1908-). *Mary was born in 1908.*
2726	James W. Cockman (1909-). *James was born in 1909.*

1113. Lewis Graham Cockman, son of William McSwain Cockman and Julia Ann Cagle, was born on May 18, 1885. He married **Dora Alma Kennedy** on December 16, 1914 in Moore County, NC. He died on September 16, 1926 and was buried in Moore County, NC at Bethlehem Baptist Church.

Dora Alma Kennedy, daughter of John William Kennedy (1872-1931) and Mary Adelaide Purvis (1874-1960), was born on April 19, 1896. She died on January 27, 1985 and was buried in Moore County, NC at Bethlehem Baptist Church. She and Lewis Graham Cockman had the following children:

2727	William Graham Cockman (1916-1935). *William was born on February 7, 1916 in Moore County, NC. He died on August 13, 1935 in Greensboro, Guilford County, NC and was buried on August 14, 1935 in Moore County, NC at Bethlehem Baptist Church.*
2728	Mary Helen Cockman (1917-1994). *Mary was born on March 16, 1917. She died on May 9, 1994 and was buried in Moore County, NC at Bethlehem Baptist Church.*
2729	Lewis "June" Cockman Jr. (1919-). *Lewis was born on June 5, 1919.*
2730	Alma Louise Cockman (1921-1923). *Alma was born on November 22, 1921 in Moore County, NC. She died on December 30, 1923 in Moore County, NC and was buried on January 1, 1924 in Moore County, NC at Bethlehem Baptist Church.*
2731	Gilbert Grier Cockman (1925-1969). *Gilbert was born on September 25, 1925. He died on October 6, 1969 and was buried in Moore County, NC at Bethlehem Baptist Church.*

1114. **Daniel Turner Caddell**, son of Tobias B. Caddell and Mary Elizabeth Cockman, was born on March 17, 1864 in Moore County, NC. He married **Peanina Louisa Maness** on September 14, 1890 in Moore County, NC. He died on May 3, 1922 in Rex Hospital, Raleigh, Wake County, NC and was buried on May 4, 1922 in Carthage, Moore County, NC at Cross Hill Cemetery.

Peanina Louisa Maness, daughter of William Armstrong Maness (1833-1895) and Rebecca E. Seawell (1833-1920), was born on January 6, 1861. She died on January 29, 1933 and was buried in Carthage, Moore County, NC at Cross Hill Cemetery. She and Daniel Turner Caddell had the following children:

2732	William B. Caddell (1891-). *William was born in March 1891.*
2733	Lessie Mae Caddell (1893-1947). *Lessie was born on May 12, 1893 in Moore County, NC. She died on December 25, 1947 in Moore County, NC and was buried in Carthage, Moore County, NC at Cross Hill Cemetery.*
2734	Cary T. Caddell (1899-). *Cary was born in October 1899.*
2735	Infant Caddell (1902-1902). *Infant was born on February 1, 1902. She died on February 1, 1902 and was buried in Moore County, NC at Friendship Baptist Church.*

1116. **Peter Thomas Hare**, son of John Russell Hare and Sarah Lee Cockman, was born on August 17, 1864. He died on April 15, 1933 and was buried in Sulphur Bluff, Hopkins County, TX at Sulphur Bluff Cemetery.

1117. **William James Hare**, son of John Russell Hare and Sarah Lee Cockman, was born on August 27, 1865. He died on January 21, 1941 and was buried in Hagansport, Franklin County, TX at Fairview Cemetery.

1119. **Isom Hegler Hare**, son of John Russell Hare and Sarah Lee Cockman, was born on October 30, 1871. He married **Katie Lou Donaghe** on March 29, 1908. He died on February 26, 1950 and was buried in Sulphur Bluff, Hopkins County, TX at Sulphur Bluff Cemetery.

Katie Lou Donaghe was born on July 29, 1883. She died on November 24, 1965. She and Isom Hegler Hare had the following children:

2736	Iva Doris Hare (1920-2008). *Iva was born on November 25, 1920. She died on January 21, 2008.*

1120. **Sarah Lee "Trannie" Hare**, daughter of John Russell Hare and Sarah Lee Cockman, was born on July 27, 1874. She died on March 21, 1922 and was buried in Sulphur Bluff, Hopkins County, TX at Sulphur Bluff Cemetery.

1122. **John Kendrick "Kinnie" Hare**, son of John Russell Hare and Sarah Lee Cockman, was born on March 15, 1880. He died on January 17, 1960 and was buried in Sulphur Bluff, Hopkins County, TX at Sulphur Bluff Cemetery.

1123. **Loretta B. Cockman**, daughter of Isham Wallace Haig Cockman and Camilla Haseltine Cagle, was born on February 5, 1873. She died on September 15, 1893.

1124. **Henrietta E. Cockman**, daughter of Isham Wallace Haig Cockman and Camilla Haseltine Cagle, was born on March 10, 1875 in Moore County, NC. She married **Clark B. Sears** on June 13, 1891 in Moore County, NC. She married **William T. Mitchell** in 1908. She died on October 16, 1917 in St. Leo's Hospital, Greensboro, Guilford County, NC and was buried on October 19, 1917 in Greensboro, Guilford County, NC at Proximity Cemetery.

Clark B. Sears, son of William Washington Sears (1829-1910) and Dorcus (1829-1890), was born in August 1872. He died in 1908. He and Henrietta E. Cockman had the following children:

2737	Male Sears (1892-). *Male was born in November 1892.*
2738	Male Sears (1894-). *Male was born in February 1894.*
2739	Corneila L. Sears (1897-). *Corneila was born in May 1897.*
2740	William S. Sears (1898-). *William was born in December 1898.*

William T. Mitchell was born in May 1865. He died on July 5, 1915. He and Henrietta E. Cockman had the following children:

2741	Anne L. Mitchell (1910-1991). *Anne was born on March 10, 1910. She died on August 5,*

1125. Robert Addison Cockman, son of Isham Wallace Haig Cockman and Camilla Haseltine Cagle, was born on July 12, 1877. He married **Lena Wetzel** on January 6, 1910. He died in September 1971.

Lena Wetzel was born on November 30, 1893. She died on August 30, 1972.

1126. Madison B. Cockman, son of Isham Wallace Haig Cockman and Camilla Haseltine Cagle, was born in April 1879. He married **Pharaby Pittman** on May 25, 1902. He died on October 13, 1918.

Pharaby Pittman was born on January 19, 1882. She died on September 19, 1963.

1129. Beretta Cockman, daughter of Isham Wallace Haig Cockman and Camilla Haseltine Cagle, was born on June 9, 1886. She died in 1974.

William Franklin Loman died in 1959.

1130. George Elisha Cockman, son of Isham Wallace Haig Cockman and Camilla Haseltine Cagle, was born on July 7, 1888. He married **Jenny Louise O. Smith** in 1924. He married **Blanche E. Alger** in 1948. He died in March 1976.

Jenny Louise O. Smith was born in 1893. She died in 1945.

1136. James Charles "Jein" Stafford, son of Jesse Parker Stafford and Nancy Jane Cockman, was born on September 17, 1876. He died on May 4, 1951.

Melissa Elizabeth \"Lizzie\" Easler was born on January 27, 1876. She died on August 30, 1920. She and James Charles "Jein" Stafford had the following children:

> 2742   Ola Stafford (1907-1979). *Ola was born in 1907. She died on August 8, 1979.*

1138. Walter Branson Stafford, son of Jesse Parker Stafford and Nancy Jane Cockman, was born on March 3, 1884. He died on June 1, 1965.

Anna Maud Hatcher was born on December 2, 1889. She died on June 22, 1962. She and Walter Branson Stafford had the following children:

> 2743   Anna Maud Stafford (1909-1999). *Anna was born on September 12, 1909. She died on September 25, 1999.*

1139. Mary Lee Williams, daughter of Richard McCoy Williams and Rebecca Francis Cockman, was born on November 10, 1875 in Moore County, NC. She married **Charles A. Stutts** on October 22, 1891 in Moore County, NC. She died on November 29, 1945 in Greensboro, Guilford County, NC and was buried in Guilford County, NC at Forest Lawn Cemetery.

Charles A. Stutts, son of George Lindsey Stutts (1846-1924) and Julia Ann Muse (1841-1910), was born on February 26, 1869. He died on March 30, 1901 and was buried in Moore County, NC at Doubs Chapel Church. He and Mary Lee Williams had the following children:

> 2744   Crissie May Stutts (1892-). *Crissie was born in December 1892.*
> 2745   Loftus Stutts (1895-1915). *Loftus was born in November 1895. He died in 1915.*
> 2746   Eugene Stutts (1896-1896). *Eugene was born on February 23, 1896. He died on October 9, 1896 and was buried in Moore County, NC at Bethlehem Baptist Church.*
> 2747   George Louis Stutts (1898-1959). *George was born on June 5, 1898. He died on November 2, 1959.*
> 2748   Cora Lee Stutts (1900-). *Cora was born in April 1900.*

1140. Charles L. "Charlie" Williams, son of Richard McCoy Williams and Rebecca Francis Cockman, was born on July 19, 1876 in Moore County, NC. He died on March 2, 1937 in Pinehurst, Moore County, NC and was buried on March 4, 1937 in Moore County, NC at Culdee Presbyterian Church.

Mary Virginia Wicker was born in 1882. She died in 1969 and was buried in Moore County, NC at Culdee Presbyterian Church.

1141. **Nannie Clark Williams**, daughter of Richard McCoy Williams and Rebecca Francis Cockman, was born on April 21, 1879 in Moore County, NC. She died on December 15, 1950 in St. Joseph of Pines Hospital, Pinehurst, Moore County, NC and was buried on December 16, 1950 in Moore County, NC at Culdee Presbyterian Church.

1142. **Jesse Bice Williams**, son of Richard McCoy Williams and Rebecca Francis Cockman, was born on May 10, 1881 in Moore County, NC. He died on September 6, 1965 in Reidsville, Rockingham County, NC and was buried in Moore County, NC at Beulah Hill Baptist Church.

> **Kate Estelle Brookshire** was born on November 11, 1896. She died on August 15, 1941 and was buried in Moore County, NC at Beulah Hill Baptist Church.
>
> **Nancy Catherine Fields**, daughter of John Fields (1861-1927) and Elizabeth Williams Fry (1863-1954), was born on October 29, 1886. She died on June 18, 1925. She and Jesse Bice Williams had the following children:
>
> | 2749 | Herbert Turner Williams (1911-1982). *Herbert was born on November 11, 1911. He died on April 2, 1982.* |
> |---|---|

1143. **Mattie Jane Williams**, daughter of Richard McCoy Williams and Rebecca Francis Cockman, was born on May 3, 1883 in Moore County, NC. She died on January 11, 1935 in Moore County, NC and was buried in Moore County, NC at Bethlehem Baptist Church.

1144. **George Archie Williams**, son of Richard McCoy Williams and Rebecca Francis Cockman, was born on September 27, 1883. He died on June 5, 1891 and was buried in Moore County, NC at Bethlehem Baptist Church.

1145. **Lillian Florence Williams**, daughter of Richard McCoy Williams and Rebecca Francis Cockman, was born on March 24, 1891. She died on August 30, 1984 and was buried in Moore County, NC at Culdee Presbyterian Church.

> **Daniel Justin McKenzie** was born on January 30, 1898. He died on January 8, 1935 and was buried in Moore County, NC at Culdee Presbyterian Church.
>
> **Fred Worth Frye**, son of James Hopkins Fry (1849-1908) and Adelaide Jane Short (1862-1918), was born on October 4, 1902. He died on July 8, 1971 and was buried in Moore County, NC at Culdee Presbyterian Church.

1146. **Myrtle Ruth Williams**, daughter of Richard McCoy Williams and Rebecca Francis Cockman, was born on July 20, 1894 in Moore County, NC. She married **Frank Edgar Lewis** on July 17, 1914 in Moore County, NC. She died on June 8, 1960 in Greensboro, Guilford County, NC and was buried on June 10, 1960 in Moore County, NC at Doubs Chapel Church.

> Frank Edgar Lewis was born on February 13, 1887. He died on June 7, 1982. He and Myrtle Ruth Williams had the following children:
>
> | 2750 | Dorothy Nell Lewis (1925-2001). *Dorothy was born on October 29, 1925. She died on September 21, 2001.* |
> |---|---|

1147. **Eugene Stephen Williams**, son of Richard McCoy Williams and Rebecca Francis Cockman, was born on November 13, 1898 in Moore County, NC. He died on July 28, 1958 in West End, Moore County, NC.

> **Vannie Lee Jackson**, daughter of William Alexander Jackson (1872-1947) and Vennie Emoline Bullard (1882-1970), was born on May 15, 1901 in Moore County, NC. She died on July 28, 1973 in Moore Regional Hospital, Pinehurst, Moore County, NC and was buried in Moore County, NC at Culdee Presbyterian Church. She and Eugene Stephen Williams had the following children:
>
> | 2751 | Margaret Marie Williams (1932-2006). *Margaret was born on December 11, 1932. She died on June 17, 2006 in Moore County, NC.* |
> |---|---|

1148. **John Huey Cockman**, son of Eli Terry Cockman and Silla Frances Horner, was born on October 29, 1880. He married **Mishie Adelaide Teague** on September 10, 1905 in Moore County, NC. He died on February 2, 1957 and was buried in Moore County, NC at Pleasant Hill United Methodist Church.

Mishie Adelaide Teague, daughter of Isaac T. Teague (1863-bef 1910) and Sarah A. Garner (1864-1931), was born on May 19, 1887. She died on May 3, 1973 and was buried in Moore County, NC at Pleasant Hill United Methodist Church. She and John Huey Cockman had the following children:

2752	Beulah Evelyn Cockman (1907-1986). *Beulah was born on May 31, 1907. She died on October 21, 1986 and was buried in Bennett, Chatham County, NC at Fall Creek Baptist Church Cemetery.*
2753	Sallie Frances Cockman (1909-). *Sallie was born on May 9, 1909.*
2754	Male Cockman (1911-1911). *Male was born on May 2, 1911. He died on May 2, 1911 and was buried in Moore County, NC at Pleasant Hill United Methodist Church.*
2755	Euliss Claude Cockman (1912-1985). *Euliss was born on September 11, 1912. He died on November 6, 1985 in Moore County, NC and was buried in Moore County, NC at Pleasant Hill United Methodist Church.*
2756	Colon Jessie Cockman (1915-2000). *Colon was born on February 1, 1915. He died on June 19, 2000 and was buried in Moore County, NC at Pleasant Hill United Methodist Church.*
2757	Carl Huey Cockman (1917-1991). *Carl was born on March 16, 1917. He died on April 4, 1991 and was buried in Moore County, NC at Calvary Baptist Church.*
2758	Johnie Roy Cockman (1919-2003). *Johnie was born on June 24, 1919. He died on September 2, 2003 and was buried in Moore County, NC at Calvary Baptist Church.*
2759	Myrtle Kathleen Cockman (1921-). *Myrtle was born on November 7, 1921.*
2760	Clara Dorothy Cockman (1924-). *Clara was born on April 8, 1924.*

1149. **Mary Clark Cockman**, daughter of Eli Terry Cockman and Silla Frances Horner, was born on February 10, 1881. She married **William Thomas Ritter** on January 12, 1901 in Moore County, NC. She died on July 6, 1957 and was buried in Moore County, NC at Flint Hill Baptist Church.

William Thomas Ritter, son of Samuel Jones Ritter (1851-1918) and Lydia Margaret Kennedy (1853-1932), was born on December 22, 1873. He died on October 8, 1934 and was buried in Moore County, NC at Flint Hill Baptist Church.

1150. **Sarah Emma Cockman**, daughter of Eli Terry Cockman and Silla Frances Horner, was born on November 24, 1883. She died on March 24, 1976 and was buried in Moore County, NC at Pleasant Hill United Methodist Church.

William Henry Brown, son of Alfred Branson Brown (1862-) and Sarah Ella Ritter (1863-1910), was born on May 10, 1888. He died on January 2, 1964 and was buried in Moore County, NC at Pleasant Hill United Methodist Church. He and Sarah Emma Cockman had the following children:

2761	William Curtis Brown (1914-1978). *William was born on June 21, 1914. He married **Rona McNeill** on January 22, 1937 in Moore County, NC. He died on September 17, 1978 and was buried in Moore County, NC at Unity Grove Baptist Church.*
2762	Henry Lester Brown (1916-). *Henry was born in 1916.*
2763	Maude Gertrude Brown (1922-1968). *Maude was born on December 1, 1922. She died on November 8, 1968 and was buried in Moore County, NC at Calvary Baptist Church.*

1151. **Martha A. Cockman**, daughter of Eli Terry Cockman and Silla Frances Horner, was born on July 4, 1885 in Moore County, NC. She married **Oscar M. Cheek** circa 1909. She died on August 5, 1974 in Moore Regional Hospital, Pinehurst, Moore County, NC and was buried on August 8, 1974 in Moore County, NC at Pleasant Hill United Methodist Church.

Oscar M. Cheek was born in 1879. He died in 1967 and was buried in Moore County, NC at Pleasant Hill United Methodist Church. He and Martha A. Cockman had the following children:

2764	William Eli Cheek (1910-2000). *William was born on February 25, 1910. He died on October 16, 2000 and was buried in Moore County, NC at Pleasant Hill United Methodist Church.*
2765	Dora Alice Cheek (1921-). *Dora was born on May 26, 1921.*

1152. **Purcilla Florence Cockman**, daughter of Eli Terry Cockman and Silla Frances Horner, was born on November 11, 1888. She died on January 4, 1943 and was buried in Moore County, NC at Pleasant Hill United Methodist Church.

William Charles Williams, son of George W. Williams (1820-1901) and Catherine L. McIntosh (1850-1914), was born on April 14, 1879 and was buried in Moore County, NC at Pleasant Hill United Methodist Church.

1153. **George Thomas Cockman**, son of Eli Terry Cockman and Silla Frances Horner, was born on June 8, 1889. He died on November 20, 1971 and was buried in Moore County, NC at Pleasant Hill United Methodist Church.

Annie Katie Maness, daughter of Reuben Addison Maness (1865-1953) and Annie Mae Maness (1875-1942), was born on September 16, 1891. She died on November 13, 1932 and was buried in Moore County, NC at Pleasant Hill United Methodist Church. She and George Thomas Cockman had the following children:

2766	Nuby Clarence Cockman (1909-). *Nuby was born on September 4, 1909.*
2767	Bertha Edith Cockman (1911-1988). *Bertha was born on January 19, 1911. She died on November 1, 1988.*
2768	Anna Frances Cockman (1912-1992). *Anna was born on June 1, 1912. She died on June 20, 1992 in Randolph County, NC.*
2769	Bonnie Jane Cockman (1914-1996). *Bonnie was born on July 2, 1914. She died on December 18, 1996 and was buried in Moore County, NC at High Falls Friends Meeting Cemetery.*
2770	Marvin Thomas Cockman (1915-1979). *Marvin was born on November 25, 1915. He married **Swannie Ellen Brown** on May 23, 1935. He died on January 2, 1979 and was buried in Moore County, NC at Rock Hill Church.*
2771	Frank Ervin Cockman (1917-2011). *Frank was born on June 4, 1917. He died on December 9, 2011.*
2772	Mary Evelyn Cockman (1919-). *Mary was born on January 16, 1919.*
2773	Ruby Kate Cockman (1921-). *Ruby was born on April 30, 1921.*
2774	George Tracy Cockman (1923-). *George was born on January 21, 1923.*
2775	Herbert Eugene Cockman (1925-2007). *Herbert was born on September 8, 1925. He married **Mary Matilda Hussey** on January 7, 1948 in Randolph County, NC. He died on July 20, 2007.*
2776	Winfred Terry Cockman (1927-). *Winfred was born on September 2, 1927.*

Maude Purvis, daughter of Nathaniel Green Purvis (1868-1958) and Aggie Norah Reynolds (1871-1919), was born on December 11, 1891. She died on December 30, 1986 and was buried in Moore County, NC at High Falls United Methodist Church.

1154. **Kenny Harrison Cockman**, son of Eli Terry Cockman and Silla Frances Horner, was born on March 21, 1891. He died on June 12, 1980 and was buried in Moore County, NC at Pleasant Hill United Methodist Church.

Aggie Donner Maness, daughter of Nancy E. Maness (1860-1943), was born on June 10, 1894. She died on July 19, 1972 and was buried in Moore County, NC at Pleasant Hill United Methodist Church. She and Kenny Harrison Cockman had the following children:

2777	Josie Mae Cockman (1914-1999). *Josie was born on May 23, 1914. She married **Earl Carter Stutts** on June 5, 1937. She died on December 25, 1999 and was buried in Robbins, Moore County, NC at Pine Rest Cemetery.*
2778	Kennie Eli Cockman (1916-1919). *Kennie was born on July 10, 1916. He died on January 17, 1919 and was buried in Moore County, NC at Pleasant Hill United Methodist Church.*
2779	Roland Harrison Cockman (1918-). *Roland was born on April 15, 1918.*
2780	Female Cockman (1919-1919). *Female was born on December 24, 1919. She died on December 24, 1919 and was buried in Moore County, NC at Pleasant Hill United*

	Methodist Church.
2781	Male Cockman (1919-1919). *Male was born on December 24, 1919. He died on December 24, 1919 and was buried in Moore County, NC at Pleasant Hill United Methodist Church.*
2782	Calvin Harding Cockman (1921-1998). *Calvin was born on March 22, 1921. He died on September 12, 1998 and was buried in Moore County, NC at Calvary Baptist Church.*
2783	Nancy Frances Cockman (1923-1998). *Nancy was born on April 15, 1923 in Moore County, NC. She died on December 4, 1998 and was buried in Robbins, Moore County, NC at Pine Rest Cemetery.*
2784	Lacy J. Cockman (1925-1925). *Lacy was born on May 23, 1925. He died on July 3, 1925 and was buried in Moore County, NC at Pleasant Hill United Methodist Church.*
2785	Donner Lee Cockman (1928-2009). *Donner was born on May 9, 1928. She married **Robert Mack Beck** on September 29, 1946 in Moore County, NC. She died on November 26, 2009.*
2786	Kerney Elbert Cockman (1930-1994). *Kerney was born on March 24, 1930 in Moore County, NC. He died on October 3, 1994 and was buried in Robbins, Moore County, NC at Pine Rest Cemetery.*
2787	Benjamin Franklin Cockman (1932-2000). *Benjamin was born on July 21, 1932 in Moore County, NC. He died on June 23, 2000 and was buried in Robbins, Moore County, NC at Pine Rest Cemetery.*

1155. Betty Jane "Janie" Cockman, daughter of Eli Terry Cockman and Silla Frances Horner, was born on November 28, 1892. She died on May 11, 1965 and was buried in Moore County, NC at High Falls First Wesleyan Church.

Causey Andrew Hussey, son of Kendrick Hussey (1855-1934) and Armetia Alice "Mishie" Purvis (1868-1930), was born on June 4, 1894. He died on October 21, 1981 and was buried in Moore County, NC at High Falls First Wesleyan Church. He and Betty Jane "Janie" Cockman had the following children:

2788	Joe A. Hussey (1919-1956). *Joe was born on May 21, 1919. He died on October 23, 1956 and was buried in Moore County, NC at Pleasant Hill United Methodist Church.*

1156. Lizzie C. Cockman, daughter of Eli Terry Cockman and Silla Frances Horner, was born on February 23, 1895. She married **John Alsey Maness Jr.** on June 30, 1928 in Moore County, NC. She died on December 27, 1975 and was buried in Moore County, NC at Pleasant Hill United Methodist Church.

John Alsey Maness Jr., son of John Alsey Maness (1856-1885) and Frances Eugenia Hughes (1856-1926), was born on August 15, 1885. He married Nancy Jane "Florence" Cockman on February 10, 1905 in Moore County, NC. He died on December 13, 1958 and was buried in Moore County, NC at Pleasant Hill United Methodist Church. He and Lizzie C. Cockman had the following children:

2789	Joe Alsey Maness (1934-2000). *Joe was born on October 20, 1934. He died on February 9, 2000 and was buried in Moore County, NC at Pleasant Hill United Methodist Church.*
2790	Lonnie Franklin Maness (1936-). *Lonnie was born on September 3, 1936.*

1157. Lula L. Cockman, daughter of Eli Terry Cockman and Silla Frances Horner, was born on August 16, 1897. She died on June 24, 1923 and was buried in Moore County, NC at Pleasant Hill United Methodist Church.

Clinton Bevin Maness, son of Reuben Addison Maness (1865-1953) and Annie Mae Maness (1875-1942), was born on November 9, 1892. He died on January 12, 1987 and was buried in Moore County, NC at Pleasant Hill United Methodist Church. He and Lula L. Cockman had the following children:

2791	Ocie Lee Maness (1914-1914). *Ocie was born on July 11, 1914. She died on July 13, 1914 and was buried in Moore County, NC at Pleasant Hill United Methodist Church.*
2792	Cella L. Maness (1916-2007). *Cella was born in 1916. She died on January 24, 2007 in Norfolk, VA.*
2793	C. Early Maness (1918-). *C. was born in 1918.*

1158. **Ruth Adlaide Cockman**, daughter of Eli Terry Cockman and Silla Frances Horner, was born on July 23, 1899. She died on June 7, 1970 and was buried in Moore County, NC at Pleasant Hill United Methodist Church.

1159. **Callie J. Williams**, daughter of Murdock M. Williams and Delphina Cockman, was born on November 30, 1874 in Chatham County, NC. She died on May 6, 1957 in Pleasant Garden, Guilford County, NC and was buried on May 7, 1957 in Greensboro, Guilford County, NC at Green Hill Cemetery.

   Jesse Ragsdale was born in 1894. He died in 1922 and was buried in Greensboro, Guilford County, NC at Green Hill Cemetery.

1160. **William M. Williams**, son of Murdock M. Williams and Delphina Cockman, was born on February 17, 1878 in Moore County, NC. He died on September 22, 1954 in Elon College, Alamance County, NC and was buried on September 24, 1954 in Greensboro, Guilford County, NC at Green Hill Cemetery.

   Maggie Self was born on November 4, 1887. She died on December 20, 1979 and was buried in Greensboro, Guilford County, NC at Green Hill Cemetery. She and William M. Williams had the following children:

2794	Ernest L. Williams (1906-1906). *Ernest was born on November 2, 1906. He died on November 5, 1906 and was buried in Greensboro, Guilford County, NC at Green Hill Cemetery.*
2795	Essie M. Williams (1909-1909). *Essie was born on October 1, 1909. She died on October 2, 1909 and was buried in Greensboro, Guilford County, NC at Green Hill Cemetery.*

1161. **Daniel W. Williams**, son of Murdock M. Williams and Delphina Cockman, was born on September 25, 1880. He died on May 5, 1965 and was buried in Greensboro, Guilford County, NC at Green Hill Cemetery.

   Rosa Bullard, daughter of William Francis Bullard (1859-1900) and Maggie Gibson (1870-1958), was born on October 6, 1890 in Scotland County, NC. She died on July 3, 1930 and was buried in Greensboro, Guilford County, NC at Green Hill Cemetery. She and Daniel W. Williams had the following children:

2796	Mary Williams (1908-). *Mary was born in 1908.*
2797	Pauline Williams (1910-). *Pauline was born in 1910.*
2798	Dean H. Williams (1913-1914). *Dean was born in 1913. He died in 1914 and was buried in Greensboro, Guilford County, NC at Green Hill Cemetery.*
2799	Clarence Murdock "Bud" Williams (1913-1988). *Clarence was born on February 13, 1913. He died on March 8, 1988 and was buried in Julian, Guilford County, NC at Pleasant Union Methodist Church.*
2800	Maggie Williams (1915-). *Maggie was born in 1915.*
2801	Clarice Williams (1917-). *Clarice was born in 1917.*
2802	Ernest Lee Williams (1919-2007). *Ernest was born on July 31, 1919. He died on July 11, 2007.*
2803	Lillian Iola Williams (1923-). *Lillian was born in 1923.*
2804	Daniel W. Williams Jr. (1923-). *Daniel was born in 1923.*
2805	Jody L. Williams (1924-). *Jody was born in 1924.*
2806	Elizabeth Williams (1926-). *Elizabeth was born in 1926.*
2807	Allene Williams (1927-1928). *Allene was born in 1927. She died in 1928 and was buried in Greensboro, Guilford County, NC at Green Hill Cemetery.*

1162. **Martha Williams**, daughter of Murdock M. Williams and Delphina Cockman, was born on November 12, 1885. She died on April 24, 1965 and was buried in Greensboro, Guilford County, NC at Green Hill Cemetery.

   Charles Roberson was buried in Greensboro, Guilford County, NC at Green Hill Cemetery. He and Martha Williams had the following children:

2808	Cabus Roberson (-)

1163. **Iola Williams**, daughter of Murdock M. Williams and Delphina Cockman, was born on July 8, 1888. She died on January 5, 1964 in Greensboro, Guilford County, NC and was buried on January 7, 1964 in Guilford County, NC at Forest Lawn Cemetery.

John Rufus Ledbetter was born on March 31, 1888. He died on November 21, 1937 and was buried in Guilford County, NC at Forest Lawn Cemetery. He and Iola Williams had the following children:

2809	Howard Loman Ledbetter (-1986). *Howard died in 1986 and was buried in Guilford County, NC at Forest Lawn Cemetery.*
2810	Julia Delfinia Ledbetter (1911-1988). *Julia was born on September 14, 1911. She died on May 3, 1988 and was buried in Guilford County, NC at Forest Lawn Cemetery.*
2811	Zadie Mae Ledbetter (1916-1994). *Zadie was born on March 24, 1916. She died on June 21, 1994 and was buried in Charlotte, Mecklenburg County, NC at Sharon Memorial Park.*
2812	Adelaide Jessie Ledbetter (1918-2004). *Adelaide was born on April 15, 1918. She died in 2004 and was buried in Guilford County, NC at Forest Lawn Cemetery.*

1164. **Lillie May Williams**, daughter of Murdock M. Williams and Delphina Cockman, was born on June 25, 1892. She died on April 9, 1965 and was buried in Guilford County, NC at Lakeview Memorial Park.

George Leslie Haithcock was born on November 11, 1885. He died on January 10, 1967. He and Lillie May Williams had the following children:

2813	Tommy Edgar Haithcock (1910-1995). *Tommy was born on November 21, 1910. He died on January 11, 1995.*
2814	Elzy Van Haithcock (1913-1974). *Elzy was born on February 4, 1913. He died on April 9, 1974.*
2815	Roy Charles "Buck" Haithcock (1915-1966). *Roy was born on August 25, 1915. He died on August 12, 1966.*
2816	Lois Irene Haithcock (1917-1976). *Lois was born in 1917. She died in 1976.*
2817	Helen Marie Haithcock (1921-2002). *Helen was born in 1921. She died on December 20, 2002.*
2818	Rebecca Elizabeth Haithcock (1923-2015). *Rebecca was born on January 29, 1923. She married **Russell Michael Murray** on November 13, 1945 in Randolph County, NC. She died on May 6, 2015.*
2819	Patricia Joanne Haithcock (1936-2002). *Patricia was born on July 11, 1936. She died on March 15, 2002.*

1165. **Walston Leonidas Cockman**, son of Charles Edward Cockman and Myca Jane "Millie" Cagle, was born on November 25, 1886. He married **Lilly Gertrude Dawson** on April 19, 1908 in Moore County, NC. He married **Minnie Belle Needham** on January 10, 1925 in Moore County, NC. He died on April 24, 1971 and was buried in Moore County, NC at Calvary Baptist Church.

Lilly Gertrude Dawson, daughter of John Bryant Dawson (-) and Mary Addie (-), was born on November 26, 1891. She and Walston Leonidas Cockman had the following children:

2820	Milly Janie Cockman (1909-). *Milly was born in 1909.*
2821	Charles Walter Cockman (1918-1973). *Charles was born on April 24, 1918. He married **Irene Patterson** on December 1, 1940. He died on August 30, 1973 and was buried in Moore County, NC at Flint Hill Baptist Church.*

Minnie Belle Needham, daughter of Eli Needham (1851-1923) and Susannah Fox (1873-1952), was born on December 16, 1897. She died on January 29, 1982 and was buried in Moore County, NC at Calvary Baptist Church. She and Walston Leonidas Cockman had the following children:

2822	Warren G. Cockman (1925-2007). *Warren was born on October 31, 1925. He died on December 22, 2007 and was buried in Moore County, NC at Calvary Baptist Church.*
2823	Harold Lee Cockman (1928-2008). *Harold was born on January 12, 1928. He died on*

	March 11, 2008 and was buried in Moore County, NC at Calvary Baptist Church.
2824	Ruby May Cockman (1933-). *Ruby was born on May 26, 1933 in Moore County, NC.*
2825	William Felt Cockman (1936-). *William was born on October 18, 1936 in Moore County, NC.*

1166. Barbara Anna Cockman, daughter of Charles Edward Cockman and Myca Jane "Millie" Cagle, was born on February 24, 1888. She died on August 26, 1974 in Seagrove, Randolph County, NC and was buried on August 28, 1974 in Seagrove, Randolph County, NC at Union Grove Baptist Church.

Rufus W. Beck Sr. and Barbara Anna Cockman had the following children:

2826	Charles W. Beck (1916-1916). *Charles was born on May 7, 1916. He died on May 7, 1916 and was buried in Moore County, NC at Flint Hill Baptist Church.*

1167. Lucy Jane Cockman, daughter of Charles Edward Cockman and Myca Jane "Millie" Cagle, was born on March 31, 1892. She married **William Linden Kennedy** on December 29, 1909. She died on July 6, 1972 and was buried in Robbins, Moore County, NC at Tabernacle United Methodist Church.

William Linden Kennedy, son of William Wesley Kennedy (1865-1918) and Etta Jane Brown (1868-1928), was born on September 30, 1888. He died on November 9, 1934 and was buried in Robbins, Moore County, NC at Tabernacle United Methodist Church. He and Lucy Jane Cockman had the following children:

2827	Louvine Kennedy (1912-1990). *Louvine was born in 1912. She died in 1990 and was buried in Robbins, Moore County, NC at Tabernacle United Methodist Church.*

1168. Peter Wesley Cockman, son of Charles Edward Cockman and Myca Jane "Millie" Cagle, was born on May 25, 1896. He died on September 20, 1973.

Alma Hancock, daughter of John Augustus Hancock (1872-1920) and Martha Ann Williams (1871-1955), was born on October 7, 1898. She died on March 19, 1944.

1169. Sarah C. Cockman, daughter of Charles Edward Cockman and Myca Jane "Millie" Cagle, was born on September 11, 1899 and was buried in Moore County, NC at Flint Hill Baptist Church.

1170. Sarah Annette Horner, daughter of William Thomas Horner and Clarkey Ann Cockman, was born on March 15, 1862 in Moore County, NC. She married **Isaac Frank Wallace** circa 1879. She died on November 20, 1913 in Randolph County, NC and was buried on November 21, 1913 in Ramseur, Randolph County, NC at First Christian Church AKA Sunset Knoll Cemetery.

Isaac Frank Wallace, son of Lochart "Lockey" Wallace (1836-1884), was born on March 15, 1856 in Moore County, NC. He died on September 5, 1925 in Danville, VA. He and Sarah Annette Horner had the following children:

2828	Ella Wallace (1886-1923). *Ella was born on February 22, 1886 in Moore County, NC. She married **Orlindo R. Kennedy** on December 20, 1903 in Randolph County, NC. She died on June 4, 1923 in Ramseur, Randolph County, NC and was buried on June 6, 1923 in Ramseur, Randolph County, NC at First Christian Church AKA Sunset Knoll Cemetery.*
2829	Sarah A. Wallace (1889-1910). *Sarah was born on February 18, 1889. She married **Alexander D. Wilson** circa 1905. She died on April 26, 1910 and was buried in Ramseur, Randolph County, NC at First Christian Church AKA Sunset Knoll Cemetery.*
2830	Aggie E. Wallace (1892-1906). *Aggie was born on October 23, 1892. She died on December 16, 1906 and was buried in Ramseur, Randolph County, NC at First Christian Church AKA Sunset Knoll Cemetery.*
2831	Leora Wallace (1900-). *Leora was born in July 1900. She married **Marshall D. Coward** on September 29, 1915 in Randolph County, NC.*

1171. Kenneth Cassidy Horner, son of William Thomas Horner and Clarkey Ann Cockman, was born on February 12, 1864. He married **Lusla Arnette** on December 21, 1892 in Moore County, NC. He died on November 10, 1931.

Lusla Arnette, daughter of David Arnett (-) and Martha (-1903), was born in 1872. She and Kenneth Cassidy Horner had the following children:

2832	Blanche Horner (1895-). *Blanche was born in 1895.*
2833	Fentress T. Horner (1903-). *Fentress was born in 1903.*
2834	Ruby M. Horner (1905-). *Ruby was born in 1905.*

1172. **John A. Horner**, son of William Thomas Horner and Clarkey Ann Cockman, was born on October 25, 1865. He died on August 30, 1882 and was buried in Moore County, NC at Cockman Cemetery #244.

1173. **George Washington Horner**, son of William Thomas Horner and Clarkey Ann Cockman, was born on December 19, 1867. He married **Mary Ann Hunsucker** on July 4, 1893 in Moore County, NC. He died on March 14, 1937 and was buried in Robbins, Moore County, NC at Tabernacle United Methodist Church.

Mary Ann Hunsucker, daughter of Clarkson Coffin Hunsucker (1846-1919) and Mary Ann Burns (1852-1878), was born on January 29, 1877. She died on May 4, 1960 in Kinston, Lenior County, NC and was buried on May 5, 1960 in Robbins, Moore County, NC at Tabernacle United Methodist Church. She and George Washington Horner had the following children:

2835	Etta L. Horner (1894-). *Etta was born in June 1894. She married **Rufus Earnest Butner** circa 1913.*
2836	William McKinley Horner (1896-1973). *William was born on September 21, 1896 in Moore County, NC. He died on May 16, 1973 in New Bern, Craven County, NC and was buried on May 18, 1973 in New Bern, Craven County, NC at National Cemetery.*
2837	Manda Stella Horner (1898-1991). *Manda was born on March 3, 1898. She died on January 20, 1991.*
2838	Fonnie N. Horner (1899-). *Fonnie was born in October 1899.*

1174. **Daniel Hopkins Horner**, son of William Thomas Horner and Clarkey Ann Cockman, was born on September 8, 1869. He married **Sarah Lavannia Brown** circa 1888. He died on January 8, 1919 and was buried in Robbins, Moore County, NC at Tabernacle United Methodist Church.

Sarah Lavannia Brown, daughter of Henry Clay Brown (1840-1910) and Mary Molsey Davis (1846-1897), was born on October 9, 1871. She died on April 18, 1934 and was buried in Robbins, Moore County, NC at Tabernacle United Methodist Church. She and Daniel Hopkins Horner had the following children:

2839	George Carson Horner (-)
2840	Bertha Lee Horner (1889-). *Bertha was born in October 1889. She married **Street Williamson** circa 1906.*
2841	Loula Belle Horner (1892-). *Loula was born in March 1892.*
2842	Daniel Curtis Horner (1894-1904). *Daniel was born on March 17, 1894. He died on August 20, 1904 and was buried in Moore County, NC at Smyrna Methodist Church.*
2843	Ethel Delena Horner (1896-1996). *Ethel was born on March 19, 1896. She died on November 17, 1996 and was buried in Robbins, Moore County, NC at Tabernacle United Methodist Church.*
2844	Cora Elizabeth Horner (1898-1962). *Cora was born on February 26, 1898. She died on April 20, 1962 and was buried in Robbins, Moore County, NC at Tabernacle United Methodist Church.*
2845	Ida Mae Horner (1898-). *Ida was born on February 26, 1898.*
2846	Oscar Cassidy Horner (1900-). *Oscar was born in March 1900.*
2847	Mamie Blanche Horner (1903-1958). *Mamie was born on March 30, 1903. She died on December 22, 1958 and was buried in Robbins, Moore County, NC at Pine Rest Cemetery.*
2848	Claude Clinton Horner (1907-). *Claude was born in 1907.*
2849	Edith Lavannah Horner (1908-1994). *Edith was born on January 30, 1908. She died on March 21, 1994 and was buried in Robbins, Moore County, NC at Tabernacle*

2850   Maida Horner (1910-1998). *Maida was born on January 21, 1910. She died on February 6, 1998 and was buried in Robbins, Moore County, NC at Tabernacle United Methodist Church.*

2851   Bessie Brown Horner (1912-1989). *Bessie was born on January 26, 1912. She died on January 4, 1989 and was buried in Robbins, Moore County, NC at Pine Rest Cemetery.*

2852   Mattie Wilma Horner (1914-). *Mattie was born on May 21, 1914.*

1175. **William Thomas "Will" Horner Jr.**, son of William Thomas Horner and Clarkey Ann Cockman, was born on August 18, 1872. He married **Cornelia Emma Ritter** on August 27, 1893 in Moore County, NC. He died on March 25, 1936 in St. Leo's Hospital, Greensboro, Guilford County, NC and was buried on March 27, 1936 in Moore County, NC at Pleasant Hill United Methodist Church.

Cornelia Emma Ritter, daughter of William Debarra "Big Foot Bill" Ritter (1835-1906) and Margaret Myrick (1837-1906), was born on February 3, 1878. She died on July 3, 1951 and was buried in Moore County, NC at Pleasant Hill United Methodist Church. She and William Thomas "Will" Horner Jr. had the following children:

2853   William Arthur Horner (1894-1971). *William was born on November 23, 1894. He died on October 13, 1971 and was buried in Moore County, NC at Calvary Baptist Church.*

2854   John E. Horner (1896-1900). *John was born on February 8, 1896. He died on August 10, 1900 and was buried in Moore County, NC at Pleasant Hill United Methodist Church.*

2855   Pearl Lena Horner (1899-1990). *Pearl was born on February 13, 1899. She died on June 29, 1990 and was buried in Ramseur, Randolph County, NC at First Christian Church AKA Sunset Knoll Cemetery.*

2856   M. M. Horner (1901-1902). *M. was born on March 21, 1901. He died on August 29, 1902 and was buried in Moore County, NC at Pleasant Hill United Methodist Church.*

2857   Mollie Horner (1904-1984). *Mollie was born on March 3, 1904. She died on September 4, 1984 and was buried in Ramseur, Randolph County, NC at Pleasant Ridge Christian Church.*

2858   G. C. Horner (1906-1907). *G. was born on June 9, 1906. He died on January 1, 1907 and was buried in Moore County, NC at Pleasant Hill United Methodist Church.*

2859   Luther Columbus Horner (1908-1964). *Luther was born on February 13, 1908. He died on September 1, 1964 and was buried in Asheboro, Randolph County, NC at Pleasant Cross Christian Church.*

2860   Infant Horner (1910-1910). *Infant was born on December 15, 1910. He died on December 15, 1910 and was buried in Moore County, NC at Pleasant Hill United Methodist Church.*

2861   Bertie Horner (1911-1958). *Bertie was born on November 10, 1911. She died on March 20, 1958 and was buried in Ramseur, Randolph County, NC at First Christian Church AKA Sunset Knoll Cemetery.*

2862   Josephine Horner (1914-1961). *Josephine was born on March 8, 1914. She died on November 3, 1961 and was buried in Ramseur, Randolph County, NC at First Christian Church AKA Sunset Knoll Cemetery.*

2863   Emma Worthy Horner (1917-2000). *Emma was born on October 17, 1917. She died on September 18, 2000 and was buried in Asheboro, Randolph County, NC at Randolph Memorial Park.*

1176. **Mary Elizabeth Horner**, daughter of William Thomas Horner and Clarkey Ann Cockman, was born on May 9, 1874 in Moore County, NC. She married **John Lee Dowdy** on September 15, 1898 in Moore County, NC. She died on July 22, 1933 in Greensboro, Guilford County, NC and was buried on July 24, 1933 in Guilford County, NC at Forest Lawn Cemetery.

John Lee Dowdy, son of Archibald Bannister Dowdy (1840-1914) and Jennett S. "Jennie" Cockman (1852-1905), was born on August 8, 1876 in Moore County, NC. He died on April 30, 1947 in Greensboro, Guilford County, NC and was buried in Guilford County, NC at Forest Lawn Cemetery. He and Mary Elizabeth Horner had the following children:

2864   Maudie Mae Dowdy (1919-2002). *Maudie was born on September 24, 1919. She married* **Silas Gray Murray** *on June 19, 1943 in Guilford County, NC. She died on January 26, 2002.*

1177. Jennie P. Horner, daughter of William Thomas Horner and Clarkey Ann Cockman, was born on December 14, 1875. She married **William Thomas "Bud" Williams** on October 7, 1894 in Moore County, NC. She died on August 4, 1927 in Broughton State Hospital, Morganton, Burke County, NC and was buried in Robbins, Moore County, NC at Tabernacle United Methodist Church.

William Thomas "Bud" Williams, son of John Spanker Williams (1842-1924) and Mary Catherine Williams (1848-1935), was born on January 12, 1873 in Moore County, NC. He died on October 18, 1932 in High Point, Guilford County, NC and was buried on October 19, 1932 in Robbins, Moore County, NC at Tabernacle United Methodist Church. He and Jennie P. Horner had the following children:

2865   Viola M. Williams (1896-1896). *Viola was born on January 17, 1896. She died on July 6, 1896 and was buried in Moore County, NC at Cockman Cemetery #244.*

2866   Mary Annie Williams (1897-1990). *Mary was born on October 29, 1897. She died on November 2, 1990.*

2867   Ida Grace Williams (1901-1982). *Ida was born on September 2, 1901. She died on October 9, 1982.*

2868   Dora Lee Williams (1904-1995). *Dora was born on September 18, 1904. She died on December 20, 1995.*

2869   Etta Elizabeth Williams (1907-1995). *Etta was born on August 8, 1907. She died on March 4, 1995 and was buried in Asheboro, Randolph County, NC at Randolph Memorial Park.*

2870   Jesse Paul Williams (1912-1914). *Jesse was born on February 8, 1912. He died on June 1, 1914 and was buried in Robbins, Moore County, NC at Tabernacle United Methodist Church.*

2871   Virginia Williams (1914-1927). *Virginia was born on November 1, 1914 in Moore County, NC. She died on May 3, 1927 in Asheboro, Randolph County, NC and was buried on May 4, 1927 in Robbins, Moore County, NC at Tabernacle United Methodist Church.*

1178. Martha L. "Mattie" Horner, daughter of William Thomas Horner and Clarkey Ann Cockman, was born on May 31, 1878. She married **William L. Stutts** on April 12, 1894 in Moore County, NC. She died on August 2, 1934 and was buried in Seagrove, Randolph County, NC at Union Grove Baptist Church.

William L. Stutts, son of Leonard C. Stutts (1815-1897) and Diannah Jane Robeson (1838-1920), was born on January 18, 1862 in Moore County, NC. He died on August 29, 1938 in Randolph County, NC and was buried on August 30, 1938 in Seagrove, Randolph County, NC at Union Grove Baptist Church. He and Martha L. "Mattie" Horner had the following children:

2872   Annie J. Stutts (1894-). *Annie was born in June 1894.*

2873   Erastus Emory Stutts (1897-1960). *Erastus was born on March 23, 1897. He died on September 29, 1960 and was buried in Midway, Davidson County, NC at Midway United Methodist Church.*

2874   Herman D. Stutts (1898-). *Herman was born in January 1898.*

2875   Mattie Vercilla Stutts (1921-1921). *Mattie was born on June 5, 1921. She died on June 5, 1921 and was buried in Seagrove, Randolph County, NC at Union Grove Baptist Church.*

1179. James Robert Horner, son of William Thomas Horner and Clarkey Ann Cockman, was born on May 16, 1880 in Moore County, NC. He married **Artimishia Marley** circa 1898. He died on December 4, 1958 in Summerfield, Guilford County, NC and was buried on December 6, 1958 in Greensboro, Guilford County, NC at Green Hill Cemetery.

Artimishia Marley, daughter of Thomas Milton Marley (1863-1923) and Sarah Emily Beck (1861-1925), was born on July 13, 1878. She died on April 16, 1948 in Greensboro, Guilford County, NC and was buried on April 18, 1948 in Greensboro, Guilford County, NC at Green Hill Cemetery. She and James Robert Horner had the following children:

2876	Estell May Horner (1898-). *Estell was born in October 1898.*
2877	Ada Horner (1900-1996). *Ada was born on July 26, 1900. She married **Charles Bernard Compton** on April 12, 1918. She died in February 1996.*
2878	Ernest Horner (1902-1903). *Ernest was born on June 9, 1902. He died on March 7, 1903 and was buried in Moore County, NC at Pleasant Hill United Methodist Church.*
2879	Ollie Horner (1905-1906). *Ollie was born on August 16, 1905. She died on August 3, 1906 and was buried in Moore County, NC at Pleasant Hill United Methodist Church.*
2880	Lorie Horner (1907-). *Lorie was born in 1907.*
2881	Margaret Horner (1909-). *Margaret was born in 1909.*

1180. **John Ransom D. Cockman**, son of Noah Wesley Cockman and Sarah Ann Cagle, was born on December 31, 1866 in Moore County, NC. He married **Zuella Jane Jeffreys** on September 10, 1902. He died on March 15, 1948 in Durham, Durham County, NC and was buried on March 16, 1948 in Durham, Durham County, NC at Maplewood Cemetery.

Zuella Jane Jeffreys was born on September 1, 1879. She died on February 28, 1910.

1181. **Joseph Islem Haglem Cockman**, son of Noah Wesley Cockman and Sarah Ann Cagle, was born on January 16, 1869. He married **Etta Lee Phillips** on March 8, 1894. He died on February 7, 1953 in Tomahawk, Sampson County, NC and was buried on February 9, 1953 in Wallace, Duplin County, NC at Well's Chapel Church.

Virginia Moore was born on January 26, 1875. She died on September 26, 1953. She and Joseph Islem Haglem Cockman had the following children:

2882	Earl William Cockman (1911-1974). *Earl was born in June 1911. He died on January 14, 1974.*

Etta Lee Phillips, daughter of John Wesley Phillips (1829-1909) and Emily Welch (1828-), was born on August 21, 1871. She died on May 21, 1905 and was buried in Robbins, Moore County, NC at Tabernacle United Methodist Church. She and Joseph Islem Haglem Cockman had the following children:

2883	Leta Ann Cockman (1894-1943). *Leta was born on December 17, 1894. She died in August 1943.*
2884	Blanche Cockman (1896-1969). *Blanche was born on March 30, 1896. She died on December 6, 1969.*
2885	Russell Cockman (1898-). *Russell was born in February 1898.*

1182. **Exer Ann Elizabeth Cockman**, daughter of Noah Wesley Cockman and Sarah Ann Cagle, was born on October 11, 1870. She married **James Commodore Beauregard Muse** on August 19, 1894 in Moore County, NC. She died on December 9, 1929 and was buried in Carthage, Moore County, NC at Cross Hill Cemetery.

James Commodore Beauregard Muse, son of Archibald Buckley Muse (1838-1903) and Martha Jane Johnson (1841-1904), was born on September 4, 1861. He died on October 26, 1931 and was buried in Carthage, Moore County, NC at Cross Hill Cemetery. He and Exer Ann Elizabeth Cockman had the following children:

2886	Glennie M. Muse (1895-1931). *Glennie was born in June 1895. She died in 1931 and was buried in Carthage, Moore County, NC at Cross Hill Cemetery.*
2887	Minnie Lee Muse (1896-). *Minnie was born in August 1896.*
2888	James Commodore Beauregard Muse Jr. (1899-). *James was born in November 1899.*
2889	Powell K. Muse (1903-1929). *Powell was born in 1903. He died in 1929 and was buried in Carthage, Moore County, NC at Cross Hill Cemetery.*

1183. **Lucretia Morndia Cockman**, daughter of Noah Wesley Cockman and Sarah Ann Cagle, was born on January 22, 1872. She married **James Thomas Powers** on October 28, 1898 in Moore County, NC. She died on October 19, 1958.

James Thomas Powers, son of John H. "Jack" Powers (1847-1925) and Cynthia America Ritter (1850-1938), was born on March 3, 1874. He died on November 6, 1966. He and Lucretia Morndia Cockman had the following children:

> 2890   Lillie Florence Powers (1899-1967). *Lillie was born on November 11, 1899. She died on September 19, 1967.*
>
> 2891   Curtis Ernest Powers (1901-1971). *Curtis was born on January 2, 1901. He died on November 17, 1971 and was buried in Randolph County, NC at Beulah Baptist Church.*

1184. Globina Hill Cockman, daughter of Noah Wesley Cockman and Sarah Ann Cagle, was born on October 17, 1874. She died on March 10, 1962.

Bud Phillips died in 1903.

1185. Abraham Rommie Cockman, son of Noah Wesley Cockman and Sarah Ann Cagle, was born on March 12, 1876. He married **Sallie Blue** on September 7, 1900. He married **Locie E. Purvis** in 1924. He died on January 5, 1949.

Sallie Blue was born in 1872.

Locie E. Purvis was born on January 10, 1901. She died on June 5, 1965. She and Abraham Rommie Cockman had the following children:

> 2892   Minnie Mae Cockman (-)

1186. Noah Wesley Cockman Jr., son of Noah Wesley Cockman and Sarah Ann Cagle, was born on May 6, 1878. He married **Addie Eunice Steel** on December 25, 1904. He died on June 15, 1943.

Addie Eunice Steel was born on May 26, 1880. She died on October 16, 1958.

1187. Magaline D. "Maggie" Cockman, daughter of Noah Wesley Cockman and Sarah Ann Cagle, was born on April 24, 1879. She married **Archibald Calhoun "Archie" Jones** on December 17, 1902 in Chatham County, NC. She died on December 11, 1960.

Archibald Calhoun "Archie" Jones, son of Emsley Jones (1845-) and Sarah A. "Sallie" Forrester (1851-), was born on April 12, 1877. He died on June 2, 1959 and was buried in Randolph County, NC at Beulah Baptist Church.

1188. Ashley Carson Cockman, son of Noah Wesley Cockman and Sarah Ann Cagle, was born on March 2, 1881 in Moore County, NC. He married **Lura Ellen Marley** on August 9, 1903 in Randolph County, NC. He died on July 27, 1963 in Greensboro, Guilford County, NC and was buried on July 28, 1963 in Greensboro, Guilford County, NC at Guilford Memorial Park.

Lura Ellen Marley, daughter of James M. Marley (1859-1931) and Lydia A. Brown (1857-1931), was born on September 4, 1886. She died on October 20, 1971 in Greensboro, Guilford County, NC. She and Ashley Carson Cockman had the following children:

> 2893   Grace Beulah Cockman (1904-1980). *Grace was born on June 2, 1904 in Siler City, Chatham County, NC. She died on November 18, 1980 in Greensboro, Guilford County, NC.*
>
> 2894   Pearl Mae Cockman (1905-2003). *Pearl was born on October 23, 1905 in Siler City, Chatham County, NC. She died on June 11, 2003 in Burnsville, Randolph County, NC.*
>
> 2895   Kathleen Virginia Cockman (1907-1993). *Kathleen was born on April 15, 1907 in Siler City, Chatham County, NC. She died on April 28, 1993 in North Myrtle Beach, Horry County, SC.*
>
> 2896   Wilbur Marley Cockman (1908-1983). *Wilbur was born on December 31, 1908 in Siler City, Chatham County, NC. He died on January 21, 1983 in Greensboro, Guilford County, NC.*

2897	Brona Gertrude Cockman (1911-2012). *Brona was born on September 23, 1911 in Siler City, Chatham County, NC. She died on November 11, 2012 in Clearwater, Pinellas County, FL.*
2898	James Edward Cockman (1913-2000). *James was born on June 20, 1913 in Siler City, Chatham County, NC. He died on August 24, 2000 in Greensboro, Guilford County, NC.*
2899	Jack Howard Cockman (1916-1995). *Jack was born on June 6, 1916 in Siler City, Chatham County, NC. He died on March 17, 1995 in Charlotte, Mecklenburg County, NC.*
2900	Ray Thomas Cockman (1918-1980). *Ray was born on October 8, 1918 in Siler City, Chatham County, NC. He died on August 21, 1980 in Greensboro, Guilford County, NC.*
2901	Sara Louise Cockman (1928-2007). *Sara was born on April 27, 1928 in Greensboro, Guilford County, NC. She died on November 4, 2007 in Greensboro, Guilford County, NC.*

1189. **Mittie Mammie Cockman**, daughter of Noah Wesley Cockman and Sarah Ann Cagle, was born on May 23, 1883. She died on November 3, 1902 in Randolph County, NC.

1190. **Jerome Cassidy Cockman**, son of Noah Wesley Cockman and Sarah Ann Cagle, was born on May 31, 1885. He died in March 1952.

Mattie Brady was born on August 19, 1888. She died on July 21, 1919.

Bessie Elizabeth East was born on October 18, 1890. She died on February 18, 1973.

1191. **Arlen Well Cockman**, son of Noah Wesley Cockman and Sarah Ann Cagle, was born on July 14, 1887. He married **Lovie Branson** on March 20, 1909. He married **Myrtle Ivey Gates** in 1915. He died on February 26, 1962.

Lovie Branson was born in 1893. She died on March 8, 1944.

Myrtle Ivey Gates was born on November 19, 1897. She died on July 8, 1977.

1192. **Ommie Cornelia Cockman**, daughter of Noah Wesley Cockman and Sarah Ann Cagle, was born on April 18, 1889. She married **Thomas Elwood Cox** on January 6, 1915. She died on May 18, 1966.

Thomas Elwood Cox was born on September 7, 1890. He died on October 20, 1955.

1193. **Mary Camilla Horner**, daughter of Thomas R. Horner and Lena Louisa Cockman, was born on June 16, 1880. She died on April 28, 1936 in Greensboro, Guilford County, NC and was buried on April 30, 1936 in Guilford County, NC at Forest Lawn Cemetery.

1194. **Norris Fulton Horner**, son of Thomas R. Horner and Lena Louisa Cockman, was born on June 18, 1881 in Moore County, NC. He married **Delphina Agnes "Della" Cox** on February 15, 1905. He died on February 28, 1952 in Greensboro, Guilford County, NC.

Delphina Agnes "Della" Cox was born on March 8, 1886 in Ramseur, Randolph County, NC. She died on June 16, 1974 in Atlanta, Fulton County, GA. She and Norris Fulton Horner had the following children:

2902	Alvania Horner (1905-1906). *Alvania was born on November 26, 1905 in Ramseur, Randolph County, NC. She died on October 3, 1906 in Ramseur, Randolph County, NC.*
2903	Florence Jeanette Horner (1907-1985). *Florence was born on March 17, 1907 in Ramseur, Randolph County, NC. She died in 1985 in Greensboro, Guilford County, NC.*
2904	Gayle Elizabeth Horner (1909-). *Gayle was born on June 25, 1909 in Ramseur, Randolph County, NC.*
2905	Bessie Louise Horner (1911-1968). *Bessie was born on November 9, 1911 in Ramseur, Randolph County, NC. She died in 1968 in Altavista, Campbell County, VA.*

2906	Norris Fonzo Horner (1913-1987). *Norris was born on December 24, 1913 in Sanford, Lee County, NC. He married **Maggie Rejean Strader** in 1951. He died on May 11, 1987 in Greensboro, Guilford County, NC.*
2907	Mary Catherine Horner (1917-). *Mary was born on March 5, 1917 in Sanford, Lee County, NC.*
2908	James Fulton Horner (1918-1973). *James was born on August 13, 1918 in Sanford, Lee County, NC. He died on July 19, 1973 in Douglasville, Douglas County, GA.*
2909	Josephine Agnes Horner (1921-2002). *Josephine was born on March 14, 1921 in Sanford, Lee County, NC. She married **Edward Donnell Johnson** on May 19, 1939 in Bedford County, VA. She died on February 8, 2002 in Fort Wayne, Allen County, IN.*
2910	Dorothy Belle Horner (1922-). *Dorothy was born on November 19, 1922 in Sanford, Lee County, NC.*

1195. Fairly Arthur Horner, son of Thomas R. Horner and Lena Louisa Cockman, was born on February 14, 1883. He died on May 10, 1951.

Frances Lucille York was born on August 6, 1883. She died on November 1, 1967. She and Fairly Arthur Horner had the following children:

2911	Helen Mae Horner (1911-1987). *Helen was born on December 30, 1911. She died on February 15, 1987 and was buried in Concord, Cabarrus County, NC at Carolina Memorial Park.*

1196. William Sampson "Bill" Horner, son of Thomas R. Horner and Lena Louisa Cockman, was born on September 23, 1884 in Moore County, NC. He died on January 12, 1952 in St. Leo's Hospital, Greensboro, Guilford County, NC and was buried on January 14, 1952 in Guilford County, NC at Lakeview Memorial Park.

1197. Chestley Paisley Horner, son of Thomas R. Horner and Lena Louisa Cockman, was born on March 12, 1886. He died on August 7, 1927 in Greensboro, Guilford County, NC and was buried on August 9, 1927 in Greensboro, Guilford County, NC at Green Hill Cemetery.

1198. Hurley Harrison Horner, son of Thomas R. Horner and Lena Louisa Cockman, was born on March 23, 1889 in Moore County, NC. He died on November 25, 1959 in Greensboro, Guilford County, NC and was buried in Guilford County, NC at Lakeview Memorial Park.

Charity Eva Finnison, daughter of John Stafford Finnison (1853-1928) and Elizabeth Ellen Councilman (1853-1909), was born on January 21, 1891. She died on December 5, 1970 and was buried in Guilford County, NC at Lakeview Memorial Park.

1199. John Lawrence Horner, son of Thomas R. Horner and Lena Louisa Cockman, was born on December 17, 1889 in Moore County, NC. He died on January 26, 1963 in Moses Cone Memorial Hospital, Greensboro, Guilford County, NC and was buried on January 28, 1963 in Guilford County, NC at Lakeview Memorial Park.

Madge Pulley was born on July 1, 1895. She died on October 13, 1971.

Nell Dagenhart was born in 1920. She died in 2008. She and John Lawrence Horner had the following children:

2912	Horner (-)

1200. Mittie Tom Horner, daughter of Thomas R. Horner and Lena Louisa Cockman, was born in 1893. She died on October 26, 1923 in St. Leo's Hospital, Greensboro, Guilford County, NC and was buried on October 28, 1923 in Greensboro, Guilford County, NC at Green Hill Cemetery.

1201. Monica Horner, daughter of Thomas R. Horner and Lena Louisa Cockman, was born on April 17, 1895. She died on December 13, 1895.

1202. Martha Jane Horner, daughter of Thomas R. Horner and Lena Louisa Cockman, was born on May 13, 1896. She died on August 5, 1896.

[Above] L-R (standing) **Arthur Horner, Josie Horner, Pearl Horner, Mollie Horner, Luther Horner, Emma Horner and Bertie Horner (seated) Will Horner and Cornelia Ritter**
(Courtesy of Will and Faye Voss Canoy)

[Right] (Back L-R) **John Lawrence Horner, Chesley Horner, Bill Horner** (Front L-R) **Harrison Horner, Fulton Horner and Arthur Horner**
[Below] **Fulton Horner and Thomas R. Horner**
(Courtesy of Janice Hullender)

1203. **Walter Wesley Horner**, son of Thomas R. Horner and Lena Louisa Cockman, was born on April 14, 1898. He died on May 30, 1898.

1204. **Jesse Horner**, son of Thomas R. Horner and Lena Louisa Cockman, was born on June 30, 1900. He died on July 23, 1900.

1205. **Marchia Alberta Lee Cockman**, daughter of James Alexander Cockman and Mary Alice Horner, was born on August 5, 1881 in Moore County, NC. She married **James Charles Wallace** on December 25, 1898 in Moore County, NC. She died on August 14, 1966 in Asheboro, Randolph County, NC and was buried on August 15, 1966 in Asheboro, Randolph County, NC at Oaklawn Cemetery.

James Charles Wallace, son of George M. Wallace (1857-1932) and Mary Lovedy Horner (1858-1884), was born on December 17, 1879 in Moore County, NC. He died on November 17, 1949 in Asheboro, Randolph County, NC and was buried on November 19, 1949 in Asheboro, Randolph County, NC at Oaklawn Cemetery. He and Marchia Alberta Lee Cockman had the following children:

2913	Cora Belle Wallace (1899-1977). *Cora was born on September 21, 1899 in Moore County, NC. She married **William Elzie Garner** on November 22, 1914. She died on July 9, 1977 in Asheboro, Randolph County, NC.*
2914	Coy Sampson Wallace (1901-1984). *Coy was born on September 26, 1901 in Moore County, NC. He married **Sallie Myrtle Purvis** on May 3, 1924 in Moore County, NC. He died on March 6, 1984 in Sanford, Lee County, NC.*
2915	James Floyd Wallace (1904-1975). *James was born on March 8, 1904 in Montgomery County, NC. He died on February 28, 1975 in Asheboro, Randolph County, NC.*
2916	Lillie Viola Wallace (1906-2001). *Lillie was born on November 22, 1906 in Montgomery County, NC. She married **Coble Maie Maness** on January 24, 1925. She died on May 28, 2001 in Randolph County, NC and was buried in Moore County, NC at Pleasant Hill United Methodist Church.*
2917	Luther Clyde Wallace (1909-1987). *Luther was born on March 13, 1909. He married **Beatrice Maness** on November 23, 1932 in Moore County, NC. He died on July 8, 1987 in Asheboro, Randolph County, NC.*
2918	Bettie Alberta Lee Wallace (1911-1969). *Bettie was born on May 16, 1911 in Moore County, NC. She married **Clinard Harrison Poole** on May 25, 1928. She died on October 25, 1969 in Asheboro, Randolph County, NC.*
2919	Beatrice Ann Wallace (1913-2008). *Beatrice was born on June 24, 1913 in Moore County, NC. She died on May 26, 2008 in Randolph County, NC.*
2920	George Carson Wallace (1916-1994). *George was born on May 18, 1916 in Moore County, NC. He married **Beatrice Thorp** on July 11, 1936. He died on August 31, 1994 in Asheboro, Randolph County, NC.*
2921	Katie Lisbon Wallace (1919-1981). *Katie was born on June 28, 1919 in Montgomery County, NC. She married **Robert Franklin Bulla** on September 16, 1938. She died on December 14, 1981 in Asheboro, Randolph County, NC.*
2922	Elizabeth Wallace (1920-). *Elizabeth was born in 1920.*
2923	Lucille Helen Wallace (1923-1994). *Lucille was born on January 23, 1923 in Moore County, NC. She married **James Nelson Whitaker** on August 23, 1941. She died on May 11, 1994 in Greensboro, Guilford County, NC.*

1206. **John William Cockman**, son of James Alexander Cockman and Mary Alice Horner, was born on October 1, 1883 in Moore County, NC. He married **Rhonie Margaret Gurley** circa 1908. He died on May 2, 1916 in Moore County, NC and was buried in Moore County, NC at Pleasant Hill United Methodist Church.

Rhonie Margaret Gurley was born on February 23, 1891. She died on June 30, 1920. She and John William Cockman had the following children:

2924	William Curtis Cockman (1908-). *William was born on December 9, 1908.*

1207. **George Charles Cockman**, son of James Alexander Cockman and Mary Alice Horner, was born on August 8, 1886. He married **Mollie Green Garner** on November 11, 1916. He died on May 29, 1959 and was buried in Moore County, NC at Flint Hill Baptist Church.

Mollie Green Garner, daughter of Duncan G. Garner (1871-1945) and Laura Luvenia Cockman (1870-1954), was born on December 8, 1897. She died on April 2, 1928 in Moore County, NC and was buried in Moore County, NC at Flint Hill Baptist Church. She and George Charles Cockman had the following children:

2925	William Fletcher Cockman (1917-1977). *William was born on August 31, 1917. He married **Bernice Jewell Davis** on January 2, 1943. He died on September 18, 1977 and was buried in Robbins, Moore County, NC at Pine Rest Cemetery.*
2926	Dora Mae Cockman (1918-2009). *Dora was born on November 30, 1918. She married **Manly K. Monroe** on November 1, 1941. She died on January 13, 2009.*
2927	Jesse James Carlton Cockman (1920-1960). *Jesse was born on May 25, 1920 in Moore County, NC. He married **Coline Maness** on November 10, 1945. He died on August 1, 1960 in Durham, Durham County, NC and was buried in Moore County, NC at Smyrna Methodist Church.*
2928	Carson Rudolph Cockman (1922-1965). *Carson was born on December 21, 1922. He died on March 17, 1965 and was buried in Moore County, NC at Flint Hill Baptist Church.*
2929	Pearlie Lee Cockman (1924-1930). *Pearlie was born on April 24, 1924. She died on August 8, 1930 and was buried in Moore County, NC at Flint Hill Baptist Church.*
2930	Male Cockman (1928-1928). *Male was born on April 1, 1928 in Moore County, NC. He died on April 1, 1928 in Moore County, NC.*

1208. **Etta Mae Cockman**, daughter of James Alexander Cockman and Mary Alice Horner, was born on March 18, 1904 in Moore County, NC. She married **William Herbert Morgan** on June 20, 1922. She died on November 4, 1933 in Asheboro, Randolph County, NC and was buried on November 5, 1933 in Seagrove, Randolph County, NC at Asbury Baptist Church.

William Herbert Morgan, son of John Thomas Morgan (1876-1939) and Laura Vandy Williams (1878-1951), was born on May 28, 1898. He died on March 6, 1923 and was buried in Moore County, NC at Flint Hill Baptist Church.

1211. **James Laborn Maness**, son of Jonah Baxter Maness and Alice Susannah Cockman, was born on February 22, 1902. He died on March 31, 1982 and was buried in Moore County, NC at Pleasant Hill United Methodist Church.

Beatrice Collins was born on January 22, 1908. She died on October 30, 1994 and was buried in Moore County, NC at Pleasant Hill United Methodist Church.

1212. **Arthur Edmund Maness**, son of Jonah Baxter Maness and Alice Susannah Cockman, was born on April 2, 1903. He died on November 14, 1989 and was buried in Robbins, Moore County, NC at Acorn Ridge Baptist Church.

Swannie Nancy Lambert, daughter of Jesse Lewis Lambert (1879-1961) and Mattie Jane Brown (1878-1951), was born on September 10, 1910. She died on June 11, 1992 and was buried in Robbins, Moore County, NC at Acorn Ridge Baptist Church. She and Arthur Edmund Maness had the following children:

2931	Cletes Arthur Maness (1929-1993). *Cletes was born on March 29, 1929. He died on September 2, 1993 and was buried in Moore County, NC at Unity Grove Baptist Church.*
2932	Colon Fred Maness (1931-2016). *Colon was born on June 27, 1931. He died on July 10, 2016.*
2933	Curtis Haven Maness (1939-1987). *Curtis was born on May 13, 1939. He married **Sylvia Jean Helms** on May 7, 1955. He died on November 13, 1987 and was buried in Robbins, Moore County, NC at Acorn Ridge Baptist Church.*
2934	Clay Lewis Maness (1943-1966). *Clay was born on April 9, 1943. He died on July 25, 1966 and was buried in Robbins, Moore County, NC at Acorn Ridge Baptist Church.*

1213. **Kenny Cassidy Maness**, son of Jonah Baxter Maness and Alice Susannah Cockman, was born on April 10, 1905. He married **Lydia Annie Wallace** on October 1, 1932. He died on March 8, 1981 and was buried in Moore County, NC at Virgil (Byrd) Wallace Cemetery.

Lydia Annie Wallace, daughter of Isham Wallace (1882-1962) and Flora Britt (1884-1946), was born on February 1, 1914. She died on January 25, 1982 and was buried in Moore County, NC at Virgil (Byrd) Wallace Cemetery. She and Kenny Cassidy Maness had the following children:

2935	Donald Cassidy Maness (1934-2005). *Donald was born on February 4, 1934. He died on July 16, 2005 and was buried in Moore County, NC at Virgil (Byrd) Wallace Cemetery.*
2936	James Paul Maness (1936-). *James was born on February 14, 1936.*
2937	Dorothy Lee Maness (1937-). *Dorothy was born on October 18, 1937. She married* **Walter Boudoin** *on February 17, 1956.*
2938	Gertrude Eloise Maness (1939-). *Gertrude was born on November 7, 1939. She married* **Robert Melvin Duguay** *on February 1, 1957.*
2939	Clyde Roger Maness (1941-). *Clyde was born on November 6, 1941.*
2940	Judy Ann Maness (1943-). *Judy was born on November 30, 1943.*
2941	Raymond Leroy Maness (1946-). *Raymond was born on April 30, 1946.*
2942	Johnnie Kenneth Maness (1948-). *Johnnie was born on March 30, 1948.*
2943	David Farrell Maness (1951-). *David was born on December 30, 1951. He married* **Lenora Ann Dupuis** *on July 8, 1973.*
2944	Roger Maness (1954-1954). *Roger was born on October 13, 1954 in Moore County, NC. He died on October 13, 1954 in Moore County, NC and was buried in Moore County, NC at Virgil (Byrd) Wallace Cemetery.*
2945	Bonnie Sue Maness (1958-). *Bonnie was born on January 10, 1958.*

1214. **Rosa Maggie Maness**, daughter of Jonah Baxter Maness and Alice Susannah Cockman, was born on July 17, 1907 in Moore County, NC. She married **Presley Parker Floyd** on April 16, 1960 in Davidson County, NC. She died on April 4, 1962 in Winston-Salem, Forsyth County, NC and was buried in Asheboro, Randolph County, NC at Pleasant Cross Christian Church.

Presley Parker Floyd was born on August 3, 1901 in Randolph County, NC. He died on July 19, 1983 in Thomasville, Davidson County, NC and was buried in Thomasville, Davidson County, NC at Holly Hill Memorial Park.

1215. **Fonnie F. Cockman**, daughter of George MDOHDIC Cockman and Lucinda Melton, was born on November 12, 1867. She died on January 30, 1915 and was buried in Rockingham, Richmond County, NC at Northam Cemetery.

1216. **Anna Jane "Janie" Cockman**, daughter of George MDOHDIC Cockman and Lucinda Melton, was born on June 18, 1869. She married **Elias "Lizard" Garner** circa 1887. She married **Josiah Turner Horner** circa 1901. She died on April 26, 1913.

Elias "Lizard" Garner, son of John Garner (1825-1905) and Sarah Ann Wallace (1830-1899), was born in 1865. He died in 1898 and was buried in Moore County, NC at Flint Hill Baptist Church. He and Anna Jane "Janie" Cockman had the following children:

2946	Kinnie Carson Garner (1888-1955). *Kinnie was born on July 15, 1888 in Moore County, NC. He died on November 3, 1955 in Hamlet, Richmond County, NC and was buried on November 4, 1955 in Hamlet, Richmond County, NC at Mary Love Cemetery.*
2947	Margaret B. Garner (1890-). *Margaret was born in August 1890.*
2948	Josephine Garner (1893-1948). *Josephine was born on August 8, 1893 in Moore County, NC. She died on May 27, 1948 in Fayetteville, Cumberland County, NC.*
2949	Sara Lucinda Garner (1895-1935). *Sara was born on September 3, 1895. She died on September 22, 1935 in Fayetteville, Cumberland County, NC.*

Josiah Turner Horner, son of James Washington Horner (1842-1921) and Lovedy Jane Wallace (1844-1916), was born in October 1869. He married Agnes Chalmers Barrett on December 25, 1892 in Moore County, NC. He married Hattie Belle McLean on May 3, 1914 in Cumberland County, NC. He died on June 24, 1923 in Cumberland County, NC.

1217. Laura Luvenia Cockman, daughter of George MDOHDIC Cockman and Lucinda Melton, was born on February 23, 1870 in Moore County, NC. She died on September 9, 1954 in Moore County, NC and was buried in Moore County, NC at Flint Hill Baptist Church.

Duncan G. Garner, son of John Garner (1825-1905) and Sarah Ann Wallace (1830-1899), was born on January 22, 1871. He died on June 26, 1945 in Moore County, NC and was buried in Moore County, NC at Flint Hill Baptist Church. He and Laura Luvenia Cockman had the following children:

2950	Mollie Green Garner (1897-1928). *Mollie was born on December 8, 1897. She married **George Charles Cockman** on November 11, 1916. She died on April 2, 1928 in Moore County, NC and was buried in Moore County, NC at Flint Hill Baptist Church.*
2951	Alexander Garner (1903-1967). *Alexander was born on May 10, 1903. He married **Lessie Jane Williams** on October 12, 1922 in Moore County, NC. He died on February 14, 1967 in Moore County, NC and was buried in Moore County, NC at Flint Hill Baptist Church.*
2952	Katie Jane Garner (1905-1952). *Katie was born on April 5, 1905. She married **Garrett Hobert Maness** on December 25, 1921 in Moore County, NC. She died on November 19, 1952 in Moore County, NC and was buried in Robbins, Moore County, NC at Tabernacle United Methodist Church.*
2953	Ashley Lee Garner (1907-1924). *Ashley was born on November 1, 1907. He died on August 4, 1924 and was buried in Moore County, NC at Flint Hill Baptist Church.*
2954	Ethel Marie Garner (1913-). *Ethel was born on April 18, 1913.*

1218. Isham Delaney Cockman, son of George MDOHDIC Cockman and Lucinda Melton, was born on November 12, 1874 in Moore County, NC. He died on February 21, 1938 in Greensboro, Guilford County, NC and was buried on February 22, 1938 in Greensboro, Guilford County, NC at Guilford Memorial Park.

Minnie Brady was born on March 2, 1872. She died on March 17, 1954. She and Isham Delaney Cockman had the following children:

2955	Charlie L. Cockman (1898-). *Charlie was born in December 1898.*

1219. Ida Delaney Priscilla Alice Cockman, daughter of George MDOHDIC Cockman and Lucinda Melton, was born on April 23, 1877. She married **Charles J. Jones** on January 21, 1930 in Richmond County, NC. She died on January 11, 1968 and was buried in Rockingham, Richmond County, NC at East Side Cemetery.

Charles J. Jones, son of Emerson D. Jones (1845-1918) and Elizabeth McIntosh (1847-bef 1880), was born on July 8, 1870. He died on August 30, 1935 and was buried in Rockingham, Richmond County, NC at East Side Cemetery. He and Ida Delaney Priscilla Alice Cockman had the following children:

2956	Thaddeus Jones (-)

1220. Delilah Cockman, daughter of George MDOHDIC Cockman and Lucinda Melton, was born on June 2, 1881. She died on December 31, 1961 in Hamlet, Richmond County, NC and was buried on January 2, 1962 in Rockingham, Richmond County, NC at East Side Cemetery.

William Lee Boone was born in 1886. He died on March 7, 1963 in Hamlet, Richmond County, NC.

1221. Dora Cockman, daughter of George MDOHDIC Cockman and Lucinda Melton, was born on August 10, 1883. She died on September 1, 1906 and was buried in Rockingham, Richmond County, NC at Northam Cemetery.

1222. Lexie Green Cockman, daughter of George MDOHDIC Cockman and Lucinda Melton, was born in September 1885. She died on July 16, 1915 in Richmond County, NC and was buried on July 17, 1915 in Rockingham, Richmond County, NC at Northam Cemetery.

John Bunyon Bullard was born in May 1879. He died on September 15, 1904 in Hope Mills, Cumberland County, NC. He and Lexie Green Cockman had the following children:

| 2957 | Margaret Myrtle Bullard (1903-1972). *Margaret was born in 1903. She died in 1972.* |

John Wesley Meacham was born on February 24, 1876. He died on June 22, 1936 and was buried in Rockingham, Richmond County, NC at Northam Cemetery. He and Lexie Green Cockman had the following children:

| 2958 | Ethel Gertrude Meacham (1912-2005). *Ethel was born on April 28, 1912. She died in February 2005.* |
| 2959 | Lillian Frances Meacham (1913-1992). *Lillian was born on July 19, 1913 in Rockingham, Richmond County, NC. She died on March 15, 1992 in Mooresville, Iredell County, NC.* |

1223. **George Hurley Cockman Sr.**, son of George MDOHDIC Cockman and Lucinda Melton, was born on July 20, 1886. He died on September 30, 1955 and was buried in Rockingham, Richmond County, NC at Northam Cemetery.

Annie Lee Mullis was born on December 8, 1889. She died on February 7, 1930 and was buried in Rockingham, Richmond County, NC at Northam Cemetery. She and George Hurley Cockman Sr. had the following children:

| 2960 | Athos Lee Cockman (1906-1978). *Athos was born on July 4, 1906. He died on June 13, 1978.* |
| 2961 | Infant Cockman (1908-1908). *Infant was born on April 5, 1908. She died on September 16, 1908 and was buried in Rockingham, Richmond County, NC at Northam Cemetery.* |

1224. **James Atlas Cockman**, son of John SSGWSQA "Jack" Cockman and Nancy Jane Melton, was born on November 5, 1868. He died on July 6, 1937.

Priscilla Williams was born on June 19, 1885. She died on October 12, 1953.

1225. **William Lockie Cockman**, son of John SSGWSQA "Jack" Cockman and Nancy Jane Melton, was born on April 15, 1871. He died on April 24, 1919 in Port Arthur, Jefferson County, TX.

Elizabeth Holton was born in 1875. She died in 1951.

1226. **Temperance Levina "Erie" Cockman**, daughter of John SSGWSQA "Jack" Cockman and Nancy Jane Melton, was born on March 29, 1875 in Moore County, NC. She married **Cornelius Henry F. "Neil" Stutts** on August 23, 1895 in Moore County, NC. She died on November 8, 1940 in Davidson County, NC and was buried on November 10, 1940 in Robbins, Moore County, NC at Tabernacle United Methodist Church.

Cornelius Henry F. "Neil" Stutts, son of Cornelius Alexander Stutts (1840-1869) and Lydia Jane Yow (1843-1920), was born on January 4, 1870. He died on January 7, 1944 and was buried in Robbins, Moore County, NC at Tabernacle United Methodist Church. He and Temperance Levina "Erie" Cockman had the following children:

2962	Arthur Ashton Stutts (1896-1948). *Arthur was born on August 21, 1896 in Moore County, NC. He died on September 1, 1948 in Broughton State Hospital, Morganton, Burke County, NC and was buried in Robbins, Moore County, NC at Tabernacle United Methodist Church.*
2963	Ollie Haywood Stutts (1898-1967). *Ollie was born on September 4, 1898. He died on June 25, 1967 in Winston-Salem, Forsyth County, NC and was buried in Lexington, Davidson County, NC at Bethany Church Cemetery.*
2964	Archie Lee Stutts (1900-1975). *Archie was born on August 28, 1900 in Moore County, NC. He died on January 4, 1975 in Lexington, Davidson County, NC and was buried in Lexington, Davidson County, NC at Forest Hill Memorial Park.*
2965	Viola Jane "Ola" Stutts (1902-1993). *Viola was born on August 30, 1902 in Moore County, NC. She married **Jonas Silas Bishop** on July 8, 1923. She died on February 24, 1993 in Davidson County, NC and was buried in Lexington, Davidson County, NC at Forest Hill Memorial Park.*
2966	Esther Mary Stutts (1904-1993). *Esther was born on July 4, 1904 in Moore County, NC. She died on October 10, 1993 in Davidson County, NC and was buried in Lexington, Davidson County, NC at Forest Hill Memorial Park.*

2967	Majorie Edith "Maggie" Stutts (1906-2000). *Majorie was born on July 24, 1906 in Moore County, NC. She died on September 27, 2000 in Wilbraham, MA and was buried in Lexington, Davidson County, NC at Forest Hill Memorial Park.*
2968	Neil Hurley Stutts (1908-1985). *Neil was born on May 1, 1908 in Moore County, NC. He married **Treva Evangeline Parks** on November 6, 1937 in Davidson County, NC. He died on May 11, 1985 in Virginia Medical Center, Salisbury, Rowan County, NC and was buried in Lexington, Davidson County, NC at Bethany Church Cemetery.*
2969	Grady Fletcher Stutts (1910-1978). *Grady was born on October 28, 1910 in Moore County, NC. He married **Bernice Rhoda Tillman** on July 6, 1933 in Charleston, SC. He died in February 1978 in Charleston, SC.*
2970	Beulah Evelyn Stutts (1913-1998). *Beulah was born on March 7, 1913 in Moore County, NC. She married **Howell Touchstone** circa 1940. She married **Jesse Michaels** circa 1951. She died on July 4, 1998 in Davidson County, NC and was buried in Davidson County, NC at Reeds Baptist Church Cemetery.*
2971	Harold Edgar Stutts (1918-2003). *Harold was born on April 18, 1918 in Davidson County, NC. He married **Esdia Reid** circa 1944. He died on December 22, 2003 in Davidson County, NC and was buried in Lexington, Davidson County, NC at Macedonia United Methodist Church.*

1227. Mary Ann "Tanie" Cockman, daughter of John SSGWSQA "Jack" Cockman and Nancy Jane Melton, was born on February 12, 1876. She married **Henry Mitchell Davis** on May 3, 1895 in Moore County, NC. She died on July 17, 1958 and was buried in Robbins, Moore County, NC at Tabernacle United Methodist Church.

Henry Mitchell Davis, son of Baxter Davis (1839-1914) and Sarah "Sallie" Yow (1841-1919), was born on February 23, 1868. He died on December 8, 1943 and was buried in Robbins, Moore County, NC at Tabernacle United Methodist Church. He and Mary Ann "Tanie" Cockman had the following children:

2972	Herbert C. Davis (1896-1950). *Herbert was born on January 25, 1896. He died on October 9, 1950.*
2973	Harvey L. Davis (1899-). *Harvey was born in April 1899.*
2974	Sherman Graham Davis (1901-1923). *Sherman was born on October 19, 1901. He died on April 21, 1923 and was buried in Robbins, Moore County, NC at Tabernacle United Methodist Church.*
2975	Harry W. Davis (1906-1977). *Harry was born on July 20, 1906. He died on January 10, 1977.*
2976	Helen Vera Davis (1911-2005). *Helen was born on March 12, 1911. She married **Robert Fulton Williams** on December 12, 1927 in Moore County, NC. She died on April 5, 2005 and was buried in Robbins, Moore County, NC at Pine Rest Cemetery.*

1228. Armittie Evelyn Cockman, daughter of John SSGWSQA "Jack" Cockman and Nancy Jane Melton, was born on May 16, 1879 in Moore County, NC. She married **Zemery Mitchell Burns** on April 25, 1895 in Moore County, NC. She died on June 10, 1954 in Baptist Hosptial, Winston-Salem, Forsyth County, NC and was buried on June 13, 1954 in Robbins, Moore County, NC at Tabernacle United Methodist Church.

Zemery Mitchell Burns, son of Henry Lindsey Burns (1844-1906) and Martha Jane Garner (1856-1933), was born on August 25, 1876. He died on October 31, 1945 and was buried in Robbins, Moore County, NC at Tabernacle United Methodist Church. He and Armittie Evelyn Cockman had the following children:

2977	Artie Mishia Burns (1896-1964). *Artie was born on October 12, 1896. She married **George Carroll Brown** on May 8, 1919. She died in 1964.*
2978	Robert Lee Burns (1897-1962). *Robert was born on August 25, 1897. He married **Ollie McGregor Jackson** on March 27, 1921. He died on November 9, 1962.*
2979	Eugenia Burns (1900-). *Eugenia was born on April 3, 1900. She married **Eddie Bryan Morgan** on September 2, 1917.*
2980	Viola Ethel Burns (1904-). *Viola was born on January 27, 1904. She married **William Eddie Tucker** on July 4, 1919.*
2981	Augusta Carlton Burns (1913-1974). *Augusta was born on October 7, 1913. He married **Lillian Frances Renfrew** on October 9, 1934. He died on January 27, 1974.*

1229. **John Wesley Cockman**, son of John SSGWSQA "Jack" Cockman and Nancy Jane Melton, was born on May 1, 1881. He married **Wilma Terry** on June 26, 1912. He died on February 22, 1920.

Wilma Terry was born on July 21, 1893. She died on October 23, 1942. She and John Wesley Cockman had the following children:

2982	Miriam Cockman (-)
2983	Wilma Terry Cockman (-)
2984	John Wesley Cockman Jr. (1914-1964). *John was born on November 21, 1914 in Rockingham, Richmond County, NC. He died on August 31, 1964 in Rockingham, Richmond County, NC.*

1230. **Noah Bethune Cockman**, son of John SSGWSQA "Jack" Cockman and Nancy Jane Melton, was born on April 4, 1882. He married **Martha Jane Lassiter** on March 4, 1904. He died on October 9, 1966.

Martha Jane Lassiter was born on June 23, 1879. She died on February 14, 1937. She and Noah Bethune Cockman had the following children:

2985	Dewey Grady Cockman (1907-1982). *Dewey was born on April 4, 1907. He died on July 8, 1982 and was buried in Rockingham, Richmond County, NC at Richmond Memorial Park.*

1231. **Nancy Jane "Florence" Cockman**, daughter of John SSGWSQA "Jack" Cockman and Lovedy Adaline Melton, was born on May 9, 1887. She married **John Alsey Maness Jr.** on February 10, 1905 in Moore County, NC. She died on August 4, 1927 and was buried in Moore County, NC at Pleasant Hill United Methodist Church.

John Alsey Maness Jr., son of John Alsey Maness (1856-1885) and Frances Eugenia Hughes (1856-1926), was born on August 15, 1885. He married Lizzie C. Cockman on June 30, 1928 in Moore County, NC. He died on December 13, 1958 and was buried in Moore County, NC at Pleasant Hill United Methodist Church. He and Nancy Jane "Florence" Cockman had the following children:

2986	Leta F. Maness (1907-1997). *Leta was born on March 20, 1907. She died on November 11, 1997 and was buried in Randolph County, NC at Beulah Baptist Church.*
2987	Claude Herbert Maness (1908-1998). *Claude was born on October 17, 1908. He married **Lydia Martha Morgan** on October 20, 1938 in Moore County, NC. He died on February 9, 1998 and was buried in Moore County, NC at Pleasant Hill United Methodist Church.*
2988	Alton Marvin Maness (1910-1970). *Alton was born on May 15, 1910. He married **Eula Bristow** on December 25, 1935 in Moore County, NC. He died on March 23, 1970 and was buried in Moore County, NC at Pleasant Hill United Methodist Church.*
2989	John Edgar Maness (1913-1984). *John was born on January 4, 1913. He died on September 4, 1984.*
2990	Nova Belle Maness (1915-1989). *Nova was born on January 20, 1915. She died on July 17, 1989 and was buried in Moore County, NC at Pleasant Hill United Methodist Church.*
2991	Norman Harrison Maness (1918-1993). *Norman was born on June 14, 1918. He married **Hattie Mae Ross** on December 24, 1942. He died on December 14, 1993 and was buried in Moore County, NC at Pleasant Hill United Methodist Church.*
2992	Theodore Houston Maness (1921-). *Theodore was born on November 8, 1921. He married **Mary Margaret Cameron** on December 23, 1960 in Moore County, NC and was buried in Moore County, NC at Pleasant Hill United Methodist Church.*
2993	Mary Catherine Maness (1924-1931). *Mary was born on August 3, 1924. She died on September 25, 1931 and was buried in Moore County, NC at Pleasant Hill United Methodist Church.*

1232. **Jennette B. "Nettie" Cockman**, daughter of John SSGWSQA "Jack" Cockman and Lovedy Adaline Melton, was born on May 8, 1891. She married **John Riland Key** on February 19, 1909. She died on October 23, 1955 and was buried in Moore County, NC at Brown's Chapel Christian Church.

John Riland Key, son of William Wesley Key (1852-1928) and Margaret Emberline McNeill (1853-1902), was born on February 28, 1884. He died on August 2, 1962 and was buried in Moore County, NC at Brown's Chapel Christian Church. He and Jennette B. "Nettie" Cockman had the following children:

2994	Carl R. Key (1910-1995). *Carl was born on December 11, 1910. He died on April 26, 1995 and was buried in Moore County, NC at Brown's Chapel Christian Church.*	
2995	Sadie C. Key (1913-1981). *Sadie was born on April 11, 1913. She married* **Charles Gustav Myrick** *on June 9, 1962 in Montgomery County, NC. She died on August 24, 1981 and was buried in Greensboro, Guilford County, NC at Guilford Memorial Park.*	
2996	Astor C. Key (1915-1964). *Astor was born on January 24, 1915. He died on December 19, 1964 and was buried in Moore County, NC at Brown's Chapel Christian Church.*	
2997	Macel Jane Key (1917-1998). *Macel was born on July 9, 1917. She married* **James Clyde Hussey** *on June 29, 1950 in Moore County, NC. She died on June 17, 1998 in Moore County, NC and was buried in Robbins, Moore County, NC at Pine Rest Cemetery.*	
2998	Mildred P. Key (1920-). *Mildred was born in 1920.*	
2999	John A. Key (1922-). *John was born in 1922.*	
3000	M. Lucille Key (1924-). *M. was born in 1924.*	
3001	Graham A. Key (1926-). *Graham was born in 1926.*	
3002	Allie J. Key (1929-). *Allie was born in 1929.*	

1233. Londia Ann "Lovedy" Cockman, daughter of John SSGWSQA "Jack" Cockman and Nancy Jane Riddle, was born on February 11, 1903.

Walter S. Hasty died on June 14, 1969.

1235. Gonzalee Cockman, son of John SSGWSQA "Jack" Cockman and Nancy Jane Riddle, was born on January 15, 1909. He died on October 17, 1956.

Rosa Nell Benton was born on January 12, 1912. She died on October 12, 1961. She and Gonzalee Cockman had the following children:

3003	Elmer Bennett Cockman (-)
3004	Betty Jean Cockman (-)

1237. William Jerome Cockman, son of Charles Riley O'Leonard Emsley Rufus Cockman and Lou Vicie Brown, was born on July 6, 1883 in Moore County, NC. He married **Alice Hunt** on April 10, 1904. He married **Dora Alice Sanders** on August 28, 1909 in Robbins, Moore County, NC. He died on July 3, 1947 in Central Falls, Randolph County, NC and was buried on July 5, 1947 in Robbins, Moore County, NC at Tabernacle United Methodist Church.

Alice Hunt was born in 1885.

Dora Alice Sanders, daughter of Malinda Sanders (1866-1905), was born on June 17, 1892 in Moore County, NC. She married Joseph Aster Kennedy on June 16, 1949 in Guilford County, NC. She died on June 30, 1983 in Randolph County, NC and was buried in Robbins, Moore County, NC at Tabernacle United Methodist Church. She and William Jerome Cockman had the following children:

3005	Ruby Mae Cockman (1910-1987). *Ruby was born on July 10, 1910 and married* **Burton Paul Smith**. *She died on December 19, 1987 and was buried in Cornelius, Mecklenburg County, NC at Mount Zion Community Cemetery.*
3006	Clyde Cockman (1913-1978). *Clyde was born on April 10, 1913 and married* **Ethel May Coble**. *He died on April 4, 1978 and was buried on April 7, 1978 in Asheboro, Randolph County, NC at Giles Chapel United Methodist Church.*
3007	Clara Aileen Cockman (1915-1986). *Clara was born on September 5, 1915 in Cumberland County, NC. She married* **Mallie Lester Wallace** *on December 19, 1931 in Danville, VA. She died on May 29, 1986 in Moore County, NC and was buried in Robbins, Moore County, NC at Tabernacle United Methodist Church.*

3008	Crissie Mon Cockman (1920-2006). *Crissie was born on August 31, 1920. She married **Charles Edward "Bud" Coble** on November 8, 1935. She died on September 15, 2006 and was buried in Asheboro, Randolph County, NC at Randolph Memorial Park.*
3009	Farley Lewis Cockman (1923-1929). *Farley was born on August 31, 1923 in Moore County, NC. He died on May 9, 1929 in Moore County, NC and was buried on May 10, 1929 in Robbins, Moore County, NC at Tabernacle United Methodist Church.*
3010	Tracy Wilburn Cockman (1926-1926). *Tracy was born on July 3, 1926 in Moore County, NC. He died on November 14, 1926 in Moore County, NC and was buried on November 15, 1926 in Robbins, Moore County, NC at Tabernacle United Methodist Church.*
3011	Esther Murial Cockman (1928-1941). *Esther was born on September 16, 1928 in Moore County, NC. She died on December 14, 1941 in Asheboro, Randolph County, NC and was buried on December 16, 1941 in Robbins, Moore County, NC at Tabernacle United Methodist Church.*
3012	Hubert Franklin Cockman (1931-2012). *Hubert was born on August 9, 1931. He married **Wilma Mae Nifong** on May 20, 1950 in Randolph County, NC. He died on May 11, 2012.*

1238. **Noah Wesley Cockman**, son of Charles Riley O'Leonard Emsley Rufus Cockman and Lou Vicie Brown, was born on June 5, 1884 in Moore County, NC. He married **Jenette Green Maness** on September 23, 1905 in Moore County, NC. He died on March 12, 1971 in UNC Hospital, Chapel Hill, Orange County, NC and was buried on March 15, 1971 in Robbins, Moore County, NC at Tabernacle United Methodist Church.

Jenette Green Maness, daughter of James R. Maness (1856-bef 1900) and Emily B. Lambert (1860-1933), was born on June 15, 1883. She died on March 10, 1939 and was buried in Robbins, Moore County, NC at Tabernacle United Methodist Church. She and Noah Wesley Cockman had the following children:

3013	Ocia Emily Cockman (1906-2002). *Ocia was born on July 7, 1906. She married **Hugh T. Brown** on July 14, 1923 in Moore County, NC. She died on November 23, 2002.*
3014	Locie Inman Cockman (1908-1999). *Locie was born on June 29, 1908 and married **Clyde Evelyn Barber**. She died on January 12, 1999 and was buried in Robbins, Moore County, NC at Pine Rest Cemetery.*
3015	Josie Jane Cockman (1910-1984). *Josie was born on December 9, 1910. She married **Hurley Lee Rouse** on October 8, 1928 in Moore County, NC. She died on July 3, 1984 and was buried in Robbins, Moore County, NC at Tabernacle United Methodist Church.*
3016	Ressie Green Cockman (1913-2008). *Ressie was born on September 23, 1913 and married **Willie Eugene McDaniel**. She died on February 15, 2008 and was buried in Robbins, Moore County, NC at Pine Rest Cemetery.*
3017	Melvin McMillan Cockman (1916-1990). *Melvin was born on April 2, 1916 and married **Alvaneal McMillan**. He died on February 15, 1990 and was buried in Robbins, Moore County, NC at Pine Rest Cemetery.*
3018	Tessie Arlene Cockman (1918-2004). *Tessie was born on October 31, 1918 and married **James Tracy Kennedy**. She died on December 19, 2004.*
3019	Mabel C. Cockman (1921-). *Mabel was born on May 15, 1921.*
3020	Julia Doris Cockman (1924-1997). *Julia was born on April 24, 1924 and married **Floyd Phillip Maness**. She died on January 13, 1997 and was buried in Robbins, Moore County, NC at Pine Rest Cemetery.*

1239. **Louis Delaney Cockman**, son of Charles Riley O'Leonard Emsley Rufus Cockman and Lou Vicie Brown, was born on February 28, 1887. He died on June 16, 1973 in St. Joseph of Pines Hospital, Pinehurst, Moore County, NC and was buried on June 18, 1973 in Linden, Cumberland County, NC at Parkers Grove Cemetery.

Lou Ellen Parker was born on October 26, 1894. She died on June 5, 1963 and was buried in Linden, Cumberland County, NC at Parkers Grove Cemetery. She and Louis Delaney Cockman had the following children:

3021	Milton Cockman (1914-1917). *Milton was born on August 24, 1914. He died on Feb 16, 1917 and was buried in Linden, Cumberland County, NC at Parkers Grove Cemetery.*
3022	Alma Cockman (1916-2002). *Alma was born on September 30, 1916. She died on December 28,*

2002.

3023   Louis Cockman Jr. (1918-1960). *Louis was born May 5, 1918. He died on March 31, 1960 and was buried in Linden, Cumberland County, NC at Parkers Grove Cemetery.*

3024   Norman Cameron Cockman (1920-1971). *Norman was born March 5, 1920. He died May 10, 1971.*

3025   Raymond Atlas Cockman (1922-2005). *Raymond was born April 14, 1922. He died November 28, 2005 and was buried in Spring Lake, Cumberland County, NC at Riverview Memorial Gardens.*

3026   Stewart Cockman (1924-1992). *Stewart was born July 27, 1924. He died October 24, 1992.*

3027   Carl Milford Cockman (1927-1981). *Carl was born August 19, 1927. He died May 3, 1981 and was buried in Spring Lake, Cumberland County, NC at Riverview Memorial Gardens.*

3028   Morris Eugene Cockman (1930-1988). *Morris was born November 5, 1930. He died February 15, 1988.*

3029   Joe Bobby Ray Cockman (1934-1981). Joe *was born in October 15, 1934. He died September 10, 1981 and was buried in Spring Lake, Cumberland County, NC at Riverview Memorial Gardens.*

[Below] **William McLenon Garner, Martha Cockman and children** (L-R) **Arthur Hugh Garner, Grace Mae Garner, and William Marvin Garner.** *(Courtesy of Wanda Davis Crenshaw, Moore County Heritage Book)*

[Left] (L-R) **Mamie Marley Hall, Nepsie Cockman Marley and Martha Cockman Garner** *(Courtesy of Paul Horner, Robbins, NC)*

[Clockwise from above] (Front L-R) **Athos Lee Cockman, Annie Lee Mullis Cockman, George Hurley Cockman** (Back L-R) **Will Boone, Delilah Cockman Boone** [Top Right] **Delilah Cockman Boone** [Bottom Right] **Lexie Green Cockman Bullard and her daughter Margaret Bullard** *(Courtesy of Roma Smith)* [Below] **Lillie Alma Maness and Laura Luvenia Cockman Garner** *(Courtesy of Billy Garner)*

[Left] **Atlas Franklin Cockman**

[Above] **Jerome Cockman and Dora Sanders**
[Below] **Jerome Cockman, Dora Sanders and children Ruby Cockman and Clyde Cockman**

[Top Left] **Altie Cockman and Mallie Wallace**
[Above and Left] **Burley Leaton Cockman and Mary Alice "Mamie" Garner** *(Courtesy of Darrel Cockman)*
[Below] **John Riland Key and Nettie Cockman** *(Courtesy of Lance Key. Lipan, TX)*

1240. Atlas Franklin Cockman, son of Charles Riley O'Leonard Emsley Rufus Cockman and Lou Vicie Brown, was born on April 16, 1889. He married **Laura A. Riddle** on April 14, 1908 in Moore County, NC. He died on May 10, 1970 in Siler City, Chatham County, NC and was buried on May 11, 1970 in Moore County, NC at Flint Hill Baptist Church.

Lizzie McIver was born on December 10, 1907. She died on July 3, 1981 and was buried in Bear Creek, Chatham County, NC at Tyson's Creek Baptist Church. She and Atlas Franklin Cockman had the following children:

3021	Arnold Webster "Bill" Cockman (1927-1980). *Arnold was born on May 9, 1927 and married* **Marie Allen**. *He died on July 25, 1980.*
3022	Allen Thomas Cockman (1929-2009). *Allen was born on March 21, 1929 and married* **Betty Allen Teague** *and* **Shelby Jean Chilton**. *He died on March 15, 2009.*
3023	Frankie Cockman (1932-). *Frankie was born on April 19, 1932 and married* **Joseph Lee Mueller Jr.**
3024	Atlas Harold "Pete" Cockman (1934-2008). *Atlas was born on May 19, 1934 and married* **Margie Gross**. *He died on March 30, 2008.*
3025	William Ronald "Buddy" Cockman (1936-2009). *William was born on September 6, 1936 and married* **Betty Wicker**. *He died on May 19, 2009.*
3026	Mary Cockman (1938-). *Mary was born in 1938 and married* **H. Hartshorne**
3027	Otis Earl Cockman (1940-2007). *Otis was born on December 12, 1940 and married* **Nellie Gordon**. *He died on October 16, 2007.*

Laura A. Riddle, daughter of Wiley Riddle (1862-bef 1900) and Sarah E. McIntyre (1872-1927), was born on December 26, 1890. She died on May 5, 1922 and was buried in Moore County, NC at Flint Hill Baptist Church. She and Atlas Franklin Cockman had the following children:

3028	Lottie Mae Cockman (1909-1982). *Lottie was born on February 15, 1909 and married* **James Harvey Moody**. *She died on November 8, 1982 and was buried in Chatham County, NC at Mount Vernon Springs Presbyterian Church.*
3029	Elbert Franklin Cockman (1911-1992). *Elbert was born on October 31, 1911 and married* **Grace H. Garner**. *He died on February 8, 1992 and was buried in Robbins, Moore County, NC at Pine Rest Cemetery.*
3030	Roy Cockman (1914-1982). *Roy was born on July 12, 1914 and married* **Betty Moore**. *He died on May 12, 1982.*
3031	Floyd Edward Cockman (1917-1981). *Floyd was born on April 7, 1917 and married* **Nellie King**. *He died on December 19, 1981 and was buried in Moore County, NC at Flint Hill Baptist Church.*
3032	June Atlas Cockman (1919-1979). *June was born on June 5, 1919. He married* **Mary Jane Dunlap** *on September 16, 1939. He died on December 31, 1979 and was buried in Robbins, Moore County, NC at Pine Rest Cemetery.*
3033	Monti Mae Cockman (1922-1982). *Monti was born on May 10, 1922 and married* **James Brock Smith**. *She died on February 24, 1982 and was buried in Bear Creek, Chatham County, NC at Hickory Grove Baptist Church.*

1242. Maggie Cockman, daughter of Charles Riley O'Leonard Emsley Rufus Cockman and Lou Vicie Brown, was born in 1893. She died in 1893.

1243. Martha Alice Cockman, daughter of Charles Riley O'Leonard Emsley Rufus Cockman and Lou Vicie Brown, was born on August 29, 1896. She married **William McLenon Garner** on August 31, 1915 in Moore County, NC. She died on February 11, 1972 and was buried in Moore County, NC at Crossroads Baptist Church.

William McLenon Garner, son of Stephen Harrison "Frog" Garner (1874-1954) and Ella Blake Wallace (1877-1950), was born on December 26, 1897. He died on May 8, 1979 and was buried in Moore County, NC at Crossroads Baptist Church. He and Martha Alice Cockman had the following children:

3034	William Marvin Garner (1916-1991). *William was born on June 23, 1916 and married* **Virginia Ruth Wheeler**. *He died March 10, 1991.*
3035	Arthur Hugh Garner (1917-1995). *Arthur was born on December 10, 1917 and married* **Elgie Mozelle Cagle**. *He died on April 4, 1995 and was buried in Moore County, NC at Crossroads Baptist Church.*

3036	Grace Mae Garner (1919-2009). *Grace was born on February 26, 1919 and married **James Marvin Jackson**. She died on May 11, 2009.*
3037	Lacy Alton Garner (1921-2013). *Lacy was born on November 15, 1921 and married **Margaret Louise Cagle**. He died on April 22, 2013 and was buried in Moore County, NC at Crossroads Baptist Church.*
3038	Dossie Louise Garner (1925-1984). *Dossie was born on November 6, 1925 and married **Durward L. Tappen**. She died on September 26, 1984 and was buried in Moore County, NC at Crossroads Baptist Church.*
3039	Tracy Elvin Garner (1927-1997). *Tracy was born on April 12, 1927 and married **Kathleen Gibson**. He died on January 7, 1997 and was buried in Moore County, NC at Crossroads Baptist Church.*
3040	Ella May Garner (1929-2004). *Ella was born on March 31, 1929 and married **Charles Wilton Watson**. She died November 2, 2004.*
3041	Cecil Ruth Garner (1932-2009). *Cecil was born on July 7, 1932 and married **Glen Louie Sanders**. She died May 11, 2009*

1244. Henry Harrison "Bud" Cockman, son of Charles Riley O'Leonard Emsley Rufus Cockman and Lou Vicie Brown, was born on November 7, 1898. He married **Wilma Lou Cox** on February 19, 1919 in Moore County, NC. He died on January 27, 1969 in UNC Hospital, Chapel Hill, Orange County, NC and was buried on January 29, 1969 in Robbins, Moore County, NC at Tabernacle United Methodist Church.

Wilma Lou Cox, daughter of Causey Cox (1862-1947) and Martha Ann Furr (1883-1932), was born on June 11, 1903. She died on February 6, 1966 and was buried in Robbins, Moore County, NC at Tabernacle United Methodist Church. She and Henry Harrison "Bud" Cockman had the following children:

3042	Annie Ruth Cockman (1921-1974). *Annie was born on November 20, 1921. She died on May 24, 1974 in Randolph County Hospital, Asheboro, Randolph County, NC and was buried on May 26, 1974 in Staley, Randolph County, NC at Staley Baptist Church.*
3043	Lucille Cockman (1925-1974). *Lucille was born on January 22, 1925. She died on December 4, 1974 in Forsyth Memorial Hospital, Winston-Salem, Forsyth County, NC and was buried on December 7, 1974 in Ramseur, Randolph County, NC at Parks Crossroads Christian Church Cemetery.*
3044	Nannie Mae Cockman (1930-1943). *Nannie was born in 1930. She died in 1943 and was buried in Robbins, Moore County, NC at Tabernacle United Methodist Church.*
3045	Giles Wilbert Cockman (1932-1988). *Giles was born on May 19, 1932. He died on July 27, 1988 and was buried in Ramseur, Randolph County, NC at Parks Crossroads Christian Church Cemetery.*
3046	Cranford Horton Cockman (1934-1976). *Cranford was born on November 18, 1934. He died on December 18, 1976 and was buried in Ramseur, Randolph County, NC at Parks Crossroads Christian Church Cemetery.*
3047	Shirley Ann Cockman (1936-2009). *Shirley was born on October 27, 1936. She died on September 23, 2009 and was buried in Ramseur, Randolph County, NC at Parks Crossroads Christian Church Cemetery.*
3048	Joe Earl Cockman (1938-2000). *Joe was born on August 25, 1938. He died on April 13, 2000 and was buried in Ramseur, Randolph County, NC at Parks Crossroads Christian Church Cemetery.*
3049	Charles Winfield Cockman (1941-2004). *Charles was born on January 19, 1941. He died on October 2, 2004 and was buried in Ramseur, Randolph County, NC at Parks Crossroads Christian Church Cemetery.*

1245. Burley Leaton Cockman, son of Charles Riley O'Leonard Emsley Rufus Cockman and Lou Vicie Brown, was born on April 27, 1901 in Moore County, NC. He married **Mary Alice Rebecca "Mamie" Garner** on April 11, 1925. He died on January 23, 1968 in Moore County, NC and was buried on January 25, 1968 in Moore County, NC at Flint Hill Baptist Church.

Mary Alice Rebecca "Mamie" Garner, daughter of Leonard Garner (1851-1922) and Mary Ella Maness (1862-1942), was born on April 11, 1905. She died on March 18, 1969 and was buried in Moore County, NC at Flint Hill Baptist Church. She and Burley Leaton Cockman had the following children:

3050	Neuby Ralph Cockman (1929-) *married Pearlie Louise Sheffield.*
3051	Janie Cockman (-)
3052	Riley Leonard Cockman (1926-2002). *Riley was born on March 6, 1926. He married Mary Elaine "Elaine" Maness on September 5, 1953. He died on March 30, 2002 in Moore County, NC and was buried in Biscoe, Montgomery County, NC at Biscoe Cemetery.*
3053	Robert Edgar Cockman (1927-1979). *Robert was born on April 2, 1927 and married Patsy Ruth Holder. He died on September 11, 1979 and was buried in Moore County, NC at Flint Hill Baptist Church.*
3054	Luella Mae Cockman (1930-2008). *Luella was born on April 5, 1930 and married Lee. R. Sullivan. She died on February 21, 2008 and was buried in Moore County, NC at Flint Hill Baptist Church.*
3055	Betty Ruth Cockman (1932-2015). *Betty was born in 1932 and married Ralph Hampton Smith. She died on July 25, 2015.*
3056	Mozelle Cockman (1933-2018). *Mozelle was born on August 2, 1933. She died on December 29, 2018.*
3057	Jessie Bell Cockman (1935-2009). *Jessie was born on November 26, 1935 and married Billy E. Holder, Daniel Holder and Melvin Pope. She died on September 21, 2009 and was buried in Vass, Moore County, NC at Johnson Grove Cemetery.*
3058	Lillie Estelle Cockman (1938-). *Lillie was born on September 25, 1938.*
3059	Mary Alice Cockman (1941-1989). *Mary was born on March 25, 1941 and married Mr. Lynthacum. She died on January 26, 1989 and was buried in Moore County, NC at Flint Hill Baptist Church.*
3060	Freddie Thomas Cockman (1943-2001). *Freddie was born on March 27, 1943. He married Alice Faye Ivey on September 19, 1964 in Moore County, NC. He died on July 30, 2001 and was buried in Moore County, NC at Flint Hill Baptist Church.*
3061	Jo Ann Cockman (1945-1945). *Jo was born on February 19, 1945. She died on February 19, 1945 and was buried in Moore County, NC at Flint Hill Baptist Church.*
3062	Billy Ray Cockman (1948-1948). *Billy was born on June 17, 1948. He died on June 17, 1948 and was buried in Moore County, NC at Flint Hill Baptist Church.*

1246. Nepsie Mae Cockman, daughter of Charles Riley O'Leonard Emsley Rufus Cockman and Lou Vicie Brown, was born on March 24, 1904 in Moore County, NC. She married **Ernest Carson Marley** on July 31, 1922. She died on April 20, 1964 in Moore Regional Hospital, Pinehurst, Moore County, NC and was buried on April 22, 1964 in Moore County, NC at Calvary Baptist Church.

Ernest Carson Marley, son of Milton Sylvester Marley (1870-1958) and Francis Perrillar "Fannie" Ritter (1875-1958), was born on September 19, 1900. He died on August 25, 1989 and was buried in Moore County, NC at Calvary Baptist Church. He and Nepsie Mae Cockman had the following children:

3063	Martha Lou Marley (-)
3064	Tracey Wilbert Marley (-)
3065	Annie Pearl Marley (-)
3066	Grady Herbert Marley (1923-1975). *Grady was born on August 17, 1923. He died on June 23, 1975 and was buried in Moore County, NC at Calvary Baptist Church.*
3067	Wilma Frances Marley (1925-2014). *Wilma was born on February 23, 1925. She died on November 17, 2014.*
3068	Milton Carson Marley (1926-1992). *Milton was born on November 18, 1926. He died on August 27, 1992 and was buried in Moore County, NC at Calvary Baptist Church.*
3069	Walter Ruffin Marley (1928-2013). *Walter was born in August 13, 1928.*
3070	Prilla Mae Marley (1932-). *Prilla was born on March 11, 1932.*

1247. Gurney Raeford Cockman, son of Charles Riley O'Leonard Emsley Rufus Cockman and Lou Vicie Brown, was born on July 8, 1906 in Moore County, NC. He married **Lillie May Crabtree** on May 12, 1927 in Moore County, NC. He died on November 19, 1966 in Moore County, NC and was buried on November 20, 1966 in Moore County, NC at Friendship Baptist Church.

Lillie May Crabtree, daughter of Andrew Jackson Crabtree (1881-1969) and Sarah Jane Sheffield (1883-1956), was born on May 6, 1905. She died on December 16, 1986 and was buried in Moore County, NC at Friendship Baptist Church. She and Gurney Raeford Cockman had the following children:

3071	Johnsie Louise Cockman (1928-). *Johnsie was born on October 4, 1928 in Moore County, NC.*
3072	Lester Gilbert Cockman (1932-2006). *Lester was born on June 16, 1932. He married* **Wanda Laverne Powers** *on December 8, 1956. He died on August 13, 2006 in Moore County, NC and was buried in Moore County, NC at Pleasant View Evangelical Church.*
3073	Richard Junior Cockman (1939-). *Richard was born on April 11, 1939 in Moore County, NC.*
3074	Helen Mae Cockman (1942-). *Helen was born on September 30, 1942 in Moore County, NC.*

1250. **Causey Belton Cockman**, son of Thomas Bias Noah Louweed Cockman and Indiana Brown, was born on August 28, 1892. He married **Dora Mae Hawks** on March 31, 1912.

Dora Mae Hawks was born on March 4, 1886. She died on December 9, 1961.

1251. **Burton Cockman**, son of Thomas Bias Noah Louweed Cockman and Indiana Brown, was born on July 3, 1895. He died on July 6, 1976.

Jennie Brown, daughter of William Wesley Brown (1863-1925) and Mary Jane "Sarah" Emmoline Camilla Hazeltine Cockman (1867-1944), was born in December 1895 and was buried in Browns Summit, Guilford County, NC at Reedy Fork Cemetery. She and Burton Cockman had the following children:

3075	Jesse James Cockman (1926-1995). *Jesse was born on April 11, 1926. He died on May 16, 1995 and was buried in Browns Summit, Guilford County, NC at Reedy Fork Cemetery.*
3076	Eugene Thomas Cockman (1927-1994). *Eugene was born on January 9, 1927. He died on June 21, 1994.*

1252. **Altie Cockman**, son of Thomas Bias Noah Louweed Cockman and Indiana Brown, was born on December 8, 1897. He married **Rosa Emma Hawks** on December 9, 1915. He died on July 10, 1975.

Rosa Emma Hawks was born on September 19, 1898. She died on September 20, 1968.

1253. **Hardin Cockman**, son of Thomas Bias Noah Louweed Cockman and Indiana Brown, was born on May 18, 1901. He died on June 15, 1962.

1254. **Mary Delila Cockman**, daughter of Thomas Bias Noah Louweed Cockman and Indiana Brown, was born on September 17, 1904. She died on January 15, 1978.

Herbert Barley was born on April 12, 1901. He died on February 4, 1977. He and Mary Delila Cockman had the following children:

3077	Barley (-)

1255. **Joe Branson Cockman**, son of Thomas Bias Noah Louweed Cockman and Indiana Brown, was born on November 26, 1907. He died on September 27, 1975.

Pearl Parrish was born on August 15, 1913.

1258. **Nettie Louise Brown**, daughter of William Wesley Brown and Mary Jane "Sarah" Emmoline Camilla Hazeltine Cockman, was born on January 12, 1886. She married circa 1899. She died on May 26, 1968 in Thomasville, Davidson County, NC and was buried on May 29, 1968 in Moore County, NC at Flint Hill Baptist Church.

1259. **Benjamin Harrison Brown**, son of William Wesley Brown and Mary Jane "Sarah" Emmoline Camilla Hazeltine Cockman, was born on October 28, 1888 in Moore County, NC. He married **Margaret Emily Cagle** on October 24, 1909. He died on January 28, 1964 in Moore County, NC and was buried on January 31, 1964 in Moore County, NC at Flint Hill Baptist Church.

Margaret Emily Cagle, daughter of John Ransom Cagle (1839-1922) and Margaret Corinne Ritter (1858-1935), was born on December 28, 1887. She died on April 15, 1965 in Greensboro, Guilford County, NC and was buried on April 17, 1965 in Guilford County, NC at Lakeview Memorial Park. She and Benjamin Harrison Brown had the following children:

3078	Robert Harrison Brown (1911-1987). *Robert was born on February 13, 1911. He died on April 21, 1987.*
3079	Mildred Margaret Brown (1914-). *Mildred was born on January 1, 1914 in Moore County, NC.*
3080	Sarah Maggie Brown (1916-1983). *Sarah was born in 1916. She died in 1983.*
3081	William Ransom Brown (b.1918, bur.1977). *William was born in 1918 and was buried in 1977.*
3082	Estella Cagle Brown (1921-). *Estella was born in 1921.*
3083	Edith May Brown (1923-). *Edith was born in 1923.*
3084	Clinton Brown (1924-). *Clinton was born on August 8, 1924 in Moore County, NC.*
3085	Linton Brown (1924-). *Linton was born on August 8, 1924.*
3086	Welford Headen Brown (1925-2009). *Welford was born in 1925. He died in 2009.*
3087	Vina Louise Brown (1928-). *Vina was born in 1928.*

1260. **James Arnold Brown**, son of William Wesley Brown and Mary Jane "Sarah" Emmoline Camilla Hazeltine Cockman, was born on August 26, 1890. He died on May 1, 1952 and was buried in Moore County, NC at High Falls United Methodist Church.

Ellen K. Mashburn, daughter of Samuel Mashburn (1851-1915) and Minnie Louella Brady (1872-1981), was born on March 18, 1901. She died on September 2, 1925 and was buried in Moore County, NC at High Falls United Methodist Church.

1261. **Neil Lee Brown**, son of William Wesley Brown and Mary Jane "Sarah" Emmoline Camilla Hazeltine Cockman, was born on May 8, 1895. He died on July 13, 1923 and was buried in Moore County, NC at Bensalem Presbyterian Church.

Effie Britt, daughter of Daniel Bethune Britt (1845-1927) and Lydia Freeman (1848-1918), was born on March 8, 1892. She died on June 18, 1967 and was buried in Moore County, NC at Bensalem Presbyterian Church. She and Neil Lee Brown had the following children:

3088	Wilbert Carlton Brown (1916-1979). *Wilbert was born on October 16, 1916 in Moore County, NC. He died on October 3, 1979 and was buried in Browns Summit, Guilford County, NC at Reedy Fork Cemetery.*
3089	Mary Lee Brown (1919-1988). *Mary was born on March 26, 1919. She died on October 30, 1988 in Moore County, NC and was buried in Moore County, NC at Flint Hill Baptist Church.*
3090	Eula Brown (1922-). *Eula was born in 1922.*
3091	Lucille Brown (1923-). *Lucille was born in 1923.*

1262. **Jennie Brown**, daughter of William Wesley Brown and Mary Jane "Sarah" Emmoline Camilla Hazeltine Cockman, was born in December 1895 and was buried in Browns Summit, Guilford County, NC at Reedy Fork Cemetery.

Burton Cockman, son of Thomas Bias Noah Louweed Cockman (1862-1942) and Indiana Brown (1864-1938), was born on July 3, 1895. He died on July 6, 1976. He and Jennie Brown had the following children:

3092	Jesse James Cockman (1926-1995). *Jesse was born on April 11, 1926. He died on May 16, 1995 and was buried in Browns Summit, Guilford County, NC at Reedy Fork Cemetery.*
3093	Eugene Thomas Cockman (1927-1994). *Eugene was born on January 9, 1927. He died on June 21, 1994.*

1263. Walter Branson Brown, son of William Wesley Brown and Mary Jane "Sarah" Emmoline Camilla Hazeltine Cockman, was born on July 10, 1897. He married **Gladys Dowdy** on July 9, 1920 in Moore County, NC. He died on November 9, 1975 in Moore County, NC and was buried in Moore County, NC at Calvary Baptist Church.

Gladys Dowdy, daughter of James S. Dowdy (1871-1948) and Sarah Elizabeth Cagle (1876-1932), was born on November 6, 1895. She died on April 16, 1988 in Moore County, NC and was buried in Moore County, NC at Calvary Baptist Church. She and Walter Branson Brown had the following children:

3094	Walter Julian Brown (1921-1987). *Walter was born on May 31, 1921. He died on May 12, 1987 and was buried in Moore County, NC at Calvary Baptist Church.*
3095	Bertha Mazie Brown (1924-1989). *Bertha was born on December 29, 1924. She died on May 25, 1989 in Moore County, NC and was buried in Moore County, NC at Culdee Presbyterian Church.*
3096	Roy Gilbert Brown (1929-1998). *Roy was born on March 16, 1929 in Moore County, NC. He died on August 26, 1998 and was buried in Moore County, NC at Calvary Baptist Church.*
3097	Sarah May "May" Brown (1931-2016). *Sarah was born on May 22, 1931. She died on March 7, 2016 and was buried in Moore County, NC at Calvary Baptist Church.*
3098	James William Wayl Brown (1933-1993). *James was born on December 1, 1933. He died on October 31, 1993 and was buried in Moore County, NC at Calvary Baptist Church.*

1264. Mittie M. Brown, daughter of William Wesley Brown and Mary Jane "Sarah" Emmoline Camilla Hazeltine Cockman, was born on October 12, 1899. She died on July 28, 1981 and was buried in Asheboro, Randolph County, NC at Oaklawn Cemetery.

John Thomas Needham, son of Alfred L. Needham (1855-1919) and Maggie Poole (1873-), was born on April 12, 1897. He died on June 14, 1953 and was buried in Asheboro, Randolph County, NC at Oaklawn Cemetery. He and Mittie M. Brown had the following children:

3099	William Norman "Tom" Needham (1922-2002). *William was born on July 25, 1922. He died on September 30, 2002 and was buried in Asheboro, Randolph County, NC at Oaklawn Cemetery.*
3100	Betty Lou Needham (1936-). *Betty was born on May 30, 1936.*

1265. Bertha Ethel Brown, daughter of William Wesley Brown and Mary Jane "Sarah" Emmoline Camilla Hazeltine Cockman, was born on June 10, 1902. She died on April 28, 1950.

Charles Glenn Needham, son of Alfred L. Needham (1855-1919) and Maggie Poole (1873-), was born on December 22, 1894. He died on June 17, 1971 in Randolph County Hospital, Asheboro, Randolph County, NC and was buried on June 19, 1971 in Asheboro, Randolph County, NC at Oaklawn Cemetery. He and Bertha Ethel Brown had the following children:

3101	Swannie Needham (1918-). *Swannie was born in 1918.*
3102	Ellen Needham (1924-2000). *Ellen was born on February 12, 1924. She died on January 12, 2000.*

1266. Arthur Edd Brown, son of William Wesley Brown and Mary Jane "Sarah" Emmoline Camilla Hazeltine Cockman, was born on October 7, 1903. He died on June 12, 1983 and was buried in Moore County, NC at Flint Hill Baptist Church.

Fronnie Agnes Morgan, daughter of Malcolm "Make" Morgan (1880-1966) and Cora Britt (1886-1953), was born on September 11, 1914. She died on January 23, 2001 and was buried in Moore County, NC at Flint Hill Baptist Church. She and Arthur Edd Brown had the following children:

3103	Clifford Albert Brown (1938-). *Clifford was born on June 24, 1938.*

1267. **Lena Brown**, daughter of William Wesley Brown and Mary Jane "Sarah" Emmoline Camilla Hazeltine Cockman, was born on June 3, 1905. She died on November 23, 1985 and was buried in Randolph County, NC at Mt. Zion Methodist Church.

John Herbert Jones, son of William Gurney Jones (1875-1917) and Mary Ellen Bridges (1878-1929), was born on March 8, 1902. He died on December 2, 1984 and was buried in Randolph County, NC at Mt. Zion Methodist Church. He and Lena Brown had the following children:

> 3104   Walter Herbert Jones (1932-1989). *Walter was born on April 15, 1932. He died on December 5, 1989.*

1268. **John Wesley Brown**, son of William Wesley Brown and Mary Jane "Sarah" Emmoline Camilla Hazeltine Cockman, was born on March 6, 1907. He died on June 16, 1985 and was buried in Randolph County, NC at Mt. Zion Methodist Church.

Mary Ida Caviness, daughter of John S. Caviness (1871-1942) and Martha Ellen Purvis (1868-1934), was born on October 29, 1912. She died on December 21, 1985 and was buried in Randolph County, NC at Mt. Zion Methodist Church. She and John Wesley Brown had the following children:

> 3105   Earl Brown (-)
> 3106   Russell Brown (1933-). *Russell was born in 1933.*
> 3107   Vera Ellen Brown (1936-1994). *Vera was born in 1936. She died on September 18, 1994.*
> 3108   Pauline Brown (1938-1998). *Pauline was born in 1938. She died on June 20, 1998.*
> 3109   Melvin Brown (1939-). *Melvin was born in 1939.*
> 3110   John Neil Brown (1945-1995). *John was born on January 20, 1945. He died on August 13, 1995 and was buried in Randolph County, NC at Mt. Zion Methodist Church.*
> 3111   Raymond Lee Brown (1947-1965). *Raymond was born on August 18, 1947. He died on June 6, 1965 and was buried in Randolph County, NC at Mt. Zion Methodist Church.*

1269. **Gurtie Cockman**, daughter of Wade Hampton Wallace and Maggie Delaney Deleeny Cockman, was born on May 25, 1909. She married **Claude Ellis Hussey** on May 9, 1954 in Moore County, NC. She died on May 9, 1962 in Lumberton, Robeson County, NC and was buried in Moore County, NC at Flint Hill Baptist Church.

William Harrison Cagle, son of John Ransom Cagle (1839-1922) and Margaret Corinne Ritter (1858-1935), was born on August 20, 1894. He died on October 25, 1959 and was buried in Carthage, Moore County, NC at Cross Hill Cemetery. He and Gurtie Cockman had the following children:

> 3112   William Velvin Cagle (1939-1978). *William was born on May 22, 1939. He died on October 13, 1978 in Charlotte, Mecklenburg County, NC and was buried in Salisbury, Rowan County, NC.*

Claude Ellis Hussey, son of Eli Jackson Hussey (1877-1938) and Sarah Alice Maness (1880-1958), was born on May 28, 1896. He married Sarah Frances Maness on March 22, 1916 in Moore County, NC. He died on September 29, 1958 and was buried in Moore County, NC at Smyrna Methodist Church.

1270. **Coy Carlton Wallace**, son of James Charles Wallace and Arnettie Maness, was born on February 21, 1882 in Moore County, NC. He married **Cornie Seawell** on January 6, 1913 in Moore County, NC. He died on July 30, 1966 in Carthage, Moore County, NC and was buried on July 31, 1966 in Carthage, Moore County, NC at Cross Hill Cemetery.

Cornie Seawell, daughter of John Wesley Seawell (1848-1926) and Emily Louise Moore (1858-1929), was born on November 4, 1895. She died on November 6, 1973 in Carthage, Moore County, NC and was buried on November 8, 1973 in Carthage, Moore County, NC at Cross Hill Cemetery. She and Coy Carlton Wallace had the following children:

> 3113   Ruth Seawell Wallace (1913-). *Ruth was born on October 22, 1913 in Moore County, NC. She married **Julian Bowden Stewart** on June 26, 1937 in Moore County, NC.*
> 3114   Coy Carlton Wallace Jr. (1915-). *Coy was born on January 24, 1915.*

3115	Mary Ivey Wallace (1917-). *Mary was born on January 24, 1917.*
3116	Rosa Lee Wallace (1918-2007). *Rosa was born on October 19, 1918. She died on September 12, 2007 and was buried in Carthage, Moore County, NC at Cross Hill Cemetery.*
3117	Henry Craft Wallace (1921-2003). *Henry was born on September 8, 1921. He died on May 26, 2003 in Wilmington, New Hanover County, NC.*

1271. Offie Doyle Wallace, son of James Charles Wallace and Arnettie Maness, was born on April 30, 1883 in Moore County, NC. He married **Agnes Bartlett** on October 23, 1923 in Moore County, NC. He died on March 4, 1945 in Carthage, Moore County, NC and was buried on March 5, 1945 in Carthage, Moore County, NC at Cross Hill Cemetery.

Agnes Bartlett, daughter of S.B. Bartlett (-) and Clara (-), was born on July 29, 1893. She died on February 18, 1954 and was buried in Carthage, Moore County, NC at Cross Hill Cemetery. She and Offie Doyle Wallace had the following children:

3118	Bettie Doyle Wallace (1925-1989). *Bettie was born on January 11, 1925. She died on June 23, 1989.*
3119	Clara Marguerite Wallace (1928-). *Clara was born on December 3, 1928. She married **Winfred Theodore Howard** on October 23, 1947 in Moore County, NC.*
3120	Offie Doyle Wallace Jr. (1932-). *Offie was born on September 20, 1932. He married **Anna Rose Williams** on December 17, 1974 in Moore County, NC.*

1272. Walter Lee Wallace, son of James Charles Wallace and Arnettie Maness, was born on February 8, 1885. He died on February 27, 1956 and was buried in Carthage, Moore County, NC at Cross Hill Cemetery.

1273. Luther Class Wallace, son of James Charles Wallace and Arnettie Maness, was born on August 29, 1886 in Moore County, NC. He married **Katie Hester Tyson** on July 21, 1920 in Moore County, NC. He died on July 27, 1968 in Moore Regional Hospital, Pinehurst, Moore County, NC and was buried on July 28, 1968 in Carthage, Moore County, NC at Cross Hill Cemetery.

Katie Hester Tyson, daughter of John M. Tyson (1865-) and Mary Jane McLeod (1875-), was born on August 30, 1895. She died on July 12, 1963 in Carthage, Moore County, NC and was buried on July 14, 1963 in Carthage, Moore County, NC at Cross Hill Cemetery.

1274. Burnie Clyde Wallace, son of James Charles Wallace and Arnettie Maness, was born on August 10, 1888. He died on January 24, 1976 in Polk County, NC.

Ethel Reid, daughter of Henry S. Reid (1864-1928) and Annie Jackson (1867-1894), was born on October 8, 1893. She died on March 8, 1971 in Moore Regional Hospital, Pinehurst, Moore County, NC and was buried on March 10, 1971 in Carthage, Moore County, NC at Cross Hill Cemetery.

1275. Loula Maude Wallace, daughter of James Charles Wallace and Arnettie Maness, was born on July 10, 1890 in Moore County, NC. She married **Jesse Fulton Sullivan** on February 2, 1916 in Moore County, NC. She died on December 24, 1943 in Moore Regional Hospital, Pinehurst, Moore County, NC and was buried on December 26, 1943 in Carthage, Moore County, NC at Cross Hill Cemetery.

Jesse Fulton Sullivan, son of John Bean Sullivan (1844-1916) and Ruth Ann McIntosh (1848-1913), was born on December 8, 1881. He died on July 6, 1961 and was buried in Carthage, Moore County, NC at Cross Hill Cemetery. He and Loula Maude Wallace had the following children:

3121	Herbert Hoyle Sullivan (1917-). *Herbert was born on July 3, 1917.*

1276. Lora Almar Wallace, daughter of James Charles Wallace and Arnettie Maness, was born on February 8, 1892. She died on June 9, 1894 and was buried in Moore County, NC at Flint Hill Baptist Church.

1277. Molly Viola Wallace, daughter of James Charles Wallace and Arnettie Maness, was born on March 13, 1894 in Moore County, NC. She married **Walter Eli Porter** on January 10, 1917 in Moore County, NC. She died on June 11, 1951 in Moore County, NC and was buried on June 13, 1951 in Carthage, Moore County, NC at Cross Hill Cemetery.

Walter Eli Porter, son of John W. Porter (1857-1935) and Nora D. Currie (1862-1916), was born on June 19, 1893. He died on May 28, 1968. He and Molly Viola Wallace had the following children:

3122   Nora Elizabeth Porter (1920-2013). *Nora was born on December 27, 1920. She died on August 5, 2013 in Union County, NC.*

3123   Walter Eli Porter Jr. (1926-). *Walter was born on June 29, 1926.*

1278. **Ruley Gart Wallace**, son of James Charles Wallace and Arnettie Maness, was born on December 18, 1895. He died on October 13, 1967 in Moore County, NC.

Margaret McIver, daughter of J. Alton McIver (-) and Mary Eppes James (-), was born on June 29, 1897. She died on April 6, 1959 and was buried in Carthage, Moore County, NC at Cross Hill Cemetery. She and Ruley Gart Wallace had the following children:

3124   Margaret McIver Wallace (1926-). *Margaret was born on April 13, 1926. She married **Steve Donald Arledge** on September 27, 1952 in Moore County, NC.*

3125   Mary Eppes Wallace (1928-). *Mary was born on June 29, 1928.*

3126   Nancy Lee Wallace (1932-). *Nancy was born on December 9, 1932. She married **Sam Hope** on June 13, 1953 in Moore County, NC.*

1279. **Lizzie F. Wallace**, daughter of James Charles Wallace and Arnettie Maness, was born on June 19, 1899. She married **John Wilbert McLeod** on November 14, 1923 in Moore County, NC. She died on May 14, 1978 and was buried in Carthage, Moore County, NC at Cross Hill Cemetery.

John Wilbert McLeod, son of J. M. McLeod (-) and Catherine Ellen (-), was born on May 20, 1900. He died on November 30, 1987 and was buried in Carthage, Moore County, NC at Cross Hill Cemetery.

1280. **Bonnie J. Wallace**, daughter of James Charles Wallace and Arnettie Maness, was born on April 9, 1904. She married **Haywood Joseph Hall** on August 1, 1928. She died on March 16, 1972 in Hill Haven Convalescent Center, Durham, Durham County, NC and was buried on March 18, 1972 in Carthage, Moore County, NC at Cross Hill Cemetery.

Haywood Joseph Hall, son of F.W. Hall (-) and Nancy (-), was born on June 3, 1902. He died on January 6, 1949 and was buried in Carthage, Moore County, NC at Cross Hill Cemetery. He and Bonnie J. Wallace had the following children:

3127   Carolyn Wallace Hall (1932-). *Carolyn was born on August 18, 1932.*

1281. **Edna Elizabeth Wallace**, daughter of William Clark Wallace and Mollie Lee Gaitley, was born on August 25, 1899 in Robeson County, NC. She died on August 4, 1977 and was buried in Fork, Dillon County, SC at Hopewell Cemetery.

Lattie Boyd Fort was born on November 9, 1880. He died on January 11, 1959 and was buried in Fork, Dillon County, SC at Hopewell Cemetery. He and Edna Elizabeth Wallace had the following children:

3128   Mollie Fort (-)

1282. **Mary L. "Molly" Wallace**, daughter of William Clark Wallace and Mollie Lee Gaitley, was born in September 1903. She died in 1981.

1283. **William Gaitley Wallace**, son of William Clark Wallace and Mollie Lee Gaitley, was born on January 29, 1907 in Roland, Robeson County, NC. He married **Anne Pennington** on February 14, 1941. He died on March 5, 1971.

Anne Pennington and William Gaitley Wallace had the following children:

3129   William Gaitley Wallace II (1941-). *William was born on December 19, 1941 in Hartsville, SC. He married **Beverly Ann Powell** on November 25, 1965.*

3130   Diane Wallace (1944-). *Diane was born on December 11, 1944.*

3131   Michael Pennington Wallace (1952-). *Michael was born on June 30, 1952.*

[Top Left] (L-R) **Robert Dall Wallace, William Gaitley Wallace and Joe. T. Wallace** [Top Right] (L-R) **William Gaitley Wallace, Joe T. Wallace, William M. Wallace, Robert Dall Wallace** [Bottom] (L-R) **William M. Wallace, Joe T. Wallace, Edna Wallace (daughter Mollie Fort), Celeste Annette Wallace, Audrey Smith (Wife of Robert Dall Wallace), Robert Dall Wallace.**
(Courtesy of Tim Anderson, LeRoy, NY)

1284. Robert Dall Wallace, son of William Clark Wallace and Gabriella "Ella" Ford, was born on June 21, 1917. He died on July 27, 1977 and was buried in Lakeview, Dillon County, SC at Lakeview Cemetery.

Audrey Smith was born on November 24, 1920. She died on September 12, 2004 and was buried in Lakeview, Dillon County, SC at Lakeview Cemetery. She and Robert Dall Wallace had the following children:

3132   Son Wallace (1942-1942). *Son was born on December 31, 1942. He died on December 31, 1942 and was buried in Lakeview, Dillon County, SC at Lakeview Cemetery.*

1287. Margaret Victoria "Peggy" Wallace, daughter of William Clark Wallace and Gabriella "Ella" Ford, was born on July 15, 1924. She married **Clifton "Cliff" Johnson** on July 7, 1945. She died on November 24, 2017.

Clifton "Cliff" Johnson died on July 21, 2008. He and Margaret Victoria "Peggy" Wallace had the following children:

3133   Cynthia Johnson (-)
3134   C. Randall "Randy" Johnson (-)
3135   Blair Johnson (-)
3136   Earl Johnson (-)

1288. Celeste Annette Wallace, daughter of William Clark Wallace and Gabriella "Ella" Ford, was born on August 6, 1926 in Florence, Florence County, SC. She married **Robert Edwin Anderson** on October 22, 1953. She died on December 5, 2013.

Robert Edwin Anderson was born on July 21, 1921 in Ellington, Chautauqua County, NY. He died on July 6, 2010 in Jamestown, Chautauqua County, NY. He and Celeste Annette Wallace had the following children:

3137   Lorinda Rea Anderson (1954-2005). *Lorinda was born on October 16, 1954 in Jamestown, Chautauqua County, NY. She died on December 30, 2005 in Buffalo, Erie County, NY.*
3138   Edwin Robert Anderson (1956-). *Edwin was born on February 12, 1956 in Jamestown, Chautauqua County, NY.*
3139   Kyle Anderson (1958-). *Kyle was born on March 12, 1958 in Jamestown, Chautauqua County, NY.*
3140   Terry Lou Anderson (1959-). *Terry was born on June 29, 1959 in Jamestown, Chautauqua County, NY.*
3141   Quinn Kipling Anderson (1961-). *Quinn was born on June 14, 1961 in Jamestown, Chautauqua County, NY.*

1289. Infant McNeill, son of Lemeul Alexander McNeill and Laura Louise Wallace, was born on April 5, 1901. He died on April 5, 1901 and was buried in Robbins, Moore County, NC at Tabernacle United Methodist Church.

1290. Ethel McNeill, daughter of Lemeul Alexander McNeill and Laura Louise Wallace, was born on February 21, 1908. She married **Odell Creswell Butler** on April 16, 1927 in Moore County, NC. She died on December 30, 1995 and was buried in Robbins, Moore County, NC at Tabernacle United Methodist Church.

Odell Creswell Butler, son of Allen Butler (-) and Melissa Core (-), was born on July 2, 1907 in Cumberland County, NC. He died on June 1, 1967 in Moore Regional Hospital, Pinehurst, Moore County, NC and was buried in Robbins, Moore County, NC at Tabernacle United Methodist Church. He and Ethel McNeill had the following children:

3142   Christine Butler (-1995). *Christine died on November 28, 1995 and was buried in Robbins, Moore County, NC at Pine Rest Cemetery.*
3143   Betty Ray Butler (1928-2002). *Betty was born on March 31, 1928 in Moore County, NC. She died on December 10, 2002 in Moore Regional Hospital, Pinehurst, Moore County, NC.*
3144   Viola Sue Butler (1930-2019). *Viola was born on March 13, 1930 in Moore County, NC. She died on January 12, 2019 and was buried in Robbins, Moore County, NC at Pine Rest Cemetery.*
3145   Odell Creswell Butler Jr. (1932-2007). *Odell was born on February 17, 1932 in Moore County, NC. He died on November 17, 2007.*

| 3146 | Dal Alexander Butler (1933-2020). *Dal was born on March 31, 1933 in Moore County, NC. He died on January 24, 2020 and was buried in Robbins, Moore County, NC at Pine Rest Cemetery.* |
| 3147 | Laura Ann Butler (1936-). *Laura was born on February 28, 1936 in Moore County, NC.* |

[Left] **Odell Butler, Ethel McNeill and Betty Ray Butler** *(Courtesy of Donald Wallace)*
[Right] **Beatrice Morphis, Donald Morphis and Rebecca Morphis** *(Courtesy of Mike Cross, Panama City, FL)*

1291. Charlie C. McNeill, son of Lemeul Alexander McNeill and Laura Louise Wallace, was born on July 10, 1911. He died on October 23, 1911 and was buried in Robbins, Moore County, NC at Tabernacle United Methodist Church.

1292. Lydia Rossie Kennedy, daughter of Elias Richard Kennedy and Maggie Elizabeth Wallace, was born on December 7, 1903. She died on December 10, 1995 and was buried in Moore County, NC at Calvary Baptist Church.

Arthur Carson Moore, son of George Thomas Moore (1879-1954) and Leta Catherine Marley (1877-1948), was born on October 11, 1904. He died on June 11, 1966 in Siler City, Chatham County, NC and was buried in Moore County, NC at Calvary Baptist Church. He and Lydia Rossie Kennedy had the following children:

| 3148 | Clara Agnes Moore (1927-). *Clara was born on October 25, 1927. She married **Harold Stewart Cole** on August 11, 1956.* |
| 3149 | E. Clayton Moore (1933-2013). *E. was born in 1933. He died on March 21, 2013 in Moore Regional Hospital, Pinehurst, Moore County, NC.* |

1293. John Wesley Raymond Kennedy, son of Elias Richard Kennedy and Maggie Elizabeth Wallace, was born on April 3, 1916. He died on July 11, 1978 and was buried in Robbins, Moore County, NC at Pine Rest Cemetery.

Cora Maness, daughter of Lewis Street Maness (1891-1949) and Laura Lee Brown (1894-1977), was born on January 11, 1924. She died on August 28, 1987 and was buried in Robbins, Moore County, NC at Pine Rest Cemetery.

Zelma Hurdy Arnold, daughter of John G. Arnold (1893-1970) and Nettie Jane Collins (1896-1967), was born on December 7, 1915. She died on December 2, 1990 in Greensboro, Guilford County, NC. She and John Wesley Raymond Kennedy had the following children:

3150	James Edward Kennedy (1936-1936). *James was born on February 19, 1936 in Moore County, NC. He died on February 22, 1936 in Moore County, NC and was buried on February 23, 1936 in Moore County, NC at Pleasant Hill United Methodist Church.*
3151	Raymond Eugene Kennedy (1938-). *Raymond was born on February 7, 1938 in Moore County, NC.*
3152	Kennedy (1940-1940). *[unnamed person] was born on March 27, 1940 in Moore County, NC. He died on March 28, 1940 in Moore County, NC and was buried on March 29, 1940 in Moore County, NC at Pleasant Hill United Methodist Church.*
3153	Ethelyn Kennedy (1941-). *Ethelyn was born on September 1, 1941 in Moore County, NC.*
3154	Maxine Kennedy (1941-). *Maxine was born on September 1, 1941 in Moore County, NC.*
3155	Kenneth Ray Kennedy (1944-). *Kenneth was born on July 29, 1944 in Moore County, NC.*

1294. Hazel Ailene Kennedy, daughter of Elias Richard Kennedy and Maggie Elizabeth Wallace, was born on March 27, 1922.

Thomas Samuel Hamilton was born on December 23, 1918. He died on April 14, 1985 and was buried in Robbins, Moore County, NC at Pine Rest Cemetery. He and Hazel Ailene Kennedy had the following children:

3156	Thomas Samuel Hamilton Jr. (-)
3157	Linda Cheryl Hamilton (-)
3158	Richard Vernon Hamilton (-)
3159	Daniel Keith Hamilton (-)

1295. Donna Inez Wallace, daughter of Jesse Lee Wallace and Mary Caroline Hilliard, was born on April 10, 1915. She died on June 12, 2006.

Wilbur Lindsay Oldham was born on December 15, 1910. He died on December 28, 1981. He and Donna Inez Wallace had the following children:

3160	Oldham (-)

1300. Fred Thomas Wallace, son of John Stellings Wallace and Pearl Phillips, was born on June 25, 1920 in Guilford County, NC. He married **Marjorie E. Self** on July 18, 1947 in Greensboro, Guilford County, NC. He died on October 22, 1965 in Atlanta, Fulton County, GA.

Marjorie E. Self was born on September 13, 1925 in Guilford County, NC. She and Fred Thomas Wallace had the following children:

3161	Janice Leigh Wallace (1948-). *Janice was born on February 25, 1948 in Greensboro, Guilford County, NC.*
3162	Fred Thomas Wallace (1950-). *Fred was born on June 17, 1950 in Miami, Dade County, FL.*
3163	John Stanley Wallace (1952-). *John was born on March 31, 1952 in Miami, Dade County, FL.*
3164	Scott Alan Wallace (1956-). *Scott was born on July 12, 1956 in Winston-Salem, Forsyth County, NC.*

1302. Jesse Edward Broadstreet, son of Oscar Azle Broadstreet and Martha Jane Wallace, was born on December 4, 1912 in Guilford County, NC. He died on June 25, 1989.

1303. **Merrill Rex Broadstreet**, son of Oscar Azle Broadstreet and Martha Jane Wallace, was born on February 27, 1916 in Guilford County, NC. He died on September 20, 2008.

Lillian Marie Blakeley was born on March 21, 1927. She died on October 20, 2008. She and Merrill Rex Broadstreet had the following children:

> 3165   Martha Jane Broadstreet (1957-). *Martha was born on June 26, 1957 in Montgomery County, NC.*

1304. **Margaret Broadstreet**, daughter of Oscar Azle Broadstreet and Martha Jane Wallace, was born on June 6, 1921 in Guilford County, NC. She died on June 15, 1998.

1305. **Catherine Broadstreet**, daughter of Oscar Azle Broadstreet and Martha Jane Wallace, was born on May 28, 1927.

Lawrence Eugene Ingold was born on August 31, 1924. He died on May 12, 1994.

1306. **Ruby Mae Wallace**, daughter of Kenneth Carson "Kennie" Wallace and Laura A. Hinshaw, was born on June 18, 1915.

1307. **Lindsay Lee Wallace**, son of Kenneth Carson "Kennie" Wallace and Laura A. Hinshaw, was born on September 6, 1917 in Guilford County, NC. He died on August 13, 1919 in Greensboro, Guilford County, NC and was buried on August 14, 1919 in Greensboro, Guilford County, NC at Green Hill Cemetery.

1308. **Carl Edison Wallace**, son of Kenneth Carson "Kennie" Wallace and Laura A. Hinshaw, was born on January 13, 1919 in Guilford County, NC. He died on February 3, 1989.

Rachel Lugenia Elkins and Carl Edison Wallace had the following children:

> 3166   Rosemary Wallace (-)

1309. **Mary Frances Wallace**, daughter of Kenneth Carson "Kennie" Wallace and Laura A. Hinshaw, was born on April 22, 1922 in Guilford County, NC. She died on December 15, 1974 in Greensboro, Guilford County, NC and was buried in Greensboro, Guilford County, NC at Westminster Gardens.

1310. **Norman Hinshaw "Stick" Wallace**, son of Kenneth Carson "Kennie" Wallace and Laura A. Hinshaw, was born on July 22, 1924 in Guilford County, NC. He died on January 18, 2007 in Greensboro, Guilford County, NC and was buried in Greensboro, Guilford County, NC at Green Hill Cemetery.

1318. **Hildred Pauline Wallace**, daughter of Edward Lee Wallace and Allie Gibson, was born on September 10, 1925 in Moore County, NC. She died on May 22, 2006 and was buried in Greensboro, Guilford County, NC at Guilford Memorial Park.

Thurston Hoover Reeder, son of Peter Jason Reeder Sr. (1890-1971) and Eula Green Scott (1896-1977), was born on June 27, 1921. He died on July 28, 1983 and was buried in Greensboro, Guilford County, NC at Guilford Memorial Park. He and Hildred Pauline Wallace had the following children:

> 3167   Thurston Hoover Reeder Jr. (1947-). *Thurston was born on January 25, 1947 in Guilford County, NC.*

1319. **Mildred Louvene Wallace**, daughter of Edward Lee Wallace and Allie Gibson, was born on September 10, 1925 in Moore County, NC. She died on May 27, 2008 in Greensboro, Guilford County, NC and was buried in Greensboro, Guilford County, NC at Guilford Memorial Park.

Dewey Wilson Moore was born on March 10, 1925 in SC. He died on May 14, 1991 in Greensboro, Guilford County, NC and was buried in Greensboro, Guilford County, NC at Guilford Memorial Park. He and Mildred Louvene Wallace had the following children:

> 3168   Donald Wallace Moore (-)
> 3169   Ray Moore (-)
> 3170   Judy Moore (-)

Fred Norman Walker was born on May 11, 1926. He died on June 5, 1981 in High Point, Guilford County, NC. He and Mildred Louvene Wallace had the following children:

> 3171   Fred I. Walker (-)
> 3172   Norma Walker (-)

1320. **Doris K. Wallace**, daughter of Edward Lee Wallace and Allie Gibson, was born on December 6, 1926 in Guilford County, NC.

1321. **Billie M. Wallace**, daughter of Edward Lee Wallace and Allie Gibson, was born on September 4, 1929 in Guilford County, NC.

1322. **William Wesley Wallace**, son of Edward Lee Wallace and Allie Gibson, was born on August 18, 1942. He died on June 6, 1999.

1329. **Rebecca Morphis**, daughter of Robert Cummings Morphis and Nannie Florence Wallace, was born on October 16, 1915. She married **William Joseph "Bill" Woodward** on November 17, 1937. She died on September 3, 1991 and was buried in Randolph County, NC at Tucker Family Cemetery.

William Joseph "Bill" Woodward was born on June 16, 1914. He died on December 17, 1986 and was buried in Randolph County, NC at Tucker Family Cemetery.

1330. **Charles Wallace Morphis**, son of Robert Cummings Morphis and Nannie Florence Wallace, was born on April 2, 1917 in Greensboro, Guilford County, NC. He died on April 30, 1917 in Greensboro, Guilford County, NC and was buried in Wentworth, Guilford County, NC at Wentworth Presbyterian Church.

1331. **Beatrice Morphis**, daughter of Robert Cummings Morphis and Nannie Florence Wallace, was born on October 29, 1918 in Greensboro, Guilford County, NC. She married **William Alexander Cross Jr.** in October 1940. She died on May 21, 2003 in Panama City, Bay County, FL and was buried on June 1, 2003 in Asheboro, Randolph County, NC at Oaklawn Cemetery.

William Alexander Cross Jr. was born on March 23, 1916. He died on July 27, 1991 in Durham, Durham County, NC and was buried in Asheboro, Randolph County, NC at Oaklawn Cemetery. He and Beatrice Morphis had the following children:

> 3173   James Michael "Mike" Cross (1941-). *James was born on August 9, 1941 in Asheboro,*
> *Randolph County, NC. He married **Sara Margaret Thomas** on August 2, 1963.*
> 3174   Nancy Louise Cross (1952-1952). *Nancy was born on November 10, 1952. She died on*
> *November 10, 1952 and was buried in Asheboro, Randolph County, NC at*
> *Oaklawn Cemetery.*

1332. **Donald Barrymore Morphis**, son of Robert Cummings Morphis and Nannie Florence Wallace, was born on August 26, 1923 in Moore County, NC. He married **Betty Jean Britt** on March 24, 1949 in Moore County, NC. He died on April 28, 1997 in Moore County, NC and was buried in Robbins, Moore County, NC at Pine Rest Cemetery.

Betty Jean Britt, daughter of Andrew Dewey Britt (1905-1985) and Essie Lena Garner (1910-1994), was born on April 27, 1930.

1333. **William Hampton "Bud" Garner**, son of Stephen Garner and Catherine Elizabeth Yow, was born on August 30, 1873. He married **Bertha Ann Fields** on April 17, 1892 in Moore County, NC. He died on April 17, 1925 in Lee County, NC.

Bertha Ann Fields, daughter of Catherine A. "Kate" Fields (1851-1923), was born on June 14, 1876. She died on October 20, 1901 and was buried in Moore County, NC at Cool Springs United Methodist Church. She and William Hampton "Bud" Garner had the following children:

> 3175   Martha B. Garner (1896-1918). *Martha was born on January 10, 1896. She died on*
> *February 6, 1918 and was buried in Moore County, NC at Cool Springs United*

Methodist Church.

3176   Henry Harrison Garner (1898-1970). *Henry was born on September 30, 1898. He died on February 14, 1970 and was buried in Sanford, Lee County, NC at Lee Memorial Gardens.*

1334. **John Marshall Garner**, son of Stephen Garner and Catherine Elizabeth Yow, was born on September 29, 1873. He married **Sarah Jane Hasty** circa 1900. He died on September 27, 1942 in Griffin Clinic, Asheboro, Randolph County, NC and was buried on September 28, 1942 in Robbins, Moore County, NC at Tabernacle United Methodist Church.

Sarah Jane Hasty was born on September 17, 1871. She died on March 23, 1943 and was buried on March 24, 1943 in Randleman, Randolph County, NC at St. Paul Cemetery. She and John Marshall Garner had the following children:

3177   Vivian Garner (1902-). *Vivian was born in 1902.*
3178   Paul Garner (1904-1917). *Paul was born on July 21, 1904. He died on July 18, 1917 and was buried in Robbins, Moore County, NC at Tabernacle United Methodist Church.*
3179   Ellen E. Garner (1907-). *Ellen was born in 1907.*
3180   Mary H. Garner (1909-). *Mary was born in 1909.*

1335. **Charles Frank Garner**, son of Stephen Garner and Catherine Elizabeth Yow, was born on February 24, 1879. He married **Letha Frances Kennedy** on December 24, 1896 in Moore County, NC. He died on October 14, 1956 and was buried in Robbins, Moore County, NC at Pine Rest Cemetery.

Letha Frances Kennedy, daughter of Enoch Spinks Kennedy (1842-1908) and Emeline F. Williams (1846-1932), was born on October 22, 1872. She died on August 24, 1965 in Moore County, NC and was buried in Robbins, Moore County, NC at Pine Rest Cemetery. She and Charles Frank Garner had the following children:

3181   Charles Lee Garner (1897-). *Charles was born in November 1897.*
3182   Pearlie Haywood Garner (1901-1990). *Pearlie was born on August 14, 1901. He died on January 2, 1990 and was buried in Robbins, Moore County, NC at Pine Rest Cemetery.*
3183   Ethel Garner (1904-1980). *Ethel was born on March 5, 1904. She died on November 2, 1980 and was buried in Moore County, NC at Unity Grove Baptist Church.*
3184   Ivey Franklin Garner (1906-1968). *Ivey was born on December 14, 1906. He died on April 22, 1968 and was buried in Robbins, Moore County, NC at Pine Rest Cemetery.*
3185   Lillie Alma Garner (1910-). *Lillie was born on April 16, 1910.*
3186   Curtis T. Garner (1913-1976). *Curtis was born on October 11, 1913. He died on April 14, 1976 and was buried in Robbins, Moore County, NC at Pine Rest Cemetery.*
3187   Irene Zadia Garner (1916-). *Irene was born on June 16, 1916.*

1338. **Myrtle E. Garner**, daughter of Stephen Garner and Catherine Elizabeth Yow, was born on October 17, 1884. She married **George Bowman** on February 20, 1929. She died on October 13, 1971 in Randolph County, NC and was buried in Randleman, Randolph County, NC at St. Paul Cemetery.

Cecil Lowe was born in 1890. He died before 1920. He and Myrtle E. Garner had the following children:

3188   Beulah E. Lowe (1914-). *Beulah was born in 1914.*
3189   Ruby A. Lowe (1915-). *Ruby was born in 1915.*
3190   Clyde E. Lowe (1920-). *Clyde was born in 1920.*

George Bowman was born on July 10, 1874. He died on May 24, 1935. He and Myrtle E. Garner had the following children:

3191   Elmer Mason Bowman (1930-). *Elmer was born on March 11, 1930.*

Myrtle E. Garner had the following children:

| 3192 | John Garner (1905-1971). *John was born on June 26, 1905. He died on November 27, 1971 in Asheboro, Randolph County, NC and was buried in Moore County, NC at Flint Hill Baptist Church.* |

1339. Nettie J. Garner, daughter of Stephen Garner and Catherine Elizabeth Yow, was born on June 5, 1887. She died on April 6, 1922.

1340. Tessa Ada Garner, daughter of Stephen Garner and Catherine Elizabeth Yow, was born on June 5, 1887. She died on August 11, 1965 and was buried in Moore County, NC at Flint Hill Baptist Church.

1341. Clem Cassidy "Cass" Garner, son of Stephen Garner and Catherine Elizabeth Yow, was born on June 2, 1890. He died on June 23, 1963.

Dorcus Hunt was born on May 7, 1892. She died on April 6, 1929. She and Clem Cassidy "Cass" Garner had the following children:

| 3193 | Garland Garner (1909-). *Garland was born in 1909.* |

1342. James Hampton B. Garner, son of Stephen Garner and Catherine Elizabeth Yow, was born on October 5, 1892. He died on October 26, 1939 and was buried in Moore County, NC at Flint Hill Baptist Church.

Fannie Chandler was born on December 23, 1895. She died on February 11, 1964 and was buried in Moore County, NC at Flint Hill Baptist Church. She and James Hampton B. Garner had the following children:

3194	James S. Garner (1911-1914). *James was born on February 2, 1911 in Moore County, NC. He died on December 13, 1914.*
3195	Jessie E. Garner (1913-1914). *Jessie was born on May 2, 1913 in Moore County, NC. She died on November 26, 1914.*
3196	Jane Elizabeth Garner (1913-1914). *Jane was born on May 27, 1913 in Moore County, NC. She died on March 27, 1914 and was buried in Robbins, Moore County, NC at Tabernacle United Methodist Church.*
3197	Hughie Edward Garner (1915-1940). *Hughie was born on May 27, 1915 in Moore County, NC. He died on September 26, 1940 and was buried in Moore County, NC at Flint Hill Baptist Church.*
3198	Henry Grady Garner (1917-2010). *Henry was born on September 9, 1917 in Moore County, NC. He died on November 23, 2010.*
3199	Fred Norman Garner (1919-1966). *Fred was born on November 20, 1919 in Moore County, NC. He died on January 20, 1966 and was buried in Robbins, Moore County, NC at Pine Rest Cemetery.*
3200	M. Margaret Garner (1922-). *M. was born on January 9, 1922 in Moore County, NC.*
3201	Pauline R. Garner (1923-1951). *Pauline was born on December 4, 1923. She died on November 7, 1951 and was buried in Whispering Pines, Moore County, NC at Yates-Thagard Baptist Church.*
3202	Virginia D. Garner (1925-). *Virginia was born in 1925.*
3203	James Hoover Garner (1928-). *James was born on September 15, 1928.*
3204	Wade Hampton Garner (1931-). *Wade was born on February 3, 1931 in Moore County, NC.*
3205	Mabel Frances Garner (1933-). *Mabel was born on January 30, 1933 in Moore County, NC.*
3206	Jimmy Landon Garner (1937-1974). *Jimmy was born on April 28, 1937 in Moore County, NC. He died on November 5, 1974 and was buried in Robbins, Moore County, NC at Pine Rest Cemetery.*
3207	Larry M. Garner (1939-). *Larry was born on September 5, 1939 in Moore County, NC.*

1343. John Fuller Williams, son of Leonard Garner and Ann Williams, was born on September 28, 1867 in Moore County, NC. He married **Elizabeth Sheffield** on July 15, 1894 in Moore County, NC. He died on October 3, 1945 in Moore County, NC and was buried on October 5, 1945 in Moore County, NC at Dover Baptist Church.

Elizabeth Sheffield, daughter of William A. Sheffield (1835-1911) and Nancy Ann Owen (1842-), was born on December 15, 1874. She died on March 13, 1956 and was buried in Moore County, NC at Dover Baptist Church. She and John Fuller Williams had the following children:

3208	William Williams (1895-1918). *William was born on June 15, 1895. He died on September 29, 1918 and was buried in Moore County, NC at Dover Baptist Church.*
3209	Mary Ann Williams (1897-1918). *Mary was born on February 11, 1897. She died on September 6, 1918 and was buried in Moore County, NC at Dover Baptist Church.*
3210	Stephen J. Williams (1899-1929). *Stephen was born on January 26, 1899. He died on December 11, 1929 and was buried in Moore County, NC at Dover Baptist Church.*
3211	Alfred Williams (1901-1958). *Alfred was born on February 24, 1901. He died on August 7, 1958 and was buried in Moore County, NC at Dover Baptist Church.*
3212	Frank Williams (1904-). *Frank was born in 1904.*
3213	Sarah Jane Williams (1907-). *Sarah was born in 1907.*
3214	Amy F. Williams (1909-). *Amy was born in 1909.*
3215	John L. Williams (1911-). *John was born in 1911.*
3216	Noah Lee Williams (1914-). *Noah was born in 1914.*
3217	Elmer Williams (1917-). *Elmer was born in 1917.*
3218	Charlie C. Williams (1918-1918). *Charlie was born on June 28, 1918. He died on July 3, 1918 and was buried in Moore County, NC at Dover Baptist Church.*
3219	Curtis Williams (1920-1970). *Curtis was born on January 23, 1920. He died on June 16, 1970 and was buried in Moore County, NC at Dover Baptist Church.*

1344. **James Frank Garner**, son of Leonard Garner and Sarah Emmaline Stutts, was born on January 6, 1878. He married **Julia Ann McNeill** on July 30, 1905. He died on December 10, 1953 and was buried in Seagrove, Randolph County, NC at Union Grove Baptist Church.

Julia Ann McNeill, daughter of Malcolm Alexander McNeill (1845-1913) and Ruth Elizabeth Lawrence (1847-1928), was born on November 2, 1886. She died on October 25, 1929 and was buried in Seagrove, Randolph County, NC at Union Grove Baptist Church. She and James Frank Garner had the following children:

3220	James Ralph Garner (1907-1967). *James was born on January 6, 1907. He died on April 30, 1967 and was buried in Seagrove, Randolph County, NC at Union Grove Baptist Church.*
3221	Wade Hampton Garner (1908-1963). *Wade was born on October 15, 1908. He died on October 9, 1963 and was buried in Seagrove, Randolph County, NC at Union Grove Baptist Church.*
3222	Theodore Garner (1909-). *Theodore was born in 1909.*
3223	Howard McNeill Garner (1910-1967). *Howard was born on March 20, 1910. He died on April 10, 1967 and was buried in Seagrove, Randolph County, NC at Union Grove Baptist Church.*
3224	Charles B. Garner (1913-). *Charles was born in 1913.*
3225	Roy A. Garner (1914-1974). *Roy was born on September 24, 1914. He died on February 16, 1974 and was buried in Seagrove, Randolph County, NC at Union Grove Baptist Church.*
3226	Lena Estelle Garner (1917-). *Lena was born on December 7, 1917.*

1345. **William G. Garner**, son of Leonard Garner and Sarah Emmaline Stutts, was born on February 18, 1882. He died on December 19, 1945 and was buried in Moore County, NC at Flint Hill Baptist Church.

1346. **Sarah Eliza Garner**, daughter of Leonard Garner and Mary Ella Maness, was born on May 18, 1891. She died on June 28, 1974 and was buried in Robbins, Moore County, NC at Pine Rest Cemetery.

James Gilbert Page, son of Gilbert Martin Page (1862-1925) and Nancy Ann "Nannie" Reynolds (1871-1954), was born on December 25, 1890. He died on August 19, 1958 and was buried in Robbins, Moore County, NC at Pine Rest Cemetery. He and Sarah Eliza Garner had the following children:

3227	Euna Belle Page (1917-). *Euna was born on April 28, 1917 in Moore County, NC.*
3228	Leonard M. Page (1920-1981). *Leonard was born on October 4, 1920. He died on September 24, 1981 and was buried in Robbins, Moore County, NC at Pine Rest Cemetery.*
3229	James Joseph Page (1923-). *James was born on July 26, 1923 in Moore County, NC.*

1347. John Thomas Garner, son of Leonard Garner and Mary Ella Maness, was born on January 23, 1893. He died on December 31, 1974 in Moore County, NC and was buried in Moore County, NC at Flint Hill Baptist Church.

Bertha Garner, daughter of William Taylor Garner (1856-1936) and Martha Ann Furr (1865-1948), was born on May 23, 1889. She died on April 23, 1972 and was buried in Moore County, NC at Flint Hill Baptist Church. She and John Thomas Garner had the following children:

3230	Marie Garner (-)
3231	Clinton Garner (1924-1992). *Clinton was born on February 5, 1924. He died on May 9, 1992 and was buried in Moore County, NC at Flint Hill Baptist Church.*
3232	Esther Garner (1925-1925). *Esther was born on July 28, 1925 in Moore County, NC. She died in 1925 and was buried in Moore County, NC at Flint Hill Baptist Church.*
3233	Howard Garner (1926-1926). *Howard was born in 1926. He died in 1926 and was buried in Moore County, NC at Flint Hill Baptist Church.*
3234	Alice Garner (1927-1927). *Alice was born in 1927. She died in 1927 and was buried in Moore County, NC at Flint Hill Baptist Church.*
3235	William Leonard "Cooch" Garner (1928-1980). *William was born on May 30, 1928. He died on May 5, 1980 in Moore County, NC and was buried in Moore County, NC at Flint Hill Baptist Church.*
3236	James Ernest "Booch" Garner (1931-1998). *James was born on December 23, 1931 in Moore County, NC. He died on January 31, 1998 in Moore County, NC and was buried in Moore County, NC at Flint Hill Baptist Church.*

1348. Edgar Addison Garner, son of Leonard Garner and Mary Ella Maness, was born on July 19, 1896. He married **Hattie Mae Simson** on March 11, 1916 in Guilford County, NC. He died on August 11, 1932.

Hattie Mae Simson was born on January 1, 1898. She died on August 25, 1981. She and Edgar Addison Garner had the following children:

| 3237 | Garner (-) |

1349. Delaney Harrison Garner, son of Leonard Garner and Mary Ella Maness, was born on May 9, 1899. He married **Etta Jennette Wallace** on January 7, 1922 in Moore County, NC. He died on October 25, 1990 and was buried in Moore County, NC at Flint Hill Baptist Church.

Etta Jennette Wallace, daughter of James Lewis Wallace (1875-1950) and Lillie Jane Maness (1884-1919), was born on March 25, 1903. She died on September 26, 1984 in Moore County, NC and was buried in Moore County, NC at Flint Hill Baptist Church. She and Delaney Harrison Garner had the following children:

3238	James Herman Garner (1922-1987). *James was born on October 15, 1922. He died on April 16, 1987 and was buried in Moore County, NC at Flint Hill Baptist Church.*
3239	Maggie Lucille Garner (1924-). *Maggie was born on September 19, 1924.*
3240	Jesse Leonard Garner (1926-2000). *Jesse was born on October 14, 1926. He died on July 19, 2000 and was buried in Moore County, NC at Brown's Chapel Christian Church.*
3241	Neuby Clarence Garner (1928-2020). *Neuby was born on December 7, 1928. He died on January 19, 2020 and was buried in Carthage, Moore County, NC at Putnam Friends Church.*
3242	Lyndon Bobby Garner (1931-1931). *Lyndon was born on March 5, 1931. He died on April 2, 1931 in Moore County, NC.*
3243	Quimby Lewis Garner (1932-2005). *Quimby was born on March 14, 1932. He died on November 1, 2005.*
3244	Maggie Ruth Garner (1934-). *Maggie was born on November 30, 1934. She married*

Daniel Lee Garner on May 17, 2001 in Moore County, NC.

3245	Thurman Winfred Garner (1937-). *Thurman was born on April 3, 1937.*
3246	Lanie Edward Garner (1940-2003). *Lanie was born on February 10, 1940. He died on November 19, 2003 and was buried in Moore County, NC at Flint Hill Baptist Church.*
3247	Delaney Harrison "Lannie" Garner Jr. (1942-2006). *Delaney was born on December 12, 1942 in Moore County, NC. He died on May 3, 2006 and was buried in Robbins, Moore County, NC at Tabernacle United Methodist Church.*

1351. **Mary Alice Rebecca "Mamie" Garner**, daughter of Leonard Garner and Mary Ella Maness, was born on April 11, 1905. She married **Burley Leaton Cockman** on April 11, 1925. She died on March 18, 1969 and was buried in Moore County, NC at Flint Hill Baptist Church.

Burley Leaton Cockman, son of Charles Riley O'Leonard Emsley Rufus Cockman (1860-1922) and Lou Vicie Brown (1863-1942), was born on April 27, 1901 in Moore County, NC. He died on January 23, 1968 in Moore County, NC and was buried on January 25, 1968 in Moore County, NC at Flint Hill Baptist Church. He and Mary Alice Rebecca "Mamie" Garner had the following children:

3248	Neuby Ralph Cockman (1929-)
3249	Janie Cockman (-)
3250	Riley Leonard Cockman (1926-2002). *Riley was born on March 6, 1926. He married **Mary Elaine "Elaine" Maness** on September 5, 1953. He died on March 30, 2002 in Moore County, NC and was buried in Biscoe, Montgomery County, NC at Biscoe Cemetery.*
3251	Robert Edgar Cockman (1927-1979). *Robert was born on April 2, 1927. He died on September 11, 1979 and was buried in Moore County, NC at Flint Hill Baptist Church.*
3252	Luella Mae Cockman (1930-2008). *Luella was born on April 5, 1930. She died on February 21, 2008 and was buried in Moore County, NC at Flint Hill Baptist Church.*
3253	Betty Ruth Cockman (1932-2015). *Betty was born in 1932. She died on July 25, 2015.*
3254	Mozelle Cockman (1933-2018). *Mozelle was born on August 2, 1933. She died on December 29, 2018.*
3255	Jessie Bell Cockman (1935-2009). *Jessie was born on November 26, 1935. She died on September 21, 2009 and was buried in Vass, Moore County, NC at Johnson Grove Cemetery.*
3256	Lillie Estelle Cockman (1938-). *Lillie was born on September 25, 1938.*
3257	Mary Alice Cockman (1941-1989). *Mary was born on March 25, 1941. She died on January 26, 1989 and was buried in Moore County, NC at Flint Hill Baptist Church.*
3258	Freddie Thomas Cockman (1943-2001). *Freddie was born on March 27, 1943. He married **Alice Faye Ivey** on September 19, 1964 in Moore County, NC. He died on July 30, 2001 and was buried in Moore County, NC at Flint Hill Baptist Church.*
3259	Jo Ann Cockman (1945-1945). *Jo was born on February 19, 1945. She died on February 19, 1945 and was buried in Moore County, NC at Flint Hill Baptist Church.*
3260	Billy Ray Cockman (1948-1948). *Billy was born on June 17, 1948. He died on June 17, 1948 and was buried in Moore County, NC at Flint Hill Baptist Church.*

1353. **Lucy Jane Garner**, daughter of James Douglas Garner and Lydia Ann Riddle, was born on April 5, 1883. She married **Lonnie Meritt Maness** on December 23, 1902 in Moore County, NC. She died on September 8, 1966 and was buried in Moore County, NC at Pleasant Hill United Methodist Church.

Lonnie Meritt Maness, son of John H. Brady (1864-) and Mary Ella Maness (1862-1942), was born on May 29, 1883. He died on August 30, 1971 in Rockingham, Richmond County, NC and was buried on August 31, 1971 in Moore County, NC at Pleasant Hill United Methodist Church. He and Lucy Jane Garner had the following children:

3261	Infant Maness (1913-1913). *Infant was born in 1913. He died in 1913 and was buried in Moore County, NC at Pleasant Hill United Methodist Church.*
3262	Wilmer Merrill Maness (1915-1994). *Wilmer was born on August 12, 1915. He died on*

November 23, 1994 and was buried in Moore County, NC at Pleasant Hill United Methodist Church.

3263   Tennie A. Maness (1919-). *Tennie was born in 1919.*

1354. **Infant Garner**, son of James Douglas Garner and Lydia Ann Riddle, was born on June 1, 1884. He died on June 1, 1884 and was buried in Moore County, NC at Flint Hill Baptist Church.

1355. **Riley Blake Garner**, son of James Douglas Garner and Lydia Ann Riddle, was born on July 4, 1886. He married **Lillie Moore** on December 11, 1916 in Linden, Cumberland County, NC. He died on May 13, 1972 in Moore County, NC and was buried in Moore County, NC at Calvary Baptist Church.

Lillie Moore was born on July 4, 1898. She died on August 29, 1958 and was buried in Moore County, NC at Calvary Baptist Church. She and Riley Blake Garner had the following children:

3264   Derotha C. Garner (1917-). *Derotha was born on December 15, 1917.*
3265   Henry Douglas Garner (1921-1973). *Henry was born on December 12, 1921. He died on March 15, 1973 in Moore County, NC and was buried in Moore County, NC at Calvary Baptist Church.*
3266   Jessie E. Garner (1923-1962). *Jessie was born on March 2, 1923. He died on January 2, 1962 and was buried in Moore County, NC at Calvary Baptist Church.*
3267   Daniel Lee Garner (1927-2013). *Daniel was born on May 26, 1927. He married **Maggie Ruth Garner** on May 17, 2001 in Moore County, NC. He died on December 27, 2013 and was buried in Moore County, NC at Calvary Baptist Church.*
3268   Sally Ann Garner (1927-2002). *Sally was born on June 5, 1927. She died on April 29, 2002 and was buried in Moore County, NC at Calvary Baptist Church.*
3269   Mary Evelyn Garner (1929-). *Mary was born on May 17, 1929 in Moore County, NC.*
3270   Clara Belle Garner (1931-1994). *Clara was born on October 20, 1931. She died on February 19, 1994 and was buried in Moore County, NC at Calvary Baptist Church.*
3271   Josephine Garner (1934-). *Josephine was born on November 7, 1934 in Moore County, NC.*

1356. **James Alfred Garner**, son of James Douglas Garner and Lydia Ann Riddle, was born on April 7, 1888. He died on June 20, 1956 in Moore County, NC and was buried in Moore County, NC at Flint Hill Baptist Church.

1357. **William Lewis Garner**, son of James Douglas Garner and Lydia Ann Riddle, was born on September 22, 1893. He died on September 10, 1969 and was buried in Moore County, NC at Pleasant Hill United Methodist Church.

Etta C. Williams, daughter of George Bryant Williams (1856-1940) and Sarah Alice Kennedy (1861-1921), was born on July 24, 1893. She died on July 26, 1961 in Randolph County, NC and was buried in Moore County, NC at Pleasant Hill United Methodist Church. She and William Lewis Garner had the following children:

3272   Mary Jane Garner (-)
3273   Etta Faye Garner (-)
3274   Dorothy Garner (-)
3275   Geneva Garner (-)
3276   Teresa Garner (-)
3277   Roy Garner (-)
3278   Archie Garner (1914-1914). *Archie was born on May 25, 1914. He died on May 25, 1914 and was buried in Moore County, NC at Pleasant Hill United Methodist Church.*
3279   Eva Alice Garner (1915-1994). *Eva was born on May 12, 1915. She died on December 31, 1994 in Randolph County, NC.*
3280   Claudie Garner (1923-1923). *Claudie was born on October 25, 1923. He died on October 25, 1923 and was buried in Moore County, NC at Pleasant Hill United Methodist Church.*
3281   Riley Garner (1931-1931). *Riley was born on February 2, 1931. He died on February 2, 1931 and was buried in Moore County, NC at Pleasant Hill United Methodist Church.*

1358. **John Earlie Garner**, son of James Douglas Garner and Lillie Alma Maness, was born on September 12, 1896. He married **Maggie Clark** on September 22, 1924 in Lee County, NC. He died on September 20, 1987 and was buried in Moore County, NC at Flint Hill Baptist Church.

Margaret Frances Marley, daughter of Milton Sylvester Marley (1870-1958) and Francis Perrillar "Fannie" Ritter (1875-1958), was born on March 3, 1904. She died on June 5, 1993 and was buried in Moore County, NC at Flint Hill Baptist Church. She and John Earlie Garner had the following children:

3282	Susie Garner (-)
3283	Marinda Garner (1940-). *Marinda was born on March 21, 1940 in Moore County, NC.*

Maggie Clark, daughter of Joshua H. Clark (1862-1918) and Ella Hart (1870-1921), was born in 1904. She died in 1936 and was buried in Moore County, NC at Flint Hill Baptist Church. She and John Earlie Garner had the following children:

3284	Lucinda "Cindy" Garner (-)
3285	Joe John Garner (1931-2010). *Joe was born on October 2, 1931. He died on September 8, 2010 in Fayetteville, Cumberland County, NC and was buried on September 11, 2010 in Moore County, NC at Flint Hill Baptist Church.*
3286	James Duncan Garner (1933-). *James was born on October 22, 1933 in Moore County, NC.*
3287	Bobby Josh Garner (1936-). *Bobby was born on March 13, 1936 in Moore County, NC.*

1359. **William Addison Garner**, son of James Douglas Garner and Lillie Alma Maness, was born on November 19, 1898 in Moore County, NC. He married **Emma Rickman** on May 7, 1922 in Pottawatomie County, OK. He died on February 28, 1965 in Moore County, NC and was buried on March 3, 1965 in Shawnee, Pottawatomie County, OK at Fairview Cemetery.

Emma Rickman was born on March 30, 1893 in Perryville, Perry County, AR. She married Fred I. Wallace on July 1, 1909 in Perryville, Perry County, AR. She died on March 18, 1928 in Shawnee, Pottawatomie County, OK and was buried in Shawnee, Pottawatomie County, OK at Fairview Cemetery. She and William Addison Garner had the following children:

3288	Ruby Mae Garner (1924-1996). *Ruby was born on February 3, 1924. She died on July 8, 1996.*
3289	Vernon Lee Garner (1926-1959). *Vernon was born on February 6, 1926. He died on May 11, 1959.*
3290	Ruth Jeane Garner (1928-1928). *Ruth was born on February 28, 1928. She died on March 30, 1928 and was buried in Shawnee, Pottawatomie County, OK at Fairview Cemetery.*

1360. **Elias Garner**, son of James Douglas Garner and Lillie Alma Maness, was born on August 2, 1901. He died on November 29, 1972 in Moore County, NC and was buried in Moore County, NC at Calvary Baptist Church.

Alene May Sheffield, daughter of Ernest Sheffield (1881-1936) and Martha Jane Morgan (1884-1941), was born on May 14, 1903. She died on July 27, 1976 and was buried in Moore County, NC at Calvary Baptist Church. She and Elias Garner had the following children:

3291	Dossie Louise Garner (1930-1970). *Dossie was born on April 17, 1930. She died on August 15, 1970 and was buried in Moore County, NC at Flint Hill Baptist Church.*
3292	Douglas James Garner (1931-). *Douglas was born on August 19, 1931.*
3293	Daisy Mae Garner (1933-). *Daisy was born on March 9, 1933.*
3294	Dora Marie Garner (1938-). *Dora was born on July 21, 1938.*
3295	Faye Lorine "Pinkie" Garner (1940-). *Faye was born on February 13, 1940.*
3296	Elias Garner Jr. (1944-). *Elias was born on November 4, 1944.*

1361. **Mary Eliza Garner**, daughter of James Douglas Garner and Lillie Alma Maness, was born on January 3, 1904 in Moore County, NC.

1362. **Lockey Merriott Garner**, son of James Douglas Garner and Lillie Alma Maness, was born on December 9, 1905 in Moore County, NC. He married **Emma Mae Wallace** on July 19, 1925. He died on July 3, 1992 and was buried in Moore County, NC at Flint Hill Baptist Church.

      Faye Akins was born on January 17, 1911. She died on December 20, 1993 and was buried in Moore County, NC at Flint Hill Baptist Church.

      Emma Mae Wallace, daughter of Isham Wallace (1882-1962) and Flora Britt (1884-1946), was born on March 22, 1908 in Moore County, NC. She died on May 17, 1995 and was buried in Moore County, NC at Big Oak Church. She and Lockey Merriott Garner had the following children:

3297	Worthy Addison Garner (1926-2009). *Worthy was born on June 30, 1926 in Moore County, NC. He married **Texie Edder Garner** on June 2, 1945. He died on July 15, 2009 in Moore Regional Hospital, Pinehurst, Moore County, NC and was buried on July 18, 2009 in Moore County, NC at Flint Hill Baptist Church.*
3298	Robert Edward Garner (1928-). *Robert was born on March 8, 1928.*

1363. **James Douglas Garner Jr.**, son of James Douglas Garner and Lillie Alma Maness, was born on January 26, 1908. He died on September 16, 1928 and was buried in Moore County, NC at Flint Hill Baptist Church.

1364. **Sarah Ella Garner**, daughter of James Douglas Garner and Lillie Alma Maness, was born on May 4, 1910 in Moore County, NC. She died on August 29, 2005 in Moore County, NC and was buried in Moore County, NC at Flint Hill Baptist Church.

      John Garner, son of Myrtle E. Garner (1884-1971), was born on June 26, 1905. He died on November 27, 1971 in Asheboro, Randolph County, NC and was buried in Moore County, NC at Flint Hill Baptist Church. He and Sarah Ella Garner had the following children:

3299	John Garner Jr. (1928-). *John was born on April 16, 1928 in Moore County, NC.*
3300	Thelma Jean Garner (1930-). *Thelma was born on September 5, 1930.*
3301	Doris Brady Garner (1947-). *Doris was born on June 2, 1947 in Moore County, NC.*

1365. **Pressley Robert Garner**, son of James Douglas Garner and Lillie Alma Maness, was born on October 5, 1912 in Moore County, NC. He died on July 13, 1994 and was buried in Moore County, NC at Flint Hill Baptist Church.

      Mary Lee Brown, daughter of Neil Lee Brown (1895-1923) and Effie Britt (1892-1967), was born on March 26, 1919. She died on October 30, 1988 in Moore County, NC and was buried in Moore County, NC at Flint Hill Baptist Church. She and Pressley Robert Garner had the following children:

3302	Billy Ray Garner (1941-1941). *Billy was born on March 8, 1941. He died on March 8, 1941 in Moore County, NC and was buried in Moore County, NC at Flint Hill Baptist Church.*

1366. **Stephen Harrison Garner Sr.**, son of James Douglas Garner and Lillie Alma Maness, was born on May 26, 1915 in Moore County, NC. He married **Doris Marie Jarrett** on February 21, 1942. He died on April 18, 1999 and was buried on April 20, 1999 in Burlington, Alamance County, NC at Pine Hill Cemetery.

      Doris Marie Jarrett was born on August 10, 1925 in Alamance County, NC. She died on March 8, 1974 and was buried in Burlington, Alamance County, NC at Pine Hill Cemetery. She and Stephen Harrison Garner Sr. had the following children:

3303	Stephen Harrison Garner Jr. (-)
3304	Billy Ray Garner (-)
3305	Gwendolyn Hope Garner (-)

1367. **Laura Alma Garner**, daughter of James Douglas Garner and Lillie Alma Maness, was born on September 17, 1917. She died on May 27, 1997 in Tomball, Harris County, TX.

1368. Ruby Helen Garner, daughter of James Douglas Garner and Lillie Alma Maness, was born on January 11, 1920. She died on August 28, 1939 in Moore County, NC and was buried in Moore County, NC at Flint Hill Baptist Church.

1369. Sarah Catherine Elizabeth Burns, daughter of Henry Lindsey Burns and Martha Jane Garner, was born on May 9, 1876 in Moore County, NC. She married **Angus Alexander "Bud" McKenzie** on October 19, 1892 in Moore County, NC. She died on January 14, 1927.

Angus Alexander "Bud" McKenzie, son of Kenneth Sidney McKenzie (1822-1897) and Mary Ellen Sanders (1844-1915), was born in 1869. He and Sarah Catherine Elizabeth Burns had the following children:

3306	Betty Florence McKenzie (1893-1967). *Betty was born on September 2, 1893 in Moore County, NC. She married **Benjamin Lee "Bud" Van Landingham** on December 27, 1911 in Black, Geneva County, AL at McKenzie Family Home. She died on September 15, 1967 in Flowers Hospital, Dothan, Houston County, AL and was buried on September 18, 1967 in Geneva County, AL at Black Community Cemetery.*
3307	Ida Mae McKenzie (1895-1982). *Ida was born on May 24, 1895 in Moore County, NC. She married **Jesse B. Cranford** in 1915 in Covington County, AL. She died in February 1982 in Mobile, AL and was buried in February 1982 in Mobile, AL at Pinecrest Cemetery.*
3308	Gertrude McKenzie (1899-1909). *Gertrude was born on August 12, 1899 in Moore County, NC. She died on October 31, 1909 in Black, Geneva County, AL and was buried on November 2, 1909 in Black, Geneva County, AL at Adoniram Cemetery.*
3309	Lavada "Vada" McKenzie (1903-1982). *Lavada was born on January 1, 1903 in Black, Geneva County, AL. She died on November 27, 1982 in Hollywood, Broward County, FL and was buried on November 30, 1982 in Dothan, Houston County, AL.*
3310	Robert Clyde "Bud" McKenzie (1904-1970). *Robert was born on December 10, 1904 in Black, Geneva County, AL. He died on May 31, 1970 in Black, Geneva County, AL and was buried in Hartford, Geneva County, AL at Hartford Cemetery.*
3311	Malcolm Comer McKenzie (1906-1939). *Malcolm was born in June 1906 in Black, Geneva County, AL. He died in February 1939 in Washington, DC and was buried in Geneva County, AL at Black Community Cemetery.*
3312	Marjorie Euna McKenzie (1909-1964). *Marjorie was born on December 4, 1909 in Black, Geneva County, AL. She died on January 3, 1964 in Black, Geneva County, AL and was buried on January 5, 1964 in Geneva County, AL at Black Community Cemetery.*
3313	John Jacob Astor McKenzie (1912-1953). *John was born on August 29, 1912 in Black, Geneva County, AL. He died on December 20, 1953 in Phenix City, Russell County, AL and was buried on December 22, 1953 in Geneva County, AL at Black Community Cemetery.*
3314	Zudora McKenzie (1914-1965). *Zudora was born on October 18, 1914 in Black, Geneva County, AL. She died on December 31, 1965 in Phenix City, Russell County, AL and was buried on January 3, 1966 in Phenix City, Russell County, AL.*
3315	Kathrine McKenzie (1920-). *Kathrine was born on July 20, 1920 in Black, Geneva County, AL.*

1370. Zemery Mitchell Burns, son of Henry Lindsey Burns and Martha Jane Garner, was born on August 25, 1876. He married **Armittie Evelyn Cockman** on April 25, 1895 in Moore County, NC. He died on October 31, 1945 and was buried in Robbins, Moore County, NC at Tabernacle United Methodist Church.

Armittie Evelyn Cockman, daughter of John SSGWSQA "Jack" Cockman (1848-1912) and Nancy Jane Melton (1841-1886), was born on May 16, 1879 in Moore County, NC. She died on June 10, 1954 in Baptist Hosptial, Winston-Salem, Forsyth County, NC and was buried on June 13, 1954 in Robbins, Moore County, NC at Tabernacle United Methodist Church. She and Zemery Mitchell Burns had the following children:

3316	Artie Mishia Burns (1896-1964). *Artie was born on October 12, 1896. She married **George Carroll Brown** on May 8, 1919. She died in 1964.*
3317	Robert Lee Burns (1897-1962). *Robert was born on August 25, 1897. He married **Ollie**

	McGregor Jackson on March 27, 1921. He died on November 9, 1962.
3318	Eugenia Burns (1900-). *Eugenia was born on April 3, 1900. She married **Eddie Bryan Morgan** on September 2, 1917.*
3319	Viola Ethel Burns (1904-). *Viola was born on January 27, 1904. She married **William Eddie Tucker** on July 4, 1919.*
3320	Augusta Carlton Burns (1913-1974). *Augusta was born on October 7, 1913. He married **Lillian Frances Renfrew** on October 9, 1934. He died on January 27, 1974.*

1371. **Barney Leason Burns**, son of Henry Lindsey Burns and Martha Jane Garner, was born on April 16, 1878. He died on July 2, 1904 and was buried in Robbins, Moore County, NC at Tabernacle United Methodist Church.

1372. **John Elsevand Burns**, son of Henry Lindsey Burns and Martha Jane Garner, was born in 1880.

Drucilla Bullard and John Elsevand Burns had the following children:

3321	Bessie Burns (-)
3322	Iris Burns (-)

1373. **Annie Jane Burns**, daughter of Henry Lindsey Burns and Martha Jane Garner, was born on December 13, 1883. She died on November 3, 1932 and was buried in Moore County, NC at Bensalem Presbyterian Church.

William Riley Lewis, son of William G. Lewis (1838-) and Sarah Jane Britt (1843-), was born on November 8, 1868. He died on December 19, 1949 and was buried in Moore County, NC at Bensalem Presbyterian Church. He and Annie Jane Burns had the following children:

3323	Leason E. Lewis (1901-1901). *Leason was born on January 10, 1901. He died on January 25, 1901 and was buried in Moore County, NC at Bensalem Presbyterian Church.*
3324	Eter Macie Lewis (1908-1999). *Eter was born on August 3, 1908. She married **Ollie Leaton Williams** on September 1, 1926 in Moore County, NC. She died on December 28, 1999.*
3325	Lessie Mae Lewis (1910-1991). *Lessie was born on October 19, 1910. She died on June 14, 1991 and was buried in Robbins, Moore County, NC at Pine Rest Cemetery.*
3326	Blennie Edna Lewis (1921-). *Blennie was born on September 11, 1921. She married **Atlas Emerson Williams** on May 26, 1937 in Moore County, NC.*

1374. **Enoch Harrison "Buddy" Burns**, son of Henry Lindsey Burns and Martha Jane Garner, was born on November 20, 1885. He married **Minnie L. D. Morgan** on August 18, 1907 in Moore County, NC. He married **Mary Britt** after 1922. He died on November 25, 1949 and was buried in Moore County, NC at Bensalem Presbyterian Church.

Minnie L. D. Morgan, daughter of Mark Allen Morgan (1854-1934) and Margaret Elizabeth "Eliza" Monroe (1862-1940), was born on February 2, 1886. She died on December 22, 1922 and was buried in Robbins, Moore County, NC at Tabernacle United Methodist Church. She and Enoch Harrison "Buddy" Burns had the following children:

3327	Clinton Burns (-)
3328	Leon Burns (-)
3329	Lonnie Burns (-)
3330	Clio Burns (1910-). *Clio was born in 1910.*
3331	Clemith Fletcher Burns (1912-1963). *Clemith was born on January 16, 1912. He died on January 28, 1963 and was buried in Moore County, NC at Brown's Chapel Christian Church.*
3332	Emery Lee Burns (1913-1960). *Emery was born on October 16, 1913. He died on February 28, 1960 and was buried in Moore County, NC at Big Oak Church.*
3333	Swannie Burns (1916-). *Swannie was born in 1916.*
3334	Henry L. Burns (1917-1917). *Henry was born on June 27, 1917. He died on June 27, 1917 and was buried in Robbins, Moore County, NC at Tabernacle United Methodist Church.*
3335	Burlie Hutton Burns (1918-1987). *Burlie was born on August 16, 1918. He died on October 13, 1987 and was buried in Thomasville, Davidson County, NC at Holly Hill Memorial Park.*

Mary Britt, daughter of Daniel Bethune Britt (1845-1927) and Lydia Freeman (1848-1918), was born on December 28, 1887. She died on February 8, 1948 and was buried in Moore County, NC at Bensalem Presbyterian Church.

1375. **Hattie Bell Burns**, daughter of Henry Lindsey Burns and Martha Jane Garner, was born on September 17, 1887. She married **Murdoch M. Stutts** circa 1904. She died on August 22, 1963 in Liberty, Randolph County, NC and was buried on August 25, 1963 in Moore County, NC at Bensalem Presbyterian Church.

Murdoch M. Stutts, son of Henry W. Stutts (1832-1904) and Mary Ann Martin (1841-1897), was born on May 20, 1866. He died on April 6, 1926 and was buried in Moore County, NC at Bensalem Presbyterian Church. He and Hattie Bell Burns had the following children:

3336	Monnie Mae Stutts (1906-1987). *Monnie was born on June 3, 1906. She married **Isham Thomas Britt** on November 2, 1928 in Moore County, NC. She died on September 8, 1987 and was buried in Moore County, NC at Bensalem Presbyterian Church.*
3337	Kenneth Martin Stutts (1908-1951). *Kenneth was born on July 26, 1908. He died on March 21, 1951 and was buried in Eagle Springs, Moore County, NC at Eagle Springs Presbyterian Church.*
3338	Albert Stutts (1913-). *Albert was born in 1913.*
3339	Roy Stutts (1916-1988). *Roy was born on March 22, 1916. He died on November 28, 1988 and was buried in Moore County, NC at Brown's Chapel Christian Church.*
3340	Robert Stutts (1918-). *Robert was born in 1918.*
3341	Paul Stutts (1920-). *Paul was born in 1920.*

1376. **Ira Nelson Burns**, son of Henry Lindsey Burns and Martha Jane Garner, was born on March 30, 1889. He died on July 30, 1889 and was buried in Robbins, Moore County, NC at Tabernacle United Methodist Church.

1377. **George Ariah Burns**, son of Henry Lindsey Burns and Martha Jane Garner, was born on August 3, 1890. He died on October 2, 1918 and was buried in Robbins, Moore County, NC at Tabernacle United Methodist Church.

1378. **Mary Ellen "Minerva" Burns**, daughter of Henry Lindsey Burns and Martha Jane Garner, was born on May 30, 1893. She died on May 30, 1893 and was buried in Robbins, Moore County, NC at Tabernacle United Methodist Church.

1379. **Sarah Jane Garner**, daughter of Sampson Delaney Garner and Lillie E. Stutts, was born on April 6, 1886. She married **George W. Brown** circa 1907. She died on August 23, 1967 and was buried in Robbins, Moore County, NC at Tabernacle United Methodist Church.

George W. Brown, son of George Rufus Brown (1862-1944) and Mary Ann Maness (1867-1942), was born on December 5, 1886. He died on November 28, 1947 and was buried in Robbins, Moore County, NC at Tabernacle United Methodist Church. He and Sarah Jane Garner had the following children:

3342	Beecher A. Brown (1907-1966). *Beecher was born on August 26, 1907. He died on September 9, 1966 and was buried in Robbins, Moore County, NC at Tabernacle United Methodist Church.*
3343	Lillie Matty Brown (1909-1963). *Lillie was born on September 11, 1909. She died on February 12, 1963 and was buried in Moore County, NC at Unity Grove Baptist Church.*
3344	Lacy Albert Brown (1912-1986). *Lacy was born on May 19, 1912. He died on April 7, 1986 and was buried in Robbins, Moore County, NC at Tabernacle United Methodist Church.*
3345	John Brown (1915-). *John was born in 1915.*
3346	Maggie Brown (1917-). *Maggie was born in 1917.*
3347	Mearl Brown (1919-). *Mearl was born in 1919.*

[Above] **Enoch Harrison Burns. Minnie L.D. Morgan and family** *(Courtesy of Jeff Burns)*

[Right] **Lillie Alma Maness Garner and Ella Garner** *(Courtesy of Lacy Garner, Jr., Carthage, NC)*

[Below] **Lucy Garner Maness, Lonnie Maness and Lillie Alma Maness Garner**
(Courtesy of Billy Garner)

1380. **Connie B. Garner**, daughter of Sampson Delaney Garner and Lillie E. Stutts, was born on September 29, 1888. She married **Beecher C. Williams** on September 12, 1907 in Moore County, NC. She died on August 3, 1979 and was buried in Robbins, Moore County, NC at Tabernacle United Methodist Church.

Beecher C. Williams, son of William Turner Williams (1848-1923) and Martha Florence Stutts (1869-1935), was born on June 29, 1888. He died on January 15, 1951 and was buried in Robbins, Moore County, NC at Tabernacle United Methodist Church. He and Connie B. Garner had the following children:

3348	Laney Carl Williams (1909-). *Laney was born in 1909.*
3349	Connie Essie Williams (1911-1987). *Connie was born on May 1, 1911. She died on May 31, 1987 and was buried in Robbins, Moore County, NC at Tabernacle United Methodist Church.*

1381. **Nancy L. Garner**, daughter of Sampson Delaney Garner and Lillie E. Stutts, was born on November 17, 1890. She died on December 8, 1972 and was buried in Robbins, Moore County, NC at Tabernacle United Methodist Church.

Thomas Jefferson Marley, son of James Ruffin Marley (1846-1909) and Lucinda A. Brown (1849-1924), was born on September 15, 1887. He died on April 25, 1967 and was buried in Robbins, Moore County, NC at Tabernacle United Methodist Church. He and Nancy L. Garner had the following children:

3350	Female Marley (1916-1916). *Female was born on June 2, 1916. She died on June 3, 1916 and was buried in Robbins, Moore County, NC at Tabernacle United Methodist Church.*
3351	Paul Jefferson Marley (1919-1977). *Paul was born on August 14, 1919. He died on January 12, 1977 and was buried in Robbins, Moore County, NC at Pine Rest Cemetery.*
3352	Robert Nathaniel Marley (1928-1989). *Robert was born on April 17, 1928. He died on April 27, 1989 and was buried in Robbins, Moore County, NC at Tabernacle United Methodist Church.*

1382. **Cornelius Robert Garner**, son of Sampson Delaney Garner and Lillie E. Stutts, was born on May 10, 1893. He died on December 14, 1917 and was buried in Robbins, Moore County, NC at Tabernacle United Methodist Church.

1383. **Katie L. Garner**, daughter of Sampson Delaney Garner and Lillie E. Stutts, was born on June 26, 1895. She died on February 2, 1988 and was buried in Robbins, Moore County, NC at Tabernacle United Methodist Church.

James Wesley Brown, son of George W. Brown (1864-1942) and Amanda Ann "Maude" McNeill (1865-1950), was born on August 20, 1891. He died on July 13, 1971 and was buried in Robbins, Moore County, NC at Tabernacle United Methodist Church. He and Katie L. Garner had the following children:

3353	Kathleen Brown (-)
3354	Annie L. Brown (1915-2008). *Annie was born on September 1, 1915. She married **Luther Clegg Williams** on April 15, 1933. She died on December 11, 2008 and was buried in Robbins, Moore County, NC at Tabernacle United Methodist Church.*
3355	Swannie Ellen Brown (1917-2007). *Swannie was born on September 3, 1917. She married **Marvin Thomas Cockman** on May 23, 1935. She died on June 23, 2007 and was buried in Moore County, NC at Rock Hill Church.*
3356	Elsie Elbert Brown (1919-1994). *Elsie was born on September 9, 1919. He died on June 3, 1994 and was buried in Moore County, NC at Rock Hill Church.*
3357	Neil J. Brown (1922-). *Neil was born in 1922.*
3358	Pauline Brown (1925-). *Pauline was born in 1925.*
3359	Charles Daniel Brown (1928-1993). *Charles was born on February 18, 1928. He died on April 30, 1993 and was buried in Moore County, NC at Rock Hill Church.*

1384. **Kinnie Carson Garner**, son of Elias "Lizard" Garner and Anna Jane "Janie" Cockman, was born on July 15, 1888 in Moore County, NC. He died on November 3, 1955 in Hamlet, Richmond County, NC and was buried on November 4, 1955 in Hamlet, Richmond County, NC at Mary Love Cemetery.

1386. Josephine Garner, daughter of Elias "Lizard" Garner and Anna Jane "Janie" Cockman, was born on August 8, 1893 in Moore County, NC. She died on May 27, 1948 in Fayetteville, Cumberland County, NC.

1387. Sara Lucinda Garner, daughter of Elias "Lizard" Garner and Anna Jane "Janie" Cockman, was born on September 3, 1895. She died on September 22, 1935 in Fayetteville, Cumberland County, NC.

1390. Mittie Jane Yow, daughter of Charles Frank Yow and Anna Margaret Garner, was born on August 15, 1890. She died on October 3, 1969.

George Daub Love was born on April 8, 1886. He died on November 8, 1967. He and Mittie Jane Yow had the following children:

3360	Julia Margaret Love (1919-2002). *Julia was born on July 22, 1919. She died on August 18, 2002.*
3361	Mary Elizabeth Love (1928-2005). *Mary was born on March 25, 1928. She died on September 23, 2005.*

1392. John Franklin Yow, son of Charles Frank Yow and Anna Margaret Garner, was born on March 11, 1897. He died on November 14, 1975 and was buried in Sanford, Lee County, NC at Euphronia Presbyterian Church.

1393. Charles Scott Yow, son of Charles Frank Yow and Anna Margaret Garner, was born on July 11, 1898. He died on March 28, 1971 and was buried in Sanford, Lee County, NC at Center United Methodist Church.

Alma Blakely was born on July 11, 1902. She died on July 4, 1989 and was buried in Sanford, Lee County, NC at Center United Methodist Church. She and Charles Scott Yow had the following children:

3362	Grace Frances Yow (1928-). *Grace was born on October 21, 1928.*

1394. Arlie Dewey Yow, son of Charles Frank Yow and Anna Margaret Garner, was born on December 3, 1908. He died on December 19, 2001 and was buried in Sanford, Lee County, NC at Euphronia Presbyterian Church.

Annie Mae Hughes was born on May 20, 1921. She died on April 15, 2010 and was buried in Sanford, Lee County, NC at Euphronia Presbyterian Church.

1395. Mollie Green Garner, daughter of Duncan G. Garner and Laura Luvenia Cockman, was born on December 8, 1897. She married **George Charles Cockman** on November 11, 1916. She died on April 2, 1928 in Moore County, NC and was buried in Moore County, NC at Flint Hill Baptist Church.

George Charles Cockman, son of James Alexander Cockman (1861-1933) and Mary Alice Horner (1865-1948), was born on August 8, 1886. He died on May 29, 1959 and was buried in Moore County, NC at Flint Hill Baptist Church. He and Mollie Green Garner had the following children:

3363	William Fletcher Cockman (1917-1977). *William was born on August 31, 1917. He married **Bernice Jewell Davis** on January 2, 1943. He died on September 18, 1977 and was buried in Robbins, Moore County, NC at Pine Rest Cemetery.*
3364	Dora Mae Cockman (1918-2009). *Dora was born on November 30, 1918. She married **Manly K. Monroe** on November 1, 1941. She died on January 13, 2009.*
3365	Jesse James Carlton Cockman (1920-1960). *Jesse was born on May 25, 1920 in Moore County, NC. He married **Coline Maness** on November 10, 1945. He died on August 1, 1960 in Durham, Durham County, NC and was buried in Moore County, NC at Smyrna Methodist Church.*
3366	Carson Rudolph Cockman (1922-1965). *Carson was born on December 21, 1922. He died on March 17, 1965 and was buried in Moore County, NC at Flint Hill Baptist Church.*
3367	Pearlie Lee Cockman (1924-1930). *Pearlie was born on April 24, 1924. She died on August 8, 1930 and was buried in Moore County, NC at Flint Hill Baptist Church.*
3368	Male Cockman (1928-1928). *Male was born on April 1, 1928 in Moore County, NC. He died on April 1, 1928 in Moore County, NC.*

1396. **Alexander Garner**, son of Duncan G. Garner and Laura Luvenia Cockman, was born on May 10, 1903. He married **Lessie Jane Williams** on October 12, 1922 in Moore County, NC. He died on February 14, 1967 in Moore County, NC and was buried in Moore County, NC at Flint Hill Baptist Church.

Lessie Jane Williams, daughter of George Bryant Williams (1856-1940) and Sarah Alice Kennedy (1861-1921), was born in 1903. She died in 1984. She and Alexander Garner had the following children:

3369	Infant Garner (-). *Infant was buried in Moore County, NC at Flint Hill Baptist Church.*
3370	Carthell D. Garner (1923-). *Carthell was born on August 29, 1923.*
3371	Louvene Ada Garner (1928-). *Louvene was born on April 16, 1928 in Moore County, NC.*
3372	Ollie Jane Garner (1934-). *Ollie was born on December 30, 1934 in Moore County, NC.*
3373	Hilda Jean Garner (1939-2014). *Hilda was born on February 11, 1939 in Moore County, NC. She died on February 27, 2014.*

1397. **Katie Jane Garner**, daughter of Duncan G. Garner and Laura Luvenia Cockman, was born on April 5, 1905. She married **Garrett Hobert Maness** on December 25, 1921 in Moore County, NC. She died on November 19, 1952 in Moore County, NC and was buried in Robbins, Moore County, NC at Tabernacle United Methodist Church.

Garrett Hobert Maness, son of Lewis Scott Maness (1855-1943) and Martha Ann Wallace (1862-1902), was born on November 21, 1896. He married Ada F. Kennedy on July 7, 1954. He died on November 12, 1981 and was buried in Robbins, Moore County, NC at Tabernacle United Methodist Church. He and Katie Jane Garner had the following children:

3374	Annie Mae Maness (1922-2020). *Annie was born on December 7, 1922. She married **Claude Cleveland Wallace** on July 2, 1937 in Moore County, NC.*
3375	Mabel Green Maness (1925-1993). *Mabel was born on November 3, 1925. She died on February 5, 1993 and was buried in Robbins, Moore County, NC at Tabernacle United Methodist Church.*

1398. **Ashley Lee Garner**, son of Duncan G. Garner and Laura Luvenia Cockman, was born on November 1, 1907. He died on August 4, 1924 and was buried in Moore County, NC at Flint Hill Baptist Church.

1404. **Sarah Sadie Williams**, daughter of Offie Alson Williams and Fannie Garner, was born on January 21, 1904 in Moore County, NC. She died on August 14, 1967 in Moses Cone Memorial Hospital, Greensboro, Guilford County, NC and was buried on August 17, 1967 in Moore County, NC at Flint Hill Baptist Church.

1406. **Clarence Williams**, son of Offie Alson Williams and Fannie Garner, was born on August 11, 1910. He died on June 20, 1997 and was buried in Moore County, NC at Flint Hill Baptist Church.

1409. **Stephen C. Wallace**, son of William Wesley Wallace and Elizabeth Jane McIntosh, was born on February 3, 1888 in Moore County, NC. He died on November 23, 1923 in Carthage, Moore County, NC and was buried on November 24, 1923 in Carthage, Moore County, NC at Cross Hill Cemetery.

Lessie Mae Caddell, daughter of Daniel Turner Caddell (1864-1922) and Peanina Louisa Maness (1861-1933), was born on May 12, 1893 in Moore County, NC. She died on December 25, 1947 in Moore County, NC and was buried in Carthage, Moore County, NC at Cross Hill Cemetery. She and Stephen C. Wallace had the following children:

3376	Lois Maybell Wallace (1912-1995). *Lois was born on September 25, 1912 in Moore County, NC. She married **Claude Smith** on December 1, 1937 in Moore County, NC. She died on February 18, 1995 and was buried in Moore County, NC at Doubs Chapel Church.*
3377	Jessie Lee Wallace (1914-2000). *Jessie was born on October 28, 1914. She died on June 27, 2000 in Moore County, NC and was buried in Moore County, NC at Beulah Hill Baptist Church.*
3378	Margie Wallace (1918-). *Margie was born on November 22, 1918. She married **Raymond Guy** on April 24, 1937 in Moore County, NC.*
3379	Montie Pearl Wallace (1921-1966). *Montie was born on March 10, 1921. She died on October 18, 1966 and was buried in Carthage, Moore County, NC at Cross Hill*

Cemetery.

3380   Aggie Pauline Wallace (1923-). *Aggie was born on August 23, 1923.*

1410. Hattie Mae Wallace, daughter of William Wesley Wallace and Elizabeth Jane McIntosh, was born on August 16, 1890. She married **Owen Patrick Priest** on November 2, 1913 in Moore County, NC. She died on January 5, 1944 in Moore County, NC and was buried in Carthage, Moore County, NC at Cross Hill Cemetery.

Owen Patrick Priest, son of Owen Priest (1840-1905) and Mary Catherine McDuffie (1842-1885), was born on May 3, 1882 in Cumberland County, NC. He died on April 27, 1930 in Moore County, NC and was buried on April 29, 1930 in Carthage, Moore County, NC at Cross Hill Cemetery. He and Hattie Mae Wallace had the following children:

3381   Mary Eliza Priest (1917-2006). *Mary was born on January 30, 1917. She died on May 18, 2006 in Jacksonville, Onslow County, NC and was buried on May 21, 2006 in Carthage, Moore County, NC at Cross Hill Cemetery.*

3382   Daniel Patrick Priest (1919-1999). *Daniel was born on January 20, 1919. He died on August 30, 1999 and was buried in Carthage, Moore County, NC at Cross Hill Cemetery.*

3383   William Owen Priest (1921-1960). *William was born on January 18, 1921 in Moore County, NC. He died on October 9, 1960 in Randolph County Hospital, Asheboro, Randolph County, NC and was buried on October 11, 1960 in Asheboro, Randolph County, NC at Oaklawn Cemetery.*

3384   Flora Ann Priest (1923-1970). *Flora was born on April 28, 1923. She died on December 26, 1970 in Asheboro, Randolph County, NC and was buried in Asheboro, Randolph County, NC at Oaklawn Cemetery.*

3385   Ruth Mae Priest (1929-). *Ruth was born on November 9, 1929.*

1411. George Quimby Morgan, son of Reuben Jackson Morgan and Nancy Wallace, was born on September 14, 1886. He died on August 28, 1966 and was buried in Vass, Moore County, NC at Johnson Grove Cemetery.

Pearl Richardson was born on June 17, 1893. She died on January 22, 1954 and was buried in Vass, Moore County, NC at Johnson Grove Cemetery. She and George Quimby Morgan had the following children:

3386   John Reuben Morgan (1911-1994). *John was born on May 16, 1911. He died on July 18, 1994 and was buried in Pinebluff, Moore County, NC at Pinebluff Cemetery.*

1412. James Martin Morgan, son of Reuben Jackson Morgan and Nancy Wallace, was born on September 9, 1889. He died on May 22, 1945 in Moore County, NC.

1415. Etta Ada Morgan, daughter of Reuben Jackson Morgan and Nancy Wallace, was born on July 2, 1896. She died on January 17, 1913 and was buried in Moore County, NC at Morgan Cemetery #418.

1417. Eli Williams, son of Elias Spinks Williams and Charlotte Wallace, was born on December 2, 1885. He died on June 11, 1960.

Ruth Coleman Garvin was born on November 17, 1900. She died on November 22, 1982. She and Eli Williams had the following children:

3387   Burke Garvin Williams (1924-). *Burke was born on May 7, 1924.*
3388   Robbie Lee Williams (1926-). *Robbie was born on April 27, 1926.*
3389   Ethel May Williams (1928-). *Ethel was born on May 31, 1928.*
3390   Ralph Carson Williams (1930-). *Ralph was born on May 25, 1930.*

Ella Florence Hall was born in February 1883. She died on May 20, 1943. She and Eli Williams had the following children:

3391   James Eli Moorefield (1919-1986). *James was born on February 14, 1919. He died on March 29, 1986.*

1418. James Rufus "Duck" Williams, son of Elias Spinks Williams and Charlotte Wallace, was born on September 9, 1888. He died on August 19, 1965 and was buried in Moore County, NC at Pine Grove Baptist Church.

Hattie Louise Williamson, daughter of Isaac Calvin Williamson (1858-1951) and Louisa Jane Deaton (1856-1945), was born on November 22, 1891. She died on May 9, 1989 and was buried in Moore County, NC at Pine Grove Baptist Church. She and James Rufus "Duck" Williams had the following children:

3392	Paul Williams (1912-1994). *Paul was born on November 16, 1912. He died on May 31, 1994 and was buried in Robbins, Moore County, NC at Pine Rest Cemetery.*
3393	Jim Williams (1914-1982). *Jim was born on April 22, 1914. He married **Gladys Burns** on April 24, 1937 in Moore County, NC. He died on December 11, 1982 and was buried in Robbins, Moore County, NC at Tabernacle United Methodist Church.*
3394	Howard Williams (1917-1968). *Howard was born on July 31, 1917. He died on October 16, 1968 and was buried in Moore County, NC at Pine Grove Baptist Church.*

1419. Robert Lewis Williams, son of Elias Spinks Williams and Charlotte Wallace, was born on December 5, 1892. He died on July 18, 1925.

Audie Farrell was born on December 22, 1896. She died on September 28, 1962. She and Robert Lewis Williams had the following children:

3395	Dorothy Lee Williams (1925-). *Dorothy was born in June 1925.*

1420. Mary Alice Williams, daughter of Elias Spinks Williams and Charlotte Wallace, was born on September 28, 1893. She married **Barney Franklin Bailey** on September 15, 1912 in Moore County, NC. She died on October 15, 1971.

Barney Franklin Bailey, son of Robert B. Bailey (1868-1942) and Naomi A. Deaton (1870-1962), was born on November 2, 1891. He and Mary Alice Williams had the following children:

3396	Jessie Lydia Bailey (1913-). *Jessie was born on June 20, 1913.*
3397	Ruby Ethel Bailey (1915-). *Ruby was born on June 2, 1915.*
3398	Swannie Mae Bailey (1918-). *Swannie was born on October 23, 1918.*
3399	Warren Harding Bailey (1920-). *Warren was born on September 1, 1920.*

1421. Eddie Carson Williams, son of Elias Spinks Williams and Charlotte Wallace, was born on October 30, 1897. He died on June 9, 1954 in Moore County, NC and was buried in Moore County, NC at Pleasant View Evangelical Church.

1422. George Branson Williams, son of Elias Spinks Williams and Charlotte Wallace, was born on January 30, 1899. He died on July 16, 1975 and was buried in Robbins, Moore County, NC at Pine Rest Cemetery.

Leta Alma Auman, daughter of Artemus R. Auman (-) and Lora Yow (-), was born on June 25, 1902. She died on February 9, 1989 and was buried in Robbins, Moore County, NC at Pine Rest Cemetery. She and George Branson Williams had the following children:

3400	Harold Branson Williams (1933-). *Harold was born on October 21, 1933.*

1423. Ocia Ometa Williams, daughter of Elias Spinks Williams and Charlotte Wallace, was born on September 16, 1904. She married **William Moore Seawell** on September 5, 1936 in Moore County, NC. She died on February 11, 1991 and was buried in Moore County, NC at Pleasant View Evangelical Church.

William Moore Seawell was born on March 13, 1899. He died on January 13, 1957. He and Ocia Ometa Williams had the following children:

3401	Emily Charlotte Seawell (1938-). *Emily was born on April 30, 1938.*
3402	Linda Lorraine Seawell (1942-). *Linda was born on September 24, 1942.*

1424. Dossie Ethel Williams, daughter of Elias Spinks Williams and Charlotte Wallace, was born on September 7, 1910. She died on October 17, 1942 in Moore County, NC and was buried in Moore County, NC at Pleasant View Evangelical Church.

J. Wiley Powers, son of William Green Powers (1871-1940) and Elizabeth Gruden "Lizzie" Phillips (1871-1926), was born on February 17, 1901. He died on December 30, 1959 and was buried in Moore County, NC at Pleasant View Evangelical Church.

1427. **James Quimby Wallace**, son of Eli Wallace and Mary Mourning Allen, was born on October 18, 1895 in Moore County, NC. He died on February 3, 1956 in UNC Hospital, Chapel Hill, Orange County, NC and was buried on February 5, 1956 in Wilson, Wilson County, NC at Maplewood Cemetery.

1429. **Oscar Lee Hooker**, son of John M. Hooker and Eliza Alice Wallace, was born on January 31, 1898. He died on March 10, 1957 and was buried in Moore County, NC at Flint Hill Baptist Church.

Lillie Ann Britt, daughter of Henry Britt (1867-1951) and Lula May McLeod (1881-1934), was born on March 25, 1911. She died on July 23, 1975 and was buried in Moore County, NC at Flint Hill Baptist Church. She and Oscar Lee Hooker had the following children:

3403	Bobby Lee Hooker (1940-1996). *Bobby was born on August 22, 1940 in Moore County, NC. He died on July 22, 1996 and was buried in Moore County, NC at Bethlehem Baptist Church.*
3404	Joyce Ann Hooker (1946-). *Joyce was born on April 27, 1946 in Moore County, NC.*

1430. **Elias Spinks Hooker**, son of John M. Hooker and Eliza Alice Wallace, was born on November 7, 1899. He died on July 30, 1975 and was buried in Robbins, Moore County, NC at Pine Rest Cemetery.

Lizzie Kirk Smith, daughter of John Newell Smith (-) and Fannie K. Kirk (-), was born on September 24, 1909. She died on August 18, 1998 and was buried in Robbins, Moore County, NC at Pine Rest Cemetery. She and Elias Spinks Hooker had the following children:

3405	William Herbert Hooker (1929-). *William was born on July 10, 1929.*
3406	Elva Grace Hooker (1934-). *Elva was born on March 20, 1934.*

1431. **Benjamin F. Hooker**, son of John M. Hooker and Eliza Alice Wallace, was born on March 9, 1902. He died on February 27, 1973 and was buried in Moore County, NC at Flint Hill Baptist Church.

1432. **Rosanna M. Hooker**, daughter of John M. Hooker and Eliza Alice Wallace, was born on November 23, 1905. She died on October 15, 1992 and was buried in Moore County, NC at Flint Hill Baptist Church.

Wade Hampton Wallace, son of Sampson Delaney Wallace (1845-c. 1893) and Missouri Coleman Hunsucker (1846-1920), was born on July 21, 1870. He died on March 15, 1947 and was buried in Moore County, NC at Flint Hill Baptist Church. He and Rosanna M. Hooker had the following children:

3407	Amaryllis Jean Wallace (1932-). *Amaryllis was born on June 8, 1932. She married* **Charles Newell Hancock** *on August 12, 1949 in Troy, Montgomery County, NC.*

1433. **Alfred N. Hooker**, son of John M. Hooker and Eliza Alice Wallace, was born on August 29, 1913. He died on November 12, 1986 and was buried in Moore County, NC at Unity Grove Baptist Church.

Bertha Lee Nalls was born on September 11, 1911. She died on December 25, 1975 and was buried in Moore County, NC at Unity Grove Baptist Church. She and Alfred N. Hooker had the following children:

3408	Infant Hooker (1938-1938). *Infant was born on January 3, 1938. He died on January 3, 1938 and was buried in Moore County, NC at Flint Hill Baptist Church.*
3409	Eva Jane Hooker (1947-1964). *Eva was born on November 7, 1947. She died on December 19, 1964 and was buried in Moore County, NC at Flint Hill Baptist Church.*

1434. **Etta Jennette Wallace**, daughter of James Lewis Wallace and Lillie Jane Maness, was born on March 25, 1903. She married **Delaney Harrison Garner** on January 7, 1922 in Moore County, NC. She died on September 26, 1984 in Moore County, NC and was buried in Moore County, NC at Flint Hill Baptist Church.

Delaney Harrison Garner, son of Leonard Garner (1851-1922) and Mary Ella Maness (1862-1942), was born on May 9, 1899. He died on October 25, 1990 and was buried in Moore County, NC at Flint Hill Baptist Church. He and Etta Jennette Wallace had the following children:

3410	James Herman Garner (1922-1987). *James was born on October 15, 1922. He died on April 16, 1987 and was buried in Moore County, NC at Flint Hill Baptist Church.*
3411	Maggie Lucille Garner (1924-). *Maggie was born on September 19, 1924.*
3412	Jesse Leonard Garner (1926-2000). *Jesse was born on October 14, 1926. He died on July 19, 2000 and was buried in Moore County, NC at Brown's Chapel Christian Church.*
3413	Neuby Clarence Garner (1928-2020). *Neuby was born on December 7, 1928. He died on January 19, 2020 and was buried in Carthage, Moore County, NC at Putnam Friends Church.*
3414	Lyndon Bobby Garner (1931-1931). *Lyndon was born on March 5, 1931. He died on April 2, 1931 in Moore County, NC.*
3415	Quimby Lewis Garner (1932-2005). *Quimby was born on March 14, 1932. He died on November 1, 2005.*
3416	Maggie Ruth Garner (1934-). *Maggie was born on November 30, 1934. She married **Daniel Lee Garner** on May 17, 2001 in Moore County, NC.*
3417	Thurman Winfred Garner (1937-). *Thurman was born on April 3, 1937.*
3418	Lanie Edward Garner (1940-2003). *Lanie was born on February 10, 1940. He died on November 19, 2003 and was buried in Moore County, NC at Flint Hill Baptist Church.*
3419	Delaney Harrison "Lannie" Garner Jr. (1942-2006). *Delaney was born on December 12, 1942 in Moore County, NC. He died on May 3, 2006 and was buried in Robbins, Moore County, NC at Tabernacle United Methodist Church.*

1435. Quimby Lewis Wallace, son of James Lewis Wallace and Lillie Jane Maness, was born on April 12, 1906. He married **Annie Savannah Barber** on July 13, 1927 in Moore County, NC. He died on December 9, 1977 and was buried in Moore County, NC at Bethlehem Baptist Church.

Annie Savannah Barber, daughter of John Andrew Barber (1869-1951) and Margaret Catherine Love (1877-1967), was born on January 6, 1902. She died on July 30, 1973 and was buried in Moore County, NC at Bethlehem Baptist Church. She and Quimby Lewis Wallace had the following children:

3420	Paul Wallace (1926-2000). *Paul was born on October 21, 1926 in Moore County, NC. He died on November 25, 2000 and was buried in Moore County, NC at Flint Hill Baptist Church.*
3421	Pauline Wallace (1928-). *Pauline was born on December 26, 1928.*
3422	Rufus Lewis Wallace (1932-). *Rufus was born on June 14, 1932 in Moore County, NC.*
3423	John Lester Wallace (1934-2017). *John was born on May 28, 1934. He died on October 27, 2017.*
3424	Margaret Murial Wallace (1936-1995). *Margaret was born on October 12, 1936. She died on February 13, 1995 and was buried in Moore County, NC at Bethlehem Baptist Church.*

1436. William Howard Taft Wallace, son of James Lewis Wallace and Lillie Jane Maness, was born on November 16, 1908. He died on November 13, 1987 and was buried in Robbins, Moore County, NC at Tabernacle United Methodist Church.

Thelma Williams, daughter of Kenneth Watson Williams (1888-1983) and Alma Rebecca McLean (1898-1920), was born on May 2, 1915. She died on April 29, 2008 and was buried in Robbins, Moore County, NC at Tabernacle United Methodist Church. She and William Howard Taft Wallace had the following children:

3425	Ricky Wallace (-)
3426	Sara Vernall Wallace (1935-). *Sara was born on October 9, 1935.*
3427	William Harold Wallace (1941-). *William was born on June 19, 1941.*
3428	Rebecca Jane Wallace (1948-). *Rebecca was born on February 13, 1948.*

1437. **Lizar Myrtle Wallace**, daughter of James Lewis Wallace and Lillie Jane Maness, was born on March 25, 1911 in Moore County, NC. She died on January 1, 1988 and was buried in Robbins, Moore County, NC at Tabernacle United Methodist Church.

Archie Daniel Horner, son of William Branson "Bud" Horner (1872-1925) and Martha Jane Garner (1881-1920), was born on June 2, 1907. He died on December 4, 1980 and was buried in Robbins, Moore County, NC at Tabernacle United Methodist Church. He and Lizar Myrtle Wallace had the following children:

3429	Wilbert Howard "Tom" Horner (1929-2010). *Wilbert was born on June 26, 1929. He married **Brenda Joyce Williams** on August 20, 1965 in Moore County, NC. He married **Sally Goad** on September 5, 1997 in Moore County, NC. He died on May 11, 2010.*
3430	Floyd E. Horner (1931-1963). *Floyd was born on May 2, 1931. He died on March 30, 1963 and was buried in Moore County, NC at Flint Hill Baptist Church.*

1438. **Montie Bertha Wallace**, daughter of James Lewis Wallace and Lillie Jane Maness, was born on February 9, 1914. She died on November 16, 1977 and was buried in Moore County, NC at Pleasant Hill United Methodist Church.

Herbert Ritter and Montie Bertha Wallace had the following children:

3431	Josie Louise Ritter (1935-). *Josie was born on February 5, 1935.*
3432	Dorothea Mae Ritter (1937-). *Dorothea was born on January 22, 1937 in Moore County, NC.*
3433	James Robert Ritter (1939-). *James was born on January 14, 1939.*

Newton C. Morgan, son of John Thomas Morgan (1876-1939) and Laura Vandy Williams (1878-1951), was born on November 23, 1902. He died on February 17, 1980 and was buried in Moore County, NC at Pleasant Hill United Methodist Church. He and Montie Bertha Wallace had the following children:

3434	Dwight Richard Morgan (1955-). *Dwight was born on August 28, 1955.*

1439. **Maggie Wallace**, daughter of James Lewis Wallace and Lillie Jane Maness, was born on November 8, 1916. She married **Harvey Franklin Ritter** on August 24, 1935 and was buried in Moore County, NC at Pleasant Hill United Methodist Church.

Harvey Franklin Ritter, son of Doctor Franklin Ritter (1874-1949) and Annie Margaret Needham (1882-1952), was born on January 8, 1911. He died on October 19, 1989 and was buried in Moore County, NC at Pleasant Hill United Methodist Church. He and Maggie Wallace had the following children:

3435	Verla Marie Ritter (1941-). *Verla was born on April 19, 1941.*

1440. **Infant Wallace**, son of James Lewis Wallace and Lillie Jane Maness, was born on October 6, 1919. He died on October 6, 1919 and was buried in Robbins, Moore County, NC at Tabernacle United Methodist Church.

1441. **Ella Wallace**, daughter of Isaac Frank Wallace and Sarah Annette Horner, was born on February 22, 1886 in Moore County, NC. She married **Orlindo R. Kennedy** on December 20, 1903 in Randolph County, NC. She died on June 4, 1923 in Ramseur, Randolph County, NC and was buried on June 6, 1923 in Ramseur, Randolph County, NC at First Christian Church AKA Sunset Knoll Cemetery.

Orlindo R. Kennedy, son of Dennis Kennedy (1862-1895) and Sarah "Sallie" Latham (1861-), was born on August 17, 1884 in Randolph County, NC. He married Betty Adelaide Caviness circa 1925. He died on August 1, 1970 and was buried in Ramseur, Randolph County, NC at First Christian Church AKA Sunset Knoll Cemetery. He and Ella Wallace had the following children:

3436	Dennis L. Kennedy (1915-). *Dennis was born on November 12, 1915 in Randolph County, NC.*
3437	Female Kennedy (1917-1917). *Female was born on October 15, 1917 in Ramseur, Randolph County, NC. She died on October 15, 1917 in Ramseur, Randolph*

County, NC and was buried in Ramseur, Randolph County, NC at First Christian Church AKA Sunset Knoll Cemetery.

3438   Female Kennedy (1918-1918). *Female was born on October 13, 1918 in Randolph County, NC. She died on October 14, 1918 in Randolph County, NC.*

1442. **Sarah A. Wallace**, daughter of Isaac Frank Wallace and Sarah Annette Horner, was born on February 18, 1889. She married **Alexander D. Wilson** circa 1905. She died on April 26, 1910 and was buried in Ramseur, Randolph County, NC at First Christian Church AKA Sunset Knoll Cemetery.

Alexander D. Wilson, son of Alexander "Sandy" Wilson (1851-1906) and Mary Adeline McManus (1849-1929), was born on June 25, 1879. He died on July 7, 1942 and was buried in Ramseur, Randolph County, NC at First Christian Church AKA Sunset Knoll Cemetery.

1443. **Aggie E. Wallace**, daughter of Isaac Frank Wallace and Sarah Annette Horner, was born on October 23, 1892. She died on December 16, 1906 and was buried in Ramseur, Randolph County, NC at First Christian Church AKA Sunset Knoll Cemetery.

1444. **Leora Wallace**, daughter of Isaac Frank Wallace and Sarah Annette Horner, was born in July 1900. She married **Marshall D. Coward** on September 29, 1915 in Randolph County, NC.

Marshall D. Coward was born on December 7, 1897. He died on May 9, 1993 in Granite Falls, Caldwell County, NC and was buried in Danville, VA at Highland Burial Park. He and Leora Wallace had the following children:

3439   James Daniel Coward (1916-2004). *James was born on March 27, 1916 in Ramseur, Randolph County, NC. He married **Lavycie Meadors** on November 30, 1935. He died on July 25, 2004 in Danville, VA and was buried on July 27, 2004 in Danville, VA at Highland Burial Park.*

3440   Edgar Lee Coward (1917-1992). *Edgar was born on June 7, 1917. He died on January 14, 1992 in Orange County, CA.*

3441   Jesse Paul Coward (1920-1999). *Jesse was born on May 11, 1920. He died on May 2, 1999 in Petersburg, VA.*

1445. **Offie Thomas Maness**, son of Lewis Scott Maness and Martha Ann Wallace, was born on November 9, 1879. He married **Mattie Ann Howard** on December 25, 1904. He died on September 2, 1951 in Moore County, NC and was buried in Moore County, NC at Smyrna Methodist Church.

Mattie Ann Howard, daughter of Benjamin M. Howard (1852-1885) and Martha Louisa Maness (1858-1885), was born on February 1, 1883. She died on March 24, 1955 and was buried in Moore County, NC at Smyrna Methodist Church. She and Offie Thomas Maness had the following children:

3442   Dewey Franklin Maness (1905-1974). *Dewey was born on November 5, 1905. He died in February 1974 in Guilford County, NC.*

3443   Mamie Flossie Maness (1907-1928). *Mamie was born on January 7, 1907. She died on July 26, 1928 and was buried in Moore County, NC at Smyrna Methodist Church.*

3444   Theodore Thomas Maness (1908-1976). *Theodore was born on February 27, 1908. He died on May 28, 1976 and was buried in Moore County, NC at Smyrna Methodist Church.*

3445   Myrtie Ethel Maness (1909-). *Myrtie was born in 1909.*

3446   Bertha A. Maness (1910-). *Bertha was born on September 3, 1910.*

3447   Essie Luola Maness (1912-1987). *Essie was born on July 5, 1912. She died on September 22, 1987 and was buried in Moore County, NC at Smyrna Methodist Church.*

3448   Lewis Clarence Maness (1914-1983). *Lewis was born on November 4, 1914. He died on May 15, 1983 and was buried in Moore County, NC at Smyrna Methodist Church.*

3449   Beulah Mae Maness (1916-1988). *Beulah was born on May 13, 1916. She died on September 15, 1988 and was buried in Moore County, NC at Smyrna Methodist Church.*

3450   Edith Esther Maness (1918-1979). *Edith was born on July 7, 1918. She died on October 26, 1979 and was buried in Moore County, NC at Smyrna Methodist Church.*

3451   Eli Darlington Maness (1920-2000). *Eli was born on March 11, 1920. He died on*

December 5, 2000 and was buried in Moore County, NC at Smyrna Methodist Church.

3452	William Herbert Maness (1922-). *William was born on March 20, 1922.*
3453	Mattie Gertrude Maness (1924-1925). *Mattie was born on December 8, 1924. She died on April 26, 1925 and was buried in Moore County, NC at Smyrna Methodist Church.*
3454	Ruth Helen Maness (1930-1994). *Ruth was born on April 1, 1930. She died on October 11, 1994 in Moore County, NC and was buried in Moore County, NC at Smyrna Methodist Church.*

1446. **Mary Alice Maness**, daughter of Lewis Scott Maness and Martha Ann Wallace, was born on April 15, 1881. She married **Sampson Delaney Williams** on March 7, 1897 in Moore County, NC. She died on April 23, 1912 and was buried in Robbins, Moore County, NC at Tabernacle United Methodist Church.

Sampson Delaney Williams, son of Noah Williams (1826-1904) and Mary Ann Davis (1833-1896), was born on August 6, 1875. He married Artie Mishie Maness on October 12, 1913 in Moore County, NC. He died on July 26, 1939 and was buried in Moore County, NC at Pleasant View Evangelical Church. He and Mary Alice Maness had the following children:

3455	Ira Radius Williams (1897-1974). *Ira was born on December 29, 1897 in Moore County, NC. He died on March 16, 1974 and was buried in Moore County, NC at Pleasant View Evangelical Church.*
3456	Arthur Lewis Williams (1899-1901). *Arthur was born on April 27, 1899. He died on November 10, 1901 and was buried in Moore County, NC at Williams Cemetery #279.*
3457	Maida Frances Williams (1901-1971). *Maida was born on March 15, 1901. She died on May 16, 1971 and was buried in Whispering Pines, Moore County, NC at Yates-Thagard Baptist Church.*
3458	William Charlie Williams (1903-1972). *William was born on February 11, 1903. He died on March 6, 1972 and was buried in Moore County, NC at Pleasant View Evangelical Church.*
3459	Jennette Vandie Williams (1904-1989). *Jennette was born on November 29, 1904 in Moore County, NC. She died on August 19, 1989.*
3460	Mamie Esther Williams (1906-1974). *Mamie was born on September 20, 1906 in Moore County, NC. She married **Hurley Clarence Yarboro** after 1939. She died on February 28, 1974 and was buried in Moore County, NC at Unity Grove Baptist Church.*
3461	Howard Taft Williams (1908-2000). *Howard was born on October 30, 1908 in Moore County, NC. He died on November 25, 2000 and was buried in Robbins, Moore County, NC at Tabernacle United Methodist Church.*

1447. **James Charles "Charlie" Maness**, son of Lewis Scott Maness and Martha Ann Wallace, was born on December 14, 1882. He married **Dora Belle Hayes** circa 1908. He died on January 5, 1959 and was buried in Moore County, NC at Flint Hill Baptist Church.

Dora Belle Hayes, daughter of John Thomas Hayes (1864-) and Almedia Eunice Fesmire (1867-1931), was born on February 1, 1893. She died on January 13, 1931 and was buried in Moore County, NC at Flint Hill Baptist Church. She and James Charles "Charlie" Maness had the following children:

3462	Pearlie Lee Maness (1909-1945). *Pearlie was born on April 8, 1909. She died on March 26, 1945 and was buried in Moore County, NC at Flint Hill Baptist Church.*
3463	Roy Thomas Maness (1913-1990). *Roy was born on April 21, 1913. He died on February 24, 1990 and was buried in Moore County, NC at Flint Hill Baptist Church.*
3464	Ray Elvin Maness (1915-1993). *Ray was born on June 15, 1915. He died on March 5, 1993.*
3465	Bennie L. Maness (1918-2003). *Bennie was born on March 7, 1918. He married **Madie Williams** on July 3, 1937. He died on September 18, 2003.*
3466	Esther Mae Maness (1920-). *Esther was born on December 26, 1920.*
3467	Tessie Edith Maness (1924-). *Tessie was born on August 20, 1924.*

3468   James Robert Maness (1929-1995). *James was born on July 15, 1929. He died on March 31, 1995 and was buried in Moore County, NC at Flint Hill Baptist Church.*

1448. Lillie Jane Maness, daughter of Lewis Scott Maness and Martha Ann Wallace, was born on September 22, 1884 in Moore County, NC. She married **James Lewis Wallace** on July 7, 1900 in Moore County, NC. She died on October 6, 1919 in Moore County, NC and was buried on October 7, 1919 in Robbins, Moore County, NC at Tabernacle United Methodist Church.

James Lewis Wallace, son of Quimby Wallace (1832-1895) and Arabella Stewart (1836-1928), was born on February 9, 1875. He married Flora Ann Garner on August 1, 1921 in Moore County, NC. He died on February 27, 1950 in Moore County, NC and was buried on March 1, 1950 in Robbins, Moore County, NC at Tabernacle United Methodist Church. He and Lillie Jane Maness had the following children:

3469   Etta Jennette Wallace (1903-1984). *Etta was born on March 25, 1903. She married **Delaney Harrison Garner** on January 7, 1922 in Moore County, NC. She died on September 26, 1984 in Moore County, NC and was buried in Moore County, NC at Flint Hill Baptist Church.*

3470   Quimby Lewis Wallace (1906-1977). *Quimby was born on April 12, 1906. He married **Annie Savannah Barber** on July 13, 1927 in Moore County, NC. He died on December 9, 1977 and was buried in Moore County, NC at Bethlehem Baptist Church.*

3471   William Howard Taft Wallace (1908-1987). *William was born on November 16, 1908 and married **Thelma Williams**. He died on November 13, 1987 and was buried in Robbins, Moore County, NC at Tabernacle United Methodist Church.*

3472   Lizar Myrtle Wallace (1911-1988). *Lizar was born on March 25, 1911 in Moore County, NC and married **Archie Daniel Horner**. She died on January 1, 1988 and was buried in Robbins, Moore County, NC at Tabernacle United Methodist Church.*

3473   Montie Bertha Wallace (1914-1977). *Montie was born on February 9, 1914 and married **Herbert Ritter** and **Newton Morgan**. She died on November 16, 1977 and was buried in Moore County, NC at Pleasant Hill United Methodist Church.*

3474   Maggie Wallace (1916-). *Maggie was born on November 8, 1916. She married **Harvey Franklin Ritter** on August 24, 1935 and was buried in Moore County, NC at Pleasant Hill United Methodist Church.*

3475   Infant Wallace (1919-1919). *Infant was born on October 6, 1919. He died on October 6, 1919 and was buried in Robbins, Moore County, NC at Tabernacle United Methodist Church.*

1449. Nettie F. Maness, daughter of Lewis Scott Maness and Martha Ann Wallace, was born on June 22, 1886. She married **Benjamin Nathaniel Marley** on November 3, 1909 in Moore County, NC. She died on February 11, 1964 and was buried in Robbins, Moore County, NC at Pine Rest Cemetery.

Benjamin Nathaniel Marley, son of James Ruffin Marley (1846-1909) and Lucinda A. Brown (1849-1924), was born on August 10, 1884. He died on March 22, 1974 and was buried in Robbins, Moore County, NC at Pine Rest Cemetery. He and Nettie F. Maness had the following children:

3476   Annie Lee Marley (1910-). *Annie was born in 1910.*

3477   Beulah Mae Marley (1911-1967). *Beulah was born on September 24, 1911 in Moore County, NC. She died on June 10, 1967 in Durham County, NC and was buried in Robbins, Moore County, NC at Pine Rest Cemetery.*

3478   Mary Gladys Marley (1920-). *Mary was born in 1920.*

3479   Benjamin Rufus Marley (1924-1996). *Benjamin was born on June 18, 1924 in Moore County, NC. He died on July 2, 1996 and was buried in Robbins, Moore County, NC at Pine Rest Cemetery.*

[Above Left] **Lillie Jane Maness** *(Courtesy of Becky Gilmore, Seven Lakes, NC)* [Above Right] **Mary Alice Maness** *(Courtesy of Dedra Routh)* [Below Left] **John Lockey Maness and Mary Lee Williams** [Below Right] **Benjamin Nathaniel Marley, Nettie F. Maness and son Benjamin Rufus Marley**
(Courtesy of Paul Horner, Robbins, NC)

1450. John Lockey Maness, son of Lewis Scott Maness and Martha Ann Wallace, was born on December 10, 1887. He married **Mary Lee Williams** on May 31, 1911 in Moore County, NC. He died on September 25, 1973 and was buried in Robbins, Moore County, NC at Tabernacle United Methodist Church.

Mary Lee Williams, daughter of John Spanker Williams (1842-1924) and Mary Catherine Williams (1848-1935), was born on August 13, 1891. She died on February 18, 1978 and was buried in Robbins, Moore County, NC at Tabernacle United Methodist Church. She and John Lockey Maness had the following children:

3480	Mazie Florence Maness (1912-2008). *Mazie was born on June 11, 1912. She died on May 21, 2008 and was buried in Moore County, NC at Unity Grove Baptist Church.*
3481	Edith Gertrude Maness (1913-1916). *Edith was born on December 22, 1913 in Moore County, NC. She died on October 8, 1916 in Moore County, NC and was buried in Robbins, Moore County, NC at Tabernacle United Methodist Church.*
3482	Floyd Maness (1915-1916). *Floyd was born on September 27, 1915 in Moore County, NC. He died on October 4, 1916 in Moore County, NC and was buried in Robbins, Moore County, NC at Tabernacle United Methodist Church.*
3483	Herman Branson Maness (1917-2000). *Herman was born on August 28, 1917 in Moore County, NC. He died on November 29, 2000 and was buried in Rockingham, Richmond County, NC at East Side Cemetery.*
3484	Doshie Catherine Maness (1920-2018). *Doshie was born on January 21, 1920. She died on September 20, 2018.*
3485	Anne Mildred Maness (1922-2019). *Anne was born on March 2, 1922. She died on January 9, 2019 and was buried in Bennett, Chatham County, NC at Bennett Baptist Church.*
3486	Dewey Winfred Maness (1924-1973). *Dewey was born on June 8, 1924. He married **Virginia Lee Auman** on January 11, 1947 in Moore County, NC. He died on November 25, 1973 and was buried in Robbins, Moore County, NC at Pine Rest Cemetery.*
3487	Eugene Garrett Maness (1926-1988). *Eugene was born on June 26, 1926. He married **Ruby Crabtree** on July 4, 1947. He died on September 14, 1988 and was buried in Robbins, Moore County, NC at Pine Rest Cemetery.*
3488	Felton Alton Maness (1929-2014). *Felton was born on June 9, 1929. He died on November 11, 2014.*

1451. William Lewis "Willie" Maness, son of Lewis Scott Maness and Martha Ann Wallace, was born on April 1, 1890 in Robbins, Moore County, NC. He married **Beulah Belle McNeill** on May 1, 1913. He died on July 1, 1985 in Alamance County, NC and was buried in Robbins, Moore County, NC at Tabernacle United Methodist Church.

Beulah Belle McNeill, daughter of Calvin McNeill (1853-1915) and Sarah Ann Leach (1859-1941), was born on April 19, 1894 in North Carolina. She died in April 1982 in Chatham County, NC and was buried in Robbins, Moore County, NC at Tabernacle United Methodist Church. She and William Lewis "Willie" Maness had the following children:

3489	Ruth Gertrude Maness (1914-2005). *Ruth was born on March 20, 1914 in North Carolina. She married **Robert Watson Elmer** on August 10, 1940. She died on August 8, 2005.*
3490	Paul Franklin Maness (1915-). *Paul was born on May 14, 1915 in North Carolina.*
3491	William Holt Maness (1916-2011). *William was born on December 16, 1916 in Ervin, NC. He married **Betty Jeanne Rowe** on January 9, 1942 in Jacksonville, Duval County, FL. He died on October 18, 2011 in Jacksonville, Duval County, FL.*
3492	Charles Edwin Maness (1918-). *Charles was born on October 4, 1918 in Parkton, Robeson County, NC. He married **Virginia Joyce Love** on November 20, 1941.*
3493	Sarah Martha Maness (1927-2005). *Sarah was born on August 9, 1927 in Siler City, Chatham County, NC. She married **Richard Edward Cramer** on December 16, 1950. She died in 2005 and was buried in Robbins, Moore County, NC at Tabernacle United Methodist Church.*

1452. Eli Carson Maness, son of Lewis Scott Maness and Martha Ann Wallace, was born on June 25, 1891. He died on January 17, 1968 and was buried in Robbins, Moore County, NC at Tabernacle United Methodist Church.

Anne Liza Covington was born on August 14, 1895. She died on February 17, 1983 and was buried in Robbins, Moore County, NC at Tabernacle United Methodist Church. She and Eli Carson Maness had the following children:

3494	James Lewis Maness (1913-2003). *James was born in 1913. He died in 2003.*
3495	Mary Elizabeth Maness (1915-1917). *Mary was born on July 16, 1915. She died on October 30, 1917 and was buried in Robbins, Moore County, NC at Tabernacle United Methodist Church.*

1453. **Lewis Rufus Maness**, son of Lewis Scott Maness and Martha Ann Wallace, was born on February 6, 1893. He died on April 25, 1974 in Watts Hosptial, Durham, Durham County, NC and was buried on April 27, 1974 in Durham, Durham County, NC at Maplewood Cemetery.

1454. **Dora Lee Maness**, daughter of Lewis Scott Maness and Martha Ann Wallace, was born on March 27, 1895. She married **Willie Lloyd Maness** on December 23, 1913 in Moore County, NC. She died on August 30, 1966 and was buried in Moore County, NC at Pleasant View Evangelical Church.

Talbert Turner Maness, son of Eliza Jane Maness (1876-1930), was born on January 8, 1896. He died on May 15, 1985 and was buried in Robbins, Moore County, NC at Tabernacle United Methodist Church.

Willie Lloyd Maness, son of W. Benton Maness (1858-1941) and Martha Euphratus "Fratus" Albright (1861-1926), was born on January 12, 1892. He died on April 11, 1953 and was buried in Moore County, NC at Pleasant View Evangelical Church. He and Dora Lee Maness had the following children:

3496	Vera M. Maness (1914-1917). *Vera was born on October 11, 1914. She died on March 12, 1917 and was buried in Moore County, NC at Pleasant Hill United Methodist Church.*
3497	Blanche Gertrude Maness (1916-1993). *Blanche was born on March 4, 1916. She died on November 7, 1993 and was buried in Moore County, NC at Pleasant View Evangelical Church.*
3498	Nora Lee Maness (1918-1986). *Nora was born on October 24, 1918. She died on April 28, 1986 and was buried in Moore County, NC at Pleasant View Evangelical Church.*
3499	Annie Ruth Maness (1921-2007). *Annie was born on January 1, 1921. She died on March 24, 2007 in Moore County, NC and was buried in Moore County, NC at Pleasant View Evangelical Church.*
3500	William Lewis Maness (1923-1997). *William was born on February 27, 1923. He died on October 12, 1997 in Moore County, NC.*
3501	Martha Lucille Maness (1926-). *Martha was born on December 21, 1926.*
3502	Vanda Edna Maness (1930-2007). *Vanda was born on May 20, 1930. She died on May 7, 2007 and was buried in Moore County, NC at Pleasant View Evangelical Church.*

1455. **Garrett Hobert Maness**, son of Lewis Scott Maness and Martha Ann Wallace, was born on November 21, 1896. He married **Katie Jane Garner** on December 25, 1921 in Moore County, NC. He married **Ada F. Kennedy** on July 7, 1954. He died on November 12, 1981 and was buried in Robbins, Moore County, NC at Tabernacle United Methodist Church.

Katie Jane Garner, daughter of Duncan G. Garner (1871-1945) and Laura Luvenia Cockman (1870-1954), was born on April 5, 1905. She died on November 19, 1952 in Moore County, NC and was buried in Robbins, Moore County, NC at Tabernacle United Methodist Church. She and Garrett Hobert Maness had the following children:

3503	Annie Mae Maness (1922-2020). *Annie was born on December 7, 1922. She married **Claude Cleveland Wallace** on July 2, 1937 in Moore County, NC.*
3504	Mabel Green Maness (1925-1993). *Mabel was born on November 3, 1925. She died on February 5, 1993 and was buried in Robbins, Moore County, NC at Tabernacle United Methodist Church.*

Ada F. Kennedy, daughter of Jonathan G. Kennedy (1860-1938) and Elizabeth Alice Brewer (1877-1951), was born in 1909.

1456. **Jerusha Annie Maness**, daughter of Lewis Scott Maness and Martha Ann Wallace, was born on July 2, 1898. She married **John Spinks Kennedy** on April 4, 1920 in Moore County, NC. She died on May 12, 1987 and was buried in Moore County, NC at Smyrna Methodist Church.

John Spinks Kennedy, son of John W. Kennedy (1856-1908) and Nancy Louisa Horner (1855-1942), was born in August 1895. He died in 1982 and was buried in Moore County, NC at Smyrna Methodist Church. He and Jerusha Annie Maness had the following children:

3505	Nannie Mae Kennedy (1921-1957). *Nannie was born in 1921. She died in 1957 and was buried in Moore County, NC at Smyrna Methodist Church.*
3506	Harold Thompson Kennedy (1922-1983). *Harold was born on July 7, 1922. He died on September 10, 1983 and was buried in Moore County, NC at Smyrna Methodist Church.*
3507	Aitha E. Kennedy (1925-). *Aitha was born in 1925.*
3508	John Lewis Kennedy (1926-1985). *John was born on May 29, 1926. He died on July 17, 1985 and was buried in Moore County, NC at Smyrna Methodist Church.*
3509	Thelma Lovenia Kennedy (1928-1928). *Thelma was born on May 20, 1928. She died on June 16, 1928 and was buried in Moore County, NC at Smyrna Methodist Church.*
3510	Harrison Carnell Kennedy (1931-). *Harrison was born on September 4, 1931 in Moore County, NC.*

1457. **Rosa Pearl Maness**, daughter of Lewis Scott Maness and Martha Ann Wallace, was born on May 10, 1901. She died on November 30, 1901 and was buried in Robbins, Moore County, NC at Tabernacle United Methodist Church.

1458. **William Walter Ritter**, son of Joseph Ritter and Rutha Jane Florence Wallace, was born on June 10, 1883. He married **Flossie E. Williamson** on March 20, 1907 in Moore County, NC. He died on August 11, 1959 and was buried in Moore County, NC at Needham's Grove Baptist Church.

Flossie E. Williamson, daughter of Eli T. Williamson (1848-1915) and Elizabeth Needham (1853-1933), was born on September 1, 1890. She died on September 15, 1969 and was buried in Moore County, NC at Needham's Grove Baptist Church. She and William Walter Ritter had the following children:

3511	Lennie Carson Ritter (1908-). *Lennie was born in 1908.*
3512	Clarence A. Ritter (1910-). *Clarence was born in 1910.*
3513	Bascom Clifford Ritter (1912-1992). *Bascom was born on May 27, 1912. He married* **Myrtie Hussey** *on February 24, 1934. He died on December 29, 1992 and was buried in Moore County, NC at Needham's Grove Baptist Church.*
3514	Ruby Ritter (1915-2001). *Ruby was born on March 22, 1915. She married* **Woodrow Wilson \"Slick\" Peurifoy** *on December 18, 1935 in Guilford County, NC. She died on August 27, 2001.*
3515	W. Kermit Ritter (1918-). *W. was born in 1918.*
3516	G. Kelly Ritter (1922-). *G. was born in 1922.*
3517	E. Edsel Ritter (1925-). *E. was born in 1925.*
3518	Vernita Annie Ritter (1929-). *Vernita was born in 1929.*
3519	Garland Ritter (1931-). *Garland was born on July 25, 1931.*

1461. **Flossie F. Ritter**, daughter of Joseph Ritter and Rutha Jane Florence Wallace, was born on November 11, 1892. She married **Artemis A. Ward** on October 7, 1909 in Moore County, NC. She died on January 7, 1955 and was buried in Guilford County, NC at Forest Lawn Cemetery.

Artemis A. Ward and Flossie F. Ritter had the following children:

3520	Walter Lee Ritter (1910-1982). *Walter was born on February 21, 1910. He died on February 21, 1982 and was buried in Guilford County, NC at Forest Lawn Cemetery.*

1464. **Maudie Ritter**, daughter of Joseph Ritter and Rutha Jane Florence Wallace, was born on December 16, 1900. She died on December 17, 1900 and was buried in Moore County, NC at Smyrna Methodist Church.

1465. Mattie Ritter, daughter of Joseph Ritter and Rutha Jane Florence Wallace, was born on October 4, 1902. She died on October 4, 1902 and was buried in Moore County, NC at Smyrna Methodist Church.

1468. Maggie S. Garner, daughter of Stephen Harrison "Frog" Garner and Ella Blake Wallace, was born on February 23, 1896. She married **Cornelius Wiley Purvis** on February 25, 1912 in Moore County, NC. She died on May 22, 1922 and was buried in Moore County, NC at Pleasant Hill United Methodist Church.

Cornelius Wiley Purvis, son of Nathaniel Green Purvis (1868-1958) and Aggie Norah Reynolds (1871-1919), was born on July 10, 1894. He married Ola Belle Seawell on October 7, 1922 in Moore County, NC. He married Ida Mae Flinchum in December 1942. He died on July 14, 1989 and was buried in Moore County, NC at Pleasant Hill United Methodist Church. He and Maggie S. Garner had the following children:

3521	James Wiley Purvis (-)
3522	Graham Harrison Purvis (1913-1967). *Graham was born on August 13, 1913. He died on January 2, 1967 and was buried in Moore County, NC at Pleasant Hill United Methodist Church.*
3523	Norman Green Purvis (1916-1988). *Norman was born in 1916. He married **Bonnie Carolyn Phillips** on December 23, 1938 in Moore County, NC. He died on February 12, 1988.*
3524	Lacy Alston Purvis (1918-1918). *Lacy was born on January 5, 1918. He died on January 5, 1918 and was buried in Moore County, NC at Pleasant Hill United Methodist Church.*

1469. William McLenon Garner, son of Stephen Harrison "Frog" Garner and Ella Blake Wallace, was born on December 26, 1897. He married **Martha Alice Cockman** on August 31, 1915 in Moore County, NC. He died on May 8, 1979 and was buried in Moore County, NC at Crossroads Baptist Church.

Martha Alice Cockman, daughter of Charles Riley O'Leonard Emsley Rufus Cockman (1860-1922) and Lou Vicie Brown (1863-1942), was born on August 29, 1896. She died on February 11, 1972 and was buried in Moore County, NC at Crossroads Baptist Church. She and William McLenon Garner had the following children:

3525	William Marvin Garner (1916-). *William was born on June 23, 1916.*
3526	Arthur Hugh Garner (1917-1995). *Arthur was born on December 10, 1917. He died on April 4, 1995 and was buried in Moore County, NC at Crossroads Baptist Church.*
3527	Grace Mae Garner (1919-2009). *Grace was born on February 26, 1919. She died on May 11, 2009.*
3528	Lacy Alton Garner (1921-). *Lacy was born on November 15, 1921.*
3529	Dossie Louise Garner (1925-1984). *Dossie was born on November 6, 1925. She died on September 26, 1984 and was buried in Moore County, NC at Crossroads Baptist Church.*
3530	Tracy Elvin Garner (1927-1997). *Tracy was born on April 12, 1927. He died on January 7, 1997 and was buried in Moore County, NC at Crossroads Baptist Church.*
3531	Ella May Garner (1929-). *Ella was born on March 31, 1929.*
3532	Cecil Ruth Garner (1932-). *Cecil was born on July 7, 1932.*

1470. Annie May Garner, daughter of Stephen Harrison "Frog" Garner and Ella Blake Wallace, was born in May 1900. She died on September 15, 1920 in Moore County, NC and was buried in Robbins, Moore County, NC at Tabernacle United Methodist Church.

Hugh T. Brown, son of George W. Brown (1864-1942) and Amanda Ann "Maude" McNeill (1865-1950), was born on October 3, 1893. He married Ocia Emily Cockman on July 14, 1923 in Moore County, NC. He died on December 29, 1987 and was buried in Moore County, NC at Brown's Chapel Christian Church. He and Annie May Garner had the following children:

3533	Myrtie Brown (1917-). *Myrtie was born on March 12, 1917 in Moore County, NC.*
3534	Pearl Brown (1920-1920). *Pearl was born on January 21, 1920. She died on September 16, 1920 and was buried in Robbins, Moore County, NC at Tabernacle United Methodist Church.*

1471. **John Spinx Garner**, son of Stephen Harrison "Frog" Garner and Ella Blake Wallace, was born on January 23, 1905. He died on May 26, 1969 in Moore County, NC and was buried in Robbins, Moore County, NC at Pine Rest Cemetery.

Lester Louise Coleman was born on June 3, 1911. She died on November 7, 1999 and was buried in Robbins, Moore County, NC at Pine Rest Cemetery. She and John Spinx Garner had the following children:

3535	Colon Grier Garner (1934-). *Colon was born on January 27, 1934.*
3536	Fay Catherine Garner (1941-). *Fay was born on April 25, 1941.*

1472. **Mandie Alma Garner**, daughter of Stephen Harrison "Frog" Garner and Ella Blake Wallace, was born on April 25, 1910. She married **Barney Lee Davis** on April 11, 1925 in Moore County, NC. She died on September 9, 1974 and was buried in Robbins, Moore County, NC at Tabernacle United Methodist Church.

Barney Lee Davis, son of Eli Davis (1869-1902) and Mary Frances "Fannie" Furr (1870-1908), was born on March 7, 1903. He died on November 11, 1981 and was buried in Robbins, Moore County, NC at Tabernacle United Methodist Church. He and Mandie Alma Garner had the following children:

3537	Annie May Davis (1926-1928). *Annie was born on April 29, 1926. She died on June 15, 1928 and was buried in Robbins, Moore County, NC at Tabernacle United Methodist Church.*
3538	Beulah Lucille Davis (1927-2001). *Beulah was born on September 16, 1927. She died on October 6, 2001.*
3539	Bobby Lee Davis (1941-2010). *Bobby was born on March 28, 1941. He died on October 18, 2010 and was buried in Moore County, NC at Crossroads Baptist Church.*

1473. **Myrtle Lee Garner**, daughter of Stephen Harrison "Frog" Garner and Ella Blake Wallace, was born on October 22, 1914. She died on February 16, 1995 and was buried in Moore County, NC at Crossroads Baptist Church.

Ellis Britt, son of General Street Britt (1874-1965) and Lucinda Frances Bruce (1873-), was born on November 9, 1904. He died on March 17, 1965 and was buried in Moore County, NC at Crossroads Baptist Church. He and Myrtle Lee Garner had the following children:

3540	Stephen Hector Britt (1933-1991). *Stephen was born on February 12, 1933. He died on December 3, 1991 and was buried in Moore County, NC at Crossroads Baptist Church.*
3541	Helen Ann Britt (1941-2013). *Helen was born on May 15, 1941. She died on June 7, 2013 and was buried in Carthage, Moore County, NC at Putnam Friends Church.*

1474. **Cornelius Blanche Garner**, daughter of Stephen Harrison "Frog" Garner and Ella Blake Wallace, was born on May 25, 1918. She married **Clarence E. Chriscoe** on August 8, 1936 in Moore County, NC. She died on October 13, 1968 and was buried in Moore County, NC at Crossroads Baptist Church.

Clarence E. Chriscoe, son of William Gurney Chriscoe (1896-1968) and Bertha Alice Kennedy (1900-1919), was born on February 16, 1917. He died on April 13, 2001 and was buried in Moore County, NC at Crossroads Baptist Church. He and Cornelius Blanche Garner had the following children:

3542	Modie Lee Edward "Clifford" Chriscoe (1938-2020). *Modie was born on March 3, 1938 in Moore County, NC. He married **Chloe Lynette Wallace** on September 7, 1954. He died on July 19, 2020 and was buried in Moore County, NC at Emsley Wallace Cemetery.*
3543	Betty Lou Chriscoe (1939-2014). *Betty was born on December 5, 1939 in Moore County, NC. She died on January 11, 2014.*

1475. **Katherine Marticia "Katie" Williams**, daughter of Baxter Williams and Elizabeth Jane Wallace, was born on February 3, 1884. She married **Norman Britt** on October 15, 1907 in Moore County, NC. She died on February 1, 1968 and was buried in Moore County, NC at Bensalem Presbyterian Church.

Norman Britt, son of Daniel Bethune Britt (1845-1927) and Lydia Freeman (1848-1918), was born on September 16, 1877. He died on April 21, 1941 and was buried in Moore County, NC at Bensalem Presbyterian Church. He and Katherine Marticia "Katie" Williams had the following children:

3544	Nettie Mae Britt (1908-). *Nettie was born on July 31, 1908. She married **Frank B. Campbell** on August 13, 1927 in Moore County, NC.*
3545	Annie Jane Britt (1916-). *Annie was born on June 27, 1916.*

1476. Walter W. Williams, son of Baxter Williams and Elizabeth Jane Wallace, was born on December 22, 1885. He died on August 17, 1951 in Lee County Hospital, Sanford, Lee County, NC and was buried in Robbins, Moore County, NC at Tabernacle United Methodist Church.

1477. Emsley Thomas Williams, son of Baxter Williams and Elizabeth Jane Wallace, was born on July 11, 1888. He died on February 4, 1963 and was buried in Robbins, Moore County, NC at Tabernacle United Methodist Church.

Martha Loucinda "Patsy" Phillips, daughter of Noah Phillips (1858-1916) and Martha Jane Spivey (1856-1922), was born on July 6, 1883. She died on June 27, 1946 and was buried in Robbins, Moore County, NC at Tabernacle United Methodist Church. She and Emsley Thomas Williams had the following children:

3546	June Melvin Williams (1911-1966). *June was born on August 20, 1911. He died on September 18, 1966 and was buried in Robbins, Moore County, NC at Tabernacle United Methodist Church.*
3547	Clarence E. Williams (1912-1912). *Clarence was born on November 26, 1912. He died on November 26, 1912 and was buried in Robbins, Moore County, NC at Tabernacle United Methodist Church.*
3548	Gurney Baxter Williams (1914-1987). *Gurney was born on March 26, 1914. He married **Mary Theresa Wadsworth** on August 29, 1936. He died on August 17, 1987 and was buried in Robbins, Moore County, NC at Tabernacle United Methodist Church.*
3549	James Frank Williams (1916-1979). *James was born on April 5, 1916. He died on November 3, 1979.*
3550	Noah Walter Williams (1918-1989). *Noah was born on May 3, 1918. He died on August 17, 1989.*
3551	Janie Elizabeth Williams (1920-). *Janie was born on February 12, 1920 in Moore County, NC.*
3552	Robert Hudson Williams (1922-1989). *Robert was born on January 10, 1922. He died in March 1989.*
3553	Johnnie Nathan Williams (1924-1984). *Johnnie was born on March 3, 1924. He died on May 18, 1984 and was buried in Robbins, Moore County, NC at Pine Rest Cemetery.*
3554	Annie May Williams (1926-). *Annie was born on January 7, 1926.*

1478. Stephen Devotion Williams, son of Baxter Williams and Elizabeth Jane Wallace, was born on April 29, 1890. He died on April 8, 1972.

Bera Mary Frazier was born on April 20, 1914. She and Stephen Devotion Williams had the following children:

3555	Ernestine Williams (1939-). *Ernestine was born on June 7, 1939.*
3556	Alwanda Williams (1940-). *Alwanda was born on July 24, 1940.*
3557	James Anderson Williams (1942-). *James was born on May 30, 1942.*
3558	Delphine Williams (1943-). *Delphine was born on September 2, 1943.*
3559	Mazel Williams (1944-). *Mazel was born on November 30, 1944.*
3560	Gilbert Wayne Williams (1946-). *Gilbert was born on January 31, 1946.*
3561	Nancy Williams (1947-). *Nancy was born on June 20, 1947.*
3562	Stephen Darrell Williams (1956-). *Stephen was born on August 1, 1956.*

Cora Bell Wallace, daughter of Virgil Spinks "Byrd" Wallace (1846-1917) and Flora Ann Garner (1877-1963), was born on May 15, 1901 in Moore County, NC. She died on June 10, 1988 in Moore County, NC and was buried in

Moore County, NC at Virgil (Byrd) Wallace Cemetery. She and Stephen Devotion Williams had the following children:

> 3563   Dora Mae Wallace (1921-). *Dora was born on August 19, 1921.*

1479. Noah Raleigh Williams, son of Baxter Williams and Elizabeth Jane Wallace, was born on October 28, 1892. He died in 1974.

> **Mary Rutledge** was born on May 6, 1895. She died on March 18, 1995. She and Noah Raleigh Williams had the following children:

> 3564   Clifton Baxter Williams (1921-). *Clifton was born on July 3, 1921.*
> 3565   Dorothy Williams (1922-1992). *Dorothy was born in 1922. She died in 1992.*
> 3566   Roger Clyde Williams (1927-1998). *Roger was born in 1927. He died in 1998.*
> 3567   Noah Raleigh Williams Jr. (1928-). *Noah was born in 1928.*

1480. Robert Henry Williams, son of Baxter Williams and Elizabeth Jane Wallace, was born on November 7, 1894. He died on January 29, 1918 and was buried in Robbins, Moore County, NC at Tabernacle United Methodist Church.

1481. Annie Cindie Williams, daughter of Baxter Williams and Elizabeth Jane Wallace, was born on February 22, 1898. She died on February 21, 1994 and was buried in Moore County, NC at Bensalem Presbyterian Church.

> **Daniel Mack Campbell**, son of Daniel Patterson Campbell (1860-1944) and Carrie McMillan (1873-1949), was born on August 27, 1892. He died on September 15, 1939 and was buried in Moore County, NC at Bensalem Presbyterian Church. He and Annie Cindie Williams had the following children:

> 3568   Clinton Patterson Campbell (1923-). *Clinton was born on March 2, 1923.*
> 3569   Baxter Zeno Campbell (1925-1931). *Baxter was born on January 25, 1925. He died on November 9, 1931 and was buried in Moore County, NC at Bensalem Presbyterian Church.*
> 3570   Ovelia Syble Campbell (1931-1938). *Ovelia was born on December 29, 1931. She died on April 28, 1938 and was buried in Moore County, NC at Bensalem Presbyterian Church.*
> 3571   Shelby Jean Campbell (1938-). *Shelby was born on July 1, 1938. She married **Bobby Lee Williams** on June 17, 1959 in Moore County, NC.*

1482. Cora Ida Williams, daughter of Baxter Williams and Elizabeth Jane Wallace, was born on August 15, 1900 in Moore County, NC. She died on September 9, 1957 in Butner Hospital, Granville County, NC.

> **Elder Van Morgan**, son of Joseph Pleasants Morgan (1853-1928) and Sarah Ann Morgan (1857-), was born on July 26, 1897. He died in March 1977 in Newport News, VA. He and Cora Ida Williams had the following children:

> 3572   Timothy Rudolph Morgan (1919-). *Timothy was born on December 30, 1919.*
> 3573   Colby Shannon Morgan (1921-1990). *Colby was born on August 15, 1921. He died on October 13, 1990.*
> 3574   Homer Elder Morgan (1923-1977). *Homer was born on September 30, 1923. He died in 1977.*
> 3575   Sara Kathleen Morgan (1925-). *Sara was born on June 26, 1925.*
> 3576   Elizabeth Mae Morgan (1927-1992). *Elizabeth was born on April 10, 1927 in Moore County, NC. She married **Wallace Needham King** on February 14, 1954 in Lancaster County, SC. She died on October 13, 1992 in Newport News, VA and was buried in Newport News, VA at Peninsula Memorial Park.*
> 3577   Bernice Cora Morgan (1929-1997). *Bernice was born on August 26, 1929. She died on January 19, 1997.*
> 3578   Paul Wendell Morgan (1931-). *Paul was born on November 23, 1931.*
> 3579   Joseph Steven Morgan (1934-). *Joseph was born on March 12, 1934.*
> 3580   Beatrice Morgan (1936-1958). *Beatrice was born on October 1, 1936. She died on April 4, 1958.*
> 3581   Ruby Morgan (1940-1971). *Ruby was born on April 10, 1940. She died in 1971.*

1484. Cora Isabelle Maness, daughter of Lineberry B. Maness and Sindy Ann "Annie" Wallace, was born on January 18, 1883 in Moore County, NC. She married **Henry Thomas Chriscoe** circa 1903. She died on December 9, 1951 in Rockingham, Richmond County, NC and was buried on December 11, 1951 in Rockingham, Richmond County, NC at East Side Cemetery.

Henry Thomas Chriscoe, son of James Alfred Chriscoe (1852-) and Margaret Emily Cole (1855-bef 1900), was born on October 7, 1877. He died on May 7, 1941 and was buried in Rockingham, Richmond County, NC at East Side Cemetery. He and Cora Isabelle Maness had the following children:

3582	Aggie May Chriscoe (1904-1988). *Aggie was born on August 7, 1904. She married **Bennie Garrett Dunn** on August 11, 1920 in Rockingham County, NC. She died on February 27, 1988.*

1485. Lewis A. Maness, son of Lineberry B. Maness and Sindy Ann "Annie" Wallace, was born on June 12, 1885. He married **Emma Huggins Bolton** circa 1906. He died on April 28, 1932 in Rockingham, Richmond County, NC and was buried on April 30, 1932 in Rockingham, Richmond County, NC at East Side Cemetery.

Emma Huggins Bolton and Lewis A. Maness had the following children:

3583	Herman Maness (1917-). *Herman was born in 1917.*
3584	Virginia Mae Maness (1921-1921). *Virginia was born on January 13, 1921 in Rockingham, Richmond County, NC. She died on December 31, 1921 in Rockingham, Richmond County, NC and was buried on January 1, 1922 in Rockingham, Richmond County, NC at East Side Cemetery.*
3585	Glenn Maness (1924-). *Glenn was born in 1924.*

1488. Josie M. Maness, daughter of Lineberry B. Maness and Sindy Ann "Annie" Wallace, was born on January 2, 1892 in Moore County, NC. She died on October 19, 1953 in Richmond Memorial Hospital, Rockingham, Richmond County, NC and was buried on October 21, 1953 in Rockingham, Richmond County, NC at East Side Cemetery.

Robert James Huggins Sr. was born on February 27, 1889 in Darlington County, SC. He died on April 3, 1954 in Richmond Memorial Hospital, Rockingham, Richmond County, NC and was buried on April 4, 1954 in Rockingham, Richmond County, NC at East Side Cemetery. He and Josie M. Maness had the following children:

3586	Robert James Huggins Jr. (1924-1992). *Robert was born on March 15, 1924 in Richmond County, NC. He died on December 10, 1992 in Charlotte, Mecklenburg County, NC.*

1492. Claude Lee Garner, son of James Poling Garner and Louisa Elafair Wallace, was born on May 1, 1893. He married **Ethel Maude Morgan** on September 25, 1918 in Moore County, NC. He died on June 10, 1967 in Moore County, NC and was buried in Whispering Pines, Moore County, NC at Yates-Thagard Baptist Church.

Ethel Maude Morgan, daughter of Noah Albert Morgan (1873-1954) and Sara Ella Shields (1869-1958), was born on March 10, 1902. She died on June 14, 1995 and was buried in Whispering Pines, Moore County, NC at Yates-Thagard Baptist Church. She and Claude Lee Garner had the following children:

3587	William Clifford "Cliff" Garner (1920-). *William was born on September 6, 1920.*
3588	Lacy Earl "Bud" Garner (1922-). *Lacy was born on November 27, 1922.*
3589	Raymond Edgar Garner (1925-1965). *Raymond was born on March 6, 1925. He died on February 20, 1965 in Moore County, NC and was buried in Whispering Pines, Moore County, NC at Yates-Thagard Baptist Church.*
3590	Ruth Mae Garner (1927-2014). *Ruth was born on August 20, 1927. She died on February 3, 2014.*
3591	Claude Ralph Garner (1930-). *Claude was born on March 15, 1930.*
3592	Virginia Doris Garner (1932-). *Virginia was born on July 8, 1932.*
3593	Walter Arnold Garner (1935-). *Walter was born on April 4, 1935.*
3594	Jewell Edna Garner (1937-). *Jewell was born on March 21, 1937.*
3595	Thelma Elizabeth Garner (1939-). *Thelma was born on September 25, 1939.*

3596	Harrison Albert Garner (1944-2017). *Harrison was born on May 15, 1944. He died on August 22, 2017.*

1493. Ira Jason Garner, son of James Poling Garner and Louisa Elafair Wallace, was born on March 3, 1895. He died on November 28, 1972 in Moore County, NC and was buried in Whispering Pines, Moore County, NC at Yates-Thagard Baptist Church.

Maida Frances Williams, daughter of Sampson Delaney Williams (1875-1939) and Mary Alice Maness (1881-1912), was born on March 15, 1901. She died on May 16, 1971 and was buried in Whispering Pines, Moore County, NC at Yates-Thagard Baptist Church. She and Ira Jason Garner had the following children:

3597	James Fletcher Garner (1920-1993). *James was born on May 12, 1920. He died on April 25, 1993 in Moore Regional Hospital, Pinehurst, Moore County, NC.*
3598	Lanie Edward Garner (1921-). *Lanie was born on August 20, 1921.*
3599	Charlie Lester Garner (1924-). *Charlie was born on January 2, 1924.*
3600	Thelma Louise Garner (1926-). *Thelma was born on July 18, 1926.*
3601	Annie Ruth Garner (1929-1929). *Annie was born on July 20, 1929. She died on July 20, 1929 and was buried in Robbins, Moore County, NC at Tabernacle United Methodist Church.*
3602	Mamie Edith Garner (1930-1975). *Mamie was born on July 28, 1930. She died on October 25, 1975 and was buried in Whispering Pines, Moore County, NC at Yates-Thagard Baptist Church.*
3603	Eula Mae Garner (1933-). *Eula was born on February 7, 1933.*

1494. Radie Florence Garner, daughter of James Poling Garner and Louisa Elafair Wallace, was born on May 10, 1897. She married **Ralph Baker Pope** on April 25, 1915 in Moore County, NC. She died on December 29, 1983 and was buried in Whispering Pines, Moore County, NC at Yates-Thagard Baptist Church.

Ralph Baker Pope, son of James P. Pope (-) and Sarah E. (-), was born on September 17, 1896. He died on November 17, 1951 in Moore County, NC and was buried in Whispering Pines, Moore County, NC at Yates-Thagard Baptist Church. He and Radie Florence Garner had the following children:

3604	Esther Lee Pope (1916-2000). *Esther was born on May 9, 1916. She died on June 9, 2000 and was buried in Moore County, NC at Pine Grove Baptist Church.*
3605	Elvin Claude Pope (1918-1982). *Elvin was born on May 18, 1918. He died on November 8, 1982 and was buried in Whispering Pines, Moore County, NC at Yates-Thagard Baptist Church.*
3606	Roy Laster Pope (1920-2008). *Roy was born on April 21, 1920. He died on July 26, 2008 and was buried in Whispering Pines, Moore County, NC at Yates-Thagard Baptist Church.*
3607	Melvin Markus Pope (1922-1996). *Melvin was born on March 3, 1922. He died on October 31, 1996 and was buried in Whispering Pines, Moore County, NC at Yates-Thagard Baptist Church.*
3608	Edith May Pope (1923-2009). *Edith was born on November 23, 1923. She died on August 27, 2009 and was buried in Moore County, NC at Calvary Baptist Church.*
3609	Raymond Pope (1927-1984). *Raymond was born on April 23, 1927. He died on April 20, 1984 and was buried in Whispering Pines, Moore County, NC at Yates-Thagard Baptist Church.*
3610	Glenn L. Pope (1930-1966). *Glenn was born on June 10, 1930. He died on August 27, 1966 and was buried in Whispering Pines, Moore County, NC at Yates-Thagard Baptist Church.*
3611	Mary Juitte Pope (1932-2000). *Mary was born on November 18, 1932. She died on December 28, 2000.*

1495. Arthur Garner, son of James Poling Garner and Louisa Elafair Wallace, was born on May 1, 1900. He married **Nannie Ada Reynolds** on January 15, 1922 in Moore County, NC. He died on January 23, 1992 and was buried in Moore County, NC at Fairview Baptist Church.

Nannie Ada Reynolds was born on March 25, 1903. She died on May 23, 1978 and was buried in Moore County, NC at Fairview Baptist Church. She and Arthur Garner had the following children:

3612   Dorothy Yvonne Garner (1927-). *Dorothy was born on September 2, 1927.*
3613   Marjorie Francis Garner (1930-). *Marjorie was born on September 29, 1930 in Moore County, NC.*
3614   Herbert Russell Garner (1932-). *Herbert was born on October 19, 1932.*
3615   Bonnie Jean Garner (1935-). *Bonnie was born on May 12, 1935 in Moore County, NC.*
3616   Arthur Leon Garner (1937-1971). *Arthur was born on August 31, 1937. He died on February 14, 1971 in Moore County, NC and was buried in Moore County, NC at Fairview Baptist Church.*
3617   Leonard Harold Garner (1939-). *Leonard was born on August 28, 1939.*
3618   Barbara Ann Garner (1942-). *Barbara was born on April 20, 1942.*

1496. Magaret "Maggie" Garner, daughter of James Poling Garner and Louisa Elafair Wallace, was born on November 1, 1901. She married **Joseph Andrew Kiser** on September 19, 1920 in Moore County, NC. She died on November 13, 1985 and was buried in Whispering Pines, Moore County, NC at Yates-Thagard Baptist Church.

Joseph Andrew Kiser, son of Robert Kiser (-) and Eliza (-), was born on January 19, 1902. He died on June 27, 1958 and was buried in Whispering Pines, Moore County, NC at Yates-Thagard Baptist Church. He and Magaret "Maggie" Garner had the following children:

3619   Grace Magdaline Kiser (1933-). *Grace was born on July 6, 1933.*

1497. Hugh Lineberry Garner, son of James Poling Garner and Louisa Elafair Wallace, was born on February 18, 1906. He died on December 6, 1987.

Shula Alma Lewis, daughter of Daniel Clayton Lewis (1871-1942) and Sarah Belle Richardson (1881-1942), was born on November 6, 1909. She died on March 7, 1995 and was buried in Whispering Pines, Moore County, NC at Yates-Thagard Baptist Church. She and Hugh Lineberry Garner had the following children:

3620   James Earl Garner (1927-). *James was born on October 12, 1927.*
3621   Mabel Beatrice Garner (1929-). *Mabel was born on February 27, 1929.*
3622   Hugh Paul Garner (1930-1998). *Hugh was born on November 3, 1930. He died on August 15, 1998 and was buried in Whispering Pines, Moore County, NC at Yates-Thagard Baptist Church.*
3623   Daniel Fred Garner (1932-1990). *Daniel was born on September 18, 1932. He died on November 2, 1990 and was buried in Whispering Pines, Moore County, NC at Yates-Thagard Baptist Church.*
3624   Monnie Alma Garner (1934-). *Monnie was born on September 27, 1934.*
3625   Irene Garner (1936-2007). *Irene was born on December 7, 1936. She died on December 27, 2007 and was buried in Whispering Pines, Moore County, NC at Yates-Thagard Baptist Church.*
3626   Larry David Garner (1940-). *Larry was born on August 8, 1940.*
3627   Darrell Newton Garner (1942-). *Darrell was born on August 10, 1942.*
3628   Judie Marie Garner (1944-). *Judie was born on March 30, 1944.*
3629   Robert Eugene Garner (1946-). *Robert was born on December 12, 1946.*

1498. Lou Minnie Williams, daughter of George W. Williams and Sarah Catherine "Kate" Wallace, was born on December 22, 1885. She married **Coy Haywood McNeill** on May 18, 1903 in Moore County, NC. She died on March 5, 1936 and was buried in Robbins, Moore County, NC at Tabernacle United Methodist Church.

Coy Haywood McNeill, son of Alexander McNeill (1822-1886) and Celia Elizabeth Yow (1838-1923), was born on March 3, 1873. He died on November 8, 1954 and was buried in Robbins, Moore County, NC at Tabernacle United Methodist Church. He and Lou Minnie Williams had the following children:

3630   Adolphus Calhoun McNeill (1904-1989). *Adolphus was born on March 22, 1904. He died on November 25, 1989 and was buried in Eagle Springs, Moore County, NC at Eagle Springs United Methodist Church.*

3631	Coy Holt McNeill (1906-1998). *Coy was born on October 21, 1906. He died on July 10, 1998 and was buried in Robbins, Moore County, NC at Pine Rest Cemetery.*
3632	George Alexander McNeill (1908-1985). *George was born on March 13, 1908 in Moore County, NC. He died on April 11, 1985 and was buried in Robbins, Moore County, NC at Pine Rest Cemetery.*
3633	Mamie L. McNeill (1910-1996). *Mamie was born on April 10, 1910. She died on March 25, 1996 and was buried in Robbins, Moore County, NC at Tabernacle United Methodist Church.*
3634	Howard Taft McNeill (1913-1996). *Howard was born on April 1, 1913. He died on November 6, 1996 and was buried in Robbins, Moore County, NC at Pine Rest Cemetery.*
3635	Roberta Mae McNeill (1915-1996). *Roberta was born on October 2, 1915 in Moore County, NC. She died on March 25, 1996.*
3636	Aggie Elizabeth McNeill (1918-). *Aggie was born on May 24, 1918.*
3637	Infant McNeill (1920-1920). *Infant was born on October 25, 1920. She died on October 25, 1920 and was buried in Robbins, Moore County, NC at Tabernacle United Methodist Church.*
3638	Leland William McNeill (1923-2003). *Leland was born on June 16, 1923. He married **Sara Leola Ussery** on July 1, 1944 in Montgomery County, NC. He died on January 23, 2003 and was buried in Robbins, Moore County, NC at Pine Rest Cemetery.*

1499. **Infant Williams**, son of George W. Williams and Sarah Catherine "Kate" Wallace, was born on October 13, 1887. He died on October 13, 1887 and was buried in Moore County, NC at Williams Cemetery #279.

1500. **Ruth Elizabeth Williams**, daughter of George W. Williams and Sarah Catherine "Kate" Wallace, was born on September 30, 1888. She married **Allen Fuller Brewer** on March 21, 1913 in Moore County, NC. She died on December 6, 1966 and was buried in Moore County, NC at Bensalem Presbyterian Church.

Allen Fuller Brewer, son of Noah Brewer (1854-1930) and Elizabeth Ann Morrison (1855-1917), was born on June 9, 1885. He died on April 2, 1932 and was buried in Moore County, NC at Bensalem Presbyterian Church. He and Ruth Elizabeth Williams had the following children:

3639	Maggie May Brewer (1913-). *Maggie was born on December 19, 1913 in Moore County, NC.*
3640	Allen Lacy Brewer (1918-1995). *Allen was born on July 5, 1918. He died on July 26, 1995 and was buried in Moore County, NC at Bensalem Presbyterian Church.*
3641	Earl Henry Brewer (1923-). *Earl was born on July 4, 1923.*
3642	Allen Fuller Brewer Jr. (1930-). *Allen was born on September 3, 1930.*

1501. **Ellis Lewis Williams**, son of George W. Williams and Sarah Catherine "Kate" Wallace, was born on March 13, 1891. He died on November 11, 1973.

Nannie Lou Britt, daughter of Daniel H. Britt (1849-bef 1910) and Minerva Deaton (1865-1920), was born on November 1, 1898. She died on April 5, 1988. She and Ellis Lewis Williams had the following children:

3643	Lucille Williams (1920-). *Lucille was born on March 28, 1920. She married **Leland Corbett Smith** on September 6, 1941 in Montgomery County, NC.*
3644	Pauline Williams (1921-2000). *Pauline was born on May 14, 1921. She died in July 2000.*
3645	Robert Eugene Williams (1924-). *Robert was born on March 27, 1924 in Moore County, NC.*
3646	Edwin Williams (1928-1929). *Edwin was born on June 27, 1928. He died on September 22, 1929 in Biscoe, Montgomery County, NC and was buried in Robbins, Moore County, NC at Tabernacle United Methodist Church.*
3647	Leon Lewis Williams (1933-). *Leon was born on January 31, 1933.*
3648	Glenn Williams (1934-). *Glenn was born on November 27, 1934.*

1502. **James Lucian Williams**, son of George W. Williams and Sarah Catherine "Kate" Wallace, was born on April 8, 1893. He died on June 14, 1970 and was buried in Moore County, NC at Bensalem Presbyterian Church.

Estella Williamson, daughter of Julius C. Williamson (1868-1950) and Harriet M. Deaton (1874-1948), was born on November 15, 1895. She died on January 4, 1972 and was buried in Moore County, NC at Bensalem Presbyterian Church. She and James Lucian Williams had the following children:

3649	Arthur Raleigh Williams (1920-). *Arthur was born on July 28, 1920. He married* **Margaret Vivian Lewis** *on December 24, 1941.*
3650	Roy Colon Williams (1922-2014). *Roy was born on September 8, 1922 in Moore County, NC. He married* **Virginia Brown Monroe** *on January 11, 1942. He died on May 30, 2014.*
3651	Viola Ethel Williams (1922-). *Viola was born on November 12, 1922 in Moore County, NC. She married* **Walter Wilson Monroe** *on April 28, 1945.*
3652	James Lucian Williams Jr. (1924-). *James was born on August 23, 1924. He married* **Geraldine Clark Bruton** *on February 12, 1944.*
3653	Foster Lee Williams (1926-). *Foster was born on May 22, 1926. He married* **Dorothy Deen Short** *on February 26, 1949.*
3654	Harold Edwin Williams (1927-). *Harold was born on December 21, 1927. He married* **Nellie Grey Monroe** *on November 19, 1949.*
3655	Treva Mynell Williams (1930-). *Treva was born on February 28, 1930. She married* **Edgar Hoyle Smith** *on June 25, 1949.*
3656	Winford Noah Williams (1931-). *Winford was born on September 30, 1931. He married* **Ruby Ann Hartsell** *on September 29, 1950.*
3657	Clinton Ray "Ruben" Williams (1933-). *Clinton was born on August 16, 1933. He married* **Geraldine Freeman** *on September 16, 1951.*
3658	Elizabeth Ann Williams (1936-). *Elizabeth was born on May 6, 1936. She married* **Joe Lee Pusser** *on June 19, 1954.*
3659	Fred Deaton Williams (1940-). *Fred was born on February 14, 1940.*

1503. **Curtis Daniel Williams**, son of George W. Williams and Sarah Catherine "Kate" Wallace, was born on February 21, 1896. He died on May 9, 1933 in Moore County, NC and was buried in Robbins, Moore County, NC at Tabernacle United Methodist Church.

1504. **Dora Lee Williams**, daughter of George W. Williams and Sarah Catherine "Kate" Wallace, was born on January 20, 1898. She died on August 31, 1982 and was buried in Moore County, NC at Mt. Carmel United Methodist Church.

Walter K. Henson, son of John Daniel Henson (1861-1950) and Margaret I. Person (1863-1951), was born on September 23, 1890. He died on September 13, 1957 and was buried in Moore County, NC at Mt. Carmel United Methodist Church. He and Dora Lee Williams had the following children:

3660	Virginia Margaret Henson (1921-). *Virginia was born on March 29, 1921 and was buried in Moore County, NC at Mt. Carmel United Methodist Church.*
3661	Juanita Henson (1924-). *Juanita was born on September 22, 1924.*
3662	Betty Jo Henson (1940-). *Betty was born on January 8, 1940.*

1505. **Callie Florence Williams**, daughter of George W. Williams and Sarah Catherine "Kate" Wallace, was born on December 22, 1900. She died on October 4, 1982 and was buried in Robbins, Moore County, NC at Tabernacle United Methodist Church.

Patrick Williams, son of John Spanker Williams (1842-1924) and Mary Catherine Williams (1848-1935), was born on June 6, 1894. He died on March 31, 1978 and was buried in Robbins, Moore County, NC at Tabernacle United Methodist Church. He and Callie Florence Williams had the following children:

3663	James Carlton Williams (1919-1924). *James was born on March 7, 1919. He died on October 30, 1924 and was buried in Robbins, Moore County, NC at Tabernacle United Methodist Church.*
3664	Willie Williams (1920-1920). *Willie was born on September 21, 1920. He died on September 24, 1920 and was buried in Robbins, Moore County, NC at Tabernacle United Methodist Church.*
3665	Jesse Wilbert Williams (1921-1975). *Jesse was born on October 12, 1921. He died on*

December 29, 1975 and was buried in Robbins, Moore County, NC at Tabernacle United Methodist Church.

3666	Paul J. Williams (1923-2020). *Paul was born on January 31, 1923. He died on May 30, 2020 and was buried in Robbins, Moore County, NC at Tabernacle United Methodist Church.*
3667	Raymond Green Williams (1924-1985). *Raymond was born on October 6, 1924. He died on May 7, 1985 and was buried in Robbins, Moore County, NC at Tabernacle United Methodist Church.*
3668	Rodger Kenneth Williams (1926-2020). *Rodger was born on March 9, 1926. He died on April 18, 2020 and was buried in Winston-Salem, Forsyth County, NC at Oaklawn Memorial Gardens.*
3669	Edith Kathleen Williams (1928-). *Edith was born on April 11, 1928.*
3670	Worthy Curtis Williams (1933-1998). *Worthy was born on March 1, 1933. He died on February 13, 1998 in Grand Rapids, Kent County, MI and was buried in Robbins, Moore County, NC at Tabernacle United Methodist Church.*

1506. **Josie Ella Williams**, daughter of George W. Williams and Sarah Catherine "Kate" Wallace, was born on January 17, 1903. She married **Martin L. Thomas** on May 14, 1923 in Moore County, NC. She died on May 28, 1924 in Moore County, NC and was buried in Robbins, Moore County, NC at Tabernacle United Methodist Church.

Martin L. Thomas, son of George W. Thomas (1862-1940) and Lydia Margaret Brewer (1866-1930), was born in June 1898. He married Alice circa 1927. He and Josie Ella Williams had the following children:

3671	Joseph Etheridge Thomas (1924-1924). *Joseph was born on May 27, 1924. He died on November 11, 1924 in Moore County, NC and was buried in Robbins, Moore County, NC at Tabernacle United Methodist Church.*

1507. **Mollie Priscilla Williams**, daughter of George W. Williams and Sarah Catherine "Kate" Wallace, was born on June 30, 1905. She married **Martin Luther Lewis** circa 1923. She died on March 4, 2001 and was buried in Robbins, Moore County, NC at Tabernacle United Methodist Church.

Martin Luther Lewis, son of Daniel Clayton Lewis (1849-1906) and Margaret E. Morgan (1855-1927), was born on April 6, 1901. He died on July 22, 1984 and was buried in Robbins, Moore County, NC at Tabernacle United Methodist Church. He and Mollie Priscilla Williams had the following children:

3672	Everette Eugene Lewis (1924-2002). *Everette was born on January 27, 1924. He died on December 19, 2002 and was buried in Robbins, Moore County, NC at Tabernacle United Methodist Church.*
3673	Doris Mae Lewis (1925-2012). *Doris was born on July 12, 1925. She died on March 18, 2012 and was buried in Fayetteville, Cumberland County, NC at Cross Creek Cemetery #4.*
3674	Willard Clayton Lewis (1928-). *Willard was born on February 17, 1928.*
3675	Robert Luther Lewis (1930-). *Robert was born on July 31, 1930.*
3676	Barbara Lewis (1938-). *Barbara was born on November 29, 1938.*

1508. **Nannie Verona Williams**, daughter of George W. Williams and Sarah Catherine "Kate" Wallace, was born on January 2, 1909. She died on August 23, 2004 and was buried in Moore County, NC at Bensalem Presbyterian Church.

John Henry Morrison, son of Alexander Morrison (1856-1919) and Lucinda Brewer (1868-1932), was born on January 21, 1899. He died on November 30, 1989 and was buried in Moore County, NC at Bensalem Presbyterian Church. He and Nannie Verona Williams had the following children:

3677	John Wilton Morrison (1926-1927). *John was born on March 11, 1926. He died on September 6, 1927 and was buried in Moore County, NC at Bensalem Presbyterian Church.*
3678	John Henry Morrison Jr. (1937-). *John was born on November 29, 1937.*

1509. **William Norman Williams**, son of George W. Williams and Sarah Catherine "Kate" Wallace, was born on October 29, 1911. He married **Minnie Helen Burns** on June 27, 1937 in Moore County, NC. He died on March 18, 2007 and was buried in Moore County, NC at Rock Hill Church.

Minnie Helen Burns, daughter of Rome H. Burns (1876-1966) and Laura L. Furr (1879-1954), was born on February 10, 1910. She died on February 15, 2009 and was buried on February 18, 2009 in Moore County, NC at Rock Hill Church. She and William Norman Williams had the following children:

3679	Jackie William Williams (1938-). *Jackie was born on June 25, 1938.*
3680	Samuel George Williams (1940-). *Samuel was born on January 8, 1940 in Moore County, NC.*
3681	Catherine Louise Williams (1941-). *Catherine was born on August 13, 1941.*
3682	Curtis Norman Williams (1943-1997). *Curtis was born on April 28, 1943 in Moore County, NC. He died on June 2, 1997 and was buried in Moore County, NC at Rock Hill Church.*
3683	Ted Williams (1947-). *Ted was born on January 12, 1947.*

1510. **Infant Wallace**, daughter of Lucian Thomas Wallace and Nancy Jane "Nan" Williams, was buried in Robbins, Moore County, NC at Tabernacle United Methodist Church.

1511. **Roscoe Greene Wallace**, son of Lucian Thomas Wallace and Nancy Jane "Nan" Williams, was born on November 1, 1900 in Moore County, NC. He died on August 10, 1960 in Moore Regional Hospital, Pinehurst, Moore County, NC and was buried on August 12, 1960 in Robbins, Moore County, NC at Tabernacle United Methodist Church.

Geneva Fogleman was born on February 18, 1897. She died on February 15, 1972 and was buried in High Point, Guilford County, NC at Oakwood Cemetery.

1512. **Hurley Carlton Wallace**, son of Lucian Thomas Wallace and Nancy Jane "Nan" Williams, was born on January 5, 1905 in Moore County, NC. He married **Beulah Mae Kennedy** on May 5, 1934 in Danville, VA. He died on April 14, 1994 in Moore County, NC and was buried in Robbins, Moore County, NC at Tabernacle United Methodist Church.

Beulah Mae Kennedy, daughter of John William Kennedy (1872-1931) and Mary Adelaide Purvis (1874-1960), was born on August 30, 1910. She died on December 16, 1997 and was buried in Robbins, Moore County, NC at Tabernacle United Methodist Church. She and Hurley Carlton Wallace had the following children:

3684	Hurley Carlton Wallace Jr. (1935-). *Hurley was born on July 15, 1935 in Moore County, NC.*
3685	Freddie Connie Wallace (1937-). *Freddie was born on November 28, 1937 in Moore County, NC.*
3686	William Lucian Wallace (1940-2005). *William was born on March 28, 1940 in Moore County, NC. He married **Sabra Diane Daurity** on July 23, 1960 in Moore County, NC. He died on April 10, 2005 in Media, PA.*

1513. **Chester Alton Wallace**, son of Lucian Thomas Wallace and Nancy Jane "Nan" Williams, was born on May 4, 1907 in Moore County, NC. He died on March 20, 1982 and was buried in Robbins, Moore County, NC at Tabernacle United Methodist Church.

Letty Jane Williamson, daughter of Julius C. Williamson (1868-1950) and Harriet M. Deaton (1874-1948), was born on December 14, 1909 in Moore County, NC. She died on April 20, 2011 in Biscoe, Montgomery County, NC and was buried on April 23, 2011 in Robbins, Moore County, NC at Tabernacle United Methodist Church. She and Chester Alton Wallace had the following children:

3687	Veona L. Wallace (1934-1934). *Veona was born on May 15, 1934. She died on May 17, 1934 and was buried in Robbins, Moore County, NC at Tabernacle United Methodist Church.*

[Left] (L-R) **Hurley Wallace, Watson Williams and Mallie Walllace**
[Above] **Hurley Wallace** [Below] (L-R) **Roscoe Wallace and Alton Wallace**
[Below Left] **Connie Wallace**

[Above Left] **Alton Wallace and Letty Williamson** [Above Right] **Jerome Cockman and Mallie Wallace** [Below Left] **Hurley Wallace and sons** (L-R) **H.C., Billy and Freddie** [Below Right] **Hurley Wallace and Beulah Mae Kennedy**

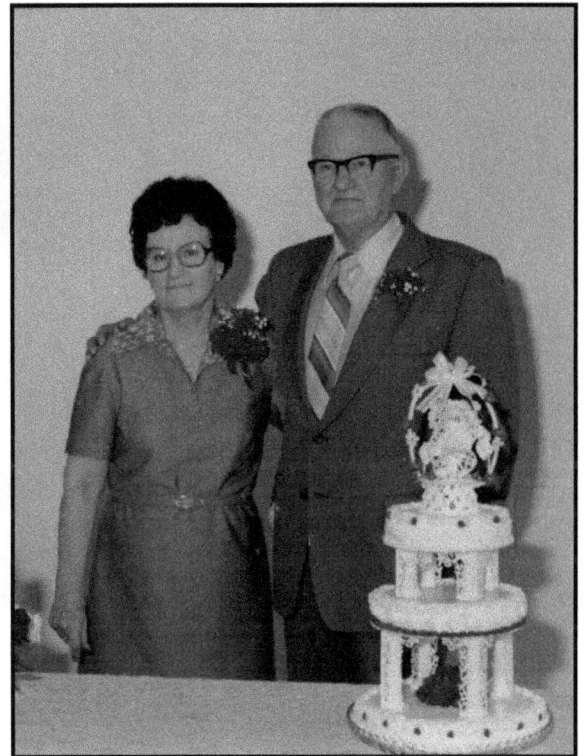

[Above/Right] **Thurman Maness and Verdia Wallace** [Below Left] **Sadie Wallace, Nan Williams Wallace and Verdia Wallace** [Below Right] **Coy Smith and Bettie Smith**

[Above] **Mallie Wallace and Clara Cockman** [Below] (L-R) **Mallie Wallace, Sadie Wallace, Verdia Wallace and Hurley Wallace**

1514. **Mallie Lester Wallace**, son of Lucian Thomas Wallace and Nancy Jane "Nan" Williams, was born on May 31, 1910 in Moore County, NC. He married **Clara Aileen Cockman** on December 19, 1931 in Danville, VA. He died on June 20, 2002 in Moore Regional Hospital, Pinehurst, Moore County, NC and was buried on June 22, 2002 in Robbins, Moore County, NC at Tabernacle United Methodist Church.

Clara Aileen Cockman, daughter of William Jerome Cockman (1883-1947) and Dora Alice Sanders (1892-1983), was born on September 5, 1915 in Cumberland County, NC. She died on May 29, 1986 in Moore County, NC and was buried in Robbins, Moore County, NC at Tabernacle United Methodist Church. She and Mallie Lester Wallace had the following children:

3688	Jacqueline Wallace (1932-2015). *Jacqueline was born on October 23, 1932 in Moore County, NC. She married **Andrew Walter Spivey** on June 30, 1952. She died on July 1, 2015.*
3689	Chloe Lynette Wallace (1939-). *Chloe was born on July 15, 1939 in Moore County, NC. She married **Modie Lee Edward "Clifford" Chriscoe** on September 7, 1954.*
3690	Doris Ann Wallace (1943-2013). *Doris was born on February 21, 1943 in Moore County, NC. She married **Anthony Elwood Parker** on November 29, 1970. She died on November 17, 2013 in Moore Regional Hospital, Pinehurst, Moore County, NC.*
3691	Patricia Louise Wallace (1946-). *Patricia was born on February 13, 1946 in Moore Regional Hospital, Pinehurst, Moore County, NC. She married **Jesse Elvin Jackson** on August 16, 1971 in Carthage, Moore County, NC.*
3692	Priscilla Lois Wallace (1946-1946). *Priscilla was born on February 13, 1946 in Moore County, NC. She died on February 13, 1946 in Moore County, NC and was buried in Robbins, Moore County, NC at Tabernacle United Methodist Church.*

1515. **Sadie Lou Wallace**, daughter of Lucian Thomas Wallace and Nancy Jane "Nan" Williams, was born on July 21, 1912 in Moore County, NC. She died on December 30, 1992 in Lumberton, Robeson County, NC.

Coy Smith, son of Lewis S. Smith (1887-1945) and Minerva J. Deaton (1883-1942), was born on December 19, 1906. He died on April 15, 1977. He and Sadie Lou Wallace had the following children:

3693	Bettie Lou Smith (1934-1999). *Bettie was born on May 26, 1934. She died on February 11, 1999 in Red Springs, Robeson County, NC.*

1516. **Verdia Lee Wallace**, daughter of Lucian Thomas Wallace and Nancy Jane "Nan" Williams, was born on August 1, 1914 in Moore County, NC. She married **Thurman Dosson Maness** on February 26, 1937 in Moore County, NC. She died on May 9, 1998 in Moore County, NC and was buried in Moore County, NC at Pleasant Hill United Methodist Church.

Thurman Dosson Maness, son of Reuben Addison Maness (1865-1953) and Annie Mae Maness (1875-1942), was born on July 27, 1909. He died on August 8, 2010 in St. Joseph of Pines Hospital, Pinehurst, Moore County, NC. He and Verdia Lee Wallace had the following children:

3694	Robert Lee Maness (1945-2013). *Robert was born on July 30, 1945 in Moore County, NC. He died on April 12, 2013 in Lawrenceville, Gwinnett County, GA.*

1517. **Connie Thomas Wallace**, son of Lucian Thomas Wallace and Nancy Jane "Nan" Williams, was born on October 26, 1916 in Moore County, NC. He died on January 18, 1972 in St. Joseph of Pines Hospital, Pinehurst, Moore County, NC and was buried on January 20, 1972 in Robbins, Moore County, NC at Tabernacle United Methodist Church.

Fonnie F. Sanders, daughter of Henry B. Sanders (1876-1959) and Ida Florence Sheffield (1891-1935), was born on April 4, 1929. She died on July 14, 1990 and was buried in Moore County, NC at Brown's Chapel Christian Church. She and Connie Thomas Wallace had the following children:

3695	Ronnie Thomas Wallace (1957-1994). *Ronnie was born on September 15, 1957 in Montgomery County, NC. He died on February 17, 1994 and was buried in Moore County, NC at Brown's Chapel Christian Church.*

1518. **Isham Thomas Britt**, son of Daniel Bethune Britt Jr. and Martha "Mattie" Wallace, was born on December 8, 1900. He married **Monnie Mae Stutts** on November 2, 1928 in Moore County, NC. He died on June 17, 1980 and was buried in Moore County, NC at Bensalem Presbyterian Church.

Monnie Mae Stutts, daughter of Murdoch M. Stutts (1866-1926) and Hattie Bell Burns (1887-1963), was born on June 3, 1906. She died on September 8, 1987 and was buried in Moore County, NC at Bensalem Presbyterian Church. She and Isham Thomas Britt had the following children:

> 3696   Libby Sue Britt (1940-). *Libby was born on March 6, 1940.*

1519. **Gertie Lee Britt**, daughter of Daniel Bethune Britt Jr. and Martha "Mattie" Wallace, was born on July 10, 1906. She married **Jeremiah Carlton Williams** on September 24, 1927. She died on December 22, 1980 and was buried in Eagle Springs, Moore County, NC at Eagle Springs Presbyterian Church.

Jeremiah Carlton Williams, son of Jefferson H. Williams (1836-bef 1910) and Mary Elizabeth Brewer (1855-1926), was born on September 20, 1892. He died on November 29, 1974 and was buried in Eagle Springs, Moore County, NC at Eagle Springs Presbyterian Church. He and Gertie Lee Britt had the following children:

> 3697   Thelma Louise Williams (1928-). *Thelma was born on August 18, 1928.*
> 3698   Harvey Irvin Williams (1931-). *Harvey was born on April 2, 1931.*
> 3699   Gordon Britt Williams (1934-). *Gordon was born on January 11, 1934 and was buried in Eagle Springs, Moore County, NC at Eagle Springs Presbyterian Church.*

1520. **Annette Barrett**, daughter of Jesse Samuel Barrett and Mary Jane Nancy Regina Ledbetter "Mamie" Wallace, was born on February 9, 1884. She married **Henry B. Dewey** on May 21, 1907 in Moore County, NC. She died on December 13, 1956 in Moore County, NC.

Henry B. Dewey was the son of William Dewey (-) and Mary J. (-). He and Annette Barrett had the following children:

> 3700   Henry C. Dewey (-)

1521. **Mary Pauline Wallace**, daughter of Isham Sedman Robert Renfro "Bob" Wallace and Bura S. Stutts, was born on November 16, 1895 in Richmond County, NC. She died on September 16, 1958 in Richmond Memorial Hospital, Rockingham, Richmond County, NC and was buried on September 18, 1958 in Rockingham, Richmond County, NC at East Side Cemetery.

1522. **Maggie Lee McLeod**, daughter of Evander Kelly McLeod and Daisy Arnold Irene Wallace, was born on July 13, 1895 in Moore County, NC. She died on August 1, 1975.

Lawrence Lowe Hinshaw was born on January 18, 1898. He died on December 26, 1986. He and Maggie Lee McLeod had the following children:

> 3701   Leon Franklin Hinshaw (1924-1974). *Leon was born on February 25, 1924. He died on December 7, 1974.*

1524. **James Samuel McLeod**, son of Evander Kelly McLeod and Daisy Arnold Irene Wallace, was born on December 14, 1900. He died on September 22, 1918 in Moore County, NC and was buried on September 23, 1918 in Moore County, NC at Union Presbyterian Church.

1525. **Mamie McLeod**, daughter of Evander Kelly McLeod and Daisy Arnold Irene Wallace, was born in 1901. She died in 1904 and was buried in Moore County, NC at Union Presbyterian Church.

1526. **Jesse Lewis McLeod**, son of Evander Kelly McLeod and Daisy Arnold Irene Wallace, was born on September 15, 1906. He died on September 30, 1949.

Mary Bell McLeod was born on April 29, 1908. She died on August 27, 1990. She and Jesse Lewis McLeod had the following children:

3702   Thelma Jean McLeod (1938-2004). *Thelma was born on September 20, 1938. She died on December 9, 2004.*

1531. Etta Bell Morgan, daughter of David Newton Morgan and Cynthia Ann "Annie" Wallace, was born on July 9, 1896. She died on February 18, 1920 in Moore County, NC and was buried in Robbins, Moore County, NC at Tabernacle United Methodist Church.

     Charles L. Garner and Etta Bell Morgan had the following children:

3703   Dora Garner (1920-1920). *Dora was born on February 12, 1920. She died on February 12, 1920 and was buried in Robbins, Moore County, NC at Tabernacle United Methodist Church.*

1532. Eli Samuel Morgan, son of David Newton Morgan and Cynthia Ann "Annie" Wallace, was born on June 19, 1897. He died on December 19, 1919 in Moore County, NC.

1533. Arthur Clemons "Offie" Morgan, son of David Newton Morgan and Cynthia Ann "Annie" Wallace, was born on May 1, 1899. He married **Minnie Lee Wallace** on January 25, 1921 in Moore County, NC. He died on September 28, 1957 and was buried in Moore County, NC at Beulah Hill Baptist Church.

     Minnie Lee Wallace, daughter of Isham Wallace (1882-1962) and Bertha Hall (1884-1906), was born on June 18, 1902 in Moore County, NC. She died on March 4, 1972 in Moore County, NC and was buried on March 6, 1972 in Moore County, NC at Beulah Hill Baptist Church. She and Arthur Clemons "Offie" Morgan had the following children:

3704   Walter Carson Morgan (1921-). *Walter was born on August 26, 1921.*
3705   Worthy Lee Morgan (1923-). *Worthy was born on April 1, 1923.*
3706   Male Morgan (1924-). *Male was born on September 12, 1924.*
3707   Alexander Morgan (1927-1980). *Alexander was born on January 13, 1927. He died on August 8, 1980 in Moore County, NC and was buried in Moore County, NC at Beulah Hill Baptist Church.*
3708   Alvin Clemons Morgan (1929-). *Alvin was born on March 5, 1929.*
3709   Faye Irene Morgan (1930-2001). *Faye was born on November 16, 1930. She died on March 23, 2001.*
3710   Eugene Hamilton "Bud" Morgan (1932-1981). *Eugene was born on August 23, 1932. He died on March 5, 1981 and was buried in Moore County, NC at Beulah Hill Baptist Church.*
3711   Lois Lee Morgan (1934-1938). *Lois was born on July 18, 1934. She died on June 1, 1938 and was buried in Moore County, NC at Beulah Hill Baptist Church.*
3712   Female 1 Morgan (1936-). *Female was born on September 14, 1936.*
3713   Female 2 Morgan (1936-). *Female was born on September 14, 1936.*

1534. Charles M. Morgan, son of David Newton Morgan and Cynthia Ann "Annie" Wallace, was born in 1901.

     Charles M. Morgan had the following children:

3714   Morgan (-)

1536. Ursula M. "Shulie" Wallace, daughter of Josiah Tay Settle Wallace and Annie Jane Sanders, was born on October 28, 1899. She died on August 6, 1901 and was buried in Moore County, NC at Brown's Chapel Christian Church.

1538. Maggie Pearl Wallace, daughter of Josiah Tay Settle Wallace and Annie Jane Sanders, was born on April 6, 1906 in Moore County, NC. She died on May 5, 1973.

     Albert Bruce Hinson was born on December 20, 1907. He died on December 29, 1961. He and Maggie Pearl Wallace had the following children:

3715   Ricky Joe Hinson (1933-2017). *Ricky was born on February 11, 1933. He died on March 3, 2017.*

1540. **Charles Evans Wallace**, son of Josiah Tay Settle Wallace and Annie Jane Sanders, was born on November 5, 1916 in Montgomery County, NC. He died on November 14, 1981 and was buried in Albemarle, Stanly County, NC at Fairview Cemetery.

   LaVina Estelle Hill was born on January 27, 1913. She died on January 29, 1992. She and Charles Evans Wallace had the following children:

   3716   Janice Sue Wallace (1938-2013). *Janice was born on April 3, 1938. She married **Richard Guy Mattox** on July 21, 1962 in Stanly County, NC. She died on December 8, 2013.*

1542. **Ila Myrtle Stewart**, daughter of Lonnie Lee Stewart and Sarah Lee Nettie Wallace, was born on May 31, 1900. She died on October 28, 1969 and was buried in Coats, Harnett County, NC at Coats City Cemetery.

   Henry Clay Stewart was born on October 4, 1885. He died on August 17, 1958 and was buried in Coats, Harnett County, NC at Coats City Cemetery.

1543. **Archie Lee Stewart**, son of Lonnie Lee Stewart and Sarah Lee Nettie Wallace, was born on August 23, 1902. He died on February 10, 1950 in Durham County, NC and was buried on February 12, 1950 in Durham, Durham County, NC at Maplewood Cemetery.

1544. **Viola Mae Wallace**, daughter of Jesse Lewis Smith Wallace and Sarah Catherine "Cassie" Hunsucker, was born on August 10, 1907 in Moore County, NC. She married **Hugh Wilton Jackson** on February 20, 1925. She died on November 17, 1994 and was buried in Sanford, Lee County, NC at Center United Methodist Church.

   Hugh Wilton Jackson, son of Archibald McGregor Jackson (1878-1934) and Mary Ann Davidson (1881-1934), was born on June 12, 1902. He died on April 20, 1990 and was buried in Sanford, Lee County, NC at Center United Methodist Church. He and Viola Mae Wallace had the following children:

   3717   Maxine Jackson (1926-). *Maxine was born on February 13, 1926.*
   3718   Hugh Donald Jackson (1936-). *Hugh was born on December 18, 1936.*

1545. **Blanche Gretchen Wallace**, daughter of Jesse Lewis Smith Wallace and Sarah Catherine "Cassie" Hunsucker, was born on June 30, 1909. She married **Earl Austin Bush** on May 23, 1958 in Moore County, NC. She died on June 5, 1991 and was buried in Moore County, NC at Union Presbyterian Church.

   Earl Austin Bush, son of Elmer Bush (-) and Bessie Detrick (-), was born in 1908.

1546. **Roberta Wallace**, daughter of Jesse Lewis Smith Wallace and Sarah Catherine "Cassie" Hunsucker, was born on June 11, 1915. She died on June 11, 1915.

1547. **Jessie Lazell Wallace**, daughter of Jesse Lewis Smith Wallace and Sarah Catherine "Cassie" Hunsucker, was born on December 28, 1922 in Moore County, NC. She married **Roy F. Burt** on May 13, 1961 in Moore County, NC. She died on October 11, 2002 in Moore County, NC.

1548. **Roland Truelove**, son of Troy Van Truelove and Eliza Rosetta Mattie Evelyn "Mattie" Wallace, was born in 1902.

1549. **Samuel Estis Truelove**, son of Troy Van Truelove and Eliza Rosetta Mattie Evelyn "Mattie" Wallace, was born on May 7, 1903 in Harnett County, NC. He died on March 15, 1957 in Raleigh, Wake County, NC and was buried in Cary, Wake County, NC at Piney Plains Christian Church.

   Maggie Stephens was born on October 18, 1904. She died on October 14, 1993 in Cary, Wake County, NC and was buried in Cary, Wake County, NC at Piney Plains Christian Church.

1550. **Pauline Truelove**, daughter of Troy Van Truelove and Eliza Rosetta Mattie Evelyn "Mattie" Wallace, was born in 1905.

1551. Alford Raeford Truelove, son of Troy Van Truelove and Eliza Rosetta Mattie Evelyn "Mattie" Wallace, was born on March 13, 1909 in Lee County, NC. He died on April 7, 1978 in Raleigh, Wake County, NC and was buried in Cary, Wake County, NC at Piney Plains Christian Church.

Addie Josephine McIver, daughter of Druary Lacy McIver (1875-1936) and Lillie Brim Riddle (1881-1935), was born on October 1, 1911 in Lee County, NC. She died on July 26, 1990 in Raleigh, Wake County, NC and was buried in Cary, Wake County, NC at Piney Plains Christian Church. She and Alford Raeford Truelove had the following children:

> 3719   Nancy Carol Truelove (1935-1980). *Nancy was born on June 13, 1935. She died on April 11, 1980.*

1553. Oscar Emerson Wallace, son of Samuel Henry Bascom "Bass" Wallace and Nettie J. Britt, was born on June 12, 1910 in Davidson County, NC. He died on September 3, 1970 in Lexington, Davidson County, NC and was buried on September 6, 1970 in Lexington, Davidson County, NC at Forest Hill Memorial Park.

1554. Floyd Lee Wallace, son of Samuel Henry Bascom "Bass" Wallace and Nettie J. Britt, was born on June 4, 1913. He died on October 3, 1997 and was buried in Lexington, Davidson County, NC at Forest Hill Memorial Park.

Leila P. Young was born in 1925.

1557. Carson Lee Horner, son of Josiah Turner Horner and Agnes Chalmers Barrett, was born on August 5, 1894. He died on September 21, 1979.

Janie McLean was born in 1906. She died in 1995. She and Carson Lee Horner had the following children:

> 3720   Madison Horner (-)
> 3721   Kenell Horner (-)
> 3722   Sonnie Horner (-)
> 3723   Billie Horner (-)

1558. Beulah Horner, daughter of Josiah Turner Horner and Agnes Chalmers Barrett, was born on February 11, 1896. She died on May 5, 1979.

John Butler was born in 1890.

1559. James Thomas "Jack" Horner Sr., daughter of Josiah Turner Horner and Hattie Belle McLean, was born on August 2, 1915 in Fayetteville, Cumberland County, NC. She died on January 31, 2013 in Durham, Durham County, NC.

1560. Mabel Agnes Horner, daughter of Josiah Turner Horner and Hattie Belle McLean, was born on December 26, 1916 in Fayetteville, Cumberland County, NC. She died on August 31, 1992 in San Pedro, Los Angeles, California.

1561. Joseph Winford Horner, son of Josiah Turner Horner and Hattie Belle McLean, was born on February 23, 1919 in Fayetteville, Cumberland County, NC. He died on October 29, 1963 in Fayetteville, Cumberland County, NC.

Martha Elizabeth Blue was born on July 26, 1925. She died on July 27, 1997. She and Joseph Winford Horner had the following children:

> 3724   Donald G. Horner (-)

1562. Hattie Pauline Horner, daughter of Josiah Turner Horner and Hattie Belle McLean, was born on October 28, 1921 in Cumberland County, NC. She died on June 15, 2008 in Cathedral City, Riverside, California.

1563. Mollie Horner, daughter of William Branson "Bud" Horner and Martha Jane Garner, was born in September 1902. She died on April 10, 1921 and was buried in Robbins, Moore County, NC at Tabernacle United Methodist Church.

1564. Mamie Horner, daughter of William Branson "Bud" Horner and Martha Jane Garner, was born on May 23, 1905. She died on April 24, 1999 and was buried in Robbins, Moore County, NC at Tabernacle United Methodist Church.

Dewey Hobson Rouse, son of Malcolm Street Rouse (1871-1948) and Rebecca Jane Maness (1869-1951), was born on April 4, 1901. He died on June 22, 1975 and was buried in Robbins, Moore County, NC at Tabernacle United Methodist Church. He and Mamie Horner had the following children:

3725	Hester Rouse (1921-). *Hester was born on July 9, 1921 in Moore County, NC.*
3726	Carl Grier Rouse (1924-). *Carl was born on October 22, 1924 in Moore County, NC.*
3727	James Colon Rouse (1927-). *James was born on February 1, 1927 in Moore County, NC.*
3728	Johnsie Louise Rouse (1929-2017). *Johnsie was born on April 20, 1929 in Moore County, NC. She died on February 3, 2017.*
3729	Cecil Edward Rouse (1934-). *Cecil was born on June 25, 1934 in Moore County, NC.*
3730	Crissie Mae Rouse (1937-). *Crissie was born on May 13, 1937 in Moore County, NC.*

1565. **Archie Daniel Horner**, son of William Branson "Bud" Horner and Martha Jane Garner, was born on June 2, 1907. He died on December 4, 1980 and was buried in Robbins, Moore County, NC at Tabernacle United Methodist Church.

Lizar Myrtle Wallace, daughter of James Lewis Wallace (1875-1950) and Lillie Jane Maness (1884-1919), was born on March 25, 1911 in Moore County, NC. She died on January 1, 1988 and was buried in Robbins, Moore County, NC at Tabernacle United Methodist Church. She and Archie Daniel Horner had the following children:

3731	Wilbert Howard "Tom" Horner (1929-2010). *Wilbert was born on June 26, 1929. He married **Brenda Joyce Williams** on August 20, 1965 in Moore County, NC. He married **Sally Goad** on September 5, 1997 in Moore County, NC. He died on May 11, 2010.*
3732	Floyd E. Horner (1931-1963). *Floyd was born on May 2, 1931. He died on March 30, 1963 and was buried in Moore County, NC at Flint Hill Baptist Church.*

1567. **James Washington Horner**, son of William Branson "Bud" Horner and Martha Jane Garner, was born on April 19, 1912. He died on November 26, 1914 and was buried in Robbins, Moore County, NC at Tabernacle United Methodist Church.

1568. **Bonnie Mae Horner**, daughter of William Branson "Bud" Horner and Martha Jane Garner, was born on March 10, 1915. She married **Hobert Lester Williams** on December 23, 1933 in Moore County, NC.

Hobert Lester Williams, son of Quincy Archibald Williams (1877-1974) and Etta Jane Morgan (1881-1963), was born on September 27, 1907. He died on June 1, 1989 and was buried in Robbins, Moore County, NC at Pine Rest Cemetery. He and Bonnie Mae Horner had the following children:

3733	Hobert Earl Williams (1934-1998). *Hobert was born on September 16, 1934 in Moore County, NC. He died on March 25, 1998.*

1569. **Dola Fonnie Horner**, daughter of William Branson "Bud" Horner and Martha Jane Garner, was born on April 6, 1918. She died on July 24, 2002 and was buried in Robbins, Moore County, NC at Tabernacle United Methodist Church.

Howard Williams, son of James Rufus "Duck" Williams (1888-1965) and Hattie Louise Williamson (1891-1989), was born on July 31, 1917. He died on October 16, 1968 and was buried in Moore County, NC at Pine Grove Baptist Church.

1570. **Rady Ora Horner**, daughter of William Branson "Bud" Horner and Martha Jane Garner, was born on November 9, 1920 in Moore County, NC. She died on May 28, 1921 in Moore County, NC and was buried in Robbins, Moore County, NC at Tabernacle United Methodist Church.

1571. **Thelma Horner**, daughter of John W. Horner and Lena Mercer, was born on February 4, 1900. She died on August 7, 1965.

Wilbur Travis Brownley was born on May 10, 1900. He died on February 7, 1969. He and Thelma Horner had the following children:

3734	John Horner Brownley (1929-2005). *John was born on September 27, 1929. He died on May 8, 2005.*

1572. Edna Williams, daughter of Kenneth K. Williams and Mary Ann Horner, was born on December 27, 1899. She married **William Lewis Kennedy** on November 8, 1928 in Moore County, NC. She died on August 1, 1972 and was buried in Robbins, Moore County, NC at Tabernacle United Methodist Church.

William Lewis Kennedy, son of Jonathan G. Kennedy (1860-1938) and Elizabeth Alice Brewer (1877-1951), was born on October 9, 1898. He died on December 20, 1959 and was buried in Robbins, Moore County, NC at Pine Rest Cemetery. He and Edna Williams had the following children:

3735	Russell L. Kennedy (1929-1942). *Russell was born on October 7, 1929. He died on October 31, 1942 and was buried in Robbins, Moore County, NC at Tabernacle United Methodist Church.*
3736	Luther Curtis Kennedy (1932-). *Luther was born on April 13, 1932.*
3737	Clyde Franklin Kennedy (1933-). *Clyde was born on June 21, 1933.*
3738	Annie Ruth Kennedy (1937-2000). *Annie was born on September 13, 1937. She died on August 27, 2000 and was buried in Moore County, NC at Flint Hill Baptist Church.*

1573. Luther Clegg Williams, son of Kenneth K. Williams and Mary Ann Horner, was born on August 7, 1909 in Moore County, NC. He married **Annie L. Brown** on April 15, 1933. He died on May 11, 1962 and was buried in Robbins, Moore County, NC at Tabernacle United Methodist Church.

Annie L. Brown, daughter of James Wesley Brown (1891-1971) and Katie L. Garner (1895-1988), was born on September 1, 1915. She died on December 11, 2008 and was buried in Robbins, Moore County, NC at Tabernacle United Methodist Church. She and Luther Clegg Williams had the following children:

3739	Margaret Frances Williams (1938-). *Margaret was born on July 11, 1938 in Moore County, NC.*

1574. Grover Williams, son of Kenneth K. Williams and Mary Ann Horner, was born on February 15, 1914. He died on February 15, 1914 and was buried in Robbins, Moore County, NC at Tabernacle United Methodist Church.

1575. Eli Ritter, son of Noah R. Ritter and Martha Louvina Horner, was born on December 28, 1907. He died on September 16, 1994.

Dorothy Lewis, daughter of Charlie Clemmons Lewis (1881-1955) and Lillie Watson Morgan (1888-1962), was born in 1917. She died in 1979 and was buried in Moore County, NC at Big Oak Church. She and Eli Ritter had the following children:

3740	Ritter (-)

1576. Eulis Alfred Ritter, son of Noah R. Ritter and Martha Louvina Horner, was born on December 8, 1909. He died on December 7, 1968 and was buried in Moore County, NC at Flint Hill Baptist Church.

Ruth Crutchfield and Eulis Alfred Ritter had the following children:

3741	Wesley Alfred Ritter (1942-1942). *Wesley was born on March 19, 1942. He died on March 19, 1942 and was buried in Moore County, NC at Flint Hill Baptist Church.*
3742	Frances Ann Ritter (1947-). *Frances was born on July 18, 1947 in Moore County, NC.*

1577. Flossie Jenettie Ritter, daughter of Noah R. Ritter and Martha Louvina Horner, was born on March 8, 1913. She died on May 7, 1988 and was buried in Moore County, NC at Flint Hill Baptist Church.

1578. Etta Agnes Ritter, daughter of Noah R. Ritter and Martha Louvina Horner, was born on October 17, 1915.

John Robert Kennedy, son of Jonathan G. Kennedy (1860-1938) and Elizabeth Alice Brewer (1877-1951), was born on June 7, 1912. He died on November 12, 1977 and was buried in Robbins, Moore County, NC at Pine Rest Cemetery.

1581. **Jesse Vander Ritter**, son of Noah R. Ritter and Martha Louvina Horner, was born on March 25, 1925. He died on April 29, 1994 and was buried in Moore County, NC at Flint Hill Baptist Church.

1582. **Amaryllis Jean Wallace**, daughter of Wade Hampton Wallace and Rosanna M. Hooker, was born on June 8, 1932. She married **Charles Newell Hancock** on August 12, 1949 in Troy, Montgomery County, NC.

Charles Newell Hancock, son of William Pliny Hancock (1891-1969) and Dora E. Britt (1891-1976), was born on July 17, 1929. He died on April 27, 1999. He and Amaryllis Jean Wallace had the following children:

>   3743   Sarah Darlene Hancock (1952-). *Sarah was born on July 13, 1952.*
>   3744   Charles Newell Hancock (1958-). *Charles was born on August 27, 1958.*

1583. **Josie Ora Moore**, daughter of Wade Hampton Wallace and Sarah Louisa Williamson, was born on March 17, 1914 in Moore County, NC. She died on January 4, 1989 in Columbia, Richland County, SC.

Josie Ora Moore had the following children:

>   3745   James Edward Moore (1939-1969). *James was born on January 23, 1939. He died on November 2, 1969 in Germany.*

1584. **Mamie Riddle**, daughter of Wade Hampton Wallace and Annie Lakey, was born on September 8, 1893. She married **Willard Graves Allred** on February 22, 1914 in Durham, Durham County, NC. She died on October 18, 1958 in Moses Cone Memorial Hospital, Greensboro, Guilford County, NC and was buried in Greensboro, Guilford County, NC at Green Hill Cemetery.

Willard Graves Allred was born on March 23, 1887. He died on December 18, 1966 and was buried in Greensboro, Guilford County, NC at Green Hill Cemetery.

1585. **Benjamin Harrison Riddle**, son of Wade Hampton Wallace and Annie Lakey, was born on April 29, 1895. He married **Brady Bell Cates** on November 2, 1917 in Durham, Durham County, NC. He died on July 19, 1949 and was buried in Greensboro, Guilford County, NC at Green Hill Cemetery.

Brady Bell Cates was born in 1901. She and Benjamin Harrison Riddle had the following children:

>   3746   Wade Hampton Riddle (1923-1929). *Wade was born on December 30, 1923. He died on August 9, 1929 and was buried in Greensboro, Guilford County, NC at Green Hill Cemetery.*

1586. **Pearl M. Wallace**, daughter of Euphernia S. "Effie" Wallace, was born in January 1898. She married **Fred Allred** on July 14, 1918 in Moore County, NC.

Fred Allred, son of William A. Allred (1863-1934) and Nancy M. Stewart (1866-1947), was born on August 31, 1899. He died on February 8, 1919 and was buried in Moore County, NC at Allred Cemetery #260.

1588. **Archie Braxton Muse**, son of Archibald Asa Muse and Catherine E. Wallace, was born on September 24, 1903. He married **Rachel Foster** in 1948.

Rachel Foster and Archie Braxton Muse had the following children:

>   3747   Archie Henry Muse (-)
>   3748   Gail Muse (-)
>   3749   Howard B. Muse (-)
>   3750   William Franklin Muse (-)

1589. **Josie A. Muse**, daughter of Archibald Asa Muse and Catherine E. Wallace, was born on June 8, 1906. She died on July 20, 1976 and was buried in Moore County, NC at Friendship Baptist Church.

1590. **Johnsie M. Muse**, daughter of Archibald Asa Muse and Catherine E. Wallace, was born on December 6, 1909. She died on August 11, 1910 and was buried in Moore County, NC at Friendship Baptist Church.

1591. **Fred Lewis Barrett**, son of Alfred Powell Hill Barrett and Flossie Alma Wallace, was born on April 9, 1906. He died on May 29, 1907 and was buried in Rockingham, Richmond County, NC at East Side Cemetery.

1593. **Minnie Grace Barrett**, daughter of Alfred Powell Hill Barrett and Flossie Alma Wallace, was born on October 25, 1909. She married **John S. Braswell** on January 1, 1928.

John S. Braswell and Minnie Grace Barrett had the following children:

>   3751   Jean Gray Braswell (-)
>   3752   Billie Braswell (-)

1594. **John Ashley Carter**, son of John D. Carter and Jerusha Francis "Ruth" Wallace, was born on October 19, 1908. He died on May 26, 1981 and was buried in Rockingham, Richmond County, NC at Richmond Memorial Park.

Bessie Mae "Becky" Howell was born on May 17, 1903. She died on February 26, 2007 and was buried in Rockingham, Richmond County, NC at Richmond Memorial Park.

1595. **Addie Webb Carter**, daughter of John D. Carter and Jerusha Francis "Ruth" Wallace, was born on December 25, 1912. She married **William Milton Hughes II** on December 25, 1937 in Robeson County, NC. She died on September 17, 2008 and was buried in Lumberton, Robeson County, NC at Meadowbrook Cemetery.

William Milton Hughes II was born on September 8, 1906. He died on March 8, 1986 and was buried in Lumberton, Robeson County, NC at Meadowbrook Cemetery. He and Addie Webb Carter had the following children:

>   3753   Hughes (-)

1596. **James Ford Carter**, son of John D. Carter and Jerusha Francis "Ruth" Wallace, was born on April 26, 1916. He died on July 7, 1983 and was buried in Guilford County, NC at Forest Lawn Cemetery.

Edith Elizabeth "Lib" Copeland, daughter of Jesse Thomas Garfield Copeland (1879-1940) and Vergie Ada Smith (1898-1980), was born on July 25, 1919. She died on February 15, 2009 and was buried in Guilford County, NC at Forest Lawn Cemetery. She and James Ford Carter had the following children:

>   3754   Anita Carter (-)
>   3755   Janet Lynn Carter (-)
>   3756   Phyllis Elaine Carter (1942-1951). *Phyllis was born on February 16, 1942. She died on November 19, 1951 and was buried in Guilford County, NC at Forest Lawn Cemetery.*

1597. **Ruth Coleman "Coley" Carter**, daughter of John D. Carter and Jerusha Francis "Ruth" Wallace, was born on May 2, 1920 in Richmond County, NC. She died on August 5, 1997 and was buried in Hickory, Catawba County, NC at Catawba Memorial Park.

Carlos Garriga was born on November 7, 1917. He died on February 1, 2008 and was buried in Hickory, Catawba County, NC at Catawba Memorial Park.

1598. **Mary Louise Carter**, daughter of John D. Carter and Jerusha Francis "Ruth" Wallace, was born on September 18, 1923 in Richmond County, NC. She married **Thurman Curtis "T.C." Oliver** on March 22, 1975 in Lumberton, Robeson County, NC. She died on May 17, 2009 and was buried in Rockingham, Richmond County, NC at East Side Cemetery.

Thurman Curtis "T.C." Oliver was born on April 16, 1904. He died on October 5, 2000 and was buried in Lumberton, Robeson County, NC at Meadowbrook Cemetery.

1599. **Billy Braxton Carter**, son of John D. Carter and Jerusha Francis "Ruth" Wallace, was born on August 23, 1928 in Richmond County, NC. He died on December 14, 2011 and was buried in Shelby, Cleveland County, NC at Cleveland Memorial Park.

Shirley Mae Wilegus was born on January 17, 1934. She died on October 31, 2018 and was buried in Shelby, Cleveland County, NC at Cleveland Memorial Park.

1600. **Mildred Hamer Wallace**, daughter of Benjamin Harrison Wallace and Ruth Mable Dawson, was born on December 1, 1913. She died on August 4, 1998 in Wilmington, New Hanover County, NC.

Clifford Belmont Jones was born on December 2, 1910. He died on February 3, 1970. He and Mildred Hamer Wallace had the following children:

      3757   Algerrie Wallace Jones (-)

1601. **Benjamin Harrison Wallace Jr.**, son of Benjamin Harrison Wallace and Ruth Mable Dawson, was born on September 9, 1915 in Lumberton, Robeson County, NC. He died on March 28, 1994 in Thousand Oaks, Ventura County, CA.

1602. **Annie Ruth Wallace**, daughter of Benjamin Harrison Wallace and Ruth Mable Dawson, was born on March 31, 1917 in Robeson County, NC. She died on April 22, 1993 in Wilson, Wilson County, NC.

1603. **Mary Missouri Wallace**, daughter of Benjamin Harrison Wallace and Ruth Mable Dawson, was born on February 8, 1919 in Stanly County, NC. She died on November 19, 1994 in Albemarle, Stanly County, NC.

1604. **Elizabeth Delaney Wallace**, daughter of Benjamin Harrison Wallace and Luna Clementine Coble, was born on February 23, 1925 in Albemarle, Stanly County, NC. She died on August 11, 2006 in Aberdeen, Moore County, NC.

Luther Almond Adams was born on May 31, 1923. He died on April 30, 2004. He and Elizabeth Delaney Wallace had the following children:

      3758   Elizabeth Coble Adams (1953-). *Elizabeth was born on April 1, 1953.*

1605. **Calvin Coble Wallace**, son of Benjamin Harrison Wallace and Luna Clementine Coble, was born on October 5, 1928 in Albemarle, Stanly County, NC. He died on December 5, 1991 in Fayetteville, Cumberland County, NC.

Esther Williams and Calvin Coble Wallace had the following children:

      3759   Valerie Marie Wallace (-)

1606. **Hattie Jane McNeill**, daughter of Alexander McNeill and Lovedy Ann "Annie" Wallace, was born on January 6, 1886 in Moore County, NC. She died on October 29, 1945 in State Hospital, Raleigh, Wake County, NC and was buried in Robbins, Moore County, NC at Tabernacle United Methodist Church.

George Baxter Davis, son of Baxter Davis (1839-1914) and Sarah "Sallie" Yow (1841-1919), was born on August 16, 1882. He died on October 22, 1958 and was buried in Robbins, Moore County, NC at Tabernacle United Methodist Church.

1607. **Archibald Daniel "Archie" McNeill**, son of Alexander McNeill and Lovedy Ann "Annie" Wallace, was born on March 24, 1887 in Moore County, NC. He died on August 2, 1965 in Butner Hospital, Granville County, NC and was buried on August 4, 1965 in Moore County, NC at Brown's Chapel Christian Church.

1608. **Effie R. McNeill**, daughter of Alexander McNeill and Lovedy Ann "Annie" Wallace, was born on August 9, 1889. She married **George A. Brown** on March 22, 1907 in Moore County, NC. She died on February 26, 1913 and was buried in Moore County, NC at Brown's Chapel Christian Church.

George A. Brown, son of James M. Brown (1856-1928) and Martha Jane Wallace (1856-1929), was born on December 5, 1887. He died on April 11, 1914 in Moore County, NC and was buried in Moore County, NC at Brown's Chapel Christian Church. He and Effie R. McNeill had the following children:

      3760   May Brown (-)
      3761   Wilbur Brown (-)
      3762   Lillian Brown (-)

3763   Hattie W. Brown (1909-). *Hattie was born in 1909.*

1609. Virgil L. McNeill, son of Alexander McNeill and Lovedy Ann "Annie" Wallace, was born on November 6, 1891. He died on February 7, 1892 and was buried in Moore County, NC at Brown's Chapel Christian Church.

1610. Nettie F. McNeill, daughter of Alexander McNeill and Lovedy Ann "Annie" Wallace, was born on December 15, 1892. She died on December 7, 1893 and was buried in Moore County, NC at Brown's Chapel Christian Church.

1611. Hugh T. McNeill, son of Alexander McNeill and Lovedy Ann "Annie" Wallace, was born in March 1895. He married **Sallie Sophia Henson** on September 22, 1917 in Moore County, NC.

Sallie Sophia Henson, daughter of John Daniel Henson (1861-1950) and Margaret I. Person (1863-1951), was born on January 31, 1898. She died on April 1, 1988 and was buried in Moore County, NC at Mt. Carmel United Methodist Church. She and Hugh T. McNeill had the following children:

3764   Kathleen Faye McNeill (1919-). *Kathleen was born on December 1, 1919 in Moore County, NC.*

1612. Grady Lester Williams, son of George Dock Williams and Hattie Jane Wallace, was born on August 24, 1901. He died on November 2, 1957 and was buried in Moore County, NC at Virgil (Byrd) Wallace Cemetery.

Annie Mae Poole was born on July 19, 1906. She died on October 27, 1994 and was buried in Moore County, NC at Virgil (Byrd) Wallace Cemetery. She and Grady Lester Williams had the following children:

3765   Dorothy Williams (1927-). *Dorothy was born in 1927.*
3766   Lester Franklin Williams (1928-2003). *Lester was born on December 11, 1928 in Moore County, NC. He died on November 22, 2003 and was buried in Moore County, NC at Virgil (Byrd) Wallace Cemetery.*
3767   Edward Leon Williams (1933-2009). *Edward was born on April 3, 1933 in Moore County, NC. He died on November 4, 2009.*

1613. Bertha Rodela Williams, daughter of George Dock Williams and Hattie Jane Wallace, was born on September 5, 1903. She died on March 23, 1977 and was buried in Eagle Springs, Moore County, NC at Eagle Springs Baptist Church.

Lyndon Edward Zachary was born on September 9, 1902. He died on August 18, 1981 and was buried in Eagle Springs, Moore County, NC at Eagle Springs Baptist Church. He and Bertha Rodela Williams had the following children:

3768   Doris Zachary (-)
3769   Barbara Catherine Zachary (1939-). *Barbara was born on February 18, 1939 in Moore County, NC.*

1614. Bertha May Deaton, daughter of George Sanderlin Deaton and Martha Elizabeth Wallace, was born on August 27, 1895. She died on October 9, 1895 and was buried in Moore County, NC at Pine Grove Baptist Church.

1615. Ida Florence Deaton, daughter of George Sanderlin Deaton and Martha Elizabeth Wallace, was born on September 14, 1896. She married **Burney Garner** on April 5, 1926 in Moore County, NC. She died on March 2, 1961 in Moore County, NC.

1616. Maudie Easter Deaton, daughter of George Sanderlin Deaton and Martha Elizabeth Wallace, was born on January 25, 1899 in Moore County, NC. She died on May 5, 1951 in Cabarrus County, NC and was buried in Moore County, NC at Pine Grove Baptist Church.

John Ed Nunn was born on July 13, 1906 in Patrick County, VA. He died on January 16, 1977 in Buncombe County, NC. He and Maudie Easter Deaton had the following children:

3770   John Frank Nunn (1927-1973). *John was born on January 8, 1927. He died in November 1973.*

3771	George Edward Nunn (1929-1982). *George was born on January 27, 1929. He died on March 7, 1982.*
3772	Marilyn Nunn (1931-1983). *Marilyn was born on November 17, 1931. She died on September 3, 1983.*
3773	Cecil Warren Nunn (1933-1988). *Cecil was born on June 13, 1933. He died on May 23, 1988.*
3774	Billy Ray Nunn (1936-2003). *Billy was born on May 30, 1936. He died on August 8, 2003.*
3775	Frances Louise Nunn (1939-1940). *Frances was born on July 7, 1939. She died on September 3, 1940 and was buried in Moore County, NC at Pine Grove Baptist Church.*

1617. **Gurney Carlton Deaton**, son of George Sanderlin Deaton and Martha Elizabeth Wallace, was born on May 22, 1902. He died on May 18, 1967 and was buried in Moore County, NC at Pine Grove Baptist Church.

Nellie Florence Williams, daughter of James Millard "Jim" Williams (1874-1965) and Laura Maness (1886-1967), was born on November 3, 1905. She died on November 1, 1988 and was buried in Moore County, NC at Pine Grove Baptist Church. She and Gurney Carlton Deaton had the following children:

3776	Meriel C. Deaton (1927-2011). *Meriel was born on May 21, 1927. He married **Iris Eldena Vickers** on October 22, 1954 in Randolph County, NC. He died on July 26, 2011.*
3777	Jeraldean Deaton (1928-1929). *Jeraldean was born on December 30, 1928. She died on May 23, 1929 and was buried in Moore County, NC at Pine Grove Baptist Church.*
3778	Doris Gene Deaton (1935-1999). *Doris was born on April 20, 1935. She died on August 5, 1999 and was buried in Moore County, NC at Flint Hill Baptist Church.*
3779	James Farrell Deaton (1936-). *James was born on July 12, 1936.*
3780	Billy Wayne Deaton (1940-1968). *Billy was born on April 14, 1940. He died on February 4, 1968 and was buried in Moore County, NC at Pine Grove Baptist Church.*
3781	Jerry Harold Deaton (1942-1989). *Jerry was born on June 12, 1942. He died on January 11, 1989 and was buried in Moore County, NC at Pine Grove Baptist Church.*
3782	Carol Lavene Deaton (1945-). *Carol was born on March 25, 1945.*

1618. **Lillie Jane Deaton**, daughter of George Sanderlin Deaton and Martha Elizabeth Wallace, was born on May 12, 1908. She died on February 7, 1972 and was buried in Moore County, NC at Pine Grove Baptist Church.

Frank Hurley Hancock, son of William Thomas Hancock (1863-1919) and Sarah Jane Williams (1866-1956), was born on July 31, 1905. He died on February 11, 1988 and was buried in Moore County, NC at Pine Grove Baptist Church. He and Lillie Jane Deaton had the following children:

3783	Frank Hurley Hancock Jr. (1932-). *Frank was born on February 9, 1932.*
3784	Marvin Ray Hancock (1933-). *Marvin was born on September 11, 1933.*
3785	Wilton Lee Hancock (1937-). *Wilton was born on May 27, 1937.*
3786	Bobby S. Hancock (1939-1941). *Bobby was born on June 10, 1939. He died on July 13, 1941 and was buried in Moore County, NC at Pine Grove Baptist Church.*
3787	Vera Mae Hancock (1941-). *Vera was born on June 15, 1941.*

1619. **John Earl Deaton**, son of George Sanderlin Deaton and Martha Elizabeth Wallace, was born on June 26, 1910. He died on February 11, 1984 and was buried in Moore County, NC at Pine Grove Baptist Church.

Meda Mae Hancock, daughter of William Thomas Hancock (1863-1919) and Sarah Jane Williams (1866-1956), was born on June 13, 1907. She married Eddie C. Greene on October 28, 1924 in Montgomery County, NC. She died on January 18, 2000 and was buried in Moore County, NC at Brown's Chapel Christian Church. She and John Earl Deaton had the following children:

3788	Paul Lee Hancock (1932-1993). *Paul was born on May 2, 1932. He died on January 26, 1993 and was buried in Moore County, NC at Brown's Chapel Christian Church.*
3789	Martha Pauline Hancock (1932-1999). *Martha was born on May 2, 1932. She died on May 16, 1999 and was buried in Moore County, NC at Brown's Chapel Christian Church.*

1620. **Virgil Pearl "Bird" Deaton**, son of George Sanderlin Deaton and Martha Elizabeth Wallace, was born on June 26, 1910. He married **Emily Niner Sheffield** on March 7, 1932 in Moore County, NC. He died on January 7, 1968 and was buried in Moore County, NC at Brown's Chapel Christian Church.

Emily Niner Sheffield, daughter of Elias Kenneth Sheffield (1895-1946) and Rosa Ellen Morgan (1898-1970), was born on July 15, 1916. She died on January 31, 1965 and was buried in Moore County, NC at Brown's Chapel Christian Church. She and Virgil Pearl "Bird" Deaton had the following children:

3790	Geneva Lorene Deaton (1935-). *Geneva was born on March 10, 1935.*
3791	Virginia Colene Deaton (1938-). *Virginia was born on October 11, 1938.*
3792	Robert Fulton Deaton (1940-). *Robert was born on December 13, 1940.*
3793	Barbara Ann Deaton (1942-). *Barbara was born on June 20, 1942.*
3794	Jesse Hilborn Deaton (1944-2006). *Jesse was born on October 24, 1944. He died on May 27, 2006 in Randolph County, NC.*
3795	Virlin George Deaton (1946-). *Virlin was born on December 29, 1946.*
3796	Rosa Ellen Deaton (1948-). *Rosa was born on September 3, 1948.*
3797	Nancy Carol Deaton (1952-). *Nancy was born on March 11, 1952.*
3798	Gail Marie Deaton (1954-). *Gail was born on March 6, 1954.*
3799	Dale Oral Deaton (1957-). *Dale was born on September 10, 1957.*

1621. **Isham Deaton**, son of George Sanderlin Deaton and Martha Elizabeth Wallace, was born on July 27, 1913. He died on December 9, 1947 in Moore County, NC and was buried in Moore County, NC at Pine Grove Baptist Church.

1622. **Lettie Ethel Deaton**, daughter of George Sanderlin Deaton and Martha Elizabeth Wallace, was born on February 3, 1916.

Charles Dolphus Ewing and Lettie Ethel Deaton had the following children:

3800	Donald Eugene Ewing (1940-2003). *Donald was born on December 28, 1940. He died on June 15, 2003 and was buried in Norfolk, VA at Forest Lawn Cemetery.*

1623. **Joseph Franklin Deaton**, son of George Sanderlin Deaton and Martha Elizabeth Wallace, was born on August 12, 1918.

1624. **Charles Hoyt Deaton**, son of George Sanderlin Deaton and Martha Elizabeth Wallace, was born on February 12, 1921 in Moore County, NC. He died on January 25, 1926 in High Point Hospital, High Point, Guilford County, NC and was buried in Moore County, NC at Pine Grove Baptist Church.

1625. **Willie Paul Deaton**, son of George Sanderlin Deaton and Martha Elizabeth Wallace, was born on May 9, 1923.

Mary Edna Hubert and Willie Paul Deaton had the following children:

3801	Janice Lane Deaton (1954-). *Janice was born on April 17, 1954.*

1626. **Minnie Lee Wallace**, daughter of Isham Wallace and Bertha Hall, was born on June 18, 1902 in Moore County, NC. She married **Arthur Clemons "Offie" Morgan** on January 25, 1921 in Moore County, NC. She died on March 4, 1972 in Moore County, NC and was buried on March 6, 1972 in Moore County, NC at Beulah Hill Baptist Church.

Arthur Clemons "Offie" Morgan, son of David Newton Morgan (1873-1943) and Cynthia Ann "Annie" Wallace (1873-1906), was born on May 1, 1899. He died on September 28, 1957 and was buried in Moore County, NC at Beulah Hill Baptist Church. He and Minnie Lee Wallace had the following children:

3802	Walter Carson Morgan (1921-). *Walter was born on August 26, 1921.*
3803	Worthy Lee Morgan (1923-). *Worthy was born on April 1, 1923.*
3804	Male Morgan (1924-). *Male was born on September 12, 1924.*
3805	Alexander Morgan (1927-1980). *Alexander was born on January 13, 1927. He died on August 8, 1980 in Moore County, NC and was buried in Moore County, NC at Beulah Hill Baptist Church.*

3806	Alvin Clemons Morgan (1929-). *Alvin was born on March 5, 1929.*
3807	Faye Irene Morgan (1930-2001). *Faye was born on November 16, 1930. She died on March 23, 2001.*
3808	Eugene Hamilton "Bud" Morgan (1932-1981). *Eugene was born on August 23, 1932. He died on March 5, 1981 and was buried in Moore County, NC at Beulah Hill Baptist Church.*
3809	Lois Lee Morgan (1934-1938). *Lois was born on July 18, 1934. She died on June 1, 1938 and was buried in Moore County, NC at Beulah Hill Baptist Church.*
3810	Female 1 Morgan (1936-). *Female was born on September 14, 1936.*
3811	Female 2 Morgan (1936-). *Female was born on September 14, 1936.*

1627. Hattie Jane Wallace, daughter of Isham Wallace and Bertha Hall, was born on April 23, 1904. She died on March 3, 1981 and was buried on March 5, 1981 in Moore County, NC at Virgil (Byrd) Wallace Cemetery.

Carson Lee Rouse, son of Lucinda Ann "Cindy" Rouse (1875-1919), was born on December 24, 1897. He died on January 12, 1965 and was buried on January 14, 1965 in Moore County, NC at Rock Hill Church. He and Hattie Jane Wallace had the following children:

3812	Dorothy Rouse (-)
3813	Arthur Carlton Rouse (1921-1978). *Arthur was born on October 26, 1921. He died on July 23, 1978 and was buried in Moore County, NC at Virgil (Byrd) Wallace Cemetery.*
3814	Ethel Lee Rouse (1924-). *Ethel was born on January 19, 1924.*
3815	Mabel Green Rouse (1926-). *Mabel was born on December 13, 1926.*
3816	Herbert Rouse (1929-). *Herbert was born on August 12, 1929.*
3817	Betty Jean Rouse (1932-2003). *Betty was born on March 6, 1932. She died on September 27, 2003 and was buried in Moore County, NC at Virgil (Byrd) Wallace Cemetery.*
3818	Margaret Rouse (1934-). *Margaret was born on February 27, 1934.*
3819	Doris Mae Rouse (1938-). *Doris was born on April 28, 1938.*
3820	Haroldeane Rouse (1939-). *Haroldeane was born on June 17, 1939.*
3821	Geraldine Rouse (1939-2005). *Geraldine was born on June 17, 1939. She died on March 29, 2005 and was buried in Moore County, NC at Culdee Presbyterian Church.*
3822	Veronica Elaine Rouse (1944-). *Veronica was born on March 4, 1944.*
3823	Valeria Eileen Rouse (1944-). *Valeria was born on March 4, 1944.*

1628. Emma Mae Wallace, daughter of Isham Wallace and Flora Britt, was born on March 22, 1908 in Moore County, NC. She married **Lockey Merriott Garner** on July 19, 1925. She died on May 17, 1995 and was buried in Moore County, NC at Big Oak Church.

Roy Cornelius Beane, son of Walter Bean (-) and Delphia Klass (-), was born on February 1, 1921. He died on June 4, 1977 in Durham County, NC and was buried in Moore County, NC at Big Oak Church.

Lockey Merriott Garner, son of James Douglas Garner (1855-1935) and Lillie Alma Maness (1880-1972), was born on December 9, 1905 in Moore County, NC. He died on July 3, 1992 and was buried in Moore County, NC at Flint Hill Baptist Church. He and Emma Mae Wallace had the following children:

3824	Worthy Addison Garner (1926-2009). *Worthy was born on June 30, 1926 in Moore County, NC. He married **Texie Edder Garner** on June 2, 1945. He died on July 15, 2009 in Moore Regional Hospital, Pinehurst, Moore County, NC and was buried on July 18, 2009 in Moore County, NC at Flint Hill Baptist Church.*
3825	Robert Edward Garner (1928-). *Robert was born on March 8, 1928.*

1631. Lydia Annie Wallace, daughter of Isham Wallace and Flora Britt, was born on February 1, 1914. She married **Kenny Cassidy Maness** on October 1, 1932. She died on January 25, 1982 and was buried in Moore County, NC at Virgil (Byrd) Wallace Cemetery.

Kenny Cassidy Maness, son of Jonah Baxter Maness (1870-1961) and Alice Susannah Cockman (1863-1949), was born on April 10, 1905. He died on March 8, 1981 and was buried in Moore County, NC at Virgil (Byrd) Wallace Cemetery. He and Lydia Annie Wallace had the following children:

3826	Donald Cassidy Maness (1934-2005). *Donald was born on February 4, 1934. He died on July 16, 2005 and was buried in Moore County, NC at Virgil (Byrd) Wallace Cemetery.*
3827	James Paul Maness (1936-). *James was born on February 14, 1936.*
3828	Dorothy Lee Maness (1937-). *Dorothy was born on October 18, 1937. She married* **Walter Boudoin** *on February 17, 1956.*
3829	Gertrude Eloise Maness (1939-). *Gertrude was born on November 7, 1939. She married* **Robert Melvin Duguay** *on February 1, 1957.*
3830	Clyde Roger Maness (1941-). *Clyde was born on November 6, 1941.*
3831	Judy Ann Maness (1943-). *Judy was born on November 30, 1943.*
3832	Raymond Leroy Maness (1946-). *Raymond was born on April 30, 1946.*
3833	Johnnie Kenneth Maness (1948-). *Johnnie was born on March 30, 1948.*
3834	David Farrell Maness (1951-). *David was born on December 30, 1951. He married* **Lenora Ann Dupuis** *on July 8, 1973.*
3835	Roger Maness (1954-1954). *Roger was born on October 13, 1954 in Moore County, NC. He died on October 13, 1954 in Moore County, NC and was buried in Moore County, NC at Virgil (Byrd) Wallace Cemetery.*
3836	Bonnie Sue Maness (1958-). *Bonnie was born on January 10, 1958.*

1632. **Clyde Grover Wallace**, son of Isham Wallace and Flora Britt, was born on December 10, 1917 in Moore County, NC. He died on January 13, 1983 and was buried in Moore County, NC at Virgil (Byrd) Wallace Cemetery.

Vada Jones was born on August 4, 1925. She died on July 3, 1997 and was buried in Moore County, NC at Virgil (Byrd) Wallace Cemetery.

1633. **Claude Cleveland Wallace**, son of Isham Wallace and Flora Britt, was born on June 18, 1920 in Moore County, NC. He married **Annie Mae Maness** on July 2, 1937 in Moore County, NC. He died on October 23, 1981 and was buried in Robbins, Moore County, NC at Pine Rest Cemetery.

Annie Mae Maness, daughter of Garrett Hobert Maness (1896-1981) and Katie Jane Garner (1905-1952), was born on December 7, 1922. She and Claude Cleveland Wallace had the following children:

3837	William Lewis Wallace (1939-). *William was born on January 1, 1939 in Moore County, NC. He married* **Nancy Louise Boyte** *on December 22, 1957. He married* **Barbara Estelle Hussey** *on May 5, 1996 in Moore County, NC.*
3838	Fred Erwin Wallace (1940-2013). *Fred was born on December 18, 1940. He died on March 17, 2013.*
3839	Bobby Stewart Wallace (1942-). *Bobby was born on December 18, 1942.*
3840	Claude Cleveland Wallace Jr. (1944-2018). *Claude was born on September 13, 1944. He died on December 7, 2018.*

1634. **Beulah Wallace**, daughter of Isham Wallace and Flora Britt, was born on April 14, 1923 in Moore County, NC. She died on April 14, 1923 in Moore County, NC and was buried in Moore County, NC at Virgil (Byrd) Wallace Cemetery.

[Left] **Grady Williams and Annie Mae Poole**
[Below Left] **Bertha Rodella Williams Zachary and Lyndon Edward Zachary**
(Courtesy of Barbara Zachary, West End, NC)

[Below Right] **Hattie Jane Wallace Rouse**
(Courtesy of Lenora Tickle, Cary, NC)

Carson Rouse, Hattie Jane Wallace and family *(Courtesy of Lenora Tickle, Cary, NC)*

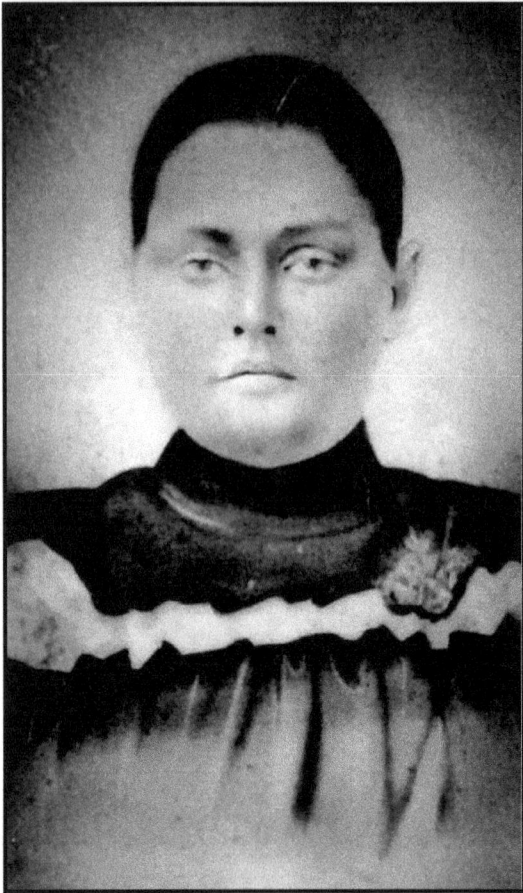

[Above Left] **Bertha Hall** [Above Right] **Clyde Wallace and Isham Wallace** *(Courtesy of Roxanne Johnson)*
[Left] **Claude Wallace** *(Courtesy of Ronnie Wallace)*

1635. **Dossie L. Williams**, son of Charles Benjamin Williams and Lula Florence Wallace, was born on January 10, 1903. He died on March 4, 1949 and was buried in Moore County, NC at Virgil (Byrd) Wallace Cemetery.

Bonnie L. Davis, daughter of George Archibald Davis (1867-1934) and Catherine Elizabeth McNeill (1870-1917), was born on January 6, 1904. She died on September 4, 1951 and was buried in Moore County, NC at Virgil (Byrd) Wallace Cemetery. She and Dossie L. Williams had the following children:

3841	Edith Lorraine Williams (1924-1998). *Edith was born on April 5, 1924. She died on July 25, 1998 and was buried in Moore County, NC at Virgil (Byrd) Wallace Cemetery.*
3842	Pattie Elizabeth Williams (1926-). *Pattie was born on May 18, 1926. She married **Roby Ellis Williams** on December 21, 1946.*
3843	Lula Mae Williams (1928-). *Lula was born on May 2, 1928.*
3844	Sally Geraldine Williams (1930-). *Sally was born on September 2, 1930.*

1636. **Regina Williams**, daughter of Charles Benjamin Williams and Lula Florence Wallace, was born on January 15, 1905. She married **Jessie Tom Sanders** circa 1926. She died on April 27, 1984 and was buried in Moore County, NC at Pine Grove Baptist Church.

Jessie Tom Sanders, son of George H. Sanders (1872-1936) and Blennie Alice Garner (1882-1958), was born on August 10, 1905. He died on March 5, 1988 and was buried in Moore County, NC at Pine Grove Baptist Church. He and Regina Williams had the following children:

3845	Floyd Sanders (1926-). *Floyd was born on December 13, 1926 in Moore County, NC.*
3846	Lucy Evelyn Sanders (1928-). *Lucy was born on December 20, 1928 in Moore County, NC.*
3847	Charlie Sanders (1931-1931). *Charlie was born on January 29, 1931 in Moore County, NC. He died on January 29, 1931 in Moore County, NC and was buried in Moore County, NC at Sanders Cemetery #274.*
3848	Elmer Sanders (1932-). *Elmer was born on March 11, 1932 in Moore County, NC.*
3849	Rose Ann Sanders (1934-1934). *Rose was born on October 24, 1934. She died on October 24, 1934 and was buried in Moore County, NC at Sanders Cemetery #274.*
3850	Pauline Sanders (1936-). *Pauline was born on January 19, 1936 in Moore County, NC.*
3851	Flossie Mae Sanders (1938-). *Flossie was born on March 26, 1938 in Moore County, NC.*
3852	Beulah Sanders (1939-1941). *Beulah was born on November 11, 1939 in Moore County, NC. She died on November 16, 1941 in Moore County, NC and was buried in Moore County, NC at Sanders Cemetery #274.*

1640. **Hazel Wallace**, daughter of Burney Leason Wallace and Bessie Lee Needham, was born on August 20, 1913. She married **Samuel Jordan Edwards** on July 23, 1933. She died on August 9, 1967 and was buried in Moore County, NC at Calvary Baptist Church.

Samuel Jordan Edwards, son of Everett Edwards (-) and Fanette (-), was born on April 11, 1912. He died on July 28, 1951 and was buried in Moore County, NC at Calvary Baptist Church. He and Hazel Wallace had the following children:

3853	Robert Lee Edwards (1932-). *Robert was born on August 15, 1932.*
3854	Jackie Francis Edwards (1934-). *Jackie was born on June 17, 1934.*
3855	Helen Edwards (1935-2020). *Helen was born on September 3, 1935. She died on August 8, 2020 and was buried in High Falls, Moore County, NC at Prosperity Friends Meeting Cemetery.*
3856	Bernie Everette Edwards (1937-1998). *Bernie was born on January 19, 1937. He died on June 30, 1998 and was buried in Moore County, NC at Calvary Baptist Church.*
3857	Margaret A. Edwards (1939-1961). *Margaret was born on March 10, 1939. She died on June 4, 1961 and was buried in Moore County, NC at Calvary Baptist Church.*
3858	Samuel Jordan Edwards Jr. (1943-2002). *Samuel was born on February 17, 1943. He died on April 29, 2002 and was buried in Moore County, NC at Calvary Baptist Church.*

1641. **Dewey Green Wallace**, son of Burney Leason Wallace and Bessie Lee Needham, was born on May 29, 1915 in Moore County, NC. He married **Pauline Hicks** on March 27, 1948. He died on October 25, 1979 and was buried in Moore County, NC at Calvary Baptist Church.

Pauline Hicks, daughter of J. Alton Hicks (1894-1978) and Iona Johnson (1899-1973), was born on March 12, 1927. She died on May 9, 2003 and was buried in Moore County, NC at Calvary Baptist Church. She and Dewey Green Wallace had the following children:

3859	Dewey Randall Wallace (1950-2007). *Dewey was born on January 6, 1950 in Moore County, NC. He died on October 4, 2007 in PA.*
3860	Janet Lynn Wallace (1952-). *Janet was born on March 30, 1952 in Moore County, NC.*

1642. **Dora Leason Wallace**, daughter of Burney Leason Wallace and Bessie Lee Needham, was born on June 21, 1918. She died on April 4, 1985 and was buried in Moore County, NC at Calvary Baptist Church.

Erskine Quince Benjamin was born on October 11, 1896. He died on August 13, 1962 and was buried in Moore County, NC at Calvary Baptist Church. He and Dora Leason Wallace had the following children:

3861	Benjamin (1942-1942). *[unnamed person] was born on October 31, 1942. He died on October 31, 1942 and was buried in Moore County, NC at Calvary Baptist Church.*
3862	Peggy Lee Benjamin (1944-). *Peggy was born on November 30, 1944.*

1643. **Essie Lee Wallace**, daughter of Burney Leason Wallace and Bessie Lee Needham, was born on February 14, 1921 in Moore County, NC. She died on November 16, 1988 and was buried in Moore County, NC at Calvary Baptist Church.

1644. **Annie Ruth Wallace**, daughter of Burney Leason Wallace and Bessie Lee Needham, was born on April 21, 1924 in Moore County, NC.

Joseph Clyde Seawell was born in 1927. He and Annie Ruth Wallace had the following children:

3863	Joseph Clyde Seawell Jr. (1943-1983). *Joseph was born on March 10, 1943. He died on August 12, 1983 and was buried in Moore County, NC at Calvary Baptist Church.*
3864	Nancy Ruth Seawell (1944-1951). *Nancy was born on September 5, 1944. She died on July 1, 1951 in Moore County, NC and was buried in Moore County, NC at Calvary Baptist Church.*
3865	Linda Gray Seawell (1947-). *Linda was born on January 27, 1947.*
3866	Johnny Leason Seawell (1947-1967). *Johnny was born on December 14, 1947. He died on January 28, 1967 and was buried in Moore County, NC at Calvary Baptist Church.*

1645. **Johnsie Grier Wallace**, daughter of Burney Leason Wallace and Bessie Lee Needham, was born on April 14, 1931.

Dempsey Edward Frye, son of Robert Clive Frye (1905-1974) and Nova Needham (1912-1982), was born on August 28, 1928. He died on April 25, 2015 and was buried in Dillon, Dillon County, SC at Evergreen Cemetery. He and Johnsie Grier Wallace had the following children:

3867	Brenda Sue Frye (1950-). *Brenda was born on February 3, 1950.*
3868	Loretta Kay Frye (1957-). *Loretta was born on July 29, 1957.*

1647. **Marjorie McNeill** was the daughter of William Thomas McNeill and Beulah Hazel Wallace.

Lassiter Hussey was the son of Jonah Marion Hussey (1887-1960) and Nancy Jane Brewer (1886-1972).

1649. **Dora E. McNeill**, daughter of William Thomas McNeill and Beulah Hazel Wallace, was born on July 1, 1920.

Harold Thompson Kennedy, son of John Spinks Kennedy (1895-1982) and Jerusha Annie Maness (1898-1987), was born on July 7, 1922. He died on September 10, 1983 and was buried in Moore County, NC at Smyrna Methodist Church. He and Dora E. McNeill had the following children:

3869	Dora Helen Kennedy (1940-). *Dora was born on March 31, 1940. She married* **Gurney**

Clinton Brewer on April 1, 1961.

1650. **Richard Thomas McNeill**, son of William Thomas McNeill and Beulah Hazel Wallace, was born on May 20, 1926. He died on December 10, 2017.

Thelma Louise Garner, daughter of Ira Jason Garner (1895-1972) and Maida Frances Williams (1901-1971), was born on July 18, 1926. She and Richard Thomas McNeill had the following children:

3870	Garry Richard McNeill (1946-). *Garry was born on November 18, 1946.*
3871	Jewelene Louise McNeill (1950-). *Jewelene was born on August 25, 1950.*
3872	Althea Doreen McNeill (1956-2017). *Althea was born on July 31, 1956. She died on December 1, 2017.*

1651. **Clarence McNeill**, son of William Thomas McNeill and Beulah Hazel Wallace, was born on May 10, 1928. He died on June 24, 2000.

Janie Estell Spivey, daughter of Eli S. Spivey (1893-1973) and Mamie Ethel Spivey (1894-1964), was born on September 29, 1929. She died on April 22, 1998. She and Clarence McNeill had the following children:

3873	Sharon McNeill (-)

1652. **Dorothy Mae McNeill**, daughter of William Thomas McNeill and Beulah Hazel Wallace, was born on March 25, 1931. She married **William Dolphia Garner** in 1968. She died on July 8, 2001 and was buried on July 10, 2001 in Burlington, Alamance County, NC at Alamance Memorial Park.

William Dolphia Garner, son of William Wesley Garner (1885-1967) and Martha L. Caviness (1895-1973), was born on May 23, 1927 in Moore County, NC. He married Doris Jean Williamson on September 27, 1947 in Moore County, NC. He died on March 17, 2012 in Burlington, Alamance County, NC and was buried on March 22, 2012 in Burlington, Alamance County, NC at Alamance Memorial Park. He and Dorothy Mae McNeill had the following children:

3874	William Mark Garner (1969-). *William was born on April 19, 1969 in Burlington, Alamance County, NC. He married* **Sherry Lee June** *on March 21, 1992 in Burlington, Alamance County, NC.*
3875	Willie Dale Garner (1970-). *Willie was born on June 1, 1970 in Burlington, Alamance County, NC.*

1653. **Annie Mozelle McNeill**, daughter of William Thomas McNeill and Beulah Hazel Wallace, was born on May 4, 1938. She died on November 22, 1940 in Moore County, NC.

1654. **Peter Paul McNeill**, son of William Thomas McNeill and Beulah Hazel Wallace, was born on May 8, 1939. He died on March 7, 2020 and was buried in Bennett, Chatham County, NC at Fall Creek Baptist Church Cemetery.

Eva Mae Phillips, daughter of Harold Cheek Phillips (1916-) and Eula Nancy Shields (1918-), was born on June 1, 1943. She and Peter Paul McNeill had the following children:

3876	Mary Murlene McNeill (-)
3877	Peter Paul McNeill Jr. (-)
3878	Janet Marie McNeill (-)
3879	Nancy Jacqueline McNeill (1962-2020). *Nancy was born on March 12, 1962. She died on May 22, 2020.*

1658. **Roy Edward Britt** was the son of Barney Edward Britt and Cora Bell Wallace.

Betty Joan Stutts and Roy Edward Britt had the following children:

3880	Bambi Shawn Britt (1977-1998). *Bambi was born on May 13, 1977 in Moore Regional Hospital, Pinehurst, Moore County, NC. She died on September 26, 1998 and was buried in Moore County, NC at Virgil (Byrd) Wallace Cemetery.*

1660. **James Robert Britt**, son of Barney Edward Britt and Cora Bell Wallace, was born on May 8, 1931. He died on August 14, 1998 and was buried in Moore County, NC at Virgil (Byrd) Wallace Cemetery.

1663. **Bettie Lou Britt**, daughter of Barney Edward Britt and Cora Bell Wallace, was born on July 22, 1944. She died on July 25, 1944 and was buried in Moore County, NC at Virgil (Byrd) Wallace Cemetery.

1664. **Dora Mae Wallace**, daughter of Stephen Devotion Williams and Cora Bell Wallace, was born on August 19, 1921.

> **Eldon Carl Cagle**, son of Jonah Franklin Cagle (1892-1972) and Mintie Lee Williams (1900-1949), was born on November 17, 1918. He died on April 21, 1971 and was buried in Moore County, NC at Unity Grove Baptist Church. He and Dora Mae Wallace had the following children:

>> 3881   Vickie Sue Cagle (1954-). *Vickie was born on September 29, 1954.*

1667. **Johnsie Elizabeth Wallace**, daughter of Steadman McLendon Wallace and Annie Boder York, was born on September 22, 1928 in Montgomery County, NC. She died on December 11, 1996 in Hamlet, Richmond County, NC and was buried in Moore County, NC at Brown's Chapel Christian Church.

> **McBride** and Johnsie Elizabeth Wallace had the following children:

>> 3882   Carlos C. McBride (-)

1668. **Irma Jean Wallace**, daughter of Steadman McLendon Wallace and Annie Boder York, was born on July 4, 1931 in Montgomery County, NC. She died in 2007.

> **Billy Lee Saunders**, son of Aaron Leo Saunders (1893-1981) and Mary Bell Lammonds (1898-1974), was born on April 5, 1932. He and Irma Jean Wallace had the following children:

>> 3883   Jeffie Jean Sanders (1958-). *Jeffie was born on November 10, 1958.*

1669. **Steadman McLendon Wallace Jr.**, son of Steadman McLendon Wallace and Annie Boder York, was born on September 6, 1934 in Montgomery County, NC. He married **Wilma Lee Simpson** on June 17, 1955 in Montgomery County, NC. He died on August 31, 1983.

> Wilma Lee Simpson was born on October 11, 1936 in Montgomery County, NC.

1670. **Dora Wilma Sanders**, daughter of Canoy Allen "Ned" Sanders and Jeanette "Nettie" Wallace, was born on January 8, 1923. She died on April 11, 1998.

1671. **Swannie Evelyn Sanders**, daughter of Canoy Allen "Ned" Sanders and Jeanette "Nettie" Wallace, was born on November 16, 1924. She died on January 15, 2001 and was buried in Moore County, NC at Virgil (Byrd) Wallace Cemetery.

> **William Ray Spivey**, son of Peter Riley Spivey (1885-1973) and Ida Jane Davis (1890-1948), was born on January 16, 1926. He died on October 13, 1985 and was buried in Moore County, NC at Virgil (Byrd) Wallace Cemetery. He and Swannie Evelyn Sanders had the following children:

>> 3884   Margaret Lorette Spivey (1941-1947). *Margaret was born on August 3, 1941. She died on June 25, 1947 and was buried in Moore County, NC at Virgil (Byrd) Wallace Cemetery.*
>> 3885   Linda Kay Spivey (1948-). *Linda was born on June 27, 1948. She married **Don Terry Maness** on December 24, 1967 in Moore County, NC at Crossroads Baptist Church.*
>> 3886   Sarah Evelyn Spivey (1949-). *Sarah was born on November 17, 1949.*
>> 3887   William Earl Spivey (1951-). *William was born on October 2, 1951. He married **Ann Key** on January 16, 1971.*

1672. Bertha Elizabeth Sanders, daughter of Canoy Allen "Ned" Sanders and Jeanette "Nettie" Wallace, was born on May 2, 1927. She died on January 27, 1988 and was buried in Moore County, NC at Brown's Chapel Christian Church.

Ernest Bruce, son of Not sure which Bruce (-), was born on July 30, 1920. He died on January 19, 1956 and was buried in Moore County, NC at Brown's Chapel Christian Church. He and Bertha Elizabeth Sanders had the following children:

> 3888   Helen Louise Bruce (1944-1996). *Helen was born on February 28, 1944. She married* ***Claude Earl Williams*** *on March 21, 1960. She died on November 30, 1996 and was buried in Moore County, NC at Brown's Chapel Christian Church.*

1673. Ethel Marie Sanders, daughter of Canoy Allen "Ned" Sanders and Jeanette "Nettie" Wallace, was born on May 7, 1929. She died on February 8, 2002 and was buried in Moore County, NC at Virgil (Byrd) Wallace Cemetery.

Arthur Carlton Rouse, son of Carson Lee Rouse (1897-1965) and Hattie Jane Wallace (1904-1981), was born on October 26, 1921. He died on July 23, 1978 and was buried in Moore County, NC at Virgil (Byrd) Wallace Cemetery. He and Ethel Marie Sanders had the following children:

> 3889   Terry Dale Rouse (1963-). *Terry was born on July 1, 1963 in Montgomery County, NC. He married* ***Tammy Elizabeth Nadeau*** *on November 3, 1994 in Moore County, NC.*

1674. Gyles Lewis "Bud" Saunders, son of Canoy Allen "Ned" Sanders and Jeanette "Nettie" Wallace, was born on August 15, 1931. He died on June 23, 2010 in Randolph County, NC and was buried on June 26, 2010 in Moore County, NC at Virgil (Byrd) Wallace Cemetery.

Celia Sue Davis was born on March 26, 1934. She died on August 24, 2004 and was buried in Moore County, NC at Virgil (Byrd) Wallace Cemetery. She and Gyles Lewis "Bud" Saunders had the following children:

> 3890   Danny M. Saunders (-)
> 3891   Sharon L. Saunders (-)
> 3892   Patricia Darnell Saunders (1956-1956). *Patricia was born on July 3, 1956. She died on July 3, 1956 and was buried in Moore County, NC at Virgil (Byrd) Wallace Cemetery.*

1675. Nora Kathleen Sanders, daughter of Canoy Allen "Ned" Sanders and Jeanette "Nettie" Wallace, was born on July 17, 1935. She died on June 23, 2000 and was buried in Moore County, NC at Virgil (Byrd) Wallace Cemetery.

1676. James Holt "Gboe" Sanders, son of Canoy Allen "Ned" Sanders and Jeanette "Nettie" Wallace, was born on August 26, 1941. He died on March 11, 1993 in Moore County, NC and was buried in Robbins, Moore County, NC at Acorn Ridge Baptist Church.

Barbara Estelle Hussey, daughter of Elam Fentress Hussey (1909-1979) and Zola Ethel Needham (1911-1990), was born on October 7, 1943. She married William Lewis Wallace on May 5, 1996 in Moore County, NC. She and James Holt "Gboe" Sanders had the following children:

> 3893   Ronald Sanders (-)
> 3894   Darin Sanders (-)
> 3895   Timothy Sanders (-)
> 3896   Rhonda Sanders (1963-). *Rhonda was born on August 19, 1963.*
> 3897   Jeffrey Duane Sanders (1969-1993). *Jeffrey was born on March 16, 1969. He died on September 11, 1993 and was buried in Robbins, Moore County, NC at Acorn Ridge Baptist Church.*

1677. Brenda Kay Wallace was the daughter of James Andrew "Jim Whit" Wallace and Mazie Florence Maness.

Ronald Colon Ritter, son of Colon Causey Ritter (1922-1991) and Bonnie Stout (1932-), was born on April 28, 1952. He died on September 2, 1987 and was buried in Moore County, NC at Smyrna Methodist Church. He and Brenda Kay Wallace had the following children:

| 3898 | James Ronald Ritter (1973-). *James was born on September 11, 1973.* |
| 3899 | Jena Kaye Ritter (1979-). *Jena was born on November 13, 1979.* |

1679. **Faye Lavone Wallace**, daughter of James Andrew "Jim Whit" Wallace and Mazie Florence Maness, was born on April 16, 1936 in Moore County, NC.

Oldham and Faye Lavone Wallace had the following children:

| 3900 | Tammy Oldham (-) |

1680. **Annie Carolyn Wallace**, daughter of James Andrew "Jim Whit" Wallace and Mazie Florence Maness, was born on November 6, 1941. She died on December 30, 2019 and was buried in Moore County, NC at Unity Grove Baptist Church.

1681. **Margaret Lee Wallace**, daughter of James Andrew "Jim Whit" Wallace and Mazie Florence Maness, was born on November 16, 1944.

Willard Darrell Cheek, son of Tilden Grant Cheek (1912-1971) and Dulcie Susan Williams (1913-1971), was born on September 22, 1938. He died on July 2, 1994 and was buried in Moore County, NC at Unity Grove Baptist Church.

1682. **Paul Brackmon Wallace**, son of Millard Fillmore Wallace and Eula Mae Garner, was born on April 24, 1936 in Moore County, NC. He died on June 10, 2009 in Moore County, NC and was buried in Moore County, NC at Virgil (Byrd) Wallace Cemetery.

Mary Magdalene Moore and Paul Brackmon Wallace had the following children:

| 3901 | Perry Brackmon Wallace (1958-). *Perry was born on July 9, 1958 in Moore County, NC.* |
| 3902 | Sheila Rosa Wallace (1961-). *Sheila was born on July 27, 1961 in Moore County, NC.* |

1683. **Daisy Lorene Wallace**, daughter of Millard Fillmore Wallace and Eula Mae Garner, was born on October 1, 1939 in Moore County, NC. She died on October 21, 2018.

Lonnie Dale Prewitt was born on May 16, 1936. He died on October 8, 1986 and was buried in Moore County, NC at Pleasant Hill United Methodist Church. He and Daisy Lorene Wallace had the following children:

| 3903 | Beverly Dawn Prewitt (1958-1980). *Beverly was born on October 29, 1958 in Moore County, NC. She died on June 14, 1980 in Lee County, NC.* |
| 3904 | Scott Dale Prewitt (1969-). *Scott was born on February 2, 1969 in Moore County, NC.* |

1684. **William Russell "Billy" Wallace**, son of Millard Fillmore Wallace and Eula Mae Garner, was born on November 30, 1942. He died on June 1, 2020.

Minnie Pearl Ownbey and William Russell "Billy" Wallace had the following children:

3905	Jackie Russell Wallace (1961-). *Jackie was born on January 4, 1961.*
3906	Johnny Ray Wallace (1963-). *Johnny was born on January 21, 1963 in Moore County, NC.*
3907	Marty Dale Wallace (1965-). *Marty was born on January 11, 1965.*
3908	Tonya Jean Wallace (1969-). *Tonya was born on July 31, 1969.*

1685. **Thelma Jean Wallace**, daughter of Millard Fillmore Wallace and Eula Mae Garner, was born on July 24, 1948. She died on July 24, 1948 and was buried in Moore County, NC at Virgil (Byrd) Wallace Cemetery.

1686. **Sandra Mae Wallace**, daughter of Millard Fillmore Wallace and Eula Mae Garner, was born on February 10, 1952.

1687. **Phyllis Ann Wallace**, daughter of Millard Fillmore Wallace and Eula Mae Garner, was born on July 12, 1956. She married **Boyd Len Garner** in 1972.

Dwain David Andrew was born on January 20, 1961 in Randolph County, NC. He and Phyllis Ann Wallace had the following children:

> 3909   Celes Tere Andrew (1982-). *Celes was born on June 17, 1982 in Moore County, NC.*
> 3910   Justin Garrett Andrew (1984-). *Justin was born on March 28, 1984 in Moore County, NC.*

Boyd Len Garner was born on December 21, 1955 in Moore County, NC. He and Phyllis Ann Wallace had the following children:

> 3911   Regina Ann Garner (1973-). *Regina was born on January 6, 1973 in Moore County, NC.*

1688. **Barbara Jean Maness**, daughter of Wiley Russell Maness and Swannie Esther Wallace, was born on February 6, 1946. She died on November 28, 2003 in Salisbury, Rowan County, NC.

1689. **David Edward Wallace**, son of Grover C. McQuargin and Swannie Esther Wallace, was born on October 12, 1936.

David Edward Wallace had the following children:

> 3912   Audrey Lynn Wallace (-)
> 3913   Teresa Ann Wallace (-)
> 3914   David Russell Wallace (1962-). *David was born on May 18, 1962.*

1690. **Lonnie Wilson Wallace**, son of Henry Clay Wallace and Camilla Drake Talley, was born on November 16, 1899. He died on April 19, 1958 in Richmond County, NC and was buried on April 22, 1958 in Rockingham, Richmond County, NC at Richmond Memorial Park.

Willie Council was born circa 1902 in Raleigh, Wake County, NC. She and Lonnie Wilson Wallace had the following children:

> 3915   Janice Wallace (-)
> 3916   Louise Wallace (-)
> 3917   Mary H. Wallace (c. 1921-). *Mary was born circa 1921.*
> 3918   Henry Clay Wallace (1923-2015). *Henry was born on March 5, 1923 in Richmond County, NC. He died on February 12, 2015 in Richmond County, NC.*
> 3919   Talmage Boyce Wallace (1924-1985). *Talmage was born on May 10, 1924 in Rockingham, Richmond County, NC. He died on December 28, 1985 in Richmond County, NC and was buried on December 30, 1985 in Rockingham, Richmond County, NC at Richmond Memorial Park.*
> 3920   Leondras Wilson "Leon" Wallace (1926-1968). *Leondras was born on April 11, 1926 in Richmond County, NC. He died on March 7, 1968 in Rockingham, Richmond County, NC and was buried on March 8, 1969 in Rockingham, Richmond County, NC at Richmond Memorial Park.*

1691. **Henry Rufus Wallace**, son of Henry Clay Wallace and Camilla Drake Talley, was born on May 8, 1905. He married **Grace May Davis** in 1924. He died on April 3, 1978 in Richmond County, NC and was buried in Rockingham, Richmond County, NC at Northam Cemetery.

Grace May Davis was born on February 17, 1905. She died on May 17, 1980 and was buried in Rockingham, Richmond County, NC at Northam Cemetery. She and Henry Rufus Wallace had the following children:

> 3921   Mary Elizabeth Wallace (1925-). *Mary was born in 1925.*
> 3922   Thelma Mae Wallace (1926-). *Thelma was born in 1926.*
> 3923   Sherman Roscoe Wallace (1926-). *Sherman was born in 1926.*
> 3924   George Henry Wallace (1930-). *George was born in 1930.*
> 3925   Douglas Darrell Wallace (1933-1989). *Douglas was born in 1933. He died in 1989.*
> 3926   Camilla F. Wallace (1934-). *Camilla was born in 1934.*
> 3927   Evelyn K. Wallace (1936-). *Evelyn was born in 1936.*
> 3928   Margaret Lucille Wallace (1938-1987). *Margaret was born on June 3, 1938 in Rockingham, Richmond County, NC. She married **James Martin Wilhelm Jr.** on*

June 10, 1959. She died on May 31, 1987 in Statesville, Iredell County, NC.

1692. **William M. Wallace**, son of Henry Clay Wallace and Camilla Drake Talley, was born on February 15, 1908. He died on May 9, 1988 and was buried in Sanford, Lee County, NC at Shallow Well Cemetery.

> **Louise L.** was born on November 17, 1911. She died on May 22, 1991 and was buried in Sanford, Lee County, NC at Shallow Well Cemetery. She and William M. Wallace had the following children:

> > 3929   William Wallace (-)

1693. **Emmett Lee Wallace**, son of Henry Clay Wallace and Camilla Drake Talley, was born on December 11, 1909 in Moore County, NC. He died on June 21, 1971 in Moore County, NC and was buried in Rockingham, Richmond County, NC at Richmond Memorial Park.

> **Virginia Lucille McIntosh**, daughter of Mason Parker McIntosh (1881-1940) and Mary Dowd (1888-1964), was born on February 11, 1913. She died on May 19, 1999 and was buried in Rockingham, Richmond County, NC at Richmond Memorial Park. She and Emmett Lee Wallace had the following children:

> > 3930   Barbara Jewell Wallace (1933-2014). *Barbara was born on September 25, 1933. She died on December 12, 2014 and was buried in Rockingham, Richmond County, NC at Richmond Memorial Park.*

1694. **Fay Dora Wallace**, daughter of Phil Earnest I. Wallace and Naomi Ester York, was born on June 8, 1906 in Perryville, Perry County, AR. She died on August 14, 1995 in Phoenix, Maricopa County, AZ.

> **David Abbott** was born on December 5, 1899 in Mena, AR. He died on May 31, 1947 in Leedey, OK. He and Fay Dora Wallace had the following children:

> > 3931   Abbott (-)

1695. **Raymond Wallace**, son of Phil Earnest I. Wallace and Naomi Ester York, was born on June 16, 1916. He died on December 26, 1975.

> **Mildred Wyonetta Brown** was born on March 25, 1914. She died on May 31, 2009. She and Raymond Wallace had the following children:

> > 3932   Paula Rae Wallace (-)

1696. **Sewell Wallace**, son of Phil Earnest I. Wallace and May Thompson, was born circa 1904 in AR. He died on June 24, 1932 in Perry County, AR.

1697. **Martha Jean Harper**, daughter of Jack McRae Harper and Jessie Nancy Wallace, was born on July 24, 1914. She died on September 6, 1993.

> **William Riley Dyer** was born in January 1908. He died in December 1969. He and Martha Jean Harper had the following children:

> > 3933   Marshall Dyer (-)

> **Albert Lloyd Brawn** was born on June 28, 1909. He died in June 1976. He and Martha Jean Harper had the following children:

> > 3934   Brawn (-)

1698. **Fred Wallace Jr.**, son of Fred I. Wallace and Blan Rickman, was born on March 27, 1920 in Oklahoma City, Oklahoma County, OK. He died on July 31, 1973 in Lakewood , Los Angeles County, CA and was buried on August 2, 1973 in Los Angeles National Cemetery, Plot 89A, F/5.

> **Joette Ellis** and Fred Wallace Jr. had the following children:

| 3935 | Linda Carroll Wallace (1942-). *Linda was born on August 12, 1942 in Los Angeles County, CA.* |
| 3936 | Robert Neil Wallace (1946-). *Robert was born on November 8, 1946 in Los Angeles County, CA.* |

1699. Thelma Dora Wallace, daughter of Fred I. Wallace and Emma Rickman, was born on August 17, 1910 in Perryville, Perry County, AR. She married **Chester Lawrence Duffield** in April 1931. She died on April 20, 2001 in Oklahoma City, Oklahoma County, OK.

Chester Lawrence Duffield was born on April 7, 1910. He died on August 16, 1979 in Oklahoma City, Oklahoma County, OK. He and Thelma Dora Wallace had the following children:

3937	Chester L. Duffield Jr. (1933-1982). *Chester was born on May 26, 1933. He married* **Kathleen Dickson** *on May 9, 1957. He died on December 4, 1982 in Virginia.*
3938	Delores Duffield (1935-). *Delores was born on August 15, 1935. She married* **James Price** *on February 5, 1960.*
3939	Juanito Ruth Duffield (1942-). *Juanito was born on August 20, 1942. She married* **Oscar Tadashi Tanji** *on May 29, 1966.*
3940	Brenda Rae Duffield (1949-). *Brenda was born on October 8, 1949.*

1700. Jessie Velma Wallace, daughter of Fred I. Wallace and Emma Rickman, was born on February 25, 1914 in Shawnee, Pottawatomie County, OK. She married **Julius Reuben Sanders** on April 18, 1936 in Seminole, Seminole County, OK. She married **B. E. Morgan** on September 5, 1946.

Julius Reuben Sanders was born on March 15, 1913. He died in 1978. He and Jessie Velma Wallace had the following children:

| 3941 | Billy Frank Sanders (1937-2008). *Billy was born on October 27, 1937. He married* **Judith Sandra Frary** *on September 30, 1972. He died on September 26, 2008.* |

1701. Georgia Baxter Wallace, daughter of Fred I. Wallace and Emma Rickman, was born on October 25, 1916 in Shawnee, Pottawatomie County, OK. She married **Tom Claude Graham Jr.** on December 23, 1935 in Hocheim, DeWitt County, TX.

Tom Claude Graham Jr. was born on April 10, 1914 in Floresville, Wilson County, TX. He died on March 20, 1966 in Houston, Harris County, TX and was buried on March 30, 1966 in Hocheim, DeWitt County, TX. He and Georgia Baxter Wallace had the following children:

3942	Tom Claude Graham III (1940-1963). *Tom was born on October 11, 1940 in Houston, Harris County, TX. He died on April 14, 1963 in Houston, Harris County, TX and was buried in 1963 in Hochheim, DeWitt County, TX at Hochheim Cemetery.*
3943	Freddie Kathleen Graham (1941-). *Freddie was born on August 27, 1941 in Abilene, TX. She married* **Clement Augustus Boulte III** *on January 29, 1966 in Fort Bend County, TX.*
3944	Wallace Wayne Graham (1942-2000). *Wallace was born on December 9, 1942 in Houston, Harris County, TX. He married* **Francesca Rodriguez** *on October 29, 1971 in Houston, Harris County, TX. He died on September 23, 2000 in Houston, Harris County, TX and was buried on October 1, 2000 in Hocheim, DeWitt County, TX.*
3945	Debra Kay Graham (1955-). *Debra was born on October 5, 1955 in Houston, Harris County, TX. She married* **Merle E. Lenfest Jr.** *on October 16, 1976 in Livingston, Polk County, TX.*

1704. Johnnie Corinne Wallace, daughter of Bertram Fleet Wallace and Amanda John Thompson, was born on September 19, 1923 in AR.

Marvin Eugene Bailey and Johnnie Corinne Wallace had the following children:

3946   Linda Jane Bailey (1947-). *Linda was born on October 11, 1947.*

Jake Q. Allen and Johnnie Corinne Wallace had the following children:

3947   Robert William Allen (1945-). *Robert was born on June 3, 1945.*

1709. **Betty Maxine Wallace**, daughter of Bertram Fleet Wallace and Amanda John Thompson, was born on December 2, 1935.

    Lowell Dean Phipps was born on August 12, 1920 in Iowa. He died on November 5, 2002 in Solgohachia, Conway County, AR.

1710. **Charles Wayne Wallace**, son of Bertram Fleet Wallace and Amanda John Thompson, was born on November 11, 1937. He married **Shirley Janelle Hardison** on November 9, 1956 in Perryville, Perry County, AR.

1711. **Julia Maggie Brown**, daughter of James M. Brown and Martha Jane Wallace, was born on January 25, 1878. She married **Andrew Sanders** on December 16, 1896 in Moore County, NC and was buried in Moore County, NC at Mt. Carmel United Methodist Church.

    Andrew Sanders, son of Brittan Sanders (1831-1913) and Ann "Spicy" Morgan (1837-1913), was born on October 30, 1868 in Moore County, NC. He died on April 26, 1960 in Moore County, NC and was buried on April 28, 1960 in Moore County, NC at Mt. Carmel United Methodist Church.

[Left] **Lillie Mae Brown Crabtree, Mary Blake Brown Richardson, Flossie Brown Richardson**
(Courtesy of Sarah Lawn) [Middle] **William Thomas Brown** *(Courtesy of Thomas Brown)* [Right]
Lurinda Brown McKenzie and Bill McKenzie *(Courtesy of Kim Malphrus)*

1712. **Margaret Lurinda "Rindy" Brown**, daughter of James M. Brown and Martha Jane Wallace, was born on August 19, 1879 in Moore County, NC. She married **Daniel Edward McKenzie** on February 7, 1897 in Moore County, NC. She died on August 24, 1957 in Richmond Memorial Hospital, Rockingham, Richmond County, NC and was buried on August 25, 1957 in Rockingham, Richmond County, NC at Northam Cemetery.

Daniel Edward McKenzie, son of John McKenzie (1817-1893) and Marian Amanda Patterson (-), was born on May 7, 1873 in Moore County, NC and was buried on March 1, 1934 in Rockingham, Richmond County, NC at Northam Cemetery. He died on March 13, 1934 in Rockingham, Richmond County, NC. He and Margaret Lurinda "Rindy" Brown had the following children:

3948	Dora Lee McKenzie (1897-). *Dora was born on November 19, 1897 in Rockingham, Richmond County, NC.*
3949	Bertie Mae McKenzie (1899-). *Bertie was born on July 26, 1899 in Rockingham, Richmond County, NC.*
3950	Margaret Belle McKenzie (1901-2000). *Margaret was born on February 13, 1901 in Rockingham, Richmond County, NC. She died on March 24, 2000 and was buried in Rockingham, Richmond County, NC at Northam Cemetery.*
3951	Amanda Jane McKenzie (1903-1991). *Amanda was born on February 20, 1903 in Rockingham, Richmond County, NC. She died on March 23, 1991.*
3952	James Leslie McKenzie (1905-1986). *James was born on March 27, 1905. He died on September 11, 1986.*
3953	Lula Dell McKenzie (1907-1995). *Lula was born on August 29, 1907. She died on September 25, 1995.*
3954	William Martin "Bill" McKenzie (1910-1995). *William was born on August 23, 1910. He died on January 8, 1995.*
3955	John Arthur McKenzie (1915-1999). *John was born on May 29, 1915. He died on September 30, 1999.*

1713. **William Thomas Brown**, son of James M. Brown and Martha Jane Wallace, was born on August 7, 1885. He married **Sara Ann Brewer** on August 18, 1904 in Moore County, NC. He married on May 23, 1918 in Moore County, NC. He died on November 29, 1977 in Richmond Memorial Hospital, Rockingham, Richmond County, NC and was buried in Rockingham, Richmond County, NC at Richmond Memorial Park.

Sara Ann Brewer, daughter of Aaron Pinkney Brewer (1859-1943) and Martha Jane Sanders (1861-1929), was born on July 5, 1884 in Moore County, NC. She died on February 9, 1918 in Montgomery County, NC and was buried on February 11, 1918 in Moore County, NC at Brown's Chapel Christian Church. She and William Thomas Brown had the following children:

3956	Alma Floyd Brown (1910-1956). *Alma was born on March 9, 1910. She died in 1956.*
3957	Thelma M. Brown (1912-1912). *Thelma was born on May 13, 1912. She died on May 13, 1912 and was buried in Moore County, NC at Brown's Chapel Christian Church.*
3958	Janie Ethel Brown (1913-1991). *Janie was born on April 4, 1913. She died on May 29, 1991.*
3959	Thomas Edgar Brown (1916-1916). *Thomas was born on March 21, 1916. He died on March 21, 1916 and was buried in Moore County, NC at Brown's Chapel Christian Church.*

William Thomas Brown had the following children:

3960	Mildred Juanita Brown (1919-). *Mildred was born on June 20, 1919.*
3961	Walter Talmadge Brown (1925-). *Walter was born on February 5, 1925 in Robbins, Moore County, NC.*

1714. **George A. Brown**, son of James M. Brown and Martha Jane Wallace, was born on December 5, 1887. He married **Effie R. McNeill** on March 22, 1907 in Moore County, NC. He died on April 11, 1914 in Moore County, NC and was buried in Moore County, NC at Brown's Chapel Christian Church.

Effie R. McNeill, daughter of Alexander McNeill (1861-1899) and Lovedy Ann "Annie" Wallace (1868-1896), was born on August 9, 1889. She died on February 26, 1913 and was buried in Moore County, NC at Brown's Chapel Christian Church. She and George A. Brown had the following children:

3962	May Brown (-)
3963	Wilbur Brown (-)
3964	Lillian Brown (-)
3965	Hattie W. Brown (1909-). *Hattie was born in 1909.*

1715. **Mary Blake "Molly" Brown**, daughter of James M. Brown and Martha Jane Wallace, was born on October 15, 1891. She died on October 1, 1979 and was buried in Moore County, NC at Mt. Carmel United Methodist Church.

H. A. Richardson was born on October 8, 1882. He died on February 3, 1935 and was buried in Moore County, NC at Mt. Carmel United Methodist Church.

1716. **Lillie Mae Brown**, daughter of James M. Brown and Martha Jane Wallace, was born in January 1895. She died in 1980.

Noah Oliver Crabtree, son of Henry Talmadge Crabtree (1845-) and Susannah Ritter (1848-1918), was born on October 14, 1885. He died on July 14, 1940 and was buried in Moore County, NC at Mt. Carmel United Methodist Church. He and Lillie Mae Brown had the following children:

3966	Oliver Glenn Crabtree (1917-1993). *Oliver was born in 1917. He died in 1993.*

1717. **Flossie Elizabeth Brown**, daughter of James M. Brown and Martha Jane Wallace, was born on October 4, 1898. She died on September 27, 1987 and was buried in Moore County, NC at Mt. Carmel United Methodist Church.

Samuel Jasper Richardson, son of Joseph Judson Richardson (1835-1916) and Martha C. Ritter (1850-1920), was born on November 18, 1884. He died on April 9, 1968 and was buried in Moore County, NC at Mt. Carmel United Methodist Church. He and Flossie Elizabeth Brown had the following children:

3967	James Judson Richardson (1918-1993). *James was born on November 17, 1918. He died on April 14, 1993 and was buried in Moore County, NC at Mt. Carmel United Methodist Church.*
3968	Grier Richardson (1920-1932). *Grier was born on September 6, 1920. He died on March 23, 1932 and was buried in Moore County, NC at Mt. Carmel United Methodist Church.*
3969	Fred Randolph Richardson (1923-2013). *Fred was born on January 3, 1923. He died on December 24, 2013 and was buried in Moore County, NC at Mt. Carmel United Methodist Church.*
3970	Samuel Jasper Richardson Jr. (1925-). *Samuel was born on January 25, 1925.*
3971	Helen Mae Richardson (1926-1930). *Helen was born on December 10, 1926. She died on December 28, 1930 and was buried in Moore County, NC at Mt. Carmel United Methodist Church.*
3972	Max Richardson (1926-). *Max was born on December 10, 1926.*

1722. **Kizzie Flowers Gordon**, daughter of William Henry Gordon and Louisa Elizabeth Wallace, was born on February 11, 1879. She married **Ira Edward Murray** on August 9, 1902. She died on December 8, 1952.

Ira Edward Murray was born on December 1, 1877. He died in 1958. He and Kizzie Flowers Gordon had the following children:

3973	Ernest Arnold Murray (1903-1995). *Ernest was born on July 9, 1903. He died on February 26, 1995.*

1723. **Laura Ann Gordon**, daughter of William Henry Gordon and Louisa Elizabeth Wallace, was born on March 31, 1883 in Moore County, NC. She died on July 9, 1961 in Greensboro, Guilford County, NC and was buried on July 11, 1961 in Guilford County, NC at Lakeview Memorial Park.

Archie Arthur Garner, son of John Harrison Garner (1840-1913) and Julia Ann Maness (1842-1914), was born on September 22, 1879 in Moore County, NC. He died on October 17, 1955 in Greensboro, Guilford County, NC and was buried on October 19, 1955 in Guilford County, NC at Lakeview Memorial Park.

Hugh T. Wallace *(Courtesy of Lucy Oakes)*

1727. Hugh T. Wallace, son of Hiram Walker Wallace and Jane Sanders, was born on March 1, 1883 in Moore County, NC. He married **Laura Cornelia Kelly** on October 5, 1902 in Hamlet, Richmond County, NC. He died on September 15, 1924 in Richmond County, NC and was buried on September 16, 1924 in Rockingham, Richmond County, NC at East Side Cemetery.

Laura Cornelia Kelly was born on April 14, 1886. She died on July 25, 1969 and was buried on July 27, 1969 in Rockingham, Richmond County, NC at East Side Cemetery. She and Hugh T. Wallace had the following children:

3974	William McKinley Wallace (1903-1993). *William was born on August 24, 1903 in Hamlet, Richmond County, NC. He died on November 29, 1993 in Rockingham, Richmond County, NC.*
3975	Mattie Evalena Wallace (1906-1981). *Mattie was born on June 1, 1906. She married* **Mack Duffie Wallace** *on October 20, 1923. She died on June 9, 1981 in Duke Hospital, Durham, Durham County, NC.*
3976	Ruby N. Wallace (1907-1908). *Ruby was born on November 29, 1907. She died on July 11, 1908 and was buried in Rockingham, Richmond County, NC at East Side Cemetery.*
3977	George Hiram Wallace (1909-). *George was born on July 14, 1909 in Kannapolis, Cabarrus County, NC. He married* **Carrie May Wiggins** *on June 10, 1933 in Hamlet, Richmond County, NC.*
3978	Mitchell Coleman Wallace (1911-1912). *Mitchell was born on July 18, 1911. He died on October 4, 1912 and was buried in Rockingham, Richmond County, NC at Mizpah Church Cemetery.*

3979	Ida Mae Wallace (1913-1997). *Ida was born on November 28, 1913 in Moore County, NC. She died on July 22, 1997 in Hamlet, Richmond County, NC and was buried in Rockingham, Richmond County, NC at Richmond Memorial Park.*
3980	Isabelle Ethel Wallace (1915-2002). *Isabelle was born on September 5, 1915 in Hamlet, Richmond County, NC. She died on June 24, 2002 in Richmond County, NC and was buried in Rockingham, Richmond County, NC at East Side Cemetery.*
3981	Hugh T. "Pug" Wallace Jr. (1917-1997). *Hugh was born on June 13, 1917 in Rockingham, Richmond County, NC. He died on February 28, 1997.*
3982	Gladys Louella Wallace (1919-2012). *Gladys was born on September 2, 1919 in Hamlet, Richmond County, NC. She died on November 8, 2012.*
3983	John Walker Wallace (1923-2000). *John was born on June 15, 1923 in Hamlet, Richmond County, NC. He died in January 2000 in Southeastern Regional Medical Center, Lumberton, Robeson County, NC.*

1728. **Julia Florence Wallace**, daughter of Hiram Walker Wallace and Jane Sanders, was born on March 31, 1885 in Moore County, NC. She married **Ira Brookshire Kelly** on June 1, 1905 in Hamlet, Richmond County, NC. She died on August 28, 1965 in Hamlet, Richmond County, NC and was buried on August 30, 1965 in Rockingham, Richmond County, NC at Richmond Memorial Park.

Ira Brookshire Kelly was born on January 26, 1886 in Hamlet, Richmond County, NC. He died on June 21, 1958 in Hamlet, Richmond County, NC and was buried on June 23, 1958 in Rockingham, Richmond County, NC at Richmond Memorial Park. He and Julia Florence Wallace had the following children:

3984	John Oscar Kelly (1906-1972). *John was born on May 10, 1906 in Hamlet, Richmond County, NC. He died on September 7, 1972 in Hamlet, Richmond County, NC and was buried on September 9, 1972 in Rockingham, Richmond County, NC at Richmond Memorial Park.*
3985	Ada Enola Kelly (1908-). *Ada was born on February 14, 1908 in Hamlet, Richmond County, NC.*
3986	Lillian Rebecca Kelly (1910-). *Lillian was born on June 3, 1910 in Richmond County, NC.*
3987	Vera Jane Kelly (c. 1912-). *Vera was born circa 1912.*
3988	Daughter Kelly (1915-1918). *Daughter was born on July 2, 1915 in Hamlet, Richmond County, NC. She died on May 2, 1918 in Hamlet, Richmond County, NC and was buried in Rockingham, Richmond County, NC at Mizpah Church Cemetery.*
3989	Julia Alma Kelly (1916-1918). *Julia was born on May 2, 1916 in Hamlet, Richmond County, NC and was buried on May 3, 1918 in Rockingham, Richmond County, NC at Mizpah Church Cemetery. She died on July 2, 1918 in Hamlet, Richmond County, NC.*
3990	Ira Brookshire Kelly Jr. (1917-1994). *Ira was born on July 3, 1917. He married **Mary Wooley** on July 10, 1970 in Rockingham, Richmond County, NC. He died on October 30, 1994 and was buried in Rockingham, Richmond County, NC at Northam Cemetery.*
3991	Edwin McPhail Kelly (1920-2014). *Edwin was born on June 15, 1920 in Hamlet, Richmond County, NC. He married **Clarice Barnett Smith** on March 16, 2002 in Rockingham, Richmond County, NC. He died on March 13, 2014.*
3992	James Chesley Kelly (1922-1982). *James was born on April 11, 1922. He died on June 16, 1982.*
3993	Virginia Colleen Kelly (1925-). *Virginia was born on December 4, 1925 in Hamlet, Richmond County, NC.*

1729. **John C. Wallace**, son of Hiram Walker Wallace and Jane Sanders, was born on March 6, 1887 in Rockingham, Richmond County, NC. He died on June 23, 1959 in Kings Mountain, Cleveland County, NC and was buried on June 25, 1959 in Cherokee County, SC at Frederick Memorial Gardens.

1730. **Camilla F. Wallace**, daughter of Hiram Walker Wallace and Jane Sanders, was born in January 1890.

Otis Tigg and Camilla F. Wallace had the following children:

3994	Maybelle Tigg (-)

1731. **Mary Alice Wallace**, daughter of Hiram Walker Wallace and Jane Sanders, was born on October 24, 1891 in Moore County, NC. She died on April 1, 1965 in Hamlet, Richmond County, NC and was buried on April 2, 1965 in Hamlet, Richmond County, NC at Mary Love Cemetery.

Arthur Pearl Martin was born on February 12, 1888 in Hamlet, Richmond County, NC. He died on May 15, 1965 in Hamlet, Richmond County, NC. He and Mary Alice Wallace had the following children:

3995	Mary Martin (-)
3996	Carl Roland Martin (1913-2002). *Carl was born on May 2, 1913 in Ghio, Richmond County, NC. He died on October 19, 2002 in Rockingham, Richmond County, NC and was buried on October 21, 2002 in Hamlet, Richmond County, NC at Mary Love Cemetery.*
3997	Linwood Martin (1919-). *Linwood was born on January 8, 1919 in Ghio, Richmond County, NC.*

1732. **Louella Wallace**, daughter of Hiram Walker Wallace and Jane Sanders, was born on October 18, 1893 in Moore County, NC. She married **James Henry Garrett** on March 14, 1909 in Rockingham, Richmond County, NC. She died on September 18, 1978 in Hamlet, Richmond County, NC.

James Henry Garrett was born on May 6, 1881 in Hamlet, Richmond County, NC. He died on December 9, 1973 in Hamlet, Richmond County, NC and was buried on December 11, 1973 in Rockingham, Richmond County, NC at Richmond Memorial Park. He and Louella Wallace had the following children:

3998	J. Reed Garrett (1910-). *J. was born on January 22, 1910.*

1733. **Ida F. Wallace**, daughter of Hiram Walker Wallace and Jane Sanders, was born on December 21, 1895 in Moore County, NC. She married **John Edward Baxley** on June 29, 1913 in Hamlet, Richmond County, NC. She died on March 9, 1966 in Hamlet, Richmond County, NC and was buried on March 10, 1966 in Rockingham, Richmond County, NC at Richmond Memorial Park.

John Edward Baxley was born in 1891. He and Ida F. Wallace had the following children:

3999	William Glenn Baxley (1914-1982). *William was born on October 15, 1914 in Moore County, NC. He died on December 21, 1982 in Moore County, NC.*
4000	Edward Fairly Baxley (1920-1988). *Edward was born on December 12, 1920 in Hamlet, Richmond County, NC. He married **Doris Lamm**. He died on October 21, 1988 in Orange County, NC.*
4001	Maryland Y. Baxley (1931-). *Maryland was born on February 25, 1931 in Hamlet, Richmond County, NC.*

1734. **Maggie Mae Wallace**, daughter of Hiram Walker Wallace and Jane Sanders, was born on November 18, 1898 in Moore County, NC. She died on April 5, 1966 in Hamlet, Richmond County, NC and was buried on April 7, 1966 in Rockingham, Richmond County, NC at Richmond Memorial Park.

John Lawrence Goodman was born on January 30, 1893. He died on June 10, 1969 in Alamance County, NC and was buried on June 11, 1969 in Rockingham, Richmond County, NC at Richmond Memorial Park. He and Maggie Mae Wallace had the following children:

4002	Raymond Wallace Goodman (1915-2007). *Raymond was born on August 23, 1915 in Hamlet, Richmond County, NC. He died on April 5, 2007 in Richmond County, NC and was buried in Rockingham, Richmond County, NC at Richmond Memorial Park.*
4003	Otis McPhail Goodman (1918-1991). *Otis was born on May 21, 1918 in Hamlet, Richmond County, NC. He died on December 28, 1991 in Richmond Memorial Hospital, Rockingham, Richmond County, NC and was buried on December 31, 1991 in Rockingham, Richmond County, NC at Richmond Memorial Park.*
4004	Fairley Odell Goodman (1920-1998). *Fairley was born on March 21, 1920 in Hamlet, Richmond County, NC. He died on July 28, 1998 in Charlotte, Mecklenburg County, NC.*
4005	Eldred Thomas Goodman (1921-). *Eldred was born on June 11, 1921 in Hamlet, Richmond County, NC.*
4006	Donald Bruce Goodman (1923-). *Donald was born in 1923.*

4007	Doris Jean Goodman (1926-). *Doris was born on August 12, 1926 in Hamlet, Richmond County, NC. She married **Thomas Lamar Simmons** on December 31, 1972 in Hamlet, Richmond County, NC.*
4008	Audrey Mae Goodman (1928-). *Audrey was born on July 4, 1928 in Hamlet, Richmond County, NC.*
4009	William Warren Goodman (1930-). *William was born on April 27, 1930 in Hamlet, Richmond County, NC.*
4010	Harrace Walker Goodman (1931-1934). *Harrace was born on December 30, 1931 in Hamlet, Richmond County, NC. He died on November 5, 1934 in Hamlet, Richmond County, NC and was buried on November 5, 1934 in Rockingham, Richmond County, NC at Mizpah Church Cemetery.*
4011	Mary Lou Goodman (1934-1935). *Mary was born on June 29, 1934 in Hamlet, Richmond County, NC. She died in 1935.*
4012	Bobby Leon Goodman (1935-2000). *Bobby was born on August 1, 1935 in Hamlet, Richmond County, NC. He died on June 6, 2000 in Anson County, NC and was buried on June 24, 2000 in Rockingham, Richmond County, NC at East Side Cemetery.*
4013	Malcolm Edward Goodman (1936-). *Malcolm was born on July 26, 1936 in Hamlet, Richmond County, NC.*
4014	Jerry Lee Goodman (1939-). *Jerry was born on February 20, 1939 in Hamlet, Richmond County, NC. He married **Beverly Ann Evans** on March 26, 1967 in Hamlet, Richmond County, NC.*
4015	Jimmy Ray Goodman (1940-1996). *Jimmy was born on September 7, 1940 in Hamlet, Richmond County, NC. He married **Sandra Ferrell Diggs** on August 5, 1962 in Hamlet, Richmond County, NC. He died in 1996 in Hamlet, Richmond County, NC and was buried in Rockingham, Richmond County, NC at Richmond Memorial Park.*

1735. **Maude Eva Wallace**, daughter of Hiram Walker Wallace and Jane Sanders, was born on February 5, 1902 in Richmond County, NC. She died on May 29, 1955 in Huntersville, Mecklenburg County, NC and was buried on May 31, 1955 in Mecklenburg County, NC at Asbury Methodist.

Arthur R. Farrell and Maude Eva Wallace had the following children:

4016	Juanita Farrell (1922-). *Juanita was born on December 28, 1922.*
4017	Herman M. Farrell (1924-). *Herman was born on April 1, 1924.*
4018	Bobby Eugene Farrell (1928-). *Bobby was born on November 20, 1928.*

1736. **Fairley Ledbetter Wallace**, son of Hiram Walker Wallace and Jane Sanders, was born on January 1, 1904 in Rockingham, Richmond County, NC. He died on January 22, 1915 in Hamlet, Richmond County, NC and was buried on January 23, 1915 in Rockingham, Richmond County, NC at Mizpah Church Cemetery.

1737. **Katherine E. Wallace**, daughter of Spinks Wallace and Martha Ann Johnson, was born on April 20, 1889 in Moore County, NC. She married **Edd D. Clark** on August 11, 1904 in Moore County, NC. She died on November 1, 1953 in Siler City, Chatham County, NC and was buried on November 3, 1953 in Chatham County, NC at Mt. Pleasant Baptist Church.

Edd D. Clark, son of Madison Clark (-), was born in 1870. He died on March 7, 1932 and was buried in Chatham County, NC at Pleasant Hill United Methodist Church. He and Katherine E. Wallace had the following children:

4019	Eddie Clark (1903-). *Eddie was born in 1903.*
4020	Sadie Clark (1905-). *Sadie was born on December 20, 1905.*
4021	Irvin Clark (1907-). *Irvin was born in 1907.*
4022	Pearl Clark (1910-). *Pearl was born in 1910.*
4023	James "Jimmie" Clark (1914-). *James was born on August 15, 1914.*
4024	Mary J. Clark (1918-). *Mary was born in 1918.*
4025	Jennie Lee Clark (1921-1996). *Jennie was born on September 6, 1921. She married **Harvey Smith** on June 19, 1943 in Moore County, NC. She died on June 15, 1996 and was buried in Siler City, Chatham County, NC at Chatham Memorial Park.*

1738. Ruth Jane Wallace, daughter of Spinks Wallace and Martha Ann Johnson, was born on June 28, 1889. She married **John Clarkston Nunnery** on April 17, 1904 in Moore County, NC. She died on April 17, 1944 and was buried in Carthage, Moore County, NC at Cross Hill Cemetery.

John Clarkston Nunnery, son of William K. Nunnery (1827-1894) and Mary Elizabeth Martindale (1839-), was born on September 21, 1877. He died on May 5, 1948 and was buried in Carthage, Moore County, NC at Cross Hill Cemetery. He and Ruth Jane Wallace had the following children:

4026	Mary Belle Nunnery (1907-1994). *Mary was born on June 9, 1907. She married **Alexander "Sandy" Barber** on December 20, 1921 in Moore County, NC. She died on October 11, 1994 in Moore County, NC and was buried in Carthage, Moore County, NC at Cross Hill Cemetery.*
4027	Jesse Clarkston Nunnery (1909-). *Jesse was born on August 29, 1909.*
4028	Daniel Bryant Nunnery (1911-2002). *Daniel was born on November 22, 1911. He died on March 6, 2002.*
4029	Ollie Mae Nunnery (1915-1976). *Ollie was born on November 27, 1915. She married **Marvin Brown** on November 19, 1932 in Moore County, NC. She died on December 29, 1976 and was buried in Moore County, NC at Brown's Chapel Christian Church.*
4030	Annie Ruth Nunnery (1918-). *Annie was born on March 22, 1918.*
4031	Mattie P. Nunnery (1922-). *Mattie was born in 1922.*

1739. William Lincoln Wallace, son of Spinks Wallace and Martha Ann Johnson, was born on January 1, 1892 in Moore County, NC. He married **Meta Moore** on May 7, 1911 in Moore County, NC. He died on September 27, 1966 in High Point, Guilford County, NC and was buried on September 29, 1966 in High Point, Guilford County, NC at Floral Garden Memorial Park Cemetery.

Meta Moore, daughter of Joe Moore (-) and Clementine (-), was born on October 19, 1892 in Moore County, NC. She died on May 4, 1974 in High Point, Guilford County, NC and was buried on May 7, 1974 in High Point, Guilford County, NC at Floral Garden Memorial Park Cemetery. She and William Lincoln Wallace had the following children:

4032	Beula Wallace (1909-). *Beula was born in 1909. She married **Richard Foster** on July 30, 1928.*
4033	Gilbert D. Wallace (1910-1981). *Gilbert was born on March 5, 1910. He married **Swannie Gean Foster** on September 16, 1928 in Moore County, NC. He died on July 10, 1981 and was buried in High Point, Guilford County, NC at Floral Garden Memorial Park Cemetery.*
4034	Willie May Wallace (1913-). *Willie was born in 1913. She married **William Hockney** on June 4, 1928 in Moore County, NC.*
4035	Josie Bell Wallace (1914-). *Josie was born on April 19, 1914.*
4036	Josephine Wallace (1916-1961). *Josephine was born on February 16, 1916. She died on April 1, 1961 in High Point, Guilford County, NC and was buried on April 3, 1961 in High Point, Guilford County, NC at Floral Garden Memorial Park Cemetery.*

1740. Daniel Isaac Wallace, son of Spinks Wallace and Martha Ann Johnson, was born on September 30, 1896. He married **Cora Lilly Yow** on April 14, 1917 in Moore County, NC. He died on September 7, 1956 and was buried in Moore County, NC at Calvary Baptist Church.

Cora Lilly Yow, daughter of James Wiley Yow (1866-1951) and Martha Ann Starling (1864-1940), was born on December 14, 1896 in Moore County, NC. She died on June 18, 1965 in Cameron, Moore County, NC and was buried on June 20, 1965 in Moore County, NC at Calvary Baptist Church. She and Daniel Isaac Wallace had the following children:

4037	Joseph Wallace (1919-). *Joseph was born in 1919.*
4038	Norman Herman Wallace (1920-). *Norman was born on February 3, 1920.*
4039	Warren Winford Wallace (1921-1996). *Warren was born on December 12, 1921. He died on September 7, 1996 and was buried in Moore County, NC at Calvary Baptist Church.*
4040	Iva Floyd Wallace (1925-1999). *Iva was born on December 15, 1925 in Moore County, NC. He died in 1999.*
4041	Ruby Dean Wallace (1927-). *Ruby was born on July 30, 1927 in Moore County, NC.*

1741. Ellen Barber Wallace, daughter of Spinks Wallace and Martha Ann Johnson, was born on May 18, 1903 in Moore County, NC. She married **Alexander Wallace** on October 26, 1922 in Moore County, NC. She died on June 30, 1975 in Carthage, Moore County, NC and was buried on July 2, 1975 in Moore County, NC at Calvary Baptist Church.

Alexander Wallace, son of Elias W. Wallace (1865-1926) and Lydia Frances Muse (1857-1927), was born on July 20, 1893 in Moore County, NC. He died on March 30, 1980 in Moore County, NC and was buried in Moore County, NC at Calvary Baptist Church. He and Ellen Barber Wallace had the following children:

4042	Carter Wallace (-)
4043	Roy Wallace (-)
4044	Margaret Francis Wallace (1924-1925). *Margaret was born on June 9, 1924. She died on August 19, 1925.*
4045	Catherine M. Wallace (1925-). *Catherine was born in 1925.*
4046	Dorothy Mae Wallace (1929-). *Dorothy was born on September 12, 1929 in Moore County, NC.*
4047	Ethel Marie Wallace (1932-). *Ethel was born on April 12, 1932 in Moore County, NC.*
4048	William Elias Wallace (1934-2014). *William was born on December 22, 1934. He died on June 26, 2014.*
4049	Norman Wallace (1938-). *Norman was born on September 9, 1938 in Moore County, NC.*
4050	Pearl Wallace (1942-). *Pearl was born on June 3, 1942 in Moore County, NC.*

1742. Fannie C. Wallace, daughter of Elias W. Wallace and Lydia Frances Muse, was born on October 18, 1885 in Moore County, NC. She married **Joe Hogan** on February 22, 1905 in Montgomery County, NC. She died on February 8, 1959 in Montgomery Memorial Hospital, Troy, Montgomery County, NC and was buried on February 10, 1959 in Candor, Montgomery County, NC at Macedonia Presbyterian Church.

Joe Hogan, son of Zacheus Huggins Hogan (-) and Mary Catherine Lamonds (-), was born on December 24, 1869. He died on April 4, 1955 in Montgomery County, NC and was buried in Candor, Montgomery County, NC at Macedonia Presbyterian Church. He and Fannie C. Wallace had the following children:

4051	Mary Gladys Hogan (1906-1945). *Mary was born on September 13, 1906. She died on July 19, 1945.*
4052	Chesley W. Hogan (1908-1981). *Chesley was born on October 8, 1908. He died on March 9, 1981 and was buried in Candor, Montgomery County, NC at Candor Town Cemetery.*
4053	Annie Lydia Hogan (1910-1999). *Annie was born on July 8, 1910 in Montgomery County, NC. She died on May 10, 1999 in Montgomery County, NC and was buried in Candor, Montgomery County, NC at Macedonia Presbyterian Church.*
4054	Johnnie Doyd Hogan (1925-1925). *Johnnie was born on June 18, 1925. He died on July 4, 1925 in Montgomery County, NC.*
4055	Eleanor Francis Hogan (1925-1925). *Eleanor was born on June 18, 1925. She died on June 23, 1925 in Montgomery County, NC.*
4056	Buster Ralph Hogan (1930-1986). *Buster was born on March 30, 1930. He died on June 19, 1986 and was buried in Moore County, NC at Flint Hill Congregational Christian Church.*

1743. William Lewis Wallace, son of Elias W. Wallace and Lydia Frances Muse, was born in January 1890. He married **Ella Green** on July 15, 1923 in Montgomery County, NC. He died on March 8, 1951 in Richmond, VA.

Ella Green, daughter of Malcolm Green (1860-1945) and Rachel Lamonds (-), was born on November 25, 1906 in Montgomery County, NC. She died on November 6, 1992 in Moore County, NC and was buried in Montgomery County, NC at Community Baptist Church. She and William Lewis Wallace had the following children:

4057	Richard D. Wallace (-)
4058	Jessie Eliza Wallace (1924-). *Jessie was born on June 20, 1924 in Montgomery County, NC.*

1744. Laura Lee Wallace, daughter of Elias W. Wallace and Lydia Frances Muse, was born on March 8, 1893 in Moore County, NC. She died on September 14, 1963 in Jamestown, Guilford County, NC and was buried on September 16, 1963 in Candor, Montgomery County, NC at Macedonia Presbyterian Church.

1745. Alexander Wallace, son of Elias W. Wallace and Lydia Frances Muse, was born on July 20, 1893 in Moore County, NC. He married **Ellen Barber Wallace** on October 26, 1922 in Moore County, NC. He died on March 30, 1980 in Moore County, NC and was buried in Moore County, NC at Calvary Baptist Church.

Ellen Barber Wallace, daughter of Spinks Wallace (1862-1930) and Martha Ann Johnson (1864-1935), was born on May 18, 1903 in Moore County, NC. She died on June 30, 1975 in Carthage, Moore County, NC and was buried on July 2, 1975 in Moore County, NC at Calvary Baptist Church. She and Alexander Wallace had the following children:

4059	Carter Wallace (-)
4060	Roy Wallace (-)
4061	Margaret Francis Wallace (1924-1925). *Margaret was born on June 9, 1924. She died on August 19, 1925.*
4062	Catherine M. Wallace (1925-). *Catherine was born in 1925.*
4063	Dorothy Mae Wallace (1929-). *Dorothy was born on September 12, 1929 in Moore County, NC.*
4064	Ethel Marie Wallace (1932-). *Ethel was born on April 12, 1932 in Moore County, NC.*
4065	William Elias Wallace (1934-2014). *William was born on December 22, 1934. He died on June 26, 2014.*
4066	Norman Wallace (1938-). *Norman was born on September 9, 1938 in Moore County, NC.*
4067	Pearl Wallace (1942-). *Pearl was born on June 3, 1942 in Moore County, NC.*

1747. Torla B. "Toadie" Wallace, daughter of Malinda "Toad" Wallace, was born in December 1888. She married **William Wesley Sheffield** on May 29, 1903 in Moore County, NC. She died before 1909.

William Wesley Sheffield, son of Benjamin Franklin Sheffield (1850-1909) and Frances Laura "Fannie" Sheffield (1859-1929), was born in May 1883. He married Mollie Downing on December 26, 1909. He married Claudia Loula Cashwell on March 4, 1916. He died in May 1941 and was buried in Moore County, NC at Friendship Baptist Church. He and Torla B. "Toadie" Wallace had the following children:

4068	Sheffield (-1905). *[unnamed person] died on July 1, 1905. He/she was buried in Moore County, NC at Friendship Baptist Church.*

1748. Ollie Leola Richardson, daughter of Isaac D. Richardson and Malinda A. Wallace, was born on December 3, 1899. She died on January 4, 1916 and was buried in Lauderdale County, AL at Canerday Cemetery.

1749. Maudie Lee Wallace, daughter of George Washington Wallace and Celia Ann McGee, was born on April 21, 1901 in Lauderdale County, AL. She died on December 8, 1901 in Lauderdale County, AL and was buried in Lauderdale County, AL at Canerday Cemetery.

1751. Ollie Irene Wallace, daughter of George Washington Wallace and Celia Ann McGee, was born on March 12, 1907 in Lauderdale County, AL. She married **Bennie Lee Beavers** on October 5, 1924 in Lauderdale County, AL. She died in May 1994 in Florence, Lauderdale County, AL and was buried in Lauderdale County, AL at Hill Cemetery.

Bennie Lee Beavers was born on June 4, 1906 in Lauderdale County, AL. He died on July 6, 1979 in Florence, Lauderdale County, AL and was buried in Lauderdale County, AL at Hill Cemetery. He and Ollie Irene Wallace had the following children:

4069	Frankie Mae Beavers (-)
4070	George Wesley Beavers (-)
4071	Joyce Elaine Beavers (-). *Joyce was born "1 MAY" in Lauderdale County, AL.*
4072	William James Beavers (1935-1993). *William was born on January 11, 1935 in Lauderdale County, AL. He married **Bonnie Nell Campbell** on June 7, 1952 in Iuka, Mississippi. He died on October 15, 1993 in Lauderdale County, AL and was buried on October 17, 1993 in Lauderdale County, AL at Hill Cemetery.*

1757. Reba Wallace, daughter of George Washington Wallace and Celia Ann McGee, was born on May 15, 1922 in Lauderdale County, AL. She died in Lauderdale County, AL.

Malachi McGee died in Lauderdale County, AL. He and Reba Wallace had the following children:

4073	Roger McGee (-)	
4074	Larry McGee (-)	

1758. **Gentry Wiley Jenkins**, son of John Wiley Jenkins and Chappel Elizabeth Wallace, was born on May 9, 1922. He died on October 11, 1993.

Bonnie Sue Gray, daughter of Alexander Newton Gray (1898-1962) and Maggie Lena Bush (1897-1971), was born on June 9, 1925. She died on February 11, 2006. She and Gentry Wiley Jenkins had the following children:

4075	Mary Elizabeth Jenkins (-)

1768. **Sarah Eveline Nall**, daughter of Joseph Allen Nall and Susanna Williams, was born on July 23, 1883 in Wise County, TX. She died on February 28, 1959 in Lockney, Floyd County, TX.

James Tollie Corder was born on December 30, 1884. He died on October 28, 1955 in Lockney, Floyd County, TX.

1769. **John Harding Nall**, son of Joseph Allen Nall and Susanna Williams, was born on November 27, 1885 in Wise County, TX. He married **Esther Eddith Smith** on July 5, 1908 in Lockney, Floyd County, TX. He died on November 15, 1966 in Amarillo, Potter County, TX.

Esther Eddith Smith was born on January 12, 1887 in Bosque County, TX. She died on June 13, 1966 in Amarillo, Potter County, TX.

1770. **Jerry Hall Nall**, son of Joseph Allen Nall and Susanna Williams, was born on December 21, 1891 in Texas. He died on August 10, 1898 in Wise County, TX and was buried in Bridgeport, Wise County, TX at Wilson Prairie Cemetery.

1772. **Walter Wilson Morrison**, son of Mackay Morrison and Nancy Margaret Williams, was born on January 13, 1892. He died on November 5, 1977.

Lola Tibbs was born on January 1, 1895. She died on February 26, 1987. She and Walter Wilson Morrison had the following children:

4076	Brenda Jean Morrison (1941-). *Brenda was born on February 10, 1941.*

1780. **Female Williams** was the daughter of Jeremiah David Williams and Samantha J. Gattis.

Coleman and Female Williams had the following children:

4077	Daisy D. Coleman (1901-). *Daisy was born in 1901.*
4078	Beatrice Coleman (1902-). *Beatrice was born in 1902.*
4079	Clara B. Coleman (1903-). *Clara was born in 1903.*

1781. **Ada Angeline Williams**, daughter of Jeremiah David Williams and Samantha J. Gattis, was born on July 26, 1873. She died on May 31, 1951.

Napoleon G. Moorhead was born on September 11, 1873. He died on January 24, 1951. He and Ada Angeline Williams had the following children:

4080	Clarence E. Moorhead (1905-1992). *Clarence was born on October 4, 1905. He died on September 21, 1992.*

1784. **Eudora Williams**, daughter of Lorenzo Dewel "Lowe" Williams and Mary E. "Mollie" Cockburn, was born on July 8, 1885. She died on December 4, 1966.

John Pinkney Keener was born on February 14, 1877. He died on May 15, 1969. He and Eudora Williams had the following children:

4081   Elvis Arlet Keener (1905-1977). *Elvis was born on August 14, 1905. He married* **Berta Edith Yancey** *on May 10, 1930. He died on June 14, 1977.*

1785. Viola Marie \"Bygie\" Medcalf, daughter of John William Medcalf and Mary Ann "Mollie" Williams, was born on January 15, 1912. She married **Bayron Harold Pennington** on April 7, 1932 in Stephens County, OK. She died on July 24, 1979.

Bayron Harold Pennington was born on November 5, 1909. He died on September 6, 1994. He and Viola Marie "Bygie" Medcalf had the following children:

4082   H. Dale Pennington (-)

1793. Mollie Williams, daughter of Hubert Andrew Williams and Henrietta Georgia Parker, was born on November 10, 1902 in Burneyville, OK. She married **Henry Olen "Jack" Barnes** in February 1925. She died on March 13, 1986 in Ardmore, Carter County, OK.

Henry Olen "Jack" Barnes was born on July 22, 1900 in Dexter, Texas. He died in July 1964 in Ardmore, Carter County, OK. He and Mollie Williams had the following children:

4083   Kathryn Georgia Barnes (1925-). *Kathryn was born on August 4, 1925.*
4084   Jack A Barnes Jr. (1927-). *Jack was born on August 27, 1927.*
4085   Richard Lynn Barnes (1930-). *Richard was born on September 22, 1930.*
4086   Eloise Jo Ann Barnes (1935-1988). *Eloise was born on June 9, 1935. She died on March 15, 1988.*
4087   Hazel Faye Barnes (1938-1938). *Hazel was born on January 22, 1938. She died on February 27, 1938.*
4088   Billy Eugene Barnes (1940-). *Billy was born on January 2, 1940.*
4089   Kenneth Wayne Barnes (1942-). *Kenneth was born on November 8, 1942.*

1794. Archie Lorenzo Williams, son of Hubert Andrew Williams and Henrietta Georgia Parker, was born on April 18, 1905 in Burneyville, OK. He married **Jewel Hudson** on August 22, 1925. He died on March 26, 1971 in Causey, New Mexico.

Jewel Hudson and Archie Lorenzo Williams had the following children:

4090   Thurman "Hudson" Williams (-)
4091   Wilbor "Hudson" Williams (-)
4092   Adrian Lorenzo Williams (1927-1927). *Adrian was born on July 13, 1927. He died on July 13, 1927.*

1795. Hardie Elisha "Boag" Williams, son of Hubert Andrew Williams and Henrietta Georgia Parker, was born on September 24, 1907 in Burneyville, OK. He married **Dalma Daley** on November 6, 1933.

Dalma Daley was born on February 12, 1912. She and Hardie Elisha "Boag" Williams had the following children:

4093   Larue Williams (-)
4094   Rebecca Williams (-)
4095   Myrtle Williams (1934-1998). *Myrtle was born on October 27, 1934. She died on May 9, 1998 in Greeneville, OK.*
4096   Vivian Leigh Williams (1936-). *Vivian was born on November 8, 1936.*
4097   John Williams (1944-). *John was born in January 1944.*
4098   James Williams (1949-). *James was born in February 1949.*

1796. Ernest Lee "Bob" Williams, son of Hubert Andrew Williams and Henrietta Georgia Parker, was born on June 11, 1910. He married **Dorothy Mae Husband** on December 7, 1935. He died on September 10, 1981 in Bakersfield, Kern County, CA.

Dorothy Mae Husband was born on January 22, 1917. She died on December 28, 2004. She and Ernest Lee "Bob" Williams had the following children:

| 4099 | Ernest Robert Williams (1936-). *Ernest was born on September 27, 1936.* |
| 4100 | Larry Lee Williams (1946-). *Larry was born on March 28, 1946.* |

1797. John Sydney Williams, son of Hubert Andrew Williams and Henrietta Georgia Parker, was born on August 23, 1912. He married **Marie Lester** on April 20, 1946.

Marie Lester was born on April 2, 1916. She died on May 16, 1981. She and John Sydney Williams had the following children:

| 4101 | John Steven Williams (1953-). *John was born on July 23, 1953.* |
| 4102 | Carolyn Ann Williams (1955-). *Carolyn was born on December 12, 1955.* |

1798. Hubert Cecil Williams, son of Hubert Andrew Williams and Henrietta Georgia Parker, was born on May 11, 1916 in Greeneville, OK. He married **Bonnie Kelly** in 1937 in Texas. He married **Eva Lee Mae Shaw** on October 20, 1941 in St. Louis, MO. He died on December 11, 2000 in Mesquite, Texas.

Bonnie Kelly and Hubert Cecil Williams had the following children:

| 4103 | Melva Ruth Williams (1937-). *Melva was born on November 20, 1937.* |

Kathren Nichols and Hubert Cecil Williams had the following children:

4104	Gary Williams (-)
4105	Beth Williams (-)
4106	Lawanda Nichols (-)
4107	Larry Nichiols (-)

Eva Lee Mae Shaw was born on April 3, 1919 in Shamrock, Creek, OK. She died on July 27, 1988 in Oklahoma City, Oklahoma County, OK and was buried in Resthaven Memory Gardens, OK City, OK. She and Hubert Cecil Williams had the following children:

| 4108 | Billy Joe Williams (1942-2005). *Billy was born on October 14, 1942 in Ardmore, Carter County, OK. He married **Elrita James Azlin** on June 23, 1962 in Wewoka, Seminole, OK. He married **Linda Renee Mahurin** on October 4, 1974 in Dallas, TX. He married **Janice Marie Orr** on September 5, 1986 in Oklahoma City, Oklahoma County, OK. He died on December 24, 2005.* |
| 4109 | Sydney Earl Williams (1944-). *Sydney was born on September 11, 1944.* |

1799. Gladys Georgia Williams, daughter of Hubert Andrew Williams and Henrietta Georgia Parker, was born on October 5, 1919. She married **Harold Gaurkee** on January 20, 1945.

Harold Gaurkee and Gladys Georgia Williams had the following children:

4110	Christine Lavelle Gaurkee (-)
4111	Charles Gaurkee (-)
4112	Catherine Marie Gaurkee (-)
4113	Kenneth Earl Gaurkee (1946-). *Kenneth was born in October 1946.*
4114	Douglas Arthur Gaurkee (1948-). *Douglas was born in April 1948.*
4115	Richard Lyle Gaurkee (1950-). *Richard was born in 1950.*
4116	Carol Ann Gaurkee (1956-). *Carol was born in September 1956.*

1800. Kathryn Marie Williams, daughter of Hubert Andrew Williams and Henrietta Georgia Parker, was born on August 12, 1922. She married **Rowe Burton Reed** on July 20, 1947.

Rowe Burton Reed was born on September 11, 1924. He and Kathryn Marie Williams had the following children:

| 4117 | Samuel Kert Reed (1949-). *Samuel was born on November 25, 1949.* |
| 4118 | Carmen Elaine Reed (1951-). *Carmen was born on August 14, 1951. She married **Walter Dean Goodner** on June 19, 1974.* |

4119	Rowe Adrian Reed (1953-). *Rowe was born on May 22, 1953. He married **Pamela Sue Lindren** on June 28, 1974.*
4120	Rowena Kay Reed (1959-). *Rowena was born on March 17, 1959. She married **Paul Tory Jhant** on March 24, 1984.*
4121	Aldera Maine Reed (1960-). *Aldera was born on July 28, 1960. She married **Brian Carey Boothe** on December 6, 1980.*
4122	Freddy Lowell Reed (1960-). *Freddy was born on December 2, 1960.*
4123	Roy Lynn Reed (1965-). *Roy was born on October 1, 1965.*

1801. **Lela Lavella Williams**, daughter of Hubert Andrew Williams and Henrietta Georgia Parker, was born on November 8, 1924. She married **Marvin Holbrook** in 1942.

Marvin Holbrook was born on May 3, 1922. He and Lela Lavella Williams had the following children:

4124	Harold Dewayne Holbrook (1943-). *Harold was born on July 18, 1943.*
4125	Hubert Doyle Holbrook (1948-). *Hubert was born on October 26, 1948.*
4126	Marvana Dinel Holbrook (1956-). *Marvana was born on November 30, 1956 in Ardmore, Carter County, OK.*

1803. **David J. Williams**, son of John W. Williams and Clarkie Ann Britt, was born in November 1891. He died in 1957 and was buried in Henderson County, TN at Palestine Cemetery.

Sis was born in 1884. She died in 1969 and was buried in Henderson County, TN at Palestine Cemetery.

1804. **Minnie Lillian Williams**, daughter of John W. Williams and Clarkie Ann Britt, was born on January 2, 1894. She married **Joe Locie McPeake** on September 12, 1909 in Henderson County, TN. She died on October 16, 1935 and was buried in Henderson County, TN at Palestine Cemetery.

Joe Locie McPeake was born on May 5, 1896. He died on July 4, 1945 and was buried in Henderson County, TN at Palestine Cemetery. He and Minnie Lillian Williams had the following children:

4127	Mary Opal McPeake (-)
4128	George Milam McPeake (1912-1986). *George was born on April 14, 1912. He died on November 6, 1986.*
4129	Elton Paige McPeake (1915-1981). *Elton was born on April 5, 1915. He died on August 7, 1981.*

1805. **John T. Williams**, son of John W. Williams and Clarkie Ann Britt, was born in January 1897.

1806. **Luther Anderson Williams**, son of John W. Williams and Clarkie Ann Britt, was born in April 1899. He died in 1967 and was buried in Henderson County, TN at Palestine Cemetery.

Vera E. was born in 1901. She died in 1949 and was buried in Henderson County, TN at Palestine Cemetery. She and Luther Anderson Williams had the following children:

4130	Alexia Jane Williams (-)
4131	Jack Williams (1923-1944). *Jack was born in 1923. He died in 1944 and was buried in Henderson County, TN at Palestine Cemetery.*
4132	Luther Williams Jr. (1924-1925). *Luther was born on December 23, 1924. He died on January 26, 1925 and was buried in Henderson County, TN at Palestine Cemetery.*

1807. **Coy Williams**, son of John W. Williams and Clarkie Ann Britt, was born in 1901. He died in 1972 and was buried in Henderson County, TN at Palestine Cemetery.

Esther M. was born in 1905. She died in 1973 and was buried in Henderson County, TN at Palestine Cemetery.

1808. **John Walter Britt**, son of William Salvage Britt and Clarkie Ann Williams, was born in September 1894. He married **Bertha Estelle Wallace** on November 14, 1914 in Henderson County, TN. He died in 1947 and was buried in Henderson County, TN at Palestine Cemetery.

Bertha Estelle Wallace was born in 1897. She died in 1984 and was buried in Henderson County, TN at Palestine Cemetery. She and John Walter Britt had the following children:

> 4133   Louise Britt (1915-). *Louise was born in 1915.*
>
> 4134   Jamie Britt (1917-). *Jamie was born in 1917.*

1809. **Amanda Elvira "Mandy" Britt**, daughter of William Salvage Britt and Clarkie Ann Williams, was born in July 1896. She died in 1966 and was buried in Henderson County, TN at Palestine Cemetery.

Sam P. Hopper was born in 1895. He died in 1957 and was buried in Henderson County, TN at Palestine Cemetery. He and Amanda Elvira "Mandy" Britt had the following children:

> 4135   James Howard Hopper (1923-1998). *James was born on January 23, 1923. He married **Helen Marie Williams** on February 28, 1945. He died on November 29, 1998 and was buried in Henderson County, TN at Palestine Cemetery.*

1820. **Flossie Ann Williams**, daughter of Joseph Park Williams and Maggie Horton, was born on April 19, 1905. She died on March 27, 1953.

Luther Washington Stewart was born on February 22, 1900. He died on December 12, 1989. He and Flossie Ann Williams had the following children:

> 4136   John William Stewart (1923-1962). *John was born on June 9, 1923. He died on December 10, 1962.*

1822. **Lala Lucille Hart**, daughter of Joseph C. Hart and Florence "Retta" Britt, was born on June 4, 1904. She died on December 22, 1941.

Sidney Thomas Holmes was born on June 28, 1902. He died on June 24, 1987. He and Lala Lucille Hart had the following children:

> 4137   Paul Hulon Holmes (1924-2009). *Paul was born on August 19, 1924. He married **Delta Mae Pollock** on March 30, 1946 in Alcorn County, MS. He died on June 15, 2009.*

1824. **Lula Britt**, daughter of Thomas Jefferson Britt and Mollie Ann Williams, was born on October 8, 1889. She died on August 18, 1896 and was buried in Henderson County, TN at Palestine Cemetery.

1825. **Casie Britt**, son of Thomas Jefferson Britt and Mollie Ann Williams, was born on September 14, 1891. He died on October 28, 1894 and was buried in Henderson County, TN at Palestine Cemetery.

1826. **Murray L. Britt**, son of Thomas Jefferson Britt and Mollie Ann Williams, was born on June 3, 1894. He died on June 7, 1918 and was buried in Henderson County, TN at Palestine Cemetery.

1829. **Elbert Anderson Britt**, son of Thomas Jefferson Britt and Mollie Ann Williams, was born in 1904. He died in 1994 and was buried in Henderson County, TN at Palestine Cemetery.

Maybelle Bramlett was born in 1909. She died in 1947 and was buried in Henderson County, TN at Palestine Cemetery. She and Elbert Anderson Britt had the following children:

> 4139   Virginia Kay Britt (1947-1947). *Virginia was born in 1947. She died in 1947 and was buried in Henderson County, TN at Palestine Cemetery.*

Lela B. was born in 1907. She died in 1991 and was buried in Henderson County, TN at Palestine Cemetery.

1832. **Hettie V. Weatherington**, daughter of William Henry Weatherington and Martha Catherine Williams, was born in May 1893. She married **Leander Edward McCormick** on September 13, 1909 in Henderson County, TN. She died in 1925 and was buried in Henderson County, TN at Center Hill Cemetery.

Leander Edward McCormick was born on March 10, 1892. He died on March 15, 1972 and was buried in Henderson County, TN at Center Hill Cemetery.

1833. **Hautie A. Weatherington**, daughter of William Henry Weatherington and Martha Catherine Williams, was born on February 17, 1895. She died on July 7, 1985 and was buried in Henderson County, TN at Center Hill Cemetery.

James Edmond Vandiver was born on September 5, 1892. He died on July 14, 1963 and was buried in Henderson County, TN at Center Hill Cemetery.

1834. **Dossie Benton Weatherington**, son of William Henry Weatherington and Martha Catherine Williams, was born in December 1896.

1835. **Toker Z. Weatherington**, daughter of William Henry Weatherington and Martha Catherine Williams, was born in 1900. She married **Murray Stewart** on December 5, 1916 in Henderson County, TN. She died in 1918 and was buried in Henderson County, TN at Center Hill Cemetery.

1836. **Milburn Otral Weatherington**, son of William Henry Weatherington and Martha Catherine Williams, was born on March 26, 1909. He died on August 11, 1998 and was buried in Henderson County, TN at Center Hill Cemetery.

1837. **Clyde Williams**, son of Dave Williams and Martha Emmaline Hart, was born in 1910. He died in 1989 and was buried in Henderson County, TN at Palestine Cemetery.

Lillian Mullins, daughter of Jim Mullins (-) and Ella L. "Nettie" Britt (1889-), was born in 1912. She died in 2001 and was buried in Henderson County, TN at Palestine Cemetery. She and Clyde Williams had the following children:

> 4140   Helen Marie Williams (1930-). *Helen was born on March 16, 1930. She married **James Howard Hopper** on February 28, 1945.*

1838. **Jerry Hubert Williams Jr.**, son of Jerry Hubert Williams Sr. and Nona Ann Green, was born on January 6, 1921. He died on July 21, 2001.

Jerry Hubert Williams Jr. had the following children:

> 4141   Tim P. Williams (1946-). *Tim was born on September 10, 1946.*

1839. **Carson Roy Black**, son of Black and Sarah C. Wallace, was born on August 20, 1904. He died on November 9, 1999 in Moore Regional Hospital, Pinehurst, Moore County, NC and was buried in Moore County, NC at Old Beulah Hill Cemetery.

Florence Cora Koon was born on October 9, 1908. She died on September 20, 2000 and was buried in Moore County, NC at Old Beulah Hill Cemetery. She and Carson Roy Black had the following children:

> 4142   Millie Black (1929-). *Millie was born in 1929.*
> 4143   Carson Roy Black Jr. (1931-). *Carson was born in 1931.*
> 4144   Charles Howard Black (1933-). *Charles was born in 1933.*
> 4145   Randolph Black (1936-). *Randolph was born in 1936.*
> 4146   Stanley Gene Black (1938-2013). *Stanley was born on August 27, 1938. He died on January 25, 2013 and was buried in Moore County, NC at Old Beulah Hill Cemetery.*

1841. **Elvira Kennedy**, daughter of John Angus Deaton Kennedy and Ella Wallace, was born on November 18, 1903. She died on February 4, 1904 and was buried in Moore County, NC at Old Beulah Hill Cemetery.

1842. **Bessie Sarah Kennedy**, daughter of John Angus Deaton Kennedy and Ella Wallace, was born on December 27, 1905. She married **Zeb Rietzel Robertson** on June 16, 1922. She died on February 3, 1989.

Zeb Rietzel Robertson was born on January 17, 1904. He and Bessie Sarah Kennedy had the following children:

> 4147   Juanita Hale Robertson (1941-). *Juanita was born on March 21, 1941. She married **Cicero Edgar Sullivan** on June 28, 1959.*

1843. **Alexander Martin Kennedy**, son of John Angus Deaton Kennedy and Ella Wallace, was born on October 4, 1908. He married **Ruth Nance** on August 12, 1935. He died on July 10, 2001 in Moore County, NC and was buried in Moore County, NC at Beulah Hill Baptist Church.

Ruth Nance was born on September 10, 1915 in Anson County, NC. She died on January 19, 1996 in Moore County, NC and was buried in Moore County, NC at Beulah Hill Baptist Church. She and Alexander Martin Kennedy had the following children:

4148	Ella Marie "Bunchie" Kennedy (1936-). *Ella was born in 1936.*
4149	Frances Lee "Sis" Kennedy (1938-). *Frances was born in 1938.*
4150	Mary Abigail "Abby" Kennedy (1943-). *Mary was born in 1943.*
4151	Marion Alexander "Bud" Kennedy (1944-). *Marion was born in 1944.*
4152	Infant Kennedy (1946-1946). *Infant was born on November 5, 1946. He/she died on November 5, 1946. He/she was buried in Moore County, NC at Beulah Hill Baptist Church.*
4153	Infant Kennedy (1946-1946). *Infant was born on November 5, 1946. He/she died on November 5, 1946. He/she was buried in Moore County, NC at Beulah Hill Baptist Church.*
4154	Ival Nance Kennedy (1947-). *Ival was born in 1947.*
4155	Inglis Ruth Kennedy (1955-). *Inglis was born in 1955.*

1844. **John Deaton Kennedy**, son of John Angus Deaton Kennedy and Ella Wallace, was born on December 26, 1910. He died on November 29, 2001 and was buried in Moore County, NC at Beulah Hill Baptist Church.

1845. **Charlie James Wallace**, son of Archibald Alexander "Archie" Wallace and Mary Jane Shaw, was born on April 27, 1904. He died on November 30, 1977 in Cumberland County, NC and was buried in Moore County, NC at Old Beulah Hill Cemetery.

1846. **John Daniel Wallace**, son of Archibald Alexander "Archie" Wallace and Mary Jane Shaw, was born on May 31, 1906. He died on December 4, 1981 in Cumberland County, NC and was buried in Moore County, NC at Old Beulah Hill Cemetery.

1847. **Lula Florence Wallace**, daughter of Archibald Alexander "Archie" Wallace and Mary Jane Shaw, was born on June 26, 1908 in Moore County, NC. She married **Benjamin Harrison Cleaver** on December 30, 1933. She died on November 27, 1983 in Brunswick County, NC.

Benjamin Harrison Cleaver, son of Isaac Cleaver (1849-1926) and Julia Ella Frye (1868-1944), was born on January 31, 1906 in Moore County, NC. He died on January 31, 1981 in Moore County, NC. He and Lula Florence Wallace had the following children:

4156	Jessie Marie Cleaver (1934-). *Jessie was born on September 23, 1934.*
4157	Benjamin Olin Cleaver (1946-). *Benjamin was born on August 28, 1946.*

1848. **Mary Ann Wallace**, daughter of Archibald Alexander "Archie" Wallace and Mary Jane Shaw, was born on January 26, 1910. She died on November 21, 1991 and was buried in Southern Pines, Moore County, NC at Mt. Hope Cemetery.

Samuel Frye and Mary Ann Wallace had the following children:

4158	Samuel Felton Frye (1931-). *Samuel was born in 1931.*
4159	Louis Fitzgerald "Tommy" Frye (1938-1984). *Louis was born in 1938. He died in 1984.*
4160	Gary Nelson "Pete" Frye (1945-1968). *Gary was born in 1945. He died in 1968.*

Leo V. O'Callahan was born on April 11, 1894. He died on April 15, 1960.

1849. **Jessie Wallace**, son of Archibald Alexander "Archie" Wallace and Mary Jane Shaw, was born on January 11, 1913. He died on September 23, 1916 and was buried in Moore County, NC at Old Beulah Hill Cemetery.

1850. **Janie Wallace**, daughter of Archibald Alexander "Archie" Wallace and Mary Jane Shaw, was born on July 17, 1915. She died on June 19, 1982 and was buried in Moore County, NC at Old Beulah Hill Cemetery.

Janie Wallace had the following children:

| 4161 | Gladys Irene Wallace (1941-). *Gladys was born on May 30, 1941. She married **Larry Dane Graham** on September 11, 1960 in Moore County, NC.* |
| 4162 | Clara Josephine Wallace (1948-). *Clara was born on January 2, 1948.* |

1851. Mack Wallace, son of Archibald Alexander "Archie" Wallace and Mary Jane Shaw, was born on October 12, 1917. He died on January 18, 1918 and was buried in Moore County, NC at Old Beulah Hill Cemetery.

1852. Evelyn Wallace, daughter of Archibald Alexander "Archie" Wallace and Mary Jane Shaw, was born on May 26, 1919.

Evelyn Wallace had the following children:

| 4163 | Betsy Jean Wallace (1942-2012). *Betsy was born on March 20, 1942. She died on January 6, 2012 and was buried in Moore County, NC at Beulah Hill Baptist Church.* |
| 4164 | Patricia Ann Wallace (1947-). *Patricia was born in 1947.* |

1853. George Wallace, son of Archibald Alexander "Archie" Wallace and Mary Jane Shaw, was born on September 21, 1921. He died on October 28, 1921 and was buried in Moore County, NC at Old Beulah Hill Cemetery.

1854. Elizabeth Wallace, daughter of Archibald Alexander "Archie" Wallace and Mary Jane Shaw, was born on February 13, 1924. She married **Keith Harvey** on February 12, 1945.

Keith Harvey and Elizabeth Wallace had the following children:

4165	Linda Kay Harvey (1946-). *Linda was born in 1946.*
4166	Flora Lynn Harvey (1952-). *Flora was born in 1952.*
4167	Teresa Ann Harvey (1957-). *Teresa was born in 1957.*

1855. Edgar Wallace, son of Archibald Alexander "Archie" Wallace and Mary Jane Shaw, was born on February 27, 1927. He died on November 8, 1930 and was buried in Moore County, NC at Old Beulah Hill Cemetery.

1856. Beulah May Wallace, daughter of James M. "Jim" Wallace and Margaret Leo Oliver, was born on August 23, 1910. She married **William Frank Lucas** on June 13, 1942 in Moore County, NC. She died on November 6, 1990 and was buried in Moore County, NC at Culdee Presbyterian Church.

William Frank Lucas, son of Wesley Lucas (-) and Emily J. (-), was born on July 28, 1888. He died on August 24, 1980 and was buried in Moore County, NC at Culdee Presbyterian Church. He and Beulah May Wallace had the following children:

4168	William Franklin Lucas Jr. (1944-2007). *William was born on October 21, 1944. He died on December 9, 2007 and was buried in Moore County, NC at Culdee Presbyterian Church.*
4169	Cleave Harrison Lucas (1945-). *Cleave was born on December 8, 1945 in Moore County, NC.*
4170	James Wesley Lucas (1947-). *James was born on April 1, 1947.*
4171	Millard Michael Lucas (1949-). *Millard was born on March 7, 1949.*

1857. Margaret Ann Wallace, daughter of James M. "Jim" Wallace and Margaret Leo Oliver, was born on January 5, 1915. She died on December 10, 1931.

1858. Chris Hugh Wallace, son of Kenneth Martin Wallace and Ella May Juline Frye, was born on April 10, 1918. He died on March 10, 1973 and was buried in Moore County, NC at Beulah Hill Baptist Church.

Emma Irene Stutts, daughter of Fred Stutts (-) and Myrtle Currie (-), was born on March 15, 1921. She died on July 27, 1983 and was buried in Moore County, NC at Beulah Hill Baptist Church. She and Chris Hugh Wallace had the following children:

4172	Irene Wallace (1946-1946). *Irene was born on July 18, 1946. She died on July 18, 1946 and was buried in Moore County, NC at Beulah Hill Baptist Church.*
4173	Dorothy Ann Wallace (1948-). *Dorothy was born on March 25, 1948.*
4174	Susan Gail Wallace (1951-). *Susan was born on October 16, 1951.*

1859. **Aretia Mae "Rita" Wallace**, daughter of Kenneth Martin Wallace and Ella May Juline Frye, was born on October 28, 1920. She married **Reuben Ernest Yow** on August 3, 1936 in Moore County, NC and was buried in Moore County, NC at Beulah Hill Baptist Church.

Reuben Ernest Yow, son of Reuben Spinks Yow (1879-1943) and Elizabeth Hicks (1891-1918), was born on September 22, 1914. He died on December 9, 1973 and was buried in High Falls, Moore County, NC at Prosperity Friends Meeting Cemetery. He and Aretia Mae "Rita" Wallace had the following children:

| 4175 | Betty Carolyn Yow (1937-). *Betty was born in 1937.* |
| 4176 | Frances Mae Yow (1941-). *Frances was born in 1941.* |

1860. **Annie Louise Wallace**, daughter of Kenneth Martin Wallace and Ella May Juline Frye, was born on December 1, 1923. She died on April 19, 1942 in Moore County, NC and was buried in Moore County, NC at Beulah Hill Baptist Church.

1861. **Mattie Frances Wallace**, daughter of Kenneth Martin Wallace and Ella May Juline Frye, was born on May 29, 1925. She married **William Lester Carpenter** on November 9, 1952 in Moore County, NC. She died on December 29, 2010.

William Lester Carpenter, son of Lester Mae Carpenter (-) and Zona Mae Bess (-), was born in 1927. He and Mattie Frances Wallace had the following children:

4177	Stanley Dean MacDonald Carpenter (1953-). *Stanley was born in 1953.*
4178	Larry Alan Carpenter (1955-). *Larry was born in 1955.*
4179	Charles Francis Carpenter (1957-). *Charles was born in 1957.*

1862. **Kenneth Charles Wallace**, son of Kenneth Martin Wallace and Ella May Juline Frye, was born on November 28, 1927 in Moore County, NC. He died on December 25, 2001 in Moore County, NC and was buried in Moore County, NC at Beulah Hill Baptist Church.

Lucille Ann Todd was born on December 10, 1933. She and Kenneth Charles Wallace had the following children:

4180	Laura Ann Wallace (1954-). *Laura was born on January 5, 1954. She married **Gerald Elon Rouse** on September 6, 1974.*
4181	Nancy Marie Wallace (1955-). *Nancy was born on March 22, 1955.*
4182	Charles Michael Wallace (1956-). *Charles was born on July 26, 1956.*
4183	Ronald Leroy Wallace (1958-). *Ronald was born on January 29, 1958.*

1863. **John Edgar Wallace**, son of Kenneth Martin Wallace and Ella May Juline Frye, was born on September 22, 1930. He married **Betty Louise McQuay** on August 11, 1959 in Charlotte, Mecklenburg County, NC.

Betty Louise McQuay was born on February 7, 1938. She and John Edgar Wallace had the following children:

4184	Teresa Lynn Wallace (1960-). *Teresa was born on December 17, 1960.*
4185	Sharon Kay Wallace (1962-). *Sharon was born in 1962.*
4186	Kenneth Price Wallace (1969-). *Kenneth was born in 1969.*

1864. **Betty Ray Wallace**, daughter of Kenneth Martin Wallace and Ella May Juline Frye, was born on September 8, 1933. She married **James Elbert Bridges** on September 10, 1956 in Bennettsville, Marlboro County, SC. She died on January 8, 2006 and was buried in Moore County, NC at Beulah Hill Baptist Church.

James Elbert Bridges was born on April 10, 1931. He and Betty Ray Wallace had the following children:

4187	Brenda Sue Bridges (1957-). *Brenda was born on February 1, 1957.*
4188	Kathy Louise Bridges (1960-). *Kathy was born in 1960.*
4189	Tammy Lynn Bridges (1963-). *Tammy was born in 1963.*
4190	Deana Marie Bridges (1966-). *Deana was born in 1966.*

1865. **Olan Curtis Richardson** was the son of William A. Richardson and Lila Leila Susannah Jones.

Olan Curtis Richardson had the following children:

4191   Olan Curtis Richardson Jr. (-)

1867. Noah J. Richardson, son of Noah Bazzel Richardson and Bessie, was born on July 6, 1902. He died on January 11, 1989.

Orlene Ella \"Punky\" Zeiler was born on April 16, 1912. She died on January 1, 2007. She and Noah J. Richardson had the following children:

        4192   Charles Jay Richardson (1936-2002). *Charles was born on April 22, 1936. He died on August 10, 2002.*

1874. Lilly F. Seawell, daughter of Archibald Winston Seawell and Mary Hadley Williams, was born in 1885.

Charlie Apples and Lilly F. Seawell had the following children:

        4193   Mary Jane Apples (-)
        4194   Audrey A. Apples (-)
        4195   Annie Lee Apples (-)
        4196   Rachel F. Apples (-)
        4197   Paul E. Apples (-)

1875. Arthur L. Seawell, son of Archibald Winston Seawell and Mary Hadley Williams, was born on September 28, 1886. He died on August 18, 1907 and was buried in Moore County, NC at Bethlehem Baptist Church.

1876. Flossie Lee Seawell, daughter of Archibald Winston Seawell and Mary Hadley Williams, was born on October 1, 1888. She died on January 8, 1936 and was buried in Moore County, NC at Bethlehem Baptist Church.

William Cicero Sullivan, son of William Lindsey Sullivan (1837-1912) and Jane McIntosh (1843-1930), was born on February 2, 1872 in Moore County, NC. He died on January 7, 1932 in Moore County, NC and was buried on January 8, 1932 in Moore County, NC at Bethlehem Baptist Church. He and Flossie Lee Seawell had the following children:

        4198   June Sullivan (1907-1962). *June was born on June 1, 1907. He died on June 11, 1962 and was buried in Moore County, NC at Bethlehem Baptist Church.*

1877. John Quincy Seawell, son of Archibald Winston Seawell and Mary Hadley Williams, was born in 1891.

Alma Dossett and John Quincy Seawell had the following children:

        4199   John Quincy Seawell Jr. (-)
        4200   Howard Dossett Seawell (-)

1878. Mamie K. Seawell, daughter of Archibald Winston Seawell and Mary Hadley Williams, was born on March 23, 1893. She died on May 14, 1945 and was buried in Carthage, Moore County, NC at Cross Hill Cemetery.

Joseph Thomas Ritter, son of Addison Worth Ritter (1849-1938) and Catherine Maness (1853-1912), was born on October 22, 1880. He died on October 16, 1923 in Sanford, Lee County, NC and was buried in Carthage, Moore County, NC at Cross Hill Cemetery. He and Mamie K. Seawell had the following children:

        4201   Josie Ritter (-)
        4202   David A. Ritter (1917-1934). *David was born in 1917. He died in 1934 and was buried in Carthage, Moore County, NC at Cross Hill Cemetery.*
        4203   Mary Catherine Ritter (1920-1964). *Mary was born in 1920. She died in 1964 and was buried in Carthage, Moore County, NC at Cross Hill Cemetery.*

1879. Fodie H. Seawell, daughter of Archibald Winston Seawell and Mary Hadley Williams, was born on October 23, 1895. She married **Robert Peter Dowd** on December 5, 1916. She died on February 17, 1971 and was buried in Moore County, NC at Bethlehem Baptist Church.

Robert Peter Dowd, son of Bryant D. Dowd (1863-1944) and Mary Elizabeth Hunsucker (1864-1932), was born on January 8, 1894. He died on February 4, 1961 and was buried in Moore County, NC at Bethlehem Baptist Church. He and Fodie H. Seawell had the following children:

4204	Herbet Bryant Dowd (1917-1917). *Herbet was born on September 9, 1917 in Moore County, NC. He died on November 4, 1917 and was buried in Moore County, NC at Bethlehem Baptist Church.*
4205	Harold Springs Dowd (1919-1992). *Harold was born on June 17, 1919 in Moore County, NC. He died on April 6, 1992 and was buried in Moore County, NC at Bethlehem Baptist Church.*
4206	Robert Peter Dowd Jr. (1922-1997). *Robert was born on January 12, 1922 in Moore County, NC. He died on February 28, 1997 and was buried in Southern Pines, Moore County, NC at Pinelawn Memorial Park.*
4207	Maude Hughes Dowd (1923-). *Maude was born on November 18, 1923 in Moore County, NC.*
4208	Henry Grossett Dowd (1926-1988). *Henry was born on March 20, 1926 in Moore County, NC. He died on August 10, 1988 and was buried in Moore County, NC at Bethlehem Baptist Church.*
4209	Frances Grace Dowd (1928-). *Frances was born on February 25, 1928 in Moore County, NC.*
4210	Elizabeth Ann Dowd (1931-). *Elizabeth was born on April 13, 1931 in Moore County, NC.*
4211	Charles Morrison Dowd (1933-). *Charles was born on January 3, 1933 in Moore County, NC.*
4212	James Russell Dowd (1938-). *James was born on December 16, 1938 in Moore County, NC.*

1881. Hattie Seawell, daughter of Archibald Winston Seawell and Mary Hadley Williams, was born in 1900. She married **Allen Lawhon McIntosh** on December 23, 1922 in Moore County, NC.

Allen Lawhon McIntosh, son of Samuel Russell McIntosh (1853-1917) and Mary Elizabeth Lawhon (1866-1935), was born on January 20, 1900 in Moore County, NC. He and Hattie Seawell had the following children:

4213	Allen L. McIntosh Jr. (-)

1882. Lettie D. Seawell, daughter of Archibald Winston Seawell and Mary Hadley Williams, was born on October 5, 1900. She died on April 20, 1910 and was buried in Moore County, NC at Bethlehem Baptist Church.

1883. Efland Archie Seawell, son of Archibald Winston Seawell and Mary Hadley Williams, was born on November 5, 1904. He died on November 22, 1973 and was buried in Siler City, Chatham County, NC at Loves Creek Baptist Church.

Willie Glenn Phillips was born on August 29, 1925. She died on June 17, 2005 and was buried in Siler City, Chatham County, NC at Loves Creek Baptist Church. She and Efland Archie Seawell had the following children:

4214	Mary Florence Seawell (-)
4215	Lois Laverne Seawell (-)
4216	Doris Myrtle Seawell (-)

1884. J. Clinton Seawell, son of John Wesley P. Seawell and Florence Jackson, was born on March 9, 1889.

1885. Gladys Gertrude Seawell, daughter of John Wesley P. Seawell and Florence Jackson, was born on June 13, 1891. She died on September 20, 1958 and was buried in Moore County, NC at Bethlehem Baptist Church.

Richard Roscoe Gordon, son of Talitha Gordon (1863-1950), was born on July 26, 1883. He died on November 7, 1958 and was buried in Moore County, NC at Bethlehem Baptist Church.

1892. Lillie D. Maness, daughter of Henry Alexander Maness and Julie Ann Johnson, was born in February 1896. She married **Arthur Thomas Harris** on May 1, 1920 in Troy, Montgomery County, NC. She died on May 7, 1952 in Biscoe, Montgomery County, NC and was buried in Biscoe, Montgomery County, NC.

Arthur Thomas Harris and Lillie D. Maness had the following children:

> 4217   Arthur Thomas Harris Jr. (-)

1893. Dillian Ruffin "Dill" Maness, son of Henry Alexander Maness and Julie Ann Johnson, was born on May 28, 1898. He married **Nancy Jane Hurley** on April 30, 1921 in Montgomery County, NC. He died on July 8, 1974 in Biscoe, Montgomery County, NC and was buried in Biscoe, Montgomery County, NC at Biscoe Cemetery.

Nancy Jane Hurley was born on February 23, 1892. She died on February 22, 1981 and was buried in Biscoe, Montgomery County, NC at Biscoe Cemetery. She and Dillian Ruffin "Dill" Maness had the following children:

> 4218   Callie Lucille Maness (1922-). *Callie was born on March 8, 1922 in Montgomery County, NC. She married **Fred McCaskill** on September 29, 1940 in Chesterfield County, SC.*
>
> 4219   Elgie Maie Maness (1923-1923). *Elgie was born on April 3, 1923 in Biscoe, Montgomery County, NC. She died on April 28, 1923 in Biscoe, Montgomery County, NC.*
>
> 4220   Robert Lee Maness (1924-1988). *Robert was born on April 29, 1924 in Biscoe, Montgomery County, NC. He died on February 19, 1988 in Asheboro, Randolph County, NC and was buried in Biscoe, Montgomery County, NC.*
>
> 4221   Carl Junior Maness (1928-). *Carl was born on June 24, 1928. He married on July 5, 1958 in Chesterfield County, SC.*
>
> 4222   James Albert (Dink) Maness Sr. (1931-). *James was born on May 13, 1931 in Biscoe, Montgomery County, NC. He married on May 17, 1953 in Chesterfield, Chesterfield County, SC..*

1894. David Willie Maness, son of Henry Alexander Maness and Julie Ann Johnson, was born on August 14, 1902 in Montgomery County, NC. He died on May 28, 1956 in Bensalem Township, Moore County, North Carrolina and was buried on May 30, 1956 in Biscoe, Montgomery County, NC.

Rosa and David Willie Maness had the following children:

> 4223   Edelle Maness (1929-1950). *Edelle was born on October 28, 1929 in Springhill Township, Scotland County, NC. She died on April 7, 1950 and was buried in Biscoe, Montgomery County, NC.*
>
> 4224   Annie Christine Maness (1932-). *Annie was born on January 12, 1932 in Biscoe, Montgomery County, NC.*
>
> 4225   Margaret Anlee (Peggy) Maness (1935-). *Margaret was born on May 29, 1935 in Biscoe, Montgomery County, NC.*
>
> 4226   David Allen Maness (1937-). *David was born on May 8, 1937 in Laurel Hill, Scotland, NC.*
>
> 4227   Katherine Maness (1937-). *Katherine was born on May 8, 1937 in Laurel Hill, Scotland, NC.*
>
> 4228   James Lee Maness (1939-). *James was born on February 13, 1939 in Biscoe, Montgomery County, NC.*
>
> 4229   Willie Junior Maness (1941-). *Willie was born on October 2, 1941 in Willianson Twp, Scotland, NC.*

1895. Henry Harris Maness, son of Henry Alexander Maness and Julie Ann Johnson, was born on July 14, 1903 in Biscoe, Montgomery County, NC. He married **Mildred Frances McCaskill** in September 1925. He died on December 10, 1971 in Biscoe, Montgomery County, NC and was buried in 1971 in Biscoe, Montgomery County, NC at Biscoe Cemetery.

Mildred Frances McCaskill, daughter of William Franklin McCaskill (1884-1960) and Minnie Iola Lomax (1891-1970), was born on November 27, 1911 in Biscoe, Montgomery County, NC. She died on August 21, 1987 and was buried in 1987 in Biscoe, Montgomery County, NC at Biscoe Cemetery. She and Henry Harris Maness had the following children:

> 4230   Rachel McCaskill Maness (1926-). *Rachel was born on October 16, 1926 in Biscoe, Montgomery County, NC. She married **Claude Alexander McCaskill** on April 20, 1946 in SC.*
>
> 4231   James Henry Maness (1934-). *James was born on February 2, 1934 in Biscoe, Montgomery County, NC.*
>
> 4232   Larry Frank Maness (1938-1938). *Larry was born on January 12, 1938 in Moore County,*

NC. He died on May 3, 1938 and was buried in Biscoe, Montgomery County, NC.

1896. **Mary Ellen Maness**, daughter of Henry Alexander Maness and Julie Ann Johnson, was born on January 12, 1905. She died on December 23, 1984 and was buried in Biscoe, Montgomery County, NC at Britt-Deaton-Greene Cemetery.

Lee Arlie Britt, son of James Patrick Britt (1869-1951) and Cornelia Ann "Nealie" Deaton (1857-1920), was born on July 26, 1895. He died on April 26, 1974 and was buried in Biscoe, Montgomery County, NC at Britt-Deaton-Greene Cemetery. He and Mary Ellen Maness had the following children:

4233	Elgie Maie Britt (-)
4234	James Edward (Ed) Britt (-)
4235	Rosa Belle Britt (-)
4236	Mary Lee Britt (1929-). *Mary was born on January 6, 1929. She married **Clayton James** on March 15, 1947 in Troy, Montgomery County, NC.*
4237	Betty Louise Britt (1936-1938). *Betty was born on October 28, 1936. She died on January 31, 1938 and was buried in Biscoe, Montgomery County, NC.*

1897. **Howard Taft Maness**, son of Henry Alexander Maness and Julie Ann Johnson, was born on October 3, 1908 in Biscoe Township, Montgomery County, NC. He died on May 15, 1965 in Biscoe, Montgomery County, NC and was buried on May 17, 1965 in Biscoe, Montgomery County, NC at Biscoe Cemetery.

Alma Suda Haywood was born on June 16, 1909. She died on June 10, 2001 and was buried in Biscoe, Montgomery County, NC at Biscoe Cemetery. She and Howard Taft Maness had the following children:

4238	Marshall Leo Maness (1931-). *Marshall was born on February 3, 1931 in Biscoe, Montgomery County, NC.*
4239	Mary Elaine "Elaine" Maness (1933-2012). *Mary was born on April 9, 1933 in Montgomery County, NC. She married **Riley Leonard Cockman** on September 5, 1953. She died on August 31, 2012 and was buried in Biscoe, Montgomery County, NC at Biscoe Cemetery.*
4240	Frances Carol Maness (1936-). *Frances was born on October 3, 1936 in Rocky Springs Twp., Montgomery County, NC.*
4241	Larry Joseph Maness (1939-). *Larry was born on August 30, 1939 in Rocky Springs Twp., Montgomery County, NC.*

1898. **Robert Paige Maness**, son of Henry Alexander Maness and Julie Ann Johnson, was born on November 29, 1910 in Biscoe Township, Montgomery County, NC. He married **Emily Carrie Maness** in 1928. He married **Myrtle Lou Batten** on August 5, 1965 in Jackson Springs, Moore County, NC. He died on November 10, 1966 in Candor, Montgomery County, NC and was buried on November 12, 1966 in Biscoe, Montgomery County, NC at Biscoe Cemetery.

Emily Carrie Maness, daughter of Mary Ann Maness (1890-1940), was born on August 13, 1914. She died on July 4, 1988 and was buried in Biscoe, Montgomery County, NC at Biscoe Cemetery. She and Robert Paige Maness had the following children:

4242	Barbara Jean Maness (1932-). *Barbara was born on July 24, 1932 in Biscoe, Montgomery County, NC.*
4243	Jo Ann Maness (1939-). *Jo was born on October 16, 1939 in Biscoe, Montgomery County, NC.*

Myrtle Lou Batten was born on June 21, 1914. She died on September 18, 1975.

1899. **Carl Samuel Maness**, son of Christopher Columbus Maness and Jennie Ervin, was born on September 11, 1893. He died on May 25, 1982 in Statesville, Iredell County, NC and was buried in Statesville, Iredell County, NC.

Carrie Bell Campbell and Carl Samuel Maness had the following children:

4244	Emma Virginia Maness (1918-). *Emma was born on April 3, 1918. She married **unk** on April 3, 1918.*
4245	Mattie Elizabeth Maness (1920-). *Mattie was born on August 9, 1920 in Iredell County,*

NC.

| 4246 | Jay Campbell Maness (1922-). *Jay was born on May 15, 1922 in Cool Springs, Iredell, NC.* |
| 4247 | Carl Houston Maness (1927-). *Carl was born on August 15, 1927 in Iredell County, NC. He married on June 10, 1950.* |

1900. Cora Lee Maness, daughter of Christopher Columbus Maness and Jennie Ervin, was born on August 29, 1896. She married **Wade Hampton Clontz** on November 12, 1916 in Barringer Twp., Iredell, NC. She died on September 16, 1974 and was buried in Mooresville, Iredell County, NC at Rocky Mount United Methodist Church.

Wade Hampton Clontz was born on December 31, 1889. He died on June 11, 1983 and was buried in Mooresville, Iredell County, NC at Rocky Mount United Methodist Church. He and Cora Lee Maness had the following children:

| 4248 | Clinton Clontz (-) |

1901. Marshall M. Maness, son of Christopher Columbus Maness and Jennie Ervin, was born on September 14, 1905 in Troutman, NC. He died on February 22, 1967 in Statesville, Iredell County, NC and was buried in Iredell County, NC.

Macy Marjorie Sherrill and Marshall M. Maness had the following children:

| 4249 | Shirley Jane Maness (1937-). *Shirley was born on November 15, 1937.* |

1905. Lou Ella Pinion, daughter of Adam Jackson Pinion and Julia Ann Maness, was born on February 21, 1894. She died on September 20, 1971 in Albemarle, Stanly County, NC and was buried on September 22, 1971 in Troy, Montgomery County, NC.

1909. Mary Elizabeth Pinion, daughter of Adam Jackson Pinion and Julia Ann Maness, was born on April 26, 1906. She died on November 10, 1992 and was buried in Troy, Montgomery County, NC at Mt. Olivet Methodist Church.

1911. Robert Lee Kellis, son of William Henry Kellis and Martha L. "Mattie" Maness, was born on January 13, 1898. He died on August 27, 1977.

Hollis Polk was born on July 15, 1917. She died on December 19, 2004. She and Robert Lee Kellis had the following children:

| 4250 | Sarah Kellis (-) |

1912. Ellis Guy Maness Sr., son of George W. Maness and Elizabeth J. Pinion, was born on September 28, 1894. He died on April 6, 1963 in Asheboro, Randolph County, NC and was buried on April 8, 1963 in Asheboro, Randolph County, NC.

Ellis Guy Maness Sr. had the following children:

4251	Ellis Guy Maness Jr. (1917-). *Ellis was born on November 15, 1917 in Ellerbe, Richmond County, NC and was buried in Franklinville, Randolph County, NC.*
4252	Cora Virginia Maness (1921-). *Cora was born on April 18, 1921 in Center Twp., Stanly County, NC.*
4253	Thomas Edward Maness (1923-). *Thomas was born on June 30, 1923 in Center Twp., Stanly County, NC.*
4254	Annie Belle Maness (1926-). *Annie was born on January 25, 1926 in Troy, Montgomery County, NC.*
4255	Edna Louise Maness (1928-2001). *Edna was born on October 21, 1928 in Troy, Montgomery County, NC. She died on December 9, 2001 in Lexington, Davidson County, NC and was buried on December 12, 2001.*
4256	George Franklin Maness (1931-). *George was born on November 19, 1931 in Troy, Montgomery County, NC.*
4257	Bobby Joe Maness (1934-). *Bobby was born on February 13, 1934 in Troy, Montgomery County, NC.*
4258	Joyce Annette Maness (1938-). *Joyce was born on May 20, 1938 in Troy, Montgomery County, NC.*

1919. **John Mack Wallace II**, son of William Wesley Wallace and Ira Lee "Arlee" Cockman, was born on September 30, 1898. He died in 1955.

Nannie Viola Rumburg and John Mack Wallace II had the following children:

4259	Frances Arlee Wallace (1928-2017). *Frances was born on August 28, 1928. She died on May 16, 2017.*
4260	John Mack Wallace III (1931-2015). *John was born on September 30, 1931 in Fayetteville, WV. He married **Yolanda Cala Garcia** in Bogota, Columbia, South America. He died in February 2015.*

1920. **Dewey Edgar Wallace**, son of William Wesley Wallace and Ira Lee "Arlee" Cockman, was born on September 6, 1900. He died on May 15, 1936 in Hope Mills, Cumberland County, NC.

Thelma J. Phillips was born on May 18, 1902. She died on November 9, 1936 in Hope Mills, Cumberland County, NC.

1921. **Bessie Wallace**, daughter of William Wesley Wallace and Ira Lee "Arlee" Cockman, was born on February 23, 1904. She died on February 26, 1904 and was buried in Hope Mills, Cumberland County, NC at Big Rockfish Presbyterian Cemetery.

1922. **Glenna Velma Wallace**, daughter of William Wesley Wallace and Ira Lee "Arlee" Cockman, was born on August 15, 1905. She married **James H. Davis** on June 20, 1929 in Cumberland County, NC. She died in 2001.

James H. Davis was born in 1908. He died on July 3, 1974. He and Glenna Velma Wallace had the following children:

4261	Dewey Davis (-)

1923. **Theodore Wesley Wallace**, son of William Wesley Wallace and Ira Lee "Arlee" Cockman, was born on April 26, 1908 in Hope Mills, Cumberland County, NC. He married **Velma Adelle Moore** on June 3, 1928 in Kinston, NC.

Margie Ella Eulah Leota Stegall was born in 1914 in Jackson County, AR. She died on August 19, 1963 and was buried in Livonia, Wayne County, MI at Parkview Memorial Cemetery. She and Theodore Wesley Wallace had the following children:

4262	Dewey Edgar Wallace (1956-). *Dewey was born on December 10, 1956 in Wayne, MI.*

Velma Adelle Moore and Theodore Wesley Wallace had the following children:

4263	Peggy Louise Wallace (1929-). *Peggy was born on March 14, 1929 in Kinston, NC.*
4264	Joanne Moore Wallace (1930-). *Joanne was born on September 26, 1930 in Fayetteville, Cumberland County, NC. She married **Robert Chubboy** in Detroit, MI.*
4265	Theodore Wesley Wallace Jr. (1932-). *Theodore was born on August 1, 1932 in Fayetteville, Cumberland County, NC. He married **Helen Ford** on December 29, 1955 in Springfield, OH.*
4266	Patricia Faye Wallace (1936-). *Patricia was born on October 12, 1936.*

1926. **James Franklin Wallace**, son of William Wesley Wallace and Ira Lee "Arlee" Cockman, was born in 1918.

Alene Prudence Lee was born in September 1926 in Wilmington, New Hanover County, NC. She and James Franklin Wallace had the following children:

4267	Linda Faye Wallace (1947-). *Linda was born on January 8, 1947.*
4268	Brenda Kaye Wallace (1947-). *Brenda was born on January 8, 1947.*

1931. **Willie May Coleman**, daughter of William Judson Coleman and Mary Blake Wallace, was born on November 3, 1906. She died on September 22, 1938 and was buried in Durham, Durham County, NC at Maplewood Cemetery.

John W. Byrd and Willie May Coleman had the following children:

4269	Byrd (-)

1932. Luther Judson Coleman, son of William Judson Coleman and Mary Blake Wallace, was born in 1908.

Luther Judson Coleman had the following children:

4270	Luther Judson Coleman Jr. (-)
4271	Lydia Coleman (-)

1933. Ruth F. Coleman, daughter of William Judson Coleman and Mary Blake Wallace, was born in 1910.

1934. John Wesley Rose, son of Isaac W. Rose and Mary Blake Wallace, was born on September 6, 1892. He died on April 10, 1970 in Watts Hosptial, Durham, Durham County, NC and was buried on April 12, 1970 in Durham, Durham County, NC at Woodlawn Memorial Park.

Eva Guess was born on February 14, 1898. She died on January 30, 1980 in Durham, Durham County, NC. She and John Wesley Rose had the following children:

4272	John J. Rose (1918-). *John was born in 1918.*

1935. Charles Anderson James Fox Rose, son of Isaac W. Rose and Mary Blake Wallace, was born on April 6, 1896 in Moore County, NC. He died on September 7, 1943 in Moore Regional Hospital, Pinehurst, Moore County, NC and was buried on September 9, 1943 in Carthage, Moore County, NC at Cross Hill Cemetery.

Allie Beatrice Caddell, daughter of Edward Harrison Caddell (1863-1957) and Lillian Jackson "Lillie" Caddell (1879-1965), was born on September 13, 1909. She died on February 24, 2000 and was buried in Carthage, Moore County, NC at Cross Hill Cemetery.

1936. John Lee Wallace, son of Henry Lee Wallace and Della Adelaide Horne, was born on June 19, 1896 in Hope Mills, Cumberland County, NC. He married **Vida Cornelia Hall** on September 7, 1928 in Cumberland County, NC. He died on December 31, 1957 in Durham, Durham County, NC.

Fleeta Streete Phillips was born on June 22, 1899 in Chatham County, NC. She died on December 20, 1927 in Durham, Durham County, NC. She and John Lee Wallace had the following children:

4273	Opal Christella Wallace (1919-2001). *Opal was born on April 18, 1919 in Durham, Durham County, NC. She died on November 13, 2001 in Durham, Durham County, NC.*
4274	Henry Franklin Wallace (1921-1965). *Henry was born on November 24, 1921 in Durham, Durham County, NC. He married **Sula Cook Allen** on October 10, 1946 in Durham, Durham County, NC. He died on May 5, 1965 in Durham, Durham County, NC.*
4275	John Lee Wallace Jr. (1924-1983). *John was born on July 3, 1924 in Durham, Durham County, NC. He married **Edith Edwards** on May 10, 1953 in Durham, Durham County, NC. He died on September 17, 1983 in Durham, Durham County, NC.*
4276	Mary Maxine Wallace (1927-). *Mary was born on November 15, 1927 in Durham, Durham County, NC. She married **Joe Dodson Burnside** on May 4, 1951 in Tampa, Hillsborough County, FL.*

Vida Cornelia Hall was born on September 17, 1903 in Hope Mills, Cumberland County, NC. She died on October 3, 1993 in Raleigh, Wake County, NC. She and John Lee Wallace had the following children:

4277	Robert Horace Wallace (1929-c. 1929). *Robert was born on July 4, 1929 in Durham, Durham County, NC. He died circa September, 1929.*
4278	Hazel Cornelia Wallace (1930-). *Hazel was born on October 20, 1930. She married **Douglas Henry Poole** on April 23, 1949 in home in Wake County, NC.*
4279	Mary Elizabeth Wallace (1931-). *Mary was born on December 30, 1931 in West Durham, Durham County, NC.*
4280	Efland Earl Wallace (1935-). *Efland was born on May 3, 1935 in Efland, NC. He married **Doris Cook** in 1953 in Washington, DC. He married **Genevieve Helen See** in November 1958 in Washington, DC. He married **Yvonne Lowery** on November 10, 1973 in Dillon, Dillon County, SC.*

4281	William Sherman Wallace (1939-2008). *William was born on July 16, 1939 in Durham, Durham County, NC. He married* **Laura Marie Jones** *on April 9, 1961 in Pompano Beach, Broward County, FL. He married* **Penny Joanne Lozon** *on December 21, 1971 in Miami, Dade County, FL. He died on August 18, 2008.*

1937. Lester Mack Wallace, son of Henry Lee Wallace and Della Adelaide Horne, was born on December 11, 1898. He died on April 14, 1970.

Rebecca Buchanan was born circa 1898. She and Lester Mack Wallace had the following children:

4282	Estelle Wallace (1920-). *Estelle was born on December 10, 1920 in Durham, Durham County, NC.*
4283	Lester Eugene Wallace (1922-). *Lester was born on August 21, 1922 in Durham, Durham County, NC. He married* **Helen Amanda Smith** *on May 16, 1942 in Dillon, Dillon County, SC.*
4284	Henry Arnold Wallace (1924-). *Henry was born on June 5, 1924 in Durham, Durham County, NC. He married* **Ora Ethel Ferrell** *on March 15, 1947 in Durham, Durham County, NC.*
4285	Rebecca Louise Wallace (1926-1997). *Rebecca was born on June 26, 1926 in Durham, Durham County, NC. She died on December 17, 1997 in Florida.*
4286	Valerie Pearl Wallace (1928-). *Valerie was born on December 13, 1928 in Durham, Durham County, NC.*
4287	Lester Mack Wallace Jr. (1941-1941). *Lester was born in 1941. He died in 1941.*

1938. Nellie Maggie Wallace, daughter of Henry Lee Wallace and Della Adelaide Horne, was born on December 29, 1900 in Cumberland County, NC. She died on March 3, 1959.

1939. Carl Clevin Wallace, son of Henry Lee Wallace and Della Adelaide Horne, was born on November 9, 1902. He died on January 23, 1994 in Southern Pines, Moore County, NC.

Sally Velena McDaniel, daughter of Robert Lee McDaniel (1877-1934) and Florence Ella Davis (1874-1958), was born on March 27, 1904 in Robbins, Moore County, NC. She died on July 13, 1992 in Southern Pines, Moore County, NC. She and Carl Clevin Wallace had the following children:

4288	Joann Wallace (-)
4289	Linda Wallace (-)
4290	Donald K. Wallace (1934-). *Donald was born on October 28, 1934 in Durham, Durham County, NC.*

1940. Jasper Conley Wallace, son of Henry Lee Wallace and Della Adelaide Horne, was born on May 8, 1904. He married **Fannie Susan Dean** on November 6, 1925. He died on June 4, 1980 and was buried in Cumberland County, NC at Judson Baptist Church.

Fannie Susan Dean was born on November 26, 1902. She died on May 6, 1985. She and Jasper Conley Wallace had the following children:

4291	Jasper Conley Wallace Jr. (1928-1928). *Jasper was born in 1928. He died in 1928.*
4292	Conley Malcolm Wallace (1931-). *Conley was born on January 29, 1931.*
4293	Stacy Lee Wallace (1934-1976). *Stacy was born on October 26, 1934. He died on May 12, 1976 and was buried in Cumberland County, NC at Judson Baptist Church.*
4294	Harold Leonard Wallace (1937-1996). *Harold was born on July 5, 1937 in Lumberton, Robeson County, NC. He married* **Annie Louise Byrne** *on April 16, 1961. He died on March 10, 1996 in Fayetteville, Cumberland County, NC.*
4295	Annie Mae Wallace (1940-). *Annie was born on September 15, 1940. She married* **Bobby Joe Price** *on April 12, 1959.*
4296	Joseph Carl Wallace (1943-). *Joseph was born on May 8, 1943.*

1942. Luther Edward Wallace, son of Henry Lee Wallace and Della Adelaide Horne, was born on April 14, 1909 in Cumberland County, NC. He married **Maggie Mae Beal** on March 12, 1934 in Cumberland County, NC. He died on August 1, 1962 in Cumberland County, NC and was buried in Fayetteville, Cumberland County, NC at McDaniel Cemetary.

Maggie Mae Beal was born on December 9, 1915 in Cumberland County, NC. She and Luther Edward Wallace had the following children:

4297	Betty Lou Wallace (-)
4298	Lillie Adelaide Wallace (1935-). *Lillie was born on December 1, 1935 in Cumberland County, NC.*
4299	Melba Jane Wallace (1938-1938). *Melba was born on January 23, 1938 in Cumberland County, NC. She died on August 24, 1938 in Cumberland County, NC.*
4300	Harvey Eugene Wallace (1941-1942). *Harvey was born on November 30, 1941 in Cumberland County, NC. He died on March 12, 1942 in Cumberland County, NC.*
4301	Edward Lee Wallace (1944-). *Edward was born on August 24, 1944 in Cumberland County, NC.*
4302	Boyd Dale Wallace (1947-). *Boyd was born on February 11, 1947 in Cumberland County, NC. He married* **Kathy Lynn Tatum** *on December 14, 1964.*

1943. Henry Clayton Wallace, son of Henry Lee Wallace and Della Adelaide Horne, was born on January 5, 1911 in Cumberland County, NC. He married **Bereatha "Bea" Cameron** on January 20, 1934 in Halifax, VA. He died on August 21, 1977 in Durham, Durham County, NC.

Bereatha "Bea" Cameron was born on September 19, 1913 in Hope Mills, Cumberland County, NC. She died on May 20, 2002 in Durham, Durham County, NC. She and Henry Clayton Wallace had the following children:

4303	Edmond Clayton "Mickey" Wallace (1937-). *Edmond was born on May 11, 1937 in Durham, Durham County, NC. He married* **Sara Ann "Sally" Rippelmeyer** *on November 26, 1960 in Durham, Durham County, NC.*
4304	James Ronald Wallace (1944-). *James was born on December 1, 1944.*
4305	Robert Lee Wallace (1946-). *Robert was born on February 19, 1946.*
4306	Judith Ann Wallace (1947-). *Judith was born on December 31, 1947 in Durham, Durham County, NC.*

1944. Polly Ruth Wallace, daughter of Henry Lee Wallace and Della Adelaide Horne, was born on December 7, 1912 in Fayetteville, Cumberland County, NC. She married **Stephen Leonard Dean** on December 8, 1928 in Cedar Creek, Cumberland County, NC. She married **Thoralf Ringdahl** on December 4, 1943 in Durham, Durham County, NC. She died on December 4, 1994 in Minot, ND.

Stephen Leonard Dean was born on August 27, 1901 in Robeson County, NC. He died in 1938 in Durham, Durham County, NC. He and Polly Ruth Wallace had the following children:

4307	Carl Forbes Dean (-)
4308	Henry Leonard Dean (1929-). *Henry was born on October 1, 1929 in Cedar Creek, Cumberland County, NC. He married* **Dolly Marlene Miller** *on December 4, 1949.*
4309	Sally Ruth Dean (1931-). *Sally was born on May 31, 1931 in Cedar Creek, Cumberland County, NC. She married* **Edward J. Kabanuck** *on October 15, 1949 in Minot, ND.*
4310	Della Love Dean (1932-). *Della was born on December 16, 1932 in Durham, Durham County, NC. She married* **John Norwood Elliott** *on December 4, 1954 in Durham, Durham County, NC.*
4311	Stephen Ellis Dean (1936-). *Stephen was born on February 22, 1936 in Durham, Durham County, NC. He married* **Mary Lynn Berwick** *on July 19, 1957 in Minot, ND.*

Thoralf Ringdahl was born on May 26, 1914 in Roseglen, ND. He died on August 14, 1982 in Minot, ND. He and Polly Ruth Wallace had the following children:

4312	Rebecca Thorine Ringdahl (1944-). *Rebecca was born on December 23, 1944 in Durham, Durham County, NC.*
4313	Richard Lee Ringdahl (1947-). *Richard was born on March 7, 1947 in Minot, ND. He*

*married **Judy Darline Fluhrer** on December 16, 1967.*

1945. Etta Mae Wallace, daughter of Henry Lee Wallace and Della Adelaide Horne, was born on January 26, 1915 in Cumberland County, NC. She died on July 19, 1915 in Cumberland County, NC.

1946. Maxine Naomi Wallace, daughter of Henry Lee Wallace and Della Adelaide Horne, was born on March 1, 1917.

Raymond Daniel Beal and Maxine Naomi Wallace had the following children:

4314	Bruce Cooper Beal (-)	
4315	Junior Beal (-)	
4316	Peggy Nell Beal (1936-). *Peggy was born on July 31, 1936 in Cumberland County, NC.*	
4317	Raymond Kenneth Beal (1938-). *Raymond was born on May 7, 1938 in Cumberland County, NC.*	
4318	Dorinda May Beal (1939-). *Dorinda was born on October 16, 1939 in Cumberland County, NC.*	
4319	Tommy Franklin Beal (1941-). *Tommy was born on December 11, 1941 in Cumberland County, NC.*	
4320	Gary Lee Beal (1944-). *Gary was born in 1944.*	

1950. Bessie Lee Wallace was the daughter of John Robert Wallace and Nora Bell Brady.

Powers and Bessie Lee Wallace had the following children:

4321	Mary Anne Powers (-)

1952. John Lucian Wallace, son of John Robert Wallace and Pauline Victoria Tew, was born on June 30, 1910 in Durham, Durham County, NC. He died in May 1977 in Durham, Durham County, NC.

Lessie Maude Hales and John Lucian Wallace had the following children:

4322	Charles Edward "Chuck" Wallace (1943-). *Charles was born on August 22, 1943 in Durham, Durham County, NC. He married **Deborah Tuplin** on May 22, 1971 in Raleigh, Wake County, NC.*

1953. Cecil Ernest Wallace, son of John Robert Wallace and Pauline Victoria Tew, was born on December 12, 1912 in Durham, Durham County, NC. He married **Ila Irene Thompson** on April 15, 1933. He died on June 22, 1965 in Durham, Durham County, NC.

Mary Lillian Williams was born on August 24, 1930 in Durham, Durham County, NC. She died on July 31, 1987 in Durham, Durham County, NC. She and Cecil Ernest Wallace had the following children:

4323	Robert Michael "Mike" Wallace (1952-). *Robert was born on January 18, 1952. He married **Diana Lynn Allison** on September 18, 1971. He married **Betty Ray Williams** on October 22, 1976. He married **Faye Allred Hutchens** on July 24, 1980.*
4324	Pamela Kay Wallace (1953-). *Pamela was born on August 23, 1953 in Durham, Durham County, NC. She married **Kurt Franz Fox** on April 3, 1993.*

Ila Irene Thompson was born on January 20, 1916. She and Cecil Ernest Wallace had the following children:

4325	Ernest Wade Wallace (1938-). *Ernest was born on November 24, 1938 in Durham, Durham County, NC.*

1954. James Fletcher Wallace, son of Charles Chalmers Wallace and Margaret Rosetta Wallace, was born on June 28, 1898. He married **Claudia Carmen Carrington** on August 2, 1919 in Durham, Durham County, NC. He died on September 16, 1979 and was buried in Durham, Durham County, NC at Maplewood Cemetery.

Claudia Carmen Carrington was born on August 3, 1898. She died on April 19, 1993 and was buried in Durham, Durham County, NC at Maplewood Cemetery. She and James Fletcher Wallace had the following children:

4326	James Wallace (-)
4327	Ronnie Wallace (-)

1955. **Daisy Mae Wallace**, daughter of Charles Chalmers Wallace and Margaret Rosetta Wallace, was born on October 18, 1901. She died on December 21, 1985 and was buried in Rocky Mount, Edgecombe County, NC at Pineview Cemetery.

Neverson Glocy Mosley was born on September 3, 1890. He died on April 14, 1959 and was buried in Rocky Mount, Edgecombe County, NC at Pineview Cemetery.

1956. **Lelia Georgia Wallace**, daughter of Charles Chalmers Wallace and Margaret Rosetta Wallace, was born on April 7, 1903. She married **Willie Lexter Harward** on September 28, 1918 in Durham, Durham County, NC. She married **Corbitt W. Carter** (1903-) on June 26, 1926 in Durham, Durham County, NC. She married **Philip Herman Galbreath** on October 26, 1945 in Richmond, VA. She died on May 12, 1997 and was buried in Paris, Lamar County, TX at Evergreen Cemetery.

Willie Lexter Harward was born on June 8, 1895. He died on October 3, 1963. He and Lelia Georgia Wallace had the following children:

4328	Chalmas Lexter "Joe" Carter (1920-1983). *Chalmas was born on June 25, 1920 in Durham, Durham County, NC. He died on June 10, 1983 and was buried in Rockford, Lamar County, TX at Rockford Cemetery.*

Philip Herman Galbreath was born on December 12, 1904. He died on October 22, 1973 and was buried in Paris, Lamar County, TX at Evergreen Cemetery.

1957. **Lawrence Craven Wallace**, son of Charles Chalmers Wallace and Margaret Rosetta Wallace, was born on August 29, 1905. He died on July 11, 1987 and was buried in Burlington, Alamance County, NC at Alamance Memorial Park.

Delia Ray Kernodle was born in 1914. She died in 2001 and was buried in Burlington, Alamance County, NC at Alamance Memorial Park.

1958. **Alvin Vernon Wallace**, son of Charles Chalmers Wallace and Margaret Rosetta Wallace, was born on February 2, 1908. He died on December 8, 1983 and was buried in Burlington, Alamance County, NC at Alamance Memorial Park.

Ava Lee Hancock, daughter of George Harrison Hancock (1876-1955) and Roxanna Elizabeth Phillips (1884-1959), was born in 1914. She died in 1977 and was buried in Burlington, Alamance County, NC at Alamance Memorial Park. She and Alvin Vernon Wallace had the following children:

4329	Jean Wallace (-)
4330	Thomas A. Wallace (1944-1969). *Thomas was born on November 18, 1944. He died on March 15, 1969 and was buried in Burlington, Alamance County, NC at Alamance Memorial Park.*
4331	Daniel Lee Wallace (1953-2012). *Daniel was born on November 17, 1953. He died on February 9, 2012.*

1959. **Forrest Lee Wallace**, son of Charles Chalmers Wallace and Margaret Rosetta Wallace, was born on August 3, 1912. He died on January 3, 1982 and was buried in Fort Pierce, St. Lucie County, FL at Hillcrest Memorial Gardens.

Martha Ruth Compton was born on August 9, 1912. She died on July 27, 1991 and was buried in Fort Pierce, St. Lucie County, FL at Hillcrest Memorial Gardens. She and Forrest Lee Wallace had the following children:

4332	Donald Lee Wallace (-)
4333	Wallace (-)

1962. **Bessie L. Wrenn**, daughter of Charlie Fletcher Wrenn and Martha Ann Wallace, was born on May 16, 1903 in North Carolina. She married **Lawton Person** on May 30, 1922 in Cumberland County, NC. She died on November 30, 1979.

1964. **Lillian Bertrude Wrenn**, daughter of Charlie Fletcher Wrenn and Martha Ann Wallace, was born on February 4, 1907 in North Carolina. She married **Clyde Canipe** on October 11, 1922 in Cumberland County, NC. She died on January 24, 2000 in Tuscon, AZ.

1966. **Ruby Juanita Wrenn**, daughter of Charlie Fletcher Wrenn and Martha Ann Wallace, was born on October 1, 1912 in North Carolina.

Tyndall and Ruby Juanita Wrenn had the following children:

        4334   Lloyd Tyndall (-)

1967. **James Fletcher Wrenn**, son of Charlie Fletcher Wrenn and Martha Ann Wallace, was born on November 16, 1914 in North Carolina. He died on January 21, 1917 in Pearce's Mill, NC.

1968. **Edna Elvira Wrenn**, daughter of Charlie Fletcher Wrenn and Martha Ann Wallace, was born on November 29, 1917 in Fayetteville, Cumberland County, NC. She married **Rupert Franklin Scarlett** on December 24, 1935 in Alamance County, NC. She died on September 9, 1990 in Hickory, Catawba County, NC.

Rupert Franklin Scarlett was born on September 17, 1912 in Hillsborough, Orange County, NC. He died on June 2, 1980 in Hickory, Catawba County, NC. He and Edna Elvira Wrenn had the following children:

4335	Wallace Elwood Scarlett (1936-). *Wallace was born on September 17, 1936 in Mebane, NC.*
4336	Carolyn Marie Scarlett (1938-). *Carolyn was born on January 8, 1938 in Orange County, NC. She married **Lester H. Hockaday** on December 21, 1958 in Hickory, Catawba County, NC.*
4337	Russell Wayne Scarlett (1939-). *Russell was born on September 9, 1939 in Mebane, NC.*
4338	Larry Nelson Scarlett (1941-1961). *Larry was born on September 2, 1941 in Mebane, NC. He died on February 23, 1961 in Conover, NC.*
4339	Martha Ann Scarlett (1943-). *Martha was born on June 11, 1943 in Alamance County, NC. She married **George Walter Hines** circa 1960 in North Carolina. She married **Beryln Dean Ledford** on June 13, 1964 in Hickory, Catawba County, NC.*
4340	Ronnie Lee Scarlett (1944-). *Ronnie was born on June 21, 1944 in Burlington, Alamance County, NC. He married **Judy Carolyn Gadfield** on December 23, 1964 in Gaffney, SC. He married **Jeannie Alyce Woodruff** on January 1, 1972 in Las Vegas, Clark, Nevada.*
4341	Brenda Anita Scarlett (1947-). *Brenda was born on February 4, 1947 in High Point, Guilford County, NC. She married **Everette Eugene Evans** on June 11, 1966 in Hickory, Catawba County, NC.*

1970. **Margaret Maxine Wallace**, daughter of Charles Mack Wallace and Gertrude Pully, was born on March 21, 1929. She married **Lilbern Randal Huddle** on September 12, 1953 in Cumberland County, NC.

1972. **Vivian Alma Wallace**, daughter of Charles Mack Wallace and Lula Ellen McKinney, was born on October 3, 1906 in Hope Mills, Cumberland County, NC. She married **James Arthur Waller** on January 5, 1926 in Raleigh, Wake County, NC. She married **Hugo William Alberts** on February 4, 1950 in Washington, DC. She died on May 2, 1998 in Alexandria, VA.

James Arthur Waller was born on August 6, 1899 in Kinston, NC. He died on February 11, 1967 in New Bern, Craven County, NC. He and Vivian Alma Wallace had the following children:

4342	Nina Pauline Waller (1926-). *Nina was born on November 5, 1926 in Rocky Mount, Nash County, NC.*
4343	Jerell Arthur Waller (1930-). *Jerell was born on September 12, 1930 in Raleigh, Wake County, NC. He married **Ruth Ellen Weaver** on December 19, 1958 in Alexandria, VA.*

Hugo William Alberts was born on March 29, 1889 in Watertown, Wisconsin. He died on February 12, 1972 in Fairfax, VA.

1973. **Oliver Lacy Wallace**, son of Charles Mack Wallace and Lula Ellen McKinney, was born on June 30, 1908. He married **Frances Henderson** on May 3, 1964 in Dillon, Dillon County, SC. He died on October 8, 1995.

Isabel (Tip) Mae Irwin was born on February 7, 1913 in Washington, DC. She died on January 11, 1963 in Fayetteville, Cumberland County, NC. She and Oliver Lacy Wallace had the following children:

>4344   Eugene Oliver "Gene" Wallace (1933-). *Eugene was born on September 11, 1933.*
>4345   Jessie Mae Wallace (1935-). *Jessie was born on November 27, 1935 in Wake County, NC. She married **James Fowler** on March 27, 1954 in Fayetteville, Cumberland County, NC.*

Gertrude Pully was born on September 30, 1912. She died on January 7, 1995 in Rural Retreat, VA.

1974. **Albert Mack Wallace**, son of Charles Mack Wallace and Lula Ellen McKinney, was born on October 5, 1911 in Rocky Mount, Nash County, NC. He died on March 24, 1992 in Potomac, MD.

Mary Grace Latham died on September 28, 1991 in Potomac, MD. She and Albert Mack Wallace had the following children:

>4346   Sherri Wallace (1942-). *Sherri was born on November 12, 1942.*
>4347   Carol Jean Wallace (1949-). *Carol was born on June 30, 1949.*
>4348   James J. Wallace (1952-). *James was born on October 28, 1952 in Chevy Chase, Montgomery County, MD. He married **Barbara Joan Neuman** on May 2, 1976 in Steubenville, OH. He married **Frances Miriam Woodham** circa November 1994 in Hagerstown, MD.*

1975. **Margaret Louise Wallace**, daughter of Charles Mack Wallace and Lula Ellen McKinney, was born on March 6, 1914 in Hope Mills, Cumberland County, NC. She died on March 29, 1955 in Washington, Beaufort County, NC.

1976. **Clyde Leroy Wallace**, son of Charles Mack Wallace and Lula Ellen McKinney, was born on June 20, 1916 in Bridgeton, NC. He died in February 1971 in Washington, DC.

Nell died on July 6, 2002. She and Clyde Leroy Wallace had the following children:

>4349   Loretta Wallace (1942-2008). *Loretta was born in 1942 in Charlotte, Mecklenburg County, NC. She died on October 15, 2008.*
>4350   Donald Clyde Wallace (1944-2019). *Donald was born on August 24, 1944. He died on November 11, 2019.*

1977. **Doris Ruth Wallace**, daughter of Charles Mack Wallace and Lula Ellen McKinney, was born on August 27, 1919 in Rocky Mount, Nash County, NC. She married **Robert Lee Shearin** on January 13, 1937 in Smithfield, Johnston County, NC. She died on June 8, 2011 in Raleigh, Wake County, NC and was buried in Raleigh, Wake County, NC at Raleigh Memorial Park.

Robert Lee Shearin was born on January 27, 1914 in Raleigh, Wake County, NC. He died on March 28, 1999. He and Doris Ruth Wallace had the following children:

>4351   Gail Andrea Shearin (1938-). *Gail was born on January 28, 1938 in Raleigh, Wake County, NC. She married **Roy Wilson Kiziah** on September 30, 1957 in Gaffney, SC. She married **Larry Eugene Wood** on November 9, 1970 in Bennettsville, Marlboro County, SC. She married **Kenneth Earl Dupree** on January 28, 1995 in Harnett County, NC.*
>4352   Phillip Lee Shearin (1949-). *Phillip was born on August 30, 1949 in North Wilkesboro, Wilkes County, NC. He married **Carolyn Green** circa 1968 in Raleigh, Wake County, NC. He married **Evelyn Clark** on January 13, 1995 in Morehead City, NC.*
>4353   Lois Ruth Shearin (1950-). *Lois was born on October 3, 1950 in North Wilkesboro, Wilkes County, NC. She married **Ronald Steven Warfield** on August 30, 1968 in Cary, Wake County, NC. She married **Edward A. Muhs Jr.** on July 3, 1982 in Richlands, WA. She married **James C. Geuder** on June 17, 1989 in Raleigh, Wake County, NC.*

1979. **Charles Kenneth Wallace**, son of Charles Mack Wallace and Lula Ellen McKinney, was born on July 23, 1922 in Rocky Mount, Nash County, NC. He died on October 28, 2011.

Kay and Charles Kenneth Wallace had the following children:

4354   Linda Wallace (1951-). *Linda was born on March 27, 1951 in Alexandria, VA.*

1980. **Iris Natalie Wallace**, daughter of Charles Mack Wallace and Lula Ellen McKinney, was born on March 10, 1925 in Rocky Mount, Nash County, NC. She died on May 27, 2007 in Clarksville, VA and was buried on May 30, 2007 in Chase City, VA.

Floyd Matthew Denton and Iris Natalie Wallace had the following children:

4355   Sandra Ellen Denton (1951-). *Sandra was born on August 5, 1951 in Raleigh, Wake County, NC. She married **Isaac Edward Yehiel** on September 8, 1973 in McClean, VA.*

1985. **Virginia Fay Grice**, daughter of William James Grice and Harriet Wallace, was born on November 5, 1926. She died on April 14, 2000 in Fayetteville, Cumberland County, NC.

Seavy M. Barefoot Sr. and Virginia Fay Grice had the following children:

4356   Janice Fay Barefoot (-)
4357   Seavy M. Barefoot Jr. (-)
4358   Walter C. Barefoot (-)
4359   David T. Barefoot (-)
4360   William G. Barefoot Sr. (1961-). *William was born on February 9, 1961.*

Marion L. Stephens and Virginia Fay Grice had the following children:

4361   Marion L. Stephens Jr. (-)
4362   Mary Ann Stephens (1946-). *Mary was born on September 9, 1946. She married **George Donald Clemons** on June 28, 1963 in Fayetteville, Cumberland County, NC.*

1990. **Edith Frances Dees**, daughter of Charles Gentry Dees and Tishi Evelyn Wallace, was born on October 21, 1923 in Hope Mills, Cumberland County, NC.

William David Pridgen and Edith Frances Dees had the following children:

4363   Glenda Pridgen (-)
4364   William David Pridgen Jr. (-)
4365   Susan Angela Pridgen (-)

1993. **Edna Maxine Dees**, daughter of Charles Gentry Dees and Tishi Evelyn Wallace, was born on October 13, 1929 in Cumberland County, NC.

Paul Wallace Smith and Edna Maxine Dees had the following children:

4366   Susan Wallace Smith (-)
4367   Lisa Kimberly Smith (-)

1994. **Robert Grant Dees**, son of Charles Gentry Dees and Tishi Evelyn Wallace, was born on December 24, 1931 in Cumberland County, NC. He died on May 11, 1996 in Fuquay Varina, NC.

Elaine P. Teeters and Robert Grant Dees had the following children:

4368   Leslie Dees (-)
4369   Robert Grant Dees Jr. (-)

2007. **Jewell Marie Wallace**, daughter of James Madison Wallace and Donnie Rachel Noble, was born on April 15, 1933 in Cumberland County, NC. She married **Burit Doyle Craven** on September 22, 1951. She married **Bobby DeLoach** in 1961. She died on September 4, 2003.

Burit Doyle Craven was born on August 18, 1932 in Randolph County, NC. He and Jewell Marie Wallace had the following children:

4370	Mark Wallace Craven (1953-). *Mark was born on August 3, 1953 in Asheboro, Randolph County, NC.*

2008. James Madison "Billy Mack" Wallace Jr., son of James Madison Wallace and Donnie Rachel Noble, was born on June 5, 1934 in Fayetteville, Cumberland County, NC. He married **Glenn Gae Harrison** on April 21, 1956.

Glenn Gae Harrison was born on May 9, 1936 in Parkersburg, IA. She and James Madison "Billy Mack" Wallace Jr. had the following children:

4371	James Madison Wallace III (1957-). *James was born on November 3, 1957 in Dunn, Harnett County, NC.*
4372	Jeanine Marie Wallace (1959-). *Jeanine was born on July 9, 1959 in Waterloo, IA. She married **Douglas Lynn Novak** on February 5, 1978.*
4373	Carol Rene Wallace (1960-). *Carol was born on November 2, 1960 in Enid, OK. She married **Eugene Phillip Brawn** in 1980. She married **Brian Douglas Meltzner** on October 3, 1992.*
4374	Krista Lynn Wallace (1966-). *Krista was born on February 7, 1966 in San Jose, CA.*

2009. Dwight Thomas Wallace, son of James Madison Wallace and Donnie Rachel Noble, was born on October 27, 1944. He married **Jan Ella Key** on June 10, 1965.

Jan Ella Key was born on January 18, 1946 in New Smyrna Beach, FL. She and Dwight Thomas Wallace had the following children:

4375	Justin Daniel Eugene Wallace Davis (1964-). *Justin was born on September 27, 1964 in Fort Valley, GA.*
4376	Dwight Thomas Wallace (1966-). *Dwight was born on March 22, 1966 in Macon, GA.*
4377	Sharon Ella Wallace (1968-). *Sharon was born on May 18, 1968 in Macon, GA.*
4378	Elizabeth Rachel Wallace (1969-). *Elizabeth was born on June 20, 1969 in Macon, GA.*

2010. Elsie Vernell Collins, daughter of Ray Thurman Collins and Lillie Al Rhoney Wallace, was born on October 31, 1931 in Fayetteville, Cumberland County, NC. She married **Winfred Glenn Cheshire** on July 21, 1950 in Cumberland County, NC.

Winfred Glenn Cheshire was born on September 26, 1927 in Cumberland County, NC. He and Elsie Vernell Collins had the following children:

4379	Winfred Glenn Cheshire Jr. (1951-). *Winfred was born on August 8, 1951 in Cumberland County, NC. He married **Rebecca Jones** on August 29, 1981.*
4380	Keith Warren Cheshire (1954-). *Keith was born on March 26, 1954 in Burlington, Alamance County, NC.*
4381	Phyllis Rae Cheshire (1956-). *Phyllis was born on March 15, 1956 in Burlington, Alamance County, NC. She married **Kyle Jeffrey Toothman** on December 18, 1977 in Cumberland County, NC.*

2011. Ray Thurman Collins Jr., son of Ray Thurman Collins and Lillie Al Rhoney Wallace, was born on December 30, 1934 in Fayetteville, Cumberland County, NC. He died on August 17, 1985 in Lumberton, Robeson County, NC.

2012. George Wayne Collins, son of Ray Thurman Collins and Lillie Al Rhoney Wallace, was born on November 30, 1944 in Fayetteville, Cumberland County, NC. He married **Linda Kay Williams** on October 14, 1967 in Fayetteville, Cumberland County, NC. He married **Diann Baker Brown** on September 4, 1971 in Charlotte, Mecklenburg County, NC. He died on October 11, 1980 in Prospect, KY.

Linda Kay Williams was born on July 5, 1947 in Charlotte, Mecklenburg County, NC. She and George Wayne Collins had the following children:

4382	Tyra Lynn Collins (1968-). *Tyra was born on May 27, 1968 in Charlotte, Mecklenburg County, NC. She married **Stephen Hideo Day** on August 29, 1992 in Charlotte, Mecklenburg County, NC.*

Diann Baker Brown was born on September 12, 1942 in Claremont, Robeson, NC. She and George Wayne Collins had the following children:

>4383 George Wayne Collins Jr. (1976-). *George was born on September 29, 1976 in Charlotte, Mecklenburg County, NC.*

2013. Linda Sue Collins, daughter of Ray Thurman Collins and Lillie Al Rhoney Wallace, was born on April 14, 1947 in Fayetteville, Cumberland County, NC. She married **Steven Milton Bunker** on January 27, 1967 in Fayetteville, Cumberland County, NC. She married **Donald Keith Forbis** on February 12, 1982 in Fayetteville, Cumberland County, NC.

Steven Milton Bunker was born on December 28, 1941 in Clinton, Iowa.

Donald Keith Forbis died on February 14, 1998. He and Linda Sue Collins had the following children:

>4384 Lori Denise Forbis (1980-). *Lori was born on August 25, 1980 in Charlotte, Mecklenburg County, NC.*
>4385 Donald Keith Forbis Jr. (1983-). *Donald was born on June 6, 1983 in Charlotte, Mecklenburg County, NC.*

2014. Patricia Ann Cannon, daughter of Nathan Joy Cannon and Sallie Adelaide Wallace, was born on July 12, 1935 in Fayetteville, Cumberland County, NC. She married **Charles Wilson Demore** on October 14, 1951 in Fayetteville, Cumberland County, NC.

Charles Wilson Demore was born on February 27, 1929. He and Patricia Ann Cannon had the following children:

>4386 Sallie Ann Demore (1955-). *Sallie was born on January 15, 1955 in Woodbury, NJ.*
>4387 David Alan Demore (1958-). *David was born on July 7, 1958.*
>4388 Charles William Demore (1965-). *Charles was born on August 17, 1965.*
>4389 Michael Robert Demore (1967-). *Michael was born on August 13, 1967.*
>4390 Alan Wayne Demore (1979-). *Alan was born on July 5, 1979.*

2015. Juanita Rhea Cannon, daughter of Nathan Joy Cannon and Sallie Adelaide Wallace, was born on November 20, 1936 in Fayetteville, Cumberland County, NC. She married **William Maurice Huff** on August 1, 1953. She died on April 17, 1988 in Fayetteville, Cumberland County, NC and was buried in Fayetteville, Cumberland County, NC at Cumberland Memorial Gardens.

William Maurice Huff died in 1996 in California. He and Juanita Rhea Cannon had the following children:

>4391 Donna Darlene Huff (-). *Donna married **Dan Thomas Nelson** on September 2, 1972 in Rosamond, CA.*
>4392 William Maurice Huff Jr. (-)
>4393 Cheryl J. Huff (-)

2016. Gwendolyn Hope Cannon, daughter of Nathan Joy Cannon and Sallie Adelaide Wallace, was born on August 16, 1938 in Fayetteville, Cumberland County, NC. She died on July 3, 1996 in Fayetteville, Cumberland County, NC and was buried in Fayetteville, Cumberland County, NC at Lafayette Memorial Park.

Lacy Black and Gwendolyn Hope Cannon had the following children:

>4394 Donald Black (-)
>4395 Charlotte Black (-)
>4396 Wesley Black (-)
>4397 Michael Black (-)

Vincent Covas and Gwendolyn Hope Cannon had the following children:

>4398 Isabell Covas (-)
>4399 Vincent Covas Jr. (-)

2017. **Nathan Joy Cannon Jr.**, son of Nathan Joy Cannon and Sallie Adelaide Wallace, was born on April 11, 1940 in Fayetteville, Cumberland County, NC. He died on May 28, 2005 in Fayetteville, Cumberland County, NC.

2018. **Brenda Carol Cannon**, daughter of Nathan Joy Cannon and Sallie Adelaide Wallace, was born on August 25, 1941 in Fayetteville, Cumberland County, NC. She died on July 21, 2015.

Paul Kenneth Bunce was born in Fayetteville, Cumberland County, NC. He and Brenda Carol Cannon had the following children:

4400	Kimberly Carol Bunce (-)
4401	Paul Kenneth Bunce II (-)

2019. **Mary Angela Cannon**, daughter of Nathan Joy Cannon and Sallie Adelaide Wallace, was born on March 26, 1944 in Fayetteville, Cumberland County, NC. She married **Robert Lambert** on December 16, 1961 in Cumberland County, NC.

Robert Lambert and Mary Angela Cannon had the following children:

4402	Brian Lambert (-)
4403	Kevan Lambert (-)

2020. **Marie Elaina Cannon**, daughter of Nathan Joy Cannon and Sallie Adelaide Wallace, was born on June 20, 1945 in Fayetteville, Cumberland County, NC. She married **Gerald Arnold Coyle** on April 16, 1965 in Las Vegas, Clark, Nevada. She married **Robert Oliver Bundy** on July 22, 1993. She died on June 21, 2006 in Fayetteville, Cumberland County, NC.

Gerald Arnold Coyle was born on May 14, 1943 in Dayton, Montgomery County, OH. He died on May 13, 1975 in Taiwan. He and Marie Elaina Cannon had the following children:

4404	Sheryl Lynn Coyle (1969-). *Sheryl was born on June 23, 1969.*

2021. **Timothy Mackins Cannon**, son of Nathan Joy Cannon and Sallie Adelaide Wallace, was born on February 24, 1947 in Fayetteville, Cumberland County, NC. He married **Alice Rebecca McMillan** on February 7, 1966 in Fayetteville, Cumberland County, NC. He married **Beverly Carol Garner** on August 3, 1979 in Dillon, Dillon County, SC.

Alice Rebecca McMillan was born on November 2, 1945 in Fayetteville, Cumberland County, NC. She died on August 12, 2008 in Fayetteville, Cumberland County, NC. She and Timothy Mackins Cannon had the following children:

4405	Alice Marie Cannon (1968-). *Alice was born on June 8, 1968 in Fayetteville, Cumberland County, NC.*
4406	Timothy Mark Cannon (1971-). *Timothy was born on January 8, 1971 in Fayetteville, Cumberland County, NC.*

Beverly Carol Garner was born on September 22, 1955 in Fayetteville, Cumberland County, NC.

2022. **George W. Brown**, son of George Rufus Brown and Mary Ann Maness, was born on December 5, 1886. He married **Sarah Jane Garner** circa 1907. He died on November 28, 1947 and was buried in Robbins, Moore County, NC at Tabernacle United Methodist Church.

Sarah Jane Garner, daughter of Sampson Delaney Garner (1863-1937) and Lillie E. Stutts (1866-1958), was born on April 6, 1886. She died on August 23, 1967 and was buried in Robbins, Moore County, NC at Tabernacle United Methodist Church. She and George W. Brown had the following children:

4407	Beecher A. Brown (1907-1966). *Beecher was born on August 26, 1907. He died on September 9, 1966 and was buried in Robbins, Moore County, NC at Tabernacle United Methodist Church.*
4408	Lillie Matty Brown (1909-1963). *Lillie was born on September 11, 1909. She died on February 12, 1963 and was buried in Moore County, NC at Unity Grove Baptist Church.*
4409	Lacy Albert Brown (1912-1986). *Lacy was born on May 19, 1912. He died on April 7, 1986 and was buried in Robbins, Moore County, NC at Tabernacle United Methodist*

Church.

4410	John Brown (1915-). *John was born in 1915.*
4411	Maggie Brown (1917-). *Maggie was born in 1917.*
4412	Mearl Brown (1919-). *Mearl was born in 1919.*

2023. Charles Worthy Brown, son of George Rufus Brown and Mary Ann Maness, was born on January 9, 1888. He married **Rosa E. Brady** on May 4, 1906 in Moore County, NC. He died on January 31, 1942 and was buried in Moore County, NC at Pleasant Hill United Methodist Church.

Rosa E. Brady, daughter of Matthew C. Brady (1869-1921) and May Ellen Phillips (1873-1945), was born on July 31, 1891. She died on April 1, 1954 and was buried in Robbins, Moore County, NC at Tabernacle United Methodist Church. She and Charles Worthy Brown had the following children:

4413	J. Edgar Brown (1912-). *J. was born in 1912.*
4414	Tessie B. Brown (1915-). *Tessie was born in 1915.*
4415	Matthew Wilson Brown (1916-1916). *Matthew was born on October 30, 1916. He died on December 7, 1916 and was buried in Robbins, Moore County, NC at Tabernacle United Methodist Church.*
4416	Charles Worthy Brown Jr. (1919-1994). *Charles was born on January 13, 1919 in Moore County, NC. He died on April 16, 1994.*
4417	Douglas Ernest Brown (1921-2004). *Douglas was born on May 10, 1921. He married **Pearl "Lorena" Robinson** on April 24, 1948. He died on February 28, 2004.*
4418	Willard O. Brown (1924-). *Willard was born in 1924.*

Sarah Ann Brown, daughter of Archibald Clem Brown (1870-1944) and Cladie Ann F. Williams (1867-1953), was born on April 23, 1898. She died on December 2, 1981 and was buried in Moore County, NC at Pleasant Hill United Methodist Church. She and Charles Worthy Brown had the following children:

4419	Swannie Marie Brown (1928-1991). *Swannie was born on July 16, 1928. She died on December 1, 1991 and was buried in Moore County, NC at Smyrna Methodist Church.*
4420	Charles Frank Brown (1932-1997). *Charles was born on November 22, 1932. He died on December 31, 1997 and was buried in Moore County, NC at Calvary Baptist Church.*

2024. William Walter Brown, son of George Rufus Brown and Mary Ann Maness, was born on April 15, 1890. He died on September 24, 1964 and was buried in Albemarle, Stanly County, NC at Fairview Cemetery.

Laura Ann Howard was born on April 6, 1900. She died on February 18, 1969 and was buried in Albemarle, Stanly County, NC at Fairview Cemetery. She and William Walter Brown had the following children:

4421	James Coleman Brown (1932-1991). *James was born on May 14, 1932. He died on April 3, 1991 and was buried in Albemarle, Stanly County, NC at Stanly Memorial Gardens.*

2026. Florence Camellia Brown, daughter of George Rufus Brown and Mary Ann Maness, was born in February 1894. She died on July 31, 1974.

Alexander J. Dunn, son of Russell Wesley Dunn (1849-1909) and Annie "Ann" Britt (1847-1907), was born on October 6, 1881. He died on December 26, 1937. He and Florence Camellia Brown had the following children:

4422	Dunn (-)

2027. James Curtis Brown, son of George Rufus Brown and Mary Ann Maness, was born on January 1, 1895. He died on October 18, 1972 and was buried in Linden, Cumberland County, NC at Parker Grove Cemetery.

Florence Ellen Parker was born on September 15, 1892. She died on December 21, 1964 and was buried in Linden, Cumberland County, NC at Parker Grove Cemetery. She and James Curtis Brown had the following children:

4423	Emma Brown (1918-1987). *Emma was born on July 3, 1918. She died on August 13, 1987.*

2030. Donnie Carson Brown, son of George Rufus Brown and Mary Ann Maness, was born on August 9, 1901. He died in August 1982.

Addie Ellen Parker and Donnie Carson Brown had the following children:

> 4424   John E. Brown (-)

2031. Bertha Loretta Brown, daughter of George Rufus Brown and Mary Ann Maness, was born on October 3, 1906. She died on June 24, 1958 in Fayetteville, Cumberland County, NC.

David Cornelius Wood was born on October 2, 1901. He died on February 12, 1976. He and Bertha Loretta Brown had the following children:

> 4425   Earnest David Wood (1931-). *Earnest was born on September 29, 1931.*

2034. Ida Louise Rouse, daughter of Malcolm Street Rouse and Rebecca Jane Maness, was born on March 7, 1890. She died on December 30, 1894 and was buried in Robbins, Moore County, NC at Tabernacle United Methodist Church.

2035. Dora F. Rouse, daughter of Malcolm Street Rouse and Rebecca Jane Maness, was born on August 15, 1891. She died on August 24, 1984.

Ira L. Davis was born on June 3, 1886. He died on July 30, 1955. He and Dora F. Rouse had the following children:

> 4426   Arthur Lee Davis (1911-1970). *Arthur was born on February 20, 1911. He died on January 20, 1970.*

2036. Effie Jane Rouse, daughter of Malcolm Street Rouse and Rebecca Jane Maness, was born on February 6, 1893. She died on September 26, 1941 in Moore County, NC and was buried in Robbins, Moore County, NC at Tabernacle United Methodist Church.

2037. Willie Marshall Rouse, son of Malcolm Street Rouse and Rebecca Jane Maness, was born on January 11, 1896. He died on June 30, 1966 and was buried in Moore County, NC at Rock Hill Church.

2038. Harrison G. Rouse, son of Malcolm Street Rouse and Rebecca Jane Maness, was born on October 13, 1898. He died on November 27, 1914 and was buried in Robbins, Moore County, NC at Tabernacle United Methodist Church.

2039. Dewey Hobson Rouse, son of Malcolm Street Rouse and Rebecca Jane Maness, was born on April 4, 1901. He died on June 22, 1975 and was buried in Robbins, Moore County, NC at Tabernacle United Methodist Church.

Mamie Horner, daughter of William Branson "Bud" Horner (1872-1925) and Martha Jane Garner (1881-1920), was born on May 23, 1905. She died on April 24, 1999 and was buried in Robbins, Moore County, NC at Tabernacle United Methodist Church. She and Dewey Hobson Rouse had the following children:

> 4427   Hester Rouse (1921-). *Hester was born on July 9, 1921 in Moore County, NC.*
> 4428   Carl Grier Rouse (1924-). *Carl was born on October 22, 1924 in Moore County, NC.*
> 4429   James Colon Rouse (1927-). *James was born on February 1, 1927 in Moore County, NC.*
> 4430   Johnsie Louise Rouse (1929-2017). *Johnsie was born on April 20, 1929 in Moore County, NC. She died on February 3, 2017.*
> 4431   Cecil Edward Rouse (1934-). *Cecil was born on June 25, 1934 in Moore County, NC.*
> 4432   Crissie Mae Rouse (1937-). *Crissie was born on May 13, 1937 in Moore County, NC.*

2040. Hurley Lee Rouse, son of Malcolm Street Rouse and Rebecca Jane Maness, was born on November 10, 1904. He married **Josie Jane Cockman** on October 8, 1928 in Moore County, NC. He died on December 3, 1986 and was buried in Robbins, Moore County, NC at Tabernacle United Methodist Church.

Josie Jane Cockman, daughter of Noah Wesley Cockman (1884-1971) and Jenette Green Maness (1883-1939), was born on December 9, 1910. She died on July 3, 1984 and was buried in Robbins, Moore County, NC at Tabernacle United Methodist Church. She and Hurley Lee Rouse had the following children:

4433	Jurlene Rouse (1929-1930). *Jurlene was born on July 20, 1929. She died on October 30, 1930 and was buried in Robbins, Moore County, NC at Tabernacle United Methodist Church.*
4434	Wilbert Lee Rouse (1930-2004). *Wilbert was born on October 8, 1930 in Moore County, NC. He died on February 9, 2004 and was buried in Robbins, Moore County, NC at Tabernacle United Methodist Church.*
4435	Donna Deloris Rouse (1940-). *Donna was born on January 23, 1940 in Moore County, NC.*

2041. **Grady Worthy Rouse**, son of Malcolm Street Rouse and Rebecca Jane Maness, was born on August 21, 1907. He died on August 18, 1982 and was buried in Asheboro, Randolph County, NC at Randolph Memorial Park.

Addie Lee Morgan, daughter of Ira Jefferson Morgan (1892-1952) and Hattie Mae Moore (1901-1926), was born on April 17, 1918. She died on January 28, 2001 and was buried in Asheboro, Randolph County, NC at Randolph Memorial Park.

2042. **Pearl Lillian Rouse**, daughter of Malcolm Street Rouse and Rebecca Jane Maness, was born on December 19, 1909. She died on September 24, 1970 and was buried in Moore County, NC at Rock Hill Church.

Nancy Wallace, Granddaughter of Everet Wallace

1841, Mar 24 -- Special to the Observer, *Fayetteville Observer* [Fayetteville, NC] Newspaper

"Mr. Hale: one of the most heart rending circumstances that has ever been witnessed occurred in this neighborhood a few days since. On the evening of the 11th instant (Mar 11, 1841), a little girl about 10 year old, though small, the daughter of Mr. Wallace, asked its mother to let her go to the old place (a place they formerly lived at) and drive the cow home. The good mother at first refused, but after some persuading, consented. The little girl set off; night soon arrived, but no news of her. The alarm was immediately given, several person hunted nearly all night (which was very rainy) without success; in the morning a goodly number of persons assembled, searched all day but to no effect; the second, third and fourth days, from fifty to seventy persons searched diligently. Late in the evening of the fourth, she was found about a mile and half from home, (had been overlooked), a lifeless corpse! the scene was indescribable. to see a human being lying in the wild woods a lifeless corpse is the most melancholy picture your humble servant ever witnessed and one I hope never again to behold. Be so good as to give the above a place in your columns. J. T. P., Temperance Hill, Moore County, Mar 18, 1841."

[*Editor's Note: Josiah T. Phillips was postmaster at Temperance Hill Post Office and Nancy Wollis Mar 1830-Mar 11, 1841 is buried at Flint Hill Baptist Church. I believe Nancy to be a granddaughter of Everet Wallace. I feel very strongly that her father was most likely Enoch or Joseph, based on the fact that both have an unaccounted daughter in the 1840 census that is listed between 10-15 years old. Nancy's birthdate (Mar 1830) on her tombstone at Flint Hill Baptist Church most likely rules out Isham (dau Sarah was born Jan 1830) and John (son Josiah was born Feb 1830). Other sons of Everet, Nathan and Nicholas, can also be ruled out based on the fact the Nicholas moved to TN before 1830 and Nathan had a daughter named Nancy who was born c1823-1828.*]

FOR THE OBSERVER.

Mr. Hale: One of the most heart rending circumstances that has ever been witnessed occurred in this neighborhood a few days since. On the evening of the 11th inst. a little girl, about 10 years old, (though small,) the daughter of Mr. Wallace, asked its mother to let her go to the old place (a place they formerly lived at,) and drive the cow home. The good mother at first refused, but, after some persuading, consented. The little girl set off; night soon arrived, but no news of her. The alarm was immediately given, several persons hunted nearly all night (which was very rainy) without success; in the morning a goodly number of persons assembled, searched all day, but to no effect; the second, third and fourth days, from fifty to seventy persons searched diligently. Late in the evening of the fourth, she was found about a mile and a half from home, (had been overlooked,) a lifeless corpse! The scene was indescribable. To see a human being lying in the wild woods a lifeless corpse is the most melancholy picture your humble servant ever witnessed, and one I hope never again to behold.

Be so good as to give the above a place in your columns.　　　　J. T. P.

Temperance Hill. Moore co., March 18, 1841.

photographed Apr 7, 2010

Descendants of Dallie Wallace

1. **Dallie Wallace** was born between 1810 and 1815. She died between 1845 and 1849. Beacom C. Britt (1804-1876) was the son of Ryals Britt (bef 1774-bef 1809) and Rhoda Parrish (1778-aft 1850). Beacom was married twice, and each time married a Wallace female. Information passed down through the Britt family identifies Beacom's 1st wife, Dallie Wallace (1810/1815-bef 1849), as a sister to his 2nd wife, Deborah Wallace (1828-1897) and daughters of Nathan C. Wallace. It is my opinion that she was probably not her sister but likely closely related. Dallie and Beacom are believed to have had ten children: Noah, Rhoda, Benjamin, Nathaniel "Nat", Mary A., Temperance, Sarah Ann "Sallie", Edward, Margaret and Patsy. Britt family history tells of Beacom Britt traveling back and forth several times between Moore County, NC and western Tennessee. Records confirm that he resided in Moore County, NC from 1828-1831, 1850-1853 and resided in Tennessee from 1836-1840 and after 1860. One story passed down said that Beacom was his family were in western Tennessee in 1833 during the Leonid meteor shower "the night the stars fell" and his mother was so frightened that she returned to North Carolina and vowed never to return.

Census records show that Beacom's first wife was born between 1810-1815, which would most likely rule out Nathan C. Wallace (1800-1884) as the father due to his age. It is much more likely that Beacom's 1st wife was a daughter to Everet Wallace or Nicholas Wallace. Everet has a daughter born between 1810-1815 that is listed in his household in the 1820 Census but had moved out by 1830. Beacom and his 1st wife appear together in the 1830 Census. Seemingly more likely but maybe less possible is that Nicholas Wallace was her father. Nicholas moved to Henderson County, TN prior to 1830. Beacom and his 1st wife moved west between shortly thereafter. It is quite possible Beacom was following his father-in-law and family. The only snag is that the unidentified daughter that is listed in the 1820 Census with Nicholas in Moore County, NC is also listed with her father in the 1830 Census in Henderson County, TN.

RECORDS OF BEACOM C. BRITT

1810, Jul 26 -- Moore County, NC Will Book A, Page 269
Will of Benjamin Britt, Dec'd. Heirs: wife Nancy (*plantation where I now live and the profits from the sale of the Harvil place*), children Behuver [Belaver], Ispthu [Jeptha], Buldu, Edwin, Tinatee [Finity] and Handay; Rodah, Widow of brother Rial Britt (*land containing Bent field*); Avington, Prulellah, Billasant [Bellison], Claramon [Cleryman], Becum and Tinsay, orphan children of brother Rial Britt (*land north and west of Mill Creek that belonged to Rial*). Executor: Joseph Allin. Witnesses: F. Bullock, Alexr. Morrison and Britin Britt. Proven Aug 1810.

1828, Aug 19 -- 1823-1831 Court of Pleas and Quarter Sessions, Moore County, NC Page 227
Ordered that Mark Allen be appointed overseer in place of Britton Britt for the road from Mill Creek to the fork East of Archd. McNeills and work the following hands: Britton Britt, Alfred Britt, Avington Britt, Daniel Munroe, Jeremiah Renolds, Joseph Allen, John Morgan, Becom Britt, Wm. Morgan, N. Lewis, John Smith, and Hiram Deaton.

1829, May 18 -- 1823-1831 Court of Pleas and Quarter Sessions, Moore County, NC Page 263
Ordered that Jeremiah Renalds be appointed overseer in place of Mark Allen for the road from Mill Creek to the fork East of Archd. McNeills and work the following hands: Mark Allen, Briton Britt, Alfred Britt, Avington Britt, Daniel Munroe, Joseph Allen, John Morgan, Becom Britt, Wm. Morgan, N. Lewis, John Smith, and Hiram Deaton.

1830 -- Census, Moore County, NC Page 449
Becum Britt
(20-30) 1M
(15-20) 1F
(0-5) 1 F

1836 -- Tax List, Henderson County, TN
Beacon Britt listed in Distict 11 (no land given)

1837 -- Tax List, Henderson County, TN
Beacon Britt listed in Distict 11 (no land given)

1840 -- Census, Henderson County, TN Page 341

Beacon Britt
(30-40) 1M
(20-30) 1F
(10-15) 1F
(5-10) 1M 1F
(0-5) 2M 1F

1850, Nov 22 -- Census, Moore County, NC Page 250
Beacom Britt 45 M, Farmer, $250 Real Estate, born in North Carolina
Deborah Britt 22 F, born in North Carolina
Benjamin Britt 15 M, born in North Carolina
Nathaniel 12 M, born in North Carolina
Mary A. Britt 10 F, born in North Carolina
Temperance Britt 8 F, born in North Carolina
Sallie Britt 6 F, born in North Carolina
Pattie Britt 1 F, born in North Carolina
Rhody Britt 72 F, born in North Carolina

1850 -- Agricultural Census, Moore County, NC Page 991
Beacom Britt listed 40 acres improved, 160 acres unimproved valued at $250

1852 -- Tax List, Moore County, NC
Becom Britt listed 200 acred valued at $250 located in District 6 on Mill Creek

1853, Apr 2 -- Deed Book 26 Page 457, Moore County, NC
Beacom Britt deeded Lauchlin B. Monroe 400 acres located on Mill Creek. J.A. McKinnon and Eli Smith were witnesses.

1860, Aug 23 -- Census, McNairy County, NC Page 450, District #8, Anderson Store Post Office
Becom Britt 56 M, Farmer, $430 Real Estate, $280 Personal Property, born in North Carolina
Debby Britt 29 F, born in North Carolina
Mary Britt 20 F, born in Tennessee
Sarah Britt 15 F, born in Tennessee
Martha Britt 10 F, born in North Carolina
Nathan Britt 8 M, born in North Carolina
Andy Britt 7 M, born in North Carolina
Avington Britt 5 M, born in Tennessee
William Britt 2 M, born in Tennessee

1862 -- Federal Tax List, McNairy County, TN
Beacom Britt listed 200 acres valued at $400

1870, Jun 18 -- Census, Henderson County, TN Page 90, District #10, Lexington Post Office
Beacom Britt 56 M, Farmer, $800 Real Estate, $500 Personal Property, born in North Carolina
Debby Britt 40 F, Keeping House, born in North Carolina
Handy Britt 16 M, Works on Farm, born in North Carolina
Nathan Britt 18 M, Works on Farm, born in North Carolina
Avington Britt 14 M, Works on Farm, born in Tennessee
William Britt 12 M, born in Tennessee
John Britt 9 M, born in Tennessee
Nelson Britt 7 M, born in Tennessee
Abe Lincoln Britt 4 M, born in Tennessee
James D. Britt 3 M, born in Tennessee

Beacom C. Britt He and Dallie Wallace had the following children:

+2   Edward Britt (-) No further information has been located on him.

+3   Margaret Britt (-) No further information has been located on her.

+4   Patsy Britt (-) No further information has been located on her.

+5   Noah L. Britt (1833-1863) married Elizabeth Brewer and they were the parents of five children, Noah served with the Union Army during the Civil War in Company K, 7th Regiment TN Calvary and died in a Confederate Prison in Richmond, VA.

+6   Rhoda Britt (1834-1891) married Carter Latham (b. 1830) and their union produced seven children.

+7   Benjamin Britt (1835-bef 1880) married his cousin Franey Wallace (b. 1828), daughter of Nathan Wallace and Finity Britt, and they were the parents of seven children.

+8   Nathaniel "Nat" Britt (1836-1871) married Amanda Jane "Mandy" Williams (1836-1907) and they had six children.

+9   Mary A. Britt (1840-) was listed in the 1850 and 1860 census records but no further information has been located.

+10   Temperance Britt (1842-) married G.W. Lee (b. 1830) and their union produced at least four children.

+11   Sarah Ann "Sallie" Britt (1843-1891) married Thomas Benton Weatherington (1843-1911) and produced seven children. The Weatheringtons are buried in Chester County, TN at Sweet Lips Cemetery.

Second Generation

5. **Noah L. Britt**, son of Beacom C. Britt and Dallie Wallace, was born in 1833. He married **Elizabeth Brewer** on September 16, 1852 in Moore County, NC. He died on October 31, 1863 in Richmond, VA.

Elizabeth Brewer was born in 1834. She and Noah L. Britt had the following children:

+12	Calvin Britt (1854-)
+13	Riley Britt (1856-)
+14	Nathaniel Britt (1857-)
+15	Henry Beacom Britt (1859-1927)
+16	Noah L. Britt Jr. (1862-1943)

6. **Rhoda Britt**, daughter of Beacom C. Britt and Dallie Wallace, was born in 1834. She married **Carter Latham** on August 12, 1845 in McNairy County, TN. She died in 1891 in Trenton, TN.

Carter Latham was born in 1830. He and Rhoda Britt had the following children:

+17	Beacom N. Latham (1846-1921)
+18	William Latham (1849-)
+19	James Latham (1851-)
+20	John T. Latham (1853-)
+21	Mary Latham (1856-)
+22	Nancy E. Latham (1859-)
+23	Carter Winfield Scott Latham (1862-)

7. **Benjamin Britt**, son of Beacom C. Britt and Dallie Wallace, was born in 1835. He married **Franey Wallace** on October 23, 1853 in Moore County, NC. He died between 1870 and 1880.

Franey Wallace, daughter of Nathan C. Wallace (1800-1884) and Finity Britt (1800-bef 1857), was born in May 1828 in North Carolina. She and Benjamin Britt had the following children:

+24	Everet Britt (1855-)
+25	Nancy J. Britt (1858-)
+26	Benjamin Britt (1860-)
+27	George Britt (1863-bef 1900)
+28	Mary A. "Mollie" Britt (1864-)
+29	Rolle Allen "Rawl" Britt (1867-1950)
+30	Deborah E. Britt (1871-1908)

8. **Nathaniel "Nat" Britt**, son of Beacom C. Britt and Dallie Wallace, was born in June 1836 in Moore County, NC. He married **Amanda Jane "Mandy" Williams** on August 26, 1857 in Madison County, TN. He died on February 19, 1871 in Henderson County, TN.

Amanda Jane "Mandy" Williams, daughter of Jeremiah Williams (c. 1775-) and Elizabeth Wallace (1808-), was born on July 16, 1836 in North Carolina. She died on July 27, 1907 in Henderson County, TN and was buried in Henderson County, TN at Palestine Cemetery. She and Nathaniel "Nat" Britt had the following children:

+31	David James Britt (1857-1953)
+32	Elizabeth Jane Britt (1860-)
+33	Henry Clay Britt (1862-1946)
+34	Thomas Jefferson Britt (1865-1942)
+35	William Salvage Britt (1868-1951)
+36	Clarkie Ann Britt (1872-1906)

10. **Temperance Britt**, daughter of Beacom C. Britt and Dallie Wallace, was born in 1842.

G. W. Lee was born in 1830. He and Temperance Britt had the following children:

+37	John W. Lee (1860-)
+38	Mary F. "Molly" Lee (1865-)
+39	Robert L. Lee (1867-)
+40	John R. Lee (1870-)

11. **Sarah Ann "Sallie" Britt**, daughter of Beacom C. Britt and Dallie Wallace, was born in October 1843. She married **Thomas Benton Weatherington** on October 13, 1865 in Gibson County, TN. She died in April 1891 and was buried in Chester County, TN at Sweet Lips Cemetery.

Thomas Benton Weatherington was born in June 1843. He married Susan J. circa 1896. He died in 1911 and was buried in Chester County, TN at Sweet Lips Cemetery. He and Sarah Ann "Sallie" Britt had the following children:

+41	John Newton Weatherington (1868-1960)
+42	William Henry Weatherington (1870-1955)
+43	Mary Lou Weatherington (1873-1955)
+44	Beacom Riley Weatherington (1875-1963)
+45	Sarah Frances Weatherington (1877-1931)
+46	Margaret Emma Weatherington (1880-1960)
+47	Thomas Cager Weatherington (1882-1903)

Third Generation

15. **Henry Beacom Britt**, son of Noah L. Britt and Elizabeth Brewer, was born on March 23, 1859 in Henderson County, TN. He died on March 11, 1927 in Graves County, KY.

Sarah L. Fields was born on December 15, 1864. She died on May 1, 1950. She and Henry Beacom Britt had the following children:

48	William Nelson Britt (1886-1962). *William was born on February 3, 1886. He died on January 26, 1962.*
49	James Allie Britt (1887-1945). *James was born in December 1887. He died on May 15, 1945.*
50	Henry Cornelius Britt (1889-1929). *Henry was born on December 9, 1889. He died on September 5, 1929.*
51	Myrtie Britt (1891-). *Myrtie was born on December 6, 1891.*
52	Clarence Orlanda Britt (1894-1926). *Clarence was born in February 1894. He died on March 21, 1926.*
53	Beulah Britt (1897-). *Beulah was born on October 12, 1897.*
54	Gladys Britt (1898-). *Gladys was born in November 1898.*

| 55 | Charlie Britt (1901-1979). *Charlie was born on March 9, 1901. He married **Agnes Genschaw** on August 17, 1934. He died on January 7, 1979.* |
| 56 | Noble Britt (1902-1985). *Noble was born on October 24, 1902. He died on March 14, 1985.* |

16. **Noah L. Britt Jr.**, son of Noah L. Britt and Elizabeth Brewer, was born on February 14, 1862. He died on April 4, 1943.

Ada Bateman was born on January 8, 1867. She died on December 28, 1954. She and Noah L. Britt Jr. had the following children:

57	Ona Estle Britt (1886-1945). *Ona was born on October 23, 1886. She died on January 25, 1945.*
58	Chester D. Britt (1889-1962). *Chester was born on November 2, 1889. He died on March 30, 1962.*
59	Henry Ray Britt (1893-1968). *Henry was born on June 27, 1893. He died on January 20, 1968.*
60	Lester Britt (1900-1990). *Lester was born on June 20, 1900. He died on May 9, 1990.*

17. **Beacom N. Latham**, son of Carter Latham and Rhoda Britt, was born on December 6, 1846. He died on March 11, 1921 in Tishomingo, Johnston County, OK.

Martha Josephine Moore was born on December 28, 1858 in Tippah County, MS. She died on June 28, 1927 in Tishomingo, Johnston County, OK.

19. **James Latham**, son of Carter Latham and Rhoda Britt, was born on May 15, 1851. He married **Lency Elizabeth "Tennsy" Williams** on April 16, 1874 in McNairy County, TN. He died in Texas.

Lency Elizabeth "Tennsy" Williams, daughter of Enoch Spinks Williams (1827-1894) and Rhoda Jane Morgan (1831-1898), was born on October 16, 1855 in Madison County, TN.

21. **Mary Latham**, daughter of Carter Latham and Rhoda Britt, was born on November 25, 1856 in Tennessee. She married **Bryant Williams** on January 27, 1874 in McNairy County, TN.

Bryant Williams, son of Jeremiah Williams (c. 1775-) and Elizabeth Wallace (1808-), was born in 1848 in Tennessee. He and Mary Latham had the following children:

61	Ella Williams (1875-). *Ella was born in 1875 in Tennessee. She married **William Melton** on December 21, 1892 in Chester County, TN.*
62	Docey Williams (1879-). *Docey was born in July 1879 in Henderson County, TN. She married **John S. Byrd** on September 28, 1895 in Chester County, TN.*
63	Dave Williams (1883-1909). *Dave was born in 1883 in Chester County, TN. He married **Martha Emmaline Hart** circa 1904 in Henderson County, TN. He died on November 7, 1909 in Henderson County, TN and was buried in Henderson County, TN at Palestine Cemetery.*
64	Jerry Hubert Williams Sr. (1886-1931). *Jerry was born on February 27, 1886. He married **Nona Ann Green** on July 6, 1915 in Crocket County, TN. He died on February 27, 1931 in Madison County, TN.*

24. **Everet Britt**, son of Benjamin Britt and Franey Wallace, was born in October 1855. He married **Frances Josephine McCarrell** circa 1878.

Frances Josephine McCarrell was born in 1858. She and Everet Britt had the following children:

65	Eliza A. Britt (1879-). *Eliza was born in 1879.*
66	Esther Francis Britt (1881-1934). *Esther was born in 1881. She died in 1934.*
67	Melvina Britt (1885-). *Melvina was born in March 1885.*
68	Robert G. Britt (1886-). *Robert was born in July 1886.*
69	Minnie T. Britt (1889-). *Minnie was born in March 1889.*
70	John W. Britt (1896-). *John was born on February 5, 1896.*

27. **George Britt**, son of Benjamin Britt and Franey Wallace, was born in 1863. He died before 1900.

Louisa M. Williams, daughter of Lorenzo D. "Low" Williams (1829-1890) and Sarah Elizabeth Hart (1844-1885), was born in February 1869. She and George Britt had the following children:

71   Ella L. "Nettie" Britt (1889-). *Ella was born in September 1889.*

72   Mary Emma Britt (1892-). *Mary was born in May 1892.*

73   Sarah Elizabeth "Bessie" Britt (1894-1973). *Sarah was born in July 1894. She married* ***Bert Lee Wallace*** *on July 18, 1911 in Henderson County, TN. She died in 1973 and was buried in Henderson County, TN at Palestine Cemetery.*

74   James Richard Britt (1896-1946). *James was born in July 1896. He died in 1946 and was buried in Henderson County, TN at Palestine Cemetery.*

29. **Rolle Allen "Rawl" Britt**, son of Benjamin Britt and Franey Wallace, was born in 1867. He married **Mary A. "Molly" Lee** circa 1887. He married **Azalee Frances "Dee" Elliot** on February 20, 1910 in Henderson County, TN. He died on May 18, 1950 and was buried in Henderson County, TN at Palestine Cemetery.

Mary A. "Molly" Lee was born in December 1869. She died before 1910 and was buried in Henderson County, TN at Palestine Cemetery. She and Rolle Allen "Rawl" Britt had the following children:

75   Felix R. Britt (1889-1909). *Felix was born in October 1889. He died in 1909 and was buried in Henderson County, TN at Palestine Cemetery.*

76   Frona Esther Britt (1892-). *Frona was born in November 1892.*

77   Franey Azilee Britt (1893-1935). *Franey was born on February 10, 1893. She married* ***Edmond R. Pollock*** *on December 9, 1909 in Henderson County, TN. She died on October 5, 1935 and was buried in Lexington, Henderson County, TN at Chapel Hill Cemetery.*

78   Hubert Jefferson Britt (1896-1969). *Hubert was born on April 3, 1896. He died on June 8, 1969 and was buried in Henderson County, TN at Palestine Cemetery.*

79   Gracie Britt (1903-). *Gracie was born in 1903.*

80   Flossie Britt (1906-1932). *Flossie was born on May 26, 1906. She died on June 19, 1932 in Henderson County, TN.*

Azalee Frances "Dee" Elliot was born in 1880. She died on February 24, 1922 in Henderson County, TN and was buried in Henderson County, TN at Palestine Cemetery.

30. **Deborah E. Britt**, daughter of Benjamin Britt and Franey Wallace, was born in January 1871 in Tennessee. She married **Louis Singleton** circa 1887. She died in 1908.

Louis Singleton was born in April 1862 in Tennessee. He died on October 21, 1930. He and Deborah E. Britt had the following children:

81   William Allen Singleton (1888-). *William was born in June 1888.*

82   Suzanne Singleton (1894-). *Suzanne was born in June 1894.*

83   Lanebury Singleton (1896-). *Lanebury was born in March 1896.*

84   Alice Singleton (1899-). *Alice was born in September 1899.*

85   Robert Sherman Singleton (1902-1929). *Robert was born on September 13, 1902. He died on December 1, 1929.*

31. **David James Britt**, son of Nathaniel "Nat" Britt and Amanda Jane "Mandy" Williams, was born on August 27, 1857 in Henderson County, TN. He married **Elvira "Kizzie" Daws** circa 1883. He died on January 8, 1953 in Henderson County, TN and was buried on January 9, 1953 in Henderson County, TN at Palestine Cemetery.

Elvira "Kizzie" Daws was born on November 8, 1857 in Tennessee. She died on June 8, 1924 and was buried in Henderson County, TN at Palestine Cemetery.

32. **Elizabeth Jane Britt**, daughter of Nathaniel "Nat" Britt and Amanda Jane "Mandy" Williams, was born in 1860 in Tennessee.

Tom Crow was born in 1860.

33. **Henry Clay Britt**, son of Nathaniel "Nat" Britt and Amanda Jane "Mandy" Williams, was born on September 26, 1862 in Henderson County, TN. He died on April 18, 1946 in Lexington, Henderson County, TN and was buried on April 19, 1946 in Lexington, Henderson County, TN at Lexington Cemetery.

      Tenie Adeline Barker was born in 1870. She died in 1922. She and Henry Clay Britt had the following children:

        86   Liston Britt (1907-1995). *Liston was born in 1907. He died in 1995.*

34. **Thomas Jefferson Britt**, son of Nathaniel "Nat" Britt and Amanda Jane "Mandy" Williams, was born on May 3, 1865 in Henderson County, TN. He married **Mollie Ann Williams** circa 1888. He died on January 19, 1942 in Henderson County, TN and was buried in Henderson County, TN at Palestine Cemetery.

      Mollie Ann Williams, daughter of James Wesley Williams (1845-) and Margaret M. Hart (1846-), was born in 1869. She died in 1962 in Henderson County, TN and was buried in Henderson County, TN at Palestine Cemetery. She and Thomas Jefferson Britt had the following children:

        87   Lula Britt (1889-1896). *Lula was born on October 8, 1889. She died on August 18, 1896 and was buried in Henderson County, TN at Palestine Cemetery.*

        88   Casie Britt (1891-1894). *Casie was born on September 14, 1891. He died on October 28, 1894 and was buried in Henderson County, TN at Palestine Cemetery.*

        89   Murray L. Britt (1894-1918). *Murray was born on June 3, 1894. He died on June 7, 1918 and was buried in Henderson County, TN at Palestine Cemetery.*

        90   Margie Britt (1896-). *Margie was born in July 1896.*

        91   Millie Britt (1899-). *Millie was born in 1899.*

        92   Elbert Anderson Britt (1904-1994). *Elbert was born in 1904. He died in 1994 and was buried in Henderson County, TN at Palestine Cemetery.*

        93   Ruby Britt (1907-). *Ruby was born in 1907.*

        94   Wess T. Britt (1909-). *Wess was born in 1909.*

35. **William Salvage Britt**, son of Nathaniel "Nat" Britt and Amanda Jane "Mandy" Williams, was born on April 8, 1868 in Henderson County, TN. He married **Clarkie Ann Williams** on December 17, 1894 in Henderson County, TN. He died on July 6, 1951 in Henderson County, TN and was buried on July 7, 1951 in Henderson County, TN at Palestine Cemetery.

      Clarkie Ann Williams, daughter of Lorenzo D. "Low" Williams (1829-1890) and Sarah Elizabeth Hart (1844-1885), was born on March 15, 1874 in Henderson County, TN. She died on April 10, 1914 in Henderson County, TN and was buried on April 11, 1914 in Henderson County, TN at Palestine Cemetery. She and William Salvage Britt had the following children:

        95   John Walter Britt (1894-1947). *John was born in September 1894. He married **Bertha Estelle Wallace** on November 14, 1914 in Henderson County, TN. He died in 1947 and was buried in Henderson County, TN at Palestine Cemetery.*

        96   Amanda Elvira "Mandy" Britt (1896-1966). *Amanda was born in July 1896. She died in 1966 and was buried in Henderson County, TN at Palestine Cemetery.*

        97   Luther T. Britt (1898-1917). *Luther was born in February 1898. He died in 1917 and was buried in Henderson County, TN at Palestine Cemetery.*

        98   Lonnie Britt (1901-). *Lonnie was born in 1901.*

        99   Ethel Britt (1903-). *Ethel was born in 1903.*

       100   Allie Britt (1906-). *Allie was born in 1906.*

       101   Bertha Britt (1907-). *Bertha was born in 1907.*

       102   Guy Britt (1909-1924). *Guy was born in 1909. He died in 1924 and was buried in Henderson County, TN at Palestine Cemetery.*

       103   Hugh Britt (1912-). *Hugh was born in 1912.*

       104   Noah Britt (1914-). *Noah was born in 1914.*

36. **Clarkie Ann Britt**, daughter of Nathaniel "Nat" Britt and Amanda Jane "Mandy" Williams, was born in April 1872. She married **John W. Williams** circa 1888. She died in 1906 and was buried in Henderson County, TN at Palestine Cemetery.

John W. Williams, son of Lorenzo D. "Low" Williams (1829-1890) and Sarah Elizabeth Hart (1844-1885), was born in July 1863 in Henderson County, TN. He died in 1903 in Henderson County, TN and was buried in Henderson County, TN at Palestine Cemetery. He and Clarkie Ann Britt had the following children:

105	William T. Williams (1889-). *William was born in September 1889.*
106	David J. Williams (1891-1957). *David was born in November 1891. He died in 1957 and was buried in Henderson County, TN at Palestine Cemetery.*
107	Minnie Lillian Williams (1894-1935). *Minnie was born on January 2, 1894. She married* **Joe Locie McPeake** *on September 12, 1909 in Henderson County, TN. She died on October 16, 1935 and was buried in Henderson County, TN at Palestine Cemetery.*
108	John T. Williams (1897-). *John was born in January 1897.*
109	Luther Anderson Williams (1899-1967). *Luther was born in April 1899. He died in 1967 and was buried in Henderson County, TN at Palestine Cemetery.*
110	Coy Williams (1901-1972). *Coy was born in 1901. He died in 1972 and was buried in Henderson County, TN at Palestine Cemetery.*

41. **John Newton Weatherington**, son of Thomas Benton Weatherington and Sarah Ann "Sallie" Britt, was born on April 8, 1868. He married **Margaret Catherine Davis** in 1890. He died on March 30, 1960 and was buried in Chester County, TN at Sweet Lips Cemetery.

Margaret Catherine Davis was born in 1868. She died in 1927 and was buried in Chester County, TN at Sweet Lips Cemetery. She and John Newton Weatherington had the following children:

111	Mary A. Weatherington (1891-). *Mary was born in October 1891.*
112	Jennie Callie Weatherington (1894-). *Jennie was born in February 1894.*
113	Thomas C. Weatherington (1895-). *Thomas was born in August 1895.*
114	William J. Weatherington (1898-). *William was born in June 1898.*
115	Brody A. Weatherington (1901-). *Brody was born in 1901.*
116	Elsie Weatherington (1904-). *Elsie was born in 1904.*

42. **William Henry Weatherington**, son of Thomas Benton Weatherington and Sarah Ann "Sallie" Britt, was born on August 9, 1870. He married **Martha Catherine Williams** circa 1892. He died on February 11, 1955 and was buried in Henderson County, TN at Center Hill Cemetery.

Martha Catherine Williams, daughter of James Wesley Williams (1845-) and Margaret M. Hart (1846-), was born on October 16, 1874. She died on April 28, 1918 and was buried in Henderson County, TN at Center Hill Cemetery. She and William Henry Weatherington had the following children:

117	Hettie V. Weatherington (1893-1925). *Hettie was born in May 1893. She married* **Leander Edward McCormick** *on September 13, 1909 in Henderson County, TN. She died in 1925 and was buried in Henderson County, TN at Center Hill Cemetery.*
118	Hautie A. Weatherington (1895-1985). *Hautie was born on February 17, 1895. She died on July 7, 1985 and was buried in Henderson County, TN at Center Hill Cemetery.*
119	Dossie Benton Weatherington (1896-). *Dossie was born in December 1896.*
120	Toker Z. Weatherington (1900-1918). *Toker was born in 1900. She married* **Murray Stewart** *on December 5, 1916 in Henderson County, TN. She died in 1918 and was buried in Henderson County, TN at Center Hill Cemetery.*
121	Milburn Otral Weatherington (1909-1998). *Milburn was born on March 26, 1909. He died on August 11, 1998 and was buried in Henderson County, TN at Center Hill Cemetery.*

Martha J. Neisler was born in 1888. She died in 1964 and was buried in Henderson County, TN at Center Hill Cemetery.

43. **Mary Lou Weatherington**, daughter of Thomas Benton Weatherington and Sarah Ann "Sallie" Britt, was born in May 1873. She died in 1955 and was buried in McNairy County, TN at Hopewell Cemetery.

Henry Messer died before 1900. He and Mary Lou Weatherington had the following children:

122	Lulu Olliebell Messer (1897-). *Lulu was born in August 1897. She married* **John Harrison Crowe** *on September 28, 1913 in McNairy County, TN.*

44. **Beacom Riley Weatherington**, son of Thomas Benton Weatherington and Sarah Ann "Sallie" Britt, was born in 1875. He married **Betty J. Hill** circa 1898. He died in 1963 and was buried in Milledgeville, McNairy County, TN at Milledgeville Cemetery.

Betty J. Hill was born in 1877. She died in 1958 and was buried in Milledgeville, McNairy County, TN at Milledgeville Cemetery. She and Beacom Riley Weatherington had the following children:

123	Teddy B. Weatherington (1899-). *Teddy was born in 1899.*
124	Ovid V. Weatherington (1900-1976). *Ovid was born on February 17, 1900. He died on March 6, 1976 and was buried in Milledgeville, McNairy County, TN at Milledgeville Cemetery.*
125	Roxie Weatherington (1901-1972). *Roxie was born in 1901. She died in 1972 and was buried in Milledgeville, McNairy County, TN at Milledgeville Cemetery.*
126	Rixy L. Weatherington (1906-). *Rixy was born in 1906.*
127	Ola Weatherington (1908-1954). *Ola was born in 1908. She died in 1954 and was buried in Milledgeville, McNairy County, TN at Milledgeville Cemetery.*
128	Susie R. Weatherington (1909-). *Susie was born in 1909.*
129	Athel C. Weatherington (1911-1990). *Athel was born in 1911. He died in 1990.*

45. **Sarah Frances Weatherington**, daughter of Thomas Benton Weatherington and Sarah Ann "Sallie" Britt, was born on August 12, 1877. She died on March 25, 1931 and was buried in Chester County, TN at Grove Springs Cemetery.

John Leander Smith was born on December 1, 1874. He died on November 21, 1953 and was buried in Chester County, TN at Grove Springs Cemetery.

46. **Margaret Emma Weatherington**, daughter of Thomas Benton Weatherington and Sarah Ann "Sallie" Britt, was born on February 23, 1880. She married **Lewis Cager Williams** on December 26, 1896 in Chester County, TN. She died on October 1, 1960 in Chester County, TN and was buried in Henderson County, TN at Palestine Cemetery.

Lewis Cager Williams, son of James Wesley Williams (1845-) and Margaret M. Hart (1846-), was born on April 23, 1876 in Henderson County, TN. He died on August 28, 1909 in AR and was buried in Henderson County, TN at Palestine Cemetery.

47. **Thomas Cager Weatherington**, son of Thomas Benton Weatherington and Sarah Ann "Sallie" Britt, was born on June 2, 1882. He died in 1903 and was buried in Chester County, TN at Sweet Lips Cemetery.

Descendants of Aaron Wallace

1. **Aaron Wallace** was born between 1818 and 1826. He died after 1880. Aaron was married to Sarah (1825-aft 1880) and they were the parents of Winnifred "Winnie", Mary, Emaline, Lauchlin B. "Lock" and Enoch Wallace. Aaron can be found in the 1850 and 1860 census in Moore County prior to relocating to the Laurel Hill community in present day Scotland County, NC. My grandfather said his grandfather, Emsley Wallace, told him that Aaron was a son of Everet (and brother to Isham, Josiah and Enoch) and moved to work in the turpentine business. Given Everet and Caty's estimated birthdates of around 1770 that would have Caty giving birth around 48-56 years old. While not impossible, it seems unlikely. It is possible that he was a "late child" of Everet but also just as likely he was a grandson (see DNA analysis page 13). If he was indeed a grandson, the potential candidates for his father would be Nicholas, Joseph or John with the most likely candidate being Joseph. Aaron is also believed to have fathered a child, William Conner Smith (1847-1920), with Fanny Smith (b. 1817/1820). William and Fanny were living next door to Aaron in 1850 and late relocated to Laurel Hill, NC near Aaron.

RECORDS OF AARON WALLACE

1848 -- Tax List, Moore County, NC
Aaron Wallace listed 1 white poll in District 3

1849 -- Tax List, Moore County, NC
Aaron Wallace listed 1 white poll in District 3

1849, Aug 6 -- Land Grant #3727, Moore County, NC
Zachariah B. Moore received 49 acres located on Martin's Suck including Edwards' Hill adjoining his own line, Kenneth Black and Jesse Hannon. Benjamin Barber and Aaron Wallace were chain carriers.

1850, Aug 12 -- Census, Moore County, NC Page 170
Aaron Wallis 24 M, Laborer, born in North Carolina
Sarah Wallis 24 F, born in North Carolina
Winnifred Wallis 4 F, born in North Carolina
Mary Wallis 2 F, born in North Carolina
Fanny Smith 30 F, born in North Carolina
William Smith 3 M, born in North Carolina

1855 -- Tax List, Moore County, NC
Aaron Wallis listed 1 white poll in District 3

1856 -- Tax List, Moore County, NC
Aaron Walace listed 1 white poll in District 3

1856, Jul 31 -- 1856-1858 Court of Pleas and Quarter Sessions, Moore County, NC Page 76
List of Non-Collected Taxes for 1855: Aaron Wallace

1857, Aug 1 -- 1856-1858 Court of Pleas and Quarter Sessions, Moore County, NC Page 261
List of Non-Collected Taxes for 1856: Aaron Wallace

1859, Fall -- 1850-1869 Superior Court Appearance Docket, Moore County, NC
#17 Aaron Wallace petitions court for restoration of citizenship

1860, Sep 13 -- Census, Moore County, NC Page 229-B, Lawhon's Hill Post Office
Aaron Wallace 35 M, Farmer, $150 Personal Property, born in North Carolina
Sallie Wallace 30 F, born in North Carolina
Winny Wallace 15 F, born in North Carolina
Mary Wallace 12 F, born in North Carolina
Emiline Wallace 8 F, born in North Carolina
Lauchlin B. Wallace 7 M, born in North Carolina
Enoch Wallace 5 M, born in North Carolina

1870, Jul 5 -- Census, Richmond County, NC Page 639-B, Williamson Township, Rockingham Post Office
Aaron Wallis 52 M, Turpentine Hand, born in North Carolina
Sarah Wallis 45 F, Keeping House, born in North Carolina
Winnie Wallis 25 F, Keeping House, born in North Carolina
Lauchlin Wallis 17 M, Turpentine Hand, born in North Carolina
Enoch Wallis 15 M, Turpentine Hand, born in North Carolina
William Wallis 6 M, born in North Carolina
John A. Wallis 2 M, born in North Carolina
Jane Jackson 20 F, born in North Carolina

1880, Jun 18 -- Census, Richmond County, NC Page 348, Williamson Township
Aaron Wallace 60 M, Head, Married, Farming, born in North Carolina, father & mother born in North Carolina
Sarah Wallace 47 F, Wife, Married, Keeping House, born in North Carolina, father & mother born in North Carolina
Winnie Wallace 34 F, Dau, Single, born in North Carolina, father & mother born in North Carolina
William Wallace 13 M, Boarder, Single, Laborer, born in North Carolina, father & mother born in North Carolina
John Wallace 12 M, GrSon, Single, Laborer, born in North Carolina, father & mother born in North Carolina
Walter Wallace 5 M, GrSon, Single, born in North Carolina, father & mother born in North Carolina
Sallie Wallace 1 F, GrDau, Single, born in North Carolina, father & mother born in North Carolina

Sarah was born circa 1825. She died circa 1889. She and Aaron Wallace had the following children:

+2   Winnifred "Winnie" Wallace (1846-1920) was the mother of six children, never married and is buried at King Cemetery at King Cemetery in Laurel Hill, NC.

+3   Mary Wallace (1849-1912) married Daniel Norton (1843-1920) and they were the parents of twelve children. Mary and Daniel are buried at a Norton family cemetery in Hamlet, NC.

+4   Emaline Wallace (1852-) was listed in the 1860 but no further record has been located.

+5   Lauchlin B. "Lock" Wallace (1853-bef 1910) married Margaret Ann Norton (1860-1929) and they were the parents of four children. Lock and Margaret lived in Marlboro County, SC and she is buried at the Adams / Newton Cemetery there,

+6   Enoch Wallace (1855-) Very few records exist for Enoch Wallace (b. 1855) and it is unclear he married or had children.

Fannie Smith was born between 1817 and 1820. She and Aaron Wallace had the following children:

+7   William Conner Smith (1847-1920) married Mary Ann Peele (1850-1917) and had one son. They are buried at Snead Cemetery in Scotland County.

Second Generation

2. Winnifred "Winnie" Wallace, daughter of Aaron Wallace and Sarah, was born in 1846 in Moore County, NC. She died on July 31, 1920 in Scotland County, NC and was buried on August 1, 1920 in Laurel Hill, Scotland County, NC at King Cemetery.

RECORDS OF WINNIE WALLACE

1850, Aug 12 -- Census, Moore County, NC Page 170
Aaron Wallis 24 M, Laborer, born in North Carolina
Sarah Wallis 24 F, born in North Carolina
Winnifred Wallis 4 F, born in North Carolina
Mary Wallis 2 F, born in North Carolina
Fanny Smith 30 F, born in North Carolina
William Smith 3 M, born in North Carolina

1860, Sep 13 -- Census, Moore County, NC Page 229, Lawhon's Hill Post Office
Aaron Wallace 35 M, Farmer, $150 Personal Property, born in North Carolina
Sallie Wallace 30 F, born in North Carolina
Winny Wallace 15 F, born in North Carolina
Mary Wallace 12 F, born in North Carolina

Emiline Wallace 8 F, born in North Carolina
Lauchlin B. Wallace 7 M, born in North Carolina
Enoch Wallace 5 M, born in North Carolina

1870, Jul 5 -- Census, Richmond County, NC Page 639-B, Williamsons Township,
Rockingham Post Office
Aaron Wallis 52 M, Turpentine Hand, born in North Carolina
Sarah Wallis 45 F, Keeping House, born in North Carolina
Winnie Wallis 25 F, Keeping House, born in North Carolina
Lauchlin Wallis 17 M, Turpentine Hand, born in North Carolina
Enoch Wallis 15 M, Turpentine Hand, born in North Carolina
William Wallis 6 M, born in North Carolina
John A. Wallis 2 M, born in North Carolina
Jane Jackson 20 F, born in North Carolina

1880, Jun 18 -- Census, Richmond County, NC Page 348, Williamson Township
Aaron Wallace 60 M, Head, Married, Farming, born in North Carolina, father &
mother born in North Carolina
Sarah Wallace 47 F, Wife, Married, Keeping House, born in North Carolina, father &
mother born in North Carolina
Winnie Wallace 34 F, Dau, Single, born in North Carolina, father & mother born in
North Carolina
William Wallace 13 M, Boarder, Single, Laborer, born in North Carolina, father &
mother born in North Carolina
John Wallace 12 M, GrSon, Single, Laborer, born in North Carolina, father & mother
born in North Carolina
Walter Wallace 5 M, GrSon, Single, born in North Carolina, father & mother born in
North Carolina
Sallie Wallace 1 F, GrDau, Single, born in North Carolina, father & mother born in
North Carolina

(photographed May 1, 2010)

1900, Jun 12 -- Census, Scotland County, NC Page 108, Upper Williamson Township
Winnie Wallace 50 F, Oct 1849, Head, Widow, 8 Children(6 Living), Farm Laborer, born in North Carolina, father & mother born in North
Carolina
James Wallace 17 M, Sep 1882, Son, Single, Farm Laborer, born in North Carolina, father & mother born in North Carolina
Charles Wallace 15 M, May 1885, Son, Single, Farm Laborer, born in North Carolina, father & mother born in North Carolina
Nettie Wallace 7 F, May 1893, Dau, Single, born in North Carolina, father & mother born in North Carolina

1910, Jun 14 -- Census, Scotland County, NC Page 147, Laurel Hill Township
Sallie Wright 35 F, Head, Widow, 3 Children(3 Living), Winder (Cotton Mill), born in North Carolina, father & mother born in North
Carolina
William Wright 11 M, Son, Single, Spinner (Cotton Mill), born in North Carolina, father & mother born in North Carolina
Esther Wright 6 F, Dau, Single, born in North Carolina, father & mother born in North Carolina
Thomas Wright 3 M, Son, Single, born in North Carolina, father & mother born in North Carolina
Winnie Walace 62 F, mother, Widow, 8 Children(6 Living), born in North Carolina, father & mother born in North Carolina
Nettie Walace 17 F, Dau, Single, Spinner (Cotton Mill), born in North Carolina, father & mother born in North Carolina

1920, Jan 24 -- Census, Scotland County, NC Page 114-B, Laurel Hill Township, Richmond Cotton Mill Village
George Chance 28 M, Head, Married, Drives Truck (Cotton Mill), born in North Carolina, father & mother born in North Carolina
Nittie Chance 27 F, Wife, Married, Run Spinner (Cotton Mill), born in North Carolina, father & mother born in North Carolina
Vance Chance 6 M, Son, Single, born in North Carolina, father & mother born in North Carolina
Frank Chance 3 M, Son, Single, born in North Carolina, father & mother born in North Carolina
Winnie Wallace 65 F, motherL, Widow, born in North Carolina, father & mother born in North Carolina

Winnifred "Winnie" Wallace had the following children:

+8	John Arch Wallace (1868-1960)
+9	Walter A. Wallace (1874-1939)
+10	Sallie J. Wallace (1879-1963)
+11	James Dozier W. Wallace (1882-1968)
+12	Charles W. Wallace (1884-1955)
+13	Nettie Wallace (1889-1928)

3. **Mary Wallace**, daughter of Aaron Wallace and Sarah, was born on October 15, 1849. She died in 1912 in Scotland County, NC and was buried in Hamlet, Richmond County, NC at Daniel Norton Cemetery.

RECORDS OF MARY WALLACE

1850, Aug 12 -- Census, Moore County, NC Page 170
Aaron Wallis 24 M, Laborer, born in North Carolina
Sarah Wallis 24 F, born in North Carolina
Winnifred Wallis 4 F, born in North Carolina
Mary Wallis 2 F, born in North Carolina
Fanny Smith 30 F, born in North Carolina
William Smith 3 M, born in North Carolina

1860, Sep 13 -- Census, Moore County, NC Page 229, Lawhon's Hill Post Office
Aaron Wallace 35 M, Farmer, $150 Personal Property, born in North Carolina
Sallie Wallace 30 F, born in North Carolina
Winny Wallace 15 F, born in North Carolina
Mary Wallace 12 F, born in North Carolina
Emiline Wallace 8 F, born in North Carolina
Lauchlin B. Wallace 7 M, born in North Carolina
Enoch Wallace 5 M, born in North Carolina

1870 -- Census, Richmond County, NC Page 640-B, Williamson Township., Rockingham Post Office
Daniel Norton 27 M, Turpentine Hand, born in North Carolina
Mary Norton 27 F, Keeping House, born in North Carolina
Simeon Norton 3 M, born in North Carolina
John Jackson 14 M, Turpentine Hand, born in North Carolina
Robert Cole 30 M(b), Turpentine Hand, born in North Carolina

1880 -- Census, Richmond County, NC Page 348, Williamson Township
Daniel Norton 30 M, Head, Married, Farming, born in North Carolina, father & mother born in North Carolina
Mary Norton 28 F, Wife, Married, Keeps House, born in North Carolina, father & mother born in North Carolina
Simeon Norton 12 M, Son, Single, Laborer, born in North Carolina, father & mother born in North Carolina
Godfrey Norton 10 M, Son, Single, Laborer, born in North Carolina, father & mother born in North Carolina
Mary Norton 8 F, Dau, Single, born in North Carolina, father & mother born in North Carolina
William Norton 6 M, Son, Single, born in North Carolina, father & mother born in North Carolina
Emma Norton 4 F, Dau, Single, born in North Carolina, father & mother born in North Carolina
Anna Norton 1 F, Dau, Single, born in North Carolina, father & mother born in North Carolina

1900 -- Census, Scotland County, NC Page 108, Upper Williamson Township
Daniel Norton 57 M, Apr 1843, Head, Married-28yrs, Farmer, born in North Carolina, father & mother born in North Carolina
Mary Norton 50 F, Oct 1849, Wife, Married-28yrs, 12 Children(10 Living), born in North Carolina, father & mother born in North Carolina
Emmer D. Norton 19 F, Jun 1881, Dau, Single, Farm Laborer, born in North Carolina, father & mother born in North Carolina
Daniel Norton 15 M, Nov 1884, Son, Single, Farm Laborer, born in North Carolina, father & mother born in North Carolina
Sarah Norton 13 F, Sep 1886, Dau, Single, Farm Laborer, born in North Carolina, father & mother born in North Carolina
James Norton 11 M, Sep 1888, Son, Single, Farm Laborer, born in North Carolina, father & mother born in North Carolina
Bart Norton 9 M, Oct 1890, Son, Single, born in North Carolina, father & mother born in North Carolina
John Norton 7 M, Sep 1892, Son, Single, born in North Carolina, father & mother born in North Carolina
Willie Norton 5 M, July 1894, Son, Single, born in North Carolina, father & mother born in North Carolina
Dave Norton 3 M, Sep 1886, GrSon, Single, born in North Carolina, father & mother born in North Carolina
Tom Norton 1 M, Nov 1898, GrSon, Single, born in North Carolina, father & mother born in North Carolina

1910 -- Census, Scotland County, NC Oage 294-B, Upper Williamson Precinct
Daniel Norton 67 M, Head, Married-1st-36yrs, Laborer(Odd Jobs), born in North Carolina, father & mother born in North Carolina
Mary Norton 63 F, Wife, Married-1st-36yrs, 13 Children(10 Living), born in North Carolina, father & mother born in North Carolina
Sarah C. Norton 22 F, Dau, Single, 1 Child(1 Living), Farm Laborer(Working Out), born in North Carolina, father & mother born in North Carolina
Annie M. Norton 4/12 F, GrDau, Single, born in North Carolina, father & mother born in North Carolina
Lawrence Deye 38 M, Boarder, Widowed, Farm Laborer(Working Out), born in North Carolina, father & mother born in North Carolina

Daniel Norton, son of Elijah Norton (1802-1865) and Eliza Walker (1806-1865), was born in 1843 in Richmond County, NC. He died on May 3, 1920 in Scotland County, NC and was buried in Hamlet, Richmond County, NC at Daniel Norton Cemetery. He and Mary Wallace had the following children:

+14	Simeon Norton (1868-)
+15	Godfrey Norton (1870-)
+16	Mary Norton (1872-)
+17	William Norton (1874-)
+18	Emma Daisy Norton (1876-1940)
+19	Anna Jane Norton (1879-1954)
+20	Daniel Mae Norton (1885-1956)
+21	Sarah Liza Norton (1886-1952)
+22	Bart Norton (1890-)
+23	James Norton (1891-1949)
+24	John Norton (1892-)
+25	W. Willie Norton (1894-1944)

5. **Lauchlin B. "Lock" Wallace**, son of Aaron Wallace and Sarah, was born in 1853. He married **Margaret Ann Norton** on December 18, 1874 in Richmond County, NC.[133] He died before 1910.

RECORDS OF LOCK WALLACE

1860, Sep 13 -- Census, Moore County, NC Page 229, Lawhon's Hill Post Office
Aaron Wallace 35 M, Farmer, $150 Personal Property, born in North Carolina
Sallie Wallace 30 F, born in North Carolina
Winny Wallace 15 F, born in North Carolina
Mary Wallace 12 F, born in North Carolina
Emiline Wallace 8 F, born in North Carolina
Lauchlin B. Wallace 7 M, born in North Carolina
Enoch Wallace 5 M, born in North Carolina

1870, Jul 5 -- Census, Richmond County, NC Page 639-B, Williamsons Township, Rockingham Post Office
Aaron Wallis 52 M, Turpentine Hand, born in North Carolina
Sarah Wallis 45 F, Keeping House, born in North Carolina
Winnie Wallis 25 F, Keeping House, born in North Carolina
Lauchlin Wallis 17 M, Turpentine Hand, born in North Carolina
Enoch Wallis 15 M, Turpentine Hand, born in North Carolina
William Wallis 6 M, born in North Carolina
John A. Wallis 2 M, born in North Carolina
Jane Jackson 20 F, born in North Carolina

1874, Dec 13 -- Marriage Certificate, Richmond County, NC
Lauchlin Wallace (age 21), son of Aaron Wallace and Sarah Wallace, and Margaret Ann Norton (age 16), daughter of Eliza Ann Norton, were married by J.P. Smith, JP. Godfrey Norton and Sarah Wallace were witnesses.

1880 -- Census, Marlboro County, SC Page 379-B
Lock Wallace 24 M, Head, Married, Laborer, born in North Carolina, father & mother born in North Carolina
Margaret Wallace 20 F, Wife, Married, Laborer, born in North Carolina, father & mother born in North Carolina
Rosetta Wallace 5 F, Dau, Single, born in North Carolina, father & mother born in North Carolina
Godfrey Wallace 3 M, Son, Single, born in North Carolina, father & mother born in North Carolina

1910 -- Census, Scotland County, NC Page 135, Laurel Hill Township
Belton J. Norton 26 M, Head, Married-1st-6yrs, Farmer(General Farm), born in North Carolina, father & mother born in North Carolina
Margaret Norton 26 F, Wife, Married-1st-6yrs, 0 Children, Farm Laborer(Home Farm), born in North Carolina, father & mother born in North Carolina
Margaret A. Wallace 50 F, motherL, Widow, 6 Children(3 Living), Farm Laborer(Home Farm), born in North Carolina, father & mother born in North Carolina
Nettie Wallace 19 F, SisterL, Single, Farm Laborer(Home Farm), born in North Carolina, father & mother born in North Carolina

1920 -- Census, Marlboro County, SC Page 278-B, Adamsville Township
John Taylor 47 M, Head, Married, Farmer(General Farm), born in South Carolina, father & mother born in North Carolina
Nettie Taylor 24 F, Wife, Married, born in North Carolina, father & mother born in North Carolina
Arthur Taylor 14 M, Son, Single, born in South Carolina, father & mother born in South Carolina
Marvin Taylor 12 M, Son, Single, born in South Carolina, father & mother born in South Carolina
Belton Taylor 5 M, Son, Single, born in South Carolina, father born in South Carolina, mother born in North Carolina
Bula Taylor 3 2/12 F, Dau, Single, born in South Carolina, father born in South Carolina, mother born in North Carolina
John T. Taylor 1 6/12 Son, Single, born in South Carolina, father born in South Carolina, mother born in North Carolina
Margaret Ann Wallace 50 F, motherL, Widow, born in North Carolina, father & mother born in North Carolina

Additional Information can be found at www.MooreCountyWallaces.com

Margaret Ann Norton was born on November 10, 1860. She died on February 20, 1929 in Marlboro County, SC and was buried in Marlboro County, SC at Adams Family Cemetery AKA Newton Cemetery. She and Lauchlin B. "Lock" Wallace had the following children:

+26	Rosa Ella Wallace (1876-1923)	
+27	Godfrey Wallace (1877-)	
+28	Margaret Wallace (1884-)	
+29	Nettie Wallace (1891-1940)	

7. **William Conner Smith**, son of Aaron Wallace and Fannie Smith, was born in May 1847 in Moore County, NC. He married **Mary Ann Peele** on December 19, 1867 in Richmond County, NC. He died on March 19, 1920 in Scotland County, NC and was buried in Scotland County, NC at Snead Cemetery.

RECORDS OF CONNER SMITH

1850 -- Census, Moore County, NC Page 170
Fanny Smith 30 F, born in North Carolina
William Smith 3 M, born in North Carolina
(living next door to)
Aaron Wallis 24 M, Laborer, born in North Carolina
Sarah Wallis 24 F, born in North Carolina
Winnifred Wallis 4 F, born in North Carolina
Mary Wallis 2 F, born in North Carolina

1860 -- Census, Moore County, NC Page 213-B
Locky Morris 29 M, Farmer, $200 Real Estate, $350 Personal Property, born in North Carolina
Margaret B. Morris 53 F, born in North Carolina
Elizabeth Thomas 39 F, born in North Carolina
Wm. C. Smith 13 M, born in North Carolina
Mary A. Thomas 7 F, born in North Carolina

1867, Dec 19 -- Marriage Register, Richmond County, NC Page 133
Conner Smith and Mary An Peele were married by Thomas Gibson

1880 -- Census, Richmond County, NC Page 345-B
Conner Smith 36 M, Head, Married, Farming, born in North Carolina, father & mother born in North Carolina
Mary Smith 30 F, Wife, Married, Keeping House, born in North Carolina, father & mother born in North Carolina
Archie Smith 2 M, Son, Single, born in North Carolina, father & mother born in North Carolina
Fannie Smith 69 F, mother, Widowed, At Home, born in North Carolina, father & mother born in North Carolina

1900 -- Census, Scotland County, NC Page 109
Conner Smith 66 M, Mar 1834, Head, Married, Farmer, born in North Carolina, father & mother born in North Carolina
Mary A. Smith 58 F, Jan 1842, Wife, Married, 7 Children(1 Living), born in North Carolina, father & mother born in North Carolina
John Smith 22 M, Apr 1878, Son, Married, Laborer(Farm), born in North Carolina, father & mother born in North Carolina
Janett Smith 23 F, May 1876, DauL, Married, Laborer(Farm), born in North Carolina, father & mother born in North Carolina

1910 -- Census, Scotland County, NC Page 295
William C. Smith 65 M, Head, Married-1st-42yrs, Farmer, born in North Carolina, father & mother born in North Carolina
Mary A. Smith 62 F, Wife, Married-1st-42yrs, 7 children(1 Living), born in North Carolina, father & mother born in North Carolina
Mary M. Cherry 21 F, Boarder, Single, Farm Laborer, born in North Carolina, father & mother born in North Carolina

1920 -- Census, Scotland County, NC Page 260
Wesley Morgan 36 M, Head, Married, Farmer(Gen. Farm), born in North Carolina, father & mother born in North Carolina
Tempest Morgan 40 F, Wife, Married, born in North Carolina, father & mother born in North Carolina
Sarah Morgan 1 9/12 F, Dau, Single, born in North Carolina, father & mother born in North Carolina
Conner Smith 73 M, Uncle, Widow, born in North Carolina, father & mother born in North Carolina

1920, Mar 19 -- Death Certificate, Scotland County, NC
William Conner Smith died in Williamson Township. Widow of Mary Ann Smith. Age: 72y 10m. Date of Birth: May 1847. Occupation: Farmer. Birthplace: More County, NC. father and mother: Unknown. Cause of Death: Endocarditis. Place of Burial: Snead Graveyard. Date of Burial: Mar 20, 1920. Undertaker: J.H. O'Brien, Laurel Hill, NC.

Mary Ann Peele was born on November 25, 1850. She died on July 27, 1917 and was buried in Scotland County, NC at Snead Cemetery. She and William Conner Smith had the following child:

+30   John Arch Smith (1877-1943)

Third Generation

8. John Arch Wallace, son of Winnifred "Winnie" Wallace, was born on April 16, 1868. He married **Martisha M. Yow** circa 1892. He married **Eva Peele** on November 30, 1920 in Scotland County, NC. He died on November 25, 1960 in Moore County, NC and was buried on November 27, 1960 in Laurel Hill, Scotland County, NC at Peele's Chapel.

Martisha M. Yow was born on June 25, 1876. She died on December 6, 1918 and was buried in Moore County, NC at Smyrna Methodist Church. She and John Arch Wallace had the following children:

31   Yancey L. Wallace (1897-). *Yancey was born on March 22, 1897.*
32   Melvin Monroe Wallace (1903-1972). *Melvin was born on February 14, 1903. He died on March 15, 1972 in Cumberland County, NC and was buried on March 17, 1972 in Aberdeen, Moore County, NC at Bethesda Cemetery.*

Eva Peele, daughter of William James Peele (-) and Eliza Jane Norton (-), was born on November 19, 1899. She died on December 18, 1972 in Moore Regional Hospital, Pinehurst, Moore County, NC and was buried on December 20, 1972 in Laurel Hill, Scotland County, NC at Peele's Chapel. She and John Arch Wallace had the following children:

33   Mattie M. Wallace (1923-). *Mattie was born in 1923.*
34   Edgar Wallace (1927-). *Edgar was born on January 21, 1927 in Moore County, NC.*

9. Walter A. Wallace, son of Winnifred "Winnie" Wallace, was born on July 9, 1874 in Scotland County, NC. He married **Mary Catherine Wright** circa 1899. He died on October 1, 1939 in Scotland County, NC and was buried on October 3, 1939 in Laurel Hill, Scotland County, NC at King Cemetery.

Hattie Hughes was born on March 16, 1867. She died on May 24, 1898 and was buried in Laurel Hill, Scotland County, NC at King Cemetery. She and Walter A. Wallace had the following children:

35   Pattie Wallace (1893-1943). *Pattie was born on March 4, 1893 in Scotland County, NC. She died on January 1, 1943 in Scotland County, NC and was buried on January 3, 1943 in Scotland County, NC at Hillside Cemetery.*
36   Clarence Murdock Wallace (1897-). *Clarence was born on July 9, 1897 in Scotland County, NC.*

Mary Catherine Wright was born on November 26, 1874 in Scotland County, NC. She died on January 28, 1921 in Scotland County, NC and was buried on January 29, 1921 in Laurel Hill, Scotland County, NC at King Cemetery. She and Walter A. Wallace had the following children:

37   Walter Thomas Wallace (1905-). *Walter was born on October 25, 1905 in Scotland County, NC.*
38   John Wallace (1915-). *John was born on January 2, 1915 in Scotland County, NC.*
39   Morris W. Wallace (1915-1916). *Morris was born on January 2, 1915. He died on June 22, 1916 and was buried in Laurel Hill, Scotland County, NC at King Cemetery.*

10. Sallie J. Wallace, daughter of Winnifred "Winnie" Wallace, was born on December 2, 1879 in Scotland County, NC. She died on September 19, 1963 in Scotland Memorial Hospital, Laurinburg, Scotland County, NC and was buried on September 21, 1963 in Laurel Hill, Scotland County, NC at King Cemetery.

Thomas M. Wright was born on November 15, 1871. He died on September 10, 1906 and was buried in Laurel Hill, Scotland County, NC at King Cemetery. He and Sallie J. Wallace had the following children:

40   William Thomas Wright (1899-1959). *William was born on August 14, 1899 in Scotland County, NC. He married **Martha Ann Gwynn** in 1918. He married **Allie Gertrude Lockey** in 1927 in Marlboro County, SC. He died on December 7, 1959 in Laurinburg, Scotland County, NC and was buried on December 9, 1959 in*

41   Mary Esther Wright (1903-1922). *Mary was born on June 14, 1903. She died on April 24, 1922 and was buried in Laurel Hill, Scotland County, NC at King Cemetery.*

42   Thomas Wright (1907-). *Thomas was born in 1907.*

11. James Dozier W. Wallace, son of Winnifred "Winnie" Wallace, was born on September 26, 1882. He married **Rebecca Jane Peele** in 1904. He died on September 24, 1968 in Scotland Memorial Hospital, Laurinburg, Scotland County, NC and was buried on September 26, 1968 in Laurel Hill, Scotland County, NC at Peele's Chapel.

Rebecca Jane Peele, daughter of William James Peele (-) and Eliza Jane Norton (-), was born on June 4, 1882 in Richmond County, NC. She died on April 17, 1942 in Scotland County, NC and was buried on April 18, 1942 in Laurel Hill, Scotland County, NC at Peele's Chapel. She and James Dozier W. Wallace had the following children:

43   Winnie Wallace (1905-). *Winnie was born on July 12, 1905 in Scotland County, NC. She married **Fred L. Carter** in 1927.*

44   Owen Wallace (1908-1984). *Owen was born on January 24, 1908. He married **Lizzie Gibson** in 1928. He died on December 19, 1984 and was buried in Laurel Hill, Scotland County, NC at Peele's Chapel.*

45   James Vester Wallace (1910-2001). *James was born on March 10, 1910. He died on August 28, 2001 and was buried in Laurel Hill, Scotland County, NC at Woodville Church.*

46   Dora Wallace (1912-). *Dora was born on May 25, 1912 in Scotland County, NC.*

47   Ella Wallace (1915-). *Ella was born in 1915.*

48   Grady Wallace (1917-2001). *Grady was born on March 11, 1917 in Scotland County, NC. He died on March 21, 2001 and was buried in Laurel Hill, Scotland County, NC at Peele's Chapel.*

49   Jane Wallace (1920-). *Jane was born in 1920.*

50   Jesse Wallace (1921-). *Jesse was born in 1921.*

12. Charles W. Wallace, son of Winnifred "Winnie" Wallace, was born on May 4, 1884. He married **Maggie English** in 1906. He married **Ethel Garner** in 1923. He died on June 2, 1955 in Hamlet Hospital, Hamlet, Richmond County, NC and was buried on June 3, 1955 in Laurel Hill, Scotland County, NC at Peele's Chapel.

Maggie English was born on January 5, 1883. She died on March 30, 1922 and was buried in Laurel Hill, Scotland County, NC at Peele's Chapel. She and Charles W. Wallace had the following children:

51   Lena Bell Wallace (1907-1948). *Lena was born on May 4, 1907 in Scotland County, NC. She married **Samuel Peele** circa 1927. She died on June 13, 1948 in Scotland County, NC and was buried on June 15, 1948 in Laurel Hill, Scotland County, NC at Peele's Chapel.*

52   Gracie May Wallace (1908-1908). *Gracie was born on August 1, 1908. She died on August 12, 1908 and was buried in Laurel Hill, Scotland County, NC at Peele's Chapel.*

53   Charles C. Wallace (1910-). *Charles was born in 1910.*

54   Lloyd Maxwell Wallace (1911-1951). *Lloyd was born on August 20, 1911 in Scotland County, NC. He died on February 23, 1951 in Scotland County, NC and was buried on February 25, 1951 in Laurel Hill, Scotland County, NC at Peele's Chapel.*

55   Edmond Wallace (1913-1914). *Edmond was born on June 2, 1913. He died on June 3, 1914 and was buried in Laurel Hill, Scotland County, NC at Peele's Chapel.*

56   Brencie G. Wallace (1916-). *Brencie was born in 1916.*

57   Annie Jane Wallace (1919-). *Annie was born on April 14, 1919 in Scotland County, NC.*

Ethel Garner was born on August 4, 1904 in Richmond County, NC. She died on January 4, 1949 in Scotland County, NC and was buried on January 5, 1949 in Laurel Hill, Scotland County, NC at Peele's Chapel. She and Charles W. Wallace had the following children:

58   James Everette Wallace (1923-1987). *James was born on December 31, 1923 in Scotland County, NC. He died on August 7, 1987 and was buried in Laurel Hill, Scotland County, NC at Peele's Chapel.*

59   John Arch Wallace (1927-). *John was born on November 16, 1927 in Scotland County, NC.*

13. **Nettie Wallace**, daughter of Winnifred "Winnie" Wallace, was born on December 28, 1889 and was buried on December 3, 1928 in Laurel Hill, Scotland County, NC at King Cemetery. She died on December 28, 1928 in Scotland County, NC.

Nettie Wallace had the following child:

60   Thomas Vance Wallace (1912-1965). *Thomas was born on September 25, 1912 in Scotland County, NC. He died on October 6, 1965 in Scotland Memorial Hospital, Laurinburg, Scotland County, NC and was buried on October 8, 1965 in Scotland County, NC at Hillside Cemetery.*

George Chance was born in 1892. He married Annie M. in 1929. He and Nettie Wallace had the following children:

61   Frank Chance (1917-). *Frank was born in 1917.*
62   Eugene Chance (1921-). *Eugene was born in 1921.*
63   Walter Chance (1923-). *Walter was born on February 10, 1923 in Scotland County, NC.*
64   Mary Elizabeth Chance (1925-). *Mary was born on April 25, 1925 in Scotland County, NC.*
65   Male Chance (1928-). *Male was born on December 28, 1928 in Scotland County, NC.*

18. **Emma Daisy Norton**, daughter of Daniel Norton and Mary Wallace, was born in 1876. She died on August 2, 1940 in Scotland County, NC and was buried on August 3, 1940 in Hamlet, Richmond County, NC at Daniel Norton Cemetery.

Henry Morgan was born on August 7, 1881 in Scotland County, NC. He died on October 28, 1961 in Scotland County, NC and was buried on October 29, 1961 in Hamlet, Richmond County, NC at Daniel Norton Cemetery.

19. **Anna Jane Norton**, daughter of Daniel Norton and Mary Wallace, was born on June 4, 1879 in Scotland County, NC. She died on May 27, 1954 in Scotland County, NC and was buried on May 31, 1954 in Laurel Hill, Scotland County, NC at Peele's Chapel.

William Franklin Peele was born on June 23, 1865 in Scotland County, NC. He died on June 23, 1921 in Old Hundred, Scotland County, NC and was buried on June 24, 1921 in Hamlet, Richmond County, NC at Daniel Norton Cemetery. He and Anna Jane Norton had the following children:

66   Samuel Peele (1896-). *Samuel was born in 1896. He married **Lena Bell Wallace** circa 1927.*
67   Lessie Peele (1910-). *Lessie was born in 1910.*

20. **Daniel Mae Norton**, son of Daniel Norton and Mary Wallace, was born on January 14, 1885 in Richmond County, NC. He died on February 17, 1956 in Scotland County, NC and was buried on February 18, 1956 in Scotland County, NC at Hillside Cemetery.

Mamie Gertrude Peele Brown was born on August 16, 1892 in Richmond County, NC. She died on September 11, 1956 in Hoke County, NC. She and Daniel Mae Norton had the following children:

68   Helen Norton (1914-). *Helen was born in 1914.*
69   Nora Elizabeth Norton (1919-). *Nora was born in 1919.*
70   Mary Catherine Norton (1921-). *Mary was born on December 5, 1921 in Scotland County, NC.*
71   Mary Norton (1924-). *Mary was born on September 17, 1924 in Scotland County, NC.*
72   Marcus Edward Norton (1930-). *Marcus was born on April 27, 1930 in Scotland County, NC. He married **Nancy Sue Steen** on October 1, 1949 in Marlboro County, SC.*
73   Martha Alma Norton (1934-1935). *Martha was born on September 26, 1934 in Scotland County, NC. She died on April 26, 1935 in Scotland County, NC.*

21. **Sarah Liza Norton**, daughter of Daniel Norton and Mary Wallace, was born in 1886. She died on May 7, 1952 in Scotland County, NC and was buried on May 9, 1952 in Scotland County, NC at Hillside Cemetery.

23. **James Norton**, son of Daniel Norton and Mary Wallace, was born on August 4, 1891. He married **Dora Lee Campbell** on June 11, 1911 in Richmond County, NC. He died on December 26, 1949 in Scotland County, NC and was buried on December 27, 1949 in Laurel Hill, Scotland County, NC at Peele's Chapel.

Dora Lee Campbell was born on September 25, 1892. She died on November 15, 1965 in Richmond County, NC. She and James Norton had the following children:

74	Walter Norton (1917-). *Walter was born on November 10, 1917 in Scotland County, NC.*
75	Emma Daisy Norton (1921-). *Emma was born on January 21, 1921 in Scotland County, NC.*
76	Janie Lee Norton (1931-). *Janie was born on July 31, 1931 in Richmond County, NC.*

25. **W. Willie Norton**, son of Daniel Norton and Mary Wallace, was born in 1894. He died on January 17, 1944 in Raeford, Hoke County, NC.

26. **Rosa Ella Wallace**, daughter of Lauchlin B. "Lock" Wallace and Margaret Ann Norton, was born on June 7, 1876 in SC. She married **Seymore M. Norton** circa 1891. She married **John H. Butler** (1866-) on September 18, 1921 in Saint Pauls, Robeson County, NC. She died on May 23, 1923 in Saint Pauls, Robeson County, NC and was buried on May 24, 1923 in Saint Pauls, Robeson County, NC at Fisher Cemetery.

Seymore M. Norton was born on June 13, 1872. He died on June 29, 1919 and was buried in Saint Pauls, Robeson County, NC at Fisher Cemetery. He and Rosa Ella Wallace had the following children:

77	Foster Shaw Norton (1894-1944). *Foster was born on June 1, 1894 in Marlboro County, SC. He died on March 22, 1944 in Saint Pauls, Robeson County, NC and was buried in Saint Pauls, Robeson County, NC at Oak Ridge Cemetery.*
78	Jesse Benjamin Norton (1896-1958). *Jesse was born on July 25, 1896. He died on February 19, 1958 in Fayetteville, Cumberland County, NC.*
79	Dora Lee Norton (1898-1964). *Dora was born on May 5, 1898. She died on June 7, 1964 in Lumberton, Robeson County, NC and was buried in Saint Pauls, Robeson County, NC at Oak Ridge Cemetery.*
80	Wade Hampton Norton (1903-). *Wade was born in 1903.*
81	Mary Cattie Norton (1904-1971). *Mary was born on April 12, 1904. She died on December 19, 1971 in Saint Pauls, Robeson County, NC and was buried in Saint Pauls, Robeson County, NC at Fisher Cemetery.*
82	Annie Ethel Norton (1905-). *Annie was born in 1905.*
83	Susie May Norton (1907-). *Susie was born in 1907.*
84	Judy Ann Norton (1909-1990). *Judy was born on November 15, 1909. She died on November 29, 1990.*
85	Anna C. Norton (1915-). *Anna was born in 1915.*
86	Rose B. Norton (1918-). *Rose was born in 1918.*

28. **Margaret Wallace**, daughter of Lauchlin B. "Lock" Wallace and Margaret Ann Norton, was born in 1884. She married **Belton John Norton** circa 1904.

Belton John Norton was born on September 21, 1882. He died on November 8, 1943 in Fayetteville, Cumberland County, NC and was buried in Laurel Hill, Scotland County, NC at King Cemetery.

29. **Nettie Wallace**, daughter of Lauchlin B. "Lock" Wallace and Margaret Ann Norton, was born in January 1891 in Scotland County, NC. She died on February 14, 1940 in Marlboro County, SC and was buried on February 15, 1940 in Marlboro County, SC at Adams Family Cemetery AKA Newton Cemetery.

John T. Taylor was born in 1870. He died on July 22, 1944 in Marlboro County, SC and was buried in Marlboro County, SC at Adams Family Cemetery AKA Newton Cemetery. He and Nettie Wallace had the following children:

87	Belton Taylor (1915-). *Belton was born in 1915.*
88	Beulah Taylor (1917-). *Beulah was born in 1917.*
89	John T. Taylor (1918-). *John was born in 1918.*

30. **John Arch Smith**, son of William Conner Smith and Mary Ann Peele, was born on September 12, 1877. He married **Jeanette Caviness** on March 18, 1900 in Richmond County, NC. He died on August 11, 1943 and was buried in Laurel Hill, Scotland County, NC at King Cemetery.

Jeanette Caviness was born on August 28, 1875. She died on December 17, 1964 and was buried in Laurel Hill, Scotland County, NC at King Cemetery. She and John Arch Smith had the following children:

90   Wavely McLean Smith (1909-1964). *Wavely was born on November 8, 1909. He died on February 8, 1964 and was buried in Laurel Hill, Scotland County, NC at King Cemetery.*

91   John C. Smith (1917-1977). *John was born on March 31, 1917. He died on August 11, 1977.*

Descendants of William Lane Wallace

1. **William Lane Wallace** was born on March 13, 1814 and died on May 6, 1886 and was buried in Little Rock, Dillon County, SC at Saint Paul's Methodist Church. [134] William Lane Wallace was one of the more colorful of the Wallace characters, spending a great deal of time in trouble with the law and rumored to have fathered at least thirteen children by multiple women. William L. was most likely a grandson of Everet Wallace through a daughter and unknown father (see DNA analysis page 15). He was involved with numerous court cases with Delphy Lakey, Elizabeth Smith & Mary Davis in the 1840's and it has been passed down through his descendants that he was living with all three and the court finally ordered him to marry one of them. William L. married Elizabeth Smith (1818-1893) around 1853. He served in Company H, 26th Regiment during the Civil War and moved to Dillon, SC soon after. [135] [136] William L. and Elizabeth are buried at Saint Paul's Methodist Church in Little Rock, SC. William Lane Wallace is also believed to have been the father of James Davis (b. 1849), son of Mary Davis (b. 1810/1815). Mary and James are listed in the 1850 and 1860 census records, but no additional information has been located.

RECORDS OF WILLIAM LANE WALLACE

1834, May 13 -- Land Grant #2989, Moore County, NC
William Barrett Senr. received 99 acres located on the drains of Buffalo Creek adjoining McLeod and his own line. John McLeod and Wm. L. Wallace were chain carriers.

1835, Aug 1 -- Deed Book 5, Page 146, Moore County, NC
William Barrett Senr. deeded William Barrett Junr. 130 acres located on McLendons Creek adjoining his own line, Person, Samuel Barrett and Jackson. William L. Wallace and M. Shaw were witnesses.

1835, Dec 1 -- Land Grant #2987, Moore County, NC
William Barrett Senr. received 25 acres located on both sides of the Juniper adjoining his own line, George Jackson and Person. Wm. L. Wallace and William Barret Jur. were chain carriers.

1835, Dec 2 -- Land Grant #2988, Moore County, NC
William Barrett Senr. received 41 acres located on both sides of Suck Creek of McLendons Creek adjoining his own line, Collin A. Munroe, McDonald, Dunlap and Samuel Jackson. Hyram Melton and Wm. L. Wallace were chain carriers.

1838, Nov -- Bethlehem Baptist Church Minutes, Carthage, NC Page 28
"Complaint against Elizabeth Smith for Bastardy and she taken up and is excluded fourth with for the same from the church."

1838, Dec -- Supreme Court Case #2744
From Moore County. Thomas Ritter and wife Margaret v. William Barrett. Regarding 300 acres located on McLendons Creek adjoining Jacob McLendon including the land that Mary Sowell resided on in 1786. The 300 acres was granted to Thomas Knight in 1760 and deeded to Jacob McLendon in 1762; deeded to Isaac Sowell in 1772; Isaac Sowell died in 1784 and land was transferred to widow Mary Sowell and oldest son John Sowell; deeded to Margaret Sowell, wife of Thomas Ritter in 1786. Deeds in the file include 1791 from Thomas Ritter and Margaret Ritter to John Sowell and 1830 from John Sowell to William Barrett Senr. In Jan 1836, Mary Smith and Wm. Wallice/Wm. Smith are associated with the land with William Barrett Senr. as landlord.

1839, Spring -- 1834-1842 Superior Court Execution Docket, Moore County, NC
#39 William Barrett Sr. v. Mary Smith. Wm. L. Wallace, Corn. Dunlap and Holden Cox were witnesses.

1841, Fall -- 1834-1842 Superior Court Execution Docket, Moore County, NC
#13 Daniel Muse v. Isham Wallace. Witnesses: Enich Wallace, Joel Lawhon, Thomas Muse, Wm. Caddell, Abram Hunsucker, Patience Muse, Leonard Furr, A. Shattuck, Polly Williams, Daniel Muse, James Melton, Shadrac Maner, Wm. Barrett Jr., Wm L. Wallace and Delphy Wallace. Continued Spring 1842 #36 -- Fall 1842 #77 -- Spring 1843 #83 -- Fall 1843 #63 -- Spring 1844 #72 -- Fall 1844 #79 -- Spring 1845 #72 -- Fall 1845 #81 -- Spring 1846 #99 -- Fall 1846 #92 -- Spring 1847 #90 -- Fall 1847 #89

1841, Fall -- 1836-1844 Recognizance Docket
#36 State v. Polly Campbell, Celia Mainer, Delphy Lakey, Betsy Smith, George Hunsucker merchant and William L. Wallace

1842, Spring -- 1836-1844 Recognizance Docket, Moore County, NC
#23 State v. Polly Campbell, Celia Mainer and Betsy Smith (A and B). William L. Wallace and Shadrack Mainer were securities.

1842, Spring -- 1834-1851 State Docket County Court, Moore County, NC Page 165
#23 State v. Polly Campbell, Celia Mainer, Delphy Lakey and Betsy Smith. William L. Wallace was security.

1843, Fall -- 1836-1844 Recognizance Docket, Moore County, NC
#5 State v. Celia Mainer and Polly Campbell. William L. Wallace was a security.

1844, Apr 24 -- 1844-1847 Court of Pleas and Quarter Sessions, Moore County, NC Page 10
Ordered that Everet Maines be appointed overseer of the road from Bear Creek to Buffalo Creek and work the following hands: John McLeod, George Cagle, Garner Maines, William Stewart, Henry Maines, Matthew Williams, Jethro Denson, Amos Bridges, William L. Wallace, Lauchlin B. Currie and Hiram Kelly.

1846/1847 -- Tax List, Moore County, NC
William L. Wallace listed 1 white poll on Locust Branch in District 9

1847, Apr 28 -- 1847-1849 Court of Pleas and Quarter Sessions, Moore County, NC Page 18
Ordered that George McIntosh be appointed overseer of the road from McQueen's Branch to the Richland Creek Bridge and work the following hands: Joseph Caddell, Quimby Sowell, Duncan McIntosh, Jesse Muse, William L. Wallace, Duncan Black, Wm. Sowell, Richardson Fry, Presly Caddell, Neill Black, Wm. R. Muse, Daniel McIntosh, Henry Muse, Elias Brewer and J. McIlwennin.

1847, Jun 2 -- Notice, The Weekly Standard [Raleigh, NC] Newspaper
Sheriff's Sale -- on fourth Monday in June next, will be sold at the courthouse in Carthage, the following tracts of land for taxes due for 1845: [selected tracts] 350 acres of Thomas McNeill on Bear Creek; 275 acres of Wm. L. Wallace on Locust Branch; 275 acres of Murdock McLeod on Buffalo Creek; 368 acres of Cheek Hardin on Deep River; William Wadsworth, Sheriff...May 1847.

1849 -- Tax List, Moore County, NC
Wm. L. Wallace listed 1 white poll in District 9

1849, Apr 27 -- 1847-1849 Court of Pleas and Quarter Sessions, Moore County, NC Page 422
Ordered that Presley Caddell be appointed overseer of the road from McQueen's Branch to the Richland Creek Bridge and work the following hands: George McIntosh, Joseph Caddell, Quimby Sowell, Duncan McIntosh, Jesse Muse, William L. Wallace, Duncan Black, William Sowell, Richson Fry, Neill Black, William Richardson, David McIntosh, Henry Muse, Elias Brewer, J. McIlwennin and Stephen Davis' hands.

1850, Nov 8 -- Census, Moore County, NC Page 237
William L. Wallis 27 M, Farmer, born in North Carolina
Josiah Wallis 16 M, Farmer, born in North Carolina
Celia Wallis 15 F, born in North Carolina
Everett Wallis 12 M, born in North Carolina
William J. Wallis 10 M, born in North Carolina
Elizabeth Smith 32 F, born in North Carolina
Mary Smith 3 F, born in North Carolina
Missouri Smith 1 F, born in North Carolina
Mary Davis 40 F, born in North Carolina
James Davis 1 M, born in North Carolina

1851, Spring -- 1834-1851 State Docket County Court, Moore County, NC Page 542
State v. William L. Wallace and Polly Davis [fornication]
State v. William L. Wallace and Elizabeth Smith [fornication]

1852 -- Tax List, Moore County, NC
Wm. L. Wallace listed 1 white poll in District 9

(photographed April 8, 2009)

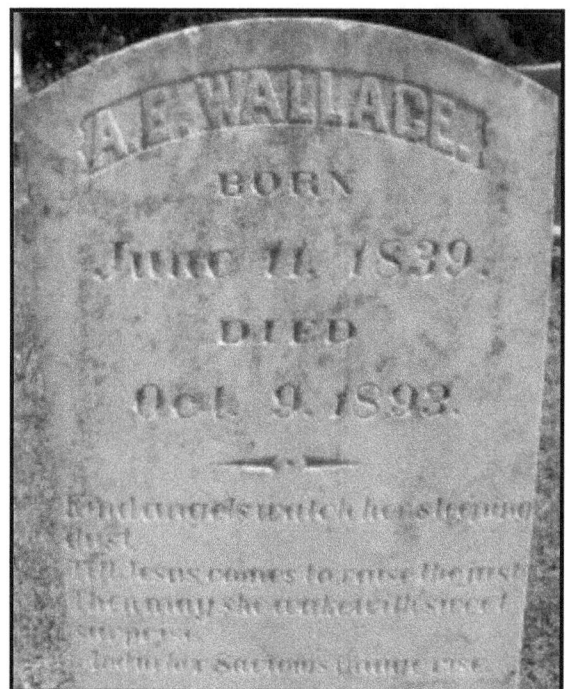

1853, Aug 27 -- Superior Court Minute Docket Book K Page 176, 178
State v. William L. Wallace and Polly Davis; State v. William L. Wallace and Elizabeth Smith. Continued Aug 22, 1854 Page 208

1854, Oct -- 1854-1856 County Court Execution Docket, Moore County, NC Page 56-57
Quimby Wallace v. John Cockman. Witnesses: George W. Horner, Robert L. Purvis, Henry Brown (of Wm.), Presley Caddell, John Garner, James Melton, Wm. L. Wallace and Isham Wallace.

1855, Jul 21 -- Teaching Contract, Moore County, NC
Artimas S. Caddell contracted with the following employers to teach a school of spelling, reading, writing and arithmetic for the term of sixty days: Jesse Muse 1 scholar, Duncan Black 2 scholars, James Dowdy 1 scholars, D.F. Muse 1.5 scholars, Miles Muse 1.5 scholars, James M. Muse 1.5 scholars, Wm. L. Wallis 1.5 scholars, Cornelius Black 1 scholar, Lemuel Sowell 1 scholar and James T. Jackson .5 scholar. [Editor's Note: Papers of Artemus Caddell, Special Collections, David M. Rubenstein Library, Duke University, Durham, NC]

1856, Apr -- Teaching Contract, Moore County, NC
A.S. Caddell contracted with the following employers to teach a school of spelling, reading, writing and arithmetic for the term of one, two or three months: Daniel McIntosh 1 scholar, Wm. Moore 4 scholars, Miles Muse 1 scholar, Duncan Black 1.5 scholars, Wm. R. Sowell .5 scholar, D.F. Muse 1 scholar, Wm. L. Wallis 1 scholar, Joseph Lawhorn 1 scholar and Neill Smith 1 scholar. [Editor's Note: Papers of Artemus Caddell, Special Collections, David M. Rubenstein Library, Duke University, Durham, NC]

1860, Aug -- Bethlehem Baptist Church Minutes, Moore County, NC Page 112
Wm. L. Wallis joined by experience

1860, Sep 1 -- Census, Moore County, NC Page 222, Mooshounie Post Office
Wm. L. Wallace 45 M, Laborer, $100 Personal Property, born in North Carolina
Elizabeth Wallace 30 F, born in North Carolina
William Wallace 20 M, born in North Carolina
Mary Wallace 13 F, born in North Carolina
Missourie Wallace 12 F, born in North Carolina
Racy Wallace 9 M, born in North Carolina
Thomas W. Wallace 7 M, born in North Carolina
Susanna Wallace 5 F, born in North Carolina
Nelson V. Wallace 3 M, born in North Carolina
Ira Wallace 2/12 M, born in North Carolina
Mary Smith 74 F, born in North Carolina
(Next Door)
1860, Sep 1 -- Census, Moore County, NC Page 222-B, Mooshaunee Post Office
Mary Davis 45 F, $50 Personal Property, born in North Carolina
James Davis 11 M, born in North Carolina

1861, Jun 3 -- Civil War Service Records
William L. Wallace (resident of Moore County, NC) enlisted in Company H, 26th Regiment NC Troops in Moore County, NC at age 50

1863, July 3 -- Civil War Service Records
William L. Wallace was hospitalized for Hepatitis, Chimborazo Hospital, Richmond, VA. He was transferred to another hospital Richmond, VA on Aug 31, 1863

1865 -- William L. Wallace moved to Hamer, SC per family notes

1880, Jun 14 -- Census, Marion County, SC Page 83-D Harleeville Township
Wm. W. Wallace 76 M, Head, Works on Farm, born in North Carolina, father & mother born in North Carolina
Betty Wallace 50 F, Wife, Works on Farm, born in North Carolina, father & mother born in North Carolina
Needam V. Wallace 20 M, Son, Works on Farm, born in North Carolina, father & mother born in North Carolina
Archie Y. Wallace 15 M, Son, Works on Farm, born in North Carolina, father & mother born in North Carolina
Elizabeth Wallace 8 F, Granddaughter, born in South Carolina, father & mother born in South Carolina
Ira Wallace 18 M, Son, Works on Farm, born in North Carolina, father & mother born in North Carolina

Delphy Lakey and William Lane Wallace had the following children:

+2   Josiah Wallace (1834-bef 1866) married Ann Miranda Muse (b. 1838) and had one daughter. Josiah served in Company J, 19th Regiment, 2nd Calvary during the Civil War and died shortly after the war.

+3   Celia C. Wallace (1835-aft 1900) had two children with Devotion D. Davis (1828-1875) and they were later married. After Devotion died, she married Jesse B. Watkins.

Annie Elizabeth Smith was born in 1818. She died on October 9, 1893 and was buried in Little Rock, Dillon County, SC at Saint Paul's Methodist Church.[137] She and William Lane Wallace had the following children:

+4   Everett W. Wallace (1837-1916) seemed to follow in the footsteps of his father, was married twice and possibly at the same time. He married Nancy Lett (b. 1843) in 1860 and had two sons. He also had four children with Martha Walker (1842-1920) during the same period of time and appears to have been married to her also. Everett served in Company I, 22nd Regiment during the Civil War. He and Martha moved to western North Carolina after the war and they are buried at Patty's Chapel Methodist Church in Henderson County, NC.

+5   William W. Wallace (1840-) married Elizabeth Jane Horner (1848-1893) and had one daughter. William served in Company D, 3rd Regiment during the Civil War. He remained in Moore County after his parents relocated to South Carolina.

+6   Mary "Duck" Wallace (1846-1926) married William Albert Hamilton (1858-1932) and they were the parents of nine children. The Hamiltons are buried at Saint Paul's Methodist Church in Little Rock, SC.

+7   Missouri Mazura "Mo" Smith Wallace (1848-1937) married John Taylor (1846-1908) and their union produced seven children. They are buried at Little Rock Baptist Church in Little Rock, SC.

+8   Thomas Walter Wallace (1853-1925) married Flora Jane Huggins (1850-1926) and they had eight children. They are buried at Riverside Cemetery in Dillon, SC.

+9   Wesley Royce "Race" Wallace (1854-1915) married Maggie Lester (1861-1905) and they were the parents of ten children. After Maggie's death, Race married Lottie Proctor (1884-1939). Race and Maggie are buried at Baker Cemetery in Dillon, SC.

+10   Susanna Wallace (aft 1855-bef 1900) married William E. Bain (b. 1851) and they produce six children.

+11   Needham Evander Wallace (1858-1920) married Hannah J. (b. 1864) later in life. He is buried at Saint Paul's Methodist Church in Little Rock, SC.

+12   Arrie Lane Wallace (1861-1938) married Nellie Wood Houston (1865-1928) and they were the parents of nine children. They are also buried at Saint Paul's Methodist Church in Little Rock, SC.

+13   Archie Young Wallace (1865-1925) married Anna Elizabeth Norton (1861-1934) and their union produced seven children. Archie and Annie are buried at Saint Paul's Methodist Church in Little Rock, SC.

Mary Davis was born between 1810 and 1815. William Lane Wallace is also believed to have been the father of James Davis. Mary and James are listed in the 1850 and 1860 census records, but no additional information has been located.

+14   James Davis (1849-)

Second Generation

2. **Josiah Wallace**, son of William Lane Wallace and Delphy Lakey, was born in 1834. He married **Ann Miranda Muse** on August 25, 1855 in Moore County, NC[138]. He served in the Company I. 19th Regiment during the Civil War and died before July 1866. [139]

1850, Nov 8 -- Census, Moore County, NC Page 237
William L. Wallis 27 M, Farmer, born in North Carolina
Josiah Wallis 16 M, Farmer, born in North Carolina
Celia Wallis 15 F, born in North Carolina
Everett Wallis 12 M, born in North Carolina
William J. Wallis 10 M, born in North Carolina

Elizabeth Smith 32 F, born in North Carolina
Mary Smith 3 F, born in North Carolina
Missouri Smith 1 F, born in North Carolina
Mary Davis 40 F, born in North Carolina
James Davis 1 M, born in North Carolina

1855 -- Tax List, Moore County, NC
Josiah Wallace Jr. listed 1 white poll on Richland Creek in District 9

1855, Feb 20 -- Superior Court Minute Docket, Moore County, NC
State v. W. L. Wallace, Josiah Wallace & Elias Moore

1855, August 25 -- Marriage Register, Moore County, NC Page 28
Josiah Wallace and Ann M. Muse by William Brewer, JP

1855, Oct 22 -- 1853-1856 Court of Pleas and Quarter Sessions, Moore County, NC Page 383
Ordered that William R. Sowell be appointed overseer of the road from the mouth of Kelly's lane to McQueen's Branch and work the
following hands: Daniel McIntosh, W.H. Muse, Neil Black, Noah F. Muse, George Williams, Bryant Caddell, Devotion Davis, John M. Davis,
Jason Sowell, Lendo Sowell, Abraham Fry, Eli Sowell, D.F. Muse, Artemas S. Caddell, Kindred Muse, Neodom Yarn, James Dowdy hands,
Jefferson Williams, Josiha Wallace and Joseph Fry.

1857, May 2 -- 1856-1858 Court of Pleas and Quarter Sessions, Moore County, NC Page 214
Ordered that Neill Black be appointed overseer of the road from the mouth of Kelly's lane to McQueen's Branch and work the following
hands: Chestly T. Horner, Daniel McIntosh, Wm. H. Muse, Noah F. Muse, George Williams, Bryant Caddell, Devotion Davis, John Davis,
Jason Sowell, Lendo Sowell, Absalom Fry, Eli Sowell, D.F. Muse, Artemas S. Caddell, Kindred Muse, Nedom Vann, James Dowdy hands,
Wm. Sowell hands, Jefferson Williams, Josiah Wallace and Joseph C. Fry.

1860, Jul 30 -- Agricultural Census, Moore County, NC Page 29, Pharrs Mill Post Office
Silas Wallace listed 10 acres Improved valued at $15

1860, Aug 1 -- Census, Moore County, NC Page 197, Prosperity Post Office
Silas Wallace 26 M, Farmer, $100 Personal Property, born in North Carolina
Miranda Wallace 22 F, born in North Carolina
Martha A. Wallace 1 F, born in North Carolina

1861, Aug-Dec -- Minutes, Bethlehem Baptist Church, Carthage, NC Page 120, 125
"One complaint against Josiah Wallas for getting drunk. [Dec 1861] Josiah Wallace's case taken up he had been cited to attend trial and
refused to come and give a straight answer to the request and the church moved and seconded that he be excluded, and he was voted out
of fellowship."

1862, Jan 24 -- Civil War Service Records
Josiah Wallace (resident of Moore County, NC) enlisted in Company I, 19th Regiment in New Bern, Craven County, NC at age 28

1863, Jan 31-Mar 9 -- Civil War Service Records
Josiah Wallace admitted to Chimborazo Hospital #3, Richmond, VA for Debililas

1866, Jul -- Superior Court Minute Docket Book M, Moore County, NC Page 215
Maranda Wallace petition for year's allowance [Editor's Note: likely meant she was a widow]

Ann Miranda Muse, daughter of James H. Muse (1802-) and Patience Fry (1802-1860), was born in 1838. She died after
1866. She and Josiah Wallace had the following child:

+15   Martha A. Wallace (1859-)

3. **Celia C. Wallace**, daughter of William Lane Wallace and Delphy Lakey, was born in 1835. She married **Jesse B. Watkins**
on January 10, 1878 in Moore County, NC.[140] She died after 1900.

1850, Nov 8 -- Census, Moore County, NC Page 237
William L. Wallis 27 M, Farmer, born in North Carolina
Josiah Wallis 16 M, Farmer, born in North Carolina
Celia Wallis 15 F, born in North Carolina
Everett Wallis 12 M, born in North Carolina
William J. Wallis 10 M, born in North Carolina
Elizabeth Smith 32 F, born in North Carolina
Mary Smith 3 F, born in North Carolina

Missouri Smith 1 F, born in North Carolina
Mary Davis 40 F, born in North Carolina
James Davis 1 M, born in North Carolina

1855, Jul 30 -- School Roster, Moore County, NC
List of school attendees and days attending during session: Artimas S. Caddell [teacher] 35 days, A.B. Muse 24 days, Cornelius D. Caddell 24 days, Ashley Muse 24 days, Commadore Muse 25 days, Ann E. Muse 34 days, Tempy Muse 30 days, Elizabeth Muse 35 days, John Muse 15 days, Maranda A. Muse 15 days, Celia Walis 16 days, Evret Walis 1 day, John Muse 26 days, Candis Muse 27 days, Archibald Dowdy 30 days, Caroline Dowdy 21 days, Jane Dowdy 24 days, Arcibal Muse 21 days, Joseph P. Sowell 15 days, Javan Sowell 22 days, Asa T. Sowell 16 days, Jefferson M. Williams 5 days, Martha Black 19 days, Wm. Black 18 days, Alexander Black 17 days, James T. Jackson 11 days and Sophia Muse 2 days. [Editor's Note: Papers of Artemus Caddell, Special Collections, David M. Rubenstein Library, Duke University, Durham, NC]

1857, Apr 28 -- 1856-1858 Court of Pleas and Quarter Sessions, Moore County, NC Page 187
State v. Devotion Davis. Bastardy. Ordered to support Cela Lakey. R.A. Cole was bondsman.

1860, Jul 6 -- Census, Moore County, NC Page 200, Carthage Post Office
Celia Wallace 21 F, Nothing(Occupation), $50 Personal Property, born in North Carolina
Devotion D. Wallace 4 M, born in North Carolina
(Next Door)
1860, Jul 6 -- Census, Moore County, NC Page 200, Carthage Post Office
Devotion Davis 31 M, Deals in Mill Stone, $1500 Real Estate, $800 Personal Property, born in North Carolina
Stephen Davis 16 M, Farm Laborer, born in North Carolina, Attended school within year
Malcolm Davis 18 M, Student, born in North Carolina, Attended school within year

1866, Fall -- 1862-1870 Superior Court Execution Docket, Moore County, NC Page 224
#18 State v. Devotion Davis and Selah Wallace. Continued Fall 1869 Page 289 #39 -- Fall 1870 Page 403 #39

1870, Jul 2 -- Agricultural Census, Moore County, NC Page 7, Carthage Township, Carthage Post Office
Celia Wallis listed 10 acres Improved valued at $100

1870, Jul 6 -- Census, Moore County, NC Page 509, Carthage Township, Carthage Post Office
Celia C. Wallis 31 F, Housekeeper, $250 Personal Property, born in North Carolina
Harrison Wallis 13 M, born in North Carolina
Mary A. Wallis 7 F, born in North Carolina
Haywood Hub 12 M (black), born in North Carolina
(Next Door)
1870, Jul 6 -- Census, Moore County, NC Page 509-B, Carthage Township, Carthage Post Office
Devotion Davis 42 M, Millstone Cutter, $800 Real Estate, $150 Personal Property, born in North Carolina

1873, Mar 14 -- Deed Book 14 Page 415, Moore County, NC
Devotion Davis deeded John McL. Kelly and James D. McIver the following land and mill stone interest: 10 acres including the quarries near Friendship Church, 12 acres including Jesse Seawell Quarry, another Quarry northeast of Seawell Quarry and mill stone interest in the Freeman land. Celia Wallace was a witness.

1873, May 19 -- Will Book D Page 66-67, Moore County, NC
Will of Devotion Davis Dec'd. Heirs: wife Ceily, son Harrison and daughter Mary Ann. Executor: James D. McIver. Witnesses: W.J. Stuart and C.T. Horner. Proven Apr 13, 1875.

1875, May 19-Jun 26 -- Orders and Decrees Book 1 Page 507-509, Moore County, NC
Celia Davis, widow of Devotion Davis, Dec'd. Application for year's allowance. Jesse Muse Esq., John Jones and Asa McIntosh appointed to review the estate.

1875, May 22 -- 1868-1876 Record of Accounts Page 518-520, Moore County, NC
Estate of Devotion Davis, Dec'd. by Administrator Celia Davis. Items were purchased by the following: W.K. Nunnery, Mary Ann Davis, Harison Davis, I.H. Caddell and Willie Ritter.

1875, Jul 6-Jul 7, 1877 -- Orders and Decrees Book 1 Page 337,398,504, Moore County, NC
S.W. Seawell, administrator of W.H.H. Davis v. John M. Davis. Celia Davis and I.H. Caddell were appointed guardian ad litem to infants Harrison, Mary A. Davis and I.H. Caddell to Charley, Edmond and Oscar Caddell.

1877, Apr 28 -- 1876-1885 Record of Accounts Page 38, Moore County, NC
Estate of Devotion Davis, Dec'd. by administrator Celia Davis. Notes were held on the following: S. McIntosh, S.D. Wallace, John Cole, M. McFarland, J.M. Davis, John H. Short, K.H. Williams and A.A.F. Sowell.

1878, Jan 10 -- Marriages, Carthaginian [Carthage, NC] Newspaper

"At the Methodist Parsonage this evening by Rev. John Tillett. Mr. Watkins to Mrs. Celia Davis"

1878, Aug 12 -- Judgement Docket, Moore County, NC
John M. Davis & S.W. Seawell v. Celia Davis, widow of Devotion Davis

1880, Jun 17 -- Census, Moore County, NC Page 302, McNeills Township, Town of Manly Station
W.H. Davis 23 M, Head, Married, Blacksmith, born in North Carolina, father & mother born in North Carolina
Alice Davis 19 F, Wife, Married, Housekeeping, born in North Carolina, father & mother born in North Carolina
Austin Davis 10/12 (Aug) M, Son, Single, born in North Carolina, father & mother born in North Carolina
Ceilie Davis 45 F, mother, Married, Housekeeping, born in North Carolina, father & mother born in North Carolina

1890, Apr 3 -- Deed Book 1 Page 509-510, Moore County, NC
Jesse B. and Celia Watkins deeded George H. Kemp 7.5 acres in McNeills Township near the Town of Manly and the Boling Spring Branch. C.W. Shaw was a witness.

1894, Mar 1 -- Deed Book 11, Page 393-394, Moore County, NC
William W. Wallace and Celia Watkins deeded John R. Lane (Chatham County) 2 tracts adjoining Hill, T.M. Fry, John R. Lane, Riley Muse. [1] 150 acres located on Richland Creek and Meadow Branch being part of George Ritter's 250 acres [2] 70 acres on Richland Creek and the Horsepen Branch being part of George Ritter's 250 acres adjoining John R. Lane, T.M. Fry, Hill and McIntosh. Leonard Lane, A.G. Ellis and W.H. Davis were witnesses.

1898 -- Bransons Business Directory, Moore County, NC
Celia Watkins (Carthage Post Office) listed as owning 33 acres valued at $115 in Carthage Township

1900, Jun 1 -- Census, Moore County, NC Page 19-B, West Carthage Precinct
Celia C. Watkins 64 F, Jun 1836, Head, Widowed, 2 Children (1 living), born in North Carolina, father & mother born in North Carolina, Farmer
Florence Huffstickler 15 F, Oct 1884, Granddaughter, Single, born in North Carolina, father & mother born in North Carolina
Laura L. Huffstickler 12 F, Jun 1888, Granddaughter, Single, born in North Carolina, father & mother born in North Carolina
Jennie D. Huffstickler 9 F, Feb 1891, Granddaughter, Single, born in North Carolina, father & mother born in North Carolina
Gracie Huffstickler 4 F, Aug 1895, Granddaughter, Single, born in North Carolina, father & mother born in North Carolina
Hattie D. Huffstickler 2 F, Apr 1898, Step-Granddaughter, Single, born in North Carolina, father & mother born in North Carolina

Devotion D. Davis, son of Stephen Davis (1793-bef 1853), was born in 1828. He died before April 13, 1875 and was buried in Moore County, NC at Davis Cemetery #72.[141] He and Celia C. Wallace had the following children:

+16   William Harrison Davis (1856-1933)
+17   Mary Ann Davis (1863-1895)

4. **Everett W. Wallace**, son of William Lane Wallace and Annie Elizabeth Smith, was born on March 8, 1837 in Moore County, NC. He married **Nancy Lett** on August 30, 1860 in Moore County, NC.[142] [143]He was also married to Martha Walker. He died on January 6, 1916 in Transylvania County, NC and was buried on January 7, 1916 in Henderson County, NC at Patty's Chapel Methodist Church.[144] Everett served Company I, 22nd Regiment during the Civil War. [145]

RECORDS OF EVERETT W. WALLACE

1850, Nov 8 -- Census, Moore County, NC Page 237
William L. Wallis 27 M, Farmer, born in North Carolina
Josiah Wallis 16 M, Farmer, born in North Carolina
Celia Wallis 15 F, born in North Carolina
Everett Wallis 12 M, born in North Carolina
William J. Wallis 10 M, born in North Carolina
Elizabeth Smith 32 F, born in North Carolina
Mary Smith 3 F, born in North Carolina
Missouri Smith 1 F, born in North Carolina
Mary Davis 40 F, born in North Carolina
James Davis 1 M, born in North Carolina

1855, Jul 30 -- School Roster, Moore County, NC
List of school attendees and days attending during session: Artimas S. Caddell [teacher] 35 days, A.B. Muse 24 days, Cornelius D. Caddell 24 days, Ashley Muse 24 days, Commadore Muse 25 days, Ann E. Muse 34 days, Tempy Muse 30 days, Elizabeth Muse 35 days, John Muse 15 days, Maranda A. Muse 15 days, Celia Walis 16 days, Evret Walis 1 day, John Muse 26 days, Candis Muse 27 days, Archibald Dowdy 30 days, Caroline Dowdy 21 days, Jane Dowdy 24 days, Arcibal Muse 21 days, Joseph P. Sowell 15 days, Javan Sowell 22 days, Asa T. Sowell 16 days, Jefferson M. Williams 5 days, Martha Black 19 days, Wm. Black 18 days, Alexander Black 17 days, James T. Jackson 11 days and

Sophia Muse 2 days. [Editor's Note: Papers of Artemus Caddell, Special Collections, David M. Rubenstein Library, Duke University, Durham, NC]

1860, Jun 14 -- Census, Moore County, NC Page 150 Long Street Post Office
Abel Kelly 56 M, Milling, $5000 Real Estate, $1500 Personal Property, born in North Carolina
Elizabeth Kelly 50 F, born in North Carolina
Martha Kelly 22 F, born in North Carolina
Delila J. Kelly 20 F, born in North Carolina
James H. Kelly 12 M, born in North Carolina
Abel A. Kelly 10 M, born in North Carolina
John M. Kelly 8 M, born in North Carolina
Jordan Parrish 17 M, Farm Laborer, born in North Carolina
Albert Wallace 23 M, Farm Laborer, born in North Carolina
Mark Kelly 63 M, Domestic, born in North Carolina
[Editor's Note: I believe that Albert is actually Everett]

1860, Aug 30 -- Marriage Register, Moore County, NC Page 73
E.W. Wallace and Nancy Lett were married by Thomas Rollins, JP.

1860, Sep 10 -- Marriages, Fayetteville Observer [Fayetteville, NC] Newspaper
"On the 30th of August, by Thomas Rollins, Esq., Mr. E.W. Walles and Miss Nancy Lett, daughter of Jas. Lett, Esq."

1861, Jun 5 -- Civil War Service Records
Everett W. Wallace enlisted in Randolph County, NC, Company I, 22nd Regiment at age 21

1861, Dec 9 -- Civil War Service Records
Everett W. Wallace received wound in thigh at Evansport, VA by "bursting of a forty-two pound gun"

1862, May 1 -- Civil War Service Records
Everett W. Wallace was discharged from Co. I, 22nd Regiment due to disability

1866, Aug 20-Feb 18, 1867 -- Superior Court Minute Docket, Moore County, NC
1867, Spring -- Superior Court Execution Docket, Moore County, NC
State v. Everitt Wallace

1870, Jul 5 -- Census, Madison County, NC Page 378-B, Township #2, White Rock Post Office
Everett W. Wallace 33 M, Farm Laborer, $300 Value Real Estate, born in North Carolina, Eligible to vote
Martha Wallace 25 F, Keeping House, born in North Carolina, Can't Read or Write
Thomas Wallace 9 M, born in North Carolina
Sarah Wallace 7 F, born in North Carolina
Mandy Wallace 3 F, born in North Carolina

1870 Census, Cumberland County, NC Page 165-B
Mary E. Lett 59 F, Keeping House, born in North Carolina
Elizabeth Lett 35 F, Domestic Service, born in North Carolina
Nancy Lett 26 F, Works in Cotton Mill, born in North Carolina
Mary Lett 24 F, Works in Cotton Mill, born in North Carolina
Levina Lett 20 F, Works in Cotton Mill, born in North Carolina
Thomas Lett 18 M, Works in Cotton Mill, born in North Carolina
Lenora Lett 5 F, At Home, born in North Carolina
James Lett 4 M, At Home, born in North Carolina
Charles Lett 2 M, At Home, born in North Carolina

1880, Jun 3 -- Census, Buncombe County, NC Page 82, Limestone Township
E.W. Wallis 44 M, Head, Married, Farmer, born in North Carolina, father & mother born in North Carolina
Martha Wallis 36 F, Wife, Married, Keeping House, born in North Carolina, father & mother born in North Carolina
Manda Wallis 13 F, Dau, Single, born in North Carolina, father & mother born in North Carolina
Lorett Wallis 10 F, Dau, Single, born in North Carolina, father & mother born in North Carolina

1880 Census, Cumberland County, NC Page 546-B, Carvers Creek Township
Nancy Walis 37 F, Head, Married, Keeping House, born in North Carolina, father & mother born in North Carolina
James A. Walis 15 M, Son, Single, Cotton Mill, born in North Carolina, father & mother born in North Carolina
Charles Walis 12 M, Son, Single, Cotton Mill Hand, born in North Carolina, father & mother born in North Carolina

1902, Oct 4 -- Voter Registration Records 1902-1908, Henderson County, NC
E.W. Wallace registered to vote in Hooper's Creek Township

Additional Information can be found at www.MooreCountyWallaces.com

Testified that he had voted in NC on or before Jan 1, 1867

1903, July 6 -- Civil War Pension Records
E.W. Wallace (age 67) applied for Pension at Lynn Post Office, Polk County, NC [146]

1906, July 2 -- Civil War Pension Records
E.W. Wallace (age 70) applied for Pension at Columbus Post Office, Polk County, NC

1910, July 2 -- Civil War Pension Records
E.W. Wallace (age 74) applied for Pension a Hendersonville Post Office, Henderson County, NC

1910 -- Census, Union County, SC Page 225-B, Union Township
Joseph A. Walker 40 M, Head, Married-2nd-1yr, Spooler(Cotton Mill), born in North Carolina, father & mother born in North Carolina
Retta Walker 29 F, Wife, Married-1st-1yr, O Children, born in North Carolina, father & mother born in North Carolina
Essie Walker 18 F, Dau, Single, Spooler(Cotton Mill), born in North Carolina, father & mother born in North Carolina
Clenon Walker 16 M, Single, Doffer(Cotton Mill), born in North Carolina, father & mother born in North Carolina
Homer Walker 14 M, Single, Doffer(Cotton Mill), born in North Carolina, father & mother born in North Carolina
Bettie Walker 13 F, Single, Spinner(Cotton Mill), born in North Carolina, father & mother born in North Carolina
Porter Walker 12 M, Single, Sweeper(Cotton Mill), born in North Carolina, father & mother born in North Carolina
Curtis Walker 8 F, Single, born in North Carolina, father & mother born in North Carolina
Everett W. Wallace 74 M, fatherL, Married-1st, born in North Carolina, father & mother born in North Carolina
Martha Wallace 72 F, motherL, Married-1st, born in North Carolina, father & mother born in North Carolina

1916, Jan 6 – Death Certificate, Transylvania County, NC
Everett W. Wallace died in Penrose, Little River Township. Married. Date of birth: Mar 8, 1842. Age: 78y 2m 8d. Occupation: farmer. Birthplace: Moore County, NC. father: William Wallace. mother: Betsy Wallace. Cause of Death: Lober Pneumonia, Vascular Disease of Heart (contributing). Place of Burial: Patty's Chapel. Date of Burial: Jan 7, 1916. Undertaker: George Phillips, Penrose. Informant: Mrs. J.L. Cannon, Penrose

1916, July 3 -- Civil War Widow's Pension Records
Martha E. Wallace (age 75) applied for Widow's Pension for E.W. Wallace at Ettawah Post Office, Henderson County, NC

1917, July 2 -- Civil War Widow's Pension Records
Martha E. Wallace (age 76) applied for Widow's Pension for E.W. Wallace at Blantine Post Office, Transylvania County, NC

1920 -- Census, Henderson County, NC Page 101, Hendersonville Township
James L. Cannon 66 M, Head, Married, Laborer-General Farm, born in North Carolina, father & mother born in North Carolina
Sarah Cannon 55 F, Wife, Married, born in North Carolina, father & mother born in North Carolina
Wade Cannon 36 M, Son, Married, Laborer-General Farm, born in North Carolina, father & mother born in North Carolina
Daisy Cannon 32 F, DauL, Married, born in North Carolina, father & mother born in North Carolina
Stella Cannon 13 F, GrDau, Single, born in North Carolina, father & mother born in North Carolina
Connie Cannon 10 M, GrSon, Single, born in North Carolina, father & mother born in North Carolina
James Cannon 8 M, GrSon, Single, born in North Carolina, father & mother born in North Carolina
Edna Cannon 5 F, GrDau, Single, born in North Carolina, father & mother born in North Carolina
Harry Cannon 3 M, GrSon, Single, born in North Carolina, father & mother born in North Carolina
E - -(sp) Cannon 10/12 M, GrSon, Single, born in North Carolina, father & mother born in North Carolina
Martha Wallace 79 F, motherL, Widowed, born in North Carolina, father & mother born in North Carolina

Martha E. Walker, daughter of John Walker (1818-) and Sarah Allen (1819-), was born in 1842 in North Carolina. She died on March 4, 1920 in Henderson County, NC and was buried on March 6, 1920 in Henderson County, NC at Patty's Chapel Methodist Church. [147] She and Everett W. Wallace had the following children:

+18	Thomas Wallace (1861-)	
+19	Sarah Wallace (1863-1938)	
+20	Amanda Louise Wallace (1867-1944)	
+21	Loretta Wallace (1870-bef 1920)	

Nancy Lett, daughter of James Lett (1800-bef 1870) and Mary McNeill (1810-), was born in 1843. She and Everett W. Wallace had the following children:

+22	James A. Wallace (1866-)	
+23	Charles Chalmers Wallace (1869-1930)	

5. **William W. Wallace**, son of William Lane Wallace and Annie Elizabeth Smith, was born in 1840. William served in Company D, 3rd Regiment during the Civil War. [148]

RECORDS OF WILLIAM WALLACE

1850, Nov 8 -- Census, Moore County, NC Page 237
William L. Wallis 27 M, Farmer, born in North Carolina
Josiah Wallis 16 M, Farmer, born in North Carolina
Celia Wallis 15 F, born in North Carolina
Everett Wallis 12 M, born in North Carolina
William J. Wallis 10 M, born in North Carolina
Elizabeth Smith 32 F, born in North Carolina
Mary Smith 3 F, born in North Carolina
Missouri Smith 1 F, born in North Carolina
Mary Davis 40 F, born in North Carolina
James Davis 1 M, born in North Carolina

1860, Sep 1 -- Census, Moore County, NC Page 222, Mooshounie Post Office
Wm. L. Wallace 45 M, Laborer, $100 Value of Personal Property, born in North Carolina
Elizabeth Wallace 30 F, born in North Carolina
William Wallace 20 M, born in North Carolina
Mary Wallace 13 F, born in North Carolina
Missourie Wallace 12 F, born in North Carolina
Racy Wallace 9 M, born in North Carolina
Thomas W. Wallace 7 M, born in North Carolina
Susanna Wallace 5 F, born in North Carolina
Nelson V. Wallace 3 M, born in North Carolina
Ira Wallace 2/12 M, born in North Carolina
Mary Smith 74 F, born in North Carolina
(Next Door)
1860, Sep 1 -- Census, Moore County, NC Page 222-B, Mooshaunee Post Office
Mary Davis 45 F, $50 Personal Property, born in North Carolina
James Davis 11 M, born in North Carolina

1861, Mar -- Minutes, Bethlehem Baptist Church, Carthage, NC Page 116
"One complaint against Wm. Wallace (Junior) for swearing, fighting and drinking and had been investigated and said Bro. acknowledged to all and said he thought he was mistaken and had no Religion and requested his name taken off of the church book. The church granted him his request by excommunicating him."

1861, Apr -- Minutes, Bethlehem Baptist Church, Carthage, NC Page 118
"One complaint against Wm. Wallace for getting drunk and dancing and he is refused baptism."

1861, Jun 20-May 16, 1865 -- Civil War Service Records
William Wallace enlisted in Company D, 3rd Regiment in Asheboro, NC on Jun 20, 1861. Present and accounted for through Jul 14, 1862. By Oct 31, 1862 was absent as he had been sent home to Randolph County due to sickness. Furloughed from Wayside Hospital, Richmond, VA on Sep 30, 1862. Admitted to Medical Director's Office in Richmond, VA on Feb 18, 1863 and transferred to Chimborazo Hospital, Richmond, VA for Rheumatism on Apr 2, 1863. Released from Wayside Hospital, Richmond, VA in Jul 1863 but did not return to duty. Wounded on May 5, 1864 by gunshot wound to the chest. Admitted to CSA General Hospital, Charlottesville, VA on Jun 6, 1864 and transferred to Lynchburg, VA. Transferred to CSA General Hospital, Danville, VA on Jun 16, 1864. Transferred to Pettigrew General Hospital, Raleigh, NC on Jun 28, 1864 then on to Greensboro, NC. Paroled as a Prisoner of War on May 16, 1865 as a result of the end of the Civil War.

1870, Aug 6 -- Agricultural Census, Moore County, NC Page 3, Ritters Township, Carters Mills Post Office
Wm. Wallis listed 8 acres Improved valued at $25

1870, Aug 9 -- Census, Moore County, NC Page 577, Ritters Township, Carters Mill Post Office
William Wallis 24 M, Farmer, $50 Personal Property, born in North Carolina
Elizabeth Wallis 23 F, born in North Carolina
Celia A. Wallis 3 F, born in North Carolina

1880, Jun 12 -- Census, Moore County, NC Page 337, Ritters Township
William Wallace 41 M, Head, Farmer, born in North Carolina, father & mother born in North Carolina
Jane Wallace 32 F, Wife, Keeps House, born in North Carolina, father & mother born in North Carolina
Annie Wallace 14 F, Dau, born in North Carolina, father & mother born in North Carolina

1880, Jun 12 -- Agricultural Census, Moore County, NC Page 9, Ritters Township
William Wallace listed renting for fixed money 4 acres Improved Fields, 5 acres Unimproved Wooded

1885, Nov 20 -- Orders and Decrees Book 2 Page 305,308-310, Moore County, NC
M.M.L. Kelly, Edmond Waddell and B.P. Phillips commissioner to partition land of George W. Horner, Dec'd. located on Meadow Branch and the Plank Road adjoining S. Cockman. Heirs: Sarah Francis Horner (Widow), G.B. Horner, James W. Horner, John and Nancy Kennedy, Eli and Frances Cockman, W.W. and Jane Wallace, heirs of George Wallace (J.C. Wallace, S.A. Wallace), A.J. and Catherine Williams and T.W. Horner.

1886, Sep 18 -- 1875-1895 Appointment of Road Overseers, Moore County, NC Page 68
Ordered that Emerson Jones be appointed overseer of the new road from Plank Road at Isham Wallace's to township line and have the following hands to work: W.J. Black, Lurrence Jones and William Wallace.

1890, Aug 2 -- 1875-1895 Appointment of Road Overseers, Moore County, NC Page 89
Ordered that W.W. Wallace be appointed overseer of the Plank Road to the township line and have the following hands to work: Ed Jones.

1891, Jul 6 -- Record of Pensions, Moore County, NC
W.W. Wallace, Carters Mills PO, Company D, 3rd Regiment, Class 4 applied for a pension for year 1891

1892, Jul 11 -- Record of Pensions, Moore County, NC
W.W. Wallace, Horners PO, Company D, 3rd Regiment, Class 4 applied for a pension for year 1892

1893, Aug 25 -- Record of Pensions, Moore County, NC
W.W. Wallace, Horners PO, Company D, 3rd Regiment, Class 4 applied for a pension for year 1893

1894, Mar 1 -- Deed Book 11, Page 393-394, Moore County, NC
William W. Wallace and Celia Watkins deeded John R. Lane (Chatham County) 2 tracts adjoining Hill, T.M. Fry, John R. Lane, Riley Muse. [1] 150 acres located on Richland Creek and Meadow Branch being part of George Ritter's 250 acres [2] 70 acres on Richland Creek and the Horsepen Branch being part of George Ritter's 250 acres adjoining John R. Lane, T.M. Fry, Hill and McIntosh. Leonard Lane, A.G. Ellis and W.H. Davis were witnesses.

1897 -- Record of Pensions, Moore County, NC
W.W. Wallace, Carthage PO, Company D, 3rd Regiment, Class 4 received pension for year 1897

1898, Jul 30 -- Record of Pensions, Moore County, NC
W.W. Wallace, Carthage PO, Company D, 3rd Regiment, Class 4 received pension for year 1898

1900 -- Record of Pensions, Moore County, NC
W.W. Wallace, Carthage PO, Company D, 3rd Regiment, Class 4 received pension for year 1900

1901, Jul 1 -- Record of Pensions, Moore County, NC
W.W. Wallace's pension application was disapproved

Elizabeth Jane Horner, daughter of George Washington Horner (1817-1885) and Mary Ann Ritter (1821-), was born on November 2, 1848. She died on January 4, 1893 and was buried in Moore County, NC at Horner Cemetery #243.[149] She and William W. Wallace had the following child:

+24   Celia Ann Wallace (1866-)

6. **Mary "Duck" Wallace**, daughter of William Lane Wallace and Annie Elizabeth Smith, was born on March 15, 1846. She died on June 12, 1926 and was buried on June 13, 1926 in Little Rock, Dillon County, SC at Saint Paul's Methodist Church.[150]

RECORDS OF MARY WALLACE

1850, Nov 8 -- Census, Moore County, NC Page 237
William L. Wallis 27 M, Farmer, born in North Carolina
Josiah Wallis 16 M, Farmer, born in North Carolina
Celia Wallis 15 F, born in North Carolina
Everett Wallis 12 M, born in North Carolina
William J. Wallis 10 M, born in North Carolina
Elizabeth Smith 32 F, born in North Carolina
Mary Smith 3 F, born in North Carolina
Missouri Smith 1 F, born in North Carolina

Mary Davis 40 F, born in North Carolina
James Davis 1 M, born in North Carolina

1860, Sep 1 -- Census, Moore County, NC Page 222, Mooshounie Post Office
Wm. L. Wallace 45 M, Laborer, $100 Value of Personal Property, born in North Carolina
Elizabeth Wallace 30 F, born in North Carolina
William Wallace 20 M, born in North Carolina
Mary Wallace 13 F, born in North Carolina
Missourie Wallace 12 F, born in North Carolina
Racy Wallace 9 M, born in North Carolina
Thomas W. Wallace 7 M, born in North Carolina
Susanna Wallace 5 F, born in North Carolina
Nelson V. Wallace 3 M, born in North Carolina
Ira Wallace 2/12 M, born in North Carolina
Mary Smith 74 F, born in North Carolina
(Next Door)
1860, Sep 1 -- Census, Moore County, NC Page 222-B, Mooshaunee Post Office
Mary Davis 45 F, $50 Personal Property, born in North Carolina
James Davis 11 M, born in North Carolina

1880 -- Census, Marion County, SC Page 195-C, Manning Township
Albert Hamilton 25 M, Head, Married, Farm Laborer, born in South Carolina, father & mother born in South Carolina
Duck Hamilton 30 F, Wife, Married, Keeping House, born in South Carolina, father & mother born in South Carolina
Mary Hamilton 8 F, Dau, Single, born in South Carolina, father & mother born in South Carolina
John Hamilton 6 M, Son, Single, born in South Carolina, father & mother born in South Carolina
Ida Hamilton 4 F, Dau, Single, born in South Carolina, father & mother born in South Carolina
Minnie Hamilton 4/12 F, Dau, Single, born in South Carolina, father & mother born in South Carolina

1900 -- Census, Robeson County, NC Page 182, Alfordsville Township
Albert Hamilton 42 M, May 1858, Head, Married-17yrs, Farm Laborer, born in North Carolina, father & mother born in North Carolina
Mary Hamilton 32 F, Apr 1868, Wife, Married-17yrs, 4 Children(4 Living), born in North Carolina, father & mother born in North Carolina
Race Hamilton 18 M, Mar 1882, Son, Single, Farm Laborer, born in North Carolina, father & mother born in North Carolina
Loler Hamilton 15 F, May 1885, Dau, Single, Farm Laborer, born in North Carolina, father & mother born in North Carolina
Kelly Hamilton 14 F, Jan 1886, Dau, Single, Farm Laborer, born in North Carolina, father & mother born in North Carolina
Evander Hamilton 10 M, Jan 1890, Son, Single, born in North Carolina, father & mother born in North Carolina

1910 -- Census, Dillon County, SC Page 112, Manning Township, Little Rock Road
Albert Hamilton 51 M, Head, Married-1st-34yrs, Farmer(Farm), born in South Carolina, father & mother born in South Carolina
Mary Hamilton 65 F, Wife, Married-1st-34yrs, 10 Children(7 Living), born in South Carolina, father & mother born in South Carolina
Evander Hamilton 19 M, Son, Single, Laborer(Home Farm), born in South Carolina, father & mother born in South Carolina
Loradine Hamilton 6/12 F, GrDau, Single, born in South Carolina, father & mother born in South Carolina

1920 -- Census, Dillon County, SC Page 185-B, Manning Township, Dillon Town
William A. Hamilton 60 M, Head, Married, Farmer-General Farm, born in South Carolina, father & mother born in South Carolina
Mary Hamilton 70 F, Wife, Married, born in North Carolina, father & mother born in North Carolina
Luadine Hamilton 10 F, GrDau, Single, born in South Carolina, father & mother born in South Carolina

William Albert Hamilton was born on November 18, 1858. He died on November 14, 1932 and was buried in Little Rock, Dillon County, SC at Saint Paul's Methodist Church.[151] He and Mary "Duck" Wallace had the following children:

+25	Mary Hamilton (1872-)
+26	John Hamilton (1876-)
+27	Ida Florence Hamilton (1877-1953)
+28	George A. Hamilton (1879-1882)
+29	Mary Hamilton (1880-1957)
+30	William Race Hamilton (1882-1952)
+31	Lola Hamilton (1885-1958)
+32	Kelly Hamilton (1886-)
+33	Evander Hamilton (1890-)

7. **Missouri Mazura "Mo" Smith Wallace**, daughter of William Lane Wallace and Annie Elizabeth Smith, was born in 1848. She died in 1937 and was buried in Little Rock, Dillon County, SC at Huggins (Little Rock Baptist Church) Cemetery.[152]

1850, Nov 8 -- Census, Moore County, NC Page 237
William L. Wallis 27 M, Farmer, born in North Carolina
Josiah Wallis 16 M, Farmer, born in North Carolina
Celia Wallis 15 F, born in North Carolina
Everett Wallis 12 M, born in North Carolina
William J. Wallis 10 M, born in North Carolina
Elizabeth Smith 32 F, born in North Carolina
Mary Smith 3 F, born in North Carolina
Missouri Smith 1 F, born in North Carolina
Mary Davis 40 F, born in North Carolina
James Davis 1 M, born in North Carolina

1860, Sep 1 -- Census, Moore County, NC Page 222, Mooshounie Post Office
Wm. L. Wallace 45 M, Laborer, $100 Value of Personal Property, born in North Carolina
Elizabeth Wallace 30 F, born in North Carolina
William Wallace 20 M, born in North Carolina
Mary Wallace 13 F, born in North Carolina
Missourie Wallace 12 F, born in North Carolina
Racy Wallace 9 M, born in North Carolina
Thomas W. Wallace 7 M, born in North Carolina
Susanna Wallace 5 F, born in North Carolina
Nelson V. Wallace 3 M, born in North Carolina
Ira Wallace 2/12 M, born in North Carolina
Mary Smith 74 F, born in North Carolina
(Next Door)
1860, Sep 1 -- Census, Moore County, NC Page 222-B, Mooshaunee Post Office
Mary Davis 45 F, $50 Personal Property, born in North Carolina
James Davis 11 M, born in North Carolina

1880 -- Census, Marion County, SC Page 83-D Harleeville Township
John Taylor 31 M, Head, Farmer, born in North Carolina, father & mother born in North Carolina
Missorie A. Taylor 30 F, Other, born in North Carolina, father & mother born in North Carolina
Margaret Taylor 12 F, Other, Single, born in North Carolina, father & mother born in North Carolina
Lizze C. Taylor 11 F, Other, Single, born in North Carolina, father & mother born in North Carolina
William Taylor 8 M, Other, Single, Works on Farm, born in South Carolina, father & mother born in North Carolina
Charlie E. Taylor 6 M, Other, Single, born in South Carolina, father & mother born in North Carolina
Adolphus Taylor 5 M, Other, Single, born in South Carolina, father & mother born in North Carolina
Jasin Taylor 4 M, Other, Single, born in South Carolina, father & mother born in North Carolina

John Taylor was born in 1846. He died in 1908 and was buried in Little Rock, Dillon County, SC at Huggins (Little Rock Baptist Church) Cemetery.[153] He and Missouri Mazura "Mo" Smith Wallace had the following children:

+34	Margaret Taylor (1868-)
+35	Elizabeth C. Taylor (1869-)
+36	William Murk Taylor (1872-1936)
+37	Charlie E. Taylor (1874-)
+38	David Dolphus Taylor (1875-1950)
+39	Jason Robert Taylor (1879-1933)
+40	Lottie Ardelia Taylor (1889-1967)

8. **Thomas Walter Wallace**, son of William Lane Wallace and Annie Elizabeth Smith, was born in 1853 in North Carolina. He died on June 27, 1925 and was buried in Dillon, Dillon County, SC at Riverside Cemetery.[154]

RECORDS OF THOMAS WALTER WALLACE

1860, Sep 1 -- Census, Moore County, NC Page 222, Mooshounie Post Office
Wm. L. Wallace 45 M, Laborer, $100 Value of Personal Property, born in North Carolina
Elizabeth Wallace 30 F, born in North Carolina
William Wallace 20 M, born in North Carolina
Mary Wallace 13 F, born in North Carolina
Missourie Wallace 12 F, born in North Carolina
Racy Wallace 9 M, born in North Carolina
Thomas W. Wallace 7 M, born in North Carolina

Susanna Wallace 5 F, born in North Carolina
Nelson V. Wallace 3 M, born in North Carolina
Ira Wallace 2/12 M, born in North Carolina
Mary Smith 74 F, born in North Carolina
(Next Door)
1860, Sep 1 -- Census, Moore County, NC Page 222-B, Mooshaunee Post Office
Mary Davis 45 F, $50 Personal Property, born in North Carolina
James Davis 11 M, born in North Carolina

1880 -- Census, Marion County, SC Page 83-D Harleeville Township
Thomas Wallace 24 M, Head, Married, Farmer, born in North Carolina, father & mother born in North Carolina
Flora Jane Wallace 26 F, Wife, Married, Works on Farm, born in South Carolina, father & mother born in South Carolina
Robt. Wade Wallace 5 M, Son, Single, born in South Carolina, father born in North Carolina & mother born in South Carolina
Lilly Frances Wallace 4 F, Dau, Single, born in South Carolina, father born in North Carolina & mother born in South Carolina
Wm. Lewis Wallace 2 M, Son, Single, born in South Carolina, father born in North Carolina & mother born in South Carolina
Flora Wallace 5/12 F, Dau, Single, born in South Carolina, father born in North Carolina & mother born in South Carolina

1900 -- Census, Marion County, SC Page 214, Manning Township
Thomas Wallace 56 M, Sep 1844, Head, Married-30yrs, Farmer, born in South Carolina, father & mother born in North Carolina
Flora J. Wallace 42 F, Mar 1858, Wife, Married-30yrs, 9 Children(7 Living), born in South Carolina, father & mother born in South Carolina
Noah W. Wallace 17 M, July 1882, Son, Single, born in South Carolina, father & mother born in South Carolina
Walter T. Wallace 14 M, Sep 1885, Son, Single, born in South Carolina, father & mother born in South Carolina
F. May Wallace 13 F, Jun 1886, Dau, Single, born in South Carolina, father & mother born in South Carolina
Archie W. Wallace 10 M, Oct 1889, Son, Single, In School, born in South Carolina, father & mother born in South Carolina

1910 -- Census, Dillon County, SC Page 114-B, Manning Township, Little Rock Road
Walter Wallace 24 M, Head, Married-1st-4yrs, Superintendent(Farm), born in South Carolina, father & mother born in South Carolina
Minnie Wallace 24 F, Wife, Married-1st-4yrs, born in South Carolina, father & mother born in South Carolina
Thomas W. Wallace 60 M, father, Married-1st-35yrs, born in South Carolina, father & mother born in South Carolina
Flora Jane Wallace 53 F, mother, Married-1st-35yrs, 6 Children(5 Living), born in South Carolina, father & mother born in South Carolina

1920 -- Census, Dillon County, SC Page 187, Dillon Town
Thomas W. Wallace 68 M, Head, Married, Carpenter-House, born in North Carolina, father & mother born in North Carolina
Jane Wallace 60 F, Wife, Married, born in South Carolina, father & mother born in South Carolina

Flora Jane Huggins was born on May 23, 1850 in Dillon County, SC. She died on May 26, 1926 in Dillon County, SC and was buried on May 27, 1926 in Dillon, Dillon County, SC at Riverside Cemetery.[155] She and Thomas Walter Wallace had the following children:

+41	Robert Wade Wallace (1874-1933)
+42	Lily Francis Wallace (1876-1882)
+43	William Lewis Wallace (1878-1955)
+44	Flora Wallace (1880-)
+45	Noah W. Wallace (1882-)
+46	Mary "Mae" Wallace (1884-1963)
+47	Thomas Walter Wallace (1884-1931)
+48	Archie Wilson Wallace (1890-1939)

9. **Wesley Royce "Race" Wallace**, son of William Lane Wallace and Annie Elizabeth Smith, was born in May 1854 in Moore County, NC. He married **Maggie Lester** circa 1885. He married **Lottie Proctor** circa 1914. He died on February 10, 1915 in Robeson County, NC and was buried on February 11, 1915 in Dillon County, SC at Baker Cemetery.[156]

RECORDS OF RACE WALLACE

1860, Sep 1 -- Census, Moore County, NC Page 222, Mooshounie Post Office
Wm. L. Wallace 45 M, Laborer, $100 Value of Personal Property, born in North Carolina
Elizabeth Wallace 30 F, born in North Carolina

William Wallace 20 M, born in North Carolina
Mary Wallace 13 F, born in North Carolina
Missourie Wallace 12 F, born in North Carolina
Racy Wallace 9 M, born in North Carolina
Thomas W. Wallace 7 M, born in North Carolina
Susanna Wallace 5 F, born in North Carolina
Nelson V. Wallace 3 M, born in North Carolina
Ira Wallace 2/12 M, born in North Carolina
Mary Smith 74 F, born in North Carolina
(Next Door)
1860, Sep 1 -- Census, Moore County, NC Page 222-B, Mooshaunee Post Office
Mary Davis 45 F, $50 Personal Property, born in North Carolina
James Davis 11 M, born in North Carolina

1880 -- Census, Marion County, SC Page 70, Carmichael Township
Murdock Smith 30 M, Head, Single, Farmer, born in North Carolina, father & mother born in North Carolina
Nancy Smith 60 F, Aunt, Single, Keeping House, born in North Carolina, father & mother born in North Carolina
Race Wallace 26 M, Other, Single, Farmer, born in North Carolina, father & mother born in North Carolina
William Wallace 20 M, born in North Carolina

1900 -- Census, Marion County, SC Page 76, Harleesville Township
Race Wallace 45 M, May 1852, Head, Married-15yrs, Farming, born in North Carolina, father & mother born in North Carolina
Maggie Wallace 38 F, Jun 1861, Wife, Married-15yrs, 4 Children(4 Living), born in South Carolina, father & mother born in South Carolina
Lizzie Wallace 14 F, Oct 1885, Dau, Single, At School, born in South Carolina, father born in North Carolina, mother born in South Carolina
Frank Wallace 10 M, May 1890, Son, Single, At School, born in South Carolina, father born in North Carolina, mother born in South Carolina
Henry Wallace 8 M, Jan 1892, Son, Single, At School, born in South Carolina, father born in North Carolina, mother born in South Carolina
Lock Wallace 5 M, May 1895, Son, Single, At School, born in South Carolina, father born in North Carolina, mother born in South Carolina

1910 -- Census, Robeson County, NC Page 29-B, Alfordsville Township
Race Wallace 58 M, Head, Widowed, Farmer, born in North Carolina, father & mother born in North Carolina
Frank Wallace 20 M, Son, Single, Laborer(Home Farm), born in South Carolina, father born in North Carolina, mother born in South Carolina
Henry Wallace 16 M, Son, Single, Laborer(Home Farm), born in South Carolina, father born in North Carolina, mother born in South Carolina
Lock Wallace 13 M, Son, Single, Laborer(Home Farm), born in South Carolina, father born in North Carolina, mother born in South Carolina
Amy McCallum 74 F(b), Servant, Widowed, 5 Children(3 Living), Cook(Private family), born in North Carolina, father & mother born in North Carolina

1915, Feb 18 -- Obituary, *The Dillon Herald* [Newspaper] Dillon, SC.
Mr. R. Wallace Dead. The community was shocked when the sad news was received in Dillon announcing the death of Mr. R. Wallace of Rowland, NC who passed away Wednesday after a long illness, although his death was not unexpected.
Mr. Wallace was a son of the late William L and Mrs. Elizabeth Wallace, who preceeded him to the grave years ago. Mr. Wallace was born and reared in Moore county near Carthrige, NC and later he moved to this county, and lived near Little Rock for a number of years. After which he moved near Rowland and spent the remainder of his life. Mr. Wallace first married Miss Maggie Lester of that place, who died about nine years ago. Of this union there, were born a number of children. Mr. Wallace lived a faithful widower until last year when he married Miss Lottie Proctor of Rowland. The unanimous verdict of his fellow citizens and friends is that he was a prosperous farmer, a faithful man and a good citizen.
Mr. Wallace leaves a young widow and four children to mourn his loss. Messrs Frank, Henry and Lock Wallace, and Mrs. Geo. Bond, all of Rowland. His surviving brothers and sisters are: Messrs Ira, Arch, Needam and T. W. Wallace, Mrs. W. A. Hamilton and Mrs. John Taylor all of Dillon and Little Rock. Mr. Wallace has long been a faithful member of Oakland Methodist church and was a Christian man. His family and friends have our heartfelt sympathy in their bereavement. The funeral service was conducted by his pastor, Rev. F. L. Glennon of Little Rock, at 4:30 o'clock, Thursday evening, and he was laid to rest at the Baker cemetery to await the resurrection. "His Niece"

Maggie Lester was born on June 13, 1861. She died on May 7, 1905 and was buried in Dillon County, SC at Baker Cemetery.[157] She and Wesley Royce "Race" Wallace had the following children:

+49	Infant Wallace (-)	
+50	Infant Wallace (-)	
+51	Infant Wallace (-)	
+52	Infant Wallace (-)	
+53	Infant Wallace (-)	
+54	Mary Elizabeth Wallace (1885-1945)	

+55	Cora Wallace (1887-1888)
+56	William Frank Wallace (1889-1963)
+57	John Henry Wallace (1893-1966)
+58	Lauch Wesley Wallace (1895-1981)

Lottie Proctor was born in 1884. She died on March 13, 1939 in Rowland, Robeson County, NC and was buried on March 14, 1939 in Rowland, Robeson County, NC at Ashpole Cemetery.[158]

10. **Susanna Wallace**, daughter of William Lane Wallace and Annie Elizabeth Smith, was born between 1855 and 1858. She died before 1900.

RECORDS OF SUSANNA WALLACE

1860, Sep 1 -- Census, Moore County, NC Page 222, Mooshounie Post Office
Wm. L. Wallace 45 M, Laborer, $100 Value of Personal Property, born in North Carolina
Elizabeth Wallace 30 F, born in North Carolina
William Wallace 20 M, born in North Carolina
Mary Wallace 13 F, born in North Carolina
Missourie Wallace 12 F, born in North Carolina
Racy Wallace 9 M, born in North Carolina
Thomas W. Wallace 7 M, born in North Carolina
Susanna Wallace 5 F, born in North Carolina
Nelson V. Wallace 3 M, born in North Carolina
Ira Wallace 2/12 M, born in North Carolina
Mary Smith 74 F, born in North Carolina
(Next Door)
1860, Sep 1 -- Census, Moore County, NC Page 222-B, Mooshaunee Post Office
Mary Davis 45 F, $50 Personal Property, born in North Carolina
James Davis 11 M, born in North Carolina

1880 -- Census, Marion County, SC Page 195-D, Manning Township
W.H. Bain 28 M, Head, Married, Farmer, born in South Carolina, father & mother born in South Carolina
Susan Bain 22 F, Wife, Married, Keeping House, born in South Carolina, father & mother born in South Carolina
Lena Bain 4 F, Dau, Single, born in South Carolina, father & mother born in South Carolina
Annie Bain 6/12 F, Dau, Single, born in South Carolina, father & mother born in South Carolina

William E. Bain was born in February 1851. He married Willie J. circa 1897. He and Susanna Wallace had the following children:

+59	Lena Bain (1876-)
+60	Annie Bain (1879-)
+61	Jim Bain (1881-)
+62	Nora Bain (1883-)
+63	Ida Bain (1888-)
+64	Iola Bain (1890-)

11. **Needham Evander Wallace**, son of William Lane Wallace and Annie Elizabeth Smith, was born on July 12, 1858. He married **Hannah J.** circa 1907. He died on April 27, 1920 and was buried in Little Rock, Dillon County, SC at Saint Paul's Methodist Church.[159]

1860, Sep 1 -- Census, Moore County, NC Page 222, Mooshounie Post Office
Wm. L. Wallace 45 M, Laborer, $100 Value of Personal Property, born in North Carolina
Elizabeth Wallace 30 F, born in North Carolina
William Wallace 20 M, born in North Carolina
Mary Wallace 13 F, born in North Carolina
Missourie Wallace 12 F, born in North Carolina
Racy Wallace 9 M, born in North Carolina
Thomas W. Wallace 7 M, born in North Carolina
Susanna Wallace 5 F, born in North Carolina
Nelson V. Wallace 3 M, born in North Carolina
Ira Wallace 2/12 M, born in North Carolina
Mary Smith 74 F, born in North Carolina

(Next Door)
1860, Sep 1 -- Census, Moore County, NC Page 222-B, Mooshaunee Post Office
Mary Davis 45 F, $50 Personal Property, born in North Carolina
James Davis 11 M, born in North Carolina

1880, Jun 14 -- Census, Marion County, SC Page 83-D Harleeville Township
Wm. W. Wallace 76 M, Head, Works on Farm, born in North Carolina, father & mother born in North Carolina
Betty Wallace 50 F, Wife, Works on Farm, born in North Carolina, father & mother born in North Carolina
Needam V. Wallace 20 M, Son, Works on Farm, born in North Carolina, father & mother born in North Carolina
Archie Y. Wallace 15 M, Son, Works on Farm, born in North Carolina, father & mother born in North Carolina
Elizabeth Wallace 8 F, Grandaughter, born in South Carolina, father & mother born in South Carolina
Ira Wallace 18 M, Son, Works on Farm, born in North Carolina, father & mother born in North Carolina

1910 -- Census, Dillon County, SC Page 121, Manning Township, Dothan Road
N. V. Wallace 52 M, Head, Married-2nd-3yrs, Farmer(Farm), born in South Carolina, father & mother born in South Carolina
Hannah J. Wallace 51 F, Wife, Married-2nd-3yrs, 2 Children(2 Living), born in South Carolina, father & mother born in South Carolina

1920 -- Census, Dillon County, SC Page 118, Harleesville Township, Little Rock Town
Neidham V. Wallace 59 M, Head, Married, Merchant-Gro Store, born in North Carolina, father & mother born in North Carolina
Hannah J. Wallace 56 F, Wife, Married, born in North Carolina, father & mother born in North Carolina

12. **Arrie Lane Wallace**, son of William Lane Wallace and Annie Elizabeth Smith, was born on March 14, 1861. He married **Nellie Wood Houston** circa 1886. He died on December 28, 1938 and was buried in Little Rock, Dillon County, SC at Saint Paul's Methodist Church.[160]

RECORDS OF ARRIE LANE WALLACE

1860, Sep 1 -- Census, Moore County, NC Page 222, Mooshounie Post Office
Wm. L. Wallace 45 M, Laborer, $100 Value of Personal Property, born in North Carolina
Elizabeth Wallace 30 F, born in North Carolina
William Wallace 20 M, born in North Carolina
Mary Wallace 13 F, born in North Carolina
Missourie Wallace 12 F, born in North Carolina
Racy Wallace 9 M, born in North Carolina
Thomas W. Wallace 7 M, born in North Carolina
Susanna Wallace 5 F, born in North Carolina
Nelson V. Wallace 3 M, born in North Carolina
Ira Wallace 2/12 M, born in North Carolina
Mary Smith 74 F, born in North Carolina
(Next Door)
1860, Sep 1 -- Census, Moore County, NC Page 222-B, Mooshaunee Post Office
Mary Davis 45 F, $50 Personal Property, born in North Carolina
James Davis 11 M, born in North Carolina

1880, Jun 14 -- Census, Marion County, SC Page 83-D Harleeville Township
Wm. W. Wallace 76 M, Head, Works on Farm, born in North Carolina, father & mother born in North Carolina
Betty Wallace 50 F, Wife, Works on Farm, born in North Carolina, father & mother born in North Carolina
Needam V. Wallace 20 M, Son, Works on Farm, born in North Carolina, father & mother born in North Carolina
Archie Y. Wallace 15 M, Son, Works on Farm, born in North Carolina, father & mother born in North Carolina
Elizabeth Wallace 8 F, Grandaughter, born in South Carolina, father & mother born in South Carolina
Ira Wallace 18 M, Son, Works on Farm, born in North Carolina, father & mother born in North Carolina

1900 -- Census, Marion County, SC Page 200, Manning Township
Ira L. Wallace 37 M, Jan 1863, Head, Married-14yrs, Farmer, born in South Carolina, father & mother born in South Carolina
Nellie Wallace 36 F, Oct 1863, Wife, Married-14yrs, 6 Children(5 Living), born in South Carolina, father & mother born in South Carolina
Alice Wallace 11 F, Oct 1888, Dau, Single, At School, born in South Carolina, father & mother born in South Carolina
Owen Wallace 9 M, Oct 1890, Son, Single, born in South Carolina, father & mother born in South Carolina
Annie Wallace 7 F, May 1893, Dau, Single, born in South Carolina, father & mother born in South Carolina

DILLON COUNTY HISTORY REVIEW—Pictured are A.L. Wallace and his youngest child, Grace Wallace McCall, a graduate of Flora McDonald College and a teacher. Wallace was a retired farmer and court crier in Dillon County since its formation in 1910.
Wallace was the son of the late William Wallace and Mrs. Annie Davis Wallace of Moore County, North Carolina. His wife was the former Miss Nellie Houston, who preceded him in death. He was survived by several daughters and sons, 21 grandchildren, and two great-grandchildren. He died at the age of 76.
His son, Ernest Wallace, and later grandson, Lynwood Wallace, followed in his footsteps, also working in the court.

(Courtesy of Buddy Altman, Latta, SC)

James Wallace 4 M, Dec 1895, Son, Single, born in South Carolina, father & mother born in South Carolina
Ernest B. Wallace 2 M, Mar 1898, Son, Single, born in South Carolina, father & mother born in South Carolina

1910 -- Census, Dillon County, SC Page 130-B, Manning Township, Buck Swamp Road
A. L. Wallace 48 M, Head, Married-1st-23yrs, Farmer(Farm), born in South Carolina, father & mother born in South Carolina
Nellie Wallace 43 F, Wife, Married-1st-23yrs, 11 Children(9 Living), born in South Carolina, father & mother born in South Carolina
Alice Wallace 21 F, Dau, Single, born in South Carolina, father & mother born in South Carolina
Owen Wallace 19 M, Son, Single, Laborer(Home Farm), born in South Carolina, father & mother born in South Carolina
Annie Wallace 17 F, Dau, Single, born in South Carolina, father & mother born in South Carolina
James Wallace 15 M, Son, Single, born in South Carolina, father & mother born in South Carolina
Ernest Wallace 13 M, Son, Single, born in South Carolina, father & mother born in South Carolina
Ruth Wallace 10 F, Dau, Single, born in South Carolina, father & mother born in South Carolina
Percy Wallace 7 M, Son, Single, born in South Carolina, father & mother born in South Carolina
Louise Wallace 5 F, Dau, Single, born in South Carolina, father & mother born in South Carolina
Grace Wallace 2 F, Dau, Single, born in South Carolina, father & mother born in South Carolina

1920 -- Census, Dillon County, Manning Township, Dillon Town
Ira Wallace 59 M, Head, Married, Farmer-General Farm, born in North Carolina, father & mother born in North Carolina
Nellie Wallace 54 F, Wife, Married, born in North Carolina, father & mother born in North Carolina
Ruth A. Wallace 18 F, Dau, Single, born in South Carolina, father & mother born in North Carolina
Percy Wallace 15 M, Son, Single, Laborer-Home Farm, born in South Carolina, father & mother born in North Carolina
Louise Wallace 14 F, Dau, Single, born in South Carolina, father & mother born in North Carolina
Grace Wallace 12 F, Dau, Single, born in South Carolina, father & mother born in North Carolina

Nellie Wood Houston was born on July 2, 1865. She died on May 11, 1928 in Dillon County, SC and was buried on May 12, 1928 in Little Rock, Dillon County, SC at Saint Paul's Methodist Church.[161] She and Arrie Lane Wallace had the following children:

+65	Alice Wood Wallace (1888-1959)
+66	Owen Lane Wallace (1890-)
+67	Annie Wallace (1893-1964)
+68	James William Wallace (1895-)
+69	Ernest B. Wallace (1898-)
+70	Ruth A. Wallace (1901-1984)
+71	Percy Michaux Wallace (1904-1948)
+72	Louise Wallace (1906-)
+73	Grace Wallace (1908-1982)

13. **Archie Young Wallace**, son of William Lane Wallace and Annie Elizabeth Smith, was born on March 15, 1865. He married **Anna Elizabeth Norton** on July 18, 1885. He died on July 17, 1925 and was buried in Little Rock, Dillon County, SC at Saint Paul's Methodist Church.[162]

RECORDS OF ARCHIE WALLACE

1880, Jun 14 -- Census, Marion County, SC Page 83-D Harleeville Township
Wm. W. Wallace 76 M, Head, Works on Farm, born in North Carolina, father & mother born in North Carolina
Betty Wallace 50 F, Wife, Works on Farm, born in North Carolina, father & mother born in North Carolina
Needam V. Wallace 20 M, Son, Works on Farm, born in North Carolina, father & mother born in North Carolina
Archie Y. Wallace 15 M, Son, Works on Farm, born in North Carolina, father & mother born in North Carolina
Elizabeth Wallace 8 F, Grandaughter, born in South Carolina, father & mother born in South Carolina
Ira Wallace 18 M, Son, Works on Farm, born in North Carolina, father & mother born in North Carolina

1900 -- Census, Marion County, SC Page 72, Harleeville Township
Archie Wallace 36 M, Jan 1864, Head, Married-15yrs, Farming, born in North Carolina, father & mother born in North Carolina
Annie Wallace 38 F, July 1861, Wife, Married-15yrs, 5 Children(5 Living), born in North Carolina, father & mother born in North Carolina
Rufus Wallace 13 M, Nov 1886, Son, Single, At School, born in South Carolina, father & mother born in North Carolina
Andrew Wallace 12 M, Jun 1887, Son, Single, At School, born in South Carolina, father & mother born in North Carolina
Archie Wallace 8 M, Sep 1891, Son, Single, born in South Carolina, father & mother born in North Carolina
Annie Wallace 4 F, May 1896, Dau, Single, born in South Carolina, father & mother born in North Carolina
Boyd Wallace 10/12 M, July 1899, Son, Single, born in South Carolina, father & mother born in North Carolina

1920 -- Census, Dillon County, SC Page 187, Manning Township, Dillon Town
Arch Y. Wallace 54 M, Head, Married, Farmer-General Farm, born in North Carolina, father & mother born in North Carolina

Annie Wallace 54 F, Wife, Married, born in North Carolina, father & mother born in North Carolina
Effie Wallace 19 F, Dau, Single, Laborer-Home Farm, born in South Carolina, father & mother born in North Carolina
Arch Anna 15 F, Dau, Single, Laborer-Home Farm, born in South Carolina, father & mother born in North Carolina
Boyd Wallace 21 M, Son, Married, Laborer-Home Farm, born in South Carolina, father & mother born in North Carolina
Maggie Wallace 20 F, DauL, Married, born in South Carolina, father & mother born in North Carolina
Gladys Wallace 3 F, GrDau, Single, born in South Carolina, father & mother born in North Carolina

Anna Elizabeth Norton, daughter of Andrew Jackson Norton (1835-1915) and Effie Malinda Williamson (1834-1902), was born on July 22, 1861 in Moore County, NC. She died on March 23, 1934 in Dillon County, SC and was buried on March 25, 1934 in Little Rock, Dillon County, SC at Saint Paul's Methodist Church.[163] She and Archie Young Wallace had the following children:

+74	Rufus Wallace (1886-1943)
+75	Andrew Jackson Wallace (1889-1961)
+76	Archie Lee Wallace (1891-)
+77	Annie Missouri Wallace (1896-1946)
+78	Boyd Wallace (1898-)
+79	Effie Malinda Wallace (1900-)
+80	Archanna Wallace (1904-1968)

Third Generation

16. **William Harrison Davis**, son of Devotion D. Davis and Celia C. Wallace, was born on December 25, 1856 in Moore County, NC. He married **Mary Emma Brown** on February 6, 1898 in Moore County, NC. He died on October 7, 1933 in Carthage, Moore County, NC and was buried on October 8, 1933 in Carthage, Moore County, NC at Cross Hill Cemetery.

William Harrison Davis *(Courtesy of Martha Wilke)*

Additional Information can be found at www.MooreCountyWallaces.com

Alice Watkins, daughter of John Watkins (1831-) and Eliza (1835-), was born in 1860. She died on January 18, 1893 and was buried in Moore County, NC at Davis Cemetery #72. She and William Harrison Davis had the following children:

81   Austin Devotion Davis (1879-1948). *Austin was born on August 8, 1879. He married **Fannie Jane Caviness** on January 15, 1908 in Moore County, NC. He died on January 18, 1948 in Moore County, NC.*

82   Lena Davis (1883-). *Lena was born in January 1883.*

83   Nellie Davis (1885-). *Nellie was born in March 1885.*

84   Jesse Stephen Davis (1887-). *Jesse was born on June 25, 1887. He married **Sallie Fuquay** on December 22, 1907 in Moore County, NC.*

85   Marge Davis (1889-). *Marge was born in February 1889.*

86   Edna H. Davis (1890-1931). *Edna was born on March 15, 1890. She married **Walter Wesley Crabtree** on October 10, 1909 in Moore County, NC. She died on November 11, 1931 and was buried in Moore County, NC at Calvary Baptist Church.*

Mary Emma Brown, daughter of Albert J. Brown (-) and S. E. (-), was born in October 1878. She died on February 25, 1934 and was buried in 1934 in Carthage, Moore County, NC at Cross Hill Cemetery. She and William Harrison Davis had the following children:

87   Blanche Davis (1899-1972). *Blanche was born on December 24, 1899. She died on January 27, 1972 and was buried in Carthage, Moore County, NC at Cross Hill Cemetery.*

88   Irvin Davis (1905-). *Irvin was born in 1905. He married **Alma** circa 1925.*

89   Herbert Lee Davis (1907-1974). *Herbert was born on June 11, 1907. He died on March 3, 1974 and was buried in Lee County, NC at White Hill Presbyterian Church.*

90   Lillian Davis (1910-). *Lillian was born in 1910.*

91   Alton Curtis Davis (1913-1917). *Alton was born on August 31, 1913. He died on February 25, 1917 and was buried in Carthage, Moore County, NC at Cross Hill Cemetery.*

92   Leana Davis (1918-). *Leana was born in 1918.*

17. **Mary Ann Davis**, daughter of Devotion D. Davis and Celia C. Wallace, was born on November 11, 1863. She died on February 7, 1895 and was buried in Moore County, NC at Davis Cemetery #72.

James Howard Huffsticker was born in May 1859. He married Margaret E. "Maggie" McKenzie on January 18, 1909 in Moore County, NC. He died in 1929 and was buried in Moore County, NC at Culdee Presbyterian Church. He and Mary Ann Davis had the following children:

93   Florence May Huffsticker (1884-). *Florence was born in October 1884.*

94   Laura Day Huffsticker (1888-). *Laura was born in June 1888.*

95   Jennie Dau Huffsticker (1891-). *Jennie was born in February 1891.*

96   Infant Huffsticker (1893-1893). *Infant was born in 1893. She died in 1893 and was buried in Moore County, NC at Davis Cemetery #72.*

97   Gracie Huffsticker (1895-). *Gracie was born in August 1895.*

19. **Sarah Wallace**, daughter of Everett W. Wallace and Martha E. Walker, was born on March 12, 1863. She married **James Lemuel Cannon** circa 1879. She died on February 11, 1938 and was buried in Henderson County, NC at Patty's Chapel Methodist Church.

James Lemuel Cannon was born on October 24, 1854 in Henderson County, NC. He died on January 6, 1940 in Henderson County, NC and was buried on January 7, 1940 in Henderson County, NC at Patty's Chapel Methodist Church. He and Sarah Wallace had the following children:

98   Eter Cannon (1881-). *Eter was born in August 1881.*

99   Wade Cannon (1881-). *Wade was born in August 1881.*

100   Lizzie Cannon (1886-). *Lizzie was born in April 1886.*

101   Robert Cannon (1888-). *Robert was born in 1888.*

102   M. L. Cannon (1890-). *M. was born in September 1890.*

20. **Amanda Louise Wallace**, daughter of Everett W. Wallace and Martha E. Walker, was born on September 11, 1867. She married **William S. Dedman** on October 13, 1882 in Buncombe County, NC. She died on October 19, 1944 in Henderson County, NC and was buried on October 21, 1944 in Henderson County, NC at Oakdale Cemetery.

William S. Dedman, son of William Dedman (1819-) and Elizabeth (1819-), was born in 1859. He died on November 12, 1932 in Henderson County, NC and was buried in Henderson County, NC at Oakdale Cemetery. He and Amanda Louise Wallace had the following children:

103	Bertha H. Dedman (1883-1953). *Bertha was born in November 1883. She married **Robert F. Reed** circa 1901. She died in 1953.*
104	William Clisby Dedman (1885-1960). *William was born in July 1885. He died on December 26, 1960.*
105	Nettie T. Dedman (1888-1981). *Nettie was born on June 1, 1888. She died on December 2, 1981.*
106	Olivia Mae Dedman (1890-1978). *Olivia was born in May 1890. She died in 1978.*
107	Dorothy Estelle Dedman (1892-1981). *Dorothy was born on March 13, 1892. She died on March 21, 1981 and was buried in Naples, Henderson County, NC at Shepard Memorial Park Cemetery.*
108	Everett Egbert Dedman (1894-1957). *Everett was born on March 25, 1894. He married **Ella Anders** circa 1920. He died on February 27, 1957 and was buried in Henderson County, NC at Oakdale Cemetery.*

21. **Loretta Wallace**, daughter of Everett W. Wallace and Martha E. Walker, was born in 1870. She married **S.W. Wilson** (1867-) on July 19, 1888 in Buncombe County, NC. She died before 1920.

Joseph A. Walker, son of John S. Walker (1847-) and Sarah E. (1850-), was born in March 1870.

23. **Charles Chalmers Wallace**, son of Everett W. Wallace and Nancy Lett, was born on September 30, 1869 in Moore County, NC. He married **Margaret Rosetta Wallace** on September 22, 1895 in Cumberland County, NC. He died on April 26, 1930 in Durham, Durham County, NC and was buried on April 27, 1930 in Durham, Durham County, NC at Cedar Hill Cemetery.

Margaret Rosetta Wallace (seated) **with her grandchildren** *(Courtesy of Katy Ibarra)*

Margaret Rosetta Wallace, daughter of John Mack Wallace (1845-1927) and Martha Ann Brown (1849-1902), was born in May 1875 in Moore County, NC. She married Walter Jackson Yates on October 14, 1933 in Caswell County, NC. She died on

July 30, 1948 and was buried in Durham, Durham County, NC at Maplewood Cemetery. She and Charles Chalmers Wallace had the following children:

109	James Fletcher Wallace (1898-1979). *James was born on June 28, 1898. He married **Claudia Carmen Carrington** on August 2, 1919 in Durham, Durham County, NC. He died on September 16, 1979 and was buried in Durham, Durham County, NC at Maplewood Cemetery.*
110	Daisy Mae Wallace (1901-1985). *Daisy was born on October 18, 1901. She died on December 21, 1985 and was buried in Rocky Mount, Edgecombe County, NC at Pineview Cemetery.*
111	Lelia Georgia Wallace (1903-1997). *Lelia was born on April 7, 1903. She married **Willie Lexter Harward** on September 28, 1918 in Durham, Durham County, NC. She married **Corbitt W. Carter** on June 26, 1926 in Durham, Durham County, NC. She married **Philip Herman Galbreath** on October 26, 1945 in Richmond, VA. She died on May 12, 1997 and was buried in Paris, Lamar County, TX at Evergreen Cemetery.*
112	Lawrence Craven Wallace (1905-1987). *Lawrence was born on August 29, 1905. He died on July 11, 1987 and was buried in Burlington, Alamance County, NC at Alamance Memorial Park.*
113	Alvin Vernon Wallace (1908-1983). *Alvin was born on February 2, 1908. He died on December 8, 1983 and was buried in Burlington, Alamance County, NC at Alamance Memorial Park.*
114	Forrest Lee Wallace (1912-1982). *Forrest was born on August 3, 1912. He died on January 3, 1982 and was buried in Fort Pierce, St. Lucie County, FL at Hillcrest Memorial Gardens.*

26. John Hamilton, son of William Albert Hamilton and Mary "Duck" Wallace, was born in June 1876. He married **Ida** circa 1896.

Ida was born in September 1869. She and John Hamilton had the following children:

115	Daniel Hamilton (1898-). *Daniel was born in January 1898.*
116	Sadie Hamilton (1903-). *Sadie was born in 1903.*
117	Kate Hamilton (1907-). *Kate was born in 1907.*

27. Ida Florence Hamilton, daughter of William Albert Hamilton and Mary "Duck" Wallace, was born on August 12, 1877. She died on August 13, 1953 and was buried in Little Rock, Dillon County, SC at Saint Paul's Methodist Church.

Andrew Jackson Norton, son of Andrew Jackson Norton (1835-1915) and Effie Malinda Williamson (1834-1902), was born on October 7, 1868. He died on December 29, 1945 and was buried in Little Rock, Dillon County, SC at Saint Paul's Methodist Church. He and Ida Florence Hamilton had the following children:

118	Neil Norton Sr. (1893-1969). *Neil was born on November 12, 1893. He died on June 15, 1969 and was buried in Little Rock, Dillon County, SC at Saint Paul's Methodist Church.*

28. George A. Hamilton, daughter of William Albert Hamilton and Mary "Duck" Wallace, was born on April 12, 1879. She died on July 6, 1882 and was buried in Little Rock, Dillon County, SC at Saint Paul's Methodist Church.

29. Mary Hamilton, daughter of William Albert Hamilton and Mary "Duck" Wallace, was born on April 23, 1880. She died on January 30, 1957 and was buried in Dillon, Dillon County, SC at Evergreen Cemetery.

John W. Brigman was born on December 5, 1873. He died on November 12, 1956 and was buried in Dillon, Dillon County, SC at Evergreen Cemetery.

30. William Race Hamilton, son of William Albert Hamilton and Mary "Duck" Wallace, was born on August 7, 1882. He married **Addie Ann Clark** on October 29, 1904. He died on October 12, 1952 and was buried in Dillon, Dillon County, SC at Riverside Cemetery.

Addie Ann Clark was born on September 12, 1884. She died on October 10, 1969 and was buried in Dillon, Dillon County, SC at Riverside Cemetery. She and William Race Hamilton had the following children:

119   Margaret Leona Hamilton (1918-2002). *Margaret was born on January 29, 1918. She died on May 5, 2002 and was buried in Dillon, Dillon County, SC at Riverside Cemetery.*

31. **Lola Hamilton**, daughter of William Albert Hamilton and Mary "Duck" Wallace, was born on September 30, 1885. She died on June 10, 1958 and was buried in Clio, Marlboro County, SC at Hebron Cemetery.

Murray Wilton Hinson was born on January 28, 1881. He died on January 31, 1949 and was buried in Clio, Marlboro County, SC at Hebron Cemetery.

36. **William Murk Taylor**, son of John Taylor and Missouri Mazura "Mo" Smith Wallace, was born on June 25, 1872. He died on March 27, 1936 and was buried in Little Rock, Dillon County, SC at Huggins (Little Rock Baptist Church) Cemetery.

Mary Elizabeth Turner, daughter of Joseph Turner (-) and Susan Cox (-), was born on September 12, 1880. She died on November 2, 1952 and was buried in Little Rock, Dillon County, SC at Huggins (Little Rock Baptist Church) Cemetery. She and William Murk Taylor had the following children:

120   Myrtle Marie Taylor (-)
121   Monroe Taylor (-)
122   Emma M. Taylor (1897-1975). *Emma was born on November 29, 1897. She died on May 15, 1975 and was buried in Dillon, Dillon County, SC at Greenlawn Cemetery.*
123   Lila Taylor (1900-1972). *Lila was born on May 24, 1900. She died on May 2, 1972 and was buried in Little Rock, Dillon County, SC at Huggins (Little Rock Baptist Church) Cemetery.*
124   Pearl Geneva Taylor (1902-2001). *Pearl was born on September 23, 1902 in Dillon County, SC. She died on January 25, 2001 in Virginia and was buried in Dillon, Dillon County, SC at Riverside Cemetery.*
125   Luther Thomas "Luke" Taylor (1908-1988). *Luther was born on April 12, 1908. He died on February 8, 1988 and was buried in Dillon, Dillon County, SC at Greenlawn Cemetery.*
126   William Murk Taylor Jr. (1911-1944). *William was born on April 9, 1911. He died on November 15, 1944 and was buried in Little Rock, Dillon County, SC at Huggins (Little Rock Baptist Church) Cemetery.*
127   Infant Taylor (1912-1912). *Infant was born on November 25, 1912. She died on November 27, 1912 and was buried in Little Rock, Dillon County, SC at Huggins (Little Rock Baptist Church) Cemetery.*
128   Thelma Taylor (1915-1916). *Thelma was born on July 22, 1915. She died on May 30, 1916 and was buried in Little Rock, Dillon County, SC at Huggins (Little Rock Baptist Church) Cemetery.*
129   Robert M. Taylor (1917-1917). *Robert was born on February 2, 1917. He died on July 18, 1917 and was buried in Little Rock, Dillon County, SC at Huggins (Little Rock Baptist Church) Cemetery.*

37. **Charlie E. Taylor**, son of John Taylor and Missouri Mazura "Mo" Smith Wallace, was born in 1874.

Sallie was born in February 1876. She and Charlie E. Taylor had the following children:

130   Eli Taylor (1893-). *Eli was born in November 1893.*
131   French Taylor (1899-). *French was born in August 1899.*

38. **David Dolphus Taylor**, son of John Taylor and Missouri Mazura "Mo" Smith Wallace, was born on November 14, 1875. He died on March 13, 1950 and was buried in Little Rock, Dillon County, SC at Huggins (Little Rock Baptist Church) Cemetery.

Mary McCormick was born on October 16, 1887. She died on December 6, 1958 and was buried in Little Rock, Dillon County, SC at Huggins (Little Rock Baptist Church) Cemetery. She and David Dolphus Taylor had the following children:

132   Newey Taylor (1910-1911). *Newey was born on November 22, 1910. He died on August 10, 1911 and was buried in Little Rock, Dillon County, SC at Huggins (Little Rock Baptist Church) Cemetery.*
133   Sadie Taylor (1920-1992). *Sadie was born on January 26, 1920. She died on October 19, 1992 and was buried in Dillon County, SC at Bermuda Cemetery.*

39. Jason Robert Taylor, son of John Taylor and Missouri Mazura "Mo" Smith Wallace, was born on March 31, 1879. He married **Nellie Long** on September 21, 1924. He died on July 5, 1933 in Dillon County, SC and was buried on July 6, 1933 in Little Rock, Dillon County, SC at Huggins (Little Rock Baptist Church) Cemetery.

Jinnie L. was born on February 1, 1880. She died on March 16, 1924 and was buried in Little Rock, Dillon County, SC at Huggins (Little Rock Baptist Church) Cemetery. She and Jason Robert Taylor had the following children:

134	Infant Taylor (-1910). *Infant died on May 5, 1910. He/she was buried in Little Rock, Dillon County, SC at Huggins (Little Rock Baptist Church) Cemetery.*	
135	Burnice V. Taylor (1916-1917). *Burnice was born on August 7, 1916. She died on May 22, 1917 and was buried in Little Rock, Dillon County, SC at Huggins (Little Rock Baptist Church) Cemetery.*	

Nellie Long was born on November 8, 1900. She died on August 23, 1977 and was buried in Latta, Dillon County, SC at Magnolia Cemetery. She and Jason Robert Taylor had the following children:

136	Lafon Hardy Taylor (1927-1975). *Lafon was born on April 27, 1927. He died on October 1, 1975 and was buried in Latta, Dillon County, SC at Magnolia Cemetery.*	
137	Carroll Jason Taylor (1930-1986). *Carroll was born on November 6, 1930. He died on April 11, 1986 and was buried in Latta, Dillon County, SC at Magnolia Cemetery.*	
138	Chester Moore Taylor (1932-2001). *Chester was born on November 29, 1932. He died on January 15, 2001 and was buried in Latta, Dillon County, SC at Magnolia Cemetery.*	

40. Lottie Ardelia Taylor, daughter of John Taylor and Missouri Mazura "Mo" Smith Wallace, was born on June 12, 1889 in Dillon County, SC. She died on September 18, 1967 in Troy, Montgomery County, NC and was buried on September 19, 1967 in Rockingham, Richmond County, NC at Mizpah Church Cemetery.

Frank D. Huggins was born on June 3, 1887 in Dillon County, SC. He died on August 30, 1939 in Rockingham, Richmond County, NC and was buried in Rockingham, Richmond County, NC at Mizpah Church Cemetery. He and Lottie Ardelia Taylor had the following children:

139	Eula Mozura Huggins (1910-1936). *Eula was born on June 23, 1910 in Dillon County, SC. She died on April 22, 1936 in Hamlet Hospital, Hamlet, Richmond County, NC and was buried on April 23, 1936 in Rockingham, Richmond County, NC at Mizpah Church Cemetery.*	
140	Joel P. Huggins (1911-1977). *Joel was born on October 27, 1911. He died in January 1977 and was buried in Rockingham, Richmond County, NC at Mizpah Church Cemetery.*	
141	Frank Darkus Huggins (1914-1976). *Frank was born on February 27, 1914. He died in February 1976.*	
142	William T. Huggins (1915-1966). *William was born on July 3, 1915 in SC. He died on December 20, 1966 in Fayetteville, Cumberland County, NC and was buried in Rockingham, Richmond County, NC at Mizpah Church Cemetery.*	
143	Plato O. Huggins (1922-1923). *Plato was born on August 30, 1922. He died on July 20, 1923 and was buried in Little Rock, Dillon County, SC at Huggins (Little Rock Baptist Church) Cemetery.*	

41. Robert Wade Wallace, son of Thomas Walter Wallace and Flora Jane Huggins, was born on September 18, 1874. He died on March 12, 1933 in Fairmont, Robeson County, NC and was buried on March 13, 1933 in Dillon County, SC at Pleasant Grove Baptist Church.

Henrietta was born on April 17, 1871. She died on March 12, 1904 and was buried in Dillon County, SC at Pleasant Grove Baptist Church. She and Robert Wade Wallace had the following children:

144	Ervin Wallace (1893-). *Ervin was born in July 1893.*	
145	Clarence Wallace (1897-1903). *Clarence was born on June 7, 1897. He died on August 26, 1903 and was buried in Dillon County, SC at Pleasant Grove Baptist Church.*	
146	Female Wallace (1898-). *Female was born in July 1898.*	

Millie Ann was born on February 11, 1878. She died on September 10, 1910. She and Robert Wade Wallace had the following children:

> 147   Charlie W. Wallace (1905-1905). *Charlie was born on April 26, 1905. He died on September 11, 1905 and was buried in Dillon County, SC at Pleasant Grove Baptist Church.*
>
> 148   French Wallace (1906-1922). *French was born on July 21, 1906. He died on March 16, 1922 and was buried in Dillon County, SC at Pleasant Grove Baptist Church.*
>
> 149   Leather S. Wallace (1908-1909). *Leather was born on June 16, 1908. She died on June 6, 1909 and was buried in Dillon County, SC at Pleasant Grove Baptist Church.*
>
> 150   Leenettie Wallace (1910-1910). *Leenettie was born on February 5, 1910. She died on June 12, 1910 and was buried in Dillon County, SC at Pleasant Grove Baptist Church.*

42. **Lily Francis Wallace**, daughter of Thomas Walter Wallace and Flora Jane Huggins, was born on March 11, 1876. She died on July 4, 1882 and was buried in Little Rock, Dillon County, SC at Saint Paul's Methodist Church.

43. **William Lewis Wallace**, son of Thomas Walter Wallace and Flora Jane Huggins, was born on June 25, 1878. He died on December 11, 1955 and was buried in Dillon County, SC at Pleasant Grove Baptist Church.

Mahaley Edginora was born on October 15, 1877 and was buried in Dillon County, SC at Pleasant Grove Baptist Church. She and William Lewis Wallace had the following children:

> 151   William H. Wallace (1898-1899). *William was born on September 26, 1898. He died on January 13, 1899 and was buried in Dillon County, SC at Pleasant Grove Baptist Church.*
>
> 152   Jane M. Wallace (1900-1902). *Jane was born on July 1, 1900. She died on May 22, 1902 and was buried in Dillon County, SC at Pleasant Grove Baptist Church.*
>
> 153   Sallie Wallace (1910-1910). *Sallie was born on April 8, 1910. She died on April 8, 1910 and was buried in Dillon County, SC at Pleasant Grove Baptist Church.*

46. **Mary "Mae" Wallace**, daughter of Thomas Walter Wallace and Flora Jane Huggins, was born on June 25, 1884 in Dillon County, SC. She died on February 13, 1963 in Lumberton, Robeson County, NC and was buried on February 15, 1963 in Dillon, Dillon County, SC at Riverside Cemetery.

Walter J. Barber was born on February 12, 1876. He died on December 26, 1960 and was buried in Dillon, Dillon County, SC at Riverside Cemetery. He and Mary "Mae" Wallace had the following children:

> 154   Leona Barber (-)
>
> 155   Ida Barber (-)
>
> 156   D. Claude Barber (1910-1980). *D. was born on June 26, 1910. He died on May 1, 1980 and was buried in Dillon, Dillon County, SC at Riverside Cemetery.*

47. **Thomas Walter Wallace**, son of Thomas Walter Wallace and Flora Jane Huggins, was born on September 13, 1884. He married **Minnie Loyd** circa 1906. He died on August 1, 1931 in Dillon County, SC and was buried on August 2, 1931 in Dillon, Dillon County, SC at Riverside Cemetery.

Minnie Loyd was born on January 8, 1885. She died on November 8, 1945 and was buried in Dillon, Dillon County, SC at Riverside Cemetery.

48. **Archie Wilson Wallace**, son of Thomas Walter Wallace and Flora Jane Huggins, was born on October 16, 1890 in Dillon County, SC. He died on July 7, 1939 in Dillon, Dillon County, SC and was buried on July 8, 1939 in Dillon, Dillon County, SC at Riverside Cemetery.

Essie Guill, daughter of William B. Guill (-) and Martha Scruggs (-), was born on August 3, 1895 in North Carolina. She died on December 31, 1939 in Dillon, Dillon County, SC.

54. **Mary Elizabeth Wallace**, daughter of Wesley Royce "Race" Wallace and Maggie Lester, was born on October 17, 1885. She died on August 7, 1945 and was buried in Dillon, Dillon County, SC at Riverside Cemetery.

George Edwards Bond was born on January 13, 1874. He died on August 24, 1955 and was buried in Dillon, Dillon County, SC at Riverside Cemetery. He and Mary Elizabeth Wallace had the following children:

> 157   Margaret Lanier Bond (1905-1987). *Margaret was born on April 25, 1905. She died on October 29, 1987.*

55. Cora Wallace, daughter of Wesley Royce "Race" Wallace and Maggie Lester, was born on August 12, 1887. She died on May 6, 1888 and was buried in Dillon County, SC at Baker Cemetery.

56. William Frank Wallace, son of Wesley Royce "Race" Wallace and Maggie Lester, was born on April 2, 1889. He died on November 19, 1963 in Lumberton, Robeson County, NC.

57. John Henry Wallace, son of Wesley Royce "Race" Wallace and Maggie Lester, was born on July 22, 1893. He died on July 27, 1966 in Southeastern Regional Medical Center, Lumberton, Robeson County, NC.

Vergie Mae McDaniel and John Henry Wallace had the following children:

> 158   Watson Wallace (-)
> 159   Thelma Wallace (-)
> 160   Ethlene Wallace (-)
> 161   Lurdene Wallace (-)

58. Lauch Wesley Wallace, son of Wesley Royce "Race" Wallace and Maggie Lester, was born on December 3, 1895. He died on October 24, 1981 and was buried in Rowland, Robeson County, NC at Ashpole Cemetery.

Annie Pearle Rogers was born on April 27, 1900. She died on July 22, 1994 and was buried in Rowland, Robeson County, NC at Ashpole Cemetery. She and Lauch Wesley Wallace had the following children:

> 162   Audrey Wallace (-)
> 163   Ruby Lois Wallace (-)
> 164   Carol Wallace (-)
> 165   Gladys Wallace (-)

65. Alice Wood Wallace, daughter of Arrie Lane Wallace and Nellie Wood Houston, was born on October 28, 1888. She died on July 12, 1959 and was buried in Little Rock, Dillon County, SC at Saint Paul's Methodist Church.

Andrew Jackson Wallace, son of Archie Young Wallace (1865-1925) and Anna Elizabeth Norton (1861-1934), was born on June 1, 1889. He died on September 26, 1961 and was buried in Little Rock, Dillon County, SC at Saint Paul's Methodist Church. He and Alice Wood Wallace had the following children:

> 166   Ira J. Wallace (1917-). *Ira was born in 1917.*
> 167   Genevieve Wallace (1919-2001). *Genevieve was born on July 8, 1919 in Dillon County, SC. She died on October 6, 2001 in Dillon County, SC and was buried in Little Rock, Dillon County, SC at Saint Paul's Methodist Church.*

67. Annie Wallace, daughter of Arrie Lane Wallace and Nellie Wood Houston, was born in May 1893. She died in 1964 and was buried in Dillon, Dillon County, SC at Greenlawn Cemetery.

Jessie Martin Altman was born in 1885. He died in 1966 and was buried in Dillon, Dillon County, SC at Greenlawn Cemetery. He and Annie Wallace had the following children:

> 168   Marie Altman (1919-2009). *Marie was born on October 22, 1919. She died on June 6, 2009.*

68. James William Wallace, son of Arrie Lane Wallace and Nellie Wood Houston, was born in December 1895.

Donnie Emily Barefoot was born in 1907. She died in 1998. She and James William Wallace had the following children:

> 169   James Ray Wallace Sr. (1927-). *James was born in 1927.*

Additional Information can be found at www.MooreCountyWallaces.com   **513**

70. **Ruth A. Wallace**, daughter of Arrie Lane Wallace and Nellie Wood Houston, was born on July 16, 1901. She died on March 4, 1984 and was buried in Little Rock, Dillon County, SC at Saint Paul's Methodist Church.

71. **Percy Michaux Wallace**, son of Arrie Lane Wallace and Nellie Wood Houston, was born on January 2, 1904. He died on December 6, 1948 and was buried in Little Rock, Dillon County, SC at Saint Paul's Methodist Church.

73. **Grace Wallace**, daughter of Arrie Lane Wallace and Nellie Wood Houston, was born on April 12, 1908. She died on May 14, 1982 and was buried in Little Rock, Dillon County, SC at Saint Paul's Methodist Church.

Clarence T. McCall was born on May 2, 1900. He died on March 23, 1982 and was buried in Little Rock, Dillon County, SC at Saint Paul's Methodist Church.

74. **Rufus Wallace**, son of Archie Young Wallace and Anna Elizabeth Norton, was born on November 24, 1886. He married **Mary L. Norton** on September 9, 1904. He died on September 11, 1943.

Mary L. Norton was born in 1887. She and Rufus Wallace had the following children:

170	Masie L. Wallace (1906-). *Masie was born in 1906.*
171	David J. Wallace (1907-). *David was born in 1907.*
172	Rufus Wallace (1909-). *Rufus was born in 1909.*
173	Annie Louise Wallace (1909-1967). *Annie was born on April 21, 1909 in Dillon County, SC. She died on August 9, 1967 in Asheboro, Randolph County, NC and was buried on August 11, 1967 in Mullins, SC at Millers Methodist Church.*

75. **Andrew Jackson Wallace**, son of Archie Young Wallace and Anna Elizabeth Norton, was born on June 1, 1889. He died on September 26, 1961 and was buried in Little Rock, Dillon County, SC at Saint Paul's Methodist Church.

Alice Wood Wallace, daughter of Arrie Lane Wallace (1861-1938) and Nellie Wood Houston (1865-1928), was born on October 28, 1888. She died on July 12, 1959 and was buried in Little Rock, Dillon County, SC at Saint Paul's Methodist Church. She and Andrew Jackson Wallace had the following children:

174	Ira J. Wallace (1917-). *Ira was born in 1917.*
175	Genevieve Wallace (1919-2001). *Genevieve was born on July 8, 1919 in Dillon County, SC. She died on October 6, 2001 in Dillon County, SC and was buried in Little Rock, Dillon County, SC at Saint Paul's Methodist Church.*

77. **Annie Missouri Wallace**, daughter of Archie Young Wallace and Anna Elizabeth Norton, was born on May 23, 1896 in SC. She died on November 12, 1946 in Raleigh, Wake County, NC and was buried on November 13, 1946 in Raleigh, Wake County, NC at Oakwood Cemetery.

78. **Boyd Wallace**, son of Archie Young Wallace and Anna Elizabeth Norton, was born on July 28, 1898.

Maggie was born in 1900. She and Boyd Wallace had the following children:

176	Gladys Elizabeth Wallace (1915-). *Gladys was born on November 3, 1915.*

80. **Archanna Wallace**, daughter of Archie Young Wallace and Anna Elizabeth Norton, was born on July 26, 1904 in Dillon County, SC and was buried on May 6, 1968 in Burlington, Alamance County, NC at Pine Hill Cemetery. She died on June 4, 1968 in Burlington, Alamance County, NC.

Nathan P. Hardwick was born in Dillon County, SC.

Descendants of Sarah Wallace

1. **Sarah "Sally" Wallace** was born in 1826, lived in the close vicinity of Everet's descendants and is very likely related. It is possible that she married into the Wallace family, but I believe that it more likely that she was a granddaughter of Everet Wallace. She had five children and was believed to have been married at least twice. She is listed in the 1850 Census as the head of household with two small children, Eli Wallace and Loveday Jane Wallace. Sally married Bazel Deaton (1823-Bef 1860) on September 16, 1851[164] in Moore County, NC and they were the parents of Joseph C. Deaton and Isaac Spinks Deaton. After Bazel's death she appears to have married a Britt between 1860-1863 and had one child, Raleigh Britt.

RECORDS OF SARAH "SALLY" WALLACE

1846, Jul -- 1785-1868 Index to Trial Docket, Moore County, NC Page 114
State v. Jonathan Richardson and Sally Wallace.

1847, Jan 30 -- 1844-1847 Court of Pleas and Quarter Sessions, Moore County, NC Page 482-483
State v. J. Richardson and Sally Wallace. Thomas Key was a witness.

1850, Nov 20 -- Census, Moore County, NC Page 246
Sarah Wallis 24 F, born in North Carolina
Eli Wallis 6 M, born in North Carolina
Loveday Wallis 1 F, born in North Carolina

1851, Sep 16 -- Record of Marriages, Moore County, NC Page 4
Bazel Deaton and Sally Wallace were married by George W. Cagle, Esq.

1860, Aug 28 -- Census, Moore County, NC Page 215-B, Caledonia Township
Sarah Deaton 33 F, Farmer, $100 Real Estate, $300 Personal Property, born in North Carolina
Elias Deaton 16 M, born in North Carolina
Lovedy Deaton 10 F, born in North Carolina
Joseph C. Deaton 6 M, born in North Carolina
Isaac Deaton 5 M, born in North Carolina
Patience Deaton 87 F, born in North Carolina

1870, Jul 21 -- Census, Moore County, NC Page 487-B, Bensalem Township, Carters Mill Post Office
Sarah Britt 43 F, born in North Carolina
Joseph Deaton 17 M, Laborer, born in North Carolina
Isaac Deaton 15 M, born in North Carolina
Raleigh Britt 7 M, born in North Carolina
Patience Deaton 93 F, Pauper, born in North Carolina

Sarah "Sally" Wallace had the following children:

+2   Eli Wallace (1844-1882) married Martha Clementine Williamson (1845-1933) and they were the parents of ten children.

+3   Loveday Jane Wallace (1849-) was married to Julius Davis (b. 1845) and had two children. She then married William Birch Morgan (1847-1922) and had five additional children.

Bazel Deaton, son of Burrell Deaton (1777-1854) and Patience Melton (1784-1872), was born in 1823. He died between 1856 and 1860. He and Sarah "Sally" Wallace had the following children:

+4   Joseph C. Deaton (1854-) is listed in the 1860 and 1870 census but no further record of him has been located.

+5   Isaac Spinks Deaton (1857-1918) married Jenny Watie Morgan (1853-1921) and they were the parents of seven children.

Additional Information can be found at www.MooreCountyWallaces.com

Britt and Sarah "Sally" Wallace had the following children:

> +6   Raleigh Britt (1863-) was listed in the 1870 census but no further record of him has been located.

Second Generation

2. **Eli Wallace**, son of Sarah "Sally" Wallace, was born on March 9, 1844 in Moore County, NC. He died on December 26, 1882 in Post Oak, Jack County, TX and was buried in Post Oak, Jack County, TX at Post Oak Cemetery.[165] Eli served in Company D, 48th Regiment during the Civil War. [166] After the war, he and Martha moved their family to Jack County, TX.

RECORDS OF ELI WALLACE

1850, Nov 20 -- Census, Moore County, NC Page 246
Sarah Wallis 24 F, born in North Carolina
Eli Wallis 6 M, born in North Carolina
Loveday Wallis 1 F, born in North Carolina

1860, Aug 28 -- Census, Moore County, NC Page 215-B, Caledonia Township
Sarah Deaton 33 F, Farmer, $100 Real Estate, $300 Personal Property, born in North Carolina
Elias Deaton 16 M, born in North Carolina
Lovedy Deaton 10 F, born in North Carolina
Joseph C. Deaton 6 M, born in North Carolina
Isaac Deaton 5 M, born in North Carolina
Patience Deaton 87 F, born in North Carolina

1862, Feb 25 -- Civil War Service Records
Eli Wallace enlisted in Company D, 48th Regiment in Moore County, NC at age 17

1862, Sep 17 -- Civil War Service Records
Eli Wallace wounded at Sharpsburg, MD

1863, Jun 4 -- Civil War Service Records
Eli Wallace sent to Hospital in Goldsboro, NC

Eli Wallace and Martha Clementine Williamson
(Courtesy of Stephen Ramming)

1880, Jun 15 -- Census, Jack County, TX Page 37-B, Precinct #3
E. Wallis 45 M, Head, Married, Farmer, born in North Carolina, father & mother born in North Carolina
Martha C. Wallis 44 F, Wife, Married, Keeping House, born in North Carolina, father & mother born in North Carolina
Catherine Wallis 14 F, Dau, Single, born in North Carolina, father & mother born in North Carolina
Thomas Wallis 12 M, Son, Single, Works on Farm, born in North Carolina, father & mother born in North Carolina
Jane Wallis 10 F, Dau, Single, born in North Carolina, father & mother born in North Carolina
James Wallis 8 M, Son, born in North Carolina, father & mother born in North Carolina
Allis Wallis 6 F, Dau, born in North Carolina, father & mother born in North Carolina
Sarah Wallis 5 F, Dau, born in North Carolina, father & mother born in North Carolina
Laney Wallis 4 M, Son, born in Texas, father & mother born in North Carolina
Emma Wallis 1 F, Dau, born in Texas, father & mother born in North Carolina
C. Williamson 55 F, Mother-In-Law, born in North Carolina, father & mother born in North Carolina

1880 -- Agricultural Census, Moore County, NC Page 13, Sheffield Township
Eli Wallace listed 75 acres Improved Fields, 200 acres Unimproved Wooded valued at $1000

Martha Clementine Williamson, daughter of Cynthia Williamson (1827-), was born on March 9, 1845 in Moore County, NC. She died on March 25, 1933 in Post Oak, Jack County, TX and was buried on March 26, 1933 in Post Oak, Jack County, TX at Post Oak Cemetery.[167] She and Eli Wallace had the following children:

> +7   Catherine Elizabeth Wallace (1866-1934)
> +8   Asa Thomas Wallace (1868-1934)
> +9   Rebecca Jane Wallace (1870-)

+10	James W. "Jimmie" Wallace (1872-1931)
+11	Cynthia Alice Wallace (1873-1935)
+12	Sarah F. Wallace (1875-1915)
+13	Laney Wallace (1876-)
+14	Emma Wallace (1879-1975)
+15	Male Wallace (1881-1881)
+16	John Franklin Wallace (1882-1961)

3. **Loveday Jane Wallace**, daughter of Sarah "Sally" Wallace, was born in 1849. A 1903 article on the murder trial of her son Asa Morgan describes a wife trade between Julius Davis and William Birch Morgan as follows *"admissions of the mother of the prisoner while she was on the stand that her husband was a Davis whom she married many years ago. After having been married to Davis for a short while there was a trade or swap made by her husband with a man by the name of Morgan. The two men swapped wives without any other formalities further than an exchange. Mrs. Morgan, as she is called, is an old woman and the mother of 12 children, four of whom were born after the exchange of wives by the two men."*[168]

RECORDS OF LOVEDAY JANE WALLACE

1850, Nov 20 -- Census, Moore County, NC Page 246
Sarah Wallis 24 F, born in North Carolina
Eli Wallis 6 M, born in North Carolina
Loveday Wallis 1 F, born in North Carolina

1860, Aug 28 -- Census, Moore County, NC Page 215-B, Caledonia Township
Sarah Deaton 33 F, Farmer, $100 Real Estate, $300 Personal Property, born in North Carolina
Elias Deaton 16 M, born in North Carolina
Lovedy Deaton 10 F, born in North Carolina
Joseph C. Deaton 6 M, born in North Carolina
Isaac Deaton 5 M, born in North Carolina
Patience Deaton 87 F, born in North Carolina

1870, Jul 21 -- Census, Moore County, NC Page 487-B, Bensalem Township, Carters Mill Post Office
Julias Davis 25 M, born in Georgia
Lovdy Davis 20 F, born in North Carolina
Eli Davis 1 M, born in North Carolina
Sarah E. Davis 2/12(Mar) F, born in North Carolina

1880, Jun 21 -- Census, Moore County, NC Page 207-B, Bensalem Township
Lovedy Davis 30 F, Head, Married, Keeping House, born in North Carolina, father & mother born in North Carolina
Eli Davis 9 M, Son, born in North Carolina, father & mother born in North Carolina
Sarrah E. Davis 9 F, Dau, born in North Carolina, father & mother born in North Carolina
William Davis 3 M, Son, born in North Carolina, father & mother born in North Carolina
Asa J. Davis 2 M, Son, born in North Carolina, father & mother born in North Carolina
William Morgan 30 M, Servant, Married, born in North Carolina, father & mother born in North Carolina

1900, Jun 18 -- Census, Moore County, NC Page 66-B, Sheffields Township
Lovie Davis 55 F, May 1845, Head, Widow, 12 Children(6 Living), born in North Carolina, father & mother born in North Carolina
William B. Davis 23 M, Jan 1877, Son, Single, Day Laborer (Saw Mill), born in North Carolina, father & mother born in North Carolina
Asa J. Davis 22 M, Jan 1878, Son, Single, Day Laborer (Saw Mill), born in North Carolina, father & mother born in North Carolina
Louise Davis 20 F, May 1880, Dau, Single, born in North Carolina, father & mother born in North Carolina
Laney Davis 14 M, July 1885, Son, Single, Day Laborer (Saw Mill), born in North Carolina, father & mother born in North Carolina
Kiser Davis 13 M, May 1887, Son, Single, Day Laborer (Saw Mill), born in North Carolina, father & mother born in North Carolina

1903, Jan 29 -- Article, *Asheboro Courier* [Asheboro, NC] Newspaper
Asa Morgan Barely Escapes the Rope "At 5 o'clock at Troy the trial of Asa Morgan closed, and the jury took the case. The trial consumed the greater part of three days. On the 25th of May 1902, Burch Morgan killed Edwin H. Reger, near Candor. Reger had served in the Cuban army and was probably from Virginia but had been at work a short time before his death at Biscoe. It appears that he had gone to Burch Morgan's to purchase whiskey on that Sunday morning. He had left Morgan's mother after some little altercation with the Morgan boys and started with Jim Wall. He had gone only a short distance from the house when he was overtaken by Burch Morgan who shot him twice from which he died without uttering a word in a few hours. James Wall, a son of Pinkney Wall, living in Tabernacle township, was the principal witness and was with Reger when Burch Morgan came toward them cursing and swearing he would kill Reger. Wall stepped behind a clump of bushes and Burch came up and fired one shot which did not seem to take effect, the second one entered the temple. Wall says that after the first firing someone in the bushes nearby, whose form looked like Asa Morgan's and whose voice he recognized distinctly as Asa Morgan's, said to his brother Burch with an oath "Shoot him again." Wall then ran. Will Carriker, another young man from Randolph County, was a witness and he and Alex Green testified that both the Morgans had repeatedly threatened to kill

Reger before during the day. There was other testimony tending to show the premeditation and deliberation on the part of the Morgans to kill Reger. The verdict was evidently a compromise verdict as was the Wilcox verdict. Wall and Carriker had gone with Reger that day and neither of them had ever seen anyone of those who were present at Mrs. Morgan's or about there that day. Liquor and women figured in the trial. Burch Morgan has not been apprehended and is still at large although there is a reward for him by the Governor of the State. Asa Morgan was sentenced to 20 years in the State's prison."

1903, Feb 3 -- Article, *Statesville Landmark* [Statesville, NC] Newspaper
"A Wife Trade That Was Allowed to Stand" Asheboro Courier (Jan 29, 1903)
"During the trial of Asa Morgan at Troy last week for the murder of Reger an account came out from the admissions of the mother of the prisoner while she was on the stand that her husband was a Davis whom she married many years ago. After having been married to Davis for a short while there was a trade or swap made by her husband with a man by the name of Morgan. The two men swapped wives without any other formalities further than an exchange. Mrs. Morgan, as she is called, is an old woman and the mother of 12 children, four of whom were born after the exchange of wives by the two men. Since the killing of Reger a son of Mrs. Morgan was killed by John Richardson. It is alleged in self defense; and since the last term of Troy court John Richardson has married a daughter of Mrs. Morgan, a full sister of the young man killed by Richardson."

1903, Mar 17 -- Article, *Statesville Landmark* [Statesville, NC] Newspaper
"Lane Morgan shot and instantly killed John Richardson near Candor, Montgomery County, Saturday. The two men were at the home of Marshal Pitman, whose wife is Richardson's sister. Morgan drew a revolver crying, "You killed my brother and I'll kill you," shot Richardson dead. A few months ago, Richardson had killed a half brother of Morgan."

1903, Mar 19 -- Article, *Asheboro Courier* [Asheboro, NC] Newspaper
Biscoe Items - "Another murder was perpetrated in Hollingsworth township, Montgomery County, near the Iola and Montgomery gold mines, about two o'clock Saturday afternoon, when Lane Morgan shot and instantly killed his brother-in-law John Richardson. It seems that Morgan wanted Richardson's wife, who is Morgan's sister to leave Richardson in no acute distress run away with Allen Richardson, a cousin of John's and for some reason it was not working to suit Morgan so he went to Marshall Pitman's house, where Richardson was and shot him with a pistol, the bullet entering the right temple. A warrant was issued for three persons who were claimed to be implicated in the crime, viz. Lane Morgan, Keyser Morgan and Allen Richardson, but they have not as yet been apprehended. This the third murder committed near this same place in the last few months. Two of the Morgans, Asa and Burch, killed E.H. Regger some months ago and John Richardson, soon after killed Eli Davis, the Morgan's half-brother and then married Morgan's sister and now the Morgan's have killed him. Murder seems to be a very common affair among these people."

1903, May 21 -- Article, *Asheboro Courier* [Asheboro, NC] Newspaper
Biscoe Items - "Lane Morgan, who killed John Richardson, his brother-in-law, near Candor, two or three months ago and Kaiser Morgan and Allen Richardson, his accomplices are now lodged in Troy jail, Montgomery County, to await the next term of Superior Court, when they will be tried for murder. Richardson was caught one day last week at or near Chesterfield, SC and when lodged in jail it seems it turned State's evidence and divulged the whereabouts of the Morgan boys and they were caught and were carried and place in jail Monday afternoon. These fellows succeeded in evading the officers of the law for quite a while and Asa and Burch Morgan, who were charged with killing E.H. Regger several months ago, are still at large."

1903, May 21 -- Article, *The Messenger and Intelligencer* [Wadesboro, NC] Newspaper
"A Bloodthirsty Gang -- Morgan Boys, who killed several people in Montgomery County, captured -- history of their crimes and capture. A Chesterfield correspondent of the Columbia, SC, State, writing under the date of Saturday, May 16th, give the following particulars of the capture and the history of the crimes of the Morgan boys, who, within the last few months, have killed several people in Montgomery County: Wednesday Messrs. D.A. and J.C. Batten arrested at their saw mill near Ruby one Allan Richardson, wanted for murder in Montgomery County, NC. Richardson came to the mills of the Messrs. Batten and hired to them as a hand. Learning that he was wanted in NC and that a reward of $50 was offered for his capture, they arrested him and carried him to Cheraw, where Mr. D.A. Batten then went on to Troy NC and had Richardson lodged in jail. This morning Sheriff D.B. Douglass, accompanied by his son, arrested at Mt. Croghan, nine mile west of here, Lane Morgan and brought him to jail here. Several months ago in Montgomery County, NC, Birch and Asa Morgan, two brothers, became engaged in a difficulty with a man named Driggers and as a result Birch Morgan shot and killed Driggers. He then escaped. Asa, his brother, was tried and found guilty of murder in the second degree and was sentenced to the penitentiary for 20 years, but subsequently escaped. Not long afterwards, a man named John Richardson killed a brother of the above mentioned Morgan. Richardson was a brother-in-law to the man Morgan whom he had killed. Two more Morgan boys, Lane and Kyser and Allan Richardson then killed John Richardson. John Richardson and Allan Richardson were half brothers and John Richardson married the Morgan boys' sister; thus the Morgan and Allan Richardson killed their brother in law and half brother, respectively. All these succeeded in getting away without capture. Rewards were offered for prisoners as follows: Birch Morgan $250; Lane Morgan $250; Kyser Morgan $50; Asa Morgan $50 and Allan Richardson $50. The first two Morgan boys were wanted as principals for their respective murders; Kyser Morgan and Allan Richardson as accessories and Asa Morgan as an escaped convict. Last week Sheriff Douglass arrested a man named Green, whom he took for Allan Richardson. Green filled the description of Richardson very well, but when Deputy Sheriff McKinsey, of Montgomery County, arrived to identify him it was found that he was not the man. Learning that several strangers were working at Mr. Oscar Taylor's saw mill at Mt. Croghan, this county and that they spent their nights in the woods, Sheriff Douglass investigated the matter and decided that they were the Morgan boys. Accordingly, he with his son and Mr. Will Ratliff this morning went to the house where the Morgans were staying, but they hadn't come out of the woods, at that hour. In a few minutes, the Morgans were seen approaching. Before the Morgans were aware of it they were arrested. But being desperate characters, they did not submit easily. While the sheriff was placing the nippers on Lane, Kyser ran and got away. In the meantime, Birch, the most desperate of them all, knocked Mr. Ratliff's gun down and started to run. Mr. Ratliff caught him and called for help. Birch pulled a pistol and shot at Mr. Ratliff but failed to hit him. He

then ran and succeeded in making good his escape. Lane was brought safely to jail. A posse is now out hunting for Birch and Kyser Morgan and everything possible will be done to apprehend them. Lane Morgan is common looking and says he is 21 years old. He acknowledges the killing of John Richardson but claims self defense. He says that he did the shooting and his brother Kyser and Allan Richardson had nothing to do with it. He says that John Richardson had a gun drawn on him when he was shot. He did not know that his brother Asa had escaped from the penitentiary. "My brother Birch is 24 years old and my brother Kyser is only 17 years old." he said. The Morgans were raised in Moore County, but for the past several years have lived in the adjoining county of Montgomery; they live seven miles from Troy, the county seat. Lane told the writer that his father left a living wife in Moore County and came to Anson County, near Wadesboro and married again, thus committing the crime of bigamy. The Morgans are a bad people and engage sometimes in making "moonshine" whiskey. Lane Morgan will be kept in jail here until Monday and will then be carried to Troy. NC. Sheriff Douglass has telegraphed to Darlington for bloodhounds to assist in trailing Birch and Kyser Morgan, who are still at large. By capturing Lane Morgan, Sheriff Douglass will secure the reward of $250 offered for him. The Messrs. Batten will receive $50 for Allan Richardson's arrest. If Birch and Kyser are captured $300 more will be forthcoming. According to Lane Morgan, Asa Morgan is not in the county and he and his brother did not know of his escape from the penitentiary. Sheriff Douglass has been at work upon this case for several weeks and has spent a good deal of money in tracking the gang. It is earnestly hoped that the others will be captured. Later -- As your correspondent was finishing this article a phone message from Ruby states that Mr. Jule Rivers has succeeded in capturing Kyser Morgan, the youngest of the Morgan boys. He is now being brought to jail. The posse is close on Birch Morgan's trail and he will probably be captured."

[Above] **Kizer Morgan** *(Courtesy of Lauren McCLure)*
[Left] **Burch Morgan and Lottie Mae Lovett**
(Courtesy of Ancestry user alimorg9)

1904, Feb 23 -- Article, *Statesville Landmark* [Statesville, NC] Newspaper
"Dangerous Criminals Who Have Escaped the Courts and the Penitentiary" Rockingham Anglo-Saxon
"In May 1903, Birch Morgan and Asa Morgan, two brothers, shot and killed a man named Reager, in Montgomery County, eight miles east of Troy. Birch Morgan did the shooting. Asa was arrested, was tried and convicted in Montgomery court, fall term, 1903, for aiding and abetting in the murder of Reager. He was convicted of murder in the second degree and sentenced to thirty years in the State penitentiary. Within six months, he escaped. Birch Morgan has never been caught. Both are at large. Last May Lane Morgan, Kiser Morgan and Allen Richardson, after making threats, went to Marshall Pittman's home, where John Richardson was employed as a farm hand and Lane Morgan shot and killed him (John Richardson). After some months all three were arrested in South Carolina and were brought to Troy for trial. Last October, Lane Morgan was convicted of murder in the second degree and sentenced to thirty years in the State prison; Kiser was sentenced to twelve years in the penitentiary. Allen Richardson was acquitted. One of our Troy correspondents notes the fact that Lane Morgan has escaped from the penitentiary authorities."

1904, Mar 15 -- Article, *The Monroe Journal* [Monroe, NC] Newspaper
"Murderer Arrested Here - Birch Morgan, a Desperado of Montgomery County, is Rounded Up by Constable Bivens After a Slow Trail Lasting Nearly a Year."

1904, Mar 18 -- Article, *Statesville Landmark* [Statesville, NC] Newspaper
"State News - Birch Morgan, a young desperado who is wanted for murder in Montgomery County and who has been at large for some time, was arrested in Monroe last week and taken to the Montgomery County jail. A reward of $250 was offered for Morgan and Constable Bivens who made the arrest will receive it"

1904, Mar 24 -- Article, *The Enterprise* [Albemarle, NC] Newspaper
"Last of the Morgan Gang -- In speaking of the arrest of Birch Morgan, in Monroe on the 10th instant, who is wanted for the murder of E.H. Reger, which occurred near Candor nearly two years ago, the *Troy Examiner* says: This is the last of that desperate family of Morgans who have become so prominent as criminals. The other three, Asa, Lane and Keyser have been convicted and sentenced to the penitentiary for 30, 20 and 12 years respectively, but Asa and Lane having escaped are now running at large. Birch is charged as being the one who did the actual shooting in the Reger murder, Asa having been convicted as an accessory. In the trial of Asa, all the evidence pointed towards Birch as the real murderer, and if the same evidence can be reproduced, he will likely follow the others to the penitentiary, should he escape the gallows."

1904, Oct 4 -- Article, *Monroe Journal* [Monroe, NC] Newspaper
"Trial of Burch Morgan. Murderer who was captured in Monroe some months ago sentenced to be hanged. A Family of criminals. Many people no doubt remember reading in The Journal about the capture of Burch Morgan in Monroe some months ago by Mr. H.J. Bivens, then constable of this township. Morgan was wanted in Montgomery County for murder. He worked on Rocky River after fleeing from his home after the murder. There it was that Mr. Bivens first began to shadow him. Then he came down to the sawmill of Funderburk and Birmingham, eight miles south of town and worked. All the time Constable Bivens was watching him for an opportunity to capture him. Morgan went heavily armed all the time. Finally, one-day last spring, Bivens succeeded in decoying him to Monroe and arrested him on the public square. Morgan was tried at Troy last week and sentenced to be hanged. The Troy correspondent of the *Charlotte Observer* gives the following account of the trial: The jury, after being out about 20 hours, returned a verdict of murder in the first degree. The worry and anxiety through which he has undergone the past few days is telling on him. His young-looking wife and his mother have been with him throughout the trial. Owing to the low social and financial standing of both the defendant and the deceased, Edwin Reger, comparatively little interest has been manifested in the trial. Judge Cooke has presided with his usual fairness to both State and defendant and is being highly commended by all who have heard the trial. The Morgan family have quite a history in Montgomery County. There are five boys in the family and within the last two years four of them have been convicted of murder and the other one has been murdered. It was developed on the trial Thursday that the husband of the mother of the Morgan boys and a man by the name of Davis swapped wives and that one paid the other a dollar and a half to boot and it seems that both were well pleased. At the Jan term 1902, Asa Morgan was convicted of murder in the second degree, for assisting Burch Morgan in the killing of Edwin H. Reger and was sentenced to twenty years in the penitentiary. At the Sep term 1903, Lane Morgan and Kisa Morgan, the two youngest brothers, were convicted of murder in the second degree for killing their brother-in-law John Richardson and were sentenced to the state penitentiary for 30 and 12 years, respectively. There was quite a sensation in the court room Thursday when Kisa Morgan, who is now in the penitentiary, was brought into court to testify in behalf of the defendant. The cries and shrieks of Mrs. Morgan reminded one more of a Holiness meeting than anything else. Judge Cooke said: "Mr. Sheriff, take that woman out of the court room. We can't' have any such carrying on as that in here. Asa Morgan and Lane Morgan who were sentenced to 20 and 30 years, respectively, have both escaped from the State prison and are now at large. There is some fear that they will attempt to liberate Burch Morgan before the day of execution."

1905, Jan 25 -- Article, *News and Observer* [Raleigh, NC] Newspaper
"Commutation Granted -- Governor Glenn Commutes Death Sentence of Birch Morgan to Life Imprisonment. Governor Glenn has commuted the death sentence of Birch Morgan, the young white man of Montgomery County, who was sentenced to hang in February, to like imprisonment. This was done upon the recommendation of the trial judge, the solicitor, and many prominent people of Montgomery County some time last year and was convicted and sentenced to die. This man Morgan come from pretty bad stock. The records of his kinsmen is one of crime. Morgan's father has had three sons convicted of murder: and by the way, the old man's record is not so clean either. During the trial of Birch Morgan it was brought out that Birch's father, while living on a farm near the town of Lilesville, in Anson County, exchanged wives with a neighbor tenant and one paid the other $1.50 to boot. A sad record for a father and his boys. Their records are worthy of serious consideration. This was Governor Glenn's first act of executive clemency"

Julias Davis was born in 1845. He and Loveday Jane Wallace had the following children:

+17   Eli Davis (1869-1902)
+18   Sarah E. Davis (1870-)

William Birch Morgan, son of Pleasant S. Morgan (1827-) and Elizabeth Williams (1830-), was born on December 22, 1847 in Moore County, NC. He married Nancy Jane Hathcock circa 1893. He died on February 10, 1922 in Norwood, Stanly County, NC and was buried on February 11, 1922 in Norwood, Stanly County, NC at Norwood Cemetery.[169] He and Loveday Jane Wallace had the following children:

+19   William Burch Morgan (1877-1952)

+20	Asa Morgan (1878-)
+21	Louise Morgan (1880-1955)
+22	Lane A. Morgan (1881-1963)
+23	Kizer Anderson Morgan (1881-1967)

5. Isaac Spinks Deaton, son of Bazel Deaton and Sarah "Sally" Wallace, was born on July 15, 1857. He died on December 18, 1918 in High Point, Guilford County, NC and was buried on December 20, 1918 in Star, Montgomery County, NC.[170]

RECORDS OF ISAAC SPINKS DEATON

1860, Aug 28 -- Census, Moore County, NC Page 215-B, Caledonia Township
Sarah Deaton 33 F, Farmer, $100 Real Estate, $300 Personal Property, born in North Carolina
Elias Deaton 16 M, born in North Carolina
Lovedy Deaton 10 F, born in North Carolina
Joseph C. Deaton 6 M, born in North Carolina
Isaac Deaton 5 M, born in North Carolina
Patience Deaton 87 F, born in North Carolina

1870, Jul 21 -- Census, Moore County, NC Page 487-B, Bensalem Township, Carters Mill Post Office
Sarah Britt 43 F, born in North Carolina
Joseph Deaton 17 M, Laborer, born in North Carolina
Isaac Deaton 15 M, born in North Carolina
Raleigh Britt 7 M, born in North Carolina
Patience Deaton 93 F, Pauper, born in North Carolina

1880, Jun 21 -- Census, Moore County, NC Page 207-B, Bensalem Township
Isaac Deaton 23 M, Head, Married, Farmer - Planter, born in North Carolina, father & mother born in North Carolina
Waity Deaton 25 F, Wife, Married, Keeping House, born in North Carolina, father & mother born in North Carolina
Sallie Deaton 6 F, Dau, born in North Carolina, father & mother born in North Carolina
James T. Deaton 4 M, Son, born in North Carolina, father & mother born in North Carolina
Lydia Deaton 7/12 (Nov) F, Dau, born in North Carolina, father & mother born in North Carolina
John A. Deaton 8 M, Son, born in North Carolina, father & mother born in North Carolina

1900, Jun 4 -- Census, Moore County, NC Page 36, Bensalem Township
Isaac S. Deaton 45 M, July 1854, Head, Married-25yrs, Farmer, born in North Carolina, father & mother born in North Carolina
Waity Deaton 49 F, Aug 1850, Wife, Married-25yrs, born in North Carolina, father & mother born in North Carolina
Lena Deaton 18 F, Jan 1882, Dau, Single, At School, born in North Carolina, father & mother born in North Carolina
James T. Deaton 23 M, July 1876, Son, Single, Laborer (Saw Mill), born in North Carolina, father & mother born in North Carolina
Aaron Deaton 14 M, Aug 1885, Son, Single, At School, born in North Carolina, father & mother born in North Carolina
Noah C. Deaton 12 M, Sep 1887, Son, Single, At School, born in North Carolina, father & mother born in North Carolina
Alma Deaton 5 F, July 1894, Dau, Single, born in North Carolina, father & mother born in North Carolina

1910, Apr 28 -- Census, Moore County, NC Page 101-B, Bensalem Township
Isaac Deaton 52 M, Head, Married(1st-30yrs), Log Cutter (Saw Mill), born in North Carolina, father & mother born in North Carolina
Waity Deaton 55 F, Wife, Married(1st-30yrs), 12 Children(7 Living), Farm Laborer (Home Farm), born in North Carolina, father & mother born in North Carolina
Mattie L. Deaton 28 F, Dau, Single, Farm Laborer (Home Farm), born in North Carolina, father & mother born in North Carolina
Noah C. Deaton 21 M, Son, Single, Log Cutter (Saw Mill), born in North Carolina, father & mother born in North Carolina
Alma Deaton 15 F, Dau, Single, born in North Carolina, father & mother born in North Carolina

1918, Dec 18 -- Death Certificate, Guilford County, NC
I.S. Deaton died in High Point. Husband of Watie Deaton. Date of birth: July 15, 1857. Age: 61y5m0d. Occupation: Mechanic. Birthplace: NC. Father: Deaton. Birthplace of Father: NC. Mother: Sallie Wallace. Birthplace of Mother: NC. Cause of Death: Pneumonia, Influenza (contributing). Place of Burial: Moore County, NC. Date of Burial: Dec 20, 1918. Undertaker: R.L. Loflin. Informant: J.T. Deaton

Jenny Watie Morgan, daughter of John Morgan (1803-1891) and Malinda Richardson (1810-), was born in August 1853. She died on September 1, 1921 in High Point, Guilford County, NC and was buried on September 5, 1921 in Star, Montgomery County, NC.[171] She and Isaac Spinks Deaton had the following children:

+24	James Thomas Deaton (1872-1955)
+25	Sarah Jane Deaton (1874-)
+26	Lydia Deaton (1879-)
+27	Mattie Lena Deaton (1882-)

+28	Aaron Deaton (1883-1922)
+29	Noah Cleveland Deaton (1887-1958)
+30	Alma Deaton (1895-1918)

Third Generation

7. **Catherine Elizabeth Wallace**, daughter of Eli Wallace and Martha Clementine Williamson, was born on June 30, 1866 in Moore County, NC. She married **Joseph D. Ritchey** on April 8, 1888 in Jack County, TX. She died on September 10, 1934 in Jack County, TX and was buried on September 12, 1934 in Post Oak, Jack County, TX at Post Oak Cemetery.

Joseph D. Ritchey was born on January 30, 1866 in Tennessee. He died on June 9, 1939 and was buried in Post Oak, Jack County, TX at Post Oak Cemetery. He and Catherine Elizabeth Wallace had the following children:

31	Martha Elizabeth Alice Ritchey (1889-1970). *Martha was born on October 9, 1889. She died on January 27, 1970 and was buried in Post Oak, Jack County, TX at Post Oak Cemetery.*
32	Sarah M. Ritchey (1891-). *Sarah was born in February 1891.*
33	William Eli Ritchey (1895-1968). *William was born on November 29, 1895 in Post Oak, Jack County, TX. He died on March 7, 1968 in Graham, Texas and was buried in Post Oak, Jack County, TX at Post Oak Cemetery.*
34	Linnie May Ritchey (1899-1899). *Linnie was born on May 16, 1899. She died on June 9, 1899 and was buried in Post Oak, Jack County, TX at Post Oak Cemetery.*
35	Infant Ritchey (1902-1902). *Infant was born on August 22, 1902. She died on August 23, 1902 and was buried in Post Oak, Jack County, TX at Post Oak Cemetery.*

8. **Asa Thomas Wallace**, son of Eli Wallace and Martha Clementine Williamson, was born on March 7, 1868 in North Carolina. He died on March 21, 1934 in Post Oak, Jack County, TX and was buried on March 22, 1934 in Post Oak, Jack County, TX at Post Oak Cemetery.

9. **Rebecca Jane Wallace**, daughter of Eli Wallace and Martha Clementine Williamson, was born on July 12, 1870 in MO. She married **Wylie Horn** on August 21, 1889 in Jack County, TX.

Wylie Horn was born in September 1865 in KY. He and Rebecca Jane Wallace had the following children:

36	Erbie Horn (1890-). *Erbie was born in June 1890.*
37	Elmer Horn (1892-). *Elmer was born in May 1892.*
38	Kelsey Marshal Horn (1898-). *Kelsey was born in June 1898 in OK.*
39	Linnie Rebecca Horn (1903-1973). *Linnie was born on April 23, 1903. She died on December 20, 1973.*
40	Lela Horn (1907-). *Lela was born in 1907.*

10. **James W. "Jimmie" Wallace**, son of Eli Wallace and Martha Clementine Williamson, was born on April 19, 1872 in Post Oak, Jack County, TX. He died on January 30, 1931 in Iowa Park, Wichita County, TX and was buried in Iowa Park, Wichita County, TX at Highland Cemetery.

11. **Cynthia Alice Wallace**, daughter of Eli Wallace and Martha Clementine Williamson, was born on September 25, 1873 in North Carolina or MO. She died on May 20, 1935 in Post Oak, Jack County, TX and was buried on May 20, 1935 in Post Oak, Jack County, TX at Kilby Cemetery.

Robert L. Dillard was born in 1877.

12. **Sarah F. Wallace**, daughter of Eli Wallace and Martha Clementine Williamson, was born on April 13, 1875 in Texas. She died in 1915 and was buried in Post Oak, Jack County, TX at Post Oak Cemetery.

Daniel W. "Tuck" Catlin, son of Eli F. Catlin (1830-1897) and Margaret K. (1834-), was born in June 1873 in MO. He and Sarah F. Wallace had the following children:

| 41 | Eli F. Catlin (1895-). *Eli was born in 1895.* |
| 42 | Flora E. Catlin (1899-). *Flora was born in 1899.* |

43	James Catlin (1906-). *James was born in 1906.*
44	Lula Maudie Catlin (1908-). *Lula was born in 1908.*
45	Cecil Catlin (1913-). *Cecil was born in 1913.*
46	Gracie Catlin (1914-). *Gracie was born in 1914.*

14. **Emma Wallace**, daughter of Eli Wallace and Martha Clementine Williamson, was born on March 20, 1879 in Texas. She died on February 27, 1975 and was buried in Post Oak, Jack County, TX at Post Oak Cemetery.

Charles Centennial Cocanower was born in 1876. He died in 1951 and was buried in Stephens County, OK at Tidwell Cemetery. He and Emma Wallace had the following children:

47	Lena Cocanower (1911-). *Lena was born in 1911.*
48	Lela Lee Cocanower (1912-1978). *Lela was born in 1912. She died in 1978 and was buried in Stephens County, OK at Marlow Cemetery.*
49	Anna Bell Cocanower (1915-2005). *Anna was born on March 22, 1915 in Jack County, TX. She died on February 20, 2005 in Calvert, Robertson County, TX and was buried in Hope, Stephens County, OK at Ramming Family Cemetery.*
50	Charles Tom Cocanower (1918-1991). *Charles was born in 1918. He died in 1991 and was buried in Hope, Stephens County, OK at Ramming Family Cemetery.*

Jim Wilson and Emma Wallace had the following children:

| 51 | Martha Clementine Wilson (1907-1997). *Martha was born on January 21, 1907. She died on November 10, 1997 and was buried in Springtown, Parker County, TX at Springtown Cemetery.* |

16. **John Franklin Wallace**, son of Eli Wallace and Martha Clementine Williamson, was born on July 3, 1882 in Post Oak, Jack County, TX. He died on October 14, 1961 in Weatherford, Parker County, TX and was buried on October 17, 1961 in Post Oak, Jack County, TX at Post Oak Cemetery.

17. **Eli Davis**, son of Julias Davis and Loveday Jane Wallace, was born in 1869. He married **Mary Frances "Fannie" Furr** on June 19, 1892 in Moore County, NC. He died in August 1902.

Mary Frances "Fannie" Furr, daughter of Mary Elizabeth Furr (1849-1922), was born on July 15, 1870. She died on November 24, 1908 and was buried in Robbins, Moore County, NC at Tabernacle United Methodist Church. She and Eli Davis had the following children:

52	Wiley Carson "Babe" Davis (1891-1953). *Wiley was born on April 19, 1891. He married* ***Mary May Britt*** *on August 19, 1916. He died on August 21, 1953 and was buried in Moore County, NC at Brown's Chapel Christian Church.*
53	Eli G. Davis (1893-). *Eli was born in April 1893.*
54	Gaston Adam Davis (1896-1976). *Gaston was born on February 15, 1896. He died on April 26, 1976 and was buried in Moore County, NC at Brown's Chapel Christian Church.*
55	Etta Mae Davis (1900-1979). *Etta was born on September 6, 1900. She died on September 13, 1979 and was buried in Armstrong County, TX at Claude Cemetery.*
56	Barney Lee Davis (1903-1981). *Barney was born on March 7, 1903. He married* ***Mandie Alma Garner*** *on April 11, 1925 in Moore County, NC. He died on November 11, 1981 and was buried in Robbins, Moore County, NC at Tabernacle United Methodist Church.*

19. **William Burch Morgan**, son of William Birch Morgan and Loveday Jane Wallace, was born on January 13, 1877 in Moore County, NC. He died on February 11, 1952 in Dillon County, SC and was buried in Lumberton, Robeson County, NC at Gunn Cemetery.

Lottie Mae Lovett, daughter of Dawson Lovett (-) and Lula (-), was born on April 3, 1894. She died on September 21, 1962 in Cabarrus Memorial Hospital, Concord, Cabarrus County, NC and was buried on September 23, 1962 in Lumberton, Robeson County, NC at Gunn Cemetery. She and William Burch Morgan had the following children:

| 57 | Rembert Dawson Morgan (1913-1977). *Rembert was born on March 9, 1913. He died on April 18, 1977 in Robeson County, NC.* |

58	Willie B. Morgan (1916-). *Willie was born in 1916.*
59	Johnny Thomas Morgan Sr. (1920-1969). *Johnny was born on April 18, 1920. He died on April 19, 1969 in Cabarrus Memorial Hospital, Concord, Cabarrus County, NC and was buried on April 22, 1969 in Kannapolis, Cabarrus County, NC at Carolina Memorial Park.*
60	Frank Morgan (1922-). *Frank was born in 1922.*
61	Pearly M. Morgan (1925-). *Pearly was born in 1925.*
62	Mina L. Morgan (1927-). *Mina was born in 1927.*
63	Freddie Morgan (1929-). *Freddie was born in 1929.*

21. **Louise Morgan**, daughter of William Birch Morgan and Loveday Jane Wallace, was born on May 15, 1880 in Moore County, NC. She married **John F. Richardson** on November 2, 1902 in Montgomery County, NC. She died on October 22, 1955 in Concord, Cabarrus County, NC and was buried on October 24, 1955 in Concord, Cabarrus County, NC at Union Grove/West Concord Cemetery.

Andrew Deese and Louise Morgan had the following children:

| 64 | Lizzie Deese (1903-1949). *Lizzie was born on August 15, 1903 in Moore County, NC. She married **Lane A. Morgan** on July 8, 1920 in Robeson County, NC. She died on April 10, 1949 in Cabarrus Memorial Hospital, Concord, Cabarrus County, NC and was buried on April 12, 1949 in Concord, Cabarrus County, NC at Oakwood Cemetery.* |

Sheffield and Louise Morgan had the following children:

65	William Bennett Sheffield (1905-1984). *William was born on December 5, 1905. He died on February 6, 1984.*
66	Ira Lane Sheffield (1913-1979). *Ira was born on May 5, 1913 in Moore County, NC. He died on August 11, 1979 in Charlotte, Mecklenburg County, NC and was buried in Concord, Cabarrus County, NC at Union Grove/West Concord Cemetery.*
67	James R. Sheffield (1914-). *James was born in 1914.*

John F. Richardson, son of David Richardson (1839-) and Elizabeth Morgan (1840-), was born in 1880. He died in March 1903.

22. **Lane A. Morgan**, son of William Birch Morgan and Loveday Jane Wallace, was born on March 14, 1881 in Moore County, NC. He married **Lizzie Deese** on July 8, 1920 in Robeson County, NC. He died on June 13, 1963 in Cabarrus Memorial Hospital, Concord, Cabarrus County, NC and was buried on June 15, 1963 in Concord, Cabarrus County, NC at Oakwood Cemetery.

Lizzie Deese, daughter of Andrew Deese (-) and Louise Morgan (1880-1955), was born on August 15, 1903 in Moore County, NC. She died on April 10, 1949 in Cabarrus Memorial Hospital, Concord, Cabarrus County, NC and was buried on April 12, 1949 in Concord, Cabarrus County, NC at Oakwood Cemetery. She and Lane A. Morgan had the following children:

68	Elizabeth Morgan (1923-). *Elizabeth was born in 1923.*
69	Lillie Mae Morgan (1925-). *Lillie was born in 1925.*
70	Ossie Morgan (1928-). *Ossie was born in 1928.*
71	Florence Marie Morgan (1936-2010). *Florence was born on March 15, 1936 in Concord, Cabarrus County, NC. She died on July 7, 2010 and was buried in Concord, Cabarrus County, NC at Union Grove/West Concord Cemetery.*

23. **Kizer Anderson Morgan**, son of William Birch Morgan and Loveday Jane Wallace, was born on March 22, 1881 in Moore County, NC. He married **Elviney Morgan** on October 29, 1916 in Anson County, NC. He died on February 24, 1967 in Concord, Cabarrus County, NC and was buried on February 26, 1967 in Kannapolis, Cabarrus County, NC at Carolina Memorial Park.

Elviney Morgan, daughter of William Birch Morgan (1847-1922) and Nancy Jane Hathcock (1868-1955), was born on March 21, 1901. She died on August 12, 1979 in Concord, Cabarrus County, NC. She and Kizer Anderson Morgan had the following children:

| 72 | Ruth Mae Morgan (1916-1989). *Ruth was born on October 5, 1916. She died on* |

September 7, 1989 and was buried in Kannapolis, Cabarrus County, NC at Carolina Memorial Park.

73   J. P. Stuart Morgan (1919-1974). *J. was born on November 17, 1919. He died on June 24, 1974 in Virginia Hospital, Durham, Durham County, NC and was buried on June 26, 1974 in Concord, Cabarrus County, NC at Oakwood Cemetery.*

74   Ruby Lee Morgan (1930-). *Ruby was born in 1930. She married **Swann McClure** on September 13, 1947.*

75   Hazel Morgan (1933-1935). *Hazel was born on June 29, 1933 in Concord, Cabarrus County, NC. She died on February 7, 1935 in Concord, Cabarrus County, NC and was buried on February 8, 1935 in Concord, Cabarrus County, NC at Oakwood Cemetery.*

76   Bobby Anderson Morgan (1937-). *Bobby was born on December 4, 1937 in Cabarrus County, NC.*

24. **James Thomas Deaton**, son of Isaac Spinks Deaton and Jenny Watie Morgan, was born on July 1, 1872 in Moore County, NC. He married **Evanna Alice Bruce** on June 19, 1903 in Moore County, NC. He died on May 18, 1955 in High Point, Guilford County, NC and was buried on May 20, 1955 in High Point, Guilford County, NC at Oakwood Cemetery.

Evanna Alice Bruce, daughter of John Robert Bruce (1846-) and Lucinda Morgan (1842-), was born in June 1880. She died on May 14, 1942. She and James Thomas Deaton had the following children:

77   Robert Lee Deaton (1906-1946). *Robert was born on November 28, 1906. He died on September 15, 1946.*

25. **Sarah Jane Deaton**, daughter of Isaac Spinks Deaton and Jenny Watie Morgan, was born in July 1874. She married **Reuben A. Allen** on June 7, 1894 in Moore County, NC.

Reuben A. Allen, son of Mark J. Allen (1836-) and Terry Graham (1836-), was born in June 1862. He and Sarah Jane Deaton had the following children:

78   Charlton L. Allen (1895-). *Charlton was born in 1895.*
79   George Z. Allen (1898-). *George was born in November 1898.*

28. **Aaron Deaton**, son of Isaac Spinks Deaton and Jenny Watie Morgan, was born on August 18, 1883. He died on February 4, 1922 in High Point Hospital, High Point, Guilford County, NC and was buried on February 6, 1922 in High Point, Guilford County, NC.

Clara was born in 1894. She and Aaron Deaton had the following children:

80   Margaret Deaton (1910-). *Margaret was born in 1910.*
81   Marvin Deaton (1912-). *Marvin was born in 1912.*
82   Edna Deaton (1915-). *Edna was born in 1915.*
83   Elizabeth Deaton (1919-). *Elizabeth was born in 1919.*

29. **Noah Cleveland Deaton**, son of Isaac Spinks Deaton and Jenny Watie Morgan, was born on July 15, 1887 in Moore County, NC. He died on December 7, 1958 in Bladen County Hospital, Elizabethtown, Bladen County, NC and was buried on December 9, 1958 in Tar Heel, Bladen County, NC at Leggett Cemetery.

30. **Alma Deaton**, daughter of Isaac Spinks Deaton and Jenny Watie Morgan, was born on July 4, 1895 in Moore County, NC. She died on December 18, 1918 in Biscoe, Montgomery County, NC and was buried on December 20, 1918.

Elvira Dunn, son of Raleigh L. Dunn (1857-) and Sarah Ann Britt (1861-), was born on February 2, 1893. He died on August 16, 1960. He and Alma Deaton had the following children:

84   Della Dunn (1913-1998). *Della was born in 1913 in Montgomery County, NC. She died on December 24, 1998 in Montgomery County, NC.*

85   Raleigh Dunn (1916-1984). *Raleigh was born on November 1, 1916 in Montgomery County, NC. He died on December 11, 1984 in Rowan County, NC.*

Descendants of Emaline Wallace

1. **Emaline Wallace** was born in 1831, married Lochart Davis (1838-1860s) and had four children: John M., Alexander, Henry T. and Margaret. She later married widower James H. Muse (b. 1802), son of Daniel Muse (1779-1846) and Susannah Ritter (aft 1780-1858). Emaline Wallace has always been a question mark. She was living with Nancy Sowell Furr (Isham Wallace and Enoch Wallace's mother-in-law) in 1850 suggesting that she was a possible daughter of Isham or Enoch. My grandfather, Mallie Wallace, remembers Emaline's son, John Davis, coming to visit his father and grandfather. His grandfather was Emsley, son of Isham, who died in 1918. But my grandfather tells a story that was told to him by his grandfather, where Lock and Emaline Davis were sharecroppers for Isham. He says that he was told that while Lock & Emaline worked on Isham's land, that Emaline had John and Alexander. But the children's father was not Lock Davis it was Isham. He said that Isham and Emaline were not related. A 1866 Moore County court case Emaline Davis vs. Isham Wallace, it was ordered by the court that John & Alexander Davis be remanded to the custody of Isham Wallace until the next county court session. This together with the fact that John and Alexander were living with Isham in 1870 is confusing. Another interesting fact is that when Isham Wallace died there was a long drawn out court case concerning his estate. All of his children, including the ones that were deceased were listed. The children that were deceased were represented by their spouses who were still living or by the guardians of their children. Emaline, John, or Alexander were nowhere to be found in these proceedings. Even John M. Wallace, the youngest son who had moved to Perry County, Arkansas was represented. That would leave you to believe that there was not a connection between them. Also, in the 1880 census John is still living with Isham and Nancy. But his relationship to the head of the household is listed as servant, not son or grandson.

In the 1890's John Davis moved to Rockingham, Richmond County with Missouri Wallace (Sampson Delaney Wallace's widow), Candace Wallace (John M. Wallace's ex-wife), and their respective families. There is some kind of a connection between John Davis and the Wallaces but I am not exactly sure what it is.

RECORDS OF EMALINE WALLACE

1850, Nov 13 -- Census, Moore County, NC Page 240
Nancy Furr 60 F, born in North Carolina
Leonard Furr 20 M, born in North Carolina
Emberline Wallis 19 F, born in North Carolina

1860, Sep 24 -- Census, Moore County, NC Page 239-B, Carthage Post Office
Lockhart Davis 26 M, Laborer Farm, born in North Carolina
Emeline Davis 26 F, born in North Carolina
John Davis 4 M, born in North Carolina
Alex Davis 2 M, born in North Carolina

1866, Aug 20 -- Superior Court Minute Docket Book K, Moore County, NC Page 440
Emeline Davis v. Isham Wallace. Ordered that John Davis and Alexander Davis be remanded to Isham Wallace's custody.

1870, Jul 9 -- Census, Moore County, NC Page 514-B, Carthage Township, Carthage Post Office
James H. Muse 68 M, born in North Carolina
Emeline Muse 33 F, born in North Carolina
Henry T. Davis 8 M, born in North Carolina
Mary M. Davis 6 F, born in North Carolina

1880, Jun 28 -- Census, Moore County, NC Page 211, Bensalem Township
Isham Wallace 80 M, Head, Married, Farmer/Planter, born in North Carolina, father & mother born in North Carolina
Nancy Wallace 67 F, Wife, Married, Keeping House, born in North Carolina, father & mother born in North Carolina

Stephen Harrison Davis 1889-1973
(Courtesy of Bruce Davis, Stanley, NC)

Candis Wallace 23 F, Dau, Married, At Home, born in North Carolina, father & mother born in North Carolina
Henry Wallace 5 M, GrSon, Single, At Home, born in North Carolina, father & mother born in North Carolina
John Davis 22 M, Servant, Single, Laborer, born in North Carolina, father & mother born in North Carolina

Lochart Davis, son of Jesse Davis (1807-1887) and Lydia Kennedy (1817-bef 1880), was born in 1838. He died in Civil War. He and Emaline Wallace had the following children:

+2   John M. Davis (1856-1925) married Julia C. Brown (1867-1936) and they were the parents of seven children. John is buried at Mizpah Church in Rockingham, NC.

+3   Alexander Davis (1858-) is listed in very few records and no further information about him has been located.

+4   Henry T. Davis (1862-) is listed in very few records and no further information about him has been located.

+5   Mary Margaret "Maggie" Davis (1864-1936) married Stephen W. Napier (b. 1847) and they had three children. Maggie is buried at East Side Cemetery in Rockingham, NC.

Second Generation

2. **John M. Davis**, son of Lochart Davis and Emaline Wallace, was born in October 1856. He married **Julia C. Brown** circa 1885. He died on January 9, 1925 in Richmond County, NC and was buried in Rockingham, Richmond County, NC at Mizpah Church Cemetery.[172]

Julia C. Brown, daughter of Henry Brown (1821-bef 1880) and Ann Francis Maness (1839-), was born on October 25, 1867 in Moore County, NC. She died on May 13, 1936 in Broughton State Hospital, Morganton, Burke County, NC and was buried on May 15, 1936 in Richmond County.[173] She and John M. Davis had the following children:

+6   Nancy Francena Davis (1886-1947)
+7   Anna J. Davis (1887-)
+8   Stephen Harrison Davis (1889-1973)
+9   John Wiley Davis (1892-1973)
+10   Alexander Davis (1899-)
+11   Ollie Mae Davis (1900-1960)
+12   Henry Lathern "Lockey" Davis (1904-1958)

5. **Mary Margaret "Maggie" Davis**, daughter of Lochart Davis and Emaline Wallace, was born on June 20, 1864. She married **Stephen W. Napier** circa 1893. She died on January 9, 1936 in Rockingham, Richmond County, NC and was buried on January 11, 1936 in Rockingham, Richmond County, NC at East Side Cemetery.[174]

Stephen W. Napier was born in April 1847 in North Carolina. He and Mary Margaret "Maggie" Davis had the following children:

+13   Archie Bennett Napier (1895-1919)
+14   William Henry Napier (1897-1975)
+15   Julian B. Napier (1899-1980)

Third Generation

6. **Nancy Francena Davis**, daughter of John M. Davis and Julia C. Brown, was born on April 29, 1886. She died on September 2, 1947 in Richmond County, NC and was buried on September 4, 1947 in Rockingham, Richmond County, NC at Mizpah Church Cemetery.

8. **Stephen Harrison Davis**, son of John M. Davis and Julia C. Brown, was born on December 23, 1889 in Richmond County. He married **Ellen Mae Stogner** on April 18, 1908 in Richmond County. He died on January 15, 1973 in Charlotte, Mecklenburg County, NC and was buried on January 17, 1973 in Charlotte, Mecklenburg County, NC at Sharon Memorial Park.

Ellen Mae Stogner was born on June 25, 1892 in Richmond County. She died on January 13, 1966 in Charlotte. She and Stephen Harrison Davis had the following children:

16   Marion Carl Davis (-)

17	Earl Davis (-)
18	Leon Davis (-)
19	Evelyn Davis (-)
20	Ethel Davis (-)
21	Nellie Davis (-)
22	Gloria Davis (-)
23	Lacy Davis (1913-1992). *Lacy was born on January 23, 1913 in Danville, VA. He died on November 14, 1992 in Charlotte.*
24	Bennie Elliott Davis (1929-1958). *Bennie was born on April 4, 1929. He died on September 14, 1958.*

9. **John Wiley Davis**, son of John M. Davis and Julia C. Brown, was born on August 21, 1892. He married **Iola Williams** on December 23, 1911 in Richmond County. He died on November 16, 1973 in Cape Fear Memorial Hospital, Wilmington, New Hanover, NC and was buried on November 18, 1973 in Wilmington, New Hanover County, NC at Greenlawn Memorial Park. He married **Beatrice Kelly**.

Iola Williams, daughter of James Thomas Williams (1862-1932) and Martha Jane Williams (1870-1931), was born on October 17, 1890. She died on May 27, 1939 and was buried in Robbins, Moore County, NC at Tabernacle United Methodist Church. She and John Wiley Davis had the following children:

25	Howard Curtis Davis (1914-2000). *Howard was born on July 13, 1914. He died on January 30, 2000 and was buried in Robbins.*
26	Beulah Mae Davis (1915-). *Beulah was born in 1915.*
27	Bertha Davis (1917-). *Bertha was born in 1917.*
28	Lloyd Odell Davis (1918-1918). *Lloyd was born on September 6, 1918 in Richmond County. He died on September 17, 1918 in Richmond County.*
29	Martha Jane Davis (1922-). *Martha was born on June 28, 1922.*

11. **Ollie Mae Davis**, daughter of John M. Davis and Julia C. Brown, was born on September 11, 1900. She died on August 11, 1960 in Richmond Memorial Hospital, Rockingham, Richmond County, NC and was buried on August 14, 1960 in Rockingham.

12. **Henry Lathern "Lockey" Davis**, son of John M. Davis and Julia C. Brown, was born on March 6, 1904. He died on September 18, 1958 in Richmond County and was buried on September 21, 1958 in Rockingham.

13. **Archie Bennett Napier**, son of Stephen W. Napier and Mary Margaret "Maggie" Davis, was born on April 16, 1895. He died on June 25, 1919 in Rockingham, Richmond County, NC and was buried on June 26, 1919 in Rockingham, Richmond County, NC at East Side Cemetery.

14. **William Henry Napier**, son of Stephen W. Napier and Mary Margaret "Maggie" Davis, was born on June 5, 1897. He died on June 21, 1975 in Richmond Memorial Hospital and was buried on June 23, 1975 in Rockingham. He married **Gertrude Benoist**.

Gertrude Benoist was born on June 12, 1910. She died on February 24, 1992 and was buried in Rockingham. She and William Henry Napier had the following children:

30	Edith May Napier (1928-1931). *Edith was born on May 15, 1928. She died on January 21, 1931 and was buried on January 22, 1931 in Rockingham.*

Descendants of Betsy Wallace

1. **Betsy Wallace** was born in 1818. I am not very clear as to the relationship (if any) between Betsy Wallace, her daughter, Sarah E. Wallace and grandson, George M. Wallace to Everet's descendants. The only record of Betsy and Sarah E. that I've found is a 1860 Census in neighboring Randolph County. Per his death certificate, George M. Wallace was born in Moore County, NC. He lived near the Moore County Wallaces and even married into a closely related family (Horner), but I am not certain as to the connection. My grandfather told a story of one of Everet's daughters moving to Randolph County and having children by a man named Whistlehunt. Unfortunately, I have not been able to locate him in any record yet. Chris Wallace, descendant of George M. Wallace, has the same Y-DNA as male Deaton descendants possibly indicating that George's father or grandfather may have been a Deaton.

RECORDS OF BETSY WALLACE

1860, Jun 26 -- Census, Randolph County, NC Page 147, West Division Township, Asheboro Post Office
Betsey Wallace 42 F, $30 Personal Property, born in North Carolina
Sarah Wallace 22 F, born in North Carolina
William Wallace 8 M, born in North Carolina
George Wallace 3 M, born in North Carolina
No Name Wallace 1/12 M, born in North Carolina

Betsy Wallace had the following children:

+2   Sarah E. Wallace (1838-)

Second Generation

2. **Sarah E. Wallace**, daughter of Betsy Wallace, was born in 1838.

Sarah E. Wallace had the following children:

+3   George M. Wallace (1857-1932)

Third Generation

3. **George M. Wallace**, son of Sarah E. Wallace, was born on May 17, 1857 in Moore County, NC. He married **Mary Lovedy Horner** on March 23, 1878 in Moore County[175]. He married **Mary Jane Muse** on December 23, 1886 in Moore County.[176] He married **Ellen Kellis** on February 9, 1896 in Moore County.[177] He died on July 23, 1932 in Albemarle, Stanly County, NC. He was buried on July 24, 1932 in Albemarle, Stanly County, NC at Salem Methodist Church.[178]

RECORDS OF GEORGE M. WALLACE

1860, Jun 26 -- Census, Randolph County, NC Page 147, West Division Township, Asheboro Post Office
Betsey Wallace 42 F, $30 Personal Property, born in North Carolina
Sarah Wallace 22 F, born in North Carolina
William Wallace 8 M, born in North Carolina
George Wallace 3 M, born in North Carolina
No Name Wallace 1/12 M, born in North Carolina

1878, Mar 23 -- Mattie Florence Wallace Yarborough Family Bible
Miss Mary L. Horner and George M. Wallace were married March 23rd, 1878

1880, Jun 16 -- Census, Moore County, NC Page 338-B, Ritters Township
George Wallace 22 M, Head, born in North Carolina, father & mother born in North Carolina
Polly Wallace 18 F, Wife, born in North Carolina, father & mother born in North Carolina
James Charlie Wallace 6/12 M Son, born in North Carolina, father & mother born in North Carolina

1883, Aug 7 -- 1875-1895 Appointment of Road Overseers, Moore County, NC Page 43
Ordered that Marshal Phillips be appointed overseer of the Buris [Boroughs] Road from Island Ford Road by B.P. Phillips' to township line and have the following hands to work: Neill Caddell, Lee Phillips, George Wallace and William May.

1884 -- Branson's NC Business Directory Page 468-474, Moore County, NC
G. Wallace listed as a farmer in Carters Mill Township

1885, May 9 -- 1875-1895 Appointment of Road Overseers, Moore County, NC Page 63
Ordered that Neill Caddell be appointed overseer of the Buris [Boroughs] Road from
Island Ford Road to township line and have the following hands to work: Leo Phillips
and George Wallace.

1885, Nov 20 -- Orders and Decrees Book 2 Page 305,308-310, Moore County, NC
M.M.L. Kelly, Edmond Waddell and B.P. Phillips commissioner to partition land of
George W. Horner, Dec'd. located on Meadow Branch and the Plank Road adjoining S.
Cockman. Heirs: Sarah Francis Horner (Widow), G.B. Horner, James W. Horner, John
and Nancy Kennedy, Eli and Frances Cockman, W.W. and Jane Wallace, heirs of George
Wallace (J.C. Wallace, S.A. Wallace), A.J. and Catherine Williams and T.W. Horner.

1886, Dec 23 -- Mattie Florence Wallace Yarborough Family Bible
Mr. George M Wallace of Carthage, N.C. and Miss Mary Muse of Carthage, NC on
December 23, 1886 at D.F. Muse's by Wayne King. Witness by I.F. Wallace and John
Horner.

1888, Feb 4 -- 1875-1895 Appointment of Road Overseers, Moore County, NC Page 75
Ordered that R.G. Gordon be appointed overseer of the Plank Road from the bridge at
McLendons Creek to Richland Creek and have the following hands to work: J.W. Sewell,
J.W. Moore, R.G. Gordan, S. Gordan, W.G. Cagel, N.W. Cockman, J.R. Cockman, Charlie Muse,
Harison Davis, George Wallace and George Sewell.

1890 -- Branson's NC Business Directory Page 457-466, Moore County, NC
G. Wallace listed as a farmer in Carters Mill Post Office

1890, Aug 2 -- 1875-1895 Appointment of Road Overseers, Moore County, NC Page 88
Ordered that W.H. Davis be appointed overseer of the Plank Road from McLendons'
Creek to Richland Creek and have the following hands to work: Jessie Horner, James
Dowdy, Joe Cockman, John Cockman, Tom Cagel, R.G. Gorden, John Seawell, James
Hufstickler, C.C. More and George Wales.

1896, Feb 9 -- Marriage Register, Moore County, NC
George Wallace (38yrs; son of Unknown and Sarah E. Wallace) and Ellen Kellis (37yrs;
dau of Calvin & Cinthia Kellis) were married by J.F. Reynolds, JP. W.M. Seawell applied
for the certificate and A.M. Ledbetter and A.W. Dockings were witnesses.

1898 -- Bransons Business Directory, Moore County, NC
George Wallace listed with 20 acres valued at $40 located in Ritters Township at
Horners Post Office

George M. Wallace
(Courtesy of Glenda Yarboro Brock)

1900, Jun 11 -- Census, Montgomery County, NC Page 224-B, Hollingsworth Township
George Wallis 44 M, Oct 1855, Head, Married-5yrs, Day Laborer, born in North Carolina, father & mother born in North Carolina
Ellen Wallis 45 F, Jun 1854, Wife, Married-5yrs, 2 Children(2 Living), born in North Carolina, father & mother born in North Carolina
Sarah N. Wallis 14 F, Jan 1886, Dau, Single, born in North Carolina, father & mother born in North Carolina
Lillie A. Wallis 12 F, Feb 1888, Dau, Single, born in North Carolina, father & mother born in North Carolina
Mattie F. Wallis 10 F, Mar 1890, Dau, Single, born in North Carolina, father & mother born in North Carolina
Frank M. Blake 23 M, Jun 1876, Boarder, Single, Day Laborer, born in North Carolina, father & mother born in North Carolina

1920 -- Census, Montgomery County, NC Page 145, Troy Township (at Boarding House)
George Wallis 63 M, Boarder, Divorced, Laborer(Cotton Mill), born in North Carolina, father & mother born in North Carolina

1932, July 23 -- Death Certificate, Stanly County, NC
George W. Wallace died in Albemarle, Stanly County, NC, Widow. Age: 75y. Occupation: Farmer. Birthplace: Moore County. Father: John
Wallace. Birthplace of Father: Moore County. Mother: Sarah Cockman. Birthplace of Mother: Moore County. Cause of Death: Hemorragia
& Paralysis. Place of Burial: Salem Church. Date of Burial: July 24, 1932. Undertaker: Palmer Funeral Co., Albemarle, NC. Informant: T.M.
Lowder.

Mary Lovedy Horner, daughter of George Washington Horner (1817-1885) and Mary Ann Ritter (1821-), was born on May
20, 1858. She died in 1884. She and George M. Wallace had the following children:

| +4 | James Charles Wallace (1879-1949) |
| +5 | Sarah Ann Wallace (1882-1971) |

Mary Jane Muse was born in 1852. She died before 1896. She and George M. Wallace had the following children:

+6	Lillie Alice Wallace (1887-1932)
+7	Mattie Florence Wallace (1890-1966)
+8	Kenneth H. Wallace (1892-)

Ellen Kellis, daughter of Calvin James Kellis (1823-1895) and Cynthia Jane Thompson (1836-1909), was born in June 1854. She died on September 11, 1940.

Fourth Generation

4. James Charles Wallace, son of George M. Wallace and Mary Lovedy Horner, was born on December 17, 1879 in Moore County, NC. He married **Marchia Alberta Lee Cockman** on December 25, 1898 in Moore County. He died on November 17, 1949 in Asheboro, Randolph County, NC. He was buried on November 19, 1949 in Asheboro, Randolph County, NC at Oaklawn Cemetery.

Marchia Alberta Lee Cockman, daughter of James Alexander Cockman (1861-1933) and Mary Alice Horner (1865-1948), was born on August 5, 1881 in Moore County. She died on August 14, 1966 in Asheboro. She was buried on August 15, 1966 in Asheboro. She and James Charles Wallace had the following children:

9	Cora Belle Wallace (1899-1977). *Cora was born on September 21, 1899 in Moore County. She married **William Elzie Garner** on November 22, 1914. She died on July 9, 1977 in Asheboro.*
10	Coy Sampson Wallace (1901-1984). *Coy was born on September 26, 1901 in Moore County. He married **Sallie Myrtle Purvis** on May 3, 1924 in Moore County. He died on March 6, 1984 in Sanford, Lee County, NC.*
11	James Floyd Wallace (1904-1975). *James was born on March 8, 1904 in Montgomery County, NC. He died on February 28, 1975 in Asheboro.*
12	Lillie Viola Wallace (1906-2001). *Lillie was born on November 22, 1906 in Montgomery County. She married **Coble Maie Maness** on January 24, 1925. She died on May 28, 2001 in Randolph County, NC. She was buried in Moore County, NC at Pleasant Hill United Methodist Church.*
13	Luther Clyde Wallace (1909-1987). *Luther was born on March 13, 1909. He married **Beatrice Maness** on November 23, 1932 in Moore County. He died on July 8, 1987 in Asheboro.*
14	Bettie Alberta Lee Wallace (1911-1969). *Bettie was born on May 16, 1911 in Moore County. She married **Clinard Harrison Poole** on May 25, 1928. She died on October 25, 1969 in Asheboro.*
15	Beatrice Ann Wallace (1913-2008). *Beatrice was born on June 24, 1913 in Moore County. She died on May 26, 2008 in Randolph County.*
16	George Carson Wallace (1916-1994). *George was born on May 18, 1916 in Moore County. He married **Beatrice Thorp** on July 11, 1936. He died on August 31, 1994 in Asheboro.*
17	Katie Lisbon Wallace (1919-1981). *Katie was born on June 28, 1919 in Montgomery County. She married **Robert Franklin Bulla** on September 16, 1938.[4] She died on December 14, 1981 in Asheboro.*
18	Elizabeth Wallace (1920-). *Elizabeth was born in 1920.*
19	Lucille Helen Wallace (1923-1994). *Lucille was born on January 23, 1923 in Moore County. She married **James Nelson Whitaker** on August 23, 1941. She died on May 11, 1994 in Greensboro, Guilford County, NC.*

James Charlie Wallace and Marchia Cockman and family
Left to Right [top row] **Beatrice, George, Lisbon, Coy, Floyd, Lucille, Betty**
[bottom row] **Clyde, Belle, James C., Marchia and Ola.**
(Courtesy of Donald Wallace)

5. **Sarah Ann Wallace**, daughter of George M. Wallace and Mary Lovedy Horner, was born on February 23, 1882 in Moore County. She died on November 27, 1971 in Stanly County, NC. She was buried on November 28, 1971 in Albemarle, Stanly County, NC at Salem Methodist Church. She married **Titus M. Lowder**.

Titus M. Lowder was born on July 7, 1885 in Albemarle, Stanly County, NC. He died on October 7, 1935 in Albemarle. He and Sarah Ann Wallace had the following children:

20	Thomas Kinnie Lowder (1907-). *Thomas was born in 1907.*
21	Mary M. Lowder (1909-). *Mary was born in 1909.*
22	Roscoe James Lowder (1917-2002). *Roscoe was born on June 12, 1917 in Stanly County. He died on April 23, 2002 in Albemarle.*
23	Sherman Lee Lowder (1919-1998). *Sherman was born on January 3, 1919 in Albemarle. He died on February 8, 1998 in Albemarle.*

6. **Lillie Alice Wallace**, daughter of George M. Wallace and Mary Jane Muse, was born on October 25, 1887 in Montgomery County. She died on September 28, 1932 in Montgomery County. She was buried on September 29, 1932 in Montgomery County, NC at Laurel Hill Baptist Church Cemetery. She married **George Sedberry**.

George Sedberry was born on June 27, 1882 in Montgomery County. He died on August 5, 1965 in Troy, Montgomery County, NC. He and Lillie Alice Wallace had the following children:

24	Minnie Sedberry (1914-1986). *Minnie was born on September 2, 1914. She died on April 28, 1986 in Troy.*
25	Lola Sedberry (1916-2001). *Lola was born on November 25, 1916 in Montgomery County. She died on June 2, 2001 in Montgomery County.*
26	Charles L. Sedberry (1928-2007). *Charles was born on March 9, 1928. He died on August 7, 2007 in Candor, Montgomery County, NC.*

7. **Mattie Florence Wallace**, daughter of George M. Wallace and Mary Jane Muse, was born on March 14, 1890 in Moore County. She married **David Franklin Yarborough** on October 28, 1913. She died on October 25, 1966 in Montgomery County. She was buried on October 27, 1966 in Montgomery County, NC at Capelsie Cemetery.

David Franklin Yarborough was born in 1890. He died on May 31, 1962 in Candor. He and Mattie Florence Wallace had the following children:

27	George Curtis Yarboro (1914-1928).	*George was born on September 24, 1914. He died in 1928 in Troy.*
28	Daniel Hughes Yarboro (1917-1917).	*Daniel was born on October 14, 1917 in Norwood, Stanly County, NC. He died on October 19, 1917 in Norwood.*
29	Carlie Glen Yarboro (1920-1978).	*Carlie was born on June 29, 1920 in Capelsie, Montgomery County, NC. He died on September 21, 1978 in Troy.*
30	David Matthew Yarborough (1922-1986).	*David was born on May 4, 1922 in Montgomery County. He died on August 30, 1986 in Montgomery County.*
31	Frank Thomas Yarboro (1930-2003).	*Frank was born on May 3, 1930 in Montgomery County. He died on December 3, 2003 in Moore Regional Hospital, Pinehurst, Moore County, NC.*

8. **Kenneth H. Wallace**, son of George M. Wallace and Mary Jane Muse, was born on May 22, 1892.

Davidson/Montgomery/Randolph County Wallaces

There were several families of Wallaces that resided on the borders of Montgomery, Davidson and Randolph counties and many of their descendants moved west and settled in western Kentucky mostly in Graves, Calloway, and Hickman counties. Like the Wallaces of Moore County, many of these Wallace families carry the given names Isham, Eli, Everet, Nathan, etc. through multiple generations. There are several Wallace families making this trip to Kentucky, and it is my belief that they are from two separate families that originate in Montgomery County, NC.

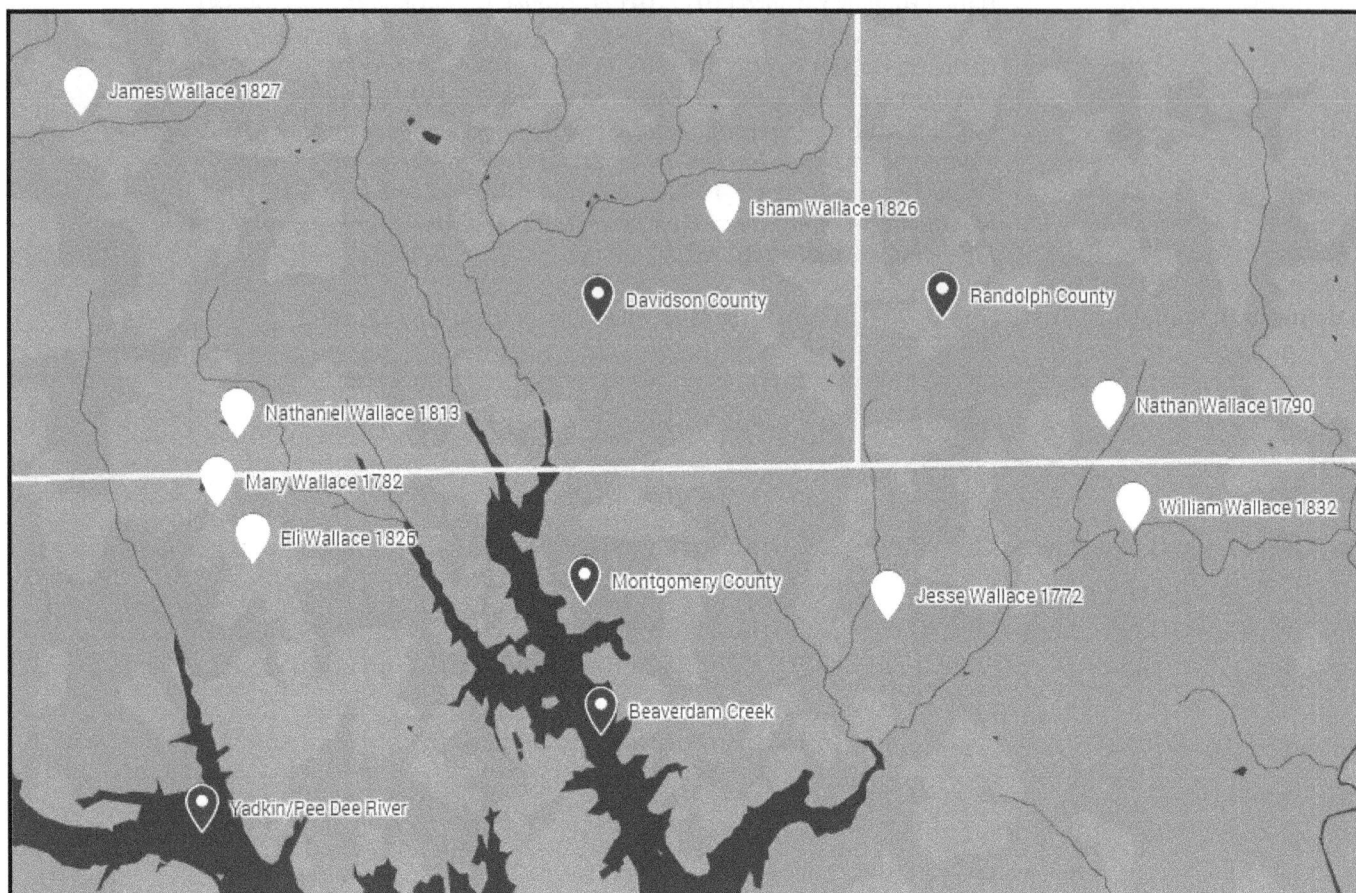

We can trace the first set of Wallaces to E. and Mary Wallace. Among their children are believed to be Isham Wallace (1778-1853), Nathan Wallace (1785-1852) and Eli Wallace (1790-1855) who lived in the area in southern Davidson County near the Montgomery County line and all migrated with their young families to western Kentucky during the late 1820's/early 1830's.

Additionally, Nathan Wallis (1806-1859) was born in North Carolina (likely Davidson County, NC) and migrated to western KY by 1840 living near the families above.

These Wallace families seems to be clearly related to Jesse Wallace (b. bef 1748). Jesse lived in the northwest section of Montgomery County on Mountain Creek [northwest of Eldorado and just east of Badin Lake Road]. This was in the same vicinity as Mary Wallace and her children. Jesse was married to Susanna during the 1770's but it is unclear if she was his only wife or 1st wife. It is possible that Mary was Jesse's widow or that she was the widow of one of his children, but not enough information is known to be clear. Jesse can be found in Montgomery County records from 1769 until at least the early 1780s. There is a Jesse Wallace listed on the 1790 Census in Montgomery County and a few other land records, but it is unclear if this is the same Jesse or a Jesse from a younger generation.

An additional Nathan/Nathaniel Wallace can be found in land records from Randolph County, NC, Davidson County, NC and Rowan County, NC beginning in 1789 concluding with an Estate being settled in 1817 in Rowan County, NC. If all these references are for the same Nathan it would place him as being born during the mid-to-late 1760's and dying in 1817. At this time, I am not sure as to his relationship to the above Wallaces but he certainly seems to be connected.

The second family of Montgomery County Wallaces is that of William Wallace (1791/1800-1843). He was married to Chaney Berry Cranford and lived most of his life near the Uwharrie River and Ophir in Montgomery County, NC and many of their children migrated to western Kentucky and can be found residing among and intermarrying with the descendants of the above clan of Wallaces. While we do not know the identity of William's parents, it has been passed down through William's descendants that his siblings were Harbard/Harbart Wallace (1796-1872), Ann Wallace (1803-1900) and Elizabeth "Betsy" Wallace (1800-1905). Harbert also moved his family to Graves County, KY in the 1830's while Ann married William Hall and remained in Montgomery County, NC. Betsy married Phillip Hagler and lived most of her life in neighboring Stanly County, NC.

Local researchers have speculated that William (II) and Harbard may have been the sons of William Wallace (I) and Ann Suggs, daughter of Rasha Suggs, and possibly the grandson of James Wallace. They suggest James Wallace was married to Mary and that he died in the Revolutionary War. They also speculate that James may not only have been the father of William (I) but also of Isham Wallace and Eli Wallace [mentioned above].[179] I have been unable to locate records that would confirm this to date, but it is certainly plausible.

Descendants of E. and Mary WALLACE

1. **E. Wallace** died before 1800 and married Mary born bef 1755. While I do not have concrete proof that these three men were brothers, and that E. and Mary Wallace were their parents – several records point in that direction. Mary Wallace (45+) and Isham Wallace (16-26) are living next door to each other in the 1800 Montgomery County, NC Census. Mary has two sons listed in her household (10-16) & (16-26) that match the ages of Nathan and Eli. Eli Wallace (1790-1855) listed his birthplace as Montgomery County, NC and his parents as E. Wallace and M. Wallace on his death certificate in Graves County, KY. Eli Wallace was granted 30 acres in Montgomery County in 1826 adjoining his own tract of 200 acres that was originally purchased by Mary Wallace from John Morris in 1794. Nathan Wallace (1785-1852) was also listed as having been born in North Carolina and in 1850 was living next door to Isham's son Isham (b. 1804) in Graves County, KY.

RECORDS OF E. AND MARY WALLACE [D. AFT 1800]

1795, Jan 27 -- Deed, Montgomery County, NC Page 99
John Morris deeded Mary Wallace 200 acres located East of the Yadkin River adjoining the county line. Neddy Pennington and Farqd. Campell were witnesses.

1795, Nov 10 -- Land Warrant #590, Montgomery County, NC
John Crump Sr. entered 250 acres located on Garr Creek adjoining Adam Davis, Mary Wallis and William Loftin. Adam Davis and Michael Fisher were chain carriers.

1800 -- Census, Montgomery County, NC Page 484
Mary Wallace
(45+) 1F
(16-26) 1M
(10-16) 1M

1855, Nov 3 -- Death Register, Graves County, KY
Eli Wallace 65 M, Married, Farmer, Resident of Graves County, born in Montgomery County, NC, Parents E. & M. Wallace, died of Fever

E. Wallace and **Mary** are believed to have had the following children:

+2   Isham Wallace (1778-1853) can be found in the 1800 Census for Montgomery County, NC, and several land records of Rowan County, NC prior to relocating to Graves County, KY by 1825. He married Fanny Jones (1774/1784-bef 1819) and had the following children: Isham, Eli, Mary and Levi W. Wallace. He later married Elizabeth (b. 1815) and they were the parents of Henry, Elizabeth, Susan, George, Eliza, and Jonathan Everett Wallace. A male descendant of Isham Wallace shares the same Y-DNA as male descendants of Everet Wallace proving they descend from a common male ancestor on their paternal line.

+3　Nathan Wallace (1785-1852) also can be found initially in Montgomery-Rowan County region prior to relocating to KY by the 1830's. He married Sarah (b. 1780) and they were the parents of Elizabeth, Isham, Eli, Mary, Nancy, John C. and Rachel Wallace. Nathan died in Pope County, IL in 1852.

+4　Eli Wallace (1790-1855) is listed in the 1810-1830 Montgomery County, NC Census and moved to KY shortly after 1830 as he is listed in several tax lists during the 1830's in KY. Eli was married twice and was the father of Temperance, Kendrick, Calvin, Lucinda, Amanda and James Lovelace Wallace.

Second Generation

2. **Isham Wallace**, son of E. Wallace and Mary, was born in 1778. He died in May 1853 in Graves County, KY[180] and married Fanny Jones, daughter of Thomas Jones (-bef 1825) and Margaret (aft 1750-1833), was born between 1774 and 1784. She died before 1819. After Fanny died, Isham married Elizabeth (1815-).

RECORDS OF ISHAM WALLACE [1778-1853]

1800 -- Census, Montgomery County, NC Page 484
Isham Wallace
(16-26) 1M 1F

1810 -- Tax List, Rowan County, NC
Isham Wallis listed 1 white poll in Capt. Jones' Company

1813 -- Tax List, Rowan County, NC
Isham Wallis listed 1 white poll in Capt. Burkhead's Company

1814 -- Tax List, Rowan County, NC
Isham Wallis listed 1 white poll in Capt. Burkhead's Company

1815 -- Tax List, Rowan County, NC
Isham Wallis listed 100 acres valued at $150 and 1 white poll in Capt. Burckhead's Company

1818, May -- 1817-1818 Court of Pleas and Quarter Sessions, Rowan County, NC
Ordered by the court that Edmon Smith act as the overseer of the road from the fork near Edward Taylors to the Randolph Line [the road called Moores Road] and have the following hands to work: Edmon Smith, Lamath Hill, Jeremiah Senton, Cornelius Loftin, John Varner, James Lacey, Ebin Lacey, John Loflin, William Loflin, Josiah Russell, Samuel Hill, Richard Loflin, Thomas Jones, Butler Taylor, John Taylor, Cabel Riley, Jeremiah Coggins, William Taylor, Jesse Boyo, Daniel Baty, Abraham Tomson, William Serrate, Richard Loflin, Daniel Wood, William Burkhead, Isam Wallis, James Tomson and Osborn Skein.

1819, Nov 6 -- Will of Thomas Jones, Davidson County NC Will Book 1 Page 40
Lists heirs as wife Margaret Jones, granddaughter Nancy Jones, three children Chattan Jones, Thomas Jones [deceased] and Isham Wallace. Executor Margaret Jones and Clement Reed. John Reed and Thomas Reed were witnesses. Probated Sep 1825.

1820 -- Census, Rowan County, NC Page 350, Lexington side [current Davidson County]
Isaam Willis
(26-45) 1M 1F
(16-18) 1M
(10-16) 1M
(0-10) 5M 1F

1826, Jul 29 -- Deed, Davidson County, NC Deed Book 3 Page 79-80
Isham Wallis deeded Jarrett Coggins 275 acres located on Beaver Dam Creek. Originally granted to George Warner as 300 acres on Oct 25, 1786. 25 acres later sold to Simon Secret. Warner sold to Henry Varner then to John Johnson then to David Sincler and then to William Adderton and then back to David Sincler. Jno. Crump and Burrell Coggins were witnesses.

1840 -- Census, Calloway County, KY Page 102
Isham Wallace
(60-70) 1M
(50-60) 1F
(15-20) 1F

1850 -- Census, Graves County, KY Page 406, District #2

Isham Wallace 65 M, $300 Real Estate, born in North Carolina
Elizabeth Wallace 35 F, born in Tennessee
Elizabeth Wallace 8 F, born in KY
Susan Wallace 7 F, born in KY
Eliza Wallace 2 F, born in KY
Henry Wallace 14 M, born in KY
George Wallace 5 M, born in KY

1852, Oct -- Death Register, Hickman County, KY
Levi W. Wallace 35 M, Widow, Farmer, Resident of Moscow KY, born in North Carolina, Parents Isham & Fanny Wallis, died of Inflammation Bowell

1853, May -- Death Register, Graves County, KY
Isham Wallace 75 M, Married, Farmer, Resident of Graves County, born in South Carolina, Parents Unknown, died of Old Age

1853, Nov 6 -- Death Register, Hickman County, KY
Mary W. Fezir 45 F, Married, Resident of Moscow KY, born in North Carolina, Parents Isham & Fanny Wallis, died of Liver Complaint

Isham Wallace and Fanny had the following children:

+5	Isham Wallace (1804-)
+6	Eli Wallace (1805-bef 1879)
+7	Mary Wallace (1807-1852)
+8	Levi W. Wallace (1817-1852)

Isham Wallace and Elizabeth had the following children:

+9	Henry Wallace (1836-)
+10	Elizabeth Wallace (1842-)
+11	Susan Wallace (1843-)
+12	George Wallace (1845-)
+13	Eliza Wallace (1848-)
+14	Jonathan Everett Wallace (1848-1907)

3. **Nathan Wallace**, son of E. Wallace and Mary, was born in 1785. He died on March 24, 1852 in Pope County, IL and married Sarah (1780-).

RECORDS OF NATHAN WALLACE [1785-1852]

1810 -- Census, Rowan County, NC Page 291
Nathan Wallace
(26-45) 1M 1F
(16-26) 1F
(0-10) 2M

1820 -- Census, Rowan County, NC Page 348, Lexington side [current Davidson County]
Nathan Willis
(26-45) 1M 1F
(16-25) 1F
(10-16) 2M 2F
(0-10) 1M 2F

1821, Mar 27 -- Marriage Register, Rowan County, NC
Jesse Redwine married Polly Davis. Nathan Wallis was bondsman; Jno. Giles was witness.

1824, Mar 10 -- Bill of Sale, Davidson County, NC Deed Book 1 Page 245
Jinney Stokes to his son William Stokes. Nathan Wallis, C.S. Adderton, J.W. Daniel were witnesses.

1824, Mar 16 -- 1823-1829 Court of Pleas and Quarter Sessions, Davidson County, NC
Alexander Shamwell, Esq., David Cox, John Davis and Nathan Wallace appointed to allot widow of Wm. Fagan one year's provision.

1827, Mar 22 -- 1823-1829 Court of Pleas and Quarter Sessions, Davidson County, NC
John Davis was appointed constable. David Cox and Nathan Wallace were securities.

1828 -- Tax List, Davidson County, NC
Nathan Wallis listed 187 acres valued at $500 in Capt. Daniels' District

1829 -- Tax List, Davidson County, NC
Nathan Wallis listed 187 acres valued at $500 in Capt. Daniels' District

1829, Aug 13 -- Deed, Davidson County, NC Deed Book 4 Page 270-271
John Davis deeded Jacob Goss and David Cos 144 acres located on the East Side of the Yadkin River adjoining Nathan Wallis and Thomas Noe. Alexr. Shemwell was a witness.

1829, Aug 22 -- Deed, Davidson County, NC Deed Book 4 Page 218
William Redwine mortgaged Nathan Wallis 187 acres located on the East Side of the Yadkin River. Redwine recently purchased the land from Wallis.

1829, Nov 13 -- 1823-1829 Court of Pleas and Quarter Sessions, Davidson County, NC
A mortgage deed from Wm. Redwine to Nathan Wallace for 178 [should be 187] acres dated Aug 25, 1829 was proven by Henry Giles

1830, Aug 9 -- 1830-1839 Court of Pleas and Quarter Sessions, Davidson County, NC
A deed from Nathan Wallace to Wm. Redwine dated Aug 18, 1829 was proven by Henry Giles

1840 -- Census, Graves County, KY Page 118
Nathan Wallace, Sr.
(60-70) 1F
(50-60) 1M
(20-30) 1M 1F
(0-5) 1M

1845, May 14 -- 1840-1846 Court of Pleas and Quarter Sessions, Davidson County, NC
A deed from Hardy Harrison to Eli Carrel for 100 acres dated Sep 10, 1826 is produced and appears that Alexander Shamwell, one of the witnesses to deed is dead and Nathan Wallis, the other witness, has removed from this state. Deed proven by Allen Newsome based on his knowledge of witness's signature.

1850 -- Census, Graves County, KY, District #2, Page 403
Nathan Wallis 65 M, Farmer, $800 Real Estate, born in North Carolina
Sarah Wallis 70 F, born in North Carolina

1852, Jul 17-Aug 3, 1857 -- Estate, Pope County, IL Book G Page 202, 277, 523
Administration of the Estate of Nathan Wallis, Dec'd. were granted to Wm. Travis Wallis and William Wood. Nathan Wallis died 24 Mar 1852. Notes held on the following: T.W Lawrence, W. Lawrence, H. Lawrence, Elsey Roach and Thos. Reed.

1852, Jul 17-Oct 19, 1854 -- Loose Estate, Pope County, IL
Administration of the Estate of Nathan Wallis, Dec'd. were granted to Wm. Travis Wallis and William Wood. Nathan Wallis died 24 Mar 1852. Estate contains land in Johnson County (IL), Pope County (IL) and Graves County, KY. Notes held on Solomon Riley, Sarah Wallis, John Wallis and Isham Wallis. Heirs widow Sarah Wallace, Elizabeth Wallace (John Kenney and wife Eliz., Travis Wallace, Nancy Wallace and one unknown), Isham Wallace, Eli Wallace (8 heirs; Elizabeth Presgrove, Sarah Punch, John Wallace, Susan Wallace, William Wallace, Eveline Wallace and one unknown), Mary Riley, wife of Solomon Riley, Nancy Wallace and husband E. Wiley Lamb and son John W. Lamb, John Wallace and Rachel Wood wife of William Wood. The following heirs received payment from the estate (1) widow (2) John Kinney (3) E. Wiley Lamb (4) Wm. T. Wallace guardian for Nancy (5) Solomon Riley (6) John Wallace (7) Wm. Presgrove of Eli Wallace Dec'd. (8) John C. Punch of Eli Wallace Dec'd. (9) Isham Wallace.

Nathan Wallace and Sarah had the following children:

+15	Isham Wallace (-)
+16	Elizabeth Wallace (aft 1800-)
+17	Eli Wallace (aft 1804-bef 1852)
+18	Mary Wallace (1810-)
+19	Nancy Wallace (aft 1810-bef 1852)
+20	John C. Wallace (1819-)
+21	Rachel Wallace (1820-c. 1867)

4. **Eli Wallace**, son of E. Wallace and Mary, was born in 1790 in Montgomery County, NC. He married his first wife circa 1810. After his first wife died, Eli married **Jemima Crowell** on January 31, 1840 in Henry County, TN.[181] He died on November 3, 1855 in Graves County, KY.[182]

1810 -- Census, Montgomery County, NC Page 540
Elias Wallis
(26-45) 1M 1F
(0-10) 2F

1826, Nov 25 -- Land Warrant #9014, Montgomery County, NC
Eli Wallis entered 50 acres located on Beaverdam Creek adjoining Davidson County Line, David Conner and Bailey. Enoch Raper and Allen Coggin were chain carriers.

1826, Nov 26 -- Land Grant #2484, Montgomery County, NC
Eli Wallis received 30 acres located Northeast of the Yadkin River adjoining his own 200 acre tract and the Davidson County line. Enoch Raper and Allen Coggin were chain carriers.

1830 -- Census, Montgomery County, NC Page 53
Eli Wallace
(40-50) 1M
(30-40) 1F
(15-20) 2M 1F
(10-15) 1M 1F
(5-10) 2F

1830 -- Tax List, Davidson County, NC
Eli Wallis listed 116 acres valued at $95 and 1 white poll in Capt. Stephens' District

1831 -- Tax List, Davidson County, NC
Eli Wallis listed 116 acres valued at $95 and 1 white poll in Capt. Stephens' District

1832 -- Tax List, Davidson County, NC
Eli Wallis listed 116 acres valued at $95 and 1 white poll in Capt. Stephens' District

1832, Aug 13 -- 1830-1839 Court of Pleas and Quarter Sessions, Davidson County, NC
A deed from Wm. Kenneday, Sheriff to Eli Wallace for 115 acres dated Apr 17, 1832 was acknowledged

1832, Aug 14 -- 1830-1839 Court of Pleas and Quarter Sessions, Davidson County, NC
Wm. Adderton v. John Cameron, principal. Eli Wallace listed as bail.

1833 -- Tax List, Davidson County, NC
Eli Wallis listed 116 acres valued at $95 and 1 white poll in Capt. Stephens' District

1840 -- Census, Graves County, KY Page 118
Eli Wallace, Sr.
(50-60) 1M
(20-30) 1F

1840, Jan 31 -- Marriage Register, Henry County, TN
Eli Wallace married Mima Crowell

1850 -- Census, Graves County, KY Page 408, District #2
Eli Wallis 60 M, Farmer, $500 Real Estate, born in North Carolina
Jemima Wallis 33 F, born in North Carolina
Lucinda Wallis 5 F, born in KY
Calvin Wallis 8 M, born in KY
Dashy Cornwell 30 F, born in North Carolina

1854, Aug -- Death Register, Graves County, KY
Amanda Wallace 3 F, Single, Resident of Graves County, born in Graves County, Died on Clarks R., Parents Eli & Jemima Wallace, died of unknown causes

1855, Nov 3 -- Death Register, Graves County, KY
Eli Wallace 65 M, Married, Farmer, Resident of Graves County, born in Montgomery County, NC, Parents E. & M. Wallace, died of Fever

Eli Wallace had the following children with his first wife:

	+22	Temperance Wallace (1806-1889)
	+23	Kendrick Wallace (1810-1865)

Eli Wallace and Jemima Crowell had the following children:

	+24	Calvin Wallace (1841-1866)
	+25	Lucinda Wallace (1845-)
	+26	Amanda Wallace (1851-1854)
	+27	James Lovelace Wallace (1851-1930)

Third Generation

5. **Isham Wallace**, son of Isham Wallace and Fanny Jones, was born in 1804. He married **Edee Reed** on December 2, 1822 in Rowan County, NC.[183] He married **Sarah "Sallie" Thompson** after 1827.

Edee Reed was born on October 11, 1800. She died on February 23, 1827 and was buried in Rowan County, NC at Reed Graveyard.[184] She and Isham Wallace had the following children:

28	Rebecca Annie Wallace (1824-). *Rebecca was born in 1824.*
29	Edee Wallace (1827-1909). *Edee was born on February 16, 1827. She died on March 29, 1909 and was buried in Graves County, KY at Burkhart Cemetery.*

Sarah "Sallie" Thompson, daughter of William Thompson (1748-1841) was born in 1799 in North Carolina.

6. **Eli Wallace**, son of Isham Wallace and Fanny Jones, was born in 1805. He died before August 25, 1879.

Sarah Smith was born in 1804. She and Eli Wallace had the following children:

30	Margaret Wallace (1825-). *Margaret was born in 1825.*
31	Mary Wallace (1827-). *Mary was born in 1827. She married **James E. Ratcliffe** on June 23, 1851.*
32	Frances Wallace (1829-). *Frances was born in 1829.*
33	William Wallace (1831-). *William was born in 1831.*
34	Henry Wallace (1835-). *Henry was born in 1835.*
35	Isham Everett Wallace (1838-1916). *Isham was born on February 9, 1838. He married **Sarah Ann Chenoweth** on August 16, 1857 in Monroe County, IL. He married **Sylvia Ann Baker** on August 3, 1865. He married **Clara Jane Green** on October 28, 1879. He died on December 15, 1916 and was buried in Calvert City, Marshall County, KY at Calvert City Cemetery.*
36	Frederick Wallace (1839-1897). *Frederick was born on June 5, 1839. He died on January 26, 1897 and was buried in Marshall County, KY at Wallace Cemetery.*
37	Levi Wallace (1843-1865). *Levi was born in 1843. He died on June 16, 1865 in Louisville, Jefferson County, KY and was buried in Louisville, Jefferson County, KY at Cave Hill Cemetery.*

7. **Mary Wallace**, daughter of Isham Wallace and Fanny Jones, was born in 1807 in North Carolina. She died on November 6, 1852 in Moscow, Hickman County, KY.[185]

William H. Feezor was born in 1805. He and Mary Wallace had the following children:

38	Jane Feezor (1830-). *Jane was born in 1830.*
39	M. Feezor (1833-). *M. was born in 1833.*
40	Elizabeth Feezor (1834-). *Elizabeth was born in 1834.*
41	Matilda Feezor (1835-1852). *Matilda was born in 1835 in Graves County, KY. She died in October 1852 in Moscow, Hickman County, KY.*
42	Adeline Feezor (1838-1852). *Adeline was born in 1838 in Graves County, KY. She died in August 1852 in Moscow, Hickman County, KY.*

43	William Feezor (1841-). *William was born in 1841.*
44	L. C. Feezor (1843-). *L. was born in 1843.*
45	John Feezor (1847-). *John was born in 1847.*

8. Levi W. Wallace, son of Isham Wallace and Fanny Jones, was born in 1817 in North Carolina. He died in October 1852 in Moscow, Hickman County, KY.[186]

Levi W. Wallace had the following child:

46	L. S. Wallis (1848-). *L. was born in 1848.*

11. Susan Wallace, daughter of Isham Wallace and Elizabeth, was born in 1843.

James Ivey was born in 1838. He and Susan Wallace had the following children:

47	Andrew Jackson Ivey (1861-1929). *Andrew was born on December 26, 1861. He died on May 26, 1929 and was buried in Sharpe, Marshall County, KY at Fooks Cemetery.*
48	Allie Ivey (1863-1939). *Allie was born in 1863. She married **William Monroe Dunagan** on August 12, 1880 in Ripley County, MO. She died in 1939 and was buried in Sharpe, Marshall County, KY at Fooks Cemetery.*
49	Georgia Ivey (1867-). *Georgia was born in 1867.*
50	Elizabeth Ivey (1868-). *Elizabeth was born in 1868.*

14. Jonathan Everett Wallace, son of Isham Wallace and Elizabeth, was born on August 27, 1848. He married **Mary M. Johnston** on January 7, 1875 in Marshall County, KY. He died on February 12, 1907 and was buried in Marshall County, KY at Story Cemetery.[187]

Mary M. Johnston was born on April 24, 1854. She died on January 22, 1929 and was buried in Marshall County, KY at Story Cemetery.[188]

16. Elizabeth Wallace, daughter of Nathan Wallace and Sarah, was born between 1800 and 1810.

Elizabeth Wallace had the following children:

51	William Travis Wallace (1822-1906). *William was born on April 5, 1822. He married **Elizabeth Susan Lawrence** on June 13, 1852 in Johnson County, IL. He married **Finetta McCaby** on October 24, 1858 in Johnson County, IL. He married **Marzee C. Bullock** circa 1889. He died on December 30, 1906 and was buried in Pope County, IL at Jackson-Brush Cemetery.*
52	Elizabeth Wallace (1831-). *Elizabeth was born in 1831.*
53	Nancy Wallace (1843-). *Nancy was born in 1843.*

17. Eli Wallace, son of Nathan Wallace and Sarah, was born between 1804 and 1810. He died before 1852.

Eli Wallace had the following children:

54	Susan Wallace (-)
55	William Wallace (-)
56	Sarah Wallace (1826-). *Sarah was born in 1826.*
57	Elizabeth Wallace (1828-1862). *Elizabeth was born on July 16, 1828. She died in September 1862 and was buried in Oskaloosa, Jefferson County, KS at Pleasant View Cemetery.*
58	Eveline Wallace (1836-). *Eveline was born in 1836.*
59	John Wallace (1840-). *John was born in 1840.*
60	Eli C. Wallace (1846-). *Eli was born in 1846.*

18. Mary Wallace, daughter of Nathan Wallace and Sarah, was born in 1810 in North Carolina.

Solomon Riley was born in 1814 in North Carolina. He and Mary Wallace had the following children:

61	Daniel J. Riley (1838-). *Daniel was born in 1838 in KY.*
62	Nathan Riley (1840-1863). *Nathan was born in 1840 in KY. He married **Jemima Bridges** on February 15, 1859 in Johnson County, IL. He died on January 20, 1863 in Memphis, Shelby County, TN.*
63	Nancy Riley (1843-). *Nancy was born in 1843 in KY. She married **Admiral Kelly** on August 24, 1858 in Johnson County, IL.*

19. Nancy Wallace, daughter of Nathan Wallace and Sarah, was born between 1810 and 1820. She died before 1852.

Edmond Wiley Lamb and Nancy Wallace had the following children:

| 64 | John W. Lamb (-) |

20. John C. Wallace, son of Nathan Wallace and Sarah, was born in 1819 in North Carolina.

Elizabeth was born in 1818 in Tennessee.

21. Rachel Wallace, daughter of Nathan Wallace and Sarah, was born in 1820 in North Carolina. She died circa 1867 in Yell County, AR.

William Wood was born in 1819 in Tennessee. He and Rachel Wallace had the following children:

65	Sarah Wood (1838-). *Sarah was born in 1838 in KY.*
66	Mary A. Wood (1840-). *Mary was born in 1840 in KY.*
67	Nancy Matilda Wood (1842-). *Nancy was born in 1842 in KY.*
68	Elizabeth Caroline Wood (1845-). *Elizabeth was born in 1845 in KY.*
69	Martha Wood (1846-). *Martha was born in 1846 in KY.*
70	Thomas C. Wood (1848-). *Thomas was born in 1848 in KY.*
71	Eveline Wood (1849-). *Eveline was born in 1849 in IL.*
72	Susan J. Wood (1852-). *Susan was born in 1852 in IL.*
73	John H. Wood (1854-). *John was born in 1854 in IL.*
74	James L. Wood (1856-). *James was born in 1856.*
75	William C. Wood (1858-). *William was born in 1858 in MO.*

22. Temperance Wallace, daughter of Eli Wallace, was born on September 24, 1806. She died on April 9, 1889 and was buried in Marshall County, KY at Feezor Cemetery.[189]

Thomas Reid was born on April 9, 1801. He died on April 22, 1879 and was buried in Marshall County, KY at Feezor Cemetery.[190] He and Temperance Wallace had the following children:

76	Eliza Ann Reid (1829-1899). *Eliza was born in 1829. She died in 1899 and was buried in Pope County, IL at Old Zion Cemetery.*
77	Joel H. Reid (1832-1912). *Joel was born on December 17, 1832. He married **Mary E. Thomasson** on September 1, 1852 in McCracken County, KY. He died on December 17, 1912 and was buried in Oak Level, Marshall County, KY at Riley Cemetery.*
78	Joyce Emeline Reid (1833-1916). *Joyce was born on May 12, 1833. She died on July 27, 1916 in Graves County, KY and was buried on July 28, 1916 in Symsonia, Graves County, KY at Symsonia Cemetery.*
79	Mary "Polly" Reid (1837-1867). *Mary was born in 1837. She married **Valentine C. Hill** on October 9, 1856 in Graves County, KY. She died in 1867 and was buried in Symsonia, Graves County, KY at Bolton Cemetery.*
80	Joseph Reid (1839-1926). *Joseph was born on May 7, 1839. He died on November 30, 1926 and was buried in Benton, Marshall County, KY at Hunt Cemetery.*
81	Isham Reid (1843-1916). *Isham was born on April 18, 1843. He married **Sarah Martha Edwards** on December 5, 1862. He died on February 14, 1916 and was buried in Woodville, McCracken County, KY at New Liberty Cemetery.*
82	John Kendrick Reid (1847-1910). *John was born on May 8, 1847. He died on December 29, 1910 and was buried in Marshall County, KY at Feezor Cemetery.*

23. Kendrick Wallace, son of Eli Wallace, was born in 1810. He died in 1865.

Tabitha Edwards was born in 1810. She died in May 1860. She and Kendrick Wallace had the following children:

83   Prudence Wallace (1838-1920). *Prudence was born on December 28, 1838 in Graves County, KY. She married* **Brantley C. Bolton** *on February 1, 1855 in Graves County, KY. She died on October 19, 1920 in Graves County, KY and was buried on October 20, 1920 in Symsonia, Graves County, KY at Bolton Cemetery.*

84   Louisa Jane Wallace (1840-1911). *Louisa was born on October 7, 1840 in Graves County, KY. She died on January 6, 1911 in Marshall County, KY and was buried in Marshall County, KY at Harrison Cemetery.*

85   Ambrose Wallace (1842-). *Ambrose was born in 1842.*

86   Edna Wallace (1844-). *Edna was born in 1844.*

87   William Phillip Wallace (aft 1847-1905). *William was born between 1847 and 1848. He died on August 17, 1905.*

88   Mary Ann Wallace (1848-1915). *Mary was born on June 13, 1848. She died on March 23, 1915 in Marshall County, KY.*

89   Green Wallace (1850-). *Green was born in 1850.*

90   Joel Kendrick Wallace (1853-1937). *Joel was born on April 19, 1853 in Graves County, KY. He married* **Belle Duncan** *circa 1884. He died on March 10, 1937 and was buried in Wickliffe, Ballard County, KY at Wickliffe Cemetery.*

91   Thomas A. Wallace (1856-1901). *Thomas was born on March 1, 1856 in Graves County, KY. He died in 1901.*

24. Calvin Wallace, son of Eli Wallace and Jemima Crowell, was born in 1841. He died on April 3, 1866 and was buried in Symsonia, Graves County, KY at Bolton Cemetery.

Sarah Bolton, daughter of Terrell R. Bolton (1809-1899) and Amelia Mary Crowell (1806-1888), was born in 1845. She and Calvin Wallace had the following children:

92   Eli Terrell Wallace (1863-1929). *Eli was born on April 2, 1863. He died on January 17, 1929 and was buried in Symsonia, Graves County, KY at Bolton Cemetery.*

93   Amelia Mariah Wallace (1865-1897). *Amelia was born on July 26, 1865. She died on March 2, 1897 and was buried in Symsonia, Graves County, KY at Bolton Cemetery.*

26. Amanda Wallace, daughter of Eli Wallace and Jemima Crowell, was born in 1851. She died in August 1854 in Graves County, KY.

27. James Lovelace Wallace, son of Eli Wallace and Jemima Crowell, was born on September 15, 1851. He died on November 21, 1930 and was buried in Symsonia, Graves County, KY at Bolton Cemetery.[191]

Belle was born on January 5, 1860. She died on March 18, 1896 and was buried in Symsonia, Graves County, KY at Bolton Cemetery.

Descendants of Nathan Wallis

1. **Nathan Wallis** was born in 1806 in North Carolina. He died on January 18, 1859 and was buried in Obion County, TN at Pleasant Hill Cemetery.[192] Nathan was married to Margaret (1807-1884) and they were the parents of Anna, Isham, Hulda, K, Jane, C.J., Levi T., Margaret, Nathan, Francis, Sara Eliza and L.S. Wallis. Nathan died in Obion County, TN and is believed to be closely related to the Isham, Nathan and Eli Wallace. Margaret died July 23, 1884 and is buried in Obion County, TN at Pleasant Hill Cemetery.[193]

RECORDS OF NATHAN WALLIS

1840 -- Census, Graves County, KY Page 103
Nathan Wallace
(30-40) 1M
(20-30) 1M 1F
(10-15) 1F
(5-10) 1M 1F
(0-5) 2M 2F

1850 -- Census, Hickman County, KY Page 10
Nathan Wallace 43 M, Farmer, $3500 Real Estate, born in South Carolina
Margarett Wallace 40 F, born in North Carolina
Isom Wallace 17 M, Farmer, born in KY
H. Wallace 15 F, born in KY
K. Wallace 14 M, born in KY
Jane Wallace 13 F, born in KY
Levi Wallace 11 M, born in KY
Margarett Wallace 10 F, born in KY
Nathan Wallace 8 M, born in KY
Franky Wallace 5 F, born in KY
Sarah Wallace 3 F, born in KY

1859, Feb 7 -- 1859-1861 Administrators, Executors and Guardian Bonds, Obion County, TN Page 36
Isham Wallis and B.S. Riley were appointed administrators of the estate of Nathan Wallis, Dec'd. with Lewis Stanley, Saml. B. Shore and John L. Guy as securities.

1860, Feb 6 -- 1859-1861 Wills, Inventories and Settlements, Obion County, TN Page 172, 377
Estate of Nathan Wallis by Administrator Isham Wallis. Items purchased by the following: Isham Wallis, C.L. Wallis, Margaret Wallis, B.S. Riley, A. Caudle, W.H. Caldwell and C.J. Wallis

Nathan Wallis and Margaret had the following children:

+2	Anna Wallis (1830-1904)	
+3	Isham Wallis (1832-)	
+4	Hulda Wallis (1835-)	
+5	K. Wallis (1836-)	
+6	Jane Wallis (1837-1882)	
+7	C. J. Wallis (1838-1877)	
+8	Levi T. Wallis (1839-)	
+9	Margaret Wallis (1840-)	
+10	Nathan Wallis (1842-)	
+11	Francis Wallis (1845-1905)	
+12	Sarah Eliza Wallis (1847-)	
+13	L. S. Wallis (1848-)	

Second Generation

2. **Anna Wallis**, daughter of Nathan Wallis and Margaret, was born on March 28, 1830. She married **Lloyd Carter** on May 29, 1848 in Hickman County, KY. She died on May 9, 1904 and was buried in Hickman County, KY at Oakwood Cemetery.

Lloyd Carter was born on August 26, 1821. He died on June 15, 1897 and was buried in Hickman County, KY at Oakwood Cemetery. He and Anna Wallis had the following children:

+14	James Loyd Carter Sr. (1849-1911)
+15	Sarah Ann Jane Carter (1852-1872)
+16	John W. Carter (1858-1923)
+17	Levi W. Carter (1861-)
+18	Robert L. Carter (1863-1934)
+19	Margaret E, Carter (1866-1872)
+20	Isham J. Carter (1869-1872)
+21	M. E. Carter (1871-)
+22	Emma F. Carter (1873-)

3. **Isham Wallis**, son of Nathan Wallis and Margaret, was born in August 1832. He married **Eliza Ann Flippo** in May 1851 in Hickman County, KY.

Eliza Ann Flippo was born on February 15, 1831. She died on November 6, 1919 and was buried in Obion County, TN at Pleasant Hill Cemetery. She and Isham Wallis had the following children:

+23	F. M. Wallace (1852-)
+24	Rachel Eliza Ann Wallace (1854-1924)
+25	Mary E. Wallace (1859-1867)
+26	Margaret Wallace (1868-1903)
+27	Martha Wallace (1871-)
+28	Elsie Pearl Wallace (1872-1885)

4. **Hulda Wallis**, daughter of Nathan Wallis and Margaret, was born in 1835. She married **William Alexander Caudle** on November 18, 1853 in Obion County, TN and was buried in Obion County, TN at Pleasant Hill Cemetery.

William Alexander Caudle, son of Absolom Caudle (-) and Mary Hainey (-), was born in 1833. He died on January 1, 1911 and was buried in Obion County, TN at Pleasant Hill Cemetery. He and Hulda Wallis had the following children:

+29	George Washington Caudle (1855-1934)
+30	William Caudle (1859-)
+31	Frederick Caudle (1860-)
+32	Edward Caudle (1862-)
+33	Jesse Caudle (1866-)
+34	Robert Caudle (1868-)
+35	Levi Caudle (1870-)

5. **K. Wallis**, son of Nathan Wallis and Margaret, was born in 1836.

6. **Jane Wallis**, daughter of Nathan Wallis and Margaret, was born in 1837. She married **B. Solomon Riley** on June 12, 1855. She married **Jesse B. Caudle** on October 2, 1867. She died on December 10, 1882 and was buried in Obion County, TN at Pleasant Hill Cemetery.

B. Solomon Riley was born in 1825 in North Carolina. He and Jane Wallis had the following children:

+36	W. R. Riley (1856-)
+37	Margaret Ellen Riley (1858-)
+38	Robert Riley (1864-)

Jesse B. Caudle, son of Absolom Caudle (-) and Mary Hainey (-), was born on March 19, 1843. He died on March 29, 1933 and was buried in Obion County, TN at Pleasant Hill Cemetery.

7. **C. J. Wallis**, son of Nathan Wallis and Margaret, was born in 1838. He married **Louisa E. Bell** on May 15, 1862 in Obion County, TN. He married **Mary E. Cummings** on November 9, 1865 in Obion County, TN. He died on December 19, 1877 and was buried in Obion County, TN at Pleasant Hill Cemetery.

Mary E. Cummings and C. J. Wallis had the following children:

+39   Mattie L. Wallis (-)
+40   Joseph J. Wallis (1864-)

8. **Levi T. Wallis**, son of Nathan Wallis and Margaret, was born in 1839. He married **Elizabeth Ferrell** on November 20, 1867 in Obion County, TN.

11. **Francis Wallis**, daughter of Nathan Wallis and Margaret, was born on November 21, 1845. She married **Malakiah R. "Mack" Caudle** on November 11, 1859 in Obion County, TN. She married **James William Robinson** on November 12, 1863 in Obion County, TN. She died on November 9, 1905 and was buried in Obion County, TN at Pleasant Hill Cemetery.

Malakiah R. "Mack" Caudle, son of Absolom Caudle (-) and Mary Hainey (-), was born in 1836. He died on April 6, 1862. He and Francis Wallis had the following children:

+41   Nancy Caudle (1862-1912)

James William Robinson was born on December 5, 1843. He died on April 5, 1925 and was buried in Obion County, TN at Pleasant Hill Cemetery.

12. **Sarah Eliza Wallis**, daughter of Nathan Wallis and Margaret, was born in 1847. She married **John E. Bell** on January 23, 1867 in Obion County, TN. She married **Robert E. Flippo** on July 25, 1867 in Obion County, TN.

13. **L. S. Wallis**, son of Levi W. Wallace, was born in 1848.

Elizabeth was born in 1847. She and L. S. Wallis had the following children:

+42   Elvira Wallace (1868-)

Third Generation

14. **James Loyd Carter Sr.**, son of Lloyd Carter and Anna Wallis, was born on August 28, 1849. He died on August 7, 1911 and was buried in Hickman County, KY at Oakwood Cemetery.

Lucy Emma Howell was born on October 22, 1855. She died on March 5, 1926 and was buried in Hickman County, KY at Oakwood Cemetery.

15. **Sarah Ann Jane Carter**, daughter of Lloyd Carter and Anna Wallis, was born on September 13, 1852. She died on April 11, 1872 and was buried in Hickman County, KY at Oakwood Cemetery.

16. **John W. Carter**, son of Lloyd Carter and Anna Wallis, was born in 1858. He died on November 23, 1923 in Memphis, Shelby County, TN.

18. **Robert L. Carter**, son of Lloyd Carter and Anna Wallis, was born in 1863. He died in 1934.

Mary F. Morris was born in 1865. She and Robert L. Carter had the following children:

43   Lula F. Carter (1884-1970). *Lula was born in 1884. She died in 1970.*

19. **Margaret E, Carter**, daughter of Lloyd Carter and Anna Wallis, was born on May 1, 1866. She died on April 13, 1872 and was buried in Hickman County, KY at Oakwood Cemetery.

20. **Isham J. Carter**, son of Lloyd Carter and Anna Wallis, was born on December 30, 1869. He died on April 12, 1872 and was buried in Hickman County, KY at Oakwood Cemetery.

24. **Rachel Eliza Ann Wallace**, daughter of Isham Wallis and Eliza Ann Flippo, was born on February 10, 1854. She married **W. Frank Callicott** on October 17, 1872 in Obion County, TN. She died on November 2, 1924 and was buried in Obion County, TN at Cane Creek Cemetery.

W. Frank Callicott was born in 1848. He died in 1924 and was buried in Obion County, TN at Cane Creek Cemetery.

25. **Mary E. Wallace**, daughter of Isham Wallis and Eliza Ann Flippo, was born on January 16, 1859. She died on February 8, 1867 and was buried in Obion County, TN at Pleasant Hill Cemetery.

26. **Margaret Wallace**, daughter of Isham Wallis and Eliza Ann Flippo, was born on May 21, 1868. She married **N. G. Buckley** on December 1, 1887 in Obion County, TN. She died on July 17, 1903 and was buried in Obion County, TN at Pleasant Hill Cemetery.

N. G. Buckley and Margaret Wallace had the following children:

> 44   Elsie Buckley (1889-). *Elsie was born in January 1889.*

28. **Elsie Pearl Wallace**, daughter of Isham Wallis and Eliza Ann Flippo, was born on July 13, 1872. She died on November 12, 1885 and was buried in Obion County, TN at Pleasant Hill Cemetery.

29. **George Washington Caudle**, son of William Alexander Caudle and Hulda Wallis, was born on December 29, 1855. He died on September 19, 1934.

Mary Saluda Taylor was born on January 9, 1867. She died on May 16, 1919. She and George Washington Caudle had the following children:

> 45   George Raymond Caudle (1885-1967). *George was born on June 25, 1885. He died on March 15, 1967.*

37. **Margaret Ellen Riley**, daughter of B. Solomon Riley and Jane Wallis, was born in 1858. She married **G. W. Holloway** on December 12, 1877 in Obion County, TN.

G. W. Holloway was born in 1844. He and Margaret Ellen Riley had the following children:

> 46   George Holloway (1879-). *George was born in 1879.*
> 47   Margaret Holloway (1880-). *Margaret was born in 1880.*

40. **Joseph J. Wallis**, son of C. J. Wallis and Mary E. Cummings, was born in 1864. He married **Henrietta Hurt** on January 5, 1881 in Obion County, TN.

Henrietta Hurt was born on March 24, 1858. She died on September 19, 1938 in Jackson, Madison County, TN and was buried in Weakley County, TN at Hurt Cemetery. She and Joseph J. Wallis had the following children:

> 48   William Cirby Wallis (1882-1952). *William was born on August 9, 1882. He died on April 12, 1952 and was buried in Jackson, Madison County, TN at Ridgecrest Cemetery.*

41. **Nancy Caudle**, daughter of Malakiah R. "Mack" Caudle and Francis Wallis, was born in 1862. She died in 1912.

Thomas Newton London was born in 1848. He died in 1931. He and Nancy Caudle had the following children:

> 49   Lucy Jane "Jennie" London (1888-1977). *Lucy was born on March 9, 1888. She died on August 3, 1977.*

Jesse Wallace (bef 1748-)

RECORDS OF JESSE WALLACE

1769 -- Regulators Petition
Anson County resident Jesse Wallas was listed as a signer

1771, Jul 10 -- 1771-1777 Court of Pleas and Quarter Sessions, Anson County, NC Page 51
A deed from John Bennett and wife to Jesse Wallace is proven by James Saunders

1772, Apr 24 -- Land Grant #3196/3699, Anson County, NC
Jesse Wallis received 295 acres located on East side of Grimes Fork of Mountain Creek adjoining Richard Adams. Jeremiah Hendrick and Wm. Adams were chain carriers.

1773, Apr 7 -- Deed, Anson County, NC, Book K, Page 84
Richard and Amey Adams deeded Jesse Wallis 100 acres located on the south fork of Mountain Creek. Jacob Cockram and Pindance Adams were witnesses.

1774, Apr 16 -- 1771-1777 Court of Pleas and Quarter Sessions, Anson County, NC Page 115
A deed from Richard Adams and wife to Jesse Wallace was proven by Jacob Cockran

1774, Sep 8 -- Deed, Anson County, NC Book K Page 271
Richard and Ann Adams deeded Thomas Mason a tract of land located on the south fork of Mountain Creek adjoining Jesse Wallis. Sampson Williams, William Adams and Elizabeth Adams were witnesses.

1774, Dec 29 -- Deed, Anson County, NC Book K Page 349
Jesse and Susanna Wallis deeded Angus McInnis 100 acres located between Dry Branch and Deep Branch on south fork of Mountain Creek. Part of an original grant from Dec 22, 1760 to Richard Adams then sold to John Bennett then to Jesse Wallis. Alexr. McLeod and Muro. McInnis were witnesses.

1775, Jan 11 -- 1771-1777 Court of Pleas and Quarter Sessions, Anson County, NC Page 98
A deed from Jesse Wallace and wife to Angus McInnis was proven by Murdo McInnis

1775, Apr 8 -- Deed, Anson County, NC Book K Page 320
Jesse and Susanna Wallis deeded Jeremiah Hendrick 295 acres located East side of Grimes Fork of Mountain Creek adjoining Richard Adams. Sampson Williams and Mary Ingless were witnesses.

1775, Apr 12 -- 1771-1777 Court of Pleas and Quarter Sessions, Anson County, NC Page 149
A deed from Jesse Wallace and wife to Jeremiah Hendrick was proven by Sampson Williams

1777 -- Petition to divide Anson County
Jesse Wallace listed as a signer on petition that led to creation of Montgomery County, NC

1779, Apr 16 -- Land Entry, Montgomery County, NC
Jesse Walles entered 50 acres located on Ceader Creek above his land where he lives

1779, Apr 16 -- Land Entry, Montgomery County, NC
Jesse Walles entered 75 acres located on the branches of Ceader Creek [sold this warrant to John Parsons prior to 1790] adjoining Butler and including Thomas Lucas' improvement.

1782 -- Tax List, Montgomery County, NC
Jesse Wallice listed with 200 acres

1782, May 17 -- Land Grant #253, Montgomery County, NC
Joshua Butler received 50 acres located on Ceder Creek. Thomas Butler and Jesse Wallis were chain carriers.

1782, May 17 -- Land Grant #296, Montgomery County, NC
James Butler received 100 acres located on Ceder Creek. Joshua Butler and Jesse Wallis were chain carriers.

1782, Aug 8 -- Land Grant #94, Montgomery County, NC
John McLanghon received 100 acres located on Riges Creek adjoining Samuel Parsons. Samuel Parsons and Jesse Wallis were chain carriers.

1782, Aug 8 -- Land Grant #252, Montgomery County, NC
Arthur Taylor received 50 acres located on branch waters of Little River. Samuel Parsons and Jesse Wallis were chain carriers.

1790 -- Census, Montgomery County, NC Page 418
Jesse Walice
(16+) 1M
3F

1794, Sep 10 -- Land Grant #1033, Montgomery County, NC
Jesse Wallis sold a land warrant for 100 aces located on Cheeks Creek to Caleb Touchstone

Nathan/Nathaniel Wallace (-bef 1817)

RECORDS OF NATHAN/NATHANIEL WALLACE [D. 1817]

1790 -- Land Grant #1557, Randolph County, NC
Nathan Wallace received 50 acres located on Big Creek adjoining Finch Carter, Rich and Millikan. Samuel Rich and Finch Carter were chain carriers.

1797, Feb 8 -- 1779, 1780, 1783-1801 Land Entries, Randolph County, NC
Nathaniel Wollace entered 50 acres adjoining Samuel Rich, Abraham Davis, and William Cranford.

1798, Jan 22 -- 1779, 1780, 1783-1801 Land Entries, Randolph County, NC
Nathaniel Wallace entered 100 acres located on Uharee River adjoining Samuel Rich and Cranford.

1799, May -- 1799-1802 Criminal Actions, Randolph County, NC
Presentment of Joel Ragsdale on a charge of assaulting Dick Hopkins. John Bean and Nathaniel Wallice listed.

1799, May -- 1799-1802 Criminal Actions, Randolph County, NC
Presentment of Dick Hopkins on the charge that he assaulted John Bean, constable, as Bean was attempting to execute the order of the court to make the sum of 5 pds and 13 shillings from the property of Hopkins and Nathaniel Wallace. This execution pursuant to a matter involving Joel Ragsdale. The incident took place 16 May 1799.

1803, Feb 23 -- 1801-1833 Land Entries, Randolph County, NC
Nathaniel Wallis entered 100 acres located on waters of McGee's Creek adjoining Samuel Rich and Cranford

1804, Mar 1 -- Estate Book C Page 306, Rowan County, NC [current Davie County, NC]
Estate of Solomon Jones, Dec'd. Heirs: Wife Elizabeth to have home plantation for life. Daughters each to have 25 pounds: Rebecca Jones, Ruth Jones, Nancy Jones and Margaret Jones. Stepson, John Tribbit 300 acres on Howard's branch of Dutchman's Creek to be leased for 5 years. Executors: wife Elizabeth, Nathan Walles, and Peter Glasscock. Witnesses: Ransom Powell, and John Powell
[Note – Solomon Jones died Apr 5, 1804 and is buried at Bear Creek Baptist Church in Mocksville, Davie County, NC. His wife, Elizabeth, was previously a widow of Mr. Trivitt/Tribbit. Solomon Jones is listed in 1800 Census of Rowan County, NC Page 451 (45+) 1M 1F (16-26) 4F (10-16) 1F (0-10) 3F]

1807, Jan 8 -- Deed Book 20 Page 27, Rowan County, NC
William Knup deeded John Isahower 114 acres located on both sides of Panther Creek adjoining heirs of Alexander Clingerman, David Woodson, Paul Powless, Adam Powless. Nathaniel Wallace and John Knup, Sr. were witnesses

1808, Sep 23 -- Deed Book 21 Page 530, Rowan County, NC [current Davie County, NC]
Elizabeth Jones and Nathan Wallis as executors of Solomon Jones Estate deeded Peter Glasscock, Jr. 307 acres located East of Howards Branch of Dutchmans Creek adjoining Pachel Stocstil and John Beeman. Scarlet Glasscock and William Moore were witnesses.

1810 -- Census, Rowan County, NC Page 291
Nathan Wallace
(26-45) 1M 1F
(16-25) 1F
(0-10) 2M

1811, Mar 4 -- 1801-1833 Land Entries, Randolph County, NC
John Cranford entered 50 acres located on Big Creek adjoining Elias Cranford, Samuel Cranford and Nathan Wallice

1812 -- Tax List, Rowan County, NC
Nathaniel Wallace listed 193 acres in Capt. Pool's Company

1812, Mar 1 -- Deed Book 20 Page 528, Rowan County, NC
Martain Hofner Sr. deeded his son John Hofner 108 acres located on Panther Creek adjoining Mathais Frick. Nathaniel Wallace was a witness

1813 -- Tax List, Rowan County, NC
Nathan Wallace listed 239 acres and 1 white poll in Capt. Bean's Company

1813, Dec 30 -- Deed Book 1 Page 92, Davidson County, NC
Nathan Wallis deeded Marvel Epps [of Montgomery County] 100 acres located on the North Side of the Yadkin River on Gere Creek. Adjoining the County Line, Edward Taylor and Look Raper. Thos. Jones and Levinah Jones were witnesses. Proven in court Jul 31, 1823.

1814 -- Tax List, Rowan County, NC
Nathan Wallace listed 239 acres and 1 white poll in Capt. Bean's Company

1815 -- Tax List, Rowan County, NC
Nathan Wallis listed 125 acres valued at $250 in Capt. Bean's Company

1815, Aug -- 1815-1816 Court of Pleas and Quarter Sessions, Rowan County, NC
A deed from Anthony Peelor to David Woodson, Senr. For 602 acres dated Dec 20, 1814 is proven by Nathan Wallis.

1815, Oct 26 -- 1801-1833 Land Entries, Randolph County, NC
James Crow entered 100 acres located on Big Creek adjoining Rich, Wallis and Willis Coggins

1817, Jan 7 -- 1801-1833 Land Entries, Randolph County, NC
James Crow entered 100 acres located on Big Creek adjoining Willis Coggins, Elias Cranford and Nathaniel Wallace

1817, May 22 -- 1817-1818 Court of Pleas and Quarter Sessions, Rowan County, NC
Administration of the Estate of Nathaniel Wallace [the widow having relinquished her right to administer] granted to Henry Harkey and he gave bond with Peter Harkey and Peter Earnheart and Adam Hoofman.

1817, Aug 18 -- 1817-1818 Court of Pleas and Quarter Sessions, Rowan County, NC
Account of Sales of the Estate of Nathaniel Walles, deceased filed

William Wallace (aft 1791-1843) and siblings

1. **Wallace**.

Unknown and Wallace had the following children:

+2   William Wallace (aft 1791-1843) was married to Chaney Berry Cranford and lived most of his life near the Uwharrie River and Ophir in Montgomery County, NC. Their union produced at least eleven children and many of them children migrated to western Kentucky.

+3   Harbard/Harbart Wallace (1796-1872) was married to Nancy Adderton and later to Docia Crowell. Harbart moved with his family to Graves County, KY during the 1830's.

+4   Elizabeth "Betsy" Wallace (1800-1905) married Phillip Hagler and lived most of her life in neighboring Stanly County, NC.

+5   Ann Wallace (1803-1900) married William Hall and lived in in Montgomery County, NC. They were the parents of at least five children.

Second Generation

2. **William Wallace**, son of Wallace and Unknown, was born between 1791 and 1800 and died in 1843 in Montgomery County, NC. William married Chaney Berry Cranford (1802-1867).[194]

RECORDS OF WILLIAM WALLACE

1832, Oct 8 -- Deed Book 24 Page 537, Montgomery County, NC
William Wallis deeded Eli Russell 200 acres on Big Creek adjoining the Randolph County Line, Richard Bean, Eli Harris, Walter Bean, and Matthew Davis. John G. Hopkins and Martin Hopkins were witnesses.

1840 -- Census, Montgomery County, NC Page 236, West Pee Dee Township
William Wallace
(40-50) 1M
(30-40) 1F
(15-20) 1M
(10-15) 2M 1F
(5-10) 2F
(0-5) 1M

William Wallace and Chaney Berry Cranford had the following children:

+6	Bascom Wallace (-)
+7	James Alvis Wallace (1821-1870)
+8	Erasmus Stimpson Wallace (1824-1901)
+9	Anna Mariah Wallace (1826-1905)
+10	Alexander Clark Wallace (1827-1889)
+11	Martha Jane Wallace (1831-1916)
+12	Nancy Caroline Wallace (1833-1907)
+13	Louisa Eliza Wallace (1836-1915)
+14	William P. "Pink" Wallace (c. 1839-1863)
+15	Leonard Harris Wallace (c. 1841-1862)
+16	Jason McKendrick Wallace (1843-1907)

3. **Harbard/Harbart Wallace**, son of Wallace and Unknown, was born in 1796 in North Carolina and died in 1872 in Kentucky. He first married **Nancy Adderton** on October 20, 1825 in Davidson County, NC[195]. After Nancy died Harbart married **Docia Crowell** in 1850 in Graves County, KY. Docia was born on October 20, 1820. She died on July 4, 1906 and was buried in Marshall County, KY at Wallace Cemetery.[196]

RECORDS OF HARBARD/HARBART WALLACE

1823, Oct 9 -- Marriage Register, Rowan County, NC
John Cooper married Peggy Kimball. Harbart Wallace was bondsman/witness.

1825, Oct 20 -- Marriage Register, Davidson County, NC
Herbert Wallace married Nancy Adderton. Henry Shemwell was bondsman.

1830 -- Census, Davidson County, NC Page 199
Harbord Wallace
(30-40) 1M
(20-30) 1F
(0-5) 2M

1830 -- Tax List, Davidson County, NC
Harbord Wallis listed 1 white poll in Capt. Daniels' District

1831 -- Tax List, Davidson County, NC
Harbord Wallis listed 1 white poll in Capt. Ward's District

1831, May 9 -- Deed, Davidson County, NC Deed Book 4 Page 762-764
William Adderton deeded his son Jeremiah Adderton 35 acres located East of Dick's Branch. Originally granted to Matthew Skeen and sold to Adderton. Harbert Wallace and Martha Adderton are witnesses.

1832 -- Tax List, Davidson County, NC
Harbard Wallis listed 1 white poll in Capt. Ward's District

1833 -- Tax List, Davidson County, NC
Herbert Wallis listed 1 white poll in Capt. Ward's District

1850 -- Census, Graves County, KY Page 406, District #2
Harbert Wallis 50 M, C. Maker, $200 Personal Property born in North Carolina
Docia Wallis 30 F, born in North Carolina
James Wallis 21 M, Farmer, born in North Carolina

1860 Census Graves County, KY Page 134, Mayfield Post Office
Harlan Wallis 65 M, Farmer, $660 Real Estate, $250 Personal Property, born in North Carolina
Dosey Wallis 40 F, Housework, born in North Carolina
Alexander Wallis 8 M, born in KY
Gemima Wallis 7 F, born in KY
Aaron Wallis 4 M, born in KY

1870 -- Census, Graves County, KY Page 247, Symsonia Precinct
Harbart Wallace 68 M, Farmer, $300 Personal Property $150 Real Estate, born in North Carolina
Dosie Wallace 47 F, Keeping House, born in North Carolina
Alexander Wallace 18 M, At Home, born in KY
Amelia J. Wallace 16 F, At Home, born in KY
Aaron C. Wallace 14 M, At Home, born in KY
Richard C. Wallace 8 M, At Home, born in KY

Harbard/Harbart Wallace and Nancy Adderton had the following child:

+17   James Lovelace Wallace (1826-1881)

Harbard/Harbart Wallace and Docia Crowell had the following children:

+18   Alexander Clark Wallace (1851-1952)
+19   Amelia Jemima Wallace (1853-)
+20   Aaron C. Wallace (1856-)

Additional Information can be found at www.MooreCountyWallaces.com

4. Elizabeth "Betsy" Wallace, daughter of Wallace and Unknown, was born in September 1800. She died in 1905.

RECORDS OF BESTSY WALLACE

1850 -- Census, Cabarrus County, NC Page 430-B
Philip Hagler 37 M, Farmer, Born in Rowan County
Elizabeth Hagler 43 F, Born in Montgomery County
Sarah Hagler 16 F, Born in Stanly County
Elizabeth Hagler 14 F, Born in Stanly County
Margaret Hagler 12 F, Born in Stanly County
Dolley Hagler 10 F, Born in Stanly County
Charles Hagler 8 M, Born in Stanly County
Daniel Hagler 1 M, Born in Cabarrus County
Mary Richey 11 F, Born in Stanly County

1880 -- Census, Stanly County, NC Page 325, Harris Township
John Heagler 27 M, Head, Married, Farm Laborer, Born in NC, Father & Mother Born in NC
Salina Heagler 26 F, Wife, Married, Keeping House, Born in NC, Father & Mother Born in NC
Adam M. Heagler 6/12(Dec) M, Son, Single, Born in NC, Father & Mother Born in NC
Elizabeth Heagler 75 F, Mother, Widow, At Home, Born in NC, Father & Mother Born in NC

1900 -- Census, Stanly County, NC Page 260, Harris Township
John Higlar 53 M, Apr 1847, Head, Married-20yrs, Farmer, Born in NC, Father & Mother Born in NC
Solen Higlar 44 F, Mar 1856, Wife, Married-20yrs, 8 Children(6 Living), Born in NC, Father & Mother Born in NC
Daniel Higlar 18 M, Jul 1881, Son, Single, Farm Laborer, Born in NC, Father & Mother Born in NC
Ella Higlar 16 F, May 1884, Dau, Single, Born in NC, Father & Mother Born in NC
Minnie Higlar 11 F, Jun 1888, Dau, Single, Born in NC, Father & Mother Born in NC
Henry Higlar 8 M, Jul 1891, Son, Single, Born in NC, Father & Mother Born in NC
Calvin Higlar 6 M, Feb 1894, Son, Single, Born in NC, Father & Mother Born in NC
Nellie Higlar 4 F, May 1896, Dau, Single, Born in NC, Father & Mother Born in NC
Betsie Higlar 99 F, Sep 1800, Mother, Widowed, 2 Children(2 Living), Born in NC, Father & Mother Born in NC
*Living next door (could there be a connection?)
Pollie Walace 60 F, Apr 1840, Head, Single, Born in NC, Father & Mother Born in NC
Tenie Walace 85 F, Apr 1815, Mother, Widow, 1 Child(1 Living), Born in NC, Father & Mother Born in NC

Phillip Hagler and Elizabeth "Betsy" Wallace had the following children:

+22   John M. Hagler (1851-1925)

5. Ann Wallace, daughter of Wallace and Unknown, was born in 1803. She died on January 19, 1900.

RECORDS OF ANN WALLACE

1840 -- Census, Montgomery County, NC Page 236
William Hall Jur.
(30-40) 1M 1F
(0-5) 3M

1850 -- Census, Montgomery County, NC Page 150
William Hall 43 M, Farmer, Born in NC
Anne Hall 40 F, Born in NC
Alexd. W. Hall 14 M, Born in NC
George W. Hall 11 M, Born in NC
Thomas W. Hall 10 M, Born in NC
Nathl. Hall 8 M, Born in NC
Eli F. Hall 5 M, Born in NC

1860 -- Census, Montgomery County, NC Page 485-B, Beans District
William Hall 52 M, Farmer, $75 Personal Property, Born in NC
Anna Hall 52 F, Born in NC
Alexdr. W. Hall 22 M, Mechanic, $100 Personal Propery, Born in NC
George Hall 21 M, Hireling, Born in NC

Thomas Hall 19 M, Farm Hand, Born in NC
Nathl. Hall 18 M, Farm Hand, Born in NC
Eli F. Hall 15 M, Born in NC

William Hall was born in 1807. He and Ann Wallace had the following children:

+23	Alexander Watson Hall (1837-)	
+24	George W. Hall (1839-)	
+25	Thomas W. Hall (1840-)	
+26	L. Nathaniel "Nat" Hall (1842-)	
+27	Eli F. Hall (1845-)	

Third Generation

6. **Bascom Wallace** was the son of William Wallace and Chaney Berry Cranford.

7. **James Alvis Wallace**, son of William Wallace and Chaney Berry Cranford, was born on April 24, 1821 in Montgomery County, NC. He married **Lavinia Bingham** on May 3, 1843 in Randolph County, NC. He died on February 23, 1870 in Montgomery County, NC.

Lavinia Bingham was born on November 12, 1827 in Montgomery County, NC. She died on September 12, 1879 in Montgomery County, NC. She and James Alvis Wallace had the following children:

28   Jane Matilda Frances Wallace (1845-1918). *Jane was born on October 12, 1845 in Montgomery County, NC. She married **Burrell Titus Coggins** on November 6, 1866. She died on June 27, 1918 in Montgomery County, NC.*

29   Chisholm Clark Wallace (1848-1932). *Chisholm was born on October 8, 1848 in Montgomery County, NC. He died on March 12, 1932 in Montgomery County, NC and was buried in Montgomery County, NC at The Forks of the Little River Baptist Church Cemetery.*

30   Cornelia Ann Wallace (1850-1913). *Cornelia was born on March 9, 1850 in Montgomery County, NC. She married **James Madison Wright** on March 15, 1868. She died on February 13, 1913.*

31   William Clegg Wallace (1852-1937). *William was born on October 27, 1852. He married **Margaret Louisa Allen** on February 3, 1881. He died on April 16, 1937 in Montgomery County, NC.*

32   Michael Rush Wallace (c. 1854-c. 1857). *Michael was born circa 1854 in Montgomery County, NC. He died circa 1857 in Montgomery County, NC.*

8. **Erasmus Stimpson Wallace**, son of William Wallace and Chaney Berry Cranford, was born on November 16, 1824 in Montgomery County, NC. He married **Folana Steed** on February 27, 1849 in Montgomery County, NC. He died on September 27, 1901 and was buried in Marshall County, KY at Wallace Cemetery.

Folana Steed was born on February 10, 1832 in Montgomery County, NC. She died on December 6, 1910 and was buried in Marshall County, KY at Wallace Cemetery. She and Erasmus Stimpson Wallace had the following children:

33   William L. Wallace (1850-). *William was born on March 3, 1850 in Montgomery County, NC.*

34   Malcolm M. Wallace (1851-). *Malcolm was born on October 31, 1851 in Montgomery County, NC.*

35   Nancy Ann Wallace (1854-1916). *Nancy was born on July 22, 1854 in Montgomery County, NC. She married **Archie L. E. Freeman** on October 31, 1876 in Graves County, KY. She died on December 18, 1916 in Graves County, KY.*

36   Emily Minerva Wallace (1855-1934). *Emily was born on June 27, 1855 in Montgomery County, NC. She died on November 29, 1934 in Marshall County, KY.*

37   Uriah Duck Wallace (1857-1938). *Uriah was born on October 19, 1857 in Montgomery County, NC. He married **Mrs. S.E. Rudd** on February 15, 1917. He died in 1938 in KY.*

38   Alexander Gray Wallace (1859-). *Alexander was born on November 9, 1859 in Montgomery County, NC. He died in Marshall County, KY.*

39   June Harrison Wallace (1862-1942). *June was born on March 31, 1862 in Montgomery*

County, NC. He married **Mariah Jane Feezor** on September 1, 1886. He died on July 24, 1942 and was buried in Symsonia, Graves County, KY at Symsonia Cemetery.

40   Mary Cassandra Wallace (1864-1904). *Mary was born on September 10, 1864 in Montgomery County, NC. She married **John Pinner Bowlin** "WFT Est 1879-1899". She died on August 29, 1904 in Marshall County, KY.*

41   Ellen Eliza Wallace (1868-1937). *Ellen was born on July 8, 1868 in Marshall County, KY. She married **Henry Burnette Feezor** on December 14, 1886. She died on April 22, 1937 in Marshall County, KY.*

42   Mattie Jane Wallace (1872-1950). *Mattie was born on November 23, 1872 in Marshall County, KY. She married **William Aron Reid** on September 11, 1895. She died on December 31, 1950 in Marshall County, KY.*

9. **Anna Mariah Wallace**, daughter of William Wallace and Chaney Berry Cranford, was born on February 11, 1826 in Montgomery County, NC. She married **John Wesley Riley** on January 7, 1847 in Montgomery County, NC. She died on July 23, 1905 and was buried in Smyth County, VA at Kell Cemetery.

John Wesley Riley was born in 1824. He died on March 17, 1903. He and Anna Mariah Wallace had the following children:

43   John Houston Riley (-). *John was born in Montgomery County, NC.*

44   Amanda Riley (-). *Amanda was born in Montgomery County, NC.*

45   Minerva Riley (-). *Minerva was born in Montgomery County, NC.*

46   William Riley (c. 1848-). *William was born circa 1848 in Montgomery County, NC.*

47   Alexander Lee Riley (1852-1927). *Alexander was born on December 5, 1852 in Montgomery County, NC. He died on September 4, 1927 and was buried in Near Texarkana, TX.*

10. **Alexander Clark Wallace**, son of William Wallace and Chaney Berry Cranford, was born on April 14, 1827 in Montgomery County, NC. He married **Sophronia Jane Steed** on January 27, 1855 in Montgomery County, NC. He died on July 17, 1889 in Graves County, KY and was buried in Marshall County, KY at Wallace Cemetery.

Sophronia Jane Steed was born on December 21, 1836 in Montgomery County, NC. She died on July 21, 1918 in Graves County, KY and was buried in Marshall County, KY at Wallace Cemetery. She and Alexander Clark Wallace had the following children:

48   James R. Wallace (1857-1878). *James was born on December 21, 1857 in Montgomery County, NC. He died on July 21, 1878 in Marshall County, KY and was buried in Marshall County, KY at Wallace Cemetery.*

49   Cornelia Camoline Wallace (1860-). *Cornelia was born on September 28, 1860 in Montgomery County, NC. She died in Marshall County, KY.*

50   Alexander Jason Wallace (1862-1885). *Alexander was born on June 28, 1862 in Montgomery County, NC. He died on February 18, 1885 in Graves County, KY and was buried in Marshall County, KY at Wallace Cemetery.*

51   Corrinia E. Wallace (1864-1888). *Corrinia was born on October 18, 1864 in Montgomery County, NC. She died on March 31, 1888 in Graves County, KY.*

52   E. Milton Wallace (1874-1905). *E. was born on January 7, 1874 in Graves County, KY. He married **Flora Feezor** in 1903. He died on May 10, 1905 in Graves County, KY and was buried in Marshall County, KY at Wallace Cemetery.*

53   Lula Ida Wallace (1877-1900). *Lula was born on October 12, 1877. She married **J.C. Edwards** on November 29, 1899. She died on June 12, 1900 and was buried in Marshall County, KY at Wallace Cemetery.*

54   Effie Wallace (1880-1899). *Effie was born on August 10, 1880 in KY. She died on March 14, 1899 and was buried in Marshall County, KY at Wallace Cemetery.*

11. **Martha Jane Wallace**, daughter of William Wallace and Chaney Berry Cranford, was born on September 17, 1831 in Montgomery County, NC. She married **Peter Cole Riley** on January 26, 1852 in Montgomery County, NC. She died on June 15, 1916 in Benton, Marshall County, KY and was buried in Oak Level, Marshall County, KY at Riley Cemetery.

Peter Cole Riley was born circa 1836 in Montgomery County, NC and was buried in Oak Level, Marshall County, KY at Riley Cemetery. He and Martha Jane Wallace had the following children:

55	Euna Riley (-). *Euna was born in Montgomery County, NC. She died in Montgomery County, NC.*
56	Amanda Riley (-). *Amanda was born in Montgomery County, NC. She married **Matt Baker** in KY.*
57	Calvin Bob Riley (1854-1932). *Calvin was born in 1854 in Montgomery County, NC. He died in 1932 in Marshall County, KY.*
58	Alice M. Riley (1865-). *Alice was born in 1865 in Montgomery County, NC. She married **Lewis E. Wallace** on May 8, 1885.*

12. Nancy Caroline Wallace, daughter of William Wallace and Chaney Berry Cranford, was born on June 6, 1833 in Montgomery County, NC. She married **Eldridge Riley** on September 5, 1855 in Montgomery County, NC. She died on January 13, 1907 in Marshall County, KY and was buried in Oak Level, Marshall County, KY at Riley Cemetery.

Eldridge Riley was born circa 1832 in Montgomery County, NC. He died on September 1, 1885 in Marshall County, KY and was buried in Oak Level, Marshall County, KY at Riley Cemetery. He and Nancy Caroline Wallace had the following children:

59	Nelson Frank Riley (1857-1931). *Nelson was born on October 23, 1857 in Yadkin County, NC. He died on December 20, 1931 in Marshall County, KY.*
60	Florence Latisha Riley (1860-1902). *Florence was born in 1860 in Yadkin County, NC. She married **Bryan Wesley Jarvis** in 1879 in Yadkin County, NC. She died on September 15, 1902 in Graves County, KY.*
61	George W. Riley (1862-1902). *George was born on October 12, 1862 in Yadkin County, NC. He married **Ada Boas** on February 13, 1890. He died on September 15, 1902 in Marshall County, KY.*
62	Joseph Commodre Riley (1868-1941). *Joseph was born on June 4, 1868. He married **Mattie May Edwards** "WFT Est 1887-1917". He died on May 5, 1941 in McCracken County, KY.*
63	Dallas Lee Riley (1870-1940). *Dallas was born on July 30, 1870. He married **Melissa Onora Baker** "WFT Est 1889-1912". He died on December 10, 1940.*
64	Peter Clark Riley (1873-1955). *Peter was born on November 2, 1873. He married **Mary Bland Holsapple** on October 13, 1913. He died on February 19, 1955 in Texas.*

13. Louisa Eliza Wallace, daughter of William Wallace and Chaney Berry Cranford, was born on October 10, 1836 in Montgomery County, NC. She married **William Reeves** in Marshall County, KY. She died on October 21, 1915 in Marshall County, KY and was buried in Oak Level, Marshall County, KY at Riley Cemetery.

Louisa Eliza Wallace had the following children:

| 65 | Shube Wallace (-). *Shube was born in North Carolina.* |

William Reeves was born on August 17, 1823. He died on May 8, 1896 and was buried in Oak Level, Marshall County, KY at Riley Cemetery. He and Louisa Eliza Wallace had the following children:

66	Absalom Reeves (-1941). *Absalom died on December 28, 1941.*
67	Izora Reeves (1871-1884). *Izora was born on June 28, 1871. She died on September 26, 1884.*
68	Robert Leonard Reeves (1874-1951). *Robert was born on July 4, 1874. He married **Addie Bethel Binkley** on July 28, 1900. He died on February 17, 1951.*

14. William P. "Pink" Wallace, son of William Wallace and Chaney Berry Cranford, was born circa 1839 in Montgomery County, NC. He died on July 1, 1863 in Gettysburg, PA in Civil War.

15. Leonard Harris Wallace, son of William Wallace and Chaney Berry Cranford, was born circa 1841 in Montgomery County, NC. He died on January 12, 1862 in Moore Hospital at Manassas Junction, VA.

16. Jason McKendrick Wallace, son of William Wallace and Chaney Berry Cranford, was born on June 10, 1843 in Montgomery County, NC. He married **Eliza Jane Waisner** on June 16, 1867 in Montgomery County, NC. He died on May 5, 1907 in Marshall County, KY and was buried in Marshall County, KY at Oakland Presbyterian Chuch.

Eliza Jane Waisner was born circa 1845 in Montgomery County, NC. She died on December 15, 1928 in Marshall County, KY and was buried in Marshall County, KY at Oakland Presbyterian Chuch. She and Jason McKendrick Wallace had the following children:

69   Jefferson Royal Wallace (1868-1946). *Jefferson was born on August 8, 1868 in Graves County, KY. He married* **Eliza Brian** *on October 19, 1892. He died on December 20, 1946 in McCracken County, KY.*

70   Bible Green Wallace (1869-1956). *Bible was born on December 18, 1869 in Marshall County, KY. He married* **Laura Belle Johnston** *on October 24, 1917 in McCracken County, KY. He died on August 4, 1956 in Marshall County, KY.*

71   Amelia Anna Thomas Neely Wallace (1874-1943). *Amelia was born on August 26, 1874 in McCracken County, KY. She died in 1943 in McCracken County, KY.*

17. Rev. James Lovelace Wallace, son of Harbard Harbart Wallace and Nancy Adderton, was born on October 9, 1826. He died on June 11, 1881 and was buried in Symsonia, Graves County, KY at Symsonia Cemetery.

Joyce Emeline Reid, daughter of Thomas Reid (1801-1879) and Temperance Wallace (1806-1889), was born on May 12, 1833. She died on July 27, 1916 in Graves County, KY and was buried on July 28, 1916 in Symsonia, Graves County, KY at Symsonia Cemetery. She and James Lovelace Wallace had the following children:

72   Nancy Cordelia Wallace (1853-1922). *Nancy was born on December 29, 1853. She married* **Joseph Surrett** *on December 20, 1874 in Graves County, KY. She died on February 10, 1922 in Graves County, KY and was buried on February 12, 1922 in Symsonia, Graves County, KY at Symsonia Cemetery.*

73   Mary Hortense Wallace (1856-1926). *Mary was born on March 12, 1856. She died on June 18, 1926 in Graves County, KY and was buried in Symsonia, Graves County, KY at Symsonia Cemetery.*

74   L. Harriett Wallace (1858-1930). *L. was born on March 19, 1858. She died on February 21, 1930 in Marshall County, KY and was buried on February 22, 1930 in Benton, Marshall County, KY at Haltom Cemetery.*

75   Bascom Adderton Wallace (1860-1943). *Bascom was born on September 14, 1860 in Marshall County, KY. He died on May 5, 1943 in Symsonia, Graves County, KY and was buried on May 7, 1943 in Symsonia, Graves County, KY at Bolton Cemetery.*

76   Joanna Wallace (1862-). *Joanna was born in 1862.*

77   Thomas Wallace (1865-). *Thomas was born in 1865.*

78   Joseph Wallace (1868-). *Joseph was born in 1868.*

79   Victoria Wallace (1868-). *Victoria was born in 1868.*

80   John R. Wallace (1872-). *John was born in 1872.*

81   Rosa Wallace (1876-). *Rosa was born in 1876.*

18. Alexander Clark Wallace, son of Harbard Harbart Wallace and Docia Crowell, was born on October 3, 1851. He died on January 31, 1952 and was buried in Oak Level, Marshall County, KY at Riley Cemetery.

M. Ellen Park was born on March 5, 1859. She died on October 9, 1919 and was buried in Oak Level, Marshall County, KY at Riley Cemetery.

21. Richard Calvin Wallace, son of Harbard Harbart Wallace and Docia Crowell, was born on June 3, 1862. He died on March 14, 1935 in Paducah, McCracken County, KY and was buried in Paducah, McCracken County, KY at Oak Grove Cemetery.

Mary F. Wallace, daughter of Rev. Isham Everett Wallace (1838-1916) and Sarah Ann Chenoweth (-1864), was born on July 22, 1861. She died on June 30, 1916 and was buried in Marshall County, KY at Wallace Cemetery. She and Richard Calvin Wallace had the following children:

82   Harvey Wallace (1884-1947). *Harvey was born in 1884. He died in 1947.*

83   Ruby Wallace (1889-). *Ruby was born in 1889.*

84   Frederick Wallace (1892-1918). *Frederick was born in 1892. He died in 1918.*

85   Herbert Wallace (1895-1919). *Herbert was born in 1895. He died in 1919.*

22. **John M. Hagler**, son of Phillip Hagler and Elizabeth "Betsy" Wallace, was born on November 17, 1851 in Cabarrus County, NC. He married **Salina Ridenhower** on August 26, 1878. He died on January 30, 1925 in Stanly County, NC and was buried on January 31, 1925 in Misenheimer, Stanly County, NC at Wesley Chapel Methodist Church.

Salina Ridenhower was born in March 1856. She and John M. Hagler had the following children:

86	Adam M. Hagler (1879-).	*Adam was born in December 1879.*
87	Daniel Hagler (1881-).	*Daniel was born in July 1881.*
88	Ella Hagler (1884-).	*Ella was born in May 1884.*
89	Minnie Hagler (1888-).	*Minnie was born in June 1888.*
90	Henry Hagler (1891-).	*Henry was born in July 1891.*
91	Calvin Hagler (1894-).	*Calvin was born in February 1894.*
92	Nellie Hagler (1896-).	*Nellie was born in May 1896.*

Descendants of John Wallace of DeKalb County, AL

1. **John Wallace** was born on January 21, 1809 in Union County, SC. He married Nancy Templeton and after her death married Lucy A. Northcutt on June 30, 1885 in DeKalb County, AL. He died on June 18, 1893 in DeKalb County, AL and was buried in DeKalb County, AL at Gilbreath Cemetery.[197] [198]

Nancy Ann Templeton was born in September 1814 in Burke County, NC. She died in August 1884 in DeKalb County, AL and was buried in DeKalb County, AL at Gilbreath Cemetery.[199] She and John Wallace had the following children:

+2	William Henry Wallace (1834-bef 1860)	
+3	John Templeton "T" Wallace (1835-1895)	
+4	Elizabeth Jane Wallace (1838-1873)	
+5	Mary Matilda Wallace (1839-bef 1850)	
+6	Martha Emeline Wallace (1842-1885)	
+7	Rachel Amanda Wallace (1843-c. 1885)	
+8	James Knox Polk Wallace (1845-1923)	
+9	Nancy Abigail Wallace (1847-1874)	
+10	Mary Frances Wallace (1849-)	
+11	Leander Andrew Perry Wallace (1851-1940)	
+12	Onias Small Wallace (1853-)	
+13	Charles Irvin Wallace (1855-1943)	
+14	Sarah Ann Wallace (1858-1892)	

Second Generation

2. **William Henry Wallace**, son of John Wallace and Nancy Ann Templeton, was born on June 18, 1834 in Alabama. He died before 1860 in DeKalb County, AL.

3. **John Templeton "T" Wallace**, son of John Wallace and Nancy Ann Templeton, was born on October 23, 1835 in DeKalb County, AL. He died on November 3, 1895 in Yell County, AR.

Elizabeth Minerva "Betty" Driskill was born on January 2, 1840 in DeKalb County, AL. She died in November 1911 in Franklin County, AR. She and John Templeton "T" Wallace had the following children:

+15	John Franklin Wallace (1862-1941)

4. **Elizabeth Jane Wallace**, daughter of John Wallace and Nancy Ann Templeton, was born on September 19, 1838 in Calhoun County, AL. She died on September 19, 1873 in DeKalb County, AL.

5. **Mary Matilda Wallace**, daughter of John Wallace and Nancy Ann Templeton, was born on November 30, 1839 in Calhoun County, AL. She died before 1850.

6. **Martha Emeline Wallace**, daughter of John Wallace and Nancy Ann Templeton, was born on May 3, 1842 in DeKalb County, AL. She died on February 6, 1885 in DeKalb County, AL.

7. **Rachel Amanda Wallace**, child of John Wallace and Nancy Ann Templeton, was born on June 9, 1843. He/she died circa 1885. He/she was buried in Crossville, DeKalb County, AL at Crossville Methodist Church.

8. **James Knox Polk Wallace**, son of John Wallace and Nancy Ann Templeton, was born on May 11, 1845. He died on October 23, 1923 and was buried in Lathamville, DeKalb County, AL at Lathamville Baptist Church.

9. **Nancy Abigail Wallace**, daughter of John Wallace and Nancy Ann Templeton, was born on November 17, 1847. She died on December 2, 1874 and was buried in DeKalb County, AL at Gilbreath Cemetery.

10. **Mary Frances Wallace**, daughter of John Wallace and Nancy Ann Templeton, was born on June 12, 1849 and was buried in DeKalb County, AL at Gilbreath Cemetery.

11. **Leander Andrew Perry Wallace**, son of John Wallace and Nancy Ann Templeton, was born on August 23, 1851. He died on April 30, 1940 and was buried in Lathamville, DeKalb County, AL at Lathamville Baptist Church.

Martha Elizabeth Carr was born on November 30, 1850. She died on December 26, 1930 and was buried in Lathamville, DeKalb County, AL at Lathamville Baptist Church.

12. **Onias Small Wallace**, son of John Wallace and Nancy Ann Templeton, was born on November 7, 1853 and was buried in DeKalb County, AL at Gilbreath Cemetery.

13. **Charles Irvin Wallace**, son of John Wallace and Nancy Ann Templeton, was born on October 25, 1855. He died on December 31, 1943 and was buried in Alabama City, Etowah County, AL at Clayton Cemetery.

Mary A. Griffin was born in 1855. She died on March 22, 1952 and was buried in Alabama City, Etowah County, AL at Clayton Cemetery.

14. **Sarah Ann Wallace**, daughter of John Wallace and Nancy Ann Templeton, was born on March 19, 1858 in DeKalb County, AL. She died on July 15, 1892 in Jefferson County, AL.

Third Generation

---

15. **John Franklin Wallace**, son of John Templeton "T" Wallace and Elizabeth Minerva "Betty" Driskill, was born on October 15, 1862 in DeKalb County, AL. He died on July 14, 1941 in Yell County, AR.

Eva Kristine Bates was born in 1866. She died on December 1, 1898 in Tuscaloosa County, AL. She and John Franklin Wallace had the following children:

> 16   James Warner "Jim" Wallace (1889-1962). *James was born on November 9, 1889 in DeKalb County, AL. He died on September 25, 1962 in DeKalb County, AL.*

Descendants of Jesse Ritter

1. **Jesse Ritter**, is believed to have been the son of John Heinrich "Henry" Ritter (-) and Sarah (-1735). Jesse was born in 1735 in Virginia and died circa 1810 in Moore County, NC. He married Susannah Wallace. Jesse Ritter, Sr. was the progenitor of the Moore County, NC Ritter family and is the earliest known ancestor to many of the Ritters throughout the south. Jesse Ritter, Sr. was born around 1735 and he can be found in numerous court records in Cumberland/Moore County, NC beginning in 1769 up until his estate was settled in c1810.

Recent discoveries from Linda Ritter of Louisiana detail the Ritter family history through personal letters as well as an oral family history written in 1910 by Murry Connie Ritter as told by his father William Young Ritter who passed the oral history down from his grandfather, Everett Ritter, Sr. The oral history and letters richly detail the beginning of the Ritter family in America through the migration of John Heinrich Ritter and two brothers from Germany to Pennsylvania in the late 1600's.

According to these letters and oral history, John Heinrich Ritter [d. 1739] and his wife Elisabeth settled in Pennsylvania where they are believed to have lived the rest of their lives. Several children continued the migration and moved south by 1732. The Ritters joined countless other families traveling down the Great Wagon Road.[200] John Heinrich "Henry" Ritter Jr. settled in Virginia and brothers Christian and Frederick migrated to the Carolina Colony near present day Salisbury, NC likely down the Great Wagon Road. Several daughters were born to Henry and Elisabeth including Margaretha, Maria, Elisabeth and Hannah. In 1734, Henry Ritter married Sarah MNU in Virginia. His parents disapproved as she was not

German. Jesse Ritter Sr. was born to them in 1735 and Sarah died during childbirth or shortly thereafter. After Sarah's death, Henry Ritter relocated to Salisbury, NC near his brother and remarried a cousin of his mother, Augusta "Gussie" Hobson Holt in 1736. She was also recently widowed. Henry and Gussie had several children but only John Ritter was named.[201]

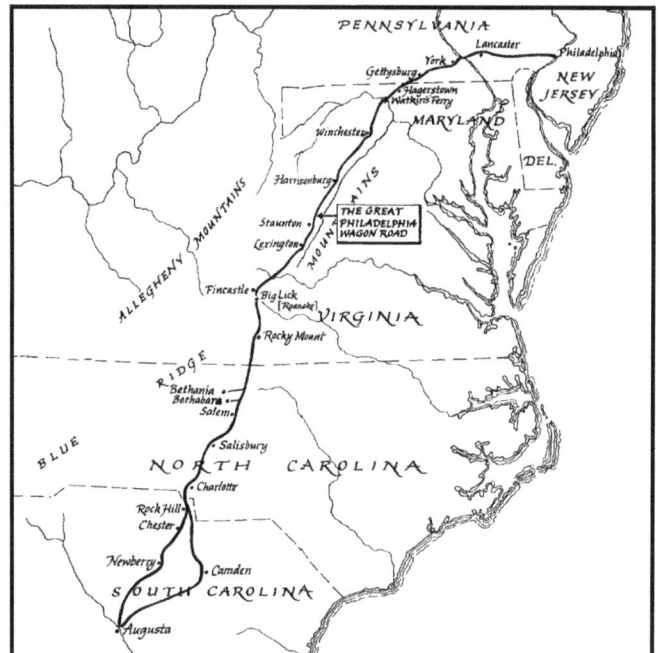

According to the oral history, Jesse Ritter and his half-brother John left the Salisbury, NC area and settled in Moore County, NC near their uncle Moses Ritter. Jesse reportedly married Susannah/Hanna/Anna and her maiden name may have been Wallace. They had Everett, John, Hannah, August [died young], Thomas, Cloey, Elizabeth, James [never married], Jesse, Nancy and Susan. Jesse's wife Susannah apparently left him, and he married Charlotte and had Hannah and Daniel. Susannah returned and "ran off" Charlotte and the kids and they left for South Carolina.[202] After Jesse Ritter died, his oldest son Everett migrated to Tennessee, Alabama and Mississippi. These letters as well as other heirlooms went with Everett and were passed down through multiple generations.

RECORDS OF JESSE RITTER

1769, May 25 -- Deed Book 3 Page 381, Cumberland County, NC
John Donahoe deeded Nicholas Newton 200 acres located on Wet Creek. Samuel Williams, Jesse Riter and Thomas Keys were witnesses.

1773, May 24 -- Land Grant #1218, Cumberland County, NC
Jesse Rutter received 200 acres located on Wet Creek adjoining Jas. Chaney and Nicholas Newton.

1774, Jan 12 -- Land Grant #0417, Cumberland County, NC
William Smith entered 50 acres located on South of Cabin Creek adjoining David Kagill and John Kagill. Jesse Ritter and Jacob Kagle were chain carriers. [note -- was not granted]

1774, Jan 13 -- Land Grant #0418, Cumberland County, NC
William Smith entered 100 acres located on Upper Buffalo Creek adjoining Leonard Kagill. Jesse Ritter and Isham Smith were chain carriers. [note -- was not granted]

1774, Jan 13 -- Land Grant #1359, Cumberland County, NC
James Stevens received 100 acres located on Horse Creek adjoining Lewis Sowell. Jesse Ritter and Robert Edwards were chain carriers.

1774, Jul 8 -- Deed Book 6 Page 279, Cumberland County, NC
Jesse Ritter deeded Nathan Smith 200 acres located on Wet Creek adjoining James Chainey and Nicholas Newton. Thos. Branford and William Manes were witnesses.

1774, Oct 25 -- 1755-1779 Court of Pleas and Quarter Sessions, Cumberland County, NC
A deed from Jesse Ritter to Nathan Smith was proven by William Manes

1778 -- Tax List, Cumberland County, NC
Jesse Ritter listed $230 of taxable property in Captain John Cox's District

1780 -- Tax List, Montgomery County, NC
Jesse Ritter listed

1782, May 18 -- Land Grant #297, Montgomery County, NC
Jesse Ritter received 156 acres on Dencen's Fork of Little River adjoining William Haltom. Spencer Alton and Robert Stephens were chain carriers.

1783 -- Tax List, Cumberland County, NC
Jesse Riter listed $210 of taxable property in Captain John Cox's District

1784, May 3 -- Petition, Apr 1784-Jun 1784 General Assembly Session Records, Box 3 Folder 41
Petition of inhabitants of the upper end of Cumberland County to divide the county beginning on the south side of the Cape Fear River at Chatham County line where it crosses the river and runs a direct course to Cole's Bridge on Drowning Creek and so to be bounded by the line of the adjacent counties to make a distinct county. Signers include Jesse Ritter.

1784, Oct 20 -- Land Grant #185, Moore County, NC
Jesse Ritter received 100 acres located on Buffalo Creek adjoining his own improvement and Matthew Ledbetter. John Ritter and Thos. Ritter, Junr. were chain carriers.

1785, Oct 9 -- Land Grant #9, Moore County, NC
Jesse Ritter received 50 acres located on Richland Creek adjoining Campbell. William Manes and Thos. Ritter were chain carriers.

1786, Feb 21 -- 1785-1794 Court of Pleas and Quarter Sessions, Moore County, NC Page 83
Jesse Writter records his mark as a swallow fork in the right ear and a slit in the left

1787 -- Marriage Licenses, Moore County, NC Will Book A Page 382
John Ritter and Elizabeth Richardson were granted a marriage license. Jesse Ritter was the surety.

1787, Feb 21 -- 1785-1794 Court of Pleas and Quarter Sessions, Moore County, NC Page 140
A deed from John Sowell and Mary Sowell to William Barrett was proven by Jesse Ritter
A deed from William Smith to May Hines was proven by Jesse Ritter

1788, Feb 20 -- 1785-1794 Court of Pleas and Quarter Sessions, Moore County, NC Page 186
A deed from Wm. Barrett and Amey/Anny Barrett to Jesse Writter was duly acknowledged by Wm. Barrett

1790 -- Census, Moore County, NC Page 159
Jesse Ritter
(16+) 2M
(0-16) 2M
5F

1795, Nov 24 -- Will Book A, Moore County, NC Page 186-187
Will of Nicholas Newton, Dec'd. Heirs: wife Meloney Newton [*298 acres between Wet Creek and Dry Creek including the plantation where I now live, 200 acres on Sings Creek, 100 acres on Horse Creek, 50 acres on Wet Creek and negro wench Mary*], son John Tucker Newton [*home tract above after his mother's death*], daughter Mary Sowel, daughter Meloney Dun, daughter Febey Melton, son William Newton, son Nicholas Smith Newton, daughter Hannah Carpenter, daughter Delaney Gibson, daughter Charity Newton, daughter Sarah Newton, daughter Elizabeth Newton. Executor: Meloney Newton. Witnesses: Jesse Ritter, John McAulay and Jesse Brown. Proven Feb 1796.

1800 -- Census, Moore County, NC Page 50

Jesse Writtor
(45+) 1M 1F
(16-25) 1M
(10-16) 1F
(0-10) 1M 1F

1810, Apr 12 -- Deed, Moore County, NC
Jesse Ritter Senr. deeded 100 acres to his grandchildren [children of daughter Susanna and husband Daniel Muse] located between Richland and McLendons Creek being part of 200 acres adjoining Jesse Sowell, Everiter Ritter, Donald McQueen, Wm. Barret, Farquard Campbell and McIver (formerly McLeod). Jesse Muse and Shadrach Manes were witnesses. [*Editor's Note: Private deed in possession of Frank Muse, Carthage, NC*]

1810 [undated estimate] -- Estate, Moore County, NC Will Book A, Page 316
Inventory of the Estate of Jesse Ritter, Dec'd. by Administrators Thomas Ritter and Jesse Sowell. [*Editor's Note: No date given on actual Inventory but Jesse Ritter Senr. can be found deeding land to his grandchildren in 1810 and is not listed in the 1810 Census likely meaning that he died during the year.*]

Jesse Ritter and Susannah Wallace had the following children:

+2   Hannah Ritter (-) The Ritter family letters suggest that she was a child but no additional information on these children have been located.

+3   August Ritter (-) The Ritter family letters suggest that he was a child but no additional information on these children have been located.

+4   Elizabeth Ritter (-) The Ritter family letters suggest that she was a child but no additional information on these children have been located.

+5   Everett Ritter (1759-aft 1850) was married to Nancy and had the following children: Nancy A., Anderson, John Newton, Elizabeth, William A., Everet Jr., James and Benjamin Franklin Ritter. After Nancy's death, Everet married Charlotte Smith (b.1790/1793) in 1822 on Jefferson County, TN and they were the parents of Susan Caroline, Margaret and Francis M. "Frank" Ritter. Everet left Moore County sometime after Jesse died and migrated to Tennessee and Alabama, where he can be found in the 1830 Census. He later migrated to Tippah County, MS where he died after 1850.

+6   John Ritter (1760-1828) married Elizabeth Richardson (1760-1841) and their union produced five children: Susanna, Thomas Wesley, John Richardson, William D. and Richardson Ritter. John was a large landowner on Buffalo Creek and at one time possessed as many as 685 acres. John, Elizabeth and several of their children are buried at a Ritter family cemetery on Buffalo Creek. Many of the Ritters in northern Moore County descend from John. His grandson Thomas Wesley Ritter (1827-1891) was elected Sheriff and a Ritter reunion is held every year at Smyrna Methodist Church dedicated to another grandson, Captain John Ritter (1816-1902).

+7   Thomas Ritter (1764-1849) married Margaret Seawell (1762-aft 1851) and they were the parents of Moses, John Thomas, George, Anna, Jennet K., William, Marvel, Dixon, Willoughby, James T., Henry B. and Burrell Ritter. Thomas and Margaret owned 500-600 acres on McLendons Creek and Thomas is buried at a gravesite near his old homeplace.

+8   Cloey Ritter (1767-1831) married Jesse Bean (b. 1757) and they had four children: Polly, Charity, Jesse and Elizabeth Bean who married into the Caddell and Fry families. Jesse served in the Revolutionary War and they lived on McLendons Creek next to Bethlehem Baptist Church.

+9   James Ritter (1769-1836) His birth and death dates were passed down by Ritter family researchers, but no additional information has been located.

+10 Jesse Ritter Jr. (aft 1770-1838) married Sarah Elizabeth "Sally" Richardson (b. 1775) and they were the parents of Drury, Richardson, Everet Solomon, Nancy, Isham S. and Mark Ritter. Jesse served in the War of 1812 and migrated west after the war to Montgomery County, MO. He later died in Marion County, AR.

+11   Nancy Ritter (1775-) married Jesse Seawell (1780-1862) and their union produced the following children: Susanna "Susie", Eleazer Quimby, Isaac McLendon, Nancy, Eli Ritter, Aaron Ashley Flowers, Jesse G., Ann M. and Joshua Lee Seawell. Jesse and Nancy lived on Richland Creek in Moore County prior to migrating west to Arkadelphia, AR where Jesse Seawell died in 1862.

+12   Susannah Ritter (aft 1780-1858) married Daniel Muse (1779-1846) and were the parents of Thomas, James H., Jesse, Daniel J., John B., Miles, Doctor Franklin, William H. and Wesley B. Muse. Daniel and Susannah lived on Richland Creek south of NC Highway 24/27 and Daniel Muse is buried nearby in a small family cemetery.

Second Generation

5. **Everett Ritter**, son of Jesse Ritter and Susannah Wallace, was born in 1759. He married **Nancy** before 1800. He married **Charlotte Smith** on September 13, 1822 in Jefferson County, TN.[203] He died after 1850 in Tippah County, MS.

Nancy and Everett Ritter had the following children:

+13	Nancy A. Ritter (-)	
+14	Anderson Ritter (1797-1873)	
+15	John Newton Ritter (1799-1855)	
+16	James Ritter (aft 1800-)	
+17	Elizabeth Ritter (1801-)	
+18	William A. Ritter (1802-1871)	
+19	Everett Ritter Jr. (1804-)	
+20	Benjamin Franklin Ritter (1815-1904)	

Charlotte Smith was born between 1790 and 1793. She and Everett Ritter had the following children:

+21	Susan Caroline Ritter (1827-1889)
+22	Margaret Ritter (1829-)
+23	Francis M. "Frank" Ritter (1834-1864)

6. **John Ritter**, son of Jesse Ritter and Susannah Wallace, was born on August 6, 1760. He married **Elizabeth H. Richardson** in 1787 in Moore County, NC. He died on July 13, 1828 and was buried in Moore County, NC at Davis/Ritter Cemetery #227.[204]

Elizabeth H. Richardson, daughter of Drury Richardson (c. 1740-1811) and Sally (-), was born on February 14, 1760. She died in March 1841 and was buried in Moore County NC at Davis/Ritter Cemetery #227.[205] She and John Ritter had the following children:

+24	Susanna Ritter (1785-)
+25	Thomas Wesley Ritter (1786-1821)
+26	John Richardson Ritter (1793-1861)
+27	William D. Ritter (1796-1860)
+28	Richardson Ritter (1803-1821)

7. **Thomas Ritter**, son of Jesse Ritter and Susannah Wallace, was born in 1764. He died in 1849 in Moore County and was buried in Moore County, NC at Thomas Ritter Cemetery.[206] He married **Margaret Seawell**.

Margaret Seawell, daughter of Isaac Sowell (aft 1740-1782) and Mary Quimby (c. 1745-bef 1808), was born in 1762. She died after February 12, 1851. She and Thomas Ritter had the following children:

+29	Moses Ritter (aft 1780-)
+30	Marvel Ritter (aft 1790-)
+31	John Thomas Ritter (1792-1869)
+32	George Ritter (1793-)
+33	Anna Ritter (1793-1865)
+34	Jennet K. Ritter (1797-aft 1880)

+35	William Ritter (1797-)
+36	Dixon Ritter (1800-1880)
+37	Willoughby Ritter (aft 1800-)
+38	James T. Ritter (1805-1898)
+39	Henry B. Ritter (1811-)
+40	Burrell Ritter (1813-1873)

8. **Cloey Ritter**, daughter of Jesse Ritter and Susannah Wallace, was born in 1767. She married **Jesse Bean** in November 1785 in Moore County. She died on April 11, 1831.

Jesse Bean was born circa 1757. He and Cloey Ritter had the following children:

+41	Polly Bean (aft 1785-)
+42	Elizabeth Bean (aft 1800-bef 1850)
+43	Charity Bean (1801-)
+44	Jesse Bean (1802-bef 1869)

9. **James Ritter**, son of Jesse Ritter and Susannah Wallace, was born in 1769. He died in 1836.

10. **Jesse Ritter Jr.**, son of Jesse Ritter and Susannah Wallace, was born between 1770 and 1780. He married **Sarah Elizabeth "Sally' Richardson** circa 1802. He died on December 15, 1838 in Marion County, AR.

Sarah Elizabeth "Sally' Richardson, daughter of Drury Richardson (c. 1740-1811) and Sally (-), was born in 1775. She and Jesse Ritter Jr. had the following children:

+45	Drury Ritter (1802-)
+46	Richardson Ritter (1805-)
+47	Everet Solomon Ritter (1810-1873)
+48	Nancy Ritter (1812-)
+49	Isham S. Ritter (1815-)
+50	Mark Ritter (1817-1864)

11. **Nancy Ritter**, daughter of Jesse Ritter and Susannah Wallace, was born in 1775. She married **Jesse Seawell** on July 5, 1807 in Moore County.[207]

Jesse Seawell, son of Isaac Sowell (aft 1740-1782) and Mary Quimby (c. 1745-bef 1808), was born in 1780. He died on October 10, 1862 in Arkadelphia, Clark County, AR. He and Nancy Ritter had the following children:

+51	Susanna "Susie" Seawell (1805-)
+52	Eleazer Quimby Seawell (1808-1893)
+53	Isaac McLendon Seawell (1810-bef 1870)
+54	Nancy Seawell (1815-aft 1860)
+55	Eli Ritter Seawell (1819-)
+56	Aaron Ashley Flowers Seawell (1822-1894)
+57	Jesse G. Seawell (1825-)
+58	Ann M. Seawell (1827-1862)
+59	Joshua Lee Seawell (1830-)

Jesse Seawell, Nancy Ritter and family *(Courtesy of Mike Cross, Panama City, FL)*

12. **Susannah Ritter**, daughter of Jesse Ritter and Susannah Wallace, was born between 1780 and 1790. She died on September 11, 1858 in Moore County.[208] She married **Daniel Muse**.

Daniel Muse, son of James Muse III (1757-1843) and Nancy (-1834), was born in 1779. He died on August 28, 1846 and was buried in Moore County, NC at Muse Cemetery #73.[209] He and Susannah Ritter had the following children:

+60	Thomas Muse (-)
+61	James H. Muse (1802-)
+62	Jesse Muse (1804-1878)
+63	Daniel J. Muse (1808-1878)
+64	John B. Muse (1813-1870)
+65	Miles Muse (1815-)
+66	Doctor Franklin Muse (1816-1891)
+67	William H. Muse (1822-)
+68	Wesley B. Muse (1827-)

Third Generation

14. **Anderson Ritter**, son of Everett Ritter and Nancy, was born in 1797. He died on December 16, 1873 and was buried in Itawamba County, MS at Little Cemetery. He married **Phebe Douglas Young**.

Phebe Douglas Young was born in 1800. She died on April 12, 1883 and was buried in Itawamba County. She and Anderson Ritter had the following children:

69	Lucy Ritter (1830-). *Lucy was born in 1830 in Alabama.*
70	John Ritter (1832-). *John was born in 1832 in Alabama.*
71	Sarah Ritter (1834-). *Sarah was born in 1834 in Alabama.*
72	Anderson Ritter (1836-). *Anderson was born in 1836 in Alabama.*
73	Martha Ritter (1838-). *Martha was born in 1838 in Mississippi.*
74	Martin Ritter (1843-). *Martin was born in 1843 in Mississippi.*

15. **John Newton Ritter**, son of Everett Ritter and Nancy, was born in 1799 in North Carolina. He died in May 1855 in Monroe County, MS. He married **Mary Young**.

Mary Young was born in 1804 in SC. She and John Newton Ritter had the following children:

75	Martin E. Ritter (1823-). *Martin was born in 1823 in Alabama.*
76	Telitha Ritter (1828-). *Telitha was born in 1828 in Alabama.*
77	William A. Ritter (1829-). *William was born in 1829 in Alabama.*
78	Lucinda Angelina Ritter (1833-). *Lucinda was born in 1833 in Alabama.*
79	Everett Ritter (1834-). *Everett was born in 1834.*
80	Narcissa E. Ritter (1836-). *Narcissa was born in 1836 in Mississippi.*
81	John Newton Ritter Jr. (1838-). *John was born in 1838 in Mississippi.*
82	Mary J. Ritter (1840-). *Mary was born in 1840 in Mississippi.*
83	Sarah C. Ritter (1842-). *Sarah was born in 1842 in Mississippi.*
84	Hardy A. Ritter (1844-). *Hardy was born in 1844 in Mississippi.*
85	Martha C. Ritter (1849-). *Martha was born in 1849 in Mississippi.*

16. James Ritter, son of Everett Ritter and Nancy, was born between 1800 and 1810. He married **Mary Ann Foster**.

Mary Ann Foster and James Ritter had the following children:

86	Benjamin Franklin Ritter (1829-). *Benjamin was born on May 22, 1829.*
87	John Newton Ritter (1847-1928). *John was born on May 23, 1847. He died on March 1, 1928.*

17. Elizabeth Ritter, daughter of Everett Ritter and Nancy, was born in 1801 in Tennessee. She married **William McBride** circa 1822. She married **Joshua Coleman** on November 24, 1855 in Hardeman County, TN.

William McBride was born on November 9, 1803 in Lincoln County, TN. He died on August 11, 1837 in Hardeman County. He and Elizabeth Ritter had the following children:

88	William McBride (1827-). *William was born in 1827.*
89	Andrew J. McBride (1833-). *Andrew was born in 1833.*
90	Pleasant Brock McBride (1837-). *Pleasant was born in 1837.*

Joshua Coleman was born in 1801 in Tennessee. He died in 1857 in Calhoun County, AR.

18. William A. Ritter, son of Everett Ritter and Nancy, was born in 1802. He died in 1871. He married **Mary Martha Young**.

Mary Martha Young and William A. Ritter had the following children:

91	John McBride Ritter (1826-). *John was born in 1826.*
92	Sealy Ann Ritter (1828-). *Sealy was born in 1828.*
93	Elizabeth Ritter (1832-). *Elizabeth was born in 1832.*
94	Phebe Caroline Ritter (1833-). *Phebe was born on September 19, 1833.*
95	Adelia Ritter (1835-). *Adelia was born in 1835.*
96	Margaret Ellen Ritter (1837-). *Margaret was born on August 4, 1837.*
97	Martha C. Ritter (1837-). *Martha was born on August 4, 1837.*
98	Marinda L. Ritter (1840-). *Marinda was born in 1840.*
99	William B. Ritter (1840-). *William was born in 1840.*
100	Sarah Elizabeth Ritter (1843-). *Sarah was born in 1843.*
101	Stephen D. Ritter (1845-). *Stephen was born in 1845.*
102	James A. Ritter (1847-). *James was born in 1847.*

19. Everett Ritter Jr., son of Everett Ritter and Nancy, was born on December 24, 1804 in Moore County, NC. He married **Jane Young**.

Jane Young was born on December 10, 1806 in Tennessee. She died on February 8, 1879 in Marion County, AL. She and Everett Ritter Jr. had the following children:

103	Thomas Ledbetter Ritter (1826-1904). *Thomas was born on May 28, 1826. He died on*

	May 27, 1904 and was buried in Smithville, Monroe County, MS at Bethlehem Cemetery.
104	Elizabeth Jane Ritter (1827-1885). *Elizabeth was born on October 1, 1827. She married* **Charles Weir Loggains** *on July 17, 1848 in Monroe County. She died on March 11, 1885 and was buried in Hartford, Sebastian County, AR at Hartford Memorial Park.*
105	Robert T. Ritter (1829-1869). *Robert was born on October 10, 1829 in Tennessee. He died on December 1, 1869 in Monroe County and was buried.*
106	John Ritter (1832-). *John was born in 1832 in Mississippi.*
107	William Young Ritter (1833-1918). *William was born on December 23, 1833 in Mississippi. He died on April 12, 1918 and was buried in Lee County, MS at Union Cemetery.*
108	Isaac A. Ritter (1838-). *Isaac was born in October 1838 in Mississippi. He married* **Lucinda C. Cody** *on January 10, 1861 in Itawamba County, MS.*
109	Everet Bayless Ritter (1841-1920). *Everet was born on April 3, 1841 in Mississippi. He died on October 31, 1920 in Hughes County, OK and was buried in Calvin, Hughes County, OK at Atwood Cemetery.*
110	Charlotte Caroline Ritter (1843-1930). *Charlotte was born on August 27, 1843 in Mississippi. She married* **George Washington Bayless** *on July 31, 1869 in Sanford County, AL. She died on August 3, 1930 in Pittsburg County, OK and was buried in Ashland, Pittsburg County, OK at Ashland Cemetery.*
111	Nancy Ann Ritter (1846-1922). *Nancy was born on February 27, 1846 in Mississippi. She died on October 22, 1922 in Le Flore County, OK and was buried in Monroe, Le Flore County, OK at Monroe Cemetery.*
112	James Henderson Ritter (1850-1906). *James was born in March 1850 in Mississippi. He died on November 2, 1906 and was buried in Calvin.*

20. Benjamin Franklin Ritter, son of Everett Ritter and Nancy, was born on January 8, 1815. He married **Nancy C. Joyner** circa 1854 in Mississippi. He married **Tranquila Waits** on October 17, 1876 in DeSoto County, MS. He died on October 1, 1904 and was buried in Pontotoc County, OK at Box X Cemetery.

Nancy C. Joyner was born on March 26, 1827. She died on September 8, 1873 and was buried in Tippah County, MS at Brannon-Joyner Cemetery. She and Benjamin Franklin Ritter had the following children:

113	Margaret Lucendy Ritter (1854-). *Margaret was born in 1854.*
114	Mary Virginia Ritter (1855-). *Mary was born in 1855.*
115	Laura E. Ritter (1858-). *Laura was born in 1858.*
116	Isaac Solomon Ritter (1859-1917). *Isaac was born on February 19, 1859. He died on March 10, 1917.*
117	Andrew E. Ritter (1861-). *Andrew was born in 1861.*
118	Benjamin Franklin Ritter Jr. (1862-). *Benjamin was born in 1862.*
119	James A. Ritter (1865-). *James was born in 1865.*
120	John Robert Ritter (1867-1934). *John was born on December 16, 1867. He died on July 2, 1934.*
121	Nancy P. Ritter (1869-). *Nancy was born in 1869.*
122	George D. Ritter (1873-). *George was born in 1873.*

Tranquila Waits was born in 1836.

21. Susan Caroline Ritter, daughter of Everett Ritter and Charlotte Smith, was born in 1827. She died in 1889 in Scott County, AR. She married **Robert Lee Bottoms**.

Robert Lee Bottoms was born on December 27, 1819 in Georgia. He died on February 27, 1907 in Jones County, TX.

25. Thomas Wesley Ritter, son of John Ritter and Elizabeth H. Richardson, was born on March 28, 1786. He died on January 17, 1821 and was buried in Moore County, NC at Davis/Ritter Cemetery #227. He married **Dolly Garner**.

Dolly Garner, daughter of Lewis Garner (1750-bef 1815), was born circa 1790. She died before May 31, 1848. She and Thomas Wesley Ritter had the following children:

123	John Ritter (1816-1902). *John was born on June 9, 1816. He married* **Sara Ann Myrick**

circa 1839. He died on November 2, 1902 and was buried in Moore County, NC at Smyrna Methodist Church.

124   Judith Ritter (1820-1900). *Judith was born in June 1820. She married **John Harrison Garner** in June 1839. She died on October 26, 1900.*

125   Elizabeth Ritter (1822-1880). *Elizabeth was born in 1822. She died in April 1880 in Moore County.*

26. John Richardson Ritter, son of John Ritter and Elizabeth H. Richardson, was born in 1793. He died in 1861. He married **Mary Kennedy**.

Mary Kennedy was born in 1802. She and John Richardson Ritter had the following children:

126   Serrepta A. Ritter (1825-1912). *Serrepta was born on May 29, 1825. She married **William M. Moore** on January 5, 1842 in Moore County. She died on August 10, 1912 and was buried in Moore County, NC at Bethlehem Baptist Church.*

127   Thomas Wesley Ritter (1827-1891). *Thomas was born on November 3, 1827. He married **Julia Ann Caddell** on July 28, 1864 in Moore County. He died on August 17, 1891 in Moore County and was buried in Moore County.*

128   John Spinks Ritter (1832-1893). *John was born in 1832. He died on June 4, 1893 in Franklinville, Randolph County, NC.*

129   Dicy Jane Ritter (1835-1891). *Dicy was born in 1835. She married **Nelson Hunsucker** on November 28, 1861 in Moore County. She died on May 31, 1891 in Moore County and was buried in Moore County.*

130   Sarah A. Ritter (1837-). *Sarah was born in 1837.*

131   Mary Margaret Ritter (1839-). *Mary was born in 1839.*

132   Exer L. Ritter (1844-1925). *Exer was born on April 9, 1844. She married **Samuel Waite Seawell** on July 31, 1864 in Moore County. She died on May 19, 1925.*

133   Ann E. A. Ritter (1846-). *Ann was born in 1846.*

134   William Lewis Ritter (1849-1918). *William was born on December 13, 1849. He died on September 2, 1918 and was buried in Moore County, NC at Friendship Baptist Church.*

27. William D. Ritter, son of John Ritter and Elizabeth H. Richardson, was born on April 18, 1796. He died on October 20, 1860 and was buried in Moore County. He married **Catherine Melton**.

Catherine Melton was born on June 4, 1800. She died on November 15, 1879 and was buried in Moore County. She and William D. Ritter had the following children:

135   Mary Ann Ritter (1821-). *Mary was born in 1821 in Moore County and was buried in Moore County, NC at Horner Cemetery #243.*

136   Elizabeth Ritter (1822-1904). *Elizabeth was born on April 15, 1822. She died on February 10, 1904 and was buried in Moore County, NC at Pleasant Hill United Methodist Church.*

137   Sarah Ritter (1827-1899). *Sarah was born on November 11, 1827. She died on July 26, 1899.*

138   Lydia Margaret Ritter (1831-bef 1853). *Lydia was born in 1831. She died before 1853.*

139   Nancy E. Ritter (1833-bef 1886). *Nancy was born in 1833. She married **Thomas Branson Cagle** in September 1861 in Moore County. She died between 1880 and 1886 and was buried in Moore County.*

140   Catherine Ritter (1835-bef 1870). *Catherine was born in 1835. She married **Ira Lane "Irely" Maness** on December 13, 1855 in Moore County. She died between 1860 and 1870.*

141   Martha Jane Ritter (1835-1907). *Martha was born on July 23, 1835. She died on May 7, 1907 and was buried in High Falls, Moore County, NC at Prosperity Friends Meeting Cemetery.*

142   William Debarra "Big Foot Bill" Ritter (1835-1906). *William was born on July 27, 1835. He married **Margaret Myrick** on January 27, 1861 in Moore County. He died on January 6, 1906 and was buried in Moore County.*

143   Emily Francis "Milly" Ritter (1840-1907). *Emily was born in 1840. She married **Asa Jones Seawell** on January 10, 1860 in Moore County. She died on March 16, 1907.*

144	John Henry Ritter (1842-1927). *John was born on April 23, 1842. He died on April 10, 1927 in Moore County and was buried in Moore County.*

28. **Richardson Ritter**, son of John Ritter and Elizabeth H. Richardson, was born on October 20, 1803. He died in March 1821 and was buried in Moore County.

29. **Moses Ritter**, son of Thomas Ritter and Margaret Seawell, was born between 1780 and 1784. He married **Mary**.

Mary was born in 1785. She and Moses Ritter had the following children:

145	Elizabeth Ritter (1810-). *Elizabeth was born in 1810 in North Carolina.*
146	Henry Ritter (1820-). *Henry was born in 1820 in North Carolina.*
147	Everett Ritter (1824-). *Everett was born in 1824 in North Carolina. He married **Rebecca Autry** on September 7, 1840 in Carroll County, TN.*

30. **Marvel Ritter**, son of Thomas Ritter and Margaret Seawell, was born between 1790 and 1800.

31. **John Thomas Ritter**, son of Thomas Ritter and Margaret Seawell, was born in 1792. He died in May 1869. He married **Mary Elizabeth Muse**.

Mary Elizabeth Muse, daughter of Jesse Franklin Muse Sr. (1759-1820) and Joyce Hill (1768-1825), was born in 1796. She and John Thomas Ritter had the following children:

148	Lewis H. Ritter (1816-). *Lewis was born in 1816.*
149	George Drathon Dickson Ritter (1823-1869). *George was born in 1823. He married **Amelia "Milly" Jackson** on October 1, 1846 in Randolph County, NC. He died in 1869.*
150	Archibald J. Ritter (1824-). *Archibald was born in 1824. He married **Cherry Ritter** on April 2, 1856 in Moore County.*
151	John D. Ritter (1826-1864). *John was born in 1826 in Moore County. He died in 1864.*
152	Thomas H. Ritter (1833-). *Thomas was born in 1833.*
153	Margaret Ritter (1834-). *Margaret was born in 1834.*
154	Dorcus J. Ritter (1835-). *Dorcus was born in 1835.*
155	Leonard H. Ritter (1838-). *Leonard was born in 1838. He married **Sarah Jane Spurlin** on January 3, 1861 in Hot Spring County, AR and was buried in Hot Springs, Garland County, AR at Greenwood Cemetery.*
156	Malcolm S. Ritter (1839-). *Malcolm was born in 1839.*
157	Christian Ritter (1843-). *Christian was born in 1843.*
158	Archibald Ritter (1845-). *Archibald was born in 1845.*

32. **George Ritter**, son of Thomas Ritter and Margaret Seawell, was born in 1793.

33. **Anna Ritter**, daughter of Thomas Ritter and Margaret Seawell, was born on September 3, 1793. She died in 1865. She married **James Bryant**.

James Bryant, son of Michael Bryant (aft 1765-) and Leah Graham (aft 1765-), was born on November 8, 1793. He died in 1869. He and Anna Ritter had the following children:

159	Margaret Ritter Bryant (1816-). *Margaret was born on November 22, 1816.*
160	Caleb C. Bryant (1821-). *Caleb was born on July 9, 1821.*
161	William Richard Bryant (1822-1885). *William was born on December 17, 1822. He died in 1885 and was buried in Moore County, NC at Harris Cemetery #45.*
162	Leandy Bryant (1825-1878). *Leandy was born on April 26, 1825. She died on November 19, 1878 and was buried in Moore County.*
163	James R. Bryant (1826-). *James was born on November 28, 1826.*
164	George Raleigh Bryant (1828-1906). *George was born on May 14, 1828. He married **Sarah A. Graham** on March 15, 1857 in Moore County. He died on July 2, 1906 in Cass County, TX and was buried in Queen City, Cass County, TX at Queen City Cemetery.*
165	Deborah Bryant (1830-). *Deborah was born on March 25, 1830.*
166	Berry Burry Ann Bryant (1833-1905). *Berry was born on May 22, 1833. She married*

James D. Thomas on May 22, 1853 in Moore County. She died on December 3, 1905 and was buried in Jackson Springs, Montgomery County, NC at Pleasant Hill Cemetery.

167   Littleton Bryant (1836-). *Littleton was born on August 21, 1836.*

34. Jennet K. Ritter, daughter of Thomas Ritter and Margaret Seawell, was born in 1797. She died after 1880. She married **Daniel H. Muse.**

Daniel H. Muse, son of Jesse Franklin Muse Sr. (1759-1820) and Joyce Hill (1768-1825), was born on April 13, 1789. He died on April 8, 1866 and was buried in Moore County. He and Jennet K. Ritter had the following children:

168   Archibald Muse (1815-1888). *Archibald was born in 1815. He married **Sarah Jane Hilton** on July 2, 1846 in Hot Spring County. He died on January 30, 1888 in Garland County, AR and was buried in Mountain Valley, Garland County, AR at Mountain Valley Cemetery.*

169   Sarah Muse (1819-1896). *Sarah was born on March 18, 1819. She married **Peter Smith** on July 22, 1838. She died on August 15, 1896 in Saline County, AR.*

170   Stephen S. Muse (1821-1876). *Stephen was born in 1821. He married **Mary "Polly" Lamb** on March 25, 1847. He died on February 12, 1876 in Montgomery County, AR.*

171   Patience B. Muse (1823-1900). *Patience was born on September 22, 1823. She married **Lemuel Whitfield Muse** on March 15, 1850. She died on October 9, 1900 and was buried in Carthage, Moore County, NC at United Methodist Church.*

172   Jesse Arnold Muse (1824-1900). *Jesse was born on October 27, 1824. He married **Mary Louise Hilton** on August 8, 1848. He died on December 10, 1900 in Garland County and was buried in Mountain Valley.*

173   Kindred B. Muse (1836-). *Kindred was born in 1836. He married **Eliza Jane Bethune** on March 21, 1861 in Moore County.*

36. Dixon Ritter, son of Thomas Ritter and Margaret Seawell, was born on November 5, 1800 in North Carolina. He died on January 2, 1880 and was buried in Sullivan, Moultrie County, IL at Smyser Cemetery. He married **Elizabeth.**

Elizabeth was born on January 29, 1810. She died on May 10, 1855 and was buried in Sullivan. She and Dixon Ritter had the following children:

174   Margaret Ritter (1829-). *Margaret was born in 1829 in Tennessee.*

175   Miriam W. Ritter (1833-1871). *Miriam was born on January 11, 1833 in Tennessee. She died on November 25, 1871 and was buried in Sullivan.*

176   William H. Ritter (1834-1900). *William was born on April 6, 1834 in Tennessee. He died on April 24, 1900 and was buried in Sullivan.*

177   John D. Ritter (1836-). *John was born in 1836 in IL.*

178   Samuel J. Ritter (1842-). *Samuel was born in 1842.*

179   Nancy Ritter (1843-). *Nancy was born in 1843.*

38. James T. Ritter, son of Thomas Ritter and Margaret Seawell, was born in 1805. He married **Margaret Caroline Ray** on December 8, 1840 in Cumberland County, NC. He died in 1898 in Cumberland County.

Margaret Caroline Ray was born in 1819. She and James T. Ritter had the following children:

180   John Thomas Ritter (1843-1918). *John was born on December 24, 1843. He died on September 23, 1918.*

181   William J. Ritter (1845-). *William was born in 1845.*

182   Mary Elizabeth Ritter (1848-). *Mary was born in 1848.*

183   Anne E. Ritter (1849-1860). *Anne was born in 1849. He died in 1860.*

184   Sereptha Ritter (1850-). *Sereptha was born in 1850.*

185   James G. Ritter (aft 1850-1895). *James was born after 1850. He died in 1895.*

186   Flora Margaret "Maggie" Ritter (1852-). *Flora was born in 1852.*

187   John R. Ritter (1856-1887). *John was born in 1856. He died in 1887.*

39. Henry B. Ritter, son of Thomas Ritter and Margaret Seawell, was born in 1811. He married **Olive Stutts.**

Olive Stutts was born in 1811. She and Henry B. Ritter had the following children:

188	Cherry Ritter (1835-). *Cherry was born in 1835 in North Carolina. She married* ***Archibald J. Ritter*** *on April 2, 1856 in Moore County.*
189	Pressley Ritter (1838-). *Pressley was born in 1838.*
190	Lindsay T. Ritter (1840-). *Lindsay was born in 1840.*
191	Betsey Ritter (1845-). *Betsey was born in 1845.*

40. Burrell Ritter, son of Thomas Ritter and Margaret Seawell, was born in 1813. He died on September 28, 1873 in Moore County. He married **Katherine Lawhon**.

Katherine Lawhon was born in 1816. She died on September 13, 1873 in Moore County. She and Burrell Ritter had the following children:

192	Elizabeth Jane Ritter (1838-1917). *Elizabeth was born on August 22, 1838. She died on January 31, 1917 and was buried in Moore County.*
193	Deborah Ritter (1841-). *Deborah was born in 1841.*
194	Margaret A. Ritter (1844-). *Margaret was born in 1844.*
195	Mary E. Ritter (1846-). *Mary was born in 1846.*
196	Susannah Ritter (1848-1918). *Susannah was born in 1848. She died on May 4, 1918 and was buried in Moore County.*
197	Samuel Thomas Ritter (1849-1944). *Samuel was born on September 10, 1849. He married* ***Prudence Ann Bryant*** *on April 13, 1879 in Moore County. He died on May 12, 1944 and was buried in Moore County, NC at Culdee Presbyterian Church.*
198	Martha C. Ritter (1850-1920). *Martha was born on October 8, 1850. She married* ***Joseph Judson Richardson*** *circa 1875. She died on April 3, 1920 and was buried in Moore County, NC at Richardson Cemetery #214.*
199	John J. Ritter (1852-). *John was born in 1852.*
200	Joel Richard Ritter (1855-1915). *Joel was born in 1855. He married* ***Mary Ann McKenzie*** *circa 1886. He died on September 12, 1915 and was buried in Moore County.*
201	Cornelius Ritter (1860-1929). *Cornelius was born on March 31, 1860. He married* ***Margaret Isabelle Thomas*** *on June 21, 1883 in Montgomery County, NC. He died on June 19, 1929.*
202	Charles Ritter (1867-). *Charles was born in 1867.*
203	Clarkson Ritter (1868-1884). *Clarkson was born in 1868. He died on March 31, 1884 in Moore County.*
204	Hattie Ritter (1870-). *Hattie was born in 1870.*

41. Polly Bean, daughter of Jesse Bean and Cloey Ritter, was born between 1785 and 1790. She married **Lochart Fry** on September 4, 1810.

Lochart Fry, son of Thomas Fry (1739-bef 1821) and Elizabeth Masters (-), was born on January 4, 1784. He died on February 9, 1853 and was buried in Moore County, NC at Lochart Fry Cemetery #209.

42. Elizabeth Bean, daughter of Jesse Bean and Cloey Ritter, was born between 1800 and 1810. She died before 1850. She married **William D. Caddell**.

William D. Caddell, son of Daniel Caddell (1761-) and Emelia (1773-), was born in 1795 and was buried in Moore County, NC at Caddell Cemetery #267.

43. Charity Bean, daughter of Jesse Bean and Cloey Ritter, was born in 1801. She married **Daniel Caddell**.

Daniel Caddell, son of Daniel Caddell (1761-) and Emelia (1773-), was born in 1800. He died on July 8, 1861 and was buried in Moore County. He and Charity Bean had the following children:

205	Lochart Caddell (1825-). *Lochart was born in 1825.*
206	Tobias B. Caddell (1826-1906). *Tobias was born on April 21, 1826. He married* ***Mary Elizabeth Cockman*** *on February 14, 1861 in Moore County. He died on January 11, 1906 and was buried in Moore County.*

| 207 | Mary E. Caddell (1829-1850). *Mary was born on March 1, 1829. She died on November 3, 1850 and was buried in Moore County.* |
| 208 | Barbara A. Caddell (1833-). *Barbara was born in May 1833.* |

44. Jesse Bean, son of Jesse Bean and Cloey Ritter, was born in 1802. He died before June 1, 1869. He married **Barsheba Fry**.

Jesse Bean had the following children:

| 209 | A. William Bean (1835-c. 1853). *A. was born in 1835. He died circa 1853.* |
| 210 | Mary Elizabeth Bean (1838-1898). *Mary was born on May 17, 1838. She married **John Andrew Barrett** on May 9, 1861 in Moore County. She died on January 26, 1898 and was buried in Moore County.* |

Barsheba Fry, daughter of Lochart Fry (1793-1875) and Nancy Hurley (1800-1870), was born in 1822. She and Jesse Bean had the following children:

| 211 | Annette Judson Bean (1847-1927). *Annette was born on March 31, 1847 in Carthage, Moore County, NC. She married **Joshua R. Brown** on November 26, 1863 in Moore County. She died on May 22, 1927 in High Point, Guilford County, NC and was buried on May 23, 1927 in High Point, Guilford County, NC at Oakwood Cemetery.* |

45. Drury Ritter, son of Jesse Ritter Jr. and Sarah Elizabeth "Sally' Richardson, was born in 1802. He married **Susannah King**.

Susannah King was born in 1809 in SC. She and Drury Ritter had the following children:

212	Maria Ritter (1830-). *Maria was born in 1830.*
213	Sylvester Ritter (1831-). *Sylvester was born in 1831.*
214	Levina Ritter (1834-). *Levina was born in 1834.*
215	Orleana Ritter (1839-). *Orleana was born in 1839.*
216	Lurinda Ritter (1841-). *Lurinda was born in 1841.*
217	Jesse Ritter (1843-). *Jesse was born in 1843.*
218	Newbern Ritter (1847-). *Newbern was born in 1847.*
219	Clarinda Ritter (1849-). *Clarinda was born in 1849.*
220	Sarilda Ritter (1850-). *Sarilda was born in 1850.*
221	Perry Ritter (1852-). *Perry was born in 1852.*
222	Felix Ritter (1856-). *Felix was born in 1856.*

47. Everet Solomon Ritter, son of Jesse Ritter Jr. and Sarah Elizabeth "Sally' Richardson, was born in 1810. He married **Anna Goodwin** on May 15, 1828 in Hardeman County. He died on December 4, 1873.

Anna Goodwin was born in 1810. She and Everet Solomon Ritter had the following children:

223	William A. Ritter (1833-1864). *William was born in 1833. He died in 1864 and was buried in Panola County, TX at Mount Bethel Cemetery.*
224	Elizabeth A. Ritter (1834-). *Elizabeth was born in 1834.*
225	Benjamin Franklin Ritter (1834-1902). *Benjamin was born on June 11, 1834. He married **Margaret A. Ball** on January 14, 1858 in Panola County, TX. He died on November 3, 1902 and was buried in Panola County.*
226	James Henry Ritter (1842-1915). *James was born on November 25, 1842. He married **Sarah Ann Ball** on January 1, 1868 in Panola County. He married **Mary Elizabeth Ball** on March 3, 1870 in Panola County. He died on January 26, 1915 and was buried in Panola County.*
227	Sarah Ann Ritter (1843-). *Sarah was born in 1843.*
228	Mary Fannie Ritter (1847-). *Mary was born in 1847.*
229	Susan Caroline Ritter (1848-). *Susan was born in 1848.*
230	Everet Solomon Ritter Jr. (1849-). *Everet was born in 1849.*
231	Martha Jane Ritter (1852-). *Martha was born in 1852.*

48. Nancy Ritter, daughter of Jesse Ritter Jr. and Sarah Elizabeth "Sally' Richardson, was born in 1812. She married **Martin King**.

Martin King was born in 1812. He and Nancy Ritter had the following children:

232	Serilda Ingleton King (1844-1918). *Serilda was born on February 26, 1844. She died on April 24, 1918 and was buried in White Deer, Carson County, TX at White Deer Cemetery.*

49. Isham S. Ritter, son of Jesse Ritter Jr. and Sarah Elizabeth "Sally' Richardson, was born in 1815 in North Carolina. He married **Mary "Polly" Marler** on March 5, 1845 in Hardeman County.

Mary "Polly" Marler was born in 1830 in Tennessee. She and Isham S. Ritter had the following children:

233	James Knox Polk Ritter (1846-). *James was born in 1846.*
234	Jacob H. Ritter (1848-). *Jacob was born in 1848.*
235	Mary Ritter (1852-). *Mary was born in 1852.*
236	Margaret Ritter (1855-). *Margaret was born in 1855.*
237	Millie Melvina Ritter (1859-1925). *Millie was born on October 11, 1859. She died on August 2, 1925 and was buried in Garland County, AR at Shiloh Cemetery.*

50. Mark Ritter, son of Jesse Ritter Jr. and Sarah Elizabeth "Sally' Richardson, was born in 1817. He died on May 18, 1864 and was buried in Ava, Douglas County, MO at Ritter Cemetery. He married **Mary Ann King**.

Mary Ann King was born in 1821. She died on July 15, 1859. She and Mark Ritter had the following children:

238	Margaret Ritter (1844-). *Margaret was born in 1844.*
239	Richardson Ritter (1844-1901). *Richardson was born on September 8, 1844. He died on March 6, 1901 and was buried in Ava, Douglas County, MO at Ava Cemetery.*
240	Nancy Ritter (1846-). *Nancy was born in 1846.*
241	Wiley Lively Ritter (1849-1896). *Wiley was born in 1849. He died on May 8, 1896 and was buried in Ava.*
242	Elizabeth M. Ritter (1852-). *Elizabeth was born in 1852.*
243	Martin Ritter (1854-). *Martin was born in 1854.*
244	Louisa Ritter (1856-). *Louisa was born in 1856.*

52. Eleazer Quimby Seawell, son of Jesse Seawell and Nancy Ritter, was born on May 10, 1808. He married **Mary Dickerson Phillips** on May 20, 1827. He died on March 15, 1893 in Moore County and was buried in Moore County.

Mary Dickerson Phillips, daughter of Eli Phillips (1785-1848) and Nancy Dowd (1787-1852), was born on July 27, 1808. She died on January 17, 1899 in Moore County and was buried in Moore County. She and Eleazer Quimby Seawell had the following children:

245	Samuel Waite Seawell (1833-1879). *Samuel was born on November 5, 1833. He married* **Exer L. Ritter** *on July 31, 1864 in Moore County. He died on February 26, 1879 in Moore County and was buried in Moore County.*
246	Virgil Newton Seawell (1839-1926). *Virgil was born on July 13, 1839. He married* **Eleanor Croom** *on September 11, 1860 in Moore County. He married* **Carrie Register** *on October 28, 1875 in Moore County. He married* **Emily Josephine Dancy** *on October 27, 1886. He died on March 31, 1926 and was buried in Moore County.*
247	Ruina Ann Seawell (1840-1886). *Ruina was born on February 14, 1840. She married* **Daniel H. Cox** *on January 28, 1872 in Moore County. She died on November 30, 1886.*
248	Cornelius Lee Seawell (1842-1868). *Cornelius was born in 1842. He died in 1868.*
249	Charles Meredith Seawell (1844-1871). *Charles was born on July 20, 1844. He died on June 14, 1871 in Moore County and was buried in Moore County.*
250	Robert Hall Seawell (1847-1899). *Robert was born on August 8, 1847. He married* **Jane Thornburg** *in 1884. He died on November 25, 1899 and was buried in Moore County.*
251	Josiah Tay Seawell (1849-1934). *Josiah was born on January 23, 1849. He married* **Margaret L. Wallace** *on December 24, 1875 in Moore County. He married* **Mattie E.**

Johnson on February 23, 1879 in Moore County. He died on June 18, 1934 and was buried in Moore County.

252   Fonnie Alice Seawell (1856-1910). *Fonnie was born on January 16, 1856. She died on October 10, 1910.*

53. Isaac McLendon Seawell, son of Jesse Seawell and Nancy Ritter, was born on October 27, 1810. He married **Catherine Patterson** on January 17, 1841. He died before 1870.

Catherine Patterson, daughter of Duncan Patterson (1782-1864) and Mary Buie (1788-1825), was born in 1815 in Cumberland County. She died circa 1875 in Moore County. She and Isaac McLendon Seawell had the following children:

253   Ann E. Seawell (1841-). *Ann was born on October 19, 1841.*

254   Jesse P. Seawell (1843-). *Jesse was born in January 1843. He married **Frances "Fannie" Seawell** on December 6, 1863 in Moore County.*

255   Nancy "Nannie" Seawell (1847-1918). *Nancy was born on February 15, 1847. She died on May 4, 1918 and was buried in Moore County, NC at Williams Cemetery #124.*

256   Ashley Seawell (1847-). *Ashley was born on September 28, 1847.*

257   William Henry Seawell (1849-). *William was born on October 24, 1849.*

258   Margaret Louise "Lou" Seawell (1857-1932). *Margaret was born in 1857 in Moore County. She married **William Wesley Wallace** on February 22, 1880 in Moore County. She died on October 18, 1932 in Greensboro, Guilford County, NC and was buried on October 19, 1932 in Greensboro, Guilford County, NC at Green Hill Cemetery.*

54. Nancy Seawell, daughter of Jesse Seawell and Nancy Ritter, was born on November 24, 1815. She died after 1860 and was buried in Toone, Hardeman County, TN at Old Sullivan Cemetery. She married **Joel Sullivan**.

Joel Sullivan, son of William Sullivan (1758-1838) and Eleanor Smith (1763-1836), was born in 1791. He married Lydia Cummings on February 20, 1810 in Guilford County, NC. He died after 1860 and was buried in Toone. He and Nancy Seawell had the following children:

259   Lydia M. Sullivan (1835-1858). *Lydia was born on February 4, 1835. She died on July 7, 1858 and was buried in Moore County.*

260   Sadie Sullivan (1836-1911). *Sadie was born on November 4, 1836. She married **Bryant Caddell** on January 13, 1857 in Moore County. She died on January 10, 1911 in Hardeman County and was buried in Hardeman County, TN at Caddell Cemetery.*

261   Isaac McLendon Sullivan (1839-1926). *Isaac was born on March 23, 1839. He married **Louisa Jane Cole** on January 13, 1862 in Moore County. He died on March 9, 1926 in Guilford County and was buried in Greensboro.*

262   Pleasant Green Sullivan (1841-). *Pleasant was born in 1841.*

263   Eli Sullivan (1842-1860). *Eli was born in 1842. He died in 1860 and was buried in Toone.*

264   Julia Sullivan (1844-). *Julia was born in 1844. She married **Presley T. Caddell** on April 10, 1873 in Moore County.*

265   Nettie Sullivan (1849-1923). *Nettie was born in 1849. She died on September 30, 1923.*

266   Jonathan Sullivan (1854-1876). *Jonathan was born in 1854. He died in 1876 and was buried in Toone.*

55. Eli Ritter Seawell, son of Jesse Seawell and Nancy Ritter, was born on December 13, 1819. He married **Nancy Patterson** on September 1, 1842.

Nancy Patterson was born in 1828. She died on May 22, 1893 in Moore County. She and Eli Ritter Seawell had the following children:

267   Frances "Fannie" Seawell (1843-). *Frances was born in 1843. She married **Jesse P. Seawell** on December 6, 1863 in Moore County.*

268   Taylor Seawell (1846-). *Taylor was born in 1846.*

269   Orrin Seawell (1850-). *Orrin was born in 1850.*

270   Malcolm Seawell (1854-). *Malcolm was born in 1854.*

271   Ella Virginia Seawell (1860-1863). *Ella was born on August 4, 1860. She died on August 30, 1863 in Moore County.*

56. Aaron Ashley Flowers Seawell, son of Jesse Seawell and Nancy Ritter, was born on March 10, 1822. He married **Jeanette Buie** in 1854. He died in 1894 in Moore County.

Jeanette Buie was born in 1827. She died in 1906. She and Aaron Ashley Flowers Seawell had the following children:

> 272   Nannie M. Seawell (1864-). *Nannie was born in 1864. She married **Thomas S. Costen** on December 30, 1896 in Moore County.*

57. Jesse G. Seawell, son of Jesse Seawell and Nancy Ritter, was born on May 27, 1825. He married **Ruth Ann McIntosh**.

Ruth Ann McIntosh, daughter of Neill McIntosh (1772-1846) and Mary Jackson (1787-1855), was born in 1829.

58. Ann M. Seawell, daughter of Jesse Seawell and Nancy Ritter, was born on May 28, 1827. She died on July 20, 1862 in Arkadelphia, Clark County, AR. She married **William N. Duncan**.

61. James H. Muse, son of Daniel Muse and Susannah Ritter, was born in 1802. He married **Patience Fry**. He later married **Emaline Wallace** (1831-).

Patience Fry, daughter of James Fry (c. 1768-aft 1850), was born on November 4, 1802. She died on June 6, 1860 and was buried in Moore County. She and James H. Muse had the following children:

> 273   Jane C. Muse (1830-1884). *Jane was born in 1830. She married **William Riley Barrett** on August 15, 1854 in Lowndes County, MS. She died on December 15, 1884.*
> 274   Sophia Muse (1835-). *Sophia was born in May 1835. She married **Edmond Holland** on October 9, 1858 in Moore County.*
> 275   Ann Miranda Muse (1838-aft 1866). *Ann was born in 1838. She married **Josiah Wallace** on August 25, 1855 in Moore County. She died after 1866.*
> 276   John B. Muse (1839-). *John was born in 1839.*

62. Jesse Muse, son of Daniel Muse and Susannah Ritter, was born on August 4, 1804. He died on May 6, 1878 and was buried in Moore County. He married **Nancy J.**

Nancy J. was born on October 14, 1810. She died on June 3, 1880 and was buried in Moore County. She and Jesse Muse had the following children:

> 277   William Riley Muse (1827-1906). *William was born on May 27, 1827. He married **Martha McIntosh** on September 4, 1862 in Moore County. He died on February 25, 1906 and was buried in Moore County.*
> 278   Candace Muse (1829-1893). *Candace was born on June 3, 1829. She died on September 8, 1893 and was buried in Moore County.*
> 279   Noah F. Muse (1834-1864). *Noah was born in 1834. He died on February 2, 1864 in Civil War.*
> 280   Susan Muse (1836-1911). *Susan was born on February 23, 1836. She married **Lochart "Lockey" Wallace** on December 27, 1855 in Moore County. She died on February 18, 1911 in Moore County and was buried in Moore County, NC at Flint Hill Baptist Church.*
> 281   Archibald Buckley Muse (1838-1903). *Archibald was born on May 31, 1838. He married **Martha Jane Johnson** on August 9, 1860 in Moore County. He died on May 6, 1903 and was buried in Moore County.*
> 282   Ashley F. Muse (1841-1863). *Ashley was born in 1841. He died on July 1, 1863 in Gettysburg, PA in Civil War.*
> 283   Commodore George Muse (1843-1865). *Commodore was born in 1843. He died on May 11, 1865 in Elmira, NY in Civil War.*

63. Daniel J. Muse, son of Daniel Muse and Susannah Ritter, was born in 1808. He died in 1878 and was buried in Chester County, TN at Estes Cemetery. He married **Elizabeth Susan Williams**.

Elizabeth Susan Williams was born on January 11, 1815. She died on October 1, 1898 and was buried in Chester County. She and Daniel J. Muse had the following children:

284	Martha J. Muse (1839-). *Martha was born in 1839.*
285	Margaret E. Muse (1840-). *Margaret was born in 1840.*
286	Susannah Muse (1842-1931). *Susannah was born in 1842. She died on August 19, 1931 and was buried in Chester County.*
287	Rebecca Muse (1846-). *Rebecca was born in 1846.*
288	William T. Muse (1857-1933). *William was born on June 8, 1857 in Tennessee. He married **Josephine F.** circa 1883. He died on March 8, 1933 and was buried in Chester County.*

64. **John B. Muse**, son of Daniel Muse and Susannah Ritter, was born in 1813. He died in 1870 in Haywood County, NC. He married **Jane Richardson**.

65. **Miles Muse**, son of Daniel Muse and Susannah Ritter, was born in 1815. He married **Priscilla Horner**.

Priscilla Horner, daughter of George R. Horner (1761-1844) and Priscilla Winslow (aft 1780-1853), was born in 1819. She and Miles Muse had the following children:

289	Not sure which Muse (-)
290	Ann Eliza Muse (1839-). *Ann was born in 1839.*
291	Temperance L. Muse (1845-). *Temperance was born in August 1845.*
292	Elizabeth C. Muse (1847-). *Elizabeth was born in September 1847.*
293	George R. P. Muse (1850-). *George was born in January 1850. He married **Melissa A. Edge** circa 1877.*
294	William W. Muse (1851-). *William was born in October 1851.*
295	Flora E. Amanda Muse (1857-). *Flora was born in August 1857.*

66. **Doctor Franklin Muse**, son of Daniel Muse and Susannah Ritter, was born on August 2, 1816. He died on June 17, 1891 and was buried in Moore County, NC at Melton/Muse Cemetery #70. He married **Jennet\Josiah Melton**.

Jennet\Josiah Melton was born in 1816. She died in 1868 and was buried in Moore County. She and Doctor Franklin Muse had the following children:

296	Archibald B. Muse (1842-). *Archibald was born in 1842.*
297	John W. Muse (1845-1915). *John was born in August 1845. He died on December 6, 1915 in Moore County and was buried in Moore County, NC at Reynolds County Home Cemetery.*
298	Candace A. Muse (1847-1929). *Candace was born on November 20, 1847. She married **Jeremiah M. Phillips** on January 17, 1866 in Moore County. She died on December 31, 1929 and was buried in Moore County, NC at Phillips Cemetery #222 (Patty Phillips).*
299	Lavina Carolina Muse (1849-1892). *Lavina was born on April 10, 1849. She died on July 28, 1892 and was buried in Moore County.*
300	Susanna "Susan" Muse (1855-1923). *Susanna was born in 1855. She died on March 24, 1923 in Moore County.*
301	Lydia Frances Muse (1857-1927). *Lydia was born in May 1857 in Moore County. She died on October 12, 1927 in Montgomery County and was buried on October 13, 1927 in Candor, Montgomery County, NC at Macedonia Presbyterian Church.*

Descendants of Moses Ritter

1. **Moses Ritter** was born in 1730. He died before May 11, 1819 in New Hanover County, NC. He married Hannah Bradbury, daughter of James Bradbury (d. 1786 Dobbs County, NC) and they were the parents of twelve children: Josiah, James Bradbury, Elizabeth, Aaron, Mary, Clementine, Moses, Thomas, Catherine "Kitsey", Rhoda, Hannah and Jesse Bradbury Ritter. Moses and Hannah's family bible listed the birthdates of all twelve children and stated that Moses lived to be 89 years old while Hannah lived to be "100 years plus 8."[210] Moses can be found in numerous records from 1753 to 1819 in eastern North Carolina. Moses and Hannah appear to have lived in old Dobbs County (current Wayne County) from 1753-1775 and in Sampson County from 1775-1785 before finally settling in present day Pender County near Moore's Creek.

RECORDS OF MOSES RITTER

1753, Apr 12 -- Land Grant #116 & 1112, Johnston County, NC
Moses Retter received 165 acres located East of Little River and on both sides of Buck Branch.

1759, Sep 1 -- Land Grant #482 & 1037, Johnston County, NC
Moses Rutter received 92 acres located North of Little River on the Head of Buck Swamp including the Goose Pond adjoining his former line.

1762, Nov 15 -- Land Patent Book 15 Page 454, Dobbs County, NC
William Grant received 140 acres located on Buck Swamp and the Mouth of Clayey Branch adjoining his own line and Moses Ruter.

1763, Mar 17 -- Land Grant #295, Dobbs County, NC
Moses Ritter received 100 acres located on Buck Swamp and the Mouth of Clayey Branch adjoining his own line and William Grant. John Regestor and Arthur Peacock were chain carriers.

1764, May 10 -- Land Grant #527, Dobbs County, NC
James Bradbury received 300 acres located East of Little River near the Goose Pond adjoining John Esterling, Henry Esterling and Moses Retter. Moses Retter and Absolem Sentos were chain carriers.

1765, Apr-Apr 1769 -- Deed Book 7, Dobbs County, NC
Page 111 - Moses Ritter to Thomas Price/Rice
Page 138 - Jesse Ritter to Drury Alldridge

1765, Sep 21 -- Land Grant #575, Dobbs County, NC
James Bradbury received 640 acres located on Lower side of Little River on Buck Marsh and Breezy Branch adjoining his own line, and William Hooker. Moses Ratter and George Bradbury were chain carriers.

1767, Aug 10 -- Land Grant #920, Dobbs County, NC
Moses Ritter received 100 acres located between Mirtle Branch and Buck Branch adjoining James Bradberry, Henerey Easterling and near Retter's own line. Wm. Waller and Isam Ellis were chain carriers.

1769, Dec 16 -- Land Patent Book 20 Page 491, Dobbs County, NC
William Worrel received 375 acres located South of Nauhunty Swamp and South of Slugh Swamp adjoining Moses Retter, Elliot and Widow Speir.

1771, Nov 28 -- North Carolina Colonial Records Volume 22 Page 414
Moses Ritter listed on Account of Sundry Firelocks Pressed into his Majesty's Service in the Expedition against the Insurgents in 1771, for the Dobbs Detachment, which were lost, broke or destroyed.

1773, Apr-May 1775 -- Deed Book 10, Dobbs County, NC
Page 420 - Jessee Ritter to Moses Ritter
Page 474 - Moses Ritter to Joshua Howell

1775, Apr 18 -- Deed Book 3 Page 502, Sampson County, NC
Edward Byrd deeded Moses Ritter 100 acres located East of Six Runs adjoining Henry MacCullows. Benjamin Bell and William Young were witnesses.

1775, Apr 18 -- Deed Book 3 Page 503, Sampson County, NC
Daniel Watkins and wife Barsheba deeded Moses Ritter 150 acres located on Run of Beaverdam Swamp adjoining Edward Byrd. David James and Jessey Watkins were witnesses.

1777, Jan-Apr 1779 -- Deed Book 11, Dobbs County, NC
Page 198 - Moses Ritter to Wilson Wadkins

1783 -- Census, Duplin County, NC [current Sampson County, NC]
Moses Ritter listed

1784 -- Tax List, Sampson County, NC
Moses Ritter listed 250 acres and 2 white polls

1785, Feb 21 -- Deed Book 20 Page 80, Sampson County, NC
Moses Ritter deeded James Spiller two tracts of land: (1) 100 acres located East of Six Runs adjoining Edward Byrd, William Blackman. (2) 150 acres adjoining David James Sr. and William Herndon. Thomas Coggins and William Harper were witnesses,

1785. Mar 23 -- Court of Pleas and Quarter Sessions, Sampson County, NC
A deed from Moses Ritter to James Spiller for 500 acres was proven by Thomas Coggins.

1786, Dec 8 -- Will, Wayne County, NC
Will of James Bradbury, Dec'd. Heirs: Wife, son Jacob Bradbury, daughter Hannah Ritter, son George Bradbury, daughter Mary Bele, granddaughter Elizabeth Bele, son Thomas Chambers Bradbury, daughter Rhoda Stanly and her eldest son James Stanly, son James Bradbury, daughter Elizabeth Grantham, son-in-law Thos. Grantham, grandson James Bradbury Ritter and grandson Aron Ritter. Executors: William McKinne, Richard McKinne and Stephen Stanly. Witnesses: Wm. McKinne Junr., Michel Buell/Bauell, Thos. Costettor and Elizabeth Auly/Orrly. Proven Jan 1787.

1787, Feb 8 -- Deed Book K Page 438, New Hanover County, NC
Bryant Buxton deeded Moses Ritter 250 acres located on Poplar Swamp of widow Moore's Creek adjoining Thomas Moore, Jeremiah Malpass, Nathaniel McGufford and Anthony Ward including plantation known as Clay Fields. John Jones, Jesse Rooks and David Jones were witnesses.

1789, Jun 15 -- Land Grant #2231, New Hanover County, NC
Moses Ritter received 100 acres located East of Moore's Creek on both sides of Poplar Branch. Thomas Lewis and Moses Ritter were chain carriers.

1789, Jun 15 -- Land Grant #2232, New Hanover County, NC
Moses Ritter received 100 acres located East of Moore's Creek, adjoining Thomas Lewis and his own line including Cuffie's Point Bay. Thomas Lewis and Moses Ritter were chain carriers.

1790 -- Census, New Hanover County, NC Page 51
Moses Rettor
(16+) 1M
(0-16) 3M
7F

1791, Dec 2 -- Land Grant #2355, New Hanover County, NC
Moses Ritter received 300 acres located East of Moore's Creek, near Moore's Creek Swamp, Cuffey's Branch and Haws Branch adjoining John Jones and his own line. Thomas Ritter and Clemmer Ritter were chain carriers.

1789, Jun 15 -- Land Grant #2270, New Hanover County, NC
Moses Ritter received 240 acres located between widow Moore's Creek and the new road South of the Clayfield Bay adjoining his own line, John Jones, A. Stakey, Huggins and Thomas Lewis. Wm. Walker and Thos. Ritter were chain carriers.

1795, Oct 2 -- Land Grant #2520, New Hanover County, NC
Moses Ritter received 70 acres located West of Long Creek adjoining R. Proby, Wm. Walker, T. Lewis and his own line. Kiah Bonham and Polly Ritter were chain carriers.

1800, Oct 11 -- Deed Book L Page 496, New Hanover County, NC
Moses Ritter deeded Nathaniel McGufford 6 tracts of land containing (1) 250 acres on Polar Swamp of widow Moore's Creek adjoining Jeremiah Malpuss, Nathl. McGufford Sr. and Anthony Ward known as the "Clayfields"; (2) 120 acres East of Moore's Creek on Pursleys Branch adjoining Anthony Ward; (3) 100 acres located East of Moore's Creek adjoining Ritter's line, Thos. Lewis and Cuffy's Point Bay; (4) 100 acres located East of widow Moore's Creek and both sides of Poplar Branch; (5) 300 acres located East of Moore's Creek, near Moore's Creek Swamp, Cuffey's Branch and Haws Branch adjoining John Jones; (6) 240 acres located widow Moore's Creek and the new road South of the Clayfield Bay adjoining his own line, John Jones, Arthur Stucky, Huggins and Thomas Lewis. William Sharpless, Pettigrew Moore and Daniel Bourdeaux were witnesses.

1800, Oct 11 -- Deed Book N Page 355, New Hanover County, NC
Nathaniel McGufford deeded Moses Ritter slaves Kim and Hages. M. Harples, Pettegru Moore and Daniel Burdeaux were witnesses.

1804, May 1 and 15 -- Wilmington Gazette, New Hanover County, NC
The following property owners were listed as being delinquent on their taxes and notified their land was going to be sold in June if the taxes were not paid: Moses Ritter for 1801: 50 acres, 1 white poll and 1 black poll; Moses Ritter for 1802: 47 acres and 1 white poll

1804, Oct 16 -- Deed Book M Page 492, New Hanover County, NC
Ajatant Mott deeded Moses Ritter 75 acres on Bever Branch. James Portevent and John Loiteevent were witnesses.

1804, Oct 16 -- Deed Book M Page 493, New Hanover County, NC
James Poitevent deeded Moses Ritter 46.5 acres North of Bever Branch adjoining Moses Ritter's line, John Walker and Daniel Burdeaux. Daniel Burdeaux and John Poitevent were witnesses.

1809, Apr 18 -- Notice, True Republican [Newspaper] Wilmington, NC
Notice: My wife Hannah has deserted my bed and board, without any provocation. I do hereby forwarn all persons whatever, from dealing with her, as I am determined not to pay, or answer any of her contracts, to which I requeit all persons to take due notice. Nevertheless, if my said wife Hannah will return to me, I will support her as usual, or procure a good house for her reception. Moses Ritter Apr 17, 1809

1809, May 4 -- Deed Book O Page 37, New Hanover County, NC
Moses Ritter deeded Nathaniel McGufford 111.5 acres located East of Long Creek adjoining Paul Overhison. James Bonham and Sam Buxton were witnesses.

1810, Aug 14 -- Deed Book O Page 99, New Hanover County, NC
Moses Ritter deeded to son Jessa. B. Ritter slaves Ann, Susannah, Fan, John and Michel. Wm. Taylor and Solon Busley were witnesses.

1812, Feb 4 -- Deed Book O Page 328, New Hanover County, NC
Jesse Ritter deeded his father Moses Ritter slaves Ann, Jack, Mike, Rachel and Fanny. Solomon Beesly and John Harper were witnesses.

1812, May 28 -- Deed Book O Page 396, New Hanover County, NC
Moses Ritter deeded Daniel Bordeaux slaves Ann, Fan, Jack, Mike and Rachel. Hugh Cowan and Spencer Stanley were witnesses.

1814, Jan 21 -- Deed Book Q Page 274, New Hanover County, NC
Moses Ritter deeded James Moore Jr. a slave named Farraby in return for another slave [not named]. John Moore and James Quen were witnesses.

1819, May 11 -- Estate, New Hanover County, NC
Robert Alexr. Henry, Joel Henry, David Smith Jur. and Wm. Jones Larkins were named Administrators of the Estate of Moses Ritter, Dec'd.

Moses Ritter and Hannah Bradbury had the following children:

+2   Josiah Ritter (1755-) is listed in the family bible but no further record of him has been located. He likely died young.

+3   James Bradbury Ritter (1757-1816) relocated to Surry County, NC, and married Anna Violet Burcham (1765/1770-aft 1830). They were the parents of twelve children: Polly, Sallie, Nancy, Rosanna, Elizabeth, Lazarus, Moses, John L., Isabelle, James, Lewis and Violet Ritter.

+4   Elizabeth Ritter (1760-1846) married Andrew Scott and after his death she migrated to Sumter County, SC and later Autauga County, AL.

+5   Aaron Ritter (1763-bef 1840) was listed in Surry County, NC in 1790 and believed to have migrated north into Virginia and then into eastern Tennessee prior to relocating Pender County, NC near his father. Ritter researchers believe that Aaron was the father of William and Moses Ritter of Claiborne County, TN.

+6   Mary Ritter (1765-) is listed in the family bible but no further record of her has been located.

+7   Clementine Ritter (1770-) married William Crawford (d. 1822) and resided in Pender County.

+8   Moses Ritter (1772-) is listed in the family bible but no further record of him has been located.

+9   Thomas Ritter (1774-) migrated to Sumner County, TN and was the father of William and Elizabeth.

+10   Catherine "Kitsey" Ritter (1776-) lived in Pender County and was married three times: Arthur Branch, Samuel Lowell and Jonathan Stanley.

+11   Rhoda Ritter (1779-bef 1855) married Revolutionary War veteran Edgerton Mott (1740-1831) and lived in Pender County. Rhoda and Edgerton were the parents of Ann Jane, Daniel W., Elizabeth and Joseph Mott.

+12   Hannah Ritter (1781-) lived in Pender County and married Vincent Walker.

+13   Jesse Bradbury Ritter (1785-) was the youngest son of Moses and Hannah Ritter and lived in the Rocky Point District of Pender County. The census records show Jesse Bradbury Ritter had a large family, but the names are not known at the present time.

Second Generation

2. **Josiah Ritter**, son of Moses Ritter and Hannah Bradbury, was born on December 8, 1755.

3. **James Bradbury Ritter**, son of Moses Ritter and Hannah Bradbury, was born on December 12, 1757. He died on September 1, 1816 in Surry County, NC. He married **Anna Violet Burcham**.

Anna Violet Burcham was born between 1765 and 1770. She died after 1830. She and James Bradbury Ritter had the following children:

+14	Polly Ritter (-)
+15	Sallie Ritter (-)
+16	Nancy Ritter (-)
+17	Rosanna Ritter (-)
+18	Elizabeth Ritter (1787-1860)
+19	Lazarus Ritter (1789-1856)
+20	John L. Ritter (aft 1790-)
+21	Moses Ritter (1796-1870)
+22	Isabelle Ritter (1800-)
+23	James Ritter (1803-1863)
+24	Lewis Ritter (1810-)
+25	Violet Ritter (1810-1858)

4. **Elizabeth Ritter**, daughter of Moses Ritter and Hannah Bradbury, was born on December 22, 1760 in Wayne County, NC. She died on December 28, 1846 in Autauga County, AL. She married **Andrew Scott**.

5. **Aaron Ritter**, son of Moses Ritter and Hannah Bradbury, was born on March 10, 1763. He died before 1840.

Aaron Ritter had the following children:

+26	William Ritter (1789-)
+27	Moses Ritter (1795-1836)

6. **Mary Ritter**, daughter of Moses Ritter and Hannah Bradbury, was born on April 27, 1765.

Mary Ritter had the following children:

+28	Daniel Biddle Ritter (1785-)
+29	Mary Jane Ritter (1789-)
+30	Jane Harvey Ritter (1791-)

7. **Clementine Ritter**, daughter of Moses Ritter and Hannah Bradbury, was born on February 20, 1770. She married **William Crawford**.

William Crawford died before November 1822.

8. **Moses Ritter**, son of Moses Ritter and Hannah Bradbury, was born on March 28, 1772.

9. **Thomas Ritter**, son of Moses Ritter and Hannah Bradbury, was born on March 31, 1774.

Thomas Ritter had the following children:

+31	William Ritter (aft 1794-bef 1850)
+32	Elizabeth Ritter (aft 1794-)

10. **Catherine "Kitsey" Ritter**, daughter of Moses Ritter and Hannah Bradbury, was born on September 15, 1776. She married **Samuel Lowell**. She married **Jonathan Stanley**. She married **Arthur Branch**.

Arthur Branch died before 1830.

11. **Rhoda Ritter**, daughter of Moses Ritter and Hannah Bradbury, was born on January 7, 1779. She died before September 14, 1855. She married **Edgerton Mott**.

Edgerton Mott was born in 1740. He died on March 20, 1831 in New Hanover County, NC. He and Rhoda Ritter had the following children:

+33	Ann Jane Mott (1806-)
+34	Daniel W. Mott (1809-)
+35	Elizabeth Mott (1810-)
+36	Joseph Mott (1812-)

12. **Hannah Ritter**, daughter of Moses Ritter and Hannah Bradbury, was born on July 17, 1781. She married **Vincent Walker**.

13. **Jesse Bradbury Ritter**, son of Moses Ritter and Hannah Bradbury, was born on July 28, 1785.

Index

Bean, Polly...563, 565, 572
Beane, Roy Cornelius...414
Bearden, Frances J...30, 75, 76
Bearden, Frances Jane...30, 77, 78
Bearden, Gertrude...174
Bearden, Myrtle...174
Beavers, Bennie Lee...437
Beavers, Frankie Mae...437
Beavers, George Wesley...437
Beavers, Joyce Elaine...437
Beavers, William James...437
Beck, Charles W...322
Beck, Effie...237, 238
Beck, Robert Mack...285, 319
Beck, Rufus W. Sr...322
Beckerdite, Catherine...206
Bell, John E...546
Bell, Louisa E...546
Benjamin...420
Benjamin, Erskine Quince...420
Benjamin, Peggy Lee...420
Bennett, Ella...166
Benoist, Gertrude...528
Benton, Rosa Nell...338
Berwick, Mary Lynn...455
Bethune, Eliza Jane...571
Biggs, Margaret Jane...255
Bingham, Lavinia...554
Binkley, Addie Bethel...556
Bishop, Carrie Ophelia...262
Bishop, Jonas Silas...335
Black...249
Black, Carson Roy...249, 443
Black, Carson Roy Jr...443
Black, Charles Howard...443
Black, Charlotte...462
Black, Donald...462
Black, Lacy...462
Black, Michael...462
Black, Millie...443
Black, Myrtle...249
Black, Nancy Jane...164
Black, Randolph...443
Black, Stanley Gene...443
Black, Wesley...462
Blair, Reece...167
Blake, Annie May...276
Blakeley, Lillian Marie...357
Blakely, Alma...372
Blocker, William L...302
Blue, Martha Elizabeth...405
Blue, Sallie...327
Boas, Ada...556
Bolton, Brantley C...543
Bolton, Emma Huggins...390
Bolton, Sarah...543
Bond, George Edwards...513
Bond, Margaret Lanier...513
Boone, Bird...67
Boone, Tabitha...28, 67, 68
Boone, Willard Webster...166
Boone, William Lee...334, 341
Booth, Audrey Mae...270
Boothe, Brian Carey...441
Boroughs, Rosanna Pearl...156
Bottoms, Robert Lee...568
Boudoin, Walter...333, 415
Boulte, Clement Augustus III...427
Bowden, Jeptha C...167
Bowlin, John Pinner...555
Bowman, Elmer Mason...359
Bowman, George...359
Boyte, Nancy Louise...415
Bradbury, Hannah...19, 578, 580

Bradbury, James...19, 578
Brady, Addie Marie...165, 287
Brady, Bradley "Red Brad"...23, 64
Brady, Charles Underwood...254
Brady, George W...165
Brady, Mattie...328
Brady, Minnie...334
Brady, Nora Bell...254
Brady, Rosa E...464
Brady, William...165
Bramlett, Maybelle...442
Branch, Arthur...582
Branson, Lovie...328
Braswell, Billie...409
Braswell, Jean Gray...409
Braswell, John S...409
Brawn...426
Brawn, Albert Lloyd...426
Brawn, Eugene Phillip...461
Bray, Abijah Herbert...274
Bray, Arthur W...274
Bray, Blanche...274
Bray, Herbert T...274
Bray, Lewis Ritter...274
Bray, Mamie Ethel...274
Bray, Shelly R...274
Brewer...6, 23, 31
Brewer, Allen Fuller...393
Brewer, Allen Fuller Jr...393
Brewer, Allen Lacy...393
Brewer, Amanda D...84
Brewer, Barbara Ann...283
Brewer, Betty Sue...283
Brewer, Dorothy...283
Brewer, Earl Henry...393
Brewer, Elizabeth...470
Brewer, Finity A...84
Brewer, Geneva F. "Jennie"...84, 183
Brewer, Geraldine...283
Brewer, Gurney Clinton...283, 420
Brewer, Harmon...33, 83, 84
Brewer, Harry P...308
Brewer, Henry Martin...84, 183
Brewer, Jennet "Jane"...230
Brewer, Joe...283
Brewer, John W...84
Brewer, Lillie...183, 308
Brewer, Lola...233
Brewer, Maggie May...393
Brewer, Margie D...183
Brewer, Marie...283
Brewer, Martha Elizabeth...281, 282
Brewer, Martin T...183
Brewer, Mary...183
Brewer, Mary E...84
Brewer, Nancy J...84
Brewer, Ruth...283
Brewer, Sara Ann...429
Brewer, Sarah C...84
Brewer, Thomas Lewis...283
Brewer, Vernon Leroy...283
Brewer, W. Vestra...265
Brewer, Walter...84
Brewer, William...84, 183
Brewer, William M...83
Brewer, William Morgan...183, 308
Brewer, Willie H...183
Brewer, Willie James...283
Brian, Eliza...557
Bridges, Brenda Sue...446
Bridges, Deana Marie...446
Bridges, James Elbert...446
Bridges, Jemima...542
Bridges, Kathy Louise...446

Bridges, Tammy Lynn...446
Brigman, John W...509
Bristow, Eula...269, 337
Britt...6, 23, 31, 516
Britt, Abraham Lincoln...82, 177
Britt, Alice E...306
Britt, Allen Emmerson...225
Britt, Allie...245, 247, 474
Britt, Amanda Elizabeth "Mandy"...176, 306
Britt, Amanda Elvira "Mandy"...245, 247, 442, 474
Britt, Annie Helen...232
Britt, Annie Jane...388
Britt, Arnold L...276
Britt, Avington...81, 176
Britt, Bambi Shawn...421
Britt, Barney Edward...232
Britt, Beacom C...33, 79, 80, 81, 82, 145, 468, 469
Britt, Beacom Nelson "Ned"...81, 176
Britt, Benjamin...31, 33, 82, 83, 468, 470
Britt, Bertha...245, 247, 474
Britt, Bertha M...177
Britt, Bettie Lou...232, 422
Britt, Betty Jean...358
Britt, Betty Louise...450
Britt, Beulah...305, 471
Britt, Billy Allen...308
Britt, Bryant...161
Britt, Burney A...277
Britt, Callie Marie...308
Britt, Calvin...470
Britt, Casie...246, 248, 442, 474
Britt, Caswell Melton...176, 306
Britt, Charles Garfield...176, 305
Britt, Charlie...472
Britt, Chester D...472
Britt, Clarence Orlanda...471
Britt, Clarkie Ann...145, 182, 244, 247, 471, 475
Britt, Clyde Wesley...305
Britt, Curtis Luke...276
Britt, Daniel Bethune...222, 231
Britt, Daniel Bethune Jr...112, 222
Britt, David James...145, 246, 471, 473
Britt, Debby Annie...176
Britt, Deborah E...83, 183, 470, 473
Britt, Edward...468, 469
Britt, Effie...348
Britt, Elbert Anderson...246, 248, 442, 474
Britt, Elgie Maie...450
Britt, Eliza A...177, 472
Britt, Eliza F...177
Britt, Elizabeth Jane...145, 246, 471, 473
Britt, Ella L. Nettie...177, 245, 307, 473
Britt, Ellis...387
Britt, Elmer D...305
Britt, Elmo Euel...305
Britt, Esther Francis...177, 306, 472
Britt, Esther Lene...232
Britt, Ethel...245, 247, 474
Britt, Eunice J...276
Britt, Everet...83, 177, 470, 472
Britt, Fannie C...187, 305
Britt, Felix R...183, 307, 473
Britt, Finity...6, 31, 33, 80
Britt, Flora...230, 231
Britt, Florence Retta...145, 246
Britt, Flossie...179, 183, 305, 306, 473
Britt, Floyd D...305
Britt, Franey Azilee...183, 307, 473
Britt, Frona Esther...183, 473
Britt, Fulton Terry...305
Britt, General Street...232

Brown, Maude Gertrude...317
Brown, May...410, 430
Brown, Mearl...369, 464
Brown, Melvin...350
Brown, Mildred Juanita...429
Brown, Mildred Margaret...348
Brown, Mildred Wyonetta...426
Brown, Mittie M...197, 349
Brown, Myrtie...386
Brown, Neil J...371
Brown, Neil Lee...196, 348
Brown, Nettie Louise...196, 347
Brown, Pauline...350, 371
Brown, Pearl...386
Brown, Raymond Lee...350
Brown, Robert...294
Brown, Robert Harrison...348
Brown, Roy Gilbert...349
Brown, Russell...350
Brown, Sallie...159
Brown, Sarah Ann...464
Brown, Sarah Lavannia...323
Brown, Sarah Maggie...348
Brown, Sarah May "May"...349
Brown, Swannie...257
Brown, Swannie Ellen...318, 371
Brown, Swannie Marie...464
Brown, Tessie B...464
Brown, Thelma M...429
Brown, Thomas Edgar...429
Brown, Vera Ellen...350
Brown, Vina Louise...348
Brown, Walter Branson...197, 348
Brown, Walter Julian...349
Brown, Walter Talmadge...429
Brown, Welford Headen...348
Brown, Wilbert Carlton...348
Brown, Wilbur...410, 430
Brown, Willard O...464
Brown, William...155
Brown, William Curtis...317
Brown, William Henry...317
Brown, William Ransom...348
Brown, William Thomas...238, 428, 429
Brown, William Walter...257, 464
Brown, William Wesley...3, 134, 196, 238, 257
Brownley, John Horner...406
Brownley, Wilbur Travis...406
Brownlow, Camilla Elizabeth...304
Bruce, Ernest...423
Bruce, Evanna Alice...525
Bruce, Helen Louise...423
Bruce, Lucinda Frances...232
Brumley...310
Brumley, Delmar Franklin...310
Bruton, Geraldine Clark...394
Bryant, Caleb C...570
Bryant, Deborah...570
Bryant, George Raleigh...570
Bryant, James...570
Bryant, James R...570
Bryant, Leandy...570
Bryant, Littleton...571
Bryant, Margaret Ritter...570
Bryant, Prudence Ann...572
Bryant, William Richard...570
Buchanan, Rebecca...454
Buckley, Elsie...547
Buckley, N. G...547
Buie, Jeanette...576
Bulla, Robert Franklin...331, 531
Bullard, Drucilla...368
Bullard, John Bunyon...334

Bullard, Margaret Myrtle...335, 341
Bullard, Rosa...320
Bullington, Louella Brown...259
Bullock, Marzee C...541
Bunce, Kimberly Carol...463
Bunce, Paul Kenneth...463
Bunce, Paul Kenneth II...463
Bundy, Robert Oliver...463
Bunker, Steven Milton...462
Burcham, Anna Violet...581
Burgess, Bill...279
Burgess, Elizabeth...229
Burns, Amanda J...215
Burns, Annie Casina...215
Burns, Annie Jane...206, 368
Burns, Artie Mishia...336, 367
Burns, Augusta Carlton...336, 368
Burns, Barney Leason...206, 368
Burns, Bessie...368
Burns, Burlie Hutton...368
Burns, Clemith Fletcher...368
Burns, Clinton...368
Burns, Clio...368
Burns, Emery Lee...368
Burns, Enoch...206
Burns, Enoch Harrison "Buddy"...206, 368, 370
Burns, Eugenia...336, 368
Burns, George Ariah...206, 369
Burns, Gladys...375
Burns, Hattie Bell...206, 369
Burns, Henry L...368
Burns, Henry Lindsey...206
Burns, Ira Nelson...206, 369
Burns, Iris...368
Burns, John Elsevand...206, 368
Burns, Leon...368
Burns, Lonnie...368
Burns, Mary Ellen Minerva...206, 369
Burns, Minnie Helen...396
Burns, Robert Lee...336, 367
Burns, Sarah Catherine Elizabeth...206, 367
Burns, Swannie...368
Burns, Viola Ethel...336, 368
Burns, Zemery Mitchell...206, 336, 367
Burnside, Joe Dodson...453
Burry, Ann Berry Bryant...570
Burt, Roy F...404
Bush, Earl Austin...404
Butler, Agnes Thelma...298
Butler, Betty Ray...354, 355
Butler, Christine...354
Butler, Dal Alexander...355
Butler, Dave M...298
Butler, Eloise...298
Butler, Elton J...298
Butler, Ina Mae...298
Butler, James M...298
Butler, John...405
Butler, John H...486
Butler, Laura Ann...355
Butler, Monroe...298
Butler, Odell Creswell...354, 355
Butler, Odell Creswell Jr...354
Butler, Ora M...298
Butler, Viola Sue...354
Butler, William Clyde...298
Butler, William Ernest...298
Butner, Rufus Earnest...323
Bybee, Luziane Annie...305
Byrd...452
Byrd, John S...249, 472
Byrd, John W...452
Byrne, Annie Louise...454

Caddell...28, 563
Caddell, Allie Beatrice...453
Caddell, Annie Cornelia Florence...159
Caddell, Artemus...113
Caddell, Artie Peoples Mishie...159
Caddell, Asa Bascom...159
Caddell, Barbara A...573
Caddell, Bryant...575
Caddell, Cary T...314
Caddell, Clement...159
Caddell, Daniel...188, 572
Caddell, Daniel Turner...188, 314
Caddell, David Bivens...262
Caddell, Dora Alice...159
Caddell, Eddie...159
Caddell, Eliza Sarah Clementine...262
Caddell, Eva Augusta...159
Caddell, George M...188
Caddell, George Washington...262
Caddell, James Bailey...158, 181, 262
Caddell, James Clyde...159
Caddell, John Spinks...159, 262
Caddell, Joseph Hurley...158
Caddell, Julia Ann...569
Caddell, Lessie Mae...314, 373
Caddell, Lily...159
Caddell, Lochart...572
Caddell, Lydia Ann...250
Caddell, Margaret Louisa...159
Caddell, Mary E...573
Caddell, Mary Emma...159
Caddell, Minnie Elsie...262
Caddell, Nona Elizabeth...262
Caddell, Pauline...262
Caddell, Presley T...575
Caddell, Robert E. Lee...262
Caddell, Sarah Otelia...159
Caddell, Tobias B...187, 188, 572
Caddell, William B...314
Caddell, William D...572
Cagle...5, 23, 57
Cagle, Abraham W....190
Cagle, Annie B...159
Cagle, Bessie Lee...159, 265
Cagle, Blake...159
Cagle, Camilla Haseltine...188, 190
Cagle, Catherine...23, 61, 63
Cagle, Clyde Jr...306
Cagle, Clyde Washington...306
Cagle, David...10
Cagle, Edna Alice...159, 265
Cagle, Eldon Carl...422
Cagle, Elgie Mozelle...344
Cagle, Eli Lee...159
Cagle, Elisha...188, 192
Cagle, Eliza Jane...176
Cagle, George...159, 187
Cagle, George Washington...187
Cagle, Johnnie Adams...187, 311
Cagle, Julia Ann...187
Cagle, Margaret Emily...347
Cagle, Margaret Louise...345
Cagle, Martha E. Patsy...177
Cagle, Mary Alma...268
Cagle, Myca Jane Millie...190
Cagle, Nancy E...176, 177
Cagle, Nancy Jane...150
Cagle, Robert...176, 177, 187
Cagle, Samantha Beulah...159, 266
Cagle, Sarah "Sallie"...176
Cagle, Sarah Ann...191, 192
Cagle, Tabitha...186
Cagle, Thomas Branson...159, 569
Cagle, Vickie Sue...422

Cagle, William Harrison...350
Cagle, William Velvin...350
Caldwell, Elizabeth...169
Callicott, W. Frank...547
Cameron, Bereatha Bea...455
Cameron, Mary Margaret...269, 337
Campbell, Baxter Zeno...389
Campbell, Bonnie Nell...437
Campbell, Carrie Bell...450
Campbell, Clinton Patterson...389
Campbell, Daniel Mack...389
Campbell, Dora Lee...486
Campbell, Elizabeth...15
Campbell, Frank B...388
Campbell, Ovelia Syble...389
Campbell, Shelby Jean...389
Canaday, Curtis...136
Canaday, Nancy Olive "Ollie"...47, 136
Canipe, Clyde...458
Cannon, Alice Marie...463
Cannon, Brenda Carol...257, 463
Cannon, Eter...507
Cannon, Gwendolyn Hope...257, 462
Cannon, James Lemuel...507
Cannon, Juanita Rhea...257, 462
Cannon, Lizzie...507
Cannon, M. L....507
Cannon, Marie Elaina...257, 463
Cannon, Mary Angela...257, 463
Cannon, Nathan Joy...257
Cannon, Nathan Joy Jr...257, 463
Cannon, Patricia Ann...257, 462
Cannon, Robert...507
Cannon, Timothy Mackins...257, 463
Cannon, Timothy Mark...463
Cannon, Wade...507
Capel, Annie T...209
Cardwell, Leslie...87
Carpenter, Charles Francis...446
Carpenter, Larry Alan...446
Carpenter, Stanley Dean MacDonald...446
Carpenter, William Lester...446
Carr, Martha Elizabeth...560
Carrington, Claudia Carmen...456, 509
Carter, Addie Webb...229, 409
Carter, Anita...409
Carter, Billy Braxton...229, 409
Carter, Chalmas Lexter Joe...457
Carter, Corbitt W...457, 509
Carter, Emma F...545
Carter, Fred L...484
Carter, Helen...256
Carter, Isham J...545, 546
Carter, James Ford...228, 229, 409
Carter, James Loyd Sr...545, 546
Carter, Janet Lynn...409
Carter, John Ashley...229, 409
Carter, John D...228, 229
Carter, John W...545, 546
Carter, Levi W...545
Carter, Lloyd...545
Carter, Lula F...546
Carter, M. E....545
Carter, Margaret E...545, 546
Carter, Mary Louise...229, 409
Carter, Phyllis Elaine...409
Carter, Robert L...545, 546
Carter, Ruth Coleman Coley...229, 409
Carter, Sarah Ann Jane...545, 546
Cash, Henry...170
Cash, Mary Henry "Mollie"...170
Cashwell, Claudia Loula...437
Cassady, Elizabeth...74
Castleberry, Glenna Faye...310

Cates, Brady Bell...408
Catlin, Cecil...523
Catlin, Daniel W. Tuck...522
Catlin, Eli F...522
Catlin, Flora E...522
Catlin, Gracie...523
Catlin, James...523
Catlin, Lula Maudie...523
Caudle, Edward...545
Caudle, Frederick...545
Caudle, George Raymond...547
Caudle, George Washington...545, 547
Caudle, Jesse...545
Caudle, Jesse B...545
Caudle, Levi...545
Caudle, Malakiah R. "Mack"...546
Caudle, Nancy...546, 547
Caudle, Robert...545
Caudle, William...545
Caudle, William Alexander...545
Caviness, Betty Adelaide...378
Caviness, Fannie Jane...507
Caviness, Glenna...271
Caviness, Jeanette...487
Caviness, Mary Ida...350
Chance, Eugene...485
Chance, Frank...485
Chance, George...485
Chance, Mary Elizabeth...485
Chance, Walter...485
Chandler, Alton B...291
Chandler, Fannie...360
Chandler, John N...291
Chastine, Temperance B...157
Cheek, Dora Alice...318
Cheek, Oscar M...317
Cheek, Willard Darrell...424
Cheek, William Eli...318
Chenoweth, Sarah Ann...540
Cherry, Betty Ann...244
Cheshire, Keith Warren...461
Cheshire, Phyllis Rae...461
Cheshire, Winfred Glenn...461
Cheshire, Winfred Glenn Jr...461
Chiffon, Nancy...35
Chilton, Shelby Jean...344
Chriscoe...115
Chriscoe, Aggie May...390
Chriscoe, Betty Lou...387
Chriscoe, Clarence E...387
Chriscoe, Henry Thomas...390
Chriscoe, John Lester...259
Chriscoe, John Thomas...259
Chriscoe, Marvin Hoyette...259
Chriscoe, Modie Lee Edward "Clifford"...387, 401
Chubboy, Robert...452
Clark, Addie Ann...509
Clark, Edd D...434
Clark, Eddie...434
Clark, Evelyn...459
Clark, Irvin...434
Clark, James Jimmie...434
Clark, Jennie Lee...434
Clark, Maggie...365
Clark, Mary J...434
Clark, Pearl...434
Clark, Sadie...434
Clayton, Charles G...50, 140
Cleaver, Benjamin Harrison...444
Cleaver, Benjamin Olin...444
Cleaver, Jessie Marie...444
Clements, Henrietta...183
Clements, Ina Inez...183, 308

Clements, John A...183
Clemons, George Donald...460
Clifton, Edith...256
Clontz, Clinton...451
Clontz, Wade Hampton...451
Coble, Charles Edward "Bud"...339
Coble, Ephriam...229
Coble, Ethel May...338
Coble, Luna Clementine...229
Cocanower, Anna Bell...523
Cocanower, Charles Centennial...523
Cocanower, Charles Tom...523
Cocanower, Lela Lee...523
Cocanower, Lena...523
Cochran, Bela...173, 302
Cochran, Charlie...172
Cochran, Columbus...173
Cochran, Dave...172
Cochran, Earnest...173
Cochran, Freeman...173
Cochran, George...172, 300
Cochran, Grady...173
Cochran, Jack C...173
Cochran, Jessie...172, 300
Cochran, Joe...173
Cochran, Julie...172
Cochran, Lehman...173
Cochran, Lena Mae...173, 302
Cochran, Leola...300
Cochran, Lester...173
Cochran, Lizzie...172
Cochran, Lorena...173
Cochran, Louvenia...173
Cochran, Marcus D...172
Cochran, N. Pete...172
Cochran, Vester...173
Cochran, Virginia...173
Cochran, William Alfred...173
Cochran, Zula...173, 302
Cockburn, Mary E. Mollie...243
Cockman...34
Cockman, Abraham Rommie...192, 327
Cockman, Adeline Haseltine...97, 194
Cockman, Alice Susannah...97, 194, 258
Cockman, Allen Thomas...344
Cockman, Alma...339
Cockman, Alma Louise...313
Cockman, Altie...196, 343, 347
Cockman, Anna Frances...318
Cockman, Anna Jane "Janie"...195, 206, 225, 226, 333
Cockman, Annette E...187, 312
Cockman, Annie May...312
Cockman, Annie Ruth...345
Cockman, Arlen Well...192, 328
Cockman, Armittie Evelyn...195, 336, 367
Cockman, Arnold Webster "Bill"...344
Cockman, Ashley Carson...192, 327
Cockman, Athos Lee...335, 341
Cockman, Atlas Franklin...196, 341, 344
Cockman, Atlas Harold "Pete"...344
Cockman, Barbara Anna...190, 322
Cockman, Benjamin Franklin...286, 319
Cockman, Beretta...188, 315
Cockman, Bertha Edith...318
Cockman, Betty Jane "Janie"...189, 319
Cockman, Betty Jean...338
Cockman, Betty Ruth...346, 363
Cockman, Beulah Evelyn...317
Cockman, Billy Ray...346, 363
Cockman, Blanche...326
Cockman, Bonnie Jane...318
Cockman, Branson...196, 344
Cockman, Brona Gertrude...328

Cockman, Russell...326
Cockman, Ruth Adlaide...189, 191, 320
Cockman, Sallie Frances...317
Cockman, Sara Louise...328
Cockman, Sarah C...190, 322
Cockman, Sarah Emma...189, 191, 317
Cockman, Sarah Lee...94, 188
Cockman, Shirley Ann...345
Cockman, Sindi Ann...94, 188
Cockman, Stewart...340
Cockman, Temperance Levina Erie...195, 335
Cockman, Tessie Arlene...339
Cockman, Thomas Bias Noah Louweed...97, 100, 196
Cockman, Tracy Wilburn...339
Cockman, Ulysses Franklin...187, 312
Cockman, Ulysses Franklin Jr...312
Cockman, Walston Leonidas...190, 321
Cockman, Warren G...321
Cockman, Wilbur Marley...327
Cockman, William Burton Ceclage...97, 100
Cockman, William Curtis...331
Cockman, William E. Sherman...97, 195
Cockman, William Felt...322
Cockman, William Fletcher...281, 332, 372
Cockman, William Graham...313
Cockman, William Jerome...196, 338, 342, 398
Cockman, William Lockie...195, 335
Cockman, William McSwain...94, 187
Cockman, William Ronald "Buddy"...344
Cockman, Wilma Terry...337
Cockman, Winfred Terry...318
Cody, Lucinda C...568
Cogdell, Dona...305
Coggins, Burrell Titus...554
Coker, Irenne L...296
Coker, James Wilson...296
Coker, Maggie M...296
Cole, Catherine...161
Cole, Harold Stewart...355
Cole, Louisa Jane...575
Cole, Nancy Jane...227
Coleman...438
Coleman, Annie Douglas...253
Coleman, Beatrice...438
Coleman, Benjamin Franklin...253
Coleman, Charles W...247
Coleman, Clara B...438
Coleman, Daisy D...438
Coleman, Joshua...567
Coleman, Lester Louise...387
Coleman, Luther Judson...253, 453
Coleman, Luther Judson Jr...453
Coleman, Lydia...253, 453
Coleman, Maggie P...253
Coleman, Ruth F...253, 453
Coleman, William Judson...253
Coleman, Willie May...253, 452
Collins, Beatrice...332
Collins, Elsie Vernell...257, 461
Collins, George Wayne...257, 461
Collins, George Wayne Jr...462
Collins, Linda Sue...257, 462
Collins, Ray Thurman...257
Collins, Ray Thurman Jr...257, 461
Collins, Tyra Lynn...461
Comer...28
Comer, D. Reese...282
Comer, Doris Blanche...282
Comer, Dossie Orlando...282
Comer, James Everette...282
Comer, Mabel...282

Comer, Melvin...282
Comer, Roy S...282
Comer, Treva Estelle...282
Comer, Wayne M...282
Compton, Charles Bernard...326
Compton, Martha Ruth...457
Cook, Doris...453
Cook, Doris Jackson...299
Cook, Nancy...157
Copeland, Edith Elizabeth "Lib"...409
Corder, James Tollie...438
Cornwell, Gurney Smith III...14
Cornwell, Jason Ritter...14
Cornwell, Margaret...14
Costen, Thomas S...576
Costins, Hannah...67
Council, Willie...425
Covas, Isabell...462
Covas, Vincent...462
Covas, Vincent Jr...462
Covington, Anne Liza...213, 384
Coward, Edgar Lee...379
Coward, James Daniel...379
Coward, Jesse Paul...379
Coward, Marshall D...322, 379
Cox, Curtis...266
Cox, Daniel H...574
Cox, Delphina Agnes Della...328
Cox, Hannah Jane "Janie"...161
Cox, Herbert...266
Cox, John Marshall...210
Cox, Joseph Arch...33, 89, 90
Cox, Louise Charity...229
Cox, Mary Ann...90, 187
Cox, Philadelphia/Rodelphia...66, 68
Cox, Rudolph...266
Cox, Sherman...266
Cox, Thelma...266
Cox, Thomas Elwood...328
Cox, Wilma Lou...345
Coyle, Gerald Arnold...463
Coyle, Sheryl Lynn...463
Crabtree, Lillie May...346
Crabtree, Noah Oliver...430
Crabtree, Oliver Glenn...430
Crabtree, Ruby...383
Crabtree, Walter Wesley...507
Craighead, Hershal...87, 185
Craighead, John Herman...87, 185
Craighead, Willie...87, 185
Cramer, Richard Edward...383
Cranford, Chaney Berry...551
Cranford, Jesse B...367
Craven, Burit Doyle...460
Craven, Mark Wallace...461
Crawford, William...582
Creed, Charles...297
Creed, Clyde...297
Creed, Gus...297
Criswell, Linnie May...185, 186
Crittenden, Elizabeth "Lizzie"...187
Croom, Eleanor...574
Cross, Henry Dock...184
Cross, James Michael "Mike"...358
Cross, Nancy Louise...358
Cross, William Alexander Jr...358
Crow, Mary T...158
Crow, Tom...246, 474
Crowe, Abner...301
Crowe, John Harrison...476
Crowell, Docia...551, 552
Crowell, Jemima...538, 540
Crumpton, Dorothy E...287
Crutchfield, Ruth...407

Cummings, Lydia...575
Cummings, Mary E...546
Currie, Sarah Ann...251
Dagenhart, Nell...329
Daley, Dalma...439
Dancy, Emily Josephine...574
Dansby...310
Dansby, Acie Willard...185, 310
Dansby, Arthur Dovard...185, 310
Dansby, Ethel Pauline...185, 310
Dansby, Isom Daniel...185
Dansby, Joanna...310
Dansby, Melanie...310
Dansby, Peggy...185, 310
Dasher...287
Dasher, John L...287
Daurity, Sabra Diane...396
Davis...28, 281
Davis, Agnes Louisa...259
Davis, Alexander...526, 527
Davis, Alsey Cleveland...163, 264, 281
Davis, Alton A...281
Davis, Alton Curtis...507
Davis, Ann Elizabeth...42, 126, 211, 215, 226
Davis, Anna J...527
Davis, Annie Mae...283
Davis, Annie May...387
Davis, Archibald McNeill...163
Davis, Arthur Lee...465
Davis, Asa Lewis...163, 282
Davis, Austin Devotion...507
Davis, Barney Lee...387, 523
Davis, Bennie Elliott...528
Davis, Bernice Jewell...281, 332, 372
Davis, Bertha...528
Davis, Beulah Lucille...387
Davis, Beulah Mae...528
Davis, Blanche...507
Davis, Bobby Lee...387
Davis, Bonnie L...419
Davis, Celia Sue...423
Davis, Charlie H...280
Davis, Clarence Webster...280
Davis, Clarkie...64
Davis, Claude Roosevelt...163, 283
Davis, Cora Helen...163, 282
Davis, Devotion D...494
Davis, Dewey...452
Davis, Dossie...281
Davis, Earl...528
Davis, Edith Pearl...282
Davis, Edna H...507
Davis, Eli...520, 523
Davis, Eli G...523
Davis, Elva C...281
Davis, Emery Lewis...281
Davis, Ethel...528
Davis, Etta Mae...523
Davis, Evelyn...528
Davis, Foster L...281
Davis, Frances...281
Davis, Frank Taft...163
Davis, Gaston Adam...523
Davis, George Baxter...410
Davis, Glennie Esther...163, 282
Davis, Gloria...528
Davis, Grace May...425
Davis, Hardy...71
Davis, Harold Edward...281
Davis, Harry W...336
Davis, Harvey L...336
Davis, Helen Vera...336
Davis, Henry Lathern Lockey...527, 528
Davis, Henry Mitchell...336

Davis, Henry T...526, 527
Davis, Herbert C...336
Davis, Herbert Lee...507
Davis, Howard Curtis...528
Davis, Howard F...280
Davis, Ira L...465
Davis, Ira Spinks...163, 281
Davis, Irvin...507
Davis, James...488, 491
Davis, James H...281, 313, 452
Davis, Jasper M...242
Davis, Jesse Stephen...507
Davis, John Archie...163, 281
Davis, John M...526, 527
Davis, John Wiley...527, 528
Davis, Julias...520
Davis, Lacy...528
Davis, Leana...507
Davis, Lelan Dawson...280
Davis, Lena...507
Davis, Lena Mae...282
Davis, Lennie Melvin...283
Davis, Leon...528
Davis, Lewis Washington...163
Davis, Lillian...507
Davis, Lloyd Odell...528
Davis, Lochart...526, 527
Davis, Lucy Ella...164
Davis, Margaret "Peggy"...104
Davis, Margaret Catherine...475
Davis, Marge...507
Davis, Marion Carl...527
Davis, Martha Jane...528
Davis, Martin D.....164
Davis, Mary...242, 243, 488, 491
Davis, Mary Ann...209, 215, 221, 494, 507
Davis, Mary M...163, 280
Davis, Mary Margaret "Maggie"...526, 527
Davis, Miriam B...281
Davis, Myrtle Nancy...309
Davis, Nancy Francena...163, 281, 527
Davis, Neil Webster...163, 280
Davis, Nellie...507, 528
Davis, Ollie Mae...527, 528
Davis, Rachel E...281
Davis, Ray Lewis...280
Davis, Rosa Lee...87
Davis, Ruth Bernice...163, 282
Davis, Sarah E...520
Davis, Sherman Graham...336
Davis, Sina...30, 71, 72
Davis, Snoten M...163, 282
Davis, Stephen Harrison...526, 527
Davis, Tallie Richard...280
Davis, Thelma A...280
Davis, Wiley Carson "Babe"...523
Davis, William...242
Davis, William Harrison...494, 506
Davs. Mary "Molly"...57
Daws, Bonnie...310
Daws, Charlie Washington...186, 310
Daws, Elvira Kizzie...246, 473
Daws, Isaac Neal "Ike"...186
Daws, Lessie...186, 310
Daws, Tempie...245, 305
Dawson, Lilly Gertrude...321
Dawson, Ruth Mable...229
Day, Stephen Hideo...461
Dean, Carl Forbes...455
Dean, Carolina...166
Dean, Della Love...455
Dean, Fannie Susan...454
Dean, Henry Leonard...455
Dean, Sally Ruth...455

Dean, Stephen Ellis...455
Dean, Stephen Leonard...455
Deaton...15, 28, 529
Deaton, Aaron...522, 525
Deaton, Alma...522, 525
Deaton, Amanda...162
Deaton, Barbara Ann...413
Deaton, Bazel...515
Deaton, Bertha May...230, 411
Deaton, Billy Wayne...412
Deaton, Carol Lavene...412
Deaton, Carson...163
Deaton, Charles Hoyt...230, 413
Deaton, Dale Oral...413
Deaton, Deborah Elizabeth...276
Deaton, Dora...164, 283
Deaton, Doris Gene...412
Deaton, Dossie...164
Deaton, Edna...525
Deaton, Eleanor...163
Deaton, Elizabeth...525
Deaton, Gail Marie...413
Deaton, Geneva Lorene...413
Deaton, George Sanderlin...230
Deaton, Gurney Carlton...230, 412
Deaton, Hattie F...164, 283
Deaton, Ida Florence...230, 411
Deaton, Ira...164
Deaton, Isaac Spinks...515, 521
Deaton, Isham...230, 413
Deaton, James Farrell...412
Deaton, James Thomas...521, 525
Deaton, Janice Lane...413
Deaton, Jeraldean...412
Deaton, Jerry Harold...412
Deaton, Jesse Hilborn...413
Deaton, John Earl...230, 412
Deaton, John M...230
Deaton, Joseph C...515
Deaton, Joseph Franklin...163, 230, 413
Deaton, Lettie Ethel...230, 413
Deaton, Lillie Jane...230, 412
Deaton, Luther...163
Deaton, Lydia...521
Deaton, Margaret...525
Deaton, Marvin...525
Deaton, Mattie Lena...521
Deaton, Maudie Easter...230, 411
Deaton, Mentie...164
Deaton, Meriel C...412
Deaton, Nancy Carol...413
Deaton, Noah Cleveland...522, 525
Deaton, Ollie...163
Deaton, Robert Fulton...413
Deaton, Robert Lee...525
Deaton, Rosa Ellen...413
Deaton, Sarah Bethune...249
Deaton, Sarah Jane...521, 525
Deaton, Tally...163
Deaton, Virgil Pearl "Bird"...230, 413
Deaton, Virginia Colene...413
Deaton, Virlin George...413
Deaton, Wiley Carr...163
Deaton, Willie...163
Deaton, Willie Paul...230, 413
Dedman, Bertha H...508
Dedman, Dorothy Estelle...508
Dedman, Everett Egbert...508
Dedman, Nettie T...508
Dedman, Olivia Mae...508
Dedman, William Clisby...508
Dedman, William S...508
Deen, Annie O...298
Deen, Ardette...297

Deen, Audry...297
Deen, Carrie E...171, 297
Deen, Ebbin O...171, 297
Deen, Floyd Virgil...171, 297
Deen, Harrison Irvin...171
Deen, Hazel...297
Deen, Jasper Arthur...171, 297
Deen, Jasper Arthur Jr...297
Deen, Jesse Randall...171, 297
Deen, Jessie C...297
Deen, Jessie Lee...298
Deen, Jewel...297
Deen, Lena...171
Deen, Leroy...297
Deen, Lessie...171
Deen, Lucille...297
Deen, Marion...171, 297
Deen, Marion Lee...297
Deen, Maxina...297
Deen, Mollie E...171
Deen, Otha...297
Deen, Randall E...297
Deen, Robert L...297
Deen, Robert Lee...171
Dees, Charles Gentry...256
Dees, Charles Gentry Jr...256
Dees, Edith Frances...256, 460
Dees, Edna Maxine...256, 460
Dees, Glenn...256
Dees, Hilda Gibsie...256
Dees, Ida Jean...256
Dees, Leslie...460
Dees, Martha Carleen...256
Dees, Robert Grant...256, 460
Dees, Robert Grant Jr...460
Deese, Andrew...524
Deese, Lizzie...524
Delaney, Florence...47
DeLoach, Bobby...460
Demore, Alan Wayne...462
Demore, Charles William...462
Demore, Charles Wilson...462
Demore, David Alan...462
Demore, Michael Robert...462
Demore, Sallie Ann...462
Dennis, Nellie...301
Denton, Floyd Matthew...460
Denton, Sandra Ellen...460
Dewey, Henry B...402
Dewey, Henry C...402
Dickens, Stella...277
Dickson, Kathleen...427
Diggs, Sandra Ferrell...434
Dillard, Robert L...522
Dixon, David...156
Dixon, Emma Ellen...156, 259
Dixon, John T...156
Dixon, Joseph...156
Dixon, Lucy J...156
Dixon, Martha Ann...156
Dixon, Mary...156
Dixon, Robert Newton...156
Dixon, Robert Newton Jr...156, 259
Dixon, Rosina S...156
Dixon, Silas F...156
Dodson...115
Donaghe, Katie Lou...314
Doss, Evie...302
Doss, Vadna...174
Dossett, Alma...447
Dowd, Charles Morrison...448
Dowd, Elizabeth Ann...448
Dowd, Frances Grace...448
Dowd, Harold Springs...448

Dowd, Henry Grossett...448
Dowd, Herbet Bryant...448
Dowd, James Russell...448
Dowd, Maude Hughes...448
Dowd, Robert Peter...447, 448
Dowd, Robert Peter Jr...448
Dowd, William...24
Dowdy, Gladys...348
Dowdy, John Lee...324
Dowdy, Maudie Mae...325
Downing, Mollie...437
Driskill, Elizabeth Minerva "Betty"...559
Duffield, Brenda Rae...427
Duffield, Chester L. Jr...427
Duffield, Chester Lawrence...427
Duffield, Delores...427
Duffield, Juanito Ruth...427
Duguay, Robert Melvin...333, 415
Dunagan, William Monroe...541
Duncan, Belle...543
Duncan, William N...576
Dunlap, Daniel A...284
Dunlap, Daniel C...284
Dunlap, Hannah Jane...69
Dunlap, Lynnie Kate...284
Dunlap, Mary Jane...284, 344
Dunlap, Nannie Lou...284
Dunlap, Oliver Max...284
Dunlap, William Alfred...284
Dunn...23, 464
Dunn, Ada L...163, 280
Dunn, Alexander J...464
Dunn, Alsey...163
Dunn, Bartholomew...163
Dunn, Bennie Garrett...390
Dunn, Daisy E...162
Dunn, Della...525
Dunn, Elvira...525
Dunn, Fannie H...163
Dunn, John Lindon...162, 276
Dunn, Lona F...282
Dunn, Martha May...163, 280
Dunn, Raleigh...525
Dunn, Wesley...162
Dunn, Wesley Thaddeus...162
Dunn, William W...163
Dunn, William Wright...163
Dupree, Kenneth Earl...459
Dupuis, Lenora Ann...333, 415
Durham, Minnie D...297
Dyer, Marshall...426
Dyer, William Riley...426
Easler, Melissa Elizabeth...315
East, Bessie Elizabeth...328
Edge, John B...267
Edge, Melissa A...577
Edge, Millie Blue...267
Edginora, Mahaley...512
Edwards, Bernie Everette...419
Edwards, Edith...453
Edwards, Frances Emily...170
Edwards, Helen...419
Edwards, J.C...555
Edwards, Jackie Francis...419
Edwards, Margaret A...419
Edwards, Mattie May...556
Edwards, Robert Lee...419
Edwards, Samuel Jordan...419
Edwards, Samuel Jordan Jr...419
Edwards, Sarah Martha...542
Edwards, Tabitha...543
Elkins, Rachel Lugenia...357
Ellice, Paley...204
Elliot, Azalee Frances "Dee"...179, 183, 473

Elliott, John Norwood...455
Ellis, Joette...426
Elmer, Robert Watson...383
Elmore...280
Elmore, Richard Turner...280
English, Maggie...484
Erice, Sam B...296
Ervin, Jennie...252
Evans, Beverly Ann...434
Evans, Everette Eugene...458
Ewing, Charles Dolphus...413
Ewing, Donald Eugene...413
Farlow, Alberta...288
Farlow, Blanche...288
Farlow, Colvin Mc...166
Farlow, Dee...288
Farlow, Dee Ette...288
Farlow, John F...288
Farlow, Maggie V...166
Farlow, Pearlie...288
Farlow, Robert Lee...166
Farlow, Thomas Kenyon...166, 288
Farlow, William Penn...166, 288
Farrell, Arthur R...434
Farrell, Audie...375
Farrell, Bobby Eugene...434
Farrell, Herman M...434
Farrell, Juanita...434
Faucette, Isabell...267
Faucette, Jesse E...267
Faucette, Leon...267
Faucette, Lonza Alexander...267
Feezor, Adeline...540
Feezor, Elizabeth...540
Feezor, Flora...555
Feezor, Henry Burnette...555
Feezor, Jane...540
Feezor, John...541
Feezor, L. C...541
Feezor, M...540
Feezor, Mariah Jane...554
Feezor, Matilda...540
Feezor, William...541
Feezor, William H...540
Ferree, David...203
Ferree, Raymond Taylor...203
Ferree, Ruth...203
Ferrell, Elizabeth...546
Ferrell, Ora Ethel...454
Fetters, Grace...291
Fields, Bertha Ann...358
Fields, George W...225
Fields, Nancy Catherine...316
Fields, Sarah L...471
Finnison, Charity Eva...329
Flinchum, Ida Mae...272, 386
Flippo, Eliza Ann...545
Flippo, Robert E...546
Floyd, Marie...203
Floyd, Presley Parker...258, 333
Fluhrer, Judy Darline...455
Fogleman, Geneva...396
Forbis, Donald Keith...462
Forbis, Donald Keith Jr...462
Forbis, Lori Denise...462
Ford, Gabriella Ella...202
Ford, Helen...452
Ford, Jewell William...306
Ford, Luther Thomas...202
Ford, Robert Lee Bud...306
Fort, Lattie Boyd...352
Fort, Mollie...352, 353
Fort, Sarah...78
Foshee, John...299

Foster, Mary Ann...567
Foster, Rachel...408
Foster, Richard...435
Foster, Swannie Gean...435
Fowler, James...459
Fox, Kurt Franz...456
Fox, Susannah...231
Franklin, Bessie Marie...283
Frary, Judith Sandra...427
Frazier, Bera Mary...388
Freeman, Amy...167
Freeman, Archie L. E...554
Freeman, Geraldine...394
Freeman, Lydia...222, 231
Freeman, Mary Ann...117
Fritz, William Abel...279
Fry...563
Fry, Barsheba...573
Fry, Elizabeth Ann "Eliza Ann"...28, 68, 69
Fry, Lochart...572
Fry, Patience...576
Fry, Salina...28, 66, 67
Fry, Thomas B. "Black Tom"...66, 68
Frye, Brenda Sue...420
Frye, Dempsey Edward...420
Frye, Ella May Juline...250
Frye, Fred Worth...316
Frye, Gary Nelson "Pete"...444
Frye, John M...250
Frye, Loretta Kay...420
Frye, Louis Fitzgerald "Tommy"...444
Frye, Samuel...444
Frye, Samuel Felton...444
Fuller, Bessie...303
Fuquay, Sallie...507
Furr...57
Furr, Charles...34, 35
Furr, Emaline...150
Furr, Malvina...5, 35, 44, 47
Furr, Mary Frances "Fannie"...523
Furr, Nancy...5, 33, 34, 35, 41
Gadfield, Judy Carolyn...458
Gaitley, Isaac...202
Gaitley, Mollie Lee...199, 202
Galbreath, Philip Herman...457, 509
Garcia, Yolanda Cala...452
Garner...28, 34, 362
Garner, Alexander...208, 334, 373
Garner, Alice...362
Garner, Anna Margaret...107, 208
Garner, Annie May...215, 386
Garner, Annie Ruth...391
Garner, Archie...364
Garner, Archie Arthur...431
Garner, Arthur...221, 391
Garner, Arthur Hugh...340, 344, 386
Garner, Arthur Leon...392
Garner, Ashley Lee...208, 334, 373
Garner, Barbara Ann...392
Garner, Bertha...362
Garner, Beverly Carol...463
Garner, Billy Ray...366
Garner, Bobby Josh...365
Garner, Bonnie Jean...392
Garner, Boyd Len...424, 425
Garner, Burney...411
Garner, Carthell D...373
Garner, Cary Alice...258
Garner, Cecil Ruth...216, 345, 386
Garner, Charles B...361
Garner, Charles Frank...204, 359
Garner, Charles L...403
Garner, Charles Lee...359
Garner, Charlie Lester...391

Additional Information can be found at www.MooreCountyWallaces.com

Harper, Minnie Kathalene...288
Harper, Rena...287
Harper, Rosa...288
Harper, Sabina...166, 287
Harper, William Elmer...166, 288
Harper, William Ernest...288
Harrell, Mary Magdalene...308
Harris...282
Harris, Arthur Thomas...448, 449
Harris, Arthur Thomas Jr...449
Harris, William Sydney...282
Harrison...174, 304
Harrison, Annie Mae...303
Harrison, Cleveland...174, 303
Harrison, Essie...174
Harrison, Glenn Gae...461
Harrison, Julia...174, 304
Harrison, Lillie...174
Harrison, Robert...174
Harrison, Ruth...303
Hart...310
Hart, Abbie May...179, 184
Hart, Acie Linn...87, 88, 185
Hart, Ambrose R...33, 78, 79
Hart, Annie May...87, 88, 185
Hart, Arie L...88, 186
Hart, Balaam Moses...87
Hart, Balaam S...86
Hart, Bennie F...88, 185
Hart, Bertie May...87
Hart, Chester...184
Hart, Edna...87, 88, 186
Hart, Edna Daisy...308
Hart, Elizabeth S...311
Hart, Ernest...87, 185
Hart, Ethel Sophronia...87, 88, 186
Hart, Eugenia Novel...87, 88, 185
Hart, Eunice...184
Hart, Gladys Lucille...87
Hart, Grady...87
Hart, Harvey Lafayette...179, 184, 309
Hart, Hattie Lee...87, 88, 185
Hart, James Cecil...87
Hart, James Columbus...33, 86, 87, 88
Hart, James Dorwin...309
Hart, James M...249
Hart, James Marion...175, 304
Hart, John Leonard...79, 175
Hart, Joseph C...246
Hart, Lala Lucille...246, 442
Hart, Leona B...184
Hart, Lula Mae...187
Hart, Luther Columbus...87, 88, 185
Hart, Luther Columbus Jr...87, 185, 310
Hart, Margaret M...51, 146
Hart, Martha Emmaline...249, 472
Hart, Mary...88, 185
Hart, Ruth...304
Hart, Sarah Elizabeth...50, 88, 144
Hart, Sidney Horace...179, 184
Hart, Thomas Benjamin...179, 184, 309
Hart, William D...78
Hart, William T...87, 88, 185, 309
Hartsell, Ruby Ann...394
Hartshorne, H...344
Harvey, Flora Lynn...445
Harvey, Keith...445
Harvey, Linda Kay...445
Harvey, Teresa Ann...445
Harward, Willie Lexter...457, 509
Hasty, Sarah Jane...359
Hasty, Walter S...338
Hatcher, Anna Maud...315
Hathcock, Nancy Jane...520

Hawks, Dora Mae...347
Hawks, Rosa Emma...347
Hayes, Dora Belle...213, 380
Haywood, Alma Suda...450
Helms, Sylvia Jean...332
Henderson, Frances...458
Henderson, Franklin...169
Henderson, Mary J...169
Henrietta...511
Henry, Mamie Jessie...184, 309
Henry, William Mattison...184
Henson, Betty Jo...394
Henson, Juanita...394
Henson, Sallie Sophia...411
Henson, Virginia Margaret...394
Henson, Walter K...394
Hester, Bonnie Lou...292
Hester, James Henry...292
Hicks, Emma Harriet...157
Hicks, Isaac Madison...157
Hicks, Julia Ann...175
Hicks, M. Eliza...252
Hicks, Pauline...420
Hicks, Sarah Frances...305
Hill, Betty J...476
Hill, Frances "Fanny"...30, 73, 74
Hill, LaVina Estelle...404
Hill, Ophelia...299
Hill, Valentine C...542
Hill, William...73
Hilliard, Mary Caroline...202
Hilton, Mary Louise...571
Hilton, Sarah Jane...571
Hines, George Walter...458
Hines, James...11
Hines, Mary...10, 11, 12, 18
Hinshaw, J.T...203
Hinshaw, Laura A...201, 203
Hinshaw, Lawrence Lowe...402
Hinshaw, Leon Franklin...402
Hinson, Albert Bruce...403
Hinson, Annie Mae...306
Hinson, John Riley Wynn...306
Hinson, Murray Wilton...510
Hinson, Ricky Joe...403
Hockaday, Lester H...458
Hockney, William...435
Hogan, Annie Lydia...436
Hogan, Buster Ralph...436
Hogan, Chesley W...436
Hogan, Eleanor Francis...436
Hogan, Elizabeth...288
Hogan, Joe...436
Hogan, Johnnie Doyd...436
Hogan, Mary Gladys...436
Holbrook, Harold Dewayne...441
Holbrook, Hubert Doyle...441
Holbrook, Marvana Dinel...441
Holbrook, Marvin...441
Holder, Billy E...346
Holder, Daniel...346
Holder, Patsy Ruth...346
Holland, Edmond...576
Holland, Janice...284
Holland, Vinoka Audrey...284
Hollie, Roxie A...171
Holloway, G. W...547
Holloway, George...547
Holloway, Margaret...547
Holmes...311
Holmes, Paul Hulon...311, 442
Holmes, Sidney Thomas...442
Holsapple, Mary Bland...556
Holton, Elizabeth...335

Hooker, Alfred N...210, 376
Hooker, Benjamin F...210, 376
Hooker, Bobby Lee...376
Hooker, Elias Spinks...210, 376
Hooker, Elva Grace...376
Hooker, Eva Jane...376
Hooker, John M...210
Hooker, Joyce Ann...376
Hooker, Oscar Lee...210, 376
Hooker, Rosanna M...210, 227, 376
Hooker, Sarah...210
Hooker, William Herbert...376
Hope, Sam...352
Hopper, Eliza Agnes...300
Hopper, James Howard...442, 443
Hopper, Sam P...442
Horn, Elmer...522
Horn, Erbie...522
Horn, John...253
Horn, Kelsey Marshal...522
Horn, Lela...522
Horn, Linnie Rebecca...522
Horn, Wylie...522
Horne, Della Adelaide...253
Horner...15, 34, 329, 529
Horner, Ada...326
Horner, Alvania...328
Horner, Archie Daniel...226, 378, 406
Horner, Bertha Lee...323
Horner, Bertie...324, 330
Horner, Bessie Brown...324
Horner, Bessie Louise...328
Horner, Beulah...226, 405
Horner, Billie...405
Horner, Blanche...323
Horner, Bonnie Mae...226, 406
Horner, Carl...226
Horner, Carson Lee...226, 405
Horner, Chestley Paisley...194, 329, 330
Horner, Chestley Thomas...194
Horner, Claude Clinton...323
Horner, Cora Elizabeth...323
Horner, Daniel Curtis...323
Horner, Daniel Hopkins...190, 323
Horner, Dola Fonnie...226, 406
Horner, Donald G...405
Horner, Dorothy Belle...329
Horner, Doxy...134
Horner, Edith Lavannah...323
Horner, Elizabeth...52
Horner, Elizabeth Jane...498
Horner, Emma Worthy...324, 330
Horner, Ernest...326
Horner, Estell May...326
Horner, Ethel Delena...323
Horner, Etta L...323
Horner, Fairly Arthur...194, 329, 330
Horner, Fentress T...323
Horner, Florence Jeanette...328
Horner, Floyd E...378, 406
Horner, Fonnie N...323
Horner, G. C...324
Horner, Gayle Elizabeth...328
Horner, George Carson...323
Horner, George R...4
Horner, George W...41
Horner, George Washington...120, 189, 190, 323
Horner, Hattie Pauline...226, 405
Horner, Helen Mae...329
Horner, Hurley Harrison...194, 329, 330
Horner, Ida Mae...323
Horner, James Fulton...329
Horner, James Robert...190, 325

Additional Information can be found at www.MooreCountyWallaces.com

McDaniel, Sally Velena...454
McDaniel, Vergie Mae...513
McDaniel, Willie Eugene...339
McDonald, Anna Jane...52, 148
McDonald, Christian...225
McDonald, Emma...305
McDonald, James William...1484
McFarland, Teddy James...299
McGee, Celia Ann...240, 241
McGee, Dollie Ann...241
McGee, Larry...438
McGee, Malachi...438
McGee, Roger...438
McIntosh, Allen L. Jr...448
McIntosh, Allen Lawhon...448
McIntosh, Christian...61
McIntosh, Elizabeth Jane...208
McIntosh, Martha...576
McIntosh, Ruth Ann...576
McIntosh, Samuel J...208
McIntosh, Virginia Lucille...426
McIver, Addie Josephine...405
McIver, Lizzie...344
McIver, Margaret...352
McKenzie, Amanda Jane...429
McKenzie, Angus Alexander "Bud"...367
McKenzie, Bertie Mae...429
McKenzie, Betty Florence...367
McKenzie, Daniel Edward...429
McKenzie, Daniel Justin...316
McKenzie, Dora Lee...429
McKenzie, Gertrude...367
McKenzie, Ida Mae...367
McKenzie, James Leslie...429
McKenzie, John Arthur...429
McKenzie, John Jacob Astor...367
McKenzie, Kathrine...367
McKenzie, Lavada Vada...367
McKenzie, Lula Dell...429
McKenzie, Malcolm Comer...367
McKenzie, Margaret Belle...429
McKenzie, Margaret E. "Maggie"...507
McKenzie, Marjorie Euna...367
McKenzie, Mary Ann...572
McKenzie, Robert Clyde "Bud"...367
McKenzie, William Martin "Bill"...428, 429
McKenzie, Zudora...367
McKinney, John Albert...255
McKinney, Lula Ellen...255
McLean, Hattie Belle...226, 333
McLean, Janie...405
McLeod, Christian...277
McLeod, Claude...223, 224
McLeod, Daniel Atlas...277
McLeod, Edgar...277
McLeod, Eliza Ellen...275
McLeod, Eliza Jane...164
McLeod, Evander Kelly...223
McLeod, Frank...277
McLeod, Grace...277
McLeod, James Samuel...223, 402
McLeod, James Wesley...223
McLeod, Jesse Lewis...223, 402
McLeod, John Wilbert...352
McLeod, Maggie Lee...223, 402
McLeod, Mamie...223, 402
McLeod, Mary...162, 163
McLeod, Mary Bell...402
McLeod, Maude Daisy...223, 224
McLeod, Robert...277
McLeod, Thelma Jean...403
McLeod, Walter...277
McLeod, William C....223
McMillan Alvaneal...339

McMillan, Alice Rebecca...463
McMillan, Maggie...278
McMillan, Onnie...278
McMurtey, Cynthia Virginia...241
McNeill, Adolphus Calhoun...392
McNeill, Aggie Elizabeth...393
McNeill, Alexander...202, 230
McNeill, Althea Doreen...421
McNeill, Annie Mozelle...232, 421
McNeill, Archibald...230
McNeill, Archibald Daniel "Archie"...230, 410
McNeill, Beulah Belle...231, 383
McNeill, Catherine...161
McNeill, Charlie C...202, 355
McNeill, Clarence...232, 421
McNeill, Coy Haywood...392
McNeill, Coy Holt...393
McNeill, Dora E...232, 420
McNeill, Dorothy Mae...232, 421
McNeill, Effie R...230, 410, 429, 430
McNeill, Elias Hector...311
McNeill, Ethel...202, 354, 355
McNeill, Garry Richard...421
McNeill, Garvin...232
McNeill, George Alexander...393
McNeill, H....34
McNeill, Hattie Jane...230, 410
McNeill, Howard Taft...393
McNeill, Hugh T...230, 411
McNeill, Janet Marie...421
McNeill, Jerome Carson...311
McNeill, Jewelene Louise...421
McNeill, John Robert...281, 311
McNeill, Julia Ann...312, 361
McNeill, Kathleen Faye...411
McNeill, Leland William...393
McNeill, Lemeul Alexander...198, 202
McNeill, Lillie Isobel...311
McNeill, Mamie L...393
McNeill, Mamie Lee...289
McNeill, Marjorie...232, 420
McNeill, Mary Elizabeth...312
McNeill, Mary Murlene...421
McNeill, Maxine Annie...232
McNeill, Mazie Lorene...232
McNeill, Nancy Jacqueline...421
McNeill, Nettie F...230, 411
McNeill, Peter Paul...232, 421
McNeill, Peter Paul Jr...421
McNeill, R. Margaret...221
McNeill, Rellie...232
McNeill, Richard Thomas...232, 421
McNeill, Roberta Mae...393
McNeill, Rona...317
McNeill, Roy Thomas...232
McNeill, Sharon...421
McNeill, Virgil L...230, 411
McNeill, William C....231
McNeill, William Thomas...231
McPeake, Elton Paige...441
McPeake, George Milam...441
McPeake, Joe Locie...441, 475
McPeake, Mary Opal...441
McQuargin, Grover C...233
McQuay, Betty Louise...446
McQueen, Nancy S...151
Meacham, Ethel Gertrude...335
Meacham, John Wesley...335
Meacham, Lillian Frances...335
Meadors, Lavycie...379
Medcalf, John William...243
Medcalf, Viola Marie...243, 439
Medlin, Avena Jane...230, 231

Melton...23, 34
Melton, Candace Ellen...5, 41, 42, 114, 130, 132, 526
Melton, Catherine...64, 569
Melton, Elizabeth...5, 41, 100, 102, 104
Melton, James...41, 100, 112, 117, 130, 195
Melton, Jennet/Josiah...239, 577
Melton, Lovedy Adaline...195
Melton, Lucinda...195
Melton, Mary Ruth...277
Melton, Nancy...23, 61, 63
Melton, Nancy Jane...195
Melton, Priscilla...5, 41, 112, 113, 114, 117
Melton, Robert...61
Melton, Temperance Levina...5, 41, 117, 120
Melton, William...248, 472
Melton, Willie Kitchen...283
Meltzner, Brian Douglas...461
Melvin, Mamie Vick...268
Mercer, Lena...226
Messer, Henry...476
Messer, Lulu Olliebell...476
Michaels, Jesse...336
Miller, Dolly Marlene...455
Miller, Dossie W...280
Miller, Lucy A...280
Miller, Martha E...280
Miller, Mary Lucille...280
Miller, Nancy E...280
Miller, Nancy Irene...280
Miller, Oscar L....280
Mitchell, Anne L...314
Mitchell, Emma...130, 132
Mitchell, William T...314
Moffitt, Julia Ann...160
Moffitt, William...187
Monroe, Manly K...332, 372
Monroe, Nellie Grey...394
Monroe, Virginia Brown...394
Monroe, Walter Wilson...394
Montgomery, Nita...291
Moody, James Harvey...344
Moore...113, 115
Moore, Arthur Carson...355
Moore, Betty...344
Moore, Clara Agnes...355
Moore, Daniel H...227
Moore, Dewey Wilson...357
Moore, Donald Wallace...357
Moore, E. Clayton...355
Moore, Elizabeth E....254
Moore, James Edward...408
Moore, Josie Ora...227, 408
Moore, Judy...357
Moore, Lillie...364
Moore, Martha Josephine...472
Moore, Mary Magdalene...424
Moore, Meta...435
Moore, Ray...357
Moore, Velma Adelle...313, 452
Moore, Virginia...326
Moore, William M...569
Moorefield, James Eli...375
Moorhead, Clarence E...438
Moorhead, Napoleon G...438
Mooring, Evelyn...290
Morgan...113, 403
Morgan, Addie Lee...466
Morgan, Alexander...403, 413
Morgan, Alvin Clemons...403, 414
Morgan, Ann "Spicy"...239
Morgan, Arthur Clemons "Offie"...223, 403, 413
Morgan, Asa...521

Northcutt, Lucy A...559
Norton, Andrew Jackson...509
Norton, Anna C...486
Norton, Anna Elizabeth...505, 506
Norton, Anna Jane...481, 485
Norton, Annie Ethel...486
Norton, Bart...481
Norton, Belton John...486
Norton, Daniel...480
Norton, Daniel Mae...481, 485
Norton, Dora Lee...486
Norton, Emma Daisy...481, 485, 486
Norton, Foster Shaw...486
Norton, Godfrey...481
Norton, Helen...485
Norton, James...481, 486
Norton, Janie Lee...486
Norton, Jesse Benjamin...486
Norton, John...481
Norton, Judy Ann...486
Norton, Marcus Edward...485
Norton, Margaret Ann...481, 482
Norton, Martha Alma...485
Norton, Mary...481, 485
Norton, Mary Catherine...485
Norton, Mary Cattie...486
Norton, Mary L...514
Norton, Neil Sr...509
Norton, Nora Elizabeth...485
Norton, Rose B...486
Norton, Sarah Liza...481, 485
Norton, Seymore M...486
Norton, Simeon...481
Norton, Susie May...486
Norton, W. Willie...481, 486
Norton, Wade Hampton...486
Norton, Walter...486
Norton, William...481
Novak, Douglas Lynn...461
Nunn, Billy Ray...412
Nunn, Cecil Warren...412
Nunn, Frances Louise...412
Nunn, George Edward...412
Nunn, John Ed...411
Nunn, John Frank...411
Nunn, Marilyn...412
Nunnery, Annie Ruth...435
Nunnery, Daniel Bryant...435
Nunnery, Jesse Clarkston...435
Nunnery, John Clarkston...435
Nunnery, Mary Belle...435
Nunnery, Mattie P...435
Nunnery, Ollie Mae...435
Oaks, W. T...309
O'Callahan, Leo V...444
Oldham...356, 424
Oldham, Tammy...424
Oldham, Wilbur Lindsay...356
Oliver, Margaret Leo...250
Oliver, Thurman Curtis "T.C"...409
O'Neal, Sarah...300
Orr, Janice Marie...440
Osborne, Rebecca...71
Owens, Esther...301
Owens, Mishie...290
Ownbey, Minnie Pearl...424
Pace, Annie...265
Pace, Catherine...265
Pace, Frank Jr...265
Pace, George Frank...265
Pace, Gertrude...265
Pace, Ruby...265
Page, Euna Belle...362
Page, James Gilbert...361

Page, James Joseph...362
Page, Leonard M...362
Park, M. Ellen...557
Parker...115
Parker, Addie Ellen...465
Parker, Anthony Elwood...401
Parker, Emma...171
Parker, Florence Ellen...464
Parker, Henrietta Georgia...244
Parker, Lillian...256
Parks, D. Houston...265
Parks, Treva Evangeline...336
Parrish, John F...275
Parrish, Maggie E...276
Parrish, Pearl...347
Parrish, Rhoda...79, 468
Parrish, William N...275
Parsons, Jane...259
Paschal...285
Paschal, Albert Everette...285
Paschal, Archie Lane...165, 286
Paschal, Arthur Garner...165, 287
Paschal, Baxter Worth...165, 286
Paschal, Donald Ira...165, 287
Paschal, Ernest Hurley...165, 287
Paschal, George Luther...165, 180
Paschal, Henry Phillips...165, 287
Paschal, Josephine...165, 286
Paschal, Julian Carr...165, 286
Paschal, Julian Carr Jr...286
Paschal, Lawrence Hughes...165, 287
Paschal, Luther George...165, 287
Paschal, Mollie Cora...165, 286
Paschal, Nancy...286
Paschal, Nannie Florence...165
Paschal, Virginia Oppie...165, 286
Paschal, Esperan...165
Patterson, Catherine...100, 575
Patterson, Irene...321
Patterson, Nancy...575
Payne, Myrtle Evelyn...294
Payne, Rome J...294
Payne, Sarah...168
Peele, Eva...483
Peele, Lessie...485
Peele, Mary Ann...482, 483
Peele, Rebecca Jane...484
Peele, Samuel...484, 485
Peele, William Franklin...485
Pendley, Bertis Belle...262
Pendley, James L...262
Pennington, Anne...352
Pennington, Bayron Harold...439
Pennington, H. Dale...439
Person, Lawton...457
Petty, Emma...204
Peurifoy, Woodrow Wilson...385
Phillips, Berry...165
Phillips, Bonnie Carolyn...386
Phillips, Bud...327
Phillips, Charles Wesley...165
Phillips, Etta Lee...326
Phillips, Eva Mae...421
Phillips, Fleeta Streete...453
Phillips, Hayes Downing...265
Phillips, Ira Glenn...265
Phillips, Jeremiah M...577
Phillips, Martha "Patsy"...159
Phillips, Martha Loucinda "Patsy"...388
Phillips, Mary Dickerson...197, 574
Phillips, Mary Elizabeth "Betty"...159
Phillips, Mary Elvia...273
Phillips, Pearl...200, 203
Phillips, Ruby Kathleen...165, 286

Phillips, Thelma J...452
Phillips, Thomas...203
Phillips, Willie Glenn...448
Phipps, Lowell Dean...428
Pigford, Mary Catherine...170
Pigford, Wright...170
Pinion, Adam Jackson...252
Pinion, Dorothy...252
Pinion, Dossie Franklin...252
Pinion, Elizabeth J...252
Pinion, James C...252
Pinion, John S...252
Pinion, Lou Ella...252, 451
Pinion, Maggie J...252
Pinion, Mary Elizabeth...252, 451
Pinion, Mittie Beulah...252
Pinion, Theodore...252
Pinner, Albert Buford...308
Pinner, Frederick Albert...308
Pinner, Russell James...308
Pittman, Pharaby...315
Plummer, Tishie Eugenia...288
Polk, Hollis...451
Pollock, Annie Bill...307
Pollock, Delta Mae...186, 311, 442
Pollock, Dorothy Victoria...305
Pollock, Edmond R...307, 473
Pollock, George...307
Pollock, George Washington...186
Pollock, James...186
Pollock, Ludell...307
Pollock, Willie...307
Pool, Andrew Ray...309
Poole, Annie Mae...411, 416
Poole, Clinard Harrison...331, 531
Poole, Douglas Henry...453
Pope, Edith May...391
Pope, Elvin Claude...391
Pope, Esther Lee...391
Pope, Glenn L...391
Pope, John Thomas Sr...299
Pope, Mary Juitte...391
Pope, Melvin...346
Pope, Melvin Markus...391
Pope, Ralph Baker...391
Pope, Raymond...391
Pope, Roy Laster...391
Porter, Nora Elizabeth...351
Porter, Walter Eli...351
Porter, Walter Eli Jr...351
Pounds, Martha...170
Powell, Beverly Ann...352
Powell, Tommie...130, 132
Powers...456
Powers, Curtis Ernest...327
Powers, J. Wiley...376
Powers, James Thomas...326, 327
Powers, Lillie Florence...327
Powers, Martha Elizabeth...176
Powers, Mary Anne...456
Powers, Nancy...176
Powers, Wanda Laverne...346
Prewitt, Beverly Dawn...424
Prewitt, Lonnie Dale...424
Prewitt, Scott Dale...424
Price, Bobby Joe...454
Price, James...427
Pridemore...310
Pridemore, Glenn...309
Pridgen, Glenda...460
Pridgen, Susan Angela...460
Pridgen, William David...460
Pridgen, William David Jr...460
Priest, Daniel Patrick...374

Priest, Flora Ann...374
Priest, Mary Eliza...374
Priest, Owen Patrick...374
Priest, Ruth Mae...374
Priest, William Owen...374
Proctor, Lottie...501, 503
Pulley, Madge...329
Pully, Gertrude...255, 459
Purvis...115
Purvis, Arthur Linton...273
Purvis, Cornelius Wiley...272, 386
Purvis, Eva Mae...272
Purvis, Flossie Adelaide...270
Purvis, Franklin...272
Purvis, Graham Harrison...386
Purvis, James Wiley...386
Purvis, Lacy Alston...386
Purvis, Lester...272
Purvis, Locie E...327
Purvis, Maude...318
Purvis, Nannie Irene...287
Purvis, Norman Green...386
Purvis, Sallie Myrtle...331, 531
Purvis, Virginia Dare...272
Pusser, Joe Lee...394
Ragsdale, Jesse...320
Raines, Annie Pearl...278
Ramsey, Louisa Carolina...86
Ratcliffe, James E...540
Ray, Catherine...148
Ray, Margaret Caroline...571
Rector, Alexander...175
Reed, Aldera Maine...441
Reed, Carmen Elaine...440
Reed, Cora Irene...130, 133
Reed, Edee...540
Reed, Erwin Winfred...309
Reed, Evelyn...309
Reed, Freddy Lowell...441
Reed, Robert F...508
Reed, Rowe Adrian...441
Reed, Rowe Burton...440
Reed, Rowena Kay...441
Reed, Roy Lynn...441
Reed, Samuel Kert...440
Reed, William Alonzo "Lonnie"...309
Reeder, Thurston Hoover...357
Reeder, Thurston Hoover Jr...357
Reeves, Absalom...556
Reeves, Izora...556
Reeves, Robert Leonard...556
Reeves, William...556
Regan, Luther...255
Register, Carrie...574
Reid, Eliza Ann...542
Reid, Esdia...336
Reid, Ethel...351
Reid, Isham...542
Reid, Joel H...542
Reid, John Kendrick...542
Reid, Joseph...542
Reid, Joyce Emeline...542, 557
Reid, Mabel Pearl...262
Reid, Mary Polly...542
Reid, Thomas...542
Reid, William Aron...555
Renfrew, Lillian Frances...336, 368
Revell, Margaret Victoria...202
Reynolds, Ervin T...274
Reynolds, Ethalene...274
Reynolds, Geneva...274
Reynolds, James...274
Reynolds, Lacy Catherine...274
Reynolds, Lucy Jane...274

Reynolds, Maggie Loretta...261
Reynolds, Martha Jane...164
Reynolds, Nannie Ada...391, 392
Reynolds, Neulan Bryant...274
Reynolds, Rufus Bryant...274
Reynolds, Rufus W...274
Reynolds, Savannah A...274
Rhodes, Elizabeth...311
Rich, Nancy Marian...231
Richardson, Alfred D...149
Richardson, Charles Jay...447
Richardson, Charles R...149
Richardson, Deborah...257
Richardson, Elizabeth H...564
Richardson, Ernest W...251
Richardson, Estella...251
Richardson, Ethel...250
Richardson, Eva B...251
Richardson, Fred Randolph...430
Richardson, Grier...430
Richardson, H. A...430
Richardson, Helen Mae...430
Richardson, Isaac D...241
Richardson, James Judson...430
Richardson, Jane...577
Richardson, John A...149
Richardson, John F...524
Richardson, Joseph Judson...572
Richardson, Maloney...223
Richardson, Margaret R...149
Richardson, Mary...41, 90, 94, 97, 149
Richardson, Matty J...149
Richardson, Max...430
Richardson, Noah Bazzel...149, 250
Richardson, Noah J...250, 447
Richardson, Odessa C...251
Richardson, Olan Curtis...250, 446
Richardson, Olan Curtis Jr...447
Richardson, Ollie Leola...241, 437
Richardson, Oscar A...250
Richardson, Pearl...374
Richardson, Samuel Jasper...430
Richardson, Samuel Jasper Jr...430
Richardson, Sarah Elizabeth "Sally"...563,
565
Richardson, Stephen O...149, 250
Richardson, Tommy F...149
Richardson, William A...149, 250
Richardson, William Zeno...53, 149
Richardson, Zeno Ellis...251
Richardson, Zeno Worth...149
Rickman, Blan...237
Rickman, Emma...237, 365
Riddle, Addie Camilla...159, 265
Riddle, Alma Estelle Clementine...159, 265
Riddle, Annie Jane...159, 265
Riddle, Benjamin Harrison...227, 408
Riddle, Frances J...262
Riddle, John W...156, 157, 159, 205
Riddle, Joseph S...227
Riddle, Laura A...344
Riddle, Laura Brantley...159, 262
Riddle, Lydia Ann...205
Riddle, Mamie...227, 408
Riddle, Margaret Mae...159, 265
Riddle, Martha Jane...157
Riddle, Mary Elizabeth...156
Riddle, Mary Louise...159, 265
Riddle, Maude Alice...159, 265
Riddle, Nancy Jane...195
Riddle, Riley Roderick...159
Riddle, Sarah Emma...159, 265
Riddle, Thomas Lee...159, 262
Riddle, Wade Hampton...408

Riddle, Wiley...195
Ridenhower, Salina...558
Riley, Alexander Lee...555
Riley, Alice M...556
Riley, Amanda...555, 556
Riley, B. Solomon...545
Riley, Bevie O...295
Riley, Calvin "Bob"...556
Riley, Dallas Lee...556
Riley, Daniel J...542
Riley, Eldridge...556
Riley, Ethel M...295
Riley, Euna...556
Riley, Florence Latisha...556
Riley, George W...556
Riley, John Houston...555
Riley, John Wesley...555
Riley, Joseph Commodre...556
Riley, Lula F...295, 304
Riley, Margaret Ellen...545, 547
Riley, Minerva...555
Riley, Nancy...542
Riley, Nathan...542
Riley, Nelson Frank...556
Riley, Peter Clark...556
Riley, Peter Cole...555
Riley, Robert...545
Riley, Solomon...541
Riley, W. R...545
Riley, William...555
Riley, William Henry Thomas...294
Ringdahl, Rebecca Thorine...455
Ringdahl, Richard Lee...455
Ringdahl, Thoralf...455
Rippelmeyer, Sara Ann Sally...455
Ritchey, Joseph D...522
Ritchey, Linnie May...522
Ritchey, Martha Elizabeth Alice...522
Ritchey, Sarah M...522
Ritchey, William Eli...522
Ritter...5, 407
Ritter, Aaron...14, 578, 580, 581
Ritter, Aaron Ashley Flowers...14
Ritter, Addison Worth...23, 61, 161
Ritter, Adelia...567
Ritter, Alvie Dewitt...13
Ritter, Anderson...563, 564, 566
Ritter, Andrew E...568
Ritter, Andrew Jackson...13
Ritter, Andy Franklin...13
Ritter, Ann E. A...569
Ritter, Anna...563, 564, 570
Ritter, Anne E...571
Ritter, Annie Aggie...214
Ritter, Arbuary Gene...14
Ritter, Archibald...570
Ritter, Archibald J...570, 572
Ritter, Aubrey Blackie...14
Ritter, August...18, 561, 563
Ritter, Bascom Clifford...385
Ritter, Benjamin Franklin...13, 563, 564,
567, 568, 573
Ritter, Benjamin Franklin Jr...568
Ritter, Betsey...572
Ritter, Bruce...14
Ritter, Burrell...563, 565, 572
Ritter, Catherine...23, 64, 66, 569
Ritter, Catherine "Kitsey"...578, 581, 582
Ritter, Cecil Franklin...14
Ritter, Charles...572
Ritter, Charles Edward...14
Ritter, Charlie Mason...227
Ritter, Cherry...570, 572

Wallace, Daniel Lee...457
Wallace, David...13
Wallace, David Edward...233, 425
Wallace, David J...514
Wallace, David Overton...12, 168, 291
Wallace, David Russell...425
Wallace, Davis Justin Daniel Eugene...461
Wallace, Deborah...6, 31, 33, 79, 80, 468
Wallace, Dempsey...34, 41, 110
Wallace, Dewey...133
Wallace, Dewey Edgar...253, 313, 452
Wallace, Dewey Green...231, 420
Wallace, Dewey Randall...420
Wallace, Diane...352
Wallace, Dimple Bernice...238
Wallace, Dock...172
Wallace, Donald...175
Wallace, Donald Clyde...459
Wallace, Donald K...454
Wallace, Donald Lee...15, 457
Wallace, Donna Inez...202, 356
Wallace, Dora...86, 114, 130, 180, 185, 233, 484
Wallace, Dora Leason...231, 420
Wallace, Dora Mae...232, 389, 422
Wallace, Doris Ann...401
Wallace, Doris K...204, 358
Wallace, Doris Ruth...255, 459
Wallace, Dorothy Ann...445
Wallace, Dorothy Mae...436, 437
Wallace, Douglas Darrell...425
Wallace, Dovie...76, 173
Wallace, Drew...166
Wallace, Dwight Thomas...256, 461
Wallace, E....16, 535
Wallace, E. Louise...186, 307
Wallace, E. Milton...15, 555
Wallace, Earl...166
Wallace, Ed...15
Wallace, Edee...540
Wallace, Edgar...250, 445, 483
Wallace, Edmond...484
Wallace, Edmond Clayton "Mickey"...455
Wallace, Edna...166, 543
Wallace, Edna Elizabeth...199, 202, 352, 353
Wallace, Edward Lee...104, 204, 455
Wallace, Edward Lee Jr...204
Wallace, Edwin E. Sr...13
Wallace, Effie...293, 555
Wallace, Effie Malinda...506
Wallace, Efland Earl...453
Wallace, Eli...5, 6, 13, 15, 16, 17, 19, 28, 30, 53, 54, 71, 74, 110, 209, 488, 515, 516, 534, 535, 536, 537, 538, 540, 541
Wallace, Eli C...541
Wallace, Eli Terrell...543
Wallace, Elias W...136, 239
Wallace, Eliza...535, 537
Wallace, Eliza Alice...110, 210
Wallace, Eliza B...293
Wallace, Eliza Rosetta Mattie Evelyn "Mattie"...120, 225
Wallace, Elizabeth...5, 20, 34, 41, 47, 67, 73, 85, 94, 169, 250, 331, 445, 531, 535, 536, 537, 538, 541
Wallace, Elizabeth "Betsy"...535, 551, 553
Wallace, Elizabeth Delaney...229, 410
Wallace, Elizabeth Jane...112, 117, 215, 217, 559
Wallace, Elizabeth M...6, 31, 33
Wallace, Elizabeth Rachel...461
Wallace, Ella...148, 170, 211, 249, 322, 378, 484
Wallace, Ella Blake...112, 215

Wallace, Ellen Barber...239, 436, 437
Wallace, Ellen Eliza...555
Wallace, Elmo LeRoy...291
Wallace, Elsie Bess...168, 292
Wallace, Elsie Pearl...545, 547
Wallace, Elva...203
Wallace, Elvira...546
Wallace, Emaline...477, 478, 526, 576
Wallace, Emerson...187
Wallace, Emerson Ethridge...89, 187, 245
Wallace, Emily Minerva...554
Wallace, Emma...517, 523
Wallace, Emma Mae...231, 366, 414
Wallace, Emmer Charity...175
Wallace, Emmerson...202
Wallace, Emmett Lee...237, 426
Wallace, Emsley Thomas...12, 15, 34, 35, 41, 42, 112, 113, 114, 115, 116, 117, 477
Wallace, Enoch...5, 16, 20, 24, 35, 44, 113, 467, 477, 478, 526
Wallace, Erasmus Stimpson...15, 551, 554
Wallace, Ernest B...505
Wallace, Ernest Joe...168, 292
Wallace, Ernest Wade...456
Wallace, Ervin...511
Wallace, Essie Lee...231, 420
Wallace, Estelle...458
Wallace, Esther Della...254
Wallace, Ethel Marie...436, 437
Wallace, Ethlene...513
Wallace, Etta Jennette...211, 213, 362, 377, 381
Wallace, Etta Mae...254, 456
Wallace, Eudora Ann...75, 171
Wallace, Eugene...291
Wallace, Eugene Oliver "Gene"...459
Wallace, Eula...169, 175, 294
Wallace, Euna...174
Wallace, Euphernia S. "Effie"...126, 227
Wallace, Eva Dee...172, 301
Wallace, Eveline...541
Wallace, Evelyn...250, 445
Wallace, Evelyn Ann...241
Wallace, Evelyn Joyce...256
Wallace, Evelyn K...425
Wallace, Everet...1, 3, 4, 5, 6, 7, 8, 9, 10, 12, 13, 14, 15, 16, 17, 18, 19, 20, 34, 35, 80, 113, 467, 468, 477, 534, 535, 588
Wallace, Everett...6, 31, 33, 84
Wallace, Everett W...15, 491, 494
Wallace, Evie Lena...304
Wallace, F. M...545
Wallace, Fairley Ledbetter...239, 434
Wallace, Fannie...293
Wallace, Fannie C...239, 436
Wallace, Fay Dora...237, 426
Wallace, Faye Lavone...233, 424
Wallace, Felix E...170
Wallace, Flavius A...253
Wallace, Flessie Bethertina...299
Wallace, Fletcher Alan...241
Wallace, Flora...501
Wallace, Flora M...69
Wallace, Florence Jane...148, 250
Wallace, Flossie Alma...126, 229
Wallace, Flossie Estelle...299
Wallace, Floyd Lee...225, 405
Wallace, Fondon...299
Wallace, Forrest Lee...254, 457, 509
Wallace, Frances...540
Wallace, Frances Arlee...452
Wallace, Frances J...72, 168
Wallace, Francis Theodore...290
Wallace, Franey...5, 6, 14, 20, 33, 52, 82, 470

Wallace, Frank...15
Wallace, Franny...6, 28, 31
Wallace, Fred Erwin...415
Wallace, Fred F...168, 292
Wallace, Fred I...132, 237, 240, 365
Wallace, Fred Jr...237, 426
Wallace, Fred Thomas...203, 356
Wallace, Freddie Connie...396, 398
Wallace, Frederick...540, 557
Wallace, French...512
Wallace, Gaston...293
Wallace, Genevieve...513, 514
Wallace, George...250, 445, 535, 537
Wallace, George Carson...331, 531, 532
Wallace, George Henry...425
Wallace, George Hiram...431
Wallace, George M...15, 529, 530
Wallace, George Reece...289
Wallace, George W...154, 255
Wallace, George Washington...136, 240, 241
Wallace, Georgia Baxter...237, 427
Wallace, Gilbert D...435
Wallace, Gladys...513
Wallace, Gladys Elizabeth...514
Wallace, Gladys Irene...445
Wallace, Gladys Lee...204
Wallace, Gladys Louella...432
Wallace, Glenna Velma...253, 313, 452
Wallace, Gloria Jacquelyn...291
Wallace, Godfrey...482
Wallace, Grace...505, 514
Wallace, Gracie May...484
Wallace, Grady...294, 295, 299, 484
Wallace, Green...543
Wallace, Hamilton...5, 44, 47
Wallace, Harbart/Harbard...535, 551, 552
Wallace, Harmon...172
Wallace, Harold L...290
Wallace, Harold Leonard...454
Wallace, Harriet...154, 255
Wallace, Harve D...89, 187, 245
Wallace, Harvey...171, 174, 300, 557
Wallace, Harvey Eugene...455
Wallace, Hattie...167
Wallace, Hattie Jane...129, 230, 231, 234, 414, 416, 417
Wallace, Hattie Mae...208, 374
Wallace, Hazel...231, 419
Wallace, Hazel Cornelia...453
Wallace, Hazel Marie...290
Wallace, Helen...204
Wallace, Helen Virginia...238
Wallace, Henry...15, 172, 535, 537, 540
Wallace, Henry Arnold...454
Wallace, Henry Calhoun...170, 295
Wallace, Henry Clay...132, 237, 425
Wallace, Henry Clayton...254, 455
Wallace, Henry Craft...350
Wallace, Henry Franklin...453
Wallace, Henry Lee...154, 253
Wallace, Henry Rufus...237, 425
Wallace, Henry W...171, 294, 299
Wallace, Herbert...557
Wallace, Herman S...15
Wallace, Hermin...89, 245
Wallace, Hildred Pauline...204, 357
Wallace, Hiram W...5, 44, 47, 133, 240
Wallace, Hiram Walker...134, 239, 240
Wallace, Homer...241
Wallace, Houston Shivers...172, 301
Wallace, Howard Houston...170
Wallace, Hugh T...239, 431
Wallace, Hugh T. "Pug" Jr...432

Wallace, Hurley Carlton...12, 219, 222, 396, 397, 398, 400
Wallace, Hurley Carlton Jr...12, 396, 398
Wallace, Ida F...239, 433
Wallace, Ida Lee...167
Wallace, Ida Mae...174, 302, 432
Wallace, Ida Victoria...89, 186, 245
Wallace, Ina Jr...295
Wallace, Inez...186, 307
Wallace, Ira J...513, 514
Wallace, Ira Leland...241
Wallace, Irene...445
Wallace, Iris Natalie...255, 460
Wallace, Irma Jean...232, 422
Wallace, Isaac Frank...112, 211, 322
Wallace, Isaac Spinks...5, 51, 52, 147
Wallace, Isabelle Ethel...432
Wallace, Isham...5, 6, 12, 13, 15, 16, 17, 19, 20, 24, 28, 30, 34, 35, 72, 113, 129, 230, 234, 418, 477, 526, 534, 535, 536, 537, 538, 540
Wallace, Isham "Ike"...5, 44, 47, 113, 134
Wallace, Isham Everett...540
Wallace, Isham Sedman Robert Renfro "Bob"...120, 222
Wallace, Ishmeal...173, 302
Wallace, Iva...295
Wallace, Iva Floyd...435
Wallace, J. Henry Calhoun...74, 170
Wallace, J. Murray...186, 307
Wallace, J. S...187, 311
Wallace, Jack...292
Wallace, Jackie Russell...424
Wallace, Jacqueline...401
Wallace, James...15, 223, 457, 534, 535
Wallace, James A...496
Wallace, James Alvis...15, 551, 554
Wallace, James Andrew "Jim Whit"...128, 129, 233, 235, 236
Wallace, James Arthur Mason Bethune...120
Wallace, James Britian...168, 291
Wallace, James Britian Jr...291
Wallace, James Charles...104, 197, 331, 531, 532
Wallace, James Dixon...289
Wallace, James Dozier W...479, 484
Wallace, James Edward...13, 170, 295, 304
Wallace, James Everette...484
Wallace, James F...172
Wallace, James Fletcher...254, 456, 509
Wallace, James Floyd...331, 531, 532
Wallace, James Franklin...253, 313, 452
Wallace, James J...459
Wallace, James Jackson...172, 301
Wallace, James Knox Polk...559
Wallace, James Lewis...110, 126, 210, 213, 381
Wallace, James Lionell...291
Wallace, James Lovelace...536, 540, 543, 552, 557
Wallace, James M. "Jim"...148, 250
Wallace, James Madison...154, 256
Wallace, James Madison "Billy Mack" Jr...256, 461
Wallace, James Madison III...461
Wallace, James Monk...71, 168
Wallace, James Oliver "Ollie"...89, 186, 244
Wallace, James Quimby...209, 376
Wallace, James R...555
Wallace, James Ray Sr...513
Wallace, James Ronald...455
Wallace, James Vester...484
Wallace, James W. "Jimmie"...517, 522
Wallace, James Warner "Jim"...560
Wallace, James William...505, 513

Wallace, Jane...85, 484
Wallace, Jane M...512
Wallace, Jane Matilda Frances...554
Wallace, Janet Lynn...420
Wallace, Janice...425
Wallace, Janice Leigh...356
Wallace, Janice Sue...404
Wallace, Janie...175, 249, 444
Wallace, Jason McKendrick...551, 556
Wallace, Jasper...75, 171
Wallace, Jasper Conley...253, 454
Wallace, Jasper Conley Jr...454
Wallace, Jasper Decaster...170, 295
Wallace, Jasper Newton Jr...173
Wallace, Jasper Newton Sr...76, 172
Wallace, Jean...457
Wallace, Jeanette Nettie...129, 232
Wallace, Jeanine Marie...461
Wallace, Jefferson Royal...557
Wallace, Jennie...172
Wallace, Jerome A...13, 67, 166, 178
Wallace, Jerusha Francis "Ruth"...126, 229
Wallace, Jesse...16, 17, 225, 228, 302, 484, 534, 548
Wallace, Jesse Lee...104, 202
Wallace, Jesse Lewis Smith...120, 224, 225
Wallace, Jesse May...294, 300
Wallace, Jessie...249, 444
Wallace, Jessie Eliza...436
Wallace, Jessie Lazell...225, 404
Wallace, Jessie Lee...373
Wallace, Jessie Mae...238, 459
Wallace, Jessie Nancy...132, 237
Wallace, Jessie Velma...237, 427
Wallace, Jewel...166, 287
Wallace, Jewell Marie...256, 460
Wallace, Jimmy...13
Wallace, Joann...454
Wallace, Joanna...557
Wallace, Joanne Moore...452
Wallace, Joel Kendrick...15, 543
Wallace, John...5, 12, 13, 16, 17, 20, 28, 231, 477, 483, 541, 559
Wallace, John Albert...241
Wallace, John Arch...479, 483, 485
Wallace, John C...74, 169, 239, 432, 536, 538, 542
Wallace, John Columbus...170, 296
Wallace, John Daniel...249, 444
Wallace, John Dixon...167, 290
Wallace, John Dixon Jr...290
Wallace, John Edgar...250, 446
Wallace, John Franklin...517, 523, 559, 560
Wallace, John Hardy...168, 293
Wallace, John Henry...503, 513
Wallace, John Lee...253, 453
Wallace, John Lee Jr...453
Wallace, John Lester...377
Wallace, John Lucian...254, 456
Wallace, John M...5, 34, 42, 76, 114, 130, 171, 240, 526
Wallace, John Mack...3, 5, 14, 52, 53, 151
Wallace, John Mack II...253, 313, 452
Wallace, John Mack III...14, 452
Wallace, John Morrison...129
Wallace, John Murriston...133, 238
Wallace, John R...557
Wallace, John Robert...154, 254
Wallace, John Spinks...5, 44, 47, 136, 240
Wallace, John Stanley...356
Wallace, John Stellings...104, 200, 203
Wallace, John Templeton "T"...559
Wallace, John W...169, 293
Wallace, John Walker...432

Wallace, John Wesley...6, 13, 28, 30, 75, 78, 174, 175, 302
Wallace, John William...172
Wallace, Johnnie Corinne...238, 427
Wallace, Johnnie Ellen...132
Wallace, Johnny...175
Wallace, Johnny Ray...424
Wallace, Johnsie Elizabeth...232, 422
Wallace, Johnsie Grier...231, 420
Wallace, Jonathan Everett...535, 537, 541
Wallace, Joseph...5, 13, 16, 20, 27, 435, 467, 477, 557
Wallace, Joseph Carl...454
Wallace, Joseph Davis...72, 169
Wallace, Joseph Garland...254
Wallace, Joseph Thomas...202, 353
Wallace, Josephine...86, 180, 184, 435
Wallace, Josiah...5, 16, 20, 42, 113, 477, 490, 491, 576
Wallace, Josiah Tay Settle...120, 223
Wallace, Josiah/Cyrus...6, 13, 28, 30, 77
Wallace, Josie...170
Wallace, Josie Bell...435
Wallace, Joyce...256, 294, 299
Wallace, Judith Ann...455
Wallace, Julia...175
Wallace, Julia Ann...168, 292
Wallace, Julia Catherine...233
Wallace, Julia Florence...239, 432
Wallace, Julia Frances...5, 52, 53, 154
Wallace, Julius...15
Wallace, June...232, 291
Wallace, June Harrison...15, 554
Wallace, K. C...293
Wallace, Katherine E...239, 434
Wallace, Katie...174, 303
Wallace, Katie Lisbon...331, 531, 532
Wallace, Kendrick...15, 536, 540, 543
Wallace, Kenneth Carson "Kennie"...104, 201, 203
Wallace, Kenneth Charles...250, 446
Wallace, Kenneth H...531, 533
Wallace, Kenneth Martin...148, 250
Wallace, Kenneth Price...446
Wallace, King Cornelius...173, 301
Wallace, Krista Lynn...461
Wallace, Kurt...15
Wallace, L. Ella...89, 187, 245
Wallace, L. Harriett...557
Wallace, Laney...517
Wallace, Larry...15
Wallace, Lauch Wesley...503, 513
Wallace, Lauchlin B. "Lock"...477, 478, 481
Wallace, Laura...168, 292
Wallace, Laura Ann...446
Wallace, Laura Lee...239, 436
Wallace, Laura Louise...104, 198, 202
Wallace, Lawrence Craven...254, 457, 509
Wallace, Lawson...75, 170
Wallace, Leander Andrew Perry...559, 560
Wallace, Leanora Helen...290
Wallace, Leather S...512
Wallace, Leenettie...512
Wallace, Lehman Grundy...172, 301
Wallace, Leigh...256
Wallace, Lelia Georgia...254, 457, 509
Wallace, Lena Bell...484, 485
Wallace, Leonard Harris...551, 556
Wallace, Leondras Wilson "Leon"...425
Wallace, Leora...211, 322, 379
Wallace, Lester Eugene...454
Wallace, Lester Mack...253, 454
Wallace, Lester Mack Jr...454
Wallace, Levi...540

Wallace, Levi W...535, 537, 541
Wallace, Lewis E...556
Wallace, Lillian Avice...170
Wallace, Lillian Gertrude...253, 313
Wallace, Lillie Adelaide...455
Wallace, Lillie Al Rhoney...154, 257
Wallace, Lillie Alice...531, 532
Wallace, Lillie Viola...260, 331, 531, 532
Wallace, Lilly...168
Wallace, Lilly Belle...172, 301
Wallace, Lily Francis...501, 512
Wallace, Linda...454, 460
Wallace, Linda Carroll...427
Wallace, Linda Faye...452
Wallace, Lindsay Lee...203, 357
Wallace, Livie...173
Wallace, Lizar Myrtle...211, 378, 381, 406
Wallace, Lizzie F...197, 352
Wallace, Lloyd Maxwell...484
Wallace, Lochart "Lockey"...5, 34, 35, 41, 110, 113, 576
Wallace, Lock T...133, 237
Wallace, Lodie...170
Wallace, Lois...203
Wallace, Lois Maybell...373
Wallace, Lonnie Wilson...237, 425
Wallace, Lora Almar...197, 351
Wallace, Loretta...459, 496, 508
Wallace, Lottie...172
Wallace, Louella...239, 433
Wallace, Louisa...170
Wallace, Louisa Elafair...112, 117, 218, 221
Wallace, Louisa Eliza...551, 556
Wallace, Louisa Elizabeth...134, 238, 240
Wallace, Louisa Jane...543
Wallace, Louise...203, 425, 505
Wallace, Loula Maude...197, 351
Wallace, Loutishie J...239
Wallace, Loveday Jane...515, 517
Wallace, Lovedy Ann "Annie"...129, 230
Wallace, Lovedy Jane...5, 34, 41, 120
Wallace, Lovena...129
Wallace, Lucian Thomas...12, 112, 113, 114, 117, 218, 219, 220, 222
Wallace, Lucille...174
Wallace, Lucille E...238
Wallace, Lucille Helen...331, 531, 532
Wallace, Lucinda...71, 167, 536, 540
Wallace, Lula Florence...129, 231, 249, 444
Wallace, Lula Ida...555
Wallace, Lummie Tanie...89, 245
Wallace, Lurdene...513
Wallace, Luther...169
Wallace, Luther Class...197, 351
Wallace, Luther Clyde...331, 531, 532
Wallace, Luther Columbus...172, 300
Wallace, Luther Edward...254, 455
Wallace, Lydia Annie...231, 258, 332, 333, 414
Wallace, M...16
Wallace, M. G...76, 174
Wallace, Mable Eunice...241
Wallace, Mack...249, 445
Wallace, Mack Duffie...431
Wallace, Maggie...211, 378, 381
Wallace, Maggie Elizabeth...104, 200, 202
Wallace, Maggie L...166
Wallace, Maggie Mae...239, 433
Wallace, Maggie Pearl...223, 403
Wallace, Malcolm M...554
Wallace, Malinda A...136, 241
Wallace, Malinda Toad...136, 241

Wallace, Mallie Lester...15, 34, 35, 112, 113, 114, 115, 222, 338, 343, 397, 398, 400, 401, 526
Wallace, Mamie Alice...293
Wallace, Manda...5, 20, 35, 51
Wallace, Margaret...204, 482, 486, 540, 545, 547
Wallace, Margaret Ann...250, 445
Wallace, Margaret Emma...86, 179, 184
Wallace, Margaret Francis...436, 437
Wallace, Margaret L...104, 197, 199, 574
Wallace, Margaret Lee...233, 424
Wallace, Margaret Louise...255, 459
Wallace, Margaret Lucille...425
Wallace, Margaret Maxine...255, 458
Wallace, Margaret McIver...352
Wallace, Margaret Murial...377
Wallace, Margaret Rosetta...154, 254, 508
Wallace, Margaret Victoria "Peggy"...202, 354
Wallace, Margie...374
Wallace, Marie...173
Wallace, Marjorie...291
Wallace, Martha...104, 545
Wallace, Martha "Mattie"...112, 117, 222
Wallace, Martha "Patsy"...72, 169
Wallace, Martha A...110, 208, 492
Wallace, Martha Ann...112, 154, 211, 212, 254
Wallace, Martha Clementine...71, 168, 291
Wallace, Martha E...78
Wallace, Martha Elizabeth...129, 230
Wallace, Martha Emeline...559
Wallace, Martha F...76, 172
Wallace, Martha J...5, 52, 53, 148
Wallace, Martha Jane...103, 104, 134, 200, 203, 238, 551, 555
Wallace, Martha Matilda...164
Wallace, Marty Dale...424
Wallace, Marvin Jackson...171, 294, 299
Wallace, Mary...5, 6, 12, 16, 17, 20, 24, 33, 83, 136, 175, 241, 294, 300, 477, 478, 480, 534, 535, 536, 537, 538, 540, 541
Wallace, Mary A...6, 31, 33, 57
Wallace, Mary A. E...148, 250
Wallace, Mary Alice...239, 433
Wallace, Mary Ann...5, 41, 52, 53, 97, 149, 249, 444, 543
Wallace, Mary Ann "Molly"...89, 186, 244
Wallace, Mary Blake...154, 253
Wallace, Mary Cassandra...555
Wallace, Mary Duck...491, 498
Wallace, Mary E...71, 76, 168, 173, 545, 547
Wallace, Mary Elizabeth...74, 166, 289, 425, 453, 502, 512
Wallace, Mary Ellis...112, 160, 211
Wallace, Mary Eppes...352
Wallace, Mary F...557
Wallace, Mary Frances...203, 357, 559, 560
Wallace, Mary H...425
Wallace, Mary Hattie...103, 104, 201, 204
Wallace, Mary Hortense...557
Wallace, Mary Ivey...350
Wallace, Mary Jane...75, 171
Wallace, Mary Jane Nancy Regina Ledbetter "Mamie"...120, 222, 224
Wallace, Mary L...168, 292
Wallace, Mary L. "Molly"...202, 352
Wallace, Mary Mae...501, 512
Wallace, Mary Matilda...559
Wallace, Mary Maxine...453
Wallace, Mary Missouri...229, 410
Wallace, Mary Pauline...223, 402
Wallace, Mary Ruth...173

Wallace, Masie L...514
Wallace, Mattie Evalena...431
Wallace, Mattie Florence...531, 533
Wallace, Mattie Frances...250, 446
Wallace, Mattie Jane...555
Wallace, Mattie M...483
Wallace, Maude Eva...239, 434
Wallace, Maude Jane...68, 167
Wallace, Maude Lee...172, 301
Wallace, Maudie Estelle...170, 295
Wallace, Maudie Lee...241, 437
Wallace, Maxie...15
Wallace, Maxine Naomi...254, 456
Wallace, Melba Jane...455
Wallace, Melford V...169, 294
Wallace, Melissa Catherine...68, 167
Wallace, Melvin Augusta...76, 174
Wallace, Melvin Eli...241
Wallace, Melvin L...186, 307, 311
Wallace, Melvin Monroe...483
Wallace, Mianna J. Annie...154, 255
Wallace, Michael Howard...13, 287
Wallace, Michael Pennington...352
Wallace, Michael Rush...554
Wallace, Mildred Doris...166, 287
Wallace, Mildred Hamer...229, 410
Wallace, Mildred Louvene...204, 357
Wallace, Mildred S...304
Wallace, Miles L...245
Wallace, Millard Fillmore...130, 233
Wallace, Minerva Mae...169, 294, 299
Wallace, Minnie Lee...231, 234, 403, 413
Wallace, Minnie Virginia...170, 296
Wallace, Miranda Idell...170, 296
Wallace, Missouri Smith "Mo"...491, 499
Wallace, Mitchell Coleman...431
Wallace, Molly Viola...197, 351
Wallace, Montie Bertha...211, 378, 381
Wallace, Montie Pearl...213, 374
Wallace, Morgan...292
Wallace, Morris W...483
Wallace, Myrtle...132, 302
Wallace, Nancy...6, 31, 33, 78, 110, 209, 467, 536, 538, 541, 542
Wallace, Nancy Abigail...559
Wallace, Nancy Ann...554
Wallace, Nancy Caroline...551, 556
Wallace, Nancy Cordelia...557
Wallace, Nancy Lee...352
Wallace, Nancy Margaret "Nannie"...112, 214
Wallace, Nancy Marie...446
Wallace, Nancy Paralee...76, 173
Wallace, Nannie Florence...103, 104, 201, 204
Wallace, Nathan...6, 13, 15, 16, 17, 19, 28, 30, 69, 534, 535, 536, 537, 549
Wallace, Nathan C...5, 6, 12, 20, 23, 31, 47, 50, 80, 468
Wallace, Nathaniel...534, 549
Wallace, Neal...13
Wallace, Needham Evander...491, 503
Wallace, Nellie Ann...254
Wallace, Nellie Maggie...253, 454
Wallace, Nettie...479, 482, 485, 486
Wallace, Nevada...295
Wallace, Nicholas...5, 10, 11, 16, 20, 23, 31, 47, 80, 468, 477
Wallace, Noah Columbus...13, 175, 304
Wallace, Noah W...501
Wallace, Norman...436, 437
Wallace, Norman Herman...435
Wallace, Norman Hinshaw "Stick"...203, 357
Wallace, Octavius...167

Wallace, Odell...172, 301
Wallace, Offie Doyle...197, 350
Wallace, Offie Doyle Jr...351
Wallace, Ola...171, 300
Wallace, Olga William...133, 238
Wallace, Oliver Lacy...255, 458
Wallace, Ollie Irene...241, 437
Wallace, Ollie Mae...166, 172, 301
Wallace, Oma...171, 300
Wallace, Onias Small...559, 560
Wallace, Opal Christella...453
Wallace, Oscar...241
Wallace, Oscar Emerson...225, 405
Wallace, Oscar Lloyd...256
Wallace, Owen...484
Wallace, Owen Lane...505
Wallace, Pamela Kay...456
Wallace, Paralee...78, 174
Wallace, Patricia Ann...445
Wallace, Patricia Faye...452
Wallace, Patricia Louise...401
Wallace, Pattie...483
Wallace, Paul...377
Wallace, Paul Brackmon...233, 424
Wallace, Paula Rae...426
Wallace, Pauline...255, 377
Wallace, Pearl...436, 437
Wallace, Pearl M...227, 408
Wallace, Peggy Louise...452
Wallace, Percy Michaux...505, 514
Wallace, Perry Brackmon...424
Wallace, Peter Sr...15
Wallace, Phil Earnest I...132, 237
Wallace, Phillip David...12
Wallace, Phillip Downy...291
Wallace, Phyllis Ann...233, 424
Wallace, Polly Ruth...254, 455
Wallace, Priscilla Lois...401
Wallace, Prudence...543
Wallace, Quimby...5, 41, 107
Wallace, Quimby Lewis...211, 377, 381
Wallace, Rachel...536, 538, 542
Wallace, Rachel Amanda...559
Wallace, Rachel Eliza Ann...545, 547
Wallace, Raleigh L...166, 288
Wallace, Raleigh S...72, 168
Wallace, Raleigh W...6, 28, 30, 74
Wallace, Raymond...237, 426
Wallace, Reba...241, 437
Wallace, Rebecca...170, 296
Wallace, Rebecca Annie...540
Wallace, Rebecca Jane...5, 52, 53, 150, 378, 516, 522
Wallace, Rebecca Louise...454
Wallace, Reuben Franklin...169, 294
Wallace, Rhoday M. "Rocky"...169, 293
Wallace, Rich...172
Wallace, Richard Albert...172, 300
Wallace, Richard Calvin...553, 557
Wallace, Richard D...436
Wallace, Ricky...377
Wallace, Robert...13, 17, 256
Wallace, Robert C...172
Wallace, Robert D...253, 313
Wallace, Robert Dall...202, 353, 354
Wallace, Robert Horace...453
Wallace, Robert Lee...455
Wallace, Robert Michael "Mike"...456
Wallace, Robert Monroe...175, 304
Wallace, Robert Neil...427
Wallace, Robert Rolland...290
Wallace, Robert Vandon...170, 296
Wallace, Robert Wade...501, 511
Wallace, Roberta...225, 404

Wallace, Rocky Leon...311
Wallace, Rodney...12
Wallace, Ronald Leroy...446
Wallace, Ronnie...457
Wallace, Ronnie Mitchell "Ron"...12
Wallace, Ronnie Thomas...401
Wallace, Rosa...557
Wallace, Rosa Bell...172, 300
Wallace, Rosa Ella...482, 486
Wallace, Rosa Lee...350
Wallace, Roscoe A...170, 295
Wallace, Roscoe Greene...219, 222, 396, 397
Wallace, Rosemary...357
Wallace, Roy...436, 437
Wallace, Roy M. Jr...302
Wallace, Roy M. Sr...174, 302
Wallace, Roy Moody...174, 302
Wallace, Ruby...241, 557
Wallace, Ruby Dean...435
Wallace, Ruby Lois...513
Wallace, Ruby M...186, 307
Wallace, Ruby Mae...203, 357
Wallace, Ruby N...431
Wallace, Ruby Pearl...253, 313
Wallace, Ruffin...5, 13, 27, 28, 66
Wallace, Rufus...110, 209, 506, 514
Wallace, Rufus Cobb...168, 293
Wallace, Rufus Lewis...377
Wallace, Ruley Gart...197, 352
Wallace, Rupert Oliver...253, 312
Wallace, Ruth...133
Wallace, Ruth A...505, 514
Wallace, Ruth Jane...239, 435
Wallace, Ruth M...170
Wallace, Ruth Seawell...350
Wallace, Rutha Jane Florence...112, 212, 214
Wallace, Ruthie Dean...186, 307
Wallace, Sadie Lou...222, 399, 400, 401
Wallace, Salina...69
Wallace, Sallie...168, 512
Wallace, Sallie Adelaide...154, 257
Wallace, Sallie J...479, 483
Wallace, Sally...78, 175
Wallace, Sampson Delaney...5, 34, 35, 41, 113, 123, 526
Wallace, Samuel Bascom...5, 34, 35, 41, 113, 117
Wallace, Samuel Henry Bascom "Bass"...120, 225
Wallace, Sandra Mae...233, 424
Wallace, Sara Vernall...378
Wallace, Sarah...5, 6, 28, 30, 51, 71, 74, 78, 136, 167, 168, 239, 496, 507, 541
Wallace, Sarah A...211, 322, 379
Wallace, Sarah Ann...5, 34, 41, 104, 114, 531, 532, 559, 560
Wallace, Sarah C...148, 249
Wallace, Sarah Catherine "Kate"...112, 117, 217, 218, 221
Wallace, Sarah E...529
Wallace, Sarah Elizabeth...86, 146, 154, 178, 183, 255
Wallace, Sarah F...517, 522
Wallace, Sarah Frances...6, 31, 33, 86, 87
Wallace, Sarah Lee Nettie...120, 225
Wallace, Sarah M...169, 294, 300
Wallace, Sarah Martha "Mattie"...75, 171
Wallace, Sarah "Sally"...515
Wallace, Scott Alan...356
Wallace, Seaborn...5, 27, 28, 67
Wallace, Sewell...237, 426
Wallace, Sharon Ella...461
Wallace, Sharon Kay...446
Wallace, Sheila Rosa...424

Wallace, Shelly R...223
Wallace, Sherman Roscoe...425
Wallace, Sherri...459
Wallace, Shube...556
Wallace, Sina...168, 292
Wallace, Sindy Ann "Annie"...112, 117, 221
Wallace, Spinks...136, 239
Wallace, Stacy Lee...454
Wallace, Stanley Newton Orville...238
Wallace, Steadman McLendon...129, 232
Wallace, Steadman McLendon Jr...232, 422
Wallace, Stella...169
Wallace, Stephen C...208, 373
Wallace, Susan...535, 537, 541
Wallace, Susan Gail...445
Wallace, Susan Sufronie...6, 31, 33, 89
Wallace, Susanna...491, 503
Wallace, Susannah...5, 20, 35, 53, 561, 563
Wallace, Susannah/Hanna/Anna...17, 18
Wallace, Swannie Esther...130, 233, 235
Wallace, Talmage Boyce...425
Wallace, Temperance...536, 540, 542
Wallace, Teresa Ann...425
Wallace, Teresa Lynn...446
Wallace, Terry Joe...311
Wallace, Thelma...513
Wallace, Thelma Devina...223
Wallace, Thelma Dora...237, 427
Wallace, Thelma Jean...233, 424
Wallace, Thelma Lorraine...255
Wallace, Thelma Mae...425
Wallace, Theodore Wesley...253, 313, 452
Wallace, Theodore Wesley Jr...452
Wallace, Thomas...6, 28, 30, 73, 74, 496, 557
Wallace, Thomas A...15, 457, 543
Wallace, Thomas Alvin...241
Wallace, Thomas Evit...136, 241
Wallace, Thomas Jefferson "Jeff"...171, 299
Wallace, Thomas Vance...485
Wallace, Thomas W...76, 174
Wallace, Thomas Walter...491, 500, 501, 512
Wallace, Thomas Wesley...78, 175
Wallace, Tishi Evelyn...154, 256
Wallace, Tom...15
Wallace, Tommy...175
Wallace, Tonya Jean...424
Wallace, Torla B. "Toadie"...241, 437
Wallace, Uriah Duck...554
Wallace, Ursula M. "Shulie"...223, 403
Wallace, Valerie Marie...410
Wallace, Valerie Pearl...454
Wallace, Vandie Lee...112, 160, 215
Wallace, Vann...129
Wallace, Veona L...396
Wallace, Verdia Lee...222, 260, 399, 400, 401
Wallace, Verle Lee...15
Wallace, Verna...168
Wallace, Verona Belle...289
Wallace, Victoria...168, 557
Wallace, Viola...168, 292
Wallace, Viola Blanche...167, 290
Wallace, Viola Mae...225, 404
Wallace, Virgil...173
Wallace, Virgil Spinks "Byrd"...5, 12, 34, 35, 42, 114, 126, 211
Wallace, Virginia...75, 171, 179
Wallace, Vivian Alma...255, 458
Wallace, W. Benjamin...85
Wallace, Wade C...167, 289
Wallace, Wade Hampton...126, 197, 227, 228, 376
Wallace, Walter...169, 293
Wallace, Walter A...479, 483

Additional Information can be found at www.MooreCountyWallaces.com

Endnotes

[1] Camp, Cordelia. *The Influence of Geography Upon Early North Carolina.* Raleigh, NC: Carolina Charter Tercentenary Commission, 1963.

[2] Merrens, Harry Roy. *Colonial North Carolina in the Eighteenth Century: A Study of Historical Geography.* Chapel Hill, NC: The University of North Carolina Press, 1964.

[3] Robinson, Blackwell P. *Moore County North Carolina 1747-1847.* Southern Pines, NC: Moore County Historical Association, 1956.

[4] Cumming, William P. *The Southeast in Early Maps*, Third Edition. Chapel Hill, NC: The University of North Carolina Press, 1998. Map 394. Retrieved from https://dc.lib.unc.edu/cdm/singleitem/collection/ncmaps/id/467/rec/110

[5] Allosso, Dan. *American Environmental History.* Minnesota Libraries Publishing Project. Retrieved from https://mlpp.pressbooks.pub/americanenvironmentalhistory/front-matter/introduction/

[6] Baxter, Angus. *In Search of your British and Irish Roots: A Complete Guide to Tracing your English, Welsh, Scottish and Irish Ancestors,* Fourth Edition. Baltimore. MD: Genealogical Publishing Inc., 1999.

[7] Will of Robert Wallace, 1800. Union County, SC Wills, Box 3 Package 13. Retrieved from www.ancestry.com

[8] Oral History written by Murry Connie Ritter as told by his father William Young Ritter, 1905. In possession of Linda Ritter, Louisiana (kikikritter42@gmail.com). Full text at https://moorecountywallaces.com/showmedia.php?mediaID=4904&medialinkID=14493

[9] Thornton, Mary Lindsay. (Oct 1964) The Price and Strother first actual survey of state of North Carolina. North Carolina Historical Review, 41(4), 477-483. Retrieved from https://dc.lib.unc.edu/cdm/singleitem/collection/ncmaps/id/520/rec/3

[10] Parker, Anthony E. *A Guide to Moore County Cemeteries.* Southern Pines, NC: Moore County Historical Association, 1976.

[11] Martin Rouse, War of 1812 Pension Application File 24992 (North Carolina), 1871. Retrieved from www.fold3.com

[12] Anthony Finley and Company, Map of Georgia, 1830. Retrieved from https://georgiainfo.galileo.usg.edu/topics/history/article/antebellum-era-1801-1860/1830-map-showing-cherokee-nation

[13] "A Remarkable Family" (1880, October 7), *The Chatham Record* (Pittsboro, NC). Page 3. Retrieved from www.newspapers.com

[14] Auman, William T. *Civil War in the North Carolina Quaker belt: The Confederate campaign against peace agitators, deserters and draft dodgers.* Jefferson, NC: McFarland and Company, 2014. Page 168.

[15] "Carolina" (1882, January 20), *The Daily Review* (Wilmington, NC). Page 4. Retrieved from www.newspapers.com

[16] Comer, James V. *Central North Carolina Collection, Volume 1.* Sanford, NC: 48hr Books, 2005. Page 458-483

[17] Judy S. Little, 5195 Hwy 22-A, Lexington, TN 38351 (jsl3851@yahoo.com), personal communication, Oct 2009.

[18] McNeill, Maxine Williams. *The Williams Family: Descendants of Noah and Mary "Polly" Williams 1725-2000.* Seven Lakes, NC: Harris Printing Company, 2000, Page 9-10.

[19] Hunt, James L. *Grandfather Clause*, 2016. Retrieved from https://www.ncpedia.org/grandfather-clause

[20] Parker, Anthony E. *A Guide to Moore County Cemeteries.* Southern Pines, NC: Moore County Historical Association, 1976.

[21] Ibid.

[22] Ibid.

[23] "Local Paragraphs" (1894, April 17), *Carthage Blade* (Carthage, NC). Page 3. Retrieved from www.newspapers.com

[24] Parker, Anthony E. *A Guide to Moore County Cemeteries.* Southern Pines, NC: Moore County Historical Association, 1976.

[25] Find A Grave. Retrieved from https://www.findagrave.com/memorial/114470200/alsey-clegg-maness

[26] Ira Mainess and Catherine Ritter Marriage, Familysearch.org. *North Carolina, County Marriages, 1762-1979*

[27] Civil War Service Records. *Ira L. Maness.* Retrieved from https://www.fold3.com/image/44692514

[28] Garner Jr., Lacy A. *Company H, 26th Regiment NC State Troops*, Retrieved from www.companyh26th.com

[29] Confederate Pension Application. *Ira L. Maness.* Retrieved from https://digital.ncdcr.gov/digital/collection/p16062coll21/id/97940/rec/5

[30] Original record in possession of Carol Smith Purvis, Bennett, NC

[31] Ruffin Wallace and Salina Fry Marriage, Familysearch.org. *North Carolina, County Marriages, 1762-1979*

[32] Civil War Service Records. *Rufus Wallace.* Retrieved from https://www.fold3.com/image/50711790

[33] Tabitha Wallace, 1914 Death Certificate. Ancestry.com. *North Carolina, Death Certificates, 1909-1976*

[34] Alex Wallace and Eliza A. Fry Marriage, Familysearch.org. *North Carolina, County Marriages, 1762-1979*

[35] Parker, Anthony E. *A Guide to Moore County Cemeteries.* Southern Pines, NC: Moore County Historical Association, 1976.

[36] Civil War Service Records. *Alexander Wallace.* Retrieved from https://www.fold3.com/image/44615743

[37] Garner Jr., Lacy A. *Company H, 26th Regiment NC State Troops*, Retrieved from www.companyh26th.com

[38] Find A Grave. Retrieved from https://www.findagrave.com/memorial/21105689/nathan-wallace

[39] Ibid. Retrieved from https://www.findagrave.com/memorial/9192108/mary-wallace

[40] Eli Wallace and Sina Davis Marriage. Ancestry.com. *Alabama, County Marriage Records, 1805-1967*

[41] Civil War Service Records. *Eli Wallace*. Retrieved from https://www.fold3.com/image/12436917

[42] Isam Wallace and Gracy A. Goodwin Marriage. Ancestry.com. *Alabama, County Marriage Records, 1805-1967*

[43] Civil War Service Records. *Thomas Wallace*. Retrieved from https://www.fold3.com/image/10021674

[44] Fanny Wallace, 1909 Death Certificate, Bibb County, AL

[45] Civil War Service Records. *Raleigh W. Wallis*. Retrieved from https://www.fold3.com/image/84627999

[46] Helen Hughes Smith (helen.smith@comcast.net), email, February 15, 2010.

[47] Rally Wallace and Elizabeth Spinks Marriage. Ancestry.com. *Alabama, County Marriage Records, 1805-1967*

[48] Find A Grave. Retrieved from https://www.findagrave.com/memorial/33444868/elizabeth-wallace

[49] Ibid. Retrieved from https://www.findagrave.com/memorial/78861479/john-wesley-wallace

[50] Ibid. Retrieved from https://www.findagrave.com/memorial/78861347/frances-jane-wallace

[51] Civil War Service Records. *Josiah Wallace*. Retrieved from https://www.fold3.com/image/7683497

[52] Find A Grave. Retrieved from https://www.findagrave.com/memorial/63366397/josiah-s-wallace

[53] Isaac Rolly and Sarah Wallace Marriage. Ancestry.com. *Alabama, County Marriage Records, 1805-1967*

[54] Tennessee State Library and Archives Blog. *The Night the Stars Fell*. Retrieved from https://tslablog.blogspot.com/2015/11/the-night-stars-fell.html

[55] Benjamin Britt and Frany Wallace Marriage, Familysearch.org. *North Carolina, County Marriages, 1762-1979*

[56] "Marriages" (1850, Sep 10), *Fayetteville Observer* (Fayetteville, NC). Page 3. Retrieved from www.newspapers.com

[57] Civil War Service Records. *Harmon Brewer*. Retrieved from https://www.fold3.com/image/66384356

[58] Ibid. *Everett Wallace*. Retrieved from https://www.fold3.com/image/76843147

[59] Find A Grave. https://www.findagrave.com/memorial/40344778/ben-wallace

[60] Benjamin Wallace and Caty Williams Marriage. Ancestry.com. *Tennessee, Marriage Records, 1780-2002*

[61] Benjamin Wallace and Holly J. Kizer Marriage. Ancestry.com. *Tennessee, Marriage Records, 1780-2002*

[62] B. Wallace and E.E. Knight Marriage, St. Francis County, AR Marriage Register

[63] Find A Grave, Retrieved from https://www.findagrave.com/memorial/40344866/eliza-elizabeth-wallace

[64] Sarah Francis Hart, 1941 Death Certificate. Ancestry.com. *Texas, Death Certificates, 1903–1982*

[65] Find A Grave. Retrieved from https://www.findagrave.com/memorial/35589362/sarah-frances-hart

[66] W. S. Wallace, 1925 Death Certificate. Ancestry.com. *Tennessee Death Records, 1908-1958*

[67] Nancy Wallace, 1945 Death Certificate. Ancestry.com. *Tennessee Death Records, 1908-1958*

[68] Find A Grave. Retrieved from https://www.findagrave.com/memorial/98907661/william-samuel-wallace

[69] Frona Cox, 1926 Death Certificate. Ancestry.com. *Texas, Death Certificates, 1903–1982*

[70] Find A Grave. Retrieved from https://www.findagrave.com/memorial/68147499/susan-saphronia-cox

[71] "Marriages" (1840, Jun 24), *Fayetteville Observer* (Fayetteville, NC). Page 3. Retrieved from www.newspapers.com

[72] "Deaths" (1892, Jul 13), *Biblical Recorder* (Raleigh, NC). Page 3. Retrieved from www.newspapers.com

[73] Shields, H.B. *Country Doctor for A Half Century*. Southern Pines, NC: The Pilot Inc. and Katherine Shields Melvin, 1976. Page 61

[74] "Local Records" (1887, Oct 27), *The Chatham Record* (Pittsboro, NC). Page 3. Retrieved from www.newspapers.com

[75] "Death of W.W. Wallace" (1906, Oct 11), *Carthage Blade* (Carthage, NC). Page 3. Retrieved from www.newspapers.com

[76] Louise Wallace, 1932 Death Certificate. Ancestry.com. *North Carolina, Death Certificates, 1909-1976*

[77] Find A Grave. Retrieved from https://www.findagrave.com/memorial/54981346/margaret-louise-wallace

[78] Quimby Wallace and Arabella Stewart Marriage, Familysearch.org. *North Carolina, County Marriages, 1762-1979*

[79] Arabella Wallace, 1928 Death Certificate. Ancestry.com. *North Carolina, Death Certificates, 1909-1976*

[80] Civil War Service Records. *Shadrack Maness*. Retrieved from https://www.fold3.com/image/52016997

[81] Garner Jr., Lacy A. *Tales from the Upper End of the County*. Raleigh, NC: Lulu, 2009. Page 188

[82] Lochart Wallace and Susan Muse Marriage, Familysearch.org. *North Carolina, County Marriages, 1762-1979*

[83] Emsley Wallace, 1918 Death Certificate. Ancestry.com. *North Carolina, Death Certificates, 1909-1976*

[84] Emsley Wallace and Priscilla Melton Marriage, Familysearch.org. *North Carolina, County Marriages, 1762-1979*

[85] *Papers of Artemus Caddell*, Special Collections, David M. Rubenstein Library, Duke University, Durham, NC

[86] *Biographical and Historical Memoirs of Pulaski, Jefferson, Lonoke, Faulkner, Grant, Saline, Perry, Garland and Hot Spring Counties Arkansas*. Chicago, IL: Goodspeed Publishing Co., 1889. Pages 700-701

[87] Samuel Wallace and Tempy Yow Marriage, Familysearch.org. *North Carolina, County Marriages, 1762-1979*

[88] William Yow and Tempy Melton Marriage, Familysearch.org. *North Carolina, County Marriages, 1762-1979*

[89] S.B. Wallace and Nancy Britt Marriage, Ancestry.com. *North Carolina, Marriage Records, 1741-2011*

[90] Lovedy Jane Horner 1916 Death Certificate. Ancestry.com. *North Carolina, Death Certificates, 1909-1976*

[91] Jas. W. Horner and Lovedy Jane Wallace Marriage, Familysearch.org. *North Carolina, County Marriages, 1762-1979*

[92] James Washington Horner 1921 Death Certificate. Ancestry.com. *North Carolina, Death Certificates, 1909-1976*

[93] Parker, Anthony E. *A Guide to Moore County Cemeteries*. Southern Pines, NC: Moore County Historical Association, 1976.

[94] Missouri Wallace 1920 Death Certificate. Ancestry.com. *North Carolina, Death Certificates, 1909-1976*

[95] Civil War Service Records. *Delany Wallace*. Retrieved from https://www.fold3.com/image/55343091

[96] Confederate Pension Application. *S.D. Wallace*. Retrieved from https://digital.ncdcr.gov/digital/collection/p16062coll21/id/150152/rec/1

[97] V.S Wallace 1917 Death Certificate. Ancestry.com. *North Carolina, Death Certificates, 1909-1976*

[98] Virgily S. Wallace and Flora Ann Garner Marriage. Ancestry.com. *North Carolina, Marriage Records, 1741-2011*

[99] Flora Ann G. Wallace 1963 Death Certificate. Ancestry.com. *North Carolina, Death Certificates, 1909-1976*

[100] Jas. L. Wallace and Flora Wallace Marriage. Ancestry.com. *North Carolina, Marriage Records, 1741-2011*

[101] Parker, Anthony E. *A Guide to Moore County Cemeteries*. Southern Pines, NC: Moore County Historical Association, 1976.

[102] Goodspeed's Biographical and Historical Memoirs of Central Arkansas Counties: Pulaski, Jefferson, Lonoke, Faulkner, Grant, Saline, Perry, Garland, and Hot Springs, Chapter 22 Perry County, Page 700-701

[103] Ibid.

[104] "J.M. Wallace Married" (1899, Apr 5), *Arkansas Democrat* (Little Rock, AR). Page 5. Retrieved from www.newspapers.com

[105] Hiram Wallace and Julia A. Williams Marriage, Familysearch.org. *North Carolina, County Marriages, 1762-1979*

[106] Civil War Service Records. *Hiram Wallis*. Retrieved from https://www.fold3.com/image/51692207

[107] Confederate Pension Application. *Hiram Wallace*. Retrieved from https://digital.ncdcr.gov/digital/collection/p16062coll21/id/150056/rec/42

[108] Julia Ann Brown 1921 Death Certificate. Ancestry.com. *North Carolina, Death Certificates, 1909-1976*

[109] Isham Wallace and Malinda Cockman Marriage, Familysearch.org. *North Carolina, County Marriages, 1762-1979*

[110] Civil War Service Records. *Isham Wallis*. Retrieved from https://www.fold3.com/image/51692250

[111] Spinks Wallis and Nancy Ollie Cannady. Ancestry.com. *Alabama, Select Marriage Indexes, 1816-1942*

[112] Find A Grave. Retrieved from https://www.findagrave.com/memorial/31945792/john-spinks-wallace

[113] Jeremiah Williams and Rebecca Kizer Marriage. Ancestry.com. *Georgia, Marriage Records From Select Counties, 1828-1978*

[114] Jeremiah Williams 1906 Death Certificate. Ancestry.com. *Texas, Death Certificates, 1903–1982*

[115] Find A Grave. Retrieved from https://www.findagrave.com/memorial/51942523/mary-williams

[116] Nathaniel Britt and Amanda J. Williams Marriage. Ancestry.com. *Tennessee, Marriage Records, 1780-2002*

[117] Find A Grave. Retrieved from https://www.findagrave.com/memorial/51942518/david-anderson-williams

[118] Benjamin Wallace and Caty Williams Marriage. Ancestry.com. *Tennessee, Marriage Records, 1780-2002*

[119] Benjamin Wallace and Holly J. Kizer Marriage. Ancestry.com. *Tennessee, Marriage Records, 1780-2002*

[120] B. Wallace and E.E. Knight Marriage, St. Francis County, AR Marriage Register

[121] James Wesley Williams and Margaret Hart Marriage. Ancestry.com. *Tennessee, Marriage Records, 1780-2002*

[122] Bryant Williams and Margaret Latham Marriage. Ancestry.com. *Tennessee, Marriage Records, 1780-2002*

[123] Find A Grave. Retrieved from https://www.findagrave.com/memorial/38680226/martha-richardson

[124] Ibid. Retrieved from https://www.findagrave.com/memorial/38680232/william-zeno-richardson

[125] A.L. Sowell and Mary A. Wallace Marriage, Familysearch.org. *North Carolina, County Marriages, 1762-1979*

[126] Henry Maness and Rebecca Jane Wallace Marriage, Familysearch.org. *North Carolina, County Marriages, 1762-1979*

[127] James M. Wallace 1927 Death Certificate. Ancestry.com. *North Carolina, Death Certificates, 1909-1976*

[128] Civil War Service Records. *John M. Wallace*. Retrieved from https://www.fold3.com/image/49861321

[129] Francis Maness 1919 Death Certificate. Ancestry.com. *North Carolina, Death Certificates, 1909-1976*

[130] Confederate Pension Application. *Marshall G. Maness*. Retrieved from https://digital.ncdcr.gov/digital/collection/p16062coll21/id/97948/rec/2

[131] James L. Wallace and Lillie Maness Marriage. Ancestry.com. *North Carolina, Marriage Records, 1741-2011*

[132] Jas. L. Wallace and Flora Wallace Marriage. Ancestry.com. *North Carolina, Marriage Records, 1741-2011*

[133] Lauchlin Wallace and Margaret A. Norton, Ancestry.com. *North Carolina, Marriage Records, 1741-2011*

[134] Find A Grave, Retrieved from https://www.findagrave.com/memorial/23498443/william-lane-wallace

[135] Civil War Service Records. *William L. Wallace*. Retrieved from https://www.fold3.com/image/44615804

[136] Garner Jr., Lacy A. *Company H, 26th Regiment NC State Troops*, Retrieved from www.companyh26th.com

[137] Find A Grave, Retrieved from https://www.findagrave.com/memorial/23498419/annie-elizabeth-wallace

[138] Josiah Wallace and Ann Miranda Muse Marriage, Familysearch.org. *North Carolina, County Marriages, 1762-1979*

[139] Civil War Service Records. *Josiah Wallace*. Retrieved from https://www.fold3.com/image/55343223

[140] "Marriages" (1878, Jan 10), *Carthaginian* (Carthage, NC). Retrieved from www.newspapers.com

[141] Parker, Anthony E. *A Guide to Moore County Cemeteries*. Southern Pines, NC: Moore County Historical Association, 1976.

[142] E.W. Wallis and Nancy Lett Marriage, Familysearch.org. *North Carolina, County Marriages, 1762-1979*

[143] "Marriages" (1860, Sep 10), *Fayetteville Observer* (Fayetteville, NC). Retrieved from www.newspapers.com

[144] Find A Grave. Retrieved from https://www.findagrave.com/memorial/50808697/everett-w.-wallace

[145] Civil War Service Records. *Everett Wallace*. Retrieved from https://www.fold3.com/image/43625541
[146] Confederate Pension Application. *E.W. Wallace*. Retrieved from https://digital.ncdcr.gov/digital/collection/p16062coll21/id/150036/rec/8
[147] Fina A Grave. Retrieved from https://www.findagrave.com/memorial/50808697/everett-w.-wallace
[148] Civil War Service Records. *William Wallace*. Retrieved from https://www.fold3.com/image/30282101
[149] Parker, Anthony E. *A Guide to Moore County Cemeteries*. Southern Pines, NC: Moore County Historical Association, 1976.
[150] Find A Grave. Retrieved from https://www.findagrave.com/memorial/23498398/mary-hamilton
[151] Ibid. https://www.findagrave.com/memorial/23498407/william-albert-hamilton
[152] Ibid. https://www.findagrave.com/memorial/27184548/mazura-taylor
[153] Ibid. https://www.findagrave.com/memorial/27184449/john-taylor
[154] Ibid. https://www.findagrave.com/memorial/27651881/thomas-w-wallace
[155] Ibid. https://www.findagrave.com/memorial/27651909/flora-jane-wallace
[156] Ibid. https://www.findagrave.com/memorial/47024363/wesley-royce-wallace
[157] Ibid. https://www.findagrave.com/memorial/47024403/maggie-wallace
[158] Ibid. https://www.findagrave.com/memorial/87693298/lottie-wallace
[159] Ibid. https://www.findagrave.com/memorial/44975394/needam-evander-wallace
[160] Ibid. https://www.findagrave.com/memorial/35396803/arrie-lane-wallace
[161] Ibid. https://www.findagrave.com/memorial/35397096/nellie-wood-wallace
[162] Ibid. https://www.findagrave.com/memorial/23521496/arch-young-wallace
[163] Ibid. https://www.findagrave.com/memorial/23521424/annie-elizabeth-wallace
[164] Bazel Deaton and Sally Wallace Marriage, Familysearch.org. *North Carolina, County Marriages, 1762-1979*
[165] Find A Grave. Retrieved from https://www.findagrave.com/memorial/30003902/william-eli-wallace
[166] Civil War Service Records. *Eli Wallace*. Retrieved from https://www.fold3.com/image/49861240
[167] Find A Grave. https://www.findagrave.com/memorial/30003632/martha-clementine-wallace
[168] "A Wife Trade That Was Allowed to Stand" (1903, Jan 29), *Asheboro Courier* (Asheboro, NC). Retrieved from www.newspapers.com
[169] William Birch Morgan 1921 Death Certificate. Ancestry.com. *North Carolina, Death Certificates, 1909-1976*
[170] I.S. Deaton 1918 Death Certificate. Ancestry.com. *North Carolina, Death Certificates, 1909-1976*
[171] Vada Deaton 1921 Death Certificate. Ancestry.com. *North Carolina, Death Certificates, 1909-1976*
[172] John M. Davis 1925 Death Certificate. Ancestry.com. *North Carolina, Death Certificates, 1909-1976*
[173] Julia Davis 1936 Death Certificate. Ancestry.com. *North Carolina, Death Certificates, 1909-1976*
[174] Maggie Napier 1936 Death Certificate. Ancestry.com. *North Carolina, Death Certificates, 1909-1976*
[175] Glenda Yarboro Brock (gyb6567@embarqmail.com), email, August 21, 2009.
[176] Ibid.
[177] George Wallace and Ellen Kellis Marriage. Ancestry.com. *North Carolina, Marriage Records, 1741-2011*
[178] George W. Wallace 1932 Death Certificate. Ancestry.com. *North Carolina, Death Certificates, 1909-1976*
[179] Ken Poole (ouch00@hotmail.com), email, August 29, 2012.
[180] Isham Wallis 1853 Death Register. Ancestry.com. *Kentucky, Death Records, 1852-1965*
[181] Eli Wallace and Mima Crowel Marriage. Ancestry.com. *Tennessee, Marriage Records, 1780-2002*
[182] Eli Wallace 1855 Death Register. Ancestry.com. *Kentucky, Death Records, 1852-1965*
[183] Isham Wallis and Edy Reed Marriage. Ancestry.com. *North Carolina, Marriage Records, 1741-2011*
[184] Find A Grave. Retrieved from https://www.findagrave.com/memorial/65965488/edee-wallis
[185] Mary Feezor 1852 Death Register. Ancestry.com. *Kentucky, Death Records, 1852-1965*
[186] Levi Wallace 1855 Death Register. Ancestry.com. *Kentucky, Death Records, 1852-*
[187] Find A Grave. Retrieved from https://www.findagrave.com/memorial/26039255/everett-j.-wallace
[188] Ibid. https://www.findagrave.com/memorial/26039262/mary-wallace
[189] Ibid. https://www.findagrave.com/memorial/28980851/temprence-reid
[190] Ibid. https://www.findagrave.com/memorial/28980859/thomas-reid
[191] Ibid. https://www.findagrave.com/memorial/37915634/james-lovelace-wallace
[192] Ibid. https://www.findagrave.com/memorial/83061608/nathan-wallis
[193] Ibid. https://www.findagrave.com/memorial/83061542/margret-wallis
[194] Wallace, Allen Maxwell. *William and Chaney Wallace and their descendants*. Lexington, KY: Privately Published, 1973.
[195] Harbert Wallace and Nancy Adderton Marriage. Ancestry.com. *North Carolina, Marriage Records, 1741-2011*
[196] Find A Grave. Retireved from https://www.findagrave.com/memorial/29184608/docia-wallace
[197] Jimmy Wallace (jim7131953@msn.com) and https://www.ancestry.com/family-tree/person/tree/9347431/person/-812647818/facts
[198] Find A Grave. Retrieved from https://www.findagrave.com/memorial/18844514/john-wallace

[199] Ibid. https://www.findagrave.com/memorial/18844526/nancy-a.-wallace

[200] Belcher, Greg. *The Great Wagon Road*. Retrieved from
http://freepages.rootsweb.com/~genbel/genealogy/augsep/thegreatwagonraod.html

[201] Ritter family letters, 1732-1739. In possession of Linda Ritter, Louisiana (kikikritter42@gmail.com). Full text at
https://moorecountywallaces.com/showmedia.php?mediaID=4905&medialinkID=14498

[202] Oral History written by Murry Connie Ritter as told by his father William Young Ritter, 1905. In possession of Linda Ritter, Louisiana (kikikritter42@gmail.com). Full text at
https://moorecountywallaces.com/showmedia.php?mediaID=4904&medialinkID=14493

[203] Averett Ritter and Charlotte Smith Marriage. Ancestry.com. *Tennessee, Marriage Records, 1780-2002*

[204] Parker, Anthony E. *A Guide to Moore County Cemeteries*. Southern Pines, NC: Moore County Historical Association, 1976.

[205] Ibid.

[206] Lacy A. Garner Jr. (lacyjoe@centurylink.net) email, (February 24, 2016)

[207] Family Bible of Jesse Sowell and Nancy Ritter. State Archives of North Carolina. NC Family Records Collection. Retrieved from https://digital.ncdcr.gov/digital/collection/p15012coll1/id/58791/rec/2

[208] "Obituary" (1858, Oct 7), *The Biblical Recorder* (Raleigh, NC). Retrieved from www.newspapers.com

[209] Parker, Anthony E. *A Guide to Moore County Cemeteries*. Southern Pines, NC: Moore County Historical Association, 1976.

[210] Family Bible of Moses Ritter and Hannah Bradbury. In possession of Edward R. Harrel, Selmer, TX as of 1991.
Information provided by Jerry Smith (jerrysmith@crosstel.net)

Wallace Surname Origins

The history of the name Wallace begins in the Scottish/English Borderlands with a family of Strathclyde-Briton ancestry. It is a name for a person who was understood to be foreign. The name is actually an abbreviation of Wallensis, which meant Welsh is derived from the Anglo-Norman French word waleis, meaning foreign. It is sometimes difficult for the layman to understand how such a renowned Scottish Clan could be called, literally, Welsh. Yet from the 3rd to the 8th century the Kingdom of Strathclyde stretched from the northern tip of France to the southern shores of the Clyde in Scotland.

This kingdom was composed of solely coastal territories, of regions including Wales, Lancashire, Westmorland and that part of southwest Scotland known as Galloway. Ironically, the first Scottish poem, dated about 1000 AD, was written in Welsh.

Hence, Richard Wallensis was a vassal in 1174 of Walter FitzAlan, the Norman/ Breton who had settled in Salop in England and then moved north to Scotland. He would later found the great line of Scottish Stewart Kings. The Wallensis were undoubtedly the original natives of the area rather than travelers who moved north from the Welsh border in the train of the Stewarts.

Early Origins of the Wallace family

The surname Wallace was first found in Ayrshire (Gaelic: Siorrachd Inbhir Àir), formerly a county in the southwestern Strathclyde region of Scotland, that today makes up the Council Areas of South, East, and North Ayrshire where in 1173 AD Richard Wallensis obtained the lands that belonged to the former kingdom of Strathclyde called Richardstoun (now Riccarton) by a grant from the King. His son, Richard Walency (or Waleis) witnessed several charters between 1190 and 1220, showing his approval of transfers of land in Molle, Kelso, Cupa and Paisley. The Chiefship passed to his grandson, Sir Malcolm Wallace of Elderslie in Renfrewshire, who had acquired those lands, the ancient Clan territories and other lands in Ayrshire. It was the younger son of Malcolm Wallace, William Wallace, born in 1275, who was Scotland's folklore hero. A knight of no small qualification and skill, throughout his life he had maintained a friendship with the House of Stewart. His many exploits started in 1297 when he killed the Sheriff of Lanark.

Wallace continued to harass the English occupying army with such skill and bewildering speed that the English were demoralized. Wallace unified the Clans of Scotland against a common invader. One of the English captains reported that Wallace was lying in Selkirk forest with his army of Clansmen.

An English force moved northwards to destroy him but found itself under siege in Stirling Castle. The Battle of Stirling Bridge was a decisive victory for Wallace, and he was awarded the guardianship of Scotland. He was probably the greatest unifying factor that Scotland ever had. But the English King once more invaded Scotland, set up his own government and Wallace became an outlaw. Betrayed by Sir John de Menteith near Glasgow, he was tried for treason in London and executed on August 23rd, 1305.

But the Clan Wallace lived on with some forty or fifty branches, most of them having their own lands and territories.

Medieval Scottish names are rife with spelling variations. This is due to the fact that scribes in that era spelled according to the sound of words, rather than any set of rules. Wallace has been spelled Wallace, Wallis, Wallys, Walace, Uallas (Gaelic) and others.

Courtesy of https://www.houseofnames.com/wallace-family-crest

www.ingramcontent.com/pod-product-compliance
Lightning Source LLC
Chambersburg PA
CBHW062020090426
42811CB00005B/908